False Necessity

POLITICS: A WORK IN CONSTRUCTIVE SOCIAL THEORY

by Roberto Mangabeira Unger

SOCIAL THEORY: ITS SITUATION AND ITS TASK

FALSE NECESSITY: ANTI-NECESSITARIAN SOCIAL THEORY IN THE SERVICE OF RADICAL DEMOCRACY

PLASTICITY INTO POWER: COMPARATIVE-HISTORICAL STUDIES ON THE INSTITUTIONAL CONDITIONS OF ECONOMIC AND MILITARY SUCCESS

FALSE NECESSITY

*Anti-Necessitarian Social Theory
in the Service of Radical Democracy*

PART I OF
POLITICS
A WORK IN CONSTRUCTIVE SOCIAL THEORY

ROBERTO MANGABEIRA UNGER

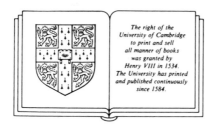

The right of the
University of Cambridge
to print and sell
all manner of books
was granted by
Henry VIII in 1534.
The University has printed
and published continuously
since 1584.

CAMBRIDGE UNIVERSITY PRESS

CAMBRIDGE

NEW YORK   NEW ROCHELLE   MELBOURNE   SYDNEY

Published by the Press Syndicate of the University of Cambridge
The Pitt Building, Trumpington Street, Cambridge CB2 1RP
32 East 57th Street, New York, NY 10022, USA
10 Stamford Road, Oakleigh, Melbourne 3166, Australia

First published 1987

Printed in the United States of America

Library of Congress Cataloging-in-Publication Data
Unger, Roberto Mangabeira.
False necessity – anti-necessitarian social theory
in the service of radical democracy.
(Politics, a work in constructive social theory;
pt. 1)
Bibliography: p.
1. Sociology. 2. Political science. 3. Philosophy.
I. Title. II. Series: Unger, Roberto Mangabeira.
Politics, a work in constructive social theory ; pt. 1.
HM24.U5354   pt. 1   320.5'312 s   [320.5'312]   86–7880

British Library Cataloguing in Publication Data
Unger, Roberto Mangabeira
False necessity: anti-necessitarian social
theory in the service of radical democracy :
part 1 of politics, a work in constructive
social theory.
1. Political sociology
I. Title
320'.01   JA76

ISBN 0 521 32975 2 hard covers
ISBN 0 521 33883 8 paperback

Contents

Contents

Contents

1

The Nature and Intentions of the Argument

EXPLANATORY AND PROGRAMMATIC THEMES

False Necessity presents an explanatory theory of society and a program for social reconstruction. The theory works toward a radical alternative to Marxism. The program suggests a radical alternative to social democracy.

As an explanatory theory of society, *False Necessity* seeks to free social explanation from its dependence upon the denial of our freedom to resist and to remake our forms of social life. It offers a relentlessly anti-necessitarian view that nevertheless generates a broad range of social and historical explanations: some comprehensive and abstract, others focused and concrete. It carries to extremes the thesis that everything in society is politics, mere politics, and then draws out of this seemingly negativistic and paradoxical idea a detailed understanding of social life.

As a program for social reconstruction, *False Necessity* shows how we may carry forward the radical project of freeing our practical and passionate dealings from the constraints imposed upon them by entrenched social roles and hierarchies. It argues that the best hope for the advancement of this radical cause – the cause that leftists share with liberals – lies in a series of revolutionary reforms in the organization of governments and economies and in the character of our personal relations. The explanatory and programmatic ideas of the book are closely connected: each supports the other, and each expresses an aspect of the vision that both share.

This vision takes the last and most surprising step in the itinerary of modern historicism. For it recognizes that the quality of our relation, as context-revising agents, to the institutional and imaginative contexts we establish and inhabit is itself up for grabs in history. We can construct not just new and different social worlds but social worlds that more fully embody and respect the creative power whose suppression or containment all societies and cultures seem to require. In this way we can break a little farther out of the tedious, degrading rhythm of history – with its long lulls of collective narcolepsy punctuated by violent revolutionary seizures. We can lift a little higher the burden of social division and hierarchy that weighs upon our efforts to gain practical, emotional, and cognitive access to one another. And we can do a little better at finding the limited circumstances that somehow express our inconformity with limited circumstances.

Explanatory Themes

The guiding concern of the explanatory theory can be described in several equivalent ways. Most of the comprehensive and influential social theories advanced in the last two centuries suffer from an internal tension. The tension is especially noticeable in the doctrines – Marxism preeminent among them – that have provided the left with its intellectual tools. All these theories, whether or not radical in their intentions, see society as an artifact. They treat every organization of social life as made and imagined rather than as given in an eternal pattern by human nature or social harmony. They therefore also emphasize the stark discontinuities among forms of social life, recognizing each such form as the expression of a different way of being human.

Yet these theories repeatedly betrayed their understanding of society as artifact by the fashion in which they turned this understanding into a concrete practice of social explanation. They pinned their theoretical ambitions to the development of a supposed science of history and society. This science presents man as the product of an evolutionary logic, or of deep-seated economic, organizational, or psychological constraints, that he is unable to alter. The weakening of the intention in the execution may be justified by the sense that without this hedging, we would fall into theoretical agnosticism, and transformative politics would lose intellectual guidance. As a result, we would become all the more subject to the influence of the social worlds we inhabit.

But the explanatory theory of *False Necessity* is meant to show that we can resolve this apparent dilemma. We *can* carry to its ultimate conclusion the view of society as artifact. Moreover, we can do so without abandoning ourselves to theoretical nihilism and without weakening our ability to resist the established social order. Thus, one way to describe the explanatory theory of this book is to say that it pushes to extremes the idea of society as made and imagined. It argues that when we go to these extremes we find theory rather than no theory.

On a second interpretation the book represents an attempt both to take sides in a dominant though largely implicit debate in modern social thought and to change the terms of this controversy. On one side of this controversy stand people – conservatives, leftists, or centrists – who claim that the currently available forms of social organization reflect deeply rooted constraints or a logic of social development. Alternatively, these people explain the institutions of each society as the cumulative outcomes of many episodes of interest accommodation or problem solving. Such outcomes, they hold, are shaped by objective facts about actual interests and possible accommodations, actual problems and possible solutions.

What do the opponents of these people mean when they claim that everything is politics? At a minimum, they mean to deny that the established forms of social organization reflect such impersonal and irresistible forces. Instead, these critics direct our attention to the particular sequence of practical or imaginative conflicts from which, they claim, established arrangements have emerged. The conflicts they have in mind are first and foremost the struggles over the uses and mastery of governmental power (politics in the narrow sense). But these conflicts also include the disputes over all the other material or intangible resources with which we make the social future within the social present. By denying that current social arrangements reflect a higher rational or practical necessity, the critics mean to argue that these arrangements can be reimagined and remade.

The slogan that everything is politics is nothing if not deflationary of the traditional claims of social theory: the received style of generalization in social thought and historical writing explains conflict by reference to institutional or imaginative structures, the fighting that goes on in all societies by reference to the framework within which it takes place. Thus, the adversaries of the people who say that everything is politics can plausibly claim that the endeavor of those whom they criticize is self-defeating. For we cannot act to change society in radical ways unless we have ideas that lay bare the pattern of constraint and opportunity in our historical situation and that illuminate the probable effects of our actions.

The explanatory theory of *False Necessity* takes sides decisively with those who say it is all politics. But in taking sides the argument of the book asserts that we can develop the everything-is-politics idea into a comprehensive set of explanatory conjectures and explanatory practices. The resulting theory remains faithful to everything the critics want, except perhaps to their characteristic hostility to comprehensive theories. But this hostility, I argue, is misplaced. Social theory can be cleansed of the qualities these antitheorists find so objectionable, so long as we are willing to accept a fundamental shift in our sense of what it means to explain a state of affairs. Indeed, the attack on the equation of prevailing social arrangements with practical necessities *must* be armed with a theory if it is to avoid trivialization and paradox.

There is yet a third way to define the main point of the explanatory theory of *False Necessity*. It may be the most telling of all these statements because it addresses permanent puzzles and concerns rather than the development of a specific theoretical tradition or the resolution of a particular contemporary controversy. The explanatory view of *False Necessity* tries to give its due to two aspects of our experience of social life that seem hard to reconcile.

In every social circumstance much of what takes place can be explained as the product of the institutional and imaginative context (order, structure, or framework) within which routine activities and conflicts occur. Wherever we look in history, we can identify a small number of basic arrangements and preconceptions that mesh together to exercise an overwhelming influence over social life. Often, we seem to be mere puppets of these frameworks or of the forces that generate and sustain them.

But our social experience also shows another face. We sometimes put these frameworks aside. We think and act, incongruously and surprisingly, as if they were not for real, as if we had merely pretended to obey them while awaiting an opportunity to defy them. We cannot live without a set of formative institutional arrangements and enacted ideals of human association, nor can we ever completely override the contrast between the things that are up for grabs in our ordinary conflicts and activities and the things that are not. But we can disrupt these established structures. We can replace them if not all at once, then piece by piece. We can even diminish the force with which they constrain and imprison us. Most importantly, this structure-disturbing and structure-inventing activity is not itself governed by a system of lawlike constraints and tendencies, certainly not by the evolutionary logic or relentless practical imperatives that the most ambitious modern social theories have traditionally invoked.

The explanatory practice developed in *False Necessity* suggests a way of imagining ourselves in society and history that does justice to these two contrasting aspects of our experience. We cannot accomplish the task merely by juxtaposing the two sets of observations – the constraints of structure and our powers of structure-disturbance – for we do not know how much credit to give each of them in any particular instance. We need a developed and supported view. A sign of the power of such a view is that it can criticize and help change both the structure-obeying and the structure-defying sides of particular societies.

The explanatory social theory developed in this book takes no stand on ultimate controversies about free will and determinism. So long as we treat all issues in social theory as reducible either to the most general problems about knowledge, reality, and value or to narrow factual and normative disputes, we cannot hope to reorient our approaches to society and history in any but the most haphazard and unselfconscious way. For we cannot resolve the metaphysical conundrums. We must try instead to factor out from the traditional metaphysical agenda the most tractable and urgent problems. Nowhere is this maxim more imperative than in the discussion of free will and determinism.

The framework-revising freedom that occupies so central a place in the social theory of *False Necessity* may be illusory from certain physicalist or theological perspectives. But it is one thing to deny this freedom in the name of forces internal to our social descriptions or explanations, and another thing to concede that these descriptions and explanations may be misleading or illusory in a view remote from our everyday experience. Our freedom remains in jeopardy until we have a normal discourse that both respects it and clarifies its sense.

False Necessity develops an antinecessitarian approach to social and historical explanation through an attempt to solve a particular explanatory problem. This problem is the origin and basis of the cycles of reform and retrenchment that characterize both the Western industrial democracies and the communist countries of the present day. Again and again, we find that partisan conflicts and attitudes about the uses of governmental power with respect to major issues, such as the direction of economic policy, move among a small number of familiar options. Thus, national governments in the industrial West oscillate between bouts of halfhearted redistribution and attempts to rekindle economic growth by concessions to big business and organized labor. Similarly, communist regimes regularly alternate between periods of economic centralism and decentralization, each swing of the pendulum complete with a detailed set of well-tried techniques and recurrent difficulties. Each traditional option is generally conceded to be a second-best solution by all the major contenders in the dispute. Only rarely is an option added to the list or subtracted from it. Why should policy keep returning to proposals that inspire so little hope? Some attribute the compulsive rounds of governmental politics to the mutual resistance of organized interests in highly fragmented societies that lack any single coherent plan of social division and hierarchy. Others emphasize the inescapable psychological, organizational, and economic imperatives that doom all imaginary alternatives to impracticality. But these comforting explanations do not work, and their failure reinstates and deepens the initial puzzle. The stubborn, mysterious cycles represent a permanent insult to societies whose official culture claims to base fundamental social arrangements upon the wills of free and relatively equal citizens and rightholders rather than upon blind drift or coercive authority.

The riddle presented by these contemporary cycles of reform and retrenchment in contemporary societies is only a special case of a far more pervasive characteristic of our social and historical experience. Wherever we look in history we see that the conflict over the use of the resources that determine the future shape of society has always moved within a narrow ambit. Prominent among the subjects of such conflict is the ongoing controversy over the relation of governmental power to social privilege and over the nature of the reforms needed to protect the established social order against its foreign and domestic enemies. But these routines of social reproduction also include all the other collective activities by which the economic or cognitive resources of society are mobilized to perpetuate or transform current social arrangements: the range of available forms of work organization or economic exchange and of acceptable moves within moral, political, or legal argument. When, for example, we consider the scope of live options in the high governmental politics of institutional reform, we find even the most powerful, determined, and clairvoyant rulers and politicians insistently returning to a small set of unpromising strategies, always unable to accomplish what they themselves consider necessary. They act as if they were in the thrall of unseen and irresistible compulsions. (An example discussed in detail later on is the repeated but futile attempts by the leaders of the agrarian-bureaucratic empires to preserve an independent class of smallholders, capable of providing the central government with a direct source of taxes and soldiers and therefore also of diminishing the government's financial and military dependence upon great landowners and warlords.)

Why should the scope of active and recognized possibility be so narrowly defined in all these theaters of conflict and choice? Explanations that appeal to the constraints of practical necessity or the balance of interests and opinions characteristically prove both too little and too much. They prove too little because the social arrangements that might satisfy basic practical needs always seem far more numerous than the institutional solutions that are actively considered; a persuasive social theory must show how and why the subset of live options gets selected. They prove too much because the range of options is sometimes abruptly enlarged, and the enlargement retrospectively deepens the puzzling quality of the previous narrowness. The attempt to understand the forces holding the cycles of reform and retrenchment in place can serve as a vehicle for the theoretical enterprise described at the outset of this chapter. For these cycles merely exemplify the more general experience of arrested and diminished possibility: the fabulously compulsive and somnambulent character of history, the long narcoleptic seizures of routine and repetition, punctuated by interludes of surprising social invention.

As the argument of *False Necessity* advances, the explanation of these narrowly defined options resolves itself into a study of the influence and the character of what I shall call the formative contexts, structures, or frameworks of social life: the basic institutional arrangements and imaginative preconceptions that circumscribe our routine practical or discursive activities and conflicts and that resist their destabilizing effects. A successful social theory must recognize the influence of these contexts. Yet it must also account for our ability not only to rebel against them but to diminish or intensify the force by which they constrain us. It must do justice to the mutual reinforcement of the institutions and beliefs that compose them. Yet it must also testify to the looseness of their internal relations. It must provide us with a way of understanding how such contexts get made. Yet it must acknowledge our inability to discover nontrivial laws, constraints, or tendencies that can explain their actual content and history.

The explanatory strategy of this book is therefore essentially simple. To explain the cycles of reform and retrenchment – and, more generally, the repetitive quality of ordinary social conflict – we need a theory of formative contexts, of how they are composed and made. An adequate theory of formative contexts, a theory capable of explaining experiences such as our experience of these reform cycles, turns out to be the theoretical enterprise I earlier described in three equivalent forms.

Given its scope, the explanatory argument of this book is largely speculative. The main purpose is to suggest a way of understanding society rather than to uncover particular facts or to test isolated conjectures. Inevitably, the discussion relies heavily on empirical work influenced by the very traditions of thought that it seeks to revise. The main test of such an explanatory argument is ultimately its ability to inspire detailed explanations more successful than the explanations made possible by current forms of social analysis.

The standards for what constitutes a successful explanation are neither unchanging nor easily malleable. They are neither an Archimedean vantage point towering above particular theories nor a subject for arbitrary stipulation by each theory. Our ideas about what constitutes a successful explanation change, slowly but significantly, as the substance of our explanatory ideas shifts. The explanatory argument of this book proposes a change in our received beliefs about what adequate social and historical explanations should be like.

It would be misleading, however, to suggest that the descriptions and explanations of this book are open to verification or falsification only at a second remove. The argument cuts across many problems and many disciplines. It advances conjectures about particular situations, processes, and events. It invokes facts, enlists familiar and less familiar learning, and proposes changes of emphasis and of approach in the understanding of many detailed affairs. Along this extended periphery of empirical implication, it remains open to more direct empirical assessment. The cumulative evaluation of these numerous and connected hypotheses casts light on the explanatory promise of the core theoretical project. Throughout, I reject any stark contrast between formulating a view and confirming it, or between considerations of theoretical coherence and appeals to scholarly research or to common experience.

Those who are wary of ambitious theories in social and historical study may feel their fears confirmed by this admission of the speculative character of the argument. But there are no uncontroversial alternatives. *Social Theory: Its Situation and Its Task* – the critical volume that introduces the present constructive work – argues that the seemingly modest practice of cumulative induction preached by much of contemporary social science cannot give its due to the central distinction between the formative institutional and imaginative contexts and the formed routines of social life. It cannot help us understand how these contexts are internally constituted, how they get remade, and how they inform a richly textured life of practical and argumentative routines. This explanatory failure has practical consequences. It disarms us before our social contexts by blinding us to their influence, their specificity, and their revisability. It tricks even the skeptical, the learned, and the disillusioned into not recognizing the makeshift, pasted-together, and alterable character of the social worlds in which they live.

The sole real alternative to the kind of comprehensive view developed here would be what the introductory volume labeled ultra-theory: a set of critical and constructive practices carefully crafted and militantly wielded to preserve their antinecessitarian power. This alternative intellectual style is not inherently better or worse than the theoretically aggressive strategy that *False Necessity* adopts. It merely presents a different mix of difficulties, dangers, and opportunities. Moreover, if this ultra-theoretical practice is to remain truly distinct from the prostrate, falsely modest versions of social science, and if it is to deal with the central distinction between formative contexts and formed routines, it must be just as bold and controversial as the unabashed theorizing practiced in this book.

Programmatic Themes

A program of social reconstruction accompanies the explanatory theory of *False Necessity*. The program addresses both the major institutions of social life – the large-scale organization of governments, economies, and workplaces – and the fine texture of personal encounters and social roles. The programmatic argument deals most directly with the practices and circumstances of the same contemporary countries that provide the explanatory theory with its focus.

Yet that argument develops an ideal and a method that may take forms very different from the proposals advanced here.

The guiding theme of the program of social reconstruction is the attempt to imagine institutional arrangements and social practices that can advance the radical project beyond the point to which contemporary forms of governmental and economic organization have carried it. By the radical project or the project of the modernist visionary I mean the attempt to realize the many forms of individual or collective empowerment that result from our relative success in disengaging our practical and passionate dealings from the restrictive influence of entrenched social roles and hierarchies. The influence of such schemes of social division and ranking depends – as the explanatory theory seeks to show – upon institutional and imaginative contexts that remain unavailable for revision in the course of ordinary social life. The program suggests how our contemporary formative contexts might be disentrenched, that is to say, how they might be more fully opened to challenge in the midst of our routine conflicts and therefore also how they might undermine or prevent rigid forms of social division and hierarchy. Against the background of almost universal disappointment with the communist revolutions of the twentieth century, the program suggests that current institutional arrangements represent merely an imperfect, initial step in the attempt to weaken the extent to which an established scheme of class, communal, gender, and national distinctions constrains our experiments in practical collaboration or passionate attachment. The weakening of the influence of this prewritten social script is to be valued not only negatively, as an occasion for a broader range of choice, but affirmatively for the forms of empowerment it makes possible. Moreover, the disruption of the script implies no lack of formed institutions or practices; it requires the invention of practices and institutions that possess certain qualities.

The empowerment that the program is meant to foster is in part the development of our practical productive capabilities. But it is also the freedom resulting from what we most prize even in current versions of democracy and community: the promise of forms of social engagement that save us from having to choose between isolation from other people and surrender to them and that describe modes of attachment that are also exercises in self-assertion. Finally, it is the empowerment that consists of conscious mastery over the institutional and imaginative contexts of our activities. The programmatic argument shows how these varieties of empowerment connect, and it explores their implications for the detailed reorganization of social life.

The commitment to advance human empowerment through institutions and practices that loosen the stranglehold of fixed schemes of social division and hierarchy over our practical and spiritual access to one another is hardly idiosyncratic. It has supplied the unifying element in the great secular modern doctrines of emancipation: liberalism, socialism, and communism. But in all these doctrines the pursuit of this aim suffers the effect of unjustifiably restrictive premises about social possibility. Just as I want to free the central insight of classical social theory – the insight into the artifactual character of social life – from its scientistic incubus, so too I want to detach the radical project from the dogmatic assumptions about possibility that represent the counterpart to this incubus. The most important of these confining assumptions are those that impoverish our sense of the alternative concrete institutional forms democracies and markets can take. Much of the programmatic argument in *False Necessity* describes ways of organizing markets and democracies that can be more useful to the radical project, and even more responsive to our received ideals, than current modes of economic and governmental organization.

The real meaning of our social ideals is largely defined by our often implicit assumptions about the institutional arrangements and social practices that realize these ideals. When, for example, we speak about democracy or community, our abstract principles and fighting words may be less telling guides to what we mean than the practical forms that realize these ideals. If someone proposes to us, or if we discover on our own, an alternative version of democratic institutions or communal life, we may be forced to confront a previously unsuspected ambiguity in our received ideal conceptions. In choosing between the alternative versions of democracy and community, we shall in effect be deciding what really matters most to us in our democratic and communal aspirations. And what holds for the understanding of ideals such as democracy or community applies to whole movements of political thought and sensibility. For the meaning of these movements also depends on the practical arrangements they are assumed to require.

The forms of governmental and economic organization proposed and defended in this book emphasize the development of practices and institutions that prevent factions, classes, or any other specially placed groups from gaining control over the key resources of a society (wealth, power, and knowledge). These same institutions and practices diminish the gap between routine conflicts within a framework of social life and revolutionary struggles about that framework. The explanatory theory of *False Necessity* explores the connections between the disruption of the mechanisms of social subjugation and the development of social arrangements that lay themselves more effectively open to challenge. The institutional proposals make good on these connections. Only from the perspective offered by these theoretical and practical ideas can we arrive at the broader under-standing of the radical project that I earlier mentioned. From the vantage point of this understanding, the struggle for social equality – the most familiar aspect of radical concerns – can be seen as a fragment of a more inclusive and complex endeavor.

The modernist criticism of personal relations and the leftist criticism of collective institutions have remained only fitfully and ob-scurely connected. This parting of the ways in the cultures of leftism and modernism has been amplified in political experience. The attack on stereotyped roles in personal relations has often proved strongest where the politics of institutional reinvention are weakest. The sep-aration between these two cultures and these two transformative movements – the most powerful of all found in the modern world – has been destructive to both. It has helped deprive leftist practice of its ability to reach direct social relations and to change their fine texture. It has also threatened to degrade the politics of personal relations into a desperate search for gratification.

The generalized understanding of the radical project presented in this book both incorporates and criticizes the personalist politics of modernism. This understanding recognizes the attack on stereotyped social roles as yet another facet of the attempt to achieve empow-erment by subverting entrenched social division and hierarchy. And it finds in the commitment to imagine a freer and richly detailed form of social life an antidote to solipsism and selfishness.

The Explanatory and Programmatic Themes Related

The explanatory and programmatic ideas of this book connect at many different levels. The most superficial link is the historical cir-cumstance that both arguments address. The explanatory view de-velops a theory of social transformation in the course of attempting to answer a particular question: Why do the cycles of reform and retrenchment in contemporary societies have the shape and the te-nacity they do? This question quickly turns into one of how to represent the formative institutional and imaginative contexts that keep these cycles going. To understand the influence of such contexts and to discover how it may be resisted we must understand how such contexts are made and what holds together their component elements. The programmatic parts of the book advance proposals designed to replace the same institutions and practices that account for the contemporary reform cycles.

There is also a more general and significant relation between the explanatory and programmatic arguments of *False Necessity*. The prevailing forms of social analysis leave no room for programmatic thought. Consider the comprehensive social theories, like hardcore

Marxism, that draw on an evolutionary and functionalist determinism. Such theories distinguish a small number of possible frameworks of social life, often ordered sequentially in a few possible trajectories of social evolution. They appeal to an inexorable logic of social transformation or to economic, organizational, and psychological constraints that are supposed to underlie this logic. For such systems of thought, programmatic argument can at best anticipate the line of historical evolution or compare the benefits and dangers of the few possible futures that lie before us. Alternatively, many forms of conventional social science deprive programmatic argument of its mission by failing to focus on the discontinuities among the institutional and imaginative frameworks that circumscribe our routine activities. Programs of social reconstruction amount to more than exercises in routine problem solving or interest accommodation, for they deal with the structures within which such exercises take place. Programmatic thought can be secure only against the background of a style of social and historical analysis that does not treat the institutional and imaginative molds of social life as inevitable or as determined by an irresistible dynamic of change.

We must develop such a style of analysis in order to possess a credible view of transformation. Until we formulate such a view, programmatic argument has no role. It is also deprived of the sense of reality that might enable it to distinguish feasible and utopian endeavors. The lack of such a sense shows in the bastardized and paralyzing criterion of political realism dominating so much contemporary ideological debate. People treat a plan as realistic when it approximates what already exists and as utopian when it departs from current arrangements. Only proposals that are hardly worth fighting for – reformist tinkering – seem practicable.

There is yet another and deeper link between the explanatory and programmatic ideas of this book. Both sets of proposals present mutually reinforcing variations on an old and central theme of our civilization: that we are an infinite caught within the finite. The finite, in this instance, is the open series of social worlds – the formative institutional and imaginative contexts – that we construct and inhabit. The infinite is the personality. It is also an inchoate, open-ended fund of the forms of practical collaboration or passionate attachment that may bind people together. Central to the whole argument of *Politics* is the notion that no one context can be our permanent home: the place where we can institute all the varieties of practical or passionate connection that we have reason to want.

The explanatory theory of society making presented here develops this theme by suggesting how we can imagine ourselves as both controlled and not controlled by our institutional and imaginative frameworks. The programmatic argument elaborates the theme by asking how we can make these finite worlds a more suitable habitation for context-revising and context-transcending agents. The explanatory theory shows how the institutional and imaginative frameworks of social life differ in the extent to which they aggravate the distinction between framework-transforming conflict and framework-respecting routine that perpetuates schemes of social division and hierarchy. Contexts may be increasingly designed to soften this distinction and undermine such schemes. The view of transformation concluding the explanatory part of the book describes the influence of such a change upon a range of forms of human empowerment. It also probes the conditions under which such a progression can occur. The programmatic argument takes up these suggestions by detailing a set of institutional arrangements and social practices that take this shift further than it has yet been carried, and do so for the sake of the many forms of empowerment that may result.

The critic may always object that he does not sympathize with this generalized version of the radical project and does not desire the varieties of empowerment it seeks. However, he must then possess either an alternative vision of social reality or a different approach to the relation between factual and normative judgments. Taken together, the programmatic and explanatory arguments of *False Necessity* illustrate the view that the relation between factual and normative issues is far more intimate than any relation the mainstream of modern philosophy since Kant and Hume has been inclined to allow. Consider the results such a view may achieve by both incorporating and changing familiar modes of prescriptive argument.

The visionary element in our ideas about self and society must ultimately always take one of two directions. It may invoke a single, authoritative arrangement of social life and human emotions. This is the direction followed by the most influential social doctrines in world history. It usually culminates in a system of sanctified social roles and ranks, echoed and sustained by a conception of hierarchical order among our faculties and dispositions. Alternatively, the visionary drive may appeal to the transcendent personality or to the opportunities of human connection that are constrained and betrayed by fixed divisions and hierarchies within humanity and by rigid rankings of subjective experience. The modernist radical or visionary prefers this second path. From this path one route leads to the "endless labor of negation": the creed of those who believe that contexts will be contexts and that true freedom lies solely in perpetual defiance to all stable institutions and conventions and in perpetual flight from one context to another. The other route, on this fork of the modernist visionary road, is the one traveled by those who argue that some contexts improve upon others in their ability to respect and to encourage the context-making and the context-transcending qualities of the self. This is the direction of *False Necessity*.

Such an intellectual enterprise must deliberately transgress the boundaries traditionally separating the intimate, the evocative, and the prophetic from the prosaic concerns of detailed explanatory conjectures and programmatic proposals. The task of making discourses that more fully combine realism, practicality, and detail with visionary fire, the moves inside the context with the moves about the context, is an integral part of the radical project. We have to strive for this confusion of discourses at every opportunity: in our most ambitious efforts at social understanding as well as in our particular practices of legal, moral, and party-political controversy.

The Explanatory Themes in Their Implicit Polemical Setting

The introductory volume (*Social Theory: Its Situation and Its Task*) presented the critical diagnosis that constitutes the point of departure for the explanatory and programmatic theory of *Politics*. In *False Necessity*, the first part of the work, this polemical setting remains almost entirely implicit; I offer here an affirmative view. In order, however, to fix more clearly the scope and the intentions of this constructive argument, it may help to make some aspects of the concealed controversial setting explicit, highlighting ideas the preliminary book left undeveloped.

Social Theory: Its Situation and Its Task distinguished two types of social analysis that jointly define the current predicament of social and historical studies: deep-structure theory and positivist (or empiricist or conventional) social science. Let me recall briefly the characteristics of each.

Deep-structure analysis represents the major though by no means the exclusive element in many of the comprehensive social theories that come down to us from the nineteenth and early twentieth centuries – the theories that contemporary social scientists often deride as "grand theory." Marxism is the most coherent and influential statement of the deep-logic style, although we can easily find in the works of Marx and his followers many ideas that not only resist assimilation to deep-structure thought but contribute to its reconstruction. Three recurrent explanatory practices distinguish this tradition of social thought.

The first characteristic operation of deep-structure analysis is the effort to distinguish in every historical situation the routines of practical and imaginative conflict from the basic framework, structure, or context that shapes these ordinary disputes while resisting their subversive effects. Deep-logic theories define such frameworks to include institutional arrangements, imaginative preconceptions, or some combination of both. The second defining operation is the identification of this framework as an example of an indivisible and repeatable type of social organization: indivisible because its elements stand or fall as a single piece and repeatable because it can emerge at different times in different societies (even if it always occurs at the same point in a sequence of stages of organization). The third typical move of deep-structure analysis is the effort to explain the identity and the realization of these indivisible and repeatable types on the basis of lawlike tendencies or deep-seated economic, organizational, and psychological constraints. These constraints or tendencies yield a list of possible social worlds or a compulsive sequence of stages of social organization. Notice, then, that this threefold description of deep-structure analysis embraces both evolutionary and nonevolutionary styles of theorizing. Marxism stands preeminent among the former. The latter has never had an elaborate statement, although economics (which has since become the model for chief variants of positivist social science) once promised to supply it.

The later history of deep-structure theories is one of attempts to deal with the difficulties of reenacting these three key mental operations in the face of inconvenient facts and resistant experience. Two related difficulties stand out; they refer to the second and third deep-structure moves. On the one hand, there does not seem to be a finite list of possible types of organization or a small number of possible trajectories of social evolution. On the other hand, the alleged lawlike tendencies or determining constraints fail to explain the actual identity and sequence of frameworks for social life. The explanatory failure of the would-be laws is obscured only when they are left so vague that they can be made, retrospectively, to explain anything.

The proponents of deep-structure social analysis deal with these difficulties by diluting their original claims. They may, for example, replace a unilinear evolution with the idea of a small number of alternative trajectories of social change. But each such loosening turns out to be both too much and not enough. It is too much to safeguard the earlier, stronger theory against a slide into vacuity. It is not enough to meet the initial objections or other objections in their spirit. The theorist finds himself driven to ever greater concessions. He holds on for fear that if he did not he would fall into theoretical nihilism and lose the intellectual basis for a critical perspective on society. The leftist experiences an additional reason for reluctance: the canonical status to which socialist movements raised Marxism often makes a repudiation of Marxist premises seem like a betrayal of the leftist cause.

The other major component of the contemporary situation of social thought is positivist, empiricist, or conventional social science. This mode of analysis sees social life as an interminable series of episodes of interest accommodation and problem solving. It denies the primacy of the contrast between the shaping context and the shaped routines and therefore also slights the discontinuities among contexts. The practical consequence of this denial is the weakening of our ability to see a whole institutional and imaginative ordering of social life as something connected, distinctive, and replaceable.

But the problem of social frameworks and of their influence upon the routine conflicts that take place within them cannot easily be avoided. Even the most prosaic activities of collective problem solving or interest balancing assume limits on acceptable solutions or compromises and procedures for identifying and ranking problems or interests. In short, they assume, under other names, the existence of a framework. The main variants of positivist social science can therefore be distinguished by the explanatory practices that enable them both to acknowledge the problem of the framework and to confine the implications of this acknowledgment.

The strategy of agnosticism (evident, for example, in the most austere branches of microeconomics) is to offer an analytic apparatus, free of independent causal content, and designed to serve disciplines expected to possess their own, independently justified explanatory conjectures. But the responsibility to come up with a view of contexts, of their genesis and internal constitution, does not go away; it merely shifts to another discipline.

The strategy of idealization treats the choice of a framework by analogy to the choice of optimal solutions or accommodations within a framework. Thus, the more propagandistic, overtly ideological forms of right-wing economics identify particular economic institutions with the free market and treat this particular version of the market as the device that makes efficient resource allocation possible. But the pure logic of maximizing choice can apply to all market or nonmarket orders, and market systems can take any number of concrete institutional forms, some of them far removed from the arrangements the conservative economists have in mind. The point can be generalized: we can never explain the making and transformation of contexts by the same relatively straightforward and uncontroversial means with which we explain decisions and outcomes within these contexts.

The strategy of hollow concession recognizes this last point in principle but fails to draw out the consequences of this recognition for the actual practice of explanation. Thus, the neo-Keynesian macroeconomists may concede as trivial that relations among aggregate economic phenomena such as inflation and unemployment depend upon particular institutional arrangements: say, the form and depth of trade unionism or the relation of national governments to organized labor and central banks. Yet the content of their discipline continues to be an analysis of economic movements against an institutional background taken as given rather than an inquiry into the interplay between economic facts and institutional constraints. Protracted stagnation in institutional reform may perpetuate certain relations among economic phenomena. It may therefore also invite the misleading conclusion that these relations are lawlike constraints, inherent in very general and vaguely defined types of economic organization, such as a regulated market economy. In fact these apparent laws depend upon very detailed and relatively ad hoc institutional configurations. As soon as any element of this institutional framework begins to change, the supposed laws start to break down.

The explanatory theory of *False Necessity* represents the constructive sequel to a polemic against both deep-structure social analysis and positivist social science. But the methods and insights available for the execution of this task come chiefly from the self-criticism and self-correction of these same two traditions of social thought. The materials and even the principles of a more tenable view are already at hand.

Neither deep-structure social analysis nor positivist social science can solve the problem that provides the point of departure for the explanatory argument of this book: the problem of explaining the content and the persistence of the cycles of reform and retrenchment in contemporary societies. Positivist social science cannot do it because the force of practical constraints and the tension among organized interests fail to explain the tenacity and the substance of these cycles until we also take into account the restrictive influence of the framework of institutions and ideas within which those interests and constraints operate. But positivist social science denies us a way to understand such frameworks: their internal composition, their genesis, and their influence upon the routines that they shape.

Deep-structure social analysis is equally powerless to elucidate the cycles of reform and retrenchment. As soon as we define the formative institutional and imaginative contexts with enough detail to explain the routines of conflict and policy that take place within them we discover that these contexts are too detailed – too mired in historical particulars – to exemplify plausibly an indivisible and repeatable type of social organization. The inability of deep-logic social theory to come to terms with the problem of the reform cycles is merely a symptom of its difficulty in squaring historical research and practical experience with belief in a list of types of social organization, ruled by an evolutionary dynamic or by deep-seated economic, organizational, or psychological imperatives.

The explanatory theory worked out in this book recognizes the shaped or structured quality of social life: the distinction between the routine moves within an institutional and imaginative context of social life and the more radical conflicts about this context. Because it takes this distinction seriously it also emphasizes the distinctiveness of the forms of social life these contexts support. But it describes and explains these contexts without resort to the ideas of a list of possible social worlds or of possible pathways of social evolution. Nor does it invoke the tendencies or constraints that might generate such a list. Though acknowledging the power that connected sets of institutional arrangements and imaginative preconceptions exercise over us, it does not turn this acknowledgment into an occasion to treat history as the enactment of a prewritten script and to treat society as a product of unmade laws. Thus, this theory accepts the first characteristic move of deep-structure analysis while rejecting the other two moves: the subsumption of the framework under an indivisible and repeatable type and the search for general laws governing the identity, the actualization, and the succession of such types. The outcome is not to abandon generalizing social and historical explanations but to transform them in content and character. The proposed view is at least as comprehensive and aggressive in its claims as the original, hardcore version of a deep-logic system such as Marxism.

Unlike positivist social science this theory recognizes the ubiquity of the contrast between transformative and routine activity. But unlike deep-structure analysis it also affirms that we can diminish the force of this contrast and enlarge the sense in which an institutional and imaginative order of social life stands open to revision. We can efface this contrast by the right social inventions. Unlike positivist social science this theory insists upon the connectedness of the elements that make up a formative context of social life. But unlike deep-structure thought it does so without falling into the prejudice that each framework exemplifies one of a series of possible social worlds or of necessary evolutionary stages. Unlike positivist social science it gives weight to the influence that entrenched institutional and imaginative contexts exert upon ordinary action and petty conflict. But unlike deep-logic theories it also does justice to our astonishing ability to act at times as if these contexts were powerless and our allegiance to them a mere ploy we were waiting to cast aside. Like deep-logic analysis it proposes a way of representing and explaining the transformation of routine-shaping or rule-producing frameworks. But unlike deep-logic argument it does not portray such changes as if they were themselves governed by a rule-bound structure. In all these ways the theory does more than offer a different explanation; it revises our received sense of what explaining a state of affairs means.

Only a theory that satisfies these demanding criteria can draw out of a view of human activity that emphasizes our ability to revise our imaginative and institutional contexts a detailed understanding of society. Only such a theory can allow us to integrate theory and historiography without forever diluting the former and distorting the latter. Only such a theory can overcome the illusory contrast between the perspective of the theorist or the historian and the quality of lived experience, a quality that includes both an awareness of messy constraints reflecting no higher rational order and a constant redis-covery of the surprising transformative opportunities that emerge in the very midst of these same constraints. Only such a theory can teach us how we may empower ourselves, and cleanse social life of some of its taint of domination and depersonalization, by gaining greater mastery over the contexts of our activity. Only such a theory can avoid the betrayal of this teaching that occurs whenever we present empowerment or equality as the predetermined outcome of a relentless historical progression.

The Programmatic Themes in Their Implicit Polemical Setting

The explanatory theory presented in *False Necessity* stands in close connection with a program for social reconstruction. The argument of the book should therefore also be read against the background of an implicit programmatic controversy. It is customary to criticize normative political theories from the angle of the substantive ideals that they enshrine and of the justificatory arguments that support these ideals. One of the many reasons why such debates are so often frustrating, and the claims of the contending doctrines so unpersua-sive, is the lack of clarity about the translation of these commitments into particular institutional arrangements and social practices. We hear an ideal attractively though vaguely described. We wonder what it will actually be like when realized in a going form of social life. We hear another ideal disparaged as unrealistic because it falsely promises to reconcile all good things and fails to acknowledge the tensions between, say, freedom and paternalism, or autonomy and community, or heartfelt engagement and critical self reflection. We wonder to what extent these tensions are indeed intractable and to what extent they may respond to changes in the practical arrange-ments of social life. There is good reason for our doubts.

Our accepted rhetoric tells us less about the content of such ideal visions than does the background of institutions and practices we implicitly imagine to realize these visions in practice. So long as we traffic in the ruling dogmas of society our doubts are kept to a minimum. If someone talks about political democracy we *know* what he means even if his litany of slogans and theories leaves us unen-lightened. We can refer to a specific tradition of constitutional arrangements and of party-political rivalry that is visible in the world we inhabit. But the more ambitious the ideal vision, the farther it departs from current solutions, the less self-evident the relation between the proposed model of social life and its practical form becomes. A theoretical understanding must then supply what established reality fails to provide. This understanding belongs at the center of normative debates and cannot be relegated to a subsidiary, informative role.

The implicit programmatic polemic of this book deals with the major modern political doctrines from the underemphasized but crucial perspective of their institutional assumptions. The conservative and centrist political movements in the Western industrial democracies usually take for granted inherited ways of organizing democracies and markets. Yet these current forms of market and democratic organization *can* be replaced. In their present forms they vitiate the very aspects of the conservative or centrist message that carry the widest and most powerful appeal.

The leftist criticism of contemporary societies, and especially of bourgeois democratic and market regimes, fails to appreciate the extent to which both markets and democracies can be radically reorganized. Preoccupied with the hierarchy-producing effects of inherited institutional arrangements, the leftist reaches for distant and vague solutions that cannot withstand the urgent pressures of statecraft and quickly give way to approaches betraying his initial aims.

The main point of the polemic may be restated in a way much more fully developed in Chapter 5 of this book. Sooner or later the conservative, centrist, and leftist parties that now exist in the prosperous democracies must resolve the tension between their programmatic commitments and the governmental and economic arrangements they normally take for granted. If the right-wing free marketeer, or the centrist communitarian, or the left-leaning redistributivist accept the established institutional order they find themselves repeatedly frustrated in the accomplishment of their professed goals. They can realize these goals only in compromised forms, and they are reduced to claiming that their proposals have never been given a fair chance. But if, on the other hand, the proponents of these movements of opinion do opt for an institutional reconstruction they tread a path for which their previous habits of thought, bolstered by the dominant styles of social analysis, have left them unprepared. They must develop elaborate institutional alternatives, a strategy for putting them into effect, and a view of social transformation to inform both their programmatic and their strategic ideas. They must also redefine their guiding ideals and their conceptions of the relation of these ideals to the aims of their political opponents. For if the real meaning of an ideal depends upon its tacit institutional background, a shift in the latter is sure to disturb the former.

These general points can now be made more concrete. The following remarks compare and contrast the programmatic orientation of the argument in *False Necessity* to some of the major familiar positions in the conflict of modern political opinions. Throughout, the central idea remains the subversive effect a disabled institutional imagination exercises upon our normative political ideas. Only a credible account of social transformation – that is, of how the formative institutional and imaginative contexts of social life are made and reconstructed – can free us from this disablement. Assumptions about the relation between our explanatory and our programmatic ideas envelop the controversy over substantive social ideals.

Consider first the classical liberal doctrine, in the form it took during its nineteenth-century heyday. The program set out in *False Necessity* shares with classical liberalism a belief in the connection between economic decentralization and political democracy. The ceaseless recombination of workers, machines, and organizational forms of production and exchange may be achieved by a centralized authority. It is certainly possible to design arrangements that render this authority accountable. But if the central power is to make and enforce allocative and recombinatory decisions, and to resist the pressures to maintain established jobs and firms and to make consumption increase faster than output, it must enjoy a considerable measure of autonomy. The combination of this discretionary authority with the direct control of matters vital to the security of the entire population makes it likely that economic centralism will first overshadow and finally undermine political pluralism.

But the program worked out in this book differs from classic liberalism by its refusal to equate political democracy and market organization with the institutional tradition of the contemporary North Atlantic countries. The traditional version of democracy combines distinctive constitutional techniques, characterized by a devotion to the dispersal of power and the distancing of mob influence, with a style of partisan conflict and organization that came into its own only several generations later. The traditional version of the market economy relies upon the more or less absolute property right – absolute in permitted usage and absolute in its temporal duration – as the primary device of economic decentralization. But I argue here that though these governmental and economic arrangements influence our whole understanding of the liberal ideal they also frustrate its realization. They help prevent a more thoroughgoing fragmentation of social divisions, hierarchies, and roles. They contribute to a social circumstance in which the principles of a liberal vision are more fully expressed in the practice of partisan politics – with its crosscutting coalitions of relatively ill defined and transitory interests – than in the quality of ordinary social life. Each person's opportunities and experiences continue to be powerfully influenced by his place in a resilient scheme of social stations.

There is a different institutional ordering of markets and democracies that further weakens the hold of collective categories over individual experience. The conflict over the mastery and uses of governmental power may be so arranged that it provides an occasion to subject every feature of the established order of division, hierarchy, and roles to the pressure of challenge. Once these alternative arrangements are worked out, in practice or in imagination, they in turn suggest a broadening of the original liberal vision. The goal of freeing men and women from subjugation can be reinterpreted as a particular aspect of what I earlier described as the project of the modernist visionary: the search for individual and collective empowerment through the dissolution of the prewritten social script. It hardly matters whether we describe the result as an extension of the liberal doctrine or as a replacement of it. The point is that we have disengaged the inherited message from its implied institutional setting and transformed its content in the process. You can already see how a similar analysis might be applied to the other familiar options of contemporary political thought.

Consider the extreme variant of classical liberalism sometimes known as libertarianism. The libertarian seeks to re-create society as a world of maximally independent agents whose collaborative relations all arise from freely bargained contracts. He wants to see government reduced to a residual role as a mutual-protection association. The program of empowered democracy defended in *False Necessity* shares with the libertarian the aim of freeing individual experience to the greatest possible extent from the overbearing influence of predetermined collective categories of class, community, or gender. But the programmatic argument of this book also reflects the belief that the way in which the libertarian proposes to accomplish this objective is misguided in two crucial respects.

For one thing, no neutral uncontroversial system of private rights is capable of defining the pure case of a market, maximally free from interference. We must choose among an indefinitely wide range of alternative sets of rules and rights, of alternative arrangements for decentralized production and exchange. Which of them are most decentralized, or most conducive to political pluralism, or even most likely to promote economic growth – these represent empirical questions that cannot be answered by the mere analysis of the concepts of a market economy or of a private order.

For another thing, the libertarian errs in his attempt to solve the problem of social coordination by in effect bombing out the state and all other large-scale or inclusive institutions. In order to increase dramatically both the decentralization of economic decisions and our freedom to experiment with the institutional arrangements for production and exchange we must devise institutions that subject capital allocation to more explicit collective deliberation and control. We can achieve this accountability of capital without abandoning the principle of market decentralization. Thus, for example, absolute property rights, still the primary device of economic decentralization, may be replaced by a rotating capital fund from which conditional and temporary disbursements or loans might be made to teams of worker-technicians and entrepreneurs. Then, government and the conflict over governmental policy would have to be arranged in ways that prevented this more deliberate method of capital allocation from serving as a tool for oppression, clientalism, or the perpetuation of vested interests. The key idea here is that we cannot come closer to the libertarian's dream of a less oppressive form of social coordination by allowing an allegedly natural private order to emerge as social interference recedes. We can more fully realize that dream only by inventing ever more ingenious institutional instruments for our objectives. There is no escape from artifice. New artifice must cure the defects of past artifice. We pursue a mirage when we seek the pure, undistorted system of free interaction. This pursuit must end either in an embittered disillusionment or in the apologetic identification of a particular market system with the abstract idea of a market.

The program advanced in *False Necessity* can also be compared and contrasted to a view that has traditionally had a more modest presence in the English-speaking countries than in other parts of the Western world. This view identifies the great wound of modern societies as the disruption of communal bonds that place each individual securely within a network of reciprocities. The wound is to be healed by the development of organizations intermediate between the individual and the state, organizations that can serve as a basis for communal life. This program is centrist in that it characteristically emphasizes the improvement of hierarchy through loyalty and self-restraint rather than through the radical subversion of hierarchical bonds. It is sometimes corporatist because the intermediate bodies, which may be productive enterprises as well as territorial entities, are to occupy a recognized place in the organization of the society. This place allows them to operate as veritable extensions of government.

The program of *Politics* shares several aspects of the centrist communitarian vision. It imagines a set of social arrangements that promise to help us reconcile more fully the enabling conditions of self-assertion: the need for engagement in group life and the effort to avoid the dangers of dependence and depersonalization that attend such engagement. Indeed, the whole program can be read as a vision of the forms and conditions of human community.

The centrist and corporatist program, however, remains ambivalent toward current institutional arrangements when it does not wholeheartedly accept them. Its proponents speak as if the existing productive and bureaucratic organizations could serve as the suitable vehicles for the communal ideal, with only minor adjustments. Workers, for example, should be given job tenure, they should participate in enterprise policymaking, and they should deal cooperatively with their employers. But the result of this acceptance of the underlying institutional framework is to both jeopardize and impoverish the communal ideal. The jeopardy consists in the intertwining of community and subjugation: so that the struggle against dominion, or even the imperative of practical innovation, is made to require the betrayal of present communal bonds. The impoverishment lies in the representation of community as a protected haven from which conflict is banished rather than as a zone of heightened mutual vulnerability in which people may entrust themselves more fully to one another, whether they conflict or agree.

A version of community less susceptible to the apology of dominion or the superstition of false necessity in social life can flourish only in an institutional framework that disrupts more effectively than current institutions the mechanisms of dependence and subjugation in social life. Such a framework must invite conflict rather than suppress it. It must weaken all the stable forms of social division and hierarchy and all the canonical sets of social roles that support community in its old, restrictive sense of a nonconflictual sharing of purposes and values. In preferring this revised institutional structure the programmatic argument of this book therefore also opts for a conception of what really matters most about community. The argument identifies this element as our ability to experiment, in a climate of equalized trust, with varieties of practical collaboration and passionate attachment that more fully reconcile the enabling conditions of self-assertion. The communitarian who begins by attempting to construct a more suitable institutional vessel for his commitments discovers that he has pushed the received communitarian ideal in a particular direction or resolved its internal ambiguities in a certain way.

Consider finally the relation of the programmatic vision of this book to the institutional program of the left. The radical left has generally found in the assumptions of deep-structure social analysis an excuse for the poverty of its institutional ideas. With few exceptions (such as the Yugoslav innovations) it has produced only one innovative institutional conception, the idea of the soviet or conciliar type of organization: that is to say, direct territorial and enterprise democracy. But this conception has never been and probably never can be worked into detailed institutional arrangements capable of solving the practical problems of administrative and economic management in large countries, torn by internal divisions, beleaguered by foreign enemies, and excited by rising expectations. Thus, the conciliar model of popular organization has quickly given way to forms of despotic government that seem the sole feasible alternatives to the overthrown bourgeois regimes.

The program of this book is a leftist program. It seeks the individual and collective empowerment that can result from the creation of institutional arrangements that undermine the forms of dependence and domination, and that do so in part by effacing the contrast between routine and revolution. Like all leftist views, it holds that only such an institutional transformation can realize in practice our ideals of freedom and community. But it differs from the mainstream of radical leftist programmatic ideas, so influenced by Marxist social theory, in several important respects. First, it assumes a background of explanatory ideas that makes the development of detailed programmatic proposals possible, legitimate, and significant. Second, it refuses to equate the market economy and the representative democracy with the particular institutional forms these principles have hitherto assumed. On the contrary, it sees in the development of alternative forms of democracies and markets the best hope for the accomplishment of leftist as well as liberal aims. Third, it draws heavily upon a tradition of institutional thought and experimentation to which the main current of leftist theory and practice has been implacably hostile: the tradition of petty bourgeois radicalism.

Thus far I have compared and contrasted the programmatic directions taken in *Politics* to a few of the major familiar positions in modern political thought. But the most significant implicit normative polemic in this book addresses an actual tendency of social transformation rather than the doctrines of a political movement. The single most attractive emergent model of social organization in the world today – least oppressive, most respectful of felt human needs, and therefore also most likely to attract the most diverse support of the most thoughtful citizens – is social democracy. The supporters of social democracy do not paint it as utopia, nor do they claim that all countries are equally ready for it. They recognize how hard it may be to achieve amid the extremes of poverty and ignorance when its achievement remains precarious in even the most favorable circumstances. They merely affirm that social democracy is the best that mankind can hope for, for an indefinite time to come. The great political issue before us is whether they are right.

As both an emergent institutional system and a familiar institutional proposal social democracy combines the following characteristics. The social democrat accepts the particular institutional versions of market economies and representative democracies that have come to prevail in the course of modern Western history. He pursues his ideals of redistribution or participation within the broad outlines established by this framework. He favors the welfare state. He wants to see the satisfaction of basic material needs guaranteed. He supports redistributive policies designed to redress gross inequalities of wealth and income. He is committed to see people more actively engaged in self-government in the places where they live and work.

But when you view social democracy as a practical experience rather than a programmatic commitment you see that these redistributive and participatory goals characteristically get realized within very narrow limits: the limits imposed by the economic and governmental arrangements that the social democrat accepts, if only because he views them as superior to all feasible alternatives. Thus, for example, the control that relatively small groups of investment managers continue to exercise over the crucial flows of investment decisions may require welfare-state programs to be repeatedly sacrificed to the demands of business confidence.

Finally, the social democrat sees the weakening of inclusive ideological struggle over the basic structure of society as something between an inevitable outcome and a desirable goal. The world of social democracy is a world where people can at last devote themselves to their practical concerns, by which the social democrat means, again, the form that people's perceived practical interests assume within the established institutional order of social life. Demobilization becomes, in this vision, the counterpart to realism and decency. Once the great ideological fevers have been spent, people can settle down to the prosaic but primary task of taking care of one another and making a practical success of their life in common.

This book can be read as an argument that social democracy is not enough and that we can establish something better than social democracy. The explanatory ideas of *False Necessity* provide an understanding of society that presents the institutional arrangements on which the social democrat relies as the relatively contingent and revisable outcome of a particular sequence of practical and imaginative conflicts. More generally, these explanatory arguments support a view of social reality within which the rejection of social democracy seems reasonable. The programmatic ideas propose an alternative to social democracy that realizes more fully the ideals that the social democrat can only imperfectly achieve and radically redefines these ideals in the course of realizing them.

But what is wrong with social democracy? The narrowest objection is that the social democrat cannot go beyond a certain point in making good on his promises of redistribution, participation, and mutual caring. He cannot go beyond the point set by his institutional assumptions and in particular by his assumptions about how market economies and representative democracies can be organized. His project, like those of the centrist communitarian or the conservative free marketeer, suffers from an incurable internal instability. The perpetuation of its institutional premises restrains the realization of its defining ideals while the reconstruction of the institutional framework invites a radical redefinition of these ideal aims.

When we view social democracy from the vantage point provided by the explanatory and programmatic ideas of this book, we can identify its key defect as the constraint it imposes upon the means of emancipation and empowerment. Once again, the constraint results from the forms of economic and governmental organization that social democracy presupposes and perpetuates. These organizational forms circumscribe our opportunities for practical innovation by limiting economic decentralization and economic plasticity. They prevent us from devising institutional means to free the practices of practical collaboration or passionate attachment more completely from the structures of dependence and domination in which these practices so easily become entangled. They keep us from affirming a more deliberate mastery over the institutional and imaginative contexts of our collective existence. We are too little under social democracy.

The force of these criticisms depends on the availability of alternative institutional arrangements that do indeed more effectively promote these connected dynamics of emancipation, arrangements described in *False Necessity* under the name empowered democracy. The objections all come down to the thesis that social democracy makes the liberal project of the enlightenment – the cause of liberty, equality, and fraternity – unnecessarily hostage to a transitory and replaceable institutional order. Once the liberal cause enlarges its sense of institutional possibility it merges into a revised and generalized version of the project of the modernist visionary and the leftist radical.

You may protest that it is perverse to hold up the image of empowered democracy when social democracy already seems a distant dream for much of mankind, abandoned to poverty and despotism. The program of empowered democracy may seem an open invitation to repeat with even more disastrous consequences the old leftist temptation to pass from a crude stage theory of social transformation to a disregard for the consequences of backwardness. But remember that many third world countries seem likely to achieve a measure of economic equality and political freedom only through the organized militancy of masses of semiemployed workers, agrarian laborers, smallholders, and radicalized petty bourgeois. Not only must they organize but they must stay organized. They and their leaders must forge institutions that sustain in the midst of routine social life a degree of civic engagement and grassroots activism that the existing democracies witness only at times of war and national crisis. The forms of economic and governmental organization developed by the Western industrial democracies do not lend themselves to this task. Designed to sustain only relatively modest levels of mobilization and conflict, they usually meet one of two fates in a third world setting. On the one hand, they may provide new ways in which to carry on the ancient game of patronage and clientalism. On the other hand, they may be used as the basis for a style of radical partisan conflict whose intensity and scope they cannot accommodate. Then, in the language of American political science, participation outruns institutionalization, and the society falls into a dissension that can end only in dictatorship or in a burst of institutional invention. Thus, the argument from backwardness may be turned on its head. For many contemporary nations social democracy may be the unrealistic choice. These countries may be able to escape governmental and social oppression only by catapulting beyond the social-democratic heritage to a style of democratic politics and of economic organization that more successfully effaces the contrast between structure-preserving routine and structure-transforming conflict.

The world looks different if you believe in the existence of an attractive and realistic alternative to social democracy. For our understanding of every historical situation expresses our tacit conception of possibility: our view of what things might become when subjected to varying degrees and forms of pressure. The explanatory alternative to deep-structure social analysis and positivist social science informs the programmatic alternative to social democracy. The ideas that inform and support the program of empowered democracy in turn advance our insight into the arrangements this program is meant to replace.

In developing the program of empowered democracy I seek inspiration in an aspect of modern Western political practice that until very recently has met with derision from centrists and leftists alike: the tradition of petty bourgeois radicalism. Historical research has produced mounting evidence of how much of the radical challenge to the emerging dominant forms of governmental and economic organization, throughout nineteenth-century Western history, came from skilled workers and artisans, technicians and professionals, shopkeepers and even petty manufacturers, rather than from the proletariat or the lumpen that have played so prominent a role in traditional leftist historiography. The program of this petty bourgeois radicalism was chiefly articulated by publicists who earned the pejorative label "utopian socialists." These publicists championed one or another version of what Marx called petty commodity production: the coexistence of a large number of relatively equal small-scale producers or productive enterprises as the mainstay of economic organization. The petty bourgeois radicals concerned themselves with the methods of cooperative production or distribution that might sustain such a system. And they sought to extend to the organization of government the same principles they applied to work and exchange.

Though the radical petty bourgeois alternative was everywhere defeated and repressed, its defeat and repression were both less complete and less directly attributable to inherent practical deficiencies than historians, entranced with a stereotype of modernization, industrialization, or capitalism, have generally supposed. Many of its proposals were in fact realized as deviant or subsidiary arrangements within economies mainly organized on different lines. These arrangements continued and continue to exercise an important economic role in the most innovative as well as the most retrograde sectors of industry. Moreover, these bids to establish a different form of industrial society were rarely put to a test that would make it possible to assess their advantages and drawbacks. Their proponents lost a long series of political and ideological wars; they did not fail at an impartial economic examination.

The practical objections to petty commodity production, shared by hardheaded centrists and radical Marxists alike, can be reduced to three main criticisms. First, petty commodity production is economically regressive. It does not permit the economies of scale and the market organization that encourage technological dynamism. Second, petty commodity production is economically unstable. The more successful petty entrepreneurs would soon drive the less successful out of business and reduce them to the condition of wage laborers. Only a corrective system of redistribution can prevent such an outcome. But such a system would then become the real economic order, and it would disrupt or dwarf the economic calculations of small-scale producers. Third, petty commodity production is politically unstable. The national governments capable of supporting such an economic regime would always be either too weak or too strong. The government, resting on a population of independent proprietors obsessed with their little worlds of property and family, might be starved of the resources that would enable it to administer and defend the society. On the other hand, if the government did obtain these resources it would soon overpower a social order bereft of large-scale organizations capable of counterbalancing its own authority. To these considerations, and to others like them, we may attribute Marx's confidence that petty commodity production is at best a transitional or a satellite mode of production.

These objections do indeed weigh against the unreconstructed version of petty commodity production: the version that presupposes economic decentralization through absolute property rights and representative democracy through the constitutionalism of checks and balances, the institutional solutions that in fact came to prevail in the course of Western history. The advocates of petty bourgeois radicalism can be faulted for having failed to appreciate the destructive implications of the emergent or established institutional order for their programmatic aims. They never entirely escaped the obsession with the thinglike image of independent, small, absolute, and permanent property, which was the downfall of petty bourgeois radicalism as of so many earlier dreams of yeoman commonwealths.

But suppose a form of economic and governmental organization that attempts to relocate a program of radical economic decentralization, social solidarity, party-political pluralism, and civic engagement within an alternative institutional framework. Such a framework might, for example, put a system of conditional and temporary claims upon a social capital fund in place of absolute property rights (the same solution anticipated in another passage of this chapter). But then to prevent the administration of this fund from serving as a means for bureaucratic domination or social conservatism, this new institutional structure would provide a far broader range of forms of accountability and participation, and of opportunities to try out radical social experiments on a large scale, than are permitted or encouraged by the inherited constitutional forms of representative democracy.

Such an institutional program might well be repudiated by the champions of petty bourgeois radicalism for giving up on the essentials of independent and eternal property. In assessing the program they would be in the same situation as all who ask themselves whether the proposed translation of an old ideal into a novel institutional form preserves what ultimately attracts them to that ideal. The program of empowered democracy can justly claim to respect the more intangible and enduring aspect of the radical, petty bourgeois cause, the aspect less tainted by the transitory experience of a particular class. For it combines respect for a sphere of vital individualized security and immunity with a promise of opening society more fully to unplanned experimentation.

The pressure under which the advanced industrial nations now find themselves to shift from an emphasis on the traditional mass-production industries to the development of more flexible and innovative enterprises, with their characteristically closer association of task-executing and task-defining activities, can provide one of many occasions to work out this alternative institutional framework. For like all shifts in organizational and technological style, this change can be accomplished in ways that either minimize or maximize the reform of established arrangements and of the vested interests they support.

The reconstructed version of petty commodity production, newly suited to the concerns of the day, can now be recognized as an inspiration to the invention of institutions that carry the radical project, the project of the modernist visionary, beyond the limit of social democracy. And the mechanism of the change – the recasting of deviant and repressed solutions as new, dominant principles of organization – is one that *False Necessity* presents as typical of the way in which we remake our contexts.

Plan of the Book

Chapter 2 of *False Necessity* begins with the analysis of an exemplary problem: the cycles of reform and retrenchment that characterize the rich Western democracies and the communist countries. Because these cycles must be understood by reference to imaginative preconceptions and institutional arrangements that are kept relatively constant, the attempt to explain them poses the question of how to think about the internal composition and the transformation of formative contexts of social life. We can then compare the contexts responsible for these particular cycles to other past or imaginary forms of social life that represent lesser or greater degrees of emancipation from false necessity. This comparison provides categories that can later be deployed in a theory of context making, and it suggests, surprisingly, a way to understand how the elements of such institutional and imaginative orders connect (Chapter 3). I then go on to analyze the genesis of the particular formative contexts identified in Chapter 2. The analysis starts with a highly schematic and interpreted narrative that both anticipates and helps justify a view of social invention (Chapter 4). The argument then turns to a program of empowered democracy, justifying the programmatic turn with a view of normative practice and of its relation to our understanding of personality and society (Chapter 5). This chapter describes and defends an institutional reconstruction of the contemporary social world that would carry farther the project of emancipation from false necessity, which is also the radical project or the project of the modernist visionary. It shows the changes in the institutional forms of markets and democracies that this advance requires. It suggests what implications the ideas that animate the institutional program have for a reordering of the fine texture of social life: the quality of direct practical and passionate relations among people. Thus, what began as an effort to free the understanding of society from superstition ends as the invocation of a form of social life that accords more fully with our character as beings who cannot be counted on to obey the rules and routines of the social worlds we make and inhabit.

A PROTO-THEORY

The Sense of a Proto-Theory

The whole social theory worked out in this book may well be seen as a development of the conception of human activity outlined at the beginning of *Social Theory: Its Situation and Its Task*. The following pages restate this conception briefly.

We must always settle down to particular social or mental worlds, the collective settings of discourse and human association. We cannot forever act as if everything were up for grabs. But neither are we justified in treating any particular mental or social world as the definitive, uncontroversial face of reason or civilization. No context can accommodate all the discoveries about the world that we might make or all the practical and passionate relations we might have reasons to establish. We can never resolve the tension between the need to accept a context and the inadequacy of all particular contexts. We can nevertheless diminish this tension by our success at inventing contexts that give us the instruments and opportunities of their own revision and that thereby help us diminish the contrast between context-preserving routine and context-transforming struggle.

This diminishment of the imprisoning quality of our contexts not only offers a partial solution to the problem of contexts but also enables us to deal with the other basic difficulty of our predicament: the conflict between the enabling conditions of self-assertion. To sustain and develop ourselves we must participate in shared forms of life. Yet all such engagement constantly threatens us with subjugation to other people and with the impersonal constraints of a social role or station. The creed of the visionary modernist is that the same practical and imaginative devices that strengthen our mastery over the established frameworks of social life also help us deal with the problem of human solidarity by purging group life of some of its evils of dependence and depersonalization.

I have shown in another book (*Passion: An Essay on Personality*) how this conception of our relation to our contexts can serve as a point of departure for a study of our intimate life of encounter and how this study can in turn inform a distinctive moral ideal or existential project. *False Necessity* develops the same basic conception in the direction of an explanatory social theory and of a program of social reconstruction.

Before the detailed explanatory and programmatic argument of *False Necessity* begins, it may help to suggest the elements of a rudimentary approach that links this abstract conception of our relation to our contexts to the social theory advanced in this book. This connecting set of notions amounts to a proto-theory: less the outline of a single, coherent theoretical system than the description of ideas that can supply a basis for many different theories. This proto-theory (i.e., not quite a theory) in turn represents but one controversial direction among the many directions that the basic view of human activity mentioned earlier can follow when applied to the explanation and criticism of social experience. Yet the proto-theory really does link the particular proposals and explanations of this book to a general view of human activity: the conception of our relation to our contexts can inspire a basic understanding of society, and this understanding can inform a social theory. The final, detailed results are what matter most.

The statement of this proto-theory serves two independent purposes. First, it elaborates the thematic and polemical introduction set out in the earlier parts of this chapter, suggesting how these ideas can begin to take shape as a coherent view. Second, it provides one way to distinguish the intention from its execution. You may reject much of the actual explanatory and programmatic argument of this book while continuing to sympathize with the rudimentary ideas sketched in the next few pages. Then, all you need do is turn the proto-theory into a theory better than the one offered in *False Necessity*.

Theses of the Proto-Theory

The initial idea of the proto-theory that anticipates the argument of this book is the existence, in every social situation, of a distinction between a set of formative institutional arrangements and imaginative preconceptions, on one side, and the routines that this formative context helps shape, on the other side. Once the elements of this institutional and imaginative context are in place, they reinforce one another. Most importantly, they bias the forms and the outcomes of the ordinary practical and imaginative conflicts through which we determine the social future within the social present. They do so in the first instance by giving different groups – classes and communities – a privileged measure of control over the means of society making: mastery over capital and productive labor, access to governmental power, and familiarity with the discourses by which we reimagine society and govern nature.

None of the routines perpetuated by a framework of social life are more striking or puzzling than the stubborn cycles of reform and retrenchment, the hapless, bungling alternation among recognizably second-best solutions to the absorbing practical problems of the day. Again and again, we find rulers and governments resorting to policy options in whose adequacy they themselves disbelieve. Practical constraints are rarely enough to account for these disheartening compulsions until their effects combine with the restrictive force of an entrenched institutional and imaginative order.

The most formidable statecraft is therefore always the one that can enlarge the range of possible solutions by changing this context. At its most ambitious, this transformative political art does not merely replace one set of institutional and ideological assumptions with another system of the same kind. It inaugurates a framework that is permanently more hospitable to the reconstructive freedom of the people who work within its limits.

Every formative context of habitual social life arises from the containment of conflict. It results from a particular, unique history of practical and imaginative struggles. It becomes entrenched, indeed it exists, only to the extent that it gains immunity to disturbance from the rivalries and challenges of day-to-day social activity. These frameworks of social life do not exist in the manner of the atomic structure of a natural object, open to observation and measurement. Nor do they merely depend upon beliefs that a changed understanding might dispel. They subsist in a practical sense, through the resistance that they oppose to a transformative will or to the back-and-forth of our petty group rivalries.

A framework of social life becomes stable only when it is reimagined as an intelligible and defensible scheme of human association: a set of models of practical or passionate human connection that are meant to be realized in the different areas of social existence. Until society has been thus reimagined, people cannot settle down to a definite context. They cannot even understand one another except as the exhausted veterans of a perennial war.

The stabilized social world that results from a containment or interruption of conflict depends for its continuance upon certain practical or conceptual activities. These activities – which go all the way from group rivalry and party politics to moral and legal controversy – constitute the most important of the routines shaped by a formative context; they renew its life and connect it with the concerns of everyday life. Yet each of these context-reproducing activities can escalate under favorable circumstances into context-disturbing conflicts. No stable, clear-cut, and rigid line separates the routine from the subversive. The basic reason why escalation cannot be precluded is the inability of any institutional and imaginative structure of social life, or even of a closed list of such structures, fully to inform our practical and passionate dealings with one another. Nothing can entirely reduce us to the condition of puppets of a formative context or of the laws and constraints that might generate a limited set or a compulsive sequence of such contexts.

One of the most important differences among formative contexts lies in the extent of their immunity to disturbance. Some formative institutional and imaginative orders make themselves relatively more open to revision than others. Some strengthen while others weaken the force of the distinction, which never entirely disappears, between the conflicts that they shape and the conflicts that shape them. Some therefore also broaden and others narrow the distance that must be traversed before a context-preserving activity turns into a context-subverting one.

The variation of formative contexts on this scale of revisability or disentrenchment appears unmistakably in the character of social hierarchies. For example, hereditary castes, corporately organized estates, and social classes mark the presence of institutional and imaginative frameworks increasingly open to challenge and revision. Beyond the social class lies the movement of opinion, organized or not as a political party. In societies distinguished by class hierarchies and by unorganized communal (i.e., ethnic) divisions, the political party has a double nature. It is both the voice of particular classes or communities and an alliance of people whose shared commitments cannot be adequately explained on the basis of their membership in particular classes or communities. In a society placed yet farther along the spectrum of disentrenchment, the party of opinion might become, in its own right, the primary form of social division. That is just what it temporarily does become whenever escalating conflict disrupts people's assumptions about collective identities and social possibilities and therefore also about their individual and group interests.

This distinction among frameworks of social life with respect to their availability to transformation accounts for only a small part of the qualities that may otherwise distinguish them. But the distinction nevertheless holds extraordinary interest for us because of its close connection with a host of ways in which we empower ourselves and make ourselves more fully available to one another. As a formative context of social life becomes more revisable or disentrenched the range of experience open to the recombining activity of practical reason broadens. The resulting development of our productive capabilities represents one sense of empowerment. Moreover, the disentrenchment of formative contexts undermines any stable plan of social division and hierarchy or any rigid system of social roles. It thereby enables us to reconcile more fully the conflicting conditions of self-assertion: the need to participate in group life and the effort to avoid the dangers of subjugation and depersonalization that attend such engagement. This more successful reconciliation of the enabling conditions of self-assertion represents another side of empowerment. But the most straightforward sense in which the disentrenchment of formative contexts empowers people lies in the greater individual and collective mastery it grants them over the shared terms of their activity. Because this range of forms of empowerment is achieved by creating formative contexts that soften the contrast between context-preserving routine and context-transforming challenge, it might be called negative capability.

People can act as more or less intentional developers of negative capability. One reason they can do so is that the achievement of a greater measure of negative capability may be implicit in the satisfaction of more particular material or ideal interests, interests more closely connected with other varieties of empowerment. Moreover, the intentional pursuit of negative capability does not imply the invention of formative institutional and imaginative contexts with fewer or less determinate characteristics, hence a leap into anarchy or pure negativity, but rather requires the creation of formative contexts with certain specifiable features. Some ways of organizing governments, economies, and families – to mention only the most obvious concerns of a formative context – lie farther along the spectrum of disentrenchment, and succeed better at producing negative capability, than others.

The advance toward negative capability can be cumulative, either because its fruits of empowerment are intentionally sought or because the social orders that favor it are more likely to survive and triumph in the competition with their rivals. However, this advance is neither irreversible in its continuance nor determinate in its implications. It is at most a possible progression, and at any given level of its development it may take an indefinite number of institutional forms. Moreover, it always interacts with another, very different type of cumulative, long-term historical causation. Each formative context not only reproduces certain routines but also makes certain trajectories of context change more accessible than others. Much happens just because of what happened before, and the more or less intentional pursuit of negative capability has to share its influence with the power of mere sequence.

A view of context making represents always just the reverse side of a conception of the internal relations among the elements that make up a context. A theory of long-term change that focuses upon the interplay between the influence of sequence and the attractions of negative capability implies a particular approach to the internal constitution of social frameworks. These frameworks are not indivisible packages that stand or fall as a single piece. They cannot be placed on a predetermined list of possible types of social organization or assigned to a stage in a master process of historical evolution. But neither are these formative contexts random juxtapositions of freely recombinable or replaceable elements. The arrangements and preconceptions that constitute them can coexist stably only when they represent similar levels of negative capability. Moreover, the institutional or imaginative materials that compose these frameworks can be harder to combine when they are drawn from very different historical sequences of context making.

Programmatic Implications of the Proto-Theory

Though the theses that define this proto-theory are extremely abstract, they have far-reaching implications for social explanation, social reconstruction, and even party-political strategy. The proto-theory suggests a way to break once and for all the link between our ability to understand ourselves and our denial of our freedom to smash and remake our contexts. This theory gives a central explanatory and programmatic role to the very fact that seems to represent the chief source of difficulty in our efforts to develop a general understanding of social life. We often seem to be helpless puppets of the institutional and imaginative worlds we inhabit. The social theorist is tempted to see in this diminishment of our freedom the condition of explanation. But the proto-theorist introduced in the preceding pages recognizes that we can always act in ways that violate the rules and assumptions of our established settings. Though some circumstances are certainly more favorable to these transgressions than others, no statable list of structures or of underlying laws and constraints can fully govern our structure-revising and structure-transcending activities. The proto-theorist invites us to take these activities as a topic for speculation and as a source of insight rather than as a limit to our explanation. The theorist who follows in his steps shows that the relation between the freedom of the agent and the constraints of structure is not a constant but itself a subject of conflict and change in history. He even argues that our ability to form contexts more congenial to our freedom is involved in all our particular efforts to empower ourselves individually and collectively and to cleanse social life of some of its evils of subjugation and depersonalization.

Such a social theory incorporates the first characteristic operation of deep-structure social analysis: the identification of a difference between the routines of conflict, exchange, or communication and the structures that shape these routines. But the significance of this operation undergoes a drastic shift when combined with the rejection of the other two characteristic moves of deep-structure thinking about society. The proto-theory points to a social theory that does not try to present each structure, framework, or context as an example of a general type: as a member of a closed list of possible social worlds or as a distinctive stage in a worldwide process of social evolution. Nor does the proto-theory invoke the kinds of developmental laws and hidden economic, organizational, or psychological constraints that could yield such a list or such a process.

The aggressive methods of deep-structure social theory have often seemed an unavoidable basis for social and historical generalization. The sole alternative has appeared to be the framework-denying practice of positivist social science, with its failure to acknowledge the importance of the contrast between routine and structure and the discontinuities among structures. The fact-battered skeptic is inclined to think that the errors of deep-structure social theory can be cured only by diluting its claims or by retreating to a posture of modest theoretical agnosticism. But the strategy of theoretical modesty turns out to be both incoherent and unnecessary. The proto-theory suggests an explanatory practice no less general in its scope and no less rich in its implications than the deep-structure theorizing it rejects.

This approach to the contemporary predicament of social thought has a special meaning for the leftist. Marxism has served the left as its main tool of explanation and criticism. And Marxism is also the clearest example of deep-structure social theory, though many of the devices that help us escape that theoretical tradition can be found in Marx's own writings. All too often, radicals have felt able to overcome the procrusteanism of a theoretically rigorous but very restrictive version of Marxism only by watering it down into a loose series of concerns, categories, and attitudes.

The argument of *False Necessity* follows a different tack. The aim here is to carry the self-transformation and dissolution of Marxism all the way, in the conviction that the outcome will be another and more defensible theory rather than a theoretical collapse. The result bears a complicated relation to Marx's own ideas, as well as to the teachings of other classic social theorists. In some ways, the view developed in this book represents an effort to vindicate the original spirit of Marxism and, indeed, of all classical European social theory – the effort to see society as made and imagined rather than as given in the nature of things – against the letter – the scientistic, necessitarian apparatus that betrayed the radical intention in the name of carrying it out. In yet other ways the theory of *False Necessity* salvages and reinterprets a wide range of Marxist ideas by taking Marxism as a special case of a more general and tenable account of social experience.

The explanatory aims of *False Necessity* are linked to its proposals for social reconstruction and political practice. The approach anticipated by the proto-theory gives programmatic thought a secure place. If our ability to explain social and historical facts depended upon the moves of deep-structure social analysis, proposals for social reconstruction would be both misguided and superfluous. History could be counted on to take care of itself; its protagonists could do little but recognize more quickly or slowly where things were heading. On the other hand, by denying us any credible view of long-term trajectories of transformation, the conventional social-science alternatives to deep-structure social theory fail to provide programmatic thought with the sense of realistic transformative possibility it requires. As a result, we are led to a bastardized and paralyzing conception of political realism: a conception that dismisses far-reaching reconstructive ideas as utopian fantasies and immediate, partial reconstructions as reformist tinkering.

The social theory developed here has a more intimate relation to programmatic thinking about social institutions than the preceding remarks may have suggested. This theory affirms that the cause of our empowerment requires us to devise institutional arrangements that advance our negative capability and that further rid social life of its mechanisms of domination and depersonalization. And it denies that current forms of social organization can be adequately understood and justified as an unavoidable stage on the road to greater negativity and empowerment.

The argument of *False Necessity* supports and develops these suggestions, drawing out their significance for the reconstruction of society. The radical project, the project of the enlightenment, the project of empowerment through the making of institutions that encourage and perpetuate the breakdown of social divisions and hierarchies, has bogged down in the face of many disappointments. The most important of these disappointments has been the failure of the twentieth-century communist revolutions to offer an attractive alternative to the institutional solutions that happen to have triumphed in the course of modern Western history. And the stultifying effects of this disappointment have been aggravated by the lack of a believable view of social transformation. Such a view is needed to account for the resiliency of contemporary forms of social organization and to supply a perspective from which to assess the realism of programmatic proposals.

We can reimagine present governmental and economic regimes, and the forms of social organization they help support, as incomplete realizations of the radical project. We can explain their stability without treating them as the necessary expressions of deep-seated economic, organizational, or psychological constraints. We can acknowledge the replaceability of inherited institutions without giving credence to the idea of a foreordained sequence that predetermines what can or must come next. Most importantly, we can formulate programs of social reconstruction that push farther the effort to achieve empowerment through the weakening of social division and hierarchy. These programs include ideas about the reorganization of governments and economies and even of our intimate life of personal encounter. They provide a basis on which to connect the leftist criticism of institutional arrangements with the modernist criticism of personal relations.

The programmatic ideas indicate an approach to political action. This approach seeks to identify opportunities for a style of political practice committed to generating small-scale or transitional versions of its more comprehensive goals. The ends must be prefigured in the means for their achievement. Nevertheless, in conformity with its rejection of deep-structure social theory, this approach denies that any one social group bears primary responsibility for the advancement of the radical endeavor. It rejects the belief that any particular class alliances or antagonisms are inherently necessary or impossible. It proposes a way to take an established logic of group interests seriously while recognizing that escalating practical and imaginative conflict weakens and shifts the influence of preexisting group interests.

The argument of *False Necessity* is doubly hopeful. It sees a hope of surprising insight in what appears to be a situation of intellectual entropy or confusion. It discovers a hope of social reconstruction in what seems to be a circumstance of blockage and disappointment. These two hopes connect. To follow this connection through its many vicissitudes in the stuff of our social experience and visionary aspirations is the central concern of this book.

2

The Making of Society Through Politics

Routine Without Reason

THE PROBLEM

IN the vast majority of historical situations, the struggle over what society will become – tomorrow or far in the future – takes the form of a tiresome repetition. Individual or collective contests over the use of the resources – of governmental power, economic capital, or technical expertise – that enable some people to set terms to other people's activities fall into a small number of set patterns. For example, political parties that remain or rotate in power constantly rehearse a small number of options in the uses of governmental authority. Even the struggle to gain office in the first place habitually falls within a narrow range of alternative strategies.

The people in such a situation may have little active awareness of constraint. They may feel an enormous gap between positions that, to an outside observer, seem barely to differ. They may detect in minor variations occurring from one moment to another cumulative changes that break the cyclical pattern. They may believe that the repertory of policies and conflicts with which they are familiar represents civilized life at its best. But the broader their knowledge and the more radical their transformative intentions, the greater will be their sense of imprisonment and even futility.

They will then search about for explanations: explanations of why the list of closed options is not bigger or smaller or just different from what it actually is, explanations of what it would take to rewrite the list. But the same insight that puzzled them in the first place is likely to undermine their confidence in accounts that show, in any strong sense of necessity, why the options have to be just the way they are. Their confidence will be undermined because it is in fact unfounded.

The problem of inexplicable routine gained its sharpest edge in a particular historical circumstance marked by the simultaneous availability of certain imaginative and practical activities. This was the circumstance of a society in which people had long become accustomed to see social life transformed through conflict. They had seen every feature of the practical or imaginative life of their society changed, even if in ways that no one had wanted or expected. People had even begun to consider everything that happened anywhere in the world as an experiment potentially relevant to actions that might be undertaken anywhere else.

Society did not cease to have a certain structure: a system of powers and rights that constantly regenerated a practical plan of division and hierarchy and expressed an enacted vision of the right and possible forms of human association. But this order had been repeatedly disturbed. Its repeated shaking had laid the basis for a special kind of insight.

Such insights and experiences invited a new understanding of society that would do more than hold up the mirror to society. It would not merely inspire men and women to seek the best possible version of the established social order. It would show people that the terms of collective existence can be remade and reimagined, more or less consciously, and that even the most stable social situation was only the temporary and precarious quieting of an endless dispute – a dispute over truth and right as well as over power and advantage. Such an approach to society confirmed and extended the experience that had originally inspired it.

Aspects of this circumstance of discovery and confusion, so favorable to an appreciation of the problems of reasonless routine, have existed at many moments in history. But the only time when it existed fully, complete with its theoretical interpretation and with the sense of collective experiments on a world scale, was in the period of the Western material and ideological assault upon the world, of the emergence of democratic mass politics, and of industrialization promoted at any cost to established ways of life. Yet the insights to be gained have long remained masked by necessitarian social theories.

Suppose you approached contemporary experience with a willingness to abandon, one by one, all the distinctive commitments of these theories. You saw social order as frozen politics. But, at the same time, you recognized that most real political situations, in both the large and the narrower senses of politics, continued to appear as the endless enactment of a small number of well-rehearsed variations. The forms of governmental and social organization that existed in the civilized countries of the world fell within a relatively narrow range of familiar alternatives. But why just these alternatives and not more? And why should each alternative present its rulers with a relatively narrow range of options for reform or retrenchment?

Where did all this constraint come from, and what kind of history did it have? In each society, it repeatedly defied both visionary intentions and practical ambitions. Its real content in any given situation and its transformation throughout world history could not derive from the formal analysis of markets and exchange systems. Nor – if the earlier criticism of deep-logic social theories is right – could it be inferred from the compulsive evolution of social forms and collective conflicts. Whatever the solution, the problem touches every period of history and every aspect of social life.

We find a similar story in societies at other times in history. Over long stretches of time, for example, the agrarian–bureaucratic empires dominating so much of world history witnessed the recurrence of certain characteristic crises and attempted solutions. These patterns reappeared so relentlessly, with so clear a felt contrast between the politically possible and the politically futile, that sometimes nobody could see them for the extraordinary restraints they were.

At any given time and place, people's enacted vision of society also turns repeatedly within a narrow area. The ordinary course of legal, political, and moral controversy stays within a set structure and stakes out familiar alternative positions. These imaginative routines help shape the course of practical conflict. To study the perpetuation and revision of such practical and imaginative constraints – and to study them where they are most striking and mysterious – is to appreciate a distinctive quality of historical experience.

In this chapter the burden of example and argument falls upon routine and cycle in the conflict over the uses of governmental power and upon the transformation of the formative contexts within which these routinized struggles take place. The main subjects discussed are twentieth-century societies where the susceptibility of social life to reinvention has been repeatedly demonstrated and recognized but nevertheless contained. People have marveled at the toughness of routines whose strength defied both explanation and effort. In the end, the argument returns to the general issue of contexts and their remaking.

The problem of routine without reason is, after all, just the same problem posed by the contrast between normal life or normal discourse and transformative conflict or transformative insight. It is the problem of trying to understand the implications of the contextual quality of our activities: we always come to rest in a provisional realm of practice or imagination but none of these resting points are the real thing – the true face of reason or of ourselves.

We cannot adequately understand the history of the remaking of such contexts through a style of analysis that explains their genealogy in the light of lawlike constraints and developmental tendencies. All the deep-logic social theories attempt just such explanations. By simplifying the pattern of suppressed and emergent deviation, of convergence and divergence, they miss the source of theoretical fascination and bafflement. But neither can we understand all the routinized settings of conflicts as variations on a total realm of possible social worlds that we can define, strongly and interestingly, beforehand. To do that, would be to treat the variations among routinized contexts as a higher-order counterpart to the variations within them: the same cyclical movements and repetitious constraints projected on a vaster scale. Any conception of possible social worlds turns out either too indeterminate to matter or too arbitrarily dependent upon a limited range of collective and personal experience.

To grasp what goes on in society and history we need a different imaginative scheme: a view of transformative variation that is no longer parasitic upon the hypothesis of convergent and indefeasible sequence or upon the definition of possible social worlds. This conception of imaginative work must show its power by generating concrete explanations. The testing ground chosen here is the explanation of the genesis and reconstruction of the contexts of routinized conflict over the uses of governmental power in contemporary societies.

The effort to address the problem of routine without reason has a practical and moral as well as a theoretical interest. Every attempt to carry out an ambitious program of social reconstruction implies an ability to identify and understand formative contexts of routine politics, in both the small and large senses of politics – the focused conflict over the winning and exercise of state power and the total struggle over the reproduction and reinvention of society in every aspect of social life. The problem takes on a higher significance from the standpoint of the vision of human freedom set forth in Chapter 1. A central theme in that vision is the progression toward a form of social practice that overrides the distinction between moving within the context and fighting over the context. This advance imparts to ordinary social life something of the quality of the imagination: its capacity to defy all sets of rules that can be formulated prospectively. Thus, the problem of routine without reason concerns both how we should imagine society and how we may recast it in the mold of the imagination.

A FIRST SETTING FOR THE PROBLEM: REFORM CYCLES AND FORMATIVE CONTEXTS IN LATE TWENTIETH CENTURY SOCIETIES

The Western Reform Cycle

Consider the experience of cycles of reform and retrenchment that took place in the rich Western democracies during the generations immediately after World War II. In each country, the struggle over governmental politics had its own forms. But all also shared to a greater or lesser extent in an experience of cyclical struggle over the uses to which state power could be put. Similar policy options were constantly exercised or combined. The endless rounds of conflict over state policy occurred against the background of a relatively stable way of organizing production and exchange that had spread to all these countries.

It was easy, at the time, to forget just how recent was this set of policy routines – and its background in the organization of production and exchange. Some of the underlying circumstances that held it in place had a long history. Nevertheless, these institutional or imaginative presuppositions had been under dangerous attack as late as the period between the two general wars of the twentieth century. They had gained a higher measure of stability only after a new arsenal of domestic and international forms of economic stabilization was built up during and immediately after the second of those wars. Until then, parliamentary democracy had not become securely established in many of these countries. Where it had, the typical policy options had not yet been clearly defined. Even the background style of industrial organization, which played a major role in the overall arrangements of the economy, was a relatively recent development. The characteristic forms of assembly-line work and of corporate organization were still being developed and diffused up to the middle of the century. Once all the formative institutional elements came together, they set the stage for routinized struggles over power. The cycles of this stabilized world proved tenacious. They resisted reform. They even defied available explanations.

One way to describe the characteristic content of this sequence is to recount the events that have habitually followed the accession to power of a political party committed to massive redistribution of income and wealth as well as to major reforms in the institutional contexts of power and production. Imagine, for example, that these reforms included attempts to gain some measure of political control over the basic flows of investment – a theme whose importance will quickly emerge from the analysis. A party with such an aim might be a labor or socialist party in a European setting.

Such a dramatic reformist intention, seriously held rather than rhetorically proclaimed by a party in power, remained a rarity in the historical circumstance I describe. For one thing, previous rounds of disappointment and defeat had already taught would-be reformers the price of vaunting transformative ambition. For another thing, the electorate's own sense of interest and opportunity had solidified in ways that made it easy to impose a majoritarian veto on any major transformative project. The political party with serious transformative intentions found itself readily pushed into an electoral ghetto. It broke out only by sacrificing, in fact, the greater part of its reconstructive aims and resigning itself to marginal redistributive adjustments. Why this happened is something my later argument must try to explain. But surely part of the reason lay in the influence the very cycles of reform and retrenchment I am now beginning to describe had upon the way people defined their interests and their best available political options.

Other facts, however, converged to create opportunities for the occasional transformative assault. One of them was the element of reconstructive fervor that had passed into the programs of the leftist parties from the wider conflicts of an earlier day. Another was the wedge opened up by the state's active subsidization of the economy in a setting of economic slowdown. Whatever the form of state support, it would create both the pressure and the occasion to assert some corresponding form of public control. This would be especially true when the subsidized were not primarily – as they had been in government-supported agriculture – a numerous mass of petty entrepreneurs.

As soon as the reforming party in office had begun to press its programs, it found its plan undercut by parallel and ultimately convergent developments.

There were relatively small numbers of people who made the major investment decisions. Any major threat of redistributionist and reconstructive reform would shake business confidence. The people with a say over major investment decisions would, then, exaggerate their habitual policy of caution and preemptive security. They would disinvest. They would promote capital flight. Or they would simply fail to undertake the bolder, riskier, and more long-term initiatives with a chance of bringing about quick and repeated breakthroughs in the overall productive capacity of the economy. All this was sure to happen quite apart from the preventive or reactive struggle that the outraged business interests might wage through their influence upon the agencies of the state and the means of communication. As soon as the economic reaction began, it exercised a destructive effect upon the designs of the people in power. It brought economic downturn. The downturn caused disillusionment in the electorate and dissension among the party militants. The politician who jumped too quickly to the conclusion that what was good for General Motors was not good for the country would soon learn the price of his exaggeration.

Another restraining process was likely to have been under way for a long time. The uncertainties, fears, and controversies that surrounded a serious reform threat would only hasten this process. Different groups in the working population would jockey for relative advantage. The better organized sectors of the work force would try to advance their wage claims: to keep ahead of an inflation already in course and to seize the opportunity, or parry the threat, posed by the transformative design. The managers would often give in to wage demands whenever they thought they could get away with it on the market: they understood the importance of a stable core work force. They could hope to survive in a product market where demand was often relatively insensitive to price and in a labor market where every group of the working population kept trying to leap ahead.

Each segment of the work force, in that sector of the economy, and eventually in the economy as a whole, would fight to keep up if it could not move forward. Some would lose. These were the less organized – the petty entrepreneurs and independent professionals and the unstably employed underclass – and the less lucky – the people stuck in declining sectors of the economy. But their economic loss would not be the end of their story. They might hope to reverse, through everything from political pressure and criminality to the very spectacle of their wretchedness, the verdict of economic defeat. The losers cried out for immediate rescue and relief: they could not wait for the state to redo society.

At the source of these problems lay an endless and uneven capacity to inflate the power of interests through organization. Both the endlessness and the unevenness were crucial to the outcome. Managers, investors, and workers alike could diminish their vulnerability to market fluctuations and change their market positions by organizing: in one case, through unions; in another case, through corporate enterprises with well-developed strategies of protection against uncertainties of the product, labor, and financial markets. But some workers and entrepreneurs could do this better than others. The inflation of interests then took a second lease on life: the interests devalued within the market could seek to revalue themselves outside it. Like the armies of Henry V at Agincourt, they could refuse to abide by the heralds' verdict of their defeat and go on fighting till victory.

Low-risk investment and unresolved bickering slowed growth, fueled inflationary instability – through both the preemptive wage contest and the pressure for governmental relief – and turned each group's attention from longer-run aims to the effort at survival and triumph in the race. Economic trouble brought political danger. The party in office might find itself out of power before it had a chance to put any of its initial program into effect. The chastened reformers or the new rulers might then turn to more modest aims: consensus over the basic lines of economic policy – and especially over wage differentials – in order to regenerate economic growth and finance the expansion of welfare services.

But whether or not the consensus they sought took the form of an articulate agreement brokered by government (an "incomes policy") or an outright wage–price freeze, it always came up against an intractable dilemma. This dilemma reflected another aspect of the inflation of interests. If the consensual or compulsory solution ben-

efited business and labor groups according to their actual ability to
disrupt the production system, the less organized would reject the
deal and strike back outside the market. If the solution tried to disregard or counterbalance economic power without in fact undermining it, it would be attacked or circumvented in the marketplace.
In either case, the deal would lack the show of moral authority: if
the experience of minute and uninterrupted conflict did nothing else,
it taught people that power, of one kind or another, produced advantage. It worked against the constant tendency to treat the frozen
power relations as embodiments of fair distribution because it kept
them from freezing completely.

In this climate of disappointment and decline, each group tried to
look out for its own. All but the most unfortunate and disinterested
withdrew into the resentful defense of privilege and possession
against rivals and the state. A party now swept into office that promised to give the investors and managers whatever they wanted and
to renounce, once and for all, the destabilizing reformist programs.
The trouble was that the government could never quite give the
businessmen enough: not enough to compensate for union militancy
or the threat of future political reversal or the newfound prudence
of the managerial class itself. Soon the audacious reformers might
have a chance to start all over again. Their chance was increased by
the coexistence of economic slowdown – aggravated by repeated
group conflict – with the lesson of the transparent connection between advantage and power, which that same conflict had taught.

Nor could the entire cycle of reform and retrenchment be bypassed
by a far-reaching breakup of concentrations of economic power. Any
strategy of competitive decentralization radical enough to break the
reform cycle would represent a transformative threat at least as severe
as the effort to seize political control of the basic investment decisions.
To break up big business and curb organized labor (so as not to save
the economy from the control of the former only to leave it in the
hands of the latter), the constitutive powers of the property right
would have to be disintegrated and redistributed. The free accumulation of capital would have to be replaced by devices that made
capital provisionally available to self-regulating enterprises and that
continuously broke up concentrations of wealth as they emerged.
The abstract idea of a market as a system of decentralized economic
decisions would have to be given a new institutional form.

In what sense were the different elements of this formative structure a single piece? Some parts of the total structure were closely
connected. All had to be at least compatible. Each bore the marks
of its coexistence with the others. Nevertheless, the formative structure was not a system that stood or fell as a whole. The change of
any of its elements had an immediate effect on the content of the

reform cycles, an effect that differed from the familiar change of position within the structure. But many elements that made up the total context might be replaced by an indefinite number of alternatives without fatally disrupting the coexistence of the rest. Each part of the whole had a history of its own. I shall argue later that this looseness of connection had remarkable theoretical and practical implications. These implications amounted to much more than the embarrassment of the deep-logic social theorist.

The Communist Reform Cycle

The same style of analysis just applied to the rich Western democracies of the late twentieth century could readily be extended to the communist countries of that same time. You might understand their characteristic reform cycles by emphasizing the boundaries that separated the outer limits of normal politics from the exceptional deviations that threatened to undermine the system, once it had taken form.

Imagine the communist regime at a moment of relative concentration of power. The whole economy stood under a coercively imposed plan. Suppose that the execution of the plan met with mounting resistance as the perceived inequities of treatment, the broken promises of leisure or consumption, and the disorienting misinformation about unrecognized bottlenecks and opportunities piled up. The rulers and planners now had two alternatives. One pushed them dangerously beyond the limits of routine politics. The other moved them toward the opposite pole of a well-known reform cycle.

They could exaggerate the centralist element and seize surplus, by brutal coercion, from any sector of the working populace that their masters had assigned to this sacrificial role. Then you had the war of the state against society. The only clear example – Stalin's war against the peasantry in 1929–31 and the years following – predated the emergence of the cycle of communist reform politics in the Soviet Union or anywhere else. It constituted part of the chain of events that had created this system of reform politics and that had helped close many alternative opportunities of social invention.

Once this routinized social world had been established, its rulers would not play lightly with the use of massive terroristic violence to impose a growth path upon a passive and frightened citizenry. State terrorism – extended to a large part of the working populace rather than limited to isolated enemies of the regime – had its own costs. It broke down communication and simple truth-telling within and outside the state. It forced the servants of the state to keep up relentless pressure at the same time they turned suspiciously against one another. It spread throughout the country the obsession with self-defense and survival. More generally, the war of government against society always threatened to become one of those episodes of escalating conflict in which everything would be up for grabs as erstwhile partners in rule turned into rival warlords and demagogues.

Thus, the rulers were more likely to respond to the problems of the centralist moment by reaching toward a relative decentralization. They did so moved by the desire to enlist some measure of collaboration with the plan. A qualified consent would have to produce what a ruthless coercion would otherwise need to exact. But it took a very special kind of decentralization to remain within the limits of this specific reform cycle. The managers of particular enterprises received additional measures of discretion to trade and produce on their own initiative and for their own account. But the ultimate authority of the central rulers over accumulation and government remained intact. The workers themselves might be allowed a limited degree of collective decision. But this collective organization of the workers could not be allowed to undermine the basic contrast between task definers and task executors lest the whole of the apparatus of control by state-appointed managers be endangered. Though "socialist legality" might be strengthened, it would not be allowed to turn into a shield for institutionalized mass conflict: the contest among parties of opinion, all the way from the heights of state power to the internal life of neighborhoods and workplaces. Decentralization within such limits invariably meant a handout of power and advantage to managers, technicians, and local authorities. They would in turn make such concessions to their own underlings as were needed to keep things going.

The decentralized moment of the reform cycle could not then be mistaken for more radical "right" and "left" deviations. The former pushed decentralization to the point where the central government – or the groups who held it – might begin by losing effective control over accumulation and end by losing control over the contest for power. The latter represented the change of guided grassroots participation into unguided mass conflict; an event that might easily arise together with its apparent opposite in the topology of the reform cycle, the war of the state against society.

Both the right and the left deviations might result from a failure to manage the reform cycle. Their immediate occasion could be the escalation of conflict within among rival segments of the party elite, some of whom would appeal to broader popular support, inspired by a blend of doctrinal commitment and factional conviction. That these deviations were always live possibilities was shown by their having anteceded the initial formation of the reform cycle. (Consider the Soviet Union of the New Economic Policy (NEP) and of the

First Five Year Plan.) They flared up, periodically, in the generations that followed the consolidation of the Soviet-style system. (Take the rebellious movements in Eastern Europe as an example of the right deviations and the Chinese Cultural Revolution during the brief period in which its instigators ceased to control it as an instance of the left ones.)

But whenever and however they appeared, these crossings of the boundaries of the reform cycle threatened to upset the established forms of power and production. They jeopardized the prerogatives of the ruling groups and (at least in the case of resurgent leftism) of the technical intelligentsia. They were repeatedly crushed by the reaction of the endangered governmental apparatus, the hesitations of their own leaders, and the military intervention of other communist powers.

Suppose then that the swing toward decentralization stayed within the permissible limits. New problems arose. The low-level authorities used every additional measure of autonomy to become still more independent from their rivals or masters. They tried to turn into vested rights the advantages they had gained for their enterprises and for themselves. The whole economy sank slowly into a welter of factional privileges and self-defensive actions within the cumbersome and resented framework of the central plan. This was a dreamless apparatchik's version of the ancient regime: freedom through privilege. Unless things got completely out of hand, a countermovement toward the reconcentration of power began. The reform cycle started all over again.

EXPLAINING THE REFORM CYCLES: THE HYPOTHESIS OF A FORMATIVE CONTEXT

The Conventional Explanations

The very existence of the reform cycles represents both a theoretical riddle and a political embarrassment. In the contemporary Western democracies these cycles bring into focus a blunt conflict between pretense and reality. For the societies in which these repetitious oscillations of policy recur are societies whose reigning dogmas of legitimacy claim to base social arrangements upon the free and equal wills of individuals, as citizens and as economic agents. Thus, the will supposedly asserts itself as majoritarian rule in the public realm and as contractual freedom in the private sphere. At a minimum, institutions, practices, and relations merely imposed by tradition or reflective of privilege are supposed to lack authority.

But the set of options that constitute the reform cycle seem to represent no group's and no party's preferred solutions to the prob-

lems of governmental policy. Their overall effect may be to leave a
particular order of privilege relatively undisturbed. Those who benefit most from this order nevertheless give every sign of favoring a
less circuitous, unstable, and anxiety-ridden route to the defense of
their interests. The reform cycles insult the primacy of the will.

The interest of the problem posed by these recurrent patterns extends beyond their challenge to a widely accepted conception of
legitimacy. For the problem turns out to be only a special case of a
pervasive feature of society and history: the existence of routines
neither chosen nor determined by deep-seated economic, organizational, or psychological imperatives. This phenomenon of routine
without reason draws attention to the nature of the social and mental
contexts we devise and inhabit. Our interests in freedom and insight
converge to give us a heavy stake in loosening the restraints these
contexts impose upon our efforts at individual and collective empowerment. But to loosen these constraints we must understand
them and to understand them we must reject the choice between
refusing to acknowledge them and attributing them to laws of social
organization or social change.

Traditional explanations of the reform cycles characteristically try
to reconcile them with the idea that current institutional arrangements
for economic decentralization and electoral representation provide a
flawed approximation to an uncontroversial mechanism for summing
up individual preferences. These explanations are compatible with
the recognition that current arrangements may be imperfect ways of
adding up choices. The imperfections may be said to result, for
example, from concentrated market influence or from the under-
organization and underrepresentation of certain groups in party politics. But such efforts to reconcile legitimacy based upon choice with
facts that seem to deny choice can play only a subsidiary role in an
approach – like the one developed later in this chapter and in this
book – that emphasizes both the formative influence of certain institutional arrangements and imaginative preconceptions upon our
practical or argumentative routines and the makeshift, revisable character of those preconceptions and arrangements.

Two strands of thought seem to reappear with the greatest frequency in the conventional accounts of the reform cycles. They usually come together: each takes explanatory pressure off the other and
makes it that much more plausible. Let me discuss them separately
and call them the argument from interference and the argument from
constraint.

According to the argument from interference the options that recur
in the course of the cycles of reform and retrenchment should not
be viewed as a list of the top preferences of groups and parties.
Instead, they represent the relatively haphazard outcomes of many

different group or partisan tendencies, coexisting in tension with one another: the resultants of the vectors that are the goals sought by the different groups. Thus what seems to be unchosen is in fact the outcome of the mutual interference among choices. For all their frustrations, the reform cycles bear witness to the vitality of democratic pluralism.

Notice that this argument can easily be reconciled with a recognition that the current forms of democratic rivalry and representation are very imperfect means for summing up individual and group interests. Some groups may be systematically underrepresented. Thus, the skeptical progressive tempers the argument from interference with an awareness of skewed representation. But the argument and the awareness can go hand in hand, qualifying each other in a familiar way, so long as the progressive believes that underrepresentation can be cured without any major overhaul of the current institutional forms of democracy.

The other strand in the conventional account of the reform cycles is the argument from constraint. According to this argument the contours of the reform cycle reflect a compromise between what individuals or groups want and unyielding practical constraints. Given current desires, expectations, techniques, and resources there are a small number of recurrent problems that policy must face and a small number of ways to deal with them. Every institutional system must come to terms with such imperatives. When the options continuously rehearsed in each cycle of reform and retrenchment are not deliberate attempts to satisfy these imperatives, they result from the futile, self-defeating attempts to disregard or escape them.

On an intellectually ambitious variant of the argument from constraint, practical requirements do not merely limit what each institutional system can do once it has already emerged. They account for the major institutional systems that exist in the contemporary world, notably the regulated market economies and representative democracies of the Western industrial countries and the economically and governmentally centralized Soviet model. Each of these systems has complex and detailed operational requirements, reflected in the reform cycles.

The argument of this book develops an alternative explanation of the reform cycles and of the many social and historical facts to which these cycles may be analogized. The centerpiece of this alternative explanation is the attempt to use the distinction between the influential frameworks of social life and the routine activities that they shape while disengaging this distinction from the necessitarian assumptions with which it has traditionally been associated. On this alternative hypothesis the reform cycles are largely shaped by the same formative institutional arrangements and imaginative preconceptions that mold many of the other routine activities and disputes of the societies in which they occur. These arrangements and pre-conceptions are loosely and unevenly connected. They resist disturbance by the ups and downs of the deals and conflicts they influence. But they nevertheless form a makeshift, pasted-together order rather than indivisible units. The collection of such past and future orders is not a closed list or a predetermined sequence, governed by lawlike constraints or tendencies. To understand the internal constitution and the occasional remaking of these orders requires a style of social analysis that breaks with the assumptions of deep-structure social theory and positivist social science. Until such an alternative mode of thought penetrates the specialized social disciplines, we cannot hope adequately to grasp the reform cycles or, indeed, any part of our practical and argumentative routines.

The alternative explanation does not deny all force to the arguments from interference or from constraint. But it demotes these arguments to a subsidiary position. Groups choose and conflict on the terms established by an institutional and imaginative structure that cannot be persuasively understood as an unbiased and therefore uncontroversial mechanism for adding up preferences. This framework determines the occasions and the instruments of organized social conflict. At a further remove, it influences the assumptions people make about collective identities – the groups to which they and others belong – and social possibilities – the alternative forms that collective action can give to social life. Through its influence on these assumptions, the framework helps shape beliefs about group interests.

The argument from constraint suffers a similar downgrading at the hands of the alternative hypothesis. There are indeed practical responsibilities to be met by any contemporary state and practical constraints on the effective ways of meeting them. But the implications of these responsibilities and constraints for policy acquire a semblance of determinacy only when we take for granted a host of institutional arrangements and assumptions about what relations among people can or should be like. These arrangements and assumptions cannot themselves be derived from practical imperatives. For though no social framework may survive unless it enables people to respect certain loosely defined practical constraints, previously untried and even unthought ways of meeting the same tests appear all the time.

In general, the more determinate the institutional implications of a practical requirement seem to be, the more reason we have to suspect that this requirement is less a test that a successful state or society must pass in order to satisfy its citizens and beat out its rivals than a restatement of what it takes to reproduce current arrangements in their present form. For example, the task of defending mass-production, "smokestack" industries in the contemporary Western democracies and of protecting the unionized labor entrenched in these industries may be shown to have implications for policy. But the exhibition of these implications begs the question of whether economic growth and the empowerment of labor (more inclusive and institutionally indeterminate goals) may not be better served by radical reforms in the organization and output of industry.

There is no simple way to show the superiority of the alternative hypothesis over explanations that play up the arguments from interference and constraint. In fact, no clear distinction exists between confirming the alternative and developing it. The appeal to the influence of a formative institutional and imaginative context does not differ sharply from notions that find a place in the repertory of confused, conventional, and unthreatening beliefs about society. That appeal gains its punch only by being connected with many other ideas to form an approach to the problems of social explanation that enables us to escape the embarrassments and equivocations of deep-structure and positivist analysis. The comparison of approach to approach rather than of isolated hypothesis to isolated hypothesis must occupy first place in a speculative work like this one.

Criticism of the Conventional Explanations

For the moment, let me outline four sets of reasons to prefer the alternative conjecture to the accounts of the reform cycles that emphasize the argument from interference and the argument from constraint. Some of the themes of this outline are worked out in detail in this or later chapters. Others are mentioned only in passing.

Criticism of the argument from interference. The established institutional forms of representative democracies and market economies do not constitute even a crude approximation to an unbiased system for adding up individual and group preferences. The first and most familiar reason why these current institutions cannot justifiably be so viewed regards access to the state. They enable certain groups to do better than others at deploying governmental power in the defense of their privileged relations to other groups. The reform cycle itself represents an example of this bias. For though reformers may periodically threaten the interests of the most privileged classes of society the overall effect of their deeds is to leave the threat largely unrealized. The existence of the reform cycles cannot, however, show that the underlying institutional arrangements favor certain outcomes and privilege certain group interests. The bias, if it indeed exists, may result from the forces adduced by the arguments from interference and from constraint, either through the direct effect of those forces upon feasible outcomes or through their more circuitous influence upon the institutional arrangements that produce the outcome.

The criticism of the argument from interference depends on the combination of a close study of the reform cycle itself with several other lines of analysis and research. One form of inquiry emphasizes the conflictual and makeshift character of the events that led to the formation of contemporary democratic and market institutions. The more these institutions are shown to be the outcomes of many loosely connected sequences of practical conflict and doctrinal controversy, intimately related to struggles over relative advantage, the less credible becomes the claim that they represent an approximation to an unbiased system of choice, or at least to the most unbiased system that practical necessities permit. The initial part of Chapter 4 pursues this theme. A second line of study uses comparative and historical analysis to explore the correlation between changes in basic institutional arrangements and changes in the distribution of group advantages and in the content and character of party-political and business cycles. (This form of research is mentioned but not developed in this book.) A third form of argument is programmatic. It shows that an alternative set of governmental and economic arrangements, with at least an initial claim to practicability, would in fact come closer than present institutions to realizing the ideal of a decision procedure unbiased among the occupants of different social stations. Here is one of the many connections between explanatory and programmatic arguments.

Criticism of the argument from constraint. The idea that practical constraints can almost always be met, and practical tasks executed, by many alternative technical and organizational means has become a commonplace of social and historical analysis. But this idea almost always takes the form of a belief in the existence of a well-defined set of solutions to a practical problem. Thus, in a society's institutional history there may be said to be branching points at which the society may adopt one of a number of clearly defined institutional responses to the practical challenges it faces. Having chosen one of these paths, the society moves down the road to the next branching. The trouble is that there rarely seem to be compelling reasons to restrict the class of feasible solutions. No wonder the theory of branching points works far better as a rationalizing retrospective gloss than as a guide to transformative practice. No wonder the set of practicable alternatives has to be constantly enlarged as new facts are discovered about the past and new solutions tried out in the present. And no wonder the idea of the multiple pathways so easily turns into a more subtle justification for the idea that history has a script although a script with many different versions.

Later in *False Necessity* I experiment with an explanatory style that dispenses in a more radical way than does the idea of the branching points with both the notion of the script and the deep-structure assumptions that guide its use. The experiment takes the form of both a schematic institutional genealogy and a view of context change inspiring this historical account. A major theme in the genealogy is the difficulty of understanding the actual content of current institutional arrangement as the product of successive approximations to an ideal of practical efficiency or of successive choices among well-defined sets of feasible responses to inescapable challenges. A major theme of the view of context change is that by ridding ourselves of the idea of the script in general, and of the conception of the branching points in particular, we increase rather than undermine the prospects for bold and comprehensive explanations in social and historical study.

The lessons of substitution. If it is true that makeshift institutional arrangements and imaginative preconceptions give a reform cycle much of its force and content, a change in those formative arrangements and preconceptions can be expected to change the cycles. If we could alter the character as well as the content of the basic institutions and ideas – the sense in which they resist transformation – we might even be able to diminish the place that unchosen compulsions such as the reform cycles occupy in social life.

A series of thought experiments begins to make the point. Suppose central governments remained tied to the gold standard or otherwise committed to sound-finance doctrine. They could not then promote redistributive measures in the distinctive mode that characterizes the particular reform cycle described earlier. The abandonment of the gold standard and the intellectual tolerance of deficit financing has in fact had a significant impact upon policy cycles and business cycles alike. (Remember Kalečki's remark that the effect of the doctrine of sound finance was to make the level of employment directly dependent upon the state of business confidence.) Suppose, on the other hand, that democratic governments had a way to prevent disinvestment or capital strikes through a more direct and less rebuttable influence upon basic flows of investment decisions than they now possess. In this event, the moments of retrenchment that characterize the particular reform cycle described previously would not exist or would assume very different form.

The changes in institutional arrangements and in business or policy facts that these thought experiments explore are not wholesale, revolutionary shifts, like the succession of modes of production in Marxist theory. Yet neither can they be assimilated to the repetitious patterns of a reform cycle. They are the stuff of what people fight about and of what they take for granted.

The Idea of a Formative Context

In every extended social situation we can distinguish a formative institutional and imaginative context that shapes ordinary deals, arguments, and conflicts while remaining largely indifferent to their destabilizing effects. The formative context – which I also call an order, framework, or structure of social life – exerts a major influence upon the form and course of social routines, including routines as important to the future of a society as the reform cycles described at the beginning of this chapter. Yet one of the hallmarks of a formative context is that it is itself hard to challenge, to revise, and even to identify in the midst of everyday cares.

A formative context of social life is partly made up of extended sets of institutional arrangements, some of them organized according to explicit norms, others less articulate. Prominent among these institutions and practices are those structuring the conflict over governmental power and the allocation of capital. A later section of this chapter discusses extensively one such group of institutions: those that help explain the particular reform cycle described previously. Chapter 4 presents a polemical genealogy of these institutional structures. The genealogy anticipates a theory of context making.

The other component of a formative context is imaginative. It consists in a set of enacted preconceptions about the possible and desirable forms of human association: assumptions about what relations among people should be like in different domains of social existence. For example, a particular conception of private community, emphasizing reciprocal loyalty, shared purposes, and the exclusion of conflict, might be seen as properly realized in the life of the family. The analysis of the formative contexts of late twentieth century Western democracies in this chapter sets this imaginative element aside. But later parts of the argument discuss its connection with the institutional aspect of a social framework.

A formative context puts a particular version of society in place of the indeterminate possibilities of social life. It shapes a complex texture of practical and argumentative routines that gain, by their continuance, an aura of naturalness and necessity. By far the most important of the routines it shapes are the conflicts over the possession and mastery of the resources that establish the terms of people's access to one another's labor and loyalty and that enable the occupants of some social stations to control the activities of the occupants of other social stations. The key resources that serve as objects of such conflicts are governmental power, economic capital, technical expertise, and the ability to enlist widely accepted ideals and normative arguments in the defense of particular interests and opinions.

A formative context guides these conflicts over the resources for society making by discriminating the occasions on which people deal and fight and the practical or imaginative tools with which they do so. It exercises a more subtle and diffuse effect by its influence on people's assumptions about social possibilities, collective identities, and group interests. The ideas about group interests that animate a set of group alliances and rivalries depend both upon people's identifications of themselves with different groups (their collective identities) and upon the agenda of live options for society, the range of social alternatives that seem to be within reach. The sense of active social possibility in turn draws life from the alternatives practically available to people: the division between what they can effectively challenge and what they must ordinarily take for granted. Similarly, collective identities need to be reaffirmed in routines of practical life, routines that an institutional and imaginative structure of social life favors or discourages.

By molding conflict over the mastery and use of key resources and by penetrating assumptions about social possibilities, collective identities, and group interests, a formative context helps sustain a set of social roles and ranks. The distinctive content of a system of social division and hierarchy depends upon the particular content of a social framework. It may seem far less obvious that the relative force of a system of social roles and ranks turns on the relative entrenchment of a formative context. By the force of a plan of social division and hierarchy I mean both the distinctness of its internal gradations and the power of its influence over people's life chances and mutual relations. By the entrenchment, immunity, or character of a formative context I mean the extent to which it resists challenge, revision, and even identification in the course of practical and argumentative routines.

A simple intuitive idea stands at the center of the conjecture that the force of a scheme of social roles and ranks depends on the relative entrenchment of the formative context that underlies it. This idea is the belief that seclusion from destabilizing conflict is a necessary if not a sufficient condition for the perpetuation of the differential allocation of advantage and the restraints upon possible action that an order of social division and hierarchy implies. The low-level animosities, rivalries, and disagreements that attend all our context-preserving activities can always escalate into conflicts that transform the context and thereby change the divisions and hierarchies it supports. For these hierarchies and divisions to be stable, things must be so arranged that the escalation is less likely to occur.

If a scheme of roles and ranks is one product of a formative context, another is a detailed set of practical and discursive routines. These routines are not just loosely defined activities. They are recurrent patterns of economic, party-political, or governmental activity like the reform cycle, or typical moral and legal arguments. Once again, the content of a formative context governs the content of the routines. The relative entrenchment of the context determines how compulsive these routines are: the extent to which they are unchosen and the degree to which they are even mistaken for the natural thing to do, the result of impersonal practical constraints, or the commands of an uncontroversial moral order.

An institutional and imaginative structure of social life gives rise to a distinction between structure-preserving routines and structure-transforming conflicts. But some frameworks generate more of a distinction than others because some make themselves less readily available than others to resistance and reconstruction.

A scheme of social roles and ranks and a detailed series of accepted, even compulsive routines are therefore the two main by-products of an institutional and imaginative framework of social life. The effects follow so directly from the cause that they could just as well be considered part of its definition. The occurrence of a detailed texture of routines, roles, and ranks is much of what it means for a formative context of social life to exist.

We should therefore expect to find that the two effects are also closely and universally linked. A stable system of social divisions and hierarchies flourishes together with a series of relatively un-challenged practical and imaginative routines like the reform cycles. The force of the former must be related to the compulsiveness of the latter, for both depend upon the relative immunity of the form-ative context on which they rest. These connections may seem un-surprising so long as they remain vague. Later arguments put them to a variety of uses and tests and give them a basis in a more inclusive approach to problems of social and historical explanation.

Implicit in this definition of a formative context is a methodological thesis with far-reaching implications. The institutional and imagi-native frameworks of social life are the hardest of social facts: not because they are easy to measure but in the sense that they are both the most resistant to transformation and the richest in the range of their effects. They may be taken as exemplary social facts: for almost everything in a social situation belongs to such frameworks, to the routinized activity that they influence, or to the anomalies of behavior and thought that resist their influence. Such anomalies often represent either residues of a past framework or raw material for making novel arrangements and preconceptions.

These exemplary social facts do not exist in the same sense as the atomic structure of a natural object. They are not just there, waiting to be identified, surveyed, and measured. Whether they exist or how much they exist is not clearly distinguishable from the facility with which they can be disregarded, resisted, or overturned.

Neither are formative contexts merely mental prejudices that survive because certain groups credit them with a specious authority. They are artifacts, and makeshift ones at that, but they are not just factitious entities that cease to exist as soon as people stop taking them seriously. They may not long be able to survive a decisive withdrawal of consent. But they can often induce in those whose life chances and daily routines they shape a blank and despairing resignation that muddies the clarity of the distinction between consent and coercion.

The primary sense in which a social structure exists is practical. It exists both because and in the sense that people cannot easily disturb it in the course of their ordinary activities. It is relatively (though never completely) out of reach, and from this position of relative immunity it exercises its wide-ranging influence on social life. Again, the quality of immunity to disturbance is not just an attribute that a formative context picks up; it results from the particular content of the arrangements and beliefs that compose it.

Formative contexts differ not only in content but in character: that is to say, in their relative degree of entrenchment or immunity to disturbance. The more entrenched they are, the sharper become the contrasts they establish and uphold between routine and transformation and the steeper, more rigid, and more influential the social divisions and hierarchies to which they give rise. Formative contexts enjoy degrees of existence. This variation matters: the disentrenchment of formative contexts is bound up with many of our most basic efforts at individual and collective empowerment.

The idea that the sense in which social structures (and social facts generally) exist is the sense in which they become relatively unreachable and unassailable, shedding some of their artifactual quality, has never been entirely forgotten by a tradition of social thought that sees society as made and imagined. But for this idea to come into its own it must enter the basic categories of social description and explanation. It must combine with the awareness that structures vary in the extent to which they provide for their own remaking.

Criteria for Membership in a Formative Context

How do we know whether a particular institutional arrangement or a belief about the possible and desirable forms of human association should be included in the definition of a society's formative context? The preceding discussion suggests two overlapping and complementary criteria. To show how each element in a formative context satisfies these criteria is also to provide a partial justification for the idea of a formative context by demonstrating that it can carry out some of the explanatory work it is meant to do.

One criterion for the inclusion of an arrangement or belief in the definition of a formative context is subjective or strategic. This standard refers to the perspective of the social actors themselves. A practice or a preconception deserves to be included within the definition of a formative context if it is regularly presupposed by the strategies with which individuals or groups advance their recognized interests and by the arguments with which they defend their goals. "Presupposed" here means taken for granted as among the conditions that an agent treats as relatively fixed when he calculates how best to promote his aims.

Consider how this subjective standard applies to the discussion of the reform cycles. From the standpoint of the social actors the reform cycles appear largely as a series of conflicting but mutually reinforcing strategies and as a set of constraints and opportunities that these connected strategies must face. The important point is what the agent does rather than what he says, for he may claim to oppose an institutional arrangement with whose indefinite continuance he actually reckons as he goes about choosing the most effective way to further his objectives.

Thus, for example, both the attempts of big business and organized labor to protect themselves through deals with each other, and the effort of the unorganized working class and petty bourgeoisie to undermine or circumvent these deals through direct pressure on governments or social conscience, operate on the same institutional assumptions. These assumptions include the beliefs that the economy and the polity represent distinct though intersecting arenas of conflict, that victories in one of these arenas can be partly reversed by triumphs in the other, that both the control of labor and investment decisions in the name of consolidated property rights and the social and technical division of labor are largely immune to attack by public officials, and that governments can nevertheless distribute benefits according to influences and principles the organized and the privileged cannot fully control. More detailed accounts of the repetitious strategies these beliefs support make it possible to identify their institutional and imaginative presuppositions with increasing precision.

The applicability of the subjective or strategic standard rests on controversial assumptions. One assumption is that the institutional and imaginative premises of different activities in a society tend to coalesce. But what certain practical or argumentative activities take for granted may be for other activities the very object of attention and controversy. Thus, in a certain society, the institutional presuppositions about the relations between business and government that are regularly taken for granted by economic enterprises in their dealings with one another may be a regular topic of dispute in party-political controversies. Or the subjects taken as given in the routine oscillations of business activity and public policy may be repeatedly subject to dispute in well-established forms of moral, legal, or "ideological" controversy. A related and equally controversial assumption of the subjective standard is that the strategic premises of different individuals and groups in the society tend to converge, not with respect to all institutions and practices, but at least with respect to the core set that makes up a formative context.

There is good reason to think that these requirements for the applicability of the strategic or subjective standard are often satisfied. Thus, for example, it would be hard for nongovernmental investment decisions and governmental policy to shift on the basis of radically different assumptions about which institutional arrangements must be taken for granted and which are up for grabs. The managers and investors would find their expectations regularly disappointed and their plans regularly upset by the policymakers, or the latter would have to forfeit any responsibility for maintaining the conditions of prosperity. Again, a society would repeatedly fall into a condition of Hobbesian strife if the classes and communities that composed it had little common ground about the institutional arrangements they took for granted and those they regarded as the very object of their typical conflicts. At a minimum, they would need to agree on the institutional procedures with which to settle their disputes.

The conditions for the application of the subjective standard may often be largely satisfied. But it is equally clear that they are never satisfied completely and that relatively stable societies differ widely in the extent to which they approximate these conditions. The subjective principle for the demarcation of a formative context occupies an important place in a social theory that draws no sharp contrast between the objective facts about society and the subjective experience of social life. But it needs to be complemented by another, more objective criterion.

This objective standard merely restates the terms of the earlier definition of the idea of a formative context. An arrangement or preconception belongs to an institutional or imaginative framework of social life if its substitution affects either of the two main hallmarks and by-products of a formative context: the scheme of social division and hierarchy or the repetitious and cyclical conflicts over the mastery and use of the tangible and intangible resources of society.

If the conjectures put forward in the preceding pages are correct, the replacement of any of the institutions or beliefs that make up a formative context alters the plan of social division and hierarchy. It also changes the form, the course, and the outcomes of routinized deals and conflicts like the reform cycles described at the beginning of this chapter. A change in the relative entrenchment or immunity of a formative context has a different effect. It weakens the compulsive force of the routines: the strength with which they drag us into the reenactment of a future we never chose. It also diminishes the degree to which our life chances and our practical or passionate transactions are molded by a predetermined order of social division and hierarchy.

Every change in the relative entrenchment of a formative context requires a modification in the distinctive institutions and beliefs that make up the context. But the reverse does not hold. There are an indefinite number of arrangements and beliefs, forming different social frameworks, that may stand at more or less the same level of relative entrenchment. They may alter the compulsive routines or the divisions and hierarchies of society without changing their relative force.

These many conjectured effects provide a way to determine whether an institution or belief belongs to the formative context of the society in which it exists. It belongs if its substitution causes any of the predicted consequences.

This discussion of the objective standard of inclusion assumes that formative contexts can be changed piece by piece. They need not be dealt with on a take-it-or-leave-it basis and replaced as indivisible units, in the fashion of modes of production in Marxist theory. Such partial substitutions amount to revolutionary reforms as opposed to either reformist tinkering within a formative context (e.g., one more move in a well-established reform cycle) or the revolutionary substitution of an entire social framework (a limiting case never more than approximated by any real-world situation). The view developed in this book sees revolutionary reform as the normal mode of context change. The thesis that contexts can be replaced part by part rather than as indivisible units immediately poses the question of constraints on the recombination and replacement of formative contexts. An approach to the problems of social theory that wants to dispense with the deep-structure assumption that such frameworks, structures, or contexts are indivisible would lose its credibility if it failed to explain why some arrangements cannot coexist stably within the same frameworks. An account of partial selective constraints on the replacement and recombination of the constituents of a formative context must be supported by a view of context making that makes sense of these constraints and holds up against historical experience.

An important qualification applies to the identification of revolutionary reform with the substitution of any part of a formative context. This qualification introduces a complexity into the use of the objective criterion for membership in a formative context. The replacement of an element in a formative context may sometimes have a restricted and focused effect – or, at the limit, no effect at all

– upon the roles and ranks, the tropisms and cycles, that a formative context shapes. Call such substitutes with marginal or narrowly targeted effects "functional equivalents." There seems no way to tell for sure just when what seemed to be a revolutionary reform will turn out in fact to be a mere functional equivalent. The occasional occurrence of functional equivalents represents yet another consequence of the nonexistence of any closed list or sequence of social frameworks.

You can therefore distinguish three ways in which an event, an activity, or a conflict may relate to an institutional and imaginative order of social life. It may remain within a formative context and occupy one of the options that this framework produces. It may revise the structure, thus changing the content or force of routines, divisions, and hierarchies, and disturbing other parts of the framework. Or it may supply a functional equivalent for an element of the structure and leave everything important intact.

The availability of the subjective and objective criteria shows that the idea of a formative context can be given empirical content. But even if we can successfully put the idea of a formative context to work, we cannot show that views of how such frameworks are internally constituted and of how they get remade represent a fruitful focus for a descriptive and explanatory social theory. After all, a different problem might be chosen as pivotal. The vantage point offered by such an alternative might lead us to view the connections and transformations of institutional arrangements or enacted social dogmas in another way. The case for this focus rests on the explanatory power and the critical and constructive uses of the theory that the focus makes possible.

The restraints upon the will that make people reproduce the present even when they want to change it and that offer them a set of choices that nobody ever really chose are riddles posed again and again in the course of ordinary social life. The mystery thickens as the theories that try to explain it away by showing how these repetitions and constraints reflect deep-seated necessities are successively discredited. Because governmental power and economic capital rank high among the means by which people create the collective future within the collective present, the limits upon their uses constitute an especially important example of unexplained constraint. As the argument develops, it will become apparent that the same puzzle reappears in different areas of social experience and that all these instances amount to special cases of the same basic issue: the nature of the conditional forms of discourse and action that we devise and inhabit. Our stakes in freedom and insight converge to give us an overwhelming interest in making these forms more hospitable to our structure-revising freedom. But to change the character as well as the content of the structures we must understand them, and to understand them we must reject the choice between refusing to acknowledge them and attributing their force and evolution to lawlike necessities.

Two Meanings of Reasonlessness

Before going on to the details of the analysis, it is worth pausing on a terminological issue. Routines like the cycles of reform and retrenchment discussed here are, I have said, reasonless. The slogan carries two distinct meanings in this book, connected in a way that helps elucidate the argument of this chapter.

The routines are reasonless in the straightforward sense that they remain unexplained. The available explanations fail to work. More precisely, the forms of thought that can identify the problem prove unable to solve it. The remedy for this brand of reasonlessness is simply the development of more successful ways of describing and explaining these closed circles of politics and policy.

Reasonlessness also carries here a second, more subtle meaning. The routines are without reason because, given current widespread beliefs, we have no good reason to acquiesce in them. Reasonlessness in this second sense may seem merely a corollary of reasonlessness in the first sense. Why – to continue with my example – should we give in to the reform cycles if we see them daily frustrate the aims of all political parties and if we cannot show that they necessarily have the form they do? Nevertheless, my argument not only severs the link between the two types of reasonlessness but turns the second type into the opposite of the first.

In the heyday of naturalistic forms of social thought, phenomena like the reform cycles were easy to accept as the perennial ups and downs of a single type of social organization. But in our time of partial emancipation from false necessity and disbelief in the sanctity of a particular hierarchical ordering of society, an explanation capable of inducing acquiescence in compulsions like the reform cycles falls into one of a few familiar patterns. Thus, it may explain the reform cycles as the undesirable consequences of something that we affirmatively desire: the outcomes of the reciprocal interference among the goals and the strategies that individuals or groups are free to pursue. The commitment to freedom of choice, the ease with which self-regarding actions check and frustrate one another, and the constraints on available resources and feasible institutions act together to bring about the result. Alternatively, an acquiescence-inducing account of the reform cycles may emphasize the influence of economic and organizational imperatives that defeat partisan programs. More ambitious explanations may present cycles in governmental policy or business activity as manifestations of the laws that govern the reproduction of a particular stage or type of organization – late capitalism, industrialized and bureaucratic mass democracies, or whatever. Such laws seem resistible, if at all, only through revolutionary change.

All these styles of explanation, however, simply fail to do the explanatory job. To explain the reform cycles and the many recurrent compulsions they resemble we must refer to the clumps of institutional arrangements and imaginative preconditions that remain stable amid the bustle of ordinary social life. These formative contexts emerge out of many loosely connected sequences of invention and conflict.

Because the formative contexts arise out of numerous intersecting trajectories of change rather than from a single, overriding dynamic, deeply rooted in practical and psychological forces, we stand a better chance of changing them. We can see how easily many of these past sequences might have turned out in other ways. We can hope to redirect many of the sequences going on now. We can change the institutional and imaginative groundwork of our societies and alter the content and force of the routines it supports.

This hopeful, open-ended message might, of course, prove illusory. As soon as the reform cycles ceased to be reasonless in the first sense – because we have found out how to explain them – they might also stop being reasonless in the second sense – because, having explained them, we would understand their necessity. The more successful accounts would uncover the driving forces behind the loosely connected sequences of events that produce formative contexts.

False Necessity claims that we can indeed move beyond the skeptical reference to the fragmentary histories of formative contexts: there are general causes and explanations beyond these histories. But they confirm rather than revoke the claim that history is open and genuine novelty possible. The general explanations advanced by the later arguments of this book suggest that formative contexts, or the recurrences and compulsions they sustain, are not necessary in any strong and interesting sense.

Thus, there emerges a quite different relation between the two senses in which routines like the reform cycles are reasonless. As the routines cease to be reasonless in the first sense, because we understand them better, they become all the more reasonless in the second sense, because we shall have all the stronger cause to credit their availability for reconstruction.

The explanatory ideas developed later in this book amplify, revise, and refine our initial sense of openness. They show how a formative context gets made and changed. They suggest that we can diminish the force of closed sets of social options, not merely replace some sets by others. They explore the nature of our interest in this achievement.

EXPLAINING THE REFORM CYCLES: THE ANALYSIS OF A FORMATIVE CONTEXT

A Simplified Description

The following pages turn back to the problem presented by the reform cycles. They offer a description of the particular formative context that helps explain these cycles. After depicting this formative context the argument explores two analogous settings that also pose the issue of routine without reason. Taken together, these explorations suggest both the importance and the difficulty of the attempt to disengage the distinction between formative structures and formed routines from the deep-structure, necessitarian assumptions with which this distinction has traditionally been associated.

Like the account of the reform cycles themselves the description of the formative contexts disregards significant distinctions among the basic institutional arrangements of different late twentieth century Western democracies. Nothing here turns on the validity of the idea of a supranational type. For the purposes of a simplified argument, designed to illustrate and develop a theoretical approach, it is enough to observe that these countries do indeed share to a very large extent the particular constellation of institutional arrangements I describe.

A more important qualification has to do with the exclusive focus on the institutional side of the formative context. A full account of the reform cycles would need to include the imaginative picture of society – the available models of possible and desirable association in the different areas of social life – that so deeply influence the course of collective conflict. The formative context must be mental as well as institutional. But to introduce this imaginative element into the analysis would be to raise the problem, right at the start, to the highest level of complexity. The view of institutional arrangements and the larger theory of transformation that this view deploys will therefore minimize references to the imaginative constraints upon action until the problem posed by these constraints can be reintroduced in a later section of this chapter.

Begin by distinguishing several clusters of institutional arrangements. The extent to which these institutional complexes depend upon one another is precisely one of the main questions to be answered in this analysis. My account of the formative context remains as general and undiscriminating as the earlier description of the reform cycle. The reason is not that the relevant institutional differences among the advanced Western countries are insignificant, much less that the existing differences can be adequately understood as variations upon a coherent institutional type; the idea of a limited list of types of social organization, each with a built-in institutional structure, should be one of the casualties of this argument. The generalization here is simply a compromise with convenience. But the very crudeness of the simplifications strengthens one of the chief implications of the description: no matter how sketchy it may be, any description of the institutional order that can actually illuminate the contemporary routines of political and economic activity brings out the particularity, indeed the oddity, of arrangements we often misunderstand as the natural institutional form of markets and democracies.

The Work-Organization Complex

The institutional arrangements that most directly affect the organization of work combine two generative principles. The first principle is the overarching contrast between two kinds of activities and the two classes of jobs associated with each of them. On the one hand lies the definition of productive tasks and labor processes; on the other hand, the more or less repetitive and specialized operations that comprise the processes and execute the tasks. The contrast between task definition and task execution remains relatively clear-cut as do the distinctions among the different operational acts that execute the tasks. Any change in production plans or processes that may be suggested by operational experience must be initiated by the task definers themselves. Material rewards and opportunities for the exercise of discretionary judgment alike are concentrated in the task defining jobs. The central contrast between task definition and task execution is, in turn, expressed and supported by a dominant organizational and technological style. It is also sustained by the legal rules and rights that allow supervisors to exercise, in the name of the property norm, an authority that combines technical coordination with an ill-defined disciplinary power.

The second generative principle qualifies the first by showing how the sectoral organization of industry affects the contrast between task-defining and task-executing activities. The largest productive (as well as administrative and military) organizations present the contrast at its most inflexible. Though these organizations may employ only a minority of the labor force, their enormous concentrations of capital and their privileged relations to government enable them to shape markets and to dominate the mainstream of industry. The detailed institutional practices protecting these economic organizations include all the legal rights and economic stratagems that allow them to protect themselves against instabilities in the capital, labor, and product markets. (For a description of some of these devices see the section on The Institutional Conditions for the Predominance of the Rigid Style of Industry in Chapter 3.) They are peculiarly vulnerable to such instabilities because of the vast scale of their investments, the relative rigidity of their processes and machinery, and the standardized quality of their products. Outside this mainstream, however, in the vanguard of high technology or in the rearguard of shoplike enterprises, a vanguard and a rearguard often barely distinguishable, a much closer interplay between task-defining and task-executing jobs or activities often takes hold.

The Private-Rights Complex

A second cluster of institutional arrangements underlying this reform cycle defines the character of subjective rights – the rights of the individual against other individuals and against the state, particularly insofar as these claims influence the control of capital. More specifically, these arrangements define the institutional context of the market. The system of subjective rights that enters into this formative context has as its pivotal device the assignment of nearly absolute claims to divisible portions of social capital: absolute in temporal duration (e.g., unbroken succession by voluntary transfer or inheritance) as well as in scope (e.g., no second-guessing of the uses to which these portions of capital are put except when they run up against the outer limits of public policy). This device for assigning capital becomes, in this institutional model, both the major guarantee and the exemplary form of all entitlements. And the many analytically and historically heterogeneous faculties that compose modern property are thought to belong, self-evidently, to a single consolidated right.

This idea of property presupposes, and is presupposed by, a particular doctrine of contract and of the sources of obligation. This view systematically plays down the genesis of obligations out of complex, only partly articulated relations of interdependence and reliance. It emphasizes, instead, the fully articulated agreement and the imposition of a duty by the state. For to allow obligations to arise out of trust and reliance would be to undermine consolidated property and the general system of rights modeled upon it. Contract and property law, of course, have never been entirely penetrated by these principles; they have always and everywhere included anomalies or counterprinciples that, though restricted to narrow areas of the law, suggest a radically different form of market organization. But these counterprinciples are easily quarantined or forgotten when it comes to defining the institutional content of a market economy.

The spirit of these dominant institutional arrangements can be defined in two complementary ways. On the one hand, the point is to measure out a prepolitical space, a set of social practices that, although theoretically open to legislative control and party-political debate, can in fact be at best marginally influenced by the course of electoral politics. This conception of a prepolitical framework of social life once received explicit support from one of the many corollaries of deep-logic theories of society: the conception of a repertory of forms of social organization, each with its built-in legal and institutional content. A country might choose, at a decisive revolutionary moment in its history, whether or not to commit itself to the combination of representative democracy with a market economy. But, once it had made this choice, the basic arrangements of constitutional, contract, and property law supposedly followed automatically. This conception has rarely been stated today as an explicit doctrine. But it continues to underlie, as an unacknowledged assumption, much of legal analysis and ideological debate. People speak of markets and democracies as if these abstract categories had a more or less self-evident institutional content.

Another complementary way to characterize the spirit of the prevailing form of contract and property is to say that this form connects a particular way of organizing a market, with all its effects of dominion and dependence, to the instruments by which the individual can defend his own sphere of autonomy. The link may be asserted self-confidently (e.g., nineteenth-century high liberalism), as when people claim that the availability of this specific style of contract and property rights belongs to the very definition of freedom. Or it may be affirmed more negatively and obliquely, as when people merely disbelieve that it is possible to organize a market on alternative principles without destroying freedom, efficiency, or both (e.g., the latter-day skeptical and disillusioned brand of liberalism). But one way or another, the fate of the idea of rights, as restraints upon what collectivities may do to individuals in the name of the collective good, is made to look inseparable from this particular style of market organization.

The importance of this institutional cluster to the reform cycle hardly needs comment. It gives bosses and investment managers the authority to organize labor in the name of accumulated property. It sets the basic terms on which disinvestment can frustrate reform. And it denies would-be reformers a tangible picture of an alternative style of economic organization.

The Governmental-Organization Complex

A third complex of institutional arrangements responsible for perpetuating the reform cycle defines the organization of government and of the conflict over governmental power.

Take first the organization of the state. The institutional arrangements that protect the individual against governmental oppression also keep the state from changing the basic arrangements of society. In particular, they prevent those in power from changing the formative context of power and production itself even when they were elected on precisely such a program. Any weakening of the restraints upon the state's reconstructive capabilities seems at the same time to endanger the basic security of the individual against oppression by his rulers. The constitutional arrangements that result in this formula for paralysis are chiefly those that constitute or extend the eighteenth-century technique of "checks and balances." These techniques characteristically multiply the number of independent centers of power that must be captured, or persuaded to consent, before state power can be effectively mobilized behind any transformative objective. Each source of consent constitutes a distinct arena of conflict with distinct procedures. And each focus of constitutional conflict creates opportunities for other quasi- or extraconstitutional restraints. Thus, the need to achieve consensus among independent powers within the state is reinforced by the need to conciliate any important bureaucratic faction or organized pressure group that may be a potential opponent. Departures from the constitutional techniques that disperse power and fragment choice seems to jeopardize individual freedom. That this link between the safeguards of freedom and the techniques of deadlock is nevertheless illusory can be directly inferred from the actual historical experience of modern constitutional systems. Thus – to take an example that will be explored later – many of the European constitutions of the interwar period were deliberately designed to enable a party in office to execute its program. Yet the traditional liberties often suffered no injury as a result. Indeed, they were sometimes strengthened.

Consider now the conflict over the uses of governmental power. The most striking feature of this conflict is the recourse to a rivalry among organized parties of opinion that is defined by the coexistence of three characteristics. First, the contest over who commands the heights of state authority remains only tenuously connected with the quarrels and concerns that occupy people in the midst of their day-to-day practical lives: partisan rivalries habitually fail to extend down into the institutions that absorb people's workaday lives. Within these institutions, people do not divide, nor do they see themselves as dividing, on the same lines that separate them when they act, episodically, as citizens.

A second characteristic of this style of party conflict is that the ideas around which parties rally are usually vague slogans, isolated moral issues, and promises of marginal material advantage to particular groups rather than serious plans for reconstructing the institutional context of power and production. This trait may seem to describe American parties of the later twentieth century better than their European counterparts. Yet the difference in the language of politics far exceeded the distinction in political practice: many of the categories and contrasts central to the language of European politics had been taken from those years after World War I when the fundamentals of social life were often genuinely up for grabs.

A third, less apparent, and more fundamental feature of this organization of the conflict for mastery of the state is the relationship it embodies and sustains between tangible material interests and programmatic opinions. In the societies whose party systems I am describing, the influence of the plan of social division and hierarchy has been weakened and the plan itself fragmented. The plan nevertheless survives, loosened but often all the more invisible and intractable. This shift in the character of social division and hierarchy – one of the many expressions of a partial break from false necessity – creates the circumstance in which the citizen typically behaves according to two contrasting logics.

First, he acts according to the logic of his place in the established plan of division and hierarchy. To this extent, he is moved by the interests and opinions of the classes, labor force factions, and ethnic, religious, or even regional communities to which he belongs. This logic is internally divided because his crude material interest as one who occupies a certain position in the division of labor may be redefined or overridden by his attachment to the ideals prevalent in communities that cut across job and class lines.

The citizen also suffers the influence of a second logic: the logic of his individual opinions, shaped by biography and character, by the voices he has heard and the options he perceives. This logic remains irreducible to the effects of his position in the hierarchical and communal scheme of his society.

The two logics constantly interfere with each other. At any given time, it is hard for the observer or the agent to tell whether generous slogans are being turned into the tools and masks of crude material interests, or whether, on the contrary, visionary aspirations are clouding the perception and pursuit of immediate material interests, and, if so, whether these aspirations derive from membership in a given group or from commitments that such membership fails to explain. Modern party politics take place in this daze of principled commitments superimposed upon opportunistic calculations. The novelty is not that this confusion should occur – for it reappears, more or less prominently, in every historical circumstance – but that it should so dominate the quality of ordinary political experience. The modern political party represents the clearest revelation of a historical circumstance in which the struggle over the state both reflects a social order that governmental politics help reproduce and reveals the inability of the social order fully to determine the ideas and decisions of individuals.

The failure to acknowledge more clearly this dazed quality of modern politics can be credited to both a conceptual ambiguity and a theoretical preconception. The ambiguity is the multiple status of beliefs about the social good as assumptions that help shape the definition of crude material interests, ideals shared within communities that are not built around stations in the social division of labor, and movements of opinion that defy the lines drawn by class and communal divisions alike. The theoretical preconception is that reasons rarely count as causes in social explanation. And the most available way of explaining adherence to political opinions is to invoke class and communal position.

The styles of governmental organization and partisan conflict I have described combine to fashion a form of popular sovereignty that can coexist with the stability of basic social arrangements. Many of these arrangements — and in particular the formative context of power and production that reproduced the plan of social division and hierarchy — remains effectively protected against attack. Radicals and conservatives alike had hoped or feared that universal suffrage, as the consummation of mass politics, would establish a state permanently at war with social inequalities. But the emergence of the governmental-organization complex outlined in the preceding paragraphs proves that popular sovereignty can be made to revolve within a well-defined circumference. A common prejudice supposes that this accommodation of the people to the settled order of social life results from a series of stubborn facts: the crisscrossing membership of the same individuals in different groups, the unavailability of realistic alternatives to the current forms of social organization, and the sheer materialism of most people's desires. But in fact the constraints upon both the partisan struggle for governmental power and the transformative efforts of reform-minded parties help prevent these assumptions from being put to the test.

To develop this idea is to describe the importance of the governmental-organization complex to the reform cycle and even to its specifically macroeconomic aspect. If the style of governmental organization and partisan rivalry were yet more hostile than they are to social experiments with coherent programmatic visions, sustained by mass support, the investors could more easily have their way. Of course, this elitist turn would not necessarily be in the interest of the investors, not at least unless extremes of inequality in the distribution of income and wealth were avoided and the economy already enjoyed a favorable position in the international division of labor. Failing the first condition, underconsumption would limit growth unless corrected by redistribution. Failing the second, national firms might find it all the harder to escape a subaltern place in the world economy. If, on the contrary, the style of governmental organization and partisan conflict were more hospitable to radical reform and collective mobilization than it now is, the reformers would not need repeatedly to bow before the investors. To be sure, this conclusion presupposes that the market and the democracy can be reorganized in ways that extend or perfect current democratic ideals. This possibility has certainly not been demonstrated by anything in the argument so far. But the first step toward supporting it is simply to grasp the distinctive character of present arrangements.

Alongside the work-organization, the private-rights, and the governmental-organization complexes, two other sets of institutional arrangements help compose the formative context of the particular reform cycle under discussion. These additional clusters reflect the combined effects of arrangements in the other institutional complexes, effects focused upon a particular aspect of social life. This is the sense in which they are derivative. But, characteristically, the combination depends upon social and intellectual compromises whose exact content could never be guessed from any amount of information about the other institutional complexes. For this reason, they deserve to be studied in their own right.

The Occupational-Structure Complex

This set of arrangements designates what classical social theory knows as the social division of labor: the distinctions among major occupational groups, distinctions connected on one side to the organization of work itself and on the other to the broader distribution of power and advantage in society. Consider some of the more general characteristics of the occupational structure in these societies.

First, the work force appears segmented in relatively distinct groups, each with its own more or less rigidly defined place in the division of labor. To a greater or lesser extent, each occupational group has a complex and cohesive social character: not only a given material standard of living and a distinctive experience of work but a set of collective self-understandings formed in a singular history of conflict and compromise. The first general characteristic of the occupational structure, therefore, is simply its surprising power to retain clarity and influence despite the absence of comprehensive religious and legal sanctions of the kind that support caste systems.

A second trait of this occupational structure is the rough but unmistakable correspondence between the place a group holds in the social division of labor and its position in the broader social distribution of power and advantage. The benefits of material rewards, independence at work, and prestige tend to concentrate in the same hands, according to the biblical slogan: to those who have, more will be given, but from those who have not, even what they have will be taken away. Indeed, this concentration of advantage seems so natural that both radicals and conservatives tend to treat it as an automatic consequence of the social division of labor.

The first two general characteristics of the occupational structure suggest a single discontinuous hierarchy. The third feature qualifies this impression by calling attention to the overriding contrast between task-defining and task-executing activities, between the jobs that allow for the open exercise of reconstructive practical intelligence and the jobs that are supposed to involve the routinized exercise of a well-defined task playing a limited role in a plan that practical intelligence has devised. The highest benefits of salary and honor usually accrue to the task-defining jobs. The force of this contrast is complicated and confused by its subtle relation to the distinction between manual (blue-collar) and nonmanual (white-collar) jobs. The white-collar job, however lowly, shares in the prestige of the highest directing social tasks, as if removal from physical labor represented, in and of itself, a sign of the dominating role of free intelligence and ensured a corresponding salary level. But a large, and even increasingly large, part of the population, all the way from humble clerical personnel to middle managers, finds itself cut off from any real experience of practical revision and invention. Many, including the low-level white-collar workers, may even be denied the material perquisites that would confirm the belief that they hold positions in the social hierarchy far above blue-collar laborers.

What relation does the occupational structure marked by these three characteristics bear to the three major institutional complexes discussed earlier? Perhaps these characteristics can all be understood as the direct results of acquiescence in the work-organization complex and in an approach to rights and government compatible with that way of organizing labor. The acceptance of the work-organization complex would explain both the preeminent contrast between task-defining and task-executing activities and the rigidity of the distinctions among occupational categories. For, as execution becomes separate from planning, each job must consist in the repetitive exercise of a step in the plan; whatever revisions of the plan the experience of trying to execute it may suggest must come from the planners rather than from the executants. Indeed, even the close correspondence between place in the occupational structure and position in the broader social hierarchy can be seen as the mere confirmation of the preference for this style of work organization.

One of the attributes that strengthened this approach to work organization in the competition with its more egalitarian rivals was precisely that it lent itself to accommodation with preexisting social hierarchies. The forms of private rights and of governmental organization that came to prevail in the course of modern Western history were compatible, as many other forms might have been, with this occupational structure. They both reflected and reproduced the social peace that guarded this structure against attack.

The view of the occupational structure just presented would deny this structure independent status as an institutional complex with an independent influence upon the reform cycle and make the occupational order appear, instead, a mere penumbra of the other institutional complexes. But this view is inadequate: it fails to provide a bridge to certain more particular characteristics of the division of labor that influence the course of routine politics and production in just the ways that merit the inclusion, in an account of the formative context, of the more or less institutionalized practices sustaining these characteristics.

The insight that underlies this initial, flawed view of the occupational structure is the thesis that politics create the division of labor. There is no self-directing history of professional techniques and organizational arrangements that could, by its own animating movement, define a system of job categories. The motion must come largely from the actions and beliefs of groups struggling over the alternative social forms that practical activity and practical progress may take. But the initial view of the occupational structure fails to take this insight far enough. The practical and imaginative strategies that generated this structure left their mark upon it. Thus, the division of labor in these as in all societies possesses further characteristics, each of which has a twofold status: the means for generating the structure, now remembered and rigidified, have become part of the structure itself. Each additional characteristic satisfies both tests for inclusion in the formative context: its continued existence is taken for granted by the habitual strategy of the parties to routine politics and exchange and its transformation would alter the content of those routines unmistakably. Consider four such features of the social division of labor.

The first characteristic describes the political transformation of artisans and of their ideological champions. For much of the nineteenth century, these groups represented a more formidable source of agitation than industrial workers. But their efforts to press for an alternative version of industrial society – a version that would give primacy to a more decentralized and fluid style of manufacturing and one less committed to the contrast between plan and execution – were repeatedly defeated. Some craftsmen turned into, or were replaced by, the skilled workers of mass-production industry. Others supplied personnel for the vanguardist sector of modern industry, the sector that allowed for more flexible production processes and less hierarchical work arrangements and that continued implicitly to offer a countermodel to the dominant version of industrialism. Any weakening of the institutional constraints or the international division of labor that support this dominant mode lent renewed force to the countermodel.

A second trait of this division of labor is the existence of a professional–managerial cadre that organizes economic activity in the name of an amalgam of property entitlements and technical imperatives. This group embodies the contrast between intellect and execution. The supervisory cadres did not perfect their present character until several developments had converged: the defeat of the early attempts to create an alternative industrial system and the reallocation of the artisans; the provisional settlement of the boundaries between governmental authority and entrepreneurial discretion; and the merger of legal and technical justifications for the exercise of authority in industry.

A third mark of the occupational structure is the existence of an organized working class that combines a specific occupational position with habitual political attitudes. The occupational position is the set of skilled and semiskilled jobs in mass-production industry, jobs relatively protected by governmental policy and labor-management agreements. One habitual political attitude is the acceptance of the existing system of industrial organization. Another is the abandonment by organized labor of the attempt to present itself as the people, a faction against the elites, and its willingness to play the role of a faction within the people, anxious to exact marginal concessions from managers, politicians, and businessmen.

A fourth feature of the occupational structure complements this third characteristic. It is the existence of an underclass charged with the most unstable and unattractive work. The underclass inhabits the periphery of the industrial system, providing industrial workers with a buffer against the cyclical character of economic activity and the society at large with the only people willing to perform the most menial services. The peripheral status of these workers becomes apparent in the style of practical reason their work exemplifies. Rather than performing a routinized task within a fixed plan, the underclass worker often shuttles among a variety of indistinct and loosely supervised activities, connected only by their contribution to a desired practical result.

Some of these more detailed traits of the occupational structure depend upon legally defined institutional arrangements, such as the rules governing union organization or the stability of the employment relation. But many more are simply rigidified definitions of group identity and opportunity, no less tenacious and influential for being only obliquely related to the system of legal rights. The revision of any one of these characteristics would suffice drastically to shift the course of routine politics. If, to take the most familiar case in point, the underclass disappeared, organized workers, compelled to face economic instability more directly, would find it harder to remain content with an industrial politics of marginal compromise. And the trade union movement as a whole, deprived of a subordinate population, would find it easier to present itself as a popular majority championing a nonfactional proposal for society.

THE HEART OF THE DIFFICULTY

I have argued that we can best understand the cycles of reform and retrenchment that characterize the governmental politics of the contemporary North Atlantic democracies as the product of a unique, richly defined institutional and imaginative order that remains largely undisturbed in the midst of ordinary social dealings. The persistence of compulsive routines like these cycles depends upon the existence of such a framework and upon its recalcitrance to challenge and revision. The particular content of the cycle turns on the distinctive content of the institutional and imaginative structure. And the relative compulsiveness of the routines in question – their unchosen quality – results from the extent to which the context remains beyond people's reach in the course of everyday practical and argumentative activities. The view that develops these related conjectures acknowledges that both practical constraints and tensions among interests affect the existence, the power, and the content of the reform cycles. But this view insists that institutional arrangements and imaginative preconceptions channel and focus the influence these additional factors exert upon the substance of policy change and partisan rivalry.

The hypothesis of the formative context, however, contributes to the solution of the intellectual problem and to the clarification of the ideological embarrassment presented by the persistence of the reform cycles only by deepening a larger puzzle. This riddle cuts to the quick of the central difficulties of social and historical explanation and confirms the inadequacy of received styles of social and historical analysis.

The arrangements and beliefs that make up a formative context are enormously important. We must consider them all the more important if we conclude that these same givens also exert a decisive influence upon other practical and argumentative routines – from the business cycle to the stock forms of legal argument. Not only are these formative institutions and preconceptions influential, they are also tenacious. They remain largely undisturbed by the rivalries, animosities, and aspirations unleashed by the conflicts they so powerfully direct. Their occasional revisions, acts of revolutionary reform, represent turning points in the history of a society.

Each such formative context exercises then an immense influence over struggles that do not ordinarily bring it into question or put it in danger. Nevertheless, the elements that compose it do not form an indivisible package, nor do they result from a universal, recurrent, or irresistible evolutionary sequence. No invincible economic, organizational, or psychological constraints, for example, decree that the stark contrast in the workplace between task definers and task executors can survive only on the basis of a particular scheme of contract, property, and unionization. In fact, the history of contemporary communist countries shows the opposite.

The closer you study these formative practices and institutions, the harder it becomes to see their history as a procession in lockstep. The constitutional plan of the state and the view of democracy it embodied gained their characteristic modern shape from late eighteenth-century controversies and inventions, combined with forms of popular party politics that first took shape in the mid-nineteenth century. Or consider the corporate form relatively secluded from political control. Even in the countries (like the United States) that adopted it soonest and perfected it most completely, it had established itself surprisingly late (as late as the Civil War in America) against other, mixed public–private forms of enterprise. It resulted from a concrete history of struggle and diffusion. This history, and not some transparent economic imperative, had prevented the more democratic Western countries from carrying forward early experiments with the political control of accumulation. It had confined such experiments to more authoritarian states, like late nineteenth-century Germany and Japan. Or consider the process by which the mainstream of production and warfare came to be marked by a relatively rigid contrast between task definers and task executors while only the vanguardist forms of productive and military activity broke down the contrast. This process had begun long before, and it had continued well after, the legal forms of the enterprise and the state had been settled. Many of the forms of factory and bureaucratic organization that we now so confidently identify with modern industrialism had not been safely established before the middle of the twentieth century. It required an act of faith to see the Fordist assembly line or the multidivisional firm structure pioneered by American corporations in the 1920s as a necessary incident in the relentless development of an indivisible type of social organization.

How can institutions and beliefs so loosely connected to one another and so much the products of many loosely connected sequences of institutional and imaginative change nevertheless stick together so firmly, remain so recalcitrant to transformative pressure, and exercise so far-reaching an influence upon social life? You can restate this larger puzzle in a way that lays bare its connection to the criticism of the contemporary situation of social and historical thought.

We cannot understand the events and conflicts that absorb most of the attention of a going social world without acknowledging the central importance of the contrast between routines and frameworks. For, like the reform cycles, each of these daily concerns draws our attention to institutional and imaginative givens that keep people acting or talking in set ways. To serve the purpose of explaining the actual content and the compulsive force of particular practical or argumentative routines, the givens have to be defined in considerable detail. The indispensable detail of their definition brings out the looseness of their connections and the complexity of their genealogy: their pasted-together and relatively accidental quality (accidental, that is, by comparison to any account that emphasizes lawlike necessities and rational justifications). The detail thereby also undermines the plausibility of attempts to understand a formative context as a flawed but nevertheless recognizable approximation to a rational norm: that is, to an uncontroversial logic of problem solving and interest accommodation. Much of conventional social science tries to dispose of the problem presented by the existence and influence of formative contexts in just this rationalistic manner when it recognizes the problem at all.

The very same reasons that make it hard for such a social science to explain the reform cycles and to imagine formative contexts also create insuperable difficulties for the tradition of deep-structure theorizing about society and history. The detail that enables the definition of a particular formative context to do its explanatory work makes it unsuitable for a role within the stories that deep-structure social analysis tells. The components of a social framework are too loosely and unevenly connected and they are too obviously the results of many loosely linked social and cultural changes to be persuasively depicted as forming one of a short list of possible types of social organization or one of a number of well-defined stages in a compulsive stage-sequence of social evolution.

Thus, for example, the particular formative context to which I attributed much of the content and force of the cycles of reform and reaction in the contemporary Western democracies is far too particular to exemplify the Marxist concept of capitalism. Attempts can be made to reconcile this particular institutional and imaginative framework with hardcore Marxist social analysis by defining it as a stage of the history of capitalism. But the difficulty persists: the revised, nuanced evolutionary story will never be detailed enough to capture the distinctive features of particular social frameworks capable of explaining particular routines until it becomes so detailed that it turns into the retrospective description of a unique historical sequence rather than the lawlike explanation of a recurrent evolutionary pattern. The arrangements and beliefs that make up the formative context described earlier in this chapter are too obviously the products of surprising events (wars, revolutions, reforms, reactions) and of unlikely practical and imaginative compromises to serve as protagonists in a tale of irresistible tendencies and practical necessities.

Though the elements of a formative context, of a social framework, or of an institutional and imaginative ordering of social life do not make up an indivisible whole, they connect with one another. We need a practice of social explanation that allows us to understand the connections. Though social frameworks do not coalesce or succeed one another according to a master logic of transformation, they produce consequences, and they have causes. We lack a way to imagine how they get made and remade. Though institutional and imaginative orders are neither unbreakable packages nor the products of lawlike tendencies and constraints, they prove to be both prodigious in the range of their effects and astonishingly recalcitrant to disturbance in the midst of ordinary social conflict. We require a form of thought that shows how such structures can exert so powerful an influence and achieve so remarkable a stability despite their jumbled and trumped-up nature.

History is discontinuous because the routine struggles that take place within formative contexts only occasionally escalate into conflicts that remake the contexts. History is surprising because these frameworks do not come from a closed list of possible frameworks or succeed one another according to a master plan. To imagine society truly is to understand how these institutional and imaginative orders of routine social existence get historically made and how they are internally composed.

ANOTHER SETTING FOR THE PROBLEM:
WORLDWIDE RECOMBINATION

The explanatory problem posed by the reform cycles takes us straight to central puzzles of social and historical explanation. I now explore these puzzles in two additional settings. Each supplementary exploration supports the claim for the exemplary status of the task of explaining the reform cycles. At the same time each exploration highlights a different facet of the explanatory task.

The first such additional setting concerns the experimental replacements and recombinations undergone by the institutional and imaginative orders of contemporary Western societies as these orders have been diffused throughout the world. By the middle of the nineteenth century, it seemed that the rich Western powers were about to conquer the world militarily, economically, and spiritually. The non-Western or economically backward countries that had not fallen under the direct rule of the Western powers were drawn into the world economic order that these powers led. The ruling elites or counterelites of the backward nations understood that their own fortunes and the fortunes of their countries depended on their ability to master the productive and destructive capabilities the Western powers had achieved. The practical test came accompanied by a spiritual assault. The doctrines of liberalism, socialism, and communism all invoked forms of association more or less emancipated from any fixed background structure of hierarchy and division and assumed an unfamiliar measure of power to change society through politics. Before the middle of the nineteenth century, the Western advantage remained far from unequivocal. Military superiority – often restricted to naval warfare – had not yet been supported and magnified by an overwhelming industrial machine. Nor had there yet developed the full array of secular doctrines of emancipation.

At first the alien elites misunderstood the threat in two opposite ways. Sometimes they imagined that the style of governmental and economic organization exhibited by the intrusive and seductive powers constituted an indissoluble whole. They could take it or leave it, but they could not remake it. At other times, they thought that a desired technological capability could be achieved without promoting any major change in the country's institutional arrangements. These two misunderstandings offered particular examples of the two most basic mistakes that can be made about an ordering of social life: the belief that the framework represents a natural and indissoluble whole and the failure to recognize that there is a framework and that its elements are somehow connected.

But time taught another lesson. The elites of the countries that had been overtaken or left behind found they could survive only by refusing to treat the institutional systems of the advanced Western powers on a take-it-or-leave-it basis. Capable reformers understood that many of the preexisting institutional arrangements and imaginative preconceptions of the society had to be given up for the sake of the development of productive and military capabilities. Instead of representing one-time innovations the most successful solutions increased the capacity to innovate repeatedly in ways of mobilizing resources and manpower, and they loosened the constraints that the established forms of privilege and rule imposed upon the organization of work and exchange. At the same time, they turned features of the backward country to competitive advantage by combining them with borrowed or invented arrangements. Typically, these redirected aspects of the "traditional" society were forms of group organization and group solidarity, like village communities, tribal associations, family enterprises, or patron–client relations, incorporated into changed practices of exchange, production, or discipline at work.

Because institutional arrangements and imaginative preconceptions support schemes of social division and hierarchy, each of these institutional recombinations or inventions implied a shift in the structure of social division and hierarchy. For the nonrevolutionary elite faction that led such reforms, the trick was to find the particular measures that would combine several features, always in actual or potential tension: to develop the minimal basis indispensable to the introduction of Western-style machines and techniques of work organization; to lay the groundwork for continued technical and organizational innovation, increasingly free from the need to anchor the most advanced military or economic capabilities in the institutions of the then leading powers; and yet, for the sake of vested interests and inherited pieties, to minimize the impact of these changes upon the society's inherited structure of social division and hierarchy. If the elite was a revolutionary vanguard, with radical transformative intentions rather than self-defensive concerns, its task was to use the pressure to catch up as an opportunity to incite broad social conflicts and to establish an institutional order that permanently weakened the hold of rigid social roles and ranks upon people's dealings and life chances.

The Japanese institutional innovations practiced during the several generations following the 1868 restoration, the administrative and economic Ottoman reforms of the mid-nineteenth century (and, indeed, the Köprülü reforms of the late seventeenth century), and the Russian reforms of the early twentieth century all provide examples of efforts at institutional recombination, undertaken by a renovating elite, largely inspired by the desire to catch up with the advanced Western countries and to avoid the radical social instability and national humiliation that the failure to catch up might produce. It is easy to exaggerate, with the benefit of hindsight, the differences between the successful and the unsuccessful attempts. The Japanese solutions had to be hammered out over a protracted period that included the massive agitation and repression of the 1920s and 1930s. The Russian and Ottoman efforts might have prospered in a less vulnerable and violent geopolitical situation.

This same search for alternative foundations to comparable levels of practical capability now goes on at a quickened pace and on a planetary scale. Revolutionary and reactionary, pluralistic and authoritarian regimes alike devote themselves to the task. You may be tempted to say that these experiments in dissociation are limited in a simple way. Countries diverge far less in the immediate technological and organizational basis of economic and military advance than in the larger settings of social and governmental order within which those bases were set. Everywhere you find not only similar machines but even kindred ways of arranging work in factories, offices, and military units. Everywhere the mainstream sectors of production or warfare are one thing, and the vanguard sectors another. It seems that the core complex of technology and enterprise organization resists dissociation more effectively than the larger setting of arrangements for the organization of government or the allocation of capital.

However, the value of this simple distinction between what can and cannot be dissociated is undercut by facts to which the argument has already alluded and later returns. Many of the characteristic Western forms of enterprise and work organization were invented and diffused when other aspects of the initial Western example had already been pulled apart and combined with alien practices in foreign lands. People had fought over these versions of industrialism in theaters of conflict as far apart as Western or Central Europe and the Soviet Union of the 1920s. No sooner did these institutional arrangements gain a measure of stability than they began to be challenged by deviant forms of organization under the pressure of forces that went from confused ideological crusades and abortive movements of mass mobilization (such as the Chinese Cultural Revolution) to market fluctuations and opportunities (such as the expansion, in advanced economies, like the Italy of the 1970s, of the vanguard sector of small-scale, experimental industry, with its own more flexible style of work organization).

As the dissociation, replacement, and recombination of the initial Western model of industrialism progresses, it may come to involve more and more of a formative context. At first, the technology and industrial organization may be imported almost wholesale from the pioneering countries but combined with approaches to governmental and economic organization unknown in the Western heartland of industrialism. At a next stage, the established forms of technology may be taken as given but combined with novel ways of organizing work and enterprises. Finally, even the principles of machine design may be revolutionized. In the end no part of the original structure is left safe from being disturbed by the experimental logic of recombination.

Where would it all end, this joining together of practices that seemed incompatible, this breaking apart of institutions that appeared inseparable? What made the worldwide experiment in dissociation so hard to understand was that it fit no apparent pattern of evolution or constraint. Many attempts at dissociation failed. Effortless and unlimited recombination described these events no better than the idea that there was a triumphant version of industrialism, with richly defined social implications, that everybody had to accept for the sake of survival and prosperity. The varieties of industrialism – economies, war machines, and supporting social orders – that occasionally emerged to compete on a world scale could not readily be understood as contemporaneous examples of a cumulative, irreversible sequence. There were too many variations. The tests of their comparative success were too many-sided and inconclusive. But neither could these experiments be accounted for as minor adjustments of some single scheme of social organization. Dissociation had already been seen to touch, with greater or lesser force, every aspect of the initial Western model. It had already gone far. There was no telling where it might not go next. If such experiments disclosed general truths about society, these truths would not have the form of a convergent sequence. Nor would they demonstrate a tight link between a society's practical success and its commitment to a single, richly defined model of social organization. The truths would need to be both more particular – the making of a particular series of live options – and more universal – an insight into what failed and successful dissociation showed about the way society gets reinvented and about the relationship of its reinvention to cumulative developments in practical capability, moral discovery, and theoretical insight.

What is the relation of this experience of worldwide institutional dissociation and recombination to the central puzzle about formative contexts that is presented by the cycles of reform and retrenchment? Each new twist in the creation of an institutional setting for the development of the practical productive or destructive capabilities of society represents an episode of revolutionary reform and inaugurates a new formative context. The experience of dissociation demonstrates that not everything can combine with everything else within a stable social framework. Some combinations do not work. But no one has yet managed to show that the constraints upon recombination are of a sort that would be capable of singling out prospectively a list of feasible formative contexts, generated by lawlike practical constraints or developmental tendencies. Reactionary or revolutionary groups that allow their conduct to be governed by such notions soon find themselves left behind by their less blinkered rivals at home and abroad.

Of course, it could be that we just have not yet discovered the right laws of social evolution or of possible social worlds and are for that reason unable to come up with the correct prospective list of practicable contexts. But the discussion of the reform cycles and the criticism of deep-structure social theory already suggest that a more promising approach may be to search for a way of thinking that enables us to identify and explain constraints upon recombination without appealing to the idea of a list of feasible social orders and without trying to find the laws or imperatives that can generate such a list.

ANOTHER SETTING FOR THE PROBLEM: CLOSED OPTIONS IN HISTORY

Generalizing the Idea of the Reform Cycle

Reform cycles and the formative contexts that shape them are no idiosyncracy of twentieth-century societies. On the contrary, in most societies of the past such cycles and contexts prevailed even more strongly. They marked with special ferocity the difference between what could be expected and what could not be realized or even conceived in politics.

The study of the dissociation of the original Western formative contexts served to bring out an aspect of the problem posed by the reform cycles: the elusive quality of the constraints upon the replacement and recombination of the elements that compose an institutional and imaginative structure of social life. So, too, this further exploration draws attention to yet another feature of the theoretical puzzle first presented through an analysis of the oscillations of reform and reaction in contemporary Western democracies. This additional consideration is the apparent relation of the compulsive character of the reform cycles to the measure of oligarchic closure upon conflicts over the mastery and uses of governmental power. *False Necessity* argues that the degree to which a formative context stands immune to challenge and revision in the midst of practical and argumentative routines contributes decisively to the rigidity and the force of the social roles and ranks that the context supports.

Just how narrowly and mysteriously defined the constraints or conflicts over the mastery and uses of governmental power have often been becomes clear when you consider societies from the standpoint of would-be reformers who, having reached high office, were anxious to meet well-known dangers to the strength and prosperity of the realm. Over enormous lengths of time and in the most varied circumstances, they felt compelled to move among a tiny number of unsatisfactory policy options.

The more narrowly and rigidly defined the scope of these live policy options, the greater the contrast between normalcy and transformation and the less the formative context of powers–rights lay open to transformative practical or imaginative activities in the ordinary course of social life. No wonder the characteristic social thought of such a world identified the established order of division and hierarchy with the inner nature of society and personality.

One counterpart to the narrowed range of policy options was some relative exclusion of ordinary people from the routine conflicts over the terms of power and production. Any approach to mass mobilization disrupts the habitual range of options even when intended to protect them. For the relations among people in the larger, escalating struggle are not predetermined by the places individuals occupy in the established order of division and hierarchy. Each round in the widened conflict becomes an occasion to discover alternative possibility: a redefinition of the interests, the identities, and the weapons. Thus, a fundamental reason for the reformers' constant return to the same policy options and their unwillingness to pursue any one of them to its utmost consequences became the conscious fear and avoidance of a conflict that would pit reforming statesmen and an aroused populace against privileged classes.

These points can now be illustrated in detail by considering two series of policy options in two kinds of societies: the agrarian–bureaucratic empires and the ancient city-states of Mediterranean (but also Asiatic) antiquity. Together, these societies represent a large part of all the forms of social life that have existed in history; their experiments with the reinvention of social life, a major element in the experience of mankind.

Closed Options in the Agrarian–Bureaucratic Empires

Consider, first, politics in the agrarian empires of antiquity. (By empire, I mean no more than a large country with a central government.) There are two major power blocks: the autocracy and its household, on one side; the landholding magnates, on the other. The system has two outside limits: revolutionary despotism, by which the autocracy would ally itself with the peasantry against the magnates, and aristocratic factionalism, by which the imperial order would degenerate into the untrammeled and unstable sectarianism of magnate warlords. Revolutionary despotism is a manifestly unpromising venture: if the autocrat is not smashed by his lordly enemies, he will be undone by his own peasant allies. Aristocratic factionalism invites the foreign invader, opens the way to the seizure of central power by one of the contending families, and weakens the shared power and authority of the landholders over the peasants. Within the boundaries defined by these two limiting situations, the autocracy and the magnates must be reconciled. The number of possible deals is severely limited; the same compromises recur constantly, though in varying combinations, throughout the history of the large, enduring agrarian states. Looking at it from the viewpoint of the autocrat, there are only three choices.

First, recruit a bureaucratic staff from men below the magnate class who will owe all to you. (This was a formative principle of Chinese statecraft at least since the rise of nonaristocratic officials in the centuries preceding the imperial unification of 221 B.C. It was also central to the Ottoman palace system and, in a radically different setting, to the state-building efforts of European absolutism.) You must then constantly shake up your own administrative apparatus in order to call up new levies of recruits; otherwise, the bureaucrats will merge with the magnates or become magnates in their own right.

Second, you may try to turn the magnates into a service nobility by involving them directly in the running of the state. By making land tenure dependent upon office, you bind them to yourself. But unless you are ever vigilant to beat them down, they will gain independence. In the end, to keep their allegiance, you will have to give them absolute dominion over the larger part of the country's land and labor. They rather than you will then be in direct control over what goes on in the countryside. An example is the gradual assimilation of *pomestye* land, held during a lifetime in return for service to the tsar, to the status of *votchina* tenure, inheritable and assured dominion, during the period from Ivan the Terrible to Peter the Great. Petrine absolutism was founded upon the consolidation of precisely the kind of ownership that Ivan's scheme had temporarily unsettled through his conditional land grants to the subaristocratic gentry. Early Yi policy in Korea suggests a variant of the same trend: at first, only the Merit Subjects, who had beholden themselves to the Crown by special services, were allowed hereditary land: as officeholders managed to wring agrarian privilege out of administrative power, this favor lost its exceptional character.

Third, you may set up a dual agrarian order. Alongside the large hereditary estates, there will be a special class of landholders who will owe you direct funds and recruits, or who will be granted claims to some parcel of the land tax in exchange for their military readiness. Remember the Byzantine military farms – *ktemata stratiotika*, the Ottoman timariots, the Mughal *zamindars*, and the Aztec military life-tenants. (This solution fades into the previous strategy to the extent that the nobility under that other policy is held to no more than occasional army service or assistance in tax collecting.) Or they may be village communities and smallholders who are expected to provide you with wealth and soldiers. (Think of the Byzantine peasant freeholds and military farms before the failure of Romanus Lecapenus and Basil II to save them had issued in the final triumph of military aristocracy and monastic landlordism.) Or they may be both powerful men with conditional land tenure and village communities with army and fiscal obligations. (The land policies of the Toba Empire and the sequel of experimentation with agrarian and military reform during the early T'ang supply an example.) When the military or economic pressure on you mounts, and you try to increase taxes and recruitment, the magnates will be able to defend themselves unless you humble them; the brunt of the burden will fall upon the small-holders themselves. Impoverished and decimated, they will seek protection from the aristocrats, and, in the next round of the contest, you will end up worse off than you were before. (This engrossment of peasant land and labor became a familiar problem for the rulers of the late Roman Empire in the West; it had its counterparts in several periods of Chinese dynastic decline, in the subversion of independent peasant proprietorship during the final centuries of the Byzantine Empire, and in the collapse of the Abbasid regime, when the ruin of many small farmers helped the central government lose control of tax collection and military power alike.)

Each of the three strategies tends to break down. For one thing, in each case there comes a moment when the successful execution of the policy would require the autocrat to throw himself decisively against the magnates. This he cannot do without courting the dangers of revolutionary despotism. For another thing, the crucial requirement of success is unbroken vigor in statecraft. But the dynastic character of the state means that a weak will may succeed a strong one by the accidents of inheritance. The indispensable continuity of rule is likely to be interrupted by succession struggles during which the contenders dole out favors in exchange for support.

These facts explain why governmental policy tends to waver confusedly among the three options and why, despairing of the possibility of carrying any one of them to its final conclusion, it muffles each in the others. All the tactics of reconciliation reappear in most of the large agrarian states: the differences lie in the relative emphasis given to the options, in the tenacity and skill with which they are pursued and combined, and in the particular institutional arrangements used to promote them. The same forces that account for the wavering also suggest why the realm must search out a career of conquest: continuous expansion binds the privileged together in a common mission, all the more important when a conquering nation rules over alien populations; provides rewards for the faithful and aspiring magnates; and wins slaves and booty with which to finance further conquest without aggravating the burden on peasants and smallholders. When the conquerors are stopped by a foreign power, by their own domestic troubles, or by the sheer unwieldiness and expense of the imperial order, the internal dangers are multiplied many times over.

In such a world, there are only a few ways in which ordinary people rise collectively to the surface of history by dealing actively with the chief power blocks in the country.

First, they may appear as a privileged urban mob, distinct from other, larger segments of the population and country. This may happen when a city-state becomes an empire or, less often, when the rank and file of a conquering people settles down in the cities of the land they have conquered. The mob is entreated and bribed, and its privilege is at best a condition of favored enjoyment, backed by a threat of riot or a memory of shared power.

Second, there are the instances in which the policy of agrarian dualism has achieved some temporary balance. One way or another, the village community manages to keep a measure of independence from the magnates and to deal, in its own right, with the central government. The village, divided internally along hierarchical and communal lines, may have to put up a common front against the outside. Forced often to accept a collective military or fiscal responsibility, it redistributes tax and war burdens periodically in order to hold together under the weight it is made to carry. The greater the pressure upon it, the more likely it is to unify and equalize itself; whenever this pressure is relaxed, the village tends to break apart into factions and ranks. (Both the eleventh-century Byzantine and the nineteenth-century Russian village communities illustrate a measure of redistributive equalization and cohesion in response to external force. The role of village officers in the Southern Sung, of the headmen of peasant-held raiyati villages in Mughal India, and of leading village families under the Tokugawa *bakufu* provide counterexamples of hierarchy when the burden imposed by an external landlord or ruler was less severe or when the outside authority strengthened the hand of already privileged insiders. Ongoing communal strife might then break out as well, whenever there was a basis for it, as in the multi-caste Indian village.)

Third, there are the occasions when despair launches the peasants into rebellion. Peasant rebellion is a normal incident of the tailspin that characteristically follows the failure of governmental policies and the disasters of foreign war. When the autocracy is forced to increase its demands upon the population and the peasantry is made to pay the price, the collapse of independent peasant proprietorship and the disintegration of village community create the atmosphere that favors insurrection. But, though the rebellious peasantry may play a decisive role for a brief moment and even establish a state for itself, it is more likely to serve as a tool of the brutal factional fighting that breaks out as the imperial order falls apart. For the peasantry to have a chance, the conditions of a regrouping of the elite power blocks must be shattered.

The agrarian empires constantly re-created, both through what their high politics did and through what it took for granted, the opportunity for maintaining societal divisions of hierarchy and com-

munal membership that enveloped almost the entirety of everyday
life and carried the blessings of a more or less assured sense of reality
and right. But this argument about agrarian empires is simply an
example of a larger problem: it would be possible to formulate a
similar description of the strict limits on politics for any particular
society. In each case, the oligarchy effect – the constraints imposed
on politics at the top of society by the need to keep the masses under
control – reinforces the rigidity of the social order and helps the
powerful understand the difference between reasonable and fool-
hardy policy.

Closed Options in the Ancient City-State Republics

The city-state republics of Graeco-Roman and Near-Eastern antiquity may often have come closer than the agrarian empires to the
features of mass politics. For the most part, however, they also
represented social worlds in which the contest for power was
hemmed in by the oligarchy effect.

They too show the existence of compulsive cycles and routines
that can be overcome only through the reconstruction of an institutional and imaginative order that cannot itself be understood as a
product of lawlike tendencies or constraints. The most frequent principle of city-state organization was the existence of a double division
between citizens and noncitizenry, and then, within the citizenry
itself, between the rank and file and a relatively well-defined hereditary elite. The oligarchy effect therefore operated at two levels: in
helping to maintain the division between citizen and noncitizen and
in supporting the distinction between the elite and the mass of citizens. Though the inner circle of power may originally have had the
character of a congregation of family elders, it was generally recast
to reflect the prominence of a relatively small number of families.
These concentrated in their own hands the instruments of wealth,
constitutional prerogative, and religious leadership necessary to keep
their fellow citizens in check. The crucial social distinction between
the city-state and the agrarian empire was that a large portion of the
country's inhabitants did have, as citizens, a claim to participate, one
way or another, in the affairs of central government. Yet the political
life of the city-states, like that of the agrarian empires, usually continued to move within a narrow space defined by two limits.

The first limit was the difficulty the oligarchy would have in dis-
enfranchising the ordinary citizenry altogether. The nobles' attempt
to throttle their fellow citizens created the danger that the oligarchic
partnership would give way to the despotism of a single ruler or
family; as long as each family could maintain its crowd of supporters
and dependents, through the normal processes of political rivalry,

there was hope of staying the threat of a supraoligarchic tyranny. The elite had reason to fear such a tyranny as much as mob rule. The mob, after all, might be easier to placate and to seduce than the prince. Moreover, unless the disenfranchisement and impoverishment of the citizenry were part of a program of imperial expansion, which would put new strains on the civic constitution, the city would have all the vulnerabilities of its imperial rivals without sharing in their strengths. It could no longer easily elicit the ingenious and passionate loyalties of a citizen army, but neither could it count on an empire's vast resources of material and manpower; the safety of the patriciate would be endangered together with that of the commonwealth. Finally, both civil solidarity and civic freedom were intertwined with the civil religion: the sacred bond between the citizenry as a corporate whole and the tutelary gods of the city. This tie would be injured and altered beyond recognition if the citizen populace were denied any residual rights of participation in affairs of state.

The other limit to the system was the difficulty of abolishing the distinction between elite and mass within the citizenry. The course of factional rivalry within the city did indeed sometimes preempt or destroy oligarchic power and push the republic toward mass politics. But the practice of demagogic reform and agitation was usually full of surprise and disappointment. Though the constitutional structure was bound up closely and transparently enough with social privilege for its revision to provoke ferocious antagonism, it was not bound up so completely that its remaking could suffice to strike at the springs of domination and dependence in the organization of work, the distribution of land and learning, and the access to different occupations. A second layer of reforms, addressed to these latter issues, would have to follow up on the reconstruction of government. Though the reforming leadership might have the clearest of visions and the most magnanimous of intentions, it was apt to be overtaken, before it could reach this level of reconstructive politics, by the factional rivalries and the new despotisms of the insurrectionary period it had inaugurated. The would-be reformers were sometimes lucky to get away without blame for the doom of the republic they had tried to rescue.

Several courses of events often avoided or destroyed the distinction between masters and servants within the citizen body but almost always at the cost of some still more pronounced disparity between the privileged citizenry and a disenfranchised or enslaved mass. One such pattern marked certain aspects of Mesopotamian city life. The members of the enfranchised corporate elite who inhabited the towns seem to have been chiefly preoccupied with the maintenance of their dominance over lands and populations outside the city's walls; the

civic association remained a loose one and was ultimately overshadowed by the emergent forms of imperial and theocratic power centered in temple–palace complexes. Second, there was the Spartan
example of a closely knit civic solidarity against a much larger subject
population, a system that required the state to be on a permanent
war footing against its enemies at home and abroad. Third, and most
importantly, there were the conflicts characteristic of late-republican
Rome and of many of the Greek city-states in their times of tyranny
and democracy. Again and again, the circle of foreign conflict and
domestic upheaval undermined the form of government and created
opportunities for restorationist or revolutionary warlords to seize
power. The attempt to gain international security, protect the trade
routes, or enrich the public treasury and the private contractors,
would overtax the military and financial strength of cities that had
to rely upon armies made up of smalltime, independent proprietors.
The disruption caused by war undermined the economic basis of the
yeoman farm. The profit and plunder of conquest produced the
money and the slaves with which to buy up the land and manage it
in a new way. The displaced citizen mass came to town as a dependent
and privileged mob or entered a professionalized army; either way,
it became available for subversive political agitation. But agitation
alone could not pay for the army nor could it satisfy the entrepreneurial backers of the factions in conflict, who needed the government to multiply, by warfare and patronage, their chances for
enrichment.

The city-states of Graeco-Roman antiquity had no easy way of
breaking out of this process once they had fallen into it. The Athenian
response, which evaded much of the sequence, was predicated upon
a unique array of strategies and circumstances: the destruction of
oligarchic rule at home; the reinforcement of citizen privileges in
exchange for relentless military obligation; the reliance on foreign
commerce and navies as well as on disenfranchised or enslaved labor;
the absence of large territorial expansion; the exaction of money,
food, and soldiers from subordinate allies; and the failed hope that
war would not be too frequent or last too long.

The other solution was Rome's transformation of the city-state
into an empire where the policy choices characteristic of large agrarian states were complicated by the residues of republican life: pseudo-
enfranchised urban mobs, the apparatus of constitutional rule, and
the occasional corporate life of the cities. These residues could never
alter the economic dependence of the cities on the countryside; the
cities produced, when they produced at all, mainly for the class of
officials and absentee landlords; and offered no serious challenge to
the imperial order. Such an order could know only the forms of

popular agitation characteristic of the agrarian empire: the peasant rebellion, the urban riot, and the military putsch.

My agrarian-bureaucratic and city-state examples show the problem of routine politics projected onto a larger screen. To grasp how such systems of live options change is to understand how history happens. For ultimately, the only other history that goes on is a history of the subjective experience and the collective imagination of social life, and this history – it will turn out – is not only inseparable from that one in content and effect but exhibits the same puzzles of reasonless routine.

THE PROBLEM RESTATED

The problem of lawless repetition in history can now be restated more precisely. Once thus restated, it becomes a point of departure for an explanatory social theory.

According to the hypothesis of a formative context we can identify in every social and historical situation a formative set of institutional arrangements and of enacted beliefs about the possible and desirable forms of human association. These arrangements and beliefs shape a broad range of practical and discursive routines. They remain recalcitrant to challenge and revision in the midst of ordinary social conflicts, although formative contexts differ crucially in the extent of this recalcitrance.

A central task of a descriptive and explanatory social theory is to provide us with a way to imagine the making and the internal constitution of these institutional and imaginative orders of social life. Our ideas about how such orders get made and remade turn out to be just the reverse side of our ideas about how they hold together.

A theory of social contexts must do justice to the largely negative lessons we can infer from the experiences of unreasoned compulsion and equally surprising freedom examined in this chapter: the reform cycles that mark the governmental politics of the North Atlantic democracies, the practice of institutional recombination on a world scale, and the overriding importance of closed sets of live policy options in past societies. The lessons come in the form of puzzles. A persuasive theory must actually explain the puzzles rather than explain them away by denying the reality of the tensions they expose.

A defensible view of how formative structures hang together must account for the reality of constraints upon the replacement and recombination of their constituent elements. But it must achieve its aim without treating these social orders as indivisible units, each of which stands or falls as a single piece. An adequate approach to context making must respect the distinction between moves within a context and changes of a context. It must identify and understand the influences and the forces that allow people to change the character as well as the content of their social orders: the extent to which these orders are presented as revisable artifacts in daily life. But it must do so without invoking laws that specify possible social worlds or necessary stages of social evolution.

Chapter 3 works out an account of constraints on the replacement and recombination of the arrangements and beliefs that compose contexts. The account develops through an attempt to formulate descriptive categories with which to compare institutions. Chapter 4 develops a view of context making, anticipated by a polemical narrative of the genealogy of contemporary institutional arrangements.

THE PROBLEM OF ROUTINE WITHOUT REASON GENERALIZED AND EXTENDED

The strategy of this chapter is to study the puzzle of the reform cycles as a special case of an issue central to our understanding and reconstruction of society. The argument concludes by generalizing the problem and extending the solution.

The Problem Generalized: The Roots of Reasonless Routine

To argue and to converse we make collectively certain assumptions about the procedures for argument and discourse. Each such set of assumptions, worked out in the discursive practices of particular human communities, puts a distinct repertory of forms of understanding and persuasion in place of the open-ended possibilities of inquiry and communication. So, too, to settle down into a social order and to deal with one another as more than belligerent or interrupted contestants in an ongoing war, we must substitute a particular, limited version of social life for the indeterminate opportunities of association.

The contrast between what we presuppose and what our presuppositions influence is never absolute. At any moment people may hit upon varieties of inquiry and discourse, exchange and community, that work although they transgress the presuppositions. If such transgressions fail to be crushed quickly, they may give us reason to change the assumptions they violated.

Though presuppositions – structures or contexts as I have called them – normally hold us captive in our everyday activity, they have a hodgepodge, pasted-together, trumped-up quality. We fail at every attempt to make one of these versions appear definitive and complete, or to enumerate higher-order rules that determine which structures of discourse are possible or which sequences of such structures must occur. When the rules that govern such lists or sequences are strong enough to be interesting, they prove too strong to hold good.

The chief root for the generality and the importance of this relation between conditioned freedom and conditioning but contingent structures lies in the disproportion between our limit-breaking capabilities and the definite, limited examples of common life and common discourse that we can fashion. We never entirely fit into these contexts. Something is left over. We can use any part of the leftover to make things new.

The disproportion between our capabilities and our shared situations would be merely ironic or tragic if we were unable to diminish it. By doing so, we change, to our benefit, the quality of our relation to our cognitive or social assumptions. As a result, we also alter, to our advantage, the quality of our relations to one another. We put more of the infinite us into the finite worlds in which we live.

We have a practical interest in this achievement. It enables us to turn our societies into less alien, delusive, and imprisoning homes and to strengthen all our more particular forms of self-assertion. *False Necessity* argues for this thesis with respect to our social contexts while suggesting that it holds true for all our contexts.

Humanity takes a long time to understand its relation to its structures of discourse and sociability. People have usually mistaken the forms of inquiry and discourse, exchange and community, to which they are accustomed for flawed approximations to the true face of reason or society. More often than not, they have cast this prejudice aside only to replace it with a more modest, halfhearted reformulation of the same belief.

The most influential and long-lived reformulation is the idea of a small set of types of cognitive or social ordering among which individuals and societies must move, whether voluntarily or not. Thus, even those who pride themselves on having discarded the superstitious belief in a single, canonical model of social organization continue to rely upon a restricted typology of social possibilities. For example, they allow their ideological choices and debates to be governed by the assumption that there are market-oriented economies, command economies, and economies that combine command and market principles. Such contrasts acquire their force and their kinship with the superstitions that they seem to replace through the tacit identification of the innocuous abstractions with concrete historical arrangements. Thus, people speak of market economies, meaning not merely the principle of economic decentralization but the distinctive forms of contract and property, and the peculiar style of government–economy relations, that came to represent economic decentralization in the course of modern Western history.

Despite its appreciation of the made-up, fought-out character of social order, classical social theory gave a major place to elaborate versions of this neonaturalistic idea of types of social organization that succeed one another, or become actual, according to higher-order laws. It compromised, again and again, between its acknowledgment of the trumped-up character of social life and its prejudices about the style of explanation that a scientific understanding of society and history supposedly requires. As a result, it remained unable to resolve, or even adequately to identify, the problems of reasonless routine with which this chapter deals. Categories like "capitalism" were gross enough to mark plausible stages in a necessary historical evolution or to identify a plausible member of a list of possible types of social organization. But, by the same token, they were too gross to explain the content of a society's repetitious conflicts over its key society-making resources.

Only when the fallback positions from faith in a single, canonical mode of inquiry or association lost their credibility did the properly modernist ideas about our relations to our contexts come to prevail. These ideas have not yet worked themselves fully into our practices of social and historical explanation. They are nevertheless responsible for many of the most original achievements of contemporary culture.

One modernist response to the problem of our relation to our contexts is the negativistic, existentialist creed. This creed sees our accepted structures of conversation and association as both imprisoning and groundless. It identifies our sole hope of freedom in the ceaseless, repetitious rebellion against such structures. The motive of the rebellion is less the hope of introducing better structures than the belief that the rebellion, while it lasts, affirms our essential freedom: our freedom to overstep the limits of the mental and social orders within which we habitually move. By this rebellion we reaffirm everything in our individual or collective selves that remains disproportionately larger than the humdrum circumstances of daily life. But we can never undertake the rebellion against structure often enough or carry it far enough to avoid the need to continue living in the real, unregenerate world – the world where we continue to rely upon all the presuppositions that we violate in the moment of defiance.

The other characteristic modernist response to the problem of our relation to the presuppositions of our life in common is an ironic acceptance of our contexts, justified by the lack of any higher standard with which to judge them. The modernist skeptic grants that we have no good reason to choose among structures of discourse or society other than reasons that already depend upon a reasonless acceptance of one such structure. We have nothing to go on but the historical societies and cultures that actually exist.

The second move of this modernist skeptic, however, is to turn this ironic proviso upside down. Precisely because each "form of life" represents a law unto itself, it is futile to look for higher justifications or higher criticisms. All we can do is to think, live, and change by the standards of the society or the tradition that we choose – or that chooses us. Thus, the modernist as resigned skeptic sees no alternative to this submission other than the paralyzing attempt to avoid engagement.

The two modernist responses to the problem of groundless and confining presuppositions repudiate the attempt to sanctify particular social and cognitive structures or to judge them by structure-transcending standards. The modernist as rebel and the modernist as skeptic also share a take-it-or-leave-it attitude toward the constraining force of our discursive and social orders. We may be able, they implicitly tell us, to replace one such order by another. But we cannot change the quality of our relation to these frameworks. We cannot weaken their power to imprison us. Structures will be structures.

This implicit premise limits the extent to which its adherents recognize our contexts to be up for grabs in history. For the premise tells us that the character of these contexts – their relation to our context-conditioned but context-revising freedom – remains constant throughout history. This unjustified and unhistorical restraint on the principle of historicity reveals the residual link between the modernist approaches to our practical or mental assumptions and the naturalistic dogmas these approaches seem to defy.

The take-it-or-leave-it view of the confining character of structures shows in a psychological dilemma. This dilemma marks both the negativistic existentialist and the resigned skeptical solutions to the problem. It is the impossibility of combining in the same experience consciousness and engagement. When we engage wholeheartedly in shared forms of life and discourse we must somehow suspend or control our sense of their groundlessness and coerciveness. When we give free rein to this sense, we stand apart and alone, in skeptical disengagement or futile though uncompromising rebellion. But to be fully the masters of our contexts we must combine consciousness and engagement. *False Necessity* argues that we can combine them, that the conditions for combining them are the same as the conditions for increasing our freedom to challenge and revise our contexts in the midst of our everyday activities, and that these conditions overlap with the requirements for other varieties of human empowerment.

The problem posed by the attempt to understand the reform cycles – the problem of understanding the genesis and constitution of institutional structures that are both makeshift and decisive – turns out to be only a special case of the more general issue posed by our relation to our mental and social contexts. The attempt to deal with this issue forces us to carry the attack on the idea of natural or uncontroversial presuppositions beyond the point reached by the familiar radicalisms of contemporary culture.

The Solution Extended: The Imaginative Side of Formative Contexts

If the problem of routine without reason is rooted in our basic relation to our contexts, we should expect to rediscover its presence in all areas of social life, not merely in the compulsive routines of conflict over the tangible resources of capital and governmental power. In explaining these practical routines the argument of this chapter has emphasized the institutional aspects of formative contexts. The institutional emphasis persists throughout this book: in the view of the internal composition of social frameworks, in the theory of context making, and in the proposals for social reconstruction that occupy succeeding chapters of *False Necessity*. The limited focus helps keep the complexity of the argument and the breadth of its themes under control.

But a formative context does include noninstitutional, imaginative components. And it does shape argumentative and discursive routines that are just as significant as the reform and business cycles studied in the earlier parts of this chapter. Material wealth and governmental power are not the only resources enabling the occupants of some social stations to set terms to the activities of the occupants of other social stations. One of these crucial resources for society making is the ability to enlist widely shared, authoritative conceptions of what the relations among people can and should be like – accepted ideals of human association – in the defense of particular interests and opinions. The stock forms of legal, moral, and ideological argument are the intangible counterparts to the routines of partisan conflict and economic exchange. The former show the same repetitiveness, the same perplexing movement among well-defined positions, as the latter.

To explain their constancy and their content we must look beyond them to the imaginative presuppositions they habitually take for granted. What are these assumptions like? What is their characteristic relation to the kinds of formative institutional arrangements that have concerned earlier parts of this chapter?

If the hypothesis of a formative context holds good, the argumentative routines depend very largely on the same institutional and imaginative assumptions that help account for party-political and economic cycles. The institutional components of a formative context influence more directly the cyclical conflicts over power and wealth. The standard forms of legal, moral, and policy discussion suffer the more immediate influence of the imaginative elements of a framework: the accepted assumptions about standards to which relations among people should conform in the different domains of practical social life.

But these are distinctions of emphasis. To explain policy and business cycles the definition of the formative context must include dominant assumptions about the styles of sociability suitable to the different areas of social life. Institutional arrangements leave open too many possibilities: too many policy solutions to recognized problems and too many ways to define individual, group, or regional interests. Only when institutions combine with preconceptions about the possible and proper shape of dealings among people do the implications of the institutional arrangements become more precise. For example, in the contemporary North Atlantic democracies, both organized labor and middle-class electorates might well think, act, and vote differently if they believed that democratic principles could and should be extended to the workplace, not merely confined to the organization of government.

Moreover, the institutional arrangements that make up a formative context must be legally defined. They must draw upon rules and principles that can be authoritatively elaborated and applied in particular instances of conflict. Every extended practice of application of law demands recourse to tacit models of human association. The lawyer clears up the ambiguities of legal materials by referring to the basic principles that help organize and elucidate whole bodies of law.

But these principles are themselves characteristically ambiguous and contradictory. To every principle there corresponds a counterprinciple that reverses its content and limits its application. Thus, the principle of freedom to contract, which establishes that people may voluntarily accept or reject a contractual relation, is qualified by a counterprinciple, which forbids people to use this freedom to undermine minimal notions of communal solidarity. It takes more basic pictures of human association to help structure the stuff of positive rules and doctrines and to determine the relative influence of particular principles and counterprinciples in each body of law.

The constitutional lawyer, for instance, relies on a conception of the democratic republic, of its defining principles, and of the parts of social life in which it is properly realized. Such a conception may remain tacit and vague. But the jurist who had no such assumptions to draw on would soon find himself at loose ends.

The following pages outline the distinctive way in which the imaginative elements fit into a framework of social life. The core idea is that a formative context includes, together with major institutional settlements, a moral geography of social life: a conception of how people can and should deal with one another in the different fields of social practice. Sometimes, this scheme of social life consists in a single, overpowering model of sociability, meant to be repeated as a theme and variations throughout social life. In other cultures, by contrast, the authoritative scheme of human association assumes the form of distinct models of sociability, each set in contrast to the others. Thus, the most influential preconceptions about sociability prevailing in the contemporary North Atlantic democracies assign radically different standards of human association to government, family life, and economic activity.

For example, in all the societies whose reform cycles this chapter has discussed, people ordinarily consider family life appropriate for a small repertory of styles of private community. These styles vary across classes and communities and, most interestingly, across families themselves. But certain themes reappear persistently. The explicit slogans, the articulate beliefs, and the oft-told stories of everyday life and pop culture present the family as an area of social experience suitable to a distinctive blend of sentiment and hierarchy: power improved by emotion, emotion harnessed to the practical responsibilities of sustaining a life together.

The family these beliefs invoke depends on shared interests and values. It cannot easily accommodate conflict, bargaining, and sharply defined entitlements. It stands in stark opposition to the principles of contract and technical necessity deemed legitimate in practical working life, and to the principles of formal equality, episodic participation, and partisan rivalry that help make up the democratic ideal.

These more or less official images of the family are largely indeterminate and partly mendacious. We fix their effective social meaning by reading them against the background of collective habits that provide the daily fare of domesticity. Such habits fail to fit the neat contrasts of more simplified beliefs about family community. They include much of the rights-mongering, the strategic negotiation, and the ill-bounded conflict that such ideals of family life exclude. They nevertheless remain close enough to the articulate beliefs to make these beliefs half credible as approximate idealizations of an obscure, unyielding experience. The complicated, partial merger of belief and practice in a particular region of social life yields a model of sociability. The coexistence of a few such dominant models of personal encounter produces an imaginative mapping of society.

Society in the family gets thoroughly permeated by the expectations, the claims, and the readings of motive that such a richly textured conception of social relations supports. The resulting cues for a life in common fall far short of a code of rules; they leave much open to idiosyncrasy, innovation, and disagreement. But they are also much more determinate than the generic idea of society. They enable people to settle into a recognized genre of social dealings, and they limit the uncertain appeal to intuition and inspiration.

No one-to-one relation holds between the institutional and the imaginative aspects of a formative context. The same institutional arrangements may be compatible with an indefinitely large number of alternative schemes of possible and desirable association. We must find the proximate explanations for the content of such a scheme in its unique history. The genealogies of the institutional components are only loosely connected; the histories of the institutions and of the beliefs must be even more loosely related.

The tightest link between the institutional and the imaginative aspects of a formative context consists in the rules and rights that largely define the major institutional settlements of a social order. For to reenact and to elaborate these rights and rules over long periods of time and extended bodies of social life, we must invoke a vision of social life.

Chapter 3 describes another, more subtle and inclusive connection between the institutional and the imaginative elements in a formative context. It argues that beliefs and institutions cannot long coexist unless they and the conceptual or practical activities that reproduce them remain comparable in at least one key respect: the extent to which they open themselves up to challenge and revision in the course of their daily use and reenactment.

To suggest more fully the character of such preconceptions about sociability and their place within a formative context, I return to the central idea of social orders as frozen politics. A simplified, fable-like version of this idea can bring out the main points. Consider the hypothetical moment when people interrupt or contain their broader struggle over the terms of human association. The settlements of this restabilized society would remain obscure and fragile if the former rivals continued to see them as mere truce lines and trophies in an ongoing social war. Exhaustion, not acceptance, would be the ruling principle of this superficially pacified social world. The disheartened but resentful or anxious contestants would continue to watch one another warily. They would view the surrounding quiescence as the barely veiled dissimulation of belligerence, as nothing more than the embodiment of a certain correlation of forces. As a result, they would lack any vision to serve as a code and a framework for their claims upon one another.

Moreover, the compromises that emerge from a bout of intensified social conflict are not just physical objects that persist, spontaneously, from moment to moment. People must patiently re-create and re-produce them in particular practical situations. A view of what the compromises signify must guide this re-creation and reproduction.

To treat the settlements as mere markers of forces is to sow disturbance as well as confusion. It is to invite people to continue the fight the better to test both what the settlements really were and what they have become.

But none of this programmed subversion really happens, at least not very long, very much, and on a very large scale. People settle down in the reordered society. They reinterpret the compromises and arrangements that emerge from a period of aggravated struggle as an intelligible and defensible blueprint for living together. They translate the indefinite idea of society into definite views of the relations and expectations suitable to the recurrent circumstances they encounter.

The reinterpretation is the easier to come by because the social war that marks the period of aggravated strife over formative arrangements is almost always partial – a revolutionary reform rather than a full-scale revolution. The converse of partiality in the war is partiality in the peace. People never resign themselves completely to the demands and the pretenses of the new order. They never entirely lose the sense that this settlement is the product of conflicts that may begin at any time. No sooner is established power jeopardized than the pieties of an inveterate prostration give way, suddenly and surprisingly, to defiance.

Each model of human association that helps constitute a plan of civilized life includes three elements: a group of ideals, slogans, and dogmas; a set of practices that, better or worse, stand for these ideals in fact; and an area of social experience to which the application of these principles remains confined. The sense of moral clarity about the fundamentals of social life depends upon the undisturbed coexistence of these three elements. This coexistence may be assailed from any of its three sides.

The most direct assault is also the rarest: an attack on the ideals that inspire and the slogans that describe a particular view of life in common, coupled with the prophetic presentation of an alternative. Thus, for example, we may repudiate an ideal of private community, held out as a model for family life, that emphasizes the exclusion of conflict and the sharing of values. We may reject this ideal as unfaithful to the deeper, inchoate, inarticulate longings that attract us to communal ideals in the first place: the hope of participating in human relations that diminish the conflict between our need for other people and our desire to avoid the threats they present to us.

The political prophet may hold up an image of community that addresses this yearning more directly: a style of communal attachments that recognizes the benefits of conflict and insists upon the priority of heightened vulnerability and mutual acceptance. In the name of this reconsidered communal ideal he may call for new forms of family life and personal intimacy. He may advocate a breaking down of the rigid contrasts between the private, personal spheres of social life to which communal standards remain confined and the public, practical areas from which they are banished.

More often, the fit among ideals, practices, and areas of application comes apart from the last two, more concrete sides. Suppose, for example, a particular model of social relations extended deliberately into a region of social life to which it had been thought unsuited. Thus, imagine democratic principles introduced into the area of industrial organization. There, those principles must be realized through practical arrangements different from the institutions that translate the reigning democratic ideal into a way of organizing government. The machinery of branches of government and of methods for coordinating their activities simply fails to fit the problems of the workplace and the enterprise. People must come up with new solutions.

Characteristically, however, there are several plausible alternatives. For example, should we maintain clear hierarchies in industry but make superiors more accountable? Or should we insist that accountability is no substitute for equality and try to keep hierarchy to whatever limits may be truly required by organizational effectiveness? The choice brings us up short, forcing us to choose as well among conceptions of what matters to us most about democracy. Thus, what began as a mere extension of familiar ideals into untried territory forces us in the end to refine and revise the ideal conceptions of human association with which we had started.

We may pretend to find the solution in a more careful analysis of our inherited view of democracy. In fact, however, we must choose among possibilities. These possibilities remained indistinct and confused so long as we failed to test the relation between our received ideals and their practical forms. The test consists in assessing alternatives – or in having them forced upon us.

Yet the pretense of finding rather than choosing is not entirely illusory. We must, however, recognize as the real subject matter of this search our inarticulate longings rather than our prized dogmas. Because the dogmas never completely shape the longings we can enlist the latter in reshaping the former.

A scheme of authoritative models of human association assumes two distinct forms in all societies that have central governments and organized legal systems.

In one register, the map of social forms exists as a set of refined assumptions and doctrines. In this high-flown mode, the scheme of models of sociability guides the interpretation or elaboration of legal rules and rights. For every extended interpretation of rules and rights must resort to guiding images of human association. From the detailed texture of rule, doctrine, and low-level analogy to the stock arguments that embody principles and counterprinciples and from these arguments to basic premises about the styles of association suitable to each area of social life – such is the itinerary of the law-applier as he moves outward from the uncontroverted to the perplexing. The last step of this trajectory may remain largely tacit in much of contemporary legal discourse. It is hard to reconcile the overt evocation of such models of sociability with the pretended contrast between restrained legal reasoning and freewheeling ideological controversy. But though it may remain implicit the final stage of the route continues to be indispensable. Without it, the lawyer loses the means to weight principle against counterprinciple in a given area of social practice or to prevent the inconclusive battle of clichés.

An argument from the need to allow government to regulate matters that condition the successful execution of its core constitutional responsibilities stands against an argument that a regime of rights requires governments not to overstep the boundaries of a tightly defined jurisdiction. An argument that security of transactions demands brightline rules is opposed by an argument that true predictability lies in the conformity of legal solutions to widely shared, flexible commercial practices. An argument that respect for the informal personalized loyalties of family life necessitates the intervention of the law in the internal life of the family runs up against an argument that people become most vulnerable and therefore most in need of protection in the intimate and unequal setting of the family. So it goes, on and on. Each of these characteristic deadlocks must be solved in practice by an appeal to detailed though largely implicit pictures of what democracies, markets, and families should be like. Such pictures combine current legal rules and doctrines with received ways of imagining society and of talking about its proprieties and possibilities.

A dominant scheme of possible and desirable association also exists in a second register, distinct from the refined though implicit dogmas of the law. In this second incarnation it persists as a set of diffuse, complicated, and even contradictory views of what society can and should be in the major characteristic situations of practical life. These preconceptions represent a silent subscript that informs people's claims upon one another and their expectations about society.

We never find a single, society-wide system of beliefs about the desirable forms of social coexistence, only the dominant ideals and the shared assumptions of particular classes and communities. Even these group-specific views fragment into countless individual life projects as people bend inherited prejudice and shared aspirations to the service of private anxieties. There are nevertheless unifying influences: the weight of established insitutional arrangements as well as the privileged hold that certain groups and traditions have upon the mass culture. Social ideals begin in present experiences, shaped by the imposing realities of current practices and institutions.

What is the relation between the two modes of a society's dominant moral geography: the implicit dogmas of the law and the diffuse preconceptions entertained by particular classes and communities? In societies, like those taken as examples in this chapter, that are not governed by foreign conquest elites, there can be no definitive, stark contrast between the two aspects of the imaginative scheme. Each gives the other cues. People find the shibboleths of the law repeated in the acts of officialdom and the slogans of government. The officials and lawyers in charge of reproducing and reinterpreting rules and rights must in turn preserve the vitality and contain the ambiguities of the authoritative ideals of association by ceaselessly reconnecting them to the imagined popular experience of social life. No wonder we find in our practices of moral and party-political controversy versions of the imaginative scheme of human association that, by their characteristics, stand midway between official dogmas and implicit convictions.

A formative context is a set of institutions and beliefs that reproduce the compulsive routines of conflict about the material or intangible resources that enable the occupants of some social stations to set terms to what the occupants of other stations may do. The cumulative, biased outcomes of such conflicts help create the social future within the social present. Remember that some components of a formative context have an especially direct bearing on some types of conflict. Thus, the elaborate, high-culture versions of the imaginative scheme of social life perform a decisive role in shaping legal controversies over rules and rights. But what key conflicts owe their force and content to the other, popular mode of the scheme of possible and desirable human association?

An Imaginative Counterpart to the Reform Cycles: Fighting the Exemplary Social Danger

Consider one such instance of compulsive routine – the way a culture singles out as primary certain dangers to social coexistence. These widely shared beliefs about the exemplary social danger are dreams turned nightmares. We have only to study them in detail to see how they reveal finely textured assumptions about the proper and possible forms of sociability. It is an example worth developing in detail as a capstone to the argument about routine without reason.

For these repeated apprehensions show the pervasiveness in social life of the problem presented earlier through the cycles of reform and retrenchment. Here, in an area far removed from rivalries over governmental power and policy, we encounter a similar, baffling compulsiveness. To explain this compulsiveness, we must uncover tacit beliefs about the right and feasible varieties of social life. This belief structure – closely associated with institutional arrangements – is too stable and influential to be confused with the routines that it helps form. But it is also too distinctive, too mired in a unique history, and too laden with a peculiar content to figure plausibly as a protagonist in a foreordained list of possible types of social organization or in a necessary sequence of such types. An understanding of the crucial assumptions requires the style of social explanation – different from both positivist social science and deep-structure social theory – that this book makes explicit.

In confirming the range of the problem of routine without reason, the following discussion of exemplary social anxieties also reveals how much is at stake in the effort to understand and to master the reasonless routines of our societies. Here, more clearly than in the experience of the reform cycles, we see how we rob ourselves of our context-breaking capabilities. As we witness the riddle of lawless constraint extended to the most impalpable aspects of social life we also discover where freedom begins. It begins, this discussion of overriding social fears suggests, when people seize on the transformative clues that both the routines and the frustration of the routines endlessly supply.

People share in preconceptions about the ultimate sources of danger to the communities they care about most. The effort to work these preconceptions out in practice and to mask or confront their failures then becomes another field for collective learning about what society is or might become.

From the Renaissance to the present day, major political doctrines have developed the idea of a civic order, animated by a particular spirit, sustained by a certain structure of institutions, and constantly endangered by a resurgent process of internal corruption that can result in subversive factionalism, bitter domestic discord, and weakness toward the foreign foe. Each major republican doctrine offers an explicit or tacit view of where the danger of corruption lies. Its institutional program responds to this peril.

The same way of thinking – the mutual adjustment between associative commitments and ideas of jeopardy – operates in our ordinary imagination of society. There is always an overriding danger and a master remedy. Each lends credence to the other, and more so as neither side is likely to be understood and described with clarity. It takes a great deal to jar people out of such presuppositions. Nonetheless, it happens, and it happens a little bit all the time.

Consider, for example, two characteristic patterns of enacted belief – one American, the other Russian – about the exemplary social danger. Though unevenly distributed among classes and communities and constantly challenged by contrasting ideas, each pattern enjoys widespread popular influence. Each finds support in the talk of elites and the conduct of officials.

The Americans worry about the horror of personal dependence. To be directly subject to the will of another person represents their most persistent idea of unhappiness. For them, the ultimate in republican degeneracy is the gangsterish manipulation of constitutional arrangements. The manipulators are less likely to be a self-serving class or party (both classes and parties are supposed to be too flaccid to be threatening, unless things get really bad) than a coterie of shameless political adventurers who turn their fellow citizens into dupes. Americans often think that the most pressing task in every well-ordered association is to factor out the element of power and then clamp down on it. They want to withdraw from the reformed but continuing reality of power the sting and the peril of personalized dependence or domination.

They resort to two main solutions. One response is to appeal to impersonal rules, impersonally applied. The other method is to bathe all associative forms, with their largely unregenerate hierarchies, in an atmosphere of pseudointimacy and mock professional colleagueship, a cheerful impersonal friendliness. By performing these two acts almost everywhere and all the time, the Americans think they are hitting the nail on the head. Once they have taken care of the main danger, they will be free to devote themselves to getting ahead in their jobs, living in their families, and, if they have done well enough, experimenting with their tastes and feelings.

Easier said than done. The move toward impersonality in the exercise of power fails to dispose of the practical costs and the social discontents of dependence. The forms of community and exchange and even the integrity of the electoral democracy itself suffer the influence of collective relations of power and advantage. But the organization of inclusive groups to fight over the structure of society might aggravate a factional bitterness with which the republic is ill-prepared to deal: a hostility of big classes rather than of crosscutting interest groups. Moreover, the use of governmental power to undermine private hierarchy may simply produce other, more formidable varieties of subjugation. That, at least, is a characteristic American apprehension.

Any entrenched advantage may yield the personalized power that Americans characteristically want to avoid. People may find it increasingly hard to believe that technical necessity or objective moral hierarchies account for the structure of social advantage. But where will the Americans draw the line between safeguarding equal opportunities in the great race and imposing equal outcomes? After all, every little victory wins a reward that means an advantage at the next stage of the contest. Besides, how can the overriding concern with the avoidance of personal dependency be squared with the widespread, stubborn allegiance to the family as the most credible experience of a social life that has become free from rigidified form? In the family, power is personal when it exists at all.

It is not enough to put such paradoxes down to those creative tensions and those tragic dilemmas that the more bookish Americans talk about. The paradoxes represent the unexpected revelations of a particular way of imagining society: a vision that hopes to tame power through markets and technical imperatives in practical life, through elections and constitutional safeguards in the state, and through natural affections in the family. To endure, the vision must at least be reconcilable with existing institutional arrangements.

Now consider the Russians. They are more inclined to believe in the futility of any attempt to disentangle personal power from the other elements of social life. They often seem to think that every form of association, starting with the family, depends on a structure of constraint and command that mixes up exploitation, exchange, and mutual love. Though the mixture makes social institutions irretrievably imperfect, its absence might make them even worse.

Everywhere, there are going to be people on top making demands on you and wrapping themselves up – with partial but only partial justification – in the garb of practical necessity and moral order. These bosses alternately bludgeon and cajole you into going along with them, in your proper sphere. They are afraid things will break down completely. They want their superiors to leave them alone.

Against this background there is cheating everywhere. People try to get away with something, sometimes for their own advantage but more often to the benefit of a community of greater concern (the family, the work gang, the local enterprise) and to the detriment of a higher authority or a rival organization. Only some of this evasive effort amounts to outright illegal activity. Only some of it gets chastised as immoral. The cheating is incurable, corrupting, and redemptive. It arises from the convergence of ordinary egotism with close collective loyalties. And it benefits from the widely shared conviction that the official scheme of things is never more than a variation on some original mess from which people can never completely get out.

The attempt to suppress the spontaneous movement of the local group, if taken to the letter, would make a bad situation even worse. Things would just stop running. Exploitation would become intolerable. The cheating is the perpetual marginal adjustment in the relations among community, exchange, and power. It both disturbs and softens the colossal burden of institutions upon the people who have to live and work in them.

Three dangers recur with cheating. There is the risk it will go too far and push the practical arrangements of society into collapse. People fear the short-run material consequences of such a collapse. Failing the surprises of war, revolution, and misery, they half accept the credentials of the established system to be the right order. The second threat is the total supression of the cheating. The result would be the closing down of the area of spontaneous adjustment, collective gusto, and nonconfrontational resistance that makes life bearable and institutions effective. The third peril is that the relatively more benign forms of cheating may cast a shadow of license and confusion favorable to more violent and destructive deeds. The former may ease the proliferation of the latter. The latter may serve as an excuse for the attempt ruthlessly to suppress the former.

At any moment, the discrepancy between daily conduct and official order can get out of hand in one of these three ways. The trouble is that this discrepancy is both an ever-present danger and a saving grace. What is there to do but to remain watchful and to bear cheerfully the rack of existence and the pretensions of power? Life, they say, has a longer history than the police.

These widespread American and Russian ideas of the paradigmatic danger in society differ widely in their qualities of vision as well as in their detailed content. The American prejudice is more revolutionary, because more openly subversive of hierarchy. It is also more absurd in the crudeness of its reductions. The Russian view is more human, because more inclusive and realistic in its image of peril. It is also, in actual effect, more tolerant of the stifling of aspiration by power. Nevertheless, both sets of preconceptions illustrate features characteristic of formative beliefs about the nature of deep jeopardy to association.

Both the American and the Russian patterns lie in a twilight zone between craziness and lack of imagination. They exemplify the insanity of the commonplace. They have some of the ideational features of obsession: they interpret a large amount of material through a scheme both highly selective and recalcitrant to falsification. That much might be true of science. But the interpretation also regularly contradicts what sensible people know about life.

The impression of a proximity to madness is justified. Experiences of blockage or liberation in personal reconciliation are crucial to the distinction between sanity and madness. To be sane is, in part, to avoid an experience of flat conflict between self-assertion and participation in community. It is also to experience your character as something that defines your self but that is nevertheless capable of change.

These confirming patterns of belief and conduct about paradigmatic social danger make experiments in reconciliation and self-transformation harder to stage. They are themselves the expression of a rigidified view of social possibility. Though they stop short of mental derangement, they survive on a diminished sense of reality and a lowered sense of the preposterous.

Both the American and the Russian idées fixes show how much beliefs about exemplary social danger take on a quality of self-ful-fillment. People end up giving them a plausible though inadequate basis of fact by acting as if they were true. Their expressed ambitions and fears start to cluster around the ability to impose or to escape personal dominion, in the American style, or to avoid being duped in the course of manipulating the connection between allegiance and cheating, in the Russian experience. The limiting image gives rise to a second-order social reality. This reality confuses and demoralizes people even in their moments of insight or invention.

Each of these sets of beliefs about the paradigmatic danger in social life has a forgotten history. This history repeats in microcosm the birth of a social world out of concrete fights and failures to fight as the institutions and doctrines that are its frozen politics win a life of their own. In each instance the particular history of conflict sets its mark upon dogma and preconception though its exact translation into ideas about exemplary peril remains tortuous and obscure. It would be difficult to exclude any part of history from the history of such assumptions, for the evolution of our authoritative models of sociability and of our haunting social fears is bound up with the outcomes of particular struggles for power. Some events nevertheless stand out in the emergence of each of these views of the source of trouble in society.

In the American experience the dismantling of corporatist society played the crucial role. (The estate-like organization of classes had still been a possibility in the colonies.) During the first generation of the Republic these events culminated in the development of a constitutional order that, with the egregious exception of slavery, combined the disauthorization of all institutionalized relations of personal dependency with republican arrangements designed to smother conflict and to perpetuate deadlock. The ideal of the independent professional, businessman, or farmer turned into a central myth of self-reliance. This myth ran little risk of being effectively challenged by an underclass made up first of slaves and disorganized dependents. Nor would it readily be defied by immigrants who thought they were passing through a purgatory of enrichment on their way back home. In a Republic in which individuals were not to be personally subject to one another, all particular bonds would rest upon the will. The basic scheme of republican life was supposed to be a once-and-for-all invention.

The failure of the Russian peasantry to free itself collectively from subjugation and the ensuing confusion of communal forms with the conveniences of governmental or landlord control had a fateful impact upon the development of the Russian idea of exemplary danger. There were few aspects of society except revolutionary agitation, religious devotion, and the subtleties of family life, in which communal attachments could significantly disengage from an entrenched hierarchical scheme. In this world of bungling centralism and broken rebellion nothing got done, beyond the daily survival of the household, that did not require the higher-ups at every rung of every hierarchy alternately to harass their underlings and to turn the other way. The inability of the Bolshevik Revolution to preserve any vestige of soviet-type conciliar institutions or to allow for conflictual mass participation ensured the persistence of this way of doing things, though changing its distributional impact and its accepted sense.

Both the American and the Russian patterns reveal an inconsolable skepticism about the experimental transformability of social life, even if Americans more often see themselves as optimists. In one instance the most that can be hoped for is to escape the nightmare of personal dependence; in the other, to keep the adjustment between allegiance and cheating under control. The skepticism reveals itself in distrust, though the target of the distrust differs in the two situations.

Trust as the acceptance of vulnerability is more than an attitude; it is also a vision of unexplored and unrealized human opportunity. Like everything in a conditional social world, beliefs about exemplary social evil limit the pressure to advance in the refinement and testing of this vision. They put people under a spell. The half-forgotten terrors of a compelling collective history live on all the more stubbornly in a diffuse atmosphere of habit and preconception.

Though such ideas of exemplary danger diminish the opportunities of society they also trivialize its horrors. The conception of an overriding threat to social life belittles the indefinite and unlimited quality of mutual need and fear, longing and jeopardy. The triviality and the skepticism grow from a common root: the concealment of the gap between the open-ended idea of society and the given, limited stock of forms of human association.

The beliefs about society enshrined in the ruling conceptions of paradigmatic danger repeatedly prove themselves inadequate in the course of everyday life. Despite all the forces that keep people from coming to an awareness of this inadequacy and acting upon it, it presses itself upon them as a dull intimation and disquiet. At any moment this disquiet may help prompt an alternative view of social reality and possibility. Practical demands or spiritual aspiration can serve equally well as the initiating impulse.

An American manager in the late twentieth century, for example, may think he can get his workers to produce more willingly and effectively if he opens up opportunities for more independent teamwork in the production process. He may see such experiments as innovations that represent no real threat to the distribution of power and profit. He may also be moved by ideas that underline the horrors of unmediated personal subjection and the lure of pseudointimacy. Once in place, these modest reforms may serve as points of departure for conflicts and inventions that not only unsettle established social arrangements but enable people to imagine untried ways of working and living together. Such discoveries highlight the gap between humanitarian delicacy or bureaucratic impersonality and civic engagement and equality. They threaten to discredit the view of how things work implicit in the reigning images of exemplary danger.

A contemporary Soviet bureaucrat and politician may feel the best way to induce workers and enterprises to execute their part of the plan is to concentrate more authority in the hands of local managers. The central government can reassert control whenever this allowance for greater decentralized discretion permits a buildup of defensive positions of privilege. The Soviet ruler may be encouraged in this posture not only by a desire for reforms that leave the basic structure of hierarchy in place but also by the conviction that the timeless interplay of cheating and allegiance can become less destructive by being partly institutionalized. But these limited freedoms and initiatives may suggest the possiblility of other, bolder reforms that change the character of the state and offer people opportunities of reconstruction rather than mere instruments of self-defense.

Nothing can stop people from experiencing disturbances that threaten their conventional ideas about the chief peril in society. If, for example, you read the high and low literature written by Americans in the two generations following World War II and studied their popular entertainments, you discovered that their fears were not as shallow as their dogmas. Americans worried about the difficulty of asserting control over the terms of their own public and private lives. They often considered themselves victims of forces they were unable to master or understand.

The less favored regarded themselves as locked into collective situations of isolation and disadvantage from which they could escape, if at all, only as resolute and lucky individuals. The more fortunate felt maddeningly defeated in their attempts at self-expression, in the midst of a heartless and hedonistic cult of personal experimentation. Many aspired to a material or spiritual power that would give the lie to the impotent privacy of their lives.

They did not find in frequent doses of the depersonalization of power or in the advance of professionalism and pseudointimacy satisfactory solutions to these problems. After the end of the Vietnam War and the civil rights movement, with a sense alternating between puzzled or cynical annoyance and fatalistic desperation, much of the citizenry gave up expecting anything from the governmental politics of their country other than the avoidance of great disasters, the defense of narrow group interests, and the assertion of national power – but not its use to disrupt basic hierarchies of power and advantage. Innocence, rather than transformative imagination and capacity, became the highest ambition of the best. When they achieved it, it corrupted them. The ordeal of frustration did not overthrow the dominant view of exemplary danger, but it did make this view less credible. It suggested the need for different ideas about how society worked, how it changed, and what it might become. That is what always happens. The closed cycles and the enslaving obsessions of society yield the first clues not just to a different world but to a world of a different kind.

APPENDIX:
ECONOMIC POLICY, REFORM CYCLES, AND
FORMATIVE CONTEXTS
IN THE SOVIET-STYLE ECONOMIES

The following discussion extends the description and analysis of the communist reform cycles and explores their connections with the institutional settings in which these cycles occur. In so doing, it shows how the distinctive problems of contemporary economies depend on the institutional arrangements that also shape the reform cycles discussed in this chapter. The overlap between the institutional conditions of the reform cycles and of economic swings should not cause surprise. For one thing, the recurrent troubles of an economy become at once topics, causes, and effects of a reform cycle. For another thing, the economic difficulties have the same quality as the frustrating rehearsal of inconclusive policy response in the reform cycles – the quality of a compulsion resulting from a presupposition. The traditional economist may be tempted to protest that such are the punishments of those who seek to replace the market by other methods of allocation. But he fails to appreciate the width of the gap between the abstract idea of a market and any particular institutional arrangements for economic decentralization, just as his Soviet counterpart may identify the principle of political control of accumulation with the centralist devices he finds at hand. The same style of analysis exemplified in this appendix can readily apply to the contemporary North Atlantic economies. Chapter 5 of this book outlines such an application in the course of presenting proposals for revolutionary economic reform. The argument of *False Necessity* shows that the task of opening economic life more fully to innovation and renewal is inseparable from the larger effort to develop formative contexts that bring framework-respecting routine closer to framework-transforming invention.

Consider once again and in greater detail certain features of the reform cycle in Soviet-model economies and polities. Some of these characteristics have to do with the seemingly technical economic difficulties that appeared at each moment of the cycle; others, with the class alliances that tended to emerge with each cyclical swing. By studying the operations of this system you learned that even the most seemingly technical phenomena of economic life became intelligible only against the background of institutional arrangements and ideas. These ideas and arrangements amounted to something much more specific than the vague idea of a planned or command economy. You also discovered that a particular relation between limits to the mobility of capital and constraints on access to governmental power played a crucial role in determining the economic and social content of the reform cycle.

Take the economic problems first and begin with the moment of maximum centralization. At such times, the communist economies were beset by the twin problems of hoarding and shortage. They were equally plagued by a tendency to exaggerate investment goals, to fall short in achieving them, and then to compensate for the difference by a series of stopgap measures that aggravated still further the simultaneous underemployment and shortage of resources. Remember the essentials of the institutional (and ideological) context within which these economic problems occurred: close control of governmental power by an elite that avoided occasions for mass militancy and mass-based partisan conflict; the claim to govern on behalf of and for the workers and, through both accelerated growth and the destruction of class privilege, to lay the basis for communism; the assumption by the central government of the authority to shape the allocation of resources (an authority that might be extensively qualified during the decentralizing moments of the reform cycle); prevalence in industry, administration, and warfare of a sharp contrast between task definers and task executors; and, consequently, the existence of managerial cadres clearly separated from the rank-and-file workers and more or less subordinate to the central rulers and planners and the entrenchment of different segments of the work force in well-defined and unequally advantaged places in the division of labor, an entrenchment subject only to the disturbances of the job hierarchy that the rulers or the managers occasionally provoked.

At the most centralized moments of this institutional system, hoarding and shortage served as weapons of managerial self-defense, closely connected to the overextension and underachievement of planning goals that represented the other characteristic problem of the centralizing phase of the cycle. The exaggeration of planning goals, at all levels of the economy, had several convergent causes. Though one or another of these pressures might be contained, it was hard to reverse all of them without changing the basic institutional arrangements of the economy.

Planners set targets with the help of information collected from enterprise managers. The more prudent managers – the managers not out to build empires – might want to minimize the tasks ultimately assigned to them by the central plan. But even these cautious managerial bureaucrats had reason, at the early stages, to overstate both how much additional capital and manpower they needed to accomplish any given task and how much the planners could get from them by giving them the maximum of financial and labor support.

For one thing, the amount of capital and manpower entrusted to the manager was likely to depend upon the expected contribution of his enterprise to the total production plan. His relative share in capital and manpower represented both a standard of success and source of tangible material advantage. It determined what he would have to work with at the anticipated moment when he would need to scale his plans down and how well he could expect to do in the next round of planning allocations. For another thing, the managers knew that the planners could not let them go out of business nor react too violently to a failure in the execution of their assigned tasks. Less production was better than no production at all, and the workers and machines had to be kept busy.

The rulers, for their part, had independent reasons to bloat the plan by pursuing a policy of heroic industrialization. The minimal legitimacy of their rule depended upon visible material success and at least apparent victory in the competition with the West. As the governmental and economic order grew more centralized and approached the extreme limit of a terroristic war by the state against society, the implicit exchange of promises of wealth for passive acquiescence became more clear-cut. At times of more moderate centralization the overstatement of the plan then became a way to fudge embarrassing allocations of resources between production and consumption or among different sectors of the productive system. In this respect it played a role similar to that of governmentally fueled inflation in the contemporary Western economies.

When the execution of the unrealistic plan started to break down, the rulers and planners found themselves compelled to make concessions to the managers in order to avoid a disastrous, economywide downswing of production. These concessions could not themselves obey any plan: their distribution remained in thrall to the sudden appearance of crucial bottlenecks that had to be broken quickly on pain of paralyzing broad sectors of the economy.

Once the plan went into operation, the motives that had encouraged the initial, heroic exaggeration of productive capacities were checked and superseded by other forces that led to underachievement. One of these forces was the recalcitrance of workers who were practically unremovable (because of job security), susceptible (because of the relative freedom to change jobs) to seduction by rival firms that promised easier working conditions, and yet incapable of being prodded forward by the promise of higher wages (because of the severity of wage constraints that resulted from the combination of job security with a commitment to avoid inflation).

Or consider the "ratchet principle," according to which future assigned tasks depended upon present performance. The pressure to underachievement that this principle generated was limited only by the fear of punishment and by the desire to keep and enlarge the quota of capital and labor assigned to the firm in the future plan. Like everything else in this tangle of problems the escape from the ratchet principle turned out to be harder and more momentous than at first appeared. To replace it the planners needed to base task assignments on long-term norms: relations of input to output for each enterprise. Suppose that such a system could have dispensed with the operation of an independent price system and that it had managed to evaluate cost and production in real rather than nominal terms. It would still have required each enterprise to be treated as an independent accounting unit that, to a larger degree, could succeed or fail on its own. Such a procedure implied decentralization with all the new problems that – as the next stage of the discussion shows – decentralization brought with it.

In Soviet-style economies the crucial constraints on additional investment lay in actual physical limits rather than in limits of effective demand. Resource constraints never exist as brute fact, somehow independent of the institutional arrangements of economic life: the scarcity you can ever actually see is always the one that a real economy, with all its defining institutional practices, has helped perpetuate. Nevertheless, the primacy of physical limits, institutionally shaped, served as one of the many links connecting the embarrassments of the bloated plans to the problems of hoarding and shortage.

Whether or not they were co-responsible for the plan's initial lack of realism the managers hoarded capital and labor. They had an unlimited thirst for resources with which to guarantee the ability to perform their assigned tasks. They therefore also had a powerful incentive to conceal, whenever possible, the extent of the resources at hand. For the size of his reserves in investment funds and manpower determined the relative ease or difficulty with which the manager would be able to keep his bosses at bay and his underlings happy. Moreover, for the reason already recalled in the earlier allusion to the ratchet principle, extreme centralization could not readily be reconciled with an attempt to reward or punish enterprises on the basis of efficiency measured by a real relation between inputs and outputs. Given the relative lack of such a measure and the prudential value of reserves there was little incentive to reveal or let go underemployed physical or human capacity.

A number of secondary forces, similarly anchored in the motivational logic of the underlying institutional system, aggravated the twin problems of shortage and slack. Thus, for example, the command of capital became an excuse to demand more labor and the command of labor to demand more capital, for what good was one without the other? The commitment to job security, combined with the determination to exercise an anti-inflationary control over wage rates and an egalitarian resistance to wage differentials, meant that salary competition among enterprises could not be used to clear labor markets.

The pervasiveness of hoarding and shortages had disastrous economic and social effects. The social consequences aggravated the economic results. One important economic effect was the vulnerability of large areas of the economy to what – from the planners' perspective – looked like largely unforeseeable bottlenecks. Another economic implication was the pressure to break these bottlenecks by forced substitutions at the enterprise or economywide level: the replacement of one physical or human input by another because – as the result of pervasive hoarding and shortage – the input of choice had become simply unavailable.

Now consider the social consequences of shortage and hoarding. The central government found itself bedeviled by an extraordinary display of economic failures that weakened its authority in every theater of its activity. The ordinary citizen as consumer had to stand endlessly in line and undertake in his domestic economy the humiliating, farcical counterpart to the forced substitutions of the national economy. At the same time, the permanent scarcity of labor produced under the communist regime the exaggerated equivalent to a Western-style market under full employment: a sullen restlessness by workers who found themselves in a permanent seller's market for labor despite the severity of the constraints on freedom, wages, and consumption. Under conditions of governmental stability this restlessness imposed on both the central authorities and the enterprise managers the need to bargain, however implicitly, with the laborers. The sole alternative to placating the labor force was to carry centralization to the forbidding, risky extreme of a terroristic war of the state against society. In a circumstance of divided and enfeebled governmental authority or inspired worker leadership, the restlessness could even flare up into an open defiance of government.

All these problems encouraged the rulers to attempt a form of economic decentralization that would harness the motivations of workers and managers alike to the goal of repeated breakthroughs in production and productivity. Such a decentralization was meant to take place within the boundaries of the basic institutional arrangements mentioned earlier. To satisfy this crucial condition it had to combine certain features. The managers gained a freer hand to invest and to organize. The enterprise became, to a significant though qualified extent, an independent unit for reckoning gains and losses. This entrepreneurial freedom in turn had to obey a series of restrictions. The workers, for example, could not be readily fired, though neither could they expect to trespass very far on managerial prerogative. Enterprise gains and losses might be translated into rewards or penalties for managers and workers. Those, however, who succeeded by skill or luck would not be allowed to go on building industrial empires. Those who failed could expect some governmental bailout, at least unless they were shown to be tangibly at fault.

The combination of the move toward decentralization with this particular pattern of institutional restraints reproduced the problems of slack and shortage in different form and elicited the same disruptive, ad hoc responses to them that these problems provoked at the moment of centralization. Take, as an example, the restrictive effect of job security. Severe institutional constraints circumscribed popular militancy for access to governmental power or economic advantage. At the same time the planners and their masters remained committed both to keep control of the basic relation between consumption and investment and to limit the inequality of incomes. For an increase in income inequality would discredit the government's socialist visage and aggravate destabilizing resentment and conflict among social groups. Both social peace and economic stability required wage restraint. Given wage restraint and the exclusion of popular power, a close to absolute job security seemed one of the few remaining ways to show the worker that he lived in a workers' state. (This inference was no more unavoidable than any other single feature of this institutional system. Thus, some Soviet-style economies, like the Chinese economy of the 1970s and 1980s, had accommodated to widespread unemployment and job insecurity.)

Once job security had been respected for a considerable time, it began to seem more like a vested right than a legitimizing expedient. Its denial to workers or managers might provoke an intense resistance that threatened to disorganize the economy and to endanger the ruling elite. To provide inclusive job security in such an institutional setting the planners had to maintain prices at a level that would keep the least efficient enterprises going while also guaranteeing that these enterprises would be able to sell their products. The desire to ensure a seller's market, combined with the anti-inflationary commitment to price and wage restraint and with the quasi-inflationary device of allowing consumers' income to rise as a whole, generated a permanent market disequilibrium. Too much demand chased too few goods. Under this particular disequilibrium, in this unique institutional context, the consumers' dearth became the producers' shortage and slack. Enterprises could not get rid of superfluous manpower and did not need to. Every additional amount of capital or inventory could either be turned into a product with guaranteed sale or hoarded as an asset whose current productive uses were undervalued in the price-fixed retail market.

There was also a second-order set of reasons for shortage and hoarding at the decentralizing moment of the communist reform cycle. On the basis of their previous experience, the managers foresaw that a bout of recentralization would eventually begin. They therefore kept all the manpower and capital they could get in anticipation of the time when physical allocations would predominate over regulated competition within a partly free price system. Thus, all the causes of economic irrationality that operated in the more centralized economy continued to act in the more decentralized system, either because they were directly applicable or because they applied by anticipation.

So far my argument has been meant to show that in its two main alternative modes this Soviet-model economy suffered from problems that seriously damaged its productive effectiveness. Problems that seemed technically economic in nature arose in fact from particular institutional arrangements. An economic order committed to combine market decentralization with the social control of accumulation should avoid these institutional practices, if only for the sake of productive effectiveness. It will become increasingly clear that much more than economic efficiency is at stake.

The economic problems I have described were sometimes considered the unconnected consequences of particular, easily reversible errors of policy and, at other times, the inherent problems of a socialist or planned economy. Both views were mistaken. The difficulties could not be corrected by a change of policy unless the change amounted to the revolutionary reform of the underlying institutional structure: the substitution of at least some of the components of the formative context. This context, however, represented something far more particular than the idea of a planned or socialist economy, just as the corresponding problems of economic management in the industrialized Western economies of the time had to be attributed to a series of practical arrangements that could not be derived from any analysis of the abstract idea of a decentralized or mixed economy.

Similar points can be made, much more briefly, about the social alliances and antagonisms that decentralizing reform encouraged. Again and again, two sets of alliances stood in opposition. The party bureaucrats and the ordinary, semiskilled workers regularly opposed such reform: the former, because it threatened their power and perquisites; the latter, because its logic of economic incentives and increased competition tended to widen the range of wage inequality. The technical intelligentsia, the managers, and the most skilled workers supported decentralization: each of these groups stood to gain from it in both power and money. This division of alliances represented more than the casual result of an easily corrigible distribution of benefits. It resulted from a convergence between the economic reforms that were feasible within the boundaries of established institutions and the collective identities and group interests these same institutions helped sustain. For a leftist the result was a Hobson's choice. For a leftist who adhered to the program of empowered democracy set out later in this book, the outcome represented a proof of failure: he wanted to find the institutional arrangements that would minimize the tendency toward the emergence of groups with entrenched places in the division of labor.

You can confirm the dependence of such economic constraints and cycles on particular institutions by performing a straightforward intellectual experiment. Consider how the embarrassments of Soviet-style economies change in a simplified version of the Yugoslav self-management system. Two key characteristics mark this alternative economic order: the transfer of property rights to the work force of each enterprise, turned into joint owners of the productive stock, and the exclusion of mass-based party conflict over the control and uses of governmental power. Thus, this approach differs from the Soviet-style economy by granting the enterprise and its work force more autonomy than they can hope to gain even in the decentralizing movement of the communist reform cycle. But it also differs from the alternative proposed in Chapter 5: first, because it keeps property rights largely intact and together, transferring them to a group of rightholders rather than dissociating the powers that compose the unified property right and attributing them to different agents and organizations; second, because it maintains central governmental power closely guarded.

The characteristic economic difficulties of such a system become apparent if you assume a more unqualified transfer of property rights to enterprise workers than the Yugoslav system in fact allowed.

That such a system cannot be reconciled with an extension and deepening of democratic ideals is clearly implied by its very definition. That it imposes severe constraints upon the mobility of capital and enables particular groups to hold capital indefinitely on terms only obliquely and sporadically related to their productive contributions is just as true though less obvious.

Imagine first a simplified version of this economy: one that pursues to the extreme the transfer of property rights to the work force of each firm. The current employees of each enterprise, benefited by almost absolute job security and with an almost unqualified power over the capital at their disposal, may produce, invest, and pay out in the way that seems best suited to their present interests. This prerogative can be exercised chiefly through two parallel though seemingly contrary policies, which might be called running up and running down capital.

To run up capital is to take advantage of past efforts and "undeserved" market windfalls so as to increase the capital intensivity and therefore the labor productivity of the enterprise. This increase in turn makes it possible both to raise wages and to widen the wage differentials among segments of the national work force or regions of the country. The central government may impose limits upon the degree of inequality. But these limits cannot amount to much; the more significant they become, the more they appear to eviscerate the self-management scheme itself. Thus, even a progressive income tax is harder to accept in such a system than in the Western-style economies.

To run down capital is to pay out the maximum in enterprise earnings to the workers or supervisory personnel at the cost of further investment. (Assume, for the sake of simplicity, no major conflict of interest among managers, technicians, and ordinary workers.) When this process is repeated throughout the economy as a whole, it prejudices future generations rather than poorer workers or regions.

You cannot count on the running up and running down of capital to cancel each other out and thereby correct the effects of vested claims over capital. Successive market advantages, often completely unrelated to worker effort or managerial skill, may translate into both the capital-intensive investment that widens the gap in productivity and income among segments of the work force *and* a lower rate of output-expanding investment than would ensure continued growth or be preferred in any number of alternative institutional systems. To be sure, each of these processes may be counterbalanced by other institutional arrangements. For example, the conditions on which the enterprise can obtain needed external finance may prompt it to resist the temptation to excessive payouts. Even then, however, other consequences of the absolute control over capital by an entrenched group are sure to appear.

In its efforts to deal with these difficulties the central government faces constraints generated by the same institutional and ideological order that had created the difficulties in the first place. Self-management, on the basis of a comprehensive property right, assigned to the enterprise work force rather than to central government or private stockholders, serves to shape and legitimize this particular institutional form of economic decentralization. Any attempt by the central government to compensate the prejudicial effects of this system on the distribution of jobs and incomes or the possibilities of innovation and growth appears as an arbitrary attack on the crucial principle of decentralization. Such an attack is all the harder to condone in a society where economic decentralization has no other available instrument and where the exclusion of democratic party conflict and effective electoral accountability leaves self-management as the only visible token of popular power. Thus, here too microeconomic constraints connect to the limits upon macroeconomic management through a series of links that include expectations about the uses of governmental power and presuppose particular institutional arrangements.

3

The Making of Society Through Politics

A Spectrum of Social Experiments

THE IDEA OF LARGE-SCALE OPTIONS

THIS chapter links the analytical description of formative contexts to a theory of their genesis and transformation. It compares the major institutional complexes that make up the formative contexts of contemporary societies to some major institutional alternatives. The sum of these comparisons suggests a larger map of possible directions that the organization of society has taken or might take. The argument focuses on only two aspects of contemporary formative contexts: first, the system of private rights, especially as it addresses the relation between government and society, and, second, the organization of work. But a more complete version of the argument would take up every aspect of the institutional orders discussed in the preceding chapter and subject them to the same style of analysis.

The strategy is simple, though its intentions are complex. I place each of the institutional complexes discussed on a spectrum whose description conforms to a single principle.

The spectrum is meant to distinguish actual and imaginary variants of social life rather than to describe a necessary historical progression. At one pole of the spectrum the contrast between the routine reproduction and the revolutionary transformation of an institutional framework reaches its point of maximum force; there is a minimum of opportunity to challenge and revise the arrangements that make up an institutional structure. At the other pole of the spectrum the contrast between routine and transformation weakens to the vanishing point; to every aspect of formative order there then corresponds an ordinarily available activity that brings it into question and opens it up for revision.

Three central ideas are developed in the course of the chapter. The first is that extended sets of institutional arrangements and the formative contexts they make up embody different degrees of advance in the denaturalization of social life: in the emancipation of our experiences of practical or passionate connection from the constraints of an entrenched scheme of social division and hierarchy and in the effacement of the contrast between fighting within a structure of social life and fighting about such a structure.

The second idea builds upon the first and constitutes the main concern of the argument. It is the thesis that the institutional orders of contemporary societies (i.e., of the North Atlantic democracies as well as of the communist regimes) represent no more than a partial move toward the denaturalization of society. We can imagine more complete realizations of the ideal of empowerment through denaturalization. The program of social reconstruction presented later makes good on this possibility.

The third guiding idea of the chapter develops the first two and represents the chief contribution of the argument to the explanatory theory of this book. Particular arrangements cannot easily coalesce within an institutional complex nor can these arrangements coexist over time if they embody very different degrees of the breaking open of society to politics. Thus, we can take a preliminary step toward a view that acknowledges the existence of constraints upon the recombination or substitution of the components of formative contexts without making these constraints depend upon the assumptions of deep-structure social theory. We can deny that these institutional and imaginative orders stand or fall together as a single piece without having to conclude that all institutional arrangements and imaginative preconceptions can be combined with all others. The thesis about the internal constitution of formative contexts justifies and develops retrospectively the descriptive approach taken in Chapter 2 toward the institutional and imaginative frameworks of routine activity. This thesis also anticipates a major theme of the view of society making to be developed in the next chapter.

Because the institutional arrangements compared and contrasted in this chapter represent different points in a spectrum of degrees of emancipation from false necessity, I call them large-scale options of social life. But notice that nothing in the following argument is meant to imply that the particular institutional arrangements discussed here represent the sole possible forms of the degrees of denaturalization they embody. By contrast to a social theory that relies on the conception of a closed list of possible social worlds (whether or not ordered in an evolutionary sequence), the argument assumes that each level of emancipation from false necessity can be realized through an indefinite range of distinct institutional forms. This variety is limited only by our institutional tradition and our reconstructive imagination. The particular forms of state–society relations or of labor organization selected for discussion in this chapter are chosen only because they are familiar. Because they are familiar, they also serve a subsidiary aim of providing categories for the comparative analysis of formative contexts. These categories are put to work in the next chapter, which draws a theory of transformation out of a schematic historical argument about the genesis of contemporary formative contexts.

By contrast to the distinctively evolutionary forms of deep-structure social theory, I presuppose no relentless march toward an ever greater emancipation from false necessity. The view of context making worked out in Chapter 4 defends weaker claims. Among these claims are the ideas that a cumulative development toward such an emancipation is possible, that such an advance has often taken place, that this possibility has often been realized, though never flawlessly or irreversibly, and that its actualization constitutes the precondition for a broad range of forms of human empowerment.

The large-scale options of social life studied in this chapter might be thought of as experiments, in the sense of the experiments Galileo and his successors introduced into modern science. Each such experiment renders accessible a reality that would otherwise remain unavailable. Thus, Galileo wanted to determine free fall and projectile motion in a void. By so doing, he could put at the center of his theory concepts that united two features. They described the most general case of motion conceivable to the thought of the time – the uniform acceleration of a freely falling body. They also allowed for mathematical treatment by constructing a circumstance in which all the parameters and variables could be specified. To reach this goal, however, Galileo had to invent a series of ingenious arguments and practical situations that revealed what would happen in a void. These arguments and situations singled out the effect of the resisting medium and generated what, taken all in all, amounted to a substitute for the inaccessible void.

Each of the large-scale options of social existence discussed here represents an experiment, in a sense similar to the Galilean idea; an experiment from the standpoint of people whose immediate experience is governed primarily by one of the other options of social life. Memory and thought rather than practical manipulation may stage the experiment. For each of these alternative directions of cumulative change turns what would otherwise be minor or residual aspects of social experience into the central themes of an entire practical or imaginative ordering of life. Remembered and analyzed, they make accessible another world – a world that seems very different from the one we are in but that is nevertheless a commentary on us as well as on its own inhabitants. If we look hard enough, we discover in contemporary society the signs of this alien reality. The principle that underlies this imaginative possibility is the same that makes a person feel, as his own insight and originality advance, that what other people do and are is also a demonstration of what he too can become or already is.

All the large-scale options together represent experiments in relation to a larger whole: the general case, the truth about humanity
and society. But here the resemblance to Galileo's experiments with
the void stops. There is no set of situations that can exhaustively
represent this general case, if only because historical experiments
help construct what they also reveal. No closed set of lawlike forces
governs this constructive activity, commanding its evolution and
determining its outer limits.

My argument orders these large-scale options according to the
degree and character of their departure from a limiting case. This
limiting case is the circumstance that consists in the near exclusion
of social experiments. In such a circumstance the arrangements and
preconceptions that constitute a formative context remain only minimally vulnerable to transformative conflict. People then come closest
to acting as if the social context of their life and thought were indeed
the context of all contexts: the true face of civilization. They live
almost as if the naturalistic premise were true.

You can then imagine several kinds of departure from this circumstance: some in the practical organization of government and
workers; others in the established vision of right and possible association. Each departure emphasizes directions that particular societies
have actually followed. Each also amounts to an experiment about
the nature of our ability to keep going when we hit against the limits
imposed upon us by our contexts.

EXPERIMENTS WITH THE STATE: PRIVILEGE
AND RIGHT

Imagine now a series of greater or lesser departures from the limiting
case of a society without experiments. Some of these departures will
have to do with the life of the state and of its public order of privilege
and right. By analyzing this life, we come to grasp some of the basic
alternative forms of rights and of the constitutional arrangements
that support these alternatives.

The System of Privilege

The first departure is hardly a departure at all; or rather it is a departure whose transformative uses are ordinarily contained as soon
as they are realized. Central governments are the most powerful of
all the instruments that can be used to transform society. But in the
circumstance of minimal experimentation that I now describe, the
state becomes little more than society constantly willing itself into
existence. Position in the state and position in society become one
and the same. A one-to-one relation must be established between

the exact form of each group's participation in governmental affairs, or of exclusion from them, and each group's power to set terms to the activities of other groups in the daily rounds of work and production. The basic form of right is then the participation in a status that directly links public office and economic privilege.

Defined abstractly, such a situation may seem to imply the thoroughgoing suppression of all transformative opportunities. The persistence of such opportunities, however, becomes apparent as soon as you consider how this restrictive correspondence between office and privilege has worked in practice.

On the one hand, there is the form of the city-state republic of Western antiquity. The citizens stand united against the foreigner and the excluded mass. A struggle goes on, however, within the citizenry. Some groups try to establish an inner civic oligarchy, and subordinate or even disenfranchise the ordinary citizenry. Other groups (the citizen people and their self-appointed captains) resist them in the name of civic condominium over the state and joint rights to the incalculable material and spiritual benefits of access to governmental power. The struggle may fall into the repetitious cycle of routine politics of city-state republics that I described earlier. But this recurrent conflict does create a permanent occasion for fighting over what society will be like. This fighting appears as a contest over the right to participate in central government, the institution that, more than any other, defines a version of civic life and defends it against all enemies within and without.

In the agrarian–bureaucratic empires, the link between public office and private privilege took the form of a hierarchy of ranks that included a ruling imperial household and a range of orders of aristocrats and notables. Such a hierarchy ties together, in the definition of each social rank, a certain measure and mode of access to governmental power, on the one hand, and particular privileged claims on social resources and human labor. But the tie-in and the hierarchy it supports tend to become indistinct and controversial at both the grass roots and the commanding heights of the social order.

The most forceful and perspicacious masters of the state strive to liberate governmental power from the constraining, destructive effect of magnate privilege. They make privilege into a precarious gift of central government, transferrable at will from one group, family, or one individual to another. In this way they try to turn both access to governmental power and privileged claims upon wealth and labor into benefits conferred from on high.

At the same time, the masses never completely participate in the order of ranks. Lacking regular access to governmental power and forced to serve as passive objects of the privileges of those who do enjoy such access, they remain outsiders to the corporate hierarchies of their oppressors. If they are allowed to go too far, through popular rebellion initiated from below or revolutionary despotism led from above, the whole hierarchical order of society collapses. Nothing and nobody within that hierarchy remains safe. But if the material security and the organizational autonomy of the working people, especially of the small-scale independent property-owners, are totally destroyed, the realm falls under the dominion of rival magnates and the central state order begins to collapse, together with the commercial economy.

So long as these twin dangers of unraveling from the top and from the bottom were held in check, agrarian–bureaucratic societies survived. But even then the fighting went on, spurred by the interplay between a recurrent opportunity and an unbounded ambition. The opportunity was the periodic weakening of the realm. The people in charge of central governments found it hard to mobilize the resources needed to manage economic or military crises. For these rulers faced severe constraints upon their ability to use governmental power for transformative purposes or to appeal directly to the class of smallholders over the heads of landowning oligarchs. The unbounded ambition that helped refuel the characteristic conflicts of these societies was each group's and each family's effort to change place in an order whose design was seen to be a product of conflict even when it was proclaimed to be a gift from heaven.

Thus, each historical example of a tight correspondence between place in the state and place in society turns out to have more room for transformative conflict than appears on the surface. Far from being a form of the life of the state and its law that belongs to a superseded moment of history, it remains an active possibility at any moment. Thus, the revolutionary state in twentieth-century societies often fell back on a new version of the radical politics of privilege, as an analysis of the formative institutional contexts of contemporary communist countries suggests. But whatever new forms the politics of privilege may assume, the chance to fight about the institutional and imaginative framework of social life remains. It remains even in this, the style of legal and governmental order that most severely represses the remaking of social life.

The System of Power and Immunity

Now imagine a society that tolerates no direct, overt correspondence between liens upon the state and advantage in society. Governmental power wins a greater freedom to maneuver. The tie between access to government and social advantage loosens. The primary basis of individual or group prerogatives becomes a background system of entitlements that the state respects, upholds, and occasionally adjusts.

The true character of this direction of development comes out most clearly in the nature of its public order of right. This order becomes, at its heart, a system of powers and immunities: a vast array of loosely connected clusters of entitlements. Each cluster defines a social position. It does so by a technique with two inseparable aspects.

The cluster of entitlements creates an island of security against the predatory or reformist actions of the state, a haven in which some material or ideal interest, and the actual person who is its bearer, can hide. So long as it remains within its protected zone, the interest cannot be struck dead. Conversely, this operation immobilizes a parcel of the state's capacity to move and shake the social world.

At the same time, each cluster of entitlement – an immunity against governmental intervention – confers a power to set terms to other people's activities. It may confer this power directly by defining a social status with certain built-in entitlements to give orders to people in other specified statuses. But, more often, it will do so indirectly by creating devices through which some become dependent upon others. Thus, certain entitlements allow for the lifelong and hereditary accumulation of capital, others for the buying of labor, and others still for the power to supervise and to make investment choices and to control the actual organization of work. When these entitlements combine with a particular technical ordering of production, complete with a distinctive organizational and a technological style and with a routinized definition of collective interests and identities in a pacified political world, they generate recurrent social positions. They do so even if they describe rights universally available to everybody rather than a hierarchy of status and prerogative.

The twofold nature of the cluster of entitlements as immunity against the state and as power over others constitutes the core of property. We commonly think of property as either a specific form of control over capital, accompanied by the power to exclude others or as a synonym for the abstract idea of right. The first idea mistakes the special case for the general one. No self-evident stable or significant distinction exists between control over the physical commodities and the material products of labor, command over labor itself, and the power to dispose of nonmaterial rights. Legal analysis quickly spiritualizes any purely material conception of property. But the second idea of property – property as abstract right – betrays an ignorance of the very different forms that a system of rights can take. Some of these forms differ radically from the rights that modern property exemplifies: different types of rightholders, different ways of marking the boundary between what falls inside and outside the scope of an entitlement, and different ways of sanctioning rights.

The most useful conception of property – the one that escapes the confusion of everyday usage while remaining in touch with the concerns and contexts of such usage – is the conception that defines property as the characteristic form of rights in the system of powers and immunities I have been discussing. The property owner, in this enlarged sense, is the person ensconced in a position in which an immunity against the state and its transformative designs is directly connected to a power to set terms to other people's activity.

The whole system of correspondences between immunity and power can pass through several levels of sanctification. It may operate through a pure state-defined legal order, subject to the ordinary forms of legislative revision. It may be embodied in constitutional arrangements, harder to change or to discredit. It may even be represented as a system of natural rights, supposedly rooted in the pieties of the collective tradition and in the highest demands of personality and immune against voracious majorities and irresponsible demagogues. Each succeeding tier of sanctification represents an additional measure of defense against the transformative powers of government and the modest surprises of routine politics.

Such a system of right can coexist with a severely restricted measure of participation in government – a restriction that may apply even to the groups benefiting most directly from the order of powers and immunities. The state may be largely in the hands of a monarch, his servants, and his closest allies in the higher ranks of society. And yet governmental initiative may be largely immobilized by the power and immunities of different ranks and communities – powers and immunities that may even be represented as barred against revision by the masters of the central governments. Such an approach to freedom as an order of status-specific powers and immunities was the single most important feature of the European absolutist state or *Ständestaat*. (The European prerevolutionary state, however, often had many of the features of the system of privilege described in the earlier section, just as the agrarian-bureaucratic empires had many of the marks of this system of powers and immunities.)

Again, the state may be in the hands of a dictatorial clique. Yet the dictatorship may exist alongside steep and stable social inequalities that use the instruments supplied by a system of formally equal and universalistic rights rather than the rank-specific prerogatives of an estatist society, whose legal form I described as the system of privilege. You can find examples in the postrevolutionary Bonapartist state and indeed all the latter-day forms of state absolutism that coexist with a private legal order similar to the kind recommended by nineteenth-century European liberalism. The crucial threat to the success of this coexistence is that governmental authority may become so far-reaching and untrammeled that the background structure of powers and immunities loses its reality. The narrowing of civic participation in governmental politics must not become the occasion to leave the state unchecked in its programmatic experiments with the social order.

The same system of powers and immunities may come to exist alongside a broader measure of popular participation in the struggle over the uses of governmental power. We find this combination in the liberal democracies of the postrevolutionary West, including the democratic states whose formative institutional context Chapter 2 described. However, just as the survival of this system of powers and immunities demands that authoritarian governments remain heavily circumscribed in the exercise of their transformative capabilities, it also requires that more democratic regimes not go too far in favoring mass militancy and mass organization. The citizen participates. But he participates in a state whose ability to revise the terms of collective existence is highly limited. It is limited by the predominance of forms of protection against governmental oppression that serve, simultaneously, as devices for shaping other people's activity, for making others dependent and turning their dependence to advantage without becoming equally dependent upon them.

Thus, the stakes of conflict must remain. Even the entitlements that most directly shape recurrent social positions may be adjusted from time to time (e.g., changes in opportunities of worker organization, or in prerogatives of management, or in legal and constitutional safeguards for foreign underclass workers). But, at any given time, most of the structure of these entitlements must be held constant. If not portrayed as constitutional natural right, it must nevertheless be seen as an indispensable basis of republican freedom. The state must be arranged in ways that help keep routine politics on this narrow path.

Right Without Dominion

The definition of rights may take still another direction. But this third direction, unlike the other two, is hypothetical: it describes the imaginary extension of tendencies that appeared as no more than minor variations and programmatic aims in all the societies that had existed up to the end of the twentieth century.

Under such a regime, the individual's safety against governmental oppression and his guarantee of effective participation in the processes that set the collective terms of his own existence no longer rely upon devices that serve private oppression. It may be a guarantee expressed in the inviolability of his immediate personal interests: his right to a job and to a change of job, his right to the satisfaction of his basic material needs, as defined by the standards of his time and place, his right to share in the construction and judgment of culture, and his right to engage affirmatively and safely in many forms of fighting about the arrangements of his social world, from the larger constitution of the society to the immediate organization of work, leisure, and family life. But none of these rights works through legal arrangements whose convergent effect is to confer an entrenched control over capital and labor or over any other basic aspect of collective existence. Therefore, nothing prevents the conflict over the uses of governmental power from touching on every aspect of the society's practical and imaginative order. The whole life of society is in fact then arranged so as to multiply the transformative practical and imaginative activities that bring every aspect of society's order into question and open that order up to conflict. The contrast between routine and transformative politics loses its force.

People who can readily put on their agenda the foundations of the world they inhabit must be haughty, high-spirited, and even reckless. They must be secure in an inviolable independence. Yet the instruments of this independence must not smother the struggles that constantly offer them visible images of the connection between the forms of their life in common and the activities from which these forms arise and that cultivate the sense of mastery suitable to men and women who are neither masters nor servants.

The movement in this direction is subject, by its very nature, to a catastrophic detour from which there is no guaranteed, automatic return. The system of powers and immunities may be followed by the overthrow of all the citizen's defenses against the state, a state whose structure of right need be no more than its own dream of absolute power. What results from this situation is never a continued terror of state against society. Such a terror would perpetuate the conflict over the fundamentals of social life, dissolve all settled contexts of power or production, and threaten to unseat and destroy the very people who brought it forth. This terror can occur only as an interlude, though a repeated and savage one, in the movement along the other two directions of state and right described earlier.

This violent interlude may end in a new example of the system of privilege, though accompanied by a greater real and rhetorical commitment to economic equality. Or it may be followed by the consolidation of clusters of entitlements that represent both defenses against governmental action and claims upon other institutions and individuals. This is a new example of the system of powers and immunities, though unaccompanied by broad-based participation in governmental decisions and though rendered precarious, at any moment, by the resurgent, recentralizing state. In this double movement toward the other directions of state and right, you have the outer limits to routine politics in twentieth-century communist regimes.

EXPERIMENTS WITH THE MICROSTRUCTURE: PATRON AND CLIENT

The Character of Patron–Client Relations

Now turn from the structure of government, with its order of privilege and right, to the detailed texture of relations among people – especially the way they deal with one another in the profane, workaday world. Under this microscope, society shows another series of departures from the polar circumstance of no experiment. Throughout history, the most common, and most limited, direction of departure has been the reenactment of an impersonal, rigid order of division and hierarchy as a series of personal, fluid deals between patrons and clients.

As patrons and clients, people excite one another's fear and gratitude in a world marked by continuing inequality. Their bond lies at some point between outright coercion and an unequal partnership. The patron and the client make a deal. The client gets some kind of protection: a bulwark against the brutal uncertainties of renewed social warfare. This guarantee begins with security in his job, his rank, or his land, but invariably includes a great deal more. The patron gets a committed laborer, follower, or hanger-on: extra hands to work, to fight, or glorify a name.

The terms of the exchange already entrench an inequality. The patron must remain the boss and leader, come what may. His is the quintessential form of rule: he offers the client a little social world from which fighting has been temporarily banished. Even when the struggle begins again in the larger world beyond – in any form from physical struggle to market fluctuations – the patron will keep it at bay. All he asks in return is obedience, industriousness, and fidelity, that lesser love.

Both exchange and dominion are transfigured by attachment. Patronage flourishes in the climate of trust. Neither patron nor client insists upon a short-term reciprocity. They refuse to exploit to the hilt their transitory advantages. They remain concerned with the long-term survival of their bond and recognize an obligation to come, in need, to each other's assistance. Their partnership, which is also a hierarchy, can never be fully codified as a system of entitlements. Thus exchange and power, confused with each other, also take on more than the color of community. To some limited and unequal but significant extent, the patron and the client put themselves in each other's hands. Their venture confirms spiritually as well as practically an authoritative form of life and the social places and activities which make that life what it is.

Thus, the patron–client tie sustains loyalties by satisfying tangible, urgent needs. But, in doing so, it assures each participant that he counts and that there is a place for him in the world. The deal he has struck acknowledges as well as threatens or bribes him. It brings out into the open the puns of calculation, mastery, and love that run through every aspect of social life.

The Core Instances of Patron–Client Relations

In certain common historical circumstances the explicit bond between patron and client became the basic form of relationship in society. These circumstances provide us with the exemplary cases of patronage: the empire-building warlord and his ex-nomadic followers who have put aside the traditions of a warrior people on the move without acquiring those of a settled agrarian oligarchy; the landowner whose dealings with his once enserfed or enslaved peasants take place in the receding penumbra of an earlier form of domination; the notable who acts as mediator between a local populace and some center of power and culture. In many societies, all these modes of patronage have intermingled. Thus, the late Roman Republic shows us the relationship of the rival warlords to their cohorts, the tie between a master's relationship to his manumitted slaves (the core context of clientship as a technical legal idea), and the bond that connected an equestrian businessman to his protector in the *nobilitas* and every successful noble or equestrian to his horde of dependents. Each of these settings brought to the fore one of the typical forms of the patron–client tie in history: patronage as the generalization of a bond between the warlord and his follower, as the edge of a vanishing system of domination, and as the transmission of advantage from a higher sphere of society.

The circumstances in which these core instances of patronage arose, and continue to arise, share something in common. Once you grasp this common element, you can see why those instances are simply the more visible representatives of a more basic and unifying movement in the fine structure of social life.

In all these circumstances, the social ranks and communal attachments that constitute the order of hierarchy and division in society were neither overwhelmingly intense and immediate, nor diffuse and discredited. (In Chapter 1, I equated the relative strength of that order with the relative unavailability, in ordinary social life, of practical or conceptual activities that bring it into question and open it up to conflict.) When the scheme of division and hierarchy becomes too fragmented, obscure, or disrespected, the patron–client relationship loses one of its background conditions: the sharply unequal measures of control over force and wealth that enable the patron to come forward as the petty despot and lord protector of a pacified social enclave. The confusion of exchange and community with each other as well as with dependence or dominion ceases to seem the natural form of social life. When, however, the order of division and hierarchy remains tangible, unquestioned, unified, and omnipresent, there is less occasion for the personal maneuvers of protection and service that represent the life of patronage and clientship. Deference, loyalty, and threat will not need to be daily reinvented in countless personal compacts that reenact the passage from uncontained fighting to the truce of mastery and surrender.

The bond between patron and client can become central and pervasive only when the social order is like a partly written script. The main plot has been given. But the details have to be improvised. This improvisation consists in constantly weaving, again, the ties of gratitude and fear. In this intermediate circumstance, the uneven reciprocities of the patron–client deal represent neither immediate reflexes of the parties' respective positions within a societywide hierarchy or a set of interlocking communal–corporate groups nor free-floating human ties only remotely connected to social rank and collective identity.

The script never *is* more than partly written. Every impersonal arrangement always must be turned into the small coin of personal relations. Every system of powers and rights must finally be enacted. If the order to be enacted is one that reproduces large-scale opportunities to start with, the little drama of the patron and the client will have its chance. When powers of command are exercised face-to-face over time, they invariably pass through the subtleties of a give-and-take that works upon the institutional shell and fills it with new content. Every letup in control, every uncertainty in the substance of entitlements and obligations, supplies another opportunity to play variations on the themes of the system of powers–rights. But these variations change from peripheral or illicit adjustments into the central constructive device of association only in that intermediate circumstance I described. The exemplary instances of the patron–client relationship to which I earlier alluded belong to an open list: open because every time we look in the past, we find new cases, and open because they can continue to occur in the future in novel forms with novel types of patrons and clients.

But for patronage to achieve this central role in the making of society, it is not enough that the order of hierarchy and division give way to an open space on which the personalized confusions of power, exchange, and attachment can be played out. It is also necessary that the open space not be occupied by a style of work organization, or by a vision of society, hostile to those confusions.

Every attempt to experiment with the organization of work carries out some conception of the relationship between task definition and task execution. Every such experiment with the ordering of work requires that the dealings between people in the collective enterprise – the bureaucracy, the army, the factory – not be entirely predetermined by their hierarchical and communal places in the outside society. The organization must generate a new repertory of relationships that can serve its own purposes of coordination and control. From the standpoint of these organizational ideals, the patron–client relationship appears as a fatal corruption rather than a constructive device. It threatens to submerge the more impersonal links between superiors and subalterns in the rivalries of would-be leaders and protectors who turn the enterprise into a midget arena for petty animosities and deal out favors and threats according to their convenience. Whenever there emerged an organization whose internal arrangements stood in some tension to the forms of hierarchy and division in the surrounding society – like the Ming–Ch'ing, Byzantine, and Ottoman bureaucracies, the Roman Church before the Renaissance, or the Theravada sangha – its leaders had to wage an endless and often losing battle against its cannibalization by patron–client deals.

Thus, for the patron-client bond to play a major role in society making, the open space left vacant by the relative withdrawal of an impersonal order of hierarchy and division must not be taken over by organizational structures with which it is at war – structures whose nature will be discussed at greater length in the next subsection. Neither must the reigning vision of society be one that rejects as paradoxical or unjustified the convergence of power, exchange, and community that the patron–client relationship constantly reaffirms.

The Peripheral Instances of Patron–Client Relations

When the experiments in work organization coincide with the imaginative denial of the joinder of calculation, attachment, and dominion, the patron–client relation continues to appear in every nook and cranny of social life. But it appears as an illicit and shadowy, though perhaps useful and even indispensable, adjustment of other practices and ideals. It then serves as the reminder of a transformative direction that has not yet been – and never is – entirely foreclosed.

This was the way that patron–client relationships appeared in the twentieth-century countries whose reform cycles Chapter 2 discussed. Everywhere in those societies you could find people who acted toward one another as patrons or clients. The white-collar worker in one of the Western democracies might expect and receive from his superior a measure of studied informality and mock equality. Despairing of the chance of changing his situation in society or the nature of his work, he looked for a boss who was also a sponsor and "friend." Outside the workplace, the underclass laborer might rely on bonds of fidelity to his protectors, bonds that gave vitality to what would otherwise remain a passive community of transients and victims. Even in his dealings with his own employer, he alternated between resentful indifference and anxious loyalty. In the communist countries of that time, countless ties of sponsorship and indebtedness paved the road to fortune and secured against the risks of disgrace. Workers teamed up with their immediate supervisors to ward off the pressures from above. The contestants for the highest offices of the state dealt in the coin of personal sponsorship and personal loyalty all the more heavily because they did not need to marshal a broader base of support in the name of impersonal policies and principles.

But though the pervasiveness of patron–client ties in all countries amounted to an open secret, it remained a shameful one: for the individual, a lesser evil; for the propagandist and reformer, a standing embarrassment; for the theorist, the mysterious reminder of something tenacious in social life.

An apparent paradox in my argument can now be resolved. The patron–client relationship, with its characteristic equivocations of power, exchange, and community, seems to be only the realization of what I described as the imaginative element in the limiting circumstance of a society without experiments. Yet I have presented the rise of patronage to a central role as one of the ways society can depart from that extreme condition of closure. Both theses hold good. The sense of their coexistence reveals the deep facts about society that are played up in this line of cumulative change.

The patron–client deal takes the order of division and hierarchy from the impersonal to the personal. It stands toward the rankings and communities of the social world as water to ice. It shows the fluid medium of personal relations from which those principles of social order constantly emerge and back into which they constantly melt, like a Buddhist aeon collapsing into its primitive moment of decay and radiance.

The replacement of the impersonal by the personal represents, whenever and to whatever extent it occurs, an opening of social life to conflict and invention. Order must now be endlessly rebuilt, through all the ploys of threat and ingratiation. The client may pit alternative patrons against each other and confuse emotions and calculations in ways that undermine his ties of allegiance. He may start by bickering over what seems to him a broken compact and end by rebelling against what he has discovered to be an unnecessary yoke.

But, so long as the patron–client relationship survives with its distinctive features, the experiment in departure from the limiting circumstance of closure cannot go far. For patronage reenacts in the form of the personal bond the essential imaginative principle that underlies every version of the subordination of the form of exchange and community to an inviolable regime of power. This subordination represents the exemplary constraint upon people's efforts to remake society and to relativize the difference between the activities that generate a social world and the activities that go on within it.

The Logic of Patron–Client Relations

The patron–client relation dramatizes some of the most basic facts about society. It reveals the correspondence between impersonal arrangements and personal relations. In so doing, it also underlines the equivocations of attachment, exchange, and power that are forever resurfacing in social life.

Every scheme of social division and hierarchy and every imaginative vision of human association represent the more or less rigidly defined subset of an open set of instrumental or passionate relations among individuals. Social hierarchies and communal attachments, sustained by powers and rights, may place people in position to make demands, pose threats, and offer help. Though this positioning may seem to carry clear implications, it still has to be seized upon and turned to advantage. The large currency of rank and force must be changed into the small coin of alliances and followings.

When the order of division and hierarchy begins to dissolve, but when its dissolution fails to be accompanied by new ways of arranging work and imagining society, the patron–client relationship becomes the dominant form of social life. Hence, the unique feature of this direction of cumulative change: the impersonal order passes into a corresponding personal form; its principles are reaffirmed rather than denied by the device of association that takes its place.

This personalization of social division and hierarchy can happen only because another group of facts about society comes into play. These facts have to do with the easy passage between mastery and ingratiation. To become stable, power must stop depending on the constant application of the whip. The brutality of armed power must be softened by habits of settled exchange and gestures of paternal care. The former confuse the maintenance of the order of dominion and dependence with the need to satisfy urgent material wants. The latter equate it with a community in which people can allow themselves a higher measure of mutual, though unequal, accepted vulnerability.

A similar personalization may take its point of departure even from a relatively equal communal or exchange relationship. Take the way the exchange may pass simultaneously into a communal order and power, until at last the same confusions I just described have been firmly entrenched in social life.

Consider these ties of alliance in their purest and simplest forms, as they may arise in relative isolation from adherence to a common cause or from some closely textured, preexisting community among the allies. At one extreme of possibilities, the catalyst of the relationship may be the posing of a threat, based upon an advantage, all the way from superior physical force to a preeminence of intellect or will. At the opposite pole, a person binds himself to another by doing him a favor and earning his gratitude.

In the first case, the starting point is mastery; in the second, ingratiation. Yet what begins in the climate of apprehension often moves into the atmosphere of gratitude, and the reverse movement is just as frequent. The ordinary condition of social relationships that call for active collaboration is the confusion of fear and gratitude. To explain why and how this happens is harder than it seems.

To be sure, the long-run stability of power requires that coercion be joined by justification. Concessions must be made to moral demands, including the demand for a measure of reciprocity between the strong and the weak – a prime instance of the spiritualization of violence. But this does not add up to an account of why, in the face of so many weapons and apologies of established hierarchy, there should also be such a forceful undercurrent reassertion of the claims of reciprocity, to the point of persistently giving rise to metaphors of paternal care and habits of settled exchange between masters and their dependents.

Again, the history of an exchange relationship that starts off on a footing of relative equality will redound to the advantage of some more than others; and the cumulative, self-reinforcing impact of these disparities is apt to produce a circumstance of hierarchy and fear. This does not, however, explain why the symbols and experiences of gratitude so often persist long after one party has asserted an indisputable superiority of power. Nor does it show why even a modest gambit of gift-giving, ingratiation, and partnership may well be met, beyond every ground for immediate suspicion, with an intimation, on the part of the supposed beneficiary, that some assault is being perpetrated against him, right then and there. These incongruous facts demand an analysis capable of tying such varieties of association to people's elementary concerns.

Start with the perception that every such alliance leads a two-sided existence. It is the outcome of precise and pressing wants. One person, for example, requires protection against constant risks to his life; another needs military followers and common laborers to safeguard his station against rival chieftains. The former offers the latter the protection afforded by membership in his cohort in exchange for service and loyalty from the hanger-on (a crude image of the genesis of Western European feudalism).

At the same time, the relationship exists in another dimension, in which the performances sought after and traded are far less capable of definition. On this other plane, every encounter is a social parallel and extension of experiences of love and hate. The encounter has to do with the terms under which one individual can win acceptance from another for the fact of his existence, as that fact is revealed in his needs and wants. The provision of benefits and the imposition of harms matter both in themselves and as signs of this larger acceptance or rejection.

For an alliance among concrete individuals to attract and sustain loyalties, it must serve as an effective way to secure tangible, urgently desired advantages among the would-be allies. It must also, in the longer run, do so in a way that assures a participant, however inferior his role in the alliance may be, that he counts, that there is a place for him in the world, and that the deal he has struck acknowledges as well as bribes or threatens him.

A shift in the character of his needs must be taken into account, at least as long as it does not alter the fundamental alignment of advantage within the pact. Thus, even the most lopsided allocation of rights and duties will be overtaken by a residual element of reciprocity. The offer of gifts and bribes, when not justified by the presence of personal love or of some compelling duty of communal obligation, will itself be feared as a danger to the maintenance of this reciprocity.

Some smaller version of love is demanded of every long-lived assertion of power. This lesser love is the solidarity by which the stronger party concedes something to the demand for reciprocity and acts as if the weaker party's interests were, to some modest extent, his own.

It may often seem that the element of solidarity has been whittled down to the vanishing point or has never emerged in the first place; take every sort of enslavement, Eastern European and Japanese "feudalism," the regimentation of mass labor in a vast array of imperial states, and even the condition of the casually employed underclass in the North Atlantic societies of the present day. This will certainly be the case when we look to these countries with a view to the way the immediate disposition of power in and outside the workplace is firmly entrenched in general principles of social organization that seem beyond the reach of its victims or even its beneficiaries to transform. Both the routines of the small-scale human encounter and the patterns of encompassing social organization may operate with such overwhelming force and self-evidence that they largely dispense with the effort to elicit loyalties and to soften the fist of straightforward coercion in the glove of reciprocity.

Even in these extreme though common cases, however, there will be intermediaries and messengers of power who, as they come into direct contact with their bosses and underlings, will be drawn into games of reciprocity. The bosses will need to count on their loyalties; they, in turn, will be able to argue that their authority over their subordinates depends upon their being treated and recognized as the forward, cutting edge of some higher order of power. Besides, each succeeding level of subordinates, down to the very lowest, will struggle to maintain a residue of group solidarity against the exactions of its masters; and the more effective it is in doing this, the more it will give rise to shadowy leaders of its own. Thus, if power becomes enmeshed in solidarity in the transactions between social ranks, solidarity must offer sacrifices to power within each rank.

This latter point draws us back to the general truth it illustrates: if one-sided dominion must give way to a dose of mutual deference, how and why is the reverse process just as universal? Offers of help and proposals of ingratiation may amount to a social metaphor of love, for they share with personal love the suggestion of accepting and valuing the other person. But they are also feared as traps.

The peril they offer has an obvious material aspect: that, in exchange for what he gets (such as military protection, salary, sponsorship, or even just some commodity he lacks), the beneficiary will be drawn into a circumstance of ever more marked subordination until he is wholly at the mercy of his alleged benefactor. The danger also has a moral side: the risk that the ingratiating initiative will not be accompanied, on the part of the putative gift-giver and seducer, by any real acquiescence in his own vulnerability. By receiving the gift, the recipient shows himself vulnerable and dependent – for he has needs that the other can satisfy – without himself being able to satisfy an equally pressing need of the giver's. The further the act of ingratiation moves away from love and trust, with their characteristic willingness to accept vulnerability, the greater this risk becomes.

When the immediate preoccupations of personal dealings are the minima of survival and security, these moral aspects of animosity and partnership may seem irrelevant or obfuscating luxuries. But this impression of superfluity comes from thinking of these anxieties about allegiance and dependence as mere additions to practical concerns rather than as yearnings that are always realized or frustrated in the way practical concerns are met. The tale about personality that is told by the down-to-earth realities of security and survival speaks more persuasively to the run of men and women than the books of their religion and laws.

Only when this ever-present reconvergence of power, exchange, and community has been avoided by forms of imagination and organization that resist it can the experimental reinvention of society gain a broader scope.

EXPERIMENTS WITH THE MICROSTRUCTURE: THE ORGANIZATION OF WORK

Clientalism and Rationalized Work

The patron–client relationship reaffirms the principles that underlie a pervasive order of division and hierarchy, and it does so in the very course of replacing or complementing that order. The need to organize collective work for practical tasks, however, may provide the occasion for cumulative changes in the fine texture of human relations that move in other directions. These changes may generate a scheme of relations at work that stands in some tension not only to a particular rigid order of division and hierarchy in society at large, but to any such order. In fact, there are at least two distinct directions of cumulative change: one of them far more subversive than the other in its effect upon the fixed order of society. As the argument is both abstract and complex, it may be helpful to summarize its main elements, though not its actual sequence, by way of anticipation.

Remember, first, some of the starting points of this view. Every impersonal, institutionalized ordering of human life in society enacts a certain version of human association. This enactment represents a selection from a larger, open set of personal relations. To the extent that fighting over the terms of people's material and moral access to one another has been interrupted or contained, this larger set appears only as a penumbra around the established order. Into this halo go the little involuntary experiments in collaboration and encounter that deviate from the institutions and ideas to whose stability, in the face of unexpected circumstance and unsatisfied need, they may nevertheless be indispensable.

The enacted version of human association always has two aspects, which correspond to the two faces of human sociability. There is the passionate aspect: the life of mutual confirmation or antagonism, in which people count for one another as more than means or obstacles to the realization of one another's ends. Its extreme associational form is the community, where people practice in their dealings a heightened vulnerability. There is the instrumental aspect: exchange and collaboration for the accomplishment of practical ends. Its extreme associational form is the work team, where personal relations are directed to the accomplishment of some practical goal. The two aspects overlap: most obviously so in the case where the work is itself a community, and the value the co-workers place on their collaboration cannot be exhausted by their concern with its practical outcome. Nevertheless, the passionate and the instrumental aspects never fully merge. Their relationship remains a troubled one, both as a theme for theoretical understanding and as an object of practical concern.

The structure of personal relations at work enacts a conception of reason at the same time that it realizes a scheme of human association in its instrumental aspect. Ways of thinking and of doing pass into each other without a break. Every account of how to go about dealing with problems includes a view of certain steps and of standard sequences and combinations of those steps. Though this view may be defined most clearly in the area of "pure" theory, it will reappear even in people's practical ideas about the collective organization of productive manual labor. Each relation among concepts or stages in reasoning can be translated into a view of links among labor operations, at various levels of physical activity. The translation is as tricky as it is unavoidable. We have just as much reason to say that a particular practice of work "embodies" a conception of reason as to claim that a conception of reason mirrors and abstracts a practice of labor.

The machine turns the same practice conception of reason into a physical object. Both in the relationship among its parts and in the way it is inserted within a larger problem solving or productive process, it reproduces both a practice of reasoning and an approach to work. For this reason, it can replace both a step in reasoning and a stage in labor.

The conceptions of reason fundamental enough to be enacted into a way of working are not infinitely numerous. In fact, history has presented us so far with only a single such fully developed practice conception, though one that can move in two very different directions, as will soon become apparent. There are many equivalent definitions of this single scheme. One of them is the idea of an interplay between abstract projects (practical or theoretical) and concrete operations.

The work that realizes this practice of reason – rational labor – is labor that executes a general, relatively predefined task. Workers can then break the task down into distinct and more or less routinized operations. Besides saving time through controlled repetition and mounting skill, this decomposition also makes it possible to reduce complicated problems to simpler, hence more manageable ones.

Moreover, once the project is laid out as a series of tangible steps, directly seen and experienced, you can spot opportunities and obstacles that would otherwise have escaped you. In the short run, this allows you constantly to improve upon your procedures for carrying out the task. In the long run, it sharpens and changes your view of what the task is: in the course of the execution you hit upon ways of redefining the project that allow you to achieve objectives you had either not articulated for yourself or dismissed as unattainable or impractical.

This practice conception of reason and labor can be seen as just a special application of the general idea of imagination. Both the task, problem, or perception, on one side, and the labor or reasoning process, on the other, undergo transformative variations in the mind or in actual activity. These variations constitute the keynote of imaginative effort. The double exercise is fully successful only when it does more than execute the task, solve the problem, or analyze the perception: it generates a changed task, problem, or image – one that lends itself to further practical or conceptual work.

This practice conception of reason and labor can develop in two different directions. The difference between the two becomes clearest in the setting of work organization. In one direction, the difference between task and execution, conception and operation, may be rigidly defined. The two kinds of activities can then be assigned to two categories of people: the task definers and the task executors. Call this the rigid variant. In another direction, the contrast between task, problem, or perception and the labor or reasoning process may be relativized. The latter is arranged and understood as a continuous revision of the former. The contrast between task definers and task executors loses its sharpness. Label this the flexible variant.

The flexible variant represents a more radical interpretation of the practice conception described; it impresses more fully upon reasoning and labor the quality of imagination. Insofar as either variant appears as a way of organizing work, it implies a departure from any established order of division and hierarchy in the society at large. At a minimum, there must be some opportunity for organizational experiment; the relations among people at work must not be entirely determined by their fixed ranks or communal attachments outside the workplace. But the flexible variant goes much farther afield than the rigid one. The rigid type can enter into some accommodation with a class order that it helps reshape. People's socially determined life chances outside the workplace help decide where they will fall in the contrast between the task definers and the task executors. Their place in that contrast in turn sustains their access to a host of advantages and prerogatives. Precisely because the flexible variant effaces the contrast between conception and execution and between the definers and the operators, it disturbs the social compromises to which its rigid counterpart lends itself so easily.

In the societies whose formative contexts of power and production

Chapter 2 analyzed, the dominant ideas and institutions of productive or military work exemplified the rigid variant of the practice conception. The flexible mode also appeared. But it remained quarantined within the vanguard areas of production and warfare: the sectors responsible for the most innovative and daring endeavors. Was this confinement a natural consequence of the inherent organizational demands and economic or technical constraints of different kinds of activities? Or did it represent just one more temporary truce line in an endless history of fighting?

The more detailed argument that follows will go through a sequence that differs from the anticipatory summation you have just read. The argument describes a whole complex style of organization, proceeding to more basic levels. Only toward the end of this account does the practice conception, with its two variants, emerge as the fundamental commitment. Like the outline that preceded, the argument is largely unhistorical. I mean it less as the narrative of an actual history than as another element in the map of large-scale options.

Task, Operation, and Hierarchy: The Organizational Style

Start by taking the complex of projects, operations, and larger social hierarchies at its most superficial but also at its most visible: the predominance of a particular way of setting up the large-scale organizations charged with the tasks of production, warfare, and administration. The analysis of this organizational style can take us through three levels of mounting importance and depth even before we try to see how this style gets placed within the hierarchical ordering of society. Each level is paradoxically related by reinforcement and subversion to the one above it.

The first level is the outward setup of the big organization and of its personnel. Here, the crucial point is the relationship between the professionalism of the personnel and, especially, of the managers, and the emergence of a divisional structure that separates the staff and the line. Professionalism, in this context, just means that the people who perform the jobs – particularly the managerial ones – are expected to promote relatively well-defined organizational objectives and claim to have the talents and skills needed to do the work. Most importantly, the officers in charge of the organizations in fact enjoy a considerable amount of independence from supervision by outsiders, whether the outsiders be property-owning capitalists, a central governmental bureaucracy, or an overtly political power. The division between the staff and the line occurs when a distinction is established between the people who direct specific functional or regional units of an organization and the officers who stand at the center, together with their advisors, assistants, and researchers, and are responsible for coordinating operations as a whole. The staff is not just the apex of the line – though it is that as well; it has distinctive responsibilities.

The staff is freed from day-to-day supervision of routine operations. It has the chance to step back and to contrast the actual layout of the enterprise with the definition of the overall tasks and with the analysis of surrounding opportunities and threats. In this way, it becomes the primary device for ongoing, deliberate reformation of the layout in view of the tasks and the circumstances, and for the redefinition of the tasks in view of the circumstances and of past experience with the working of the layout. The staff is the self-conscious spearhead of the belief that it is possible to seize the initiative of events and to subject them to the discipline of a well-informed will. In its execution of this purpose, it wants to make professionalism all the more serious a matter, for the professionalism of the staff is a claim to ally specialized knowledge and capacity with an insight into the principles that govern the way specialization gets defined within the organization and for the organization as a whole.

It is striking that the full-fledged development of these organizational characteristics in the areas in which they have developed most – armies and business – is extremely recent. The professionalization of officer corps – frequently limited, in any event, by the effort to keep high military rank in the hands of certain classes of notables – was not capped by an unequivocal distinction between staff and line in the major European armies before the turn of the century. And it took the multidivisional firm structure, pioneered by big American corporations in the 1930s, to introduce that distinction into the professionally managed business enterprise.

On the other hand, governments, which started to experiment with this combination of organizational characteristics long before armies and business, have always kept an ambivalent attitude toward those traits. Take the history of ministerial administration in Western Europe. From at least the fourteenth century on, after the thirteenth-century halt in administrative development, we find many forces collaborating toward professionalization of the high bureaucracy: the separation of narrower and narrower royal councils, distinct from the general aristocracy; the crucial role played by the secretaries of state, who acted as liaison between council and king; and the expert staffs put together by these high servants of government. It was a style of centralization that has to be carefully distinguished from the initial English tendency to use local gentry to do governmental work and from the early French tactic of multiplying lower bureaucratic offices. It was constantly limited by the need of strong and weak monarchs alike to compromise with the possessing classes, to involve them in running the central government, and to allow them to turn to private use offices already defined as public. To grasp the real meaning of the continuing limit on professionalization even when the compromise with the possessing classes is eclipsed and the entire civil service professionalized, you have to understand what happened to the governmental counterpart of the staff–line distinction.

Here, too, a broad line of development can easily be discerned. The initial condition was one in which the functional powers of ministers of state were mixed up with responsibilities for particular territorial units, major affairs were dealt with by shifting groups of high-office holders, and the cabinet as a whole lacked ministerial solidarity. The end point is one in which the functional has been separated from the territorial, and collective solidarity coincides with individual responsibility. Together, these features transform the cabinet and its immediate auxiliaries into a staff distinguished from the line of regional or functional offices farther down the bureaucracy. But here the ambivalence of politics toward organization intervenes to check and, occasionally, to reverse this dynamic. The central power holders – princes, party leaders, mass politicians – both want and fear the transformation of the highest administrative offices into a staff. What the change brings to them in heightened resources of control, it seems to take away in an increased resistance of the high ministerial staff to political guidance from the center. This ambivalence comes to a head in the posture of presidents toward their cabinets (needed as an instrument for controlling the bureaucracy, feared as a screen between bureaucracy and president). But it is also crucial in the relationship of parliamentary cabinet governments to the high professional bureaucracy.

Standard Operating Procedures and Continuous Hierarchy

The division between staff and line and the professionalization of personnel turn out, from another standpoint, to be the preferred devices of a more intangible set of organizational ideals. These ideals are at best limits that are never reached, but it is impossible to understand the temper and the hesitancies of large-scale organizations in our day without taking them into account. Again, the distinctive quality of these organizations consists not in their having invented the ideals but in having given them an unprecedented degree of free play and sustained attention.

One cluster of these deeper organizational aims consists in the effort to assimilate a major part of what the organization does to a group of standardized operating procedures. The spirit of the system of standardized operating procedure is best defined by contrast to ad hoc instrumental judgments and rigid rules, on the one hand, but also to communities of shared purposes, on the other.

The standardized operating procedures represent a compendium of well-established ways of dealing with the recurrent demands faced by the people who hold different jobs within the organization. The procedures ride on a double justification: their responsiveness to the overall tasks and the changing circumstances of the organization – a responsiveness supported by past experience but subject to constant reassessment – and their ability to fit in with other standardized operating procedures in a way that respects the basic structure of power and coordination within which decisions are made. The second justification keeps the standardized operating procedures from falling apart into a medley of dissociated instrumental judgments about what to do and how to do it, made by each jobholder on his own initiative. The first justification is meant to keep the procedures from being petrified into a system of rules that have lost touch with their instrumental uses. For, when such dissociation occurs, the rules are taken as the basis of privileges that each specialized segment of the organization uses as shields with which to jostle against the other segments to the detriment of the organization as a whole. Viewed from this perspective, the devotion to formal rules, far from being the apogee of organizational efficiency, represents its decline into factional indiscipline and collective rigidity.

The other half of the spirit of the standardized operating procedures is highlighted by their relation to the alternative ideal of a community of purpose. An army or a party on the verge of combat may be able to act, under inspired leadership, at the motion of a widely shared and intensely felt set of aims. Even then, however, it must have another structure to fall back on when the doubts and the disagreements break out. A sign of the vitality of a system of standardized operating procedures would be its capacity to exercise a unifying influence in the absence of any significant sharing of ends; and it is on this capacity that the propagandists of this organizational ideal pin the hope of defeating communities of shared purpose at their own practical games.

Another major organizational ideal of the same importance is a conception of what hierarchy within the organization should look like – at least the hierarchical relations among those who stand at the upper rungs of the ladder. Call it continuous hierarchy. The subordinate should be allowed a significant though varying amount of discretion in the performance of his job. Yet, at each crucial juncture, he should be accountable to a vigilant supervisor. The interplay of supervision and discretion is meant to bring under control a familiar oscillation of organizational life: the swing between the subordinates' efforts to transform every measure of independence into an occasion for developing vested interests and self-defensive habits, and the periodic lashing out of the supervisors in their half-futile attempt to quash the unruliness below.

In their more developed forms, the ideals of continuous hierarchy and of standardized operating procedures fit tightly together. The hierarchy helps keep the standardized operating procedures from being petrified into rigid rules without allowing them to fly apart into ad hoc instrumental judgments. The standardized operating procedures provide the practical criteria that allow the continuous hierarchy to work: the balance of supervision and discretion is set, in each case, by the needs of fidelity to the procedural system itself.

Even this summary account of the organizational ideals is enough to suggest that they have a paradoxical relation to the surface characteristics of professionalism and the staff–line distinction. In one sense, they bring these traits to fruition by suggesting how the impulses toward professionalism and planning can be translated into a way of going about the organization's day-to-day activities. But in another sense they can be read as a subtle, undercurrent condemnation of the distinction between the staff and the line within the commanding elites and, more generally, of the very distinction between the managers and the managed. For both these sets of distinctions impose constraints upon the responsiveness of the procedures to task and circumstance as well as upon the interplay of supervision and discretion throughout the hierarchy. The basic differentials of power are not treated as up for grabs in the same way that other features of the organizational setup are; they do not require renewed justification and experiment in the light of changing opportunity. Instead, they are taken as the horizon that defines a world.

This disturbance in the relation between different levels of the organization already serves to anticipate one of the ways in which the internal order of the enterprise links up with the surrounding hierarchy of the society. The shackles placed upon the free working out of continuous organizational hierarchy and standardized procedures of operation represent, from the standpoint of the organization, a requirement that derives its force and its authority more from that outside order than from anything that goes on within the organization.

Analytical Reason, Machine Production, and Rationalized Labor

Beneath these stubborn organizational ideals, there is still another level of formative influences: the overlapping spheres of analytical reason, machine production, and rationalized labor.

These large-scale organizations have been built in an age that has witnessed the triumph of a particular image of analytical reason and the transformation of that image into a basis of practical as well as scientific activity on a worldwide scale. Understood in this light, the core of reason is a particular tie between analysis and abstraction.

At the most immediate level, abstraction means simply the attempt to break every comprehensive intellectual task into discrete, more manageable components until what seemed vulnerable solely to unproven inspiration can be mastered by careful probing. The more important side of analysis, however, lies in its tacit ontological message rather than in its explicit methodological program. Commonsense perception comes in conventional chunks, the traditional ways of viewing the world that are rooted in the relatively unmediated experience of the senses, the conveniences of everyday activity, the habits of language, and the vulgarized science of previous ages. Analytical reason insists upon disrespecting that way of dividing up the world and of understanding the relationship among its parts, for it denies the claim of that mental geography to be a testing point of reality. The disrespect goes in two directions. It moves toward the disintegration of those chunks of perception into smaller pieces or, in any event, into pieces whose boundaries fail to map those of the conventional world. The disrespect for the unexamined view of reality also moves toward abstraction – the reunification of these revised categories, descriptions, and explanations into wholes more comprehensive than the ones that convention and common sense might allow. These wholes can in turn be subject to analytical pulling apart, and the entire process begins anew. Because synthesis works through abstraction, it involves a widening gap between the richness of the concrete world of experience and the austerity of the simplified world of science. We cannot fill this breach by using science to both explain and conceal perceived differences among things in the world if only we were willing to go through the trouble.

The program of analysis and abstraction rests upon a willingness to treat the entire world as potentially homogeneous for the purposes of explanatory laws. We can, in principle, translate what we see and know about a certain level of explanation – biological, for example – into a more basic or general level – say, particle physics. We may still be interested in the more detailed and superficial modes of explanation because, by filtering out irrelevant information, they are less cumbersome. We may also, for one reason or another, be unable to carry out in fact the reduction from the more limited to the more generic. But, whatever the obstacle to practicing our principle might be, we forswear the possibility of its lying in inherent differences among kinds of things, differences that would in turn require distinct varieties of understanding, each untranslatable into the others.

The resolute break with the commonsense world and with the habit of conventional individuation may be distorted into a plot to suppress alternative modes of reason. It may leave open the crucial question of the standards by which the success of analysis and abstraction is to be judged. But it promises a deeper understanding of reality and mastery of the secret forces of the universe.

To grasp the extraordinary social impact of this idea of reason, you must understand how it gets embodied in a special practical relation to the world. The chosen instrument of this relation is the machine; but less the machine as such than the machine as the model, the product, and the occasion of a certain type of working relationship among people. The solution of a production problem by mechanical means calls for two related tasks. The problem must be redefined in a way that lends itself to a mechanical solution; the inventor must hit upon a convenient abstraction. He must then build a device that decomposes the abstract task into a set or sequence of operations with maximum economy of effort. In fact, the two sides of the inventor's job may be all but indistinguishable. The definition of the mechanical task is guided by a presentiment of what is technically viable. Then, the actual machine presents a visible image of the decomposed task. As he watches the machine work, the inventor can get new ideas about how to have the same task performed more efficiently by introducing new elements or rearranging the existing ones. But he can also go farther and see in such rearrangements and innovations the stimulus to a redefinition of the projects to be accomplished.

This concept of the machine has an affinity to the idea of reason as analysis and abstract synthesis. Machines have existed long before that idea of reason gained its present degree of power and elaboration. But when analytical reason comes together with the mechanical transformation of labor, each is enormously strengthened by the other. The latter receives from the former a constant flow of projects to carry out. The former gets from the latter both a vehicle with which to transform its material environment and a way with which to test its dreams against the resistance of the world. The machine is reason's call to arms; it is analysis on horseback.

Analytical reason and machine production come fully into their own only when they enter into partnership with the practice conception of a rationalized collective labor. Collective labor is rationalized to the extent that the deliberate and constant interplay between project and operation – the formulation of tasks and the planning of execution – becomes the decisive influence upon the organization of work. The point to stress is, once again, the two-way flow of this interchange. The definition of jobs and, at the limit, the assignment of individuals to those jobs become conscious responses to programs and opportunities. Conversely, by seeing the work unit in motion, people (but which people?) learn to redefine the program themselves in more practicable ways and to discern new opportunities for carrying them out.

The basic principles that underlie rationalized labor are the same as those that stand at the root of machine production. For this reason, it becomes possible to integrate human labor tightly with machines and to treat the question of which parts of work should be done by human hands and which by machines as entirely open to judgments of technical, economic, and social advantage. Indeed, the relative ease with which this substitution can be carried out is another mark distinguishing rationalized labor.

Rationalized labor never exists in more than a compromised position. Far from being transitory or peripheral, this compromise is an enduring and deeply set trait of the organization of work as it in fact exists in the contemporary world. Job definitions, for example, are shaped by the interests of managers and commanders in controlling the people under them as well as by the efforts of different sectors of the managed to preserve the job classifications they associate with security and fairness. But the impulse of rationalization is still there, however qualified it may be by functional calculations of power and profit, and it has a potentially subversive influence on the ordering of the work group.

The Rigid and the Flexible Variants of Rationalized Collective Labor

There is a central ambiguity in the concept of rationalized labor, an ambiguity best understood in the language of a spectrum rather than of sharp contrast. At one pole of this spectrum lies a rigid form of rationalized labor. A clear distinction is made between the work of defining the more or less abstract projects that are to be carried out by the group and the actual work of execution. The definition of the tasks includes decisions about the structure of jobs, hierarchies, and perhaps even material rewards within the organization as well as decisions about how to reassess both the layout of work and the understanding of the collective tasks in light of the group's concrete experience. The clearer the line between projects and operations, the greater the pressure to distinguish the operations (and the people responsible for them) from one another. Each element in planning has a counterpart in execution. These counterparts get their meaning and justification from their direct relation to the plan and, in principle, should be changed only when the plan itself changes. This rigid classification of operational acts, tied in with an independently defined plan, is the core contemporary meaning of routinization at work.

The rigid style of work organization can be realized by any number of alternative institutional arrangements. Do not mistake the general scheme for any of its concrete instances. In the industrial organization of the countries whose formative contexts of power I described at the outset, the most familiar examples were the Ford-type and Taylorist assembly line arrangement of the plant and the multidivisional-firm structure of the enterprise. But these inventions, like the larger formative contexts themselves, had been invented and diffused relatively recently. Moreover, the organizational practices differed from country to country and from sector to sector of the economy. In some places (e.g., France) the contrast between conception and execution was reinforced, paradoxically, by the abundance of intermediate cadres of supervisors and foremen who transmitted orders and imposed discipline. In other countries (e.g., Germany), the contrast was softened by the relative absence of these cadres and the devolution of greater amounts of discretion and skill to bottom-level workers. Some of these variations arose from the particular settlements struck among sections of the work force and of the entrepreneurial classes. Some of them could be traced back to those imaginative ideas, enacted in personal relations and developed by abstract ideas, that we call national culture.

In warfare, you could find the typical instance of rigid rationalization in the standard infantry unit. The unit belonged to an army based upon semiskilled conscripts or hirelings commanded by a professional officer corps. And it was deployed in the confrontational style of fighting I soon describe. There were the officers and the men; the more or less fixed battle plans and the more or less familiar bag of tactical routines; and the clear assignment of distinct responsibilities to different segments of the army in motion. The same basic variations that existed in the industrial sphere reappeared in the military one and for the same general reasons.

Take now the flexible form of labor. It relativizes the difference between formulating tasks and executing them. The project becomes simply the provisional and sketchy anticipation of a collective effort. Each operational act represents the project on the march: an adaptation of the plan to circumstances that is also both a step toward greater detail in the understanding of what the project is and a proposal for its redefinition. Because the moments of formulation and execution tend toward merger and simultaneity rather than separation and sequence, the boundaries among operations are themselves more elastic. Each operative step gains meaning and guidance from its direct relation to the other steps as well as from its link with the provisional and progressively enriched plan. The foremost difficulty of organization becomes the need to maintain direction and unity without abandoning the impetus toward flexibility.

In the economies of twentieth-century societies, the major examples of the flexible practice conception could be found within the sectors most responsible for innovation. Sometimes the relevant institutions were separate units of an enterprise whose main body ran on principles of rigid rationalization. Sometimes they were smaller, independent firms. The designers of new processes and products had to collaborate closely with their customers, their skilled workers, and even with their own competitors outside their firms. They had to work with their customers to define practical needs in the light of opportunities for innovation and lines of innovation in the light of practical needs. They had to work with one another to pool resources and protect themselves against the effect of market instabilities. Most significantly, they had to collaborate intimately with their own skilled laborers. The skilled workers who made the new products with the help of fluid processes and general-purpose machines had to understand the objectives at close hand. To make the inevitable adjustments as they went along, they needed to distinguish the central elements in those goals from the peripheral ones. They found themselves in something like the position of a judge tied to the lawmaker by a community of purpose. The designer, for his part, had to reconceive product and process in response to the difficulties and opportunities people discovered when they actually set out to pull apart and rearrange existing products and the machines or processes for building them.

The kind of organization that flourished in these innovative enterprises had its numerous, less explicit counterparts in early forms of petty manufacturing and artisanal corporations. In these earlier experiments, the contrast between conception and execution had been softened, more often by the commitment to corporate-communal solidarity than by the demands of accelerated innovation.

Warfare also had its cases of flexible rationalization. The stock examples turn up in conflicts that fall under the greatest pressure to economize force and rely on maneuver such as tank warfare during World War II or revolutionary warfare and counterinsurgency in the years thereafter. It will soon become clear that the same style of fighting can be introduced – and sometimes has been – in almost any imaginable military circumstance, once an army overcomes certain barriers that are social and imaginative rather than technical.

When the distinction between the rigid and the flexible forms of rationalized labor is brought out into the open, you can trace parallel, but less obvious, ambiguities in the ideas of machine production and analytical reason.

The machine may be thought of as a tool whose uses are defined wholly from the outside, first by the inventor, then by the owner or the operator. The connections among its component parts are set, and the lessons to learn from its operation are those that inspire the invention of new machines and the reordering of human labor. But the machine may also be a largely self-correcting device, able to make marginal adjustments and to switch the relations among its component parts. Such a machine reflects, in its conception and functioning, the flexible interpretation of rationalized labor. It also dramatizes that the distinction between abstract task and concrete operation may be less significant than another distinction that arises within the sphere of abstract tasks itself. This additional distinction is the contrast between choosing the presuppositions of work (what work is for and what relations among people it can legitimately adopt) and deciding how to go forward once these presuppositions are set. The self-correcting machine may do the actual work; it cannot choose the assumptions.

Similarly, there are two different ways to view the relation of particular intellectual tasks to an effort of understanding. You may draw a clear distinction between theorizing and modes of experiment, inference, and induction that are meant to probe the limits of established theory. But you may also, with greater fidelity to Cartesian precept, conceive these lesser acts of the intellect as small-scale theorizing, indistinguishable in kind from what goes on when more general hypotheses are strung together.

The whole cluster of analytical reason, machine production, and rationalized labor has an ambivalent relationship to the organizational ideals of continuous hierarchy and standardized operating procedures, just as these ideals themselves have a two-sided relation to the surface traits of professionalism and the staff–line distinction. Moreover, the nature of the ambiguity suggests other ways in which the internal structure of the organization may be linked with the larger hierarchy of society.

To the extent that the rigid form of rationalized labor – and therefore also of machine production and analytical reason – is preferred, methods of continuous hierarchy and standardized operating procedures seem to be reinforced. The continuous hierarchy has a basis in the need to distinguish project definition and reassessment from project execution and to separate the special skills required by definition from the more ordinary capacities demanded by execution. The standardized operating procedures are made relatively determinate: they must satisfy the need to preserve a certain kind of internal organization setup, to which the distinction between the task definers and the task executors is central, as well as the need to meet practical exigencies through coordinated effort. Similarly, political options in governmental politics become clear when the people who are able to act understand not only what practical demands have to be met (e.g., fiscal and military strength) but also what form of state must be preserved (e.g., dynastic control of monarchic power in the course of maintaining a condominium of autocrat and magnates).

To the extent that the flexible variant of rationalized labor prevails, continuous hierarchy has no obvious support or apology. Even when it does, it loses the power to serve as an antidote to politics. Nothing is inherently a matter of task definition as distinguished from execution, except for the choice of the basic assumptions: the aims of work, the permissible personal relations through which it can be carried out, and the rewards it can win. That the layout of jobs depends upon, and in turn is shaped by, decisions about these matters reveals clearly the nontechnical element in work organization, and helps distinguish expert counsel, everyday supervision, and political choice from one another. The standardized operating procedures may now well be underdetermined: there are likely to be different ways to accomplish the practical objectives of the enterprise, depending upon the internal structure of the work group through which you want to achieve these aims. Because the structure is not given, because it is recognized to be a matter for group politics as well as for instrumental calculation, the ideal of standardized operating procedures becomes incomplete.

The Institutional Conditions for the Predominance of the Rigid Style of Industry

My examples already suggest that the rigid and flexible variants of the practice conception in the societies whose formative contexts of routine politics I described at the start of this chapter appeared as, respectively, the mainstream and the vanguard of production and warfare. This disposition was the outcome of a particular history of practical and imaginative struggles, a history whose general character the next section of this chapter and the second part of this book investigate. This sequence of disputes shows both how the practice conception could take hold of the organization of work and how its more radical, flexible form came to be confined to the vanguard of industry. For the moment, you can understand the disposition of the mainstream and the vanguard, unhistorically, as the result of certain conditions. Whenever these conditions failed to be satisfied, the rigid variant lost its hold over the mainstream. The unhistorical and historical accounts can readily be translated into each other: the latter shows the sequence of conflicts that made it possible to satisfy, over a broad range of social life, the conditions described by the former. The very statement of the conditions already incorporates a compressed reference to the history. Take production and warfare, one by one.

The predominance of the rigid variant in the production system has both a technical–economic and a social basis. The economic basis is the mass production of standardized goods. The machines are product-specific and the production processes are themselves rigid. Indeed, the production process and the machinery together very largely determine what will be produced. Changes in this productive structure are costly except when they involve no more than marginal adjustments or recombinations of a small number of elements. The organizational and technological apparatus absorbs successive infusions of capital. Very quickly, a stage is reached where the productive stock pays for itself only at high levels of production. The consumers make no specific requests, nor is there any close collaboration between the makers and users of products. People buy, passively, among batches of standardized products and are either unwilling or unable to pay large premiums for distinctive commodities.

Most importantly, perhaps, the relevant product, labor, and financial markets must be stable. Major and uncontrollable instability in any of these markets threatens the rigid and expensive production apparatus with disaster. In the communist states, the governmental control of accumulation and of access to consumption warded such instability off and thereby maintained the economic basis of the rigid variant. But in the contemporaneous Western economies, there had to be for each kind of instability a corresponding compensatory mechanism: the internal generation of corporate investment funds for financial instability; subcontracting or the hiring of unorganized underclass workers to reconcile product instability (variable levels of demand) with labor instability (the need to maintain a pacified, permanent, and proficient core labor force).

The destabilization of markets and of mass production does not guarantee the triumph of the flexible variant in any sector. The response to such destabilization may run from the relatively decentralized enterprise or plant to the despotically managed artisanal shop. Initiatives like these still represent variations on the rigid mode. In this sense, what I have described as the economic requirement of the flexible style is less a necessary or sufficient condition at all than a favoring circumstance.

But the hold that the rigid version has over the mainstream rests on a social as well as a technical–economic basis. The fulfilment of this social condition requires that both a negative and an affirmative task be accomplished. The negative work is to defeat, contain, or destroy the movements that champion an alternative organization of production. This defeat can never occur in the marketplace alone. It must occur also – and often previously – on a series of battlefields, domestic and international, practical and imaginative. Like the conquest of an agrarian empire by nomadic invaders, this is a victory that must keep being rewon. It was won every time an early modern European state suppressed minor guilds and petty manufacturers; won in the nineteenth century when artisanal corporate organization was more or less openly suppressed; and won in the Soviet Union of the late 1920s or the China of the late 1960s, in the course of violent factional quarrels that went from the oligarchies to the masses. Some of these deviations might have eventually altered the relationship between mainstream and vanguard more than others. But all had to be defeated before their societies could be made safe for the predominance of the rigid variant within the mainstream.

The affirmative task that must be performed in order to guarantee this safety is the creation of a system of powers–rights that enables the rigid variant to operate. That system must entitle certain people to occupy the role of task definers in the name of property, or of technical expertise, or of the government that appointed them. It must also shape and contain the routine contests over the uses of governmental power in ways that do not put that entitlement in constant jeopardy.

Even the relative stability of the product, labor, and financial markets and the availability of countermeasures to the instabilities that do occur depend upon that system of powers–rights. For though volatility in a market may occasionally arise from demographic or natural variations, it is the system of powers–rights that determines who will suffer and who may benefit from these oscillations.

More often, this dependence is still more direct: market instability turns out to be only another name for an unresolved conflict over the terms of powers and rights on which exchange will take place and labor will be offered up and controlled. This struggle may be fought among states, or among any combination of governments, entrepreneurs, workers, and consumers. The point is not that market forces fail to operate. It is rather that the kind of market that exists – and the system of legal entitlements and of extralegal but customary dependencies shaping that market – are never themselves the spontaneous products of such forces. The market-defining rights and practices exhibit and reproduce a particular social settlement. The distinctive contours of such a settlement can never be inferred from the abstract conception of a market.

The argument does not and cannot prove that the flexible approach to work, with its softening of the contrast between plan and execution, can apply to the whole economy. But the analysis does multiply reasons to believe that the actual boundary between the mainstream and the vanguard, and the relative importance of these sectors of the economy, depends upon struggles and resolutions that "neutral" economic or organizational imperatives cannot persuasively explain.

The Institutional Conditions for the Predominance of the Rigid Style of Warfare

Now take the predominance of the rigid variant in the mainstream of warfare. There, too, you can identify a technical-economic and a social condition. The analysis of warfare turns out to complement neatly the argument about production. Where one is inconclusive, the other carries more weight; each covers the other's defects.

The technical-economic condition is the predominance of warfare as a direct confrontation of forces over warfare as indirect maneuver. Although both elements exist in all military operations, they may exist in strikingly different proportions. Moreover, although both styles of warfare require at some point an actual shock and resistance, each aims for a different kind of encounter with the enemy. Although both styles require intelligence as well as force, one requires more of it than the other – or rather it requires that the intellectual conception of the battle be related to the actual fighting of it in a more immediate way.

Warfare as confrontation looks to the measure of force against force. The enemy must be engaged on a broad front. The closer the struggle comes to being a "total war," the more this front involves the adversary's entire population and economy as well as the soldiers thrown into battle. On this broad front, the enemy will be worn down by cumulative infusions of manpower and materiel. Battle plans can be essentially simple. Tactics can be reduced to a well-defined repertoire of standardized procedures. The soldiery must be willing (in the circumstances) to stand up and fight. It must have the technical proficiency demanded by the weaponry. Beyond this, however, no great amount of discretion is required of the ordinary combatants.

In this confrontational style of warfare, the rigid variant can operate. The plan of battle can be distinguished, step by step, from the repetitive tactical procedures. Each battle plan will include, as one of its elements, a definition of the appropriate tactical mix. The makers and transmitters of orders can be relatively distinguished from the executors. The contrast breaks down only for the junior officers who must maintain the cohesion and morale of the small groups under their command while carrying out their part of the overall combat plan. Higher up in the hierarchy, everything may transpire in an atmosphere of managerial impassiveness or controlled anguish.

Contrast all this to the style of indirect maneuver. The goal here is to win, through intelligence, precision, daring, and opportunism what cannot be secured by a clear superiority of resources. The enemy's more powerful forces – both his armies and their support structures – must be hit and disorganized before they can be brought to bear on focused, important points of encounter. Careful preparation, patient avoidance, the instinct for the vital weakness, the rapid strike, the dazzling movement, the relentless pursuit, often of a more numerous but disorganized and demoralized enemy – these make up the devices of warfare as indirect maneuver.

Under such conditions, the battle must be planned to take advantage of shifting opportunities and dangers on the field. The tactical repertory of fighting must be indiscriminate and open-ended. The commanders must communicate and coordinate in the midst of violence and uncertainty. But they must also allow the fighting crews in place to deviate and to improvise. The battle plan itself becomes a continuous interplay between the overall conception and these localized decisions.

An army that wages war in this fashion has its hierarchy of command. But it knows no firm contrasts between the definers and the operators. Its success depends upon the union of trustworthiness with tactical insight at the lowest rung of the ladder; its soldiers are small-time generals. Here the flexible variant must prevail.

Thus, the mainstream of warfare can be held by the rigid mode of rationalized collective labor only when direct confrontation predominates over indirect maneuver. But this predominance in turn depends on several circumstances, each of them indispensable. First, the fighting force must be able to count on decisive superiority over the adversary in manpower and materiel. Second, the enemy must not be in a position to respond successfully by employing the style of indirect maneuver. For example, his demographic and economic heartland may be threatened with invasion or destruction. Third, the struggle must not be so unlimited in scope and intensity that the ability to survive, to move, and to invent in the midst of inconceivable destruction becomes the paramount requirement of victory. Such destruction makes the conditions of struggle from one moment to the next radically different and unforeseeable and puts a premium on the capacity to re-create organization and momentum in the midst of this violence. The survivors – soldiers or civilians – must then act like members of an army committed to the indirect maneuver and to the interplay between conception and operation. It is the sort of circumstance that might follow an all-out nuclear war. But it also exists, in germ, wherever people find themselves shaken by violence.

If all these requirements can indeed be met, the style of direct confrontation has its advantages, especially for an army that, on other grounds, wants to adopt the rigid mode of rationalized collective labor. It is a way to fight that minimizes risks, dispenses with exceptional ingenuity, and makes possible straightforward calculations. If it is prodigal in manpower and materiel, it economizes on command skills. Besides, it provides planners with a counterpart to rationality in a stabilized market: you invest each military resource in the way that maximizes the marginal return to the army's overall confrontational power.

But there is the danger that the preference will be carried over to the situations in which the requirements of success fail to be met. For they may indeed fail to be met not just in the periphery but in the center of the struggle. The apparent course of prudence will then spell disaster.

The reasons for believing that the flexible practice conception could pass from the vanguard to the mainstream of production are all inconclusive. Some have to do with the abstract analysis of organizational ideas; others, with the vagaries of the experiments that have taken place in history. But the parallel argument about warfare leaves much less room for alternative approaches. If military activity and insight have a core, it lies in the style of indirect maneuver, which realizes, to a higher degree than the confrontational approach to fighting, the economy of force through the primacy of intelligence. The warfare of direct confrontation can best be understood as the departure from this ideal that becomes affordable when circumstances relax the imperative to economize force. Once you accept the idea of a significant relation between indirect maneuver and the flexible practice conception, the confinement of the indirect style to the vanguard of warfare stops looking natural.

The provisional or special quality of the technical–economic conditions for the predominance of the rigid form are, then, clearer in the military theater than in the productive one. The reverse happens when you pass to the social conditions of that primacy. Even the rigid variant of rationalized collective labor in warfare presupposes a professional organization where superiors and subalterns can deal with each other in ways not fully shaped by an overarching social hierarchy and division nor easily reducible to the habits of patrons and clients. However, if conception and operation, task definers and task executors, stand apart in the economy, it may seem inevitable for them to stand apart in the army. The reproduction of this contrast will in turn reinforce its strength in its original or primary productive context. It is not only an aristocracy but a class of professionals, managers, and higher technicians who may appear as the natural source of an officer corps. Conversely, the broader application of the flexible mode in warfare, under the pressure of military emergency, may serve as a localized experiment that people can later extend to the economy.

THE SENSE OF THE LARGE-SCALE OPTIONS

The Institutional Embodiment of Negative Capability

Reconsider now, in the light of the comparative analysis worked out in the preceding pages, the three general ideas this analysis supports. The first thesis is that different institutional arrangements reflect varying degrees of advance in the denaturalization of society. Society becomes denaturalized to the extent that its formative practices and preconceptions are open to effective challenge in the midst of ordinary social activity; the gap between routine moves within the given framework and radical conflicts about this framework narrows. The concept of denaturalization or of emancipation from false necessity includes the idea of a weakening of rigid roles and hierarchies. It therefore also refers to the development of forms of production, exchange, and passionate attachment that are less marked by such rankings and divisions. The social theory that deploys the concept of denaturalization argues that these different senses of emancipation from false necessity are connected as a matter of empirical fact. I use the term negative capability to suggest the variety of forms of empowerment that denaturalization makes possible.

Not only whole formative contexts but the particular clusters of arrangements and assumptions that constitute them embody higher or lower levels of the development of negative capability. Only because of this fact does it make sense to claim that similarity in the level of negative capability can operate as a constraint upon the recombination or substitution of different practical or imaginative elements to constitute a stable formative order. Among the directions of labor organization compared in this chapter, the rigid form of rationalized collective labor is more experimental than either the patron–client relation or the more impersonal forms of division and hierarchy from which clientship descends. But it is less experimental than the flexible form of rationalized collective labor. Among the varieties of private entitlement compared here, the system of power and immunity – the classical style of modern Western contract and property rights – is less rigidifying than a system that grants to organized ranks or estates a distinctive measure of access to governmental power as well as to land or labor. But it is more rigidifying than another system – hypothetical yet capable of being constructed with institutional and conceptual materials already available – that would assign temporary and conditional claims to the divisible portions of social capital by means other than the consolidated property right.

The Intimation of a Greater Negative Capability

The second major idea supported by the argument of this chapter is directly related to the program put forward in the final chapter of this book. The particular varieties of private entitlement and work organization that characterize contemporary societies can be contrasted to other arrangements that represent a lesser measure of denaturalization. But they can also be contrasted to institutions that embody a yet higher level of the development of negative capability. These more experimental and emancipatory alternatives are in part imaginary orders. Their realism must be tested by practical experience and their formulation guided by a credible view of transformation. But these imagined alternatives also have roots in the anomalies of contemporary social experience. The arrangements that are more or less denaturalized than their modern-day counterparts do not represent extreme points on a finite spectrum of emancipation from false necessity; no such well-informed spectrum exists. Such comparisons draw a penumbra of remembered experience and anticipated possibility around present social reality. They never set limits to the possible variety of social life.

The same point about the availability of more denaturalized alternatives holds for the formative contexts of contemporary societies, not just for the particular elements of these contexts discussed in this chapter. The significance and justification of this point must await both the program of social reconstruction and the theory of context making presented later in *False Necessity*. The program develops the details of a more emancipatory alternative. The theory informs the programmatic argument while emphasizing the accidental, trumped-up quality of our inherited institutions.

Similarity in the Level of Negative Capability as a Constraint on Context Making

The third thesis of this chapter is that practices or preconceptions can combine to form a stable formative context only when they exemplify and offer a similar level of development of negative capability. This idea provides a direct link between the descriptive analysis of formative contexts in Chapter 2 and the view of context making presented in Chapter 4.

In the course of the argument of Chapter 2, it became clear that an adequate description of formative contexts, and therefore also of the repetitious patterns of conflict they help reproduce, must satisfy two distinct standards. It must recognize the existence of constraints upon the institutional or imaginative elements that constitute a formative framework. Historical experience suggests that some juxtapositions just do not work. As we discover that more and more combinations can be made, we also gain new insight into the instability of other combinations. It is only because of such constraints upon recombination or substitution that the elements of a formative context can truly be said to reinforce one another or to stand apart from the routines they perpetuate. We must therefore recognize these constraints in order to overcome the distortions of conventional social science and naive historiography.

But it is not enough to acknowledge the constraints upon substitution or recombination. A tenable view must also deny that the elements of a formative context can stand or fall only as an unbreakable whole, or that there is a finite list of formative contexts. (The former of these denied theses might be upheld without the benefit of the latter, though not very persuasively: formative contexts would then be represented as an open-ended collection of Democritean atoms. But it is hard to see how the idea of a finite list of types of social organization can survive unless supported by a belief in the indivisibility of each of these types.)

Particular institutional arrangements (or imaginative preconceptions) cannot easily come together into a cohesive cluster of institutions nor can such clusters coalesce into a stable formative context if they embody very disparate measures of emancipation from false necessity. What gives this constraint its force? Institutionalized social arrangements must be reproduced by practical and conceptual activities. The extent to which the arrangements are disentrenched – that is, available for effective challenge – influences the character of the activities that reproduce them. In the most general terms, the less entrenched or naturalized a set of arrangements becomes, the more the activity of reproducing these arrangements resembles the practice of subjecting them to permanent review and occasional transformation. There is no limit to the variety of practical forms that the denaturalization of any given domain of social experience may take. There is no predetermined set of possible institutional vehicles for any given level of negative capability.

Consider an example. A system of entitlements to capital, labor, and governmental power must be put to work by a conceptual activity, legal analysis. We can distinguish styles of legal analysis with respect to the naturalistic quality of their assumptions or effects even though we cannot explain everything about them in this way or determine in advance what forms a more or less emancipated style of legal analysis may assume. Thus, in many societies characterized by well-defended schemes of social division and hierarchy and by widespread acceptance of a particular exemplary model of human association, legal doctrine merged freely into theology and political theory. The jurists made open use not only of low-level statutes, precedents, analogies, and of rationalizing policies and principles, but also of an explicit scheme of the possible and desirable forms of human association. In other societies, such as the North Atlantic democracies of today, legal doctrine scrupulously avoids explicit reference to this third level of analysis. It does so precisely because prescriptive models of social life have come to be seen as more radically controversial. To make legal analysis depend upon argument about such models of human association would be to undermine the cherished distinction between legal doctrine and open-ended ideology. This distinction is in turn justified by the equation of the legal standpoint with the judicial role and by the peculiar responsibilities that traditional liberal states assign to judges. But a different style of legal analysis, in a different institutional setting, might abandon the contrast to open-ended ideology and reincorporate argument about models of social life in an openly tentative and controversial manner.

The varied conceptual and practical activities required for the reproduction of different sets of institutional arrangements influence and invoke one another in several ways. They express ways of imagining society. Institutional arrangements that embody widely different levels of denaturalization also require operational activities that express incompatible views of what society is like and of what it can and should become. The clash is all the more likely to be destabilizing because these assumptions are not merely speculative hypotheses. They are urgent guides to practice that shape lived-out attitudes of submission or resistance to established social practices.

Now that the idea of similarity in the level of disentrenchment, denaturalization, or emancipation from false necessity as a constraint upon context making has been made explicit, it is easy to see how this idea connects with the specific arguments and examples of this chapter. Consider first the variations in the organization of work, so often inseparable from the more general character of social life. A style of work organization that depends on the rigid form of rationalized collective labor can coexist, as it does now, with a market order that uses the absolute property right as its device of decentralization. It can also be reconciled, as in present-day communist regimes, with the replacement of proprietary prerogative by centralized bureaucratic control. But it cannot live together with the more entrenched and naturalistic style of legal entitlements – called in this chapter the system of prerogative – that directly and overtly arranges society into a hierarchy of corporately organized ranks, each with characteristic jobs and with a distinctive relation to economic resources and governmental power. For rationalized collective labor, as it has been defined in this argument, requires a relatively open space within which numerous economic agents can experiment with the form of their practical, productive relations at work or exchange. Labor becomes rationalized to the extent that it provides a visible image of practical reason, trying things out, recombining, and renewing. Nor, conversely, can a microstructure of social life dominated by patron–client relations supply a basis for the system of classical property and contract rights, unless these legal entitlements remain mere slogans without effective application to social life.

On the other hand, the rigid form of rationalized collective labor would be hard to reconcile with a system of rights that establishes economic decentralization through institutional devices such as rotating capital funds that allow for more decentralization and plasticity than absolute property rights can permit. The classic proprietary route to economic decentralization enables the task definer to exercise an authority that merges a narrower task of technical coordination with a broader, disciplinary authority. The absolute property right is implicated in many of the particular devices, such as the internal corporate generation of investment funds, by which mass-production industry, organized according to the rigid model of labor rationalization, maintains its hold over the mainstream of the economy. The development of a decentralizing alternative to consolidated property facilitates more intense and open collective conflict by denying to limited elites of property holders and property managers (or to their bureaucratic successors) a veto over the terms of economic prosperity.

Consider, by way of further example, the relation of private rights to the organization of government. The style of contract and property rights that rose to prominence in the course of modern Western history can certainly coexist with the liberal democracies that owe their basic structure and techniques to the traditions of late eighteenth and early nineteenth century constitutionalism. These traditions established democracies committed both to an ideal of maximum representative legitimacy with minimal mobilization and to procedures that ensure accountability by encouraging deadlock. This same style of property and contract rights can also be reconciled with an authoritarian regime in which the power holders are not accountable to a mass electorate but in which they respect a private order founded upon principles radically different from the principles that shape the organization of government. Thus, the European absolutist monarchies provided the terrain on which modern contract and property rights first developed.

But these rights cannot live with a caste or estatist regime that closely links degrees of access to governmental power with degrees of control over labor and capital. Nor, less self-evidently, can this system of private entitlements combine with a mobilizational dictatorship or a mobilizational democracy. By a mobilizational dictatorship I mean a dictatorship that pushes an aggressive plan of social reconstruction rather than accepting a private order as more or less given; by a mobilizational democracy, the more effective subjection of ever wider areas of social life to broadly based collective challenge and conflict. (Empowered democracy, described and defended in Chapter 5, is such a regime.) Both the mobilizational democracy and the mobilizational dictatorship would be frustrated by a system of rights that effectively secludes a great deal of economic life from their influence and that drastically limits opportunities to innovate in the organizational settings of production and exchange.

These arguments and examples flesh out the idea that the pressure toward similarity in the extent of denaturalization or revisability acts as a constraint upon the substitution or recombination of the practices and ideas that compose a formative framework. But in order not to be misread, this thesis must be both extended and qualified.

The Constraints of Sequence and the Constraints of Negative Capability

I remarked earlier that a view of constraints upon the recombination or substitution of the elements that compose an institutional framework is always just the reverse side of a thesis about how these frameworks are made and revised. Thus, the theory of context making presented in the next chapter must show how a move toward institutional arrangements that embody greater degrees of negative capability can come about. The theory includes the thesis that people can act more or less intentionally to achieve the many forms of empowerment that more denaturalized arrangements make possible.

There is another, equally important form of historical causation, which is simply the influence that each formative context exercises upon the contexts that succeed it. By definition, a formative order makes certain moves easier than others; it facilitates the repetition of certain routines while hindering challenges to them. Less obviously, but no less importantly, it favors some lines of context revision over others. For one thing, the practical problems caused by the very repetition of the privileged routines become urgent and focus attention on the aspects of the institutional framework most directly involved in these problems. For another thing, some aspects of an established institutional and imaginative order may be more resistant to challenge than others. But because formative contexts can be replaced piece by piece (subject to the constraint that the newly combined elements do not represent widely differing degrees of negative capability) and because a given context can do no more than make certain paths of transformation more accessible than others, no context can predetermine its own sequel.

If some such theory of cumulative historical change is correct, similarity in the level of negative capability cannot be the sole constraint upon the joinder of formative institutions or preconceptions. Another constraint is the sharpness with which any new element departs from the sequence of previous formative contexts, the foreignness and unassimilability of the invention into a given tradition of ideas and practices. A particular institutional arrangement may be hard to accept and to fit with other established arrangements, not because it embodies a higher or lower level of negative capability but simply because it makes use of materials that resist translation into a familiar idiom of social understanding and practice. More specifically, the institutional innovation may fail because it cannot be grasped and dealt with as an intelligible transformation of remembered sequences or current arrangements. The interplay between the possible development of negative capability and the influence of sequence constitutes one of the major concerns of the approach to context making developed in Chapter 4. So, too, the interaction between these two forces is crucial to an understanding of how the elements of a formative context reinforce one another.

Constraint Without Deep Structure

The thesis that similar levels of negative capability impose a constraint upon the recombination or substitution of the elements of a formative context can easily be mistaken for a version of the belief in a limited list of possible social worlds. The analysis of institutional variations distinguished by the degree of negative capability that each group of institutions embodies seems to suggest the idea of a multidimensional map of social possibilities. The position a society occupies on one dimension of the map – its forms of right, its organization of work, the shape of its government, and the preconceptions about social ideals and transformative opportunities that accompany each of these – influences its position on the other dimensions. It seems that by making the map more and more detailed, you can end up with a short list of possible forms of social worlds. Thus, by a roundabout route, you would have returned to a stringent although nonevolutionary version of deep-structure social theory.

Such a reading would misinterpret the argument of this chapter. At any level of negative capability and with respect to any domain of social life, there are an indefinite number of possible institutional solutions. The feasible options are circumscribed by the difficulty of combining arrangements or preconceptions that reflect widely different degrees of emancipation from false necessity. The practical and intellectual materials generated by a particular tradition also limit the solutions actively considered. Thus, the institutional examples just discussed all come from modern Western history. Nevertheless, even these two sets of constraints fail to yield the type of closed list that a theory of possible social worlds requires.

You have seen how the attempt to compare and contrast the institutional arrangements that make up the formative contexts of certain contemporary societies leads beyond itself to an account of how context change takes place and to a vision of the changes worth undertaking. This vision and this account – intimately connected – are the major themes of *False Necessity*.

4

The Making of Society Through Politics

Imagining Transformation

THE MAKING OF CONTEMPORARY FORMATIVE CONTEXTS: AN INSTITUTIONAL GENEALOGY

THE GENESIS OF FORMATIVE CONTEXTS AND THE THEORY OF CONTEXT MAKING

THE argument of Chapters 2 and 3 started from a particular explanatory problem: the attempt to understand the tenacity of the reform cycles that characterize the governmental politics of late twentieth century Western industrial democracies.

This problem led to an effort to understand how the formative institutional contexts that shape these reform cycles change and how they are put together. The analysis of one of these contexts suggested that neither the perspective of naive historiography and positivist social science nor the standpoint of deep-logic social theory would suffice to do the job. The one, by denying the distinction between structure-preserving and structure-transforming events, cannot even pose the question. The other, by insisting upon the idea of a limited list of possible social worlds or stages of social transformation, gives an answer that is implausible on its face: a definition of the formative contexts sufficiently detailed to account for the reform cycles also reveals their hodgepodge character and makes it hard to think of them as cohesive wholes occupying a predefined place in a catalogue of social possibilities or historical stages. Moreover, it soon became apparent that the riddle exemplified by the reform cycles can be found in every period and facet of social life: over and over again, we must understand routine by postulating a formative institutional or imaginative context that shapes it. Over and over again, we discover that styles of social thought insensitive to the shaped and compulsive quality of social life cannot account for either the internal composition or the historical making of formative contexts. Nor can either be elucidated by theories appealing to the idea of a deep structure that singles out types and stages of social organization. A social theory capable of satisfying these minimal, negative needs gives a concrete form to the view of human activity presented at the outset of *Social Theory: Its Situation and Its Task.*

Chapter 3 carried the argument forward by locating the formative institutional contexts of late twentieth century North Atlantic and communist countries on a map of large-scale variations in social life. The analysis showed that much in these societies and in the character of their formative contexts can be understood as marking an intermediate position between the maximization and the minimization of experimental freedom in social life, between the strengthening and the weakening of the contrast between transformative conflicts about the contexts and routine moves within them. At the same time the argument suggested a way to understand the constraints upon substitutions in the elements of formative contexts that does not presuppose deep-logic social theory. There is the constraint of sequence: an institutional or imaginative framework makes certain sequels easier than others. Indeed, if it makes sense to speak of such a framework having a point, this consequence is its point. But there is also another constraint irreducible to the effects of sequence: the difficulty of combining within a single institutional context elements that represent very different degrees of facility for revision. This suggestion can be justified, made precise, and properly distinguished from deep-logic social analysis only within a view of how social contexts get made and remade.

The present chapter develops an account of transformation that avoids the errors of naive historiography and deep-logic social theory, gives a social-theoretical interpretation to the modernist view of human activity, and seeks to explain the construction and revision of formative contexts. As the problem selected for intensive focus earlier was to explain the reform cycles in certain contemporary societies, the immediate subject matter of the theory of transformation is the genesis of the formative contexts that account for those same reform cycles. The argument advances by two large steps: a schematic and polemical history of the formative contexts of contemporary Western industrial democracies and the account of context making that this institutional genealogy foreshadows.

The historical narrative mobilizes both familiar and controversial knowledge in behalf of a view of transformation made explicit toward the end of this chapter. The explicit view of context making offered there gives a more precise theoretical interpretation and defense of the explanatory approach implicit in the narrative, but it is not the only plausible defense or interpretation. You can agree with the general form of the theory while finding its narrative realization faulty. Conversely, you can sympathize with the intentions of the narrative approach while rejecting the particular version of it represented by the theory. The narrative is both the loose anticipation of a theory and the specification of a pretheoretical puzzle that requires a theoretical solution.

The historical argument focuses successively upon three of the major institutional clusters that compose the characteristic formative contexts of late twentieth century industrial democracies: the work-organization cluster, the private-rights cluster, and the governmental-organization cluster. For the sake of simplicity, I disregard the occupational-structure cluster. More significantly, the view of context making focuses on the institutional rather than the imaginative components of formative contexts. The final section of the chapter indicates the general way in which the theory of social frameworks and of their remaking would be altered by the reintroduction of this crucial imaginative element.

You can take as your topic any formative institutional structure at any moment of relative quiescence. The arbitrary termination point of the narrative – in this case, the situation of particular countries in the late twentieth century – determines how far back it makes sense to go. Moreover, the different elements of the formative context whose genesis you want to explain do not crystallize at the same rate. Thus, although the constitutional and administrative structure of contemporary Western democracies has been developing uninterruptedly since the High Middle Ages, the particular institutional practices I emphasize took their form during a very brief period: for the pioneering countries, the second and third quarters of the nineteenth century. Before this time the work-organization or private-rights aspects of the institutional orders described in Chapter 2 had a degree of ambiguity of developmental possibilities they have rarely achieved since. Once the rules of party-political conflict and constitutional structure had been more or less set, the system of private rights and the organization of work became more fixed than they had been before. The attempt significantly to change them would now require a reform of the arrangements that define the structure of the state and the conflict over governmental power. The point can be generalized: the structure of society does not become secure until the relation between state and society has taken a defined form and social divisions have been entwined with degrees of government-supported privilege. Remember therefore in reading this narrative that the genealogy of the work-organization and the private-rights complexes might well have been broken up into two distinct phases, divided by the consolidation of the governmental-organization cluster.

The narrative argument takes as its target what it calls a mythical history of the formative contexts of contemporary Western societies. This mythical history, still so prominent in the historical and social-science literature, retrospectively rationalizes the emergence of current formative contexts as the necessary expression of deep-seated economic, organizational, or psychological imperatives. Its liberal–conservative form is the belief in the triumphant emergence of market institutions and of the more efficient forms of economic production and the more democratic forms of governmental organization that supposedly accompanied those institutions. The proponents of this thesis characteristically acknowledge that the market is a necessary but not a sufficient condition of political democracy. They tacitly identify the abstract conception of a market with the particular market institutions that came to prevail in Western Europe and North America. The Marxist variant of the mythical history accepts all these beliefs while making them relative to a specific stage of historical development. For the Marxist, the mythical history becomes the account of the emergence of capitalism and of the types of bourgeois democracy or Bonapartist authoritarianism that the capitalist mode of production tolerates. Both the liberal–conservative and the Marxist formulations play up a particular stereotype of English history as the exemplary route to the unprecedented wealth and power of the world-conquering Western nations. Deviations from the English prototype are thought to require special explanations.

The polemic that my narrative conducts against the mythical history involves three main theses. The first thesis is that the mythical history drastically underestimates the variety of institutional forms that competed for acceptance in the course of the events with which it deals. Many alternatives, once defeated, came to occupy an important though limited place within the triumphant order. The second thesis is that of all these alternatives the most formidable and persistent rival of the now dominant institutional order was a version of what Marx disparagingly called petty commodity production. The critics of this alternative are right in claiming that it could not have succeeded within the institutional structures we now implicitly equate with markets and democracies. But they fail to appreciate that in a drastically revised institutional form the alternative not only had a promising future but continues to have one today. Thus, the historical argument presented here is frankly connected with a view of programmatic opportunities in the present. The third thesis is that to the extent certain institutional forms of economic and governmental organization did win out their victory cannot be credited to their inherent practical or moral superiority. They did not win thanks to a self-propelling dynamic of organizational, economic, and psychological imperatives. Their triumph resulted in large part from a much more complicated and accidental history of practical and imaginative conflicts, of missed opportunities and failures of information. Yet the way of exploring this largely negative thesis will already suggest that its point is less to emphasize accident, variation, and particularity than to come up with an alternative strategy of generalizing explanation.

The highly schematic and polemical character of my narrative inevitably makes it to some extent unhistorical. There is no easy escape from partiality of perspective: a history of formative contexts is the greater part of history *tout court*, even with the drastic simplification involved in focusing on institutional arrangements rather than imaginative preconceptions. Occasional plunges to a level of richer historical detail offer only a limited corrective. There is, nevertheless, an important sense in which the historical authenticity of an argument has to do less with its wealth of detail than with its fidelity to the quality of lived historical experience. The prestige of the mythical history, endlessly elaborated in countless historical monographs, testifies to the difference between historicity and detail. Surely we lose the historical sense if we allow understanding to be controlled by the perspective of naive historiography, which cannot do justice to the sharp discontinuities between social worlds and between the types of subjective experience they harbor. And we lose the historical sense just as much if we surrender to deep-logic social analysis, which makes the possibility of explanation depend upon the denial of surprise and contingency and thereby opens an unbridgeable gap between the experience of living in history and the practice of explaining history. I want a more concrete historiography too, but I want one that does not have to rely upon bad, antihistorical theories.

A SKEPTICAL PROLOGUE: PRIVATE ENTERPRISE AND GOVERNMENTAL POLICY

Before turning to the genesis of the major institutional complexes described, consider, by way of preliminary example and admonition, the history of a subordinate, derivative, and eclectic institutional practice: the division of decisional responsibilities between central governments and large-scale business enterprises. In one sense this division merely extends the private-rights complex: the corporate institution, relatively insulated from public control and public controversy, takes its place alongside the system of contract and property rights. But it is also closely connected both with a style of governmental politics that limits the assertion of collective control over the basic shape and pace of economic growth and with an approach to the organization of work that mixes technical coordination with a generic disciplinary authority and thereby makes possible a stark contrast between task-defining and task-executing activities.

The massive network of governmentally granted subsidies, incentives, and privileges, the overt partnership between government and business in some sectors, and the domination of public enterprise in others, do not eviscerate the division between government and business of its force. Large concentrations of capital and labor are realized in the form of separate realms governed by managers in the name of the property norm. The mythical history would have us believe that this arrangement is a necessary consequence of the attempt to reconcile economic decentralization with economies of scale. But is it? A little bit of history suffices to make you wonder. Consider how this solution came to prevail in the country with which it is now most closely identified.

In early nineteenth century America, government and business stood in a multiplicity of relations, and many doctrines about the proper association between governmental and corporate power competed with each other. You appreciate this variety best when you focus on policy debates at the state level. The institutional situation was one in which enterprises under mixed public–private control and ownership played an important role; the right of incorporation, often closely guarded, became an instrument for bestowing and receiving illicit favor, and a justification for exercising a potentially high degree of control over the corporation in exchange for those powers of government (like the power of eminent domain) that were delegated to it. Three main doctrines of incorporation struggled for influence; the first, responsive to a populist vision, was hostile to all incorporation, invoking an ideal of individual enterprise; the second proposed to develop those aspects of the current situation that involved a major overlap of governmental and corporate powers and that therefore opened the internal structure and the external activities of the corporation to control by the agencies of government; the third view wanted to make the privilege of incorporation more readily available and to build a thicker wall between corporate discretion and governmental authority. By the start of the Civil War, this third doctrine had triumphed in practice, and its victory was consolidated by the 1880s. In the end, the corporate form became a device that allowed large concentrations of economic power over workers and markets to operate at a crucial remove from the risks of partisan democratic conflict. The reform movements of the late nineteenth and the twentieth century, from Progressivism to the New Deal, took the structure generated by the earlier contest for granted. Whether the theme of restraint upon business or that of organization in the service of business prevailed in these latter-day movements, neither the restraint nor the rationalization ever went so far as to endanger the fundamental screening of business from national politics that had been settled upon at an earlier date.

The facts that converged to this end were of very different kinds. One of them was the division of the forces opposed to autonomous private incorporation between the populist critics of corporate business and the proponents of a broader overlap of the spheres of corporate and governmental power. Another was the economic influence exercised by the businessmen themselves: though cliques of insiders stood to benefit from the favoritism of closely guarded incorporation, a much larger group was anxious both to incorporate more easily and to rid their incorporated businesses of tight governmental interference. More often than not, they had the material means and the personal connections to translate this anxiety into political influence. Moreover, the self-operating, relatively unpoliced corporation might well seem to involve less of a break from established practice than the attempt to deepen the relations between government and business; the latter would force upon state institutions and party politics a mounting burden of responsibility. For that burden to be discharged the forms of political action and organization would, sooner rather than later, have to be transformed.

An additional decisive cause of the outcome, however, had to do with the ascendancy of a doctrine of freedom and efficiency, forged by lawyers and publicists who often regarded themselves, and were regarded in their own time, as hostile to the business interests whose legal and conceptual underpinnings they helped cement. The core of their conception of freedom was the unwarranted identification of the abstract idea of decentralized market decision with a concrete system of contract and property rights organized around spheres of absolute discretion in the control of labor and commodities. The core of the related idea of economic development was belief in the existence of an unbreakable natural link between economic growth – including repeated breakthroughs of the capacity barrier – and the security in vested rights that inheres in the chosen system of contract and property. This belief represented a double mistake: first, by supposing the existence of security *tout court* as distinguished from security for some against others; second, by failing to deal adequately with the constraints that vested rights impose on innovation. What these doctrines of freedom and development had in common was the effort to depoliticize the basic structure of rights and economic policy.

Once the earlier conflicts and uncertainties had been forgotten, their settlement took on a specious semblance of naturalness and necessity. The structure that emerged, however, was no more necessary and natural than the interests and the illusions, the tactical achievements and the tactical failures, that accounted for its initial consolidation and avoided its later disruption. An aspect of that structure was the definition of a tight stranglehold of powers over the flow of basic investment decisions: by the time mass party politics came into its own and the protective shield of sound finance doctrine had been cast aside, a characteristic dilemma of macroeconomic policy emerged: the need not to surrender totally to business interests for fear of losing elections and even of undermining the conditions of prosperity itself; and the contrasting need not to forfeit business confidence entirely in order to avoid disinvestment. The emerging system also existed in the imagination: in the clear-cut separation between an area of social life, governmental politics, to which democratic principles applied, and a larger world of work and exchange, to which they did not apply. In the end, the weight of these richly textured though largely tacit conceptions of what ideals fitted where turned out to be more important than the naive doctrines of freedom and security that had once been their polemical spearhead.

The full significance of these developments becomes plain when they are placed in a broader comparative historical setting. Western countries, like the United States or Britain, that were to have a relatively ample experience of democratic conflict had chosen a growth path that accepted a strong barrier between business and government, each marked by contrasting principles of organization. On the other hand, later industrializing countries, like Germany and Japan, that experimented with a deeper mutual involvement of government and business did so in the setting of a more authoritarian national politics: for the commitment to economic growth and the chosen route to it were, in both Japan and Germany, part of a conscious strategy of building national power under the aegis of a revamped and reunified elite. The third option was missing: the combination of democratic mass politics with a close and varied net of relations between state and enterprise. The absence of this combination – easier to achieve perhaps in the pioneering instances of industrialization than in the cases when an elite could present itself as the custodian of a collective effort to catch up – was decisive for the whole later course of politics and economy in the West and in the world at large. Yet it never did follow any immanent, unstoppable logic.

This American episode suggests two points of more general interest. First, the controversy over the proper institutional form of economic decentralization may have characterized other aspects of economic history as well. Recovering the structure of this controversy may help us shake loose the misleading identification of the market form of economic order with the particular kinds of markets we know now. Second, as soon as we try to understand in greater detail the emergence of a particular institutional arrangement in a particular place we discover not the smooth operation of developmental compulsions and lawlike constraints but messy struggles, punctuated by surprising turns and conducted by people who often helped to frustrate their own confused objectives. We should think vice before concluding that these events and personalities were just the unwitting agents of objective and inescapable imperatives, such as the imperative that supposedly determines a unique set of market institutions capable of combining economic decentralization with economies of scale. The invocation of such requirements may seem the only alternative to theoretical agnosticism. But we may find a way to save the appearances – the detailed texture of historical life – and to vindicate our reconstructive freedom while nevertheless continuing to explain the facts.

THE GENESIS OF THE WORK-ORGANIZATION COMPLEX

The Mythical History of Work Organization

The dominant form of work organization in the advanced Western societies is characterized by the prevalence of the rigid form of rationalized collective labor in the mainstream of industry and by the confinement of the flexible form to the industrial vanguard. Remember that the rigid form accentuates the contrast between task-defining and task-executing activities while the flexible form softens it. This allocation of approaches to the organization of work depends upon the prevalence of mass-production industry, manufacturing standardized products through rigid production processes, product-specific machines, and large, centralized concentrations of capital and labor. The prevalence of the mass-production style is sustained by favorable institutional conditions and by a particular international division of labor.

The point of much traditional historical, economic, and sociological work, conservative and radical alike, has been to show that this particular compromise of styles of economic organization was necessary whether or not, as the radicals claim, it represented only a necessary stage to something else. This explanatory aim is ordinarily pursued through an argument central to the mythical history of work organization. The argument claims that the English path to industrial growth – or, rather, what is commonly identified as the English path – represented the preferred if not the only road to early industrial development. The stereotype of the English experience includes the replacement of the small family farm and independent peasantry by large-scale agrarian businesses owned by aristocratic magnates or rising peasant proprietors who often produced for a foreign market; the eventual substitution of artisanal guilds by mechanized factories and corporate enterprises as the end result of a passage through ever more centralized versions of the putting-out system; the reorganization of work as a system of well-defined and repetitious tasks

within the new large-scale industries and their nonindustrial counterparts, all the way from bureaucracies to hospitals, in other sectors
of practical life; and the reorganization of the entire world economy
as a machine to reproduce this industrial style on a worldwide scale
through the specialization of entire national economies.

This story forms the core of the mythical history of industrialized
market societies and of that confused entity, capitalism, at once a
historical universal and a historical particular. It is the trajectory of
economic development exposed by *Capital* as a diabolical but prov-
idential drama and presented in numberless textbooks as the most
natural thing in the world. The social counterpart to this path of
economic growth has been the continued existence of prosperous
families that have a good chance of bequeathing from generation to
generation their privileged control over labor, capital, culture, and
governmental power. The mythical history is therefore also a story
about them and an assurance that their interests were on the right
side of social evolution.

Here, as in later sections of this interpreted narrative, I argue that
this view of industrial development drastically underestimates the
degree of deviation from the mainstream that occurred even in such
prize exhibits of the mythical history as the economic and social
transformation of England. In fact the deviant forms reveal more of
what was distinctive to the West and what made it incomparably
revolutionary than do the dominant ones. I also claim that the traditional view gives a mistaken sense of the degree of prevalence that
the more rigid type of work organization in fact achieved. According
to the mythical history the deviations appeared for special reasons –
the idiosyncracies of the regions where they arose – but failed for
general ones – the inherent imperatives of industrial development.
But there are grounds to conclude that the now dominant institutional form of Western industrial society won and maintained its
preeminence over its rivals for reasons that have little to do with its
intrinsic productive capabilities. One set of reasons for this conclusion
has to do with the many ways in which state power was mobilized
against the deviant forms and in support of the hegemonic ones.
Another reason is the threshold effect of early and still precarious
success. Machine design, organizational practices, and even technical
and economic ideas began to consolidate around the emergent style
of work organization and to bestow upon it a second-order necessity.
Deep-logic social analysis itself and the historical interpretations it
has inspired contributed to this fabulous bootstrap. For they helped
form a restrictive view of historical possibility that aggravated rather
than qualified the sense of naturalness that always surrounds victorious settlements and solutions.

One particular line of deviation from the mainstream of industrial development stands out by its ubiquity. A discussion of it brings into focus the issues at stake in the larger controversy. In every period of modern Western history some controversialists denied that the canonical style of industrialization had to prevail, even as part of the transition to an alternative economic order. They took sides with those who defended an economy of family farms and cottage industry, of technological revolution and cheap production without armylike factories, of market decentralization without the license to concentrate wealth, and of more cooperative forms of labor and exchange. Their advocacy has been traditionally derided as the program of petty bourgeois sentimentalism, engaged in a losing debate with tough-minded radicals and conservatives. Their critics point out that the petty bourgeois alternative would have been both self-destructive and inefficient. It would have been self-destructive because the more successful petty enterprises would soon have expanded into large-scale businesses unless they were constantly restrained and dispossessed by a state that would have then become the real power in the economy. It would have been inefficient because the alternative system could never have accommodated the enormous economies of scale that made continued economic revolution possible.

But these critics turn out to have no larger a share of the truth than their petty bourgeois adversaries. The tough-minded are right in the sense that the alleged alternative would have been both self-destabilizing and inefficient *unless* it built for itself institutional arrangements for markets and democracies different from the arrangements that have in fact come to prevail. Petty commodity production had no long-term future within property-based market economies and American-type democratic institutions. It would have required a different institutional framework. And this framework would have radically altered its social meaning and consequences. But the petty bourgeois romantics are right to insist that their alternative has been repeatedly suppressed rather than defeated in an impartial Darwinian competition. They are also correct in claiming for their program the status of a feasible point of departure toward an alternative industrial society. They even have a point when they argue that in fragmentary form this alternative industrialism has played a much larger role in the actual industrialization of the West than the mythical history acknowledges.

This debate has practical importance because the alternative has never been definitively discarded. Continuously reasserted in the course of modern economic history, it remains today, in altered form, a serious possibility of industrial organization. The case for the alternative is of theoretical and practical interest because it suggests a different approach to modern economic history and prefigures a theory of transformation free from the errors that beset deep-logic social thought.

My discussion advances in three stages. It begins with the early forms of industrial development, then turns to their agrarian counterparts, and finally takes up the latter-day manifestations of the contest between dominant and deviant variants of industrialism.

The Conflict over the Organizational Form of Manufacturing

The most powerful intellectual tool of the mythical history of manufacturing and agriculture in early modern Europe has been the proto-industrialization theory. The most significant polemical result of this theory is to define the petty bourgeois deviation as an unstable transitional form that turns into a blind alley of economic development when it does not quickly give way to the high industrial road. The main elements of the proto-industrialization thesis are the following. Because of the relative poverty of their soil or the pastoral character of their agriculture, certain regions started out with large amounts of underemployed labor. These regions were the star candidates for those early bursts of country-based industrialization whose uses and ultimate failure the proto-industrialization thesis purports to describe. The advance of agricultural techniques in the more fertile regions resulted in still greater underemployment in the poorer ones. The peasant household, like most economic agents in the preindustrial world, was more concerned to preserve a customary way of life than to maximize a rate of return. The peasants of the impoverished and overcrowded regions therefore clung to their land and sought additional employment. They provided the cheap labor that the putting-out system could exploit. Thus there began simultaneously in many regions of Europe a flurry of decentralized manufacturing activity, closely linked with agricultural work and held together by merchants primarily engaged in long-distance trade.

At first the merchant may have served merely as the commercial intermediary and the purveyor of raw materials to a household that continued to own the instruments of its own labor. But the residual independence of domestic industry was eventually doomed by the destruction of its agrarian base. The spread of small-scale rural industry undermined the Malthusian constraints upon early marriage. The resulting abrupt rise in the population of regions that already suffered from an impoverished agricultural base helped fragment peasant landholding. Peasants who had once been both smallholders and independent contractors often found themselves landless wage employees, working for an entrepreneurial landowner or merchant.

The story did not end there. From the standpoint of the merchant, now in charge of the production process, the rusticated industry of the putting-out system suffered from several incurable defects. It confronted the master with formidable problems of control over the efficiency of workers whom he could not directly oversee. It ran into the resistance or unreliability of laborers who would work only the time necessary to safeguard their accustomed standard of living (a backward-bending labor supply curve). And its decentralized character imposed transportation costs that limited the expansion of putting-out networks.

These problems, the proto-industrialization argument continues, could be solved only by the concentration of workers in centralized factories. The factory system therefore preceded and made possible the mechanization of industry and the extreme, technical division of labor. The attempt to prolong the life of decentralized, rural industry either failed or generated satellites to the central form of productive activity. This central form became the mechanized, mass-production industry, operating against the background of a countryside emptied of most of its population and given over to large-scale agricultural business.

It is embarrassing to the broader social and historical ideas supported by the proto-industrialization thesis that many of the features we now regard as intrinsic to the dominant model emerged only recently and ran into trouble only a few generations after their original introduction. The Fordist, assembly line production process and the divisional structure pioneered by some of the large American corporations of the 1920s and 1930s may serve as examples. This belated development suggests that even after the events described by the students of proto-industrialization had run their course, the contemporary form of market organization was very far from being in the cards. For the moment, however, consider only how much the proto-industrialization thesis understates the degree of deviation and conflict in the history of early European industrialization. Most of the anomalous experiments and trajectories that the proto-industrialization argument fails to accommodate illustrate the career of that petty commodity variant of industrialization whose condescending dismissal by mainstream theory and historiography I earlier recalled.

In early modern European history many regions witnessed the development of manufacturing complexes that exemplify this alternative industrial path. These industrial ventures were distinguished by their relative smallness of scale, their resourcefulness in using flexible production processes to satisfy particular, varying needs rather than rigid processes to fulfill standardized needs, and their efforts to organize work in ways that allowed for a closer interplay between supervision and execution. In all these respects, these early industries were forerunners of what has since become the vanguard sector of the advanced Western economies. Indeed, in many cases they survived to become part of the vanguard sector, though in others they either disappeared or assimilated to the dominant industrial model.

Among the instances of deviation were the woolen industry of the West Riding, the Birmingham hardware trade, the cutlery industries of Sheffield in England and Solingen in Germany, and the textile industry of Lyon. These and other experiences of industrial development have benefited from an increasing number of studies by both historians and social theorists. A close reading and comparison of these studies suggests an account of the reasons for the failure or success of these experiments that cannot be reconciled with the mythical history. The pattern of success and failure does not support the premise that most sectors of an economy are inherently more suited to what we now consider the mainstream or the vanguardist forms of production: the deviant experiments succeeded and failed in distinct sectors as well as in different regions and at different times. The deviations were more likely to flourish when governmental power was not used exclusively to institute legal rules and economic policies that consolidated the dominant model and when the deviant entrepreneurs themselves responded to periodic economic crisis in ways that exploited the flexibility of their enterprises.

Compare, for this purpose, the experience of the Sheffield cutlery industry with that of the Lyonnaise textile producers. The general line of governmental policy and market organization in England unequivocally favored large-scale merchants and manufacturers in their generations-long struggle against artisans and petty entrepreneurs and helped force these petty producers into the role of economic reactionaries or satellites. Against this already hostile background, the cutlery makers of Sheffield responded to the economic crisis of the 1870s and 1880s, to higher tariffs, and to competition from their more resourceful Solingen counterparts by the classic defensive maneuvers of cottage industry under attack. These maneuvers drastically restricted the potential economic significance of the deviant mode even when they ensured the marginal economic survival of the petty entrepreneurs themselves. A few of the cutlery makers found a niche in the narrow market for custom-made luxury goods. In this way, they gave up the battle to occupy a portion of major productive activity, resigning themselves to economic insignificance. Others switched to the economic, organizational, and technological methods of the dominant model. They began using product-specific machines, rigid production processes, and a more pronounced hierarchy of the supervisors and the supervised in order to make specialty steels. Burdened by the inflexibility of big business without its advantage of scale or governmental favor, they became easy prey to the next changes in market conditions.

Contrast this outcome to the history of Lyonnaise textile manufacturing. There the manufacturing of textiles by artisanal cooperatives and petty entrepreneurs had been pursued, with occasional interruptions, from the seventeenth century onward. After having been disorganized during the years of the revolution, this style of manufacturing was reconstituted at the outset of the Orleanist regime. Its most characteristic organizational device was the subcontracting of weaving to master artisans.

Two successive shifts in taste jeopardized the textile manufacturing of Lyon. The first was the change from more intricate fabrics, prized for the texture and design of their weaving, to the cheaper cloths, admired for the vividness of their colors. This shift in demand resulted in a massive transfer of contract orders to less expensive and less proficient subcontractors, which in turn brought on, in the Lyon uprisings of 1831 and 1834, one of the great artisanal revolts of the nineteenth century. The second such change was the surge, during the 1870s and 1880s, of a taste for still cheaper cotton-and-silk-waste fabrics. This might well have caused the downfall of the Lyonnaise *fabrique* had the manufacturers and artisans not played upon the economic and technological ambiguities of their situation to draw strength out of weakness. The small-scale manufacturers used mixed fabrics and new forms of printing and dyeing. The high instability of demand in the textile markets, the diffusion of electricity as a cheap decentralized power source, and the relatively low wages of rural weavers all favored the *petite fabrique*. Moreover, the larger setting of French national policy had never ceased to be more congenial to the alternative style of manufacturing than its English counterpart. The survival of artisanal or petty entrepreneurial cadres in much of France, as in the other European regions where they flourished, found support in the vitality of independent smallholding agriculture. This vitality in turn reflected the continuing ability of French peasants and petty bourgeoisie, from the consolidation of absolutist government to the successive postrevolutionary regimes, to enlist governmental power in their own favor. At their most successful, the smaller entrepreneurs and proprietors mobilized governmental power not only to obtain narrow material advantages but to safeguard whole ways of life. By the 1960s, the cottage industries dominated the textile manufacturing of Lyon: 55 percent of weaving and 70 percent of spinning were in the hands of the *petite fabrique*. By a continuous series of self-transformations, punctuated by major crises and ingenious responses, petty commodity producers, the ridiculed reactionaries of industrial history, had secured a prominent place in the most advanced sectors of industry.

At a minimum, success stories like this one show that there is no natural allocation of economic activities to the dominant and the deviant types of industry, the rigid and the flexible forms of work organization. The kinds of textiles produced in Lyon by the latter-day version of cottage industry were made in many other parts of the world, from Great Britain to Taiwan, by mass production, with product-specific machines, rigid production processes, and stark contrasts between planning and execution.

The successful alternatives exemplify a continuity between artisanal manufacturing or petty commodity production and vanguardist industry. They suggest how national styles of industrialization, acquired capacities to enlist state power, and collective strategies influenced the boundaries between the two types of industrial organization. They even demonstrate a surprisingly frequent link between the artisanal rearguard and the high-tech vanguard of Western industrialization. But they do not prove that the alternative industrial type could have then, or can now, gain a dominant place in the economy and impart to it a different social character. Even the successful cases were, in another sense, failures: in no instance was the consolidation of the alternative style in one sector of the economy followed by changes in the defining institutional. form of markets and polities that might have permitted a more drastic shift in the character of Western industrialism.

The attempt to assess the larger promise of the deviant cases must therefore be indirect. One approach is to study the dependence of the dominant industrial style upon a variety of extraeconomic institutional arrangements that were themselves subject to constant struggle. The study of this dependence could then be complemented by an attempt to imagine the institutional conditions under which the alternative industrialism could have flourished more widely. This is a theme pursued throughout this interpretive history of contemporary formative contexts as well as in later parts of *False Necessity*. Another, much narrower approach is to consider how the rivalry between the dominant and the deviant models relates to early modern struggles over agriculture and to contemporary conflicts about economic organization. In this way what has usually been seen as a highly localized and long-settled quarrel can be shown to be part of a general and continuing dispute.

The Conflict over the Organizational Form of Agriculture

The parallel to the deviant model in the history of manufacturing was a style of agricultural development that gave a preeminent role to the family farm and to cooperative relations among smallholders. The significance of the parallelism is hardly self-evident. Cottage industry sometimes flourished, as in the heyday of the Birmingham and Sheffield metal trades, against a background of land concentration. Conversely, family-scale agriculture was occasionally accompanied by the near absence or the stagnation and involution of manufacturing activities, as in Piedmont, Catalonia, and some parts of the Netherlands. Nevertheless, the deviant agricultural style did have broader economic and social implications. The proto-industrialization thesis, put in its place, shows the economic implication: the destruction of small-scale ownership or tenancy played a decisive part in the particular trajectory of manufacturing history studied by the exponents of that thesis. Their mistake was only to see this trajectory as the preferred or even the necessary route to the maximum development of productive capabilities. The broader social implication becomes clear when you consider that the dominant and deviant models of manufacturing and agriculture favored, or injured, the same social groups. Cottage industry was quickest to escape the role assigned to it by the proto-industrialization thesis wherever there flourished a class of small-scale producers. Yet, factorylike manufacturing and land concentration never abolished this class nor did they create a polarized society of magnates and dependents. The large and rigid enterprises needed the buffer of small-scale production against economic instability. For reasons still to be discussed, the legal arrangements that defined these more concentrated market systems and the polities that protected them never allowed the repetition of the deadliest crisis known to the agrarian-bureaucratic empires of antiquity: the reduction of small-scale producers to servile status and the consequent shrinking of the market in labor and in goods.

Modern Western agricultural history supports two main conclusions about the practicability of relative agrarian decentralization. These conclusions illustrate the elements of falsehood and truth in the polemic against petty commodity production.

The first conclusion is that the family farm turned out to be as efficient, by the measure of acreage and even labor productivity, as the more concentrated forms of agriculture. This style of agricultural development prevailed in many of the regions that proved to be most successful in the earlier phases of the approach toward industrialization. Where ownership was concentrated, the form of agricultural exploitation often continued to resemble that of familial production in most other respects. And in many of the instances in which this productive style gave way to larger-scale units, tilled by laborers under centralized control, the active alliance of national governments with landowning magnates, exerted through law, policy, and calculated omission, was largely responsible for the result.

A second conclusion, however, qualifies this first one. In those instances where small-scale production flourished well into more advanced stages of industrialization and agricultural mechanization, it proved to be unstable or else to depend upon a special deal between government and the family farm. This deal enabled the small producers to resist the risks of agricultural instability while cordoning off the agrarian sector from an economy largely organized on different principles. This second conclusion suggests once again that a more secure and influential place for small-scale agriculture would have required a change in the institutional character of markets and polities. The following paragraphs use a variety of allusions to European history to illustrate the first conclusion and the experience of nineteenth-century France and America to exemplify the second.

A comparison of agricultural regions in sixteenth-, seventeenth-, and eighteenth-century Europe shows that the most flourishing areas were often the ones characterized by family-scale agriculture, whereas the concentration of ownership and management prevailed in many of the more backward regions. Piedmont and Lombardy in contrast to Sicily and Naples; Catalonia in comparison to the rest of Spain; Flanders and Holland as against Germany beyond the Elbe – all tell, in this one respect, the same story, though each brings out a distinct facet of the common problem. Thus, the history of Catalan agriculture clearly shows how access to governmental power (e.g., the Catalan representative assembly) and to a vital urban market benefited family-scale agriculture. And the example of Flanders, where highly specialized, labor-intensive farms coexisted with large grain-producing estates, demonstrates that smallholding could continue to flourish in a milieu of precocious industrialization.

The significance of these early modern European experiences comes out most clearly when they are placed in a world-historical context. The most populous and enduring societies before the revolution of techniques and ideas that radiated out of the North Atlantic were the great agrarian-bureaucratic empires. A characteristic crisis repeatedly jeopardized the prosperity and even the survival of these societies, narrowing markets, sapping the authority of central governments, and cutting off opportunities of advance toward irreversible commercialization and industrialization. Whenever unforeseen economic or military dangers required the central state to demand additional fiscal or military contributions, the landowning magnates, largely thanks to their control of local public administration, managed to shift the brunt of the burden onto the smallholders and other petty producers. These small folk, ruined by exactions they could not meet, then voluntarily sought, or were compelled to accept, a status of personal dependence upon the very potentates who had undone them. This surrender to lordly protection shook the most important support of market activity. The sphere of exchange narrowed to the dealings among larger domains that tended toward

economic autarky and hierarchical discipline. The central government, dangerously weakened, found itself even more beholden to
the great landholders than it had been before. No wonder the most
acute statesmen and reformers in these societies were obsessed with
the attempt to preserve the smallholding and petty mercantile sectors
as a basis for the government's fiscal and military strength.

Why they repeatedly failed, why Europe, less deliberately, escaped
the destructive cycle of those empires, and why both questions can
best be answered by an antinecessitarian social theory are issues to
be taken up in another part of this volume. What matters for the
moment is the suggestion that the most distinctively European form
of agricultural development was the supposedly deviant and regressive agriculture of smallholders. The remarkable feature of the standard, "English" model of agrarian concentration – a feature that
requires further elucidation – was its ability to move as far toward
concentration as it did without provoking the market-destructive
crises that had frequently accompanied superficially similar movements in other societies.

But given that the family-run farm represented a practicable alternative to agrarian concentration in the economic circumstances of
early modern Europe, could it continue to play a progressive role in
the era of industrialization and mechanized agriculture? The answer
to this question lies – surprisingly – less in technical-economic considerations than in the uses of governmental power. In France – with
its densely settled land and strong traditions of alliance between the
state and the peasantry – legal rules and governmental policy helped
safeguard the relatively labor-intensive tillage of middle-sized and
small-sized farms. The resulting style of agricultural development
was almost by definition less labor productive than its more concentrated English counterpart. Yet recent studies have demonstrated
that, at least in the nineteenth century, the total economic effect was
only negligibly prejudicial if it was prejudicial at all. If output per
worker remained lower in French than in British agriculture, it was
consistently higher in French than in British industry. And during
the entire 1815–1915 period, commodity output increased at the rate
of only 1 percent per annum less in France than in Britain. It seems
doubtful that any significant portion of this differential could justifiably be attributed to a contrast in the form of agricultural organization. And to the extent that it could the difference might well be
considered a low price to pay for avoiding British extremes in the
destruction of peasant-provincial life and in the creation of a desperate
urban mass.

By contrast, the nineteenth-century American family farm – located in a land of receding frontiers, less defined social classes, and
more meager communal traditions – had to survive in a less protected

environment. From the 1830s and 1840s on, the farmer needed constant technical innovation and crop specialization to survive in his struggle to pay off the bank creditor and compensate for the unlucky harvest. The counterpart to a more highly mechanized and relatively larger farm was the emerging division between a successful rural petty bourgeoisie and a mass of landless laborers. The former provided a major market; the latter, the initial work force for the manufacturing sector. Only with the price-support and agricultural-extension programs of New Deal and World War II years was this style of family-run agriculture stabilized at a higher level of productivity than its French counterpart.

The French and American cases present contrasting but complementary examples. In the United States, competition leading toward concentration was allowed to go farther than in France. The American government took longer to settle with the small farmer, the whole period between the relatively ineffective Homestead Act and the much more effective technical and price-support systems. The less successful farmers were weeded out. The American and French experiences show that the critics of petty commodity production are right to this extent: given the general character of the polities and markets in which these farms have existed, competition produces concentration and empties out the land. For it is the large producer who can most readily mobilize capital, secure access to distant markets, and outlast a bad harvest. In both France and the United States, special governmental action was essential to preserve the family farm as the dominant form of agricultural production. And in both countries, this action took a form that drastically curtailed the exemplary significance of decentralized production for the economy as a whole while preserving it in its isolated, agricultural sector.

Governments did not reformulate the legal categories of property and contract in ways that might have ruled out absolute and permanent control over large accumulations of capital. Nor did they reorganize their own constitutional arrangements and methods of party-political rivalry in order to facilitate popular-democratic control over the main lines of investment and accumulation. They merely helped a particular form of productive activity survive despite the institutional conditions that, together with the inherent risks of agriculture, constantly threatened to destabilize it. In manufacturing, petty commodity appeared as either the rear guard or the vanguard of an industrial system organized on alternative principles. In agriculture, it emerged as an anomaly justified by its peculiar social charm and undeniable practical efficacy. In both areas, its potential significance remained fragmented and obscured, and its possibilities of development were sacrificed to a hostile institutional system.

Contemporary Debates

No institutional structure of governmental or economic activity emerged in the West that might have turned petty commodity production into a realistic form of social organization capable of carrying economies to ever higher levels of productive output. Nevertheless, the alternative possibilities signaled by the deviations in the history of early modern European manufacturing and agriculture continued to reappear at later moments in the social and economic history of the West. These later experiments with the basic form of work organization fell into two main clusters. The first group consists in the revolutionary attacks of the nineteenth and the early twentieth centuries, typified by the 1848 revolutions and the years immediately after World War I. The second group comprises the recent forms of vanguardist industry. To understand the relationship between the early and the late deviations is also to take a first step toward seeing how closely connected the two latter-day types of deviations really are, despite the absence of an apparent connection.

There is a continuum between the simple despotism of the early factory and the advanced forms of assembly line organization. In this assembly line approach to work, the supervisors continued to exercise a disciplinary power that far outstripped the functions of technical coordination. This system served accelerated growth by its facility for appropriating surplus and for moving men and machines around. But its basic economic disadvantage – and the disadvantage of the institutional arrangements that sustained it – was to subordinate the opportunities of economic experimentation to the interests of economic privilege. A real relation also exists between the artisanal or family-farm team and the flexible, commando-type organization that characterizes the vanguardist sectors of modern industry, administration, and warfare. The essential shared trait is the fluidity of work plans. If the strength of the commando style lies precisely in its practical opportunism, its weakness is its difficulty in adapting to the requirements of scale and complexity.

In each of these parallel lines of economic and organizational development, the most recent phase – the Fordist plant or the vanguardist work group – represents the more rationalized one. It is more rationalized in the sense that the relations it creates among people at work embody more fully a conception of the interplay between abstract productive tasks and concrete operational acts. Each of the two lines of development – I have already shown – gives a different interpretation to this interplay.

But what of the link between the popular insurrectionary challenges to the dominant form of manufacturing and the axis that leads from artisanal shop to commando-style industry? To be sure, many of the revolutionary movements were often fought out in the name of doctrines that derided these deviations as the sentimental or reactionary commitments of the petty bourgeoisie. Yet such slogans are belied both by the nature of the social forces that sustained many of the radical protests and by the actual content of many of the revolutionary experiments.

Contemporary historians have repeatedly emphasized the key role that skilled workers and sentimental petty bourgeois ideologists played in the insurrectionary movements of the nineteenth and early twentieth century. Not only did these groups resist, more fiercely and consistently than any others, the development of the dominant model of industrialism but they often served as the chief organizers of revolutionary alternatives. Indeed, the classic form of these alternatives in the economy and the polity – the cooperative work group and the soviet or council-type of administrative body – can best be understood as idealized versions of the organizational forms that the petty producers and their sympathizers were trying to defend. This origin explains the striking mixture, in these experiments, of archaic and even neofeudal characteristics with visionary commitments. It also sheds light on the continuing failure of these insurrectionaries and ideologists to come up with schemes of economic and administrative organization capable of reconciling their aspirations with the requirements of large-scale production and administration. Thus, the revolutionary experiments repeatedly failed to bequeath the elements of an institutional scheme that might have provided a realistic alternative to the ruling styles and conceptions of industrialism and democracy. And this failure, with its sequel of smug or embittered disenchantment, contributed further to the entrenchment of the dominant approach to work organization.

To interpret the latter-day manifestations of the deviant style from this perspective is, once again, to deny that their extinction or confinement can be explained by the necessity of the institutional arrangements that they were meant to displace. But it is not, in any simple sense, to disprove that the proposed alternative was incompatible with social requirements for the accelerated development of practical capabilities of production (or of administration and warfare). For the alternative mode of economic organization remained incompatible with those requirements so long as its advocates failed to come up with institutions that would have perpetuated economic decentralization without permitting large and permanent accumulations of private capital and that would have established governments capable of supporting and administering these economic arrangements. Just what such alternative institutions might have looked like in the past or should look like in the future is a subject of Chapter 5.

You can now put together the elements of a way of accounting for the relative defeat of the deviant mode of work organization that rejects the mythical history and dispenses with the hypothesis of deep-logic social theory and with the prejudices of unreflective conservatism. Though this revised account is constantly strengthened by new historical findings and new social experiments, it expresses less a revolution in ground-level empirical studies than a reinterpretation of familiar but underplayed or misunderstood events.

Proceeding along this route, you would observe that the revolutionary experiments in work organization were all forcibly suppressed before they had been tried out for any extended period or revised in the course of their application. You would then go on to emphasize that the activists and theorists of these deviant movements were consistently misled by prejudices about possible class alliances and possible institutional alternatives to the existing or emergent forms of market and democratic order. These prejudices prevented them from using their brief moments of experimental opportunity to develop the elements of realistic alternatives. In this way, the would-be architects of a reconstructed society were defeated in part by their inability to free themselves sufficiently from the intellectual authority of the world they had set out to destroy. This inability often encouraged them to seek refuge in an ideological fantasy that merely turned upside down a reality it had failed to understand or to escape.

Turning to the exceptional status of the flexible vanguardist form of industrial organization, you would argue, along lines previously suggested, that the predominance of mass production is not the direct result of superior economic efficiency. Rather, this predominance depends upon the institutionally guaranteed ability to ward off instability in the product, labor, and financial markets as well as upon an international division of labor that prevents either cheap-labor or technologically innovative economies from disrupting stable world markets. If these conditions failed to be satisfied, mass-production industry, with its stark contrast of task-defining and task-executing activities, might not suddenly crumble in all sectors of the economy. But it could be expected to lose its secure hold over many areas of production.

Nevertheless, the resulting extension of the flexible, vanguardist type of industry might simply make way for a competition among new economic enterprises. The more concentrated businesses might once again evolve into new versions of the old mass-production industries and use their influence over markets and governments to protect themselves against economic instability and foreign competition. Indeed, such an outcome might be expected to follow as a matter of course unless the most fundamental economic arrangements of the economy had been revised: the arrangements that establish an equivalence between the means for decentralizing economic decisions and the devices for concentrating capital.

Because such changes in the character of economic institutions might involve the overtly political administration of capital (e.g., a national rotating capital fund), they would in turn require changes in the organization of government and of the conflict for governmental power. An authoritarian, revolutionary state would merely create a class of people obsessed with the exercise of social control and with the interests of their own clients and creatures: bureaucrats, managers, and technical personnel. On the other hand, a demobilized liberal democracy would lack both the governmental structures and the civic militancy required to subject the basic form of economic accumulation to effective partisan rivalry.

This counterfactual fable has a double point. It shows how the problems confronted by the initial forms of petty commodity production – the inability to gain a more than peripheral place within the established institutional framework – might reappear as a dilemma faced by the distant but still recognizable counterparts of those early deviations. This lesson suggests another. The availability and the identity of alternative forms of work organization have depended largely upon the prospects for imagining and establishing alternative ways to organize markets and democracies. How should we understand the genesis of the forms of market and democratic organization that have in fact achieved primacy?

Note that the preceding argument against the mythical history of work organization does not deny force to technological and resource constraints. It does invoke and support the assumptions: (a) that at any given time those constraints significantly underdetermine the style of work organization; (b) that technological constraints are as much the result as the cause of social settlements, codified in institutional arrangements such as forms of work organization; and, more suprisingly than (a) or (b), (c) that we cannot comprehend either in advance or in retrospect the range of feasible organizational responses to technological or resource constraints. We do not need to define the range of possible alternatives in order to understand the history of economic organization. So, too, on a larger historical scale, we do not need to predefine branching points in the history of formative institutional contexts in order to understand how contexts get remade.

THE GENESIS OF THE PRIVATE-RIGHTS COMPLEX

Its Elements Reviewed

The private-rights complex consists in the arrangements that define the institutional character of the market. These arrangements are largely sets of legal rights. One of their more striking features is the ability to structure the basic framework for non-economic dealings (other than those of party politics and public administration) in the very course of defining the market. But why should the legal categories that shape the market provide the model for all entitlements? The answer to this question is far from self-evident; it is one of the facts that an account of the emergence of the private-rights complex must explain.

Remember that the central feature of this complex is a system of property rights that ensures economic decentralization by distributing nearly absolute claims to divisible portions of social capital – absolute in scope of exercise and in continuity of temporal succession. The contractual counterpart to this property system is a structure of contract rights that denies legal force to those relationships of personal interdependence and mutual reliance that cannot be characterized either as the fully deliberate undertaking of an obligation by a rightholder or as the unilateral imposition of an obligation by the state.

The spirit animating this private-rights complex – it will be remembered – is the search for a pure, prepolitical logic of free human interaction. To a surprising extent the system of contract and property is presented – and, even when not so presented, it is implicitly understood – as the legal structure inherent in private ordering. Autonomous self-regulation may not, it is conceded, be good for everything. The main points of the private-rights system can be varied in many ways. And some people may be better placed to exercise their rights than others. But such qualifications do not prevent the identification of these private entitlements with the general project of setting up a system for private coordination. This identification is no mere theoretical afterthought. Nor can it even be adequately understood as simply a requirement of legitimation. It orients the understanding and application of private rights. It prevents people from asking anew, at each crucial turn in ideological or legal controversy, what institutional form the market in particular and private ordering generally can and should have.

There is a mythical history of the private-rights complex that seconds, in style and effect, the traditional way of accounting for the development of the work-organization complex. Few would subscribe to this historical approach in its crudest form. But, like the broader habits of social and historical study that it exemplifies, it continues to inform much of our actual thinking about legal entitlements and the institutional arrangements they define. A testimony to the authority of this conception is its influence upon liberals and Marxists alike. The liberals see the gradual development of a market structure – its gradual emergence from the feudal and neofeudal restrictions that so arbitrarily and expensively restricted the free play of self-interested exchange. As the market order expanded only gradually into wider areas of social life, so too its inherent legal structure was discovered only step by step. This structure was made up in large part by the modern system of contract and property. Thus, liberals and Marxists alike view the private-law arrangements and ideas of early modern Europe as necessary points on the continuum that led to current contract or property law, a law that could in turn be seen as an indispensable prop to the market system. In its conception of the relation between this market order and political freedom, the dominant liberal view has spanned the gamut between the confident conviction that the two cannot be separated (for each is both the condition and the extension of the other) and the more negative and skeptical belief that any attempt to replace this market order entirely will produce arrangements that jeopardize freedom.

Marxists have traditionally dissented less than might have been expected from this additional element in the mythical history. The market economy makes three highly controlled appearances within Marxist-influenced 'eft social theory. First and primarily it is the central institutional device of capitalism – a well-defined stage of world-historical evolution. Second, it supplies the institutional framework for petty commodity production, an unstable social order, destined to pass into capitalism or to perform a subsidiary role within it when it does not disappear altogether. In both these appearances, the basic market structure is assumed to be identical with the familiar contract and property system. Third, the market may reappear under communism, relieved of the burden of oppression and scarcity that has weighed upon it until now. But because communism represents less a well-defined program than the far beckoning culmination of class-ridden history, its institutional arrangements remain in the shadows. Its advocates fail to give practical detail to the idea of an exchange system that presupposes neither the traffic in human work nor a stable social and technical division of labor.

The Marxist ambivalence toward the market carries over into an ambivalence toward private rights, which appear sometimes as an incident in the commodified world of capitalism and, at other times, as a feature of any tolerable social regime. Thus, the Marxists, like the liberals, accept the fundamental tenets of the mythical history of private rights: the certainty that the development of contract and property institutions in modern Europe embodied the emergence of the market order as one of the necessary stages or permanent possibilities of social life. Liberals and Marxists differ only in how they propose to correct the defects of the market system: by combining it with alternative forms of allocation (planned social democracy) or by reducing it to a peripheral role.

The argument of the following pages attacks this mythical history at its root premises, the premises that Marxists and liberals share. It pursues this attack by discussing three seemingly paradoxical features of the private-rights complex and its formation. To set these paradoxes side by side is to underline the specificity of our contract and property system. More particularly, it is to confirm that the dominant system of contract and property rights constantly struggled with alternative principles of social organization and that some of these principles even suggest elements for the successful institutional reshaping of petty commodity production. But the most telling implication of the view able to replace the mythical history is the suggestion that this system of contract and property could inform social life only by combining with arrangements that negated and even reversed the professed aims of the private-law order. Conversely, success in the attempt to bring practical economic life closer to the ideal conception of an exchange of goods and labor among free and deliberate agents would have required a radically different legal basis for economic decentralization.

The Paradox of Origin

The development of private legal entitlements in the specific form in which we have come to know them did not smoothly accompany the gradual formation of a society of free rightholders confronted with a submissive and accountable government. Those entitlements and theories emerged, instead, as part of a particular social settlement that included as one of its incidents or results the formation of an absolutist state. The contract and property rights fashioned and systematized by the jurists of early modern Europe supplied instruments for the familiar process by which the consolidation of absolute rights (especially in land) could advance hand in hand with the strengthening of a unified governmental sovereignty. Tax (as governmental finance) and rent (as the private rightholder's charge for the use of allodial property) became clearly separated. At the same time governments altered what had, up to that point, been their characteristic ways of dealing with gainful economic activity. Sometimes states had treated manufacturers and merchants (especially in long-distance commerce) as pliant victims to be milked for all they were worth. In more settled and ambitious empires, this predatory attitude gave way to the more aggressive tutelage of economic production and exchange with a view to maintaining the conditions of social harmony. This attitude characteristically prevailed in agrarian policy even when not applied to commerce and industry. In early modern Europe the most successful governments pioneered a new approach to economic activity: they deliberately manipulated governmental authority and military force, domestically and internationally, in order to promote economic growth. Thus, the same pattern of retrenchment and partnership that characterized the relationship between government and allodial property in land carried over to public policy toward trade and industry. Ways were thereby found to protect wealth-making activities without stifling or starving them through the very devices of protection.

These institutional innovations were both the products and the instruments of a particular social compromise. In countless variations, a redefined elite of enterprising nobles and successful commoners gained a more unchecked control over land, labor, and movable capital while governments won greater administrative cohesiveness, broadened their area of maneuver, and deliberately subordinated the maintenance of harmony to the acquisition of wealth. Much in this outcome can be understood as the expression of a straightforward deal: the state would grant the elites a more untrammeled control over land, labor, and commercial wealth while the elites would in turn allow the managers of the new state – at once weaker and stronger than many of its counterparts in non-European civilizations – to dispose more freely of taxes and troops, to develop an aggressive administrative apparatus, and even to experiment with different approaches to the relation between the creation and the protection of wealth. The contract and property system represented merely the first half of the exchange, the half that permitted the consolidation of private control at the ground level. To recognize this deal is not to suppose that central governments were staffed by other than members of the elites or were devoted to nonelite objectives. You need only assume that, against the double background of a relative fragmentation of the elites and an irreversible commercialization of the economy, the masters and agents of the new-model state won the power to pursue their narrower aims more freely. They owed part of this freedom to having never had pervasive responsibilities or powers in the management of the national economy.

The uniqueness of this institutional solution can be inferred from a comparison with the experience of the agrarian–bureaucratic empires of antiquity. In those societies, the assumption by elites of a more unchecked control over land, labor, and commercial wealth typically signaled the decommercialization of the economy and the ultimate fragmentation of governmental authority. Thus, a superficially similar tendency possessed in context an entirely different meaning. For in the early modern West, this proprietary victory of the elites took place in a society that had already been transformed by the irreversible commercialization of the economy and the thoroughgoing diversification of the elites, phenomena that in turn reflected the relative success of Western European peasants and artisans in resisting complete subjection to great landholders and local potentates. Although this resistance was less successful in some places than in others (compare again England to France or Catalonia to the rest of France), it was almost uniformly more successful in Europe west of the Elbe than in the great agrarian-bureaucratic empires of premodern and non-European history.

The argument about the paradox of origin permits a tentative conclusion. The contract and property system represented an important element in the emergence of a social order and a social vision radically at odds with the ideas we now attribute to this system. Of course, it might have outgrown these marks of origin. But this preliminary insight already suggests that contract and property rights are not what they seem. The remainder of the discussion shows that they could never close this gap between appearance and reality: the idealized market vision could be more fully realized only by legal arrangements that departed drastically from those that have come to define market regimes in modern Western history.

The Paradox of Specification

A second paradoxical feature of the private-rights complex generalizes and deepens the lesson taught by the first paradox. If we are tempted to dismiss the first paradox as having shown merely that the legal structure of the market has an incongruous origin, we now discover that this legal structure was constantly and mysteriously bound up with alternative principles of social order that altered, and even inverted, its apparent significance. This inversion reflects less an ideologically motivated dissimulation than the inability of the contract and property system to govern crucial features of the practical dealings among people without the help of arrangements antagonistic to the manifest spirit of that system.

The traditional Western form of contract and property has proven unable fully to penetrate at least two aspects of social life – one central and the other tangential to practical economic life. The central aspect is the actual organization of production, in particular the effort to coordinate labor in the pursuit of practical objectives. A practical organization cannot operate effectively if the relations among its members are predetermined by a regime of rigidly defined entitlements and obligations demarcating zones of unchecked discretion. The rationalization of collective labor means precisely that the work team can become a visible embodiment of practical reason, with its relentlessly opportunistic calculation of means to ends and its accelerated interplay between task definitions and operational acts. The strength of the flexible variant of rationalized collective labor is to carry to the extreme this opportunism and this freedom from the constraints imposed by any preexisting plan of social division and hierarchy. Conversely, to bind every practical decision about the organization of production to the absolutes of right and obligation is to ensure practical failure. As soon as you concede the need for discretionary maneuverability, you face the problem of deciding who exercises the discretion and under which restraints. The pure system of contract and property provides no answer to this question because, though it may legitimate certain exercises of power, it remains in its form merely a legal structure of coordinate relationships.

The other aspect of social life that the modern regime of contract and regime cannot fully penetrate may be peripheral to much of productive activity in its most characteristically modern variants. But it has always been vital to our practical experience of society, and it has always persisted as an undercurrent theme in our workaday lives. This is the domain of communal relations where mutual ties are valued as ends in themselves, the effects of action upon one's fellows really matter, and an acceptance of heightened mutual vulnerability overtakes the punctilious reckoning of tit for tat.

Both practical and communal life resist the procrustean limitations of the classical rights-regime. The private-rights complex simply cannot go far enough in specifying these practical or communal arrangements without appealing for help to other methods of social organization. This demand for further specification creates the possibility of something we in fact observe: the private-rights order takes on an entirely different social significance once it operates alongside the ideas and arrangements that provide it with its necessary complement of specification.

Two main sets of complementary principles of social organization have, in succession, given private rights their indispensable wedge into practical social life. The first such body of principles simply generalized and restated the particular social settlement in which the modern system of contract and property originally figured. This was the corporate-estatist society (*Ständestaat*) of early modern Europe. This approach to social organization saw society divided into well-established divisions and hierarchies. A particular group or institution was visibly defined by the place it occupied in this social map, visibly because the communal–hierarchical unit often possessed an explicit corporate identity. The most notorious examples were the Church and the standing army – organizations that, together with many others, were considered to perform natural functions in society and to cement the social order. People had prerogatives – or duties – just by virtue of belonging to one of these corporate entities in their societies.

The mythical history of the private-rights complex would have led you to expect early modern legal doctrine to be overwhelmingly preoccupied with the single-minded defense of the canonical contract and property system. And indeed you may find such a defense in the writings of later publicists like Bentham, Beccaria, von Humboldt, or Stuart Mill. But when you turn instead to the most influential jurists, such as Blackstone or Christian Wolff, concerned to systematize and justify the details of the institutional order, a different and more interesting picture emerges. Their major intellectual ambition was to synthesize or, when synthesis failed, merely to juxtapose the legal arrangements of the *Ständestaat* with those of the liberal contract and property system. Quite correctly, they viewed this reconciliation as a crucial element in the legal description of a defensible social order rather than as a tactical and temporary compromise between the archaic and the modern. The *Standestaat* was no mere hangover of feudalism; it arose simultaneously with the rudiments of the private-rights complex. Thus, the favored classifications of rights in general and property in particular typically included both the rank-specific prerogatives of an estatist legal order and the formally universalistic rules of contract and property. Jurists repeatedly failed to develop a general conception of right capacious enough to include these two species of entitlement yet sufficiently narrow to exclude all others.

The second set of specifying principles of social order to have complemented the contract system consists in the extralegal techniques of order and control that characterize large-scale organizations in the societies where the private-rights complex continues in force. To a large extent these are the techniques intrinsic to the work-organization complex and supported by the distinctive links between state and society that the governmental-organization helps explain. Take the basic employment relation in the sectors of the economy marked by large-scale organizations. Even in those legal systems that continued to define employment contractually, individual contract was only the beginning in the regulation of labor. The individual agreement was first set in the framework of a system of collective bargaining meant to reestablish the reality of contract on a terrain otherwise marked by a contract-subverting degree of group inequality and personal dependence. The agreements that issued from this special contractual process could set only the most general terms for the exercise of supervisory authority. Even if submission to this authority could be treated as a manifestation of choice (what choice in a worker's world of few and similar jobs?), the actual process of supervising work could not, for the reasons earlier described, be fully turned into material for rigidly defined obligations and entitlements. It therefore became necessary to invoke, explicitly or implicitly, the technical necessity, the practical inevitability, of these work arrangements. And because everything, from the design of machines to the idea of rationality, had been influenced by this approach to the organization of labor, the claim acquired a semblance of plausibility. The mistake was only to credit the claim with an ultimate truth, a truth that transcended the actual sequence of conflicts and truces that had produced these results. The less well founded the appeal to technical necessity and the more the underlying social reality involved outright subjugation, the starker the contrast established between the picture of social life conveyed by the contract and property system and the daily reality of work.

A straightforward example of the conceptual and political embarrassments engendered by this contrast can be found in the legal issue known in American labor law as the problem of retained rights and familiar, under different names, in all modern Western legal systems. To what extent are the matters not covered by prior collective agreements a proper subject for collective bargaining and to what extent, on the contrary, are they properly reserved to managerial discretion (reserved rights of management)? To narrow the scope of retained rights is to enhance the applicability of the revised contract scheme (i.e., the framework of collective bargaining) at the cost of jeopardizing both the necessary practice of managerial discretion and the particular set of institutional arrangements (i.e., the work-organization complex) through which this discretion is currently exercised. Thus, the attack on these arrangements can be parried by the justified but only partly pertinent observation that a margin for discretion must be preserved in the interests of practicality. What routine legal and political thought cannot recognize is the distinction between the undoubted practical imperative and the contingent institutional means for satisfying it.

A great deal of legal-doctrinal argument in the advanced Western countries – perhaps most such argument in the area loosely known as private law – devotes itself to problems of the same order as the question of retained rights. By this I mean problems that arise from the attempt to reconcile the contract and property system with the actual institutional practices of exchange and production, practices perpetuated against the backdrop of highly developed links between social privilege and governmental power. This is Blackstone's and Wolff's task all over again; though the identity of the specifying complement has changed, its subversive force upon the private-rights order it completes remains the same.

The alternative to the mythical history gives rise to a readily testable hypothesis about the history of modern Western law and legal thought. The dominant legal controversies have been about what I have described as the danger of inversion through specification. The primary task the jurists set themselves was to reconcile the content and vision of the legally defined market order with alternative principles of social organization. These alternative principles were needed for the private-rights complex to penetrate production and community and to accommodate the real institutional framework of society. Yet, in each of the major instances, the complement threatened to compromise and even reverse the original liberal message supposedly expressed by the private-rights complex. To manage this irreconcilability became the continuing preoccupation of legal doctrine. If this hypothesis is true we should expect to find the familiar, liberal version of private rights – the one that the mythical history sees as "rising" and "falling" throughout these events – most prominently displayed in the relatively brief interlude when estatist principles were on the wane and contemporary styles of work organization had not yet crystallized. Even then we should expect the liberal ideas and arrangements to be stated more aggressively by propagandists and philosophers than by lawyers who had to make sense of the detailed structure of institutions.

The criticism of the mythical history gives rise to the suspicion that *no* complement of the private-rights system could do other than reverse its supposed significance. This suspicion would turn into a persuasive argument if it could be shown that an alternative legal definition of the market suffers from no such instability, precisely because it departs in certain specified ways from the received institutional definition of a market. To show that some elements of this alternative were prefigured in deviant aspects of past experience and that they escaped the instability is a step toward the explanatory goal and a concern of this institutional genealogy.

The Paradox of Superfluity

There is one final paradox to consider in the history of the private-rights complex: the classical theory of contract and property continues to be upheld although it accounts for increasingly less law. Consider the general theory of contract, the very model of analytic purity in modern Western law, the supreme technical achievement of the nineteenth-century jurists, and the part of legal thought that most perfectly expresses the assumptions of liberal political philosophy. What did classical contract theory still govern by the end of the twentieth century? Some of the limitations upon the applicability of core contract theory had been there from the start.

First, there were the exceptions to the dominant principles. Freedom to choose the contract partners and the contract terms had always been restricted by counterprinciples. The freedom to choose the partners would not always be allowed to operate in ways that undermined the communal aspects of social life. Thus, for example, reliance or enrichment in fact might generate legal obligations that had not been voluntarily assumed and the manipulation of the rules and presumptions governing intent to be legally bound kept intra-familial relations from subjection to the logic of contract theory. The freedom to choose the contract terms hit against the limits imposed by the counterprinciple that unfair bargains would not always be enforced. The unfairness might consist either in a gross disparity of real values (including a disparity that arose from unexpected changes in market conditions) or in a measure of inequality and dependence that effaced the difference between a contract regime and a power order. No higher set of principles governed the relation between principles and counterprinciples. When principles and counterprinciples lost distinct institutional agents, such as courts of law and courts of equity, there ceased to be any simple way to draw the boundaries between the dominant principles and the exceptional counterprinciples; no one could or can say for sure just how far the exceptions reach.

The reach of the ruling contract theory had always been qualified by repressions as well as by exceptions. The categories of this theory were far better suited to one-shot, arm's-length transactions than to continuing business relationships that occupied a position midway between deals among strangers and the internal arrangements of an organization. Despite the importance of these continuing relationships to the real workings of the economies that contract law governed, they were left without adequate legal regulation. Part of the difficulty lay in the assumptions and implications of a contract law centrally addressed to extended and close business dealings. Such a law would have to deny the stark contrasts between contract and organization and between contract and community and to recognize partly articulate relations of interdependence as sources of obligations. This recognition would in turn imply a view of law and obligations dangerous to the idea that absolute property provides the very model of legal right, and incompatible with the view of law and obligations embodied by the private-rights complex.

Over time, the constant repressions and exceptions of classical contract theory were aggravated by outright exclusions. At the zenith of its influence, contract theory had appeared capable of absorbing the better part of the law. But one by one whole bodies of rule and doctrine were removed from its purview and subject to special rules and categories, incompatible with the general theory. These rejects included commercial law, labor law, antitrust, family law, and even international law.

Adding up the exceptions, the repressions, and the exclusions, classical contract theory seemed to have become, more than ever, an irrelevancy. There simply was very little of the law that it still actively informed. Such was in fact the trivializing conclusion drawn by the exponents of the mythical history: freedom of contract had risen and then fallen, a victim to the twofold assault of legal skepticism and social democracy.

But this conventional explanation fails to account for two striking features of modern law and legal history: one explicit, the other subjacent. The subjacent trait supplies the key to an understanding of the former. The explicit feature is the persistent obsession with classical contract law: the excluded bodies of law continue to be worked out by opposition to the supposedly defunct model, without, however, generating any alternative general theory of the sources of obligation and the nature of rights. The subjacent feature is the negative significance of the classical contract theory: any alternative, systematic approach to private rights and obligations, even by judicial extension from the principles implicit in the specialized bodies of law that had been excluded from contract, would have threatened the established form of market organization. Thus, for example, to apply throughout the private-rights system even the limited revisionist methods of labor law would be to ask at every turn just when a given situation resembled a power order more than it did a contract regime. To revise contract bargains too often or too drastically, in response to an inequality of bargaining power, would be to replace contract by a noncontractual method of allocation. But not to revise them frequently or radically enough would be to court the danger that a vast range of contractual transactions represented merely a cover for allocation by command. Nothing guarantees that in any particular institutionalized version of the market the minimum of correction needed to secure the reality of a contract regime falls below the maximum of correction compatible with the decentralized decision making such a regime requires. It might well happen that, over a vast range of economic life, you could never correct enough by one criterion without correcting too little by the other. Even if the solution of labor law – the special framework for collective bargaining – were adequate on its own ground, it could not be generalized to the entire economy without drastically changing the institutional form of the market.

The point of the seemingly irrelevant contract theory was simply to occupy the space that might have been occupied by an alternative scheme of contract and property rights and therefore by an alternative institutional version of the market. In this ghostly and prophylactic role, contract theory did not merely fade away or merge comfortably with more progressive ideas, as the mythical history suggests. It stood there, and would continue to stand there, until a different market order had been developed. The shared assumption of its defenders and critics was that if it failed, nothing that rivaled it in generality could succeed.

Yet here lay one of the unrecognized dilemmas in the history of modern law. The core of contract theory remained defensible only if many areas of law and social practice were excluded from its scope of application, while legal principles that opposed classical theory survived within the central body of contract as exceptional or repressed elements. But each of the exclusions, exceptions, and repressions showed in its own way that exchange and production might be set within a different institutional framework and conducted under different rules. Some of these deviant possibilities, once generalized, recombined, and reformulated in the course of the revision, might significantly diminish the degree of revisionary intervention needed to preserve the distinction between contract regimes and power orders. Contract law included deviant elements that pointed toward a private-rights order that gave legal force to relations of reciprocal dependence and confined both the fully articulated act of will and the unilateral imposition of a duty by the state to anomalous roles as sources of obligations. Other deviant tendencies changed the institutional identity of the bargaining partners or revised actual markets by reference to the operations of a preferred, imaginary market. But a real turning point would come if these particular deviations could be overtaken by a restructuring of the basic legal form and setting of decentralized economic decisions: a restructuring that could replace the absolute control of divisible portions of social capital with a mechanism of rotating, divided, or otherwise conditional access to capital. Without such a redirection the fundamental relation between the need to correct transactions and the need not to correct them could not be changed. Nor could there be hope of building an institutional framework that would interpret and develop the major alternative to the dominant form of work organization. Such an alternative would create the practical means with which to distinguish more effectively the conditions for scale and continuity in production from the circumstances that starkly contrast task executors and task definers, mass-production and vanguardist industry, the prerogatives of concentrated, self-reproducing capital and the claims of innovation and experiment.

THE GENESIS OF THE GOVERNMENTAL-ORGANIZATION COMPLEX

Its Elements Reviewed

Arrangements for the organization of government and for the conflict over governmental power make up a third part of the formative institutional context.

The chief feature of the constitutional structure of the state in this institutional order is its combination of popular sovereignty, through representative democracy and universal suffrage, with devices that disperse power among different agencies of the state and different arenas of constitutional conflict. These devices limit governmental power and render it accountable only by subjecting it to constant deadlock. The opportunity for deadlock increases, under this constitutional regime, in direct proportion to the disturbances in the settled pattern of institutional arrangements and group deals that a proposed use of state power threatens to effect.

The central trait of this style of conflict over governmental organization is the method of competition among political parties or among factions of a dominant party. These partisan conflicts sometimes map and at other times disregard the major communal and hierarchical divisions of the society. From this ambivalent relation of partisan strife to social order – the mark of a society whose categories of division and hierarchy have been weakened, fragmented, and yet preserved – all other leading characteristics of modern party politics follow. The conflicts of party politics remain only tenuously related to the quarrels dividing people in everyday life. The issues on which these partisan conflicts get fought out are characteristically a hodgepodge of vague ideological commitments and cynical, mercenary promises to organized interests. Because these two components are only rarely connected by coherent and developed programs, it is often hard to tell to what extent a party platform requires or even intends a change in the formative institutional context. In the ensuing confusion the individual elector or politician may find it hard to know when his ideological slogans are serving to mask cruder and more immediate interests and when, on the contrary, these interests have been irretrievably confused by an ideological haze.

The confusion is no mere fault of insight or skill; it is rather the sign of a society whose experience of governmental politics is at odds with important features of its social order. Politics, in the narrow and traditional sense, have become largely a matter of shifting alliances among vaguely defined groups with crisscrossing memberships. But social life continues to be marked by a relatively stable and historically unique division of labor that resists disturbance and helps reproduce a scheme of social division and hierarchy.

These styles of constitutional organization and partisan rivalry produce a regime whose commitment to the free combination of free wills, though supposedly limited only in the interests of its own continuing freedom, is in fact powerfully restricted. Major areas of social practice and organizational life – including the basic form of the division of labor – remain secluded against the disturbances of party politics and reformist ambition. Meanwhile, a civically inactive populace, divided into stabilized classes and communities, expects from governmental politics little but occasional threats or sops to its habitual standard of living or its received moral ideas. The skeptic will say that this circumstance is the best that can reasonably be hoped for and that it is far better than the most probable alternatives. Though historical understanding cannot refute him it may help shake some of the assumptions that make his view plausible.

Two Chronologies

The governmental-organization complex is the element of the formative context of contemporary North Atlantic societies with the longest unbroken history. The style of constitutional organization just recalled, if not the method of partisan rivalry with which it was eventually combined, had been developing continuously since the late Middle Ages. The formation of central chancelleries, the emerging contrast between territorial and administrative specialization, the relation of central governments to a fundamental law they could adjust but not radically disturb or disrespect, and even the distinctive characterization of the administrative, judicial, and legislative bodies – all this formed part of an institutional tradition that new doctrines of popular sovereignty took as an unavoidable starting point.

In another sense, however, the governmental-organization complex has the shortest history of any component of the formative context. It developed in brief and distinct spurts from the late eighteenth century to the late nineteenth century. The first spurt was the development of liberal constitutionalism in the late eighteenth and early nineteenth centuries. These constitutional schemes sought to grant rule to a cadre of politically educated and financially secure notables, free from both clientalistic dependence and untrammeled factionalism and fully able to safeguard the polities they governed against mob rule and seduction by demagogues. Thus, this early liberal constitutionalism added to its techniques for the dispersal of power and the fragmentation of conflict, methods for filtering out unwanted or excessive popular or demagogic influences. These methods, often justified by the desire to keep civil life in the hands of independent people, included restrictive suffrage, a prodigal use of intermediate levels of representation, and a variety of precautions and prejudices directed against the emergence of popular factions capable of disrupting local notable leadership.

The second major spurt of institutional inventions occurred in the second and third quarters of the nineteenth century in leading Western countries – notably Britain, France, and the United States. Its distinctive feature was the replacement of the filtering-out techniques by universal suffrage and by a new practice of mass-based political parties. These parties rarely approached the condition of mass movements. But neither were they merely electoral syndicates, enlisting popular support opportunistically the better to succeed in a fight for access to privilege-sustaining governmental power. They were simultaneously fragile alliances of office seekers and spokesmen for the recognized interests and ideals of particular classes and communities, simultaneously such spokesmen and advocates of causes that joined people across class or communal lines. No institutional artifact expresses as perfectly as the modern political party the paradoxes of a partial freeing of social life from rigid division and hierarchy.

Among the decisive events in this second spurt were the realignment of voting rules and party organization in the period of the two English reform bills, the development by Martin van Buren and his contemporaries of a doctrine and practice of party politics, and the change in the character of national and local contests for governmental power brought about by such associates of Napoleon III as Persigny, Ollivier, and Morny. The special interest of the late nineteenth century German experience is to show how extensively the new party-political practice could be realized even though the first moment of liberal constitutionalism had remained drastically truncated.

Why did this remarkable shift take place? Credit must be given to the continual demoralization of overt hierarchical exclusions in societies that had already tasted a relative disengagement of governmental power from a hierarchy of social ranks and that had experimented, in all the ways described by other parts of this institutional genealogy, with the partial emancipation of society from false necessity. Against this background the normal temptation of an elite faction to promise more power to the people in exchange for greater popular support became harder to resist. An additional cause of the shift toward a new style of party politics was the pressure to secure mass loyalty and to transcend regional rivalries in a period of national conflict, a pressure that increased dramatically when the system of limited wars began to break down. But it is hard to think these causes could have produced such rapid and decisive effects if the ruling and possessing classes had not discovered that the filtering-out techniques and the prerogatives of notables could be abolished without giving way to all-out social agitation and to the radical redistribution of wealth and power. This discovery was surprising, in fact the single biggest surprise in nineteenth-century political history. What we still mean by representative democracy is the outcome of this unforeseen merger of an earlier constitutional scheme with a set of mid-nineteenth century innovations. Like all the other achievements with which this institutional history deals, this merger may seem the uncontroversial outcome of an irresistible progression. Yet it was a cut-and-paste job if there ever was one.

The products of these two quickly paced moments of institutional invention, and the dogmas that made them intelligible and authoritative, eventually spread throughout the rich Western world. The consolidation of these institutional arrangements and imaginative preconceptions greatly altered the terms of conflict over the other aspects of the emerging formative context. Before this change, the work-organization and the private-rights complexes had been far more effectively up for grabs than they became after it. The new way of arranging governmental power and partisan conflict effectively channeled institutionalized disputes away from more radical threats to the institutional framework and to the plan of social division and hierarchy that this framework helped reproduce. It lent a semblance of authority to the most influential half-truth of modern politics: the need to choose between reformist tinkering and all-out revolution. A successful attack against other parts of the formative institutional context now came to require a prior reckoning with the governmental-organization complex: if not its all-out replacement at least its partial displacement by unorthodox styles of collective organization and collective conflict. It is on this shorter and more dramatic, rather than on the longer and more subtle, chronology of the government-organization complex that the following sections concentrate.

The Mythical History of Democracy

A mythical history of modern representative democracy goes side by side with the mythical histories of industrial organization and private rights. Once again, liberals and Marxists share its key elements though giving them very different senses. The view of the outcome colors the understanding of the process. The exponents of the mythical history combine curious anecdotes and allegedly unavoidable developments to tell how the masses were gradually incorporated into polities and how freedom-guaranteeing constraints came to be imposed upon governmental power. The actual forms of constitutional organization and party conflict that made this result possible had a tangled and often surprising history. But, according to this mythical history, the trials and errors of modern political experience, and the undoubted failure of many proposed alternatives, have confirmed that the emergent institutional solutions were much more than flukes. They represented the strongly determined and perhaps even necessary compromise among the main constraints of size, complexity, administrative efficacy, legal restraint, and popular accountability that a contemporary democracy must satisfy. For all practical purposes, they *are* the real meaning of democracy.

The ideal outcome of this democratization is the circumstance in which all major social arrangements fall under the control of simple or qualified majorities acting through elected representatives and competitive political parties. Though some minorities may be effectively excluded from the political nation, their apprenticeship in familiar methods of group organization and group pressure may suffice to draw them in. At a minimum, in this view, the contest among elites and parties for control of the state must be crucially influenced by the relative success with which each group elicits mass support. Of course, if the majorities use their power to undermine the system for combining free and equal wills – by destroying, for example, the method of rotation in office – democracy ceases to exist; the democratic republic is a definite structure, not just the popular verdict.

Why, if social life under democracy tends toward such an outcome, do we so often find stability and even stagnation in democratic politics? Why does governmental policy characteristically revolve in such a narrow circle through all the reversals of electoral politics? Why, in particular, do relatively deprived majorities not use the suffrage to award themselves the wealth and the power that remain so unequally divided in their societies? To these questions, the mythical history and the view of democracy it supports give one of two answers. The first answer claims that the live options of current policy represent, in fact, the solutions with the best chance of commanding majority preference, albeit a preference formed reluctantly, in the light of disappointment with many unrealistic and dangerous alternatives. The second available answer is that, though these active options would not head any particular faction's list of preferred policies, they describe the resultants of many vectors of deliberate group or individual choice, the unintended, movable compromise among many group interests coexisting in tension with one another.

A view of the relation between democracies and markets completes the mythical history. This view recognizes that market economies and the richly defined systems of private right that accompany them can develop outside a democratic framework. They have often been reconciled with limited authoritarian regimes that respect the contract and property rights of the citizenry. But the mythical history tells us that the reverse does not hold. Democracies have never survived and cannot persist without markets. For the allocation of goods and services by central authorities or princely overlords would undermine the independence indispensable to the authentic exercise of democratic citizenship. Nothing in the standard versions of this thesis is necessarily incompatible with a recognition that markets and the entitlement systems that define them might assume forms entirely different from the forms that have in fact come to prevail. But the practical force of the argument depends on the assumption that the market system that democracy requires is the same market system that has in fact prevailed in the course of modern Western history. The thesis that democracy depends upon markets, like so much else in the mythical history and in the broader social ideas this history exemplifies, turns out to be true only in senses very different from those in which it is usually intended. The emergent style of democratic politics did and does depend upon the existence of some kinds of market organization just as it was and is incompatible with other market systems. A more radical democracy – one that carries to a further extreme the authority of combinations of will over social arrangements – would also have to give a large role to decentralized economic decision. But it would do so under different institutional auspices.

One approach to the criticism of the mythical history is to attack the mythical characterization of the outcome: the idea that current forms of democracy approximate the ideal of government by free combinations of free wills, or, at least, that they offer no insuperable obstacle to an approach toward that ideal. The discussion of the reform cycles that set the stage for the present analysis has already explored this task. Another approach is to dispute the actual picture of the genesis of democracy that the mythical history paints. This is what I now do by examining two aspects of the developments of modern representative democracies that the traditional historical account cannot adequately explain.

Objections to the Mythical History:
The Surprise of Universal Suffrage

The mythical history fails to accommodate the surprising effect of universal suffrage. The central assumptions underlying the mythical history might lead you to sympathize with the view, common to most nineteenth-century conservatives and radicals, that universal suffrage would revolutionize society. The vote, it was feared or hoped, would give the mob and its leaders the means with which to wreak havoc with the established structure of authority and advantage in social life. Both the moderates (classical liberals, modernized conservatives, and outright cynics) and the radicals came up with explanations for why this expected result did not in fact occur. These explanations made only minimal dents on the mythical history, and they revealed just how many assumptions the radicals share with the moderates. But the explanations do not work. Their failure indicts the ideas they were meant to save.

Thus, the moderates emphasized that, with the economic success of the advanced countries, increasingly large sectors of the population had won a stake in the preservation of the established order. The moderates underlined the fragmentation of estates and classes into countless factions composed of overlapping and incompatible memberships. They reasserted the nonexistence of realistic alternatives to existing institutional arrangements. The primary test of realism here became simply the interaction between constant human desires and the inherent organizational requirements for satisfying and reconciling these desires at given levels of scientific knowledge and technical capability.

Before examining the merits of these attempts to deal with the consequences of electoral democracy, remember that the early radicals and conservatives were not entirely wrong about the vote. They were at least more right than our anachronistic sense of the inevitability of present forms of democracy can readily acknowledge. In many of the advanced countries, the incorporation of the masses did turn out to be full of danger: it often seemed that deprived or resentful electorates, entranced by right-wing or left-wing demagogues, would use the party pluralism of liberal democracy to advance partisan causes and popular leaders subversive of the liberal-democratic system. The ultimate defeat of these threats was due less to the foreordained triumph of democracy than to the forcible defeat of these rightist and leftist alternatives, a defeat imposed in the course of the civil wars and the world wars of the nineteenth and twentieth centuries.

But, though the remembrance of these events serves as an important corrective to a contrived sense of natural progression, it is neither here nor there on the basic theoretical issues at stake in the present controversy. The moderates will still want to claim that once these perils are met, democratic republics have an inherent institutional structure, although one that only collective trial and error can reveal. And they will still insist on explaining the relative tranquillity of these democratic republics in ways compatible with the basic conception that such an inherent structure exists and that it ensures to the extent possible (even if it is a modest extent) the government of society by free combinations of free wills.

The traditional explanations for the surprise about universal suffrage run up against two objections – one, crude and seemingly straightforward; the other, more subtle and controversial. The force of the former, however, depends on the truth of the latter. The crude objection begins by conceding that the lower orders may be satisfied by the gradual rise of their material standard of living and that each individual hopes to escape, through himself or his children, from his place in the social hierarchy. But the objection states that even these admissions fail to explain why electoral majorities continue to tolerate the extremes of inequality in wealth, income, and power that have persisted through the age of mass politics. This passive majoritarian response would begin to appear reasonable or natural only when the hope for material advancement is combined with the disillusionment with the practicability and the benefits of alternative forms of social organization.

The more subtle and controversial objection to the traditional attempts to reconcile the surprises of the suffrage with the mythical history of democracy addresses precisely this experience of disillusionment. It is one thing to accept a series of options as the only ones readily available in a historical situation. It is another, entirely different matter to attribute to these options a deep practical necessity and to treat them as the sole possibilities that economic, organizational, or psychological imperatives make practicable. On the first of these two interpretations the task becomes to explain how these limiting options acquired and maintained their force, an inquiry that proceeds from assumptions already antagonistic to those of the mythical history. But the second interpretation, with its invocation of unyielding practical necessities, implies a thesis that much of this interpreted narrative and indeed much of this book has been meant to criticize.

Marxist and non-Marxist radicals alike have often shared much more than might be expected of this mythical-historical gloss on the tamed suffrage. They have often attributed the stability of partisan conflict to "false consciousness." In this view, people live under the spell of ideas that make the established institutional order intelligible and authoritative; they mistake the regularities of a pacified social order for the eternal laws of society and human nature. But perception and sensibility are never as completely at the mercy of established preconception and power as they would have to be for the false consciousness argument to explain the taming of universal suffrage.

Once open conflict over any element of a formative context has been contained or interrupted the pacified order begins to win a second-order necessity; the routines that it shapes influence people's assumptions about the possible and the real. To this extent the false consciousness thesis is correct. But the proponents of the thesis go wrong whenever they forget that this influence over people's assumptions is never stronger than the framework of institutions, practices, and preconceptions on whose continued stability it depends. The order, I have argued, is subject to an endless stream of petty disruptions that can escalate at any moment into more subversive conflicts. Indeed, as soon as this escalation begins, people may abandon with surprising alacrity the pieties that until then had seemed to bewitch them. This observation applies with redoubled force to the disturbed and only half-trusted formative contexts that can subsist in the age of mass politics, world politics, and enlarged economic rationality. We therefore need to explain why the sense of possibility in modern democracies continues to be so narrowly constrained and why the context-preserving quarrels so rarely grow into context-disturbing struggles. If the general argument of this essay is correct, a satisfactory account must not rely on the notion that the context resists transformation because it embodies built-in necessities of social organization or historical evolution.

The more extreme the false consciousness thesis, the harder it becomes to distinguish it from the liberal approach to the surprises of universal suffrage. These extreme views still see the live options that dominate political experience as direct expressions of individual or group preferences rather than as the unintended consequence of the reciprocal interferences among organized group interests. Only the choices are now thought to be made under the influence of compulsions the agents themselves barely grasp. These compulsions supposedly establish a sharp contrast between the illusions of the participants in historical struggles and the insight of theoretical observers.

The radical steeped in Marxism, in the tradition of deep-structure social analysis, and in the habitual practice of the European left will characteristically assert that only a very different institutional system could truly embody the free combination of free wills. But the idea that social systems are inseparable wholes, the belief that each of these wholes represents a moment in a foreordained sequence, and the polemical opposition of true and false consciousness – the paralyzing legacies of deep-logic social theory – collaborate to deny constructive programmatic thought the resources it needs. On these inherited radical assumptions, the inauguration of an authentic democracy appears to require an all-or-nothing, cataclysmic regeneration of society, perhaps even of all societies throughout the world. The actual institutional proposals, though laying claim to "scientific" foundations, often turn out to be little more than an imaginative reversal of existing institutional arrangements. This reversal puts direct democracy in the place of parliamentary representation, and a strenuous all-encompassing political life in the place of the reluctant and episodic activity of the modern citizen. Its characteristic product is the soviet or conciliar style of organization that has been constantly re-created, and just as constantly abandoned, in the course of modern insurrections. This attempt to construct through mere inversion is less an exercise of programmatic thought than a manifestation of despair at the ability to think programmatically. It remains overawed by the very social reality that it pretends to escape. Its implicit intellectual conservatism is the reverse side of a disengagement from a social reality whose transformative opportunities are mixed together with resistances to transformation.

Objections to the Mythical History:
Parties and the Conditions of Stability

Another embarrassment to the mythical history refers to the relation among the assumptions that normative democratic theory makes about the conditions of governmental stability. This argument against the mythical history connects with the earlier argument focusing on the failure to explain the domestication of the vote. For both objections develop the implications of the divergence between actual social life and the promised subjection of social arrangements to the will. Moreover, a crucial part of this second line of criticism builds upon the conclusions of the earlier line.

Throughout the early modern period, as indeed in much of earlier Western political history, the organizations and movements most closely resembling modern political parties remained objects of intense suspicion. This suspicion went beyond the residual but vague belief that partial interests were inherently dangerous and illicit. It expressed the belief that all such factions would be nefarious in one of two ways. On the one hand, these factions might be no more than predatory syndicates of office holders, of seekers after office, and of hangers-on, organized to pillage the state or to prostitute its authority to the syndicate's private interests. On the other hand, the faction might participate in an all-out struggle between large social classes or confessional groups. Such a struggle would inevitably prove incompatible with the minimal conditions for stability in society as well as in government. Though Machiavelli had seen the running quarrel between patricians and plebeians as a source of strength in the Roman Republic, his view remained more persuasive as a criticism of the simpleminded equation of communal cohesion and social strength than as an analysis of the relation between partisan conflict and institutional continuity.

In the liberal democracies of the modern West both popular sovereignty and the restraints upon it worked through the rotation of political parties. A major task of the fabulous history of democracy therefore became the attempt to show how political parties had ceased to be mere predatory syndicates without becoming the instruments of ferocious social or religious warfare. It was also important to show that this result had come about in a manner compatible with the government of society by the free combination of free wills – or at least that it had come as close to this ideal goal as could reasonably be hoped for.

To these ends, three conditions had to be satisfied. First, the parties had to adopt programs for the exercise of governmental power. These programs had to be animated by ideal conceptions of public policy, social welfare, or the content of rights as well as by promises to accommodate the narrowly selfish interests of particular groups. The programmatic element distinguishes the modern party from a gang of pillagers. The second condition to be satisfied was the privatization of religion. Religious differences had to become matters for the intimate forum. Confined there, they had to lose some of their intense and immediate relevance to secular conflicts over the structure of society. The third condition was the creation of a more fluid and fragmented society, made up of groups who select their membership on criteria that overlap at some times and are incompatible at others. Each group – a segment of the work force, ethnic or national collectivities, regional cultures – influences only a limited part of the lives of its members. And the total array of groups fails to generate any cohesive system of social divisions and hierarchies.

The third condition, operating in conjunction with the first, does for class differences what the second condition is meant to do for confessional antagonisms. Religious antagonisms cannot be murderous because they have been privatized. Secular ideological contests cannot be destructive because the stark class oppositions that might make them dangerous have been defused by a far-reaching change in the character of society.

But suppose that the account of this change – that is, of the events alleged to satisfy the third condition – is so exaggerated as to be largely false. Suppose, more specifically, that this account confuses the quality of party politics in modern democracies with the characteristics of actual social life. A truth that radical social theorists influenced by the idea of the epiphenomenal character of "politics," have always had trouble acknowledging, but that ordinary experience and empirical study have regularly confirmed, is that electoral behavior, party affiliation, and professional-political divisions very often defy any obvious logic of social order. To study an election in, say, the America of Jackson or the America of the late twentieth century is to discover the severe limits of the attempt to understand partisan differences as the predictable results of particular social stations. Even when you move beyond class analysis to include considerations of ethnic origin, religious persuasion, and regional milieu, the explanations characteristically suffer from a retrospective, makeshift quality; the next coalition at the next election discredits it. And this shifting and unreliable quality of divisions in the electorate is usually accentuated in the realignments of the parties or party factions and of the professional politicians who lead them. Only the idea of politics as epiphenomenal could explain the facility with which these familiar characteristics of party-political rivalry are attributed to society itself.

But the actual divisions and hierarchies of contemporary Western societies are hardly the mirror of liberal party-politics. Class positions, ethnic identities, and segmentations of the work force are often a great deal more stable than the electoral antagonisms and alliances of liberal-democratic politics. To take seriously the idea that liberal society is like liberal politics we would have to see existing social life as marked by an easy freedom of movement among social stations that were themselves subject to constant revision. But though such a view may occasionally be implied by the self-congratulatory rhetoric of conservative politicians, it accords neither with ordinary experience nor with the common assumptions and conclusions of empirical social study.

The argument of this book suggests an explanation of the disparity between the quality of politics and the character of social life. The practices of party politics in the advanced Western democracies belong to a distinctive style of governmental organization and partisan rivalry. Rather than embodying, together with the market, a pure method for the free combination of free wills, this style helps reproduce a distinctive organization of society, rich in particular divisions and hierarchies and committed to a particular scheme of possible and desirable association. Parts of the explanatory argument in *False Necessity* are designed to show this constraining influence at work, while other parts emphasize the relatively accidental character of the underlying institutional settlements. The programmatic arguments complete the attack by presenting an alternative better suited than existing liberal institutions to traditional liberal ideals. Thus, liberal society differs from liberal politics (in the narrow and traditional sense of the term politics) precisely because liberal politics are what they are. To recast society in the image of liberal politics, we would have to change political life; liberal-democratic society can become what it is supposed to be only if liberal-democratic politics become different from what they currently are.

This argument requires no radical revision in our ordinary observation of social life. Apart from its closeness to a social theory free from the assumptions of deep-structure theory and positivist or social science, its strength is simply to account for a disparity between the acknowledged qualities of partisan conflict and social life. The major available liberal and Marxist approaches to politics deny this disparity by reducing one of its terms to the other.

In the light of these considerations the reconciliation of partisan conflict with indispensable stability becomes an embarrassment to the mythical history of democracy and to liberal-democratic theory. The contest among parties of opinion that share an ambivalent relation to the system of social divisions and hierarchies works both to open society up to democratic politics and to put society beyond the reach of democratic politics. Many of the fundamentals of the social order remain relatively immune to the types of conflict and controversy that this established regime permits.

The skeptical, minimalist liberal may acknowledge these points while trying to avoid their force. He may claim that the partial deflection of conflict from basic arrangements and preconceptions, even from those generating social divisions and hierarchies, is necessary to secure the degree of individual freedom and economic efficiency that is realistically possible. A satisfactory response of this defense ultimately requires a discussion of the possible alternative forms of economic and governmental organization. The institutional program presented in Chapter 5 promises to secure individual liberties and civic peace through a style of governmental organization and party strife that helps weaken both the hold of rigid hierarchies or roles and the contrast between context-respecting routine and context-transforming conflict.

But there is one aspect of this debate with the skeptical democrat that can be separated out for early, tentative treatment. This aspect is the problem presented by the idea of stability, which from the outset has been the guiding theme in the debates about party politics. One of the assumptions of the original hostility to parties was that fundamental disagreements about society destroy the indispensable minimum of civic peace because such disagreements cannot be compromised. The latter-day defenses of party politics have drawn novel conclusions from this premise only because they have seen practical possibilities for the reorganization of state and society that had previously gone unrecognized. Thus, the optimists who view society in the mirror of liberal politics claim that with the privatization of religion and the supersession of entrenched hierarchies and divisions fundamental disagreements have been made superfluous. The skeptics are content to observe that to design politics for more fundamental disagreements would be to court an intolerable level of strife.

But the underlying equation of the nonnegotiable with the fundamental (which we can now interpret as all those matters that have to do with the formative institutional or imaginative context of social life) gains its plausibility from a further, untenable assumption. This assumption is the idea, characteristic of deep-structure social theory, that social systems (restrictively interpreted, once again, as formative contexts) represent indissoluble wholes. They stand or fall as a piece. Moreover, the identification of the fundamental with the nonnegotiable conflicts with an ordinary political experience. Comprehensive approaches to social reconstruction are a great deal harder to combine or compromise when stated as abstract doctrines than when translated into concrete strategies of transition or detailed social practices. The very same institutional devices that might make the dispute over fundamentals more readily available in the course of ordinary life might also root that dispute more firmly in the immediate concerns of ordinary life. Such devices might therefore weaken the conditions that leave fundamentals resistant to compromise and recombination. The programmatic argument of the next chapter follows up on these suggestions. The final vindication of a different view of stability and conflict would be actually to relate stability and conflict in ways that current democratic theory and practice rule out.

THEMES OF THE INSTITUTIONAL GENEALOGY

Provisional Conclusions

This section gives a provisional summary of the argument about the genesis of the formative and institutional context of the rich North Atlantic democracies. The view of context making worked out in the second half of this chapter makes the sense of the account more general and precise.

The basic, minimal theme has been negative and cautionary: the claim that the dominant forms of industrial society to have emerged in the course of Western history cannot be correctly understood as required by the inherent constraints of practical organization or economic necessity. At successive points in the history of these institutional arrangements, solutions containing the elements of alternative institutional schemes were proposed or tried out. The deviations emerged repeatedly; each step toward the consolidation of a dominant style of economic or governmental organization created new opportunities to break away from it. There is no end in sight to the rearrangements nor – if the general view of society developed in this study is correct – can there be. One of the most important reasons for this continuous recurrence of alternatives is that no set of institutional practices or conceptions of social life ever wins a complete victory. More often than not, the deviations persist. They reach an accommodation with the victorious organizational arrangements, which they both complement and jeopardize, and assume a subsidiary or anomalous role within an order constituted on other principles. At any moment these anomalies of organization or belief may be treated as points of departure for fundamental reconstruction. Thus, the imagination may find in current reality the materials it needs for even its most subversive efforts.

What I have described as the vanguardist sector of industrial organization presents an instructive example. Vanguardist industry has traditionally operated outside the areas of the economy in which the institutionally guaranteed stability of product, labor, and financial markets, on a domestic and a world scale, makes mass production profitable. Nevertheless, both the early and the late forms of this rearguard and vanguard sector suggest an alternative way of organizing the entire economy and of relating the economy to government.

This minimalist, negative theme of the narrative may seem too modest and commonsensical to deserve objection or approval. It merely insists upon the relative contingency of the particular forms of industrial society that happen to have carried the day up to now. The student of society may be content to hold on to the remnants of a theory of necessary historical sequence or possible social worlds while diluting it until it ceases to appear controversial. Attractive as this solution may appear it would remain vacuous if it did not derive partial meaning from the intellectual-historical setting in which it is proposed. Contingency and necessity are conceptions that lack a self-evident content; they merely summarize the picture of reality and the strategy of explanation presented in a body of thought. An emphasis on the contingency of the prevailing forms of industrialism indicates a willingness to depart from inherited, deep-structure versions of social theory. This willingness does not in itself produce an alternative basis for theoretical understanding. Yet my polemical narrative contains, more or less implicitly, the rudiments of just such a basis.

To anticipate the main lines of this theoretical conception, consider a second, more specific and controversial theme of the narrative. This theme is the thesis that the dominant mode of industrialism, which resulted in the formative contexts discussed in Chapter 2, had a major rival. This rival was the style of economic organization I have described at various points as the revised version of petty commodity production or the system of decentralized and flexible production and dissociated property. At the outset this alternative pathway would have represented little more than an exaggeration of the forms of petty commodity production that reappeared, with varying prominence, through modern Western agrarian and industrial history. To survive, however, such a system would early have had to undergo a major institutional redefinition. The necessary changes would have required, among other things, an extension into the mainstream of industry of the forms of industrial organization that characterize the vanguard of industry, an alternative style of market order (i.e., dissociated property and its contractual counterparts), and a version of representative democracy that would have allowed central governments to be intimately involved in the management of the economy without crushing the new market forms under new orders of privilege. Though such an industrial society has nowhere emerged as a cohesive system, fragmentary elements toward its construction have regularly reappeared in modern history.

In assessing the practicability of this rival style of industrialism, two different objections must be distinguished. In one view, the alternative could never have arisen in the first place; the real conditions of European society supposedly ruled it out. In another view, such an alternative could not have remained stable once it had been introduced; it would have undergone a process of self-destruction. But many of the aspirations that inspired it could have been fulfilled in an alternative style of governmental and economic organization. Though the two objections overlap, they have different implications. It matters whether the alternative lost out because it collided with deeply rooted constraints of social organization and material progress or whether its exclusion was due to particular triumphs and defeats reflecting no such deeper determination. If, as the narrative has already suggested, the truth comes closer to the latter proposition than to the former, the institutional frameworks of contemporary industrial economies lack any higher authority.

Truth and Error in the Polemic Against Petty Commodity Production

The main target of the argument that alternatives to the dominant form of economic organization were bound to fail has been petty commodity production – the economic and social order of small-scale, independent producers and traders, the eternal dream of petty bourgeois utopias, of the well-meaning but woolly-headed votaries of social solidarity, and of the righteous but small-minded apostles of a society of independent yeomen. This traditional proposal should be sympathetically interpreted to include a provision for cooperative organization by the petty producers. A minimum of institutional innovation would allow for at least some of the advantages of scale without subverting the distinctive character of the petty bourgeois economy. Certain arguments reappear in the polemic against this program for social reconstruction; all try to demonstrate its impracticality.

The first element in the polemic emphasizes the inability of such an economic order to sustain continued growth and innovation. Even if the formidable obstacles to taking advantage of economies of scale could be overcome, the petty producers would be perpetually tempted to superconsumption. Nothing could counterbalance the pleasures of immediate consumption except hope for the large accumulations of private wealth that such an economic order cannot permit. Moreover, this alternative economy would suffer from the absence or the weakness of a class of people capable of exercising managerial responsibilities at levels intermediate between central governments, on one side, and the household, shop, or cooperative, on the other. Above all, petty commodity production would fail to secure the economies of scale indispensable to cost cutting and accelerated technological innovation.

A second strand in the criticism of the petty bourgeois economy singles out the self-destabilizing character of this alternative. Under a regime of petty commodity production, market competition would soon result in economic concentration: some independent producers would prosper while others would go under. This social polarization could be avoided only by a relentless governmental supervision that would undermine both the independence and the efficiency of economic agents. Thus, the argument goes, petty commodity production would fall victim to either competition or intervention.

Yet a third argument identifies an instability in the governmental framework of petty commodity production. It claims that such an economic order would be incompatible with the existence of a state capable of defending it against internal crisis or foreign threat. The state would always be either too weak or too strong to preserve the economy. On one hand, faced with a population of jealously independent and self-absorbed petty producers, the central government might find itself unable to extract the economic and manpower resources needed for long-term infrastructural investment or effective protection against the predatory designs of rival states. On the other hand, if the government managed to overcome these obstacles to its effectiveness it would tower over a society of powerless producers. These producers would be unable to resist the encroachments of public officials or to prevent them from turning access to governmental power into a new basis for economic privilege.

These arguments do indeed tell against the traditional program of petty commodity production and against all the radical utopias formulated in the image of that program. For all the reasons its critics emphasize, such a system would be self-destructive as well as incapable of guaranteeing accelerated material progress. But the radical and conservative critics of the petty bourgeois alternative share a key assumption with its defenders. This assumption is the thesis, evoked and attacked so often in this book, that there exists a narrow set of types of social organization, each with its built-in legal–institutional structure. Thus, the defenders of petty commodity production resemble its adversaries in accepting the idea that the market and the democracy have a self-evident form. Though the scale of economic organization they have in mind may be different and though this difference is sure to have far-reaching distributive consequences, they propose no radical change in the legal organization of a market economy and the constitutional structure of a democratic government. This same premise unites Marxists and conservatives when they imagine that we must either accept the market economy and representative democracy in the peculiar forms that have become dominant in the course of modern Western history or else embrace the institutional order inaugurated by the Russian revolution.

The critics of petty commodity production fail to consider that the archaic or deviant economic form they criticize can undergo a cumulative change in its institutional foundations. Such a change would drastically alter the detailed institutional content of this alternative while preserving the social sense of its deviation from the arrangements that triumphed in the course of modern Western history. Conversely, the traditional advocates of decentralized and flexible production fail to recognize that their proposal is impractical for just the reasons the critics have pointed out.

Which institutional changes might have given and may yet give a revised version of petty commodity production a chance to succeed? To answer this question is to establish an initial, tenuous link between the view in this chapter of how formative contexts developed and the program for context change presented in Chapter 5.

The organization of the economy would have had to have reconciled seemingly incompatible objectives: the advantages of scale and concentration, the opportunity for entrepreneurial initiative, and the constant redistribution of property needed to make capital available to emerging teams of workers and entrepreneurs and to break the stranglehold of concentrated capital holdings over the forms of exchange and production. Unless this third objective could be achieved, the social sense of the deviation of petty commodity production from the prevailing style of market organization would have been lost. But the third objective seems to conflict with the first, the ability to exploit advantages of scale.

That the conflict may not be as intractable as it appears is suggested by the second objective, which seems to presuppose both the first and the third goals without being unrealistic or incoherent as a result. The emancipation of entrepreneurial initiative requires the ability to launch undertakings with the complexity that large-scale concentrations of capital and labor make possible. But the need for entrepreneurial flexibility also argues for arrangements that avoid the effective monopolization of such capital concentrations by privileged groups. How well a particular market system avoids these twin dangers becomes an empirical question once you accept that markets can assume different institutional forms, each with its own unique consequences for the distribution of wealth, power, and technical expertise.

The key to a solution would be a mechanism capable of guaranteeing rotation in the access to capital. Teams of workers, technicians, and entrepreneurs would be allowed access to portions of social capital under fixed terms and at a stipulated rate of interest, to be charged by the public capital fund. There would be limits on the extent to which these teams could use the capital at their disposal to enrich themselves or to gain control over other economic activities. Political decisions would settle the basic terms of access to the rotating capital fund. These decisions might include a commitment to seclude from close supervision entrepreneurial discretion in broad sectors of the economy. But the extent and form of entrepreneurial autonomy would emerge from conscious collective debate and choice rather than from the supposedly automatic operations of a prepolitical market. The fundamental principles of property law and the corresponding categories of contract would have to be reconstructed. The different faculties that now compose the property right would be dissociated and assigned to different entities: the central democratic institutions responsible for ultimate decisions about the social form of economic accumulation, competing investment funds that these institutions might establish, and the teams of workers and entrepreneurs who would be the ultimate capital takers.

Such an economic regime undermines the props to the dominance of the rigid variant of rationalized collective labor in the mainstream of industry. For it destroys and even reverses the many institutional devices that enable inflexible, mass-production industries to defend themselves against market instabilities. As a result, the flexible style of industrial organization, with its more intimate contact between task-executing and task-defining activities, escapes its confinement to the experimental vanguard of industrial organization and invades a portion of the mainstream of industry.

The implications of such an economic reordering for social hierarchy are even more dramatic than its consequences for industrial organization. Though stable social hierarchies would not necessarily disappear, they would be weakened and transformed. For one thing, the inheritance of major capital assets, the basis for the continuity of prosperous families, would disappear once the property right had been broken up into component rights granted to different kinds of rightholders. For another thing, the extension of the flexible variant of rationalized collective labor into the mainstream of industry would subvert one of the most important incentives to the perennial renascence of social hierarchy: the ability to set terms to other people's activities by means that remain sheltered from the risks of a broadly based accountability.

Such an economic regime and the social order it would help sustain would be quickly perverted if it were unaccompanied by a suitable way of organizing government and the conflict over governmental power. Government must be able to serve as a locus for effective controversy over the entire range of economic activities. Yet, for this very reason, it must be all the more open to participation and control and all the more subject to restraint against despotic ambition and resurgent privilege. The constitutional techniques for limiting governmental power must not be restricted to the armory of eighteenth-century institutional devices that control government only by disabling it from ambitious reform. Moreover, the partisan conflict over the mastery and uses of the state must be arranged so as to incorporate more easily the concerns and controversies of everyday life.

These remarks merely suggest the general direction the alternative form of market order might take and the general way in which the impetus of petty commodity production can survive in a radically altered institutional environment. To explore the problems of such an alternative regime and to justify this regime on grounds of practicality and desirability are concerns of the programmatic discussion undertaken in Chapter 5. Enough has been said, however, to suggest that such an alternative is at least conceivable, that it suffers from no obvious incoherence, or instability, and that it can best be understood as the extension and transformation of a series of related institutional deviations that have in fact recurred at many moments of modern Western history.

We can then imagine an alternative organizational setting for a democratic and relatively decentralized industrial society. This alternative is not self-destructive on its face. The prospects for a feasible alternative weaken the case for attributing the marginalization of this recurrent petty bourgeois challenge to its inherent impracticability, or to its incompatibility with either an objective logic of economic constraints or an implacable stage sequence of social evolution. An independent, less controversial reason to disbelieve in the thesis of the practical necessity of the dominant form of industrialism and democracy is the evidence of all those occasions when central governments and privileged groups intervened to crush or restrict the deviant forms of economic organization before these forms had a chance to operate and to compete with rival institutional solutions. The preceding narrative accounts for the defeat of the petty bourgeois alternative without appealing to deep-structure explanations of why petty commodity production was doomed to failure from the start. We simply do not need the standard necessitarian explanations.

Certain social hierarchies were already in place as the struggle over these institutional arrangements developed. The emergent style of market organization challenged the interests and ideas of these favored groups far less than either the archaic or the reconstructed versions of the petty bourgeois alternative. From this perspective what became the dominant institutional forms of polities and economies can best be understood as the outcomes of an accommodation between the interests and identities of preexisting elites, on one side, and the practical advantages or spiritual attractions of more revisable and hierarchy-subverting institutions. For the reconstructed alternative would have represented a higher degree of experimental freedom and allowed for a still more relentless development of productive powers, a greater disengagement of the forms of exchange and community from the vitiating constraints of dependence and dominion, and a more complete emancipation of insight into society and personality from the constraints of false necessity.

It often happens in biological evolution that an adaptation succeeds by responding to an environmental threat while minimizing the genetic and mechanical break with existing biological forms. Yet the price of this minimalist adaptation is a rigidity that makes the species all the more vulnerable to its next environmental challenge. Something similar holds for the success of the formative institutional context whose genesis the preceding pages have discussed.

The Minimalist and the Maximalist Interpretations of the Institutional Genealogy

Thus, two salient theses emerge from this schematic genealogy of contemporary formative contexts. One, a negative and minimalist thesis, emphasizes the multiplicity of institutional forms that industrial society might have assumed. The other, more focused and controversial claim affirms that the fragmentary elements of petty commodity production and the cooperative efforts of small-scale manufacturers, artisans, and farmers might have served as a point of departure for an alternative style of economic and governmental organization.

Taken in concert these two theses lend themselves to a systematic misinterpretation. The criticism of this misunderstanding further fixes the sense of the preceding narrative and prefigures themes in the theory of transformation advanced later in this chapter. It is tempting to see the two theses as merely a diluted version of the deep-logic idea of a compulsive sequence of stages of social organization that exhibit a coherent program for the development of practical capabilities or moral aspirations. History, on this view, consists in a series of branching points; at many junctures, developments can proceed in two or more directions. The complete science of history describes the sequence of branching points. The system and sequence of these branches reveals both the driving forces of history and the range of possible forms of social life. Subsidiary, relatively more contingent and particularistic factors explain why at each juncture one alternative prevails over another. On this theoretical interpretation of the polemical narrative, the formative institutional context of power and production in early modern European societies could have developed in either of the directions I have labeled dominant and deviant. This picture, however, is misleading in two crucial respects.

First, it suggests that as our understanding of society improves we can pass more and more smoothly from the statement of general facts about society to the analysis of the sequence of branching points and even to the explanation of why, at a certain time, one alternative triumphs over another. In fact, however, we cannot complete this passage, not just because we always need to collect more facts but because the very character of historical experience eludes this explanatory style. The more entrenched a formative context, which is to say the more immunized from the disturbances of routine practical or imaginative conflict, the greater the influence it exercises upon its sequels. The entrenchment of an institutional system can be measured by the extent to which it makes some transformations of itself harder to achieve than others as well as by its imperviousness to disruption by routinized group conflicts that it helps shape. The particular content of any such institutional context, the influence it suffers from the institutions that preceded it and the influence it exercises upon the arrangements that succeed it, all have an irreducible particularity. They resist deduction from general facts about society or general tendencies of historical change.

Every institutional system becomes entrenched, however, at the cost of a restraint upon the many practical powers, moral aspirations, and theoretical insights that depend upon the freeing of human connections from the constraints imposed by a particular plan of social division and hierarchy. The development of these powers, aspirations, and insights requires the repeated effacement of the institutional and imaginative barriers that distinguish conflict within an established order from conflict over the remaking of an order. Success or failure in seizing opportunities to reach a higher level of experimental freedom has consequences. These consequences have effects of their own. The preexisting character of European society may have made the now dominant institutional arrangements of North Atlantic societies easier to establish than the alternative of revised petty commodity production. Yet these victorious arrangements may also have been less promising than their principal rival as a basis for achieving what I shall describe as negative capability: the sum of advantages made available by institutional arrangements with the double characteristic of weakening the hold of rigid roles and hierarchies and effacing the contrast between reform and revolution. This point has more than antiquarian interest. Here, as always, the discarded alternatives may be resurrected in new forms once the special conditions that protect the dominant solutions have been eroded.

The picture of social history as a series of branching points is also misleading in another, related respect. It suggests that we do or might possess a master vision of the multiple trajectories that are possible in history. By gaining such a vision the theorist hopes for an understanding that the historical agent never achieves. For the agent, critical and generalizing insight consists largely in the effort to imagine what existing or remembered anomalies would be like if they turned into organizing principles. The losers and the lost causes of the past and the outlawed or restrained elements in the present arm the subversive imagination with its weapons. The social theorist cannot replace this style of thought with a radically different understanding. He can at best compensate for his removal from immediate action by longer memory and broader observation. His picture of multiple pathways and branching points simplifies and makes transparent the record of our attempts to empower ourselves both by establishing orders of social life and by refusing to take those orders as final definitions of our collective possibilities. His favored materials are all the deviant organizational and imaginative schemes to have arisen in history, including the deviations that have temporarily achieved dominance. He offers not a master blueprint of all possible developments but an interminable reweighting of the elements that make a trumped-up history.

THE GENESIS OF ANOTHER FORMATIVE CONTEXT: THE COMMUNIST ALTERNATIVE

Applying the Spirit of the Institutional Genealogy to the Non-Western World: Two Examples

The institutional genealogy shows that what at first seem to be governmental, economic, and legal arrangements strongly determined by a combination of inexorable technical requirements and irresistible social influences turn out, on closer inspection, to have been a series of complicated and precarious settlements, the outcomes of many loosely connected lines of invention and habit, compromise and coercion, insight and illusion. As soon as we shake loose the dogmas of liberals, Marxists, and modernization theorists, we begin to recognize the astonishing variety of forgotten, suppressed, or subordinated institutional notes silenced under the din of the triumphal march toward the contemporary mixed economy and parliamentary democracy. The din, like the triumph, was always greater in the books than in real life. One cluster of institutional alternatives – labeled here petty bourgeois – reappeared insistently in a wide variety of forms and settings. In a radically revised institutional translation, it holds special promise today.

The historical polemic of this chapter closes with a discussion of two episodes in the making of, and in the failure to remake, the Soviet-style institutions described in Chapter 2: the decisive events of the late 1920s and the early 1930s in the Soviet Union and the Chinese Cultural Revolution of the late 1960s. This close to my admonitory narrative serves both a general and a particular purpose. The general aim is to show how the same haphazard and hodgepodge processes that provided Western industrial democracies with their distinctive institutions also worked elsewhere in the world to produce radically different institutional systems. An antinecessitarian approach does not apply merely to the details of an institutional tradition; it also illuminates the fashioning of new traditions.

The special purpose of this final twist on the institutional genealogy is to suggest the significance of a revised version of petty commodity production for conflicts and controversies far removed from the North Atlantic world. No party ever actually proposed such an alternative in Russia. Yet the alternative could have done – and can yet do – justice to much in the defeated Bukharinist and Trotskyist causes, revealing their hidden common ground and the changes they would have needed to undergo to ensure rapid economic growth and strengthen mass participation in government.

No faction of Chinese cultural revolutionaries ever advocated such proposals. Indeed, the failure of the cultural revolutionaries, from above or below, to come up with any detailed program of institutional reform helped abandon that mass conflict to violent and sterile frustration. Yet if the militants had freed themselves from their initial sponsors and translated their antibureaucratic intentions into plans with a wider appeal, they might well have moved in the direction of something like the institutional program insinuated earlier and discussed more fully in Chapter 5.

There may at first seem to be inconsistency in a way of thinking that emphasizes how much institutions are mired in unique histories of conflict and compromise, ungoverned by any master plan, and yet sees similar institutional arrangements as relevant to the problems of widely different societies. Why are the solutions not as particularistic as the histories, each unique and uniquely suited to a particular situation? The answer, in a nutshell, has two parts: our concerns are not as unique as our situations, and our situations, in an age of partial emancipation from false necessity, enable us to treat anything proposed or tried out in one place as potentially applicable, with adjustments, everywhere else.

Institutional histories are accidental and idiosyncratic in the sense that they obey no ready-made or universal script. Each such history is a record of missed opportunities, including opportunities to realize the radical ideas, now circulating all over the world, that invite societies both to seek wealth and might and to empower the individual by smashing the roles and ranks that belittle and enslave him. The more we manage to weaken the influence formative institutions and beliefs exercise over their own remaking, the freer we become to take our cues from wherever we like and to respond in similar ways to similar ambitions and anxieties.

Understanding the Soviet Alternative
Without the Help of Deep-Structure Social Theory

Chapter 2 described a formative institutional context of late twentieth-century communist countries that both differs from the basic institutional order of contemporary Western industrial democracies and resembles it. The Soviet institutional system appeared when its Western counterpart had not yet assumed its contemporary form: each suffered, if only by reaction, the influence of the other. The immediate ideological origins of the Soviet alternative lay, after all, in two reactions to an earlier version of the same Western institutional system whose consolidation my schematic narrative has tried to analyze. One reaction was proudly professed: the commitment to overthrow the economic and political subordination of the working classes. A Western-style institutional system seemed capable of being realized in the conditions of economically and culturally more backward countries only in a form that would perpetuate indefinitely the oppression of the masses. The other reaction remained largely unacknowledged though it was no less powerful: the attempt to achieve Western levels of national prosperity and power in countries traditionally burdened by the intimate partnership between a repressive bureaucracy and a predatory oligarchy.

It was crucial that both these objectives were in the end carried out by a centralized state whose power found no counterbalance in an alternative system of economic decentralization or popular sovereignty. The soviet or conciliar style of organization was the only alternative of which the Soviet revolutionaries and their followers in other countries were aware. And it represented less a serious attempt to establish government and the economy on a new basis than a utopian inversion of established institutions and an escape from the task of dealing with the problems of the large scale. The repeated failure of this stubborn revolutionary dream left in place only the cold reality of a central government concerned to survive domestically and internationally, at any cost. Access to this new source of power came to mean everything. The contrast between task definers and task executors had never been starker, though the former lorded it over the latter in the name of governmental authority rather than the property norm. And the familiar system of Western property and contract was maintained for small-scale property, especially in the agrarian sector, while the centralized and unaccountable government exercised undivided economic sovereignty over the major forms of productive and financial capital. The communist reform cycle assumed its characteristic structure: its recurrent moments of decentralization came to mean merely increased opportunities of initiative on the part of lower-level bureaucrats and managers. So long as this reform cycle kept its distinctive shape, decentralization never produced a genuinely new way of allocating access to capital. Nor did it undermine the contrast between task-defining and task-executing activities or threaten the oligarchic control of governmental power.

How did this institutional system emerge? The methods and ideas that inspire the mythical history of the Western institutional order have a comforting answer: it says that the Soviet model represents, in broad outline, the only possible alternative to the triumphant Western solution open to industrialized or industrializing societies in the circumstances of modern life. If the analyst is out to be sympathetic, or to express a pessimistic and worldly realism, he may go on to observe that only some combination of bureaucratic and entrepreneurial dictatorship – the forcible exaction and reinvestment of a surplus – can lift today's poor countries out of their poverty. This interpretation of the Soviet model draws an additional halo of justification around Western institutional arrangements. For who could want the alternative unless driven to it by desperate circumstances?

The polemic against the mythical history should therefore include a reinterpretation of the genesis of the Soviet model. This restatement makes two central claims. Its first thesis is that we can account for the emergence, diffusion, and tenacity of the Soviet-style formative context in ways that dispense with the appeal to deep-logic constraints of organizational, psychological, or economic necessity. We do not have to suppose that the Soviet system is one of the few options among which humanity must choose at its present level of wealth and knowledge. In fact, a convincing analysis of the origins of the Soviet model must emphasize factors that cannot be connected with the types of causes dear to deep-logic social theory, not at least without postulating a long and fabulous series of intermediate links between these causes and the actual events.

A second thesis of this reinterpretation is that we can identify at least one major realistic alternative to the institutional system that triumphed in the modern West. This alternative represents a counterpart to the institutionally revised system of petty commodity production discussed in earlier sections of this chapter, a counterpart specifically suited to the circumstances of a backward country. Such a solution would have required yet more audacious institutional inventions than its successful rival. But it would also have had many practical advantages further down the line: all the benefits that can result from institutions carrying forward the task of emancipation from false necessity.

The argument develops in two phases. The first discusses the most important turning point in the development of the Soviet-style system. The second phase analyzes the failure to break out of the Soviet model during the Chinese Cultural Revolution, an episode in which the communist reform cycle got out of hand.

The Origins of the Soviet Model

The war between the Soviet state and the Russian peasantry that began in the winter of 1930–31 exercised a decisive influence on the making of the Soviet model. This war, with its immediate antecedents and sequels, was the occasion for the final defeat of both the Bukharinist "right" and the Trotskyist "left" within the party. It gave determinate form to a relationship between state and society that had been left open by the November revolution. It settled for a long time to come what large numbers of people could expect in their material lives and what government could demand from them. The terms of accumulation and collaboration that grew out of this series of encounters were changed only slowly and marginally in later periods of Soviet history. They became the practical groundwork for a communist regime that would be reproduced elsewhere and that elsewhere, as in the Soviet Union itself, would scarcely change for several generations.

In the late 1920s the Soviet government faced an unmistakably difficult situation. To stay in power and accomplish its minimal programmatic objectives, it had to achieve rapid economic growth. It could not rely on foreign capital: met by the hostility of the Western industrial powers, it could not avoid a high degree of economic autarky even if it had wanted to. Nor could it readily obtain capital by a sharp and lasting depression of industrial wages. Such a policy would have alienated a social group whose active support or grudging acceptance was crucial to the leadership for reasons that were as much doctrinaire as practical. These considerations accentuated what would in any event have been true for any economy with the relative backwardness and dimensions of the Soviet economy in the 1930s: a major part of the capital for stepped-up accumulation would have to come from the transfer of agricultural surplus in the form of cheap food goods for urban populations and industrial workers, and of agrarian exports that could be used as payment for needed machine tools and industrial inputs.

The severity of the situation was masked during the early years of the New Economic Policy by the existence of a large margin of underutilized capacity in the Soviet economy's productive stock and especially in its industrial plant. As long as this margin continued to exist, the pressure on the agrarian sector remained relatively moderate: manipulation of the terms of trade between agrarian and industrial goods might be enough to effect a transfer of value from agriculture to industry without disrupting the agrarian economy or provoking violent resistance by the peasantry. Such manipulation had proved able to overcome the "scissors crisis" of 1923–24. The result of this temporary success was to lend a semblance of plausibility to the Bukharinist slogans of the NEP period: the ideas that the terms of commodity circulation were enough to determine value and value transfers and that economic growth could be spontaneously assured by the reciprocally reinforcing influence of agrarian and industrial accumulation within a structure of limited market freedom.

But the policies that worked when there was underemployed capacity could not and did not work as the capacity barrier was approached and broken. The squeeze on the agrarian economy became stronger. Other devices had to be found to supplement pricing policy. In this sense, NEP policy resembled Keynesianism, and it shared some of Keynesianism's limitations. A doctrine relevant to particular conditions of underemployed capacity broke down when carried over to the task of achieving repeated breakthroughs in productive capacity.

To be sure, confused, widely fluctuating price policy helped disorganize the agrarian economy. But a system of stable, intelligible administered prices would almost certainly not have been enough to avoid the problems that had surfaced by the time of the procurements crisis of 1927–28. If the state wanted to avoid dependence on the kulaks (the larger farmers) and to expand agricultural production rapidly, it needed to pursue an alternative agrarian policy.

One such alternative would have required the Soviet government to gain a foothold in cooperative farming by millions of smallholders. It would have had to create marketing and procurement structures that would make these farming cooperatives dependent upon the state while giving them priority in technical and financial assistance. Such a program, however, could not be easily carried out by a rigid, authoritarian government. It called for a government that would be willing and able to promote grassroots collective organization on the part of a large segment of its citizenry and that would open itself to the deals, pressures, and risks such organization would inevitably spawn. Such an alternative would have represented something like the reconstructed version of petty commodity production outlined earlier.

The policy of coerced collectivization and violent dekulakization that was in fact pursued involved the Soviet state in an unprecedented revolutionary campaign against a peasant society of twenty-five million households. This campaign, for all its fits and starts, did in fact achieve an increased and prolonged transfer from the agrarian to the industrial sector, and generated rapid though discontinuous growth. But it did so at many costs. Soviet agriculture was left scarred for an indefinite time to come: the autonomy that peasants and agricultural laborers had failed to achieve in the form of significant collective organization reappeared in the multiple stratagems of a rearguard struggle against coerced collectivization and the forced appropriation of the agricultural surplus.

Besides, the decision to disrupt millions of households called for a state and a leadership that would stop at nothing in the techniques of revolutionary despotism. The alternative conceptions of communist democracy represented, halfheartedly, by the right and left factions in the party were among the victims of the struggle. Thus, there was a tight connection between the way the problem of economic growth was solved and the development of the state. The whole period from the November revolution to the war against the peasantry could be seen as a time when both the mechanism of accumulation and the organization of government had been left undefined. The counterpart to the economic reprieve of underemployed capacity was the political limbo of unresolved factional rivalry.

Both the Bukharinist right and the Trotskyist left had failed to understand what was happening and what was needed. The Bukharinists did not understand the extent of the accumulation problem until the procurements crisis of the late 1920s was already in full swing. The Preobrazhensky leftists allowed themselves to be pushed into a mock Faustian language of heroic industrialization without specifying the concrete institutional forms for enlisting the collaboration of the working masses with the economic plans. Both sides raised the issue of democracy within the party and the state only when driven from power, and therefore they did so alone and at different times rather than in concert. Neither faction had grasped the extent to which the forms of accumulation and of government were bound up with each other. Each faction consistently mistook the other for its most dangerous adversary when in fact they had many aims and ideas in common. Among these shared concerns was the central issue of how to structure collaborative economic arrangements in such a way that a market mechanism (in the sense of some system of economic decentralization) could be combined with central political control over the direction and rate of accumulation. An emerging alliance of agrarian or industrial entrepreneurs and party bureaucrats had to be dismantled without precipitating the state into a revolutionary war against society. In the event, the Bukharinists joined with Stalin against the supporters of Trotsky. The remaining leftists had failed to join hands at the right time and to translate their democratic slogans into the organization of mass constituencies.

To understand the outcome, we have to take into account the severity of the available options and the strategic errors of the right and left factions. But, even then, the events lack any irresistible logic of their own. The personalities of the leaders – Trotsky's and Bukharin's vanities and illusions, Stalin's mastery of the bureaucratic apparatus, his surefire instinct for the kill, his genius for dosage, and his luck – played an immeasurable part. The turning points in the history of stabilization policy represent an encounter with the impersonal, intractable forces of material life. Yet even there, the full range of contingencies comes into play, as if to remind us that history never stops being political in either the largest or the smallest ways.

The elements of the outcome determined what the Soviet system would be like in the immediate future. They therefore also established the starting point for other communist regimes. The solution that emerged had two decisive features. Whereas one aspect followed directly from the strategy of coerced collectivization, the other was more obliquely linked with it.

The decision to wage war on the peasantry and to crush the right and left factions within the party meant that the preferred structure of accumulation would minimize the role of cooperation and autonomous organization from the bottom up. Instead, it would emphasize the imposition, verging on systematic state terrorism, of a coercive order. The government and leadership that could manage to do this with the vast millions of peasants would be likely to do it with the industrial work force as well, no matter what the ruling ideological preconceptions might be. The combination of remorseless centralism with the violent shattering of the way of life of a large part of the people and the destruction of almost every remnant of the agrarian populations' independent associative life meant the triumph of a kind of state and leader that would see in every sign of communal autonomy and resistance an indication of conspiracy and breakdown. These were institutions and attitudes that could not be easily turned on and off to deal with different parts of the population. Thus, the Soviet experience confirmed, once again, the fateful importance of the relationship between the presence or absence of collective mobilization and the particular ways in which governmental power is used.

The oblique counterpart to this system of accumulation without mobilization was the emerging partnership between the ruling elites in party and bureaucracy and the technical intelligentsia of managers and professional or scientific personnel. The process of mutual though unequal acceptance (the technical intelligentsia was never coequal with the top cadres) had begun even before the start of the

NEP. It had been deepened during the NEP years. Despite the traumatic effect of the purges, it survived Stalinism. Its survival reflected a straightforward fact of reciprocal advantage and dependence. As the regime became increasingly committed to imposition of an order in town and country, it could not afford to fight simultaneously, on a second front, against the technical intelligentsia. The technicians, after all, had the power to disrupt the existing production system until another system could be devised and other technical cadres could be trained.

The regime had something to offer the technical intelligentsia in exchange for its collective support. Though Bukharinist ideas might be rife among the managers, engineers, and other professionals and though the terroristic aspects of revolutionary despotism might be especially hated, there was a basis for minimal agreement. That basis included the desire to preserve a style of work organization distinguishing between the people who formulated general productive tasks, or controlled their execution, and the people who did the routine work. The technical intelligentsia might not rule in the state, but at least it ruled (under watchful eyes) in the bureaus, factories, collective farms, army, schools, and hospitals.

The ruling elites and the technical intelligentsia had in common more than a crude interest in power and its perquisites. They also shared, with increasing clarity, a conception of efficiency and rationality and of the style of organization that would embody them. This conception minimized the break with the style of organization prevalent in the Western industrialized powers of the time (e.g., Lenin's celebrated interest in Taylorism). It also presupposed the foreclosure of widening collective conflict and escalating collective mobilization in every major sector of the economy. Thus, the two elements of the Soviet solution – accumulation without independent collective association, and accommodation with the technical intelligentsia by maintaining the sharpest contrast between task makers and task appliers – were implicated in each other.

The result of this crucial episode in Soviet history was related to the suppression of the soviets after the November revolution. The relationship brings out a special connection between the Western and the communist experiences. It also illuminates the general link between radical conflicts over the mastery of the state and the structure of society and the more subtle or detailed settling of accounts that takes place when new terms are laid down for economic growth and stability.

The soviets were put down almost immediately after the November revolution. They were deprived of their original role as devices of collective mobilization and became, instead, mere instruments of governmental control. In this respect, their history resembled that of peasant communes that had been transformed into passive tools of some agrarian empire's fiscal policy. The suppression of the soviets had created the opportunity to orient the state and the economy in a way that would restrict all independent collective organizations. But the destruction of the soviets did not make this result inevitable, nor did it tell on just what terms accumulation would go forward. Only the conflicts of the late 1920s and their sequels set these terms. In a similar way, the defeat of radical movements in Western Europe after World War I had created an opportunity to minimize the changes in the established forms of power and production that would be necessary for lasting civil peace as well as economic stability and growth. That opportunity was later realized by the forms of economic policy developed during World War II and by the domestic and international economic arrangements and governmental alliances of the postwar era.

In fact, there was more than a generic parallel between the events in Western Europe (or, more generally, in the Atlantic zone) and those in the Soviet Union; there was a direct mutual influence. The failure to create an alternative style of work organization and of democracy in one area of the world made the failure in the other area seem that much more unavoidable. The development of organizational structures (e.g., the multidivisional firm structure) was going on in the advanced Western countries after the soviets had already been untoothed, and each refinement of those structures suggested to the masters of Soviet Russia the need to find the closest counterpart compatible with their own forms of rule and property. The war effort added to the plausibility of this selective emulation by making it important to achieve the most rapid possible mobilization of resources and labor with the fewest risks and discontinuities.

The settlement of the late 1920s and early 1930s determined the ground on which later conflicts would be fought in the Soviet Union and other communist countries. There were an outer circle and an inner circle of struggle.

The outer circle presented occasional flare-ups of the defeated "right" and "left" tendencies. An example of the rightist resurgence would be the rebellious movements in Eastern Europe; an example of the leftist, the Chinese Cultural Revolution. They had in common the impulse to reverse the strategy of accumulating without allowing independent collective mobilization. They represented, and were understood to represent, an assault upon this strategy that threatened to upset the established forms of power and production. They jeopardized the prerogatives of the ruling groups and (at least in the case of resurgent leftism) of the technical intelligentsia. They were repeatedly crushed thanks to the reactions of the endangered governmental apparatus, the hesitations of their own leaders, and the military intervention of other communist powers.

The inner circle of conflict was represented by struggles that went on chronically because they arose out of a congenital weakness in the stabilization settlement. There was a limit to the state's use of terroristic violence against society in the effort to impose a growth path upon a passive and frightened citizenry. Terrorism would have its own costs in the breakdown of communication and of simple truth-telling, in the government's need to keep up the remorseless pressure, and in everyone's obsession with survival and self-defense. Once there was a letup in state terrorism, the rulers and planners would have to win a greater measure of active collaboration by the working population at every level of hierarchy. To enlist this collaboration and to compensate for their own relative ignorance of difficulties and opportunities, the central planners periodically felt pressed to allow for greater decentralization in the production system. The loosening of central control, however, could not be permitted to fall into open-ended collective conflict or grassroots mobilization. It could not be allowed to threaten the basic hierarchy of rule within the society at large or the large-scale enterprise. It could not be set free to undermine the barrier between the task makers and the task appliers. Decentralization within these limits invariably meant a greater concentration of power in the hands of managers, technicians, and local authorities. They would in turn make such concessions to their own underlings as were needed to keep things going.

But the decentralizing movement brought dangers of its own. Low-level authorities used every additional amount of discretion to build up more autonomy from dependence upon their rivals or their masters. They tried to turn the advantages they had gained for their enterprises and for themselves into vested rights. The whole economy would then start to sink into a welter of factional privileges and self-defensive actions within the cumbersome and resented framework of the central plan. This was a dreamless apparatchik's version of the ancien régime: freedom through privilege. Correctives milder than revolutionary despotism sufficed to stop it.

No point along these epicycles was satisfactory from even the narrowest perspective of accumulation. At each point, muddling through seemed the best that could be hoped for. Nevertheless, there was no way to avoid the turns and about-turns. They arose from the difficulty an order of the kind that had emerged in the Soviet Union at the decisive point of the late 1920s would inevitably have in coming to terms with the consensual requirements of a production system.

To see what is most revealing about these events, we need to push the comparison between the twentieth-century Soviet and the Western settlements to a more general level. In both cases, the accepted solution resulted in a persistent limit to the government's capacity to push the economy repeatedly into the high gear of accelerated innovation. This is just a particular way of saying that neither settlement did justice to the exigencies of the modern formula for worldly success.

In both instances, the limitation had the same fundamental structure. The dominant stabilization policies, and the formative contexts of power and production these policies helped sustain, enabled a more or less closed and privileged group to exercise a stranglehold over the conditions of collective prosperity. In one case, this group was the party and bureaucratic elite with its allies in the upper rungs of the technical intelligentsia. In the other case, it was the managers and officials who controlled the crucial flows of investment decisions. In both cases, the other groups dug in their heels. They attempted to organize themselves for self-defense and advancement. They tried to turn every new advantage into a vested right. More often than not, they hardened the criteria of group membership and alliance rather than effacing these lines by a strategy of expanding alliances. They sought and received benefits according to their power to disrupt: whether by the slowing down of the production system in a narrower sense or by the withholding of partisan support in a larger sense. There was certainly no general proportion between each group's ability to blackmail and its actual productive contributions to the economy.

The basic obstacle to ever renewed innovation was then the constraining interplay between an elite certain to confuse social opportunity with factional interest and a larger world of groups armed with uneven degrees of collective organization and devoted to the stratagems of preemptive security. Here was an example of the way the same forces that go into the remaking of a social world – the interplay between collective mobilization and the transformative uses of governmental power – turn into the protective shell that helps defend this world against attack.

The outcome of these constraints upon collective material progress was not definitive economic crises. It was an endless stream of squabbles and a recurrent entropic movement toward hardened factional privilege. Most worldly people thought that things had always been and would always be this way.

A Failed Attempt to Break Out from the Soviet Model: The Chinese Cultural Revolution

The Chinese Cultural Revolution offers a contrasting case: the failure to achieve in fact what at one point had looked like a possible breakthrough into a different style of industrial society strengthened by the very forms of production and control that were initially jeopardized. For a while at least, reconstruction for the sake of economic growth – an objective whose relative importance had been one of the very subjects of the contest – was achieved as inconclusive rivalry among proposals gave way to the reassertion of preexisting institution, with a familiar decentralizing twist. The events by which an entrenched system temporarily rids itself of its domestic challengers and emerges with new strength from a battle for survival are among the most important and the most common ways in which the relation between institutional forms and practical needs gets played out: reaction, like revolution, is not easily separable from reform.

The experience of the Chinese Cultural Revolution also holds a more specific interest for an institutional genealogy that anticipates both a theory of context making and a program for social reconstruction. I have suggested that the "right-wing" Soviet deviationists of the 1920s raised once again the problems posed by the institutional arrangements that eventually became dominant in the West. The fulfillment of what was most original in their program would ultimately have required the realization of the reconstructed, economically dynamic and internally stable form of petty commodity production: hence a novel institutional ordering of market economies and democratic regimes. The Chinese Cultural Revolution highlights the difficulties encountered in the course of an equally confused and halfhearted attempt to establish a stabilized order capable of perpetuating a higher measure of collective mobilization and context-challenging conflict in the midst of everyday social life. The petty commodity and mobilizational ideals may seem only loosely connected. Yet they are indeed linked through the requirements that must be satisfied in order to rescue a radically decentralized economy from instability, perversion, and regressiveness. This argument, first advanced during the discussion of certain turning points in European institutional history, becomes clearer in Chapter 5, which develops a program for institutional reconstruction responsive to both the mobilizational and the decentralizing ideal.

Consider the basic march of events. The first stage was one in which Mao and his faction attempted to execute an internal coup within the elites. Their initial motives for stepping up the controversies that led to the Cultural Revolution were surely complex: they included, in some blend the participants themselves could hardly have decomposed, an unvarnished power interest – the desire to humble rival centers of power in the state apparatus and the party – and a visionary commitment – the will to escape from the consolidation of bureaucratic power in the manner already perceived as indicative of the Soviet vice. Even at its most radical, however, this commitment seems never to have allowed for the possibility of reorganizing power on a radically new basis and institutionalizing popular participation on an unprecedented scale.

The second stage of the events started when the faction that had begun the quarrel within the elites attempted to enlist broader mass support in order to do its will – a variation on the characteristic mechanism by which the recruitment of mass constituencies shakes up an oligarchy's inward-turning squabbles. The call for mass agitation became progressively more shrill, as befitted the confused, halfhearted assault upon bureaucratic power. The popular response, however, soon began to exceed the expectations of its architects. Its major source of support lay in the dispossessed (such as the temporary and contract workers – the Chinese underclass) and in the youth that had not yet acquired the knack of discounting the value of words. Its centers were a few cities. Its major forms of action were the mass demonstration and the transformation of self-criticism techniques. Self-criticism had been a subtle method for reasserting consensus and control through contained conflict – the very image of routine politics, drawn into the microcosm of the enterprise, the work gang, or the neighborhood and supplemented with a subtle psychology of the way an individual can be made to render himself transparent to his fellows. The fundamentals of power at every level would remain out of bounds to conflict and complaint. In the hands of the practicing cultural revolutionaries, however, self-criticism became a device for humiliating alleged enemies and bureaucratic superiors; the boundaries of what could be done to people, who could be reached, and what could be attacked, began to fall apart. This evolution, a paradigm of the way the very instruments of routine politics may turn into the agencies of political intensification, was symbolized by the assault on Liu Shao-chi, at once leader of the party elites and consummate theorist of the mainstream tradition of self-criticism. The widening conflict forced the politicians behind the Cultural Revolution and their allies in the army to choose between two options, which presented themselves in ever starker and more dangerous contrast as agitation grew. One option was to support the insurrectional movement unequivocally, attempting to lead its temper. The other was to reassert control so that the basic structure of party leadership at the top levels and managerial authority at the lower ones would not be destroyed; the popular tumults would then not depart too far from the purpose originally meant for them: that they should serve as a weapon of intimidation in an elite conflict. Not all surprises would be allowed to happen.

The definitive choice of the latter option inaugurated a third stage: the effort to bring events under control once again started with the "seizure of power" movement of early 1969. The new "revolutionary committees" installed in the enterprises, with the participation of local workers, party cadres, and army representatives, served as the crucial device by which mass participation was whittled down to the point of harmlessness. In this way, too, the more radical factions among the political elites lost any independent channel by which to communicate with their potential supporters below. The extent of the loss became clear only later. The nonarmy radicals found themselves reduced to the condition of favorites at court with a tenure dependent upon the survival of their master.

The fourth stage of the conflict was the period of settling scores among the erstwhile radical allies in light of the largely successful decision to reestablish control. It was also the phase in which the relationship between the domestic and the foreign policy aspects of these conflicts became clear. The two issues came together in the Lushan Plenum of 1970, when Lin Piao and the radical army faction were attacked for failing to swallow the new line of antagonism to the Soviet Union. The main points of the deal were the acceptance by the party and state bureaucracies of the emerging program of international realpolitik in exchange for a guarantee of minimal security made all the more credible by the annihilation of the radical army faction. Yet it would be a mistake to see in the quest for this reorientation to world politics a cause of the earlier reassertion of control. The masses might also have been mobilized for the new foreign policy, but once they had been demobilized, the issue of the terms on which the reinstated elites would agree to the desired international aims became pressing.

The fifth stage of events was the aftermath of restoration, reaction, and reform: after Mao's death even the appearance that his line was the predominant one could be denied and his favorites could be discarded.

The ending of the story suggests the paradox whose resolution in turn uncovers the deeper meaning of the plot. Mao and his immediate friends and supporters seemed to be in charge of events from the start: they began the agitation; they succeeded in controlling it; and they set the terms on which compromise would be struck after rebellion had been put on a leash. Yet in the end their initial enemies sat in the seats of power and judgment. A program of economic growth was organized around a more clear-cut chain of managerial and party hierarchy than had existed before. Concessions to "socialist legality" left little real substance to popular participation. Decentralizing reform respected the limits of the communist reform cycle.

The explanation of the paradox lies in the choice between the two options of continuing mobilization or demobilization. The unequivocal choice in favor of the latter had taken place before any real alternatives in the organization of production or power had had a chance to consolidate. Indeed by its very nature, the success of such a reassertion depended upon its anticipating the emergence of any alternative logic of power and production, capable of making an economy run and a polity stick together. In the end, the alternative modes of organization remained, at best, half-baked compromises or growths upon a body constituted on different principles. None of the participatory schemes had passed the threshold points at which they might have started to pay off and surmount the opposition. In the absence of a developed alternative scheme of enterprise organization and coordination, the equivocal participatory concessions, such as the "revolutionary committees," became at most an annoying and costly though ineffective hindrance to restrengthened managerial authority; a similar problem arises in the Western economies when efforts are made to push through redistributive or regulatory programs without changing the fundamental pattern of powers over investment. So too, as long as no novel system for governmental decision, control, and communication has begun to appear, departures from established practice in the name of the mass line – or any other line, for that matter – will appear as gestures toward chaos. Their fate will depend upon an unequal battle in which well-organized powers are pitted against sinking enthusiasms.

So, once the reassertion of control had taken place, the Cultural Revolution as a mass movement was lost. But so were the elite factions responsible for its beginning and its later paralysis. To survive as a power bloc they would not only have had to dissociate themselves from the personality of the leader: they would also have had to define themselves in terms other than the ones that had set them on course. Their erstwhile enemies, the governmental and party bureaucracies, found themselves in charge of the real machines of administration and production and discovered as well that, in the newly clarified circumstance, their own power interests coincided with the practical needs to get things done and deliver the goods. To admit this much, you do not have to believe that anyone in the Cultural Revolution – elites or masses – was close to coming up with workable alternatives, or even that such plans of association as they might have found would have represented a change for the better. The point is that no alternatives were really put to the test and that the collective process of searching for them was paralyzed close to the start.

Here, then, is a case of failure in breakthrough toward an alternative mode of socialism and industrialism, unless the breakthrough is defined as a return to a clearer version of preexisting institutions, a return permitting limited decentralizing experiments and achieved at the cost of a protracted ordeal of provoked, uncontrolled, and suppressed insurrection.

Surely a background condition of the whole development was the tilt toward restabilization inherent in the available technologies and organizational forms – the ones that China had largely imbibed from the West. For these favored bright lines between subordinate, routine operations and controlling, task-defining activities, in every sphere of production, administration, and warfare; in the not very long run, a strategy of radical participation would have demanded radical disaggregation and reinvention of the existing technologies and organizational practices.

A much more immediate factor in the outcome, however, was the illusion of an elite faction that thought it could have it both ways with mass mobilization, that it could use the agitated populace at will as a club with which to beat its enemies at the center of power, and yet keep this mass following from posing any serious challenge to the basic structure of power. It is the most paradigmatic of illusions to which mass politics can give rise, for it lies at the very origins of mass politics. It goes to the terms on which collective allegiances can be won and collective aspirations contained. It deals with the way in which the development of organization and technology is steered so as to allow for a more free-playing involvement in productive tasks while maintaining a stable hierarchy of spiritual authority and material advantage.

Just as the liberal identification of freedom and efficiency with a very detailed system of vested rights played a crucial part in the nineteenth-century American events discussed in an earlier section, so too the equation of the impersonal needs of organized power and national development with the maintenance of a concrete system of vested rights performed an equally important role in this episode of twentieth-century Chinese history. But whereas the American belief was largely a mistake that helped cause the result it did not describe, the Chinese belief more truly described a situation. This truth, however, had been brought into being by an illusion, the illusion of those who tried to play fast and loose with mass mobilization. The economy remained as if subject to built-in forces but only because, at the moment of opportunity, its two-hearted political enemies had not dared invade it in the name of possibilities it excluded.

A THEORY OF CONTEXT MAKING

THE AGENDA OF THE THEORY

The Implicit Theoretical Polemic Recalled

This second part of Chapter 4 develops a theory of context making. The theory suggests an account of how we remake the institutional and imaginative frameworks of social life and therefore provides the dynamic counterpart to the earlier steps of the explanatory argument of *False Necessity*, which explore the character of formative contexts and their internal constitution. More particularly, it makes explicit the view of context change implicit in the institutional genealogy presented in the first part of the chapter.

Unlike the polemical narrative that anticipates it, the theory is meant to have general application. Moreover, it deals with the imaginative as well as the institutional aspects of contexts and their reinvention. Nevertheless, only by synecdoche may this account be called a theory of social transformation. For it addresses solely the major, discontinuous change that occurs when formative institutions and preconceptions are revised.

An adequate view of context making must satisfy the criteria set by the earlier stages of the explanatory argument. It must reject the competing positions of positivist social science (or naive historiography) and deep-structure social theory.

Remember that positivist social science refuses to take seriously the individuality of different social worlds: the ways in which both the institutional shape of society and the subjective experience of personality differ sharply from one society to another. Positivist social science ignores any ultimate distinction between the routine events that take place within a mental or practical context and the struggles that revise this context. These two failures of insight – the failure to distinguish structure-respecting disputes from structure-changing conflicts and the failure to treat seriously the specificity of societies and cultures – arise from the same premises and produce the same results.

The standpoints of positivist social science (or naive historiography) and deep-structure theory represent two facets of the refusal to take the historicity of the social world seriously. Paradoxically, though the two refusals appear to move in opposite directions, they both end up making the same mistake: they understate the extent to which our experiences and projects are at risk in history. In one instance the limitation takes the form of denying the seriousness of the distinctions between societies. It disregards the power of insight and action to change the basic terms of subjective experience and collective organization. In the other case the refusal appears as the conviction that history already has a basic script. The struggles that go on in history may provide minor variations of content and pace (the evolutionary variant of deep-structure theory). They may determine which of several possibilities will be actualized (the non-evolutionary variant). But they can never rewrite the script itself. By contrast, in the view for which I argue here, we write this script both by fighting and by failing to fight. The formative contexts that result from this fighting not only shape our practical and passionate dealings but also determine the extent to which peace requires prostration.

A satisfactory approach to context-making has as its reverse side a defensible view of the internal constitution of the institutional and imaginative frameworks of social life. Such a view must recognize that the constitutive arrangements and ideas of a formative structure develop separately and can undergo piecemeal replacement. (The deep-logic theories have trouble recognizing or explaining this part-by-part replaceability.) At the same time, it must acknowledge the staying power of these constituents: the components of a social framework do somehow support one another and they do prove hard to change in the course of routine practical or imaginative conflicts. (Positivist social science has a hard time making sense of this staying power.)

The idea of historicity has been one of the greatest and most distinctive achievements of modern thought. Yet the historical perspective does not become secure until the standpoints of both naive historiography and deep-logic theory have been replaced. This replacement does not occur until we actually formulate and deploy an alternative style of social and historical explanation. Until then, we cannot carry the principle of historical consciousness to its final conclusions. Until then, we cannot know how to historicize the relation between freedom and structure by showing how the force with which formative contexts imprison us is itself one of the things up for grabs in history.

The Theory Outlined

The theory of context change presented here is divided into four parts. This subsection outlines by anticipation their topics and themes. Each part describes a distinctive influence upon context making. Because these influences fail to merge together into a single, lawlike scheme, it is all the more important to develop little by little a view of the complex relations among them.

Each of the four sets of ideas can be fully understood, developed, and supported only when placed alongside the other three. Each reflects a basic feature of social life. And each can be translated into a thesis about the implications of having to live in contexts that are less than natural or absolute.

The first part of the theory considers the ordinary workings of an institutional and imaginative framework of social life. It discusses how such a framework gains a measure of stability and a semblance of necessity, despite its haphazard, ramshackle origins. The containment or interruption of conflict suffices to give a context an initial measure of stability. Yet even relatively disentrenched contexts – like the institutional and imaginative orders of contemporary societies – have hardened faces. They effectively prescribe routines and resist transformation.

The argument explains this exorbitant stability. But it does so without appealing to deep-seated economic, organizational, and psychological constraints or to irresistible and determinate tendencies of development. Nor does it understand the problem-solving and interest-accommodating activities of a routinized social world as approximations to a context-transcending norm of rationality. It insists that the particular content and relative entrenchment of a framework determine the vital terms on which problem solving and interest-accommodation take place.

The key claim of this first part of the theory is that each of the forces that bestow a higher stability on formative contexts also generates an endless series of opportunities for the destabilization and reconstruction of the established order. The link between stability and destabilization is built into the detailed practical and imaginative activities that reproduce a social world. The small-scale disharmonies these activities regularly excite can always escalate into context-subverting conflicts. When they do so they also make possible the operation of the long-run influences on context change that provide the next two parts of this view with their subject matter.

The second part of the theory deals with the influence upon context change that results from the many advantages – varieties of empowerment – offered by less entrenched contexts: that is, by contexts that weaken the hold of rigid roles and hierarchies upon our experiments in practical collaboration or passionate attachment and do so by bringing framework-transforming conflict and framework-preserving routine closer together. The central thesis of this aspect of the view of context making is that the varieties of empowerment produced by more revisable and hierarchy-subverting frameworks help explain how a cumulative move toward more disentrenched contexts may occur. The mechanism by which advantages of empowerment explain the appearance of more empowering frameworks may be intentional. (The agents deliberately and voluntarily establish the disentrenched context so that they can gain its advantages.) Alternatively, the connection may be unintentional, by a social counterpart to Darwinian natural selection. (The more disentrenched contexts outlast their rivals.) But for the most part the style of agency has a distinctive and intriguing character that fails to fit the extremes of intentional and unintentional action.

Whether it is more intentionally or less intentionally pursued, the attractions of negative capability – for that is what I call empowerment through disentrenchment – remain relatively indeterminate in their practical implications. Those attractions are reversible. They are qualified by countervailing forces such as the benefits provided by a coercive surplus extraction that relies upon entrenched roles and hierarchies. Above all, they work largely with materials generated by histories – sequences of contexts – they only partly shape. This aspect of the explanatory argument holds the most immediate interest for the radical project – the enterprise of liberals and leftists. For the aims of the radical cause represent a version of the cumulative changes whose possibility the argument about negative capability helps explain.

A third part of this view of context making deals with another influence upon long-run, cumulative context change. Each institutional and imaginative order of social life influences its sequel by giving a bias to the outcomes of order-transforming conflicts. These biases may be overridden and even inverted. But they may also push context change in a certain direction: a direction of substantive arrangements and preconceptions and a direction of relative entrenchment or disentrenchment.

The main interest of this third part of the theory has to do with the relation it suggests between the two long-run influences on context change: the push of sequential effects and the pull of negative capability. The advance of negative capability diminishes the force of sequential effects by limiting the power of formative contexts to bias the outcomes of practical or imaginative struggles over context change. Conversely, however, the institutions, practices, and ideas generated by concrete histories of context change provide the materials on which the attractions of negative capability can work.

Thus, the two long-term influences cannot be reduced to each other. A particular historical sequence of contexts or context states is not just an expression of higher-order developmental tendencies, as in the evolutionary brands of deep-structure social theory. Such a sequence suffers the influence of forces – the advantages of negative capability preeminent among them – that make cumulative change in the content and quality of social frameworks possible. The sequence is nevertheless more than the product of such influences. Moreover, it generates the relatively accidental and particularistic stuff that those influences (or rather the people who enlist them) may sift, compare, and transform.

The fourth part of the view of context change describes the factors of disturbance that further prevent the forces identified by the previous three parts from coming together to impose a grand scheme of context change. One factor of disturbance is the inability of formative contexts fully to shape the practical or passionate dealings among people. The individual resists becoming the complete puppet of his contexts. He resists even if he does not want to resist or know that he is resisting, and even when the structure of social life is most deeply entrenched. The residues of past frameworks and the anomalies of present practice survive to supply the starting points of defiance and reconstruction.

Another factor of disturbance is the partly self-fulfilling character of our ideas about social reality and social change. We can never distinguish clearly and definitively between the descriptive accuracy of a theory (its success as a representation of reality) and its transformative effect (the practical consequences of acting as if the theory were true). Though we can partly control this effect, through comparison and analysis, retrospective control never suffices to dispel the confusion. We would have to try to control prospectively by reversing or varying our practices and projects. But we could not achieve this prospective compensation for the self-fulfilling effect without a degree of detachment from our practical concerns and our ideal commitments that would once again change us.

The two factors of disturbance – the residual recalcitrance of our practical or passionate relations to the frameworks that partly shape them, and the self-fulfilling character of our ideas about social life – share the same basis. This basis is the absence of a natural context, or of a context of all contexts, or of a system of laws capable of determining which contexts or sequences of contexts are possible.

Guiding Intentions

Three general remarks further connect this theory of context change with the broader explanatory view of *False Necessity*. These remarks may help clarify the intentions and thereby dispel the ambiguities of an intricate argument. For the intelligible connections this argument emphasizes presuppose a conception of order more subtle and inclusive – less starkly contrasted to brute accident and particularity – than any acceptable to deep-structure social theory. These initial observations also serve, in miniature and fragmentary form, a purpose similar to the proto-theory presented in Chapter 1. They describe different aspects of an intellectual project. You may accept the project while rejecting the version of it worked out in the rest of this chapter. Then, even the flawed materials of the failed attempt may be serviceable in the development of a better alternative.

Like the entire explanatory argument to which it belongs, the view of context change presented here has a two-sided relation to Marxist social theory. Marx's original doctrines, and much of the work conducted under their aegis, represent the most comprehensive statement of deep-structure theorizing – and of the deep-structure use of functional explanation. The following theory stands in opposition to those doctrines. But other parts of Marx's writings and of the Marxist tradition as a whole are irreducible to the amalgam of deep-structure and functionalist ideas. For Marxism also represents the single most powerful statement of the antinaturalistic conception of society. The self-criticism of the Marxist tradition provides both general inspiration and particular aid to those who would carry forward the view of social order as frozen politics.

Thus, you can begin to understand what may otherwise seem a surprising and even paradoxical feature of the view of context making offered here. The salvageable part of the Marxist theory of social change represents a special case of the approach for which I argue. But it is not a special case in the traditional scientific sense of an account that applies in the presence of local or temporary boundary conditions. It is, rather, a special case in a looser, psychological sense. Much of the view worked out in the following pages can be mapped onto Marxist theory so long as the Marxist relaxes certain unjustifiably restrictive assumptions about social possibility. In particular, these are the assumptions represented by what were previously described as the second and third moves of deep-structure explanation: the belief in a short list or compulsive sequence of indivisible social frameworks and the appeal to the lawlike constraints and tendencies that can generate such a sequence or list. But it is no easy matter to lift these restrictive assumptions, for they influence the categories, explanations, and theoretical attitudes that give Marx's doctrine its distinct identity and that hold together his intellectual followers.

The view of context making to be developed here is, in a special sense, antideterministic. The overriding aim is less to dilute than to revise the sense in which context change is determined. To be sure, the view makes context change much less determined prospectively – and much less subject to a predefined master plan – than it is, for example, in Marx's theory of history. But it is one thing to take a theory like historical materialism and dilute its claims by multiplying, mediating, or qualifying causes or sequences, and it is another thing to change the style of explanation.

The theory worked out in the rest of this chapter does not make social and historical explanation depend on a denial of our ability to shatter and revise our contexts in ways that no higher-order laws have fully determined. It seeks a style of transformative explanation compatible with our subjective experience of living in history. For in this experience the sense of constraint and compulsion coexists with the recurrence of surprise and discovery.

Such an explanatory practice can more readily make use of historical learning and inform historical narrative. A style of historical writing that has only positivist social science or deep-structure explanation to inspire it must either keep theory at an ironic distance or discount the open-ended variability and uniqueness of whole forms of social life and the radical uncertainty of the course of social conflict.

Finally, this view of context-making gives a secure place to programmatic thought. By reaffirming the context–routine distinction while dispensing with the idea of higher-order laws that govern context change, it makes room for programmatic inventions that cannot be dismissed as the handmaidens of foreordained tendencies or constraints. By recognizing that contexts can be remade part by part, not just all at once, it justifies taking revolutionary reform rather than either inconsequential tinkering or full-scale revolution as the standard topic of programmatic argument. By providing a credible view of context revision it gives to our thinking about social reconstruction the perspective needed to avoid measuring the realism of proposals by their closeness to current arrangements.

These last considerations suggest yet another general point important to understanding the aims of this argument. The view of context change focuses, first and foremost, on the features of social reality and social change that provide opportunities for the radical project: the project of seeking human empowerment through the invention of institutions, practices, and ideas that more fully emancipate social life from rigid roles or hierarchies and that make themselves more easily available to revision in the midst of everyday life. Moreover, it does not merely show how the project may be most effectively carried out. It also contributes to the redefinition of the project, free from arbitrarily restrictive assumptions about the possible forms of social order and personal experience.

Chapter 5 argues that explanatory and programmatic ideas are far more intimately related than our traditional ideas about facts and values would countenance. But the value of a theory of context change that informs the radical cause does not depend upon a commitment to this cause. There is a special cognitive interest in a view of social change that considers society from the vantage point of the radical project. This project is distinguished by its commitment to weaken rigid divisions among roles, genders, classes, communities, and whole societies and to free us from the compulsions of unrevisable contexts. By subjecting these divisions and compulsions to the maximum of transformative pressure – in fact or in imagination – the pursuit of the radical cause puts their necessity, indeed their reality, to the test. For we understand a state of affairs by trying to change it or by imagining how it would change as a result of varying types and degrees of intervention or by entering into the transformative and countertransformative efforts of other minds, remote or long dead.

The cognitive value of the radical standpoint may be restated in a more general form. Once we free the radical project from indefensibly limiting preconceptions about how contexts change, which contexts can exist, and what contexts can be like, we can reinterpret the project. It must be seen to include a commitment to change the very nature of our relation to the institutional and imaginative framework of social life. To study society and history from the radical perspective – if only as a stratagem of discovery – is to force ourselves to confront the chief sources of trouble in social explanation: the failure of our social contexts fully to determine our ideas and actions, and the failure of higher-order constraints and tendencies fully to govern the content and sequence of these contexts.

STABILITY AND DESTABILIZATION
IN THE WORKING OF FORMATIVE CONTEXTS

The Core Conception

The first set of ideas in this view of context change deals with the normal life of an institutional and imaginative framework, the life that goes on in the interludes of revolutionary reform. The point is to understand how the ordinary workings of a formative context make context change possible. This initial group of conjectures represents, then, something like a statics of the minute structure of social life. But it is a statics of a peculiarly antistatic type. For its central themes are the dependence of stability upon artifice and illusion rather than necessity, and the constant reemergence of the opportunities to remake a social world that result from the very means used to defend this world.

Here, by anticipation, are the major claims and assumptions of this part of the argument. There are two moments to distinguish in the stabilization of a formative context. The season of heightened and intensified conflict over some part of the framework must be brought to an end and conflict contained or interrupted. This social peace may be achieved either through an acceptance of the preexisting institutional arrangements and imaginative preconceptions or through their partial replacement. (The total substitution of the framework is the unrealistic, limiting case.)

This peace must be imposed. It must result from a series of violent or nonviolent, practical or imaginative struggles, fought out against the background of antecedent arrangements and preconceptions biasing the result of the struggles without determining it. There must be a victory and a defeat, however modest its dimensions and imperceptible its forms. Only then can the second moment of context stabilization begin. The imposed contexts become the beneficiaries of the stabilizing forces this section of the argument examines.

Consider three sources of the second-order necessity of formative contexts. One is the consolidation of an organizational and technological style of economic activity. Especially when it is realized within a system of nation-states at uneven levels of wealth and power, such a style reinforces the institutional settlement on which it was originally superimposed. A second source is the hardening of assumptions about collective identities, group interests, and social possibilities and of correspondences between the privileges each group enjoys and its relative access to governmental power. A third source of derivative necessity is the transformation of the imposed or accepted institutional order into a set of authoritative models of human association meant to be realized in different areas of social existence. Such an imaginative scheme lives both in the more pliant and organized form of official legal and moral dogma and in the more elusive and ambivalent form of implicit, widely shared assumptions about what the relations among people should be like in the different domains of social existence.

The forces operating at this second moment of stabilization presuppose the interruption or containment of fighting over fundamentals. The stabilizing mechanisms cannot account for the distinctive content of a formative context; they operate whatever this content may be. Their work is not to steer institutions and beliefs in any particular direction but rather to give them a degree of stability that they would otherwise lack. They alter the subjective quality of people's experience of formative contexts. This shift in turn has practical consequences.

The stabilizing forces can therefore be said to lend a second-order necessity to the social orders on which they exercise their influence. The term second-order necessity should be understood by analogy to the traditional idea of custom as a second nature, a distinctive and compulsive nature superimposed upon our indeterminate species nature. The forces of stabilization produce the tropisms in which a routinized form of social life so largely consists. Each force generates opportunities to destabilize the formative context in the very course of bestowing upon it an additional level of stability. It thereby also provides an opportunity for the operation of forces, discussed in later parts of this theory, that make possible long-run cumulative changes in the constraining power as well as in the distinctive content of formative contexts.

The transformative opportunities resulting from the operation of the context-stabilizing opportunities are just that: opportunities. They may or may not be turned to advantage. Each one takes the form of a series of petty disturbances. To be put to transformative use these disturbances must be made to escalate into broader and more intense conflict. We can describe circumstances that usually encourage or discourage this escalation, that make it harder or easier. But we cannot draw up a list of the necessary and sufficient conditions under which such escalation occurs. The obstacle to making such a list does not arise from a mere localized, remediable defect in our understanding of society. Rather, the search for necessary and sufficient conditions rests on mistaken assumptions about what social life is like: the assumptions common to deep-structure social theory and positivist social science.

This part of the view of context change develops through an analysis of the three forces contributing to the second-order necessity of formative contexts. The point is to show how each stabilizing influence regularly produces opportunities for destabilization.* There is no magic to these three. Others may be added, and even these may be divided up or combined in other ways.

The Second-Order Necessity of Formative Contexts: The Organizational and Technological Style

A stabilized set of formative institutional arrangements becomes the basis for an organizational and technological style of economic activity. This style then exerts a retrospective stabilizing influence upon the arrangements it has taken for granted and upon the group divisions and hierarchies these arrangements support. The adversaries of the newly established institutional settlement find they cannot go far in challenging this settlement without jeopardizing the dominant approach to technological design and the ways of organizing production and exchange that have been superimposed upon this approach.

The genealogy of current forms of work organization presented earlier in this chapter provides an extended example. The events that led up to the consolidation of the forms of economic organization characterizing contemporary formative contexts included a vast range of group conflicts, fought out in changing circumstances and with unexpected outcomes. Elites were redefined and their relation to the central and local powers of government was reshaped. Governmental authority was actively enlisted against alternative lines of development in ways that spanned the distance between the most violent methods of repression and the slow, subtle accumulation of legal rules and economic policies. The results of these conflicts favored the rigid form of rationalized collective labor, with its sharp contrast between task-executing and task-defining activities. Varieties of work organization that softened this contrast were relegated to the commercial and technological rearguard and vanguard of the

---

* In *Social Theory: Its Situation and Its Task*, the idea of the link between stability and destabilization was presented through the discussion of the survival, identity, and oligarchy effects. Now, however, I need categories that can serve the aims of a more detailed analysis, specifically concerned with context change.

economy. The dominant style of work organization in turn became the basis for distinctive approaches to industrial organization and machine design, closely adapted to each other. Mass-production industry conflated disciplinary and efficiency aims. It developed a panoply of defenses against market instability. And it adopted purpose-specific machines, meant to function in a rigidly organized production process. General-purpose or metamachines were confined to the industrial vanguard, and became for a long time the exceptional rather than the standard form of machine design. Thus, in the end, the institutional arrangements and the group hierarchies became the basis for complex managerial and technological conventions. All but the most discerning identified these conventions with economic rationality.

The climb to a higher order of stability did not happen all at once: no clear break or time lag separated the crystallization of institutional arrangements and of group divisions and hierarchies from the development of this organizational and technological complex. But once the complex had formed, it offered an additional layer of protection to the underlying institutional order. A different order would require different organizational and machine-design techniques. For example, a reconstructed, practicable version of the petty bourgeois alternative to the dominant industrial style must break down the stark contrast between task-defining and task-executing activities. Such an alternative cannot accept a tradition of machine design presupposing a passive worker, pegged to an isolated, discretionless role. The practicality of the proposals will be disputed, all the more so because adversaries of the established order must often appeal to little more than a speculative possibility of practical organization. Thus, for example, the idea of a metamachine long remained a purely speculative conception, suggested by the theory of machine design, before it became actualized in the vanguard sector of industry.

But even if the ultimate practicality of an alternative style were beyond dispute, its development must still overcome formidable difficulties of transition. One technological and organizational order must be disrupted before another can be established. The disruption exacts a real economic toll. Moreover, the established technological and organizational style ends up influencing people's intangible assumptions about social possibility and, through them, about group interests.

The preceding discussion of this stabilizing mechanism presupposes a hypothesis introduced in Chapter 3 and developed later in this chapter. Functionalist social theories are right to see connections between the forms of social organization and the ability to exploit technological opportunities for productive or destructive, economic or military purposes. The organization of teamwork imposes constraints upon the ability to develop and deploy practical techniques and machines. The larger institutional environment (and, specifically, the part of it I call the formative context) in turn shapes the forms of teamwork. We must recognize these constraints. But we must also understand that there is no one-to-one relation between arrangements at these different levels of technological capability, work organization, and institutional arrangements, and no list of solutions at one level that are required by a particular solution at another level.

An organizational and technological style acquires an additional stabilizing power when it begins to spread throughout a system of interdependent states at unequal levels of economic growth and military strength. (It does not matter for the present purpose whether such a state system actually includes the whole world. But assume that if it occupies a lesser portion of the globe, it is both economically and militarily autarkic.) The state enjoying the greatest economic and military capabilities may be able to impose upon weaker or more backward countries many of its favorite arrangements and dogmas. It may indulge the most primitive of ideological impulses, which is the desire for self-reproduction.

But imposition is hardly necessary. Success remains the best persuasion. It takes time for the ruling or possessing elites of the more backward powers to discover that the practical capabilities achieved by the more advanced countries can be developed through methods of work organization different from the methods prevailing in the pioneering nations of the state system. Only slowly do the relatively backward nations find out that they can combine the same imported ways of organizing work with governmental or economic arrangements completely unknown in the dominant countries. At first, the practical capabilities seem inseparable from their organizational and institutional setting. The setting in turn seems available on a take-it-or-leave-it basis.

The persuasive authority of the organizational and institutional solutions that have achieved preeminence in the dominant powers often gets reinforced by the most influential ideas about practical progress and its enabling circumstances. Cultural ascendancy habitually accompanies practical triumph: the ruling doctrines of statecraft and economic management in the dominant countries represent the established amalgam of a technological and organizational style with a formative institutional and imaginative context as if this amalgam were a prerequisite of worldly success. Thus, for example, many of the ideas about economic policy and management emanating from the universities of the rich North Atlantic countries in the years after World War II presented mass-production industry and its technological complement as the condition of industrial development. Those prestigious theories also treated the contemporary Western forms of regulated market economies and representative democracies as the sole possible institutional basis for industrial mass production outside a modernizing fascist or communist dictatorship. The same gospel, with a slightly different message, had been preached by the liberal political economists and publicists of the early nineteenth century. At that time, the institutional genealogy I labeled the mythical history was already beginning to dominate our understanding of how we came to be what we are.

Illusion, however, is not the necessary basis for the added stabilizing force a technological and organizational style achieves when it begins to spread throughout a state system. Even if the rulers of the more backward nations understand the looseness of the connections between industrial or military capabilities and ways of organizing work, or between such organizational styles and the larger institutional environment, they may well feel they lack the time to develop an alternative. For in the course of the attempt, they might be overcome from abroad or overthrown from within. Given these many inducements to imitation, it is no wonder the follow-the-leader sequence within a state system can so easily be mistaken for a spontaneous convergence, driven forward by the universal influence of the same objective constraints.

Thus far I have described how an organizational and technological style gives a second-order necessity to the institutional settlements on which it is superimposed. Let me now turn the argument around and show how this same stabilizing force creates opportunities for destabilization. To this end I begin with the international twist just discussed and then return to the core phenomenon.

The more widely diffused an organizational or technological style becomes, the greater the variety it is likely to encounter in the social and cultural environments in which it must function. The differences are bound to make the mechanical imitation of the imported technological and organizational style impractical. The institutional order and the methods of work organization in the backward country may be incapable of supporting the technological, economic, or military developments that would allow the country to catch up. Failure to promote revolutionary reform consigns the latecoming country to an ever more dependent position within the state system to which it belongs. But the effort merely to reproduce, lock, stock, and barrel, both the foreign organizational and technological style and its whole institutional setting is equally unrealistic. A practical and imaginative ordering of social life cannot be replaced, and certainly not suddenly, just because a revolutionary leadership wants to replace it in order to revise the position its country occupies within a world order. Successful imitation requires reinvention.

Consider the very common situation in which an elite of renovating reformers and discerning conservatives wants to introduce the changes needed to permit the economic development and military strengthening of their country while minimizing the disturbance to established institutions and to the group divisions or hierarchies these institutions support. This is the situation in which we would expect the stabilizing effect of the proliferation of an organizational and technological style within a state system to be at its strongest. It is therefore also the best circumstance in which to put to the test the hypothesis that this stabilizing force has destabilizing implications.

The renovating elite must identify the connections between the desired practical capabilities and their immediate setting in a form of work organization and machine design. It must also establish that accommodation between this managerial and technological style and the country's basic institutions which requires the least possible deviation from the current arrangements of the backward country. The reformers must invent the counterpart to the foreign organizational and technological style that will bring their country up to the level of the leading nations while minimizing disruption at home.

The most ingenious solutions capitalize on the distinctive characteristics of the backward country and turn what appeared to be archaic obstacles to practical use. But remember the looseness of the connection between an industrial style and an institutional order and the difficulty of developing from scratch a new approach to technology and work organization. Given this looseness and difficulty, renovating reform commonly produces two-sided results. Its managerial and technological approach may remain relatively close to the solutions favored in the original leading powers of the state system while its broader institutional settlements may be far more distinctive. The renovated formative context differs both from the old order of the reformed society and from the alien order of the foreign rivals. It represents an original creation.

The age of world history offers many examples of such national experiments in economic and military strengthening through stabilizing invention. The agent has often been a faction or a coalition of factions within the elite that identifies its own interests with the affirmation of national power and prosperity. Such reforms have continuously occurred both within and outside the West and with varying degrees of deliberation and central guidance. Thus, Wilhelmine Germany developed an organizational and technological style that differed only modestly, though tellingly, from the English original. The German economy followed the broad lines of the rigid variant of rationalized collective labor and embraced the new style of mass production. However, it also incorporated a relatively greater element of artisanal practices into industrial organization itself. It softened the contrast between task-defining and task-executing activities and multiplied intermediate work roles. At the same time the continuous processing industries in which the Germans soon came to specialize encouraged the development and deployment of less purpose-specific machines. Together with this subtle and modest originality in technological and industrial style went governmental institutions and practices that differed far more sharply from the English route to wealth and power. In Germany a more authoritarian constitution came to coexist with practices more conducive to mass mobilization to a greater extent than anything seen in nineteenth-century Britain after Chartism.

Japan provides the most notoriously successful example of conservative reform outside the West. There, the policies of the post-restoration regime were far more deliberate, and the deviations, when contrasted to the English original, far more extensive. The preexisting devices of communal organization and patron–client relations were reconstructed and superimposed upon the rigid variant of rationalized collective labor. At the same time the institutional reorganization of government assured a position of privilege to a reconstituted elite.

The German and Japanese developments exemplify the conservative absorption of a technological and organizational style by late-coming countries within a state system. Yet even this conservative style of diffusion constantly generates transformative opportunities. The successful conservative reform requires changes in the organization of labor. It even alters the basic institutions and beliefs that constrain the forms of practical collaboration in work or warfare. Shifts like these in turn suppose and produce a realignment in the definition and ranking of interests, in the character and composition of the ruling and possessing elites, and in the access of rulers and ruled, possessors and dispossessed, to governmental power. Such a realignment can never be wholly predesigned. It creates uncertainty. It generates conflict. Some groups within the elites or the working masses resist the change. Other groups quarrel over place within the new order. Such transitional disputes can easily grow in intensity and scope, and turn the conservative episode in more radical directions. The conservative reformer reckons with the existence of such struggles. Because he cannot prevent them, he must try to contain them.

It is easy to forget how conflictual even the most successful instances of conservative absorption really were. Thus, for example, the violent mass strikes and social conflicts that shook Japan in the first two decades of the twentieth century are submerged under the retrospective gloss of an institutional outcome supposedly predetermined by the cultural peculiarities and psychological predispositions of the Japanese people. In Japan, as everywhere else, the relatively conservative outcome had to be fought for long and hard before it could assume its deceptive patina of naturalness and necessity. So, too, the cases of national economic and military regression, sometimes labeled "failed modernization" (e.g., mid-twentieth century Argentina), may often best be understood as instances in which the conflict over the institutional and distributive equation of the national catching-up failed to be resolved decisively one way or another.

Pass now from the international dimension of the stabilizing aspect of the organizational and technological style to the core phenomenon itself. Even apart from its diffusion through a variety of social and cultural circumstances, the consolidation of an organizational and technological style produces opportunities for context change. An approach to management and machines never arrests completely the perception of practical productive opportunities, any more than an established scientific theory can fully block out perceptions and discoveries that threaten it. The designers of machines, the managers of work teams, and the heads of businesses have reasons of their own to seize on some of these opportunities and to begin innovating at the boundary of the current managerial and technological tradition. The significance of small-scale, opportunistic experimentation becomes clear when connected with a central hypothesis of this argument. According to the hypothesis a formative context constrains – loosely but significantly – ways of organizing work. Forms of work organization in turn limit people's ability to seize practical productive opportunities. If this hypothesis is correct, the experiments performed on the technological and organizational style must, as they accumulate, put pressure on aspects of the established institutional and imaginative framework of social life. The experiments invite yet larger experiments and, in so doing, they also create opportunities for conflict over basics.

A subsequent part of the theory of context making offers another reason to link such conflict with the progress of industrial or military capabilities. The next section of this chapter argues that under certain conditions the pressure of practical opportunity has a cumulative, directional quality. The constraints that preestablished social roles and hierarchies impose upon the forms of production and exchange must occasionally be lifted if particular classes or whole nations are to avoid defeat or eclipse at the hands of their rivals. Consequently, we must invent institutional arrangements that weaken the hold of social division and hierarchy upon our experience of sociability and soften the contrast between context-preserving routine and context-transforming conflict. The internal development of technological and organizational insight may itself make a modest but real contribution to the recognition of these larger possibilities and connections. It may therefore also help destabilize the very order that it once reinforced.

Later sections of this transformative argument play a series of variations on a practical example that illuminates the case for linking practical opportunity with institutional destabilization. This example looks to the future rather than to the past of the transformations covered by the institutional genealogy.

The changing international division of labor, with the industrialization of the top tier of third world countries, threatens the emphasis on mass-production industry and on the rigid form of rationalized collective labor in the more advanced economies. A similar effect results in the gradual change of consumption expectations and worker attitudes within the richer nations. Finally, the independent development of technology, with the invention of (computerized) general-purpose machines, both relatively cheap and able to make relatively cheap goods, pushes in the same direction. These pressures suggest the need for a greater emphasis on a type of production, work organization, and machine design hitherto largely confined to both the most advanced (capital-intensive and technologically sophisticated) and the least advanced sectors of the economy. The alternative organizational and technological style more nearly approaches the description of the flexible form of rationalized collective labor, softening the contrast between task-defining and task-executing activities.

We can imagine this shift in style accomplished under the aegis of conservative intentions, with a minimum of disruption of established institutions, just as the approach this new style is meant to displace was once absorbed, conservatively, by the elites of relatively backward countries. But the lesson remains the same. No matter how successful the conservative brand of industrial reconstruction, it requires institutional readjustments. Such readjustments disturb the established pattern of implicit accommodation among classes, communities, or segments of the work force and between these groups and national governments.

Consider an example. The erosion of traditional mass-production industry threatens the position of organized labor, entrenched in that sector of the economy. It therefore poses the issue of whether unionized labor is to continue to rely on unionization or whether labor is to be represented and empowered in an entirely different way. The conflicts invariably ignited over the forms and effects of such adjustments can be seized on and broadened by movements with more radically transformative aims. Or they can simply get out of hand and produce institutional results that none of the contenders foresaw.

The Second-Order Necessity of Formative Contexts: *The Logic of Group Interests*

A formative institutional and imaginative framework produces and supports a set of roles and ranks. The people who inhabit it settle down not just to particular social stations but to an order of stations, daily reaffirmed in the routines of practical collaboration and passionate attachment. These stations and routines cannot be reenacted without also being imagined. The resulting assumptions help close a social world in upon itself.

Some of the assumptions address the boundaries of collective identities. They tell each individual what groups he should consider himself a member of – what *we's* he should identify with – on the basis of his practical roles and life history. They conjure up a series of incomplete and partly contradictory but nevertheless connected and mutually reinforcing pictures of what the relevant *we's* in society are. They define and elucidate the relative authority and necessity of the many ways in which people are divided up into groups and in which groups are ranked.

Other assumptions deal with social possibilities. Such assumptions teach the individual what he may reasonably expect for himself and his family. They describe the live options among which society and therefore the groups within it must choose. They separate the practicable from the utopian, thereby also demarcating the social terrain on which – barring the unforeseeable or catastrophic – the individual knows he must move.

Yet other premises describe the content of group interests. These preconceptions define what each group's interests are and how they clash with the interests of other groups. Different groups need not – they generally do not – agree on how to define clashes of interest. But, once again, for this higher-order stability to be achieved, the disagreement must not be too radical or pervasive. It must not prevent different classes and communities from sharing the sense that they can fight for their interests without quarreling over the reconstruction of basic institutional arrangements or over the distinction between the practicable and the utopian.

The logic of group interests is the most ostentatious and operative part of these assumptions. Yet it depends for its semblance of clarity upon the other premises about social possibilities and collective identities. Only when such beliefs about possibilities and identities have begun to harden can the routinized push and shove about group interests take place.

Once assumptions about collective identities, social possibilities, and group interests have begun to form, they lend a new measure of necessity to the stabilized formative context. A world is constituted in which people know what their interests are because they take for granted all the things that make interest analysis possible. Each person becomes an informal version of the positivist social scientist, speaking the prose of a routinized social world while both invoking and concealing the institutional and imaginative framework he has come to accept unquestioningly.

An example drawn from the earlier historical narrative may help make the point. The narrative repeatedly used the pejorative label petty bourgeois to describe the single most significant set of alternatives to the institutional order that eventually became dominant in the North Atlantic countries. But this label has to be applied with many reservations. Old craft groups, new skilled workers, and small-scale proprietors, tradesmen, and farmers figured prominently in these movements. Yet the dominant self-images of these continuing insurgencies portrayed a resistance of the people against their bosses and rulers that overrode distinctions among corporate estates, classes, or segments of the work force. The subjective acceptance and construction of the gross divisions among petty bourgeois and workers did not fully take hold until the most serious early nineteenth century challenges to the ascendant institutional order had long been crushed. An additional wave of social agitation and institutional invention during the years immediately following World War I saw the development of both collective-bargaining and corporatist labor regimes. Only after these further agitations and inventions occurred did the distinction between the organized working class and the precarious or disenfranchised underclass become part of the way people understood the conflict of group interests.

An alternative approach to the hardening of group interests has to do with tangible compromises rather than intangible assumptions. It describes the development of a detailed set of explicit or implicit accommodations among social groups and of the habits and expectations, privileges and duties, that give each group a distinctive measure of access to the exercise and use of governmental power. The forging of deals among groups and between groups and governments may be no more than parallel refinements of the initial moment of context stabilization, when institutional arrangements cease to be challenged and rough compromises are worked out. But the involvement of the two refinements in each other makes a distinctive contribution to the second-order necessity of a system of group interests.

Public power becomes private privilege: governmental authority is actively enlisted in the defense of a particular allocation to groups of positions within and outside the social division of labor. At the same time, each group uses its overt or covert transactions with other groups – classes, communities, segments of the work force – to maintain a lien upon a parcel of governmental power. Neither the group bargains nor the correspondences between governmental access and factional privilege develop smoothly, free of reversals or ambiguities. Their effects cannot be counted on to harmonize. After a while, however, the two processes become entwined; each compensates for the fragility of the other. Jointly, they help shape both the concerns and the weapons of collective rivalry. The petty fears and ambitions they encourage help keep other aspirations at bay.

So long as the social peace fails to be absolute – and it never really is absolute – people continue to fight both about their perceived interests and about the institutional and imaginative framework within which those interests acquire meaning. Groups join together in ways not determined by the preexisting context, and pass from the normal struggle over interests within a structure to fighting over an aspect of the structure itself. This circumstance represents the prototype of collective mobilization.

The relation of governmental power to private interests always remains at least partly up for grabs. In all but stateless societies the disturbance of the relation between governmental power, on one side, and the system of social roles and ranks, on the other, is an indispensable part of context-transforming conflict. In collective mobilization the controversy over interests extends into conflict over the institutional and imaginative framework for interest accommodation. Similarly, in this framework-disturbing struggle over the state, the effort to harness governmental power to different factional objectives merges into a quarrel over the precise way in which governmental power should be connected or opposed to a differential ordering of group privileges.

When, at the initial moment of stabilization, context-transforming conflict is contained or interrupted, collective mobilization turns into collective contractualism: the practice of partly bargained-out and partly imposed deals between groups. These deals soon begin to seem only marginally revisable. The broadest contest over the state changes into the politics of privilege: the jockeying to move slightly up or down the ladder of access to governmental favor. The key moment of second-order stabilization takes place when the politics of privilege and the politics of collective contractualism begin to fit tightly together and thereby acquire a steadying influence that either would lack if deprived of support by the other.

Thus, for example, the position the unionized and relatively privileged sector of the labor force has come to occupy in contemporary Western democracies depends upon a long series of events that combined deals with governments and accommodations with other groups. These events include: the defeat of the more radical segments of the labor movement, sometimes by violent military action; the self-definition of the labor movement as a defense of factional interests rather than as a campaign for the general reorganization of society; the emergence of a precarious understanding between union leaders and the owners or managers of large-scale enterprise; the acceptance by organized workers of basic distinctions among job categories, each category defined by relative reward and status as well as by the content of work duties; the development of a negative solidarity against both the manager–owners and the excluded, unorganized, less advantaged segments of the work force; and active governmental involvement in the making of laws and policies that fostered the uneven organization of the working class and allowed the better organized segments of the labor force to inflate their organizational advantage by translating it into additional claims upon state power and public largesse. The key point is that from the content of the emergent institutional arrangements you could never have inferred the content of these deals and accommodations. They added something else: a new measure of naturalness and constraint.

Consider now how the hardening of a logic of group interests may generate opportunities for destabilization even as it helps stabilize a formative context. The basic reason why a logic of group interests creates transformative opportunities is that even the most routinized and closely defined assumptions about such interests suffers from persistent substantive and strategic ambiguities. These may be used to put recognized interests at odds with the established institutional and imaginative framework of social life.

The interests discriminated by such a set of assumptions are substantively ambiguous in the sense that they are never unified or detailed enough to provide the occupants of any given social station with a single uncontroversial view of their interests. Thus, similarly situated individuals and groups, or the same groups and individuals at different times, may act on distinct views of their interests. Together with the ordinary clash of interests, these uncertainties fill society with an endless petty agitation. Some conceptions of interest asserted in the midst of this Brownian motion of social life are harder to satisfy completely within the existing institutional and imaginative frameworks than others. Some therefore go farther than others in redefining current arrangements as constraints upon the fulfillment of recognized interests. There are, for example, any number of intermediate beliefs between the idea that industrial workers' sole interests are to secure their jobs, earn more money, and work less and the contrasting view that these and other interests can be fully assured only by a far-reaching reorganization of government and the economy.

Interests are ambiguous strategically as well as substantively. Alternative strategies, with very different implications for the wider social peace, promote even the most precisely defined group interest. Thus, for example, a group may pursue a narrowing tactic of preemptive security that treats all groups one rung down the ladder as rivals and adversaries. As a result, the prerogatives of the better placed group become hostage to the continued impoverishment of its immediate subordinates. Alternatively, the group may adopt a policy of broadening alliances that enlists immediate subordinates and potential rivals in the common struggle against the higher-ups. The broadening and narrowing strategies may be relatively more or less feasible and relatively harder or easier to reconcile with the received view of group interests. But there is no general reason to believe that one of the two strategies will always be more effective than the other.

Yet the strategies have radically different implications for the perpetuation of interest conflict within a social framework as opposed to conflict about the framework itself. The narrowing strategy encourages each group to cling to its established position. It thereby reinstates the received premises about identities, possibilities, and interests, and leaves unchallenged the institutional and imaginative framework on which these assumptions have been overlaid. But the broadening strategy leads back from collective contractualism to collective mobilization. What begins as a tactical alliance ends up as an enlarged collective identity. What starts as a purely instrumental effort ultimately broadens the sense of possibility. For as conflict widens and intensifies, the militants awake to the constraints that current arrangements of power and production impose upon the fulfillment of their objectives. They may even begin to experiment with small-scale versions of alternative arrangements, established by their own initiative or by the parcels of governmental power they and their allies manage to win. The fusion of collective identities and the enlargement of the sense of social possibility in turn change the preexisting definitions of group interests. The new definitions of interests encourage new conflicts and new challenges to the established context. Thus, the strategic ambiguities of interests clarify, extend, and dramatize the substantive ambiguities discussed earlier.

Consider now the promise of destabilization as it appears from the perspective of the alternative description of this source of second-order necessity: the description that emphasizes the hardened merger of governmentally supported privilege with collective contractualism. Implicit or explicit group deals and privileged liens upon governmental power are no more precise in form and unequivocal in implication than are the more intangible assumptions about identities, possibilities, and interests. They will be resisted at the margin, and what is marginally contentious can soon become more fundamentally controversial. The attempt to revise the deals and redesign the liens shades into the defiance of the formative context. If institutional changes occur, they in turn may shake up the bargains and the privileges.

The arrow of destabilization can also move in the reverse direction, from localized institutional change to fighting over the translation of institutional reform into particular deals. The readjustment of a formative context need not come from escalating conflict. It often results from more or less deliberate responses to an internal or foreign crisis. These changes from on top may be modest; but they are also common if only because formative contexts impose constraints upon the ability to seize practical productive opportunities. Thus, modest institutional reform, introduced reluctantly and belatedly to support a shift in the dominant organizational and technological style, shakes up the pattern of state-supported privilege and collective contractualism. It adds uncertainties and sparks conflicts that may be redirected to more transformative goals.

My earlier example of industrial reorganization also illustrates this form of reverse destabilization. The shift from mass production to a greater emphasis on the organizational and technological methods of vanguardist industry threatens the traditional form of unionization. It raises the question of how labor is to be empowered, whether by unionization or by alternative devices, and whether in ways that reaffirm the traditional contrasts between independent, skilled, organized workers, and underclass laborers, or in ways that override these contrasts. The new relations that need to be established among governments, business, and labor may ultimately be accomplished with a minimum of disturbance to established institutions and to the deals and privileges, the roles and hierarchies, these institutions support. But this triumph of conservative statecraft will nevertheless be conflict-ridden. The resulting disputes may serve as points of departure for wider struggles that can help change the basic forms of market economies and representative democracies.

The Second-Order Necessity of Formative Contexts: The Imagination of an Intelligible and Defensible Scheme of Human Association

Still another source of second-order necessity is the reinterpretation of a stabilized formative context as an articulate plan for human coexistence. Because the same theme is taken up again by the programmatic argument of Chapter 5, discussion of this additional link between stability and destabilization can be brief.

People come to define the restabilized arrangements and the rough compromises distinguishing the initial moment of context stabilization as a plan for coexistence in society. The plan exchanges the abstract and indeterminate idea of society for a particular model or set of models of human association. It establishes what relations among individuals can and should be like in different areas of social life.

The imaginative scheme bestows moral authority on a corrected or idealized version of current arrangements, justifying the strong

in the enjoyment of power and privilege and excusing the weak from
the continuation of struggle. But its contribution to the intelligibility
of a pacified social order is even more basic than its support for the
moral authority of this order. The imaginative scheme does not
merely tell the occupants of different social stations what to expect
from one another. It also provides them with an elementary grammar
of social action. It enables them to participate in complicated interdependencies, practices, and institutions without having to spell out
all the assumptions about the ways people are expected to act, and
the meanings that actions carry, in a particular domain of social
existence. The imaginative plan of social life thereby keeps people
from having to deal with one another as contract partners who share
little common experience or allegiance and therefore try to regulate
their dealings with as much prospective detail as possible. To make
a social world in this way both authoritative and intelligible is part
of what is implied in giving up the fight over the further reconstruction of a formative context.

The acceptance of this intelligibility and authority comes easily.
For one thing, the disturbance that precedes the initial moment of
stabilization is usually localized. Many practices and preconceptions
remain unchallenged. Rather than inventing a new normative practice
or even an entirely new imaginative scheme, people need only continue an old practice and revise an old scheme. For another thing,
the reigning view of the realistic and desirable forms of human association does not merely redescribe brutal impositions and accidental
compromises. It promises to hold up an improved standard of what
things should be like, a standard that can be used to criticize as well
as to justify, to soften as well as to strengthen. Though the inhabitants
of a stabilized social world have surrendered, even their surrender is
halfhearted. Onto the revised arrangements and beliefs that emerge
from the new settlement they project all their vague, confused longings for happiness and empowerment. The authoritative image of
civilization into which the truce lines and trophies of conflict have
been recast becomes the vehicle for aspirations left unexamined, undeveloped, and unfulfilled.

The imaginative plan may take the form of a single, exemplary
model of human association, meant to be realized with suitable adjustments throughout all areas of social practice. We usually find
such a unitary, recurrent standard of sociability accepted in societies
with very entrenched frameworks and in cultures that enshrine highly
restrictive assumptions about the possible forms of personal and social experience. The characteristic content of this one-model scheme
is the patron–client ideal that seeks to combine, in the same relations,
practical exchange, communal loyalty, and outright subjugation.

In societies less submissive to the constraints of false necessity the dominant ways of imagining the possible and desirable forms of human association characteristically assign different models of human coexistence to distinct realms of social practice. Thus, in the late twentieth century North Atlantic countries whose formative contexts I have earlier studied, people thought of practical exchange, communal loyalties, and nonreciprocal power as mutually repellent forms of experience. They credited an ideal of private community, meant to be realized in the life of family and friendship; an ideal of democratic participation and accountability, addressed to the organization of government and the exercise of citizenship; and an amalgam of voluntary contract and impersonal technical hierarchy or coordination, suited to the practical world of work and exchange. Moreover, they implicitly identified each of these ideals with particular practices and institutions. Thus, people meant by democracy not only the ill-defined aspirations that their slogans and speculative theories proclaimed but a historically unique way of organizing governments and partisan conflict.

The relation of legal doctrine to beliefs about the possible and desirable forms of human association is instructive. In societies less cracked open to politics legal doctrine can openly refer to a background scheme of models of human association, which are alleged to be inscribed in the permanent requirements of human nature and social order when they are not also mandated by divine authority. But in societies that have moved farther toward disentrenchment and antinaturalistic skepticism, such a style of legal doctrine becomes unacceptable. For the explicit invocation of such overarching standards of possible and desirable human association is now feared to embroil the legal analyst in the open-ended controversies of the ideologue or the propagandist. It therefore threatens to reopen the conflict over the basic terms of social life. Under these circumstances, legal analysis can neither avow nor avoid relying upon such assumptions about the possible and desirable forms of human association. For lawyers cannot relinquish such assumptions without either presenting the law as merely an expression of interest-group or class conflict or attempting to keep legal reasoning very close to narrow precedent and narrow construction. Those who would use legal doctrine to give the social order the gloss of a higher-order rationality now face a more formidable obstacle.*

The imaginative scheme of models of possible and desirable association also lives, in a looser and messier form, in popular consciousness. The classes and communities that make up society give their own distinctive twists to the dominant vision of possible and

---

* See *The Critical Legal Studies Movement*, Harvard University Press, Cambridge, 1986.

desirable human association. Much in their professed ideas or implicit assumptions about what relations among people should be like in different realms of social existence may be incompatible with the beliefs of other groups or with the legal, moral, and partisan discourse of the wealthy and the powerful. But unless the country is ruled by a conquest elite alien to the native inhabitants, or unless insulated and antagonistic groups coexist with an imposed structure, we can expect to find a more subtle and contradictory imaginative scheme – or rather a series of overlapping and analogous schemes. The difference between the informal vision of authoritative models of human coexistence and the vision presupposed by elite discourses such as legal doctrine usually resembles the relation of a natural language to an impoverished computer language. Yet the substantive themes of the richer language will carry over, truncated and biased, into the poorer counterpart.

Whether the imaginative scheme is unitary or pluralistic and whether it takes its more elitist and systematic or more popular and contradictory forms, it exercises a retrospective stabilizing influence upon a social order. Any marked deviation by an individual from social norms begins to appear selfish and antisocial whatever its actual motives. Any conflict that defies the scheme seems to threaten civilization itself, if not in the large then in the small, in the detailed pieties by which people evaluate one another and in the implicit assumptions that sustain trust and permit communication.

But, like its counterparts, such a stabilizing force generates destabilizing opportunities. To show how these opportunities arise, take an imaginative ordering of social life at its clearest and most coherent, as it can be found in the elite discourses of legal doctrine or speculative moral and programmatic controversy. Ideal images of human association can always be plausibly interpreted in different ways. These ambiguities remain concealed and contained so long as each such image is represented by distinctive practices or institutions in well-defined areas of social life. The amalgam of ideal understandings, representative practices, and domains of application supports the sense of assurance.

But there is always at least a residual uncertainty about the practical forms that properly represent a model of association and the exact domain of social practice in which it can realistically and suitably be applied. Moreover, different classes, communities, and movements of opinion believe themselves to have an interest in seeing these marginal uncertainties resolved in some ways rather than others. Thus, people quarrel about the resolution of the ambiguities. They quarrel by the crude and open methods of factional or class rivalry and in the refined, secluded forms of legal and philosophical controversy.

This small-time bickering can escalate, either because it simply gets out of hand or because a transformative movement deliberately exploits and aggravates it. The result is to disturb the apparent fit among the authoritative images of coexistence, their practical representations, and their areas of application. Such disturbances force people to choose among different interpretations of the antecedent, largely implicit ideals of human association. Some interpretations fit with the current institutional order and reaffirm the dominant models of human coexistence; but others can inspire challenges to the institutional order and begin to unravel the imaginative scheme. For the meanings we confer on these received and enacted conceptions of sociability are never fully exhausted by the practices and institutions that stand for them in particular compartments of social life. Beliefs about how people ought to deal with one another in particular areas of society are more than readily applicable dogmas. They also serve as bearers of ill-defined aspirations for empowerment and mutual acceptance. They are therefore instruments of a mental reservation by which people who seem to have surrendered unreservedly to a particular institutional and imaginative framework continue to nurture a measure of secret independence and unfulfilled yearning. Two analytically distinct but ordinarily overlapping processes can play out this potential ambivalence in the relation of a scheme of authoritative models of association to a stabilized formative context.

First, there are horizontal conflicts. Uncertainty and disagreements always persist about the exact range of social practice to which different models of human coexistence should apply. The great amount of practical and imaginative material resisting assimilation to the formative context adds to the confusion. The resulting border disputes – conflicts over where to draw the line between different ideals and between the domains of social life to which they apply – become topics of speculative moral and ideological debates or of factional conflicts and social experiments. Such border disputes produce a constant pushing and shoving of familiar ideals onto slightly unfamiliar social territory. As such projections or displacements multiply, people begin to disagree about the practical forms that a given image of human association should assume when enacted in an area of social practice from which it has hitherto been excluded. This disagreement exposes the hidden ambiguities of the traditional models and the multiplicity of framework-preserving and framework-transforming uses to which they may be put.

Consider, for example, the implications of attempting to extend the democratic ideal into industrial organization. Whatever democracy may mean in this setting it cannot mean carrying on with the traditional forms of the tripartite state or with the current mechanisms of democratic representation and accountability. If industrial democracy is interpreted to mean a limited level of worker participation in business decisions it may be accommodated without major disturbance to the established institutional and imaginative framework. Suppose, however, it is understood to require a shift in the basic form of capital allocation and of control over investment decisions. It will then also shake up the imaginative vision that contrasts an area reserved for democratic principles with a realm governed by voluntary contract and technical hierarchy. This imaginative disturbance may radiate outward, challenging every part of the dominant vision of social proprieties and possibilities.

There are vertical as well as horizontal conflicts. Even within the core area of social practice traditionally assigned to a particular model of human association, discrepancies and doubts will arise about its appropriate practical form. The marginal conflicts that seize on these disharmonies may be further aggravated by the sense that all the established practical realizations of the ideal fail to do it justice, that they betray its promise. There is always an indefinite penumbra of aspiration that intimates more – more by way of empowerment or solidarity – than can be found in public dogma and established practice. Such variations and tensions feed conflict. And the conflict once again reveals the ambiguities of the received models of sociability and demonstrates their ambivalent relation to the institutional arrangements they ordinarily help justify.

Thus, in the contemporary industrial democracies the blend of technical hierarchy and voluntary contract takes different forms in sectors of the economy that either strengthen or soften the contrast between task-defining and task-executing activities. Widely recognized moral assumptions identify personal subjugation as the exemplary social evil. Neither individual and collective contract nor alleged technical necessity suffice to lift the experienced burden of subjugation from the experience of work in the areas of the economy that most starkly contrast task definers and task executors. Workers continue to suffer strongly felt experiences of powerlessness and humiliation. The vanguard sectors of the economy offer a visible though limited example of an alternative style of work organization. Radical critics have argued that this alternative can be extended and generalized through much of the economy. But extension and generalization cannot ultimately succeed without a series of cumulative changes in the organization of power and production. Nor, once realized, can they be reconciled with ruling beliefs about the proper contrast between the domain of representative democracy and the realm of contract and technical hierarchy.

The Escalation of Conflict: The Unavailability of Necessary and Sufficient Conditions

The main theme of the preceding discussion has been the tightness of the link between stabilization and destabilization, the transformative opportunities generated by the very forces that impart a retrospective, second-order necessity to a stabilized context. An endless series of petty quarrels, a permanent Brownian motion, keep even the most pacified social world in contained but irrepressible agitation. The deep-structure social theorist dismisses these low-level disturbances as trivial, identifying in them either a random and unproductive strife or a confirmation of the lawlike routines of an established social order. He sees a basic discontinuity between these controversies and the conflicts that accompany the replacement of one order by another. The positivist social scientist, on the contrary, exalts this constant bickering as the true stuff of social life: the exercise of problem solving and interest accommodation that plays so large a role in his understanding of society. But because he systematically disregards or avoids the distinction between routines and frameworks and the influence of frameworks and framework revision on the problems that chiefly concern him, he cannot see the Brownian motion for what it is. He cannot recognize the nature and extent of its transformative promise or achieve a comprehensive and unified view of its many forms.

The small-scale, contained fighting engendered by each form of second-order necessity may escalate at any time. The subjective sign of escalation is the growing intensity of the fighting. The more tangible, external sign is the widening scope of the conflict: both by the involvement of more groups in the struggle and by the concern with an ever broader range of issues. The special meaning of escalation, however, is the step-by-step passage from context-preserving to context-transforming conflicts. The quarrels about practical adjustments, collective identities, and moral ideals that take the framework for granted pass into struggles that bring the framework into question.

The escalation may be the work of a movement that sees its opportunity in the extension of petty bickering. Or it may be the involuntary consequence of conflicts getting out of hand. In this event, the expanded struggle shows its transformative significance only retrospectively. Much more often, foresight and accident combine to cause escalation.

A critic may object that we have explained little until we have established the necessary and sufficient conditions for escalation. But a corollary of one major thesis of this book is that we cannot draw up such a list of necessary and sufficient conditions. The problem does not result merely from a limited and remediable defect in our knowledge, as if we could approach the desired outcome by thinking a little harder or discovering a little more. The facts about social reality and social change condemn this search to disappointment. To believe in the existence of such a list, or in the possibility of gradually revealing it, we have to believe in something that at least resembles deep-structure social theory. We have to believe that context change, and therefore also context selection, are governed by lawlike constraints or developmental tendencies. (The polemic against the style of explanation by necessary and sufficient conditions continues, in different form, later in this account of society making.)

Instead of necessary and sufficient conditions, the view presented here recognizes that some circumstances regularly encourage escalation while others discourage it. Prominent among the escalation-favoring circumstances are middle-level crises, such as those provoked by the need to reform basic institutional arrangements in response to military and economic rivalry from abroad or to shifts in the relative size and wealth of different sectors of the population. A skillful and lucky transformative practice, however, may cause escalation to take place even in the absence of such favoring conditions. Conversely, the most favorable opportunity may be squandered. Most importantly, the antecedent institutions and preconceptions and the schemes of social division and hierarchy they support never predetermine the outcome of escalating conflict, any more than they predetermine its occurrence or scope. The underdetermined choice of trajectories by different groups and governments and the relative insight or illusion, skill or ineptitude, with which people pursue these chosen trajectories help shape the final result. (The programmatic argument of Chapter 5 considers the favoring and disfavoring circumstances of escalation. This consideration establishes one of many links between the explanatory and programmatic ideas of *False Necessity*.)

Convinced determinists may resist this defense of the refusal to describe the necessary and sufficient conditions for the extension of conflict and the transformative use of the Brownian motion. They may argue that when we look more closely we always find causes that explain the occurrence, scope, and outcome of escalation, causes that range from the momentary situation of a society to the details of individual biography. They may even insist that all these causes connect, at least from the idealized standpoint of a Laplacean mind. Nothing in this or any other part of the explanatory argument of *False Necessity* depends on the refutation of such determinists. It is unnecessary to take a position with respect to their claims. The narrower aim of the approach to context change taken here is to free social explanation from the assumptions of both deep-structure analysis and conventional social science: to respect the distinction between structure and routine while denying that the identity, actualization, or succession of formative contexts is governed by higher-order laws or by deep-seated economic, psychological, and organizational constraints.

Of course, this view of context change would lose much of its authority if our subjective experience of reconstructive freedom were illusory (though remember that there is always the habitual hedge of the speculative monist, who holds that phenomenal distinctions are only *ultimately* illusory). But it is no part of this argument to deal with the metaphysical conundrums of free will and determinism and to show in precisely what sense the experience of freedom harmonizes with the practice of causal explanation. We already do something to vindicate our reconstructive powers when we loosen the link between our interest in the generality of our social explanations and the habit of portraying ourselves as the passive objects of social worlds. We do even better when we are able to show that such worlds differ radically in the constraints they impose upon their own remaking.

The Brownian motion of social life – the emergence of destabilizing opportunity out of stabilizing methods – provides the occasion for influences that may shape long-term context change. These influences, working in concert or in opposition, account for a remarkable possibility. Contexts may change in quality as well as content. They vary in the force with which they imprison the people who move within them. The discussion now turns to the sources of possible long-term, directional change.

NEGATIVE CAPABILITY

The Core Idea

The very devices that stabilize formative contexts endlessly produce the occasions and instruments of destabilization. The escalation of framework-preserving routines into framework-transforming conflicts creates an opportunity for two great influences upon context making. These influences differ from the mechanisms of stability and destabilization just discussed in that they account for the *possibility* of cumulative context change in a certain direction, not just for the precariousness of every established order. In particular, they give us the prospect of changing over time the quality as well as the content of our formative institutional and imaginative structures: the relation of these structures to our structure-revising capabilities. These long-term influences upon context change share with the mechanisms of stability and destabilization the power to present the transformative will with opportunities as much as with constraints. They certify that no ultimate incompatibility holds between the radical project and the nature of social reality.

Consider what would happen if such long-term influences did not exist and if we were left with only the mechanisms of stability and destabilization and with an open list of circumstances that either favor or discourage the escalation of framework-preserving conflict. We would have trouble explaining how or why the component elements of each formative context stick together and reinforce one another. For our ideas about the internal constitution of social orders are always just the reverse side of our beliefs about how such orders change. We might even find it hard to resist the slide into positivist social science, with its disregard for the significance of the distinction between framework and routine and its picture of social life as a series of exercises in interest accommodation and problem solving.

If we nevertheless managed to rescue the distinction between the forming structure and the formed routines, we would have no basis for believing in selective constraints upon the replacement or recombination of the elements composing a formative context. Thus, we might be drawn to a truncated version of deep-structure social theory, seeing the institutional and imaginative frameworks of social life as indivisible but ultimately arbitrary – there, but there for no good reason. If in turn we succeeded in avoiding this conclusion we would still have no reason to hope to become more fully the masters of the social orders that we construct. History would be a procession of conditional social worlds: each a law unto itself, each conditional in the same sense as the others. The radical project would therefore be based upon an illusion, at least if it is true that the disengagement of social life from structures of dependence and domination requires that no major aspect of social organization remain shielded against challenge and conflict.

This section is devoted to the most controversial of the two long-run influences upon context change, which is also the influence most directly relevant to the attempt to change the relation between freedom and structure. Formative contexts and the extended sets of arrangements and preconceptions that constitute them vary with respect to the quality I called disentrenchment, denaturalization, or emancipation from false necessity. This quality has two aspects; that these aspects are connected is an empirical claim.

One aspect of disentrenchment is the degree to which a formative context can be challenged in the midst of ordinary social life. A structure is entrenched or naturalized to the extent that it prevents such challenge, and it is disentrenched or denaturalized insofar as it facilitates the challenge. On an equivalent definition, disentrenchment implies a shortening of the distance to traverse before our context-preserving activities can become context-transforming activities. It is the relative facility with which we can interrupt the oscillation between the narcoleptic routines and the revolutionary interludes of history and achieve conscious mastery in the midst of civic peace. Moreover, a more disentrenched structure designs this greater opportunity for revision into the very activities on which its reproduction depends.

The other aspect of disentrenchment is the relative disengagement of our practical and passionate dealings from a preexisting structure of roles and hierarchies. In this sense, disentrenchment is the diminishment of the influence that the social station of the individual – of the place he occupies in the contrast of categories, classes, communities, and genders – exercises over his life chances and experiences. It is the lifting of the grid of social division and ranking from our practical and passionate relations to one another.

The connection between the two sides of denaturalization is far from self-evident. There are no scripts for particular social roles and ranks until the institutional and imaginative assumptions that define a particular version of social life become secure. Such assumptions cannot in turn become secure unless they provide for their own relative immunity to attack. They do so by forming routines – of economic exchange, factional conflict, and normative controversy – that take established institutions and preconceptions for granted. Earlier discussion has emphasized that the contrast between stabilizing and destabilizing activities can never be absolute. The concept of disentrenchment implies that the contrast is variable as well as relative.

These clarifications help introduce the main thesis of this part of the view of context making. Disentrenchment of formative contexts provides societies with a range of material and intangible advantages, all the way from the encouragement of the development of productive capabilities to the exercise of a more conscious mastery over social circumstance. In fact, all the varieties of individual and collective empowerment seem to be connected in one way or another with the mastery the concept of disentrenchment or denaturalization describes. I call these varieties of empowerment "negative capability" when considering them in relation to the context change that makes them possible. Thus, we may use the poet's turn of phrase to label the empowerment that arises from the denial of whatever in our contexts delivers us over to a fixed scheme of division and hierarchy and to an enforced choice between routine and rebellion.

It should already be clear from the definition of disentrenchment that the route to negative capability is not a leap into anarchy, permanent flux, or mere indefinition. The institutional and imaginative frameworks that strengthen our negative capability are no less particular and no less capable of being described than frameworks relatively lower on the scale of disentrenchment. Thus, for example, the actual institutions and guiding doctrines of the liberal bourgeois democracies are less entrenched and more favorable to negative capability than the arrangements and dogmas of the European absolutist monarchies they succeeded. The hypothetical institutions and doctrines of the empowered democracy described by the later programmatic arguments of this book are in turn just as distinctive as the versions of representative democracy and market economy they are intended to replace.

To be sure, the less entrenched structures are by definition more open to revision in the midst of ordinary social life. But they are not therefore more unstable, except in the very special sense in which a circumstance of frequent, partial adjustments can be said to be more unstable than a situation of rigid structures, periodically disrupted by sudden, major transformations. Rigidity is not stability, nor does the increased transparency and revisability of our practices mean we will want constantly to revise them. The liberal bourgeois democracies have been no less stable – though stable in a different sense – than the absolutist monarchies before them. Moreover, because disentrenchment involves a weakening of the mechanisms of dependence and domination, ordinary working men and women have been more rather than less secure in these democracies.

The attractions of negative capability account for the possibility of a cumulative movement toward greater disentrenchment. In some instances this movement may result from a more or less deliberate striving for the advantages of denaturalization. In other instances the movement may be explained by a social counterpart to Darwinian natural selection: societies achieving the advantages of greater disentrenchment are that much more likely to survive in the economic and ideological struggle with their rivals, and their styles of organization and vision are therefore also that much more likely to proliferate. But by far the most common way in which the advantages of disentrenchment account for the emergence and persistence of more denaturalized formative contexts does not fit into either the intentionalist or the Darwinian mold. This most common and distinctive form of agency requires special analysis.

The idea of negative capability as an influence represents a frankly functionalist or ideological element in the theory of context making. The appearance and propagation of less entrenched institutional and imaginative orders is explained by the consequences they may produce – the development of negative capability. But qualifications, soon to be discussed, diminish the functionalist character of this idea. For one thing, countervailing forces may override the attractions of negative capability. The most important of these is the ability of coercive surplus extraction, based on relatively more entrenched orders and on the hierarchies they sustain, to serve as a rival basis – and in certain circumstances even a stronger basis – for the development of productive or destructive capabilities. Moreover, the forms of empowerment summarized under the heading "negative capability" can advance through alternative packages of institutional arrangements. Some alternatives jeopardize other noneconomic varieties of empowerment. The most important consequence of such qualifications is that every advance toward greater negative capability is precarious and reversible, not just susceptible to being deflected into a minor and temporary epicycle.

The influence of negative capability operates on the institutional and imaginative materials generated by particular historical sequences of context making. These sequences in turn constrain only loosely and fitfully our capacities of resistance and invention. Thus, there is no limited list of institutional systems that consitute the necessary vehicles of any given level of negative capability. To speak of an advance in negative capability is not to specify the particular institutional and imaginative forms the advance must take. Nor does a cumulative movement toward less naturalistic orders imply any preestablished evolutionary sequence of institutional systems and social dogmas awaiting a chance to advance to the next step.

When you add up all these qualifications, the result is not to take back the thesis about negative capability but, rather, to detach the thesis from the prejudices of evolutionary, deep-structure social analysis. What emerges is the conception of a possible progression, which presents the radical project with its chance. The ideas that make sense of the notion of a possible move toward more revisable and hierarchy-subverting structures run together with the ideas that justify a commitment to the radical project. For the thesis of negative capability has a prominent role in a view of the conditions of human empowerment and of the means by which we may limit more successfully the part played by dependence and depersonalization in our dealings with one another.

From the vantage point of this preliminary statement, look back once again to the polemical genealogy in the first part of this chapter. Emerging economic, legal, and governmental institutions were all less naturalistic than the arrangements they replaced. The advantages they made available may help explain their appearance and success. Further analysis must specify the mechanisms by which these advantageous consequences helped bring more denaturalized contexts into being.

The institutional and imaginative materials with which such transformations worked were unique to European history. But the solutions developed out of such materials proved exemplary. The dominant institutional and imaginative orders of the world-conquering Western powers appeared as the setting for a quantum leap in the development of economic and military capabilities. They also provided a basis for a relatively greater emancipation of communal life and individual self-expression from preexisting roles and hierarchies. No wonder that conquest often proved unnecessary to spread European arrangements. Reforming elites anxious to secure similar benefits for themselves and their countries accomplished what conquerors did not. It took time to discover that such benefits could be given institutional and imaginative foundations radically different from the formative contexts of the pioneering Western countries. But the classic European social theorists wrote at a time when these alternative possibilities had not yet become apparent. They were therefore tempted to misunderstand the triumphant European settlements as the necessary form of a stage in world history.

Remember also that these prevalent European solutions were far from secure or self-evident within the European world itself. Throughout the history of their development they had to accommodate to rival institutional ideas. In fact, the most significant rival – the alternative whose economic aspect I have been calling petty commodity production – might well have gone farther than the now dominant economic and governmental arrangements in promoting negative capability. But to make their cause practicable, the advocates of the petty bourgeois alternative would have had to find new ways to organize representative democracies and market economies.

From this initial exposition it should already be clear that the thesis about negative capability requires two key analytical refinements. The first is to distinguish the varieties of empowerment the idea of negative capability encompasses and to show how each aspect of empowerment depends on the invention of more disentrenched, revisable institutions. The second refinement is to solve the problem of agency. We must describe how the ability of certain arrangements to encourage an advance in negative capability helps cause their emergence and persistence. We need to understand the mechanisms by which the functional consequence or advantage becomes an explanatory cause.

The Practical Advantages of Disentrenchment

The most tangible instance of negative capability is the development of the productive and destructive powers of society. The idea of a connection between institutional disentrenchment and practical empowerment merely appropriates and generalizes a familiar belief about requirements of practical progress. The narrower and relatively precise version of this idea is the thesis that economic rationality or efficiency requires the freedom to combine and substitute to best advantage the factors of production. The relatively broader and vaguer form of the notion is the idea that maximum flexibility serves practical success.

Our practical activities are opportunistic. They require the constant substitution of resources and the revision of technical and organizational means in the light of changing circumstances. To be sure, they also demand a framework of shared understandings and practices so that not everything has to be constantly reinvented or fought over. But to ensure worldly success we must be able to revise this framework in the light of emergent practical opportunities. We must not allow it to predetermine the way we combine with one another and with machines in our joint practical endeavors. More specifically, the keynote of practical reason and of rationalized collective labor is the continuous interplay between the definition of ends and the choice of means, the setting of tasks and the operational activities designed to carry them out. The organization of human labor and its coordination with the material and technical resources at its disposal should become a visible image of practical reason. Conversely, the idea of practical reason translates a view of flexible, self-correcting teamwork into a conception of individual mental activity. In order to make our practical collaborative ventures a more faithful image of practical reason, we must weaken the influence of preestablished social roles and hierarchies upon the relations among co-workers. We must not allow fixed rules to predetermine the ways in which the holders of particular jobs, or the members of particular communities or ranks, may deal with one another. We must crack the routines of practical life open to the recombinational activity of practical reason. The same changes that enable a formative institutional and imaginative context to loosen the hold of social roles and hierarchies also diminish the contrast between context-preserving routine and context-transforming conflict.

Consider from another angle the link between disentrenchment and the development of practical productive and destructive capabilities. The organizational style of economic or military teams limits the full development and exploitation of a technological capability. The broader institutional setting of governments and economies in turn constrains the organization of the work group. The work team cannot be flexible unless its internal life comes partly out from under the influence of a scheme of social stations. Practical empowerment requires institutions and preconceptions that permanently weaken social divisions and diminish the arbitrary, recalcitrant just-thereness of our social orders.

Here is a typical, narrowly focused example. The decades preceding the French Revolution saw the development of lighter and more accurate artillery pieces. The armies of revolutionary France were able to take the fullest advantage of these new weapons by innovating in battle tactics and troop deployment. The dense military formations then in use favored rigid forward marching procedures. Such units could not deploy on the field with the flexibility needed to take maximum advantage of potential combinations of infantry and light artillery. At the same time traditional military formations offered an easy target for the more accurate guns, manned by more flexible adversaries.

The prerevolutionary social situation influenced the preferred tactics and deployments of the prerevolutionary armies. In an army like the German one, of sullen serfs and near serfs, pressed into dynastic wars whose aims they did not share or even understand and lacking nationalist ardor, officers feared their men would break and run away as the moment of battle approached. Often, a row of special soldiers with stretched bayonets had to walk at the back of each unit, literally propping forward the reluctant warriors. The armies of revolutionary France found it relatively easy to adopt thinner formations and more supple tactical procedures. They had better reason to count on the discretion and loyalty of soldiers who were called to defend a national and popular revolution beleaguered by absolutist monarchies.

Thus, successful use of the new technological opportunity required a new organizational style. The institutional and spiritual inventions on which the style depended convinced the soldiery that the army belonged to the nation and that the nation did not just belong to privileged elites. Multiply this particular example many times over, to cover other aspects of military technology, organization, and strategy, and you can begin to see that the armies of revolutionary and Napoleonic France had at least one major advantage in their wars with their Continental adversaries.

The story does not end here. The enemies of France could not exploit the new technological and tactical opportunities presented by such developments as the improved artillery pieces without changing the institutional form of the state and the relation of the ruling and possessing elites to the working people. But France's rivals did not need to change the ancien régime as much or as violently as the French revolutionists had set out to do. They required only the measure of popular reform needed to justify a sense of national community (even right-wing nationalism had to make concessions to egalitarianism) and to enlarge the influence of merit-based recruitment and promotion in military and governmental organization. In the age of Stein and Hardenberg, the Prussian military reformers demonstrated what successful conservative reformers rediscover: that they can have their cake and eat it too. They can reconcile the measure of institutional disentrenchment needed to take advantage of current technological and organizational opportunities with a suitable version of the present plan of social division and hierarchy. The jeopardized elites fail when they feel compelled to choose between trying to reproduce a foreign institutional example and rejecting reform outright, for fear it may inevitably shake the established social order to the ground. Thus, for example, the Mamluk state in Egypt lost its ability to resist Ottoman attack when it refused to shift its military emphasis from cavalry to armed infantry. As an alien, corporately organized ruling class, the Mamluks (or, rather, the Mamluk leaders) felt unable to disengage their apparatus of rule and their collective identity from a cavalry-based military organization.

Some may object that the example of the light artillery pieces lacks broader significance. Other productive or destructive faculties might not make any demands on the broader institutional and social environment. Such powers might even require more rigidity and hierarchy rather than more flexibility and equality. The thesis of negative capability in the practical domain does indeed presuppose a belief in the possible preeminence of cumulative disentrenchment as an enabling social condition of the development of practical capabilities. A defensible version of the thesis of negative capability must recognize that the coercive extraction of resources and manpower, supported by more entrenched contexts and more rigid roles and hierarchies, can provide an alternative basis for the development of productive or destructive forces. The question is whether this entrenchment-based alternative can be given its due weight within a theory that nevertheless continues to see in cumulative disentrenchment at least a possible axis of practical progress.

Institutional arrangements that help reproduce rigid roles and hierarchies can certainly serve as a basis for coercive surplus extraction. Hierarchical duties, enforced and sanctified by challenge-resistant institutions and arrangements, encourage the near automatic transfer of material and manpower resources to limited elites. This device has the formidable practical advantage of making the confiscation of resources appear to be the unavoidable implication of a moral or natural order rather than a result of will and conflict. After all, the human sense of institutional entrenchment is to make the order of social life appear more like a natural fact than like a political artifact. In the relatively more entrenched order the concentration of claims to capital and labor is that much more likely to be taken for granted and that much less likely to be disturbed by threats, deals, and challenges. But the cost is to limit the capacity of experimenting with combinations of resources, machines, and labor and with alternative forms of exchange and production.

Surely in certain historical situations the practical advantages of disentrenchment fall below the practical benefits of coercive surplus extraction. But what are these situations? They seem to be ones in which the creation of a surplus of labor and capital over current consumption remains the overriding practical problem of society, towering over the problems of technological innovation and organizational flexibility.

You may be tempted to say that such is precisely the condition of all societies, at least until they achieve prodigious wealth and come close to eliminating economic scarcity. But in fact it seems to be the circumstance only of very poor countries – of countries poorer than the more prosperous agrarian-bureaucratic empires of world history or than early modern European nations before the onset of the industrial revolution. Economists and historians have repeatedly shown how hard it is to explain sudden surges in productive output and productivity – such as the series of events we call the industrial revolution – by reference to differences in social-savings rates. Often, both the general rate of saving and the amount of surplus coercively appropriated by economic or governmental elites seem to have been even higher in economically stagnant societies than in countries making a quantum leap in their productive capabilities. The main point about nineteenth-century England in contrast to, say, Ch'ing China, is not that the English saved or skimmed off more than the Chinese but that they used resources, performed activities, ran organizations, and recombined factors of production in different ways. The need for surplus extraction does not disappear but becomes subsidiary to the manner of use.

We have an additonal reason to think that the practical advantages of entrenchment are more limited than they may at first appear. Not all coercive surplus extraction depends upon rigid social roles and hierarchies, nor is the route to emancipation from false necessity always uncoercive. The opening of social life to practical experimentation may occur through consensual, decentralized, and participatory methods or through centralized command and coercion. The institutions that make this opening possible may advance toward a radical democracy that destroys privileged holds upon the resources for society making. But such institutions may also move toward a mobilizational dictatorship that relentlessly subjects social life to plans imposed by a central authority, willing and able to recombine people and resources. From the narrow standpoint of encouraging the development of practical capabilities, the risk of the consensual path is that decentralized, participatory claims will harden into a system of vested rights that narrows the area of social life open to practical innovation. From the same limited perspective the risk of the dictatorial route is that the willingness to exploit practical productive opportunities will be sacrificed to the power interests of the central authorities.

A mobilizational despotism should not be mistaken for an entrenched order of division and hierarchy, although each of the two may serve as a basis for the development of practical capabilities and although many societies in the age of mass politics have regularly combined aspects of both. The mobilizational dictatorship reaches for negative capability through coercive means. It therefore attempts to crush all intermediate corporate bodies, all independently organized social ranks, communities, and local governments. Its distinctive economic ambition is not merely to extract a surplus but to recombine and reorganize and to keep reorganizing and recombining. Long ago social theorists such as Tocqueville understood that a new breed of democracies and despotisms shared both a hostility to stable orders of social division and hierarchy and a willingness to treat social relations as subjects for practical experiment. Modern planning dictatorships characteristically engage in a quest for greater negative capability. Forced recombination rather than naturalistic entrenchment is their thing. Once we understand their distinctiveness the historical role of the search for practical progress through entrenchment begins to look much more limited.

Compare the thesis of negative capability to the Marxist thesis about class society and the development of the productive forces. The sequence of modes of production depicted by Marxism portrays all historical societies as driven forward by the logic of coercive surplus extraction based upon class hierarchies and upon the institutionally defined relations of production that such hierarchies require. Primitive communism is egalitarian. But under primitive communism people remain enslaved to both material scarcity and unreflective tradition. Mankind must undergo the immense, painful detour of class society and class conflict before it can attain through communism a higher because freer form of the equality it possessed under primitive communism.

Yet the evolutionary scheme of historical materialism includes a significant minor theme that we can reinterpret as a special case of the thesis of negative capability. The sequence of modes of production is also a series of steps toward the assertion of the free-floating, unitary, universal quality of labor. The divisions and hierarchies of class society mask and constrain this quality. Thus, though capitalism may aggravate many aspects of class oppression and working-class misery, it also reveals more clearly than its predecessor modes of production the interchangeable character of all human labor power. The despotism of capital may take charge of the modern factory. But this despotism tears down barriers to the free recombination of men and machines. At the same time the primacy of exchange values over use values in the sphere of circulation, combined with the relentless treatment of labor as a commodity, emphasizes the convertibility of all forms of productive activity into all other forms.

In Marx's writings these ideas, so close to the thesis of negative capability, remain imprisoned within an evolutionary variant of deep-structure social theory. Moreover, Marx fails to draw the distinction between coercive surplus extraction, based upon entrenched hierarchies, and experimental recombination, premised on institutional disentrenchment. The absence of any counterpart to this distinction is, to use the language of his followers, no accident. For historical materialism sacrifices the insight into negative capability to the belief that the emergence of communism represents the single decisive and definitive turn from necessity to freedom.

A Comparative Historical Perspective on the Thesis of Negative Capability

Consider how this discussion of the development of the economic aspects of negative capability relates to the character of the institutional arrangements whose emergence the earlier schematic narrative studied. The new forms of agrarian and industrial organization exhibited aspects of coercive surplus extraction. The legal rights and governmental institutions sustaining them made possible a basic continuity of the elites. In their historical setting, the engrossment of leaseholds and the factory system represented advances in the degree of command over large pools of land, capital, and labor that could be exercised by large-scale enterprises.

However, once you locate these organizational shifts in a broader comparative-historical background it becomes clear that the refinement of coercive command was only part of the story. The new coercive arrangements did not merely embody new forms of entrenchment. They also reflected more disentrenched arrangements. Agrarian concentration was a qualitative as well as a quantitative process: the single, consolidated right to a piece of land replaced the coexistence of many claims, vested in different rightholders. If the quantitative side of this shift contributed to the development of the factory system by making more labor available, the qualitative side contributed by helping destroy the constraints of clientalistic relations between social superiors and subalterns. The qualitative shift took place even where the quantitative change remained modest: in the regions where smallholding and small-scale manufacturing achieved their greatest vitality.

I have emphasized that the new system of contract and property rights coexisted first with estatist prerogatives, specific to a particular social rank or corporate body, and then, increasingly, with methods of organizational discipline and surveillance that were justified in the name of technical necessity. The classical system of private rights allowed the persistence of entrenchment-based coercive surplus extraction. The latter-day disciplinary techniques, on the contrary,

stood for coercive forms of practical experiment and disentrenchment. The universalistic system of property and contract rights provided a legal structure for recombining resources, people, and
practices, even though it was worked out and compromised in ways
that remained biased toward an authoritarian contrast between task
definers and task executors. The early liberal and utilitarian propagandists of the new order were correct to see a promise of free social
experimentation in the ascendancy of the new system of universalistic
rights. Their mistake was to sanctify the particular form and content
of these rights and to misunderstand the compromises that qualified
and even inverted the real social meaning of the entitlements.

Every major aspect of early modern European society confirms
the reality of this heightened availability of social life to willful experimentation. The early factory was not only an organization for
controlling workers; it was also a method for rearranging people and
machines in ways not predetermined by any social script. You can
say the same, on a larger scale, when you look beyond the early
factory to the society in which it appeared. The absolutist monarchies
of the period, and the people who staffed the emerging central governments, may seem to have been only barely capable of acting with
a measure of independence from landowning or mercantile elites.
Yet when you compare these states to the central governments of
the major agrarian–bureaucratic states of past history, you see that
the new Western regimes had become immensely less vulnerable to
the crises that periodically fragmented the agrarian bureaucratic empires and delivered disintegrated polities and economies into the
hands of warlords and magnates. The new Western states were better
able to maintain a direct fiscal and military link to smallholders and
small-scale traders and manufacturers. These low-level producers
preserved their independence more successfully. The commercialized
agrarian economy became less prone to the recurrent catastrophe of
decommercialization. Such changes laid the institutional and economic basis for persistent group conflict. The possessing and ruling
elites never became so united that they were able to close off institutional experimentation from the bottom up or from the top down,
not at least to the extent that experimentation had been regularly
closed off in the agrarian–bureaucratic states.

Remember that before the new European arrangements could exist
as a stable order, they had to live as a fluid series of conflicts. The
circumstances in which the Roman order in the West broke up allowed collectively organized peasants to fight it out with local landowners and overlords on more equal terms, for there was no
governmental apparatus to tilt the scales in favor of the nobles. The
"crisis of feudalism" merely sealed a result that had been achieved
through continuing group struggle. Where grassroots collective or-

ganization was weakest and centralized noble reaction strongest – as in Eastern Europe – the same demographic crisis led to enserfment rather than to a freer peasantry. As centralized governments emerged they usually strengthened the hands of local elites. But they did so more in some countries and regions than in others. A few states approached the antimagnate alliance between smallholders and central governments that had eluded even the most successful and determined reformers in the agrarian–bureaucratic empires. Even where the alliance between central governments and landowning or mercantile elites proved strongest in Western Europe, it respected a measure of free movement by the working mass, of decisional autonomy by the governmental apparatus, and of elite conflict and fragmentation. No great agrarian and bureaucratic state of the past had done as well.

The Noneconomic Varieties of Negative Capability

The development of practical abilities to produce or to destroy is not the only form of empowerment that can be advanced through the invention of more disentrenched formative contexts. Another variety of empowerment is the diminishment of the conflict between the enabling conditions of self-assertion. Our basic experience of freedom of action requires that we be engaged in a broad range of forms of group life: a practical division of labor in which we exchange commodities and labor, communities in which we value engagement as an end in itself and seek reciprocal engagement, and shared cultures that provide us with the means for self-reflection, self-expression, and communication.

But all these varieties of engagement pose a double threat of subjugation and depersonalization. They threaten to involve us in structures of dependence and domination. Thus, we may find that our participation in the division of labor pegs us at a fixed station in a rigid hierarchy. We may see our communal loyalties misspent on patron–client relations that represent the fluid, personalized form of social hierarchies. Even a culture secretly entangles us in hierarchies of value that translate, more or less obliquely, into hierarchies of actual people. At the same time that he risks dependence, an individual risks becoming the passive object of a rigid social role, his life chances and experiences and finally his very character determined by the station he occupies.

But the sole alternative to disengagement on these punishing terms is no engagement at all and thus the denial of all the practical, emotional, and cognitive resources we need in order to affirm a presence in the world. We require not only the material advantages of the social division of labor but the assurance of acceptance that we may receive in a community and the means for self-expression and self-reflection we gain from a shared universe of discourse. The most fundamental experience of blockage we can undergo is the sense of an irresolvable conflict between the need for engagement and the need to avoid the dangers of dependence and depersonalization. Conversely, an aspect of empowerment is our relative success at moderating this conflict between the enabling conditions of self-assertion. Free, empowered people are those able to develop styles of practical collaboration and passionate attachment that also represent occasions to form and advance individual life projects.

A major theme of the social theory of this book is the ability to change the character of our relation to our collective contexts. The more disentrenched social orders keep the resources and powers of society making from being confiscated by privileged groups. More generally, they prevent our practical and passionate relations from falling subject to a single sanctified version of social life. By undermining fixed roles and hierarchies, they weaken the pressures of dependence and depersonalization that accompany our efforts at engagement in group life. Disentrenchment can thereby help empower us by moderating the conflict between the enabling conditions of self-assertion.

Negative capability includes yet a third, related aspect of empowerment: our success at gaining mastery over our formative institutional and imaginative contexts. This variety of empowerment lets us participate in our social worlds without suspending our critical faculties or surrendering to the hallucinatory identification of the actual with the necessary. We no longer have to choose either a futile rebellion against all institutions and conventions or a resentful, bad-faith acceptance of the outward forms of society as the sole alternatives to the compulsive reenactment of established routines. The ordinary efforts through which people seek to realize their perceived interests broaden into an experience of effective participation in the collective criticism and remaking of the institutional and imaginative structures within which people define and satisfy their interests.

This instance of empowerment is one most directly linked with the creation of less naturalized contexts. Yet it merely generalizes the aspect of negative capability that consists in diminishing the conflict between the enabling conditions of self-assertion. For this third variety of negative capability does to our relation toward whole forms of social life what the second aspect of empowerment does to our relation to particular social roles and hierarchies. The thesis of negative capability illuminates the connection between the character of our relations with one another and the quality of our relation to the shared contexts of our actions.

Consider how these two noneconomic forms of negative capability connect with the first side of negative capability – the way disentrenchment encourages the development of practical productive forces. The thesis of negative capability does not presuppose a necessary convergence among these aspects of empowerment. In fact, the discussion of practical progress through disentrenchment has already suggested how and why they may conflict. The opening of social life to the opportunism of practical reason and practical experiment may come about through despotic as well as consensual means. The centralized, dictatorial forms of disentrenchment liquefy fixed social roles and hierarchies just as much as the more liberal forms. But they replace such modes of social division and ranking with the imposed, unstable hierarchies of ruthless planners anxious to impose their will upon the social order. This route to disentrenchment puts one type of dependence in place of another. It may make social life even more hostile to a reconciliation of the enabling conditions of self-assertion. Moreover, it concentrates in the hands of the central authorities the freedom to remake the institutional and imaginative assumptions of a social order. The powerless subjects of a mobilizational dictatorship may no longer be tempted to equate their social world with the built-in logic of social life. But neither do they win power over their contexts. The will that turns society into an artifact is not their will.

The thesis of negative capability requires us to believe only that no *unavoidable* conflict exists between the practical and the nonpractical forms of empowerment. In every situation we can search for the forms of practical disentrenchment that also help reconcile the enabling conditions of self-assertion and that increase our mastery over the shared contexts of our actions. The search may be facilitated or hindered by the available institutional and imaginative tools. But the effort does not have to fail.

What place does the development of these noneconomic modes of negative capability occupy in the events dealt with by the schematic narrative presented in the first part of this chapter? The new forms of work organization and private rights struck a compromise between disentrenchment and a form of coercive surplus extraction based upon entrenched roles and hierarchies. The disentrenchment that did take place therefore had authoritarian as well as consensual aspects. Thus, the power to make social relations more fully the subject of an experimental will was at first largely confined to bureaucrats and entrepreneurs. Yet the greater freedom to recombine was there, clearly expressed in the more universalistic aspect of the system of private rights: the effort to define the basic legal relations among people without regard to the particular social stations that the rightholders occupy. The style of liberal democracy that began to take shape in the early decades of the nineteenth century started to democratize an experience of mastery over the context that already existed in more authoritarian forms. The doctrines of utilitarianism and classical political economy explicitly recognized the link between the primacy of will over custom and the conditions of economic progress.

It may seem less persuasive to claim that the emergent formative contexts of the modern European societies provided a backdrop favorable to experiments in a fuller reconciliation between the enabling conditions of self-assertion. Yet this hypothesis becomes more plausible once you remember the very different despotic and participatory forms that emancipation from false necessity can assume. The lives of workers in early factories, swollen cities, and concentrated "capitalist" estates may have been as oppressive as anything in earlier European history. But oppression was not the whole story. The new varieties of workers' self-defense and of popular communal and religious life often took on an archaizing and pseudomedieval form. Yet these experiments in collaboration and community also witnessed the emergence of styles of association relatively free from the implicit hierarchies of patron–client relations.

Nowhere is this freedom more striking than in the character of the petty-bourgeois challenge to the emergent forms of economic and governmental organization. The advocates of the petty-bourgeois alternative may have failed to come up with the institutional structure that might have cured petty commodity production of its economic and political instabilities. But with the help of a hodgepodge of pre-liberal and liberal legal conceptions, they did envisage forms of work and community more fully emancipated from rigid roles and hierarchies.

The significance of disentrenchment for the quality of collaboration and community becomes even clearer when we turn from the conflicts of early modern Europe to the experience of contemporary societies. The cultural-revolutionary politics of personal relations may be far more firmly established in the domains of domesticity, leisure, and consumption than in the organization of practical life. It may still flourish more strongly among the educated professional classes than among ordinary working people. Its war against the tyranny of roles and hierarchies may be perverted by a lack of institutional imagination. Yet its achievements are real. We cannot understand them merely as a series of episodes in the confined life of high culture. We can often trace the ideas of this cultural-revolutionary politics of role jumbling to the work of small numbers of thinkers, artists, and professional outsiders. But the diffusion of these ideas through the medium of popular culture, and the sympathy with which they have been greeted by ever larger sectors of the population, would have been inconceivable without a prior transformation of social life. As always, people had to see enacted before their eyes a fragmentary example of the connection between the freedom to revise social arrangements and assumptions and freedom from dependence and depersonalization. Only then could they want more of the same and believe more possible.

The Problem of Agency: The Intentional and the Unintentional Development of Negative Capability

The thesis of negative capability is a species of functional explanation. Its development therefore poses the key issue presented by all varieties of functional explanation. How does the functional consequence come to exercise a causal influence? How do the economic and noneconomic advantages produced by less entrenched structures help explain the emergence and persistence of these structures?

The easiest instance for functional explanation is the setting of successful intentional conduct: the consequence becomes a cause by serving as the goal of an activity. Darwinian theory provides a spectacular example of functional explanation in a wholly nonintentional setting. The functional advantage or explanatory consequence of reproductive success in the environment turns into a causal influence through a distinctive mechanism of transformation: the interplay between random genetic recombination and natural selection against a background of purely physical or mechanical constraints. The causal influence of negative capability upon long-term, cumulative change in the content and quality of formative contexts is therefore easiest to grasp in two cases: either when the causal influence can be attributed to fully intentional action or when it can rely upon a social counterpart to natural selection. Such a counterpart exists if the formative institutional and imaginative contexts that encourage advances in negative capability have a better chance of surviving in the economic and ideological competition with their rivals, whatever the independent causes that may explain the initial appearance of these more revisable formative structures.

Some aspects of the development of negative capability approach the standard of fully intentional action. Other aspects provide counterparts to natural selection. But much in the causal influence of negative capability fails to fit either the intentionalist or the Darwinian model. Events and transformations drawn from the earlier institutional genealogy can illustrate each of these modes of intentional, nonintentional, and special agency.

The aspects of the reach for negative capability that most closely approach the pure case of intentional action are circumstances involving retrospective practical wisdom, prospective ideological aspiration, or some combination of the two. The thesis of negative capability is merely the controversial explication and generalization of a practical lesson that becomes clearer as the number of worldwide experiments in the achievement of negative capability multiplies. In the long series of events covered by the earlier institutional narrative, the latecomers had the benefit of hindsight. The later they came, the greater the benefit. The most telling instances of the deliberate pursuit of practical empowerment through institutional disentrenchment are often successful movements of national renovation and reform led by elites concerned both to improve their own positions within their societies and to bring these societies up to the levels of economic prosperity and military strength achieved by the leading Western powers.

In each successful example of renovating reform the reformers arrived at a new understanding of social life and acted upon this understanding. They discovered that the exploitation of technological and organizational opportunities required a loosening of the constraints that rigid roles and hierarchies imposed upon both the recombination of factors of production and the practice of technological and organizational innovation. The weakening of those constraints was not merely a condition for freedom in practical experimentation. It was also an indispensable basis for awakening and strengthening the sense of nationhood that could bind different classes, communities, and regions together in shared economic and military endeavor and render the great mass of the people less open to the blandishments of foreign or domestic subverters. This weakening of the structure of social division and hierarchy invariably turned out to require a change in governmental and economic arrangements.

Another common discovery qualified this first set of insights and showed how empowering reforms could be reconciled with a commitment to defend a reinterpreted version of elite interests. The reformers even understood that the primary beneficiaries of an economic order that emphasized coercive surplus extraction could emerge richer and stronger when recast as authoritarian experimentalists and recombiners. To make discoveries such as these was to grasp the practical aspect of the development of negative capability. To act successfully on this understanding was to show how negative capability can be developed by intentional action.

A case in point is my earlier example of the response of the Prussian reformers to the threat posed by the French revolutionary army and government. The examples become clearer as we move ahead in time: to, for instance, the reforms sponsored by German, Japanese, and Russian elites during the later part of the nineteenth century. In the course of the twentieth century, the insight into the links connecting economic and military success to the partial liquefication of the social order as well as to the establishment of more disentrenched institutions has become a worldwide possession. This insight may be concealed in some instances under a show of reverence for tradition and in other circumstances under revolutionary pretensions. But it never lies far from the concerns of practical statecraft. The rulers and the ruling classes that fail to take it seriously become easy targets for overthrow by other, more resolute groups better able to connect their factional interests with the cause of national development.

Additional examples of the conscious and deliberate pursuit of negative capability concern the teachings of liberal, socialist, and communist doctrines rather than latecomers' anxieties over practical statecraft. The revolutionary ideologies of liberalism, socialism, and communism all seek to develop forms of empowerment through the subversion of rigid roles and hierarchies and through the subjection of social life to the transforming will. The social ideals and the social theories informing these doctrines are marred in traditional liberalism by the implicit identification of representative democracies and market systems with forms of government and economy that in fact frustrate the fulfillment and distort the definition of liberal aims. Orthodox Marxism sees the nexus between the ideal of empowerment and the advance of disentrenchment through the narrowing lens of deep-structure social analysis.

To find the fragmentary signs of a more inclusive understanding we must look to a loose amalgam of tenets about freedom and efficiency that classical liberals often shared with utilitarian propagandists and writers on political economy. But in every one of the major traditions of social criticism the insight into the connection between empowerment and disentrenchment was prejudiced by a failure of institutional imagination, which was in turn provoked by the lack of a credible social theory. Nevertheless, each secular doctrine of emancipation did embrace something like the thesis of negative capability, though in versions either unjustifiably narrow or excessively vague.

Political movements in power have repeatedly acted upon radical liberal, socialist, and communist doctrines. To this extent their actions exemplify the intentional promotion of negative capability. We should not allow the diversity of their more particular aims and the disparity of their social basis to conceal the extent to which they have all shared in the same quest. This quest is the search for the advantages resulting from a loosening of the constraints that an institutionally determined logic of social division and hierarchy imposes upon our experiments in practical collaboration and passionate attachment.

Nor should an emphasis on the radical promise of alternative, deviant pathways of institutional change permit us forget how much the dominant solutions were themselves influenced by the modern revolutionary social doctrines. Early forms of the work-organization and the private-rights complexes, discussed in the polemical institutional genealogy of this chapter, certainly preceded the formulation of liberal and socialist theories. The practical and imaginative conflicts from which those early forms emerged helped produce the expanded sense of social possibility that the secular doctrines of emancipation later codified and developed. But the doctrines in turn set their mark upon the later versions of such legal and economic arrangements. They did so both directly, through their influence upon the conditions of legitimate authority in the private order (e.g., the system of collective bargaining for workers), and indirectly, through their effect upon the character of representative institutions.

There is less of a gap than may at first appear between the two aspects of the intentional encouragement to negative capability: the high-minded programmatic aspiration to emancipate social life from the constraints of a rigid scheme of division and hierarchy, and the self-interested efforts of reforming elites to make their relatively backward countries catch up with the most advanced contemporary levels of economic prosperity and military strength. For one thing, the ideological programs included a commitment to the development of practical capabilities through the invention of more revisable and hierarchy-subverting institutions. For another, the emancipatory ideologies often served as the legitimating vocabulary of reform-minded elites in relatively backward countries.

Consider now nonintentional agency in the development of negative capability. There is a social counterpart to natural selection. Formative contexts permitting a relatively higher level of negative capability may have, for this reason alone, a better chance to survive in the economic, military, and ideological competition with their rivals, whatever the causes that explain the initial creation of these more denaturalized contexts. The practical advantages disentrenchment offers to the exploitation of technological and organizational opportunities may outweigh the countervailing benefits of coercive surplus extraction based upon entrenched frameworks of social life. The relative emancipation of both the division of labor and the experience of community from predefined roles and hierarchies may make a more denaturalized formative context attractive to the leaders of mass movements around the world. Thus, through a combination of practical advantages and ideological prestige the more disentrenched structures may proliferate and drive out more rigid and hierarchical arrangements.

The analogy to natural selection remains imperfect because the intentional and the unintentional realization of negative capability can be only roughly contrasted. The success of the relatively more disentrenched arrangements is soon recognized, and what began as an unpremeditated experiment may eventually turn into a deliberate goal. Moreover, even the least intentional approach to negative capability works less by circumventing people's conscious desires and intentions than by applying to them the pressure of an enlarged sense of social possibility.

When we take an overview of a long historical process, like the one discussed earlier in this chapter, we may be tempted to exaggerate the unintentional element in the development of a more disentrenched structure. But the impression of the complete estrangement of the historical agents from the effect of their creation begins to dissipate as soon as we go into greater detail. The closest that people ordinarily come to the unintentional development of negative capability is better described as the fragmentary anticipation of broader possibility. People more or less deliberately pioneer an advance in negative capability in a narrow area of social life. In this experiment they later discover principles with broader application. Indeed, the whole thesis of negative capability can best be understood as just such a retrospective extension, its subject matter being the entire experience discussed by the institutional genealogy. This style of partly deliberate agency fits into the circumstance of intermediate intentionality described next.

The part of the genealogy that comes closest to exemplifying the nonintentional, quasi-Darwinian form of agency is the long chain of improbable events that allowed the European countries to escape the endless reform cycles of the agrarian–bureaucratic societies. No breakthrough to the early forms of the institutional arrangements that have become dominant could have occurred if the familiar developmental pattern of the agrarian–bureaucratic empires had remained undisturbed. Remember that this pattern included: the central government's inability to maintain a direct fiscal and military link to a class of independent smallholders and to safeguard them against the encroachments of landowning elites; the success with which these elites and their minions or representatives in the lower rungs of the bureaucracy undermined or circumvented policies designed to defend the smallholders and forced onto these petty producers and tradesmen the full burden of emergency fiscal or military support; the ensuing ruin of the small-scale producers compelled to seek protection from the grandees who had plotted their destruction; the formation of huge estates and independent armies; and the consequent breakdown of both the commercialized economy and the administrative unity of the state until a reforming elite managed to reestablish the institutional conditions of governmental strength and economic vitality. I have argued that the single most important factor in the medieval European evasion of this pattern was the absence of a central state able to tilt the scales in favor of landowning elites against the smallholders, independent laborers or tradesmen, and village communities. Thus, the little people could fight it out with their immediate local superiors in conditions where they had a chance – not a chance to escape their subordinate status but a chance to retain a variable measure of collective independence. These conditions encouraged the emergence of social groups (such as the merchants of independent towns) less dependent upon a landowning elite, the change in the relation between town and country, and the eventual emergence of central governments better able to act independently. The social changes in turn provided an environment favorable to further institutional disentrenchment: the institutionalized weakening of rigid roles and hierarchies and of a contrast between framework-preserving routine and framework-transforming conflict was preceded by the more fluid, conflictual enactment of this weakening. No such institutional invention was *intended* to promote any aspect of the link between disentrenchment and empowerment. Yet the societies in which the inventions took root proved able to stage additional institutional experiments and to develop further practical capabilities that set them on the path to world primacy.

The most interesting and distinctive aspect of agency in the development of negative capability fails to fit the extreme instances of intentional or unintentional action. This intermediate mode of agency has both a familiar and an unfamiliar aspect. The familiar one is the idea of the innovator's advantage. A group within a society pioneers in the development of a limited form of negative capability, in a restricted domain of social life. If, for example, these innovators are developing a new form of economic enterprise they must see a chance to reap rewards from a more flexible recombination of labor, expertise, and capital rather than merely from a more successful effort at coercive surplus extraction based upon preexisting roles and hierarchies. They must imagine a style of production or exchange that not only differs from current ways of doing business but also brings people together in ways foreign to the logic of the established social order. The immediate incentive is the chance of capturing for themselves the profits or privileges that others will only later be able to achieve. What holds for pioneering groups within a society may hold as well for an entire society within a system of national economies or world powers. The best-known protagonists of such innovations are entrepreneurs whose rewards are measured in wealth. Other protagonists may include bureaucratic innovators whose success produces wealth for themselves and their countries, or even propagandists and ideologists whose achievements lie in the transforming effect of a broader sense of social possibility upon established group interests and collective identities and whose reward is influence.

The innovators have a motive to act. But they may not at first have more than the dimmest understanding of the general relation between empowerment and disentrenchment. If all that could be said about these pioneers is that their self-interested experiments happened to coincide with the requirements for the development of negative capability, these examples would hardly differ from the situation of unintentional agency, with its social counterpart to natural selection. But here is where the other, less familiar part of the intermediate case of intentionality comes in. Once a set of more disentrenched institutional arrangements or preconceptions about possible and desirable human association gains acceptance, it must be run. The institutions or preconceptions must be reproduced by practical or conceptual activities: routinized styles of conflict, exchange, and argument. Such activities differ from those needed to operate more inflexible and hierarchy-producing institutional arrangements or to elaborate and apply more naturalistic forms of legal, moral, and political thought. Moreover, the procedures required for the successful operation of complex institutional arrangements invariably imply a view of the problems with which the arrangements deal. Such an implicit view must include at least a partial understanding of the thesis of negative capability. Thus, if the innovators do not have to grasp the whole truth of negative capability in order to introduce their innovations, they or their successors and imitators must achieve a measure of insight into this truth if they are to operate and to reproduce the initial innovation in changing circumstances. This indispensable insight ensures the element of intentionality in the intermediate case of agency. Examples drawn from each of the three major institutional complexes addressed by the institutional genealogy illustrate this halfway situation.

The entrepreneur and the manager who ruled a modern factory had to develop a style of production, marketing, and labor control that guaranteed stability, or compensated for instability, in the key capital, product, and labor markets while maximizing opportunities for flexibility and recombination. As the coercive element in the new forms of work and market organization diminished, the importance of entrepreneurial and managerial skills increased. The successful manager in the new institutional environment had to sacrifice a measure of flexibility in work organization the better to safeguard his interest in maintaining a secure work force. He had to use techniques that have historically spanned the full gamut between a violent factory despotism and a policy of friendly deals with unionized labor to the detriment of temporary or jobless workers and occasional subcontractors. The sacrifice of flexibility in work organization was enshrined in what I have described as the rigid variant of rationalized collective labor, with its sharp contrast between task-defining and task-executing activities. Too severe a restraint upon flexibility in work organization was, however, as dangerous as no restraint at all.

For it put the manager at a disadvantage in the competition with his more flexible competitors and encouraged a sullen resistance from his laborers. As mass production developed, the manager also had to forego a measure of flexibility in product and production design and in creating or managing market opportunities in order to satisfy the requirements of a style of industrial organization that depended upon a concentration of resources and that remained especially vulnerable to market instabilities. But this further sacrifice of flexibility also had to be balanced against a countervailing need to make continuing technological and organizational innovation possible.

The whole art of management came to lie in the achievement of the maximum of flexibility compatible with maintaining both a structure of control over workers and preemptive defense against market competitors. The prize goes to the manager who either can loosen the restraints on innovation that are imposed by the needs for control over workers and for preemptive defense against competitors, or who can multiply opportunities for innovation within those restraints. Such a manager acts on an implicit theory amounting to a qualified version of the thesis of negative capability.

Similarly, efforts at practical reform by bureaucrats and politicians require a capacity to see beyond the established logic of group interests and collective identities and to envisage deals and experiments that collapse distinctions enshrined by this logic. The emancipatory doctrines of liberalism, socialism, and communism have often functioned as vague, elastic normative justification for a statecraft of recombination that has its own claims to being taken seriously.

Like economic and governmental institutions, systems of private rights must be applied and elaborated by an activity. This activity is legal doctrine, taken both as a substantive conception of social organization and as a method of analysis. The substantive conception of social life that inspires modern legal thought takes for granted the incompatibility of both contractual and communal ideals with rigid and pronounced inequality. Rather than accepting the patron–client relation as the exemplary form of all social life, this conception seeks to realize radically different models of human association in different areas of social existence. In each area it seeks a distinctive way to tame the dangers of power: accountability, representation, and legal restraint in the constitution of the state; voluntary agreement and impersonal technical necessity in the organization of work; and the solace of intimacy and parenthood in the life of the family. From a more searching critical perspective this conception may appear both apologetically naive and unjustifiably restrictive. It nonetheless presupposes a newly broadened sense of social possibility and institutional diversity. To move within its boundaries is, at a minimum, to recognize that exchange systems and forms of communal life have a controversial relation to each other and to hierarchies of power and advantage.

Consider now the characteristic methods of modern Western legal analysis as distinguished from the dominant conception expressed in substantive law and doctrine. The prevailing genre of legal justification is characterized by an embarrassment to commit itself to any scheme of possible and desirable association, even to the scheme it in fact presupposes. Thus, the legal analyst wants to contain legal analysis at the level of rules, or principles, purposes, and policies, rather than appealing to the inclusive normative views of society and personality that occupied so prominent a position in earlier, classical styles of legal doctrine. Much in modern legal analysis can best be understood as a half-conscious attempt to resolve a particular contradiction: the contradiction between the impulse to treat the law as a haphazard, confused body of transitory outcomes to particular conflicts among organized interests and the opposing tendency to represent the authoritative materials of the law as an approximation to a defensible scheme of human association. The desire to achieve a higher form of consistency and justification leads in the latter direction but the effort to represent society as an artifact of legislative will pushes in the former direction. Such are the hesitations of legal analysis in an age of partial emancipation from false necessity. The embarrassments, contortions, and stratagems of this style of legal thought all presuppose a partial acceptance of the idea that we raise ourselves up by overthrowing the tyranny of a prewritten social script over our social experience. They therefore exemplify a half-intentional agency in the making of negative capability.

The Thesis of Negative Capability Qualified and Reinterpreted

The preceding discussion of negative capability has focused on the varieties of empowerment that may result from the creation of more disentrenched institutions. It has gone on to examine how the emergence and persistence of more disentrenched contexts come to be influenced by the capabilities that disentrenchment permits. But the full sense of the thesis of negative capability can be appreciated only after it has passed through a series of qualifications. The preceding discussion has anticipated almost all these qualifications. But when they are brought together, they clearly indicate how much negative capability differs from the deep-structure style of evolutionary explanation. The point of the qualifications, it soon appears, is less to weaken the thesis than to fix the sense the thesis acquires outside the framework of deep-structure analysis.

A first qualification is that coercive surplus extraction, based upon rigid roles and hierarchies and upon the institutions or preconceptions that sustain them, may rival and outdo the practical benefits of more hierarchy-subverting and more freely revisable arrangements and ideas. We must assess the force of this reservation in the light of the empirical hypothesis that entrenchment-based, coercive surplus extraction is likely to have the upper hand only in relatively poor societies. In such societies the promise of innovation pales in comparison to the difficulty of generating savings. If this hypothesis is true, denaturalization – the creation of formative contexts that both undermine stable roles and hierarchies and efface the contrast between context-preserving routine and context-transforming conflict – has a more general and enduring influence than coercive restraints on consumption or leisure.

A second qualification is that the three aspects of negative capability I have distinguished do not necessarily go hand in hand. The development of productive or destructive capabilities through disentrenchment may occur through coercive as well as consensual means. It may be the handiwork of a ruthless command system, committed to impose its transformative plan upon a recalcitrant society. When institutional invention takes this tyrannical direction, it may harm rather than benefit a widespread experience of empowerment in the sense either of greater mastery over context or of fuller reconciliation between the enabling conditions of self-assertion.

This observation has an important corollary. The fragmentary development of negative capability may not be an unqualified good even within an argument, such as the one developed here, that attributes normative authority to a view of human empowerment and its conditions. (See the discussion of facts and values in Chapter 5.) At best, the thesis of negative capability encourages us to search for the particular enabling forms of practical empowerment that do coincide with our larger human interests. It teaches us that nothing in the demands of practical social life condemns this search to failure. It thereby holds before us the hope that by a change in the character of our relations to our contexts we may partly free our relations to one another from the taint of dependence and depersonalization.

A third qualification is that any cumulative advance toward greater levels of negative capability is reversible. At no point does the development of more denaturalized structures become safe. The single most important source of reversibility is the ambiguity of the state. Governmental power may serve as the master tool of context smashing. However, the access to the strengthened state may become a basis for the reconstitution of social divisions and hierarchies. The explicitly imposed character of such state-based divisions and hierarchies and the revolutionary ideas under whose aegis mobilizational regimes conduct their affairs, the memory of upheaval and reconstruction, and even the requirements of worldwide economic and military competition may all seem to limit the renaturalization of social life. But what was once experienced as an artifact may gradually come to be mistaken for the way things are. A society may suffer a slow decline into rigidity and ineptitude before being brought up short by an unforgiving rival.

A fourth qualification, which goes farthest toward distancing explanation through negative capability from evolutionary accounts in the deep-structure style, has been anticipated by the analysis in Chapter 2 of the internal structure of formative contexts. It will soon be further developed through the discussion of the influence of formative contexts upon their own remaking, as a second source of long-run, directional change in the character and content of frameworks of social life. The point of this final reservation is that the influence of negative capability works with the materials generated by particular institutional and imaginative sequences or traditions as well as with our fitful efforts to escape the limits of these traditional materials. There is no short list of the possible institutional and imaginative forms among which mankind must choose at each step in the development of negative capability. For there is no grand scheme of possible types of social organization or necessary institutional and imaginative forms of social evolution underlying mankind's experiments in context making. There is no closed set of suitable formative contexts waiting to be deployed at the right evolutionary turn. Thus, the question – what institutional and imaginative forms can and should a particular advance in negative capability take? – never has an uncontroversial answer. Much depends on the materials, opportunities, and obstacles of a particular circumstance or tradition. Even the imponderables of resistance and invention have their place, for no structure of social life fully determines its own sequel.

These several qualifications may at first appear to eviscerate the thesis of negative capability. In fact, however, they serve only to emphasize the distance separating this thesis from evolutionary explanation in the deep-structure mode. Once the thesis has absorbed all these qualifications it turns into a claim about the *possibility* of a certain precarious, indeterminate, reversible but nevertheless cumulative and momentous change in the character of our formative contexts as well as in their content. In particular, the thesis shows, if it is true, the fundamental realism of the radical project: the effort to diminish the influence of dependence and depersonalization upon our experience of social life by changing the quality of our relation to the institutional and imaginative frameworks of our existence.

Like any conception of happiness and ennoblement, the radical project draws upon certain assumptions about social reality and social possibility. But we must look to past and present experience to test and correct these assumptions. We must see whether something in the nature of social reality dooms this cause. Here, then, is the practical sense of the thesis of negative capability. The thesis represents less a claim that the history of context making is oriented in a particular direction than a claim that we can act on the radical project if we want to. The thesis does not merely support the fundamental realism of this transformative commitment. It forms part of a set of descriptions and explanations that help refine and revise our understanding of what the commitment is and that show us what obstacles we must face in order to realize the commitment in practice.

It is true that you do not need to share an allegiance to the radical project in order to evaluate or even accept these descriptive and explanatory ideas. Nevertheless, I shall later argue that our basic programmatic choices and explanatory views have a far more intimate connection than traditional ideas about the divide between factual and normative judgments lead us to suppose. For the moment, it is enough to emphasize that what we understand as social reality depends on the deliberate or involuntary, the real or imagined transformative experiments we perform upon it. If we were both long-lived and indifferent enough to push these experiments in all conceivable directions simultaneously, we might end up with a conception of social reality more truly neutral among particular transformative endeavors. But we do not in fact have either the time or the indifference, and our exercises in social explanation are anchored, implicitly if not explicitly, in attempts to maintain or remake our social worlds, attempts that our explanatory ideas in turn help elucidate and criticize. The explanatory argument of this book, and the thesis of negative capability within it, is the work of a mind anxious about the realism of the radical cause.

Applying the Thesis of Negative Capability: Classes and the State

The thesis of negative capability has far-reaching implications. Let me now briefly illustrate these implications in two important areas that may appear to be strangely undervalued by this view of context change: social classes and the state.

Formative arrangements and beliefs generate a system of social stations: of roles and hierarchies, group interests and collective identities. They do so by influencing the claims people can make upon one another's labor, wealth, help, and loyalty and by shaping people's ability to command the economic and noneconomic resources of society making. One of the many implications of deep-structure social theory for analyzing social hierarchies is that such hierarchies always have the same fundamental nature, however much they may differ in content. Marxist social theory, for example, recognizes that the class systems of capitalism and feudalism differ in the type of connection they establish between power in the state and power over labor and capital. But both the relation of class interests to social conflict and the lawlike, dynamic tendencies of history (the interplay between forces and relations of production) always remain the same. According to Marxism, only under prehistorical, primitive communism or posthistorical, developed communism do class division and class conflict fail to appear or cease to exist. Moreover, just as there is a necessary, well-defined sequence of modes of production, so there is a clear-cut, inescapable logic of class interests that corresponds to each mode of production. Ideological obfuscation and self-deception may temporarily conceal this logic of interests. But continuing conflict will eventually make it clear.

The explanatory approach developed in this book weakens the allegedly determining force of objective class interests. By denying that there is a necessary sequence or short list of indivisible formative contexts the theory also undermines the basis for any strong claim about the need for a particular logic of class interests. A related idea emphasizes that escalating conflict progressively disorganizes an entrenched logic of group interests and collective identities. The implications underline the importance of alternative approaches to social explanation in general and to the possibility of cumulative context change in particular.

An important corollary of the point just stated is that class-based explanations (or explanations appealing to hierarchies or divisions other than classes) cannot be expected to account for long-run, cumulative context change. They do far better at illuminating the normal operation of a particular social world. They are more helpful in revealing the content and mechanisms of stability than in accounting for the occurrence or direction of destabilization. They are also better at explaining a single, historically located episode of context change than at showing how or why several such changes can produce a cumulative effect and stake out a certain direction. This corollary sheds retrospective light on the relative absence of class analysis from the earlier, general discussion of negative capability.

The shift in the sense of class analysis that comes closest to the thesis of negative capability is the redefinition of class as a distinct species of hierarchical ranking. Class hierarchy is not the sole or exemplary form of social hierarchy. Formative contexts can be placed on a spectrum of disentrenchment. The farther along on this spectrum they stand, the weaker the stereotyped hierarchical positions they generate: weaker in the greater openness of their institutional and imaginative foundations to challenge, weaker in their diminished influence over both context-respecting routine and context-transforming conflict (which in any event come closer together), and weaker even in the extent of the inequalities of wealth, power, and prestige they establish. The familiar descriptive vocabulary of social hierarchy can be easily related to this spectrum. Thus, the caste, the estate, the class, and the party of opinion (whether or not organized as a political party in the modern Western sense) are characteristic hierarchical forms of social frameworks whose hierarchies are progressively weaker in all the senses indicated.

The caste or estate comes closer to the limiting case of a society whose hierarchies are not only represented but also treated in practice as beyond the reach of the transformative will. Of course, this characterization focuses on only part of the historical reality to which the vocabulary of caste habitually applies. The actual Indian *jatis*, for example, as opposed to the scriptural Hindu *varnas* that supposedly subsumed them, were always locked in conflict with one another. They always jockeyed for access to governmental power. The experience of living under what may appear to be the most naturalized hierarchy invariably includes a fragmentary awareness of the dependence of stereotyped hierarchical systems upon social conflicts and institutional artifacts. Here, as almost always, the comparative differences of experience (between, say, living under Hindu castes and living under modern Western-type classes) are far smaller than the differences of dogma. That the experiences nevertheless *are* different justifies the application of the spectrum idea to the varieties and vocabularies of social hierarchy.

The interpretation of the caste idea as an approximation to a limiting case of entrenched hierarchy is also simplified in another way, which brings out more clearly what a view of context making like the one presented here can contribute to the comparative study of social hierarchies. A particular form of social hierarchy can never be adequately understood as merely a more or less rigid and determining principle of ranking, based upon more or less naturalistic arrangements and assumptions. It carries a weight of connotation rich with the practices and beliefs of a unique historical tradition. It can be relieved of these meanings only by an exercise in drastic historical simplification. The same can be said of the corporately organized estates of the prerevolutionary absolutist monarchies of Europe or of the social classes of the postrevolutionary West. The general point illustrates rather than qualifies a view that sees negative capability and the sequential effects of current contexts as two distinct but interlocking influences upon long-run context change. The former influence works with the materials provided by the latter.

At the opposite pole of disentrenchment lies the party of opinion. The party can similarly be understood as an approximation to an ideal, limiting circumstance in which the free alignment of people among organized movements of opinion replaces entrenched divisions and hierarchies. Of course, political parties as they have in fact developed are never just free alignments of opinions. They are advocates for the recognized interests of particular classes and communities. They are defenders of programs that do not easily correlate with class or communal position (the free-alignment aspect). And they are syndicates of office seekers.

But if it is possible to imagine and establish more revisable and antihierarchical formative contexts than those now existing, it is also possible to conceive of a situation in which stable classes and communal divisions have weakened further. In such a situation the role of the party as an embodiment of opinions that override class and communal divisions becomes more important than its role as a voice for classes and communities or as a partnership of professional politicians. The division of society into fluid movements of opinion that fail to follow class or communal lines becomes the primary principle of social organization. In such a society social life in fact approaches the liberal image. It does so, however, only by revising the institutional assumptions and guiding conceptions of the liberal cause.

Remember also that the freedom invoked by the idea of free alignment is not freedom in the sense of uncaused action. It is merely freedom from the determining effect of current social stations upon the stands people take in the struggle over the future form of society. For the creation of more disentrenched contexts never immunizes us against causal influences. It merely diminishes the extent to which we are at the mercy of the established frameworks of social life. One of the aims of the explanatory theory of *False Necessity* is to show just how much is involved in this "merely."

Even the most entrenched formative context, productive of the most rigid, determining, and inclusive hierarchies, can be dissolved by escalating practical and imaginative conflict. One outcome of this dissolution may be all-out social warfare: the violent, merciless struggle for security and advantage at any cost. Another outcome is the increasing supersession of castes, estates, or classes, as well as of communal or ethnic groups, by movements of opinion whose membership and orientation cross preexisting lines of social division and hierarchy. The two experiences often coexist and combine. The more disentrenched the formative context becomes, the more the dissolution of social stations into parties of opinion (or, rather, of parties of opinion based upon particular social stations into parties not based upon them) carries over into the routine experience of social life.

Between the caste or the corporately organized estate and the emancipated movement of opinion stands the social class: a characteristic form of hierarchy in societies partly emancipated from false necessity. The interplay between classes or communities and political parties that both do and do not represent these communities and classes has become the dominant form of conflict over the mastery and uses of governmental power in the West ever since the mid-nineteenth century. It may be useful to employ the class concept in this sense as a term of art, indicating one of a number of varieties of hierarchy, distinguished by their relative position on a spectrum of disentrenchment. But if you want to keep the concept close to its core setting of familiar, richly defined connotations, you have to particularize it still further, drawing into its descriptive significance a multitude of imaginative and institutional assumptions that form part of the modern Western experience of class.

Any number of other actual or not manifestly unfeasible inter-mediate forms of hierarchy differ significantly from this more richly defined experience of class. Consider, for example, a society in which independent family position or tradition is relatively less important than meritocratic advancement (as in contemporary Japan), or in which relative access to the state apparatus is combined with meri-tocracy (as in the contemporary Soviet Union) as a basis of position and advantage. Whether or not you take this final step toward the historical particularization of the class concept, you will have come to recognize that class analysis is most powerful when applied to short-run, context-specific problems of social explanation. In the study of such problems, class analysis plays a derivative though im-portant role.

Consider the speculative history of the state suggested by this approach to division and hierarchy. This narrative seems to be com-patible – so far as it goes – with familiar ethnographic and historical observations. It develops a latent theme in the earlier treatment of negative capability. And it anticipates the ideas of the later program-matic argument about government. Such a speculative history may appear unjustifiably evolutionary. But I hope to have shown already that evolutionary explanations may shift in sense drastically once we disconnect them from deep-structure assumptions.

Stateless societies – societies without central governmental insti-tutions able to tax or redistribute wealth, to recruit soldiers and wage war, to adjudicate disputes and define enforceable norms – seem usually to have stood very far toward the extreme naturalistic pole of the spectrum of entrenchment. The institutions and preconcep-tions constituting such formative contexts were only minimally avail-able to revision in the midst of ordinary social life. The absence of a central government itself helped to weaken the experience of society as artifact. For throughout history the state has been the single great-est tool for remaking the social order. Central governments focus on an identifiable point the collective power to make and remake society. They establish a visible connection between human will and the social order, no matter how much society's ruling practices and ideas may conceal and constrain the treatment of society as artifact.

In such entrenched but state-free formative contexts, division prevailed over hierarchy. Such societies were what the language of modern anthropology describes as segmented rather than stratified, or their forms of stratification were subordinate to their methods of segmentation. Moreover, real or fictive kinship usually played the major role in segmentation. Each segmented unit (clan, tribe, village commune, or whatever) had its internal hierarchies and elites: its dominant families, for example. But the higher-ups could not draw capital and manpower on a societywide basis. Even within their small worlds they found their cupidity and ambition restrained by the demands of kinship-based solidarity as well as by the poverty of their societies.

Imagine, then, that a combination of unusual crises, opportunities, and institutional inventions required and permitted the societywide mobilization of material and human resources: for example, a need for defense against invaders or rivals or the hope of conquest and plunder, against a background of increased surplus, denser population, and greater technological sophistication. The leaders or leading families of certain segments into which society was divided might step forward as the leaders of the entire constellation of segments. They would then assert a largely personal control over capital, land, laborers, or soldiers drawn from many of the divided units of society. Eventually, what had once been an exercise of personalistic authority, practiced in a crisis situation, would become an institutionalized arrangement for normal social life. Both the desire of the power holders to perpetuate their power through their descendants and the commitment to preserve the newfound levels of economic and military capability may have contributed to the result. The state would have now come into existence. For a state exists when there are effective institutions and widely shared ideas that enable a group – the people who staff the state or who are the state – to exercise a significant influence over the use of the economic and noneconomic resources with which we create the social future within the social present.

The process I have described is certainly not the sole route to the emergence of the state. But all the different routes resemble one another. Besides, this particular form of state making has continued to recur well into historical times in the experience of pastoral or nomadic peoples, who may owe much of their success as conquerors and empire builders to the closeness between their methods of governmental organization and the perennial experience of fluid collective mobilization.

Once a central government had come into existence, its power could be used to help build up privileged degrees of "private" control over land and labor. The disparities among social ranks became closely identified with degrees of more or less privileged access to governmental power. The emphasis of the social order shifted from segmentation or division to hierarchy. Formative contexts may then have become both more entrenched and less entrenched than in their stateless form: more entrenched because they came to be defined and supported by agencies with the power to command people and resources on a societywide basis; less entrenched because the exercise of a commanding governmental authority implied a partial recognition of the artifactual quality of the social order.

If the thesis of negative capability is correct, the entrenched formative contexts that characterized these early state societies put restraints upon the development of productive capabilities and other forms of human empowerment. The pressure to overcome such constraints might for a long time be overridden by the countervailing advantages of coercive surplus extraction based upon rigid roles and hierarchies. But the pressure nevertheless made itself felt through the several modes of intentional, unintentional, and half-intentional agency discussed earlier.

The organization of government and of the conflict over governmental power represents one of the extended institutional complexes that make up a formative context. Like the context as a whole, it can vary in the extent to which it remains open to challenge in the midst of ordinary social life and in the degree to which it encourages the formation of fixed roles and ranks. A particular level of disentrenchment in the organization of the economy or in the system of private rights does not necessarily require any particular form of governmental organization. But according to the argument of Chapter 2, a formative context cannot become stable unless all its constituent elements occupy similar levels of negative capability.

The structure of the state has remained controversial throughout history. Central governmental institutions have been both the major support of private privilege and the chief instrument for the disruption of privilege. In modern times some doctrines have attempted to resolve this dilemma by seeking the nearly complete abolition of governmental institutions. An uncoercive private order of free coordination would reduce governmental institutions to a residual role. But no such uncontroversial uncoercive order exists. The problem is not only that choices must be made among alternative ways to define such a free order. It is rather that the economic and the noneconomic resources of society have to be constantly redistributed, and their redistribution fought about, for disentrenchment to progress. Compare, for example, a market economy based on conditional and temporary claims to capital, allocated by publicly regulated capital funds, to a market economy committed to absolute property rights. The former economy does more than the latter for economic decentralization, plasticity, and equality. As the argument about the reconstruction of petty commodity production has already suggested, the effort to preserve this alternative market order from authoritarian perversion may in turn require a change in the inherited institutional forms of representative democracy. Such a reorganization is in fact independently required if we are to realize more fully any of the goals of freedom and decentralization, community and concerted action, participation and equality, that have come to dominate the rhetoric of contemporary party politics. Those whose hopes depend upon our further emancipation from false necessity cannot bypass the state; they must rebuild it.

THE SEQUENTIAL EFFECTS OF FORMATIVE CONTEXTS

The Idea of Sequential Effects

A second influence upon context change is the effect an institutional or imaginative framework has upon the frameworks or framework changes that may succeed it. A formative context exists in the sense that it resists being disturbed by everyday tensions and that it helps shape a richly defined set of routines; the sense of its existence is parasitic upon the sense of entrenchment. It is harder to change the framework or to challenge the roles and hierarchies the framework supports than to fight, exchange, or converse within the framework. Of course, people may soon discover that they cannot advance very far in the pursuit of their material or ideal interests without confronting established institutional or imaginative assumptions. But they must then begin to change the quality of their efforts and ideas. They must overcome a higher order of resistance.

As context-preserving conflict escalates into context-transforming conflict, the contestants move into the broader and more intense struggle with stronger or weaker weapons. A formative context shapes the means and opportunities of struggle. It gives some groups – as defined by their place in the system of social divisions and hierarchy – an advantage over others. It makes certain conceptions, programs, or ideals easier to justify and even easier to comprehend than others.

Moreover, the different institutional complexes and imaginative preconceptions that make up a formative context are unlikely to be equally open to revision. Some will be harder to replace. The relatively greater recalcitrance to revision from which some parts of the structure benefit may result from the greater support these parts receive from the other components of the framework. Remember that a formative context is neither an indivisible whole nor a freely recombinable collection. Some of its elements may be relatively easier to change without having to change the institutions and beliefs with which it connects. Other parts, however, may be harder to disconnect. Their substitution may require more extensive revolutionary reforms. When you combine the uneven vulnerability of the elements forming a context with the uneven opportunities each context affords to different social groups or movements of opinion, you can begin to see how a framework may influence its own sequel.

This sequential influence never determines particular outcomes. At most it makes certain lines of transformation more likely than others. Given the complexity of the circumstances involved in each instance of context change and the difficulty of comparing such instances, we have little prospect of ever being able to quantify these probabilities. No wonder we can explain a context change retrospectively much better than we can predict it, although an element of prediction is required for the intellectual guidance of transformative practice.

An additional qualification is that the sequential effect remains time-bound. We may be able to understand (at least retrospectively) how a formative context shapes its immediate sequel. But we cannot easily trace the effects of this influence at later moments of context change. There are too many possible combinations: any number of parts of the new, revised formative context that may be revised farther down the road; any number of possible replacements for the revised parts; any number of reasons why the easiest transformations may be spurned in favor of more difficult results; any number of alien contexts and traditions that may be drawn upon as sources of transformative inspiration; and any number of ways in which all these causes may be further shaken up by the imponderables of invention and insight, of war and economic crisis.

Thus, a chain of sequential effects is, if not randomly aligned, at least extremely sinuous. The point is not that it is uncaused but rather that so many and such various causal influences act upon it. For by abandoning the pretensions of deep-structure social explanations we also give up all hope of discovering a master set of dynamic tendencies underlying sequences of context change. Sequential effects must be understood apart from other long-run influences upon context change that are less directly time-bound: the attractive force of negative capability and the subsidiary, countervailing influence of coercive surplus extraction. The sequential effects are not epiphenomena; they have their own life, and their messiness is just the reverse side of their relative autonomy.

Within the limits just outlined, the sequential effects should nevertheless be viewed as possible long-term, cumulative influences upon context making. They do not have to push in any particular direction except to the extent that they may interact with the influence of negative capability. But a tilt toward one line of transformation can build upon a previous tilt, and what began as a slight inclination to change in a particular direction may become an orientation harder to redirect.

The whole contentious narrative with which this chapter began provides a striking example of sequential effects. The conflicts that produced the dominant forms of governmental and economic organization and of private rights did not take place in a social and institutional vacuum. They occurred against the background of institutions and beliefs that favored certain groups and disfavored others. The reigning institutional arrangements discussed in earlier parts of this chapter implied a change in the structure of social division and hierarchy and in the distribution of the key economic and noneconomic resources of society. A standard topic of European history-writing is the reconstruction of economic and governmental elites that attended the transition from "feudalism" to "capitalism." But the alternative of petty commodity production stood in far sharper tension with preexisting elites and their progeny than did the styles of economic organization that came to prevail. This greater conflict with established interests would have applied even to the naive, unstable, and unreconstructed form of petty commodity production. The formative contexts of late medieval European societies tilted the scales in favor of what later became the dominant approach to agriculture and industry. The reality of the tilt is hardly a speculative hypothesis. The petty bourgeois challenge was usually defeated or contained even before its internal instabilities had become manifest. The instruments of its suppression went all the way from outright repression to legal rules and economic policies that disfavored smallholders, petty manufacturers, and small-time traders.

Even with this bias, however, you can imagine a series of events, not radically different from other actual occurrences, that might have overcome this tilt. After all, from a larger world-historical perspective the entire European development represented an improbable exception to the recurrent patterns of the agrarian–bureaucratic empires. The deviant petty bourgeois economic forms did occupy a larger place in many European regions where smallholders and minor manufacturers were able to cement alliances with stronger and more independent central governments. It might be objected that these regional variations merely give further proof of the bias. But the vitality of collective peasant, artisanal, or petty-manufacturing organizations was often more the outcome than the cause of particular sequences of group conflict.

Moreover, other aspects of the institutional genealogy reviewed in this chapter demonstrate the limits rather than the force of the tilt. The authority of preexisting elites may help account for the contours of liberal constitutionalism. But that authority cannot explain why these elitist liberal polities nevertheless opened themselves to universal, unrestricted suffrage, mass parties, and trade unions. To appreciate the biases of sequence correctly, you must combine them with the other influences upon context change examined by this view of context making.

The Interplay Between Negative Capability and Sequential Effects

The most interesting problems about sequential effects concern the relation between such effects and the influence of negative capability. In the evolutionary variant of deep-structure social explanation the influence of a context upon its own transformation has no independent force but is merely the detailed expression of the lawlike tendencies governing context change. For the politicized social theory developed in this book, however, the indeterminacy, complexity, and reversibility of dynamic tendencies, such as those resulting from the advantages of negative capability, give sequential effects an independent life. This independence in turn renders both puzzling and significant the relation between the time-bound force of sequence and the less focused attractions of negative capability.

One side of the relation has already been discussed. The influence of negative capability works with and through the materials generated by particular sequences of context change. To be sure, the pressure of negative capability (and of the countervailing forces that qualify its operation) may have influenced the course of context change. But such pressure counts as only one of many influences.

There is never a well-ordered list of the possible institutional or imaginative forms society may assume at a given level of emancipation from false necessity. The new forms are built with the institutional and imaginative materials at hand. The materials at hand are in the first instance the ideas and arrangements of the context being changed. They also are all the intellectual and practical resources to be recovered from the past history of that context or of other frameworks. As disentrenchment progresses traditions of context change intersect more readily and overtly. The recombination of elements drawn from different traditions becomes easier so long as they embody comparable levels of negative capability.

The system of absolute property rights, for example, developed through a reworking of the same doctrinal categories that had served the rank-specific or corporate-style prerogatives of an estatist society. The discontinuities between estatist and liberal jurisprudence may impress a mind formed by the conventions of Western legal culture. But once we reexamine the same problems from a broader comparative historical perspective, we become aware of how these different legal styles depend upon the continuous stretching and reinterpretation of civilian and common-law categorical schemes or argumentative habits.

What is true of the system of private rights also holds, though less obviously, for economic and governmental institutions. The emergent forms of economic and governmental organization constituted recognizable transmutations of an institutional vocabulary many centuries in the building. Even the institutional program of empowered democracy presented in Chapter 5 merely takes off from a particular historical approach to the organization of market economies and representative democracies.

It may seem that the givens and starting points of reconstruction hardly matter so long as we continue to reconstruct endlessly. But reconstruction takes time to learn and to execute, and it is often unintentional. Moreover, we can never tell for sure to what extent our results have been influenced by our working materials. For we lack a secure, uncontroversial Archimedean point outside particular sequences of context change from which to assess the proximity of particular traditions to a universal ideal. Even our bolder efforts at the speculative understanding of social experience are never more than the penumbral enlargement of our actual, recollected, and intimated experience of life in particular social orders and of fights about particular revolutionary reforms.

Thus far I have discussed the constraints that sequential effects impose upon the workings of the search for negative capability. Consider now the reverse relation: the consequences of an advance toward greater disentrenchment for the sequential effects of formative contexts. A more disentrenched framework is a framework less resistant to challenge and revision in the midst of ordinary social activity. To the extent that our context-making freedom can be partly institutionalized and thereby exercised without the violent accompaniment of a Hobbesian social war, to that extent we cease to be the passive automatons of our contexts. Just as the more disentrenched framework imposes less of a grid of preestablished division and hierarchy upon our ordinary dealings, so too it enforces less of a bias upon its own transformation.

One way cumulative advances in negative capability may influence the passage from one context state to the next is the outright exclusion of institutional solutions or social visions embodying a lower measure of negative capability. The cumulative growth of negative capability may also diminish what I have called the sequential effect. Because complete disentrenchment represents an idealized limit rather than a goal we can envisage actually reaching, the sequential effect never entirely disappears. But the thesis that this effect can vary in force follows directly from the thesis that social orders differ in their power to imprison us within a particular version of sociability.

The same developments that diminish the power of sequential effects also influence the countervailing forces of stability and destabilization that besiege an ongoing formative context and the regularity with which transformative opportunities arise from the very circumstances that lend a second-order necessity to social frameworks. In the more denaturalized structures, there is less distance to cross before a context-reproducing practice becomes a context-destabilizing activity. The opportunities counterbalancing the spurious, second-order necessity of formative contexts lie more clearly at the surface of social life.

The institutional genealogy presented in the initial sections of this chapter describes, among other things, a passage from a circumstance in which sequential effects were relatively stronger to another state of affairs in which they became relatively weaker. The preexisting arrangements, preconceptions, and elites of early modern European society tilted the scales in favor of what became our dominant styles of economic, governmental, and legal organization. Undoubtedly, contemporary formative contexts continue to bias change in certain directions as well as to impose the recurrent, unchosen patterns described by the cycles of reform and retrenchment. But the tilt – at least the tilt in any direction other than the direction of further disentrenchment – has become smaller now than it was then.

How do we find out whether such a change has in fact occurred? How do we measure the tilt or even infer its existence? We can try to do with our recent past and contemporary experience what historical argument does with more distant events. We can consider the extent to which preexisting arrangements and assumptions, and the divisions and hierarchies they support, fail to explain the institutional experiments that take place in particular societies. In our own practical efforts at transformation we can try to judge the role these antecedent circumstances have played and will play in the success, the failure, or the redirection of our plans.

Imagine this condition of cumulative disentrenchment extended to its outermost, idealized limit. The chief form of ordinary social conflict becomes the clash and combination of parties of opinion – organized or unorganized movements of thought and sensibility whose commitments cannot be explained by the place its supporters occupy in a preexisting system of social roles and ranks. The ideals and programs of these movements do not remain within the limits set by any shared scheme of the models of human association meant to be realized in different domains of social existence. Nothing in this description implies that people's beliefs and actions become somehow uncaused. In fact, the metaphysical determinist may continue to claim that such beliefs and actions remain entirely determined. The point is, however, that they can no longer be explained as the products of a fundamental, unchallenged framework of institutions and assumptions.

At the times when the sequential effects retain their importance and the attraction of negative capability prevails over the countervailing advantages of coercive surplus extraction, a characteristic tension may arise. Some context changes may promise more for the development of negative capability while other, rival institutional or imaginative proposals may accommodate more easily the preexisting institutional order and the group interests it supports. Thus, the dominant institutional forms of Western industrialization were easier to reconcile with the interests of the richest and most powerful groups of early modern European society than any suitably revised version of the petty bourgeois alternative. The institutional inventions needed to cure the petty bourgeois program of its internal instabilities would only have aggravated its unacceptability to the dominant interests. Yet this program would have been more promising to the development of negative capability. Thinking that the bolder but ultimately more promising solution had no chance from the start, because it threatened the rich and the powerful, would not do justice to the many intentional and unintentional ways in which the more disentrenched and empowering approach may triumph.

Reconsider, from the vantage point of a speculative conception of world history, the preceding discussion of the relation between the two sources of cumulative, long-term context change. If history were the history of a single society, if it were, from the outset, world history in the strongest sense, there would be no way to tell apart the cumulative development of negative capability and the influence of a particular context upon its sequels. There would simply be an occasional or even cumulative weakening of the restrictive force of imaginative and institutional frameworks in social life. On the other hand, if there were simply separate societies, each with its own series of sequential constraints and opportunities, these parallel and separate sequences would never cross. Everything would then happen as if history were marked by many independent chains of sequential effects. In fact, however, neither view describes what history is like.

Several circumstances converge to account for the link between the sequential influence of formative contexts and the causal significance of negative capability. History, to be sure, is the history of different societies, with their distinguishing formative contexts. Even at their most entrenched, however, the contexts never fully determine the deeds and thoughts of the people who move within them. Moreover, the degree of their determining influence may itself wane. Because different social worlds do in fact collide, materially and spiritually, these causal sequences may be jumbled. They may even merge, ultimately, into a single process: that would indeed be world history.

Such a world history may emerge because one formative context or sequence of formative contexts has taken the others over. It may also come about because all distinctive contexts and sequences of context change have been mixed together. Insofar as world history emerges by this second route, its emergence dissolves the force of sequential restraint. But because social life never entirely escapes from dependence upon a limiting and shaping context, the sequential effect never disappears completely.

Thus, the basis for the influence of sequence also explains the many-sided relativity of this influence. It draws its force and direction from a particular social order. The very subsistence of such an order depends in turn upon the temporary suppression of the conflicts whose containment enables a textured form of life to subsist. Explanations appealing to the force of sequence must do justice to all the things that enable people to limit and resist this force.

THE FACTOR OF DISTURBANCE: TRASHING THE SCRIPT

Resistance to the Context

The final set of ideas in this view of context change deals less with a general influence upon the remaking of our social orders than with a limit upon all other such influences. This limit is the resistance the individual opposes to determination by his context, or by a list or sequence of contexts, or by the forces shaping the content and history of these contexts. Our recalcitrance turns out to be closely connected with another source of disturbance in history and in our efforts to understand history. The additional cause of uncertainty is the partly self-fulfilling character of our conceptions of social reality and possibility.

More than any other fact, our resistance to determination by our contexts accounts for the surprising and paradoxical quality of social experience. But though this stucture-defying resistance represents an anomaly in relation to all other fixed structures or structure-shaping forces, it is no mere residue of unexplained fact in this view of context change. On the contrary, it has an integral role to play in a theory, like this one, that unties the possibilities of social explanation from the appeal to all-determining and wholly determined structures.

This factor of disturbance makes explicit the basic circumstances that prevent all the other forces invoked in the narrative or the theory from meshing to form a closed and compulsive pattern. Its presence becomes more obvious as historical reconstruction or social description gain details. Moreover, its significance grows at the extremes of the spectrum of disentrenchment. At the farthest limit of emancipation from false necessity, it turns into a pervasive quality of ordinary experience. At the opposite pole of maximum entrenchment, it accounts for our capacity to overcome the constraints and redirect the forces that seemed to hold us in thrall.

The Context-Transcending Imagination and the Factor of Disturbance

The resistance of the individual to the institutional and imaginative framework of social life appears in two distinct forms that at first seem related only by opposition. On the one hand, the source of disturbance is the individual's partiality, the ultimate basis of which is his residual sense of being the center of the world – at least of his own world. No matter how entrenched the practical and imaginative order of society may be, it never turns him into its pliant agent. To some marginal but significant extent, he has ideas and goals of his own. He can never quite grasp the social order from a perspective that wholly transcends his place within it. Even when his intentions become altruistic, his knowledge remains fragmentary. The collisions between these partial perspectives, of will or understanding, give rise to an instability still more basic than the instability inherent in the very mechanisms that help stabilize formative contexts.

The element of disturbance appears, as well, in another, bolder and often more generous guise, the visionary impulse, the capacity to imagine – and to try out – forms of practical or passionate connection and of subjective experience that transcend the divisions and hierarchies of social life. It is the ability, which the individual never quite loses, to do the things that fail to fit.

The two faces of the element of disturbance look in opposite directions: one, toward self-centeredness, the other, toward prophetic hope. They are nevertheless faces of the same thing. Observe, first, their negative connection. They both presuppose the individual's resistance to the influence of a formative context. Even this negative relation, however, fails to do justice to the strength and significance of the link. Remember that the opportunity of the visionary appeal is precisely the individual's experience of forms of subjectivity and connection that override the constraints of the established order. Both aspects of the element of disturbance begin with the real, embodied, never quite capturable person whose antagonism to the dogmas and institutions of society takes the dual form of quarrelsome self-concern and visionary detachment.

To acknowledge such a two-sided element of disturbance is to take no position on the metaphysical issue of free will and determinism. It may or may not be true in some ultimate sense that to explain something is to give its sufficient conditions and that failure to do so represents a failure of explanation itself. The thesis central to this set of ideas takes its stance one step down from the metaphysical controversy. It tries to separate out from this controversy the more limited dispute whose resolution is essential to its concerns. The minimal form of the thesis is the claim that however human conduct may be determined, it cannot be determined exclusively by the institutional and imaginative design of society.

The element of disturbance operates with very different effect according to the level of exploitation of negative capability that has in fact been achieved. At the lowest levels – when formative contexts are relatively entrenched – it increases the chances for breaking out of a rigid order. It ensures that even the framework most carefully and successfully immunized against fighting can again be broken apart. At the contrasting limit of maximum emancipation from false necessity, the role of the factor of disturbance may be exactly reversed. It may now become a force that provokes the resurgence of an entrenched social order.

People who find themselves in a more or less extreme situation of loosened structure may act in ways that draw them back into a circumstance of straitened constraint. They may do this more or less deliberately, finding their freedom too troublesome, too dangerous, too costly, or too unholy. They may also reach the same result under the influence of selfish motives and shortsighted ideas.

Even in a circumstance of maximum disentrenchment, governmental power or group strategy may create the first elements of a resurgent order of social division and hierarchy. As soon as a system of differential social stations begins to crystallize, people may start to cast their conceptions of interest, identity, and possibility in its terms. They may adopt a strategy of preemptive security and narrowing alliances. They may simply fail to grasp the consequences of their actions for the reconsolidation of entrenched arrangements.

Our recalcitrance to thoroughgoing determination by the established institutional and imaginative structure of social life is a source of disturbance and surprise. But it need not represent an anomalous or subversive factor within the type of explanatory social theory argued for here. All other parts of this view of context change require this addition. The forms of destabilization built into the methods for stabilizing social contexts depend, in each instance, upon the structure-resisting quality of individual action and insight. The sequential influence of an order is only relative: one of the causes and corollaries of its relativity is precisely the individual's ability to act and think in ways this order can neither control nor countenance. The cumulative move toward higher levels of negative capability presupposes the possibility and the effectiveness of structure-breaking action and in turn widens the area available for its operation. Here at last is a view of transformation that need not treat the most obvious feature of ordinary social and historical experience as a mysterious inconvenience, nor conclude that reason must lose where freedom wins.

The Self-Fulfilling Quality of Our Theoretical Conceptions

Our views about society have an irremediably self-fulfilling quality. The effect of our conceptions of social reality and possibility upon the very experience they describe and explain means that our social theories have an ineradicable element of contestability, which is nowhere more evident or important than in our ideas about the existence, composition, and reconstruction of formative contexts. This incurable lack of assurance touches history itself, for it condemns us to disagree and struggle about our understanding of social life as well as about our material and ideal interests.

The self-fulfilling quality of our ideas about contexts is closely connected with our resistance to the influence of context. This quality is much more than the result of a localized interference of a measuring procedure upon measured phenomena. If we were indeed fully determined by our contexts or by a system of lawlike tendencies and constraints underlying the realization or succession of these frameworks, social reality might indeed be isolated from the effects of any particular account of it. Our conjectures would represent only better- or worse-informed approximations to the understanding of objective influences upon contexts and their revision. Because no system of context-produced or context-producing laws can fully govern us or limit our possibilities, we cannot by appealing to a closed system of laws determine what our contexts can become. Yet the answers we explicitly or implicitly give to this question influence our goals and actions. They end up changing what society is like and even what we are like.

We develop, probe, and test our ideas about social reality and possibility by doing transformative or conservative things to social situations. Our ideas about what can be done and what can happen influence both the way we define our interests or ideals and the actions by which we attempt to safeguard or advance them. In both ways our views of society – and about the character and transformability of social frameworks – inform our conservative or transformative projects, which in turn push social organization and personal experience in certain directions. Thus, our explanatory ideas leave their mark upon the reality for which they attempt to account. Beliefs about society or social possibility may actually become truer (i.e., easier to apply to experience) just by having been acted upon.

Some of our projects may fail and by their failure may cast a critical light on the descriptive and explanatory assumptions that informed them. But we can never be entirely sure that these same projects might not succeed under slightly different circumstances or with the help of slightly different methods. Even when we can draw persuasive inferences from success or failure, we face a more basic difficulty. We can never be sure how much our views of social reality or possibility would be changed if we had chosen to subject our inherited social experience to different transformative pressures. We have neither the time nor the indifference required to act upon a random and comprehensive set of transformative projects. If, absurdly, we tried to act in such a manner in the hope of overcoming the bias in our beliefs about society we would once again change the subject matter – ourselves – in the very course of attempting to grasp it.

We can, indeed, go a long way toward making a view of social reality and possibility more independent of the revelations produced by current or remembered collective efforts to preserve or transform our forms of social life. We can try to develop a conception drawing upon the revelations of many such efforts, undertaken by many classes, communities, and peoples in many different eras. A social theory compensates for its relative removal from a particular setting of conflict by recollecting a rich experience of reaffirmed and broken constraint and by drawing around this recollected and interpreted experience a penumbra of intimated possibilities. In this way, it hopes to achieve something of the cognitive effect of seeing society and history from the standpoint of a numerous and varied set of transformative or conservative projects.

But there is a limit to the efficacy of this cure. Each project is itself partly the product of certain beliefs about what people can and cannot do to their societies and to themselves. It takes an all–out rationalistic optimism to suppose that these inspiring ideas or inspired endeavors cancel out one another's biases. If much of history is the product of bad theories that have become less bad merely because people took them seriously, then it is hard to know how much of this made-up reality can be changed just by taking different theories for granted.

The implication of this discussion of the self-fulfilling quality of social theories is not that social reality is an artifact of our speculative ideas about society and social transformation. It is rather that we are unable to separate out with assurance the aspect of past, present, or future experience that is a product rather than a test of our speculative views. Nor does the argument lead to the conclusion that a social theory represents merely the elaborate rationalization of a transformative or conservative precommitment. The conclusion is, instead that we cannot separate, clearly and definitively, the part of a speculative social theory that represents a successful attempt at a more detached understanding and the part that can succeed only as a self-fulfilling myth, even a myth of emancipation and enlightenment.

THE USES OF THE THEORY OF CONTEXT MAKING

The Complete Job

How can the theory of context making presented in the second part of this chapter be used? From the outset, you should be careful not to treat this view the way you would a comprehensive theory in natural science: as a closed system of ideas that can be tested only at its periphery of empirical application. Rather, the view inspires a loose collection of explanatory practices and informs an equally loose group of transformative activities.

What would it mean to do a complete explanatory job on a social situation with the help of this account of context making? There would rarely be reason to attempt the complete job, but it may be helpful to imagine what it would look like. For the effort to do so provides an occasion to recapitulate the chief theses of the theory and emphasizes its twin central intentions. One intention is to break the link between the methods of social or historical explanation and the appeal to context-produced or context-producing laws and constraints. The other is to historicize the relation between structure and freedom: to explain stability and change in a way that not only recognizes but elucidates our capacity to diminish the force with which our frameworks deny us the ability to remake and rethink them.

Imagine, then, a complete job performed on a complicated social circumstance with the aid of the theory developed in this and preceding chapters. It may seem odd to apply a theory of context change to a social situation rather than to an episode of revolutionary reform. But this application simplifies the argument and underlines the continuities between the explanatory conjectures of this chapter and the descriptive or comparative categories of Chapters 2 and 3. Remember that a major theme of the explanatory argument of *False Necessity* has been that the way we describe and explain the workings of a social framework and of the whole social world it shapes already implies a view of framework change. Remember also that the polemical narrative beginning this chapter anticipates the application of the theory to an extended and connected series of social changes.

The first step in the complete job is to distinguish in the situation being studied the formative context and the formed routines. Actually, the attempt to select out the institutions and preconceptions that deserve to be included in the framework already presupposes a view of past transformations and future possibilities. We can state with assurance that a practice or preconception belongs to a context only when we know that its appearance has redirected, and that its substitution would rearrange, the ways in which people use the tangible and intangible resources of society to set terms to one another's activities and to determine the conditions on which some people can enlist the practical aid or allegiance of others.

The second step is to analyze the internal composition of the formative context and the particular practical and imaginative activities by which this context is regularly reproduced. The analysis must take into account that some parts of the framework are more tightly embedded in the whole they compose, and therefore harder to replace piecemeal, than others. It must describe the connections among the components of the context in ways compatible with the theory of context making, recognizing that our ideas about the internal constitution of a framework and our ideas about how the context gets remade are always just the reverse side of each other. It must show how the arrangements and preconceptions constituting the formative structure are constantly reenacted and defended by certain practical or conceptual activities, all the way from the form of commodity exchange to the prevailing method of moral and legal controversy. The executor of the complete job must show how each context-preserving activity draws shape and guidance from the framework it helps reproduce. He must also describe the particular devices of containment or truncation that prevent each context-respecting activity from turning into an occasion for context-transforming struggle.

The third step of the complete job is to place the institutional and imaginative framework in a double history. There is a history of sequential effects: the effects of earlier context or context states upon the present framework, and the effects of this framework upon its own transformative sequel, the bias it imposes upon the direction of change. Then, there is a history of the attractions of negative capability and of the forces that may counterbalance or override them. The established context must be placed on a spectrum of entrenchment and disentrenchment, and its emergence or subsistence must be interpreted as an episode in the relation of empowerment to emancipation from false necessity. If either of these two histories – the history of negative capability or the history of sequential effects –

existed alone, the formative context might be or seem to be the passive product of a determinate evolutionary dynamic. But the reciprocal interference of the two histories prevents any cohesive set of forces from becoming predominant, and makes room for surprise.

An important part of the attempt to locate the framework in this double historical setting is the commitment to understand how the context fails to fit into the sequence from which it emerged and how it in turn coexists with deviant modes of practice and sensibility that fail to fit into it. These incongruous elements may often be used as material with which to resist and to revise the framework. They may even prefigure institutions and conceptions that empower us more fully by pushing back farther the restraints of false necessity. But the passage of deviant practice into a more dominant position is never a smooth operation; it is likely to require the invention of novel institutional forms and the reinterpretation of familiar ideals. To execute the complete job we must see how much the present framework is indebted to a record of past, surprising deviations, and we must study the anomalies and the resistances that may play a similar role in relation to the established order.

The fourth step of the complete job is to consider what the present context might become under different directions, degrees, and circumstances of transformative pressure. Part of this exercise involves analyzing the opportunities for destabilization that result from the very activities that constantly restabilize the formative context. Another part is to examine the characteristically paradoxical relation of received ideals and recognized interests to the established institutional arrangements of society. The current institutional arrangements help shape the definition of these interests and ideals while frustrating their more complete fulfillment. Yet another part of this final step of the complete job is to anticipate the alternative institutions and conceptions that may realize such interests and ideals more fully while changing their recognized content in the course of realizing them. The last step in the complete job may even seek to describe the transformations of current practices and preconceptions that would contribute to a further measure of empowerment through disentrenchment. You would probe for the points of convergence between these changes and reforms required to realize given ideals and interests.

This book can be read as an attempt actually to do this complete job on the formative contexts of certain contemporary societies while developing and defending the theory under which the job is to be done. But the tentative and sketchy character of the result in a work already long and complicated shows that the complete job is a limiting case and a dangerous one too. For the standard explanatory uses of the theory we must look elsewhere.

The Normal Practice of a Politicized Social Theory

The more accessible alternative to the complete job is the revision of familiar genres of explanatory, critical, and programmatic writing. The view of contexts and context change presented in *False Necessity* can be used to support, connect, develop, and reconstruct these genres, to mix them together, and even to create others like them. At a minimum the view can serve as an antidote to dangers that beset these inherited ways of thinking and writing. *False Necessity* incorporates – and revises in the course of incorporating – each style of thought and explanation enumerated in the following paragraphs.

Consider first the genre of antinecessitarian explanation. This style of analysis criticizes an evolutionary stereotype, such as the identification of a simplified view of the English route to economic growth with the universal characteristics of "modernization" or "capitalism." The critic puts the stereotype in its place. He may hesitate to reject it entirely. But he reinterprets it against a background of forgotten conflict, of repressed or contained alternatives, and of continuing and continuingly promising deviations from the supposed norm. He emphasizes the relatively accidental quality of the events that resulted in the prevalence of the once or currently dominant arrangements. He takes the losers seriously even when he does not side with them.

The weak point of the antinecessitarian explanation is its characteristic lack of foundation for the claim that the alternatives were realistic, that they were not in fact ruled out by deep-seated economic, organizational, or psychological imperatives. This weakness is often aggravated by the temptation to disregard the external obstacles or internal instabilities that the defeated or contained alternatives confronted. The failure to recognize these instabilities and obstacles in turn invites a recurrent historiographic put-down: the counter-revisionist historian shows that the would-be radical prophets were in fact archaizing malcontents. Thus, for example, the petty-bourgeois radicals of the nineteenth century may be dismissed as the last-ditch defenders of a doomed artisanal dream. The politicized social theory for which *False Necessity* argues provides conjectures, categories, and methods that prevent an interest in explaining social and historical facts from being confused with an interest in vindicating the deep necessity of actual outcomes and triumphant arrangements. Moreover, by its emphasis on the importance and the variability of institutional forms, the theory shows how we can acknowledge the difficulties that the defeated alternatives faced in their original institutional form while nevertheless continuing to claim that these difficulties might have been – and may yet be – superseded once an alternative acquires a new institutional character.

A second, related genre is the analysis of a whole social world from the standpoint of its hidden tensions and vulnerabilities. The statecraft of reform and subversion habitually relies upon just such an analysis. When written at all, this genre is characteristically written episodically and for a practical purpose. Yet the historical reconstruction of a past situation may aspire to the same quality when its concern is to see beyond the distortions of hindsight to the many oppositions and possibilities in a world that is past, and thereby to recover the ambiguity and openness in what is now dead and gone. The practitioner of this genre wants to understand the situation as a whole rather than as a linear series of episodes of interest accommodation or problem solving in the manner of positivist social science. But he also wants to avoid the denial of multiple tensions and multiple possibility that has traditionally characterized the emphasis on the whole in deep-structure social explanation and in the earlier tradition of nationalist and romantic historiography. He seeks to recognize the detailed mechanisms of stabilization and constraint that lend a second-order necessity to the established order while also identifying the transformative opportunities to which each mechanism gives rise. He appreciates the shaping and constraining influence of the dominant arrangements and assumptions while also searching for the residues and anomalies they fail to crowd out.

This analysis of stability and destabilization, of precarious dominance and promising deviance, is in constant danger of taking too much of the current institutional and imaginative framework for granted. It may take the framework for granted whether it understates the presence of deviance and the prospects for destabilization or whether it overstates them. For the subtle and delicate part of the exercise is understanding how recognized group interests, collective identities, and received ideals may change as practical or imaginative conflict escalates and as practices and institutions are replaced. To offer a way of imagining such changes is the main contribution this politicized social theory can make to the analysis of stability and destabilization.

A third genre focuses on the interplay between routine activities and institutional or imaginative assumptions within a particular domain of social existence. Its concern is to reform a specialized branch of social analysis and turn it into the living image of a less superstitious understanding of social life. It seeks to develop an understanding less likely to mistake particular artifacts for social laws. Take economics as an example. *Social Theory: Its Situation and Its Task* discussed the distinct techniques of evasion by which the different styles of contemporary economic analysis evade the problem of the framework. Thus, to recall only the most striking instance, the macro-economist concedes in principle that the relations among aggregate economic phenomena (such as savings, investment, and employment) he seeks to study and establish depend upon very particular institutional assumptions such as the form and extent of unionization, the instruments with which governments may influence the economy, and the style of industrial organization and enterprise finance. Yet, having made this concession of principle, he hastens to return to a style of analysis and explanation that connects the aggregates directly to one another against an institutional background that he rarely makes crucial to the internal content of the economic account. Implicitly, he begins to treat the economic regularities he observes as if they were the laws of a general type of economic organization (i.e., the "regulated market economy"), irreplaceable except by distant, unrealistic, and undesirable alternatives. He fails to treat these regularities as the expression of a highly particular, temporary, and loosely connected series of social institutions and preconceptions. In a period of quiescence, when basic arrangements remain unchallenged, such an approach may achieve a measure of apparent success. This macroeconomist, however, attributes the wrong sense to the correlations that do hold in such a period of stagnation. For he sees deep necessity and general law where there are only the grinding routines reproduced by a makeshift and unique set of formative arrangements and beliefs. He will be caught by surprise as soon as the formative context changes again.

In economics, the genre of reformed, specialized analysis inspired by this antinaturalistic social theory would put the interplay between economic activities and the institutional and imaginative framework of social life at the center of its concern. It would recognize the pure system of equilibrium analysis or choice theory for what it is: a useful but empirically empty analytical apparatus. It would therefore also ascribe a much diminished and qualified sense of lawfulness to economic phenomena. It would not make its explanatory hopes depend upon the discovery of more determinate and universal economic laws. Every other branch of positivist social science can be reformed in a similar spirit.

The literature of social science includes many fragmentary examples of this genre. Economics, for example, has the tradition of nineteenth-century German and twentieth-century American institutionalism. Even the writings of mainstream economists have contributed to this mode of economic thought. But such examples dramatize all the more clearly the risk of an unguided eclecticism that compensates for its lack of theoretical direction by snatching ideas from incompatible styles of analysis. The result has often been to confirm the adepts of orthodox economics (or of its counterparts in other branches of positivist social science) in the conviction that their critics lack a coherent alternative. For, indeed, all coherent alternatives in any particular area of social science either presuppose or prefigure an escape from the confines of positivist social explanation, with its evasion of the framework problem, and of deep-structure social theory, with its reification of formative structures and its misguided search for structure-producing laws. The politicized theory of this book offers a principle of criticism and guidance that can help rescue such intellectual and political dissent from confusion and marginality.

Still another genre (or set of genres) appropriated, informed, and revised by a politicized social theory like the one developed in *False Necessity* is the programmatic proposal: the description of ways to reorganize social arrangements and institutions. In its contemporary forms programmatic thought suffers from a double disturbance: it lacks confidence in a way to argue about ideals and interests or about their implications; it also has no credible conception of social reality and transformation, no persuasive way to think about contexts and context change. The explanatory argument of *False Necessity* is most directly relevant to the second trouble.

In one guise, programmatic writing searches for minor adjustments, exercises in tinkering. Its proposals may then appear realistic, but their semblance of realism depends entirely on their making few or no changes in the established formative context of social life. (It is easy to appear realistic when you accept almost everything.) This style of programmatic thought takes interests and ideals as they are, with whatever authority they are assumed to possess, and looks for a more effective way to realize them. It has no prepared answer to the critic who asks, But why should we credit these recognized interests and ideals with any force? The normal element of such a style is practical controversy within a particular political community rather than abstract debate among speculative thinkers. (There is, of course, no a priori reason why ambitious theoretical claims cannot be advanced to support a marginally adjusted version of current practice. Such a combination, however, is today almost exclusively an artifact of the academic political philosophers.)

The other common contemporary genre of programmatic writing is utopian. It describes ideal arrangements distant from current realities. The utopian may not even pretend to have a practical way to reach this goal from the position he and his society now occupy. He nevertheless hopes that his radical proposals may inspire transformative practice in the here and now. However, the absence of a credible view of transformation exacts its price. The utopian proposal often turns out to be little more than the inverted image of current reality. Its content betrays the failure of the utopian thinker to reconstruct or even reimagine the very social order he appears to have overcome in an act of admonitory fantasy. Whether presented evocatively or discursively, the utopian vision speaks for interests and ideals that transcend the standards of a present political community. Yet the latter-day utopian (unless, once again, he is an academic political philosopher) has no prepared way to support the authority of his proposals. Though he speaks to frustrated parts of current experience, he lacks a developed view of the role these repressed aspects of sensibility and sociability ought to play in our imagination of a reordered social world.

The social theory for which this volume argues can help fuse the two genres of programmatic thought by providing both with a tenable way to deal with contexts and context change. So long as we lack the means for such a synthesis we remain condemned to the surrogate and arbitrary conception that measures realism by the closeness of proposed practice to current practice. (Even such an approach, however, rests on assumptions about transformative possibility, for how do we know what is close?) As a result, we are torn between dreams that seem unrealizable and prospects that hardly appear to matter. The aim must be, instead, to replace the criterion of closeness with a conception of realistic trajectories of context change. Along each trajectory, proposals may be cast in terms ranging from narrowly focused and short-run plans to distant and comprehensive reconstructions. Yet we need not present even the most radical proposal as a timeless blueprint, nor identify it with perfectionist aspirations, nor make it merely invert or negate the institutional and imaginative vocabulary of current society. The argument of Chapter 5 shows how a version of programmatic thought that overrides the contrast between the tinkering and the utopian genres of programmatic argument also effaces the contrast between taking for granted received ideals or recognized interests and searching for a more transcendent perspective. The explanatory theory that informs this revised approach to programmatic writing extends into a view of normative practice.

A politicized social theory must do its work through the reform of established genres like these, and through the invention of yet other ways of thinking and writing. The reform of each genre offers a new opportunity to reopen the issues raised by the attempt to sever the link between our practices of social explanation and the denial of our ability to remake our contexts. It enables us to undertake localized intellectual interventions in the spirit of comprehensive and radical intellectual reconstruction.

A CODA: FUNCTIONAL AND
COUNTERFACTUAL EXPLANATION IN THE
THEORY OF CONTEXT MAKING

The theory of context making set out in the second part of this chapter becomes more precise when reconsidered in the light of two well-known philosophical issues: the debate about functional explanation and the controversy over counterfactual explanation. For the most part, this work takes up methodological issues as an integral part of substantive debates; a methodological program always transcribes obliquely a substantive vision. Occasionally, however, the explicit analysis of methodological issues serves to dispel crucial ambiguities in a substantive argument.

Functional Explanation in the Theory

The view of context making seems to rely, in certain respects, on functional explanation, especially when it explains events according to their contribution to the development of negative capability. It therefore seems vulnerable to the criticisms leveled against functional hypotheses in social thought.

Functional explanations account for the emergence and continuance of a state of affairs by the consequences it produces and are therefore a species of causal explanation. They treat the power of something to generate certain effects as the cause of that thing. Whatever the difficulties in justifying the deployment of functional argument in particular explanatory settings, the structure of this explanatory approach is no more controversial than any other version of causal analysis. It fits easily into received schemes of scientific explanation, such as the deductive-nomological model.

G. A. Cohen has usefully distinguished functional explanations both from the study of functions and from those schools of twentieth-century anthropology and sociology that have been labeled functionalist. The study of functions is merely the inquiry into the consequences of states of affairs and, particularly, into the effects of these states upon one another. It implies no commitment to functional explanation, much less to the thesis distinguishing the functionalist schools. Functionalism, on the other hand, holds that everything in a society is connected and that the components of a social or cultural order must be explained by the contribution these components make to the whole that they constitute. If the study of functions is less than required for functional explanation, the functionalist thesis is more. Functional accounts can be legitimately deployed by those who see societies and cultures as largely made up of conflicting elements or who attribute explanatory force to consequences that imply the disruption rather than the maintenance of established orders.

The greatest difficulty posed by the use of functional explanation in social and historical studies consists in the failure to achieve clarity about the precise mechanism through which the consequence produces the cause. Deliberate action may provide this connecting mechanism. People set out to achieve certain objectives, and the foreseen consequences of their actions, as purposes or motives, become the causes of these actions. In these circumstances, functional explanation offers few difficulties. More precisely, the core context of functional explanation consists in situations that combine several attributes. There must be a cohesive source of action – an individual or, more debatably, a movement. Deliberate action cannot be plausibly attributed to a collection of individuals who have no active awareness of working toward a common goal. The individual or collective agent must remain largely in control of the environment of their action. When this control fails, the power of the unintended consequences of intentional actions to cause those actions requires a special, nonobvious elucidation. As Jon Elster has argued, the course of action explained must be brief. The longer the duration the less likely that cohesive and deliberate agency can be ensured and the more likely that purposive action will have to be replaced by other, more obscure and dubious ways to turn consequences into causes.

When functional explanations are used in social and historical study beyond the boundaries of the easy case defined by intentionality, effective control, and short-term duration, the mechanism by which consequences acquire causal force requires additional definition. The functional explanations advanced in this more uncertain territory are often equivocal: they invoke a vague analogy to purposive action without either specifying or justifying their departures from the scheme of purposive explanation. More often than not, the confusion matters not only for its own sake but because it denies social experience much of the quality of surprise and possibility that accompanies intentional action. To a greater or lesser extent, it encourages us to picture people as the half-conscious objects of forces explained by consequences that nobody actually ever chose and that barely anyone, other than the theorists in the know, really understands. Thus, an abyss opens between lived experience and retrospective or theoretical judgment.

Yet social and historical experience seems repeatedly to justify functional explanations that go beyond the core case of intentional action. There does seem to be something to the search for an equivalent in social studies to the Darwinian mode of functional explanation. The problem is to find the equivalent to Darwinian explanation that renders precise the more than intentional connection between consequence and cause while respecting the sense of historical contingency.

Consider first, for the sake of the comparison, how core evolutionary theory (by which I mean here the "modern synthesis" of Darwinism and genetics) fits the model of functional explanation. The explanatory consequence is reproductive success in the environment. The mechanism that turns this consequence into a cause is the interplay between random genetic recombination and natural selection. This interplay operates against the background of additional constraints such as the mechanical limits to the building of alternative bodily forms with the biological materials at hand.

The part of the preceding theory of context making that deals with the long-term development of negative capability represents the historical parallel to the style of biological explanation. It nevertheless avoids the two main objections to the use of supraintentional functional accounts in social study: imprecision in describing the link between consequence and cause, and retrospective or contemplative fatalism in the appreciation of historical events and social arrangements.

The counterparts, in this aspect of the theory, to the goal of reproductive success are the three distinct forms of development singled out by the theory of negative capability: the growth of the practical powers of production (or destruction), the potentially cumulative emergence of forms of practical collaboration or passionate attachment less circumscribed by the restraints of a fixed pattern of dependence or dominion, and the advance of theoretical insight into the truth about false necessity. It is important to remember that these distinct cumulative developments remain always mere reversible possibilities. Moreover, in their most general form, they draw their authority in part from the contribution they all make to a freedom whose value is itself controversial: the freedom that consists in resisting imprisonment by a particular structure of life or discourse. The third, theoretical expression of the development of negative capability highlights this special sense of moral progression and reveals what the other two expressions have in common. The development of practical powers, or the creation of forms of exchange and communities less constrained by a preexisting hierarchical order, often proceeds in advance of what available theoretical insight considers possible. But these new social forms can continue to operate only because the participants in them understand their principles of operation and grasp how such principles exhibit a more capacious sense of social possibility and reality than had been available before. The consequences of negative capability are more complex than the relatively straightforward goal of reproductive success. They nevertheless possess a unity: the individual and collective empowerment made possible by repeated departures from a fixed logic of recombination in society or culture.

But what of the mechanism that would give causal force to this threefold structure of consequences? The most remarkable feature of this instance of functional explanation, in contrast to the examples found in the natural sciences, is its resistance to a clear-cut contrast between the strictly intentional and unintentional transmutations of consequences into causes. Actions that bring about a development of negative capability may be undertaken for the very purpose of developing this capability. Thus, reformers in high office may deliberately attempt to achieve the minimal weakening of the established order of social division and hierarchy that allows for a more remorseless recombination of material and human resources. Alternatively, some actions bringing about a development of negative capability may be performed without foresight of the consequences. Yet this lack of foresight is compatible with a relation to negative capability that the contrast between intentional and unknowing action cannot capture. Consider some examples. A small-scale experiment in deviation from the established forms of business organization, for example, may be undertaken merely for the sake of the immediate advantages it promises its authors. A model of human association at odds with ruling social ideals may remain quarantined in a limited area of society, without any apparent general reach.

The public or private entrepreneurs who want to initiate and extend a practical innovation must be able to replace or recombine the components of the novelty; the original innovators must themselves constantly reinvent their own invention if they want to stay ahead. Every way of organizing work, no matter how self-contained it may appear, relies on preexisting social relations and accepted assumptions in order to fill out its ambiguities. A shift in this background would itself suffice to require the rearrangement of the initial innovation if changes in particular market conditions and institutional settings did not.

Similarly, the ideological critic who wants to extend an anomalous model of human association to areas of social life it had previously left untouched must reinvent it. For every enacted picture of human association involves a transaction between a more or less indeterminate conception and a set of context-specific practices that give the conception its richly defined meaning and are in turn illuminated by it. Thus, when ideals of family community or of a democratic republic are extended into the realm of practical work and exchange, they cannot continue to mean just what they meant before.

The businessmen or ideologists who follow the leaders in these examples may have neither a commitment to the development of any aspect of negative capability nor any extended insight into how their actions advance it. In this sense, they are unintentional agents. They must nevertheless practice the art of recombination. To practice it repeatedly and successfully, they must, to some extent, understand it. The art of recombination required involves rearranging the constitutive elements of a set of institutional practices or imaginative pictures. It also implies rearranging them in a particular direction, however circuitous and halting the pattern may be: the direction of disentrenching institutional or imaginative structures and making them more susceptible to criticism and revision in the midst of ordinary social life. To practice repeated recombination people must master at least an implicit and truncated version of the insights developed by a full-fledged theory of negative capability.

The same point can be restated in more general form. The characteristic method of social invention in general and of the development of negative capability in particular is to seize on deviant, subsidiary, or repressed elements in present or remembered experience and to push them toward a dominant position, all the while changing them in the course of this extension. The transmutation of the deviant into the dominant may amount to no more than a change in the composition of an established order of life or discourse, a change that preserves the relation between what the order incorporates and what it excludes. But if the theory of negative capability is true, the most successful transmutations over the long run – the ones least vulnerable to subversion by practical rivalry, moral indignation or aspiration, and theoretical insight – are likely to be those that permit or invite further tinkering. Thus, they may be repeatedly corrected rather than entirely replaced. Such innovations preserve to a higher degree, in their own workings, the practice of recombination that created them in the first place. The social innovator may neither want nor comprehend the development of negative capability as a general goal. But he will be more likely to fail unless he grasps the principles of accelerated recombination that help explain the workings of his most successful inventions. If his contribution to the development of negative capability is not entirely intentional and conscious, neither is it wholly compulsive and unknowing.

Compare this view of the way consequences may operate as causes in history and society to the neo-Darwinian idea of the interplay between natural selection and random genetic recombination. The counterpart to genetic recombination here is the more or less conscious and intentional innovation whose character has just been described. The counterpart to natural selection is the greater vulnerability of the less developed forms – the ones that fail to embody a higher measure of negative capability – to practical, moral, or theoretical challenge and defeat. The difference is that this test of failure and success, rather than operating blindly, already bears the imprint of the minds like those that devise the innovations. For a set of institutions and discursive practices gets in trouble by failing to achieve the flexibility that embodies or perpetuates the practice of recombination. Thus, innovation and vulnerability to subversion connect far more intimately than genetic variation and natural selection; each is partly internal to the other. A related consequence is that the possible cumulative development of negative capability may achieve a directional movement and rapidity that biological evolution can never attain, not at least unless Lamarckianism is true.

Counterfactual Explanation in the Theory

A major feature of the theory of context change set out in these pages is its effort to dissociate success in explanation from the attempt to show that an event had to have occurred as it did. This theory devalues the necessity of what exists. Thus, the earlier polemical genealogy of the current formative contexts of power and production emphasizes how the distinct social and institutional versions of industrialism to have emerged in the course of modern history suggest a yet wider range of possible variation. Indeed, insight into lines of development that were halted or reversed is crucial to understanding the main direction events in fact took. We see a social order differently according to how much of its content we attribute to deeply rooted practical, psychological, or moral imperatives and how much to the precarious, haphazard exclusion of alternative arrangements and preconceptions.

The alternatives this theory invokes fit into no well defined set of possible forms of social organization or possible pathways of social change. They represent, instead, the imagined extension of deviations that have in fact emerged and been contained: a penumbra of variation around actual societies and actual events rather than an a priori scheme of social and historical possibility. No single criterion traces the limits of possibility or distinguishes the realistic alternatives from the futile approaches. We must determine the extent to which particular deviations failed because they were suppressed by force and guile and the extent to which they failed because they were outdone by their rivals on the multiple terrain of practical, moral, and theoretical needs. And we must be guided in this judgment by a general view of context making that tries to make sense of the entire historical record of successful or failed deviation.

Though social and historical alternatives in this theory remain parasitic upon actual events, they lose explanatory value if they cannot serve as the antecedents in hypothetical judgments of cause and effect. They must figure in arguments of a type that has proved central to my institutional narrative: thus, for example, if petty commodity production had been the chosen path to industrialism, it would either have failed or have needed to undergo the institutional redefinition described earlier. The making of claims like these introduces into the heart of this theory of transformation the famous problem of counterfactuals and lays the view open to the criticisms leveled against counterfactuals.

A counterfactual argument draws out the consequences of a hypothetical state of affairs. Typically, the argument is used to make a point about events that did occur. Given the character of social experience and social thought, it is hardly surprising that all but the most narrowly necessitarian students of history and society find themselves repeatedly tempted to rely upon counterfactual explanations. The importance of such explanations to social and historical analysis is habitually obscured by the failure to make them entirely explicit.

Recent critics have distinguished two main objections to the common uses of counterfactual argument. (See, especially, Brian Barry's discussion, cited in the notes.) Such objections can best be understood as expressing strong and weak versions of the same test for the validity of counterfactual claims.

The strong version states that the theory violated by the hypothetical existence of the counterfactual antecedent must not be the same theory used to pass from the antecedent to the consequent. The causal passage from antecedent to consequent must not depend on laws violated by the hypothesis of the antecedent itself. For such an ambivalence creates the danger of a speculative free-for-all masquerading as rigorous explanation. Consider the following example. If the Aztecs, possessing the social organization they in fact developed, had produced the steam engine, the technical division of labor in the Aztec economy would, within two generations, have resembled the one prevailing in England around 1840. We cannot simultaneously pretend to have a theory of technical or social change capable of determining precise connections between technological innovation and social arrangements and suppose that the Aztecs might have developed the steam engine without first reconstructing their society. The reason why this first criterion of legitimacy in counterfactual explanation may nevertheless be too severe is that it discounts the possibility that an apparently unified body of explanatory ideas may be broken apart into distinct elements, some of which may then be incorporated, with the help of counterfactual speculation, into another set of ideas. Counterfactual argument may be a tool for pillaging one theory to build another.

The other, looser version of the test for the validity of counterfactual explanations criticizes those counterfactual explanations where the change in preexisting reality dwarfs in importance the further move from antecedent to consequent. If the Aztecs, while retaining more or less the society and culture we know them by, had possessed a highly industrialized economy and a mechanized army, they would certainly have defeated the Spanish invaders. At first, the objection seems to be merely one of triviality. If the Aztecs had industrialized, the course of world history that brought Cortés to the Yucatán might well have been entirely different, and the outcome of those battles beside the point. On a closer view, however, the weak test states, more diffusely, the same basic problem posed by the strong test. The more we disrupt our understanding of reality by suspending part of our beliefs about how things happen, the more uncertain become the calculations informed solely by the beliefs we have chosen to retain. The problem is not merely that we have fewer assumptions to go on but that we are unsure about how to use the assumptions we have kept.

How well does the counterfactual element in the view of context making presented here hold up under this double test? Take, as an example of the use of counterfactual conditionals in this theory of transformation, the particular hypothesis that has played so large a role in the institutional genealogy put forward in the first part of this chapter. According to this hypothesis, there existed a major alternative to the dominant form of industrialism. This alternative might have arisen out of the actual impulses toward and beyond petty commodity production in the history of modern Western industry and agriculture. Such impulses, however, would have failed unless petty commodity production had undergone something like the institutional redefinition outlined earlier and described more fully in Chapter 5. The redefinition would have resulted in a fuller development of negative capability than the forms of production and exchange that in fact prevailed. Rather than having been defeated once and for all, the alternative remains a live possibility once new circumstances (e.g., changes in the international division of labor) bring pressure to bear against the established styles of industrialism.

This set of ideas has no trouble passing the weaker test for the validity of counterfactual explanations. The shift in preexisting reality represented by the counterfactual antecedent certainly does not dwarf the long chain of consequences derived from it. For here the antecedent – the further development of deviant tendencies that in fact emerged – differs only by gradual and almost indistinguishable steps from actual occurrences, on one side, and from the first links in the chain of consequences, on the other. Even the institutional redefinition that might have nurtured these aberrations was prefigured, however fragmentarily, in social thought and practice.

But what of the other, more severe and precise test? Do these counterfactual claims depend upon the very theories suspended by the counterfactual antecedent? The exact reverse can be said. The same ideas that guide insight into the chain of counterfactual consequences also support the historical realism of the counterfactual antecedent and inform the way it is defined. The same conceptions link the institutional genealogy of the first part of this chapter to the theory of the second part of the chapter. They emphasize that similar practical powers (such as those implied by an incipient industrialized economy) can be realized by alternative institutional orders, that these orders differ in the degree of negative capability they embody, and that such differences can be ascertained by analyzing specific features of formative institutional contexts of power and production. More significantly and controversially, the same animating ideas suggest criteria for choosing the deviations with a better or worse chance of taking hold. We must look to the preexisting situation and take into account its sequential effects and its distinctive opportunities for stabilization and destabilization. We must examine the conduciveness of the rival alternatives to negative capability. We must not forget to reckon with the factor of disturbance represented by the perspicuity, guile, tenacity, or sheer luck with which one or another alternative is pursued.

The ideas supporting both the antecedent and its consequences may seem too loose to be considered a theory of any kind. And indeed the theory to which these ideas contribute neither resembles natural science nor supports confident predictions. The theory aspires only to broaden and to refine, not to replace, the pre-theoretical self-reflection of historical agents. Its claims, including its counterfactual claims, resemble far more the arguments of plain people about what to expect and what to do than they resemble the structure of covering law and deductive inference in natural science. They are contentious but defensible grounds for argument rather than knockdown proofs or statistical generalizations. But by abandoning the quest for a certainty it cannot achieve the theory gains the countervailing explanatory advantages suited to its character. *Politics* is an effort to make good on these distinctive strengths.

5

The Program of Empowered Democracy
The Remaking of Institutional Arrangements

FROM EXPLANATIONS TO PROGRAMS

PLAN OF THE DISCUSSION

THIS chapter sets out a program for reconstructing the large-scale institutional structure of society: the constitution of government, the organization of the economy, and the system of legal rights. This institutional program is extended by a program for remaking the fine texture of social life: the style of direct, person-to-person relations.

The immediate subject of the programmatic argument is the institutional structure of contemporary societies and in particular the formative institutional context of the Western industrial democracies, the very context whose origins the argument of Chapter 4 explored. The program is not meant as a timeless blueprint, to be applied with appropriate variations to any historical circumstance. It responds to a particular situation with particular measures and beliefs, drawn in large part from a particular institutional and imaginative tradition. Just as the interpretive genealogy of Chapter 4 anticipated a general theory of transformation, so the program presented in this chapter and the following exemplifies not only an approach to the social ideal but a view of the possibilities of programmatic argument.

How does the programmatic vision connect with the account of context change developed in the preceding parts of this book? After all, the dominant tradition of modern philosophy since Hume and Kant has emphasized the difference between the *is* and the *ought*. Modern social thought affirmed its identity in part by the resoluteness with which it tried to overcome the loose confusion of normative and explanatory ideas. The initial section of this chapter elucidates and justifies the suspect turn from explanation to program making.

The argument moves through three steps. First, it considers the narrowest link between the programmatic and the explanatory ideas. The institutional program includes a feasible version of petty commodity production, the most stubborn rival of the style of economic organization that became dominant in the course of modern Western history.

The second step goes on to consider the relation between the larger theory of transformation that informs my polemical genealogy of dominant and deviant styles of industrial society and the conception of the ideal that inspires this entire institutional program. Both the program and the explanatory theory take as their point of departure the same fundamental account of our relation to the contexts of our activity. In particular, they discover both a practical and an epistemological interest in the paradox of contextuality: our need to settle down to a particular context and our inability to accept any context in particular as fully satisfactory. The programmatic argument sees the change of our relation to the contexts of our activity as the basis for a broad range of forms of empowerment.

The third step in the effort to establish a link between the explanatory and the programmatic arguments examines the sense in which a vision of human empowerment can possess prescriptive authority. Views that define both the meaning of empowerment or self-assertion and the causal conditions for its promotion should be seen as the most common form of a historically located practice of normative argument. Such a fundamental practice cannot be in any simple sense true or false, right or wrong, though we may have reasons to change it or even to abandon it. Our ways of assessing the normative weight of conceptions of self-assertion ultimately reflect views about our relation to our fundamental practices.

THE RESCUE OF PETTY COMMODITY PRODUCTION

My highly interpreted account of the genesis of the contemporary formative context of power and production in the advanced Western countries emphasized the abundance of deviant forms of organizations failing to fit the dominant "English" route to development. The argument also suggested that many of the deviations that took root, and an even larger portion of those that did not, represented variations on the theme of petty commodity production: the economy of small-scale, relatively equal producers, operating through a variable mix of cooperative organization and independent activity. Elements of this alternative were never completely suppressed, although the suppression went further in some countries than in others, influenced industry more than agriculture, and excluded the cooperativist varieties of small-scale production more than the recourse to small-scale, independent property. The smallholding alternative continues to characterize the agriculture of many industrializing Western countries. The centralized factory and the multidivisional enterprise coexist everywhere with a multitude of manufacturing and commercial shops that employ most of the work force. Many of the economy's most technologically advanced as well as its most technologically retrograde sectors depart from the model presented by mass-production industry and display features of petty commodity production. Moreover, the working masses in the advanced West and throughout the world stubbornly maintain the petty bourgeois dream against the almost universal advice of their centrist or radical betters, who insist that history has condemned this dream to frustration.

Nevertheless, as a principle for the organization of the economy, the program spearheaded by the artisanal classes and by the "utopian" propagandists of cooperation has been repeatedly defeated in the course of modern Western history. A major point of the polemic in Chapter 4 against the stereotype of Western development is to argue that this defeat cannot be plausibly understood as the result of inescapable economic, organizational, or psychological constraints. The early versions of the alternative were defeated before they had a chance to fail. The alliance of central governments with preexisting and emergent elites generally sufficed to ensure that the dominant style of economic organization won out. At times, this alliance supported the use of outright military force against the proponents of the alternative (e.g., the crushing of the experiments barely begun by the 1848 revolutionaries). More often, economic policies and legal rules tilted the scales against the alternative.

But the argument about origins in Chapter 4 also showed that had the alternative been tried out on a larger terrain, it would have run into basic dilemmas. To solve these dilemmas it would have been necessary to invent an institutional framework for power and production very different from the one that has come to prevail in the course of modern Western history. In the absence of this invention, petty commodity production would indeed have proved economically regressive and economically and politically unstable. But from its indispensable institutional reconstruction it would have emerged with a character very different from the one its champions had sought to impress upon it. To this limited extent the conservative or radical opponents of petty commodity production *were* right, though not in the sense they supposed.

The alternative production system seemed bound to die through either economic concentration or economic stagnation. The more successful independent producers would eventually reduce the less successful producers to the condition of dependent wage labor. Thus, something like "capitalism" or, more precisely, something like the dominant style of modern Western economic organization would result. But suppose that concentration failed to occur and that independent, small-scale, and relatively equal producers and traders continued to dominate markets. Then, petty commodity production would preclude the economies of scale in production and exchange that are vital to technological dynamism. The society would vegetate in economic stagnation or regression, until its institutional order collapsed under the pressure of domestic discontent or foreign rivalry and conquest.

The dilemma of concentration or stagnation besetting the alternative cannot be resolved so long as the chief mechanism of economic decentralization remains the consolidated property right: the claim to divisible portions of social capital that is relatively unlimited in both scope and duration. For this method of market decentralization achieves economies of scale precisely by permitting proprietary concentration – a concentration that may persist so long as the property owner avoids too many mistaken investment decisions. Antitrust law and policy simply take for granted the existence of a fixed trade-off between economies of scale and competitive fragmentation, as if any particular degree of interference between competition and scale were required by the laws of economic reality.

The dilemma of concentration and stagnation can be broken only by a method of market organization that makes it possible to pool capital, technologies, and manpower without distributing permanent and unqualified rights to their use. Claims upon the divisible portions of social capital have to be made temporary and limited: temporary, to prevent the ongoing accumulation of economic power in particular hands; limited, to stop accumulated capital in some enterprises from being used to gain control over other enterprises or to reduce large numbers of propertyless workers to wage-dependent status. Such limitations must be merely the reverse side of an allocational system that makes substantial resources available to teams of workers and entrepreneurs and thereby achieves the indispensable economies of scale. But if such a system is to retain a plausible link to the spirit of petty commodity production, it must compensate and more than compensate for the required limitations of time and usage with more economic deconcentration and greater facility to try out new ways of organizing work and exchange than can be hoped for under property-based market regimes. Above all, the alternative institutional definition of markets must work.

Suppose that, by narrowly economic standards, it does work. The dilemma of concentration and stagnation would then give way to another problem, about the relation between government and the economy, that the revised version of petty commodity production would have to solve. Even under existing market regimes, the rules of property and contract law, which describe the basic means for the allocation of claims to capital, are the results of conflicts over the uses of governmental power. And legal analysis shows that, on however small a scale, these rules contain the elements of conflicting approaches to market organization. But the types of market organization they enshrine operate to a large extent as if they had an inner logic barely distinguishable from the logic of a general coordination of private interests. The preconceptions of legal and political theory further aggravate the sense that the rules of private law are somehow apolitical; politics decide whether to have a market at all and even how much of a market to permit but not what a market should look like, legally and institutionally. This choice among radically different styles of economic decentralization is not supposed to exist.

The reconstructed form of petty commodity production requires a much more overtly political administration of the social capital fund. It does so even if the allocation of capital claims emphasizes general rules and conditions rather than discretionary judgments. The deliberative processes of a democratic government must gain the scope, continuity, and decisiveness required for effective social control of accumulation. Unless this more explicit economic influence of government is counterbalanced by new forms of participation and accountability, governmental power can be used all the more effectively to entrench some private interests at the expense of others or to subordinate all these interests to the will of the groups in control of the state. The new-model economic alternative would then prove incapable of coexisting with a form of governmental organization that can sustain it. The current style of liberal-democratic thought and practice seems inadequate to this task. It makes central power accountable only by helping to stalemate it. It disperses power in order to slow it down, and it seeks to combine representation with demobilization. Its characteristic devices are ill-suited to the demand for governmental processes both more present in the economy and more pliant to the citizenry.

Thus, the attempt to give the repressed alternative form of industrial organization a chance requires nothing less than the reinvention of the institutional framework of markets and democracies. The program of institutional reconstruction explored in this chapter can be understood in part as the description of such a framework. One aim of the programmatic argument advanced here is to suggest the radical and comprehensive institutional redefinition that the repressed alternative would have to undergo in order to become feasible. But why should we be interested in this return of the repressed?

My earlier discussion of the origins of contemporary formative contexts has already emphasized the many lives of the alternative. Remember its most recent incarnations in the Western industrial democracies and in their third world periphery. The changing international division of labor threatens the stability of mass-production industries in the richer countries and underlines the importance of a greater emphasis on the vanguardist industries, with their characteristically more flexible interplay of task-defining and task-executing activities. This change of emphasis can be accomplished by either more conservative or more subversive means. Its more restrained form would resort merely to economic incentives and manpower training. Its more radical variant would begin by depriving mass-production industries of the legal-institutional devices by which they protect themselves against potentially fatal instabilities in the product, capital, and labor markets. This more transformative sequel would culminate in a capital-allocation system more supportive of the teams of technical workers and manager–technicians that typically do the main work of vanguardist industry. The reconstructed mode of petty commodity production represents just such a system.

In many contemporary third world countries, popular forces search for a more equal and less authoritarian growth path. These forces want redistribution with agrarian reform, the redirection of the production system to mass needs, and a relatively greater measure of autarky from the world economy. They seek a program that frees them from having to choose between either passive collaboration with the national bourgeoisie, in the name of a blind faith in the dialectic that supposedly leads from capitalism to socialism, or commitment to the cause of an industrial proletariat that turns out to be a relatively small labor aristocracy, lost amid a far more numerous petty bourgeois and underclass populace. The growth path and the class alliances these popular movements are in search of require both a broad range of decentralized economic activity and a pooling of large-scale resources, under a regime of governmentally guided accumulation. The acceptance of decentralized forms of production and exchange saves the popular state from having to wage war against its actual petty bourgeoisie and aspiring working classes. It therefore also prevents the economic disruption and governmental authoritarianism that such a war brings in its wake, as Soviet experience so dramatically testifies. Such economic arrangements in turn call for a practice of government that expands both the scope of public decisions and the means for holding public officials accountable. Once suitably adapted to third world conditions, the remodeled framework of petty commodity production promises to satisfy this combination of objectives.

The recurrence, over so long a period and across such varied circumstances, of occasions and attempts to try out one or another version of the alternative suggests it must have more going for it than its suitability to an odd series of particular historical circumstances. The genealogical argument of Chapter 4 implies that this deeper basis of the recurrence is the promise to carry the development of negative capability in practical life farther than our established ways of organizing power and production have hitherto permitted. The point of the preceding paragraphs has been to describe a first link between the explanatory and the programmatic arguments of this book, not to present the primary inspiration of the program. To anticipate: an entirely different inspiration to connect the explanations and the proposals is the desire to rescue the modernist theory and practice of personal politics – the war against rigid social roles and canonical orderings of the emotions – from its disastrous anti-institutional and privatistic bias and to do so by imagining an instituted form of life that does justice to modernist ideals. Once you grasp the deeper and more general connection between the explanatory and the programmatic ideas developed here, you can begin to see how the same program serves such seemingly unrelated objectives as the rescue of modernism from privatism and the defense of petty commodity production against impracticality.

THE ADVANTAGES OF NOT FITTING

The relation between the explanatory and the programmatic aspects of the argument can be reformulated in a manner that emphasizes the shared grounding of programs and explanations in a picture of human activity. The theory of transformation in this book gives a constructive use to what might otherwise seem a mere explanatory embarrassment: our irrepressible ability to think, act, and connect beyond the limits imposed upon us by any existing or denumerable list of social or mental frameworks. We can not only step outside these structures but also limit their imprisoning force and draw from this limitation a range of varieties of empowerment. The constraining force of the formative contexts helps explain much of our routine behavior and even a great deal of the actual sequence of institutionalized social worlds. But our ability to stand outside these structures and eventually to change the relation between their constraining force and our power to resist them introduces another possible source of long-term, cumulative historical transformation. The interaction between the consequences of our membership in stabilized social worlds and the consequences of our ability to escape those consequences produces a practice of social explanation incompatible with deep-structure social analysis. The new practice emancipates us from the suspect contrast between the lived sense of openness and contingency in history and the retrospective appeal of the theorist to lawlike constraints that underlie the surface agitation of history. It does so by attacking simultaneously both sides of this opposition. Theoretical insight and political prophecy need no longer seem inexplicable exceptions to structural determinism.

Just as the earlier view of context change confers an affirmative explanatory value on our structure-transforming capability, the program outlined in this chapter gives this capability an independent normative interest directly connected to its explanatory value. The empowerment produced by the development of negative capability has explanatory value because it serves our individual and collective projects of self-assertion and because we can act, more or less perspicuously and intentionally, to create the social orders that strengthen our negative capability.

The whole program for the reconstruction of institutional arrangements and personal relations that is developed here takes as its point of departure the improving effect a greater mastery over the contexts of our activity may have upon our relations to one another. In particular, this change in our relation to our habitual frameworks promises to moderate the conflict between the enabling conditions of self-assertion: between our need to participate in shared forms of practical, emotional, and cognitive life and our struggle to escape the threats of dependence and de-individualization that seem inherent to all forms of collective engagement.

Nothing in the program worked out here represents a sharp break with the shared ground of the modern secular ideologies of emancipation: liberalism, socialism, and communism. All these doctrines emphasize the link between individual or collective empowerment and the dissolution of social division and hierarchy. All hold that such dissolution depends upon the remaking of practical institutions. They differ, of course, in their understanding of institutional reconstruction (a voluntary act? a reflection of underlying forces?), in their specific institutional proposals and their resulting evaluation of present society, and therefore also in their way of characterizing the content of empowerment.

The programmatic argument worked out here contrasts with those doctrines in relying upon a far more inclusive view of the possible institutional forms of human coexistence, a view focusing upon the conditions and consequences of our ability to alter the basic character of our relation to our established frameworks. One result of this enlargement of the sense of social possibility is to change the way we define the empowerment we hope will result from the further effacement of the contrast between context-preserving routine and context-transforming conflict. It then becomes possible to grasp with greater precision both the distinctions and the connections among varieties of empowerment – the development of productive capabilities, the escape from passive imprisonment within a framework, and the moderation of the conflict between the enabling conditions of self-assertion – and to take each aspect of empowerment seriously as a concern of social reconstruction. The hope of limiting the conflict between structures and freedom by changing the content and character of structures, the broadening of the range of imagined alternatives to current forms of social organization, and the specification of the ideal of empowerment all help prepare the way for a reconciliation between the leftist and the modernist criticism of contemporary societies, between the social-revolutionary politics of institutional reconstruction and the cultural-revolutionary politics of personal relations.

The intimate and fundamental connection just described between the explanatory and the programmatic arguments takes for granted another, looser but no less important relation. Deep-structure social theory makes programmatic thought superfluous. There is no point in asking ourselves what society should become if history will tell us in the end what it must become.

The weakening of ambitious, deterministic claims, through the dilution or abandonment of deep-logic social theory, and the rise of conventional social science have had a paradoxical effect upon the status of programmatic thought. They have undermined the most extreme necessitarian objections to the enterprise of programmatic thought; but they have also failed to produce any credible theory of transformation and, more especially, any persuasive account of the remaking of formative contexts and of the limits to their recombination and renewal. The more compromised versions of deep-structure social theory circumscribe necessitarian claims without offering persuasive reasons not to restrict them even more drastically. Though they erode belief in the lawlike constraints to which the hard-core variants of deep-logic analysis appeal, they supply no alternative basis for social-theoretical generalization. Conventional social science fails just as clearly to present any coherent approach to the substitution of frameworks. (Remember its characteristic stratagems: profess total agnosticism about all nontrivial causal connections, as in the most rigorous branches of microeconomics and choice theory; or assimilate the choice of frameworks to the choice of the most efficient solutions within a framework, as in the cruder, more propagandistic versions of microeconomics; or concede the historically specific and contingent character of a framework while searching for stable correlations and causal sequences within the framework, as if it were not so makeshift and transitory after all, as in much of macroeconomics.)

The failure to produce a credible account of the remaking of our institutional and imaginative frameworks and of the relations among their component elements deprives us of any standard by which to distinguish realistic and unrealistic transformative projects. The sole criterion left is the relative closeness of a given project to the established order. In this way, there arises the typical dilemma of programmatic theory in an era of theoretical agnosticism. If a proposal is distant from current reality it is a futile utopian dream not worth thinking about. If, on the other hand, the proposal lies close to the established framework it represents mere reformist tinkering not worth fighting about. The perpetuation of this false dilemma is the direct consequence of a bastardized conception of political realism. This conception reflects less the wrong ideas about transformation than the failure to entertain seriously any ideas about transformation at all or the tongue-in-cheek allegiance to ideas that are literally incredible.

The mere abandonment of strong necessitarian claims is not enough; the practice of programmatic argument requires credible ideas about society making. It demands that we distinguish, however tentatively, between more realistic and less realistic trajectories of transformation. We can then ask not whether a particular proposal is close to what already exists or distant from it but whether it can be placed along a realistic trajectory. We can continue to press short-term and long-term proposals without feeling compelled to choose between utopian irrelevance and marginal adjustment. The defense of this intellectual opportunity is a major objective of the explanatory theory presented in this book.

THE NORMATIVE FORCE OF CONCEPTIONS OF EMPOWERMENT

A familiar objection can be made to the preceding attempt to establish a general and intimate connection between the explanatory and the programmatic arguments of this book. The way of establishing the connection seems to assume that a view of human empowerment, or of the conditions of individual or collective self-assertion, can exercise normative authority, that it can guide us in organizing a life or a society. But how can it? It seems that a set of descriptive and explanatory ideas can teach us how most effectively to pursue a given ideal of self-assertion. But it cannot persuade us to value that ideal more or less than a competing goal we might pursue. And it cannot even convince us to accept or reject a particular picture of empowerment or self-assertion, except to the extent that a definition of empowerment implicitly incorporates a strategy for its own realization, or makes factual assumptions that prove to be untenable or inconsistent. Though this objection holds good in a very limited sense, there is another, very important sense in which it remains false.

There is no unique, distinctive form of thought or experience to which we can confidently append the label "normative argument," just as there is no uncontroversial method for explaining the constitution of the physical world. All we have are a series of historically produced practices of inquiry, invention, collaboration, or production. The procedures and concerns that distinguish these practices change, though they may change only slowly and imperceptibly, according to the substance of the ideas and actions we use them to produce. Some of the practices are fundamental in the sense that they influence broad reaches of our experience and generate other, more short-lived or narrowly focused activities.

We are our fundamental practices. But we are also the permanent possibility of revising them. It is hardly surprising to find our twofold relation to contexts reproduced in our relation to our basic ways of acting. For these contexts consist both in a set of arrangements and preconceptions and in a series of conflictual activities, standard procedures for conflict over individual or group positions in the division of labor and individual or group rights under the law. Such activities ordinarily keep an order going but may, once they get out of hand, transform it. Fundamental practices differ from many of these activities only because they often have a longer, slower, and more universal history than the formative contexts they help perpetuate or disrupt. As a result we are often tempted to forget that even our most basic practices are relatively accidental ventures, whose success remains at risk in history.

One of the most common and influential of such practices is the attempt to draw guidance for action from factual conceptions of personality or society. The guidance consists both in the definition of certain ideals of individual or collective striving and in hypotheses about how these ideals may be most effectively realized. The ideals and the hypotheses cannot be clearly distinguished. Such a characterization, however, has the drawback of placing too much emphasis on the passage from the empirical (the substantive conception of personality or society) to the normative (the aims of individual or collective striving), a passage that constitutes the obsessive concern of much modern moral philosophy.

On an alternative characterization, the core of the practice I have in mind is the attempt to describe the conditions of empowerment or self-assertion. We simultaneously define a conception of self-assertion and an account of the requirements for its realization in the life of the individual or the society. Once again, we cannot neatly divide the definition and the strategy. We must recognize that the view of self-assertion counts less as the depiction of a limited, contentious value, to be weighed against competing values, than as a summation of our strivings for happiness. If the effort to formulate such views of self-assertion has a central theme, it may be the struggle to resolve the conflict between the imperative of engagement in shared forms of life and the dangers of dependence and depersonalization such engagement brings.

The views of self-assertion just mentioned support existential projects and social visions. Existential projects are an individual's plans to live his life so that the best and most important things will occupy their proper place; they are most often attempts to attain a happiness that does not depend on the instability of illusion or the surrender to routine. Social visions are efforts to imagine an intelligible and defensible ordering of a life in common. Each such vision trades the indeterminate conception of society for a unique model of human association or for several distinct models, meant to be realized in different areas of social life.

There is no closed list of ways to test a view of human self-assertion or empowerment or the existential projects and social visions it generates. Almost everything in our understanding and experience may be relevant. These numerous clues may even regularly contradict one another. When we focus on the more general aspects of the view – the ones presenting a picture of society or personality – the most suitable tests may be empirical and may emphasize the compatibility of the view with our factual discoveries about self or society. But they may also include the lessons of an educated introspection. We can compare the view to our immediate experience, so long as we also judge this experience by trying to assess how much of it results merely from the routines and preconceptions of a particular stabilized society.

Alternatively, we may turn to the existential projects and social visions resulting from a general view of self-assertion and apply more practical tests to their evaluation. Is the vision or project unstable in the sense of unleashing or perpetuating forces that frustrate the realization of its professed goals? Do our attempts to realize it diminish rather than strengthen our sense of empowerment, perhaps by aggravating the conflict between the benefits and the dangers of engagement in shared forms of life or shared universes of discourse? All such practical tests rely on the resistance our pretheoretical sense of empowerment puts up against unrestrained theoretical manipulation.

The practice I have just described might be called normative argument, so long as we are careful to avoid an easy misunderstanding. Many practices have existed in history and exist today that offer to guide us in our attempts to reconstruct or criticize social relations. Some practices focus on individual conduct or social institutions; others may convey only oblique and unacknowledged messages about the society we ought to organize or the lives we ought to lead. Do not suppose that all these procedures are versions of the same thing. They are at best overlapping and analogous. Such analogies and overlaps are all you can reasonably expect once you understand the historical, made-up quality of all our practices and resist the temptation to treat those we deploy as constituents of a permanent organon of human knowledge and activity.

Nevertheless, this cluster of styles of normative discourse has been extraordinarily tenacious and widespread. The programmatic argument of this book uses them, and revises them in the course of the use. In what sense can the deployment of these familiar forms of normative discourse produce conclusions with prescriptive weight? To what degree do these evaluative practices presuppose or exclude the distinction between factual and normative claims that has come to occupy so central a role in modern thought? To what extent can the family of inherited normative styles be rejected by someone who claims merely to subordinate the goal of self-assertion to a different objective? These questions may best be answered by responding to two types of critics. There is no simple way to characterize the status of the fact–value dichotomy within the practice, except by redefining this status as the sum of our answers to these and other critics.

Consider first the person who accuses the traditional practice mentioned in the preceding paragraphs of disrespecting the crucial distinction between facts and values and who insists on a style of argument that claims to derive normative conclusions solely from normative premises. We may accuse him of mistaking the practice he rejects for a particular metaphysical interpretation of it, such as Aristotle's teleology. We can criticize him for sharing, unreflectively, the teleologist's metaphysical realism: the assumptions that all our practices rest on presuppositions making more or less implicit claims about what the world is really like, and that all these claims must converge toward a single coherent picture of reality. We can then go on to point out that the modern philosophical attempt to draw a rigid distinction between the factual and the normative has largely failed. To the extent that the styles of normative moral or political thought produced by this attempt escape emptiness they do so only by resorting to implicit conceptions of personality and society, conceptions all the more dangerous because they are neither brought to light nor subject to criticism. Thus, the wants and intuitions some philosophers use as the raw material of moral theorizing may already compose a picture of the self and its overriding concerns. And the methods of choice other philosophers invoke may be more or less tacitly identified with institutional arrangements – such as particular ways of organizing markets and democracies – that help to perpetuate unique forms of life and to enact distinctive ideals of personality.

Of course, the rejection of the metaphysical-realist perspective and its replacement by a practice conception are themselves contentious.

The merits of the solution must be compared with the advantages of rival approaches. Moreover, the status of the practice conception within the world it describes is puzzling. For what is the practice by which we survey all other practices from a historicizing angle? Perhaps it is a reformed philosophy: a philosophy that refuses to close the list of our practices, or to interpret the list we have as the expression of a higher necessity, or to identify the list with our very selves.

Now consider a very different critic. His quarrel is with the point of departure rather than the method. He protests that he sees no reason to credit human empowerment, or individual and collective self-assertion, with any authority, or at least with anything more than a very limited authority. He hears our story about self-assertion and says: So what? First, we must assure ourselves that he understands just how we are characterizing the dispute. The aim is not to exalt a discrete value at the cost of others but to present a detailed vision of the strengthening of human life. We must remind him that such a vision combines a picture of the aims of our striving with an argument about the conditions for realizing these aims. He may claim to understand this combination but persist in rejecting the authority of the aim of self-assertion. If he moves far enough toward a radical skepticism, we cannot refute him. What we can do is to show how much must be given up in order to occupy this extreme and irrefutable position. And we can attack on their merits the intermediate positions that seem to escape the limits of a project of self-assertion without falling into this all-out skepticism. We can try to persuade him that he must choose between involvement in the controversy over alternative views of human empowerment and the paralyzed outsiderdom of the unqualified skeptic.

Suppose, for example, that our interlocutor embraces a variant of the philosophies that teach the ultimate unreality of the phenomenal world of individuation and that exhort the individual to sacrifice the life of subjectivity and encounter to the quest for the absolute. I am not interested in theories of self-assertion, he may say, if my primary aim is to overcome the illusions and sufferings that inevitably accompany the insistence on selfhood. (It is actually harder than it may first appear to find examples of this critic; the development of the experience of subjectivity and encounter keeps being introduced – in Buddhist moral psychology, for instance – as a secondary aim or as an indispensable condition to the transcendence of self.) We may argue that he cannot in fact suppress his selfhood and that his futile attempt to overcome the self in order to conquer self-centeredness will produce unexpected and perverse effects (e.g., cranky obsessions rather than a participant mind). On the other hand, we may argue that his message fails to do justice to his driving concerns. He values as spirit that which transcends the limitations of particular contexts.

But he fails to see it is precisely personality or consciousness that most clearly possesses this context-transcending power. He does not recognize that the institutional and imaginative settings of our lives may differ in the degree to which they give play to context-transcending capability. He fails to understand that only through engagement in personal relations and social movements can we change our settings and enlarge the part of our lives graced by the qualities he most prizes.

A critic, however, may occupy a position farther along the spectrum of disengagement from efforts at individual and collective self-assertion. He may simply refuse to give any weight to human striving and its success. He cannot be proved mistaken. And the impossibility of proving him mistaken defines one of the residual, revised senses in which a practice conception of evaluative activities presupposes the fact–value distinction rather than repudiates it.

The response to the critic who rejects the point of departure rather than the method suffers from a crucial weakness. A vision of human empowerment and its conditions describes a form of life rather than a discrete value. But what is its relation to the ideal of love – the acceptance of the concrete other – and to the many forms of commitment and concern that often seem to represent the diluted counterparts of love? Surely, at least this form of striving must resist assimilation to an argument that ostentatiously employs the language of empowerment? Only the substance of the programmatic argument can answer this doubt. The answer will not have been formulated until the program for institutional reconstruction extends into a vision of the transformed relations among individuals.

THE JUSTIFICATION

INTERNAL AND VISIONARY ARGUMENT

This part of Chapter 5 shows how the program of empowered democracy may be justified and how the justifications anticipate the outline of the program. Programmatic ideas, when they remain in touch with a close sense of social reality and present controversy, are always just the reverse side of the criticisms, visions, and strategies that can generate them. Thus, when we study the normative arguments or the ideal conceptions supporting a program and the style of political practice that can realize it, we study the program itself.

Our normative ideas can move in two main directions. By far the most common of the two is what might be called internal argument or internal criticism. We take a particular tradition – or a particular community of sense or value – as our starting point. The abstract, indeterminate idea of society gets translated into a particular model or set of models of human coexistence, meant to be realized in the different domains of social life by distinct sets of institutions and practices. In some societies, a single model of human association is intended for application, as a theme and variations, to every domain of social life. Typically, this recurrent scheme of human coexistence builds inequality, exchange, and communal loyalty into the same human connections; the patron–client relation is its obsession and its ideal. But in many other societies, and especially in the societies addressed by the institutional program of this chapter, sharply distinct models of human association are meant to be realized in different areas of social practice. Thus, we have an ideal of representative democracy for the organization of government and for the realm of citizenship, an ideal of private community for the life of family and friendship, and a blend of contractual exchange and technical hierarchy for the workaday world. The most ambitious models are the communal and the democratic, for they hold up the promise of a fuller reconciliation between the enabling conditions of self-assertion: the image of a development and of an expression of self that can be achieved through engagement and attachment. The willingness to tolerate a far more instrumental style of personal relations and a much weaker and looser relation between the enabling conditions of self-assertion is justified by the belief that attempts to extend the democratic and communal ideals into practical, daily life would be futile and self-defeating. The practical failures of such attempts and the despotic tendencies they would unleash – so the argument goes – would end up endangering democracy and community in the areas of social life where they belong.

Internal argument forswears the search for ultimates. It takes place within a tradition of accepted moral and political ideals largely defined by a scheme of models of human coexistence, made actual by institutional arrangements and social practices, in areas of social life considered suitable to each of these ideals of association. The interlocutors in an internal controversy probe the uncertainties, ambiguities, and tensions in the imaginative world defined by their shared points of departure. The exact boundaries of the models of human association – of the areas marked out for democracy and for private contract or technical hierarchy, for example – may be disputed. Or there may be a disagreement about whether established practices and institutions represent an adequate realization of a given model of human association: over whether, for example, the constitutionalism of checks and balances does justice to our ideal of representative democracy. Such disagreements over the scope and the practical form of received models of association expose tensions within these models that may previously have been concealed and force us to choose the direction in which we want to develop each model.

Many of our most common forms of normative disagreement may at first seem unrelated to any overarching and assumed map of images of human association. No such map seems involved in an argument over whether a particular act is justifiable in a particular setting. Yet the evaluative premises and ideals we bring to bear on these arguments over the legitimacy of isolated deeds characteristically draw on a repertory of conceptions of what the relations among people can and should be like in characteristic situations of social life. Indeed, when we turn from the favored conundra of the modern moral philosophers to the stuff of actual moral assurance and anxiety we discover that much of this stuff has to do with socially recognized roles, with the obligations and aspirations we attach to these roles, and with the extent to which we believe ourselves justified in defying role expectations. Reciprocally related social roles are merely models of human coexistence translated into detailed scripts for dealings among individuals.

Like all practices that help reproduce a stabilized social world, internal argument can escalate into a broader conflict over the fundamentals of this world. What began as debate that took for granted a scheme of models of possible and desirable human association can end as a controversy over the scheme itself. In fact, when we examine detailed internal arguments in legal, political, or moral controversy, we find that they avoid this escalation only by sleights of hand and arbitrary truncations. Much of modern legal, moral, and political theory tries to give such truncations a semblance of rational necessity, the better to contrast legal doctrine, moral casuistry, or political criticism with open-ended and supposedly arbitrary ideological warfare. This theoretical effort to circumscribe the scope and the revisionary effect of normative reasonings finds unexpected support in a widespread philosophical teaching: because only particular historical communities of sense and value exist in the world, we *must* choose one of these communities and play by its terms. But despite the formidable array of intellectual justifications enlisted in its defense, the attempt to ensure internal normative argument against the dangers of escalation characteristically produces the opposite of the results it is designed to achieve; it increases rather than diminishes the element of sheer assertion and arbitrary juxtaposition in our received forms of political, moral, and legal analysis. In the course of justifying the program outlined in later parts of this chapter, I want to illustrate a practice of internal argument whose insights and persuasiveness depend precisely on the ease with which it escalates into more basic controversy.

This initial characterization of internal argument already suggests how escalation takes place and why it cannot easily be prevented. The vocabulary we use to invoke our accepted models of human association is typically vague and contradictory, so that a stranger to our social practices would be baffled by these familiar descriptions of our ideals. But we know what we are talking about because we understand these models against the background of specific social practices and institutional arrangements, realized in particular areas of social life. We know what representative democracy, for example, means because we more or less implicitly equate the democratic ideal with certain constitutional techniques and styles of partisan rivalry inherited from the eighteenth and nineteenth centuries. So long as our sense of the fit among the models, practices, and domains of application remains undisturbed we feel assured. Though we may disagree about particular legal, moral, or political decisions, we preserve an implicit confidence in the broader imaginative framework within which such decisions must be made.

But suppose a model of human association is extended to an area of social life to which it did not previously apply: say, representative democracy to the internal organization of a productive enterprise. Such a displacement of a familiar model onto unfamiliar territory may be motivated by practical or ideal concerns (the need to elicit worker cooperation or the belief that neither technical necessity nor private contract adequately legitimate the type of power that managers exercise over workers). After all, the boundaries of application of distinct models of human association are never entirely clear-cut. The projection of a model into an unfamiliar domain of application merely extends the boundary disputes that proliferate in even the most stable ideological situations.

Once the old model is applied in new settings it must be realized by untried practical or institutional forms. Representative democracy in the workplace cannot mean the tripartite state and the traditional style of partisan rivalry. But what then should it mean? In choosing the new practical forms we not only confront the constraints and opportunities presented by the new area of application; we also disclose ambiguities in our ideal that remained concealed so long as the image of association, the practical forms, and the domain continued to fit together uncontroversially. Is the most important point about democracy the refusal to privilege anyone's interest over anyone else's? Or is it the experience of participation in decisions about the basic terms of a collective activity? Or is it something that neither of these aims fully captures?

We cannot answer such questions merely by analyzing more closely our received conception of democracy. For there is no permanent archetype underlying this conception: no canonical order of social life that settles, once and for all, the core meaning of democracy. If the explanatory arguments of this book are correct we cannot fix the meaning of democracy by appealing to an inherent logic of a type of social organization such as capitalism, because no such types exist. Our inherited ideal of democracy is nothing but a particular set of practices, applied to a particular group of problems, and invested with an indiscriminate range of aspirations whose relation to their practical forms we have left largely unexamined. In fact, the implicit awareness that there are no archetypes to our models of human association is what drives us to avoid the escalation of internal argument in the first place. We cannot merely decide what democracy already means; we have to decide what we want it to mean. And the meaning we impart to it in this new setting is likely to react upon our conception of democracy in its original core domain and to heighten our sense of the discrepancy between the pretensions of political rhetoric and the realities of our political experience. Thus, we may have moved, step by step, into a discourse that puts established ideals of association up for grabs.

Although we cannot find conclusive guides in the circumstance of heightened imaginative struggle, neither are we reduced to silence or to an unreasoning assertion of will. For our practice of normative argument can move in an alternative visionary direction. Our thinking about ideals becomes visionary or external to the extent that it holds up a picture, however partial or fragmentary, of a radically altered scheme of social life and appeals to justifications that do not stick close to familiar and established models of human association. The visionary is the person who claims not to be bound by the limits of the tradition he and his hearers or interlocutors are in; at least he does not support his cause by advocating the gradual extension or clarification of shared assumptions about the possible and desirable forms of human association.

Visionary thought can arise from the escalation of internal argument, or it can begin as independent activity that collides with internal argument. Moreover, we know the visionary in two forms so different that their similarity becomes apparent only in contrast to internal argument. In the cold form he is the philosopher who ascribes normative force to a conception of personality or society, to a method of choice that supposedly relies on no such conception, or even to an entire metaphysical or religious picture of the world. In the hot form he is the political prophet who evokes a reordered social world in which all the major forms of individual and collective self-assertion may be promoted and all our practical and passionate connections may be cleansed of some of the perils that make us shrink from them. Both the rationalizing theorist and the political prophet speak to us as people whose insights and judgments are not limited by the dogmas and institutions of our societies and cultures. When they take the visionary turn, both emphasize the sharpness of the break between their teachings and our realities.

Notice that visionary thought is not inherently millennarian, perfectionist, or utopian (in the vulgar sense of the term). It need not and does not ordinarily present the picture of a perfected society. But it does require that we be conscious of redrawing the map of possible and desirable forms of human association, of inventing new models of human association and designing new practical arrangements to embody them.

Notice also that the concept of visionary thought implies no particular view of how visionary proposals may be supported. In particular it does not require the search for self-evident or metaphysically justified first principles. On the contrary the historical experiences and the intellectual attitudes that place internal argument and visionary thought in tension with each other are also characteristically hostile to this philosophical foundationalism. Internal argument is controversial because it takes certain social ideals and practices for granted: if not as the limit of prescriptive judgment, at least as its starting point. Internal argument benefits from the detailed texture of an assumed and accepted imaginative world. But it invites an objection: Why give any weight to this tradition? Visionary thought proclaims a more self-conscious independence from any society or culture in particular. It therefore raises a question: What support is there for this claim to transcend tradition?

There is no uncontroversial way to characterize the sense of the authority that internal and visionary arguments may possess, or the proper relation between the internal and external perspectives. Whatever characterization we accept is sure to influence the form and content of our actual argument. It seems clear, however, that our relation to imaginative schemes of possible and desirable forms of human association is simply a facet of our relation to the imaginative and institutional contexts of our activity. I therefore propose to view internal and visionary arguments and their relation to each other in the spirit of the same thesis about our relation to the formative contexts of social life that animates all the explanatory and programmatic ideas of this book.

The resulting conception recognizes two inherently controversial and inconclusive activities that inspire and correct each other but never succeed in emptying our normative ideas of a large, ineradicable residuum of choice, commitment, and faith. My arguments for the program of empowered democracy are meant to exemplify this approach to normative arguments. But the approach is less a response to the normative skeptic than an attempt to show how we can incorporate into our practices of criticism and justification the insights proclaimed by all but the most uncompromising forms of skepticism about values and ideals.

The development of a view of the varieties of normative argument and of their relation to each other may at first seem a strange diversion from the task of elaborating a program of social reconstruction, even given the relation of program to justification and of justification to views of what counts as a justificatory argument, idea, or impulse. But the program is not just an institutional proposal. It is also an advocacy of practices that reproduce these institutions and keep them faithful to the spirit that inspires them. One such practice is normative argument. If part of the larger ambition of this program of empowered democracy is to narrow the distance between context-preserving routine and context-transforming conflict, a similar approximation must take place between the style of normative controversy that takes an established context for granted (internal argument) and the style that transcends this context and claims to judge it from an independent standpoint (visionary thought). For the routines that reproduce and respect a context include our habits of moral and social controversy.

The program of empowered democracy is merely the next step in a trajectory: not the millennium but the further emancipation of our practical and passionate attachments from a predetermined script, the further subversion of a fixed plan of social division and hierarchy, and the further reach toward the forms of individual and collective empowerment this context smashing may produce. So, too, the development of methods of normative argument that more fully combine the detailed texture of internal argument with the greater transcendence of visionary thought represents merely the development of a tendency we already see at work all around us.

There is no permanent canon of forms of normative argument. Our ways of arguing about ideals are, like all our other practices, the mutable products of a specific history and the expressions of our ideas about society and thought. Where a naturalistic understanding of society prevails the particular distinction between internal argument and visionary thought sketched at the outset of this section does not exist. Some normative controversies may have a narrower and others a broader scope. But, within a naturalistic view, there is no question of having to choose between claims within a scheme of models of human association and claims about such schemes. Only one legitimate scheme is supposed to exist, though its practical manifestations may pass through countless episodes of corruption and regeneration. The contrast between the internal and the visionary already presupposes an acute sense of the specificity and discontinuity of the imaginative worlds within which we may argue. Once we accept this presupposition, we are assaulted by two feelings of arbitrariness: that of the internal arguer who takes for granted an imaginative map of forms of possible and desirable association, and that of the visionary who claims to step outside any particular tradition but has no uncontroversial foundation on which to rest his arguments and proposals. The following sections suggest how this twofold arbitrariness may be simultaneously recognized, contained, and included in a constructive practice of normative criticism and justification.

THE VISIONARY JUSTIFICATION FOR EMPOWERED DEMOCRACY

Empowerment and Context Smashing

The visionary justification for the institutional program worked out in this chapter is postponed to the final sections, which present it as the spirit animating the whole body of institutional proposals. This part of Chapter 5 is therefore mainly concerned with the program's internal justification. The aims of the whole program, however, may be better understood if parts of the visionary justification are anticipated. Moreover, when it is seen to interact with the visionary justification, internal argument becomes stronger and less indeterminate than it would otherwise be. The composite result of the two kinds of arguments is still inconclusive in its detailed implications and still depends upon an irreducible element of commitment or faith. But both the uncertainty of the implications and the shakiness of the ground are less than they would be if either type of justification had to stand alone.

The vision offered by this program is that of a society in which people are more fully empowered through the development of institutional arrangements that both diminish the gap between framework-preserving routine and framework-transforming conflict and weaken the established forms of social division and hierarchy. It is a program of empowered democracy because it promises to serve a range of forms of individual and collective empowerment, in part by empowering democracy itself: that is, by extending the subjection of social life to democratic participation and conflict. As always, the effort to project a received image of human association into an unfamiliar terrain requires that the ideal be reconceived. Indeed, the conception of democracy presented here merges into the idea of the next best thing to the absolute or natural context that we can never possess. This second best is a set of artificial arrangements that both better ensure their own availability to challenge and more effectively emancipate from a prewritten script our experiments in practical collaboration and passionate attachment. It is the vision of a society in which individuals are freer to deal with one another as individuals rather than as placeholders in the system of class, communal, role, or gender contrasts. The point of the vision is not chiefly to enlarge our field of choice but, rather, to imagine and defend a certain change in the quality of our experience of subjectivity and sociability and to describe the institutional conditions of this shift.

The change I have in mind consists in the interaction among three varieties of empowerment, all to be encouraged by the same institutional devices, all familiar from the earlier discussion of negative capability. One variety consists in the development of our practical capability through the openness of social life to the recombinational and experimental activities of practical reason. Another type of empowerment is the exercise of a more complete and deliberate mastery over the imaginative and institutional contexts of our activities. And still another lies in our success in escaping both submission and isolation and in diminishing the conflict between the enabling conditions of self-assertion: between our need to participate in group life and our effort to avoid the dangers of dependence and depersonalization that accompany such engagement.

These varieties of empowerment have convergent or overlapping institutional requirements and a shared human significance. Some institutional solutions may privilege one type of empowerment at the expense of the others. For example, the way of opening social life more fully to practical experimentation may aggravate certain forms of domination. To that extent it may also heighten rather than diminish our experience of conflict between the enabling conditions of solidarity. But a major thesis of the explanatory theory that forms part of the background to this political vision is that no necessary or permanent conflict exists among the enabling institutional conditions of the several modes of empowerment. It is up to us to discover in our historical situation which conditions of each variety of empowerment also satisfy the other varieties. We cannot be sure to find this subset or, having found it, to establish it in practice. But neither is there any general reason to expect that we must fail.

The shared human significance of these aspects of empowerment is our success at making the world – the whole social and even natural setting of our lives – more fully into a home and a garden. The transformed world becomes a place whose limits and patterns bear a closer relation to our felt concerns. In it, our sense of being at home becomes less dependent upon our service as placeholders in a preestablished system of social stations.

Although this vision includes the idea of enabling individuals to develop and pursue their life projects, it does not pretend to be neutral among all possible projects. It emphasizes whatever in the experience of the individual enables him to treat others and himself as an original, to fashion practical and passionate attachments less vitiated by dependence and depersonalization, and to move within his social contexts with the heightened self-consciousness and engagement of a context-revising agent.

It is not surprising that the first two varieties of empowerment should share the same institutional requirements. Both Marxism and mainstream economics prepare us for the idea that the development of productive capabilities depends on the weakening of the resistance that fixed orders of social division and hierarchy impose upon the organizational forms of exchange and production. But the relation of the first two kinds of empowerment to the third is less familiar, and it brings us closer to what gives the program of empowered democracy both its distinctive message and its claim upon the visionary imagination. Our relative success at moderating the conflict between the enabling conditions of self-assertion is one of the root experiences of freedom. It is one of the basic ways in which we make the world into a home and avoid the conflict between our sense of who we are or of what we want and our understanding of the social situation in which we find ourselves. The consequences of our ability or our failure to limit the contest between the enabling conditions of self-assertion help determine the quality of much of our cognitive, emotional, and political experience. The explanatory theory developed in the earlier parts of *False Necessity* supports the thesis that the favoring institutional conditions of the third variety of empowerment overlap with the institutional requirements of the other two. The same devices that open up society to practical experimentation and recombination and that strengthen our self-conscious mastery over the institutional and imaginative frameworks of our social experience also help cleanse group life of some of its capacity to entangle people in relations of dependence and domination and to turn them into the faceless representatives of predetermined roles.

The Radical Project and the Vision of Empowered Democracy

The idea that the development of our practical capabilities and of our mastery over our collective contexts is connected, through its shared institutional requirement, with the cleansing of dependence and depersonalization from group life has always been central to the radical project. The great secular ideologies of emancipation – liberalism, socialism, and communism – agree in affirming the importance of this link. They are all committed to the making of institutional arrangements that simultaneously turn us more completely into the authors of the social worlds we inhabit and free us from the need to choose, at every turn, between isolation and submission. But the understanding of society and history that informed

these ideologies suffered the effects of unjustifiably restrictive assumptions about the possible shape of social organization and in
particular about the possible institutional forms of markets and
democracies. The program of empowered democracy *is* the radical
project, restated and revised in the light of an enlarged sense of social
reality and possibility. To achieve this enlargement it is not enough
to change the way in which we describe and explain the formative
contexts of social life; it is also necessary to imagine institutional
arrangements that in fact carry the radical project farther than it has
been taken by the institutional systems now available in the world.
Our broadened sense of the practical forms that the radical project
can assume, a sense inspired both by a credible view of social change
and by an actual exercise in programmatic imagination, reacts back
upon our understanding of what the radical cause is for. The ideas
set out in the preceding paragraphs express this changed understanding.

To say that empowered democracy represents the next step in the
advancement of the radical project is to emphasize that it does not
stand for an ideal of social perfection. The claim of this program to
be a political vision and to draw on a visionary justification does not
depend on promising heaven. What the program does hold up is the
image of a society in which the shaking up of institutional arrangements and the redrawing of our imaginative map of possible and
desirable association allow us to carry forward the stalled endeavor
to which the modern emancipatory ideologies are committed. One
intention of the programmatic argument of this book is to illustrate
the twin theses that we must be realists in order to become visionaries
and that we can be visionaries without being millennarians.

Facts and Values in the Vision of Empowered Democracy

It should be clear that just as the program of empowered democracy
does not depend upon perfectionist assumptions, so too it is not
meant to remain neutral among contrasting visions of the good or
among competing conceptions of personality and society. It takes
sides with the radical project and reinterprets it in a certain way. The
program refuses to follow the main line of modern moral and political
philosophy in the futile attempt to make normative argument independent of particular conceptions of self and society.

But to acknowledge the commitment to particular factual and ideal
conceptions is to invite an objection: What then, other than a gratuitous act of commitment, constitutes the basis of this political vision? The acceptance of this program does indeed require a real and
irreducible element of pure commitment. The sense in which the
programmatic vision depends upon such a groundless choice is the

sense in which a sufficiently thoroughgoing normative skepticism is irrefutable. It is also the revised, limited sense in which we should accept the traditional idea of a discontinuity between the *is* and the *ought*, between factual and normative claims. But the irreducible commitment is not to a richly textured group of ideals, values, and arrangements. It is not even to the radical project exemplified by the modern liberal, socialist, and communist doctrines. It is merely to a much broader and looser range of goals of empowerment, freedom, or self-assertion. All the rest depends upon claims that, though always controversial and inconclusive, are nevertheless empirical.

To say the claims are empirical is not to assert that they describe and explain isolated features of our experience or that they can be corroborated or falsified one by one. It is merely to state that they do depend upon ideas about the possibilities of our experience and the constraints of our situation and that we have reasons, though controversial and inconclusive ones, to prefer some of the ideas to others. Modern philosophy has taught us to broaden our understanding of what counts as an empirical claim: the ontological assumptions of a scientific theory, the "laws" of logic and the truths of mathematics, and almost all the propositions traditionally placed on the analysis side of the contrast between the analytic and the synthetic. The ideas informing a political vision like the program of empowered democracy also belong to this broadened domain of empirical beliefs.

What makes it difficult to assess this particular category of empirical beliefs is that we have too much rather than too little to go on: too many arguably relevant forms of discourse, sources of observation, and facets of experience. We have no reason to believe they all add up to one coherent picture; they are much more likely to lend themselves either to many such pictures or to none. But notice that to say a political vision is contestable, because its informing ideas have these characteristics, is very different from saying that its detailed conclusions and assumptions rest on no more than an act of partisan faith. The claim that they do not is central to a major concern of this book: the effort to break down the rigid contrast between social explanation and political vision.

In particular, the program of empowered democracy, taken as an instance of visionary thought, depends upon three large sets of empirical claims. Each set of ideas stands more or less closely connected to the explanatory theory advanced in earlier parts of *False Necessity*. Each draws part of its empirical status and persuasive force from this link with a body of explanatory ideas that can be put to work and judged, verified, or falsified, at many points along its periphery of detailed explanation and implication. Each represents the result of an interaction between preexisting intuitions or experiences and their theoretical reinterpretation and revision.

The first set of sustaining empirical ideas has to do with those of our most tenacious desires that are also most relevant to the task of institutional reconstruction. The argument for empowered democracy depends on the belief that our ordinary demands for security, freedom, and connection do have the internal relations and the institutional implications invoked in my discussion of the aspects of empowerment and that there is little in our experience of longing that cannot be related to one of these varieties of empowerment. The understanding of these implications and relations changes the direction and the sense of our desires, because all our desires are informed by ideas. This group of empirical assumptions is the one most directly connected with the view of context making presented in Chapter 4.

The second set of empirical claims addresses the status of normative argument itself. Here, the aim is to propose an understanding of normative argument as a diverse and mutable series of historically located practices: practices that, like our elementary desires themselves, change under the influence of an altered understanding of society and personality, of thought and language. The particular style of interaction between visionary and internal argument represents a proposal to revise the way in which we engage in normative argument and to do so under pressure from a host of empirical ideas about the nature of institutional and imaginative contexts and the ways they change. These contexts are perpetuated by activities that normally reproduce them but that may, through escalation, destabilize and transform them. Our practices of normative argument, in moral, legal, and partisan-political controversy, are themselves examples of these stabilizing–destabilizing activities.

But the effort to bring internal and visionary argument more intimately and explicitly together does not follow directly from the willingness to see normative argument as a loose group of historically specific and revisable collective practices. It results, instead, from the commitment to empowered democracy itself. If an empowered democracy is the institutional order that softens the contrast between moving within a context and fighting about its terms, then all the forms of practical and imaginative conflict on which it depends must also make their stable, routine forms more like their exceptional, destabilizing manifestations. Our inherited practices of internal argument (in legal doctrine, moral casuistry, and partisan debate) must incorporate more of the characteristics we traditionally attribute to visionary thought. Our justifications of empowered democracy must, in turn, serve a dual purpose: they must be both a discourse addressed to the unconverted and a discourse we ourselves might practice under the arrangements whose establishment we advocate.

Implicit in this practice orientation to normative argument is an invitation to abandon the perspective of metaphysical realism. Metaphysical realism may be defined as the thesis that all our practices presuppose hypotheses about the world and that if these hypotheses are true they must all add up to a coherent world picture at some ideal limit of all-inclusive insight. For the metaphysical realist the relation of human goals to factual observations must be a fact about the world. We must not have two practices – one, normative argument, the other, natural science – that make incompatible assumptions about the same fact. From the standpoint of metaphysical realism the traditional criticism of the normative uses of empirical ideas about society or personality (i.e., the criticism somewhat inappropriately blamed on Hume) may be irrefutable: we must choose between the way *is* and *ought* connect in our scientific explanations and the way they connect in other forms of discourse. But once you abandon the metaphysical-realist prejudice the traditional criticism becomes largely irrelevant. We *can* criticize our practices but not merely by assuming that one of them (i.e., modern natural science) can limit what may justifiably be said and how it may be said within another (i.e., a particular style of normative argument).

The third and narrowest set of empirical assumptions deals with the relation of the program of empowered democracy to other versions of what I have called the radical project and indeed with the existence of the radical project itself. Here, as always, a newly envisaged possibility of social reconstruction leads us to reinterpret a past history of transformative effort and thought. It prompts us to reassess the aims and relations of liberal, socialist, and communist doctrines. These intellectual-historical claims are the least closely connected to the explanatory theory of *False Necessity*. Although no less controversial than the other empirical assumptions previously mentioned, they are the easiest to assess.

THE INTERNAL JUSTIFICATION OF EMPOWERED DEMOCRACY: THE STATE NOT HOSTAGE TO A FACTION

The following sections describe three convergent lines of internal justification for the program of empowered democracy. Each argumentative strand reveals a distinctive way of getting from our received models of possible and desirable association to the ideals that inspire the institutional proposals. Each underlines a different aspect of the program's intentions. And each draws attention to the most interesting feature of internal argument: its ability to push us from relatively less controversial starting points to relatively more controversial conclusions. This ability is vastly strengthened when the practitioner of internal argument draws on a social understanding that expands his sense of the institutional forms that received ideals of human association can take. It is also reinforced when he spurns the devices of argumentative truncation that attempt to enforce a rigid contrast between internal criticism and visionary thought.

At least one important route of internal criticism I postpone to a later section: arguments from the failure of current economic and governmental institutions to ensure the conditions for economic growth and stability. Prosperity represents both an aim in itself and a condition for the successful realization of received democratic ideals or party-political programs. The economic variety of internal criticism, however, may best be considered in direct connection with the parts of the program of empowered democracy that propose a reorganization of the economy.

The first line of internal justification starts from a minimalist version of the democratic ideal and from the contrast between the requirements of this ideal and the contemporary forms of democratic politics. The conception of democracy as the regime that subjects social relations to the wills of free and equal citizens has often been disparaged by the more skeptical democratic theorists as an unrealistic idealization. But even these skeptics, when they do not characterize democracy as merely disguised oligarchy, insist upon the authority and the practicality of a narrower ideal of democracy: the goal of preventing the state from becoming hostage to a faction. The faction may be a class, a community, or a party. Governmental power must not be exclusively and permanently exercised by such a sector of the population nor used for its primary benefit. Elites may share much of public office among themselves. The authority of the state may regularly serve some classes and communities better than others. But the power elites must compete for office. Their success in gaining office and in keeping it must depend to a significant degree upon their ability to enlist mass support, within the electoral process and outside it. The people who win governmental power under these conditions must in fact be able to set policy over the major issues of social life. They must not find their programs regularly circumvented or undermined by a faction of the population, entrenched in positions of privilege that elected officials and representatives are unable to disturb. Such an ideal of democracy is more than an artifact of theory; in less articulate form it lives in even many of the more cynical popular conceptions of democratic polities.

Democracy, for the citizens of North Atlantic democracies at the close of the twentieth century, *is* this ideal. It is also, however, a detailed set of institutions and practices, such as the constitutional techniques that deliberately multiply hurdles to the execution of any bold program and the style of party rivalry and rotation that first assumed its modern identity several generations after the earliest liberal constitutions had been invented. All but the most self-conscious radicals see democracy as both that minimalist ideal and these distinctive practices. But you do not have to be a radical to see how far the experience of democratic politics fails to make good even on the seemingly modest commitment to prevent the state from falling hostage to a faction. The recognition of this straightforward disparity between an accepted ideal and a familiar reality represents the beginning of the style of internal argument this discussion is meant to exemplify.

Consider first the ability of relatively small groups of people – financial and enterprise managers – to exert a crucial degree of control over the basic flows of investment decisions, the decisions that most directly shape the rate and character of economic growth. These investment controllers play a disproportionately important role in determining the response of the economy to public policy. Parties in office bent on economic redistribution and institutional reform quickly discover the negative economic consequences of plans that jeopardize business confidence – as most serious transformative projects do. The ability of the investment managers to respond to the distant threat of reform with the immediate answer of disinvestment, less productive, long-term investment, or outright capital flight compels the reformers to limit their aims. It perpetuates the reform cycles discussed in Chapter 2. It places the conditions of collective prosperity largely beyond the reach of democratic control.

Clearly, the privileged control that small cadres of entrepreneurs and financiers can exercise over key investment flows is simply the most dramatic instance of a more pervasive problem: the capacity of specially endowed or organized groups to withdraw major areas of policy from the effective jurisdiction of elected governments and to hold these governments hostage to the perceived interests of narrow factions. The key lies in the combination of a measure of factional or nonreciprocal privilege with the insulation of such privilege against disturbance or redistribution in the normal rounds of partisan rivalry and policy change. Viewed from this broader perspective the beneficiaries may be as much organized labor and bureaucratic or technocratic elites as private entrepreneurs and investors. Their ability to hold the state hostage may therefore survive a gradual expansion of the public sector of the economy that is not accompanied by a more fundamental shift in the methods of decentralized capital allocation and in the institutional forms of production and exchange.

Consider next the consequences of the influence large-scale business and administrative organizations exercise upon the quality of everyday social life. These organizations seem to be indispensable instruments of economic and administrative efficiency because they permit the large-scale pooling of financial, technological, informational, and manpower resources. Yet they pose a double threat to

The State Not Hostage to a Faction

the minimalist ideal of preventing the state from becoming hostage to a faction. On the one hand, they endanger the integrity of democratic elections and democratic representation by the pressure they are able to exert upon the financing of elections, the attitudes of the mass media, and the career backgrounds and prospects of officials. On the other hand, they create vast domains within everyday practical life that are not themselves organized on principles analogous to those shaping democratic governments. They appear, in the prosaic world of work and exchange, as the sole alternative to isolated petty property. In this capacity they help make the promises of citizenship seem a largely irrelevant exception to the inevitable demands and characteristics of practical life.

The single most powerful source of these contrasts between the minimalist democratic ideal and the realities of democratic politics is the reliance on absolute property rights as the primary device of economic decentralization. These rights provide the institutional shell within which those who act as delegates of the property owners are entitled to organize work on nondemocratic principles. They enable relatively small numbers of businessmen to maximize the constraining effect of business confidence. They constitute the means for accumulating influence over the instruments of mass communication. More subtly but no less importantly, they help sustain a style of industrial organization that privileges mass-production industry, with its sharp contrast between task-defining and task-executing activities, and its incalculable value as a citadel from which managers, investors, and union leaders can hold reform-minded governments to ransom. These mass-production enterprises could not contain the otherwise fatal threat of instability in the capital, labor, and product markets on which they depend without resorting to a range of devices, all of which (as argued in Chapter 3) presuppose absolute property.

The evidence for believing in the existence of a strong link between democratic pluralism and economic decentralization is persuasive. Moreover, the traditional alternatives to a property-based market economy do indeed threaten us with bureaucratic despotism, massive inefficiency, or a combination of both. But notice that these familiar alternatives – the nationalization of the private means of production and the bestowal of such means upon the work force of each enterprise – do not alter the character of the property right; they merely transfer it – in one case, to central planners, in the other case to the people who happen to have the jobs at the time the transfer takes place. Their negative consequences, discussed in the appendix to Chapter 2, may make the subversive effects of absolute property rights upon democratic politics seem modest by comparison.

But imagine a way of organizing a decentralized economy that dissociates and assigns to different entities the faculties that now compose the property entitlement. Teams of workers, technicians, and entrepreneurs would make conditional or temporary claims upon competing capital funds, whose administrators would in turn be accountable, for their resource base and their overall capital-allocation policies, to the elected governments and representative assemblies of the democracy. Such a reorganization of the institutional form of a market economy might enable us to fragment markets and enterprises, to reconcile enterprise fragmentation more easily with economies of scale, and to encourage experimentation and diversity in the organization of production and exchange. This alternative would also pose dangers of its own. Its deliberative processes might be perverted by increasingly explicit deals among particular groups of capital takers, capital fund managers, and politicians. To guard against this danger, the forms of democratic accountability and participation might have to be extended – extended beyond what the inherited constitutional techniques of the liberal state can readily countenance. The conflict over the mastery and uses of governmental power would have to be reorganized in ways that more effectively subjected to challenge and conflict every emergent situation of privilege.

Suppose we confront the resigned democrat with both the criticism and the proposal outlined in the preceding paragraphs. He may reject the proposed alternative as impractical or dangerous and insist that the present form of democracy, with all its imperfections, is preferable to any feasible alternative. But if he pursues this tack we can at least hope to sharpen his sense of the contrast between present realities and a minimalist version of his own ideals. We can draw him into empirical controversies over the probable consequences and conditions of alternative arrangements. We can shake his sense that the democratic ideal has a self-evident institutional content.

He may reject our program not because he believes it to be unfeasible but because he thinks it fails to respect that aspect of the democratic ideal we should care about most. But then in choosing either to reject the alternative or to accept it he gives greater clarity to his understanding of what democracy is for. Although the new institutions may have been justified or motivated by the narrow goal of rescuing the state from the control of a faction, they require from those who would operate them or reason from them a revised idea of democracy. This idea extends the notion of a state not hostage to a faction into the notion of a society not hostage to any entrenched version of itself and not designed to make its citizens hostage to predefined places in a plan of social division and hierarchy.

If internal argument is defined narrowly as taking its points of departure from received empirical understandings of society as well as from inherited ideals of human association, we cannot expect it to persuade anyone to accept proposals for alternative institutional definitions of markets and democracies. It can merely heighten our sense of ambiguity and prevent us from staying, imaginatively, where we are. Its focus is sharpened and its force strengthened, however, when it can draw upon an enlarged sense of social possibility (such as the explanatory theory of this book seeks to justify) and upon visionary justifications of its arguments. The internal discussion then provides the materials and opportunities on which the visionary can seize, while vision gives the internal arguer a stronger measure of corroboration and clarity. In the end the visionary and the internal justifications may even merge into a single mode of discourse.

THE INTERNAL JUSTIFICATION
OF EMPOWERED DEMOCRACY:
SOCIETY AS AN ARTIFACT OF WILL

The dependence of internal argument upon both social theory and visionary thought becomes all the clearer in a second line of criticism. This alternative version of the case for empowered democracy also plays on the contrast between acknowledged ideals and experienced realities. But it starts from an ambitious rather than a minimalist version of the democratic idea, and it highlights disharmonies between aspiration and experience that the first line of internal argument leaves unexplored.

Democracy, in this more ambitious view, is a regime in which the basic arrangements of social life are chosen by the wills of free and equal citizens. The more ambitious ideal connects with the minimalist goal because the circumstance in which the state remains hostage to a faction amounts to a situation of privilege in the authorship of social arrangements, a confiscation of the society-making power the democrat believes ought to reside more or less equally in all. The more ambitious ideal goes farther because it requires that we be able affirmatively to trace our most important institutions and practices to democratic choice. (In the light of the explanatory theory of *False Necessity* the most important arrangements may be defined, more precisely, as those composing the formative context of social life.) Moreover, this more demanding ideal outlaws unchosen tradition as well as nonreciprocal privilege; it insists that our society be our artifact.

In our democratic aspirations the commitment to bring society under the rule of free and equal wills never stands alone. It is tempered and complemented by an expectation about the type of social order these free and equal wills establish. This expectation constitutes the distinctively liberal element in our thinking about democracy. A democratic social order is one in which no majoritarian choice destroys the framework that enables new majorities to emerge and to change or reverse earlier decisions. It is also one in which majorities do not choose to abandon individuals to a circumstance of dependence or subjugation that mocks the claim of the abandoned to be the free coauthors of the social worlds they inhabit.

One way of clarifying the relation between democracy as a procedure (the triumph of the will) and democracy as an outcome (the effective respect for the continuing autonomy of the individual and for the continuing emergence of new challenges to old decisions) is to say that only those outcomes count as democratic that do not jeopardize the procedure. But the relation between procedure and outcome gains a higher order of generality when we reinterpret both the procedure and the outcome as complementary expressions of the same effort to free our practical and personal dealings from any imposed arbitrary or domination-tainted grid.

The feature of democratic politics that contrasts most clearly with this exigent and internally complex ideal is the persistence of the reform cycles discussed in Chapter 2. Caught in these cycles, democratic polities alternate among a small number of policy options that are almost no party's favorite solutions. Why must we be condemned endlessly to rehearse economic or social policies that are widely viewed as halfhearted and second best? And why should we find the range of feasible alternatives so narrowly defined when we did not democratically choose the list or trace its limits?

There are two familiar ways to reconcile these facts with the more ambitious democratic ideal. We often find these two tactics combined. The composition of the narrow list of viable alternatives can be attributed to the pressure of inexorable practical constraints, such as the requirements of satisfying the material expectations of large populations against a background of limited resources and limited technological and organizational capabilities. Alternatively, the rigidity and recurrence of the options may be put down to the inevitable effects of the mutual resistance that many organized interests impose upon one another in socially and culturally pluralistic societies. The repeated solutions are the few resultants of far more numerous vectors. But the argument of Chapter 2 has already suggested that neither practical constraints nor pluralistic tensions suffice to explain the shape and tenacity of the reform cycles unless we also take into account the independent influence of a formative institutional and imaginative context such as the one described there.

Now suppose someone objects that even this institutional and imaginative framework results largely from the combination of free and equal wills. A liberal-democratic constitution not only provides for its own revision but also enables suitably constituted and represented majorities to revise any social arrangements, subject only to the revisable constraints imposed by the constitution itself and to the limitations in the content of legislation that inhere in a commitment to the democratic ideal. Remember, however, that a formative context consists in detailed institutions and beliefs, not just in an explicit constitutional scheme. Much or most of the formative context may never be mentioned, directly or indirectly, in the constitutional document. Conversely, many things found in a written constitution may not deserve to be included within the description of a formative context. Unlike the written constitution the formative context is not chosen. And the whole point of its existence and entrenchment is to resist the ordinarily available forms of challenge and disturbance. Moreover, if we attributed the content of the unwanted reform cycle to the formative context while continuing to insist that the context is chosen, we would be driven to conclusions that are either unpersuasive or embarrassing. When we choose the context we must be unaware of its real consequences for the course of routine conflict and policy. In this event our allegiance to the framework depends upon ignorance. Alternatively, we may appreciate the consequences but regard them as the unavoidable price for the gaining of benefits and the defense of ideals that only this framework can ensure. But then we make an empirical claim about the feasibility and consequences of alternative institutional means to achieve those goals. We find ourselves drawn into the very controversies about the merits of alternative regimes that this internal argument is designed to bring to the fore.

What changes in the content and character of the contemporary democracies would diminish the discrepancy between the more ambitious democratic ideal and the experience of democratic politics? The changes required would disrupt not only these but any other reform cycles. At the very least, they would prevent whatever part of these recurrences cannot in fact be attributed to the tensions of pluralism or the constraints of practical necessity. And they would succeed in this objective only to the extent that they weakened the force of formative contexts by narrowing the distance of context-preserving routine from context-transforming struggle.

One such set of changes might replace constitutional techniques of fragmentation and planned deadlock (such as the checks and balances of presidential regimes) with methods better suited to enable a party in power to try out far-reaching programs of social transformation. Another group of reforms would ensure, in the organization of governmental politics, occasions and methods with which to bring every important feature of the social order into question. The structure of government and the style of party-political rivalry would provide opportunities to destabilize any privileged hold over the material and cultural resources with which the social future is created within the social present. Still another set of reforms would put the decentralization of economic decisions on a basis that prevented small numbers of capital controllers from setting the social terms of economic growth. This altered institutional basis for economic decentralization would also help open the ordinary world of work and exchange to collective conflict and deliberation.

There is no a priori reason to believe that reforms of this kind and with these goals would converge with the institutional changes suggested by the previous line of internal criticism. The convergence between the requirements of the effort to prevent the state from being hostage to a faction and the requirement of the attempt to ensure the rule of free and equal wills is an empirical hypothesis. But it is one made plausible by a major theme of the explanatory theory of this book: the idea that privilege becomes stable only by being insulated from the effects of routine conflict. It is a conjecture vindicated by the detailed institutional proposals and supporting arguments presented later in this chapter.

By confronting the democrat with such a combination of internal criticisms and responsive proposals, we may hope to unbalance his self-assurance and force him to choose between a retrenchment or an extension of his commitments. He may reject our proposed alternative as unfeasible or dangerous. But if he accepts our empirical claims about the nature and basis of the reform cycles, we have at least taught him to understand the constraints present institutional forms impose upon his version of the democratic ideal. We have drawn him into particular controversies about the conditions and consequences of alternative governmental and economic arrangements. If, in the end, he remains faithful to the current institutional scheme, we can even expect to make him concede that they support only a far more modest conception of democracy than he had previously been inclined to profess. He can then hardly blame a disillusioned citizenry from seeking in other aspects of their experience (such as the politics of personal relations or of large-scale organizations) the satisfactions they have failed to find in citizenship.

Suppose, on the other hand, that the democrat accepts if not our proposals, the route of institutional transformation they exemplify. As he moves along this route he must enlarge his preexisting view of the democratic ideal. The changed institutions require from those who operate them, or reason from them, a new democratic theory. For this theory the goal of subjecting social relations to the wills of free and equal citizens can be achieved only by arrangements that weaken the practical and imaginative force of the contrast between the pursuit of private interests within a framework and the self-conscious fighting over the content of this framework.

Here, as before, the power of internal criticism not merely to expose problems and ambiguities but to support a particular resolution of them depends upon the extent to which internal argument incorporates into its own practice the other forms of discourse explored in this book: the expansion of the sense of social possibility that an antinecessitarian social theory permits, the higher confidence in the rightness of the cause that visionary thought inspires, and the awareness of alternatives that programmatic thinking awakens.

THE INTERNAL JUSTIFICATION OF EMPOWERED DEMOCRACY: THE FRUSTRATION AND FULFILLMENT OF PARTY-POLITICAL PROGRAMS

A Different Version of Internal Argument

The two possibilities of internal criticism explored in each of the last two sections differ in the relative ambition of the democratic ideal from which they start. They nevertheless illustrate the same basic method. Both exploit the tensions between an accepted conception of democracy and the realities of democratic politics. Both suggest changes in the institutional form of governments and markets that, once accepted, require an enlargement of the initial democratic ideal. Both show how this enlargement goes hand in hand with an effort to apply democratic principles to social relations previously considered unsuited to them. Both suggest that the alternative to this redefinition of democratic ideals and democratic institutions is a heightened sense of the disharmonies between received ideals and current institutions and a more active engagement in the discussion of possible alternatives. Both demonstrate that the ability of internal argument to push us to surprising conclusions, and not merely to explicate ambiguity, depends upon the extent to which it is informed by critical social theory, reinforced by political vision, and enriched by detailed institutional proposals and experiments.

My final line of internal criticism presents a variation on this method. Instead of taking the ideal of democracy as a point of departure, the exercise focuses on the main types of party-political programs advanced in the Western industrial democracies, the societies that represent the immediate setting for the programmatic arguments of this chapter. The party programs can be understood both as interpretations of democracy and as efforts to reconcile the democratic ideal with other goals and values. They make somewhat different assumptions about the models of possible and desirable human association that ought to be realized in different areas of social existence. But they rarely make these assumptions explicit, in part because they view enacted ideals of human association solely as objects of governmental policy.

Once again, however, the crux of the internal argument lies in the relation of the distinctive ideals of each party program to the formative contexts of the societies in which they are upheld. Here, too, attention focuses on established and alternative institutional definitions of market economies and representative democracies. The argument is cast in the form of a dilemma. If the proponent of the program continues to accept the existing institutional framework, he finds himself repeatedly frustrated in accomplishing his objective. He can realize it up to a certain point but there he hits against a barrier he finds himself unable to overcome. The discussion of the reform cycles in Chapter 2 suggests the nature of these barriers and offers a hypothesis about their institutional and imaginative basis. The comparative classification of Chapter 3 probes their distinctive identity and effects. The schematic narrative of Chapter 4 explores their historical origins. Faced with the obstacles dramatized by the reform cycles, the champion of a current party program may continue to press his plans, complaining that they have never been given a fair trial. Alternatively, he may give up the pretensions, though not necessarily the rhetoric that expresses them, and embrace present arrangements as practical necessity.

Suppose, on the other hand, that the adherent to the party program recognizes the need to reform the current institutional structure the better to realize his goals. Once he has established the alternative arrangements, or even just imagined them in significant detail, he discovers that they require of him a revised understanding of his programmatic aims and their relation to the aims of his adversaries. Internal argument does not merely force the proponent of the program to confront this choice between the retrenchment and the transformation of his ideals. It gives him reasons to choose the second horn of this dilemma over the first and, having done so, to move in the direction of the program of empowered democracy laid out in detail later in this chapter and already anticipated in earlier arguments. The reasons are inconclusive and controversial but gain greatly in force if the interlocutor comes to accept the conclusions of an explanatory social theory like the one offered in this book and hears the visionary message this theoretical understanding helps inform.

Three programs are discussed here: the conservative (or classical-liberal) program of free markets and decentralization, the corporatist–centrist program of encouraging communities focused on organizations such as business enterprises or local governments that lie between the central government and individual citizens, and the social-democratic program of egalitarian redistribution and grassroots participation in workplaces and local governments. Clearly, the three programs do not come close to including the important programmatic differences among political parties in contemporary democracies. Nor are they neatly divided among different party movements. To this day, for example, many of the European Christian Democratic parties hesitate between the second and third orientations I have distinguished. The extreme leftists of the labor or socialist parties sometimes advance programs that resemble ideas associated with the most radical free-market ideas, and if my argument is correct they are right to do so.

Nevertheless, despite the remoteness of my classification of programs from the fine texture of party differences in particular countries, the main point of this version of internal argument finds frequent corroboration in contemporary experience. The troubled relation of institutional assumptions to programmatic aims is not just the teaching of an alien experience, addressed to people who have never thought along such lines. It is a dimly understood but pervasively felt anxiety of party-political practice. The conservative free-market parties do hesitate between serious efforts to advance economic and governmental decentralization and outright pandering to the business interests. They fail to appreciate the constraints the current forms of markets and democracies impose upon their partisan ideals because they do not envision the alternative institutional forms that representative governments and decentralized economies might assume. Similarly, left-leaning reformers in high office regularly hesitate between advocating economic redistribution within an unchanged institutional framework and seeking changes in the framework. They vaguely understand the difficulties that current institutional arrangements create for large-scale redistribution. But they have little to put in place of the current market forms except nationalized industry, central planning, and brokered deals among big business and organized labor and nowhere to look for an alternative to current constitutional methods except impractical ideas of direct democracy and selfless civic engagement. The confusion is there all right; we lack the insights with which to dispel it.

The Conservative (Classical-Liberal) Program of Governmental Decentralization and Economic Competition

One characteristic partisan program has free markets and governmental decentralization as its watchwords. Its extreme form is the libertarian commitment to consign the state to a residual role as a mutual protection association and a provider of essential services.

The illusion it never unequivocally abandons is the idea of an un-controversial system of free human interaction, complete with a sys-tem of contract and property rights, that we can establish if only we manage to discipline government and prevent it from playing fa-vorites among individuals or groups.

The devolution of governmental power to small territorial units is a major plank in the conservative platform. But territorial decen-tralization immediately presents the issue of economic decen-tralization. The traditional objection to devolution is that it delivers working people into the hands of local notables and elites. Its real social significance must therefore be largely determined by the char-acter of local society, and this character in turn bears the imprint of the country's economic regime. Even in societies that do not exhibit an ostentatious class hierarchy the emancipatory effect of territorial deconcentration depends very largely on the quality of relations among people in their everyday, practical lives. The forms of pro-duction and exchange help shape this quality.

Thus, the nature and extent of economic decentralization is crucial to the conservative program. The institutionally serious conservative wants to maximize the independence of economic agents and the competitiveness of product, labor, and capital markets. But he con-fronts two obstacles to the achievement of his goals.

First, he must face the tension between the breakup of economic units and the practical advantages of economies of scale. A shrinkage of the size of the economic units and an extreme market fragmen-tation can be expected to drive up unit costs. It may prevent the concentration of resources and the organization of markets that en-courage technological dynamism by making technologically pro-ductive investments physically possible and financially rewarding. Thus, the conservative feels compelled to temper his goals of de-concentration for fear of exacting an economic cost that the society would not and should not pay.

A second obstacle to the program of economic decentralization has to do with a tension within the competitive ideal itself rather than with the constraints that economies of scale impose upon this ideal. Disparities in market influence and in economically relevant information are the very stuff of market transactions. Economic suc-cess is measured in the accumulation of capital and in the financing of technical, organizational, and informational capabilities allowing the agent to be that much more influential at the next round of transactions. If these inequalities of power and knowledge are allowed to accumulate without limit, the market system would soon become a power order because the psychological reality of autonomous eco-nomic decision making would be destroyed. But if the transaction-shaping inequalities resulting from earlier transactions were canceled out by a higher redistributive authority as soon as such inequalities arose, the market would in effect have been sacrificed to an overriding method of redistributive allocation. The thoughtful conservative or classical liberal recognizes this problem as a disharmony inherent in the market ideal and as still another reason to restrain his decentralizing goals.

The tension between market competitiveness and economies of scale and the disharmony within the market idea itself between the requirements of decisional autonomy and the restraint on corrective redistribution are endemic to all market systems. What the conservative fails to understand, however, is that market systems – the arrangements for decentralized capital allocation, production, and exchange – may differ sharply in the extent to which they resolve or aggravate these tensions. Under some institutional settlements the economies of scale needed to sustain a high level of technological dynamism may be unattainable. The minimum of case-by-case correction needed to prevent the market from remaining a power order may be more than a maximum of correction beyond which the corrective system of allocation replaces the market. Under other systems economies of scale may be reconciled with a far-reaching fragmentation of agents and markets, and the pressure for case-by-case corrective redistribution may greatly diminish. That market economies do vary along these lines is a historical fact, though one whose dimensions and implications remain misunderstood. The more speculative and controversial claim is that the actual historical variations represent but a portion of the indefinitely wider range of possible variations. The significance of the speculative claim is brought into focus by a proposal to reconstruct, in the here and now, the institutional basis of a decentralized economy.

The conservative does not recognize these actual or possible variations in the institutional form of a market economy, or if he recognizes them in the abstract, he fails to appreciate the consequences of the recognition. His first impulse is to equate the abstract idea of a market, as a system that enables many economic agents to bargain on their own initiative and for their own account, with particular economic institutions and legal rules. When he says "market" he means not only a market based upon absolute property rights but the unique system of contract and property rules that prevailed in the course of modern Western history. He may believe that part of the two tensions described can be resolved by such measures as the repeal of unnecessary governmental regulation. Whatever part of the tensions results from the established institutional framework of capital allocation, however, he attributes to the very nature of a market.

Suppose we point out to him the distinction between the abstract idea of a market and its concrete historical forms. We follow up on this distinction by proposing an institutional redefinition of the market regime. We advocate a version of the idea of rotating capital funds and disassociated property rights that later parts of this chapter develop and that the earlier lines of internal criticism have already evoked. It may now be helpful to restate the suggestion in slightly greater detail. Such an alternative system would, remember, pull apart and assign to different entities powers that the property right brings together and grants to the same rightholder. Teams of worker-technicians and entrepreneurs would make conditional and temporary claims upon one of a number of competing, semi-independent social capital funds, oriented to different kinds of investments and social needs. The ultimate constraints under which both capital takers and capital givers would operate would be determined by the central representative bodies of the democratic republic. These constraints would presumably include limits on the accumulation of capital by a team, the distribution of profits or the acquisition of other enterprises and services, and the permissible levels of wage and income inequality. Such constraints might be designed to prefer the rotation of both manpower teams and capital resources over the maintenance of long-lasting enterprises and a labor force bound to particular enterprises. But even these preferences might occasionally be reversed in some sectors of the economy for the sake of experimentation and comparison. The basic and sector-specific rates of interest charged by the central capital funds to the lower-tier competing funds and passed on by these funds to the capital takers would constitute the mainstay of governmental finance. Each aspect of the proposed economic regime would be implemented by a broad range of intermediate arrangements and transitional strategies, leading gradually from current institutions to the desired alternative.

We might try to persuade the free marketeer to move in the direction of our proposal by showing him that, if feasible, it would dramatically limit the tensions plaguing his efforts to achieve a fuller measure of economic decentralization in social life. Under the proposed system the entrusting of vast amounts of capital to managers who act as the delegates of the absolute property owners would cease to be the indispensable means for taking advantage of economies of scale. Nor would the breakup of large-scale enterprises endanger practical efficiencies. The competing capital funds would be able to give large amounts of resources to particular teams and several teams would be able to join in certain endeavors. Yet this pooling of manpower, technological, and financial resources would remain both temporary and conditional. Moreover, the alternative regime would deprive the mass-production industries of the major devices with which they protect themselves against instability in their product, capital, and labor markets (see the argument about rigid and flexible production in Chapter 3). It would thereby encourage the extension into the mainstream of industry of an organizational style and scale characteristically associated with the high-tech and service vanguard of the economy. Because the proposed system would prevent the accumulation of private fortunes (through strict limits on the accumulation and hereditary transmission of wealth and through the development of the right to satisfy basic material needs), ensure the diversification of access to capital, and sever the link between entrepreneurial success and cumulative market influence, it would also distance the exchange system from a power order. The need to correct transactions and redistribute their outcomes would greatly diminish because a much higher measure of equality (or of the prevention of permanent inequality) would be built into the defining rules of the market order. In brief, the new system would encourage both more economic deconcentration and more innovation in the organizational forms of production and exchange, though it would do so by abandoning the relatively absolute and unified property right.

These economic arrangements would in turn require changes in the organization of government and of the conflict over governmental power. If only to compensate for the dangers that attend a more overtly politicized allocation of capital, the forms of participation and accountability in governmental politics would need to expand. The conflict over the mastery and uses of governmental power would have to provide the occasions and instruments to destabilize emergent alliances between cadres of politicians or bureaucrats and groups of capital takers. The more mobilizational and conflictual style of politics that can be expected to emerge from such constitutional changes may have independent appeal to a classical liberal. For the earnest liberal wants to establish a society in which individual experience, opportunity, and initiative are not overshadowed by social station and in which the devolution of power to local governments does not mean surrendering to local elites.

The conservative as classical liberal might reject these proposals as unfeasible, inefficient, or dangerous to civic freedoms. But if he could be engaged in the effort to respond to this sequence of critical arguments and constructive suggestions he would gain a more acute sense of the difference between the abstract idea of a market and its varied institutional forms. He would have to assess more self-consciously the constraints current forms impose upon his ideals and to explore more seriously the empirical assumptions that lead him to reject this or other alternatives. And he might be led to make explicit the reasons that prompt him to subject the ideal of economic and governmental decentralization to the special requirement of the absolute property right.

If, on the other hand, he moved toward the proposed arrangements he would experience a transformation in his self-conception and in his understanding of his relation to his political adversaries. His view of the market would become disengaged from the commitment to small-scale property and his conception of democracy would no longer remain attached to the specific constitutional techniques of the contemporary liberal democracies. Most importantly, he would alter his sense of his disagreement with centrists and leftists. From his newfound vantage point many of the traditional differences among these ideological tendencies would be overshadowed by the dispute about whether to take the established institutional framework for granted or to reconstruct it along the lines suggested.

Here, as always, the persuasive force of internal argument – its ability to go beyond the exposure of ambiguity to the justification of a particular direction of institutional change – depends upon how much it is allowed to incorporate. It can neither convince the interlocutor to confront the ambiguity it exposes nor lead him toward the particular resolution it desires if it must work solely with received ideals and widespread empirical assumptions. But its direction sharpens and its base broadens to the extent that it draws upon a credible view of social transformation and institutional invention, a visionary message, and detailed programmatic proposals. To be sure, all these informing ideas are controversial. But each new focus of controversy is an opening through which further varieties of relatively corrigible and partly empirical insights can be brought to bear on our programmatic controversies.

The Centrist Program of Corporatism and Community

The centrist program of corporatism and community may seem much less important than the other two discussed here. Certainly, it has always been less strongly represented in the English-speaking countries than in continental Europe or Latin America. Even in the countries where it has exercised the strongest influence, it has lost the specificity it once possessed in, for example, the social teaching of the Catholic Church in the period between the wars, a teaching that resonated in the programs and rhetoric of the center Christian parties. Today, the centrist program of community has largely become a vague aspiration in search of an explicit ideological form.

But it continues to repay internal criticism as much as its more influential rivals. Its predicament of institutional disorientation merely makes explicit a problem shared less self-consciously by free marketeers and social democrats. Centrist communitarianism provides an opportunity to probe the relation of our inherited communal ideals to current institutional arrangements. And it corresponds to a powerful undercurrent of disappointment and longing even where it fails to be articulated as a distinct political program. The identity of this program may best be understood from the angle of its diagnosis of the ills of modern society. According to this diagnosis the primary evil of daily life in contemporary society is the breakdown of the bonds of communal solidarity and the abandonment of the individual to self-reliance, loneliness, and selfishness. The isolated individual confronts the government and other large-scale organizations with very little, except the obsessional nuclear family, by way of communal sustenance.

The centrist communitarian may gladly acknowledge that the disruption of the texture of sustaining reciprocal loyalties resulted from changes that also made societies both more equal and more productive. But he does not believe that the situation of universalized estrangement constitutes the inevitable counterpart to economic growth and social equalization. Moreover, he also recognizes that there is no return, desirable or possible, to the earlier more naive, more impoverished, and often more oppressive and hierarchical situation. He seeks a response that respects the conditions and achievements of modern life.

His prescription begins with the effort to define the intermediate organizations – intermediate between the state and the individual – that can serve as practical settings for a modernized communitarian ideal. But the centrist communitarian characteristically displays a pattern of hesitation and equivocation when he tries to define these institutional settings. He does not advocate a radical reconstruction of current institutions; the idea of alternative institutional definitions of market economies and democratic representation forms no part of his doctrinal repertory. But neither does he fully accept established institutional practices. Typically, he wants to transform existing institutions – businesses and bureaucracies, shops and factories – from within and to do so less by dramatic transfers of power or institutional inventions than by nurturing habits of mutual allegiance, communal harmony, and restraint on individual or factional self-interest. Insecurity and extreme inequality must be avoided. But he does not see entrenched hierarchies of advantage as themselves an insuperable obstacle so long as the relations between superiors and subalterns are infused by a sense of continuing mutual loyalties and of devotion to the common good of the group. Economic security and coparticipation in collective decision-making may help sustain this devotion and these loyalties. But the widespread acceptance and enactment of certain moral ideas are likely to be just as important.

Where is the centrist communitarian to look for the practical realization of his aims? The most richly developed versions of the centrist communitarian program often place their hope in the effort to impart to modern enterprises some of the characteristic forms of the guild: the association of employers and employees on a basis of security and mutual commitment. This association requires from both the workers and their supervisors a willingness not to push to the hilt each party's advantage on the labor market. The leading right-of-center version of this idea is the repudiation of class conflict and union militancy and the redefinition of existing businesses as a locus for community. Because the intermediate organization was often supposed to occupy a well-defined and regulated place in the social order and perform some of the functions reserved by liberal theory either to individuals or to governments, this right-of-center communitarianism sometimes presupposed a corporatist reorganization of society. In this corporatist guise it served as an inspiration to fascist theory. Yet the doctrine of guild socialism showed that the same idea could be reinterpreted in a left-of-center manner.

The explicitly corporatist devices of the centrist communitarian program may have lost their attraction. But the practical compromises and moral concerns that inspired these ideas persist in vaguer and more credible forms. On the one hand, they surface in the advocacy of consensual deals between workers and employers in mass-production industries and large-scale organizations. These pacts characteristically rely upon the distinction between a stable, organized labor force and the transitory, unprotected workers or the independent subcontractors who enable the enterprise to respond to demand cycles without having to enlarge its permanent work force. The deals also require national governments to be actively engaged in promoting the more cooperative style of labor–management relations. On the other hand, the same ill-defined communitarian concerns reappear in forms unrelated to work. Such forms go all the way from the willful and factitious development of ethnic or national identities to the attempt to reconstruct the family as a refuge from the experience of egotistic self-interest. These versions of the quest for community gain urgency from the awareness that their work-related counterparts amount to hardly more than strategies for more effective practical cooperation and leave the communitarian aspirations unfulfilled. But the question is precisely: What would it take to fulfill them?

The centrist communitarian program is defined in part by its refusal to break decisively with the established institutional forms of democracies and markets. The result of this refusal is to frustrate the realization of the communitarian ideal. One aspect of frustration is the division of the communitarian ideal into practical solutions that lack emotional force and psychosocial experiments that lack connection to humdrum practical life. Another, more fundamental aspect is the entanglement of the communal ideal in social relations of dependence and domination. I earlier argued that present institutional arrangements both realize and block the radical project of fashioning institutions that weaken the influence of preestablished social division and hierarchy over our practical and passionate dealings with one another. This argument is implied in the recognition of the failure of current institutions and dogmas to prevent governments from remaining hostage to a faction, for privileged access to governmental power is the single most important tool for the entrenchment of group prerogative.

Consider what happens to the communal ideal when it must be realized in a setting of recalcitrant but also resented inequality. Every rebellion against dependence and domination takes on the character of a betrayal of communal bonds, whereas fidelity to these communal bonds requires submission to a hierarchical order. Yet the societies in which these varieties of dependence and domination persist are not like the societies in which the ideal of patron–client relations, with their combinations of exchange, dominion, and allegiance, reigned unchallenged. The coexistence of community with inequality is recognized, half-consciously, to require special excuses and to generate special problems. People fear that this coexistence will turn the communal ideal into little more than the softening halo of a brutal power system. They fear it will sacrifice to the preservation of this system their chances for greater practical and emotional access to one another. This subversive though imperfectly articulated insight poisons the subjective experience of communal life. Allegiance becomes deference, and deference is vitiated by an undercurrent of resentment, contained by apathy, escapism, and willed naiveté. When the resentment produces actual rebellion it must be repressed. However anodyne a form the repression may take, it is experienced as particularly nasty because it occurs against the background of so troubled a sense of entitlement and possibility.

At the same time, the continuing entanglement of communal ideals in structures of dependence and domination distances the ideal and the experience of communal life from the basic problem of solidarity: our effort to moderate the conflict between the enabling conditions of self-assertion and to free our experiences of attachment and engagement from some of their perils of dependence and depersonalization. The higher-ups are preoccupied with the maintenance of control; the underlings, with the anxieties of resentment and rebellion. Neither superiors nor subalterns can readily move toward the heightened mutual vulnerability that represents the most immediate spur to the advancement of solidarity. Moreover, both masters and mastered find their attempts to deal with one another as individuals constrained by the roles each person occupies within the hierarchical structure of the group.

Suppose we propose to the centrist communitarian that he follow the trajectory of institutional change anticipated in preceding sections and worked out later in this chapter. We argue to him that these institutional inventions help undermine the obstacles to the realization of his communitarian ideals. They do so primarily by contributing to the disruption of the mechanisms of privilege and to the undermining of entrenched social roles and hierarchies. Moreover, because factional advantage can easily turn into cultural hegemony, the proposed arrangements make it harder for any one group to present its distinctive way of life as a model for society although they may also help destabilize the pattern of inherited communal, ethnic, or national identities. Finally, they vastly expand the opportunities for individual engagement in collective life.

Even if the centrist communitarian believes in the feasibility of some version of the proposals for empowered democracy, he may reject them as subversive of his communitarian aspirations. He may insist that their appeal to conflict and mobilization jeopardizes the cultivation of group harmony and of shared values that he sees as the core of communal life. He may repudiate the emphasis on challenge to all nascent forms of privilege as a disguise for factional selfishness and animosity. But if he pursues this tack he may still be led to confront the constraints that existing institutional arrangements impose upon his communitarian objectives. He may become more conscious of the specific quality of the communities that can flourish within the institutional framework he refuses to abandon. And he is put on notice that this framework is at least not the self-evident vehicle of the communitarian program and that if our proposal does not seem preferable to present arrangements, another may well be.

If the centrist communitarian does agree to move toward this proposed revision of our basic institutional arrangements, he soon finds himself redefining the communitarian ideal. He now comes to see the promise of a fuller reconciliation between the enabling conditions of self-assertion as more important than group harmony or than the sharing of values and opinions; his idea of community begins to incorporate conflict as a condition rather than an evil. At the same time he begins to abandon the view of community as a distinctive model of human association to be realized in narrowly defined domains of social existence. He starts to see community instead as a variable aspect of social life, more fully realized in some areas of social practice than in others but never definitively excluded from any area.

These shifts in his preexisting definition of community are not the results of tricks we spring on him. They merely exemplify the interplay between images of association, their practical forms, and their domains of applications that represents the essential dynamic of internal argument. The more fully the centrist communitarian allows the visionary and social-theoretical supports of this programmatic direction to inform the moves of internal argument, the more likely he is to join us in our campaign.

The Social-Democratic Program of Redistribution and Participation

The third program considered here has the strongest manifest affinity with the proposals of empowered democracy. Moreover, when it is considered less as a partisan platform than as the idealized agenda of a certain tendency of social transformation, it represents the most attractive alternative to empowered democracy. But it is also the party orientation that I shall discuss most briefly. Almost everything I have to say about its ambivalent relation to present institutional arrangements has already been anticipated by the criticism of the other party orientations or by the analysis of contemporary reform cycles, or will later be developed more fully in the course of presenting the plan of empowered democracy.

The program of social democracy is distinguished by its commitment to diminish inequalities of wealth and income, to guarantee through tax-and-transfer schemes the satisfaction of welfare needs, and to establish the economic and social conditions for full employment. Together with this major theme of redistribution and stabilization, the social-democratic program incorporates a minor theme of grassroots involvement: the active participation of ordinary men and women in the governance of their workplaces and localities. In the internal evolution of social-democratic attitudes this minor theme has come to play an increasingly prominent role either because traditional economistic demands become less pressing or because participation is seen as a basis for practical cooperation and for avoiding costly and unnecessary economic strife.

The social democrat is often straightforward in expressing his ambivalence toward the institutional framework he finds in place. He frequently speaks of modernizing economic and governmental institutions, of making them more accountable and participatory in their operation and more egalitarian in their effects, and of bringing them closer to the experience of ordinary men and women. But he does not advocate radical institutional inventions. He is likely to insist that mixed economies and representative democracies are infinitely better than available alternatives like the Soviet style of organization. He, too, implicitly identifies markets and democracies with the institutional forms he sees around him even though he professes an open-minded attitude toward institutional experimentation.

The social democratic program often finds its champions in labor or socialist parties with a radical Marxist past. But the commitment to the proletariat regularly encourages an uneasy, favored relation to organized labor, entrenched in mass-production industry. The two main variants of social democracy reflect clashing but equally nonradical attitudes toward this special connection. One approach maintains the privileged link to the organized industrial working class; but it treats organized labor increasingly as a well-defined interest group, with a stake in the perpetuation of a certain style of industrial organization, rather than as a powerless, national mass unified not only by its present position but by its devotion to a new ordering of society. Another approach wants to sever the increasingly onerous connection and seeks support in a more amorphous middle-class constituency. Both approaches lack a transformative institutional vision. The social democrat ends up being someone who always promises a little more within the present institutional order, discovers that these promises are hard to keep, and attributes the difficulty of keeping them to the complexities of interest group politics and the intractability of practical constraints rather than to the formative institutional and imaginative context he half-consciously accepts.

The analysis of the reform cycles in Chapter 2 has already indicated ways in which current institutional forms of markets and democracies frustrate the achievement of the social-democratic goals of redistribution and participation. Thus, for example, the threat of serious redistribution encourages disinvestment and economic crisis wherever relatively small numbers of capital managers are able to exercise a major influence upon basic investment flows. To change this situation without merely transferring economic sovereignty to central planners or tenured enterprise labor forces would demand an alternative to absolute property as an instrument of economic decentralization. It would also require a style of governmental organization that could prevent this alternative from turning into an instrument of renascent privilege.

The participatory ideal faces similar constraints. It is certainly possible to expand the range of grassroots involvement in local administration and workplace governance without any change in the institutional structure of democratic governments and market economies. But this framework-respecting style of collective participation involves little real transfer of power. It is easily criticized as an exercise in human relations, and it often disappoints both its champions and its beneficiaries. As soon as the social democrat tries to give real force to the participatory ideal, however, he comes up against the limitations imposed by the established formative context. If workers participate more actively in the organization of the enterprise, can their power reach the point of overriding managers and stockholders?

If not, the participation amounts to little more than a consultative technique. If yes, we must make the workers into the new collective capitalists and property owners or revise the fundamental methods of capital allocation. If citizens are to participate more fully in local government, how can the approach toward techniques of direct democracy be reconciled with a system of public office and specialized bureaucracy that runs on entirely different principles? Until it hits against the limits set by these principles the participatory movement threatens little and offers less.

If the social-democratic program remains within the boundaries of current economic and governmental arrangements, it can hope to realize its participatory and redistributive goals only in the marginal and fitful manner described. The reflective social democrat who has grasped the constraints current market and democratic institutions impose upon his objectives but who has rejected available alternatives as impractical or dangerous must emulate the chastened classical liberal or centrist communitarian. He must retrench in his claims while holding himself open to examine such other proposals for institutional reconstruction as may be advanced.

If, on the other hand, the social democrat agrees to move toward the program of empowered democracy, his sense of what a more participatory and egalitarian society is like begins to change. The empowered democracy, for example, achieves a greater measure of economic equality through its basic methods of capital allocation and constitutional organization rather than through the tax-and-transfer correction of market outcomes. It therefore implies a far more intimate connection between civic engagement and outcome egalitarianism than the traditional social democrat envisages. We can hardly expect him to take internal criticism in this direction unless he comes to accept, in whatever fragmentary or implicit form, the visionary aspirations and the understanding of social reality and possibility that inform the program of empowered democracy.

The Radical Direction of the Internal Argument

In what sense does the internal criticism of party-political programs outlined in the previous sections have a leftist direction? The program of empowered democracy, anticipated by these lines of internal argument, is presented here as a leftist program of social reconstruction. In a real sense it does stand to the left of any of the three programmatic orientations discussed in the preceding sections. Yet I have also claimed that under certain assumptions the program of empowered democracy represents the fulfillment of each of the party tendencies. This claim makes the desired outcome look like a synthesis of current partisan opinions rather than a position to their left. How can the apparent paradox be resolved?

You cannot capture in any one hierarchical ordering of values and policies the continuing identity of the leftist idea. What distinguishes and unites the left over the course of its modern history is the commitment to carry forward what we can now retrospectively recognize as the radical project: the effort to establish institutional arrangements that more fully emancipate our practical and passionate dealings from a preestablished and recalcitrant structure of social division and hierarchy and do so in part by the facility with which such arrangements lay themselves open to revision in the course of ordinary social life. The implications of this shared endeavor can be clarified by substituting for the three party tendencies discussed the revolutionary slogans of freedom (for the classical liberal program), fraternity (for the communal corporatist program), and equality (for the social-democratic program). To understand the leftist as the person who values equality over freedom and fraternity is to miss the main point of the leftist undertaking, though leftists have often laid themselves open to this misrepresentation, particularly when accused of not facing up to the insoluble disharmonies among competing values.

In fact, however, it is their accusers who are confused. The confusion arises from the failure to appreciate one of the most important features of normative argument: the way in which ideals of human association draw their meaning from the combination of an open-ended aspiration with concrete practices and institutions realized in particular areas of social existence. Because of this interplay among abstract ideals, practical forms, and domains of application, vague ideals like autonomy and community cannot have a stable core of meaning. But if the effective human meaning of such ideals varies according to their practical forms, so must the extent to which the ideals contradict or complement one another. Much of traditional modern moral and political argument, with its stock arguments about the conflict of values, fails to understand this characteristic of our moral and political opinions.

Once we do understand it, however, we are that much less likely to mistake leftism for the assertion of a particular value over other competing values and are much more open to an interpretation that accords more fully with the actual campaigns and the felt aspirations of the left. On this interpretation, the leftist is the person who believes that the most important elements in our ideals of liberty, equality, and fraternity cannot be adequately realized through present institutional arrangements. More specifically, he believes they can and should be realized through the direction of institutional change described by the revised understanding of the radical cause.

The emphasis on the radicalism of the reconstructive effort elicited by these internal arguments and by their explanatory and visionary supports may aggravate another concern. If the direction is in fact that radical, if it stands clearly to the left of any major party orientation alive in the contemporary democracies, how can it be expected to have a chance?

The response to this concern comes in the detailed programmatic proposals, their supporting justifications, and their explicit relation to the explanatory ideas worked out in the earlier parts of this book. The presentation of the proposals for institutional reform includes a consideration of the transitional forms they may assume and of the favoring circumstances on which they may seize. It is preceded by a description of the style of political practice they would both require and perpetuate. Consider, first, by way of anticipation, the most general reasons for insisting that the radicalism of the program should not be equated with a lack of realism.

To many it may seem that social democracy is the best future that mankind may reasonably expect. By social democracy in this setting I mean a way of life more complex than the social-democratic program discussed in the preceding pages. This way of life includes: the perpetuation of the current institutional forms of mixed economies and representative democracies; the halting, partial development of the welfare state and of the social-democratic program of economic redistribution and grassroots participation within the limits tolerated by the institutional framework; the management of crises and shifts such as the decline of mass-production industries in ways compatible with the maintenance of that same institutional order; the continued disengagement of the citizenry from practical or imaginative conflict over the formative context of society; and the search for happiness through a mixture of experiments in material consumption, personal relations, and communal diversity. How could the program of empowered democracy hope to compete with a direction of change that fits so easily with existing assumptions about self-interest, collective identity, and social possibility because it respects the institutions and preconceptions that help to shape these assumptions and renew their life?

Once the argument for empowered democracy goes beyond the constraints imposed by received ideal and empirical preconceptions, its force depends upon the thesis about empowerment that has been restated in so many forms in these pages. If this thesis is correct the basic advantage of empowered democracy over social democracy is its ability to carry farther than its more established rival the varieties of self-assertion or negative capability. This advantage may compensate for the greater remoteness of empowered democracy from present economic and governmental institutions, if only feasible combinations of transitional arrangements and favorable circumstances can be found.

One aspect of the conception of advantage deserves special attention because of its responsiveness to the objections of the self-professed realist. The earlier account of context change claims that the development of productive and destructive capabilities requires a cumulative loosening of the constraints imposed by preestablished social roles, divisions, and hierarchies upon the organizational forms of production and exchange. At some levels of technological development the constraints that entrenched social divisions and hierarchies impose upon practical experimentation may be overshadowed by their use as an instrument for coercive surplus extraction. But at higher levels of resource availability and technological development, coercive extraction of surplus becomes less relevant and less difficult to ensure than permanent organizational and technological innovation. Remember also that the theory of transformation claims that the breaking open of social life to higher measures of practical recombination can be achieved by either more despotic or more consensual means. But among these practical solutions we usually find some that also advance the empowerment resulting from the creation of forms of communal life and practical collaboration less plagued by the risks of dependence and depersonalization. The program of empowered democracy is put forward as an example of just such a special solution in the historical circumstance to which it is addressed. It presents a vision of solidarity that simultaneously contributes to the enabling conditions for the development of practical capabilities. If this claim can be supported, it justifies the realism of the program. At least it does if the obstacles to the initial acceptance and introduction of empowered democracy are not themselves insuperable.

The issue of realism takes on an added poignancy in a third world setting. Although the institutional proposals detailed later in this chapter are designed with the contemporary Western democracies chiefly in mind, these proposals have their third world counterparts. Yet how, it may justifiably be asked, can countries that often remain far from the achievements of social democracy aspire to the more ambitious goals of empowered democracy? The answer lies in what I earlier called the catapult argument. In the absence of the great accidents of war and invasion many of these countries can expect to attain Western levels of economic equality and democratic pluralism only through the militant organization of the oppressed, the excluded, and the angry. It is not enough for these sectors of society to mobilize; they must remain mobilized. They and their leaders must use the favoring circumstances of crisis, revolution, and radical enthusiasm to establish economic and governmental institutions that help perpetuate in the midst of humdrum social routine somethı of the transitory experience of mass mobilization. The program empowered democracy represents a plan to establish institutions wiι.. this more mobilizational character. For many third world countries the route of empowered democracy may represent less the bolder alternative to social democracy than the sole practical means by which even social-democratic goals can be achieved. To escape the predatory rule of their elites and the subordinate status of their economies these peoples must catapult themselves forward to a more extreme version of the radical project than the richer nations have yet achieved. They must become empowered democracies in order to become democracies at all.

THE PRACTICE

THE PROBLEMS OF TRANSFORMATIVE PRACTICE

The Task of a View of Transformative Practice

The institutional ideas presented in this chapter have two sources: one is intellectual; the other, practical. The intellectual source is a practice of normative criticism and construction: exceptionally as visionary thought but more often as normative argument from within a tradition. In the sequence of exposition such visionary conceptions and internal criticisms anticipate the outline of the program they help to justify. But, in the actual psychological experience of formulating programmatic ideas, institutional proposals and ideal commitments develop simultaneously. Surprising turns in internal normative argument – our ever-present ability to deduce controversial conclusions from relatively uncontroversial premises – may suggest departures from current institutional arrangements. And the fragmentary description of these institutional proposals, together with our ideas about realistic trajectories of transformation, may in turn awaken us to unsuspected tensions between our ideal models of human association and the institutional arrangements that realize these models in fact.

The institutional program has a basis in political practice as well as in normative argument. The institutional ideas have to be realized by collective action. They remain unpersuasive and dreamlike until we have complemented them with a view of the social activities that might establish them. Our ideas about transformative practice and our programmatic commitments exhibit the two-way relation we find in our experience of the interplay between justificatory argument and institutional invention. Program and practice form a single vision; each can be inferred from the other, given a certain background view about the remaking of formative contexts. (The background view invoked here is the explanatory theory presented in earlier parts of this book.) The correspondence between practice and program comes out even more clearly in the small-scale politics of personal relations than in the large-scale politics of institutional arrangements.

By imagining a style of practice that prefigures a desired programmatic outcome we deal with the demonic problem of politics: the tendency of means to create their own ends, or the difficulty of realizing our chosen ends except through means that bring about results we do not want. A programmatic vision that cannot rely on a corresponding style of practice remains unstable: its proponents must choose at every turn between inaction and betrayal. The indispensable prefigurement of the ends within the means may refer to the social character of the transformative movement. The movement may embody a living, fragmentary, compromised image of the future it advocates for society as a whole. Alternatively, the prefigurement may take the form of localized experiments in novel styles of social organization, experiments that the transformative movement helps stage in the surrounding society. The practical solutions and the enacted ideals that distinguish these small-scale foreshadowings must be revised when those ideals and solutions extend to broader areas of social life. But the revised forms may still be recognized as transformations of the early, anticipatory experiments.

The following pages present a view of the style of transformative practice that can establish and reproduce the programmatic arrangements discussed later in the chapter. The ideas about justification and those about practice converge to support the institutional proposals. And the view of transformative practice establishes yet another link between the explanatory and the programmatic themes of *False Necessity*.

It may seem that nothing that is not trivial could possibly be said about the generalities of transformative practice. For the realm of practice is the domain of the constraints imposed by each unique context. Nevertheless, the theory of social change and the program for social reconstruction presented in this book help support an approach to problems of transformative practice. Indeed, if they did not, we could hardly hope to establish the necessary correspondence between program and practice. For the program itself is pitched at a level of generality beyond the distinctive problems of individual nation states. Success at speaking cogently about practice even at this transnational level lends support to a central thesis of this book: that we not only can break out of particular formative contexts or sequences of formative contexts but can also change the character of the relation of these frameworks to our freedom as agents. The generality of the programmatic and practical ideas is more than a convenience of exposition; it is a corollary of a whole view that refuses to give the constraining influence of context the last word and that promises to alter the sense in which our societies imprison us.

Two great problems must be confronted by the transformative practice described here. The portrayal of the practice begins with a discussion of these problems and an anticipation of the way the following argument resolves them.

Reconstructing Institutional Arrangements and Revising Personal Relations

The first major problem of transformative politics has to do with the relation between the effort to reconstruct social arrangements and the attempt to change the character of the direct practical or personal dealings among individuals. Neither endeavor can prosper without the other. Yet they cannot easily be integrated into a single undertaking.

The ultimate stakes in politics are the qualities of the direct relations among people. As the practical and visionary fighting over the content of social life gets contained or interrupted, as a formative context of power and production settles into place, as the routines of work and domesticity grind on in the protective climate of the social peace, as men and women learn to give to their abstract moral slogans a meaning compatible with the recurrent experiences of their everyday lives, the styles of personal relations harden. Among these habits of personal dealings are the available forms of friendship and marriage, the things that people expect from one another's company, and the methods they use to cope with conflict and disappointment and to express their wants and feelings in the conventions of society. These habits also include the manner and degree in which, in the different circumstances of social life, people reconcile self-assertion and attachment and deal with the significance of hierarchy for community. In all these ways, men and women show how they hope to achieve a measure of redemption through their dealings with one another. This fine texture of routinized human relations is the primary social reality. Even the boldest transformative efforts often take it for granted or, having acknowledged its importance, fail to alter it.

People understand differences in material standards of living, they care about them, and accept or reject them, largely for what these differences reveal about the ordering of human relations and the place each person occupies within it. To be sure, an individual may desire more material goods simply as a means to realizing his independently chosen ends. Short of the most basic needs for security and survival, however, the ends people entertain are commonly shaped by a background scheme of images of feasible and justified human association and by the desire to hold a certain place within this scheme. Even when, through exceptional insight, faith, and courage, an individual defines and pursues goals that seem to contradict the ruling vision of collective life, his aims make sense only in relation to some other view of human association, whose sovereignty he recognizes or desires to establish. The chief objects of human longing are other people and the character of dealings with them. The whole world of material things is like a stack of poker chips that people use to signify the ups and downs in the great game they play about the nature of their relations to one another.

For all its importance, however, the politics of personal relations cannot advance unless it is accompanied by the reconstruction of the formative context of power and production. This institutional framework helps shape the routinized dealings and preconceptions that constitute the fine texture of social life. It defines the occasions, and tilts the scales, of the ordinary individual and collective conflicts that take place just because people want to remain who they are and to keep what they have. It enables some people to set terms to other people's activities.

This pinning down of the collective power to remake social life affects, more or less obliquely, every aspect of people's relationships to one another. Even the seemingly most private aspects of love and marriage, of religious devotion and intimate ambition, bear the marks of the experience of each individual's power or powerlessness in the face of the circumstances of social life. The available forms of practical collaboration or passionate attachment hit against the limits of preconceptions and institutions that, in turn, obey and sustain the larger order of the society. By these means, both the powerful and the powerless are denied opportunities to discover the indefinition of self and society. Each institutional order denies these opportunities in a different fashion and to a different degree.

The formative context of power and production influences people's elementary dealings with one another in another, more subtle way. The stabilization of a social world requires the spiritualization of violence. The haphazard sequence of truce lines in the ongoing group struggle must be reinterpreted as an intelligible and defensible scheme of human association: a canon of the possible and desirable models of human association to be realized in different areas of social life. The ability to assign relatively stable meanings to a system of legal rights requires at least a tacit reference to such a scheme. Even people's effort to make sense of everything in society, from the appropriate use of different buildings to the expectations that attach to different roles, must appeal to another, vaguer version of this imaginative scheme of social life.

Our immediate experience of practical and passionate attachments always includes more than is dreamt of within this implicit map of possible and desirable forms of human association. The exorbitant elements in our experience, the elements that fail to fit the established context, provide us with an endless flow of incitements to reimagine and remake society. But this reconstructive opportunity can be taken advantage of only to the extent that people manage to redefine their enacted ideals and establish a new relation between actual social practices and the assumptions about possible and desirable association that support and authorize these practices. Until the marriage of presupposed meaning and realized institutionalized practice has been achieved, our incongruous experiences remain anxieties without a message and rebellions without a legacy. Transformative struggle must then proceed without the incalculable prestige and credibility that a model of human association acquires just by being realized in a routinized practice.

The history of the world religions has repeatedly shown the price of the failure to embody a novel vision of personal interaction in a changed institutional ordering of practical life. The religious movement submits to the state. Often this submission takes place under the delusive appearance of a religious conversion of the power holders. The votaries of the religion limit rather than push the struggle over the formative institutional context and over the routinized personal dealings and preconceptions that take place within it. The iconoclastic spiritual vision strikes a compromise with the established forms of behavior and perception: not just the deal inherent in the slow process of changing people's most elementary habits and ideas but the additional accommodation that arises from the willingness to take a large portion of social life more or less for granted. Then, the thing the religion forgets perverts the thing it remembers. The untransformed social order ends up taking its revenge against the vision of transformed personal relations.

Just as the attempt to change the character of direct personal relations soon requires a transformation of fundamental institutional arrangements, so the enterprise of institutional reconstruction calls for a vision of the transformed personal relations that the new institutional arrangements are meant to sustain. It even demands anticipatory examples of the realization of this vision.

For one thing both the persuasiveness and the realism of an institutional program require that gross institutional arrangements be changed into the small coin of personal relations. The human sense of institutional proposals depends in the end on their implications for the social microcosm. Only when we reach in thought and practice this level of personalized detail can we see a radically reconstructive program chastened by its confrontation with the stubborn, daily cares of ordinary people.

For another thing the vision and anticipatory experience of transformed personal relations encourage the self-restraint vital to successful institutional reconstruction. When the government's active engagement in the defense of established institutional arrangements has been shaken by violent or peaceful means and when settled assumptions about collective identities, interests, and opportunities have come partly unstuck, institutional reinvention enjoys its favored moment. This opportunity can, nevertheless, be squandered if redistribution over material advantages takes priority over institutional reconstruction. Redistribution may exercise a mobilizing effect by granting larger numbers of people the security that enables them to give themselves more wholeheartedly to escalating conflict. But both rapid redistributive and institutional change disrupt routines of production, exchange, and administration. The need to contain the disruptions of the transition period often requires that institutional aims be given priority over redistributive goals, except to the extent that these goals result immediately from those aims. When the tide of enthusiasm recedes and the opportunities for revolutionary reform shrink, a changed formative context must already be in place. The ability to see institutional transformation as part of an attempt to change the character of our most elementary personal interactions pushes conflict over the form of society beyond the instrumental struggle over material advantages. It extends strategic prudence into visionary ardor, thereby offering the incitement to sacrifice and self-restraint that cold calculation is rarely enough to ensure.

But though the transformation of personal relations and the reconstruction of institutional arrangements depend upon each other in all the ways described, they cannot easily be combined. The two undertakings seem to require devotion to divergent and partly conflicting aims. The effort to reorder institutional arrangements demands the churning up of the social practices in which personal attachments are embedded, and it turns the imagination away from the delicate and intricate texture of personal interdependencies. The dangers appear vastly to increase when the reconstructive program aims to carry society to a circumstance of heightened plasticity. Moreover, efforts to combine, in a single programmatic vision, proposals for institutional change and ideas about the transformation of personal relations have traditionally been associated with a naturalistic view of society and personality.

The intellectual solution to this first overriding problem of transformative practice is given by the many links of thematic analogy and mutual dependence that the programmatic argument of this chapter establishes between the reform of institutional arrangements and of personal relations. The argument integrates the two concerns on the basis of a radically antinecessitarian view of society and of a corresponding commitment to reduce the extent to which society is just there, as a set of entrenched roles or stations, beyond the reach of the will. The two practices of revolutionary institutional reform and of transformation in personal relations can reinforce each other despite the conflicts sure to arise between them.

Transformative Practice from the Top Down and from the Bottom Up

A second great problem of transformative political practice is internal to the attempt to reconstruct the formative institutional structure of power and production. Stated in the most general terms and with respect to the broadest range of projects of social reconstruction, the problem is the tension between the importance and the dangers of using governmental power in order to transform society in the image of a programmatic vision.

The use of centralized, coercive state power to impose a plan of social life is likely to be both futile and dangerous unless it is prepared by a less willful change of habits and sentiments. The masters of the state will soon find themselves waging war against a resistant society. The results of the interplay between the transforming will and the social resistance may bear little relation to the initial program. The commitment to carry this program out may soon take second place to the struggle to hold on to an isolated and rebuffed authority.

The attempt to gain control over an aspect of governmental power and use it for transformative purposes cannot, however, be left to take care of itself. For the control of governmental power exercises an overwhelming influence upon the course of conflict over the basic form of society. Those who postpone to the end the bid for governmental power may find their enemies holding the cards.

Like the first great problem of transformative practice, this second is a special case of the conflict and mutual dependence between means and ends. Like the earlier problem, it takes on a peculiar intensity because of the distinctive goals the program outlined here assigns to transformative action. In one description, the program of empowered democracy seeks to diminish the gap between framework-preserving routine and framework-transforming conflict. It does so by increasing the mastery we exercise over our contexts in the midst of our normal activities. Our practical and passionate dealings and our relations to the social worlds we inhabit are to be improved by our success in putting the basic arrangements of society within reach of ordinary collective conflict and decision and thereby breaking the hold of factional privilege over the resources needed to remake society. The style of transformative effort most closely anticipating this programmatic goal is the same style earlier labeled as collective mobilization. The second problem of transformative practice is therefore the tension between the strategy of changing social life through the capture and use of governmental power and the attempt to change society by gradually heightening collective mobilization. Governmental power may indeed be used both to enlarge opportunities for grassroots collective militancy and to consolidate its achievements. Nevertheless, the imposition of a reconstructive plan from the top down seems to be the very opposite of what a practice emphasizing collective self-mobilization and self-organization requires.

Before developing in detail this program-specific formulation of the second problem of transformative practice, remember the defining characteristics of collective mobilization. It is the coming together of people in ways that already differ from the kinds of relations that exist in the surrounding society and for the purpose of changing aspects of these relations. At first, the aims may be narrow and the innovations modest. But as the mobilizational movement presses forward, with its mixture of disciplined organization and organization-denying militancy, the goals become bolder. The gap between society as currently established and as recast within the movement widens. People broaden their sense of the groups to which they belong and of the possibilities of social experimentation. Their conception of the interests worth fighting for change accordingly. At every stage of its progress collective mobilization offers people an experience of reinventing the terms of their social existence. It undermines the clarity of the distinction between the aspects of life surrendered to a prosaic calculus and the areas in which personal relations matter for their own sake. It draws defined impersonal institutions back into the undefined personal realities from which they arise. It may do all these things faintly or strongly. But it does them always. Collective mobilization is thus more than a weapon for the remaking of social life; it is the living image of society dissolved, transformed, and revealed, in the course of the fights that take place over what society should become. Mass mobilization occurs when collective mobilization turns into the experience of large numbers of ordinary men and women.

Ideally, the capture and use of governmental power would be the last step in the gradual transformation of society. Mastery of the state would represent only the final consolidation of a victory achieved by other means; governmental power would be like ripe fruit falling from the trees. One domain of institutional life after another – connected areas of social practice and the internal arrangements of large-scale organizations – would be transformed by an exercise of collective mobilization inspired by a programmatic vision such as the one later sections of this chapter discuss in abstract and systematic terms. A shared feature of the new arrangements would be to preserve more fully in routinized social practice some of the qualities social experience assumes in the moment of collective mobilization.

It is not absurd to think that these many moves of collective mobilization might take a predominant programmatic direction, even though no one has written this program down and no one has orchestrated in detail these many experiments in social change from the bottom up. To admit this possibility of shared direction you have only to accept a number of assumptions that have already been presented and will be further justified. You must believe that this trajectory of transformation can be imagined and justified in bits and pieces, through the interplay between received social ideals and more inclusive understandings of social possibility. You must think that the normative doctrine of the program is not radically different from the ideal conceptions to which we already resort in our fragmentary attempts to criticize or justify particular institutions. You must concede that the connected reforms advocated by the program represent at least one possible route to the varieties of empowerment earlier discussed. And you must recognize that the logic of group interests, and of group alliances and antagonisms, begins to lose its clarity and its determining influence as soon as conflict starts to escalate.

Consider the dangers of the attempt to reverse the sequence that puts escalating grassroots mobilization first and the use of centralized governmental authority last. For the sake of clarifying the stakes, focus initially on the extreme case. A revolutionary vanguard seizes the central government and the military apparatus through force, guile, or luck, and attempts to impose its program by coercive means. We may even assume their take-over has been facilitated by mass agitation. Yet nothing but the experience of agitation itself has established anticipatory, fragmentary versions of the programmatic aims. In such a circumstance, two forces may easily converge to foreclose opportunities to realize any program resembling empowered democracy. These forces show two ways in which means may overtake ends.

On the one hand, the rulers may commit themselves to a project that finds little echo in the vague discontents and tangible wants of the populace. They rightly feel themselves threatened by rejection from within if not by invasion from abroad. To hold on to power becomes, in this precarious situation, their paramount concern. The obsession with the maintenance of power at any cost gains a semblance of justification from the need to keep custody of the supposed means of transformation. The effort to hold on to power in the circumstance of isolated and rebuffed authority is itself an all-consuming project. It requires the containment of conflict, the exaction of obedience, and the exercise of a vigilant distrust. It tempts its votaries to violence and rhetoric – those "two ways of denying reality." And it brings to the fore men skilled at perpetuating and strengthening an apparatus of control. Those rulers who take the prophetic dogmas at the heaviest discount will rise most quickly. The moment to carry out the program of empowered democracy will never come. Alternatively, the program will be carried out with so many concessions to the imperatives of the apparatus and to the power interests of those who staff it that little of its original content will remain.

On the other hand, plain people will fail to see in the professed aims of the revolutionary regime the elements of an alternative order of life. Once secure in power, the willful regime may succeed in promoting economic growth and material welfare. But it cannot credibly stand for the ideal of a society broken open to everyone's will or for the varieties of individual and collective empowerment permitted by the opening of privileged holds on the resources of society making. Faced with a mixture of unbelievable slogans and unmistakable coercion, ordinary men and women will withdraw into their families and careers in search of whatever tangible advantages they can secure. From these havens, they will emerge, because they must, only to engage in a sullen wrangling with their bosses and rulers.

These dangers stand out most clearly in the extreme instance of a revolutionary vanguard that attempts to impose a radical plan upon a resistant populace. But the same perils reappear, on a more moderate scale, whenever the struggle over governmental power as the master tool of social reconstruction takes precedence over the reform of one domain of institutional practice after another through escalating collective mobilization. The struggle for governmental power imposes a relentless discipline of its own. Militants and supporters must be converted through a language they can understand. Battles must be fought in circumstances where they can be won. Such tactical imperatives may require compromises and self-restraints incompatible with the conflictual style of a mobilizational strategy. In all these ways the effect of focusing on the struggle to win governmental power is to tempt partisans of the transformative movement to take for granted current assumptions about collective interests, identities, and possibilities.

The effort to cling at any cost to whatever measure of governmental power has been won presses the would-be reformers to depart farther and farther from their initial aims. Thus, for example, institutional reforms may be subordinated to immediate redistributive goals, and the reformers' time in office may come and go before they have had a chance to alter the formative institutional context of power and production. First the cause of partisan victory and finally the concern with partisan survival may prompt the sacrifice of one programmatic aim after another. The growing disparity between the slogans and the achievements of the reformers may provoke their disappointed supporters into ever greater degrees of withdrawal from militancy at the grass roots.

Despite all the dangers of anticipating the attempt to gain governmental power and use it for transformative ends, state power cannot in the end be treated as the final, spontaneous trophy of collective mobilization and institutional reform. The risks of leaving the take-over of governmental power to the end are even greater than the perils of using public office to reconstruct society. To begin with, governmental power may decisively influence the opportunities and obstacles of an organized, structure-revising militancy. It may do so through all the ways the state reproduces society. Government may enlarge or constrict the freedom to organize and proselytize. By redistributing wealth, it may free people from the extremes of a demobilizing poverty. It may counterbalance factional privileges even before it has abolished them.

Moreover, although a programmatic vision and a distinctive trajectory of transformation may emerge from the dispersed activities of many movements, this activity is unlikely to maintain a minimal cohesion and continuity of direction unless the grassroots efforts interact with at least occasional help from those who determine the most important rules and policies. The institutional reforms must enjoy sustenance in law and economic policy. The policy and legal obstacles to their further expansion must be overcome. And in all these ways tentative experiments and visionary routine must find an anchor in alternative, emergent structures.

The very attempt to win governmental office may prove almost as important as its exercise. The electoral or extra-electoral contest to gain position in government shakes the many links that connect access to the power of the state and entrenched privilege in society. The pattern of public intervention in favor of factional prerogatives gets disturbed. This disturbance in turn helps put the established definitions of collective identities, group interests, and human possibility up for grabs.

Even if your party were to arm you with an endless patience and propose to wait many generations for a slow but solid victory, you would find opportunities lost and lost forever. You would watch your enemies renew the life of institutional arrangements that would help shape future wants and self-descriptions. You would see people give to your party's slogans a meaning in accord with practical experiences you were powerless to influence. You would stand by while the aspirations of your movement withered in isolation. Why would these results surprise you if you had truly abandoned faith in the dialectic of history and learned to recognize how closely the dealings among groups connect with their relation to government?

The second key problem of transformative political practice may now be restated in formulaic terms. Collective contractualism (the explicit or implicit bargains among groups entrenched in the division of labor) changes into collective mobilization. This change encourages and depends upon the process by which the hardened links between private privilege and governmental power turn into a more intense and less defined struggle over the state. Yet each process makes voracious demands of its own. Each, followed to the end, threatens to disrupt and displace the other.

The ready antidote to this danger may seem to be an interplay between the pursuit of governmental power and the propagation of self-guided collective mobilization. Each move forward in the capture of parcels of state power can be used to improve the conditions for autonomous grassroots militancy. Each successful change of stabilized deals into an open-ended fight over the redefinition of ideas about collective identities, interests, and possibilities can help prevent the power of the government, and the quest for governmental office, from becoming an instrument of demobilization.

The allusion to this interplay, however, represents the name of a solution rather than its description. The description comes in the form of a view of transformative practice or, rather, of the limited insight into the problems of such a practice that can be achieved outside a particular setting of conflict. The ideas and maxims constituting this view are formulated here at two hypothetical moments of transformative practice: a moment when the movement, still far from the heights of governmental power, has only just begun to take root in society and a moment when it wins the highest offices. This view of practice should be general enough to apply to transformative movements that culminate in either the peaceful or the violent seizure of state power. The wager is that even at this level of generality, so remote from the problems of any individual circumstance, we can discover principles of action that illuminate the task of transformative practice.

Who are the agents of this program? They are the people whom I sometimes call the radicals, the transformers, or the transformative movement and, at other times, the defenders of empowered democracy. By radicals I mean the adherents to the radical project as previously defined: the men and women who seek to promote specific varieties of human empowerment by developing economic and governmental institutions that both diminish the conflict between framework-preserving routine and framework-transforming struggle and loosen the constraints of established social hierarchies and roles upon the forms of production, exchange, and personal attachment. The program of empowered democracy represents a proposal, informed by a view of social reality and social transformation, to develop the radical project in a certain direction. As a version of that project, it addresses a distinctive historical circumstance (the circumstance of contemporary industrial democracies and their rivals). But like any other social vision of comparable generality it embodies ideals, methods, and assumptions intended to have a broader reach.

This preliminary loose identification of the transformative agents should be read against the background of a refusal to treat any particular class, community, or nation as the natural proponent of this or any other program, even though it is possible to identify the strata, parties, and even countries most likely to be receptive to it. The explanatory theory of *False Necessity* has already justified this refusal. The programmatic argument justifies it some more. The relation of the transformative movement to existing parties and classes and the relation within the movement among cadres, rank and file, and potential supporters are taken up in the course of the following discussion of transformative practice.

THE TRANSFORMATIVE MOVEMENT IN QUEST OF POWER

The First Task: Linking Grassroots Mobilization with the Contest for Governmental Power

The first and most persistent task of the transformative movement is to maintain the connection between grassroots mobilization and the contest over governmental power. The allusion to the importance of maintaining this link merely restates the basic problem of transformative practice discussed in the preceding pages. But the first principle of practice describes the organizational basis for a successful solution to the problem.

The point of departure for this strategic approach is a recognition that neither the effort to capture parcels of governmental power nor the attempt to develop collective mobilization must be allowed to crowd the other out. Each must be practiced with an eye to the requirements of the other. At every juncture of activity the participants in the movement ask: Which grassroots organizations are most likely to be useful in the contest for governmental power and what style of engagement in this contest can encourage militant collective self-organization? Nevertheless, the two contending goals of transformative practice are characteristically served by two different types of organizations. To insist on an immediate synthesis of the two types is to risk creating a political enterprise unable to perform either role effectively. The conditions that would allow for the organizational synthesis cannot be assumed; they must be created.

In the contemporary Western democracies the primary tool for the conquest of governmental power is the political party, often little more than an electoral syndicate held together by a strange combination of transitory interest-group alliances, vague but powerful affinities of vision and sensibility, and career ambitions of professional politicians. The poverty of the institutional imagination regularly makes for an incongruous, shaky fit between tangible promises to particular groups and ideal commitments to social reconstruction. The same lack of clarity about the relation of formative contexts to routine policy options helps prevent the parties from breaking or even understanding the cycles of reform and retrenchment that so greatly influence their electoral fortunes. Such an electoral syndicate ordinarily takes for granted current definitions of group interest, collective identitities, and social possibilities. It is tempted to seek the broadest possible alliance of interests and opinions it can achieve consistently with these assumptions and with its sense of its historical identity. It understandably resists challenges to such assumptions, which risk sacrificing its chances for high office. It tends to defer to organizations, like labor unions or ethnic associations, that claim to represent its prospective constituents. And it usually confines its activities out of power to planning for future electoral campaigns or to the ritual reassertion of its distinctive identity. All these proclivities make it ill-suited to the work of grassroots collective mobilization. The available experience of partisan struggle, directed to central power, may bring people together. But it is much less likely to bring them together in ways that already begin to defy this context and to overstep the assumptions about the interests, identities, and possibilities the context helps sustain.

To the extent that the work of collective mobilization is carried on at all in the contemporary industrial democracies it is undertaken by a medley of nonparty organizations: the more militant and less economistic labor unions, social activists committed to organize as well as to defend the unorganized poor or oppressed minorities, and citizens' movements devoted to social interests perceived to fare poorly in mainstream governmental politics. Each variety of popular extrapartisan militancy can remain detached from any general program for social reconstruction, or it can make common cause with the social-democratic parties and reinterpret its commitments from a social-democratic perspective. But if its participants accept the internal criticism of the social-democratic program outlined earlier, they will come to believe that their objectives cannot adequately be accomplished within the institutional frameworks to which social democracy remains committed. They will also be more ready to see the campaign for empowered democracy as a fulfillment of their own efforts.

This shift in the self-definition of extrapartisan grassroots activity may be paralleled by a reorientation of any of the existing political parties or by the creation of a new party committed to empowered democracy. The internal criticism of contemporary party-political programs has shown how the established institutional forms of market economies and representative democracies frustrate the realization of the classical liberal, the centrist communitarian, and the social-democratic programs. The program of empowered democracy can persuasively claim to realize the part of existing party-political platforms the established institutional framework excludes. But, of course, abstract commitments are one thing, and represented interests are another. The program of empowered democracy has a far better chance of taking root in the reform, labor, socialist, and communist parties of the industrial democracies than in the centrist and conservative parties.

The initial concern of the defenders of empowered democracy, then, must be to work loosely within the political parties and the extrapartisan grassroots movements most open to their vision. Success in influencing the programmatic orientation of these movements and parties can in turn be expected to bring about a shift in the conception of the relation between partisan politics and social activism. The convert to the program of empowered democracy wants to develop the style of political practice whose character I am now beginning to describe. Because he seeks to tighten the link between collective mobilization and the quest for governmental power, he also desires to bring together the grassroots organizations and the political parties that most fully represent each side of the transformative effort. But it does not follow that he should try to abolish the contrast between the political party and the extraparty organization as quickly as possible. For the result might be to harness the grassroots social activism to the short-run perspective and the consensus-building concerns of the electoral syndicate while exposing this syndicate to the risky, long-term experiments and aggravated factionalism of the grassroots activities.

So you can imagine the friends of empowered democracy working, at first, with a loose sense of their shared identity, within political parties and nonparty social movements. They work both to change the direction of the party or movements to which they belong and to prepare the day when party and movements can safely unite. The picture here is not one of a conspiratorial organization that sends its militants out as secret agents and partners. It is rather an image of people who from several points of departure and in different theaters of activity gradually converge toward the sense of sharing in a common undertaking.

The interplay between social activism and party campaigns can be vastly reinforced by the presence of a third element, distinct from both traditional partisan rivalry and collective mobilization. The task of this third element is to detach a parcel of governmental, economic, or technical authority from service to the reproduction of the existing formative context and to turn this fragment of power, instead, into a floating resource – a resource that can be fought over and converted to transformative uses.

In countries with a strong statist tradition the lower rungs of the governmental bureaucracy constitute the most likely agents for the development of such floating resources. For example, in many Latin American nations whole sectors of the economy (e.g., agriculture) are closely supervised and coordinated by economic bureaucrats: public-credit officers and agronomists. Such countries often provide for corporatist union systems that compulsorily include most of the labor force. The unions may be staffed, guided, or manipulated by public lawyers and agents of the Ministry of Labor. Normally, these forms of state activity seek social harmony in the form of submission to economic and bureaucratic elites. But the bureaucracies are typically mined by a multitude of more or less well-intentioned, confused, unheroic crypto-leftists – middle-class, university-trained youth, filled with the vague leftist ideas afloat in the world. The ambiguities of established rules and policies and the failures of bureaucratic control can supply these people with excuses to deny a fragment of governmental protection to its usual beneficiaries and make it available to other people, in new proportions or new ways. A tiny flaw is then introduced into the manner in which the state apparatus fits into the social order. The result is to create a floating resource – one the transformers can appropriate or fight about.

In countries with a weak statist tradition (such as the English-speaking democracies) reliance on state-provided resources is dangerous. For the welfare-state programs that enable social workers or public-interest lawyers to carry on their organizing efforts tend to be precisely the programs sacrificed first during the retrenchment phases of the reform cycle. In these countries, however, the learned professions are often proportionately stronger than in the societies with a more marked statist heritage. A vast area of social practice is effectively withdrawn from the scope of party-political conflict and treated as a subject for the application of professional expertise, when in another country some of the same subjects might be handed over to bureaucratic supervision. The outcomes of fighting and of the containment and interruption of fighting reappear as, say, the structure of legal rights inherent to a democratic market system or the style of work organization necessary to the management of an advanced industrial enterprise. The rights-defining practice of lawyers and the efficiency-defining practice of managers and engineers represent the two most prominent professional methods for the depoliticization of social decisions. But such depoliticization invariably depends on violent truncations of analysis: on the creation of a fictive sense of determinate rational constraint at the cost of arbitrariness in defining the methodological and institutional assumptions that make this determinacy possible. As a result, the depoliticization can be reversed. The domain of professional expertise can be turned into one more arena for carrying on, under special though contestable constraints and with special though revisable tools, the struggle over the formative institutional and imaginative assumptions of social life. A fragment of the power exercised by the efficiency experts and rights specialists becomes a floating resource: a society-making capability whose uses and beneficiaries are not predefined.

Whether the floating resource results from a bureaucratic betrayal or from a politicization of professional discourse, it serves the alliance of grassroots mobilization and state-oriented party politics. It turns the attention of both party and extraparty activists toward the immense depoliticized area of social practice that stands between them. It also provides those who begin to agitate and organize in this area with an opportunity to enlist resources, previously devoted to the reproduction of the existing social world, in the construction of enclaves and countermodels: enclaves for further experiments in the blend of grassroots mobilization and party politics; countermodels to a portion of the current formative context of social life. The point of the next principle of transformative practice is to explore the relation between enclaves and countermodels.

The Second Task: The Experimental Anticipation of Empowered Democracy

The need to prefigure the goals of empowered democracy in the means for its attainment does not merely require that collective mobilization and the struggle for governmental power be allowed to reinforce each other. It also demands that the transformative movement succeed in establishing small-scale, fragmentary versions of the future it advocates for society. Without these experimental anticipations of the program, there would be no way to bridge the gap between reformist tinkering and wholesale revolution and no way to pass from one set of assumptions about group interests, collective identities, and social possibilities to another.

Several features of the explanatory theory of this book suggest the characteristics of social reality that make such experimental anticipations possible. One characteristic is the looseness of the relations among the constituent elements of a formative context: despite the existence of constraints upon the institutional or imaginative elements that can be successfully combined, formative contexts can be changed piecemeal. Another enabling feature of social reality is the relativity of the distinction between the practical or imaginative activities that respect and reproduce a formative context and the activities that challenge and transform it.

Each fragmentary anticipation must satisfy two basic requirements. First and fundamentally, it must represent a step on a possible passage from the present formative order to the desired order. Like the situations it connects, and despite its limited scope, this step always has a double significance. It involves institutional changes. It also requires a shift in the assumptions about group interests, collective identities, and social possibility that help sustain, and receive sustenance from, current institutional arrangements. The correspondence between institutional order and the logic of group interests holds good for parts of a formative context, not just for a formative context as a whole. An act of experimental anticipation should satisfy another requirement: it should contribute to the solution of the overriding problem of means and ends by serving both as an anticipatory image of broader transformations and as a strategic tool.

As an anticipatory image the experiment embodies a partial, tentative, transitional version of part of the program. As a strategic tool it constitutes an enclave within which people may collect forces in order to engage in further episodes of grassroots mobilization and further efforts to win parcels of governmental power. When the anticipatory experiment goes well, its instrumental and expressive uses cannot be clearly distinguished. It then resembles the type of artwork (say, a late romance of Shakespeare's) that invokes a higher, renewed order of human life and demands an assent which is also a redemptive complicity. It gives people a more tangible and therefore more persuasive sense of what the desired transformation of social life would be like. As a result, the vision that inspires the transformers stands a better chance of enticing the will and the imagination to collaborate in making it come true.

No anticipatory experiment can maintain its content unchanged when extended to another area or transposed to another scale. The fragmentary version of the program is never just the program in microcosm. It is a transaction between an established and imagined reality and an effort to work out the implications of a complex program for particular problems.

One form the anticipatory experiment can assume might be called the movement as model. The movement as an organized political party or as a loose confederation of grassroots activities seeks to be an image of the future it advocates for the society as a whole, a picture of the true republic within the false republic. The relations between superior and subalterns, or between centralized collective decision and individual or factional initiative, the merger of democratic and communal ideals with each other, and their extension to ordinary practical dealings, must all turn the movement into a living icon of its program. To be sure, the fidelity of this image to the societywide program is limited both by the constraints of current institutional arrangements and current perceptions of group interest and by the distinctive problems of a political party or a grassroots organization. The opportunity nevertheless exists because it arises from the very nature of collective mobilization. For remember that collective mobilization occurs when people come together for transformative aims in ways that defy, however modestly, established hierarchies and roles. Collective mobilization can hope to change the formative context of social life only because it already escapes the pattern this context prescribes.

The success of the method of movement as model depends in part on an ability to capture some of the legal and financial support that normally goes to organizations with no transformative aims. To this end, it helps to exploit the structural similarities between the passive and the militant organization and to take advantage of the difficulty of distinguishing them in the eyes of the law. For example, a unitary, all-inclusive, corporatist union structure, such as can be found throughout much of Latin America, may have originally been designed by pseudopopulist authoritarian regimes as a device of controlled mobilization. Yet once the union structure is established it may be susceptible to gradual, piecemeal take-over from within. The "liberated" parts of the union system may become just such fragmentary models of the desired society. And the work of liberation may be facilitated by the failure of existing labor-law rules (if not of the people who administer them) to discriminate clearly enough between passive and radical unions or union militants.

The other factor on which the success of the movement as model chiefly depends is its ability to break down the distinction between the work of organization and agitation and the ordinary responsibilities of practical life. The prospects for prefiguring a reordered formative context increase as the activity of the movement goes beyond a narrow focus on conflict with bosses or bureaucrats and turns into a setting where people can go about their ordinary activities. At that point, engagement in the work of the movement ceases to compete with practical concerns or to be the special province of professional agitators and politicians. Clearly, this objective can be far more easily attained by the movement as a loose confederation of social activities and organizations, conducted both within and outside established institutions, than by the movement as a political party. The importance of this goal suffices to ensure the inadequacy of a party model of transformative practice.

The movement as model is not the sole form of the anticipatory experiment. Its other, even more important method can be labeled the exemplary conflict. Every society plays host to an endless series of petty practical conflicts, constantly renewed by the ambiguities in the accommodations struck between different groups or between these groups and governmental policy. The transformative movement must seek out the more promising of these disputes and intervene in them on the side of its present or potential allies. It must attempt to solve the disputes in ways that foreshadow a portion of its broader program. A sign of success in this work is that the intermediate solution provides a link between current assumptions about group interests, collective identities, and social possibilities and the form these assumptions would take if the program of empowered democracy were to be fully accepted and established. Such conflicts are thus doubly exemplary. They exemplify the ordinary controversies that proliferate throughout the society. And they can be met with solutions that prefigure, on a modest dimension, alternative institutional arrangements.

Once again, an example may help bring the method into focus. The example is all the more revealing because of its distance from the conventional picture of social agitation. Consider the economic tensions between small-scale and large-scale producers. At one extreme of contemporary economic and technological sophistication the small-scale producers may be peasants working at the periphery of capitalized agribusinesses or on relatively unmechanized plantations. At the other extreme, they may be high-tech "cottage" manufacturers, working for and against mass-production industry, as a permanent vanguard and an occasional rival. As rearguard or as vanguard, the petty producers work in an economic and institutional environment that disfavors them, if only by forcing them to do business in markets mainly organized by the large-scale producers. The small-scale producers may embrace the subaltern and dangerous role and accept whatever work the large-scale producers allot to them. They may press for governmental support in the form of fiscal policy or financial, commercial, and technological assistance. Alternatively, they may couple this pressure upon government with cooperative organization among themselves. Cooperative financial, marketing, and machine-sharing arrangements may help them capture economies of scale, diminish their vulnerability to market fluctuations, and escape the role to which the large producers want to confine them. Thus, some form of competitive partnership among the smaller and more flexible firms may emerge from an implicit or explicit contest with the dominant businesses. As the small-scale enterprises expand their experiments in resource-pooling they begin to develop a version of the rotating capital fund – a major principle in the economic organization of empowered democracy. As they combine this flexible pooling arrangement with various forms of state support they establish a preliminary model for dealings among many tiers of governmental capital givers and private capital takers. They pioneer in methods for using governmental assistance to change the character of markets rather than to supplant the market principle. In all these ways they give a little object lesson in the establishment of a reconstructed, dynamic version of petty commodity production. By participating in the problems of petty producers and by promoting the types of solutions just described, the transformative movement practices the method of exemplary conflict. The sense of incongruity this example may cause reflects the influence of unjustifiably restrictive views of what context-transforming conflict may be like and of who may serve as its executors.

The practice of exemplary conflicts may become more powerful when the radicals learn to connect the practical solutions they advocate with the ideals implicit in the most morally ambitious models of human association: the models that promise to reconcile more fully the enabling conditions of self-assertion. Representative democracy and private community are the most important of these models in the societies the program of empowered democracy most directly addresses. The exemplary solutions to exemplary conflicts – the solutions that most faithfully anticipate the transformative program – are also characteristically the ones that extend democratic or communal ideals and practices to areas of social life from which they had previously been absent and that reconstruct these ideals in the course of extending them. By such means the practice of exemplary conflict gains the element of visionary intensity it might otherwise lack.

The Third Task: Recruiting and Managing the Cadres

No problem of transformative practice is more important, or less studied, than the recruitment and management of cadres. The inequalities in existing societies combine with differences of temperament to maintain the distinction between the cadres and the rank and file. The cadres, activists, or militants are the people whose relatively privileged social circumstances and intimate psychological identification with the movement enable them to devote themselves to its work. Distinct from the ordinary supporters or sympathizers of the movement, they are also not its leaders although the leaders are usually recruited from their midst. These militants make the movement, and they can break it.

The further the movement goes along the spectrum of escalating mobilization, the more its fate depends on the cadres. For the sporadic exchange of favors or the occasional show of support must then be increasingly replaced by experimental deviations from existing arrangements, with or without the use of governmental authority. The militants supply the personnel to staff the experiments and keep them faithful to the program.

A politician who is good at everything in practical politics may find himself frustrated and defeated by the problem of the cadres. With luck, it is even possible to go a long way by being good at cadre management though bad at almost everything else. (Remember Mussolini.) The visionary leader and the egalitarian participatory movement are especially apt to be undone by trouble with the cadres. For the visionary leader who begins by fearing that too close an association with the recruitment and management of activists will compromise his moral authority may end up transformed into a symbol, manipulated by other, more astute politicians. (Contrast Gandhi's failures to Saint Paul's achievements.) And the radical movement, embarrassed by the social and psychological realities of leadership, may find itself destroyed or perverted by the very tensions among leaders, militants, and supporters it has failed to acknowledge and control.

In the practice of the movements that can serve as vehicles of a fuller democratization of social life the problem of the cadres comes to a focus on a single issue. Although no aspect of the techniques of radical politics has greater practical importance, none is more consistently disregarded in the literature of social activism. The problem consists in the range of difficulties presented by two types of cadres that, coexisting in very different proportions, tend to dominate the political movements that have arisen from the radical traditions of modern politics. Each major type of agitator and organizer suffers from deficiencies of vision directly reflected in failures of action. Such defects have been the ruin of many a radical campaign. They must be corrected or contained by something other than the good intentions of the militants themselves or the restraining influence each type exercises upon the other. For the coexistence of the two kinds of activists is just as likely to aggravate the dangers of each as to balance them out.

Consider first the sectarian cadre. He is obsessively concerned with the fidelity of the movement to the right line: to just the right programmatic objectives and social alliances. Although he may speak incessantly of the corrective value of practice, his tendency is to refer every major controversy about practice to a preestablished scheme and, particularly, to the kind of scheme congenial to deep-logic social theory. He treats a specific set of group (i.e., class or community) alliances as given in a predefined type or stage of social organization. If hard-core Marxism did not exist, he would need to invent it; the pompous subtleties of a hairsplitting scholasticism provide his natural element.

The truths he fails to appreciate are the insights the criticism of deep-structure social theory makes explicit. He does not understand the extent to which the reconstructive program can and must be chosen rather than found in a preexisting list of options. Nor does he recognize how much the apparent clarity of a calculus of class interests, class alliances, and class antagonisms depends on the very stagnation his movement seeks to interrupt.

The illusions of the sectarian result in two related habits of action and thought. On the one hand, he stands ever ready to split the movement for the sake of the line. He delights in internal antagonism, seeing in it the confirmation of his political seriousness. His energies are consumed in an endless and unproductive infighting rather than in a cumulative, outward-turning struggle. On the other hand, the divisions he provokes, expressed as they are in an idiom of manipulable political rhetoric and superstition, easily become the vehicles of personal or factional rivalries that are driven by baser motives. The very starkness of the gap between the categories to which the sectarian appeals and the content of practical politics makes the confusion between correctness and malevolence all but inevitable. Indeed, the sectarian may switch lines sharply and frequently, and change them all the more abruptly because the ideological contrasts that absorb his attention have so tenuous a foothold in practical experience.

The typical rival of the sectarian is the consensualist, coalition-building cadre. He nurtures a moralistic, antistrategic view of politics. He envisions a struggle between the rich and the poor or, more simply, between the good and the bad. He stands ready to fight in the battle of the little people against their masters. He therefore exudes confidence in his ability to tell who his allies and adversaries are and what must be done in the given situation. But this confidence rests on a naive and sanctimonious moralization of the social order rather than on an allegiance to the dogmatic prejudices of deep-logic social theory. He repeats, in modernized form, the oldest and most universal pattern of social criticism, for he imagines politics as the reenactment of a drama, outside historical time, that tries to preserve or restore the rightful order of society. He is an inveterate goody-goody.

What the consensualist cadre fails to grasp is the controversial and conflictual character of social life. He does not appreciate that the cause of the little people can reasonably be understood in different and incompatible ways, and that these alternative interpretations imply, and are implied by, divergent trajectories of institutional reform and coalition building. He does not recognize the need for fundamental choices that are also gambles. He does not admit that these choices entail and legitimate a large measure of internal factionalism.

These illusory assumptions also take their toll in a misguided strategy. The consensualist cadre often imposes a particular line under the mistaken impression that there is nothing particular about it. He thereby barricades himself against the lessons of experience. Because he thinks he knows who the friends and enemies of the movement are, he fails to manage existing divisions or to exploit potential alliances that are not self-evident. Because he believes that the demands of his cause are clear he fails to develop arrangements capable of replacing established practices. And because his naiveté is supported by a sanctimonious disposition he can be as repulsive to the outsider as the most bigoted sectarian.

Theoretical enlightenment would seem to be the necessary and sufficient cure for the inadequacies of the two types of cadres. Have the right ideas about politics, and you are on the way to being the right kind of cadre. But, in the short run, theoretical criticism is not enough. For the perversities of the sectarian and the consensualist result from a circumstance of divided loyalties as well as from a legacy of mistaken ideas. The consensualist and the sectarian alike are caught between the leaders and the rank and file. Both kinds of cadres accept leadership and in turn perform a custodial role that cannot easily be acknowledged and legitimated within the tradition of radical politics. Moreover, sectarian and consensualist cadres alike can exercise power and submit to it in the name of impersonal ideological rectitude or uncontroversial popular solidarity. Neither type of activist has to confront the discretionary, controversial character of the choices he makes or has made for him. For it is discretion that gives power its most painful edge.

There is a realistic, second-best solution to the problem of the cadres, an alternative to full theoretical enlightenment. The first step of the solution is to create another manner of cadre, one who does not share the complementary illusions and defects of the consensualist and the sectarian and who is animated by the view of transformative practice these pages describe. This better cadre is able to play the other two against each other. The creation of a third style of cadre represents a far more modest accomplishment than the total renovation of the corps of activists. For this achievement not only dispenses with the total substitution of the cadres but can also draw on the reinforcement of insight by ambition. The third type of cadre can turn to his own advantage the resistance that the consensualist and the sectarian are almost sure to provoke in the rank and file and in the populace among which the movement does its proselytizing work.

The next stage of the second-best solution plays out the rivalry among the sectarian, the consensualist, and the "enlightened" cadres for the favor of the rank and file. The leaders who emerge from this new group of militants or who have helped create them provoke the rebellion of the ordinary activists against the ideological purists and the goody-goodies. They hardly need to fabricate occasions for this rebellion; it is enough for them to await the frequent occasions when the beliefs of the consensualists or sectarians suggest strategic decisions that endanger the movement.

The final stage of the next-best solution is to complete the rebellion both by propagating a more defensible understanding of transformative practice and by effacing the starkness of the contrast between who is and who is not a cadre. The situation in which all members of the movement are simultaneously cadres and noncadres will be realized more fully and easily when the ideas animating practice no longer resemble an esoteric science or a sacred creed and when they develop rather than deny the uncertainties and opportunities that inform ordinary political life. (Remember that the social theory underlying this conception of practice rejects any sharp contrast between the subjective experience of the agent and the insight of the theorist.) The ideal of maximum possible confusion between cadres and noncadres can also be approached more easily when the dogmas of a mistaken style of practice do not defeat at every turn efforts to carry forward the work of emancipating society from false necessity and entrenched order.

The three-step solution to the problem of the cadres can never be easy. It must contend with limitations of insight and generosity against which no theoretical rectification can guarantee us. It must be performed again and again, rather than once and for all; the three steps must be made to overlap and to recur. At least, however, this approach to the problem of the cadres remains in close touch with the ideas that inspire this whole view of transformative practice and the program of social reconstruction this view anticipates and confirms. Moreover, it makes no demand of extraordinary selflessness or privileged knowledge.

*The Fourth Task: Recognizing and Devaluing the Logic of
Group Interests*

The theory of society that underlies the view of transformative practice presented in this section implies a certain view of the agent's
relation to the logic of group interests. By the logic of group interests
I mean the overall constellation of positive and negative aims that
seem to inhere in the distinct places that every system of social division and hierarchy generates.

Both deep-structure social theory and conventional, empiricist social science encourage belief in the clear and determining influence
the logic of group interests exercises over the course of conflict in
social life. The deep-structure theorist in his hard-core Marxist guise
believes a system of class interests to be implied by the structure of
a mode of production and by the forces commanding the succession
of modes of production. He believes, as confidently as he believes
anything, that escalating conflict reveals the system of underlying
class interests and that those who persist in making or disregarding
the class alliances this system requires will be destroyed. Hence, he
enters political practice with a clear sense of the alliances that are
necessary and of the antagonisms that are unavoidable.

The positivist social scientist or the routine politician (remember
the affinity between routine politics and positivist social science) gives
a different sense to similar conclusions. He may concede a significant
element of give and ambiguity in the established logic of group
interests. He may even acknowledge that the clarity of this system
of alliances and animosities depends entirely on the persistence of
institutional arrangements that can be challenged and replaced. But,
having made this acknowledgment of principle, he then wants to get
back to ordinary politics and ordinary thought. He has no way to
represent to himself the transformation of group interests that is
brought about by a change in their institutional framework. The
moment of rupture is, for him, a limit to thought and action rather
than a central problem to be explained or an objective to be achieved.

The activist who has understood the problems of transformative
practice in the light of the social theory developed in this book must
respect the constraints that group interests impose upon collective
action. Yet from the outset he must also act in the spirit of one who
sees these collective interests as dependent upon institutional frameworks that are not themselves guided by higher-order laws. This
determination to recognize the immediate realities of class or communal interest while denying that they are for keeps is no ad hoc
reconciliation of clashing attitudes toward the force of class and communal interests. It is, rather, the direct expression in practice of a
certain theoretical understanding of society. And this understanding

turns what would otherwise be a vague prudential formula into an approach to the problems of political practice.

The narrower the range and the dimmer the intensity of conflict over the institutional and imaginative framework of routinized social life, the more transparent, rigid, and influential the system of class and communal interests will appear. This clarity of the system of collective interests will grow stronger when the institutional framework provides for its own insulation from destabilizing strife. For a system of group divisions becomes secure when it is constantly regenerated by the institutional arrangements that shape our routine activity and that allot the economic and cultural resources for society making. These arrangements in turn achieve safety when they stand protected against the disturbing effects of ordinary conflict.

If the transformative militant finds himself in such a situation, he must strive to understand it and to mold his actions according to its dictates. He must identify the groups that will most easily support his cause given their preexisting view of their own interests. He must not pursue group alliances or antagonisms that frontally disregard the constraints that currently perceived group interests impose. Nor must he propose objectives that cannot readily be translated into the language of such interests. (Even the political prophet, who ostentatiously breaks with the system of group interests, must appeal to the anomalies of current personal experience.)

But the subversive activist entertains a mental reservation even when he seems to be bending to the stabilized social world and its active repertory of interests and possibilities. He sees its stability as predicated upon the temporary interruption and containment of broader conflict and the partial realization of negative capability. He is committed to an alternative institutional order he sees as capable of pushing farther the emancipation of social life from false necessity. Moreover, as the next maxim of this view of transformative practice emphasizes, he understands that even the most rigidified social situation is rich in ambiguities that can be exploited by the resolute transformer.

At moments of extreme closure the whole art of the transformer consists in the attempt to find in the modest opportunities that never entirely disappear a foothold for larger conflict. He must take everything *almost* as given: *almost*, because the relation between the uncertainty about just what is given and the vision of something beyond the given create the possibility of movement.

As conflict escalates, the institutional niches and collective identities that lend a real but superficial clarity to group interests begin to fade. It now becomes clear that choices must be made among alternative routes along which each preexisting group interest may be both fulfilled and redefined. Each path involves a commitment to a set of institutional arrangements – or, rather, to a sequence of institutional reforms – that is just the reverse side of a group of social alliances. Each sequence ends up changing how people see their interests. The possibility was always there. But now it can begin to be lived out. And this living out gives the thesis of the provisional, redefinable quality of group interests a credibility it would otherwise lack.

Consider, for example, the situation of the labor or socialist parties in the industrial democracies of the late twentieth century. They might continue to define themselves as spokesmen for the organized work force, entrenched in the mass-production sector of the economy, while speaking with another voice to a larger, indistinct constituency outside the traditional working class. Following this strategy, they would seek no drastic alteration of the established institutional arrangements for government and production: only the incremental redistribution of wealth and income, the gradual development of social assurance schemes, the extension of nationalized industry, and the occasional experiments with more participatory methods of decision in workplaces and neighborhoods. But these parties might also well conclude that there was no future in the privileged commitment to a shrinking part of the work force (i.e., the unionized workers of the mass-production industries), anchored in a declining sector of national industry. Prudence alone might lead them to cast about for an alternative program that could turn them into representatives of a larger coalition: an alliance of people committed to novel or archaic forms of small-scale entrepreneurship and professional independence as well as of the unemployed, the unorganized, and the poor. One candidate for such a program would be the reconstructed version of the suppressed alternative in Western history: revised petty commodity production, with its many consequences for the regimes of governmental organization and capital allocation, consequences the program of empowered democracy spells out.

As the execution of this program advanced, the distinctions among the underclass, the skilled workers, the old and the new petty bourgeoisie, and the independent technical or professional cadres would weaken, not because a single homogeneous work force would emerge but because the surviving distinctions within the labor force would be numerous, fragmentary, and volatile. Each stage in the trajectory of institutional reconstruction would be both preceded and followed by a shift in the way people imagined the groups they belonged to and the interests that were theirs.

At the extreme of escalation of conflict all rigid social relations collapse into the twofold circumstance earlier described. On the one hand, society passes into the Hobbesian conflict of all against all. Each person grabs whatever he can and gives himself to the relentless search for preemptive security. On the other hand, the contest of class and communal interests dissolves into a struggle of parties of opinion, animated by alternative programmatic visions. On the one hand, the man in tooth and claw steps outside the social station: all are equalized by the brutal struggle for defense and self-defense. On the other hand, the successor to the interest-determined agent is the individual as a context-transcendent being whose commitment to certain ideals and opinions is not determined by his membership in particular classes and communities. The strongest assertions of spiritual independence resemble the most brutish contests for material advantage in their power to weaken the constraints that social stations impose upon the will and imagination of the individual. In this circumstance of maximum conflict the perspective of the transformative militant becomes, in part, the standpoint of the theorist and the prophet.

Thus, at each stage of escalation, the transformative activist must change his attitude toward the established system of group interests: first finding his allies within the constraints this system imposes and then helping to overthrow such constraints. His apparently incompatible attitudes, however, are motivated by the same theoretical conception; what seems to be a shift in assumptions turns out to be faithfulness to the same ideas. At the beginning of the process the enlightened militant may easily be mistaken for the traditional leftist, content with deep-structure social analysis, or for the conventional, interest-group politician, who shares the premises of conventional social science. But from the outset he recognizes that moral and political intelligence requires you to see in real people *more* than examples of a social category and in social categories *no more* than the expression of a conditional social world, with its definitions of interest and identity, of associative reality and possibility.

His ultimate aim is not merely to replace one set of collective interests by another but to change the sense in which society making remains at the mercy of a preexisting system of group interests. The program of empowered democracy that this view of transformative politics anticipates and supports seeks to undermine the basis of fixed social stations in a formative institutional order effectively protected against recurrent challenge. The normal experience of politics (both in the narrower sense of conflict over the mastery and uses of governmental power and in the broader sense of struggle over the remaking of society) must more fully embody the dissolution of classes and communities into parties of opinion. The attitude toward group interests that characterizes the moment of escalation must become the normal attitude. But the further dissolution of social classes into parties of opinion must be achieved without the Hobbesian search for preemptive security. For the dissolution that is sought results from the adoption of particular institutional arrangements rather than from a violent anarchy, and these arrangements ensure the vital security of the individual. However, the institutional means for ensuring this security must not, like consolidated property, allow any one group to gain a privileged hold on the resources for society making. They must minimize the rigidifying implications of individual security upon the surrounding social order. (See the later discussion of immunity rights.)

The Fifth Task: Identifying and Exploiting Transformative Opportunity in the Midst of Stability

The transformative movement must learn to identify and exploit opportunities for practical and imaginative destabilization even when the current formative context seems most stable and entrenched. (Remember that entrenchment designates the extent to which the formative institutions and preconceptions make themselves unavailable to challenge and revision in the midst of routine social activity. Stability, on the other hand, refers to pressure or danger, such as economic or military crisis, at any given level of entrenchment. To adopt a contrast beloved of leftists whose minds have been formed by deep-structure analysis: entrenchment is an attribute of structure, whereas stability describes a conjuncture.)

The fifth task is merely an extension or a special case of the fourth task. The preceding principle of transformative practice describes an approach to prevailing assumptions about group interests, collective identities, and social possibilities. It teaches a way to take these assumptions seriously while denying them the last word. The present maxim of practice explores the implications of this same approach for the circumstance in which the approach is hardest to apply and easiest to forget.

The discussion focuses on three characteristic instances of transformative opportunity that persist in even the most stable moments of societies like the contemporary North Atlantic democracies. For this purpose I choose examples of practical collective conflict, although I might just as well have selected situations drawn from the routines of, say, legal controversy. The analysis of these transformative opportunities draws upon several basic themes of the social theory worked out in this volume: the close connection between perceived group interests or identities and institutional arrangements, the failure of any institutional or imaginative framework to accommodate all emerging opportunities for practical or passionate human connection, and the irrepressible ability of context-preserving activities to escalate into context-transforming struggle. In each instance the analysis of transformative opportunity shows how the response to a relatively minor crisis or disharmony may be achieved in contrasting ways. These responses may either maximize or minimize the disturbance to formative institutional arrangements, or to formative ideas about possible and desirable human association and to the assumptions about interests, identities, and possibilities that these ideas or arrangements help support. The transformers must recognize the initial opportunity. They must master the practice of the disturbance-maximizing response. They must turn each success in the pursuit of this response into an example of the fragmentary anticipation of their program.

One irrepressible source of transformative opportunity arises from the relation between the enlistment of governmental power in the service of private privilege and the more or less negotiated or coercive accommodations private groups make to one another. The place that each class, community, or segment of the labor force occupies in the scheme of social division and hierarchy depends in large part upon its relative success at securing direct or indirect governmental protection for its interests. The protection may take the form of legal rules, of economic policies, or even merely of a refusal to upset an established pattern of group advantage or compromise. The influence thus gained and secured can in turn be used to renew a measure of privileged access to governmental power: if not through hereditary claims upon office then through economic and cultural influence upon elections, policies, or even assumptions about the appropriate and inappropriate uses of public authority. Every group must engage in this struggle unless it resigns itself to the lowest social positions. Every group must fight to stay ahead in order not to fall behind.

But the translation of governmental power into group advantage and of group advantage into governmental power is a trick that must be constantly repeated. The less immediate the connection between the power and the advantage, the greater becomes the attention that must be devoted to it and the less predictable the results it may produce. While government personnel and policies shift, the relative economic, organizational, or demographic strength of different groups also changes. The structure of government-supported prerogatives and disabilities within which groups must operate is therefore incurably unstable. This low-level, contained instability results in an endless series of petty conflicts and anxieties that the transformers must learn to recognize and exploit. For what may seem from one standpoint an annoyance without a message may be reconceived from another perspective as a revelation. If the boundaries of recognized group interests and identities can be shaken by conflicts over the mastery and uses of governmental power, then perhaps everything in the current logic of group interests and identities may be changed by this or some other type of conflict. The transformative agents must do all they can to carry this insight into the subjective experience of the fighting over group advantage and governmental privilege. To this end they must play upon two other major transformative opportunities that persist in the presence of stability.

One such opportunity arises from the existence of an irreducible strategic ambiguity in the requirements for the defense of group interests. Suppose that the formative institutional and imaginative context of society is very clearly defined and largely uncontested. Each segment of the work force occupies a well-marked place in the social division of labor: characteristic jobs, complete with a distinct relative level of wages and discretion, a shared style of life, and many shared attitudes, ambitions, and apprehensions. (The segmentation of parts of the labor force is only one aspect of the logic of group interests. But it suffices to illustrate the point now under discussion.) Each segment of the work force may pursue either of two strategies in the defense of its interests. It may adopt a narrowing strategy. It then seeks to hold on to its current position and prerogatives strictly conceived. It defines the groups just below it or most similar to it as its rivals and adversaries. The resistance it opposes to its superiors is tempered by the fear that they might make common cause with its inferiors to prejudice its interests and its place. This strategy has the advantage of minimizing short-run uncertainties and risks. But aside from making it difficult for a group to achieve a significant improvement on its current position, it also makes each group hostage to the continuing inferiority of its immediate subalterns. The group will hesitate to engage in acts of defiance for fear that such acts might incite its own inferiors to rebellion.

The alternative is an expanding strategy. The group and its leaders seek to ally themselves with the closest coordinate or inferior groups against their common superiors. They may do so at first in a spirit of mere tactical alliance. But what begins as a tactical partnership may slowly turn into a broadened definition of collective interests and identities, a definition cemented by alternative institutional arrangements or by the experiments that prefigure them.

Even if you suppose that the logic of group interests, collective identities, and social possibilities is both well defined and unchallenged, this logic provides no general reason to prefer either the narrowing or the expanding strategy. Each has its advantages and its risks. The relative persuasive force of each depends on specific traditions and circumstances of collective action. Although both strategies may be equally compatible with such rigid assumptions, they have radically different implications for the future of those assumptions. The narrowing strategy encourages the perpetuation of assumed interests, identities, and constraints on possibility. The expanding strategy leads directly to their subversion. The militants of the transformative movement must seize on this strategic ambiguity. They need to argue and act whenever possible in favor of the expanding strategy, even if they have to begin by doing so on the basis of received views about interests, identities, and possibilities. In so arguing and acting they await the first chance to show how the enlargement of alliances for the sake of currently perceived group interests may help bring about a redefinition of these interests.

The coexistence between a more conservative and a more radical response to the same problem reappears in another situation, the most promising of the transformative opportunities likely to appear in a circumstance of seemingly unshakable stability. Societies and their governments regularly face middle-level crises brought on by the need to adapt their institutional arrangements to unexpected economic or military challenges. To exploit an opportunity for the development of practical productive or destructive capabilities they must revise an aspect of their current formative context. If they fail to carry this revision out they risk economic decline or diplomatic and military defeat. Either is likely to spark conflict over current institutions. But if they go ahead and execute the reforms, they must face the prospect of conflict nevertheless. The institutional arrangements to be changed or preserved support complex accommodations among groups or between groups and governments. The practical objectives may be satisfied with minor institutional adjustments. But it is important to understand that these goals can invariably be realized through alternative institutional adjustments, each with its distinctive effects upon the relative positions of contending groups or their relation to the state. The crisis-diverting reforms are unavoidably productive of conflict both because they disturb existing deals and because, depending on their content, they can upset these deals in very different ways. Once the conflict arises, it can widen in scope and intensity. The aim of conservative crisis-managers is to seek the reforms that meet the immediate practical danger while minimizing the disturbance to established institutions and recognized interests. The goal of the transformative movement is just as clearly to exploit the controversies that will inevitably take place: to expand and intensify them and to meet them in ways that also represent steps in the direction of the transformative program.

By way of example, consider again the rich industrial countries who now find themselves under pressure to adapt to changes in the international division of labor by changing their style of industrial organization. They must move from an emphasis on traditional mass-production industries (the favored ground of the rigid variant of rationalized collective labor) to greater strength in the more flexible, vanguardist forms of high-tech manufacturing and provision of services. This shift can be staged in forms that scrupulously avoid challenge to the current institutional forms of capital allocation and representative democracy. But even in this modest version they require new arrangements and new deals. They therefore also produce new conflicts. Thus, for example, a labor movement traditionally entrenched in the mass-production industries may find its inherited forms of representation threatened. It may then seek alternatives that redefine the relation of organized labor both to governments and to the previously unorganized sectors of the labor force. Such alternatives may also change the balance between union militancy and participatory representation in enterprise decision making. Managers and bureaucrats may find that a haphazard pattern of covert subsidies and transfers has to be replaced by a more organized relation between public policy and entrepreneurial decision. Large-scale enterprises may come under pressure to reconstruct their internal divisions in the image of the smaller businesses that had previously flourished as their junior trading partners, subcontractors, or unofficial research departments. All these changes are compatible with what can be broadly described as a conservative route to industrial reconstruction. Yet none of them can be accomplished without offering alternatives and generating conflicts.

The advocates of the program of empowered democracy may seize upon these conflicts. They may do so all the more easily because they can justifiably claim to favor institutional arrangements that push the same shift farther. The system of capital allocation they support deprives the mass-production industries of the devices by which these industries have traditionally protected themselves against instability in the product, labor, and capital markets. It also gives the more flexible vanguardist enterprises the institutional advantage previously reserved to their mass-production rivals.

Middle-level crises like these provide the standard occasion for revolutionary reform and are the stuff with which conservatives and radicals alike must chiefly work. No wonder the frequency and the importance of such crises have been dramatically understated by both positivist social science and deep-structure social analysis: the former insensitive to the distinction between solving problems and changing frameworks, the latter obsessed with the idea of total and sudden framework change.

The ideas implicit in the discussion of this final source of transformative opportunity become both more general and more precise when they are related to three theses of the explanatory social theory developed earlier in this book.

The first relevant thesis is the existence of a relation between the development of practical capabilities and the making of institutional arrangements that loosen the constraints imposed by a preestablished scheme of social division or hierarchy upon the organization of work. (Remember that at certain levels of resource availability and technological development this relation may be temporarily overridden by the service that entrenched hierarchies and roles render to coercive surplus extraction.) The thesis shows why a series of middle-level crises and of responses to them may result in a cumulative creation of institutional arrangements that weaken rigid social roles and hierarchies while narrowing the gap between context-transforming and context-preserving activities. Thus, the thesis draws attention to the special interest such crises hold for a political practice committed to the program of empowered democracy.

A second pertinent thesis of the social theory advanced here is that any move toward greater negative capability can be accomplished through alternative sets of institutional arrangements and therefore also through alternative effects upon the wealth, power, and prestige of different groups. The particular content of existing institutions, available ideas, and traditions of group action may limit the range of existing solutions. No solution is likely to succeed if it requires too sudden an advance in negative capability or if it draws upon materials too far removed from the unique history that produced a formative context. But such limits remain loose and ambiguous; they fail to specify a unique solution to any given middle-level crisis or even a well-defined set of possible solutions. Because such a crisis can always be met by alternative institutional reforms and because any such reform disturbs vested group interests, conflict is sure to result. The conservative must try to contain it. The radical must attempt to turn it to his purposes.

A third implicated thesis of the social theory is the frequent existence of an inverse relation between the contribution an institutional reform makes to the development of negative capability and the ease with which it fits into a received history of institutional reinvention. The radical (by whom, remember, I mean the champion of the radical project as earlier defined, not just the person who wants more change) has the strategic disadvantage of demanding – at least ultimately – a bigger break with current assumptions about group interests, collective identities, and social possibilities. But if he thinks and acts correctly, he may gain the countervailing advantage of plausibly claiming to make the organization of social life more hospitable to the further development of practical capabilities and the further management of middle-level crisis. He even promises to turn this speculative future benefit to present use. By understanding and respecting the affinity of the radical cause to the practical interest in social plasticity, he helps to even the odds in his contest with the conservative.

The Sixth Task: Formulating a Visionary Language

Success in executing all the tasks of transformative practice previously discussed will not ensure the availability of a language in which to discuss practices and programs. The forms of discourse now available to radical transformative movements are largely unsuited to the program of empowered democracy. Some represent the sloganlike versions of deep-structure social theory. Others merely appeal to established conceptions of group interest. Some have a utopian content almost entirely devoid of institutional specificity. Others describe institutional reforms without making explicit their connection to any general program of human empowerment or emancipation. In a very real sense the movement must talk itself into power, and its talk, like its more worldly stratagems, must be both a tool of persuasion and a device of discovery.

The first standard an appropriate mode of discourse must satisfy is the ability to combine an appeal to recognized group interests (i.e., the recognized interests of the groups composing the initial coalition of program supporters) with a reference to a sequence of institutional reforms that move in the desired direction. A suitable discourse enables people to reflect upon the interplay between definitions of group interests and successive adjustments of the institutional framework within which these interests get defined and satisfied.

Consider the habits of thought and expression on which such an interaction depends. In order to prefer the forms of satisfying preexisting groups that require institutional reconstruction to those that do not, it will be necessary to anticipate in the earliest and most prosaic discussions something of the visionary impulse that underlies the program. Strategic calculation alone never suffices to tilt the scales in favor of an unmistakably risky course of action.

The institutional proposals, for their part, must be stated in terms that are modest and concrete enough to allow for linkage with current debates and concerns. But they must also be sufficiently far-reaching to exercise a visionary pull. The solution to this apparently intractable dilemma is to focus on a whole sequence of cumulative institutional changes going from minor reforms to major reconstruction. It is the trajectory that matters rather than any single place along it. Thus, the language of the movement must speak of right and wrong routes, of realistic and unrealistic paths. It must repudiate the exclusive contrast between reformist tinkering and all-out revolution. It must bring to bear on the identification of realistic paths of change the applied version of an entire understanding of social transformation. In these, as in so many other ways, the discourse of the movement should represent the practical extension of the style of social theory for which this book argues.

The preceding considerations already suggest that the language of the reconstructive movement must be prophetic as well as institutional. It must achieve a visionary freshness and immediacy to enlist energies on the side of the institution-challenging forms of interest satisfaction and to maintain the instructive and encouraging connection between present experiences and ultimate programmatic aims. These aims are the subject of political prophecy *because* they promise a better solution to the problems of solidarity and contextuality: a better opportunity to diminish the conflict between the enabling conditions of self-assertion and to make our social contexts less arbitrary and imprisoning.

Thus, the language may play on aspects of our current ideals and practices of democracy or private community that, however flawed, offer a more complete experience of self-assertion through attachment than we can find in the everyday world of work and exchange. The talk of the transformer then suggests how these higher experiences of solidarity may be extended to broader areas of social life and how they would be revised in the course of this extension. Alternatively, the discourse of the transformer may make use of whatever in pop culture emphasizes the idea of the adventurer, at once ordinary and extraordinary, who is able to fight back against his context and to triumph over the belittling routines of humdrum practical life. The purpose is to show how this fantasy can be made real, which is to say how it can be actualized in a form that is both collective and institutionalized.

But whatever the rhetorical strategy pursued, the emphasis of language must always fall on the subtleties of personal experience rather than on the more impersonal aspects of dogma and practice. For one thing, only the reference to detailed, person-to-person relations can give the discourse of the movement an intelligible and persuasive immediacy. For another thing, only the test of personal experience, as shaped by changing institutional context and as interpreted by theoretical analysis, can ultimately validate our ideas about possibility and empowerment. There can be no real conflict between the rhetorical uses and the intellectual value of the appeal to personal experience. The exercise of political prophecy presupposes the failure of established dogmas and institutions fully to inform our direct practical or passionate dealing. The prophetic vision takes the anomalies resulting from this failure as points of departure for the regeneration of social life.

A political language couched in this spirit will not easily be produced or accepted by militants formed in the tradition of deep-structure social theory. Until the cadres are transformed and the theory is replaced, many compromises may have to be made with theoretical prejudice. It may take time before what seems merely a concession to the demands of popular understanding can be accepted as a requirement of true insight.

THE TRANSFORMATIVE MOVEMENT IN POWER

A Second Moment of Transformative Practice

The preceding discussion deals with the problems faced by a transformative movement when it remains distant from governmental power and struggles to gain a foothold in social life. Consider now the problems faced by that same movement when it comes to exercise a fragment of central state authority, that great and perilous lever of transformation.

Once again, the analysis treats simultaneously the peaceful winning of power by electoral and parliamentary processes and the violent seizure of the state against a background of revolutionary action. Here, even more than at the earlier moment of practice, the analogy may seem misleading. Yet here, even more than previously, it pays off. Although it presents distinctive problems the revolutionary situation also simplifies and dramatizes the difficulties transformative practice must confront in the evolutionary circumstance.

The following discussion of practice at the moment of governmental power makes explicit a pattern only implicitly present in the analysis of the moment of relatively powerless agitation. Once again, the overriding goal is to use methods that both anticipate and produce, both express and serve, the desired outcome. Once again, the aim requires that centralized collective decision combine, in both its practical methods and its transitional results, with decentralized, grassroots engagement and decision. The program of empowered democracy, which this style of transformative practice is meant to suit, rejects the one-way imposition of institutional solutions from the heights of state power. But it also repudiates, as misguided and self-defeating, any attempt to do without large-scale governmental and economic institutions and to replace institutional arrangements with an uncontroversial system of pure, uncoercive human coordination. A premise of the program is that no such system exists and that the development of less coercive systems of coordination is bound up with the transformation – not the abolition – of governmental institutions.

The Primacy of Institutional Reconstruction over Economic Redistribution

The transformative movement in office must affirm the primacy of institutional reform over the redistribution of wealth and income. It must also prefer the forms of economic distribution that result from institutional reconstruction to those that leave basic institutional arrangements unchanged.

Both major redistribution (meaning, in this setting, economic redistribution) and institutional reform have disruptive effects. They provoke resistance and dislocation and do so in the parliamentary as well as the revolutionary situation. Both redistribution and institutional change must go forward in the face of opposition from those whose advantages they threaten and whose beliefs they insult. Moreover, both can disorganize practical activities of production, exchange, or administration and cause an opposition that arises from the fear of disorder and jeopardy. The resistance-provoking effects of redistribution may be even stronger than those of institutional reforms whose redistributive effects are delayed or unclear. They may take the form of disinvestment and capital flight as well as of overt antagonism to the party in office. But these "nonpolitical" consequences may soon produce "political" results; if they are allowed to persist too long they will quickly erode any government's base of popular support or tolerance. On the other hand, institutional reform is sure to provoke major disruption even if its redistributive consequences are not overt and immediate. A transitional period exists during which part of the established formative context ceases to operate – a series of arrangements for production, exchange, or administration – before the intended replacement is secure. The transitional difficulties may well be further aggravated and prolonged by the need to make the new institutions fit with the arrangements that are left unchanged, and to reconstruct them so they can fit.

The transformative movement in office inevitably runs a race against time. No matter how successful it may be in its policies, it must count with disappointment on the part of many of its supporters. This disappointment is in part psychological. The hot moment of social life – the moment of escalating collective mobilization and public enthusiasm – cannot be permanently sustained. To recognize that it cannot is not to introduce an ad hoc claim about motivations but merely to emphasize the subjective side of the whole view of human activity that animates the explanatory and programmatic argument of this book. Alhough we can transcend our contexts, we cannot pursue any of our ordinary human concerns outside a context.

The radicals want something of the quality of the hot moments of social life – the periods of accelerated collective mobilization – to pass into the cold moments – the ordinary experience of institutionalized social existence. Thus, the whole program of empowered democracy can be seen, from a limited but nevertheless illuminating perspective, as an effort to capture in a stable context part of the heightened freedom from false necessity that is discovered in the course of our activities of context making.

The uncertainties and resistances of the transition increase the pressure to establish the alternative arrangements as quickly as possible. Here the relative priority given to redistributive and institutional aims becomes crucial. If the transformative movement attempts to pursue all its redistributive and institutional aims simultaneously, it aggravates the disruptions and antagonisms and increases the likelihood of being voted out of office, overthrown, or perverted from within before it has had a chance to carry out its plans for institutional reconstruction.

Suppose, however, that the movement decides to give priority to noninstitutional redistribution. The difficulties of transition will still occur, and though disruption may be less than it would be if the focus remained fixed upon institutional reforms with delayed or implicit redistributive effects, resistance may be even greater. The people threatened in their most tangible interests will organize to agitate against the party in power. Even if they remain entirely passive, the nearly automatic response of investment capital to heightened risk will ensure the occurrence of economic difficulties that will jeopardize support for the government. If it has come to power by democratic parliamentary means, the transformative movement in office will soon find itself under pressure to abandon its more ambitious redistributive goals, to content itself with a program of economic growth and restabilization, and to assuage the very business groups it previously assaulted. If the radicals in power fail to retrench, their tenure in office may well be shortened. But whether they retrench or not they risk leaving office without having executed any part of their institutional program. Redistributive tax-and-transfer measures, which require the constant correction of outcomes generated by the ordinary arrangements for production and exchange, can more easily be reversed. Even when they prove lasting, they may turn out in retrospect to have at best redistributed a little for the sake of not reconstructing much. The radicals would have unwittingly contributed to keeping politics at the limit of marginal redistribution within an unchallenged institutional framework.

When the transformative movement holds power by revolutionary means, the danger of giving priority to redistribution presents itself in a different way. The quickened resistance excited by the redistributive plans may tempt the regime to retrench or drive it out of power. But resistance may also provoke the radicals into the relentless centralization of authority. The redistributivist emphasis then becomes an episode in a series of events culminating in the dictatorial perversion of the movement and its program.

These arguments suggest the importance of emphasizing the primacy of institutional reconstruction over redistribution. Whether their situation is parliamentary or revolutionary, the transformers generally come to power on a wave of urgent redistributive de mands. To resist these expectations the transformative movement must rely on many sources of help: the preference for redistributive policies resulting from institutional reforms rather than for those supplanting these reforms; the long-term development of insight into transformative practice; the careful sustenance of the ardor attending the experience of collective mobilization; the concern with the per-sonalist, noninstitutional parts of the program, which help inspire this ardor; and the active engagement of ordinary men and women in the emergent economic and governmental arrangements.

In the most extreme revolutionary situations the primacy of in-stitutional reform over noninstitutional redistribution may hardly be a matter of choice. An institutional order has already been disrupted. No distribution or redistribution can take place until an institutional framework for production, exchange, and administration gets con-solidated. The only question is, which framework? The revolution-ary government must do its best to resist the tendency of some of its peasant, worker, or petty bourgeois constituents to demand re-distribution according to notions of fairness and right embedded in the prerevolutionary order.

In parliamentary circumstances these distinctive reasons to assert the priority of institutional reform over economistic redistribution no longer hold. But the government has a countervailing reason to struggle against the tendency of some of its constituents to adopt a clientalistic attitude to the state: to await passively the benefits it may shower upon them. By engaging people in the conflicts and exper-iments required for the development of new institutions, the move-ment gives them a focus of concern other than immediate redistribution. It thereby establishes a bond with ordinary working men and women stronger than the gratitude or love that people may be expected to show a paternalist welfare state. It also keeps alive the type of relation between central government and decentralized social action that the whole program of empowered democracy is designed to encourage.

The principle of the primacy of institutional change must be qual-ified in several ways. Some forms of economic redistribution are needed to tear people out of the misery and fear that effectively prevent them from mobilizing. Such situations – pervasive in third world countries and common to the underclass in even the richer Western nations – trump institutional goals. But it may still be pos-sible to pursue these goals in ways that combine institutional and redistributivist effects.

The significance of this qualification becomes clearer in the light of another qualification, already present in the initial statement of the principle. Almost all forms of institutional reconstruction produce long-run redistributive effects. Some institutional reforms, however, have dramatic consequences for the redistribution of wealth and income, while some forms of redistribution presuppose no change in the society's institutional arrangements. Consider the difference between a mere tax-and-transfer mechanism, on one side, and, on the other side, the broader involvement of workers' delegates in salary-setting and investment-making decisions or a change in the terms on which capital is made available to workers and small-scale entrepreneurs.

A particularly favorable and instructive case for early redistribution is presented by agrarian reform, especially when it seeks to replace the large, relatively unmechanized, plantation-style estates that still flourish in many third world countries with family-style farms, organized in a cooperative financial, marketing, and technological network, with governmental support. Such an agrarian reform illustrates the qualifications to the principle of priority of institutional change over economic redistribution, while also serving as the exception that proves – or, rather, elucidates – the rule. It alleviates the single most important source of extreme poverty and clientalistic subjugation in the countries to which it is suited: the condition of the landless agrarian laborers and of migrants and marginal smallholders. At the same time it provides an occasion to anticipate a major theme of the program for economic reorganization. The collaboration among small-scale and medium-scale farmers on the basis of government-supported arrangements for the pooling of financial, marketing, and technological resources modestly prefigures the multitiered system of rotating capital allocation the program of empowered democracy embraces.

Notice, however, that agrarian reform is the easiest case in which anticipatory institutional experimentation combines with economic redistribution and long-run programmatic commitments converge with short-run practical needs. It is, in the terms of earlier arguments, a relatively unreconstructed form of petty commodity production. The industrial counterparts to such agrarian solutions require more far-reaching institutional changes and therefore demand from the radicals in power a more careful balancing of redistributive and institutional methods. It is then all the more deplorable when the special opportunity offered by this style of agrarian reform is sacrificed either to the dogma of agricultural collectivization or to a strictly privatistic and proprietary form of smallholding.

The Combination of Central Decision with Popular Engagement

In both the revolutionary and the parliamentary situation the transformative movement needs to combine a change in the methods, forms, and uses of central governmental power with a heightened degree of popular engagement in ground-level economic and administrative institutions. In its most general form the commitment to achieve such a recombination simply restates the basic principle of prefiguring the ends in the means. But here this commitment takes a specific form, suited to the moment of arrival in central power, when the passage from means to ends is most visible and the tension between means and ends most dramatic.

The need to combine a reorientation of central power with an increased popular involvement in the organization of production, exchange, and local government and administration breaks down into two tasks: one governmental, the other economic. The two problems often come to a head at different moments: the governmental first, the economic later. A common but fatal error of transformative movements is to suppose that they have solved the latter when they have disposed of the former. Then, the failure to understand and to accomplish the economic task quickly undoes the governmental achievement.

The governmental task is to work toward a mutually reinforcing relation between effective use of the central governmental apparatus and popular participation in local government and administration. By effective use of the central governmental apparatus I mean in part the ability to press forward toward the reconstruction of governmental institutions the program of empowered democracy advocates (see the discussion in later sections of the chapter). Top priority must be given to replacing the traditional constitutional techniques that guarantee freedom and pluralism only by preventing bold transformative projects. A later part of the programmatic argument describes how full-blown empowered democracy accomplishes this objective.

Effective use also means that the radicals in high office do whatever possible to act within present governmental institutions as they would act if their desired governmental reforms had been achieved. This attempted conversion of established institutions to a new style and new uses is not an exercise in political bad faith or a mere tactical gamble, though its use must be tempered by an awareness that it may be seen as both of these. It is, on the contrary, a consequence of the perspective of internal normative argument, which sees the constitutional and legal order as a disharmonious conversation between controverted ideals of human association and the practical arrangements supposed to embody them in different domains of social existence. Theories of the constraints appropriate to different institutional roles – including the roles of such officeholders as cabinet ministers, parliamentary representatives, and judges – are not self-evident parts of present arrangements; they presuppose a view of the ideals that present institutional arrangements should be considered to serve. Many views may be excluded as plausible candidates. But the closure comes from the rough, loose continuum of a constitutional and legal tradition and the larger climate of opinion within which it developed, not from the practical arrangements standing alone. Thus, for example, ideas about the proper limits of the judicial role are likely to depend upon a conception of the kind of democracy the constitution establishes. Though the choice of this conception is not a free-for-all, neither can it be kept entirely separate from the question of what kind of constitution people now living would like to have. The separation becomes harder to establish when (as in the United States) the constitution is treated less as an easily replaceable artifact than as a structure within which the nation, with the help of occasional amendments, can endlessly renew itself.

The incongruous use of existing institutions grows in importance relative to the development of new institutions when the setting is parliamentary rather than revolutionary. In parliamentary situations incongruous use is most important when the inherited constitutional structure of the state possesses a special sanctity. But it is never an adequate substitute for reconstruction, only a diminished though real possibility of action. If there is enough popular support to prevent a putschist vanguardism, there must also be enough support to change the constitutional arrangements.

There is one aspect of the effective use of central government that no movement can avoid, whether it comes into power by peaceful elections or by violent revolution: the effort to prevent the permanent bureaucracy from silently undermining its plans. In the revolutionary situation the inherited bureaucratic and military structure must be replaced. The failure to do so with sufficient relentlessness has been the bane of many a revolutionary experiment. (Consider the experience of some of the revolutions in Central Europe immediately following World War I.) In the parliamentary circumstance the need is just as great though both opportunities and risks are more modest. The movement in power must discipline its inherited bureaucrats – if it cannot rid itself of them – by a combination of political will from the top and popular engagement at the grass roots. The preservation of a nonpolitical civil service is compatible with such an approach so long as technocratic authority is not allowed to masquerade as administrative neutrality and civil servants continue to be pressed by resolute politicians and an engaged populace.

The principle of transformative practice now under discussion requires the reorientation of central government combined with the active engagement of ordinary men and women in ground-level government and administration. In both revolutionary and parliamentary situations the achievement of this objective may require the widespread use of rotation as well as party-political pluralism and the partial deprofessionalization of lower administrative positions. Popular engagement succeeds best in its purpose when it can seize on the opportunities created by the central government for decentralized collective decision-making. The mass of actively engaged citizens must in turn press the central reformers not only to decentralize power but to decentralize it in ways that prevent its devolution to inherited oligarchies.

The primacy of institutional reform over economic redistribution and the preference for redistributive measures that presuppose institutional reconstruction are vital to the successful interplay between grassroots engagement and the reorientation of governmental policy. The preferred policy must make the redistributive program depend upon the activities of local governments and the internal transformation of large-scale productive enterprises. The byword "No redistribution without militancy" must be incorporated into the design and work of institutions.

Notice that the combination of a reoriented central policy with intensified grassroots engagement has both a programmatic sense and a strategic use. The combination is successful to the extent that the tension between the sense and the use disappears. A basic premise of the program of empowered democracy is that the diminishment of the contrast between context-preserving routine and context-transforming conflict cannot be achieved either by bombing out the state and putting a pure system of human coordination in its place or by submerging fixed institutional arrangements in personal charisma. Nor, on the other hand, can it result from solutions imposed by a self-appointed vanguard upon a recalcitrant and sullen populace. Empowered democracy attempts instead to change the relation between large-scale, inclusive institutions and noninstitutionalized collective action, to make the former into a more congenial home for the latter. The closer the movement comes to its moment of power – and therefore also to its hour of institutional definition – the less room there is for discrepancy between means and ends. The key themes of the program must be directly and faithfully represented in the relation between what the movement does with central power and what it does with local or nongovernmental organizations.

A government committed to revolutionary reform needs active grassroots engagement to stand strong against its foreign and domestic enemies, to replace untrustworthy bureaucrats, and to prevent the disruption of essential services. To the objection that a major part of the population may be hostile to the government's intentions, the answer must be that plans without broad support are bad plans to execute; at least they are not plans that can produce the institutions of an empowered democracy. The government must retrench to whatever extent necessary to maintain broad support at the ground level, so long as it continues to respect, in its retreat, the principle of the primacy of institutional change over economic redistribution. A parliamentary government stands less in need of active popular support than does a revolutionary regime under siege. But the importance of preventing an attitude of passive clientalistic dependence upon a redistributive state becomes correspondingly greater.

An economic as well as a governmental task must be accomplished to secure the interplay between the reorientation of central policy and grassroots popular involvement. This economic mission can be dealt with summarily, in part because its difficulties are similar to those of the governmental task and in part because such difficulties can be better understood in the context of specific proposals for the reorganization of the economy. The reformers in power must attempt to combine a measure of political control over the basic flows of investment decisions with the active engagement of the working population in the basic activities of production and exchange.

The central government should try to consolidate as soon as it can the degree of control over investment decisions that is necessary to prevent the destabilizing trauma of economic crisis. It should prefer the forms of control that foreshadow the system of capital allocation defended by the program of empowered democracy. The nationalization of a range of large-scale enterprises may represent in many countries the easiest way to secure a public nucleus of capital accumulation that provides the minimal conditions for economic stability and growth at a time of heightened social and ideological conflict. But nationalization is far less promising as a transitional experiment than any number of ways in which central governments may begin to explore procedures for allocating capital, conditionally and temporarily, to smaller and more flexible enterprises while preserving, through pooling devices, the economic advantages of scale. (A number of such transitional forms of reconstructed capital allocation are discussed later, in a section on transitions, alliances, and opportunities.)

Just as the emergency form of central political guidance of the economy is nationalization, so the corresponding emergency method at the grass roots is the actual occupation by workers of factories, shops, and farms. In such a revolutionary circumstance the alternative market order – with its several tiers of capital givers and capital takers – must ordinarily be built within a dominant, semiautarkic state sector. But reform governments that come to power by parliamentary means in a contemporary mixed economy must employ a more subtle and varied range of techniques. Instead of the actual occupation of the productive stock by workers, they must press for checks upon private investment policy – and in particular upon the power to invest or to disinvest in ways that maximize financial return rather than productive advantage. They must link these checks from the top down with a cumulative transfer of parcels of capital access and decision-making power not only to the labor force of existing enterprises (many of which would eventually be broken up into smaller, more flexible units) but also to teams of workers, technicians, and entrepreneurs who want to go into business. The objective is to come closer to a situation that is neither that of an economically sovereign government facing powerless workers nor that of tenured workers who have succeeded private capitalists as the joint holders of absolute property rights. It is to approach a circumstance in which economic access, decentralization, and flexibility advance through the disassociation of consolidated property into several different faculties, allocated to different types of capital givers and capital takers, rather than through the transfer of consolidated property to a new absolute and permanent rightholder – the central government or the enterprise labor force.

The programmatic sense and the strategic use of the combination of central control and grassroots engagement run closely parallel to the sense and use of the governmental counterpart to this economic task. The economic program of empowered democracy must be prefigured in the early, partial realization of its key commitment: the social control of economic accumulation must be achieved in ways that promote rather than supplant decentralized economic access, discretion, and organizational flexibility. The revolutionary regime must guarantee production and distribution lest a disappointed populace seek protection from old elites or new rulers. But it must do so in ways that do not tempt it to denature its program on the pretext of carrying it out. The parliamentary reform government must break out of the cycle of reform and retrenchment by preventing the capital strike while engaging working men and women in an active, non-clientalistic relation to its economic proposals.

THE INSTITUTIONS

THE IDEA OF AN INSTITUTIONAL PROGRAM

The critical arguments and the forms of political practice discussed in the preceding sections represent two parallel lines of approach toward a program of social reconstruction. This program takes the contemporary formative contexts analyzed in Chapter 2 as its point of departure, in particular the institutions of the rich Western democracies. It describes how these institutions might be remade in light of the internal and visionary arguments rehearsed in an earlier section of this chapter. It depicts the arrangements that could suit –

both as feasible product and as favorable circumstance – the style of politics just examined. The easy intellectual passage, back and forth, between criticism or practice, on the one hand, and program, on the other, shows that the proposals presented here respect the maxim that the ends must be prefigured in the means. For the criticism of existing arrangements and the methods of practical organization represent the basic instruments of political action.

The exposition of the program distinguishes three main spheres for institutional reconstruction: the constitution of government, the organization of the economy, and the system of rights. These areas correspond very roughly to the major institutional complexes singled out in my earlier analysis of the Western formative contexts. But the major domains of programmatic reform are designed to emphasize the importance of the organization of government and of the struggle over governmental power as the chief means for the stabilization or destabilization of society. Lawmaking and discretionary economic policy are the chief tools with which the state goes to work on social life, just as rights definition and economic organization are the most important results this action helps produce. Moreover, by defining the agenda of institutional reconstruction in ways that do not neatly fit the categories deployed in the analysis of the contemporary Western formative context, I also want to underline that this program might be realized through a transformation of other institutional systems, including those of contemporary communist countries.

Each section of the institutional programs begins with critical remarks. These remarks establish a link between the more general ideas and arguments supporting the program as a whole and the detailed content of the institutional proposals. Characteristically they draw attention to an evil brought out by an aspect of our traditional way of organizing democracies or rights, or of understanding the nature of legal entitlements – an evil that despite its distinct identity points to a more general defect in the contemporary formative contexts.

Nothing in modern political or intellectual life gives much hope to those who would devote themselves to the task of programmatic thought. All over the world the most politically conscious and active elements claim to be interested in alternatives to established institutions. The most common objection to those who criticize contemporary institutions is that they have nothing to put in place of what they seek to destroy. Yet if a person who hears these professions of interest in alternatives were to go around looking for the constructive proposals such an interest might be expected to produce he would soon be disappointed. What programs do we have? The platforms of the political parties usually consist of a blend of vague slogans and cynical promises. The slogans illustrate a rhetoric of feeling. The promises hold out the hope of entrenching a private interest through rights definition or economic policy. The coexistence of the promises and the slogans expresses the peculiarly somnambulant quality of so much of modern politics: the remorseless contest of narrow material interests gets disoriented by muddleheaded ideological aspirations while the ideologies may seem at any moment the nearly transparent rationalizations of selfish factional goals. What the platforms most conspicuously lack are, precisely, large-scale proposals for reordering major aspects of the institutional structure of society.

To turn from the party platforms to the political writings of the left is to encounter a similar poverty of ideas. Both the illusions of deep-logic social theory and the faith in the spontaneous creative powers of revolutionary action have disarmed the constructive political imagination of the left. The major constructive institutional theme of leftist thinkers has been the idea of direct democracy in the form of conciliar, worker-council government. Rather than offering a credible alternative, this institutional conception has more often served as a reverse image of contemporary society, the revenge of a secretly hopeless mind upon a political reality that it cannot imagine pulled apart and reconstructed through a series of conceptual and practical adjustments that we can actually make. And this imaginative failure – I earlier argued – is itself partly responsible for the institutional forms that twentieth-century communism in fact assumed.

The few who try to work out alternatives more considered than those found in the party platforms or in the mainstream of leftist literature are quickly dismissed as utopian dreamers or reformist tinkerers: utopians if their proposals depart greatly from established arrangements, tinkerers if they make modest proposals of change. Nothing worth fighting for seems practicable, and the changes that can be readily imagined often hardly seem to deserve the sacrifice of programmatic campaigns whose time chart so often disrespects the dimensions of an individual lifetime. If all this were not enough, the would-be program writer still has a final surprise in store for him. He will be accused – sometimes by the very people who told him a moment before that they wanted alternatives – of dogmatically anticipating the future and of trying to steal a march on unpredictable circumstance, as if there were no force to Montaigne's warning that "no wind helps him who does not know to what port he sails."

What are we to make of this astonishing gap between the alleged interest in alternatives and the lack of any tangible sign that this interest is real? The problem is not merely that programmatic ideas lack the immediate excitement of both theoretical controversies and practical politics and require repeated acts of faith. The difficulty also lies, I have argued, in a troubled conception of social reality and social transformation that deprives us of any sensible way to distinguish the utopian from the realistic and seduces us into identifying political practicality with the willingness to take for granted almost all the institutions and beliefs that matter. (A practical man, said Disraeli, is a man who practices the errors of his ancestors.) All the more reason to join a programmatic proposal to an explanatory approach.

The program outlined in the following pages represents the application of internal and visionary arguments to a particular circumstance. Viewed from the standpoint of internal criticism, it is no more than an imagined moment in the interplay between ideal conceptions of human association and particular institutional arrangements. Even when this program is taken as an exercise in visionary thought, its image of empowerment works with the materials provided by a distinctive institutional tradition.

To many the result may seem both too deviant from established reality to be of much practical interest and too clearly located in a particular historical setting to have a more general intellectual appeal. Yet to those who see this program as at best a hortatory dream, I protest that we can realize each of its facets bit by bit, through a series of more modest reforms for whose realization practical politics constantly create new occasions. To those who see the program as of only transitory interest, I answer that it exemplifies an intellectual practice whose significance outreaches its immediate scope of application. The program adds retrospective support to an understanding of contemporary societies as placed in a middle position on an imaginary spectrum of degrees of emancipation from false necessity. The programmatic argument shows what it means to take the capacity to revise our contexts as both an ideal to be pursued and a fact to be recognized. And it suggests the style of constructive social thought that can achieve a more than tenuous link with social explanation.

AN EXPERIMENT IN CONSTITUTIONAL REORGANIZATION: THE EXAMPLE OF THE DUALISTIC SYSTEMS

The program begins with a discussion of the constitutional structure of central government. In no area of the institutional order is our dependence upon a unique tradition more striking. For our views about the organization of democratic governments are very largely beholden to a small stock of ideas that come to us from the end of the eighteenth century and the beginning of the nineteenth. We have long ceased to appreciate that those ideas were once regarded as rivals for a primacy that seemed anything but certain and as instruments of specific social goals that would now be regarded as suspect and even shameful. This protracted exercise in forgetting, buttressed by the stabilization of the social world we inhabit, has persuaded us that these techniques of governmental organization represent the very nature of liberal democracy. The act of persuasion has been all the easier because of the inability of the recurrent socialist dream of worker-council government ever to outlast the briefest revolutionary interludes and the failure of the communist-style popular democracies to provide a respectable alternative to the liberal-democratic institutions that we have.

So complete has been the suppression of historical experience, we seem hardly to remember that these same liberal institutions of government changed their real social meaning, while maintaining their outward forms, at least once in the course of their history. In the pioneering democracies, this change took place during the mid-nineteenth century, when the system of universal suffrage and mass-based political parties first took its modern form. Until then, liberal constitutionalism seemed to be the instrument of a republic of notables that carefully filtered out the fickle mob and the dangerous demagogue. And the sole alternative to such an overtly elitist polity seemed to be the peril and chaos of a radical democracy. Few, if any, foresaw that the same liberal constitutionalism would, in conjunction with the emergent style of partisan conflict, shape the mass democracies we now know.

Given our delusive tendency to equate representative democracy with a very distinctive constitutional tradition, it may be helpful to consider the one significant wave of constitutional reforms this tradition has in fact witnessed. At a minimum these reforms remind us of the artifactual and revisable character of our ways of organizing central democratic governments. But I have another, stronger reason to discuss them. They prefigure, in a limited setting, many of the concerns and techniques of the parts of the program defended here that deal with the organization of the state, just as the vanguard sector of contemporary industry anticipates much of what the program advocates for the reorganization of work and industry.

I have in mind the series of constitutional innovations introduced by the post–World War I constitutions in Europe and developed further by some of the post–World War II ones. You have to distinguish two aspects of this wave of constitutional innovations: the ideas and practices originally championed by the theoreticians of the constitutions adopted in the immediate aftermath of World War I and the quite different set of constitutional conceptions and arrangements that emerged, piecemeal, when those earlier approaches were abandoned or revised.

Many of the constitutions promulgated in the wake of World War I – like the German, the Austrian, and the Polish, or, for that matter, the constitutional program of the Russian provisional government –

arose from the reciprocal effect of two forces: the predominance of a hesitant, embarrassed left in the constitutional conventions or cabinets of that almost revolutionary era, and the teachings of the legal theorists who identified themselves, more or less explicitly, with this political faction, men like Hugo Preuss or Hans Kelsen. The social-democratic majorities had even less of a conception of a radically new governmental structure than they had of an alternative industrial organization. To their left, they saw only the revolutionary tradition of conciliar-type government (the commune, the soviet) constantly revamped and reabandoned in the history of popular insurrections. Their main concern was simply to react against the immediate past. As their characteristic political experience had been the struggle against an authoritarian executive, their primary constitutional objective became to ensure the obedience of the executive to the parliament. The legal theorists added the goal of "rationalizing" government: of identifying every aspect of governmental power and creating the legal form that would shape and discipline it. In pursuing this aim they continued to be guided by the implicit equation of accountability with the techniques of dispersion of power and distancing among branches and levels of government. The force of their commitment to these techniques seemed to be undercut by the theoretical concentration of almost unbounded power in the parliament and by the use of the popular initiative and the referendum alongside electoral representation. The commitment was nevertheless reaffirmed by the weight of the constraints upon the governing ministry that actually had to carry out legislative policy.

The collapse of many of the European democracies of the interwar period cannot be attributed primarily to defects in their constitutional structures. It took place in the setting of the unresolved challenges to the emergent formative context of power and production, the very same setting that, at an earlier moment, had allowed the new constitutionalism to take hold. Nevertheless, the relative immobility to which those constitutional arrangements often condemned the government sometimes helped hasten the downfall of republican institutions.

The new constitutions, however, did not stay put. They were revised. Most of these revisions had two immediate causes: the change in the balance of political forces, from left to right, and the desire to give the executive decisional mobility in a domestic and international circumstance of perpetual insecurity. Some revisions, like the amendments to the 1921 Polish constitution, almost completely reversed the original spirit of the constitutional plan and established a plebiscitarian presidency with all-inclusive powers. Other shifts, however, like the Austrian reforms of 1929, the Portuguese constitution of 1933, or even the changing constitutional practice of the Weimar Republic, contained the elements of an alternative, though highly limited, constitutional program. This program proved insufficient to rescue states that had already been caught up in the deadly struggles of the interwar period. But it did contain the elements of the dualistic structure developed later, more explicitly, by constitutions like the Icelandic of 1944, more lopsidedly by the French of 1958 and 1962, and most fully by the Portuguese of 1978.

Two closely connected arrangements distinguished this emergent constitutional scheme. One was the establishment of two governmental powers elected by direct universal suffrage – the parliament and the presidency, whence the core meaning of the term "dualism." The other was the decision to make the active government – the parliamentary cabinet – dependent upon both those powers, yet for that very reason not entirely dependent upon any one of them. Three leading institutional ideas worked in this dualistic system.

One was the effort to maximize the popular aspects of indirect democracy. The plebiscitarian features of the presidential regime, subversive of party oligarchies, would be joined to the vital partisan conflicts of a parliament elected under proportional representation.

The second idea was the attempt to give the acting government decisional initiative by allowing it to lean on either the president or the parliament and not to fall automatically or immediately because it had lost the support of either. The goal therefore became to permit the rapidity and continuity of governmental action by making the ability to act effectively independent of a consensus among all the powers of the state. (Think, for example, of the impact in a presidential regime of the antagonism between president and legislature; in a parliamentary one, of the effect of fragile party coalitions in a wider social context of frantic but petty collective bickering.)

The third institutional idea put limits on the second one and allowed it to operate without jeopardizing the primacy of the appeal to the mass electorate recognized by the first idea. It consisted in the use of devices that allowed different powers in the state to resolve deadlocks by provoking immediate general elections at which they themselves would be at risk. This technique had already been used in some of the European constitutions of the immediate post–World War I years. For example, the parliament might be able to remove the president on purely political grounds, dissolving itself by that very act. The president might simultaneously be allowed to bring about an electoral confrontation with a hostile parliamentary majority.

The significance of these parallel rights of appeal to the mass electorate increased when combined with a more general duplication of functions among branches of government. More than one power might be allowed to perform the same acts: to propose or even provisionally pass certain laws. If one of the duplicated powers in the state failed to obtain some required agreement on the part of its twin, there would be a deadlock that justified new elections.

These devices had an ambiguous relation to the mainstream constitutional tradition. On the one hand, they might be seen as minor adjustments to practices they did not displace. Examples of the dualistic revision coexisted with the older constitutional arrangements, and most had been initiated by moderate reformers or even by conservatives, uninterested in any radical reconstruction of state and society. On the other hand, the shift in the constitutional tradition could also be seen as the small-scale, limited version of a more drastic change. This alternative interpretation seemed to be supported by the internal analysis of some of the professed or tacit goals that motivated the dualistic experiments. Instead of disciplining power through the perpetuation of impasse, constitutional dualism disciplined it by the rapid resolution of deadlock. In the place of the techniques of distancing and dispersion, it put devices that replicated functions, focused conflicts, and broke up political oligarchies. No wonder the Portuguese constitution of 1978 – the only one of the late-twentieth-century constitutions to show an explicit commitment to aspects of institutionalized collective mobilization – was also the one to adopt most unreservedly the institutional ideas worked out through the dualistic experiments. In fact, the alternative constitutional structure presented in the next section of this chapter generalizes the principles already exhibited by the dualistic reforms.

There is no cause for surprise at the ambiguous relation of the dualistic system to the earlier constitutionalism: such an ambiguity marks all significant reforms. More specifically, dualism resembled those changes in industrial organization that, in the course of the twentieth century, introduced aspects of the flexible form of rationalized collective labor into sectors once dominated by the traditional assembly line and the other trappings of the rigid approach to industrial organization. Constitutional dualism shared with these industrial innovations its substance and historical circumstance as well as the ambiguity of its relation to the tradition within which it arose. Constitutional and industrial reforms could either remain minor variations on the established formative context of power and production or become steps toward the inauguration not just of another context but of a new measure of freedom over contexts.

THE ORGANIZATION OF GOVERNMENT: THE MULTIPLICATION OF OVERLAPPING POWERS AND FUNCTIONS

The attempt to emancipate social life more fully from false necessity can succeed only if our ordinary social experience gives us the occasions and the means to challenge and revise every aspect of the basic institutional structure of society. To every major feature of this structure there must correspond a practical or imaginative activity that puts it up for grabs, and this activity must be available to us in the midst of our routine conflicts and concerns. Among these routines none are more important, as a domain for context-challenging activities, than those that respect the struggle over the mastery and uses of governmental power. For this struggle directly influences the terms on which we conduct all our other disputes. A main point in my earlier criticism of the established version of democracy was precisely that by placing much of the established institutional order effectively beyond the reach of democratic politics, that mode of democracy fails to give adequate application to even the most modest conception of inherited democratic ideals.

Viewed from this standpoint, the classical liberal technique of dividing central government into a small number of well-defined branches – executive, legislature, and judiciary – is dangerous. It generates a stifling and perverse institutional logic, and it does so whether the division of powers takes the rigid, tripartite form of presidential systems or assumes the more flexible style of parliamentary regimes. The effort to put every aspect of the social order on the line will characteristically require many ways of using governmental power – or of fighting over its use – that find no suitable setting in the existing order. Would-be reformers may be told, for example, that the reconstructive activity they have in mind does not quite fit either the legislature or the judiciary. So it should not be done at all, for fear of distorting the system of institutional roles that supposedly helps define the inherent constitutional structure of democracy. But the result of abstaining is typically to leave a faction of society with an inordinate measure of control over the human and material resources by which we create the future society within the present one: money, expertise, and governmental authority itself.

The program that seeks to empower democracy in order to empower people must therefore multiply the number of branches in governments while attributing overlapping functions to agencies of the state. The multiplication of powers in the state should obey two overlapping criteria: first, that when the total system of powers and functions has been established, it will work to prevent any section of society from gaining a lasting stranglehold over the material or human resources that can be used to generate the future form of society; second, that the same system provide an opportunity for the exercise of every major variety of transformative activity, practical or imaginative. The first criterion looks to the result; the second, to the means. Each may predominate in the design of a particular power.

Another reason to multiply the number of powers in the state with overlapping functions is the usefulness of increasing the number of governmental authorities that are chosen, one way or another, by a general electorate. The point is to transfer to the relations among governmental institutions the same device by which mass politics loosen the oligarchy effect: the effort to enlist increasing mass support in the course of rivalries over the mastery and use of state power. One of the many reasons why this loosening of the oligarchy effect remained so imperfect had to do with the defects of the institutional means by which the loosening was achieved. The fewer the lines of access to the grass roots of popular involvement, the greater the likelihood that oligarchic tendencies will assert themselves within the institutional order and thereby constrain or defeat the wider intentions of the constitutional plan.

Consider two examples of the creation of new powers in the state. Each illustrates one of the two criteria cited earlier. And each displays, in a more focused setting, a more general concern of the whole constitutional scheme. The commitment to avoid a monopoly over the resources of society creation may justify the establishment of a branch or agency of government especially charged with enlarging access to the means of communication, information, and expertise, all the way from the heights of governmental power to the internal arrangements of the workplace. The effort to control the sources of technical knowledge and expertise is the natural ambition of unresponsive power. It becomes all the more attractive as wealth comes to consist, in ever increasing measure, in the capacity to undertake instrumental activities on the basis of specialized knowledge, routinized at its core and flexible in its applications. It is vital to the enlarged democracy that the tendency, at every level of social life, to gain an entrenched, uneven access to this capacity be constantly resisted. The power able to resist this tendency cannot be a mere instrumentality of any other power or a limited governmental organization. For the struggle about what exactly it should do would be a major form of conflict over the uses of governmental power and a chief determinant of the terms on which people can collaborate practically.

Such a branch of government must be legally and financially qualified to oversee the basic arrangements separating technical coordination and managerial advice from a generic disciplinary authority in the workplace. (See the later discussion of the regime of capital.)

It must be able to make know-how available to those who, under the conditions I shall describe, set up new productive enterprises. It must be able to intervene in all other social institutions and change their operations, by veto or affirmative initiative. Its power to intervene must be directly related to the task of securing the conditions that would maximize information about affairs of state and achieve the maximum subordination of expert cadres to collective conflicts and deliberations. The officers of such a branch would be selected by joint suffrage of the other powers in the state, the parties of opinion, and the universal electorate.

Now take an example of the prevalence of the other criterion by which to multiply branches of government: the commitment to give every transformative practice a chance. The order of right – the laws generated by the joint, constitutionally regulated collaboration of all the other powers of government – constitutes a repository of social ideals. Though these ideals never form a cohesive whole or justify a single imaginative scheme of right and possible association, they stand in greater or lesser tension toward the internal life of particular institutions.

There is a practical and imaginative activity that works out the implications of such prescriptive models of association for the remaking of institutional life. Its imaginative aspect consists in understanding and elaborating a large body of law as a project to advance a certain vision of life in common. Its practical aspect lies in the series of procedural devices that involve some far-reaching intervention in an area of social practice. These devices aim to strike down obstacles to the advancement of the ideal, to prevent such obstacles from arising in the first place, and affirmatively to reconstruct the chosen area of social life in conformity to the guiding vision. Such interventions may involve the institution that undertakes them in the ongoing administration of major institutions: productive enterprises, schools, hospitals, asylums. (Think of the complex, collective injunctions afforded by American law in the late twentieth century, and imagine their radical extension.)

As the governmental power moves forward in its attempt to reconstruct a body of social practice, it finds inducements to go still farther. First, the partial execution of the reconstructive effort reveals new causal connections: more or less remote social forces that prevent the fuller realization of the ideal pursued. These causal links extend, continuously, in all directions. Only standards of institutional limitation and reservations of institutional prudence, or the qualifying force of other powers in the state, could keep every instance of this procedural intervention from expanding, bit by bit, into a complete remaking of society. Second, each step forward in the application of an ideal to social life reveals new ambiguities in its content and new disharmonies between it and established social practice. Even a well-defined and seemingly limited reconstructive project never ends: each new occasion for its realization reveals both new ambiguities in its meaning and new requirements.

The imaginative aspect of the activity I have described – the understanding of bodies of rule and principle as expressive of ideals of human association – is universal to all forms of legal doctrine. Indeed, I shall argue later that any extended practice of legal doctrine failing to render explicit this reference to ideals of common life degenerates, by virtue of this truncation, into a pseudorationality, an arbitrary choice of results that the ambiguous body of law cannot support and that only a broader exercise of social criticism could justify. But the practical aspect of this activity is another story. When the implementation of the broadened conception of doctrine involves a systematic intervention in large areas of social practice and the consequent disruption of major institutions, it does not seem to lend itself easily to any of the branches of government admitted by the received constitutional traditions of democracy.

The characteristics of the traditional judiciary – devoted, as it primarily is, to the settling of more or less focused rights and wrongs under the law – make it a less than ideal instrument for far-reaching and systematic intervention in social practice. The ajudication of localized disputes over the boundaries of rights may best be conducted by officals removed from the pressures of conflict over the uses of governmental power and expert in the entire body of law, or else by ordinary laymen involved in the life of a community (popular tribunals). Neither type of adjudicative corps may be well suited to conduct a radical extension of complex procedural intervention. The expert judges, with their vaunted immunity from direct influence by the other powers in the state, or even by the general electorate, would, with such procedural weapons in hand, turn into a nearly absolute censorial authority. They would hover over the republic, like a Lycurgus who had forgotten to go away after completing his work of state building. The popular tribunals of ordinary laymen are equally disabled from the performance of this task because both their inexpertise and their fragmentation prevent them from acting effectively as the agents of a systemic reconstructive intervention in social life.

If the traditional judiciary seems ill-qualified for the purpose so does the conventionally understood legislative body. Preoccupied as it is with the struggle over more or less marginal adjustments to the existing law and with the support or subversion of the party in power, it cannot be easily expected to undertake the ideal, long-range, and systematic interventionism that would provide such a power with its mandate. There would always be the danger that a legislature's attempts at such an engagement would become subordinate to short-term partisan rivalries, and the reasonable suspicion that it had been so tainted would, even if unjustified, rob it of authority. The point is not that the activity of such a power should be or seem unpolitical, but that it should represent politics carried on by somewhat other means and to a somewhat different end. The conventional legislature is defective in another way as well. Though its members may be expected to be proficient in the more general styles of political persuasion, most may lack firsthand familiarity with the more specialized forms of normative argument – religious, moral, and technically legal – that flourish in the society. An enlarged conception of legal doctrine weakens these distinctions but does not abolish them.

These arguments suggest that the power responsible for systematic interventions should be a branch apart, staffed and organized according to the principles most suitable to its overriding task. Like the power responsible for rescuing know-how from privilege, its members may be selected by the other powers, the parties of opinion, and the universal electorate. They should be drawn from activities that have acquainted them with the different modes of normative thought important in the society. They should have at their disposal the technical, financial, and human resources required by any effort to reorganize major institutions and to pursue the reconstructive effort over time.

Such a branch of government must have a wide latitude for intervention. Its activities embrace, potentially, every aspect of social life and every function of all the other powers in the state. If the other powers could not resist and invade the jurisdiction of this corrective agency, it would become the overriding authority in the state. The broad-based selection of its members would not compensate for this evil: the control of a primary access to the general citizenry, the very circumstance the technique of overlapping powers and functions wants to avoid, would have reappeared under the new constitution. The resistance the other powers impose must not, however, exemplify the rigid distribution of functional competences, the checks and balances, of the tradition inherited from the eighteenth century. The paralyzing impasses such devices favor, hostile to the aims of a constitutionalism of decisive experiments and broadened participation, would become all the more deadly when many more branches of government coexisted and collided. Thus, the effort to describe the appropriate workings of this reconstructive power nicely illustrates the problem addressed by the constitutional technique of multiple and overlapping branches of government.

THE ORGANIZATION OF GOVERNMENT: SHAPING AND RESOLVING THE CONFLICT OF POWERS

A main way in which the received constitutionalism tried to discipline power was its appeal to an automatic mechanism of containment: any branch that went beyond its proper sphere would be automatically stopped by all the other branches. This banal system of checks and balances has a meaning that does not become apparent until you understand both the problems that it was originally designed to solve and the effects it continues to produce long after those problems have changed beyond recognition.

In the prerevolutionary Europe of corporatist and estatist polities the different powers in the state were often identified as representing particular segments of a hierarchically ordered society. The attempt to create a state set up without regard to the internal divisions of society, in a society whose disorganized classes replaced corporately organized estates, meant that the powers of the state had to be defined by reference to one another. And as the division of government into different departments (branches) with specialized functions achieved greater fixity, it also became more important to establish a mechanism that would hold these departments to their assigned tasks and keep them from invading one another's domains. One device would be appeal to an outside umpire. If this umpire were an unaccountable sovereign claiming to stand for the collective good (such as a monarch), he would pose a serious threat to the form and spirit of a republican constitution. But neither could a universal electorate serve as the arbiter every time power clashed. For such a procedure would be dangerous as well as cumbersome. It would run counter to the liberal aim of establishing a representative regime that would minimize the opportunities for popular agitation and for the scheming of demagogic agitators. Thus, it became important to invent a built-in method of mutual restraint that would avoid the need to turn to the outside umpire.

It is remarkable that as the republican order became more democratic, the constraining effect of the system of "checks and balances" continued to operate. When first devised, the system was subsidiary to another, more ostentatious method of restraint: a filtering-out technique that both restricted the suffrage and established many levels of intermediate representation between grassroots electorates and central governments. In time this technique – once justified by the commitment to ensure that electors be independent and informed – proved both an intolerable insult to popular sovereignty and a superfluous guarantee of social stability.

The founding liberal myth of a constitutional mechanism and a system of rights that tower above the hierarchical and communal divisions of society has since become true in an unacknowledged and embarrassing sense. Liberal-democratic politics and the society in which it is practiced have indeed become separate: a social order that consists largely of groups entrenched in fixed niches within the division of labor and occupying stable places in the established scheme of social hierarchy coexists with a political practice that plays up to shifting coalitions of interest formed by groups with crisscrossing and unstable membership. A major thesis of my explanatory and programmatic arguments has been that liberal politics – and its defining institutional framework – help perpetuate a form of social order that can be remade in their image only by a transformation of the liberal conception and practice of political life. To make society resemble what liberal politics to a considerable extent are already like, we would have to change the institutional form of the state and of the conflict over governmental power and push the liberal vision beyond the point to which its creators have up to now been willing to take it.

The classical technique of checks and balances is only a small part of the structure that would have to be changed. But it exemplifies in a particularly heavy-handed way the constraints imposed by the larger structure to which it belongs, just as the arguments deployed in its favor illustrate with peculiar clarity the vision we must replace.

Because of the system of checks and balances, a faction bent on an ambitious program must capture more or less simultaneously the different departments of government. And the leaders of each branch of government can usually be counted on to be so jealous of the prerogatives of their offices that pride of place becomes identical with resistance to every bold plan. Indeed, the most noticeable feature of the system is to establish a rough equivalence between the transformative reach of a political project and the obstacles that the constitutional machinery sets in its way.

Some say this method of mutual restraint and deliberate deadlock serves as a necessary defense of freedom. But a program that proposes ways to extend the enjoyment and meaning of public freedoms while avoiding the paralysis of experimental capability in politics helps discredit belief in this necessity. Others say the pattern of stalemate is an unavoidable consequence of the conflict among narrow organized interests in societies in which most people remain reasonably satisfied most of the time. But this view is a principal target of a theory that wants to show all the ways in which a contingent, revisable institutional order forms the occasions and instruments of conflict and shapes assumptions about identities, interests, and possibilities.

A constitutional program committed to the empowerment of democracy therefore has many reasons to replace the inherited strategies of automatic and reciprocal institutional constraint. The multiplication of overlapping governmental powers and functions lends added urgency to such an innovation.

Three principles may concurrently govern the conflict of powers under the reformed constitution. The first – and the only one of the three widely used in the established liberal bourgeois democracies – is the absolute restraint one power may impose upon another. This restraint can be overcome only by the reciprocal influence the different branches may exercise upon one another's composition. Suppose that a party succeeds to office on a platform of far-reaching distribution of wealth and power, reforms directed against the institutional framework of the economy. Imagine, further, that the new rulers keep the support of the highest representative assemblies, which also form part of the decisional center of government. (See the next section, on the organization of the center.) Some of the innovations may involve an attack upon the basic rights guaranteeing the individual's security and his access to conflict over the mastery and uses of governmental power. An agency in the state, isolated from the immediate effects of the struggle over governmental power, must be able to hold back such assaults. It hardly matters whether it is the same judiciary that settles particular controversies or some distinct constitutional authority. What does matter is that the nature and basis of this individual immunity change. (See the later discussion of immunity rights.)

The second principle to govern the conflict of powers is one of priority among the different branches. The third is the use of the immediate or delayed devolution of constitutional impasses to the general electorate. These two principles qualify each other. When the branches of government are few and the constitution limits power by perpetuating impasses, it is natural to treat the branches as equal. The force of this conclusion vanishes together with its premises. The test of a power's relative hierarchical position lies precisely in its right to impose its will upon other powers. The two most important justifications of higher hierarchical place are the breadth of the composition of the branch or agency (the extent to which its members are chosen by an organized societywide struggle) and the scope of its responsibilities (how far into the social order its central constitutional responsibilities allow it to reach). By these criteria, for example, the interventionist power responsible for vindicating the ideals that underlie the entire legal system is more important than the power charged with maintaining the integrity of access to information. The decisional center of government is more important than both.

The constitution may establish circumstances in which a conflict between powers justifies an immediate devolution to the general electorate. This will be peculiarly appropriate to circumstances in which the contest arises within the decisional center and indicates a failure of popular support for the party program. A prodigal use of this technique, however, would paralyze the state's capacity for action just as surely as a commitment to the method of restraining power by perpetuating impasses. Thus, the normal method for resolving conflicts between unequal powers will be delayed devolution (referendum) to the electorate. Suppose, for example, that the party in office enters into conflict with the power responsible for disrupting established institutions in the name of the systematic ideals attributed to the legal order. If the party is acting in the execution of its program, and if it has not been stopped in this course by the judicial protection of individual security, it would be allowed to proceed. But the dispute would be set for debate and resolution at the next general election.

No one of these constitutional procedures is essential to the constitutional scheme. The particular institutional proposals represent no more than a plausible interpretation of the project of an empowered democracy. Which of these interpretations works best, in the spirit of that project, cannot be inferred conclusively from general arguments. The same loose connection between the details and their reasons holds for the relationship between the entire institutional plan and the conception that underlies it.

THE ORGANIZATION OF GOVERNMENT: THE DECISIONAL CENTER

Just as the multiplication of overlapping powers and functions threatens to worsen the paralytic effect of the system of checks and balances, so too it threatens to submerge the decisional center of government under a confusion of clashing agencies. This result would be fatal to the aims of the revised constitutional order, which must give a party of opinion, supported by a broadly based social movement, a chance to try its program out. The instruments at its disposal for doing this must be even more effective than those available to the ruling parties of the established style of democracy. They must be able to reach the sources of private power this style ordinarily leaves untouched. They must be proportionate to the intentions of collective movements capable of linking struggles at the heights of state power to the rivalries of everyday life. They must be able to deal with the complexities introduced by the presence of many branches of government. Moreover, so long as the state exists in a world of rival states, it must have at its head an authority capable of decisive diplomatic and military action.

The decisional center of government includes the executive and the legislature foreseen by received constitutional doctrine. It hardly matters whether these are conceived as two distinct branches of government, in the context of a presidential regime, or as something close to a single power, under a parliamentary system. For the new-model constitution may either include an elected president or dispense with him. The powers forming this decisional center are those most immediately responsible for the implementation of a partisan program that may address the overall structure of society and for the ultimate control over the state's dealings, in peace and war, with other states. It may not seem self-evident that these two concerns should be joined in the hands of the same public agencies. But those governmental institutions that stand closest to the citizenry and that provide the broadest scope for popular decision must also be the ones to make the choices that involve most dramatically the lives and fortunes of the people. The powers that stand outside this decisional center are the ones charged with a more focused responsibility and removed, to a relatively greater degree, from immediate partisan rivalry.

In order to understand the place of the decisional headquarters within the constitution of the empowered democracy, it helps to consider its nature and responsibilities in earlier constitutional schemes. In these schemes, it often amounted to almost the entire constitutional system.

Start with a simplified version of the medieval European constitution. The central constitutional task – usually performed by a king in parliament – was the occasional declaration or restatement of the law, conceived as a body of sanctified custom that determined the rights and obligations of each estate in the realm. For this conception to become dominant, the origin of these customary arrangements in a history of particular conflicts had to be forgotten or denied, and the conflicts themselves interrupted or contained. The other, subsidiary constitutional function was the power of the prince to deal with the unexpected by taking emergency measures that might involve some ad hoc revision of the customary order. Without this power of princely correction the stability and survival of custom might be jeopardized by every significant change in circumstance. The corrective function – the *gubernatio* by contrast to the *jurisdictio* – could not easily be assimilated to the system of thought that informed the central vision of right. To exercise or to accept it was to acknowledge, even if only marginally and implicitly, the failure of the established order to exhaust the possible forms of social life. Whether the prince claimed to act by divine inspiration or secular wisdom, he, his advisers, and his critics made use of a faculty of inventing measures that might endure, turning into custom.

The liberal-democratic states of the modern West did not alter this picture as much as at first appeared. The nostrums of the dominant political rhetoric might proclaim a popular sovereignty limited only by the sanctity of individual and minority rights. Under a presidential regime, the president and the legislature were able, in conflict or cooperation, to work out the implications of party programs for existing social arrangements. Under a parliamentary regime, this conception of a sovereign decisional center stood out even more clearly. The occupants of the highest executive offices became the instruments by which an electorally successful party could act upon the principles for which it had stood in the elections. The head of state turned, at most, into an official responsible for overseeing the mechanism by which rival parties fought for power.

Even with the reforms introduced by the dualistic system, the reality of constitutional practice qualified the idea of programmatic initiative to the point of radically changing its understood meaning. All the traits of a demobilizing constitutionalism made it hard for a victorious party to seize the state or, having seized it, to execute its program rapidly and decisively. The link made by the legal system between the means of immunity against government and the forms of control over individuals meant that the attempts to carry a partisan program into the reconstruction of the private order appeared as more or less direct threats to individual or minority freedom. Reigning opinion and constitutional principle conspired to ward off these threats. Thus, even under the most flexible parliamentary regime, with the greatest measure of unity between cabinet and parliament, policy making and legislation by the decisional center rarely amounted to more than marginal and fragmentary interventions in a social and legal order with a tenacious structure of its own. Thus persisted the older constitutional idea of a legislature that debates and enacts occasional changes in the laws. Despite its seeming archaism and unsuitability to the structure of a dynamized parliamentary regime, it expressed the reality of constitutional practice. For just as the larger attempt to realize the idea of a state hostage to no faction would require a major change in the organization of government and in its relation to society, so too, on a smaller scale, the idea of a government organized to make and implement a coherent party program would demand a change in the conception of the decisional center, in its structure, and its relation to the other agencies of the state.

Suppose, for the sake of simplicity, that the new constitution includes a qualified parliamentary regime (which provides for a popularly elected president, independent of the parliament, with significant powers of his own, as in the dualistic system). The supreme representative assembly must carry out two tasks, neither of which can be easily assimilated to the traditional idea of legislation. On the one hand, it must supervise and ensure the fidelity of the party or parties in office to the program to which they committed or came to commit themselves in the course of their campaign or of their tenure in office. On the other hand, the assembly should serve as the maximum level of a series of forms of popular representation that spread out through society. In this second role, it may work, in an interlocutory capacity, as the agency responsible for settling conflicts among the other branches of government. Its task will be most important in those cases of lesser importance when the solution is not immediately entrusted to the universal electorate. It must also provide the vehicle by which these lower-level representative bodies can stop the ruling government in its tracks and go to the country.

These two tasks – the supervision of the party in office and the interlocutory representation of the larger electorate – need not be performed by the same representative body. A smaller council within the larger one may represent the parties in office and supervise the execution of the program. This program-supervising work may seem like a job done anyway under existing democratic institutions. But its delicacy and importance increase dramatically when the partisan conflicts at the summit of governmental power extend down to the disputes that occur on the familiar ground of work and leisure and when the entire structure of society is at stake in this struggle.

Under such a scheme, the whole idea of legislation undergoes a change. The laws and directives embodying the program are worked out together by the cabinet and the smaller supervisory council. No hard-and-fast distinctions exist between the different kinds of norms thast result from the process. The supervisory partisan council performs a role that could be called jurisdictional as much as legislative: it judges in each instance the conformity of enactment to program. The large representative body, to which this smaller council may belong, serves to stop rather than to initiate or enact measures of state. At the same time, thank's to its size, the multiplicity of the forms of election and representation that generate it, and the closeness of its ties to lower-order representative assemblies, this more inclusive body provides a running preview of the broader electoral struggle.

The cabinet and council govern subject to the restrictions imposed by this greater assembly and the other powers in the state. Thus, there will be conditions under which the power designed to preserve the integrity of communication, or to vindicate by interventionist procedures the imputed ideals of the legal order, or to adjudicate individual disputes and safeguards, can impede the exercise of governmental power in a particular instance, or reserve a matter for later electoral decision, or even provoke an impasse requiring immediate devolution to the electorate. But the cabinet need not necessarily count on a majority in the larger organization. In circumstances of party fragmentation and intense partisan rivalry, a method may be devised that allows a minority force to rule so long as it can win compensatory support from other powers in the state or from lower-level representative bodies.

THE ORGANIZATION OF GOVERNMENT: MAKING MINICONSTITUTIONS

There are limits to the extent to which any particular set of institutional arrangements can embody a principle of permanent self-revision. By its very existence in a particular form, it excludes other constitutional arrangements. By excluding other such schemes, it also rules out certain modes of practical or passionate association that people may come to want. No constitutional system can be perfectly elastic in relation to all possible instances of collective life. Nor can this limitation be adequately remedied by a conventional power of constitutional amendment. For the exercise of such a power can rarely change more than an isolated fragment of the established constitutional order.

The normal constitutional system must include among its own precepts the opportunity to establish special constitutional regimes for limited contexts and aims. These special regimes amount to miniconstitutions. At the most modest level, the party in office may have as part of its program to set up institutions able to act in anomalous ways, with exceptional degrees of power, in particular sectors of the society. (See, for example, the later discussion of a regime of extreme entrepreneurial freedom within an economy whose main lines remain subject to direct political control.) At the highest level, the leaders of a party may appear before the universal electorate requesting some special regime of power – a temporary change in the arrangements and prerogatives of the decisional center – that can be reconciled with the crucial constitutional safeguards for individuals, minorities, and oppositions. In this event, the election becomes, simultaneously, a conflict over the form of the state and the identity of the highest officeholders.

Whatever the scope of the miniconstitution, its use always requires a specific precautionary method. To each special venture in the establishment of an extraordinary power there should correspond a special venture in control. Thus, the higher power that institutes an anomalous lower power must provide for the special independent board that will supervise the anomalous agency's actions and regulate its connections to the other, normal parts of government. The party that appears before the electorate in search of special arrangements and prerogatives must at the same time come with a proposal for the institution of a special supervisory authority, an ad hoc branch of government. Thus, every special power, under the exceptional constitutional regime, has a shadow power in its pursuit. The shadow grows longer in proportion to the dimensions of the special power it follows.

THE ORGANIZATION OF PARTISAN CONFLICT: POLITICAL STABILITY IN AN EMPOWERED DEMOCRACY

The most obvious objection to the constitutionalism of permanent mobilization defined by the preceding techniques is its apparent inability to guarantee a minimum of stability. Everything in such a constitution might seem explicitly designed to reduce state and society alike to bitter strife and paralyzing confusion. Carried to the extreme, such an instability would deny people the practical and moral benefits of all lasting, secure forms of association. It would disrupt the social basis for the development of productive or destructive capabilities just as much as if it had allowed a principle of vested rights to preclude all innovation in social life. In the end, a regime of extreme instability would turn out to destabilize itself and to give way, at whatever cost, to a stabilized order. People would cry out for firm leaders and peacemaking institutions. Their freedom would seem intolerably burdensome to them if they could keep it only by accepting an uncertainty that disturbed every aspect of life and an antagonism that always stood ready to turn from programmatic disagreement to bitter quarreling and from quarreling to violence.

The attempt to explain the nature and bases of stability under the transformed constitutional regime requires us to consider the role to be played by organized parties of opinion under such a regime. More generally, it serves as an invitation to imagine the actual dynamic of central political struggle that would characterize such a reordered society. Once again, our ability to make reasonable conjectures about the workings of adjusted social practices puts to the test our understanding of the practices we actually have. For once this understanding goes beyond the most external and mechanical descriptions, or the most ambiguous correlations, it requires ideas about the difference it would make to change particular arrangements or enacted beliefs.

Remember first that the emancipation of society from false necessity takes in part the form of a dissolution of social classes into parties of opinion. To some extent, this dissolution has already taken place: it is always reemerging through history, and the liberal-democratic polities of the present day have carried it to an unprecedented point. The classical liberals who have betrayed their early radical vocation claim society has already reached this condition. But if the early analysis is correct the relatively rigid quality of social life differs fundamentally from the comparatively fluid organization of politics, and our political ideas and institutional arrangements are partly responsible for the results. The institutional program outlined here seems calculated not only to propose carrying this dissolution of social classes into parties of opinion still further but to aggravate its destabilizing effects. The problem of instability has its focus in the relation between an extended partisan strife and the constitutional and social conditions that seem to turn this strife in a dangerous direction.

The ancient hostility to factional struggle always had a double foundation. One basis was the conviction that factions would be inherently selfish and thus subversive of the common good. The other was the fear that contending parties would destroy the civic peace.

Factional struggle seemed incompatible with the stability of any polity so long as it cut to the most basic matters of life. Chief among these, in an age of belief, were the terms of salvation. Thus, parties of religious opinion seemed to be the exemplary case of factions that would tear a commonwealth apart. Their differences could not be compromised, and their partisans would rest only with the complete defeat of their adversaries. At least, this uncompromising demand would persist so long as the religious principle demanded a privileged if not universal community of belief.

The closest secular equivalent to religious controversy was all-out ideological disagreement. When the major factions defined themselves by sharply opposing secular visions of what society should become, or pitted the tangible interests of one large class against those of another, the republic would be equally in trouble. The normal conflicts for and over governmental power might quickly slide into a social warfare that put everything up for grabs. For the sake of realizing nonnegotiable goods, all restraint in the use of means would soon be forgotten.

Partisan rivalry became safe, in this view, when it came to be characterized by two related features. The principles and interests to which each major party was committed no longer fitted into a single cohesive vision, sharply and clearly contrasted to the visions championed by the other leading factions. At the same time and for the same reasons, a multiplicity of crosscutting factions – if not parties, then segments of parties and other collective bodies – would organize for the prosecution of particular goals. The citizens would find themselves divided in many contradictory ways rather than enlisted into two or three civic armies ready to do battle, first figuratively and then literally, over the organization of society. In such a circumstance, partisan conflict would rarely seem to be about society's formative institutional context or its enacted imaginative scheme of association. It would be largely about the marginal advances of certain groups within that context. Any change in the defining institutional arrangements or the embodied vision of social life would normally come about as a by-product of the struggle over fragmentary goals and interests. It is precisely because of this relative deflection from the fundamentals that, on this view of minimal stability, partisan rivalry appears compatible with republican life.

Notice that this received conception of the sources of stability and instability depends upon two crucial identifications. The first is the equation of instability, understood as a heightening of the intensity and a broadening of the scope of conflict over the uses of governmental policy, with instability, interpreted as a resurgent threat to the individual's most vital interests in material security and welfare. This link presents instability in the image of Hobbesian civil strife, as the nightmare from which people must and will escape at any cost. My later argument about the reorganization of the system of legal rights suggests how to uncouple these two types of jeopardy so that the basic security of the individual is guaranteed and even strengthened in a mobilizational democracy.

There is another identification at least as central to the received view of stability: the equivalence established between fundamental conflicts and nonnegotiable disputes. The concept of a formative institutional and imaginative context provides a more precise interpretation of what is fundamental and permits restating the classical approach to stability in the following terms: an institutional order deliberately designed to favor repeated controversy over the formative context will, if it succeeds in its objectives, inevitably result in an escalation of nonnegotiable demands that will tear the civil peace apart. It will create precisely the style of partisan strife that the mainstream of Western political thought has always considered intolerable.

It is tempting to see a refutation of the equivalence between fundamental conflict and nonnegotiable practice in the partisan rivalries of many Western European democracies in the two or three generations since World War II. There you found major parties committed to radically different programs for the organization of society and of its relation to the state. Large numbers of partisan cadres treated this program as the articles of an intransigent faith and managed, with varying degrees of success, to draw the larger electorate into their own vision of fundamental differences. Yet these states remained stable by any plausible test of stability you might care to propose.

The actual practice of party politics and administration, however, told a different story from the programs and the speeches. For the most part, this party-political activity continued to revolve in the toils of the reform cycles described in Chapter 2. No matter how bold their intentions upon arriving in office, reformers typically found themselves dragged down by the cumulative force of resistances that undermined their hold on the state before allowing them to establish the basis for an alternative organization of power and production. Thus, in practice, the system of partisan rivalry departed much less from the conventional model of stability-preserving partisanship than the contenders' rhetoric seemed to indicate. For the rhetoric came from periods, such as the aftermath of World War I, when a formative context had been in jeopardy or had failed to achieve a determinate form. But the reality was that of a stabilized social world where wide swings in governmental policy were much more likely to end as costly disturbances than as lasting innovations. In all the ways described, the very structure of institutions had been, more or less intentionally, rigged against too many surprises.

The real trouble with the traditional identification of conflicts over fundamentals with conflicts not lending themselves to compromise is its failure to appreciate that the relation between what is negotiable and what is fundamental changes according to the beliefs people entertain about society and the institutional structure of party conflict. As a result, the classical approach to stability in politics disregards the possibility of a circumstance distinct from both marginal, peace-preserving and basic, peace-destroying disputes: a style of factional rivalry that regularly questions the practical and imaginative foundations to the established social order.

The feature of the conflict over the basic arrangements of society that most directly makes it resistant to compromise is, paradoxically, its characteristic vagueness, its elusive and almost dreamlike quality. The less the abstract vision championed by the contending parties is worked into a texture scheme of social life, the flimsier the basis for any compromise. In the absence of a detailed plan for a reordered society, the only sure sign of victory becomes the triumph of an exclusive allegiance: the defeat of the disbelievers and the rise of the orthodox. At the same time, whenever a factional program combines vagueness of definition with intensity of feeling, it easily becomes hostage to whatever interpretations of its airy, murky promises may, for wholly secondary reasons, come to prevail. The temporary circumstances of a movement, the choices made by a leadership, or the mere desire to contradict an adversary lead the faction to embrace one particular version of its commitments over others. This almost accidental preference is then invested with all the devotion that had been reserved to the abstract conception. It is as if these details, rather than counting for their own sake, represented surrogates for the faction's image of its own identity and fortunes. In this substitute capacity, they again refuse compromise: there are no standards, other than the crassest material ones, by which to judge the cost of concessions, and any concession may seem to jeopardize the faction's essential identity.

Even the feared quarrels of confessional parties confirm this idea. These disputes become uniquely venomous in one of two circumstances. In the absence of any worked-out view of the implications of religious truth for the secular life of society, the relative preponderance of competing allegiances may be all there is left to fight about. Or the religion may include a detailed program of social life that pretends to prescribe almost every important feature of collective existence down to the last detail. The personal quality of the relation to God – the deepening in the relation to Him of all the claims and emotions that may exist among individuals – is falsified by the arbitrary, inscrutable character of the link between the central points of revelation and the unrevisable details of sacred laws. The detailed plan begins to look untouchable precisely because it is arbitrary. People lack the criteria by which to judge whether a similar vision could be realized, more perfectly, by different arrangements. There is, in this view, no underlying vision to be discovered and stated apart from the details of sacred law.

The more the conflicting partisan visions get translated into detailed schemes of collective life, down to the lowest levels of work and leisure, the less likely it becomes that these visions will seem impenetrable to one another. The force of concreteness changes the relation between the depth and the deadly intransigence of a partisan struggle. The deeper a programmatic position, the closer it comes to offering a revision of society's basic institutional arrangements and, even, of the fine structure of elementary personal relations. Take, then, a number of practical ways of doing things: of getting work done and assigning incomes and jobs, or organizing exchange and distribution; of living in families and dealing with superiors, subordinates, and equals. Impose the sole restriction that each competing scheme have the qualities allowing it to carry conviction for its specificity rather than for its vagueness (and consequent openness to the free play of connotation). Within its circumstance, it must seem practicable. It must appeal to an established, though inchoate, sense of personal realities, needs, and longings. Views with such characteristics are likely to be, and to appear, deconstructible and recombinable in many different ways. They will have the same features that theory shows societies themselves to possess, for they are nothing but social worlds, or variants of the existing social world, prefigured in the imagination. Moreover, the requirements of practicability and of responsiveness to personal aspiration impose constraints upon the extent of the divergence of the proposals from actualities.

That these views must seem practicable in the near future, or that they must be capable of immediate though partial realization, makes persuasion depend if not upon insight then upon the appearance of insight. Despite the inexistence of any metascheme that sets limits to possible societies or determines their unique sequence, the actual experience of transformative effort shows that some features of the existing order resist pressure more than others. The persuasive force of a program depends in part upon its success in incorporating into the definition of its aims and strategies a view of these differential pressures that ongoing events continue to confirm. Fidelity to personal experience exerts a similarly restraining influence. For the prophetic dogmas of politics, like the images of the self in world literature, differ more than do the actual wants of people.

The argument of the social theory developed in this book offers a justification for these common observations. It does so by working out the idea that each imaginative and institutional form of society represents an attempt to freeze, into a particular mold, the more fluid experiences of practical and passionate relationship characterizing the immediate, relatively unreflective, uninterpreted, and undisciplined life of personality. The dogmas and arrangements inform this life and alter it. But they do not completely overcome its recalcitrance or determine its inner nature. The visionary impulse in politics draws much of its persuasive force from the appeal to this defiant experience. The competing programmatic visions that, by dint of both their depth and their concreteness, touch people's ordinary concerns and inward longings do not thereby set themselves on the track to some ultimate convergence, any more than do whole societies under the negative impact of the dissolution of their rigid schemes of hierarchy, division, and associational possibility. But they do find the lines of divergence blurred by the presence of overlapping themes.

Both the political ideas and the actual institutional organization of the conflict for power in present-day liberal democracies discourage the alliance of scope and specificity. They do so, most directly, by denying opportunities for a continuous connection between the disputes of official politics and the quarrels of everyday life. They do so, more generally, by adopting institutional arrangements that make the choice between reform cycles and revolutions seem the normal condition of civic life. Thus, every radical vision has to be imagined as an abrupt and total deviation from existing society and nurtured without the chastening influence of practical experience and responsibility.

This circumstance does not merely enforce a constrained view of stability and reassert the dilemma of routine and revolution. It also accounts, in significant measure, for the strange, dreamlike quality of a politics that serves, at the same time, to accommodate the crassest interests and to express a struggle among abstract opinions. The experiences defining the situation of mass politics, world history, and enlarged economic rationality deprive all but the crudest interests of their appearance of self-evidence and make explicit their dependence upon opinion. Were it not for this disturbance of concreteness, party politics in the modern sense could never have emerged, for one of its crucial elements, from the start, was the commitment to speculative principles. These principles, however, remain, for the most part, both fragmentary and abstract, or they become only sporadically concrete. Thus, even in the circumstance of routine and reform cycles people act as if dazed by abstraction. Their political conduct has something of the arbitrariness of confessional factions clinging all the more woodenly to literal prescriptions, or lurching all the more haphazardly among conceptions of the ideal, because people lack any developed vision of a transfigured human reality.

To organize the conflict for and over state power in a way that encourages the combination of depth and concreteness, you need both ideas and institutions. Without the institutions, the ideas would lack transformative influence. You could expose the arbitrarily narrow assumptions of the received account of social peace and invoke the possibility of another style of stability. But you would be unable to deny the reality of the dilemma posed by this account within the institutional framework it took for granted. Your proposals would seem like proposals for another time. Without the ideas, however, the reformed institutional arrangements would lack a vision that made them intelligible and linked them, by a series of mediating connections, to an understanding of social reality and social transformation. The fuller and truer account of the varieties and conditions of stability must do the same work for the revised constitution that the more truncated and misleading view of tolerable stife did for the earlier democracies.

The ideas necessary to inform such a revised style of partisan conflict can be developed and supported by a social theory freed from the preconceptions of naive social science and deep-logic thinking. The two most important contributions such a theory can make to the intellectual climate of this practice of fundamental but negotiable disputes are the view that formative contexts can be replaced piecemeal and the thesis that the deviant elements in any social order have a subversive and reconstructive potential. Because revolutionary reform – defined as the substitution of any element in a formative context – is possible, a conflict can deal with fundamentals while stopping short of a confrontation of ultimate views. Not only can schemes of social life – proposals for alternative formative contexts – be recombined, but they can be recombined in different ways.

Because new dominant solutions must typically begin as attempts to extend an already existing deviant principle of organization or imagination, we can usually translate even the boldest vision into proposals that work with familiar and intelligible materials.

The ideas that inspire this approach to social stability and invention gain practical influence upon the style of partisan rivalry only when combined with a change in the institutional setting of party conflict. Such changes proceed outward in a net of mutually reinforcing measures revealing the connections between the narrowly constitutional proposals discussed in earlier sections and the ideas about economic organization and legal rights put forward in later pages.

The most significant practical reform addresses the relation of political parties to the organizations that absorb everyday life. In the midst of daily experience, the forms of practical or passionate association must be subject to methods of collective deliberation and conflict that connect with the most general issues of national politics. People must be able to see the positions they take within this more intimate circle as partial but recognizable extensions of their stand in the largest national sphere and vice versa. To this end, the partisan conflict needs to be fought in terms of programs combining breadth of scope with concreteness of intention: these programs should address structures of authority and advantage within and outside large-scale organizations.

The other institutional changes are the enabling conditions of this shift. They contribute to the connection between central political conflict and everyday concern. They keep this connection from taking the spurious form of the reduction of the societywide parties of opinion into the weapons of social classes or of segments of the work force rigidly defined by the niche they occupy in the division of labor. Frequent devolution to the universal electorate and the maximization of opportunities for factional propaganda and agitation at all levels of society bring many major conflicts before the citizen in a manner that penetrates his awareness of the immediate concerns of life even when it occupies only a modest portion of his time. The guarantee of welfare rights enables the individual to accept these conflicts without feeling they jeopardize his basic safety. His conception of minimum stability shrinks to the extent that his most intimate interests in material and moral security for himself and his family get disentangled from a system of vested proprietary rights that turns the forms of immunity from governmental power into the means of control over other people. (See the later discussion of the system of rights.)

The single most important condition to the linkage between conflict at the grass roots of social life and conflict at the heights of governmental power is the reform of the reigning practical institutions that allow small groups of people to exercise a general disciplinary power over everybody else in the name of the property norm, of the state's control over the economy, or of the inherent imperatives of organizational life. The arrangements and preconceptions of these institutions systematically confuse technical or managerial expertise with a more indiscriminate capacity for ultimate decision and command. To the extent that collective conflict and choice gain a significant role within major organizations and that expertise and coordination are distinguished from the ultimate choice of goals and methods, to that extent the opportunity arises for partisanship in the midst of humdrum practical activities. (See the later discussion of the regime of capital for an analysis of how, concretely, to create this opportunity while maintaining both the primacy of national politics over the national economy and the chances for bold entrepreneurial innovation.)

These practical institutions, broken open to collective conflict and deliberation, would also have to take on many of the tasks and characteristics previously attributed to the state. Thus, they should be drawn into the forms of popular representation and administrative responsibility. They should not become exclusive channels for the distribution of essential welfare benefits, for such a role would give them a formidable power of intimidation over their members and jeopardize the integrity of welfare rights. Law and policy, for their part, should give priority to the varieties of distribution and redistribution that strengthen militant collective organizations rather than replacing them: that prefer, for example, the cooperative, public–private offer of services to lump-sum transfers.

The institutional arrangements outlined in the preceding pages remain dangerously compatible with an outcome inimical to the aims of empowered democracy. The national political parties get entrenched in the organizational settings of everyday life. There, at the grass roots, people divide up in ways that help constitute and reflect their divisions at the societywide level. But each party of opinion merely serves in the end as the instrument of a large social group or class or work force segment defined by a relatively stable place in the division of labor. In such a circumstance, a politics of preemptive security, petty bickering, and marginal adjustment would again be likely to dominate the greater part of civic life. The logic of fixed collective interests, rigid definitions of collective identity, and arbitrarily narrow assumptions about historical possibility would again gain an independent force that, though ultimately false, was true relative to its circumstance. Programmatic specificity would turn out to be the enemy of depth and scope in political struggle.

The entire constitution, rather than any one of its features, is designed to prevent such an outcome. By relativizing, through all its provisions, the contrast between an original formative struggle over the basic order of society and the routine contests that go on within this order, the empowered democracy would counteract emergent schemes of rigidly defined interests, identities, and ideas of possibility. Insofar as the attempt to extend the vulnerability of structure to conflict and choice succeeds, the source of partisan division among people becomes to an ever greater degree the diversity of their opinions rather than the nature of their stations. This diversity will be to an ever lesser extent the mere surface expression of some underlying scheme of independently defined collective interests. Opinion will instead be nothing but each individual's partly corrigible interpretation of the meaning of his experience: of what he needs and wants and thinks possible for himself and for other people.

It is important to understand just how this condition compares with the conventional idealized picture of the social basis of the "liberal-bourgeois" democracies: the existence of crosscutting groups that never agglutinate into coherent, long-lasting, and potentially dangerous factions. For one thing, the reformed constitution wants to realize in fact the circumstance described by this picture and, indeed, to carry it to extremes rather than to reverse it in favor of a fantasizing, sentimental, archaic, tyrannical prospect of devotion to a shared vision of the common good. The point is not just that groupings on the basis of collective interest will be fuzzy and unstable but that they will constantly be exploded as soon as they begin to harden. For another thing, precisely because the destabilization of the collective positions gets pushed so far, the individual's commitment to a party of opinion cannot be based primarily upon the material advantages of groups defined by a stable niche within the social division of labor. It must depend, increasingly, upon a combination of immediate, tangible personal interests and personal vision or conversion. The citizen becomes more and more an individual rather than a puppet of collective categories of class, community, or gender, or a player in a historical drama he can neither understand nor escape.

Suppose all these changes in ideas and institutions were realized. Minimal stability might still seem threatened in another way. A society organized under a regime such as this would appear peculiarly subject to a virulent form of the invidious comparison that already characterizes the established democracies. Because mass politics denies people the experience of a more or less naturally assigned and stable place in the division of labor, everyone compares his advantages to those of everyone else. To this degree, almost everybody has to judge himself a relative loser. The reformed and empowered democracy seems to aggravate the situation by undermining still further the sense of natural social place and hierarchy. Thus, the citizenry of such a republic would be thrown into an endless anguish of envy and longing. This anguish might itself be a source of radical instability in the life of the republic. The citizens might always alternate between a paralyzing self-contempt, when they felt they had failed and deserved to fail, and a resentful hatred of the constitution, when they blamed their institutions for their discontent. Their minds might be totally absorbed in petty deals and comparisons of advantage. They would find themselves unable ever to accept any collective provision for the distribution of jobs, opportunities, and material benefits, unable to accept it, at least, as anything more than the transitory triumph of some factions over others.

The way the constitution avoids this instability is basically the same as the way it prevents the entrenchment of partisan divergence in everyday life from turning into the mere self-defensive jousting of groups defined by relatively fixed places in the division of labor. The social conditions that generate the dynamic of invidious comparison in the existing democracies must be radicalized. Three connected reforms fix the meaning of this radicalization.

First, all the institutional arrangements that sustain a high level of collective mobilization in normal social life prevent the dynamic of invidious comparison from focusing upon the differential relations among relatively fixed social places. They dull and disorient indignation. They help liberate the contest of opinions from obsessional concern with disparities of advantage.

Second, the disconnection of the forms of immunity against the state from means of control over other people – a disconnection carried out primarily by the regime of capital outlined in the following pages – presupposes and makes possible a major equalization in the material circumstances of life. It opens up ultimate issues of income differentials, job access, and educational opportunity to the centers of national decision. At the same time, however, it enables ground-level organizations to provide a series of variations on the minimal levels of equality mandated from above. This second series of institutional revisions does not necessarily moderate the experience of invidious comparison. Such a comparison may seize all the more fiercely upon the most modest material inequalities or upon the more intangible but ultimately more important differences of honor and achievement. But it helps separate out from this experience of invidious comparison the distinct element of class struggle over the organization of material life. By so doing, it draws attention to the more general problems of envy, equality, and the acceptance of differences. Here, as elsewhere, the aim is less to suppress fighting than to liberate it from the exclusive and bitter obsession with confined aspects of the structure of society.

Yet a third effect of these constitutional changes upon the dynamic of invidious comparison has to do with the power of the reformed constitution to increase the importance of aims to which that dynamic simply fails to apply. For the force of such comparative judgments depends in part upon the exclusivity of the struggle for relative advantage within an order taken as given. But the more the duel over relative place within the order gets mixed up with a conflict over the order itself, the more the dynamic of invidious comparison is likely to be overshadowed and transformed from within by other motivations. (A later section comes to terms with the relation between institutions and motivations.)

Consider, by way of example, the likely effect of such changes upon what was known in the North Atlantic democracies of the late twentieth century as the problem of incomes policies. To ensure economic stabilization through continued economic growth and the control of inflation, governments needed a minimum of broadly based acquiescence in the distribution of the benefits and burdens imposed by any coherent recovery program. From the pure standpoint of economic growth, it often seemed less important to decide which of several possible recovery paths would be taken than to settle on one path in particular and to remain on it for some time. One aspect of the ability to stay the course was the capacity to secure some basic agreement to the established distribution of income shares among segments of the work force and, more generally, of the entire population. Without such a minimal consensus, the better-organized or more protected segments of labor and business constantly tried to cash their organizational advantage into additional income. Everyone else attempted to catch up. Those who lost our (unorganized workers, independent professionals, proprietors, and rentiers) sought, one way or another, for compensatory help from government (through manipulation of the tax burden or of welfare rights). In such an atmosphere, enterprise investment strategies were skewed by the overwhelming concern to maintain a stable, core labor force. The downward rigidity of the wage structure helped keep markets from clearing and inflation from correcting itself. Group wage and income differentials were unstable both because groups remained unevenly organized and because their power to defend themselves in the marketplace did not coincide with their ability to pressure governments. This disparity perpetuated an inconclusive, paralyzing bickering among social ranks or work force segments with fixed niches in the division of labor.

The deeper historical situation that underlay these tendencies reflected the coexistence of two facts. The first was that the hierarchy of collective positions in the division of labor had been shaken to the point of undermining its appearance of naturalness and its claim to moral authority. The idea that customary wage differentials were fair just because they were customary coincided with an active sense of the arbitrariness of the entire scheme – of its vulnerability, in the large and in the small, to renewed collective conflict. No group had any reason to accept the place assigned to it within the job and income hierarchy if it could hope, by rebeginning the fight, to do better. At the same time – here entered the other defining fact – the hierarchy of collective places had been only partly disturbed. Though too weak and fragmented to guarantee acquiescence in a particular pattern of distribution, it was strong and unified enough to regenerate the system of collective stations people would fight over.

The reformed constitution acts upon this circumstance by altering the second of these two facts. The system of stations is more thoroughly fragmented. This fragmentation occurs less by a once-and-for-all redistributive fix than by the deepening and enlargement of the conditions that make the passage of collective contractualism into collective mobilization an ongoing rather than a sporadic and anomalous feature of social life. The result should be not to guarantee a spontaneous consensus over income shares but to strike at the basis of the resentful collectivism and unbroken, grubby impasse that the failure of income policies exemplified.

BREAKING THE RULES: THE FORMS OF DECENTRALIZATION

The program of empowered democracy requires that power be decentralized in a way that resolves a familiar dilemma. Central governmental power is the greatest lever for the transformation of social life. But to put all hope in central power holders and in the forms of accountability that may be imposed upon them is to sacrifice social experimentation to a single-minded plan. It is to focus civic engagement on a distant, barely visible point and to concentrate in the hands of the few the short-term authority taken away from the many. Empowered democracy would be an illusory, self-contradictory program if this dilemma were indeed intractable.

But the dilemma need be no more insoluble than any other tension between abstract institutional commitments. The tension is real enough. What is illusory is the fixity of the antagonism between the two aims. Both centralism and decentralization can assume an indefinitely wide range of institutional forms. Some forms aggravate the tension, whereas others mollify it.

The traditional program of decentralization relies upon the two basic principles of subsidiarity and functional specialization. The principle of subsidiarity requires that power to set rules and policies be transferred from a lower and closer authority to a higher and more distant one only when the former cannot adequately perform the particular responsibility in question. Of course, everything depends upon the standard of adequacy. Nevertheless, against the background of a view that sees established institutions as uncontroversial, the principle works to justify the maximum possible decentralization. It draws force from the commonsense notion that the authority or group closest to the individual ought to be the most involved in the resolution of his problems. And it merges into the liberal conviction that the ultimate residual authority is the individual himself. Functional specialization, the other plank in the traditional platform of decentralization, requires that the same task not be performed by two competing or overlapping authorities. It is the logic of entrepreneurial efficiency extended to the organization of the governmental hierarchy in both unitary and federal states.

The program of subsidiarity and functional specialization is what contemporary right-wing and centrist parties have in mind when they defend the decentralization of governmental power. But this style of decentralization merely disarms central governments before an untransformed society. It hands decision over to local elites. It respects entrenched privilege. For all these reasons, it aggravates the dilemma mentioned earlier.

An alternative road to decentralization should leave room for major swings in the emphasis different political parties may give to either greater centralized authority or more decentralized experiment. But it should also place these swings within a framework that upholds the broader commitments of empowered democracy. Such a framework must prefer the forms of centralization and decentralization that are less likely to immunize privilege against effective challenge. Imagine, then, a constitutional order that provides for two complementary methods of decentralization. The relative weight to be given each method depends upon the programs of the political parties in office. The system composed by the two strategies applies to both federal and unitary states, and it changes the relation of legal rules to individual conduct.

The first method is the conditional right to opt out of the norms established by higher authorities. Under this approach, the central representative agencies lay down rules governing a broad range of social situations. But a minimum of two individuals, or a larger group of people, can opt out of these rules and establish an alternative charter. The opting parties must satisfy two key conditions. First, when they set up the alternative structure they must stand in a relation of relative equality, whether as individuals or as enterprises. Second, the optional charter must not have the effect of casting one of the parties into a relation of enduring subjugation. The first condition is primary. The criteria that give it content can take current private-law doctrines of economic duress as their point of departure.

Such an approach may still rule out certain innovations simply because they conflict with the minimal standards of conventional morality. Nevertheless, the spirit of this form of decentralization is to permit a much broader range of deviation from public rules than we are now accustomed to: a range broad enough to include both economic and family matters.

The other method of decentralization, the qualified devolution of power, reallocates power among the levels of the governmental hierarchy rather than between government and people. The qualified devolution of power seeks to transfer power from higher to lower governmental authorities in just the way the traditional principle of subsidiarity recommends. But it differs from the traditional, right–center style of decentralization by attaching to every episode of devolution a corresponding guarantee.

The point of the guarantee is to prevent the devolution from helping to entrench old or emergent privileges. More specifically, the transfer of authority and resources must be prevented from serving to build up a local citadel of hierarchy, strengthened against both internal challenge from the disfavored and external challenge from the broader politics of the republic.

The form of the safeguard is proportional to the extent and duration of the transfer of authority. An example at the highest level of government is the special branch, described earlier, that would disrupt and reconstruct whatever organizations and practices condemned people to a circumstance of subjugation subversive of their role as citizens of the empowered democracy. Many other safeguards may apply to more local or transitory forms of devolution. Among these mechanisms, the empowered democracy may use ad hoc supervisory boards, special rights of challenge and appeal, and the practice of transferring authority or resources to overlapping and competing bodies.

THE ORGANIZATION OF ANTIGOVERNMENT: THE STRUCTURE OF VOLUNTARY ASSOCIATION

The program of empowered democracy for the reorganization of government has its counterpart in a scheme to facilitate the self-organization of society outside government. The point of this plan is twofold. The negative aim is to organize a parallel state or even an antistate. It is to form a set of institutions that, without canceling the opportunities for government-sponsored social experiments, diminishes the risk of despotic perversion: the danger that the governmental arrangements of the new-model democracy may be used to initiate a concentration of power unrestrained by independent social organizations.

An analogy and a distinction may help bring out what is at stake. According to a familiar theme in modern political thought, predemocratic ancien régimes enjoyed a complex, differentiated structure of privileges and power. This scheme of group prerogatives and disabilities limited both popular sovereignty and centralizing despotism. The destruction of the tissue of intermediate association in the name of democracy creates opportunities for a more thoroughgoing despotism than any practiced under the ancien régime. If the contemporary liberal democracies have stood fast against this danger – so the conservative–liberal argument goes – they have done so by incorporating more of a system of differentiated collective prerogatives and immunities than the more naive apologists of liberal democracy like to acknowledge.

The negative work of this part of the program of the empowered democracy can be redescribed, with the help of this skeptical argument, as the attempt to establish a style of restraining social counterweights. These brakes, however, no longer take the form dear to conservative–liberal propagandists and aristocratic–corporate politics. They cease to be anchored in institutions that help establish privileged strangleholds on society-making resources and that reproduce a scheme of fixed social roles and ranks.

The affirmative point is to turn the organizational instruments of nongovernmental association into better means of discovering, questioning, and revising each formative institutional and imaginative context of social life. The ways people have of coming together to pursue individual and group interests within a framework left both undisturbed and unremarked should draw closer to the ways they can challenge such frameworks. We should abandon the futile or self-defeating attempt to superimpose upon the factional pursuit of private interests an activity of selfless or enlightened devotion to the common good. Instead we can create practical institutional conditions that enlarge the scope and the sense of our prosaic, self-regarding efforts. The conflict over interests can always escalate into struggles over the preconceptions and arrangements that help define the interests. Let us institutionalize the escalation, depriving it of its supposed terrors. And let us do so for the sake of the forms of empowerment served by the whole program of institutional reconstruction outlined here.

Consider the issue of union organization as a setting in which to formulate ideas that can later be generalized. The legal setting of union organization in the advanced Western democracies follows, more or less resolutely, a contractarian approach. This approach seeks to reestablish in the employment relation the minimal degree of freedom from economic duress required to make of labor contracts between employers and employees something more than a cover for outright subjugation. The remedy against such duress is to ensure an opportunity for collective organization and collective bargaining. This opportunity enables workers to counterbalance the overweening pressure employers might be able to exercise if they could deal with the workers on an individual basis. The law must make an exception to contractual forms the better to uphold the essentials of contract. What counts is not that most workers in fact unionize and avail themselves of collective bargaining – individual labor bargains may continue to preponderate – but that workers can unionize if they find themselves under contract-subverting duress.

Two master principles work out this idea. A principle of freedom from government requires that unions remain under only the minimal form of public control inherent in the establishment, elaboration, and application of the labor laws. A principle of structural pluralism commands that the law impose no unitary scheme of union classification: no system for determining which unions are to represent which workers or how the labor force is to be divided up for the purpose of union representation. Certain dominant principles of classification may emerge. But the union structure looks like a collection of fragmentary pieces of different puzzles, with the fragments forming no single, coherent picture.

Only in a few countries, and often due to fascist influence, do we find elements of a corporatist model of labor relations. Under this contrasting approach, unions represent an extended part of the structure of government. By their power to establish and tutor labor organizations central governments gain a chance to practice controlled mobilization. Governmental control replaces autonomy from the state. At the same time, the corporatist labor regime follows a principle of unitary classification. This principle affirms that the entire work force should be divided up into a single, coherent classificatory scheme: all the fragments should in fact be pieces of the same puzzle.

Any democrat must oppose the governmental-control aspect of the corporatist model. But the principle of pluralistic classification, characteristic of the contractarian approach, has defects of its own. It forces union organizers and militants to expend much of their efforts in the attempt to unionize. It absorbs them in the peculiarly inconclusive factional struggles a pluralistic union system encourages. The struggles remain indecisive because the contenders need not fight for place and join issue within a single structure. They can simply inhabit different, hostile but noncommunicating union hierarchies. Moreover, both the dispersive pluralism of the contract regime and its treatment of collective organization as a mere surrogate and safeguard of private bargaining encourage a sharp contrast between worker–employer and worker–government relations. The result is to discourage workers from treating workplace disputes and conflicts in national politics as parts of the same continuum.

No wonder the quasi-contractual organization of labor seems to favor a purely economistic style of militancy, relatively unconcerned with the organization of the work force, even less interested in the larger institutional structure of the economy and the polity. When the core economic basis of the unions in the mass-production industries declines, the union movement formed under the contract model comes to be perceived, and to perceive itself, as just one more interest group. It ceases to speak as the voice of all working people and as the bearer of a message for the whole society.

By contrast, the corporatist approach may better serve the extremes of repression and mobilization. When administered by a strong, authoritarian government, it represents – just as its authors intended – a formidable tool of industrial discipline. But against the background of governmental weakness or openness, its unitary organization facilitates an institutionally committed militancy. The work force is already unionized and unionized in a single framework. This structure need not be created from scratch. It can be taken over by those who see the conflict over interest-defining structures as the continuation of fights over structure-defining interests. Their work is made easier by an institutional and imaginative tradition that dramatizes rather than conceals the links between the domains of government–worker and worker–employer relations.

Why not then join together, in the interest of empowered democracy, the contractarian principle of autonomy from governmental control and the corporatist principle of unitary classification? Different currents of opinion – linking the organized political parties to the distinctive problems of the workplace – would contend for place in this unified structure of labor organization, just as the political parties themselves compete for position in the unified structure of government. And the workers in the labor movement as a whole or in particular job categories may even initiate changes in the classification scheme, subject to veto by the national legislature.

The familiar role of unions will change as the style of industrial organization shifts. It would change all the more under the economic program of empowered democracy, outlined later in this chapter. But a role for the organization and representation of people on the basis of job categories will remain long after workers cease to confront managers imposed upon them by an alien and unaccountable authority.

The same combination of autonomy and unity that applies to unions can also extend to territorial organization. A unitary system of neighborhood associations may also be established, at least at the local level, as a stimulus to popular engagement in local government and as an independent control upon local authorities.

On the solid ground of this organization of people in the places where they work and live, a host of other forms of association may flourish, pluralistic and fragmentary in structure as well as free from governmental control. Legal opportunities, public resources, and free access to the means of communication support these additional groupings. But such open-ended associational experiments complement rather than replace an associative structure established by law and made, by law, independent from government. This antistate helps keep the state humble and the people proud, inquisitive, and restless.

THE ORGANIZATION OF THE ECONOMY: THE CURRENT MARKET REGIME AND ITS COSTS

A second domain for reconstruction is the institutional framework of economic life. The major theme of this part of the program is the attempt to imagine an alternative institutional definition of the market just as the major theme of earlier parts of the program lies in the proposal of an alternative institutional setting for democracy. This part of the institutional scheme anticipates the outline of a theory of the enabling conditions of material progress that extends the central social theory of this book into an area of life that may seem peculiarly resistant to its intentions.

In any society the organization of government and of the economy depend upon each other. But the character of the institutions, and of the forms of thought that explain and justify them, often make the connection both indirect and obscure. In the constitution outlined here, the link becomes, instead, direct and transparent. This shift represents far more than an accidental and minor feature of the institutional proposal; it exemplifies a general truth about society, a truth to which the social theory underlying the proposal attaches great importance.

Collective mobilization is the exemplary form of the collective creation of society, of society making conceived as an ongoing and deliberate event, intentionally undertaken by particular people, rather than as a definitive foundational act or a permanent, unknowing drift. A constitutional order that tries to multiply the occasions for collective mobilization gives immediate practical effect to the hidden truth that any given institutional and imaginative order both arises out of practical or visionary fighting and depends upon its partial and provisional containment. The segments of social life that appear to operate by some distinct logic of their own do so only on sufferance from a peace whose continuation they can never themselves guarantee. To the extent the peace gets broken, it becomes evident that what seemed to be distinct spheres of social life governed by laws of their own are in fact only temporary versions of some larger, inchoate realm of practical or passionate association whose unity is more important than its temporary internal differentiations. A constitution that perpetuates mobilization in the moment of normalcy brings this unity out; the distinctive self-operating laws of different spheres of social life begin to lose their appearance of even relative autonomy. Contemporary cosmologists have pointed out that a universe approaching its higher-energy moment of maximum collapse and density would exhibit directly the symmetries and connections that, in the cooler stages of its history, had to be discovered scientifically and represented mathematically. The constitution of the empowered democracy produces in the social world the effect of that moment of greatest transparency.

This section prepares the description of an alternative institutional framework for economic life through a criticism of existing economic arrangements. The criticism emphasizes the unity of the explanatory and normative ideas that can help guide a constructive effort. The immediate target of the criticism is the private-rights complex of the advanced Western countries, especially insofar as it influences the organization of production and exchange.

The private-rights system establishes a practical and imaginative equation between the abstract idea of a market and a historically unique group of institutional arrangements. The abstract concept of a market means no more than the existence of a large number of economic agents able to bargain on their own initiative and for their own account. The historically specific arrangements with which this abstract market idea gets improperly identified have as their core the consolidated property right: a more or less absolute entitlement to a divisible portion of social capital – more or less absolute both in its discretionary use and in the chain of voluntary transfers by successive property owners. Once this initial identification has been established, the market economy is often further assumed to imply a particular style of industrial organization: the style that puts standardized mass production in the mainstream of industry and flexible production in its vanguard. Indeed, if we accept the identification of the market with the system of relatively decentralized consolidated property, we also have some reason to further assume that an industrialized market economy will favor this method of industrial organization. For the system of consolidated property does contribute to the conditions that allow mass-production industries to arrange markets and to counteract what might otherwise be instabilities in the product, labor, and financial markets. Rigid, highly capitalized enterprises could not hope to survive such oscillations.

It may seem surprising that the consolidated property system and the mass-production style of industrial organization also characterize the major contemporary alternatives to the economic systems of the advanced Western countries. Yet consolidated property and mass production are also at home in the socialist-bureaucratic and workers' ownership models whose distinctive business cycles the appendix to Chapter 2 analyzes more fully. In one case, the consolidated property rights are transferred to a central government; in the other case, to the workers who have secure jobs within a given enterprise when the transfer takes place. Though the immediate target of my critical arguments is the economic regime of the advanced Western countries, many of these arguments carry over, with only slight adjustments, to the main rival economic systems. The present section suggests this carry-over and the more detailed discussion of the appendix to Chapter 2 develops the thesis. To deny that the available alternatives are the necessary options among which we must choose, to show what these alternatives have in common, and to suggest how this common element might be replaced all form part of the view.

Consider first a series of criticisms of the established forms of democracies and markets. These criticisms fall into two main categories, anticipated by the earlier discussion of reform cycles. Some are arguments about the effect of established economic arrangements upon freedom. Others address the influence of existing or alternative institutional arrangements upon economic efficiency and growth. I do not assume that what contributes to material progress always enhances freedom. There is nevertheless an element of truth in the superstitious belief that the two go together. Liberation from poverty and drudgery is one of the chief forms of empowerment. Moreover, it depends as much as the other forms on a partial lifting of the constraints an entrenched plan of social division and hierarchy imposes upon our collective experiments in the organization of exchange and production.

Our current version of market institutions jeopardizes freedom on both a large and a small scale. On a large scale it leaves a restricted number of people with a disproportionate influence over the basic flows of investment decisions. It thereby withdraws the basic terms of collective prosperity from effective democratic choice and control. As a result, the plans of reform governments are easily frustrated in precisely those areas that so often matter most to the reformers. Any attempt to assert governmental control over the main line of economic accumulation seems both to undermine the effective decentralization of economic decisions and to enhance the authority of bureaucratic officials. The difficulty of imagining an alternative governmental structure both more capable and more democratic makes all the more fearsome such a strengthening of central authority.

At the same time the current market form undermines freedom

on a small scale. It does so, diffusely, by generating and permitting inequalities of wealth that reduce some people to effective economic dependence upon others – those who occupy the supervisory positions. It does so, more precisely, by helping to prop up a style of industrial organization that thrives on the relatively rigid contrast of task definers and task executors.

The earlier stages of the programmatic argument suggest yet another sense in which our present mode of economic organization limits freedom. The empowered democracy outlined in earlier parts of this program represents a requirement of freedom. Yet such a democracy cannot flourish if the everyday world of work and exchange is organized in ways that not only differ from the principles of democratic government but limit their scope, undermine their influence, and disrupt their workings. If markets cannot be given a different institutional form, if the only practical alternatives to the established economic regimes are the socialist-bureaucratic and the worker-ownership models, the program of empowered democracy is doomed from the start, and with it our hope of extending the meaning of freedom.

Take now a series of arguments about the constraints the established market system imposes upon economic progress – that is upon the ability to sustain repeated breakthroughs in productive capacity and productivity. (Remember that these same criticisms apply in a different sense, but with redoubled force, to the major acknowledged alternatives.) After enumerating these critical arguments, I make explicit the basic view of the enabling conditions of economic progress that underlies them.

The first criticism focuses upon the absolute degree of economic decentralization. Within the established regime of capital, economies of scale seem to require almost by definition the consolidation of property rights over large amounts of capital in a single decisional center, even if – as in many large stock corporations – shares of ownership are widely distributed. A centralized management acting in the name of fragmentary shareholders supervises the large-scale pooling of manpower and capital resources. These managers can then act almost as if they held their power by the accumulation of personal wealth. An apparent fragmentation of the consolidated property system may thus end up preserving the essential features of this system. The most important of these traits is precisely the legally protected faculty to organize production and exchange in the name of a more or less absolute claim to a divisible portion of social capital.

Without an extreme dispersion of business power, the breakup of trade unions in turn appears intolerable, at least in the absence of an alternative way of asserting the power of the labor force to resist business authority. But the alternative devices that respect the principle of consolidated property while changing its locus – greater central governmental control over economic accumulation or outright workers' ownership of enterprises – seem to aggravate the threat to efficiency and freedom, or both. Conversely, the unacceptability of breaking up the trade unions provides an additional excuse to accept as inevitable the current degree of economic concentration. Attempts to encourage economic decentralization can therefore be derided by tough-minded publicists as sentimental reveries.

A second economic criticism addresses the plasticity of the current market economy rather than the absolute degree of decentralization it permits. Plasticity is the generalized form of economic rationality: the ease of recombining the components of the institutional context of production and exchange as well as of combining factors of production within a given context. The point of plasticity, broadly speaking, is to increase the opportunity for experiment and innovation in social life. The move toward more plastic economic arrangements loosens the predetermination of exchange and production relations by rules and regularities that remain unavailable for revision in the light of emergent practical opportunities.

The economic value of this loosening may seem uncontroversial when the constraints to be weakened are those of a social order that arranges production and exchange according to noneconomic standards and subordinates the logic of restless practical reason to respect for entrenched social divisions and hierarchies. But the case for plasticity may seem a great deal less persuasive when the constraints to be loosened are universal rules that seem to cast everyone in the same position of formal equality. For, it may be objected, the interest in experimentation must stop at the limit dictated by the even more fundamental need for a stable and generally understood framework for practical dealings. To this objection there are two answers. One response, implicit in a general thesis of the social theory developed in this book, is that the only assurance that fixed arrangements will not generate new systems of entrenched social division and hierarchy is precisely that they be open to challenge and revision at all levels of activity. The other answer, specific to the present economic arguments, is that alternative economic regimes and indeed alternative market systems, though equally stable, may differ in the extent to which they permit variation in the social forms of exchange and production. Relative openness to organizational innovation, like relative conduciveness to economic decentralization, is a feature of discrete institutional systems, not a characteristic of economies or markets in the abstract. The idea that the functioning of a competitive price will automatically ensure that over time the most efficient innovations prevail has been traditionally criticized for not taking account of market failure. But this criticism misses the more fundamental point that a competitive price system is institutionally indeterminate. Precisely because of its indeterminacy, no automatic identification exists between allocative efficiency relative to a particular price system and the encouragement of continued breakthroughs in productivity and productive output – all facts that would be too trivial to mention were not their implications almost universally disregarded.

A third economic objection to the present market system, seen in its broader governmental and social setting, has to do with the constraints it imposes upon a growth-oriented macroeconomic policy. A strategy for economic growth may be realized through any number of alternative patterns of distribution: differential wage, tax, or subsidy levels. It is vital, however, that one such distribution be made to stick, at least to the extent necessary to avoid an inconclusive conflict over the proper distribution. For even when such conflict fails to cause major disruption, it prevents governmental policy from being decisively marshaled in favor of any given strategy of economic growth.

In the rich North Atlantic democracies we find two correlations of forces in two relatively distinct domains. In the market arena, big business and organized labor, both entrenched in the rigid, mass-production sector of industry, exercise a disproportionate influence over the organization of markets and production. Through investment and disinvestment policies, through the disruption of the core productive system, and through their influence upon the means of mass communication or the financing of politics, they can strike back against any distributive deal that fails to respect their position of strength. On the other hand, the groups relatively weak in the economic arena – petty proprietors, independent professionals, and the unorganized underclass – will seek to overturn through the vote, through social agitation, and even through appeals to conscience and prudence the distributive bargains that do them in. No distributive bargain can respect both correlations of forces and none can preserve itself against the destabilizing effect of the powers it devalues.

To be sure, this inconclusiveness might be avoided by many possible institutional changes: if, for example, the government had dictatorial powers ("authoritarian capitalism"), thereby enabling it to impose a solution, or if unionization extended to the entire labor force, thereby bringing the two correlations closer, except insofar as big business retained a broad measure of independent decisional authority. But each institutional change would produce more far reaching and disturbing consequences for society. Thus, if an authoritarian, nonrevolutionary state is not the relatively passive instrument of a particular class, it must reach a modus vivendi with different classes. It will find itself continually pulled among conflicting claims: the desire to pander to established elites, the effort to win wider popular support, and the attempt to assert an independent power interest, justified in turn by the strengthening of the nation-state. The competing claims may maintain the effect of deadlock while drastically changing its causes and content. On the other hand, the general unionization of the labor force and the overcoming of the distinction between the working class and the underclass would, at a minimum, put pressure on the established style of industrial organization by denying the rigid, mass-production industries one of their instruments of defense against oscillations in demand: sub-contracting work or hiring temporary workers. To the extent the unionization was militant and led the unions to define themselves as the people rather than as an interest group, the resulting mass mo-bilization would be far more consequential. For either it would be suppressed or it would lead to yet more drastic changes in the basic institutions and enacted beliefs of society.

Consider now the general view of the enabling conditions of eco-nomic progress that underlies such criticisms. The statement of this view suggests the broader range of ideas within which the critical arguments would have a secure place. It reveals the basic unity of those arguments. It provides a perspective from which to criticize the major available alternatives to economic regimes of the contem-porary Western democracies. It supplies a basis on which to imagine the reconciliation between enlarged political freedom and accelerated economic growth.

Economic progress occurs through the acceleration and deliber-ateness of leaps in productivity and productive output. To this end, the relations among people at work must become as much as possible an embodiment of practical reason: they must give expression to the free interplay between problem definitions and problem solving. In this interplay, new definitions suggest new solutions; and new so-lutions, new problems. Presuppositions – such as the rules governing inference and the idea of what counts as a solution or as the instrument of a solution – are gradually dragged into the interplay. As a result, the boundary becomes increasingly fluid between what is treated as a problem and what is accepted as a presupposition. In the organi-zation of production and exchange these presuppositions may be the limited stock of associative and technical ideas that people bring to economic activity, the practices that compose the institutional set-ting of production and exchange, or the social divisions and hier-archies generated by an entrenched formative context of social life, predetermining how people can deal with one another at work or in trade. The last point is especially important: economic relations cannot become practical reason on the march so long as they remain subject to a closed logic of the social stations that are possible and the activities that occupants of these stations may undertake.

How does this view of a basic condition of economic progress relate to the familiar idea that economic growth requires that particular groups combine innovative capability with access to capital? So long as we continue to accept the naive view of the market as possessed of an inherent institutional structure, we can count on the price system to channel capital automatically to those best able to use it. But once we abandon the idea of inherent institutional structure of the market, the identification of the most productive users becomes, like everything else about an economy, a matter of experimental fact. The institutions and the people responsible for setting the ultimate framework of economic life must compare the results of different institutional arrangements. Such a comparison becomes more valuable as the experiments compared become more numerous; and they become more numerous as the framework itself becomes more flexible, enabling economic agents to renew and recombine the arrangements making up the institutional context of production and exchange. The transformation of economic life into an embodiment of practical reason describes both the expected outcome of this ongoing experiment and the means for carrying it out.

Such a transformation of economic organization may take two main directions. One direction is coercive. A commanding will, ordinarily ensconced in the central government, repeatedly shatters the constraints that old or reemergent routines and privileges impose upon the dynamic of problem solving and the renewal of institutional arrangements. In particular, it disrupts social divisions and hierarchies and the institutional arrangements that give life to them, at least to the extent necessary to prevent these institutionalized roles and ranks from closing down the range of social life left open to economic experimentation. The basic problem with the coercive approach is the tendency of the institutional center that exercises this directing function to subordinate the practice of the problem-solving dynamic to the power interests of those who hold this power or serve as the agents of the powerholders farther down the command ladder. The crucial practical difference among institutional versions of the coercive approach is, therefore, the relative facility with which they lend themselves to such abuse.

The alternative direction is consensual. The economic order takes the form of a decentralized framework for interaction by parties able to bargain on their own initiative and for their own account. The characteristic problem of such market solutions is their tendency to define economic positions or the claims upon capital and labor that make them possible, as vested rights. Interest in the perpetuation of these claims, sanctioned by law and keyed into current styles of economic organization, takes precedence over the seizure of emergent productive opportunities, and the resulting price system confirms a rationality that remains only loosely connected with its productive economic uses. Market systems differ in the extent to which they avoid this difficulty and encourage both absolute decentralization and institutional plasticity., These decisive differences are rooted in the institutional arrangements defining the context of production and exchange, including the detailed texture of contract and property law. The crucial point is the legal-institutional device for decentralizing claims of access to capital. The belief that this device must always amount to a variation on the consolidated, relatively absolute property right represents a groundless prejudice, but one from which even the most subtle forms of political economy have only partly freed themselves.

Neither the coercive nor the consensual realization of the problem-solving dynamic can ever prevail to the complete exclusion of the alternative. Even the most coercive system must count on voluntary collaboration, on pain of resorting to a runaway governmental terrorism that both disrupts the production system and overtaxes the capabilities of the state. Every working collaboration in turn implies settled expectations and partial reciprocities that imply a significant measure of de facto consensual decentralization. Conversely, every consensual market system requires the degree of centralized direction needed to establish basic guidelines and other rules governing the power to vary those fundamental norms of exchange.

From the pitiless standpoint of developing practical capabilities to produce or to destroy, the problem is not to choose between coercion and consensus. It is rather to invent the consensual or coercive solutions that go farther than do existing economic regimes toward freeing economic initiative from the constraints of administrative or proprietary privilege. Many nineteenth-century utilitarians and liberals thought they had solved this problem once and for all by discovering the pure system of market coordination, just as they also claimed to have expounded the built-in institutional structure of a democracy. But they were mistaken, having drastically understated the ambiguity of the institutional arrangements that might both realize and redefine market economies and democratic governments.

Notice also that although the coercive and consensual realizations of problem solving and plasticity may be equally promising or troublesome when viewed in the narrowest practical terms, an important difference between them emerges as soon as they are placed in a broader setting. The consensual emphasis in economic life fits with the broader program of an empowered democracy, whereas the coercive one does not. The objection to be made against current market systems from this wider perspective is the same one they deserve on narrower economic grounds: their failure to move far enough along the consensual path and to heighten the plasticity of economic life.

This sketch of a general approach to the enabling conditions of material progress suggests why the available alternatives to the mixed economies of the rich North Atlantic countries of the present day are inadequate, both as machines for accelerated economic growth and as integral parts of an empowered democracy. Each alternative system establishes a balance or an oscillation between the prerogatives of those who exercise a directing will and the vested rights of those who represent the lowest significant rung of effective decentralization. In the Soviet-type model, the prerogatives of the central rulers and bureaucrats are balanced against the settled positions of the managers in charge of economic enterprises. In the Yugoslav "worker-control" model, they are balanced against the vested rights of the workers who occupy an entrenched position within an enterprise. (Even this distinction loses its force to the extent that effective job security becomes an accepted constraint within the Soviet model.) The reform cycles characterizing each system show the outer limits within which both the most coercive and the most consensual moments of these economic systems remain, limits that prevent either the coercive or the consensual approaches from achieving a form more congenial to the ceaseless renewal and recombination required by accelerated economic progress.

An alternative economic order must minimize the constraints current economic systems impose upon the free interplay of problem definition and problem solving. It must do so both to make a practical success out of the experiment in a more empowered democracy and to create a form of economic life that extends and sustains the social ideal underlying the whole constitution. The scheme of economic life must emphasize the consensual interpretation of organizational experimentation over the coercive one. This emphasis requires an attempt to imagine a mechanism of economic decentralization more radical in its bias toward decentralization and plasticity than the classical property right. Nor should we imagine that transferring economic sovereignty to a central state apparatus or to the enterprise work force represents the sole alternative to the familiar version of a market system. But what then might a better market structure be like? And how would it connect with the exercise of effective democratic conflict and control over social resources?

Before considering an answer to these questions, reflect on two clues for construction implied by the preceding critical arguments.

The first hint has to do with the shape of the property right. The

economic systems discussed in the preceding pages all maintain consolidated property: they keep together the many heterogeneous powers that compose this right, and they assign all these powers to the
same rightholder. The systems differ solely in the way they define
the identity of this major rightholder: the freely accumulating individual and the beneficiaries of his inheritance, the state and its delegates and favorites, or the work force of each enterprise. The consolidated property entitlement serves as the most striking instrument of the privileged control over capital. The reason why it does
so is not self-evident: it appears, after all, to be compatible with
substantial equality. Nevertheless, the attempt to combine substantial
equality with the consolidated property right turns out to be both
paradoxical and impractical. It is paradoxical because it can be
achieved only through some independent institutional mechanism
that eviscerates the significance of the consolidated property right by
drastically limiting its exercise and its accumulation by the rightholders. It is impractical because the immediate effect of such limitations is to undermine the market principle in the legitimate abstract
sense of economic decentralization and to impede the mobility of
capital. The severance of the link between politics as organized group
conflict and politics as privilege or stalemate seems to require a systematic breaking up of the property right.

The other clue in the criticism of existing economic systems refers
to the relation between the regime of capital and the organization of
government. The critical discussion suggests that the idea of a connection between the market and freedom holds good, although not
in the sense in which it has been ordinarily understood. We find the
legal tools of privileged hold over capital reciprocally linked, through
a series of mediating institutions and preconceptions, to the forms
of privileged access to state power. The trouble comes from mistaking democracy and the market with some marginally adjusted
version of the institutional arrangements already established in the
advanced Western countries. I have shown how, in the Soviet-style
economies, even the most technical microeconomic constraints on
the operation of a market mechanism related, directly or indirectly,
to the failure to bring the control of state power into question. (See
the appendix to Chapter 2.) Thus, to take one of the more oblique
examples, you could not understand the force of the nearly absolute
job security constraint without taking into account the implications
of the attempt to uphold the pretense of a workers' state in a society
where workers had few powers. Such powers as they might have –
like the claim to job security (by no means acknowledged in all
communist economies) – depended upon their ability to play on the
unintended consequences of existing institutional arrangements (such
as the tightness of the labor market, under conditions of severe wage

control, a situation giving the workers shop-floor power while also helping establish job security). In the Western-style economies, the analogous connections were more subtle. The microeconomic constraints in markets connected to macroeconomic constraints that included the need of elected governments to accommodate to the relatively small groups controlling the major flows of investment decisions. Conversely, the stability of the established institutional arrangements, including the arrangements that defined markets, depended upon a long-lasting social demobilization that had in turn been encouraged – and at one time deliberately sought – by the constitutional organization of government.

THE ORGANIZATION OF THE ECONOMY: THE ROTATING CAPITAL FUND AND ITS DEMOCRATIC CONTROL

The Core Conception

A regime capable of working out the implications of the clues described in the preceding section brings the structure and direction of economic life into the domain of central conflicts over society's alternative futures, a domain in which no segment of society and no cadre of experts can easily gain the upper hand. Such a regime constantly resists and reverses the subjection of capital to the more or less permanent and unrestricted dominion of particular rightholders. It pushes the economy farther into becoming a perpetual innovation machine and increases the freedom of economic relations from predetermination by a challenge-resistant scheme of social life.

The key idea of the institutional proposal is the breakup of control over capital into several tiers of capital takers and capital givers. The ultimate capital giver is a social capital fund controlled by the decisional center of the empowered democracy: the party in office and the supporting representative assemblies. The ultimate capital takers are teams of workers, technicians, and entrepreneurs, who make temporary and conditional claims upon divisible portions of this social capital fund. The central capital fund does not lend money out directly to the primary capital users. Instead, it allocates resources to a variety of semi-independent investment funds. Each investment fund specializes in a sector of the economy and in a type of investment. The central democratic institutions exercise their ultimate control over the forms and rates of economic accumulation and income distribution by establishing these funds or by closing them out, by assigning them new infusions of capital or by taking capital away from them, by charging them interest (whose payment represents the major source of governmental finance), and, most importantly, by setting the outer limits of variation in the terms on which the competing investment funds may allocate capital to the ultimate capital takers. The investment funds may take resources away from one another, thus forming in effect a competitive capital market, whose operations are also overseen by the central representative bodies of the democracy. The investment funds in turn allocate resources to the primary capital takers – teams of entrepreneurs, technicians, and workers – under two different regimes. The funds set the terms on which financial and technological resources may be obtained. The capital users pay an interest charge to their investment fund just as the latter pays a charge to the central social fund. Within the limits laid down by both the central governmental bodies and the competing investment funds, these direct capital takers buy and sell. Within those limits they, too, may bid resources away from one another. They profit from successful enterprise and suffer from business failure. But they never acquire permanent individual or group rights to the capital they receive. Nor does success entitle them to expand continuously, to buy out other enterprises, or to introduce into their own business a special category of relatively disadvantaged and voiceless workers. Success merely increases their income.

Thus the proposed regime provides for three tiers of capital givers and capital takers, the second tier being both a taker and a giver. The precise balance of economic power among these levels represents a major topic of political conflict under the empowered democracy. The discussion of the following pages strikes a particular balance only in order to clothe the central intuitive idea in more tangible dress.

The basic legal principle of this alternative economic order is the disintegration of property: its breakup into distinct powers, vested in different agents. To be sure, much in the design of this alternative may already be recognized in germ in the interplay between consolidated property and relatively haphazard governmental regulation as well as in the subtleties of contemporary capital markets. You can hardly expect otherwise from a programmatic argument that draws on internal criticism, addresses a particular historical circumstance, and eschews a millennarian utopianism while nevertheless claiming to express a visionary impulse. Yet the proposed regime offers an institutional framework within which the principle of deliberate social control over the forms and consequences of economic accumulation can be more fully reconciled with decentralized economic decision making than it can be within a market order using consolidated property as its device of decentralization and occasional administrative regulation as its means of control. The economic order of the empowered democracy is both more a socially responsible economy and more a market economy than the system it is meant to replace; the impression of paradox results from a failure to grasp the effect of institutional variation upon the tensions between general principles. It is more of a socially responsible economy because the means for collective review of the arrangements and results of economic life are deeply integrated into the institutional order rather than dependent upon a relatively haphazard pattern of governmental intervention. It is more of a market economy because it promises to increase both the absolute degree of economic decentralization and the revisability of the organizational settings of production and exchange, although, admittedly, it does so at the cost of circumscribing both the duration and the absoluteness of individual capital claims. Consider now, in greater detail, each of the three major tiers of capital givers and takers.

The Central Capital Fund

The first tier, the social investment fund, falls under the control of the central executive and representative bodies of the empowered democracy. The central social fund establishes the competing investment funds, which form the second tier of the system. It occasionally opens new funds or closes old ones and shifts resources from some to others. But its single most important task is to draw the limits of variation within which the competing investment funds must operate. Some limits are institutional; others, parametric. The institutional decisions set boundaries to the permissible organizational forms of production and exchange. The parametric decisions influence the employment and cost of capital, most notably through the interest charged for its use. Rules and policies that restrict either wage and authority disparities or the right of enterprise personnel to distribute business gains as current income share institutional and parametric characteristics.

Among the key parametric or institutional decisions to be made by the fund are: the basic underlying rate of interest to be charged to all specialized investment funds; the choice between forced reassignments of capital and variable rates of interest as alternative ways to control the relative size of the specialized funds and the relations among gross sectors of the economy; the alternative regimes or terms under which the second-tier, specialized funds may give out capital; the minimal restraints upon accumulation, reinvestment, investment in other enterprises, distribution of profits as income, preference for capital-intensive technology, and exclusion of outside workers that must be respected either in the economy as a whole or by particular funds and sectors; the extent to which the specialized funds may allow the enterprises they deal with to insulate managerial and technical prerogatives from the collective decisions of its members and thereby establish a hierarchy of privilege among segments of its labor force; and the outer limits to wage (or other income) inequality that must be respected by enterprises in the economy as a whole or in particular sectors.

Some decisions may take the form of economywide rules and policies, others may be written into the charters of particular investment funds, and still others may be left entirely open to the discretion of these funds or of the enterprises and teams that receive capital from them. The correct balance among these options, as more generally the relative power of the three tiers of capital givers and capital takers, constitutes a major concern of governmental party-politics under the empowered democracy. The evisceration of the second and third tiers of the system, through the making of increasingly detailed and intrusive decisions, would destroy the distinctive character of this economic regime. The disintegration of property would give way to the transfer of property to the central government. But the abdication of decisional responsibility by the central democratic institutions, and its resulting concentration in the specialized funds and the primary capital takers, would be equally subversive of the regime. For one thing, the democracy would lack effective means to assert ultimate collective control over the two aspects of economic life that are crucial to the character of a society: first, the direction and rate of economic growth, and the consequent balancing of economic and noneconomic goals and of the claims of different generations; and, second, the relations of equality and inequality, of joint responsibility and mutual distancing, allowed to exist in the organization of production and exchange as well as in the distribution of their benefits. For another thing, the division of property rights between the specialized investment funds and the primary capital takers would not long survive if these two levels of the regime were left on their own. A new system of consolidated property rights, in the service of a new plan of entrenched social division and hierarchy, would emerge from an economy reorganized by the more successful funds or enterprises.

The Investment Funds: Capital Auctioning and Capital Rationing

The second tier of the capital regime consists of investment funds established by the national government or the social fund through which government sets economic policy. The investment funds hold capital from the social fund and give it out to the primary capital takers, who represent the third tier of the economic system. Without this intermediate level – at once capital taker and capital giver – the central democratic entities would be forever tempted to exercise a roving, ad hoc economic clientalism, and the prospects for extreme decentralization and organizational diversity would greatly diminish. The investment funds, chartered by the central government, specialize in a sector of the economy or a type of investment (short-term or long-term, low-risk or high-risk, oriented to small ventures or large ventures). But these specialties are not meant to peg the funds at fixed positions in the economic order. Their areas of operation intersect; many funds may compete within the same sectoral or functional area. In fact, within the limits established by the top tier of the system, they may even bid away one another's assets on an investment-fund capital market placed under the control of the central social fund.

The special funds are semi-independent bodies, much like contemporary central banks or even philanthropic foundations in contemporary Western societies, with their technical personnel chosen by a combination of appointment from above and election from the sectors in which they operate. The method of appointment should vary, as later discussion suggests, with the specific aims of each fund and the nature of the system by which it allocates capital. The definition of this system is by far the most important issue to be faced in designing the second tier of the capital order.

In their capital-allotment policies the funds operate with a mixture of general rules and discretionary judgments. The danger that a promising entrepreneur may be turned away is diminished by the existence of numerous overlapping and competing funds. And if this opportunity seems insufficient remember that even under the regime of consolidated property an entrepreneur must either already be rich or succeed in convincing others to give him money.

Each fund conducts its activities under one of two regimes: capital auction and capital rationing or rotation. The choice between them, set by the fund charter, has far-reaching consequences for the role of the fund in the economy and for the structure of its dealings with other funds and with the primary capital takers. The interaction between the two regimes influences the whole character of the economic order of an empowered democracy.

The key feature of the capital-auction system is that, within certain gross limits, the primary capital takers can buy one another's resources by offering to pay the capital-auctioning fund more for the employment of these resources than their current users. If the value of the resources has been run up, part of this added value may be paid to the current users as a reward, though it may then be subject to capital, income, and consumption taxes designed to restrain the resulting economic inequality. (Notice that the tax system, which becomes subsidiary to state-charged interest as a source of governmental finance under empowered democracy, must reappear as a constraint on inequality in the capital-auctioning area of the economy.) To guard against the continued depletion of assets, on the other hand, the capital-auctioning fund must use a blend of screening, guarantees, penalties, limits on the distribution of profits, and provisions for repossession.

The capital-rationing or rotation system, by contrast to the capital-auction system, largely avoids the buying-out of some capital takers by others. Instead, it emphasizes the conditional and temporal limits to the capital taker's employment of the resources placed at his disposal. It demands a much heavier use of parametric constraints than can be reconciled with the capital-auction regime: the setting of standards about the minimal levels of permissible reinvestment and maximum levels of allowable profit distribution. The capital-rationing fund must be ready to take the initiative in pooling financial and capital resources, in bringing teams of worker-technicians and entrepreneurs together for large-scale, durable enterprises, in redistributing capital from time to time to new teams, and in designing incentives and disincentives.

As under the capital-auction system, successful enterprises cannot be allowed to build industrial or financial empires. Once certain limits of personal enrichment and enterprise investment are reached, the additional capital goes back to the original capital fund for reassignment. But much more clearly than under the capital-auction system, continuing enterprise decline must be met by fund intervention, followed by the recovery and reassignment of the residual capital and the reentry of a retrained enterprise work force into the labor market, a blow softened though not annulled by the welfare rights described later in this chapter.

The advantage of the capital-auction system is that it maximizes opportunities for the trial and error of entrepreneurial decisions. Its danger, for the program of empowered democracy, is that it jeopardizes social control over economic accumulation and economic inequality. The advantages and disadvantages of capital rationing are just the reverse.

To identify this dilemma may seem tantamount to recognizing the persistence of the tension between social control and market decentralization under the economic regime of empowered democracy. But remember that the point of this whole programmatic argument is less to abolish the basic tensions familiar to our vocabulary of ideological controversy than to change their sense and moderate their force. Both capital auctioning and capital rationing reconcile market decentralization and social control more fully than the inherited combination of property-based markets and administrative regulation, although they do so by different means and in different proportions. The auction and rationing regimes encourage this reconciliation more effectively through their combination than either could alone.

Some capital funds, possibly in the more standardized sectors of the economy, would operate primarily on the model of rationing, whereas others, possibly in the more experimental areas of manufacturing and services, would follow the capital-auction model. In this way the whole economy would benefit from an ongoing experiment with these alternative styles of market organization.

Because a rationing fund exercises a much stronger influence over the economic fortunes of its capital takers than does a capital auctioning fund, it should give them a major role in its decision making. The fund and its recipients may form a veritable industrial confederation, subject to both the pressure of conflicting interests within the confederation and the demands of the central democratic agencies. By contrast, an auctioning fund may be expected to keep more clearly apart from its capital takers. It stands in some ways in the position of an investment bank dealing with its clients and in other ways in that of a governmental agency supervising a capital market, except that here no one exercises absolute and permanent control over any portion of capital. These last remarks carry the discussion from the second to the third tier of the system: the primary capital takers with whom both auctioning and rationing funds deal.

The Primary Capital Takers: Problems of Scale and Incentives

Within limits set by the capital-giving fund, the capital users transact freely with one another. Theirs is a market system, though the specific quality of their decision-making autonomy depends upon the extent to which they operate under the auction or the rationing regimes. Either regime, however, provides the enterprise work force with the conditions for exercising a crucial say about the organization of work and about the range of income and power disparities. It is only required that these decisions remain within the ample boundaries established by the higher tiers of the economic order.

Under the auction regime the power to organize production is evident: the auctioning fund can more easily leave its users to their own devices. It is more concerned with long-term rates of return and organizational or technological breakthroughs and experiments than with the maintenance of any particular system of work organization. Under the rationing regime the independence of capital takers is more restricted. But the counterpart to these restrictions becomes greater engagement of the capital takers in the governance of their fund.

Under both regimes the capital-taking unit is a team that, as a whole, receives capital grants or bids capital away from other users.

Within ample bounds it remains free to govern its internal relations. Moreover, the entire economic order of dissociated property deprives the mass-production industries of the instruments
with which they protect themselves against instability in their
product, capital, and labor markets. It thereby favors extending
into the mainstream of the economy a style of organization previously confined to the economy's experimental vanguard and
distinguished by a closer and more continuous interplay between
task-defining and task-executing activities.

Neither the auction nor the rationing regime, however, turns its
clients into new individual or collective property owners. The economic system of empowered democracy is not worker corporatism.
(For a partial criticism of the worker-corporatist alternative, sometimes called the Yugoslav model, see the appendix to Chapter 2.)
The individual worker does not even have an absolute or permanent
right to job tenure within his enterprise or team, and the enterprise
or team has no absolute or permanent right to the resources temporarily put at its disposal or to the wealth it accumulates through
their use. But every citizen does have an unconditional right to the
satisfaction of his legally defined minimal welfare needs (see the later
discussion of immunity rights), qualified only by the size of the
welfare fund available to government, which is in turn influenced
by the price charged for the use of capital and by the decisions made
about the basic desired rate of economic growth.

The discussion of the third tier of the reformed economy raises
two problems deserving more detailed analysis and influencing the
operation of the economy as a whole. One problem is the compatibility of the proposed system with economies of scale. The other is
its probable effect upon the motivation to work.

Many forms of economic activity will always require the pooling
of large-scale resources in manpower, technology, and financial capital and the continuity of enterprises over long periods. But the
resulting concentration of workers, capital, and machines need not
have the familiar characteristics of contemporary mass-production
industry, operating under a system of absolute property rights.

Large-scale enterprises may be relatively loose confederations of
teams or units that move in and out of a particular enterprise, just
as an entire capital-rationing fund may be a loose confederation of
these enterprises. Such an organizational scheme would combine
flexibility with pooling to an extent still uncommon in the contemporary practice of mass-production industry. Yet it would merely
exaggerate an already discernible tendency in some of the more innovative large-scale businesses. Many such enterprises have organized themselves into small-scale, tenuously integrated units, each
emulating the organizational style of the smaller, more flexible, van-

guardist enterprises that proliferate in the high-technology and service sectors. The influence of technological evolution favors this tendency while the managerial and financial interests generated by property-based market and work-organization systems continue to frustrate it. We cannot reasonably expect to tell in advance exactly which current characteristics of large-scale and continuous enterprise would change under an institutional reform like the one proposed here, and which would prove to result from more intractable economic, organizational, or psychological constraints.

There is at least one other foreseeable effect of the dissociation of property rights for the conduct of large-scale business. Such a system prevents managers from exercising a broad-ranging discretionary authority over their workers that confuses the requirements of technical coordination with the right to act in the name of property (whether the private property of stockholders or the public property of an economically sovereign state), a right fitfully restrained by explicit or implicit collective bargaining. Nor may the enterprise work force under the proposed system entrench itself against disadvantaged or jobless workers from outside or hire them to occupy a subordinate status. The common association of mass-production industry with a distinction between a core, almost tenured work force and a variable periphery of unstable workers or subcontractors violates the spirit of the economic system described here. Such a distinction would quickly generate a hierarchy of vested interests, benefiting workers entrenched in the more successful sectors and enterprises. And it would constrain the opportunities for organizational innovation and ceaseless recombination.

There is indeed a price to pay for avoiding such privileges and constraints. Neither individuals nor groups would be able to nurture distinctive forms of life that are based upon the permanent occupancy of stereotyped positions in the social division of labor. But there are compensations. The attempt to develop varieties of practical collaboration less dependent upon a preestablished set of social roles, hierarchies, and divisions is more than a practical goal; it is a major aspect of the ideal underlying this entire argument for empowered democracy. It would not be a powerful ideal if it did not also promise a special sort of happiness. I explore the character of this happiness when dealing, in the final part of this chapter, with the spirit that inspires this whole institutional program.

Consider, finally, the effect of these economic institutions upon the motivation to work. The economic system outlined in the preceding pages allows for a large range of variation in the income rewards to particular capital takers. Under both the auction and the rationing regimes the individual prospers with the economic success of his team and suffers with its economic failure. Moreover, within the limits established by the central and specialized funds each team is free to establish economic rewards and penalties.

The conflict between incentives to diligence, on one side, and egalitarian or welfare goals, on the other, is not abolished. At the very least, however, it becomes a subject of explicit collective experiment and discussion at each tier of the capital-allocation system. The reformers may even hope to moderate the conflict by diminishing the dependence of work incentives upon stark inequalities of wealth and income. For many aspects of the proposed regime are calculated to universalize within society the conditions encouraging people to shift the focus of their ambitions from the accumulation of a patrimony to the shape of a career and to the slightest nuances in the semblance of worldly success. The result is not spiritual redemption. But it does help push motivations beyond the obsessions peculiar to a society in which people feel unable to distinguish their most vital interests from their continued hold upon a particular type of job.

This eclectic and open-minded approach to the problem of incentives and inequality illustrates the general attitude of the whole programmatic argument toward the mutability of human nature. The view of society and personality that informs this argument refuses the consistently disappointing and misleading attempt to distinguish a permanent core and a variable periphery of human nature. It takes into account the loose, contradictory, and complex set of motivations and aspirations that people demonstrate in the societies it wants to reform. It recognizes that even the most intimate and seemingly unyielding of these propensities are influenced and cumulatively remade by the institutional and imaginative context in which they exist. But it rejects as unrealistic any institutional scheme whose success requires a sudden and drastic shift in what people are like here and now.

Contrast with an Inheritance-Free Property System

The whole character of the democratized economy stands out by comparison to a system that preserves the traditional mix of property-based markets and ad hoc regulation but that limits private fortunes by abolishing inheritance and levying a heavy capital tax. The economic program of empowered democracy also abolishes the hereditary transmission of substantial assets. Each individual would be given instead a wide range of minimal welfare guarantees, including support during job transfers and opportunities for ongoing reeducation and retraining. What the mere abolition of inheritance cannot do, however, is to develop an economic order congenial to the spirit of empowered democracy. It cannot open ordinary social life to the same practice of collective conflict and deliberation that people experience in the exercise of citizenship. It cannot turn the arrangements of production and exchange into subjects of deliberate social experimentation and thereby give a practical as well as an ideal sense to the conception of a formative context more freely open to revision in the midst of ordinary social life. It cannot knock the institutional props out from under a style of industrial organization that continues to emphasize the discontinuity between task-defining and task-executing activities. It cannot cleanly sever the link between the ability to take advantage of economies of scale and the opportunity to command large numbers of workers in the name of property: for while an inheritance-free system does away with magnates, the managers of great businesses may have all the freer a hand as the fictive delegates of countless petty holders of equity. It cannot overcome, though it may diminish, the conflict between the rewards for economic achievement and the methods for ensuring basic social equality. The redistributive state would still have to intervene through tax-and-transfer policies. Thus, the logic of rough equality and the flow of actual market outcomes would remain far more starkly opposed than the need for incentives to work requires or than the economic order of a radical democracy permits.

Supplementary Ideas

A number of subsidiary or qualifying ideas help fill out this institutional picture. Remember first that the proposed regime should not be misunderstood as a compromise between a centralized ("command") and decentralized ("market") economy. It should be taken instead as a proposal to provide both the market economy and the social control of economic forces with alternative institutional definitions. From the mere fact that this alternative system provides for the central institutional and parametric decisions I have described, you cannot legitimately infer it would result in markets less decentralized (i.e., with fewer and less independent decision-making agents) than the Western-style economies of the late twentieth century. Such central institutional and parametric decisions are also made in those economies, only in a fashion more fragmentary, invisible, and invidious because susceptible to being either manipulated or overridden by privileged social groups. The forms of this decision making range from the unstable conduct of discretionary economic policy within the institutional limits described to the marginal legislation of a system of contract and property falsely equated with the very nature of a market. Such choices are also made within a constitutional structure that disempowers collective action and deliberation in the many ways pointed out by the internal arguments explored at the beginning of this chapter. Moreover, by their selective character, their underlying vision of what a market has to be, and their mistaken assumptions about the requirements of industrial efficiency, these decisions permit the emergence of vast centers of private power that also represent constraints upon decentralization.

But once you set aside the polemical comparison between the Western-type economies and the alternative system, you still have to acknowledge the presence of powerful centralizing tendencies within the economic regime of empowered democracy. Unless compensated, such tendencies can pervert the democratizing program. (The next section discusses both these tendencies and their antidotes.)

A second clarifying idea is that the fidelity of the regime of capital to its goals depends closely upon the implementation of the other, more narrowly constitutional part of the republican program. Only such a reformed government can be technically capable of performing these enlarged responsibilities. Only such a government can resist more effectively the risk of becoming the instrument by which particular groups transform temporary advantage into lasting privilege.

The third auxiliary idea is that the realization of such a regime of capital presupposes a different background order of right. In particular, it presupposes the disaggregation of the consolidated property right. This disaggregation takes place in two related ways. First, the different powers that appear merged within the consolidated property right get pulled apart. To take the single most obvious and important point, the employment of large amounts of capital is always conditional and temporary and the recipients' powers of use always coexist with the powers of the administrators of the social capital fund and of the competing investment funds. The other aspect of the disaggregation of property is therefore the assignment of these separated powers to different entities: the three tiers of capital givers and capital takers. There is nothing novel about disaggregation in either of these senses; the consolidated property right, after all, represents an artifact of particular traditions. In most legal orders, in most historical periods, property always has been disaggregated in both these senses. What matters for the program, however, is that the disaggregation takes the particular form that suits a democratized economy.

THE ORGANIZATION OF THE ECONOMY: THE DANGER OF CENTRALIZATION AND ITS ANTIDOTES

The capital regime just outlined has certain centralizing tendencies that, if left unchecked, would pervert the whole system. The presence and peril of these tendencies become the more obvious once you enlarge the ideas of centralization and decentralization. Decentralization refers, at a minimum, both to the number of agents who are able to trade and produce on their initiative and for their own account and to the extent of their independence. This second element may be expanded to include the extent of variety in the conduct of economic affairs: variety in the ways of doing business, organizing work, variety even in the results of labor, variety measured chiefly by the margin of departure from what most other economic agents do. This is the sort of decentralization that the normal regime of capital chiefly endangers.

It does not help to say that this recentralizing impulse is no more hostile to economic pluralism than are contemporary economic systems. Whatever comparison may show, the centralist tendencies are noxious in themselves. They undermine the economy's capacity to achieve repeated breakthroughs in output and productivity, a capacity that depends largely upon the persistent exercise of an almost frenzied inventiveness applied to the very context and structure of productive activity. The centralizing tendencies also threaten the basic aims of the constitution. Once the internal arrangements and external strategies of economic organizations stabilize into a single dominant mode, they favor the emergence of well-defined groups, formed on the basis of rigid conceptions of collective interest, identity, and opportunity. Each organization, each segment of economic life, becomes a little world whose structure mirrors the arrangements of all the little worlds with which it coexists and collides. That repeated pattern, supported by central power, supplies the mold in which the group divisions and hierarchies can form.

Apart from any genuine technical constraints of economy by scale and repetition, two main centralizing forces operate within the normal regime of capital. One centralizing dynamic merely works out the implications of the threat that the reemergence of well-defined groups poses to the constitution. The normal regime of capital applies in principle throughout the economy. It establishes a distinctive style of control and decentralization. However indeterminate the institutional implications of this style may be and however significant the margin of autonomy allowed to the individual enterprises, this approach to the relation between central economic authorities and decentralized economic agents may become the basis for a dominant type of enterprise organization and enterprise dealing. A casual combination of biases and transitory market circumstances may turn into an enduring mode of industrial organization. The parties elected to office may then adjust the parametric and institutional decisions so as to favor this dominant type and thereby further consolidate its ascendancy. With this, a renewed, subtle version of the politics of privilege emerges. The dominant enterprise type readily becomes a system of niches in which economic groups can form. The most favored and the most numerous, if they are also most numerous or most favored in the society at large, can then attempt to use governmental power to entrench their advantages. Thus, the state would become an enemy to deviant types of business organization and once again help turn the occasional disadvantages of some segments of the work force into continuing subordination. This outcome would jeopardize both the specific goal of avoiding unconditional claims upon capital and the general commitment to avoid the reappearance of a stabilized plan of social division and hierarchy.

The other dynamic of centralization is internal to the government itself. The governmental bodies that make the institutional and parametric decisions belong to a scheme designed to perpetuate, multiply, and extend collective mobilization. This mobilizational context, however, may be insufficient to prevent the assertion of a bureaucratic interest in the transparency and stability of the economic order. Once the basic decisions about the parametric and institutional bases of economic activity stop being fragmentary and implicit, they become all the more subject to a characteristic bias. The administrative foundation of this bias is everyone's desire to cover his tracks in a realm where public scrutiny and controversy are intense. Its general form is the tendency to treat variation first as folly and then as an immoral assault upon the collective interest. Its economic manifestation is the intolerance toward radical disagreements about the risks that are reasonable for a business to take, disagreements whose very occurrence represents one of the conditions of continued economic progress. The chosen institutions and parameters may be more or less deliberately rigged against deviant risk schedules and systematically increase the dimension of risk relative to the margin of deviation. Many kinds of risk taking may even be intentionally prohibited as irresponsible or indirectly excluded by their incompatibility with the institutional or parametric requirements imposed from on high.

No constitutional scheme can guarantee itself, once and for all, against the renascence of a politics of privilege. Conflict produces winners and losers. The winners will try to keep their own prizes and abolish their own example, and so long as a central state exists, they will find ready at hand an instrument with which to do so. It would be unwise, even if it were possible, to destroy a central government if you understand such a government simply as the terrain on which people can fight about the basic terms of collective life and carry their opinions into practice. For the risk of a mutual reinforcement between privileged access to the state and privileged advantage in society is overshadowed by the danger that a structure of social life may emerge that cannot be revised by any readily available means at all: the naturalization of society is the peculiar risk of statelessness. To justify the destruction of a distant central government, a circumstance would have to arise in which people's material and moral connections to one another were so completely contained in a narrow social and geographical area that the structure of their social existence would be wholly determined by what went on within this circle. But this reduction of the polity to a metaphorical if not a literal village would mean the naturalization of society with a vengeance: the turning away from the larger clash of alternative visions and versions of society, the eternal dream of those who want to get off the roller coaster of history.

Short of statelessness, no society can protect itself against the reappearance of the politics of privilege. So, too, as institutions become the explicit contexts and instruments for revising the basic terms of social life, the reorganized economy confronts the other centralizing danger: that parties and governments, armed with new opportunities to try out their proposals, may exclude too much random or dissident variation. The result may be to impoverish the practical and imaginative resources available to the programs of another day. The generic antidote the constitution of the reformed republic gives to these perils is the twofold effort to achieve the maximum incitement to conflictual collective mobilization outside governmental institutions while obtaining the greatest permeability of governmental institutions to the results of this mobilization. An approach to voluntary association that draws its strength from mere opposition to the state cannot be secure – for it lives under threat from rulers at home and powers abroad. Nor can it freely transform social life in its own image – for it comes up against institutional limits it can overcome only by perennially defeating or neutralizing the state. Thus, the need to imagine a state with a built-in bias toward the self-organization of society.

The preceding discussion has shown that the generic risks of the appeal to an empowered democratic state take distinctive forms in the economic domain. The compensations must be correspondingly specific. One such compensation is the provision for an extraordinary regime of capital, to exist alongside the ordinary one. The most basic antidote, however, is the existence of the intermediate tier of the capital-allotment system: the specialized competitive investment funds, which shield the primary capital takers from ad hoc or detailed governmental control. They operate with a vast array of different sets of investment policies and different combinations of institutional and parametric constraints. They span the distance from maximal guidance to minimal checks. Moreover, the auction or rationing regimes they follow represent two radically different versions of market organization.

THE ORGANIZATION OF THE ECONOMY: THE DESIGN OF WORK

There is another compensation to the perils of centralism and monotony: the effect of the constitution upon the organization of work. The importance of such an effect goes far beyond the problem of decentralization. The organization of the workplace represents the area in which the striving for social control of economic activity and permanent collective mobilization must most clearly confront the demands of practical effectiveness in a highly mechanized and industrialized economy. The character of ordinary work experience also either strengthens or undermines the psychological dispositions on which the constitution depends; more than any other aspect of social existence, except the family, it serves as the school of everyday life and teaches the only lessons that ordinary people in ordinary times cannot easily forget.

The proliferation of the flexible version of rationalized collective labor matters to this enriched idea of decentralization in several ways. The flexible style of work organization, with its softening of the contrast between supervisors and supervised, can flourish in large enterprises and plants (offices, stores, outlets) or small ones. But the rigid type favors the large enterprise and the large plant or office: large enterprises, to permit and justify successive infusions of capital; large plants or offices, to organize the work force in the fashion of a conventional army. Moreover, the flexible mode encourages the proliferation of divergent forms of production by making it unnecessary to subordinate experiments in the organization of work to the maintenance of a fixed structure of control. In this sense, it does for the organization of work what the breakup of oligarchic control of government does for the society as a whole.

Each economic system criticized in the preceding section enshrines the rigid variant of rationalized collective labor as the mainstream form of work organization and relegates the flexible variant to the vanguard of industry, administration, and warfare. In Chapter 2, I argued that the overwhelming predominance of the rigid variant cannot plausibly be understood as a consequence of the inherent organizational requirements of technologically advanced, large-scale industry and warfare. It depends, on the contrary, upon the fulfillment of certain social and technical-economic conditions. It may help to recall briefly what these conditions, in the industrial sphere, are, and how they came to be satisfied by the Western-style economies of the post–World War II period.

The social conditions include both a negative and a positive element. The negative element was the defeat of the social movements that threatened to overturn, at a single stroke, the constitutionalism of permanent demobilization, the quasi-oligarchic control of basic investment decisions, and the rigid contrast between task definers and task executors at work. The positive element was the development of an order of right that – in the name of both property and technical necessity (each covering for the other) – distinguished the task definers from everybody else. In so doing, this order also conflated technical coordination with a broad disciplinary authority, limited only by the collective contracts struck by an unevenly organized work force. The technical-economic condition was the avoidance of the various forms of economic instability that would jeopardize the large-scale, mass-production industries operating largely with product-specific machines and relatively inflexible production processes. In these industries, the rigid variant of rationalized collective labor prevailed. They sank successive amounts of capital into product lines, production processes, and even work arrangements that could not easily be altered. The combination of deepening capital investment with structural inflexibility made these enterprises all too vulnerable to the disruptive effects of instability in the financial, product, and labor markets. Against the instability of financial markets they employed the generation of internal investment funds. Against the convergent effect of instability in labor and product markets, they developed ways to reconcile the maintenance of a relatively privileged and pacified labor force (working to produce for the unstable part of demand) with the deployment of outside subcontractors or occasional, unorganized laborers, who absorbed, on the front line, the shock of downturn and helped fill burgeoning orders during booms.

The economic order of the reformed republic knocks the props out from under each of these social or technical-economic encouragements to the prevalence of the rigid variant of rationalized collective labor. It does so as an automatic consequence of the institutional arrangements it establishes. The attack upon the stabilizing conditions of the established style of work organization does not guarantee that the flexible variant will prevail throughout the economy. It merely destroys the bias in favor of the rigid mode and facilitates different versions of the continuous interplay between task definition and task execution to take hold in many sectors of the economy. Consider just how the proposed economy system subverts each of the conditions mentioned; the argument moves in the reverse order of the earlier enumeration.

Take the technical-economic conditions first. The recourse to internally generated investment funds is drastically curtailed by the overall method of assigning capital conditionally as well as by the limits on enterprise accumulation. In fact, the assignment of capital will even be subject to terms that affirmatively require efforts to moderate the contrasts between task-defining and task-executing activities and among job categories in general. The interconnected defenses against instability in the labor and products markets cannot survive the measures designed to limit job exclusivity within the enterprise, the shift in the fundamental status of workers, and the open-minded favor to all manner of small and medium-size enterprises.

Consider now the affirmative element in the social conditions for the predominance of the rigid style of work organization. The whole constitutional scheme takes away the legal basis for concentrating in a few hands the power to direct other people's labor: its goals, forms, and rewards. To prevent the emergence of economic entitlements that enable individuals to control large amounts of labor, property must be disaggregated in the sense defined earlier: not handed over lock, stock, and barrel to the capitalist, the government, or the enterprise work force. Disaggregate property (rather than transfer it) is what the reformed regime of capital does.

Finally, take the negative aspect of the social conditions of contrasting styles of work organization. The inauguration of such a radical democratic program would mean reversing the defeat of the revolutionary movements and leftist experiments that took place throughout Europe in the aftermath of World War I. Despite the relative crudity of their programmatic ideas, these experiments and movements came closer than any other episode of collective conflict to articulating the very vision this transformative program develops. The program represents, in a sense, the development of what they left vague and confused. Its implementation presupposes the victory of which they were robbed. The previous discussion of transformative practice and the later analysis of transitional institutional arrangements suggest how this victory may be won.

THE SYSTEM OF RIGHTS

Redefining Rights

The system of rights represents a distinctive domain for institutional reconstruction. By a system of rights I mean simply an institutionalized version of society, which is to say, a form of social life acquiring a relatively stable and delineated form and generating a complicated set of expectations. The stability and the expectations are not merely those of the prison camp: a system of rights defines arrangements that many people (how many?) treat as the expression of a defensible scheme of human association. The organized social world that a system of rights describes is not presented and understood primarily as a collection of mere truce lines or trophies in ongoing social and party warfare. Each such social world seeks to provide the exclusive setting of human life and, though it invariably fails in its attempt at exclusivity, it succeeds enough, while it survives, to shape beliefs and motivations as well as opportunities and practices.

We have come to think of the vocabulary of rights as ordinarily limited to the legal definition of institutions and practices and therefore to state-described and state-enforced law. The following discussion presupposes this narrower conception of right while effacing the clarity of its boundaries. For the system of rights described here is meant to transcribe an institutional structure that weakens the contrast between state and civil society just as it softens the opposition between devotion to the common good and the pursuit of private interests.

The remaking of the system of rights is not a separate task of institutional reconstruction, as if we could change the constitutional form of government, the style of conflict over the control and uses of governmental power, the regime of capital, the organization of work, and *then* the content and form of legal entitlements. It is rather the indispensable expression of all those other changes. But this expression is not transparent or automatic. It poses specific problems and clarifies hidden connections.

Consider two objections radicals frequently make to any program for the redefinition of legal entitlements. To anticipate a response to these objections is to indicate the direction taken by this stage of the programmatic argument.

One source of hostility to theories of legal rights is the belief that rights, any rights, are inseparable from a particular type of social and economic organization – such as "capitalism" – that can and should be overcome. In a more inclusive variant of the argument, legal rights become a form of social regulation inherently suited to a particular social practice – such as the market exchange of commodities and of labor. Though the critic acknowledges that this law-sustaining practice may exist in a broad range of societies, he insists it cannot be reconciled with other types of social organization and especially not with the type (e.g., communism) to which he is committed. All versions of this objection rely upon the idea of a limited and well-defined list of possible types of social organization, a characteristic theme of deep-logic social theory. They depend even more directly on the unjustified identification of rights with a particular style of entitlement, with what I earlier called the consolidated property right.

These critics know perfectly well that every body of law includes entitlements that differ in content from consolidated property rights. They may even acknowledge that differences in the content of rights and in the character of the social activity to which rights apply influence the ways in which entitlements are created and interpreted. But they drastically underestimate the extent to which legal entitlements may differ, in form and content, in different legal systems. Like their conservative adversaries, they allow themselves to be beguiled by the imaginative dominance of the consolidated property right as a model to which all entitlements in all legal systems must conform. The programmatic argument about rights developed here claims that the construction of an empowered democracy requires the elaboration of types of legal entitlements differing, in form as well as content, both from one another and from the consolidated property right, that there are no obvious insuperable conceptual or practical obstacles to development of these alternative models of rights, and that the rudiments of such alternatives can already be found in current legal thought and practice.

If this first objection to rights theories reflects a sociological radicalism preoccupied with the built-in constraints of social types, a second objection arises from a modernist or existentialist radicalism. It denounces rights not for serving a particular institutional order but simply for establishing any institutional order. The radicalism that underlies this objection believes we achieve freedom only by a ceaseless struggle against all institutional routines. Such a vision recognizes the disproportion between our capabilities and the limited social or mental contexts in which we attempt to exercise them. But its great weakness is its failure to come to terms with the imperative of contextuality. We must in the end inhabit a particular social world, and we can never perform the act of denial often or quickly enough to prevent individual and social experience from being largely, though not entirely or ultimately, governed by the practices and assumptions of the world we live in. Nevertheless, the argument for the empowered democracy and for its system of rights rescues something from the wreck of this self-defeating ideal. It preserves the conception that formative contexts of power and production vary in the extent to which they respect and encourage our context-smashing abilities and enable us to exercise a vigilant and self-conscious mastery over the collective settings of individual activity. The system of legal rights outlined here defines a society that diminishes the dazed, narcoleptic quality of routinized social life and does so for the sake of a vision of individual and collective empowerment. Each detail of this set of legal entitlements connects back to this seemingly empty but in fact inspiring ideal.

The Trouble with the Established System of Legal Rights

What is the trouble with the established system of legal rights? From the standpoint of the criticism and the vision that underlie this whole institutional program, the trouble can be summarized by a single fact: the practical and imaginative ascendancy of the consolidated property right. The consolidated property right that exercises this overwhelming influence can be defined by both its content and its form. In content it is the principle of economic decentralization that consists in the allocation of more or less unrestricted claims to divisible portions of social capital: unrestricted both in the chain of temporal succession and in the scope of permitted usage. To be sure, the law has always recognized limits to this absolute discretion, just as in the counterpart area of contract it has always tried to restrain the dominant principles of freedom to choose the partner and the contract terms. But these qualifications remain anomalies. They acknowledge the existence in current society of forms of human association irreducible to the central categories of property and contract. They show that the coexistence of absolute property rights generates practical problems that cannot be solved by more absolute property rights. But they do not present alternative, developed models of entitlement.

Consolidated property right works its restrictive influence most directly through its relation to a version of the market economy that stands in the way of an advance toward greater economic plasticity and even toward greater degrees of economic decentralization. The result is not only to circumscribe unnecessarily the opportunity for permanent economic innovation but also to reproduce an ongoing conflict between the practice of democracy and the organization of the economy. Democratic control over the forms, pace, and result of economic accumulation is undercut while the contrast between task-defining and task-executing jobs turns the workplace into a permanent countermodel to the exercise of democratic citizenship.

The continuing authority of consolidated property also exercises a more indirect influence. By identifying the abstract principle of economic decentralization with a particular version of market institutions, it drastically restricts our vision of the possible alternatives to current market systems. The imagined alternatives – the transfer of undivided economic sovereignty to central governments or the attempt to cast the workers in each enterprise as the holders of consolidated property in their own business – jeopardize public freedoms and economic dynamism in all the ways previously discussed. And the basic institutional choice seems to be the selection of a mix of economic centralism and decentralization. But the radical who has freed himself from the vestiges of deep-logic social theory and the spell of a particular theory of rights knows that any given mix of centralism and decentralization can assume different institutional forms. Thus, the functional and imaginative centrality of consolidated property within the system of rights contributes to the negative prejudice that underlies some of the paradoxes discussed in my earlier account of the genesis of the private-rights complex. Though the received system of private rights provides some people with the instruments with which to reduce other people to dependence, though it coexists with other rights that pose no such threat (welfare and civic entitlements), and though it needs to be combined with methods of organizational surveillance and hierarchy that nullify or reverse its overt meaning, it may nevertheless seem indispensable. Any attempt to replace it may seem bound to cause tyranny and inefficiency. The polemic against this negative prejudice can be completed only by a proposed system of rights that defies the negative prejudice on which the "realistic" defense of current institutions depends.

The prejudicial effect of the influence exercised by the consolidated property right does not stop at the direct and indirect contributions of consolidated property to a certain organization of the economy. It also exercises a broader, more intangible influence because it readily becomes a model for rights dealing with matters far removed from the methods for economic decentralization. It provides a form that, once abstracted from its specific content, is reproduced in almost every area of thinking about rights. The absolute portion of capital delineates a zone within which the property owner may act as he pleases, no matter what the consequences of his actions, and outside of which he may expect no protection, no matter how appealing his claim. The boundaries of such a right are primarily defined, at the moment of its creation, by law or contract; the relational setting in which the right is to be exercised remains largely irrelevant to its definition; thus, the discretionary action constituting the heart of this model of entitlement may be circumscribed but cannot be eviscerated. The definition of the right must be connected to its application by a rulelike or principled method of adjudication that can keep under control both open-ended normative controversy and complex causal analysis. The source of the right must be suited to the decontextualization that characterizes its later life: the unilateral imposition of a duty by the state, the fully articulated act of will, or some combination of the two.

The effect of attempting to cast all rights in this mold is to force large areas of existing social practice into incongruous legal forms. Thus, the obligations arising from relations of mutual interdependence are governed by contractual and delictual incrustations upon

a body of law obsessed with instantaneous contracts and confrontations between hypothetical strangers. The organization of work in
large-scale institutions is treated either as the beneficiary of a paternalist police power or as the parallel to a regime of free contract.
The need to combine widespread supervisory discretion with at least
the facade of a regime of contract is in turn justified as a requirement
of impersonal technical necessity.

Why does the legal form of the consolidated property right exercise
the influence I have just described? You need not conjecture that this
influence betrays a conspiracy of judges and jurists to maintain the
property regime or that it demonstrates the unconscious subjection
of motives and beliefs to the functional requirements for the
reproduction of an established social order. Each type of legal right
represents, even in its most formal aspects, the incomplete but significant picture of a certain model of human association. The stubborn understatement of existing, much less possible, diversity in the
form and substance of legal rights is a version of the idolatry of the
actual. It shows a failure to grasp the extent to which the models of
human association already accepted in the less practical parts of social
life (the exercise of democractic citizenship and the life of family and
friendship) offer imaginative points of departure for the remaking of
practical institutions.

The Generative Principles of a Reconstructed System of Rights

Two basic constructive principles inform a system of rights that gives
legal form to the governmental and economic institutions of an empowered democracy and escapes, once and for all, the confining
example of consolidated property.

The first and basic constructive principle is that the security of the
individual should be established in ways that minimize both the
immunity of institutional arrangements to challenge and conflict and
the ease with which some individuals can reduce others to dependence. The meaning of this principle can be brought out by a brief
discussion of its elements: the security of the individual, the avoidance
of social petrification, and the antidote to dependence.

The security of the individual is his justified confidence that the
conflicts of the republic will not put at risk his most intimate concerns
with physical security, minimal material welfare, and protection
against subjugation by any public or private power. The individual
remains secure only if he enjoys basic freedoms to express himself
and to combine with other people, most especially to combine with
them for the purpose of influencing the future form of society. Security requires that the individual feel assured that overwhelming

practical need will not periodically threaten him with poverty or force him to submit to a superior power.

The commitment of empowered democracy to expand the scope of context-revising conflict makes it all the more important to assure the individual that his basic security, and the security of those closest to him, will be protected. If he lacks this assurance, the institution-alized controversies and reinventions of social life will quickly be-come intolerable to him and he will see each as a threat to himself. Of course, nothing can ensure that the institutions guaranteeing the immunity of the individual will not be undermined, but only in the trivial sense that nothing can entirely prevent any institutional ar-rangement from being changed.

If the attempt to give the constitution a transcendent basis may prove temporarily useful, it may also turn out to be dangerous once transcendent justifications go out of fashion. If an antimobilizational style of politics seems to diminish the risk that any arrangements, including those that guarantee immunity, will be altered, it does so only by producing dangers of its own. No contribution to public freedoms is more important than the attempt to make them rest on a basis that puts the fewest possible constraints upon experimentation with the institutional forms of social life. In this way, they need not be jeopardized every time conflict produces change. And because the entrenchment of practices and arrangements that cannot easily be challenged and altered usually goes hand in hand with the devel-opment of structures of dependence and domination, the rebellion against these structures can easily turn into an attack upon the pro-tections of immunity.

Though the constitution of the empowered democracy requires an effective defense of immunity, it is not compatible with all possible views of security. The individual may, for example, feel that his vital sense of protection requires that he live in a quiescent polity and that he have at his disposal private wealth in the form of consolidated property rights. He may even feel he is secure only if he has a lifelong guarantee to occupy a particular job or to live in the manner cus-tomary to a certain caste. The constitution of the empowered de-mocracy expresses a social and personal ideal incompatible with this version of the ideal of security. Like all our other ideas about our-selves, subjective conceptions of security are stubbornly held, and no single set of facts serves to disprove them. But if the ideals and understanding underlying this institutional program hold up, people will have reason to change their views of what essential security consists in. They and, if not they, their children will discover that the security that matters does not require the maintenance of a nar-rowly defined mode of life. They reach this conclusion in part by finding senses and varieties of security compatible with an ever greater jumbling up of distinct styles of life and in part by awakening to a conception of the personality as both dependent upon context and strengthened through context smashing.

It may be objected that any arrangement for securing immunity, must be, by definition, an institutional practice not open to revision. But this objection misses the key point. The institutional interpretations and foundations of security differ in the measure of their abstractability: that is to say, in the extent to which they can be disengaged from a complex texture of social life. At one extreme, the safeguard of individual immunity may consist in the intangibility of a particular way of life, defined by the position a group occupies within a well-defined communal and hierarchical order. At the other extreme, it may consist in a set of rights whose main demand upon the other parts of the social order is that they lay themselves open to challenge and revision and that they contribute to the overcoming of the gap between contextualized routine and context revision. Along the spectrum defined by these two poles, the rights afforded by empowered democracy have the same relation to a property-based rights system that absolute property has to inherited ranks. The point is to diminish the extent that safeguarding security rigidifies social life and thereby helps reproduce inflexible roles and ranks. A major theme of the programmatic argument developed here is that, in a particular circumstance, with its available stock of available institutional practices and models of human association, this seemingly vague ideal can be made to yield affirmative proposals. And so, too, one task of the system of rights is to give a distinct content to the seemingly empty idea of a more abstractable immunity right.

From even the little that has been said it should be clear that differences in the abstractability of the institutions that establish the immunity of the individual are not just isolated technical features of certain arrangements. They represent both rival interpretations of the meaning of security and causal conjectures about the most effective way to realize in fact this particular ideal of security. In both guises they exemplify the general views of society and personality they help sustain.

Just as the forms of immunity differ in the extent to which they bar social life against transformative pressure, so too they differ in the ease with which they lend themselves to use as instruments of domination. To recognize this difference, it is enough to recall an earlier comparison between two kinds of rights within existing legal systems. The property owner can use consolidated property rights, freely accumulated and transferred by inheritance, to diminish his dependence upon other people (or rather upon their discretionary decisions) while increasing their dependence upon him. But welfare entitlements and civic or public rights do not lend themselves to this use except through a far more indirect chain of deliberate manipulations or unintended effects. This imbalance between the subjugation-producing effects of the legal forms of immunity within a legal system can extend into differences between entire legal systems, according to the way each legal order goes about protecting individual security.

Immunity guarantees in the reformed constitution should satisfy two negative standards: they should not supply instruments of subjugation and they should not help protect the social order against effective challenge and revision. A major theme of this book has been that a necessary condition for maintaining a system of communal and hierarchical divisions is that these divisions be generated and regenerated by institutional arrangements protected against the risks of the routine practical and imaginative conflicts of social life. Precisely this seclusion from conflict represents the surest sign of triumph in the social warfare. It would also be a sufficient condition of structures of dependence and domination, were it not for the following qualification: society may be highly routinized in a fashion that gives communal division primacy over social hierarchy. The social order may then appear as a confederation of relatively equal and rigidly separate communities, although foreshortened hierarchies may appear within each community or group. In such a circumstance institutional arrangements, sanctified by slowly changing custom, may aggravate the contrast between context-preserving routine and context-transforming conflict. Something like this situation is said to exist in many tribal societies. Moreover, the longing for such a circumstance marks a long succession of political utopias from the idea of a republic of relatively equal yeoman farmers to the unreconstructed versions of petty commodity production. But even when such a rigidified system of communal divisions (sometimes called a segmented society) can be realized in fact, it suffers from a peculiar instability. If the view of the enabling conditions of material progress presented in earlier parts of this book is correct, the development of productive or destructive capabilities requires a shifting around of people, jobs, and institutional arrangements. It even demands that the organization of work represent a visible embodiment of practical reason, understood as a method for the continuous interplay between task definitions and operational acts. Whenever the rigidified society as a whole or a group within it faces a practical emergency (or an exceptional opportunity), its leaders must mobilize resources and manpower in ways not predetermined or even tolerated by the established institutional order. Those who take the lead in this extraconstitutional mobilization find themselves with a floating quantum of power in their hands: the power represented by the emergency resources. They may then fashion arrangements that transform this exceptional control over free-floating capital and manpower into an institutionalized part of the social order. Notice how this line of argument suggests a speculative conjecture about the genesis of social hierarchies out of relatively egalitarian tribal societies. The larger view of the enabling conditions of material progress that this hypothesis presupposes explains why the combination of rigidity with equality fails to recur at higher levels of the development of productive capability. The segmented tribal society is a historical fact, whereas the idea of the yeoman republic is an archaizing fantasy.

The first generative principle of a system of rights for the empowered democracy is the commitment to establish the individual's position of immunity in a way that minimizes both the rigidification of the institutional order and the risks of personal subjugation. But though this principle represents the most important constructive idea of a system of rights suitable to the empowered democracy, it can generate this system only when complemented by a few subsidiary principles. One of these auxiliary ideas is that the legal devices for granting access to divisible portions of social capital should contribute to the making of a decentralized economic order; which is to say, of an economic order that privileges the consensual route to the development of negative capability. The legal form of economic decentralization, however, must carry negative capability beyond the point it can reach under a regime of consolidated property rights and mass-production industry. Market rights must therefore be created that combine certain features of consolidated property with other traits that consolidated property lacks. Thus, under the reformed constitution, the terms of access to capital emphasize the provisional and conditional character of all proprietary control. But within these terms and for this period, the discretionary use and transfer of the resources may be nearly absolute and may resemble, to that extent, consolidated property. Indeed, the clearer the assertion of ultimate collective control over the forms, rate, and fruits of accumulation, the stronger the justification for property and contract rights similar to the most unforgiving versions of nineteenth-century private law. This subsidiary principle requires no further discussion here; the arguments that support and elaborate it have already been worked out in the course of discussing the proposals for economic reorganization.

Another subsidiary idea does require more extended analysis because its foundations and aims outreach those of the institutional program. This principle is the effort to affirm legal rights that, by their form and content, suit the obligations of interdependence that characterize communal life. And these rights, when viewed in their interaction with the other types of entitlements constituting the system of rights, should embody and promote a certain prescriptive vision of communal relations.

The program for institutional reconstruction worked out here does not exhaust the reach of the vision that inspires it. The ultimate stakes in politics are the fine texture of personal relations. The institutions of the empowered democracy matter not only for the heightened freedom, prosperity, and self-consciousness they promise but also as the framework for a style of personal attachments. At the center of this revised approach to direct personal relations stands a conception of community as a zone in which the increased acceptance of mutual vulnerability makes it possible to multiply ways of diminishing the conflict between attachment to other people and the claims of self-consciousness and self-possession. Overcoming this conflict represents but another facet of the project of human empowerment.

Traditional legal thought has accustomed us to think of communal life as almost beyond the proper scope of legal rights. If the jurists are to be believed, legal regulation appears in the domain of intimate and communal relations as the hand of Midas, threatening to destroy whatever it touches. But this supposed antipathy between rights and community reflects both a rigid view of rights and an impoverished conception of community. Its actual effect is often to leave communal life all the more subject to the forms of self-interested exchange and domination from which the policy of legal abstention is expected to protect it.

A legal theory under the spell of consolidated property imagines rights to establish sharply demarcated areas of discretionary action. But the rigid related contrast of right and no-right, the refusal to take into account the effect that an exercise of right has upon the associates of the rightholder, and the insistence upon explicit bargain or unilateral state imposition as sources of obligation are all inappropriate to communal life. In fact, they are even unsuitable to continuing business dealings that involve significant collaboration between business partners. Communal and collaborative relationships demand that the scope of a right be contextually defined in the light of standards and judgments about the effect the exercise of the right might have upon other people. The legal penetration of community and collaboration also requires the legal acknowledgment of obligations that arise from half-articulate and half-deliberate relations of interdependence rather than from either completed bargains or unilateral impositions of duty. Though current law occasionally protects such interdependencies, it characteristically does so through a haphazard sequence of subordinate principles and exceptional bodies of doctrine. The effect is to make the protection depend upon mechanical distinctions.

The policy of legal abstention reveals an inadequate view of community as well as a single-track conception of rights. It sees community as the exclusion of conflict or the restraint on self-interest and, in either instance, as a contrast to the quality of workaday life. Because the received vocabulary of legal rights is associated with both conflict and self-interest, it appears here as an alien and subversive presence. But the imagined contrast between a communal idyll and the everyday world of work and exchange is both unrealistic and corrupting. It fails to recognize the element of conflict that inevitably arises from the development of independent subjectivity. It does not see that the restraint on self-interest retains its vital connection to the communal ideal only to the extent that it remains subordinate to a principle of radical mutual acceptance. However, the strongest argument against the stark contrast of communal harmony and practical activity is that this antithesis forms part of a scheme of social life that harms both the elements it so rigidly opposes. It abandons practical life to unrestrained self-interest and technically justified hierarchy and reduces private community to a futile refuge against the brutality of the outside world. To the extent that the forms of dependence and domination remain undisturbed, the communal ideal becomes the softening mantle of a power order. Every attempt to assert equality in the distribution of trust requires a betrayal of existing communal attachments.

The generative principles discussed in the preceding pages connect the other parts of the institutional program to the reconstruction of the system of rights. They suggest the creation of distinct types of entitlements, distinguished along lines that, in fainter and more tortuous outline, can already be discerned in modern law. These types of rights differ both by their operational characteristics and by the particular areas of the institutional program to which they give legal form. The distinguishing operational features concern the relation between the right at the moment of its initial formulation and the right at the moment of its legitimate exercise. They also include the modes of argument and analysis most relevant to the passage from formulation to exercise. The aspect of the institutional program to which each type of right refers presents less a distinct model of human association than part of a scheme designed to prevent such rigid distinctions from taking hold. Within such a view, the operational characteristics of entitlements cease to be seen as the inherent features of rights, just as rights themselves are no longer thought to mark the built-in structure of an institutional type of governmental, economic, or communal organization. Now the form of a right can be made to reflect, deliberately and directly, its programmatic role.

Market Rights

Market rights are the rights employed for economic exchange in the trading sector of the society. They come into their own within a fully realized version of the reconstructed economy: the economy that allows teams of workers, technicians, and entrepreneurs to gain conditional and temporary access to portions of social capital and that thereby develops both the absolute degree of economic decentralization and the extent of economic plasticity.

Market rights show two different faces, according to whether we focus on the relation between the capital takers and the capital fund or on the dealings among the capital takers themselves. In the relation to the capital fund, what stands out, by contrast to the existing market systems, are both the general commitment to a scheme of conditional and provisional rights of access to capital and the turn to explicit collective decision making to set the precise terms of use. These terms may fix the time for which capital may be available, the interest charged by the fund for its resources, the uses to which capital may be put (e.g., the extent to which it may be employed to expand the enterprise), and the outer limits that must be observed in experiments with the form of work organization. They may leave a broad and nearly unlimited scope for entrepreneurial discretion in certain sectors of the economy while circumscribing this discretion severely in other sectors.

The key legal significance of the new relation between the capital fund and the capital takers is brought out by its impact on the traditional contrast between private and regulatory law. This contrast typically combines and confuses two ideas that should be kept distinct. First, there is the opposition between the rules and practices defining a particular type of market and those correcting its results in particular transactions. This distinction, though never entirely clear-cut, has its justifications. The reformed market and the revised theory of market rights would not abolish the difference between market definition and contract correction. It would simply make this difference less important by weakening, for reasons soon to be remembered, the felt moral and social need to correct particular deals.

But implied in the contrast of private and regulatory law there is another, indefensible idea. This idea, rarely confessed but even more rarely abandoned, is the distinction between the rules and practices establishing a market (the content of private law) and those correcting the operations of the market economy as a whole, or of broad sectors of this economy, rather than the results of particular transactions. This supposed general correction may be motivated by social policies, such as distributional fairness, that market institutions are supposedly unable to accomplish (the task of regulatory law). The contrast between market definition and general market correction makes no sense as a distinction between two inherently different activities or topics. The market may indeed substitute nonmarket for market forms of organization. But nonmarket forms are just as likely to represent fragments of a different style of market organization – one at odds with the style enshrined in the established rules of private law. Received economic and legal thought has trouble recognizing these exemplary deviations because of its habitual confusion of the market with one particular version of market institutions. Under the reformed economic system, however, such confusion would lose its props; the basic norms of contract and property would be seen to be no less "political" than the distributional issues fought out in the categories of regulatory law. The resulting advance in intellectual clarity would also be a gain in our effective mastery over the terms of practical social life.

Consider now the second side of market rights: the side that refers to the dealings among the economic enterprises themselves. Here firms are free to transact with one another within the limits of time and use prescribed by the central political decisions. The constraints on entrepreneurial discretion are certainly more overt than in the current style of market institutions. But I have already suggested several reasons to expect that the overall workings of such a system would actually broaden the opportunities for the exercise of entrepreneurial initiative. One such line of reasoning deserves further development here because of its close bearing on the form and effect of economic rights.

A transactional system retains its character only so long as it can be distinguished from a power order in which some people make decisions at the behest of others. Yet market transactions constantly produce inequalities of wealth, and they commonly presuppose inequalities of information. Success in the market appears, first and foremost, as the acquisition of advantages that can be used to secure further advantages in the next rounds of market transactions. If all such inequalities are canceled out as soon as they have been gained, the market is reduced to little more than the facade to an overriding method of redistributive allocation. But if these inequalities are allowed to accumulate too much, the market is gradually replaced by a power order. We cannot deduce from the abstract idea of the market an ideal reconciliation between the imperatives to correct and not to correct. We cannot even expect that there will be such a reconciliation for all possible versions of market institutions. For a given economy, or sector of the economy, the minimum of correction needed to prevent it from collapsing into a power order may be greater than the maximum of correction compatible with the autonomy of market decisions. Market systems, and the broader formative institutional contexts of power and production to which they belong, differ crucially in the extent to which they realize the idea of a structure of decentralized bargaining, without having constantly to correct or compensate the outcomes of particular transactions.

Legal systems often appeal to a stratagem that moderates or obfuscates, rather than solves, the problem of overcorrection and undercorrection. This stratagem replaces outright redistributive correction by rules and standards that distinguish between contractual situations according to the degree to which the parties are allowed to treat one another as unrestricted gamblers. The antigambling theme includes the notion that the parties had in mind a rough equivalence of performances. It also incorporates the idea that they are engaged in something of a collaborative venture and may not exploit to the hilt one another's unexpected misfortunes or guileless mistakes. Both because it characteristically works through presumptions of intent and because it singles out only certain transactions, the antigambling impulse softens and conceals the subversive force of redistributive correction. Yet it does in effect circumscribe the scope of decentralized economic decision. The frequency with which it appears in the setting of significant disparities of power between the contract partners suggests that one of its major, half-conscious uses is to protect the weak from the strong.

An economic system that dispenses with consolidated property as the principal mechanism of economic decentralization may increase the constraints of time and usage on the employment of capital, although even these constraints may be set very differently in different sectors of the economy. Within these limits, however, it lessens the need for ad hoc redistributive corrections. In the core area of the dealings among takers of capital from the rotating capital fund, it diminishes the pressure to restrict initiative in all the ways suggested by the antigambling impulse. For this reconstructed system is designed precisely to encourage decentralization and plasticity and to undercut all the devices enabling entrenched economic organizations and accumulators of capital to protect themselves against the effects of market instabilities. The provisional teams of capital takers, secure in their basic welfare entitlements, can be treated to a very large extent as unrestricted gamblers.

What follows for the operational characteristics of market rights? Such rights would have the basic operational features of contract and property entitlements in current private law. In fact, for the reasons previously considered, these characteristics may be realized in an even more untrammeled form. Property, to be sure, would be disaggregated, as it has been in so many periods of its history, into a series of distinct powers assigned to different entities or rightholders: central representative bodies of the democracy, the competing investment funds, and the capital takers who have access to the fund on explicitly temporary and limited terms. But within these limits the capital takers would benefit from market rights with all the formal characteristics of current contract entitlements. The limitations of time and use could be absorbed, as conditional terms or public policy prohibitions, without damage to the three basic operational traits of the consolidated property right itself.

First, the source of obligation must be either the unilateral imposition of a duty by the state or a fully articulated agreement. The half-deliberate relations of interdependence and reliance that occupy so prominent a place in our ordinary views of moral obligation have no force here.

Second, the boundaries of the entitlement are primarily defined at the moment of its initial formulation. The specific relational context in which a market right may be exercised has only a limited bearing on the definition of how the rightholder may or may not use his right. To be sure, the commitment to demarcate the scope of the right at the moment of its birth must inevitably be fudged in a system of judge-made law, just as it unavoidably weakens even in a system of legislated law that has cast doctrinal conceptualism aside. But there a distinction must be drawn between the reinterpretation of entitlements in the light of general purposes, policies, and principles and the willingness to make this reinterpretation depend upon the detailed relational setting in which the right is exercised.

From this second characteristic there follows a third: a bright line separates the areas of entitlement and nonentitlement. Within the boundaries of the entitlement, the rightholder may act as he pleases, deaf to the effect that the exercise of the right may have upon other people. Outside those boundaries, however, he cannot expect to be protected, no matter how appealing his claim may seem morally. This bright line between the zones of right and nonright keeps the rightholder in the circumstance of a gambler.

The market rights of the reformed constitution do not bring about any major change in these operational characteristics, which already apply to the consolidated property rights of existing economies. The number of legally imposed conditions and prohibitions increases while the direct or indirect correction of transaction outcomes diminishes. Yet the practical effects and the imaginative message of the rights that possess these familiar structural features are radically transformed by the institutional reconstruction of the economy.

Immunity Rights

Immunity rights protect the individual against oppression by concentrations of public or private power, against exclusion from the important collective decisions that influence his life, and against the extremes of economic and cultural deprivation. They give him the justified confidence of not being fundamentally endangered by the expanded conflicts of an empowered democracy. This confidence encourages him to participate fearlessly and actively in making collective decisions about the organization of society. This initial definition of immunity rights requires several clarifications.

The interests to be protected by such entitlements may not always be identical to the ones people may themselves define as crucial to their security. But neither are these interests the expression of an independently defined and externally imposed view of what vital security requires. The theory of immunity rights rests, in part, on the empirical hypothesis that freedom from violence, coercion, subjugation, and poverty (defined in both absolute and relative terms) enters into people's ordinary conception of essential security. These goods are rivaled in importance only by the more intangible sense of being accepted by other people as a person, with a place in the world. But, to a varying extent, people have also always put their sense of basic security in the maintenance of particular social roles, jobs, and ways of life. Any attempt to indulge this conception of security would prove incompatible with the institutions of the empowered democracy and with the personal and social ideals that inspire them. The case for the reformed constitution draws heavily on the argument that people can and should wean themselves away from a restrictive, rigidifying view of where they should place their sense of protection.

Modern history has abundantly showed that motivations can be changed in just this way. The triumph of liberal or authoritarian mass politics has weakened the system of fixed social stations that might enable people to seek their essential safety in the performance of a precise social role and in the claims upon resources and support that may accompany these roles. The experience of world history, with its headlong recombination of institutional practices and ways of life, has forced whole peoples increasingly to disengage their abstract sense of collective identity from their faithfulness to particular customs. The play of economic rationality has taught everyone that an insistence upon the perpetuation of rigid social stations and ways of life exacts a formidable cost in economic sluggishness. The constitution of an empowered democracy merely carries these tendencies farther while harnessing them to a liberalizing rather than a despotic cause.

The chief goal of the system of immunity rights is to afford the citizen a safety that encourages him to participate actively and independently in collective decision making. The point is not to favor public engagements by contrast to the pursuit of private interests, a choice that would confront the individual with real dangers and unattractive options. The institutional arrangements and the animating ideas of an empowered democracy progressively weaken the antithesis between civic participation and the pursuit of private interests. Immunity rights encourage the citizen to share in an activity combining features of both, within a more integrated experience of mastery over the social contexts of activity.

The idea that individual security must be strengthened if individual involvement in expanded collective conflicts is to be encouraged also rests on straightforward empirical assumptions. Unless the citizen feels secure in the most vital matters, he will live in constant fear of the controversies in which the life of an empowered democracy abounds. He will soon try to escape from what will appear to him an intolerably perilous situation. He may try to flee the anxieties of this free-for-all by throwing himself under the protection of whatever aspiring strongman may offer to shield him. The republic would soon degenerate into a battle of demagogues or warlords in command of frightened retinues.

Freedom as participation presupposes freedom as immunity. The critics of traditional democratic theory go wrong when they polemically contrast positive and negative freedom to the advantage of the former and treat participatory opportunities as a more than satisfactory substitute for immunity guarantees. But the defenders of conventional liberal democracy are mistaken to treat the narrow forms of participation available in a demobilized democracy as an adequate complement to the safeguards of immunity. They also err in viewing consolidated property rights (which they mistakenly identify with the market form of economic organization) as an indispensable condition of freedom, indispensable if only because their replacement would destroy liberty.

Note that the suggested relation between immunity and participation merely appropriates and develops a familiar theme of classical republican thought. Thus, one traditional justification of the property qualification to the suffrage was the conviction that the poor elector would become dependent upon patrons for physical protection and economic support. This traditional fear has in fact been borne out by the perversions of universal suffrage in contemporary third world countries.

We are accustomed to think that the legal means for assuring individuals a sphere of inviolable security necessarily impose a measure of rigidity on social life. Thus, there may arise the false belief – so characteristic of the diluted, modern versions of social necessitarianism – in an inevitable tension between the desire to secure an area of protected individual safety and the commitment to leave the shape of social relations open to experimental innovation, especially when innovation comes through governmental policy.

A minimum of tension is unavoidable; here as elsewhere we do not have to become perfectionists when we stop being fatalists. Any solution to the problem of immunity requires that some rules remain stable and some resources be set aside. But there is no fixed inverse relation between individual security and social rigidity. You can have more, or you can have less, of both at the same time. A caste system affords individuals a mode and a measure of security, in a fashion bound up with the entrenchment of dependence and dominion and at the cost of an extreme rigidification of social life. Absolute property rights give security too: a protection that leaves more room for movement, and condemns fewer people to gross oppression, than does caste. The immunity rights of an empowered democracy have the same relation to consolidated property that property has to caste.

Immunity rights safeguard two main sets of vital interests. They secure against governmental or private oppression especially insofar as such oppression may threaten or circumscribe the opportunity to participate, actively and equally, in major decisions about the organization of society and the disposition of social resources. They protect against economic or cultural deprivation, especially insofar as it makes the individual dependent upon governmental officials or private patrons. Each major direction of the immunity right requires further discussion.

The narrowly political and civic freedoms that a more democratic constitution must protect do not differ in kind from the freedoms already upheld by conventional democratic practice. They include freedom of expression and association and freedom from arbitrary imprisonment or imprisonment for subversive activity. If the wealth of society permits, these liberties may well incorporate a freedom to opt out of ordinary, gainful social activity and to lead, with a minimum guaranteed income, what many may view as a self-absorbed and parasitic existence. Society stands to benefit from the alternative social visions that may be dreamt up and enacted by these internal exiles or by the countercommunities they form. And the individual's awareness that he may at any time withdraw from society into a proud independence may make it easier for him to display this self-possession within society. But the special quality of political and civic freedoms under an empowered democracy depends less on such additional entitlements than on the enlarged opportunity to exercise the ordinary freedoms and on the many features of the institutional plan that contribute to protect these liberties.

Under this institutional proposal, the exercise of public freedoms ceases to be either a last-ditch defense against despotic governments or an ecstatic deviation from the tenor of ordinary social life. For example, the freedom to associate politically gains new force when institutional arrangements make it easier to establish a connection between disputes at the center of governmental power and debates inside the grassroots organizations that absorb much of people's everyday lives. Even the vote for the central representative bodies and higher offices of the state takes on a greater authority when constitutional arrangements no longer deliberately link the safeguards of freedom to the obstacles that stand in the way of institutional experimentation.

The constitutional scheme contributes to the stability of these essential freedoms by the beliefs that it exemplifies and confirms, by the motivations it reinforces, and by the methods of institutional design it deploys. These contributions help define the distinctive quality of the traditional political and civic freedoms under an empowered democracy.

Remember, first, that these immunity rights do not lend themselves to the exercise of domination and that they impose a minimal rigidity upon the organization of society. For these reasons, no part of the essential security of the individual is made to rest upon the exercise of consolidated property rights. Thus, the rebellion against domination and the attempt to experiment need not endanger – as they so often have – the indispensable safeguards of liberty.

Consider also that the institutional structure of the empowered democracy shares with the traditional version of democracy a commitment to avoid the concentration of governmental power into a small number of offices. Indeed, the proposed constitution multiplies the spheres of institutionalized conflict over the resources for society making. The aim is to avoid associating this multiplication of independent parts of government with constitutional techniques that encourage and perpetuate deadlock and thereby help insulate social arrangements against effective challenge. But because there are many arenas of conflict, the take-over of the state by a faction determined to pervert the constitution, or the withdrawal of the citizenry into a dangerous passivity, cannot be sudden or invisible. Such events would result in the derangement of the relations among governmental institutions and in the stultification of these many, independent centers of institutional experimentation. No constitutional plan can save citizens who have lost the desire for self-direction. It is nevertheless possible to devise institutions that give us many chances to discover the perversion of our political ideals.

Other psychological and intellectual forces complement the stabilizing effect of these methods of institutional design upon the arrangements that secure the immunity of the individual. The institutions of radical democracy increase opportunities of empowerment that merge the sense of satisfying a private interest into the experience of mastery over the social contexts of individual action. Such experiences of empowerment have an addictive force, and the longing for self-assertion becomes attached to the complex of institutions that presuppose and guarantee the security of the individual.

Just as the motivations encouraged by a more democratized constitution are tenacious, the insights on which this constitution draws are irreversible. The programmatic vision defended and developed here has many connections to descriptive and explanatory ideas. But it is important to distinguish the more affirmative and contentious aspects of these ideas – such as the particular theory of transformation presented in Chapter 4 – from the initial negative conceptions on which the affirmative ideas try to make good – such as the theses that institutional systems do not fall into a predefined list or sequence and that they differ in the extent to which they aggravate or efface the contrast between context-preserving routine and context-transforming conflict. These more elementary and largely negative ideas form a proto-theory: a body of ideas that can serve as point of departure for different views of social reality and possibility. They represent an advanced form of skeptical disenchantment with attempts to present particular social orders as either holy or necessary. From the perspective of this proto-theory, deep-logic social thought can be recognized as only a halfhearted version of the experience of seeing through false necessity. The conventional democratic creed of the present day can be seen to continue the superstitious and unargued identification of markets and democracies with the forms of democracies and markets that happen to exist. Freedom is intangibly but immeasurably strengthened when its safeguards no longer depend on such superstitions and when seemingly nihilistic insights can be enlisted in the cause of a liberalizing program.

Freedom against governmental or private oppression represents only one of two major sets of immunity rights. The other set consists in welfare entitlements: guarantees of access to the material and cultural resources needed to make a life. These include provision for nourishment, housing, health care, and education, with absolute standards proportional to the wealth of society. The right to opt out of gainful social activity can be viewed as an extension of these welfare entitlements rather than as a development of the traditional civic liberties.

The key point is that under the proposed regime welfare entitlements must provide a minimal, equal amount of resources, whether as money or as services in kind, rather than respect a claim to keep particular jobs or positions. The enforcement of such claims to specific social places would undermine a program of democratization that puts its hope, and the hope for developing the productive capabilities of society, in the cumulative opening of social life to revision and recombination. The rejection of job tenure as a major direction for welfare entitlements highlights the contrast between the program of empowered democracy and traditional proposals for re-communalizing social life.

The economic institutions of an empowered democracy help generate the resources to fund the welfare entitlements and encourages individuals to make their conceptions of material welfare more independent of tenure in particular jobs. The arrangements of an empowered democracy contribute to the development of productive capabilities and thus promise to increase the absolute amount of wealth available to finance welfare rights. Those arrangements also diminish the familiar conflict between the bias toward economic growth and the commitment to satisfy welfare needs. Collective and individual choices – between consumption and saving, and between short-term and long-term or safe and risky investments – must still be made. But the basic flows of investment decisions are no longer critically influenced by relatively small numbers of investors, managers, and entrepreneurs who may be frightened into disinvestment by every concession to the poor or every advance toward greater equality of circumstance. Moreover, together with the sharp curtailment of inheritance, the rejection of consolidated property rights as the chief vehicle of market decentralization makes it unnecessary for the welfare system to serve as a relatively futile and disruptive means to moderate inequalities that the operation of the economy constantly re-creates and sharpens.

At the same time, the institutions of the empowered democracy weaken the fixity of special social roles, or stations in the social division of labor, and restrain the allegiances that attach people to these fixed places. In this way, the institutions help stabilize a type of welfare entitlement that minimizes the creation of vested rights in particular jobs.

Welfare entitlements and civic freedoms have the same operational features, readily inferred from the preceding discussion of the social ideals and empirical assumptions underlying the theory of immunity rights. Discussion of these structural characteristics can be summary, because in all but minor respects they coincide with the formal traits of consolidated property. But the social significance of the structural features changes radically with the shift in their institutional setting.

First, the source of the immunity right is the situation of ongoing connection to the society – the mere circumstance of continuing involvement in its institutional arrangements. The importance of a clear-cut dichotomy between citizenship and residency diminishes when decisional processes within grassroots or productive organizations resemble and amplify decision making in the central representative bodies of government. Note that the source of the immunity right is a situation – and, indeed, a situation that transcends all particular engagements. Yet the specificity of this source does not make the other structural features of immunity rights any different from the operational characteristics of traditional rights of contract or property, whose sources are articulated agreements or state-imposed duties.

The immunity rights are defined as rigidly as possible at the time of their initial formulation. There is no more latitude for their redefinition at the moment of exercise than inheres, inevitably, in the interpretive freedom of the law applier. The particular relational circumstance in which the right is to be exercised is largely irrelevant. For the immunity rights define the safeguards – the minimal defenses – with which the individual enters all the dealings in which he does participate.

Consequently, a bright line circumscribes the boundaries of each immunity right. The rightholder can expect to distinguish confidently between the factual circumstances in which the law protects him in the asserted exercise of such an entitlement and those in which it does not. He need not subject the use of his right to a calculus of its effects upon other people. All the entitlements that make up the system of rights must be developed and enforced without prejudice to these safeguards, which secure each individual in a proud and jealous independence and enable him to experiment with contract and community without the fear that he may become another person's dependent.

Destabilization Rights

Destabilization rights protect the citizen's interest in breaking open the large-scale organizations or the extended areas of social practice that remain closed to the destabilizing effects of ordinary conflict and thereby sustain insulated hierarchies of power and advantage. The combination of immunity rights with destabilization rights gives legal expression to the central institutional mechanism of the whole constitutional plan. The destabilization entitlement ties the collective interest in ensuring that all institutions and practices can be criticized and revised to the individual interest in avoiding oppression. The empirical basis for this connection is the role that closure to effective challenge plays in the entrenchment of factional privilege.

The primary respondents to the citizens who claim a right to have an organization or an area of social practice destabilized are the nongovernmental organizations or the actual individuals who are legally competent, or actually able, to reconstruct the objectionable arrangements. The subsidiary respondent is the state, perhaps even a special branch of government. Governmental action to disrupt and reconstruct the overprotected and subjugation-producing arrangements may be needed not only because the people in charge of the organizations or practices at issue may be the biggest beneficiaries of the insulated hierarchies but because there may be no people visibly in charge. Such a situation is especially likely to occur when the claimant seeks to disrupt an area of social practice rather than a discrete organization.

Consider now in greater detail the content of destabilization rights. They encompass both a negative and a positive use. Their negative aim has already been described as the attempt to deny protection against destabilizing conflict to either institutions or noninstitutional arrangements whenever this immunity to conflict seems to generate stable ties of domination and dependence. The destabilizing conflict that must be kept open may come from within a particular institution, if such an institution is the target of the right. It may result from the ordinary activities of a sector of the society or the economy. Or it may even take place in the central deliberative processes of the republic. What matters is that the arrangements in question be available to *some* mode of attack. When the focus falls on the evil to be remedied rather than on its cause, the destabilization entitlement can be redescribed as the citizen's right to prevent any faction of the society from gaining a privileged hold upon any of the means for creating the social future within the social present. The destabilization right can also be depicted in a way that draws attention to the process by which immunity to conflict arises and gives rise to power and privilege. The two descriptions overlap because the exercise of a privileged hold over the resources for society making allows those who exercise the hold to subjugate those who do not.

The voluntary passivity of potentially affected publics may be the original cause of an entrenchment of prerogative. But the turning point that justifies the exercise of a destabilization right takes place only when a new burst of collective activity by the immediate victims of the newly entrenched prerogatives can no longer easily overcome the entrenchment-producing effects of this political withdrawal.

Destabilization is not enough; intervention provoked by the exercise of a destabilization right must change the disrupted practice or institution. The entire argument of this book supports the idea that susceptibility to revision is not a merely negative characteristic. Some sets of institutional arrangements go farther than others toward overcoming the contrast between context-preserving routine and context-transforming struggle. What is true of large constellations of practices must also hold, though less clearly, for particular, relatively isolated practices. But the search for the affirmative content of the seemingly negative idea of a structure-revising structure must be tempered here by a concern not to circumscribe unnecessarily the freedom to experiment either with the content of the general laws or with the design of particular institutions. The reconstructive activity unleashed by the exercise of a destabilization right must therefore obey a negative presumption. It should aim at the minimum of reconstruction required to satisfy the negative aims of the entitlement rather than at the form an institution or practice would take if it were to make the greatest possible contribution to the development of negative capability. Instead of being used to force men and women to be free, it should give them a second chance before they decide to enslave themselves.

The destabilization right whose negative and affirmative content I have just described has counterparts in variants of the complex injunctive relief found in contemporary law. Such relief frequently has courts intervening in important institutions, such as schools and mental asylums, or in major areas of social practice, such as electoral organization, and reconstructing them in the name of democratic ideals said to inspire complex bodies of law. The character of the relief afforded by destabilization rights can be brought out all the more clearly by contrast to these established remedies. On the one hand, the destabilization entitlements go farther than anything available in current law. Freed once and for all from the restrictive model of consolidated property, they can develop unashamedly as devices of institutional disruption and reconstruction. The exercise of these rights brings into question a part of the collective structure of society rather than serving merely as a means to vindicate a transitory interest within that structure. Because they do not suit standard judicial or legislative settings they may even have to be elaborated and enforced by a special branch of government. (Recall the suggestion, in the section on the organization of government, as to how such a branch might work.) On the other hand, however, the destabilization rights have a more precise focus than the complex injunctions of present law. They serve not to embody specific ideals of human association but to ensure that, whatever the enacted forms of human association may be, they will preserve certain minimal qualities: above all, the quality of being readily replaceable.

The whole theory of destabilization rights outlined in this section rests on a key empirical hypothesis: the belief that treats insulation against destabilizing conflict as a necessary condition for the entrenchment of structures of domination and dependence. The explanatory social theory helping sustain this program of empowered democracy emphasizes the connection between freedom from subjugation and freedom as mastery over context. The legal practice of destabilization rights must itself become one of the principal ways of testing and developing this hypothesis experimentally.

To gain a sense of the practical settings in which to deploy the abstract ideas discussed up to now, consider an example of a situation calling for the exercise of destabilization rights under a fully mature version of the proposed constitution. Suppose some of the enterprises trading under the capital fund are unusually successful, thanks to a combination of exceptional diligence or skill and unforeseen market conditions. They succeed in using economic influence, electoral pressure, and policy persuasion to change the terms on which capital is made available. Under the new terms they are allowed to gain control of other, subordinate enterprises and to hire workers for temporary, dead-end, and underpaid jobs shunned by the stable, relatively privileged labor force of the enterprise. Once established in this new situation, they can extend their wealth and influence still farther. They increase the autonomy of the capital fund from the central deliberative processes of the democracy, leaving technocrats, beholden to the favored enterprises and groups, in effective charge of crucial financial decisions. The subversion of the nascent privileges now requires something between a mere shift in policy and a constitutional revolution.

In such a circumstance, the agency of government responsible for developing destabilization rights may move to rob the nascent prerogatives of their defenses. The law may provide that some of these interventions take effect unless and until reversed by a combination of other branches of government. Thus, the enforcing authority may order the enterprises in question to moderate their internal hierarchy or relinquish some of the devices by which they exclude new workers or relegate them to a permanently inferior status. Other destabilizing interventions may come closer to jeopardizing the democracy's freedom to experiment. Although taking effect immediately, they may need to be reconfirmed, within a short time, by other branches of government or by the general electorate. Such a procedure might be suitable, for example, when the responsible agency of government intervened to prevent the bodies directly responsible for administering the rotating capital fund from using their discretion in a systematically biased fashion to favor a certain group of enterprises in ways not adequately justified by the importance of support for up-and-coming innovators. Other types of intervention would not take effect at all until confirmed by the electorate or by a broad range of intermediate representative bodies. This suspended application might be called for whenever the asserted destabilization right came into conflict with decisions of the democracy's major representative assemblies: the privilege-entrenching measures might, for example, have been laid down by the national parliament.

The example of the perverted capital fund already suggests the importance of developing standards that give specificity to the abstract ideal inspiring the theory of destabilization rights. There are two ways in which the ideals underlying the theory of destabilization rights gain the concreteness that enables them to produce practical consequences. Analyzing these processes serves to link the basic conception of destabilization rights with the distinctive operational characteristics of such rights. Each form of specification affects the other types of entitlement, and each has an established place within the reigning styles of legal doctrine. Yet their importance undergoes here a hypertrophy that imprints special features on the right.

The first method of specification is the advance of the abstract idea of availability to criticism and challenge toward increasing concreteness. The subsidiary standards required by the march toward particularity may be drawn to some extent from the developing body of explanatory and normative ideas that lends sense and justification to the entire constitutional plan. But because a constitution must gain a life independent of the doctrines that may have originally inspired it, the criteria must also rely upon the laws and arrangements of the society. For the bulk of the arrangements and laws of an empowered democracy must give a range of concrete expressions to the vague notion of a structure-revising structure. No legal theory or legal practice can keep this ideal alive once it has lost its hold on the conscience of the citizenry and has ceased to be realized, however imperfectly, in the actual organization of social life. Experience, recorded in a tradition of institutional practice, must show how far the quest for negative capability has gone, what distinctive problems it must face in different areas of society, and which of its varied social meanings it takes at each moment of its history and in each area of its application.

The other, complementary method of specification consists in treating self-revision not as an abstract ideal to be made more concrete by a series of contextual definitions but as a goal to be advanced by suitable causal means. Empirical questions must be asked and answered with respect to each major area of application of the destabilization rights. Which institutional practices are in fact most immunized against challenge and revision? When is this immunity to attack most likely to generate stable relations of dominion and dependence? And when does it in fact generate them? Which forms of disruption and reconstruction will promote most effectively and economically the goal of openness to revision? And which will minimize the danger of continuing intervention by external authorities? The empirical difficulty of answering these questions and the administrative difficulty of acting upon the answers are two reasons why traditional court institutions may be unsuitable to develop and enforce the entitlements.

The operational characteristics of destabilization rights result directly from the two modes of specification just discussed. First, the immediate source of the right is neither a fully articulated agreement nor the unilateral imposition of a duty by the state but the interplay between a basic commitment of the constitutional plan and the emergent practices that place the commitment in jeopardy. Second, the initial, legislative definition of the entitlement must always be complemented by an important element of specification at the moment and in the circumstance of the claimed exercise of the right. Legislation may go some way toward codifying the two processes of specification: it may distinguish situations and remedies in ways that implicitly answer the relevant causal questions and that implicitly provide contextual definitions of the abstract ideal of freedom from subjugation through availability to revision. Both sets of issues, however, must be reopened at the moment of the asserted exercise of the right if contextual definition and causal investigation are to do the work required by the theory of destabilization rights. A third operational characteristic follows from the second. Because the redefinition of the entitlement must pass through the surprises of causal investigation and the shifts of contextual analysis, no bright line surrounds the area of the protected legal claim. The point of destabilization rights is not to demarcate a fixed zone of discretionary action, within which an individual rightholder may do whatever he pleases, but to prevent recurrent, institutionalized relationships among groups from falling into certain prohibited routines of closure and subjugation. So the controlling image is the mandated, context-specific disruption of complex collective arrangements rather than the vigilant defense of a zone of untrammeled individual discretion.

Solidarity Rights

Solidarity rights give legal form to social relations of reliance and trust. The aims of the theory of solidarity rights extend beyond the limited goals of the institutional program to the transformed communal and personal relations an empowered democracy may help generate and sustain. The establishment of a system of entitlements that gives an explicit place to solidarity rights represents part of a plan of institutional transformation. But it also serves the cultural-revolutionary transformation of personal relations that goes hand in hand with the plan to empower democracy.

Solidarity rights form part of a set of social relations enabling people to enact a more defensible version of the communal ideal than any version currently available to them. This reconstruction of the idea of community does not rest content with either the commitment to exclude conflict from a charmed circle of group harmony or with the willingness to limit the play of self-interest. Both altruism and harmony are deemphasized in this reconstructed image of community. Insofar as they continue to play a role, they do so for the sake of their contribution to the view of community as a zone of heightened mutual vulnerability. In this zone people may experiment more freely with ways to achieve self-assertion through passionate attachments.

A later section develops this communal ideal and argues its superiority over altruism and harmony as the nub of the communal ideal. This revised conception of community relates the communal ideal to the central concern with empowerment instead of relegating it to the role of refuge against the brutality of workaday life. It encourages people to recognize and use the element of conflict that marks even the closest personal connections.

This changed understanding of community helps resolve an apparent paradox: an institutional program that seems to exalt collective militancy, with all its conflictual consequences, is claimed to support a communal ideal. But the paradox fades once each of its supposed elements is put in its place. For one thing, the ideal of community invoked here is no longer defined by contrast to conflict. For another thing, the institutional program is oriented less to the perpetuation of struggle than to the emancipation of social life from the automatisms and hierarchies with which the rigid contrast of conflict and community is invariably associated. Only through the softening of the opposition between context-preserving routine and context-transforming conflict can the mechanisms of domination and dependence be subverted. Only through this subversion can communal attachments be rescued from their traditional status as mere reprieves from the brutality of everyday life or mere restraints upon the untrammeled exercise of privilege.

Solidarity rights apply to relations within distinct communities and to relations of trust and reliance that take hold outside a well-defined communal setting. (Compare to destabilization rights, which encompass relations within and outside an organization.) The domain of solidarity rights is the field of the half-articulate relations of trusting interdependence that absorb so much of ordinary social life but remain troublesome aberrations for a legal theory devoted to the model of consolidated property. The situations calling for the exercise of such entitlements include family life, continuing business relationships (as distinguished from one-shot transactions), and the varied range of circumstances falling under fiduciary principles in contemporary law. The trust such relations require may be voluntary and reciprocal or half-deliberate and unequal, usually in the setting of disparities of power or advantage.

The chief practical legal expression of the refined view of community underlying the theory of solidarity rights is the legal protection of claims to abide by implicit obligations to take other people's situations and expectations into account. By contrast to traditional contract law, the obligations are only partly explicit and the expectations refer to detailed, continuing relational positions rather than to instantaneous arm's-length transactions. The restraints these entitlements impose on individual self-interest matter solely as a by-product of the effort to vindicate a delicate texture of interdependencies and representations. It is through an analysis of this texture that the central categories of the law of solidarity rights must be developed.

It follows that solidarity rights should not be misunderstood as claims to a subjective state of mind on the part of the person who owes the rightholder a duty. The point is not to ensure that the owner of the duty has a benevolent and concerned frame of mind. Pursued to its ultimate conclusions, such a subjectivist goal would result in a stifling and hypocritical despotism of virtue, obsessed with invasive yet futile methods. The immediate aim, instead, is to accomplish just the reverse of what consolidated property offers the rightholder. People bound by solidarity rights are prevented from taking refuge in an area of absolute discretion within which they can remain deaf to the claims others make upon them. Thus solidarity rights deny the discretionary action both immunity rights and market rights seek to protect. Wherever such entitlements apply, people must answer to the claims arising from the usual blend of reliance-in-fact, half-made promises, and customary role-dependent standards of obligations. Subjective motives are to be influenced, if at all, only in the long run: the theory and practice of solidarity rights represents but a small part of an institutional program that enacts certain ideas about society and personality and favors some impulses over others.

The operational characteristics of solidarity rights can be inferred from the theory and practice of their more limited counterparts in contemporary law. These counterparts include the law of fiduciary relationships, the contractual and delictual protection of reliance, the doctrines of good faith and of abuse of rights, and the many doctrinal devices by which private law supports communal relations while continuing to represent society as a world of strangers.

The first structural feature has to do with the sources of the obligations protected by solidarity rights. Such obligations arise from partly articulate relations of interdependence rather than from either fully bargained agreements or the unilateral imposition of a duty by the state. The obligations covered by solidarity rights resemble the vast majority of the duties people have traditionally recognized in the most diverse societies, even in the few societies refusing to give such duties substantial legal protection. But the characteristic quality of these obligations is transformed by an institutional order that encourages the jumbling up of fixed social roles and the disruption of systematic hierarchical and communal contrasts.

The second operational trait of solidarity rights refers to the relation between the entitlement as initially defined and the entitlement as redefined at the moment of a claimed exercise. General principles and discriminating standards must be developed, along the lines previously suggested, to single out the recurrent situations suitable for the enforcement of these entitlements. And other, complementary standards and principles must distinguish between such situations in order to determine the legal consequences of recognizing a particular solidarity right. For example, an unequal relation may require the imposition of a greater duty of self-restraint on the advantaged party, whereas a more equal common endeavor may justify reciprocity in the allocation of duties. But the very standards deployed in this initial definition of the right invoke an additional definition in context. For only the specific relational context, analyzed in detail, can reveal a structure of interdependence and show its complex blend of reliance-in-fact, semiexplicit representation, and equality or dependence. The program of empowered democracy increases the particularity of relations of interdependence because it undermines rigid role systems and the moral expectations such systems produce. It therefore also makes the contextual redefinition of solidarity entitlements all the more important.

The third operational trait of solidarity rights follows directly from the second characteristic. No bright line divides the area of conduct in which the holder of a solidarity right may claim protection and the area in which he may not. Instead of contrasting a zone of unquestioned discretion to an area of no protection, this class of entitlements favors a nuanced grading of degrees of legal support for the rightholder. The determination of where the rightholder stands along this spectrum of legal protection depends in every instance upon an analysis of his prelegal relation to the person against whom he wants to assert the right.

It does not follow from the establishment of solidarity rights that they ought to be coercively enforced nor from the commitment to enforce them that they should be overseen by the same judicial bodies responsible for administering, in last resort, immunity and market rights. I have argued that destabilization rights should be applied by a distinctive branch of government. Similarly, many of the solidarity rights may best be enforced, when they are enforced at all, by more informal means of mediation, with more ample participation from parties, families, communities, or work teams, depending on the subject matter of the dispute.

But many solidarity rights may best remain unenforceable, as a statement of an ideal. The mere threat to let black-robed officials or officious companions enforce them might fatally injure the quality of reciprocal trust they require. The most serious candidates for exclusion from coercive enforcement are the relations in which a rough equality of power coincides with the central importance of trust to the success of the association.

It may be objected that an unenforceable right is no right at all and that merely to speak of such entitlements is to disinter the illogical language of natural rights with its implicit but halfhearted allusion to a natural, absolute context of social life. But it is a mistake to identify the positivism of governmental enforcement and the idea of innate and eternal entitlements as the only two senses that rights language may bear. A system of rights, in the sense employed by this discussion of all rights, is fundamentally the institutionalized part of social life, backed up by a vision of possible and desirable human association. The limits to rights are the limits to institutionalization itself. Not everything in a system of rights need be enforceable, on pain of being treated, if it is unenforceable, as either a natural right or a meaningless gesture. The rights that governmental or other institutions may not enforce remain a public declaration of a public vision, extending, qualifying, and clarifying the ideals embodied in other, enforceable parts of the system of rights.

To be sure, the refusal to enforce certain rights weakens the sense in which the part of social life those rights address is institutionalized at all. But such a weakening fits well with the idea of solidarity rights as a point of passage from the institutionalized to the personal, non-institutionalized aspects of social life. The vision underlying these rights, and inspiring the system of rights as a whole, is partly a conception of how the institutional and the noninstitutional realms should connect.

OPPORTUNITIES, ALLIANCES, AND TRANSITIONS

Empowered democracy is not meant to be a utopian blueprint, good for all time. Instead, it interprets the implications of a social ideal, intimately connected with a method of social explanation, for a particular historical circumstance. An important part of the programmatic argument therefore is made of ideas that suggest the occasions on which such a program might be implemented, the class alliances that might sustain its initial application, and the transitional forms that might constitute intermediate steps between its proposals and current varieties of governmental or economic organization.

These subsidiary ideas are even more tentative and loosely connected than the programmatic arguments they complete. Their value is to exemplify a way of thinking rather than to replace a judgment of the distinctive demands and opportunities of particular historical situations. The impossibility of reducing the implementation of a program to theoretical formulas is less a limitation of theoretical discourse than a consequence of features of social and historical life that an adequate theory helps us understand. According to deep-logic social theory (in its evolutionary variant), programmatic thought, when possible at all, consists in the effort to anticipate a higher stage of social evolution or to work out the secondary problems each new stage brings in its wake. The same assumptions underlying this approach to programmatic thought also make it possible to ask such questions as, What are the occasions, the class alliances, and the intermediate institutional arrangements necessary and sufficient to the inauguration of a new form of social life? But if formative contexts of power and production fit into no well-defined sequences or lists and if they can be pulled apart and recombined piecemeal, any search for a theoretically based formula of transition must be misguided. What can be legitimately said about implementation and transition must take a far more open form. If the results seem disappointingly tentative, at least they are not illusory and make no sharp break between theoretical insight and the subjective experience of transformative effort. Moreover, the looseness of these ideas does not make them theoretically insignificant. On the contrary, they bring out aspects of this view of society that would otherwise remain implicit. These aspects tighten the link between the explanatory and the programmatic arguments of *False Necessity*.

Opportunities

Deep-logic social theory is obsessed with the contrast between reformist tinkering and all-out revolution. The concept of revolution has traditionally equated two events that do not always or even often go together: a style of action – the violent seizure of the state by a revolutionary mass led by a conspiratorial vanguard – and an outcome – the radical substitution of an entire formative context. Whatever the teachings of official doctrine, the basic conditions in modern times for episodes that come close to combining these two characteristics have been the division of the elites and the paralysis of the heavy arm of officialdom. As the forces that watch over the stability of the social world are temporarily checked, pieties that seemed unshakable begin to shake and inherited assumptions about social possibility may suddenly expand. If a well-organized movement, with a realistic plan, is waiting in the wings, something may actually happen.

By far the most important favoring circumstance for the occurrence of such subversive conditions has been defeat at war, with its fearsome burden of slaughter and disappointment and its tangible evidence of the remaking of social relations through wartime mobilization. In the third world, the attempt to overthrow an unpopular dictatorship has proven a distant runner-up. But war or subversion produce these subversive effects only when combined with a real and consciously felt contrast between the elites and the masses.

In the circumstances the world had reached by the late twentieth century these classic conditions of revolution had dwindled in subversive potential. War had become too terrible to serve as the normal midwife to revolutionary upheaval except along the periphery of conflict between the great powers. The overthrow of clumsy tyrannies was an activity restricted to parts of the third world. The force of the contrast between elites and masses had been steadily eroded in the industrial democracies by the practice of an antimobilizational mass politics and by the strengthening of a popular culture that overrode the distinction between high culture and folk culture. If deep-logic social theory was to be believed, significant transformation had become steadily more impossible, save as a by-product of catastrophic and unforeseeable events.

In the course of modern history, however, there have been at least two other circumstances or tendencies that have regularly created opportunities for the more or less deliberate reconstruction of formative contexts. The type of reconstruction they permit typically falls far short of the all-out change envisioned by the idea of revolution. But both despite this limit and because of it, such favoring circumstances are especially relevant to the implementation of the institutional program outlined here.

One circumstance is the periodic need to realign institutional arrangements for the sake of continued economic growth. Viewed over the long run, the development of collective practical capabilities requires a heightening of the plasticity of social life. This heightening can take either predominantly coercive or predominantly consensual forms. It can also be achieved by reforms that either minimize or maximize the break with the preexisting social order. Often a solution easier to accept in the short run, because it accommodates more readily the established structure of organized interests, turns out to be less promising in the long run, for precisely the same reason. The emerging formative institutional context of power and production, when contrasted to its major petty bourgeois rival, represents just such an option on the largest historical scale. But a similar choice reappea~s on more modest dimensions.

Thus, the style of industrial organization and the pattern of dealings between government, on one side, and the entrepreneurial and working classes, on the other, has changed discontinuously in the course of modern Western history. Each discontinuity originates in large social conflicts as well as in the pressure upon entrepreneurial groups and national governments to escape the doom of a superseded specialization. Each discontinuous break also allows for both more conservative and more daring solutions.

For the advanced Western countries of the present day, the pressure for realignment takes the form of the need to overcome the special pattern of constraint upon economic growth analyzed earlier: the institutional stimulus to an organizational gigantism that economies of scale cannot justify, the inability to settle on a scheme of rewards and burdens that permits a coherent macroeconomic policy, and the failure to give a larger role to the vanguardist, flexibly organized industries that might allow the older industrial economies to deal more successfully with the changing international division of labor.

These problems might be solved in ways minimizing the break with established institutional arrangements and with the conceptions of interest and collective identity these arrangements help shape. Thus, for example, a distinctive deal might be reached that merely splits the differences among opposing forces in the production system and in the electoral contests of the democracy. Public policy might make funds, incentives, and skilled labor more readily available to the flexible, vanguard industries without changing any of the legal-institutional arrangements that enable rigid, mass-production industries to protect themselves against market instabilities.

But similar results may also be achieved by means that imply a more drastic departure from current practice. The institutional means for protecting mass-production industries against market instabilities might be abolished, a move that would imply far-reaching changes in the system of private rights as well as in the style of work organization. The core consensus necessary to the conduct of a coherent macroeconomic policy might be achieved by a more aggressive deconcentration of the industrial system. Thus, the power of big business and organized labor would be undermined; the correlation of forces in the productive system would more nearly approach its counterpart in the economic arena. Beyond a certain point, such a deconcentration would require a way to make large amounts of capital available to teams of entrepreneurs and workers that nevertheless prevented these teams from building a permanent industrial empire. It would also imply a way of protecting and representing workers different from the traditional mass-constituency union, whose fate seems indissolubly bound up with large-scale mass production industry. An advanced version of this alternative route to worker empowerment would encourage a more fluid contrast between workers and entrepreneurs: against the background of extended welfare entitlements, all could look to membership in a team with a defeasible claim upon the social capital fund. Thus, one thing would lead to another, and the more radical version of industrial realignment would create a string of opportunities to change, piece by piece, the formative institutional context of power and production.

You need not imagine this more radical realignment as the execution of a plan imposed from above. The adoption of a different style of economic policy and industrial organization means that established interests must find new instruments and even new definitions in an institutional structure that has been at least marginally revised. Such a transfer can never be smooth; it engenders conflict. Success in passing from one moment of economic organization to another, with only a minimum of social and institutional change, represents a triumph of conservative statesmanship. For if conflict is allowed to get out of hand, some of the contenders may come to see their interests as lying in a more radical version of the shift, depending upon the ideas they and their leaders adopt. The immediate concerns that might favor a more reconstructive strategy and the transitional forms it might take are topics for later discussion.

The need for realignment in economic policy and industrial organization is not the sole occasion to choose between more conservative and more radical revisions of the established institutional order. The search for ever more ambitious forms of personal expression in the setting of continuing economic dissatisfaction, provides another occasion to choose between more conservative and more radical revisions of the formative institutional context. Of the revolutions in sensibility that have accompanied the history of mass politics, none is more remarkable than the vague though universal cult of self-fulfillment. The self-fulfillment that serves as the object of this piety is one that, unlike most of its predecessors or counterparts in the history of feeling, cannot be defined as a happiness gained from performing the duties of a particular social station. Indeed, the newfangled happiness depends, to a large extent, upon experiences of self-expression and association that escape the dictates of preestablished social roles and even depend upon a willingness to violate such role expectations.

This cult of self-fulfillment is intimately bound up, in the age of mass politics and world history, with the practice of invidious comparison. All may readily compare their advantages with those of everyone else, and imagine their own lives as graced, on a smaller scale, with the material or spiritual benefits that accrue to the most successful. No longer do envy and ambition move within the narrow confines of the inequalities existing within a particular social rank or community, with its distinct way of life and unique standards of propriety and success.

Invidious comparison applies to the more spiritual benefits of social life as well as to crude economic advantage. People do not wait to be secure and well cared for before pressing their claim to varieties of self-fulfillment that might have been thought luxuries of the rich, leisured, or overrefined. On the contrary, they advance this claim as soon as they feel even a modest reprieve from the pressure of material need.

The new moral message is conveyed by an ever more universal popular culture that combines in a single mode of discourse the ancient themes of romance, reenacted in countless folk cultures, with the fancy gospel of high modernism, not perhaps as originally stated by philosophers and writers but as lived out in the politics of personal relations. This popular culture crosses the boundaries of all civilizations, insofar as distinct civilizations still exist. To the millions intent on their television or movie screens, in their moments of bored or exhausted leisure, it offers something midway between an entertainment and a revelation.

The message purveyed on this world scale and with such relentless insistence can be read as an offer to let everyone participate in the material and spiritual advantages of a particular way of life: the existence of the educated middle classes of the rich North Atlantic countries, with its security, comforts, and gadgetry, its democratic safeguards and private joys, and its titillating flirtation with the quasi-modernist popular culture whose excesses may still occasionally shock. On an alternative reading, however, the point of the message is to evoke a form of life that allows people to experiment with varieties of practical collaboration, personal attachment, and individual self-expression that obey no preestablished logic of social roles. The two interpretations differ less than might appear: the Western way of life so coveted by the propaganda of self-fulfillment has gone further than its predecessors in liquefying entrenched structures of social division and hierarchy and in creating the institutional and imaginative conditions for a more free-floating experience of exchange, attachment, and subjectivity.

Like the need for realignment in economic policy and industrial organization, the pursuit of self-fulfillment can be undertaken in ways that minimize the pressure to change the formative institutional context of social life. Indeed, the dominant practice of the cultural-revolutionary politics of personal relations, and of the vision of intimate success that inspires it, has been privatistic: a flight into private enjoyments that require no fundamental reconstruction of institutional arrangements and of the social divisions and hierarchies that these arrangements sustain. Thus, the willingness to put the fine structure of social life up for grabs and subject it to modernist tests is often accompanied by a prostrate acquiescence in the established order of society, while the leftist attack on current social organization just as often goes together with a failure to reimagine and reconstruct the microstructure of personal relations. But the privatist and fatalist pursuit of self-fulfillment has its disappointments, which create an opportunity to redirect the search for happiness toward an alliance between the politics of personal relations and the politics of institutional reconstruction.

First, the established institutional systems impose upon both economic growth and egalitarian redistribution the many constraints earlier discussed. They therefore make it hard to support the dazzling life-style required by even the more privatistic and hedonistic versions of this ideal of self-fulfillment. Although these dominant institutions and interests may encourage the consumerist rapture of a privatistic hedonism, economic life suffers from the subversive effect of this hedonism on diligence at work.

Second, the ease with which the modernist teaching gets compartmentalized into private life is balanced against the constant temptation to pass from the private to the public domain. The relation between superiors and subalterns in the organizations in which people spend their working lives provides the bridge between private concern and public stance. The subversion of deference, the demand to share in discretionary authority, and even the pretense of egalitarian camaraderie cannot finally be satisfied without reforming these organizations – offices and factories, shops and schools – in ways that push present economic arrangements to their limits of tolerance.

Third, the privatist solution exacts a heavy cost even when it can be successfully stabilized. Private enjoyments that remain unconnected to a broader solidarity or to a collective historical project soon take on the quality of a desperate and obsessional narcissism. Because they offer the individual no sense of participation in something greater and more lasting than himself, they belittle him in his own eyes.

Such troubles create an opportunity for a version of the pursuit of self-fulfillment congenial to institutional reconstruction. For the program outlined in this chapter shows how the institutional structure of society must be changed if the cultural-revolutionary ideal is to be more fully realized in social life. Such change requires, and can best begin, through the remaking of basic arrangements and enacted beliefs rather than through the redistribution of resources within an unchallenged order.

The preceding pages have described two very different types of occasions that contemporary social life opens up for revolutionary reform along the lines sketched earlier. Less dramatic than the sequel of war and occupation, they are also less rare or risky. Located at the most humdrum and ethereal extremes of social experience, they suggest the variety of points from which the reconstructive effort may depart. But in the end they are no more than the most obvious examples of a pervasive principle, namely, that the opportunity to destabilize and to reconstruct is always built into the very devices that perpetuate the existing social peace.

Alliances

You may object that the discussion of opportunities for institutional reconstruction is superfluous until you are told who will find it in his interest to support such a program. Few aspects of the programmatic discussion can be so likely to disappoint a mind formed either in worldly ambition or in theoretical study than the failure to specify who could be expected to support such a program and for what reasons. To answer correctly the question about interests we must first define the sense in which it can be legitimately asked. Such a definition is implicit in earlier arguments about the contrasting assumptions that deep-structure social theory and the alternative defended in this book bring to class-interest or interest-group analysis.

In its illustrative Marxist version, deep-structure theory claims that escalating conflict makes explicit an underlying logic of group interests that is ordinarily concealed by the compromises and equivocations of the social peace. To each mode of production there supposedly corresponds a system of conflicts among objective class interests, including the interest of the class whose particular stake in the inauguration of the next mode of production coincides with the universal interest of mankind in developing the productive forces of society. Though class interests may be understood with greater or lesser clarity, and though such triumphs or failures of insight may have fateful consequences for particular classes in particular countries, they cannot alter the basic facts about class goals.

This approach to the political consequences of group interests has encouraged disastrous mistakes even on the part of those who pride themselves on their detachment from theoretical dogma. As the basic terms of social life open up to transformative conflict, the baneful influence of these ideas upon the political practice of radicals becomes more visible. Thus, this influence has become most evident in the third world, whereas its European heyday was the period between the wars.

Remember now the main tenets of the alternative approach to

group interests suggested by the social theory worked out here. The strategic implications of this approach will soon become clear. The stabilization of a social world may occur at different levels of permanent plasticity, that is to say, with different degrees of contrast between context-preserving routine and context-revising conflict. Assumptions harden about collective identities, social opportunities, and group interests. Each group takes more or less for granted its position in the entrenched scheme of social hierarchy and division – its distinctive niche in the social division of labor or its communal way of life, which may or may not be closely related to occupational position.

But even in the circumstance of maximum hypothetical rigidity, the perception of group interests must deal with ambiguity and allow for the influence of opinion and persuasion. For one thing, the order of division and hierarchy never becomes entirely cohesive, just as the contrast between routine and revolution never becomes absolute. The agent cannot reconcile the contradictory clues to his "real interests" without recourse to a partly independent set of ideas that resolves ambiguities and sets priorities. For another thing, the promotion of a predefined interest can always follow two alternative tacks: a narrowing strategy that clings to a niche and defends it against the closest rivals (and especially the immediate inferiors) or a broadening strategy that seeks to enlarge alliances against more fundamental common adversaries (e.g., the bosses). What begins as a tactical partnership can easily turn into a redefinition of collective identities.

As conflict escalates in scope or intensity and questions more and more of the terms of social life, the hardened logic of group interests undergoes a contradictory change. On the one hand, the concern for security and preemptive defense amid the tumults of the social world leads each group to dig into its present threatened situation all the more firmly and to strike out all the more fiercely against perceived enemies. On the other hand, the predetermination of interests by social position loses its force. For not only are established arrangements disturbed, but the imagination of realistic alternatives penetrates everyday experience. People come to be divided increasingly by differences of opinion that antecedent position or experience predict with increasingly less accuracy. Social classes (as well as all other hierarchically or communally defined groups) dissolve, to a greater extent than before, into parties of opinion.

Thus, the dissolution of classes into parties of opinion is not a once-and-for-all event taking place at a single moment at the end of history. It is, rather, a tendency always present even in the most rigid social circumstances and rapidly accelerated whenever context-preserving quarrels turn into context-subverting struggles. A major aim of the program of empowered democracy is to make this dissolution stick: to turn it into a permanent feature of ordinary social life. Such an ambition generalizes the meaning of the attempt to make social life resemble what, to a considerable degree, liberal politics are already like.

This view of the relation between interests and opinions has important implications for the strategic practice of transformative movements. Such a practice must be inspired by a double vision. It must identify the groups that in a given stabilized social situation are most likely to favor a given transformative practice. To accomplish this task it must understand correctly the logic of organized interests as it exists, neither exaggerating nor understating its ambiguity. But, at the same time, it must anticipate how escalating conflict may change the content of this logic and weaken its force. To this extent the reformers must treat one another as members of parties of opinion that override and redraw the fault lines of the social order. They must see in themselves and in those whom they seek to seduce the protagonists of a humanity that must choose its assumptions about identities and interests.

Notice that the two modes of vision – the one accepting and the other defying established definitions of group interest – cannot be just sequentially ordered; the second mode must be deployed from the very beginning to complement and to discount the calculus of interests, even though its initial role may be greatly restricted. Notice also that the two modes do not contrast as realism and idealistic aspiration; they both belong to the analysis of social reality. This last fact throws light on the perspective from which the whole programmatic argument has been developed. The appeal to the universal conscience of humanity expresses here a thesis about the unique and provisional character of any given logic of group interests: its relativity to a particular degree of constraint upon the recombination of ranks or cultures and its inability to define an indispensable stage in a universal progression.

Focus now on how the first mode of vision might be exercised in an attempt to define the groups with the most immediate interest in executing the type of program for which I have argued. For the purposes of this argument, consider only the rich North Atlantic countries and the richest fringe of the third world, as they were toward the end of the twentieth century, and disregard the important variations in social structure and culture between countries. For each of the groups to be singled out as potential short-run supporters of the program, the recognition of interest was far from automatic; it required an act of persuasion. This requirement testifies to the inevitable overlap between the two approaches. And in each instance, successful persuasion would involve an interplay between the political leaders and the rank and file of the respective classes.

The first group of likely supporters would be the most obvious losers in the current social order, those whose exclusion from task-defining authority combined with the greatest lack of economic welfare and job security. These primary losers included both the underclass and the less skilled and less organized sectors of the working class. Their conversion to such a program would depend on a recognition of the enormous constraints the established institutional structure imposed upon both social equality and economic growth. These limits are made patent by the cycles of reform and retrenchment that periodically threaten and circumscribe welfare entitlements and full-employment policy.

A second group of potential adherents to the program would be the old and new petty bourgeoise: the small-scale proprietors, technicians, and professionals as well as the technical cadres who move in and out of large-scale organizations and wanted opportunities for independent initiative. Their conversion to the institutional program requires them to understand a version of a thesis defended in the historical argument of Chapter 4: the impossibility of realizing the petty bourgeois dream of easy access to initiative and capital without a major shift in the institutional assumptions with which this dream had been traditionally associated. So long as the present institutional forms of markets and democracies and the present system of legal entitlements remain in place, small-scale private or cooperative enterprises, however numerous, would prove to be an incrustation upon an order constituted on principles fundamentally antagonistic to their prosperity and prominence. All plans to achieve a significant increase in either the deconcentration or the plasticity of economic life would prove futile. By comparison, the program outlined here represents, among other things, an effort to redefine the petty bourgeois program in ways that would save it from self-destabilization and enable it to connect with the aspirations of other sections of society.

A third group of potential supporters would be the class of fancy staffers, calculators, and rhetoricians – the restless and overeducated who lived uncomfortably with the contrast between cultural revolution and institutional stagnation and suffered from a chronic shortage of access to opportunities for experiment, influence, and decision. The initial sympathy to such an institutional program among these cadres might be sparked by the awareness that its implementation would vastly multiply the number of independent settings for organizational experiments and combine, in each of these settings, ideological controversy with technical problem solving.

As the conflict over institutional transformation persisted and intensified, this particular calculus of group interests would lose its relevance. Each succeeding experiment might give rise to new divisions and hierarchies, suggesting new combinations of interest. Or it might, on the contrary, simply diminish the significance of an analysis of preexisting group interests as a guide to possible alliances and interests. People vying for allies would then have to address one another in more of the spirit in which I must address you, reader, not knowing your social station or the fate that it is supposed to have reserved for your political opinions.

Transitions

Many aspects of the theoretical approach worked out in this book highlight the importance of institutional arrangements that can serve as bridges between the programmatic goals and current practices. First, remember the rejection of the all-or-nothing attitude encouraged by deep-logic social theory and the emphasis on revolutionary reform as the normal way of revising formative contexts. Second, bear in mind the commitment to a transformative practice that anticipates its ends in its means, treats existing deviations as the favored raw material of major reconstructions, and uses conflict both to accumulate influence and to anticipate a desired future. Third, recall the thesis that normative argument, even in its visionary mode, transcends a context or a tradition only by first reappropriating it.

The following pages enumerate, in each of the major domains touched by the program, a series of conceivable institutional arrangements that could serve as transitional forms. Examples are given with the rich North Atlantic world of the late twentieth century in mind, and their sketchiness results in part from the inability of programmatic generalities to solve the strategic problems of transformation in a particular national setting. Sketchy or not, these illustrations serve to demonstrate the existence of a spectrum connecting the most modest and the most radical examples of the programmatic vision.

The politics of transition obey a principle of uneven development: transitional forms may advance in one direction more rapidly than in another. Ultimately, the level of advance in one realm imposes limits upon the degree of progress that can be achieved in another. The reason for such constraints is not that all parts of the program form a single indivisible whole in the sense of indivisibility that deep-logic social theory attributes to necessary stages of social evolution or possible types of social organization. The basis of the mutual dependence is, instead, the looser connection that derives from the impossibility of continuing coexistence among institutional arrangements that reflect sharp differences in the development of negative capability. This alternative conception of mutual dependence has been extensively discussed in Chapter 2.

In the organization of government, the task of the transitional arrangement is to establish a state that can serve both as a more effective instrument for the destabilization of entrenched plans of social division and hierarchy and as a more pliant object of collective conflict and controversy. One relatively far-reaching form such a transition can take is a general constitutional reform of the kind exemplified by the dualistic system discussed earlier. Such a reform increases the decisional mobility of the center of government, strengthens methods of accountability that do not deliberately encourage constitutional stalemate, and multiplies the points of contact between the heights of state power and the general electorate. Another, more limited transitional method is the creation of a new branch or quasibranch of government, such as the administrative agencies under the American constitution, that may exemplify a novel and anomalous relation between state and society. (Note that in the case of the administrative agencies the increased power of government to champion social experiments is not matched by a greater power of organized society to assert effective control over the bureaucratic apparatus.) Still another transitional method is an established branch of government's assuming activities that anticipate practices and preconceptions of the new-model constitution. Thus, the judiciary may forge complex interventionist remedies allowing for the destabilization and reorganization of large-scale institutions or major areas of social practice, even though such remedies may be irreconcilable with the received view about the appropriate institutional role of the judiciary (or of any other branch of government).

The performance of such incongruous functions by an established branch of government cannot be repudiated as merely the bad-faith manipulation of a constitutional plan. A doctrine of appropriate institutional roles cannot be persuasively deduced from any unique group of arrangements for the organization of government, because the conception of a democratic republic or a democratic political process, which such a doctrine of roles inevitably expresses, cannot itself result from such a deduction. Otherwise, we would have to believe there is a hard and fast distinction between reasons to prefer a given normative view of democracy and grounds to prefer this view as an interpretation of an existing democratic constitution. A people may treat its constitution either as a rigid but easily replaceable commitment to a particular conception of democracy or as a permanent set of detailed arrangements compatible with a range of descriptive and normative political conceptions. But a nation is headed for trouble if it treats its constitutional plan as both definitive and inseparable from a particular theory of democratic politics. For it will then have denied itself the means to adapt to changes in circumstance and shifts of faith.

With respect to the organization of conflict over the control and uses of governmental power, a transitional practice might take its point of departure from a style of political action that combines two features. Its subject matter consists in the problems of hierarchy, inequality, and coordination in large-scale organizations or in particular areas of social practice. Its method is workplace solidarity and collective mobilization at the grassroots level. Step by step, this practice can be linked with the contest over the heights of governmental power. Such a combination may occur through the extension of these experiments in internal institutional politics. Or it may occur through the adoption by conventional political parties of a mobilizational style that does not accept the simple contrast between a reformist politics of petty deals and a revolutionary politics of escalating confrontation. Whatever the specific route, the crucial point is to combine a way of connecting grassroots and governmental politics with a program that seeks to deprive all areas of social practice or institutional life of their effective immunity to conflict and challenge.

The reorganization of the economy provides the richest and most familiar area for the discussion of transitional forms, if only because greed and ambition may suffice to produce here what imagination is insufficient to suggest elsewhere. The desired transitional arrangements should conjoin the assertion of more effective political control over the basic terms, pace, and direction of economic growth with a change in the microstructure of production that undercuts the rigid contrast between task-defining and task-executing jobs and activities.

In the circumstances of late twentieth century industrial democracies – the illustrative setting of this treatment of transitions – there are two complementary occasions for the development of transitional forms of economic organization with this characteristic. Both these occasions arise from the terms on which governments try to protect economic stability and growth. One focus is reactive: the willingness to subsidize industry in the face of domestic and international pressure or, more generally, to guarantee profitability and employment. The other focus is innovative: the attempt to encourage changes in the structure and direction of production (industrial policy) or, more specifically, to facilitate the expansion of the vanguardist sector of industry. The reactive strategy tries merely to limit the effects and slow the rate of economic decline. The active response seeks to guarantee the conditions for the continued success of the national economy as a whole.

Take first the reactive, subsidization issue and consider how it presents itself in two characteristic situations. In one situation, governments accustomed to overt attempts to maintain the profitability of industry and the stability of large-scale enterprises confront a strong labor movement. Such a movement almost invariably supports wage solidarity among segments of the labor force: respect for the customary wage differentials and job categories that result from a long history of collective conflicts and deals as well as of market relations.

Incentives and infrastructural investments geared only to the most efficient industries undermine wage solidarity and are therefore resisted by the labor movement. But if the support policy is calculated to reach even the least efficient enterprises of a given sector of the economy or of the economy as a whole, it produces for their more efficient counterparts what are perceived as windfall profits. The very circumstances and attitudes that inspired the broad-based subsidization policy in the first place generate pressure to exact a quid pro quo for these government-created riches. Thus, strong labor movements and left-leaning governments may demand greater public and worker participation in basic investment decisions and changes in the organization of work that progressively soften the contrast between task-defining and task-executing activities. Participation in basic investment decisions may operate through joint public–union pension funds that buy into enterprise equity through agreements to invest in particular innovations. Or it may take a form that respects entrepreneurial initiative more fully while anticipating the basic principle of the rotating capital fund; part of the windfall profits may be taxed away and made available, conditionally and provisionally, to new teams of petty entrepreneurs and skilled workers. These small-scale rotating capital funds may be administered by independent public banks or agencies.

In another typical variant of economic and political life in the rich North Atlantic countries, more passive and conservative governments and relatively weak trade-union movements coexist with a strong petty bourgeoisie, with the continuing authority of the dream of petty proprietorship and small business, and with a greater respect for what are imagined to be the inherent rules of market economies. The least controversial form of subsidization in this circumstance is government support of agriculture. Widespread family ownership and the overt instability of agricultural production contribute to make farm subsidies palatable. (The United States provides the classic example.)

Against such a background, the characteristic dramatic instance of industrial subsidization is the rescue of a failing large-scale industry. The underlying impulse may be to avoid a major loss of jobs, to prevent an economically disruptive and strategically dangerous gap in the production system, or to satisfy influential interest groups.

But whatever its motive, the industrial rescue creates special embarrassments. It both violates free-market doctrine and lacks the special justification of support for family-scale enterprise. Thus, it may allow for more modest versions of the same institutional experiments that become feasible in the other, more broadly based circumstance of subsidization.

Turn now to the active, industrial-policy issue: the attempt by governments to seize the initiative in helping reorient the structure of industry. For the industrial economies of the late twentieth century part of this reorientation consists in attempting to extend the area of economic life open to the vanguardist sector of industry. But this particular theme of industrial reorganization is no more than the occasional form of the more fundamental and permanent need to increase the plasticity of economic arrangements.

The earlier discussion of transformative opportunities has already suggested this effort may be carried out in ways that either minimize or sharpen the break with preexisting institutional arrangements and social practices. The more reconstructive tack requires legal and organizational changes that would deny rigid, mass-production industries the institutional devices with which they protect themselves against market instabilities. Thus, for example, the strategy of hiring temporary, relatively unprotected workers during upturns in a demand cycle and then firing them as soon as business declines might be frustrated either by the unionization of the entire work force or by a connected series of legal prohibitions and fiscal disincentives. Capital must be made available to existing vanguardist enterprises as well as to groups of entrepreneurs, technicians, and workers willing and able to found new firms. The availability of needed finance might be ensured by the same anticipatory forms of the rotating capital fund suggested in my earlier discussion of subsidization policy: independent public agencies or banks lending money and technical assistance conditionally and provisionally, with an initial endowment derived from the direct or indirect taxation of mass-production industry and renewed with the proceeds of their own operations. Success would require further initiative in organizing cooperative technological and marketing arrangements among the innovative enterprises. Thus, the idea of a technologically advanced and institutionally redefined form of petty commodity production would begin to be realized together with the conception of a rotating capital fund. To the extent that all these experiments were carried forward, the economy would gradually see the proliferation of enterprises that began to overcome the contrast between task-defining and task-executing jobs or activities.

The final domain for the development of transitional institutional forms is the reconstruction of the system of legal rights. In this realm, transitional strategy must combine a methodological and a substantive approach; the former represents the indispensable instrument of the latter.

The methodological approach is the development of an expanded version of legal doctrine, a version that overrides the simple, polemical opposition between restrictive legal analysis and freewheeling ideological controversy. As a positivist rule-formalism loses its credibility, legal argument begins to appeal more openly to impersonal purposes, policies, and principle, as necessary complements to rules and rule analysis. But the line cannot easily be held at this point. The incorporation of these nonrule elements may be treated as simply a step toward the incorporation into legal reasoning of debate over the models of social relations applicable to different areas of social practice, models we take for granted when deploying argument from purpose, policy, or principle.

The practice of legal analysis creates many opportunities to enlarge in this direction the character of legal doctrine. There is the conflict among models of human association, which goes on more or less tacitly in the form of inevitable choices between principles and counterprinciples, or between alternative ways of relating principles and counterprinciples, in any extended body of legal doctrine. There is the impulse to organize and justify a set of legal ideas by making ever more explicit a set of assumptions about the possible and desirable forms of social relations, a process that opens both the ideas and the assumptions to further criticism and broadens the habitual range of legal argument. And there is the disharmony between acceptance, in the legislative setting, of the cynical rhetoric of interest group politics and the appeal, in an adjudicative context, to the priestly language of impersonal ideals. To seize on these many opportunities is to create a legal and political discourse that overrides the contrast between the routine and the revolutionary in normative argument. Such a discourse will often be unsuited to judges. But to the citizenry it offers a medium in which to advance the interplay between received ideals and established practices, whatever the role constraints of particular officials. It gives us a way to discuss, in the course of our everyday disputes, the remaking of the institutionalized scheme of social life.

The substantive aspect of the transitional forms of rights is the attempt to develop the elements of modern law and legal thought that rebel against consolidated property as the unique model of entitlements. Contemporary law already provides materials for each of the categories of right discussed in the institutional program. Thus, the point of departure for the development of the immunity rights lies in existing public freedoms and welfare entitlements. Market rights are most legitimately exemplified by dealings between enterprises of roughly equal influence, trading in a setting of deliberately assumed risk. Such rights would begin to operate, in the manner suggested by the program, as the transitional forms of economic organization, with their anticipations of the rotating capital fund, began to be implemented. The germ of solidarity rights already exists in the aspects of modern law that recognize the genesis of legal obligations out of only partly articulate relations of reliance and interdependence. Even destabilization rights are prefigured by the ideas underlying many complex judicial remedies. These remedies often seek to reconstruct major institutions or distinct areas of social practice for the sake of a legally supported ideal of association that society continues to betray.

THE CULTURAL-REVOLUTIONARY COUNTERPART TO THE INSTITUTIONAL PROGRAM

The Idea of a Personalist Program

The institutional program of empowered democracy has its counterpart in a program for the transformation of personal relations. Call this program cultural revolution. There are both causal and justificatory links between the institutional proposals and their personalist extension. Like any institutional order the institutions of empowered democracy encourage certain changes in the character of the direct practical or passionate relations among individuals, and they depend for their vitality upon the perpetuation of these qualities. At the same time the ideals inspiring the cause of empowered democracy also support a criticism of the fine texture of social life.

The correspondence of institutional and personalist proposals should not, on reflection, prove surprising. The qualities of our direct practical or passionate dealings always represent the ultimate object of our conflicts over the organization of society. No institutional structure or system of social dogma informs these dealings completely; the inability to do so guarantees in even the most entrenched and coherent frameworks the possibility of anomaly and rebellion. But only insofar as a formative structure does influence these subtle personal relations can it show its mettle. All the routines of practical and imaginative conflict that every such framework helps perpetuate must ultimately take the form of person-to-person encounters, even though they may be encounters in which practical aims and institutionally defined roles prevail. But although institutional arrangements matter because of their influence upon personal interaction, the task of presenting a view of transformed personal relations cannot be accomplished by the mere statement of an institutional program. The links between institutional order and personal behavior are –

though real – loose, complex, and obscure. Moreover, influences upon the character of our encounters with one another go far beyond the institutional framework of social life; they include not only biological or technological constraints but also ideas, habits, and attitudes that never quite crystallize into institutions. The institutional agenda must be complemented by a personalist program.

There is also a narrower, tactical reason for the need to make this addition. Successful institutional transformation requires a willingness to subordinate redistributive aims to institutional goals. The subordination implies a sacrifice; the sacrifice must be inspired by a vision; and the vision must address the thing people care about most – their immediate experience of practical collaboration and passionate encounter, of self-assertion and solidarity. A visionary ideal must draw much of its force from its personalist immediacy, whether or not the ideal takes the form this book advocates.

Just as the institutional program needs a personalist vision, so the latter cannot dispense with the former. Personal relations must move within a context that is, to a large extent, institutionally defined. If this framework is not brought into closer accord with the spirit of the personalist vision, it will exact a price in the frustration or perversion of the ideal.

The effort to combine the institutional and the personal was known at earlier moments in the history of Western political thought as the attempt to unite the political and religious, a union Tocqueville recognized as the hallmark of the greatest revolutions. For religious creeds enter this secular realm largely as articulations of a prescriptive phenomenology of subjective experience and personal encounter and as bearers of existential projects containing a social message. The revolutionary need not, indeed he should not, put his faith in the total transformation of an established formative context, recognizing instead that these contexts can be and ordinarily are changed bit by bit. But even revolutionary reform must manage over time to link transformation in the domain of institutions with change in the "pianissimo" of the personal in order to attain its objectives.

The classical liberal would nevertheless object to this personalist extension of the institutional program. You can imagine him reasoning in the following way. An explicit aim of the project of empowered democracy is to deny authority to any entrenched scheme of authoritative models of human association, enacted in the different domains of social life. To advocate a particular style of direct personal interaction, and to support this advocacy with social pressure if not coercive force, is to betray the spirit of the institutional program rather than to extend it. It is also to impose a despotism all the more oppressive because it meddles even with the areas of intimacy that despots are ordinarily content to leave alone. If, however, the program of cultural revolution is not to be backed up by organized or informal coercion, why should it be so closely linked with proposals to reform social institutions?

This objection reflects a double misunderstanding: first, about the sense in which institutional orders can be neutral among styles of social interaction; second, about the nature of the cultural-revolutionary program itself. The classical liberal is right to object to an institutional program if it embraces a highly defined and restrictive view of what people – and relations among people – should be like. Thus, even the program of empowered democracy would lose much of its persuasive force if its success turned out to depend on the presence of the ever-ready, selfless citizen of classical republican myth.

But the classical liberal is wrong to think – if he does think – that an institutional order can be neutral among all possible styles of personal interaction or to draw a watertight distinction between the public institutions of a people and the forms of close association or intimate experience to which the people are drawn. The futile quest for institutions that are unbiased among all possible manners of association can only impede the search for arrangements that in fact free people more effectively from a closed canon of associative practices and models. The insistence on absolute neutrality can also keep us from appreciating the full extent of what we choose when we choose an institutional program. It can thereby lull us into commitments we might otherwise prefer to avoid.

Once we recognize the impossibility of perfect neutrality we are more likely to acknowledge the inadequacy of the neutrality standard as a guide to the criticism and invention of social forms. The authority of the radical project lies in its vision of the individual and collective empowerment we may achieve by cumulatively loosening the grip of rigid roles, hierarchies, and conventions upon our experiments in practical or passionate association. We can lift the burden of dependence and depersonalization, in part by changing the character of our relations, as individuals and as collectivities, to the institutional and imaginative frameworks of social life.

This conception of empowerment – of its meaning and conditions – incorporates a version of the neutrality ideal, both as an end and as a means. It does so in the form of a commitment to free social life from the compulsions of a ready-made script. But it does not claim to be indifferent to the choice among alternative styles of association. Nor does it produce an institutional or moral blank; it is rich with implications for both the design of social institutions and the character of personal dealings.

This two-sided attitude toward the ideal of neutrality stands closely connected with an approach to the vexing question of human nature, its relative determinacy, diversity, and mutability. The institutional and personalist program should not depend upon a narrowly and dogmatically defined account of human nature. The programmatic arguments and proposals must reflect an awareness that in changing our institutions and practices we also change who we are; no motivations and drives are cast in so rigid a mold that their form, intensity, and experienced significance remain uninfluenced by the transformation of the social world. But we also know, as a matter of individual experience and historical memory, that many of our predispositions toward one another resist manipulation. Rather than attempt neatly to separate an unchanging core and a variable periphery of human nature, we can simply impose an ad hoc, loosely defined constraint. The successful realization of the program must not require any abrupt or drastic change in the predispositions we now experience. A programmatic vision could be justly criticized for requiring all-out public-spiritedness or altruism. We *can* choose who or what to become, but only so long as we go step by step, never expect to move very far at any one time, and resist the temptation to mistake our strongest current desires for a permanent kernel of human nature.

Thus far, I have discussed the part of the classical liberal objection to the idea of a cultural-revolutionary program that rests on a mistake about the sense in which institutional arrangements can and should be neutral. Consider now the part of the objection that reflects a more limited misunderstanding of the nature and scope of the cultural-revolutionary cause. You will soon see that this cause does not specify an inclusive, detailed picture of desirable personal relations and communal forms. It merely indicates certain minimal qualities that such forms and relations should possess. Morever, by its very nature this personalist program cannot be coercively implemented, either by central governments or by other organizations. What governments and organizations can do to assist the cultural-revolutionary endeavor is to subvert socially enforced roles and hierarchies and to help the individual feel secure in a core of vitally protected interests. The rest depends on the politics of personal relations and decentralized institutions, carried out within these institutions and relations by their participants. Such a politics draws on the devices of fiction and enactment: to tell stories about yourself and others, to represent through these stories untried possibilities of association, and to try these possibilities out.

Despite the many reasons to extend the program of empowered democracy into a vision of transformed personal relations, this book cannot carry the extension out in detail. Both *Social Theory: Its Situation and Its Task* and *False Necessity* have argued that programmatic ideas must be intimately informed by an imagination of reality and possibility. Only then can such ideas suggest credible solutions. Only then can they cut through the false dilemma between the prostrate acceptance of current orderings of social life and the depiction of utopias that merely deny and invert a reality we feel powerless to reimagine and reconstruct.

But the explanatory argument of this book moves at the level of the large-scale institutional structure of society. The understanding it provides is too gross to serve as a capable guide to the formulation of such an intimate personalist program. A successor volume to *False Necessity* will explore the implications of the antinecessitarian thesis for an understanding of the microstructure of social life: the realm of direct practical and passionate relations. The more subtle insight into social and personal possibility to result from that exploration can inform a more persuasive ethic – for an ethic, in an enlarged, loosened, and partial sense of the term, is what the program of cultural revolution ultimately amounts to.

The following pages merely suggest the outline of a vision that needs to be worked out later, with better tools. The argument advances in three steps. First, it suggests a definition of the general theme of the cultural-revolutionary program. Second, it describes two planks in the cultural-revolutionary program: two connecting sets of qualities that this program seeks to impart to our direct dealings. Finally, it lists some of the truncated but rich materials that lie at hand, ready to assist us in our efforts to develop this part of our programmatic ideas and of our transformative practice.

A Unifying Theme of the Cultural-Revolutionary Program: A Transformed Conception of Community

Social theories offering a radical criticism of society have often held out the vision of a regenerate style of personal relations. But all too often the conception of a perfected human community put forward by these doctrines has been literally incredible. The view of the ennobled form of human solidarity has been little more than the reverse image of current experience: the dramatization of a wish to avoid all the dangers of conflict and inaccessibility that result from the independence of our wills and minds. The leftist contribution to this persistent fantasy has often been the hope that the banishment of subjugation from social life would put an end to our self-absorption and our antagonisms.

An impoverished and unbelievable idea of community emphasizes the exclusion of conflict and the sharing of values and opinions. In any society like the societies we know in history this ideal of communal life can gain a semblance of reality only in certain privileged corners of social experience, such as the intimacy of the family. Even then, it often depends for its force upon the polemical and delusive contrast established between this idealized exception to the quotidian and the character of a workaday world surrendered to the heartless exercise of dominion and the unrestrained calculation of advantage. The claim to mark out a privileged circle of communal relations frequently conceals the devolution of these purified areas of private community to the very experiences of oppression and malevolence from which they are supposed to offer a reprieve. When this ideal of community is used to inspire a vision of the transformation of all social life, the opposition between the privileged zone of harmony and the brutal, prosaic world of conflict gets replaced by a contrast between the purgatory of historical experience and the dream of a liberation from history.

The implications of this presumed rupture between history and the escape from history comes out in a comparison with a typical narrative strategy of the early romantic novel. A man and a woman fall in love with a passion whose subjective quality depends upon the vehemence with which it hurls itself against the social obstacles set in its way. Often the lovers spring from different classes, an advance over the romances of an earlier day when a legitimate love and a sound social hierarchy were regarded as inseparable and could diverge only temporarily and thanks to mistaken identities or forgotten origins. The authorities of the family, the church, and the social order are ranged against the lovers' union. The narrative revels in the story of the adventures the lovers undergo as they confront and finally overcome these many resistances. The end is the marriage, the goal and justification of all the preceding struggle and the inauguration of a higher example of human community. The trouble is that the typical romantic novel has nothing to say about what life under the new dispensation is actually like, nothing that would not make the ideal of marital felicity seem both unrealistic and unattractive. Silence becomes its alibi: let me not bore you, reader, with the indescribable felicities of this happy union. Only in novels that have a more or less deliberately ironic relation to the early romantic ideal of marital community can the marriage be portrayed in credible terms.

A similar narrative structure appears in the radical and millennarian versions of social thought that promise a cleansed community (e.g., communism) as the reward for an immemorial fighting. Mankind, like the romantic lovers, must pass through a many-staged ordeal of class and national conflicts so that it may arrive at a form of life free from at least these forms of conflict. But, like the romantic marriage, this final reconciliation cannot be portrayed in a way that makes it seductive or even believable.

The vision of a perfected community, successful at overcoming the antagonism of its members, would not be so persistent if it did not so often seem the only available alternative to certain familiar doctrines. These doctrines identify the inadequacies of a particular form of social organization with the inherent limitations of social life, or they portray a small number of alternative forms of social organization as the repositories of incompatible sets of ideals among which we must choose. The view of social life that animates the explanatory and programmatic arguments of *Politics* rejects these apologetic doctrines without embracing the millennarian and perfectionist assumption. This view enables us to complement the institutional proposals with an ideal of direct, individual relations that is imaginatively credible. At least, the alternative proposed here does not require a sudden rupture in our prior experience of social life; it merely extends to the domain of the personal the same conception of social reality and the social ideal developed in the parts of *False Necessity* that deal with the institutional structure of society.

The result is a transformed ideal of community. Like any proposal to change an inherited evaluative notion, this revised conception of community draws its tacit meaning from the institutionalized and noninstitutionalized social practices that are meant to realize it. Having revealed, through these novel forms of practical realization, an unsuspected ambiguity in an inherited ideal, it invites us to resolve this ambiguity in a particular direction. It takes a stand on the issue of which aspects of that ideal really do or should matter most to us. (Recall the earlier discussion of the internal, standard mode of normative argument.)

The kernel of this revised ideal of community is the notion of a zone of heightened mutual vulnerability, within which people gain a chance to resolve more fully the conflict between the enabling conditions of self-assertion: between their need for attachment and for participation in group life and their fear of the subjugation and depersonalization with which such engagement may threaten them. Success at these experiments in accepted vulnerability gives us moments of ardor and empowerment, and the quality that life attains at these privileged moments can under favorable circumstances be perpetuated in lasting personal commitments and diffused through a broader social experience. This notion of community shifts the gravitational center of the communal ideal away from the sharing of values and opinions and the exclusion of conflict. Here is a version of community that, although jeopardized by conflict, also thrives on it.

The ideal of community can be most fully realized in the noninstrumental areas of social experience, where constraints imposed by the calculation of practical advantage are relaxed. But it no longer presents itself as the privileged possession of a charmed circle of private existence, contrasted polemically to the rest of social life. It becomes instead a quality that all social relations can enjoy to a greater or lesser extent.

The argument of the following sections suggests that this abstract and seemingly empty conception of community in fact points to a particular line of transformation in the subjective experience of social life. The distinctiveness of this line is brought out by its message about the performance and the betrayal of our received social roles.

A Plank in the Cultural-Revolutionary Platform: Role Defiance and Role Jumbling

A social role is simply a typical place in a recurrent social relation. Roles come in sets, and these sets of roles exist so long as there are recurrent positions some people hold in relation to others and so long as these positions exercise normative authority as well as factual influence upon the practical or passionate relations among the individuals who occupy them. The role requires discrete, repetitious, and normatively charged stations.

Any major change in the formative institutional context of social life has a transformative impact upon established roles. The effect is all the greater when the institutional program aims not merely to replace one set of roles by another but to diminish the force of roles, the influence they exercise over our experience of human connection. The loosening of roles is, in fact, just one more corollary of the softening of the contrast between structure-preserving routine and structure-transforming conflict.

One way to understand the sense of the cultural-revolutionary attack on rigid roles is to ask what it would take for some characteristic ambitions of modern moral thought to be realized. Just as classical liberal theory treats the social world it helps elucidate and support as a fluid mass of free and equal citizens and rightholders, so the dominant styles of moral speculation treat duty and obligation in the language of universalistic, role-neutral precepts. But just as the stuff of social conflict continues to be dominated by the realities of social division and hierarchy, so we expend much of our moral scruple in taking a stand about the obligations, aspirations, and expectations that mark the roles we continue to occupy. We argue about what our role duties are and how we may reconcile them, as well as about the weight we should attach to roles in general and the persistence with which we should rebel against them. Just as the attempt to actualize liberal ideals requires ideas and arrangements unfamiliar to liberals, so the effort to make our moral experience resemble more closely what so much of moral thought already supposes it to be like calls for a practice of role defiance and role jumbling that has little place in traditional moral doctrines.

The cultural revolutionary wants to show how roles can be stretched, pulled apart, combined with other roles, and used incongruously. He acts out a loosened sense of what it means to occupy a role. In this way he helps disrupt frozen connections among social stations, life experiences, and stereotyped forms of insight and sensibility. He thereby carries into the drama of everyday personal relations the effort to free sociability from its script and to make us available to one another more as the originals we all know ourselves to be and less as the placeholders in a system of group contrasts.

The roles that deserve to be targets of this cultural-revolutionary subversion are, above all, those that mark a place within a preestablished scheme of class, communal, or gender divisions: what an older sociological tradition used to call ascriptive roles. Specialized work roles are neither inherently suitable nor intrinsically unsuitable as subjects for role defiance and role jumbling. The more the technical and the social divisions of labor present themselves in everyday life as a rigid grid of functional allocations, the more they deserve to be smashed up at the microlevel of cultural-revolutionary defiance and incongruity as well as at the macrolevel of institutional innovation.

A Plank in the Cultural-Revolutionary Platform: The Confusion of Expressive Means

A striking mutual dependence exists between what people feel about the situations they are in and the means by which they communicate to other people these subjective experiences. There are stock situations and – at least so far as these current means of expression go – stock responses to them. A table of correspondences arises between what people feel, or are supposed to be capable of feeling, in the recurrent circumstances of social life and the combined ways of acting, talking, and looking that convey the subjective response. The basis of these correspondences is an accommodation between subjectivity and society.

The differences in the ways that people use these available expressive means are not so great and numerous as to belie the vision of possible and desirable association enacted by society. So long as men and women believe themselves able to communicate to one another what the experiences of social life are like, and to communicate it by some recognizable variation on the repertory of standard expressed response, they continue to accept some of the crucial, realized dogmas of society. The social order may thwart both their ambitions and their ideals but it does not leave any part of their subjectivity without a voice. It therefore does not seem to enshrine assumptions about possible experience that they already know to be false. Far more than a natural language, this social code shapes what it is supposed to convey. By using it faithfully enough, you become a certain kind of person. You fulfill in yourself the implicit prophecy about human possibility the institutions and dogmas of society proclaim. Every naturalistic social doctrine has understood this truth and developed on the basis of this understanding a method of educating the passions through the constant reenactment of the proper social forms and the constant reinstatements of the proper personal responses to the typical situations of social life.

One of the aims and methods of cultural revolution is the disorganization of these codified affinities between subjective experience and expressive means. The cultural revolutionary begins by taking the fullest advantage of the incongruous aspects of all social experience: the fact that people always do feel more than the social code enables them to express. Many of these voiceless experiences may seem to have no bearing on the struggle over the collective structure of society. Yet all represent some opportunity of subjectivity and relationship whose very possibility the available code denies. In following the line of the incongruous, the cultural revolutionary has two aims. When considered in tandem, these goals suggest a method of action.

The cultural revolutionary wants to develop the varieties of relation and subjectivity that a fixed scheme of association denies, subjectivity and relationship being reverse sides of each other. Among these suppressed human opportunities are all the experiences evoked by the other elements in the work of cultural revolution. They, too, must gain vehicles of expression, for, without such vehicles, they cannot develop.

The cultural revolutionary, however, is not content to put one range of expressible subjectivity in place of another. He also wants permanently to loosen the connection between the subjective experience of personal encounters and its symbolic representation. All experience must be capable of expression, and all expression must influence the content of experience. A way must nevertheless be found to keep the life of subjectivity from becoming entirely hostage to a closed list of symbolic forms.

These two aims may seem at first contradictory: the effort to express novel experiences and the struggle to loosen the link between experience and expression. What resolves the apparent paradox is that the experiences to be expressed are primarily those described by the other parts of the program of cultural revolution. All the modes of relationship and subjectivity invoked by this program have in common some incorporation of the indeterminacy of society and personality into the minute episodes of ordinary life. The theoretical affinity between the two seemingly contradictory aims is confirmed by the power of the same practical methods of action to advance both of them.

The most important method is the displacement and combination of expressive forms originally meant to designate supposedly uncombinable subjective responses to the circumstances of social life. There is hardly an alternative: all expression must begin with the stock of available signs. Such mixing does not take place as a mere transitory expedient, to be cast aside once new appropriate symbols emerge. It keeps going on. The continued recourse to it serves to perpetrate the permanent confusion of social or sexual roles and of prescriptive models of association. It carries into the normal course of social life something of the implicit boundlessness of personal subjectivity and relationship. It keeps alive the acknowledged tension between the reach toward the unconditional and the pervasiveness of context.

The disruption of the stock forms of subjective response is accompanied by a particular spiritual anxiety, which reveals yet another side to the ambiguities of cultural revolution. The sense of having enlarged the range of expression and experience alternates with the awareness of speaking a disordered social language and of undergoing incompletely formed and expressible responses to the ordinary incidents of life. The cultural revolutionary drags the element of incongruity between experience and expression from its unmentioned corner into the center of daily existence. The ordinary person becomes to that extent more like the poet, whose visionary heightening of expressed emotion may border on unintelligibility and aphasia.

The Available Points of Departure: Two Truncated Versions of Cultural Revolution

Like the institutional program of empowered democracy that it extends, the personalist program of cultural revolution must start from the arrested and truncated versions already at hand. We need to identify them and to understand the opportunities and dangers they present.

We have witnessed two main movements of practice and sensibility in the twentieth century that approach, by their ideas and their methods, the program of cultural revolution. On one side stands the radical experimentation with personal relations that characterizes in varying degrees the industrialized democracies of the North Atlantic world. Its self-reflection is the culture of high and popular modernism. On the other side, you can find in the surrounding poorer and largely non-Western world occasional radical projects for transforming the fine structure of elementary personal relationships and the ideas about self and society that underlie them. But these projects usually remain subsidiary to leftist efforts at institutional reconstruction. In different ways and for different reasons, each of the two movements falls short of the program of cultural revolution. The defects of one provide a reverse image of the flaws of the other. Either form of failure stops cultural revolution dead in its tracks after giving it an initial impulse. But each stops it in a different way.

Consider first the approach to cultural revolution in the advanced Western countries. There, the progress of a cultural-revolutionary politics of personal relations has roughly coincided with the stabilization of the formative institutional structure of society. In fact, this familiar, limited version of cultural-revolutionary practice seems to thrive on passive acquiescence in the established institutional order. Nevertheless, to speak of cultural revolution in this setting is not to grasp at metaphor or to mistake the mere struggle over personal relations for the particular programmatic vision outlined in earlier pages. Each theme in that vision is tenaciously pursued today, not just by small numbers of vanguardist critics but by ever larger multitudes. In fact, by the end of the twentieth century, the program of cultural revolution has seeped into popular culture.

But though all the themes surround us, all appear subject to a characteristic truncation. It is as if cultural revolution had been suddenly arrested in its momentum while continuing to collect details and adherents. With this concealed paralysis comes a distortion of commitment – a distortion, that is, by reference to the personalist program outlined earlier. The most general mark of this mistake lies in the tendency to treat each aspect of cultural revolution as a pretext for endless self-gratification and self-concern. Every part of the cultural-revolutionary program is interpreted negatively as a license to withdraw not only from the particular, rigidified hierarchies of value and power implicit in fixed assignments of role or schemes of association but from the very experience of larger connections and responsibilities, from the possibility of self-transcendence, and from the claims of self-sacrifice. No wonder the emancipation of personal possibility from preexisting institutions and dogmas is so often taken, in the manner of the neoromantic attitude toward love and marriage, as an opportunity to deny the permanence or the exclusivity of any personal relation. For exclusivity and permanence might imply responsibility and renunciation. No wonder the most important attachments begin to seem incompatible with any lasting social form. For a public presence would turn the intimate connection outward toward broader communal engagements. The enemies of this version of cultural revolution are right to denounce such tendencies as a gospel of despairing selfishness, promoted in the disguise of moral enlightenment.

Earlier discussion suggested that the main source of these distortions is the cutting off of radicalism in the sphere of personal relations from any practical experience of struggle over the collective structure of society, from any developed vision of a regenerate life in common. As a result of this severance, people find it hard to recognize, in any but the most abstract sense, the constraints that collective institutions in fact impose upon even the most seemingly radical experiments in personal relations. All the less role-dependent personal relations that require a novel institutional setting or a more generous set of social involvements and responsibilities run up against the limits laid down by the quiescent social world. A failure of vision completes the work of the institutional constraints. Without an active sense of engagement in the remaking and reimagining of society, people feel absolved of responsibility for the larger collective contexts of their existence and irresponsible to any shared enterprise that can precede and outlast them. The illusions of endless gratification and casual intimacy then become less a voluntary choice than an almost irresistible imaginative compulsion.

The poorer and more turbulent countries of the world have witnessed many attempts to alter the basic character of personal relations as part of a larger struggle over the collective structure of society. When these attempts have won a broader popular allegiance, they have in fact established a connection between conflicts in the most intimate and the most public spheres.

Nevertheless, the practice of cultural revolution often emerges in these settings as if distracted and even obsessed by anxieties far narrower and more focused than the concerns embraced by the radicalism about personal relations that has spread throughout the North Atlantic countries. Thus, the link between the remaking of institutions and the transformation of personal relations has been established in a mutilated form that drastically limits and vitiates the significance of the achievement.

This other practice of cultural-revolutionary politics has had two obsessional targets: the contrast between the mass and the elite, and that between the pure and the impure. Sometimes one, sometimes the other, stands at the forefront of concern. The Chinese communist practice of "criticism and self-criticism" and Gandhi's method of pedagogic defilement neatly exemplify each.

The technique of criticism and self-criticism, first conceived by Liu Shao-ch'i and his collaborators, was reinterpreted and revised under the impact of the "mass line." This technique had roots that long predated the communist take-over of state power. It had been a device for reaffirming common purpose, discipline, and hierarchy within an in-group of beleaguered revolutionaries. The victim recanted. The group of cadres readmitted the deviant. All rearticulated and reaffirmed the doctrinal and organizational essentials of their movement. Under the influence of the mass line, pioneered by Mao Tse-tung and his coterie and then accepted and enlarged by zealous agitators, the method changed its form and purpose. In the hands of its most radical practitioners, it became part of an attempt to chasten and, if possible, to destroy the established bureaucracies of party and state and to produce a new man or woman, new above all in their attitude toward authority. The victim now appeared often as the mere pretext for the reenactment of a collective denunciation of every trace that the inherited contrast of masses and elites had imprinted upon the style of direct personal relations. Because that contrast had amounted to a hierarchy of value as well as to a system of control, its subversion had all the seductive and liberating force of an attack upon the distinction between the pure and the impure. The crudest allocations of personal role, or the most rigid conceptions of the style of association suitable to each domain of social life, could be accepted so long as they did not overtly involve the feared contrast between elite and mass.

Recall, by comparison, Gandhi's teaching and agitation in India. Consider the aspect of his activity that comes closest to the status of cultural revolution: not passive disobedience against the imperial master but the attempt to form a man who can be the citizen of a single nation, capable of common allegiance and even compassionate solidarity, across the frontiers traced by the norms of caste and ritual purity. In Gandhi's world, the distance among castes appeared bound up with the ritual contrast of the pure and the impure. To disrespect caste lines was the exemplary form of impurity. The position of each group within the caste hierarchy could be justified, though not explained, by the group's relative closeness to the purest or the most impure activities. The most cultural-revolutionary aspect of Gandhi's politics was his practice of defilement and his recruitment of others to share this practice with him: to reach out to the forbidden person, to undertake the most humiliating work, to touch the dirtiest thing (though exalting cleanliness and continence as high forms of virtue). The empowered person was the person who had emancipated himself, through repeated practice, from the fixed hierarchies of value that stood in the way of mutual responsibility and shared nationhood. Insofar as the caste system represented the chief locus of this ranking of values, the defiance of the values included an attack upon the system. But no more developed vision of cultural-revolutionary practice or program emerges from this relentless, focused concern. Even the longing for a civilization of self-reliant, communal villages represents less a deliberate rejection of the ideals that inspire the program of empowered democracy and cultural revolution than an avoidance of the need to describe in detail the face-to-face relations a suitably empowered individual should hope to experience.

The ideas, attitudes, and power relations implicated in the contrasts between mass and elite or the pure and the impure do indeed act as a bar to the realization of the cultural-revolutionary program. But the single-minded focus on these concerns to the exclusion of others narrows the front on which cultural revolution can be staged and leaves untouched much of the established structure of social life. Stubborn fighting over the mastery of the state and the organization of the economy often occurs side by side with the rebirth of styles of personal association characteristic of an earlier, destroyed social order. The radicalism in the sphere of intimacy that has spread throughout the Western industrial democracies and penetrated its world-seducing popular culture combines insight and illusion, both empowering and disabling its practitioners. But it has often been dismissed by the militants and theoreticians of third world cultural revolution, forgetful of their own disabilities, as the autumnal and luxurious self-indulgence of dying classes and civilizations.

In one view, the advanced Western countries represent the privileged terrain for the execution of the cultural-revolutionary program. Their more thoroughgoing supersession of the contrast between masses and elites, and their wider acquaintance with the transvaluation of hierarchies of values, has freed them from constrictive obsessions and enabled them to practice the politics of role defiance and role jumbling on the broadest front. In another view, the poorer and more tumultuous places where the collective structure of society seems more fully up for grabs, represent the favored theater for cultural revolution. There, people fight out the conflict over personal relations, in depth, as part of a questioning of the whole social order. Larger collective involvements and responsibilities sweep aside the corrupting illusions of self-gratification. Both views are one-sided and even impertinent. The point is to connect the revolutionary reform of institutional arrangements with the cultural-revolutionary remaking of personal relations. In this effort there is no uniquely favored terrain and there are no clearly anointed champions of the cause.

THE SPIRIT

THE SENSES OF SPIRIT

Consider now the spirit that inspires this whole institutional program. Suppose someone were to hear the program expounded and defended in just the terms adopted in the preceding sections. He might still remain unsure of the point of it all and press upon the obsessive proponent an insistent question: Yes, but what do you really want? The spirit of the constitution is the restatement of its animating ideal in a manner sharp enough to count as an answer to such a question. This ideal – at once a vision for society and a project for individuals – connects directly with a view of social reality, and its formulation exemplifies the anomalous genre of normative argument I termed visionary thought.

The spirit of the institutional proposal can also be restated with greater psychological immediacy. In this more experiential mode, the spirit is the set of motivations and attitudes that the constitutional scheme relies upon and that it in turn helps sustain. The most relevant attitudes and motivations are those that connect (or disconnect) the individual to the many collective settings of his existence and that express what he hopes to get, or fears to receive, from a life in society. The psychological dynamic implied by the institutional scheme must be realistic, and the inevitable bias of this dynamic toward certain personal ideals and against others must be defensible. Realism in turn implies stability. An unstable set of motivations is one that, once in operation, will change in ways so radical as to undermine the connected sets of institutional arrangements depending upon its continuance. The unstable spirit may disregard an irrepressible element of ordinary experience and yearning. Or it may encourage ambitions that cannot be made to coexist for long without a shift of impulses and objectives.

To define the spirit of the constitution is therefore to make clear that the entire institutional program can claim no neutrality among social or personal ideals. To a significant extent, it must be defended as both an account of the meaning of self-assertion and a hypothesis about the social conditions under which individual self-assertion may best be achieved. On both these scores the program implies a theory – an explanatory view of society. To claim for a particular set of institutional arrangements a strict neutrality among ideals of personality and society is to claim the impossible. It is to abandon the effort to invent social orders that are in fact less biased and more corrigible in exchange for a fantasy of detachment.

Nevertheless, the constitution and its spirit benefit from a special sense of neutrality. Like so much of social life in an age of partial emancipation from false necessity, this institutional program represents the theory and practice of a jumbled experience. It draws upon, and attempts to encourage, forms of practical and passionate human connection that recombine and redivide activities traditionally associated with different nations, classes, communities, and roles. More generally, its goal is to bring something more of the underlying indefinition of personal and collective existence into a workable mode of life. Thus, the skeptic who disbelieves all large theoretical arguments for particular social ideals, but who, for that very reason, wishes all the more to weaken the tyranny of the present over the future, may nevertheless commit himself to this program.

It is a disputable commitment, for it rests on at least two arguments, each of which remains open to attack. The first is the value given to openness toward the uncreated forms of experience, a value that does not follow self-evidently from the premises of a general political skepticism. The second argument is that the constitutional scheme I have described can in fact serve this openness more than rival systems. But, though the skeptic's reason to accept the program of empowered democracy may be controversial, it is plausible, and its plausibility shows the breadth of the sympathies on which the constitutional program might draw.

The adversaries of the program must therefore fall into one of two groups. They must have a different general view and this view must favor an institutional structure less exteme in the pursuit of the radical cause. Or, if they want to avoid any such structure, they must believe that definite structure can best be avoided by some means other than those provided by this program. I have argued, though indirectly, against both these positions: against the first by presenting the grounds of political iconoclasm and against the second by describing the workings of the constitution and by defending its empirical assumptions. More detailed and direct arguments you, reader, will easily be able to supply.

THE SPIRIT OF THE CONSTITUTION: THE STRUCTURE-DENYING STRUCTURE

The following pages define the spirit of the institutional proposal in two equivalent ways. One definition describes the point of a social vision; the other brings out the ideal of personality and the psychologic dynamic that correspond to this collective ideal and help inspire and justify it.

The spirit of the constitution can be described in another still more general way. The constitution is a superstructure: distinct from the remaining institutions of society not only because it sets the terms on which they may be revised but because, of all parts of the social order, it is the most obviously invented. The artifactual quality that applies, in greater or lesser degree, to all social life, appears concentrated in it. This superstructure, however, has a remarkable property. It is designed to prevent any definite institutional order from taking hold in social life; there lies its structure-destroying effect. In this respect, it is the precise opposite of the eighteenth-century prerevolutionary idea of the constitution as a device by which to exhibit and sustain some determinate scheme of social division and hierarchy. At the extreme, each rank or sector in society was to be represented by a particular agency of the state so that to study the constitution would be like looking at a Renaissance building whose facade discloses the plan of its interior. By contrast, the constitution of the reformed republic pushes social life toward an approximation to the ideal of an order that preserves in its determinate existence the marks of an original indefinition and that thereby loosens the constraints of context. A few analogies amplify the meaning of this alternative description of the spirit of the constitution.

Compare, first, the constitution to the flexible variant of rationalized collective labor, whose extension it promotes, if only by undercutting the institutional props to the predominance of the rigid variant. The normal forms of discourse and relationship maintain a relative distinction between the structure of activity and the activity itself. Only when insight or conflict have reached a certain threshold is the structure of activity brought explicitly into question. In the flexible variant of rationalized collective labor, however, the structure of work – the definition of the job categories, the hierarchy of discretion, the standardized operating procedures – changes frequently according to the demands of the task at hand and the results of collective deliberation. Activity within the frame of reference carries over, by constant gradations, into activity about the frame. The revised constitution extends this mode of practice to the whole of social life. It describes the meta-arrangements instituted by people to the end that their activities may more effectively subject their practices and institutions to scrutiny and revision.

But there is a difference. The goals of work are always given by some act of will, even if it is the will of the workers themselves, and even if the definition of the ends shifts with each new step of operational experience. In this sense every work system resembles a machine. But there is nothing external to the democratic republic that might supply these ends of action – nothing except the fantasies of its citizens. So the description of the enlarged democracy cannot be complete until it includes an account of the relation of individual fantasy to public order.

Compare now the program of the revised republic to a characteristic ambition of twentieth-century art. Take an example from painting, though the same point, in different form, might be illustrated by any of the arts. The disintegration of the picture plane in cubism can be understood, in one way, as a deliberate subordination of the representational to the expressive. The wrenching apart of the forms in the picture disturbs their reference to the external world and facilitates the use of these disturbed forms as references to a hidden subjective experience that lacks any natural or readily constructible language of its own. But one way to understand this stylistic event cuts across the distinction between the expressive and the representational. So long as the different clues contained in the painting can be reconciled within some possible – that is to say, conceivable – world, the imagination can assign a more or less definite referent to the work. It does not matter whether this reference points to the external world. (Compare to the nature of consonance and resolution in music.) After having tried out a certain number of variations and finding one or a few that fit, the reimagination of what you see stops. It stops at the price of adding some defined artifact to all the other defined artifacts that already exist in the world but that, strangely, arise out of an imaginative activity whose very nature is the endless denial of all settled determinations. Suppose, however, that the clues in the work of art contradict one another in every imaginable world. The imagination cannot then come to rest; it must continue to spin out variations in its understanding of the work. None of these variations fit for sure. The effort of the viewer, if it does not merely stop out of exhaustion, boredom, or despair, reenacts the endless travail of the imagination that produced the work. At first, it may seem that the external forms and colors (or sounds and words) merely provide the excuses that allow art to deal with itself. But this is still a superficial view. The imagination – including the artistic imagination – is nothing but the search for reality through the perpetual multiplication of schemes of transformative variation, reaching toward the unconditional through the discovery of the less conditional. The art concerned with itself is also and primarily concerned with the original truth of indefinition and with the quest for the unlimited. When it determines to provide visible signs of its own power to break all rules, the imagination pursues the paradoxical ambition of giving a finite form to the infinite.

The project of the reformed republic is the political parallel to this artistic aim. In place of the contradictory clues that deny rest to the imagination, it puts the institutional arrangements that help keep collective deals and state-supported privilege from congealing into a cohesive order and from lending support to a definite enacted vision of social life. Instead of the always unfinished labor of the beholder, forced to repeat the permanent spin of the constructive imagination, it favors collective practices of experimentation and innovation that never fall into planned quiescence and that encourage people to rediscover the gap between institutional order and the undefined opportunities of practical or passionate attachment.

But the difference between the artistic and the political context is that the latter deals with a focused content: the dense, intractable material of personal connection. The program of a republic cannot be fully defended on narrowly political grounds or even by reference to an overarching social ideal. The republic is also a stage on which some possible progression in the forms of human encounter can take place. To know how good a stage it is, you have to come to an understanding of the nature and possibilities of human encounter, the proper subject matter for a view of the passions. Unenlightened by such a view, the program of the restored republic remains crucially incomplete.

The most illuminating analogy may well be religious rather than technical or artistic, for it shows most clearly the relation of the republican program to the truth about the conditional and the unconditional. Imagine a religion in which all people are both priests and prophets and in which the priestly and the prophetic work coincide. The prophetic work is the denial of the absolute character of any set of social arrangements. The priestly one is each individual's and each group's renewed sacrifice of the acceptance of any one situation as a permanent element in the definition of its identity. The priestly, sacrificial emptying out is just the reverse side of the prophetic iconoclasm. This priestly and prophetic activity makes possible the emergence of fuller forms of self-assertion and attachment, and enables people to hold themselves open to the signs of the unconditional or the less conditional. But because the waiting and sacrifice have to do with the most ordinary, profane, and constant realities, they must, even more than do religion and art, contain a promise of happiness. To be credible, this promise must begin to be kept as soon as it is made.

THE SPIRIT OF THE CONSTITUTION: THE IDEAL OF EMPOWERMENT

An alternative definition of the spirit of the constitution emphasizes an ideal of personality and a psychological dynamic. Its distinctive character may be brought out by considering the response it offers to a particular experience of disbelief and submission. This experience is so intimately connected with the partial emancipation of social life from false necessity that every attempt to realize a stronger freedom must grapple with it.

In democratic and nondemocratic states alike, wherever relative education and privilege allowed people to participate actively and consciously in the experience of mass politics, world history, and enlarged economic rationality, a familiar attitude toward society became harder and harder to recapture. This was the sense that the actual design of social life embodied some higher, value-giving and self-justifying reality. To the extent that people could share in such a view, society would have the radiance of a perpetual revelation.

Imagine two kinds of sacred reality. The first is a foundational reality or transcendent personal being; the second, the experiences of personality and personal encounter that, multiplied many times over, make up a social world. Whereas the first of these two sacreds is elusive and disputable and requires, to be recognized, the power of vision, which is the ability to see the invisible, the second seems near and palpable. Whenever they can, men and women try to identify the first of these two sacreds with the second. They want to see the social world graced with the authority of an ultimate reality. But the progress of insight and the disclosures of conflict prevent this bestowal of authority. If there is a common theme in the history of thought and of politics, it consists precisely in failure to sustain claims of unconditional authority on behalf of particular ways of talking, thinking, living, and organizing society. As the two sacreds lose their contact with each other, the distant one fades away into an ineffable, longed-for reality without any clear message for understanding and conduct. The nearby one becomes profane and arbitrary.

The farther this process goes, the more it seems to threaten the experience of belief itself. The relation between the two sacreds is only the most acute form of the link between immediate contexts of thought or action and the wider contexts in terms of which the former can be understood, criticized, and justified. The remote sacred is the context of all contexts, if there can be one, and not simply the next widest context to the one we are in. The same parallel and connected events in the history of mind and society that disrupt the identification of the two sacreds also create obstacles to mistaking any context for a context of all contexts. The only beliefs people can readily have in such a situation are beliefs incident to some particular conceptual or social practice to which they deny any ultimate foundation.

Under the influence of this experience, people become like a priesthood that has lost the secret of its mysteries; their devotions and dogmas become pretenses and ploys. Looked at from afar, they could easily be mistaken for those who still share the naive euphoria of the identification of the conditional with the unconditional. But what appears, superficially, to be the same behavior proceeds from a different motive, has a different meaning for those who do it, and opens up different opportunities of action. Now their very lack of belief tempts them to capitulate all the more readily to the demands and opinions surrounding them. Resistance to these surroundings would exact sacrifice. Sacrifice can be offered willingly only by those who see some reality or value that would give it sense and make it worthwhile.

What their moral wills cannot accomplish, their imaginations can also not reach. When they try to conceive some alternative social world, they find only another conditional reality, just as arbitrary and exacting in the demands it makes upon its participants as the one that already exists. Nothing is left to them but to choose one of these worlds and to play by its rules. Each such world is both ultimately groundless and definitive of the terms of people's practical, passionate, and cognitive dealings with one another. By a perverse but logical implication, the decisiveness of its influence arises precisely from its lack of any place within a hierarchy of contexts. There is no larger defining reality to which it can serve as the vehicle or from whose standpoint it can be criticized.

The loss of strong belief in the ultimate rightness and necessity of established arrangements and opinions does not suddenly put current social arrangements at issue, nor does it make the reinvention of beliefs and practices any easier. The more common effect runs in the opposite direction. The lack of a sacrificial or imaginative impulse to transformative action means that existing ideas and institutions fail to be subject to the pressure that might reveal their workings, their limits, their hidden weakness, and their chances of replacement. Thus an involuntary skepticism and a craven fatalism may confirm each other.

In such a circumstance, many people may begin to regain a mock version of the naive–naturalistic view of social life. They do not merely want the distant sacred. They want it in a form that specifies and justifies the content of the nearby sacred. Theirs is the sentimental attitude: the wish to repeat and to believe in order to repeat. If the great imposter is the one who fools himself, the little imposter is the one who cannot quite carry it off. To this role of the petty imposter, the sentimentalist of strong belief is almost always condemned.

Individuals and even entire nations may manage for a while to convince themselves. They will imagine that a particular system of detailed social relationships and opinions is mandated – by God, by history, or by some other supreme authority. Their task will be easier if, out of lack of education or experience, they never quite abandoned the naive–naturalistic view in the first place. To the others – their disillusioned contemporaries – these people will seem slaves to an obsession that is also an illusion, and indeed they are.

Disbelief joined to fatalism, the sentimental longing for the naive and vicious confusion of the conditional with the unconditional, and the occasional obsessional living out of this spurious equation – these experiences are doubly hostile to the program of empowered democracy. They express preconceptions about self and society incompatible with the beliefs that justify this program and that incite people to carry it out. They display and generate emotions that, if allowed to hold the field, would quickly undermine the institutions the program describes. Unless the constitution is protected against the rule of such emotions, it cannot stand: only disappointment and failure would come of putting a machine for permanent iconoclasm in the hands of people who alternated between the listless acceptance and the idolatrous worship of social forms.

One antidote to these subversive emotions is the diffusion of a better, less superstitions understanding of society. The emotions I have described represent the psychological counterpart to a philosophical doctrine: the thesis that all we can do is to select a social world or a tradition of discourse and play by its rules. Precisely because all forms of social life are groundless, we must choose between a radical and paralyzing skepticism and an acceptance of the criteria of sense and value with which one such form of social life furnishes us. Thus, we must perform, though with heightened historical consciousness, the Humean operation of using an irresistible social engagement to crowd out an irrefutable mental anxiety. (When I go out into the street, my skepticism vanishes, driven out by involvements rather than by arguments.) We can never hope to change the character of our relation to the contexts of our ideas and activities by weakening the power these contexts hold over us and strengthening the power we exercise over them.

A central argument of this book, however, has been that only a social theory that recognizes and explains this possibility enables us to imagine society and history richly and truly. Such a theory shows how the power to loosen the bonds of contextuality without ever breaking them once and for all constitutes the most basic character of progress in thought and politics, of realism in the former and freedom in the latter. This insight does not, by itself, determine the content of a theoretical system or an institutional order. But it excludes certain beliefs as false. What is more relevant to the cognitive element in the emotions I described, it gives another sense to certain ideas and experiences. Thus, for example, it discredits the interpretation of the alternative forms of social or governmental organization that happen to exist at a particular time as humanity's compulsory option list. It enables people to criticize their own achievements in science or art, cultural or social revolution, by discovering the extent to which the structure they created in each realm suppresses the very activity of making and destroying structures.

The diffusion of an element of correct belief cannot, by itself, suffice to generate the emotions that sustain the constitution. The education that counts most is the one that daily life ministers. People may have a theoretical insight into the truth about the conditional and the unconditional. This insight may alter the character of all their views of self and society, of the secular and the sacred. But unless this insight gets somehow reconfirmed by the events of everyday life, it will fail to receive the testimony of the emotions. There must be a recurrent practice in ordinary social life that provides the reconfirmation and ensures the testimony.

This recurrent practice is the ability to entertain fantasies about possible forms of self-expression or association and to live them out. Its goal is the strenuous enlargement of enacted possibility. It misses the point to suppose that the reason for this commitment is merely a desire to increase the range of the choices open to us. It is, rather, to do justice to the offended and forgotten greatness of the ordinary human heart and to strengthen all those varieties of individual or collective self-assertion that depend upon active mastery over the contexts of our action.

The citizen of the empowered democracy is the empowered individual. He is able to accept an expanded range of conflict and revision without feeling that it threatens intolerably his most vital material and spiritual interests. The struggles in which he engages challenge or transform not only the material circumstances of his life but the nature and structure of the groups to which he belongs and even his preexisting sense of personal identity. This perpetual readiness for renunciation amounts to less than a sacrifice. The citizen renounces because he knows that, whatever happens, he will not be abandoned, humbled, or oppressed and because his concessions are transfigured by the affirmative inclinations and achievements I shall soon describe. The constitutional basis for this willingness to accept the risks of expanded conflict lies in the guarantee of immunity afforded by a system that precludes entrenched dependence or dominion and keeps every issue open for another day. Its higher spiritual significance consists in the assertion of transcendence as a diurnal context smashing. The citizen lives out in practice what the foundational view of human activity proclaims: the truth that his connections, desires, and insights cannot be definitively contained by the conceptual or institutional framework within which they provisionally operate. He denies the choice between resignation and escape, between treating these worlds as the end of the story and refusing wholehearted participation in any of them. He has learned the secret of how to be in them without being entirely of them.

Put more affirmatively, the ideal effect and demand of the constitution upon personality consists in the accumulation of three mental tendencies, all of which meet in the practice of fantasy and enactment. The first tendency is the accentuation of desire, of its scope and intensity. This goal holds for desire in general, whatever its specific aim or relative weight. It applies, however, with special force to those desires that aim at particular aspects of freedom itself. For such desires differ from others in contributing directly to the central experience of human empowerment. They do not – at least not inevitably – destabilize the regime within which the ordinary person can experience this enhancement of the will nor do they have the quality of an obsessional fixity that crowds out other desires. The second mental disposition is the enlargement of the imagination. The person imagines a broader spectrum of circumstances within which desires can be satisfied. The stronger the imagination becomes, the more it transfuses desire, sloughing off the elements that focus upon mere satiation or obsession and emphasizing the experience of active deliberation and reconstruction itself. The third mental tendency is the broadening of the actual opportunities to realize in practice the transformed desires produced by the first two tendencies. Such expansion saves the enhancement of the will and the imagination from issuing in a self-destructive experience of constantly frustrated insatiability.

This ideal of empowerment, and the practice of fantasy and enactment that most directly embodies it, may seem at first almost empty. They do not tell us what particular forms of human connection we should establish. The appearance of emptiness is, however, illusory. The previous stages of this programmatic argument have shown that the seemingly negative ideal of a context more fully open to challenge and revision can be made to yield very detailed institutional implications. To be sure, the citizens of such a democracy must still choose which forms of association to dream up and to enact within the institutional structure they have established, accepting some and rejecting others. The points of departure for these projects in association are inevitably local: the varieties of association enshrined by established practice and dogma as well as the incongrous experiences of practical or passionate connection suggestive of opportunities this order denies. But the more we succeed at the task of remaking society on the model of an empowered democracy, the more directly our particular forms of association can be tested against the several aspects of self-assertion I earlier distinguished: the development of practical capabilities and of the enjoyments they make possible, the diminishment of the conflict between the enabling conditions of self-assertion (the need for engagement and the avoidance of subjection), and freedom from the superstitions of false necessity.

As the contrast between context-preserving routine and context-revising conflict dissipates, the idea of a canonical list of forms of association also loses its force.

Nevertheless, insofar as the contrast between context-respecting and context-challenging activities persists, we find that all our associational practices and ideas remain subject to a two-layered standard of judgment. The normal standard is the conformity of these practices to inherited, enacted ideals of association. The exceptional, visionary standard comes from the turn we give to our basic longings for empowerment and solidarity, which, together, compose a more complex project of self-assertion.

The change in our relation to our contexts that the program of empowered democracy exemplifies may seem to deprive us of the normal standard, first by undermining our confidence in its authority and then by jumbling up the distinct models of association that represent its working materials. But, in exchange, that movement begins to turn the exceptional standard into the ordinary one: it enables us to experiment, more constantly, freely, and self-consciously with the relation between ultimate aspirations and social practices. And it thereby encourages us to develop a richer, more subtle, and more prosaic discourse about matters that too easily seem to be beyond words.

THE SPIRIT OF THE CONSTITUTION: EMPOWERMENT IMAGINED AND PERVERTED

In the industrial democracies of the late twentieth century the ideal of empowerment lives a strange double life. This ideal has already been realized in the important but truncated form of an experience of rightholding open to large numbers of ordinary men and women. Here is empowerment as the ability to move within the discretionary zone of entitlements defined on the model of the consolidated property right. The achievements and deficiencies of this version of empowerment, as well as the alternatives to it, have already been discussed.

The felt inadequacy of this experience of rightholding becomes evident in the fantasies of adventure and mastery. These fantasies are not even meant to be lived out. When, in exceptional circumstances, people have taken them seriously and acted upon them, the results have often been disastrous.

The hidden, second life of the empowerment ideal shows the extraordinary force of this longing and the perverse forms it assumes when left unrealized in the ordinary lives of ordinary men and women. Consider a typical example of the aestheticized presentation of empowerment in the twentieth century: Abel Gance's cinematic extravaganza about Napoleon Bonaparte (1934). There he is – the great hero, the man of will, embodying the highest degree the rage of transcendence and the transformative vocation. He refuses to take the established contexts of action for granted and repeatedly smashes, or threatens to smash, them. He combines an acute insight into the opportunities and dangers of his situation with an ability to imagine possibilities that the logic of this situation excludes. He conducts himself within the established world as if he possessed secret knowledge, and indeed he does.

The context smasher puts himself into situations that others would regard as ridiculous and demeaning (e.g., Napoleon's awkward and self-deceiving pursuit of the philanderer Josephine). He doesn't feel tainted; he just doesn't give a damn. For one thing, his efforts are all turned toward his great enterprise and away from the petty ambitions and fears of ordinary life. For another thing, he transvalues the hierarchies of his contemporaries: his greater freedom from the context enables him to judge by another hierarchy of value. Therefore, he appears to be shameless when he is in fact guided by an alternative moral vision. This vision does not merely replace one hierarchy of values by another; it partly liberates moral judgment from the constraining effect of any clearly defined hierarchy.

The same forces that free him from the fear of being laughed at also emancipate him from small-minded vanities and resentments. (Remember that all this is part of the myth presented in the film rather than of the actual psychological reality of these individuals.) Though he may be ruthless in his treatment of particular individuals and loyalties, he never indulges in revenge for its own sake, nor can he be manipulated through vanity. After all, he is on more important business and has greater pleasures.

Then there are the piercing eyes, the intense, wild expression that the man of will shares with all the secondary characters and even the ordinary mobs drawn into the momentous events he commands. It reminds you of those books of nineteenth- and early twentieth century photographs of Chinese, Japanese, and Russians. The subject looks into the camera with the same crazed expression. Perhaps his disquiet comes from the unfamiliarity of the camera, which seems to puncture the shell of social routine and produce a moment of dazed incongruity in which the familiar limits and aims of action fall away and deeper, wordless concerns rise up. Perhaps the surprise given by the machine serves both to exemplify and to portray the larger shock administered by the Western intrusion. Perhaps, however, these circumstances merely precipitated a distinctive, ambivalent experience of human empowerment. The fierce-eyed subjects, amid their ornate or ragged trivia, look as if they had seen beyond the photographer and their circumstance to a reality previously hidden from their eyes. They had seen something of the God who says, No man sees me and lives. Similarly, in the Gance film, the actors looked at the moving camera as the exotic photography subjects had looked at the still one. The revolutionary interlude replaced with advantage the Western shock. All the way from the transcendent man of will to the agitated crowds, the participants seem in touch with another, higher reality, with the things you see and feel when one conditional world has been destroyed and another not yet emerged, as if this crack in the finite provided a glimpse into the absolute. At any moment, this context-breaking brio might be converted into an idolatrous delusion: people might treat their particular historical endeavors as if these undertakings were themselves the absolute. Such were the risks and complications of a more radiant vitality.

All these aspects of human empowerment – the frenzied pursuit of the transformative vocation; the freedom from the fear of the ridiculous, from the compulsion of mean-minded concerns, and from the "narcissism of petty differences"; the ability to impart to worldly action the ardor that accompanies the loosening of the constraints of context – all this appeared bound up with a special union between leader and followers. At a still more concrete level, it seems inseparable from particular forms of mass organization. The leader achieved empowerment in a basically different fashion from the other people. He alone took events by the hand and thereby realized the transformative vocation in all its purity. He required no teachers or mediators and promised no equality with himself: on the contrary, equality among his followers depended upon their acceptance of his special role. When, for example, he freed himself from the fear of the ridiculous, there was never a suggestion that they could do the same, except perhaps unconsciously as the result of a spell he cast on them and they on one another.

The exceptionalism of the leader was connected, obscurely but significantly, to the form of his historical enterprise. In different degrees and in different ways, pseudorevolutionary nationalism and its surrogates involved the superimposition of a communal ideal upon social hierarchies that this ideal simultaneously adjusted and preserved. Such movements often embraced the cult of warlike force, wielded by the collectivity under the guidance of the leader. Thus, the psychological experience of empowerment was to be realized through social forms that constrained or negated the different aspects of freedom. Yet empowerment meant freedom if it meant anything. Here was a social experience at war with itself: a monstrous equivocation, already prefigured in the circumstance of followers whose access to the sense of empowerment paradoxically depended upon their submission to a leader or upon their absorption in a crowd. Nevertheless, the film presented the experience of empowerment as if it were inseparable from these offensive manifestations.

The audience at the cinema stood at a second, safer remove from the man of will. They responded with barely suppressed fascination to the representation of greatness while ashamed and even repelled by the social forms that greatness took. They got no help in distinguishing the former from the latter, nor could they readily imagine any alternative way by which society might extend the availability of empowerment.

The epic grandeur evoked by such a film did for the audience what the bewitching force of a more or less consciously staged collective drama did for the participant crowds and the secondary characters within the film: it provided their admiration with an alibi. But the apparent alibi ended up calling attention to the crime. The aesthetic of empowerment – the worship of an imaginative power to transform reality unaffected by ordinary human longing, the substitution of art for religion and even for love – ran through much modern art. In the antinovelistic style of works of art like these, it reached its most crudely and overtly political but also most revealing form.

To comprehend what attracted the audience, however ambivalently, to this display of impenitent grandeur, you need to understand some crucial aspects of the circumstance people lived in. The less advantaged ranks of society might be almost entirely preoccupied with the need to find work, to support a family, and maintain a position within a residual local or ethnic community. Many might still adhere to an ideal of the honorable calling that made them relatively immune to larger conceptions of empowerment. But whenever the compulsions of material need loosened, or people's actual or imagined experience of social and personal possibility broadened, the conception of empowerment underwent a corresponding change. All the varieties of happiness that involved the experience of transforming a context emerged alongside the longing to exist safely within a context. There was little chance of a naive return to the mere acceptance of place within an unquestioned world. Return, under these conditions, would produce a sentiment of defeat and self-compromise, poisoning the more limited happiness that people knew and cherished. The extraordinary and lucky individual – the leader, the artist, the thinker, the mover and shaker – might satisfy his aspiration. But he satisfied it in a way that excluded other people and that perpetuated, in some less dramatic form, the paradoxes of empowerment that exclusion produced. Neither the privileged nor the excluded could imagine, much less realize, an alternative social form of empowerment. The character of their fantasies emphasized the nature of their constraint.

A driving force of the constitutional program is the desire to do justice to the human heart, to free it from indignity and satisfy its hidden and insulted longing for greatness in a fashion it need not be fearful or ashamed of. To this end, the experience of empowerment must be made real rather than vicarious. It must be reconciled with the ordinary needs and attachments of ordinary people. And it must be freed from its corrupting association with the cult of leaders and of violence. The program outlined here describes the institutional requirements for achieving these objectives.

THE SPIRIT OF THE CONTITUTION
REDEFINED BY CONTRAST

The spirit of this institutional proposal becomes clearer by contrast to other, familiar doctrines of the present or the past that superficially resemble it.

In the contemporary world, the most persistently attractive program of social reconstruction has often been described as social democracy or as the welfare–corporate state. Its most developed forms have emerged in Western Europe and Japan. To be sure, even in the advanced industrial democracies, it has prospered far more in some places than in others. But its influence, at least among the industrial democracies, is shown by the failure of more left-wing or right-wing political parties to make a major dent on its achievements or to find a political creed of comparable authority.

Recall the major tenets of the social-democratic program. First, it upholds the particular variant of constitutional democracies whose instruments were first perfected in the crucial period from the late eighteenth to the mid-nineteenth century – though its proponents may say this institutional structure is merely the best one around, rather than show much interest in looking for significantly different alternatives. For they believe that the main problems and concerns lie elsewhere. Second, this doctrine holds that government must actively supervise a regulated market economy organized along just the lines of the formative institutional context whose content and genesis Chapters 2, 3, and 4 described. The democratic state must encourage investment in the most promising sectors of industry. It must seek to place the national economy in a favorable place within the international division of labor. And it must broker with big business and organized labor, as well as with other sectors of the population, distributive deals that enable all to turn from disruptive conflict to productive collaboration. Third, people's basic material needs must be taken care of. This objective may be accomplished through either a recognition of universal welfare claims independent of job position, or an emphasis on job security, accompanied by a tie-in of welfare benefits to job position. Fourth, people should be encouraged to participate in the organization of the workplace and the management of their local areas. These local engagements should help blur the distinction between public and private order and revitalize the sense of citizenship. Fifth, both welfare guarantees and local participation should be achieved in ways minimizing conflict about the social order as a whole. Such conflict gives free reign to ideological posturing, utopian illusions, and selfish defensiveness that draw people away from the collaborative undertakings needed to solve practical problems.

Two mutually reinforcing impulses underlie the social-democratic program and make clear why it is simply the most recent version of the desire to deny or contain the political character of social life. One such impulse is the perennial desire to retreat from the violent connotations of history into a stable life of practical concerns and communal engagement. The other impulse is the effort to discover the objective structure of practical requirements and organizational constraints that the loose talk of the ideologists disguises.

The argument for empowered democracy sees this social democratic program as practically, spiritually, and theoretically inadequate. It is practically inadequate because the development of productive or destructive capabilities requires a more thorough subversion of the hold of privilege over the means of society making than the established institutional versions of markets and democracies allow. It is spiritually inadequate because this same liquefaction of established social structures is needed to develop the richness of our subjective life and to advance our attempts to reconcile more fully the enabling conditions of self-assertion. It is theoretically inadequate because it relies upon yet another diluted residue of the naturalistic idea: it still draws on the idea of a latent structure of flexible coordination and collaboration that is waiting there to be discovered, if only we could get rid of the distractions of ideological conflict.

The program defended here diverges from the social-democratic ideal in its advocacy of radically revised ways of organizing market economies and democratic governments, in its search for the institutional arrangements that further soften the contrast between context-preserving routine and context-revising conflict, in its preference for the styles of welfare guarantees that presuppose these institutional reforms rather than compensating for their absence, and in its effort systematically to connect involvement in local and workplace self-government with conflict over the basic terms of social life.

If social democracy conceived in these ample terms represents the closest counterpart and rival to the program of empowered democracy, civic or classical republicanism may seem to be one of its sources. But the genealogy is no more accurate than the comparison. The civic republicanism to which I refer has been the single most important rhetorical weapon of many who oppose both the selfish privatism and the rampant inequality they see as continuing to vitiate contemporary Western forms of economic and governmental organization. The characteristic republican trope is the need to recapture the selfless devotion to collective ends that supposedly distinguished the ancient republics. Its ambition is to ensure an equality of material circumstance and to enlist a selfless devotion to the common good. Equality is to be ensured by granting each citizen a roughly equal unit of property. Prohibitions of alienation (e.g., of land) and constant redistributions must prevent exchange from undermining this fundamental equality. Devotion to the common good is to be won by requiring the citizens, from childhood on, to participate in public responsibilities and by deploying all the varieties of education and example that may coax them out of their tendency to withdraw into narrow attachments and material pleasures. The tenacity with which some partial version of this doctrine has been upheld under the most diverse historical circumstances is matched only by the regularity of its failure whenever it has been allowed to influence, even obliquely, actual policy.

The material cost of the classical republican doctrine lies in the paralysis of the power to innovate. For, as earlier stages of the argument have repeatedly emphasized, the development of practical capabilities depends upon the ability to recombine and renew, by consensual or coercive means, not only the factors of production but the arrangements that constitute the organizational setting of productive activity. A country nailed to the constraints upon recombination that classical republicanism requires could not survive in the military, economic, and ideological rivalry of nation-states. Nor could it provide its citizens with the many opportunities for individual and collective experimentation that enrichment opens up.

The spiritual cost of the classical republican program is even more terrible. The equal rightholders live in a circumstance of self-conscious austerity. This austerity is not due merely to the constraints such a system of right imposes upon material progress; it results as well from the spiritual incompatibility of this regime with luxury. Luxury means, in part, the surfeit and variety of sensual pleasure, particularly insofar as this pleasure is directed away from personal attachment to material things or symbolic representations. The psychology of variation and surfeit cannot easily be reconciled to a circumstance requiring the quiescence of basic social arrangements, a basic sameness in the outward conditions of life, and the comparative isolation of each rightholder within his separate sphere of right. In such a circumstance, the individual readily falls victim to two contrasting sets of emotions, which sometimes coexist and at other times replace each other. He may wallow in a torpor of narrow routine (after all, how much can the yeoman or his latter-day counterpart find to do in his little plot?), while he jealously watches over his shoulder to see that nobody gets ahead of him or trespasses on what is his own. The adherents to this social doctrine have always claimed that the citizen of their desired republic can be expected to put the collective good over private interest. But the content of this collective good is exhausted in the defense of the system of inviolable spheres of right against all domestic or foreign enemies. The sameness of different subjectivities must be ensured by their shared emptiness; any richness of subjective experience creates the danger of cumulative discord or hopeless self-absorption. The citizens may disguise their indignation at any departure from this sameness in the language of a pompous and unforgiving virtue. These emotions will sometimes give way to others: no social order can entirely submerge longing in routine. The individual fantasizes fabulous wants and satisfactions. If his own imagination is inadequate to generate these yearnings, he may receive them from other societies, or from the rebels and deviants he ostentatiously condemns but secretly envies, or even from the mere exaggeration of the satisfactions and desires he already experiences. Such longings can be counted on to be both persistent and forbidden. When openly flaunted, they will antagonize the regime. When denied, they may linger on, as resentment and self-contempt, to poison it.

The program of empowered democracy avoids these material and spiritual costs by redefining both the character and the forms of equality and participation. The rough equality of material circumstance that it seeks is meant to arise as the convergent effect of absolute claims to the satisfaction of minimal material needs (claims that rank among the immunity rights), the temporary and conditional character of access to capital, and the openness of the formative context of power and production to challenge and change. The participation in public life that it proposes is not the cult of altruistic goals rigidly contrasted to private ends, nor is it the fatal mania of meetings that invariably ends in boredom for the many and manipulation by the few. What it wants, instead, is to extend the scope and the clarity of private ambitions by enlarging our sense of the possible forms of association through which they may be realized and redefined. In this way, it seeks to superimpose upon the delights of private enjoyment the pleasures – neither private nor public – of creating, within society, distinctive but shared forms of life that permit shared but distinctive activities.

The radical democratic program outlined here is therefore less a sequel to the classical republican vision than a superliberalism. It pushes the liberal war against privilege and superstition to a point that requires the abandonment of the forms of governmental, economic, and legal organization with which liberalism has traditionally been associated. Having made its peace with modernity, it no longer needs to prepare the future by pretending to restore the past. This superliberalism is also the defensible form of a leftist ideal that breaks the spell of deep-logic social theory, confronts the need to think institutionally, refuses to define itself by reference to class interests shaped by the very institutions it wants to reconstruct, and seeks to further both freedom and equality by turning subversion into a practical way of life.

THE MEANING OF IMPERFECTION

Consider now three apparent dilemmas that, if true, would prove fatal to the programmatic argument. Each is false in its initial form. But each apparent dilemma can be reformulated as the description of a real risk. To acknowledge both the reasonableness and the seriousness of this risk is to emphasize the antiperfectionist character of the program. All that can be claimed for the institutional platform of the empowered democracy is that it represents an advance over the available forms of governmental and economic organization.

Self-Reproduction and Stability

A first apparent dilemma has to do with the self-reproducing quality of the constitution. On the one hand, the constitutional scheme may guarantee its own perpetuation by the success with which it informs motivations and shapes the occasions and instruments of conflict. But such a success at self-defense would discredit the authority of the institutional scheme, for it would show this scheme to be in flagrant violation of the animating ideal of revisability. The formative context of power and production would have become more rather than less entrenched, and the entrenchment would be all the more insidious for being largely automatic and invisible.

Suppose, on the other hand, that the institutional structure could be as easily revised as its claim to legitimacy requires. Imagine that the scope of conflict over the basic terms of social life were as ample as the programmatic argument implies. Then, any political party elevated to office that failed to share the vision underlying the institutional scheme would set out to change it. The decisional mobility the proposed style of governmental organization seeks to strengthen would make such changes all the easier to effect. Only a party that precisely shared the spirit of the constitution could be counted on to develop it according to its ideals.

Clearly, the dilemma draws attention to the relation between disentrenchment and institutional stability. The staying power of a formative context seems to depend to a large extent on its unavailability to revision. It therefore also depends on the failure of written constitutions or legal rules to make this structure entirely explicit. To explicate the formative context while undermining all other obstacles to its revision seems to be a formula for transience.

The flaw in the description of this dilemma is the assumption that only the entrenchment of an institutional plan – only its protection against the destabilizing effects of ordinary conflict – can ensure its continuity. There is not, nor is there meant to be, any guarantee that this particular institutional plan will, once established, be perpetuated. The plan merely interprets, for a particular historical circumstance, an approach to the project of individual and collective empowerment. The institutional implications of the approach must change constantly and unpredictably. These changes will in turn suggest new interpretations of the animating ideas of the institutional plan. Moreover, parties may rise to power that are radically unsympathetic to the spirit of the proposed constitution. They may undo the constitutional plan. And the experiment in empowered democracy, once interrupted, may never be repeated. But do not suppose that an institutional plan can continue, or that its animating ideals can be upheld, only if it remains hard to revise. The argument for the new-model republic includes the hypothesis that once the increased opportunities for individual and collective self-assertion opened up by the empowered democracy are tasted, they will not easily be forgone. The hypothesis may prove wrong. But the spirit of empowered democracy requires us to put it to the test; every obstacle to institutional change takes something away from the distinctive design and ambition of this institutional program. The point is to undertake an experiment, an experiment in whose success we have reason to hope but whose integrity we wish above all to preserve. Here is a style of institution making that presupposes no contrast between an omniscient and benevolent Lycurgus (the founders, the revolutionaries, the fathers of their country) and the ordinary historical agents who live in the world Lycurgus has set up.

Militancy and Empowerment

A second dilemma refers to the psychological attitudes needed to avoid a perversion of the constitutional scheme. The institutional program, it seems, can achieve its desired objectives only if the citizens throw themselves ardently into the organized conflicts of the republic, conflicts whose resolution influences every facet of the institutional order and whose occasions recur in every domain of social life. In the absence of broadly based and wholehearted civic engagement, empowered democracy might suddenly turn from the freest constitution to the most despotic. As the citizens withdrew, out of boredom or frustration, into their immediate concerns, the group in power would find in these institutional arrangements an unrivaled opportunity to turn transitory advantages into vested rights. The connections among spheres of social life, the ease with which programmatic experiments could be tried out, at least in the early years of the regime, and the weakening of independent centers of power able to stand up to these initiatives from the center – all this may open the way for the architects of a new order of privilege. The work of entrenchment and enserfment may be all the more dangerous by benefiting from the citizens' impression that they lived under the most free (though, unbeknown to them, also the most fragile) of constitutions.

If, on the other hand, only a constant militancy could prevent these perverse consequences, empowered democracy would depend upon unrealistic and indefensible assumptions about conduct and motivation. The implicit ideal of human existence would be too narrow and biased to carry authority. It would harm or downplay all those forms of subjective experience and practical problem solving that depend upon the containment of civic militancy, which threatens to consume the time of those whom it does not bore, or whom it does not intimidate into privatistic withdrawal.

But we have reason to downplay both horns of this apparent dilemma. The constitution of empowered democracy does not oppose private desires and collective devotions. Instead, it robs this polemical contrast of its force. It does so by enabling people more easily to extend the humdrum practice of pursuing interests within a framework of unquestioned institutional and imaginative assumptions into the extraordinary activity of questioning this framework. Thus, the practice of fantasy and enactment that the institutional program encourages is less a public militancy than an extension of the ordinary activity of defining goals and pursuing them. Its chosen expression is not civic pomp and heroic striving but the activity of a working life. And its favorite devices are conversations rather than meetings, conversations that continue when the meetings end.

On the other side, the constitutional plan eases the formation of a large number of perceived group interests in tension with one another. It multiplies the arenas in which the citizens may engage in organized conflict over the organization of social life. It breaks down the rigid roles and ranks that give stability to conceptions of group interest. It dissolves such conceptions into the more fluid crisscrossing lines of parties of opinion unanchored in social stations. It makes actual social life more closely resemble what, to a considerable extent, democratic party politics are actually like. Moreover, although the program of empowered democracy undermines the independent centers of social authority that a petrified division of labor or a stable corporatist organization of society sustains, it brings into existence other constraints upon central power.

Thus, what initially seemed an intolerable dilemma turns into a calculated risk. There is no assurance that empowered democracy will provide adequate safeguards against the danger that people may withdraw from civic life and through their withdrawal permit a new and more thoroughgoing entrenchment of factional interests. I claim only that the guarantees and benefits of the constitutional plan make it reasonable to run these risks. Indeed, we must reach toward a regime such as empowered democracy if we are to reconcile freedom as empowerment with the practical drive toward plasticity in social life, the condition of collective wealth and power. Both our happiness and our virtue depend upon the particular institutional forms we give to the search for plasticity. Just as the quest for empowerment through plasticity may enable us to live out more fully our context-transcending identity, so, too, it may subject us to a despotism less messy or violent but more thoroughgoing than any yet known.

Solidarity and Empowerment

A final dilemma refers to the relation between the spirit of the constitution and the social ideals this spirit seems to antagonize. The programmatic argument would make no sense if the spirit of the constitution were neutral among all credible accounts of the meaning and requirements of our project of individual and collective self-assertion. For this argument assumes that neutrality is possible only in the highly limited sense defined earlier. But once we abandon the hope of neutrality we can recognize more frankly the bias and insufficiency of empowered democracy. Of all the values this institutional program downplays, the weightiest is the commitment to communal attachments and to the transforming virtues of personal love and of faith and hope in individual people. To the extent that the ideal of empowerment means something more limited than the general effort to achieve individual and collective self-assertion, it seems to value the development of individual and collective capabilities more than the continuance of particular loyalties to individuals and groups. It slights the customary practices in which such loyalties are inevitably embedded.

Empowered democracy represents only a partial vision of a form of life designed to help us to carry forward our efforts at self-assertion. The details of this vision reflect the legacy and the problems of a particular historical circumstance. The defense of the vision invokes a particular normative and explanatory approach. The content of the vision needs to be complemented by a conception of transformed personal relations.

The ideal of empowerment fails to make up the whole of a defensible social ideal. Taken in isolation, it does indeed threaten to submerge concern with trust under the power-mad or narcissistic flaunting of the will and the heartless cult of magnificent capability.

But the program of empowerment through institutional invention and cultural-revolutionary practice refines as well as threatens our experiences of solidarity. The reinvention and advancement of the radical project, in the form of empowered democracy, make it easier for us to give our attachments the qualities of love: the achievement of a heightened mutual vulnerability; the imaginative acceptance of other individuals that tears through the screen of stereotyped images, roles, and ranks; and the effacement of the conflict between our need for others and our fear of the jeopardy in which they place us. These qualities of love represent the least illusory and most durable aspect of our communal ideals: the part best able to outlast the disappointments of life and the surprises of history.

In many convergent ways the program of empowerment reinforces the ideals of solidarity that it also jeopardizes. The proposals extend a series of social changes that shake up and leave permanently weakened all roles and ranks. The more rigid and influential such divisions and hierarchies are, the more do our attachments and animosities stay entangled in a vitiating dilemma. Every allegiance remains susceptible to confusion with craven role playing or with the exchange of exploitation and servility between oppressors and oppressed. Conversely, every attempt by the subjugated to win more independence seems to require the betrayal of loyalties that represent the strongest available examples of community. The institutionalized destabilization of the hierarchical and divided order of society diminishes the opportunities for this equivocation. It allows us to attach ourselves to others without accepting subservience and to become more free without turning against those to whom we feel closest.

The program of empowerment makes a second contribution to the improvement of solidarity. It strengthens the liberty of the individual to forgive the harms other people do him. The record of these wrongs tempts him to search for preemptive security against other people. It freezes him into strategies of distancing and defense. The empowered are freer to be generous. They can more readily lift the burden of frustration and resentment and imagine themselves related to others in untried ways – especially in ways that diminish the conflict between attachment and independent self-assertion.

The result is a benefit to society, in the form of a boost to collaboration. Above all, however, it is a gain to the individual. For that conflict blocks human capability – to be, to do, to produce, and to connect.

In yet a third and most significant way the program of empowerment helps better our relations to one another. The institutionalized breakdown of rigid ranks and roles continues the work of democracy: it saves us from remaining placeholders in a system of predefined social stations. As the grip of these stations upon individual experience loosens, we become more able to deal with one another, imaginatively and practically, as individuals rather than as stand-ins for collective categories of class, gender, nationality, or race. This opportunity to address the other as a concrete individual never completely defined by the coordinates of his place on a social map is a mark of love. The style of solidarity favored by empowered democracy draws our communal relations closer to love just as it undermines sharp contrasts between the communal and the noncommunal aspects of life in society.

Some may object that they prefer the old version of community, the version based on the opposition of insiders and outsiders, on the intolerance of conflict within the group, on the jealous defense of exclusive communal traditions, on the commitment to outward, even inherited signs of joint identity, and on the insistent sharing of values and preconceptions. But this antique style of solidarity is less capable of reconciliation with other basic goals of ours, less likely to outlast the illusions of false necessity, and therefore also less capable of making us happy. For the happiness it grants us requires special circumstances of social tranquillity and unchallenged prejudice and depends on the maintenance of conditions that hinder the development of our powers.

Considerations like these – informed promises of happiness – rather than assessments of conformity to ready-made standards of right and wrong are what do and should matter to us in the criticism and justification of forms of social life. Such considerations exemplify the methods employed by political argument under the impact of enlightenment about false necessity. They also complement and correct the more closely textured varieties of social criticism that contrast our distinct, received ideals of human association with the practical arrangements supposed to realize these ideals in fact.

Two great constructive forces work upon social life. One force is restless experimentation with institutions, ideas, and techniques for the sake of enhancing our practical capabilities. This search for growth in worldly power shades into the quest for another, less tangible empowerment: the ability to question and revise our shared institutional and imaginative assumptions as we go about the daily business of life. It is the opportunity to join engagement with self-consciousness, and to avoid the choice between alienation and stupefaction, to act confidently within a society or a culture without becoming its puppets. The overlap between the conditions for these two modes of empowerment is a surprising fact rather than a self-evident truth.

The other major constructive force is our acceptance of one another across the barriers of division and hierarchy that keep us apart. We want access to relations and communities that limit the conflict between our need to affirm ourselves in one another's presence and our struggle to escape the incalculable dangers we pose to one another. We want something better than the middle distance, and we know that failure to find it leaves us homeless in the world.

The reformed democracy directly serves the search for empowerment both as practical capability and as mastery over context. Its point is to secure capability to the individual as well as to the society. This aim connects the program to the liberal tradition. But because the commitment to empower individuals – not just societies or groups – sees through the eyes of a theory that looks beyond false necessity, it requires us to break with institutional arrangements that liberals have traditionally identified with their cause. To complete this rupture, we must free ourselves from the received contrast between liberal and socialist programs, which depends upon the same superstitions.

The program of radical democracy has a more troubled relation to the strengthening and cleansing of solidarity. The fulfillment of its proposals does not ensure us of coexisting in peace. It does not take away our hearts of stone and give us hearts of flesh. But it does enable us to live out more fully the tense, ambiguous, ennobling connection between solidarity and empowerment, between the experience of mutual acceptance and the development of our faculties, between our longing for one another and our efforts to find particular expressions for the impulse within us that rebels against all particularity. What more could we ask of society than a better chance to be both great and sweet?

Bibliographical Notes

AIMS AND NATURE OF THESE NOTES

THESE bibliographical notes have four aims. The first is to acknowledge direct debts for ideas, arguments, and observations. The second objective is to compensate for the lack of a detailed intellectual-historical or polemical setting in a book that is almost entirely constructive. (For a more extended view of the intellectual background to the argument, refer to *Social Theory: Its Situation and Its Task*.) The third goal is to point to scholarship that explores in greater detail some of the past and present social situations mentioned in the text. The fourth and controlling purpose is to recruit and to help co-workers in a common endeavor by sharing with them elements of a study plan.

Remember that this work is frankly speculative. The bibliographical references are therefore meant to elucidate, guide, and connect, not to prove by induction or persuade by exegesis. Traditional footnotes would not serve the main purpose of this commentary. They also seemed inappropriate for two additional reasons. On the one hand, there was no reasonable point at which to stop; an informative citation could always be added to a citation already included. On the other hand, a massive apparatus would increase the danger of mistaking examples for proofs.

Some parts of the book, especially those dealing with historical events, are annotated at greater length. Others, particularly the long chapter that offers a program of social reconstruction, have few annotations. Titles appear in English if an English translation is readily available. A particular list of references departs from chronological order whenever another sequence seems preferable. The text page numbers to which this commentary refers appear at the outside margin. Themes that key in with the text are in italics.

1. THE NATURE AND INTENTIONS OF THE ARGUMENT

Explanatory and Programmatic Themes

For a statement of the intellectual and practical-political settings of the argument see the text and notes of *Social Theory: Its Situation and Its Task*.

A few clarifications may be helpful here. I characterize *deep-structure social theory* and *positivist social science* as tendencies defined by the recurrence of particular explanatory moves. No one thinker or book ever fully exemplifies any such tendency, nor is the most interesting exposition of a tendency usually found in the thinker who remains most faithful to it.

Thus, Marx and the Marxist tradition supply the most powerful instances of deep-structure analysis. Consider the core account of the system-preserving and system-transforming laws of capital in *Capital* and the broader evolutionary ideas about the succession of modes of production presented in *Introduction to the Critique of Political Economy, The German Ideology,* and the *Communist Manifesto.* Yet Marx's writings also include some of the most useful points of departure for the construction of a practice of explanatory social theory that carries the conception of society as artifact beyond the constraints imposed on it by deep-structure assumptions. See, for example, the criticism of political economy worked out in the *Poverty of Philosophy,* the *Grundrisse,* and the discussion of "the fetishism of commodities" in *Capital,* vol. 1, chap. 1, section 4.

Although later Marxists have elaborated the deep-structure tenets, they have also developed the contrasting themes in Marx's work. See especially the political Marxists mentioned in item 3 of the list of general influences in the later notes to this chapter.

A social theory may give a less prominent role to deep-structure assumptions without coming any closer to a developed alternative. Weber's intellectual trajectory confirms the point. Some of his work conforms to the evolutionary variant of deep-structure theory and even exhibits the particular merger of deep-structure premises and functional methods discussed in *Social Theory: Its Situation and Its Task.* See *The Agrarian Sociology of Ancient Civilization* and the treatment of bureaucratic rationalization in *Economy and Society.* Major portions of Weber's work fail to fit this model without, however, providing an explanatory alternative. Some, like *The Protestant Ethic and the Spirit of Capitalism,* remain close to a causally agnostic scrutiny of meanings and intentions. Others, such as large parts of *Economy and Society,* provide a similarly agnostic typology of social forms.

Notice that much recent work defends or criticizes Marxism and other comprehensive social theories as views that assign a central role to functional explanations: to explanations that account for a social situation or process by appealing to the consequences it tends to produce. See G. A. Cohen, *Karl Marx's Theory of History: A Defense,* Princeton, Princeton, 1978, pp. 249–296; Jon Elster, "Marxism, Functionalism, and Game Theory: The Case for Methodological Individualism," *Theory and Society,* vol. 2 (1982), pp. 453-484; G. A. Cohen, "Reply to Elster on 'Marxism, Functionalism and Game Theory,' " *Theory and Society,* vol. 2 (1982), pp. 483–496.

In *Social Theory: Its Situation and Its Task,* however, I have argued that in these theories functional explanations gain their characteristic

structure and generate their characteristic problems only when combined with deep-structure assumptions about the distinction between formative contexts of frameworks and formed routines, about
the indivisibility of those frameworks, and about the lawlike constraints or developmental tendencies that supposedly govern them.

The key to *positivist social science* (and to its counterpart, naive
historiography) is not hostility to general explanations that cannot
be directly verified or falsified – the most prominent theme in the
polemic about positivism in social and historical studies. Nor is it
the appeal to reductionist or economistic views of personality and
social relations. It is, rather, the failure to recognize the centrality, variability, and implications of the contrast between the formative institutional and imaginative frameworks of social life and the practical or
argumentative routines these frameworks help shape. The varieties of
positivist social science may therefore be usefully distinguished by the
way in which each disposes of the framework–routine distinction.

Consider contemporary American economics as an example.
There is an austere general-equilibrium analysis that seeks to cast
economic theory beyond and above particular institutional contexts
of production and exchange. See, for instance, Gerard Debreu,
Mathematical Economics: Twenty Papers of Gerard Debreu, Cambridge,
Cambridge, 1983. There is an ideologically aggressive economics
that represents a particular institutional framework as mandated by
efficiency requirements (e.g., the Chicago School and its successor,
rational-expectations theory). And there is a policy-oriented economics that acknowledges in principle the decisive importance of
particular institutional arrangements while in practice eviscerating
the significance of the acknowledgment (e.g., the American
Keynesians, like the later Samuelson, Tobin, and Solow). This third
variant of economics as positivist social science studies the direct
relation among large-scale economic aggregates of, say, investment
or unemployment as if an existing set of institutional arrangements
– however revisable, accidental, and recombinable they may be –
could produce or tolerate lawlike economic regularities.

The text defines *the radical project* inclusively. On this definition,
John Stuart Mill, Alexander Herzen, Karl Marx, P.J. Proudhon,
and Virginia Woolf were all champions of the cause. Whether so
inclusive a definition makes sense depends at least in part on what
we can do prospectively to develop and unify the radical project.
It depends on our success at carrying forward the interplay between
the speculative themes that distinguish and often oppose these varieties of liberal, leftist, and modernist radicalism and the practical
social arrangements that are made to represent these themes. So
the message, at least in this initial chapter is: Suspend judgment.

The Proto-Theory

The statement of the proto-theory provides a convenient occasion
to enumerate some of the major influences on the development of

the theoretical view presented here. The same list appears at the outset of the notes to *Social Theory: Its Situation and Its Task*. The ideas and arguments of this book do not represent a synthesis of the conceptions contained in the following sources. But neither are the components of the list a random assortment of ideas, linked only by the accidents of one individual's intellectual trajectory. They rank among the materials available today to whomever wants to combine, as *Politics* does, the reconstruction of social thought along antinecessitarian lines with the anticipation of practical forms of social life that can more fully realize the radical project. Each of the nine sets of ideas, themes, or forms of intellectual practice contained in the list can be, and has been, used in ways that conflict with the intellectual program advocated in this book. Yet all nine together can be enlisted in the execution of this program. Their availability lends support to the claim that we already have at hand the building blocks of an antinaturalistic social theory able to give new life and new meaning to the cause that leftists, liberals, and modernists share.

1. The theme of the rigid and the fluid, the hot and the cold, moments of social life. This theme has been present, in one form or another, in virtually every period and tradition of social thought. Its most famous formulation in classic European social theory can be found in Durkheim's discussion of the moments of collective ecstasy (*The Elementary Forms of Religious Life*, trans. J. W. Swain, Free Press, 1969, pp. 240–242) and in Max Weber's treatment of charisma and routinization (Economy and Society, eds. Guenther Roth and Claus Wittich, Bedminster, New York, 1968, vol. 3, chap. 14, pp. 1111–1155). It reappears as a central idea in Sartre's late work; see *Criticism of Dialectical Reason*, trans. Alan Sheridan-Smith, New Left Books, London, 1976, pp. 256–404. It plays a prominent role in the writings of Victor Turner; see *The Ritual Process: Structure and Anti-Structure*, Cornell, Ithaca, 1977. Francesco Alberoni has given this idea its most elaborate and rewarding contemporary formulations. See particularly *Movimento e Istituzione*, Il Mulino, Bologna, 1981.

2. Karl Marx's criticism of English political economy, particularly as evidenced in the *Poverty of Philosophy*, the *Grundrisse*, and the early sections of *Capital*. This criticism represents an example of how the portrayal of an extended area of social practice as an expression of eternal laws of social organization may be attacked with the purpose of changing the content and character of social and historical explanations. The task is to find an affirmative explanatory voice more responsive to the spirit of this critique than Marx's affirmative explanations, with their search for the "laws of motion" of capital and their story about the succession of modes of production.

3. The writings of Marxists, or of writers sympathetic to Marxism, who emphasize and explore the autonomy of politics, in both

the narrow and the inclusive senses distinguished in the note at the beginning of Chapter 1: the conflict over the mastery and uses of governmental power and the strife over any of the formative terms of social life. Some are thinkers and activists who attempted to theorize transformative political practice. See Antonio Gramsci, "The Modern Prince" and the "Critical Notes" on Bukharin, in *Selections from the Prison Notebooks of Antonio Gramsci*, trans. Quintin Hoare and Geoffrey Nowell Smith, International Publishers, New York, 1971, pp. 123–205, especially 136–145, and 419–473. Others are contemporary historians who have studied traditions of collective organization and class consciousness. See, for example, E. P. Thompson, *The Making of the English Working Class*, Vintage, New York, 1963; Robert Brenner, "Agrarian Class Structure and Economic Development in Pre-Industrial Europe," *Past and Present*, no. 70 (1976), pp. 30–75, and "The Agrarian Roots of European Capitalism," *Past and Present*, no. 97 (1982), pp. 16-113; Gareth Steadman Jones, *Languages of Class: Essays in English Working-Class History, 1832–1982*, Cambridge, Cambridge, 1983. Still others are sociologists who have probed comparatively the relations among class structure, state conflict, and governmental politics. See, for example, Barrington Moore, Jr., *Social Origins of Dictatorship and Democracy*, Beacon, Boston, 1966; Theda Skocpol, *States and Social Revolutions: A Comparative Analysis of France, Russia, and China*, Cambridge, Cambridge, 1979.

These varieties of political Marxism should be distinguished from the related tendency to put in place of the privileged causal connections emphasized by Marx a notion of generalized reciprocal causation. See the classic expositions in Georg Lukács, "Reification and the Consciousness of the Proletariat," in *History and Class Consciousness: Studies in Marxist Dialectics*, trans. Rodney Livingstone, MIT, Cambridge, 1968, pp. 83–222; Karl Korsch, "Marxism and Philosophy" (1923), in *Marxism and Philosophy*, trans. Fred Halliday, Monthly Review, New York, 1978, pp. 29–97.

At times the political Marxists have sacrificed the development of their insights to the desire to retain a connection with the central theses of historical materialism. To them these tenets have seemed the only available basis for theoretical generalization and for critical distance from the arrangements and circumstances of the societies they lived in. At other times, the political Marxists have simply given up on theory. See, for example, E. P. Thompson, "The Poverty of Theory or an Ornery of Errors," in *The Poverty of Theory and Other Essays*, Monthly Review, New York, 1978, pp. 1-210. They have then paid the price in the loss of an ability to convey a sense of sharp institutional alternatives for past, present, and future societies. The constructive theory of *Politics* just keeps going from where the political Marxists leave off. It does so, however, without either renouncing theoretical ambitions or accepting any of the distinctive doctrines of Marx's social theory.

4. A loose and apparently unrelated set of forms of twentieth

century social analysis that has emphasized the institutional indeterminacy of abstract types of social organization such as a pluralistic
democracy or a market economy and that has demonstrated the
dependence of supposed economic or social laws upon unique,
transitory institutional arrangements. I have found the most interesting discussions of the interplay between institutional arrangements and social or economic regularities in the writings of interwar
economists. One group of writings concerns the strategies of
economic recovery in the West (Keynes, early Kalečki, Hayek).
Another body of literature grows out of the Soviet industrialization debate, so intimately connected to the formative events
of the late 1920s (Preobrazhensky, Bukharin). On the other
hand, the idea that there can be markets or democracies radically
different from the democratic or market systems we normally
take for granted or imagine possible has been most extensively
explored by the critical legal studies movement in the United
States. See the discussion in Roberto Mangabeira Unger, *The
Critical Legal Studies Movement*, Harvard, Cambridge, 1986, pp.
5–8, 22–40, 97–99. Once you get the point of institutional indeterminacy, the old-fashioned literature of German, French, and
English institutional history becomes a priceless storehouse,
providing countless illustrations of the unique character of different institutional arrangements, of their made-up and pasted-
together quality, and of their decisive effects.

Political thinkers and practical politicians alike have always
understood "that what are called necessary institutions are only
institutions to which one is accustomed and that in matters of social
constitution the field of possibilities is much wider than people
living within each society imagine" (Alexis de Tocqueville, *Recollections*, trans. George Lawrence, Doubleday, Garden City, 1970,
chap. 2, p. 76). The point is to turn this ironic proviso into a
principle of insight.

5. The ideal aspirations of nineteenth-century liberal thinkers,
like Benjamin Constant, Alexander Herzen, Wilhelm von Humboldt, Alexis de Tocqueville, John Stuart Mill, and T. H. Greene,
reinterpreted from the standpoint of a continuing though submerged strand in Western social thought. This strand relates political pluralism, in the narrow sense, to the prosperity,
empowerment, and collective self-organization of the "little people." Three stages in the evolution of this tradition of thought can
be found in James Harrington, *The Oceana*, in *The Oceana and Other
Works*, (reprint of the London 1771 edition), Scientia Verlag, Aalen,
1980, especially the second part of the preliminaries, pp. 57–72;
Henry Summer Maine, *Village Communities in East and West*, Murray, London, 1871, which should be read together with Henry
Sumner Maine, *Lectures on the Early History of Institutions*, Murray,
London, 1875; and Barrington Moore, Jr., *Social Origins of Dictatorship and Democracy*. The classical liberal creed supplies a motivating impulse. But the other mode of thinking, with its focus on the

practical bases of pluralism, helps save the impulse from unwarranted identification with the institutional commitments of nineteenth-century liberals. The help doubles in force when the resulting insights combine with the ideas about institutional arrangements – their trumped-up character and their crucial influence – suggested by the sources mentioned in item 4 of this list.

In this connection, there is much to learn from the study of the recurrent problems of social reform in the great agrarian–bureaucratic empires that shaped so much of world history. The boldest reforming statesmen in these empires repeatedly tried and failed to preserve the independence of a class of smallholders who might provide central governments with a direct fiscal and military base and counterbalance the influence of landowning magnates. Such efforts were undoubtedly inspired by a policy of state security and social stability rather than by a devotion to pluralism and equality. But few things can better strengthen a sense of the relations between the vitality of social pluralism at the grassroots level and the particular institutional design of a society than a study of the attempts of, say, the Toba regime during the period of disunity between the Han and T'ang dynasties in China or the Macedonian dynasty in Byzantine history to make an intensely hierarchical society safe for a class of state-serving smallholders.

6. The tradition of petty bourgeois radicalism. The importance of this tradition has been borne out by a renewed appreciation of the continuing role played in modern Western history by predominantly petty bourgeois movements and publicists in challenging the dominant form of Western industrialism. Publicists like Proudhon, Louis Blanc, and Lassalle tried to combine practical proposals and speculative conceptions in ways that resisted the archaizing impulse.

An encouraging development in contemporary historical writing has been the appearance of studies that emphasize, against the shibboleths of orthodox liberalism and orthodox Marxism alike, the significance, tenacity, and suppressed potential of challenges to what eventually became the system of mass production and of property-based markets. Some of these writings are plangent in tone, underlining the ties that bound the radicals to social aspirations and forms of rights consciousness current in preindustrial and prerevolutionary Europe. See, for example, Fernand Braudel, *Afterthoughts on Material Civilization and Capitalism*, trans. Patricia M. Ranum, Johns Hopkins, Baltimore, 1977; William H. Sewall, Jr., *Work and Revolution in France*, Cambridge, Cambridge, 1980; Craig J. Calhoun, *The Question of Class Struggle: The Social Foundation of Popular Radicalism During the Industrial Revolution*, Chicago, Chicago, 1982. But other studies have demonstrated the continuity of the alternative that has been pejoratively labeled petty or simple commodity production, its reemergence under new guise in the most advanced sector of modern manufacturing, and its value as a model for more far-reaching industrial reconstruction. See Charles

Sabel and Jonathan Zeitlin, "Historical Alternatives to Mass Production," *Past and Present*, no. 108 (1985), pp. 133–176. Whether despondent or hopeful, this literature supplies an alternative to the traditions of conservative or radical necessitarianism that have dominated thinking about the history of the institutional forms of production and exchange. But it does so without embracing the simple and sentimentalized story of big bad people eating up good little people that has too often appeared to be the sole available alternative. See, as an example of the earlier challenge to the conservative or radical mainstreams, R. H. Tawney, *The Agrarian Problem in the Sixteenth Century*, Harper, New York, 1967 (reprint of the 1912 edition).

7. Ultra-leftist ideas about collective mobilization and grassroots organization, current today through the third world. These ideas are relevant to the effort undertaken in this book not only as points of departure for programmatic thinking about social reconstruction but also as examples of attempts to think about social contexts and context change in a way free from the confining assumptions of deep-structure social analysis. Though often clothed in Marxist language, their distinctive concern is better described as the attempt to perpetuate in ongoing, routine activity what the sources mentioned in item 1 of this list would call the fluid or hot moment of social life and to do so for the sake of a vision of the individual and collective empowerment that may result. There is no handy doctrinal source in which to study these ideas. Yet they are everywhere. Sympathy for them may appear irreconcilable with an interest in the revival and reconstruction of the petty bourgeois alternative mentioned in item 6. But the impression of irreconcilability begins to dissipate with the help of two intellectual transformations encouraged by the approaches evoked in items 2 through 6 of this list.

The first such change results from the conclusion that the program of petty bourgeois radicalism cannot succeed until and unless it abandons the stubborn dream of privatistic withdrawal into a protected domain of family property and local concerns. In the place of this dream it must put forms of decentralized economic and governmental organization that can prevent concentrations of power and wealth more effectively than current representative democracies and regulated market economies are able to do.

The second indispensable transformation is to disabuse ultra-leftism of its prejudice against detailed programmatic proposals and institutional commitments. If the vague ideals of contemporary ultra-leftists have a chance of being partly realized in the world, the reason is that formative institutional and imaginative contexts differ in the extent to which they impart to routine social existence the qualities of the fluid, context-revising moments of social life.

8. The portrayal of human nature in such modernist writers as Proust, Joyce, and Beckett and the discursive counterpart to this image of man in the writings of such philosophers as Heidegger and Sartre. That such a modernist image of man in fact exists, that

it can be understood as a recognizable transformation of the Christian-romantic tradition of thinking about personality, and that it can be weaned away from its habitual indifference or hostility to political concerns and from its disbelief in the possibility of changing the relation between freedom and structure are all theses argued in *Passion: An Essay on Personality*, Free Press, New York, 1984. The view of personality and personal relations developed in that book and the account of society and society making presented in *Politics* are meant as parallel explorations, different in focus and level of detail but mutually reinforcing.

9. The philosophical attack on the belief in privileged methods and representations – that is to say, in representations and methods whose privilege consists in their insensitivity to changes in our empirical beliefs. This attack has been carried out by the second generation of analytic philosophers, led by such thinkers as Quine and Putnam. Their work helps free social and historical thought from the prejudice that received views about necessity and contingency, causality and explanation, enshrined in the natural sciences, must be dealt with on a take-it-or-leave-it basis. Moreover, as polemically interpreted and extended, this attack on the unavowed remnants of the synthetic a priori becomes easy to connect with the assault on comprehensive, necessitarian historical narratives that has been mounted from a very different philosophical tradition. See Richard Rorty, *Philosophy and The Mirror of Nature*, Princeton, Princeton, 1979. The combined criticism of privileged beliefs and metanarratives serves as a source of encouragement in the attempt to free radical social criticism from deep-structure assumptions.

Politics is also the product of two very different experiences. One experience is the exposure to the rich, polished, critical and self-critical but also self-consciously disintegrated and Alexandrian culture of social and historical thought that now flourishes in the North Atlantic democracies. This social-thought culture suffers from the influence of a climate of opinion in which the most generous citizens hope at best to avert military disasters and to achieve marginal redistributive goals while resigning themselves to established institutional arrangements. The other shaping experience is practical and imaginative engagement in the murky but hopeful politics of Brazil, a country at the forward edge of the third world, where, at the time of writing, at least some people took seriously the idea that basic institutions, practices, and preconceptions might be reconstructed in ways that did not conform to any established model of social organization.

Much in this work can be understood as the consequence of an attempt to enlist the intellectual resources of the North Atlantic world in the service of concerns and commitments more keenly felt elsewhere. In this way, I want to contribute toward the development of an alternative to the vague, unconvinced, and unconvincing Marxism that now serves the advocates of the radical project as their lingua franca. If, however, the arguments of this book are correct, the transformative focus has intellectual uses that transcend its immediate origins and motives.

2. THE MAKING OF SOCIETY THROUGH POLITICS: ROUTINE WITHOUT REASON

The Western Reform Cycle

There is a considerable literature about the reform cycles in the 44–49 contemporary North Atlantic democracies. It provides one of many links between positivist social science and a style of social analysis 51–82 concerned with the institutional foundations of routine policy decisions. For early formulations, see W. Nordhaus, "The Political Business Cycle," *Review of Economic Studies*, vol. 42 (1975); D. Hibbs, "Political Parties and Macroeconomic Policy," *American Political Science Review*, vol. 71 (1977), pp. 1467–1487; G. D. MacRae, "A Political Model of the Political Business Cycle," *Journal of Political Economy*, vol. 85 (1977), pp. 239–263. The most comprehensive formulation can be found in Edward Tufte, *The Political Control of the Economy*, Princeton, Princeton, 1978. For later writings that both develop and criticize the earlier statements, see R. Winters et al., "Political Behavior and American Policy: The Case of the Political Business Cycle," in *Handbook of Political Behavior*, vol. 5, ed. S. Long, Plenum, New York, 1981; D. Hibbs and N. Vasilatos, "Macroeconomic Performance and Mass Political Support in the United States and Great Britain," in *Contemporary Political Economy*, ed. D. Hibbs and H. Fossbender, Elsevier, Amsterdam, 1981; T. Brown and A. Stein, "The Political Economy of National Elections," *Comparative Politics*, vol. 14 (1982), pp. 49–97; James K. Alt and K. Alec Chrystal, *Political Economics*, Univ. of California, Berkeley, 1983, pp. 103–125.

The criticism in these writings addresses a view emphasizing the coincidence of the reform cycle with the business cycle. The formulation in this book focuses not on the coincidence between these two recurrent swings but rather on the extent to which both can be explained as products of the same or overlapping institutional arrangements and imaginative preconceptions. Furthermore, the discussion in the text implies a very informal definition of the reform cycle. The existence of the phenomenon that this definition describes requires no extended corroboration other than the facts readily available to an active, informed citizen in the contemporary democracies.

For an attempt to relate the reform cycle to particular institutional arrangements, see Claus Offe, "Competitive Party Democracy and the Keynesian Welfare State," in *Contradictions of the Welfare State*, ed. John Keane, MIT, Cambridge, 1984, pp. 179–206.

For an interesting case study of two moments of the reform cycle in the same country, see Nigel Harris, *Competition and the Corporate*

Society: British Conservatives, the State and Industry, 1945–1964, Methuen, London, 1972; Leo Panitch, *Social Democracy and Industrial Militancy: The Labour Party, the Trade Unions and Incomes, 1945–1947*, Cambridge, Cambridge, 1976.

The Communist Reform Cycle

49–51   The discussion refers to the Soviet model: the Soviet Union itself and, to a lesser extent, the East European countries. This com-
51–82   munist reform cycle may seem to be more narrowly economic in character than its Western counterpart. But that is only because the economic and the narrowly political considerations connect more tightly and transparently. Not suprisingly, the best analysis appears in writings that discuss problems and oscillations of economic policy and production. See David Garnick, *Enterprise Guidance in Eastern Europe*, Princeton, Princeton, 1975; Janos Kornai, *The Economics of Shortage* (2 vols.), Elsevier, Amsterdam, 1980; Janos Kornai, *The Dilemmas of a Socialist Economy*, Economic and Social Research Institute, Dublin, 1979. On the relation of the economic and the political-control aspects of the communist reform cycle, see Moshe Lewin, *Political Undercurrents in Soviet Economic Debates*, Princeton, Princeton, 1974; Marc Rakovski, *Towards an East European Marxism*, St. Martin's, New York, 1978, pp. 18–38, 73–104. For a clearer sense of the relation between economic constraints, instabilities, or recurrences and institutional conditions, you have to look to an earlier body of work growing out of the Soviet industrialization debate of the 1920s. See the later notes to the discussion of the genesis of the Soviet model in Chapter 4.

Closed Options in the Agrarian-Bureaucratic Empires

88–92   For a general discussion of pluralism and conflict in agrarian-bureaucratic empires, see S. N. Eisenstadt, *The Political System of Empires*, Free Press, New York, 1969.

For an economistic analysis of the typical crisis and tailspin of the agrarian-bureaucratic empire, see Carlo M. Cipolla, *The Economic Decline of Empires*, Methuen, London, 1970, pp. 1–15. For a case study of the crisis and tailspin, see A. H. M. Jones, *The Later Roman Empire 284–602*, Univ. of Oklahoma, Norman, 1964, vol. 2, pp. 773–788, 813–872; A. H. M. Jones, "Over-Taxation and the Decline of the Roman Empire," *Antiquity*, vol. 33 (1959), pp. 39–43.

Despite the importance of the policy options discussed in this section and their recurrence in so many societies, no general comparative discussion seems available. In the fragmentary, monographic literature the most inclusive treatments I have encountered are: Stefan Balázs, "Beiträge zur Wirtschaftsgeschichte der T'ang-Zeit (618–906)," *Mitteilungen des Seminars für Orientalische Sprachen zu Berlin, Osiasiatischen Studien*, vol. 34 (1931), pp. 1–92, vol. 35

(1932), pp. 1–73, vol. 36 (1933), pp. 1–62; George Ostrogorsky, 88–92
"The Peasant's Pre-emption Right: An Abortive Reform of the
Macedonian Empire," *Journal of Roman Studies*, vol. 37 (1947), pp.
117–126. The Byzantinists often demonstrate the best grasp of the
reform options, perhaps because of the remarkable continuity of
these problems and debates in Byzantine history. I discuss these
matters in greater detail in *Plasticity into Power: Comparative-Historical Studies on the Institutional Conditions of Economic and Military
Success*, Cambridge, Cambridge, 1987. The following notes cite
specialist studies that have proved especially helpful in understanding each standard policy option to which the agrarian–
bureaucratic empires regularly resorted.

    1. The policy of *recruiting a bureaucratic staff from groups directly
below the landowning aristocracy*. On the *Chinese experiment in weakening the link between the bureaucratic staff and local landowning elites*
through the reforms of the late T'ang and the Sung, see James T.
C. Liu, *Reform in Sung China: Wang An-Shih (1021–1086) and His
New Policies*, Harvard, Cambridge, 1959; Denis Twitchett, "The
Composition of the T'ang Ruling Class," in *Perspectives on the
T'ang*, ed. Arthur F. Wright and Denis Twitchett, Yale, New Ha-
ven, 1973, pp. 47–85; Brian E. McKnight, "Fiscal Privileges and
the Social Order" in *Crisis and Prosperity in Sung China*, ed. John
Winthrop Haeger, Univ. of Arizona, Tucson, 1975, pp. 79–100;
David G. Johnson, *The Medieval Chinese Oligarchy*, Westview,
Boulder, Colo., 1977, pp. 19–20, 149–152; Patricia Ebrey, *Aristocratic Families in Early Imperial China*, Cambridge, Cambridge, 1978.
To Professor Timothy Brook of the University of Toronto I am
indebted for accounts of writings of Niida Noboru and other Japanese historians of China. On the repeated failure of attempts clearly
to sever the connection between bureaucracy and landowning elites
and on the consequences for the constraints within which policy
had to move, see E. A. Kracke, Jr., "Family vs. Merit in Chinese
Civil Service Examinations," *Harvard Journal of Asiatic Studies*, vol.
10 (1947), pp. 103–123; Victor Lippit, "The Development of
Underdevelopment in Chinese History," *Modern China*, vol. 4,
(1978), pp. 251–328. But for a view that emphasizes the role of
official status as a source rather than a consequence of landowning
status, see Ping-Ti Ho, *The Ladder of Success in Imperial China*,
Columbia, New York, 1967.

    On the *Ottoman palace system* as an attempt to achieve through
very different measures objectives similar to the aims of the Chinese
examination system, see Joseph von Hammer, *Geschichte des Osmanischen Reiches*, Hartleben, Pest, 1828, vol. 2, pp. 218–249 (at the
time of the death of Mohammed II); Norman Itzkowitz, *Ottoman
Empire and Islamic Tradition*, Knopf, New York, 1972, pp. 49–60;
Stanford J. Shaw, *History of the Ottoman Empire and Modern Turkey*,
Cambridge, Cambridge, 1976, vol. 1, pp. 113–139.

    For a representative study of the use of this technique by the
prerevolutionary absolutist monarchies of Europe, see Otto Hintze,

88–92   "The Commissary and His Significance in General Administrative History: A Comparative Study," in *The Historical Essays of Otto Hintze*, ed. Felix Gilbert, Oxford, New York, 1975, pp. 267–301. See also Martin Göhring, *Die Amterkäuflichkeit im Ancien Régime*, Ebering, Berlin, 1938; Roland Mousnier, *La Vénalité des Offices sous Henri IV et Louis XIII*, Presses Universitaires, Paris, 1971; Eckart Kehr, "Zur Genesis der Preussischen Bürokratie und des Rechtstaates," in *Moderne Deutsche Sozialgeschichte*, ed. Hans-Ulrich Wehler, Kiepenheuer, Cologne, 1973, pp. 37–54.

2. The policy of making the *nobility dependent for land tenure upon service to the state*. On the system of *pomestye* land in Russia and its assimilation to *votchina* tenure, see Jerome Blum, *Lord and Peasant in Russia*, Princeton, Princeton, 1961, pp. 170–188, 252–255. On the *Korean system of Merit Subjects* and the comparable development it underwent, see Edward W. Wagner, *The Literati Purges: Political Conflict in Early Yi Korea*, Harvard, Cambridge, 1975, pp. 19–21; Susan S. Shin, *Land Tenure and the Agrarian Economy of Early Yi Korea*, 1973, doctoral dissertation on file at Yenching Library, Harvard University.

Consider as a further example the status of "bannermen" within the Manchu conquest elite in China. See Jonathan D. Spence, *Ts'ao Yin and the K'ang-hsi Emperor, Bondservant and Master*, Yale, New Haven, 1966, pp. 2–18; Robert B. Oxnam, *Ruling from Horseback: Manchu Politics in the Oboi Regency, 1661–1669*, Chicago, Chicago, 1975, pp. 38–40, 47–49, 124–126, 170–175. Compare to the Mughal *mansabdars* (rank holders) and *jagirdars* (land-revenue assignment holders). See Stephen P. Blake "The Patrimonial – Bureaucratic Empire of the Mughals," *Journal of Asian Studies*, vol. 39 (1979), pp. 77–94, and the Mughal studies cited later.

3. The *policy of agrarian dualism*.

a. The *reliance of central government upon landlords who, although not involved in central administration, have special fiscal and military obligations*. On the Byzantine *ktemata stratiotika*, see Hélène Antoniadis-Bibicou, *Etudes d'Histoire de Byzance à propos du "Thème des Caravisiens*," Services d'Edition et de Vente des Production de l'Education Nationale, Paris, 1966, pp. 99–114; Arnold Toynbee, *Constantine Porphyrogenitus and His World*, Oxford, London, 1973, pp. 134–145. On the Ottoman timariots, see Stanford J. Shaw, *History of the Ottoman Empire and Modern Turkey*, vol. 1, pp. 125–127; Gyula Kaldy-Nagy, "The First Centuries of the Ottoman Military Organization," *Acta Orientalia Scientiarum Hungaricae*, vol. 31(2), (1977), pp. 147–183. On the Mughal *zamindars*, see Irfan Habib, *The Agrarian System of Mughal India (1556–1707)*, Asia Publishers, London, 1963, pp. 136–189; M. Athar Ali, *The Mughal Nobility Under Aurangazeb*, Asia Publishing House, Bombay, 1966; Norman Ahmad Siddiqui, *Land Revenue Under the* Mughals, Asia Publishing House, Bombay, 1970, pp. 21–40. On the Aztec military lifetenants, see Nigel Davies, *The Aztecs: A History*, Univ. of Oklahoma, Norman, 1980, pp. 80–81. On the Byzantine *pronoia*, see

Georges Ostrogorsky, *Pour l'Histoire de la Fléodalité Byzantine,* 88–92
trans. Henri Gregoire, Institut de Philologie et d'Histoire Orientales
et Slaves, Bruxelles, 1954.
    b. The *reliance on state-obligated smallholders and peasant
communities.*
    On the exemplary Byzantine developments and debates, see Paul
Lemerle, "Esquisse pour une Histoire Agraire de Byzance," *Revue
Historique,* vol. 219 (1958), pp. 32–74, vol. 219 (1958), pp. 254–
284, vol. 220 (1958), pp. 43–94; George Ostrogorsky, "The Peasant's Pre-emption Right," pp. 117–126, and *History of the Byzantine
State,* trans. Joan Hussey, Rutgers, New Brunswick, N.J., 1969,
pp. 269–276; Arnold Toynbee, *Constantine Porphyrogenitus and
His World,* pp. 122-134. For the aftermath of the failure to uphold
the policy of smallholder protection, see Angeliki E. Laiou-
Thomadakis, *Peasant Society in the Late Byzantine Empire,* Princeton,
Princeton, 1977.
    On the policy of agrarian dualism at its most successful and
aggressive in Chinese history, see Wolfram Eberhard, *Das Toba-
Reich Nordchinas: Eine Soziologische Untersuchung,* Brill, Leiden,
1949, pp. 206–221, which should be considered against the background of Eberhard's "Zur Landwirtschaft der Han-Zeit," *Mitteilungen des Seminars für Orientalische Sprachen zu Berlin, Osiasiatische
Studien,* vol. 35 (1932), pp. 74–105; Denis Twitchett, "Lands Under
State Cultivation Under the T'ang," *Journal of the Economic and Social
History of the Orient,* vol. 2 (1959), pp. 162–336 (on the connection
of agrarian dualism with the system of military colonies); Denis
Twitchett, *Land Tenure and the Social Order in T'ang and Sung China,*
Oxford, Oxford, 1962. For the Northern Dynasties and Sui versions of the *fu-ping* system (divisional militia based on smallholders
with military responsibilities), see Arthur F. Wright, "The Sui Dynasty (518–617)," in *Cambridge History of China,* vol. 3, *Sui and
T'ang China, 589–906,* part 1, ed. Denis Twitchett, Cambridge,
Cambridge, 1979, pp. 96–103; and for the T'ang version, see Howard J. Wechsler, "T'ai-tsung [reign 626–49] the Consolidator," in
the same volume, pp. 207–208. See also Philip A. Kuhn, *Rebellion
and Its Enemies in Late Imperial China: Militarization and Social Structure,* Harvard, Cambridge, 1970, pp. 15–20. On the effect the failure
of the policy of agrarian dualism had on agrarian structure in the
subsequent Sung period, see for two somewhat contrasting views:
Mark Elvin, *The Pattern of the Chinese Past,* Stanford, Stanford,
1973, pp. 69–83; Joseph McDermott, *Land Tenure and Rural Control
in the Liangche Region during the Southern Sung* (doctoral dissertation
on file at Cambridge University, 1978). It is important to distinguish the policy of support for smallholders from the vaguer and
looser set of anticoncentrationist agrarian ideals present at all stages
in Chinese history. See Hsü Chung-shu, "The Well-Field System
in Shang and Chou," in *Chinese Social History,* trans. E. Tzu Zen
Sun and John de Francis, Octagon, New York, 1972, pp. 3–17;
Mark Elvin, *The Pattern of the Chinese Past,* pp. 47–51, 59–63; Denis

88–92   Twitchett, *Financial Administration Under the T'ang Dynasty*, Cambridge, Cambridge, 1970, pp. 1–11; Joseph Levenson, *Confucian China and Its Modern Fate: A Trilogy*, Univ. of California, Berkeley, 1968, vol. 3, pp. 16–43.

In *Plasticity into Power: Comparative-Historical Studies on the Institutional Conditions of Economic and Military Success*, Chapter 1, I argue that the failure of the policy of support for smallholders and of the other standard reform options condemned the agrarian-bureaucratic empires to revolve in certain well-defined cycles of commercial vitality and decommercialization, administrative unification and fragmentation. Only a few societies broke through these cycles, enlarged the range of social possibilities, and revolutionized the world as a result.

4. *The agency of the common people in a social world that revolves within the limits set by the rehearsal and frustration of the reform options previously discussed.*

a. The *privileged urban mob.* See *Paul Veyne, Le Pain et le Cirque: Sociologie Historique d'un Pluralisme Politique*, Seuil, Paris, 1976.

b. The *temporary stabilization of the policy of agrarian dualism.* On the Byzantine peasant commune, see Georg Ostrogorsky, "Die Ländliche Steuergemeinde des Byzantinischen Reiches im X. Jahrhundert," *Vierteljahrschrift für Sozial- und Wirtschaftsgeschichte*, vol. 20 (1927), pp. 23–108; George Ostrogorsky, "La Commune Rurale Byzantine," *Byzantion*, vol. 32 (1962), pp. 138–166. For a comparative discussion emphasizing the link between the redistributive and the control aspects of the peasant commune, with the eventual substitution of smallholding by enserfment, see G. I. Bratianu, "Servage de la Glèbe et Régime Fiscal: Essai d'Histoire Comparée, Roumaine, Slave et Byzantine," in *Etudes Byzantines d'Histoire Economique et Sociale*, Geuthner, Paris, 1938.

On the nineteenth-century redistributive Russian village community, see Geroid Robinson, *Rural Russia Under the Old Regime*, Univ. of California, Berkeley, 1972, pp. 117–128; Francis W. Watters, "The Peasant and the Village Commune," in *The Peasant in Nineteenth-Century Russia*, ed. Wayne S. Vuanich, Stanford, Stanford, 1968, pp. 133–157; Jerome Blum, *Lord and Peasant in Russia*, pp. 504–535.

On village communities and the role of village officers under the Southern Sung, see Brian E. McKnight, *Village and Bureaucracy in Southern Sung China*, Chicago, Chicago, 1971.

On peasant-held *raiyati* villages in Mughal India, see Irfan Habib, *The Agrarian System of Mughal India*, Asia Publishers, London, 1963, pp. 111–135; Ishtiagi Husain Qureshi, *The Administration of the Mughal Empire*, N. V. Publications, Lohanipur, pp. 281–294.

On the village and the leading village families under the Tokugawa *bakufu*, see Thomas C. Smith, *The Agrarian Origins of Modern Japan*, Stanford, Stanford, 1959, pp. 1–11.

c. On peasant rebellion as a confirmation of the structure it

defies, see the discussion of the Japanese experience in Irwin Scheiner, "Benevolent Lords and Honorable Peasants: Rebellion and
Peasant Consciousness in Tokugawa Japan," in Tetsuo Najita and
Irwin Scheiner, eds., *Japanese Thought in the Tokugawa Period, 1600–
1868*, Chicago, Chicago, 1978, pp. 39–62.

Closed Options in the Ancient City-State Republics

The discussion of closed options in the ancient city-state republics 92–95
has been chiefly influenced by the following writings. Taken together, these studies present a striking series of explorations in the
relation between constraints on the range of feasible governmental
policies and limits to mass participation in governmental politics.
A. Andrewes, *The Greek Tyrants*, Harper, New York, 1963; Victor
Ehrenberg, *The Greek State*, Methuen, London, 1969; Victor Ehrenberg, *From Solon to Socrates*, Methuen, London, 1973; Jacqueline
de Romilly, *Problèmes de la Democratie Grecque*, Herman, Paris, 1975;
M. I. Finley, *The Ancient Economy*, Univ. of California, Berkeley,
1973; M. I. Finley, "Athenian Demagogues," in M. I. Finley, ed.,
Studies in Ancient Society, Routledge, London, 1974; Paul Veyne,
Le Pain et le Cirque; E. Badian, *Foreign Clientelae (264–70 B.C.)*,
Oxford, Oxford, 1958, pp. 192–225; E. Badian, *Publicans and Sin-
ners: Private Enterprise in the Service of the Roman Republic*, Blackwell,
Oxford, 1972, pp. 82–118; Christian Meier, *Res Publica Amissa:
Eine Studie zur Verfassung und Geschichte der Späten Römischen Re-
publik*, Steiner, Wiesbaden, 1966; Mathias Gelzer, *The Roman No-
bility*, trans. Robin Seager, Blackwell, Oxford, 1975; P. A. Brunt,
Social Conflicts in the Roman Republic, Norton, New York, 1971;
Claude Nicolet, *Le Métier de Citoyen dans la Rome Republicaine*,
Gallimard, 1976.

A close study of the Gracchan reform period, of its social aftermath and agrarian setting, illustrates the twin limits to the politics
of the city-state republics discussed in the text. See J. Carcopino,
"Les Lois Agraires des Gracques et la Guerre Sociale," *Bulletin de
l'Association Guillaume Bude* (January 1929), pp. 3–23; G. Tibetti,
"Ricerche di storia agraria Romana," *Athenaeum*, vol. 38 (n.s., vol.
28), (1950), pp. 183–266; G. Tibetti, "Il latifondo dall'epoca grac-
cana all'impero," *Relazioni del X. Congresso Internazionale di Scienze
Storiche*, Rome (1955), vol. 2, pp. 235–292; Arnold J. Toynbee,
Hannibal's Legacy, Oxford, London, 1965, vol. 2, pp. 190–210, 486–
517; E. Badian, "Tiberius Gracchus and the Beginning of the Roman Revolution," in Hildegard Temporini, ed., *Aufstieg und Nieder-
gang der Römsichen Welt*, Gruyter, Berlin, 1972, vol. 1, pp. 668–
731; David Stockton, *The Gracchi*, Oxford, Oxford, 1979.

On the failure to assimilate mass politics, see also Gaetano de
Sanctis, *La Guerra Sociale*, La Nuova Italia, Florence, 1976; Emilio
Gabba, *Republican Rome, the Army and the Allies*, trans. P. J. Cuff,
Univ. of California, Berkeley, 1976, pp. 20–37, 154–161.

Appendix: Economic Policy, Reform Cycles, and Formative Contexts

115–124 On the relation between economic regularities and institutional arrangements in the Soviet-type model, see the books of Kornai, Lewin, and Rakovski cited earlier and the commentary on the discussion of the making of the Soviet model in Chapter 4.

On the same relation in the self-management (i.e., Yugoslav) system, see Ljubo Sirc, *The Yugoslav Economy Under Self-Management*, pp. 133–137, 173–178; Włodzimierz Brus, *Socialist Ownership and Political Systems*, trans. R. A. Clarke, Routledge, London, 1975, pp. 62–93.

Much can be learned about incomes policies, corporatism (i.e., deals among central governments, organized labor, and big business), and other characteristic moves of policy in the current Western economies by studying – with an eye both to what they say and to what they do not even discuss – policy-oriented reports such as Paul McCracken, *Towards Full Employment and Price Stability: A Report to the OECD by a Group of Independent Experts*, Paris, OECD, 1977.

3. THE MAKING OF SOCIETY THROUGH POLITICS: A SPECTRUM OF SOCIAL EXPERIMENTS

The Idea of Large-Scale Options

125–128   Many remote counterparts to the idea of the large-scale options of
social life can be found in the literature of social theory. But some
164–171   of these counterparts (the types of modes of production in Marxism) are part of the machinery of deep-structure social theory. Others (Weber's typology of forms of domination, Parsons's pattern variables) oscillate between being a classification without clear explanatory uses or presuppositions and serving a residual evolutionary role. The theory served by the descriptive categories presented in Chapter 3 includes evolutionary themes. But the evolutionary sense is transformed by the thoroughgoing rejection of deep-structure assumptions. Moreover, a single generative principle commands the formulation of these categories: the extent to which different practices, institutions, or beliefs possess the quality of denaturalization or disentrenchment.

Experiments with the State: Privilege and Right

128–134   For analogy and contrast, see Karl Marx, "On the Jewish Question," in *Early Writings*, trans. Rodney Livingstone and Gregor Benton, Vintage, New York, 1975, pp. 212–241; Georges Gurvitch, *L'Idée du Droit Social*, Scientia Verlag, Aalen, 1972 (reprint of the 1932 edition).

These two analyses share in common the concern with the separation and the rapprochement of the formal legal status of the individual and his social circumstance. The idea is that liberalism, for all its achievements, has a cost. See, in the same regard, Louis Dumont, *Homo Hierarchicus: An Essay on the Caste System*, trans. Mark Samsbury, Chicago, Chicago, 1970, pp. 231–234; Louis Dumont, *Homo Aequalis: Genèse et Epanouissement de l'Idéologie Economique*, Gallimard, Paris, 1977.

By contrast, the classification in the text is written from a perspective that wants to redeem liberalism through more liberalism. The crucial conceptual move here is the disengagement of the liberal impulse from the institutions and practices to which it has been committed. The criticism of rights in modern legal thought has made this disengagement possible. See Roberto Mangabeira Unger, *The Critical Legal Studies Movement*, Harvard, Cambridge, 1986. The programmatic argument of Chapter 5 makes good on the notion that another set of entitlements might be less rigidifying and hierarchy-creating than the classical liberal system of contract and property rights.

On the European *Standestaat* as an example of what the text calls *the system of privilege*, see Roberto Mangabeira Unger, *Law in Modern Society: Toward a Criticism of Social Theory*, Free Press, New York, 1976, pp. 155–166.

Experiments with the Microstructure: Patron and Client

For a general view of patron–client relations that contrasts with the 135–144 approach taken by the text, see L. Grazziano, *A Conceptual Framework for the Study of Clientalism*, Cornell University Western Societies Program Occasional Papers, no. 4, New York, 1975; S. N. Eisenstadt and Louis Roniger, "Patron-Client Relations as a Model of Structuring Social Exchange," *Comparative Studies in Society and History*, vol. 22 (1980), pp. 42–77.

On clientship in the Roman Republic, see Christian Meier, *Res Publica Amissa*, pp. 24–63.

On the generalized patron-client relations between the prince and the mob especially in the Hellenistic states, see Paul Veyne, *Le Pain et le Cirque*, especially pp. 689–690.

On patron–client relations in contemporary Mediterranean settings, see E. Gellner and J. Waterbury, eds., *Patrons and Clients in Mediterranean Societies*, London, Duckworth, 1977.

On patron–client relations in a Latin American (Brazilian) setting, see Vítor Nunes Leal, *Coronelismo, Enxada e Voto*, Alfa-Omega, São Paulo, 1975; Roberto Schwartz, *Ao Vencedor as Batatas*, Duas Cidades, São Paulo, 1977.

On the extension of patron–client relations beyond the situations in which they are publicly recognized as legitimate, see Vincent Lemieur, *Le Patronage Politique: Une Etude Comparative*, Laval, Quebec, 1977.

Experiments with the Microstructure: The Organization of Work

144 For an interpretation of bureaucratic organization that emphasizes, in a French setting, *the effort to avoid personal, clientalistic dependencies* and studies the paradoxical consequences, see Michel Crozier, *The Bureaucratic Phenomenon*, Chicago, Chicago, 1964, especially pp. 193–194, 220–224.

145–147 The *analogy between styles of reasoning and ways of organizing work* has two quite distinct sources. One is the so-called kinematic theory
151–154 of machinery as expounded in Franz Reuleaux, *Theoretische Kine-*
156–158 *matik: Grundzüge einer Theorie der Maschinenwesens*, Braunschweig, 1875. This approach to machine design suggests and exploits links between styles of reasoning and of work organization. The history of this tradition of thinking about machines is explored in Theodor Beck, *Beiträge zur Geschichte des Maschinenbaues* (2nd ed.), Springer, Berlin, 1900. The links among view of reason, principles of machine design, and approaches to the organization of work stand out even more clearly in Leonardo da Vinci's pioneering work. See Ladislao Retti, "Elements of Machines," in Ladislao Retti, ed., *The Unknown Leonardo*, McGraw-Hill, New York, 1974, pp. 264–287. On the special way in which classical political economy recognized these connections, see Maxine Berg, *The Machinery Question and the Making of Political Economy, 1815–1848*, Cambridge, Cambridge, 1980, pp. 75–110. Another spur to the formulation of the practice conception of reason and labor developed in the text is Kant's transcendental deduction, with its heavily operational language. See *Critique of Pure Reason*, trans. Norman Kemp Smith, St. Martin's, New York, 1965, pp. 129–176. Piaget's developmental psychology picks up on this Kantian theme. See *Genetic Epistemology*, trans. Eleanor Duckworth, Columbia, New York, 1970.

147–149 The discussion of *the staff and the line* is indebted on the business side to an American tradition of writing about business history. See especially Alfred D. Chandler, Jr., *The Visible Hand: The Managerial Revolution in American Business*, Harvard, Cambridge, 1977, pp. 415–468. See also Alfred D. Chandler, Jr., and Herman Daems, eds., *Managerial Hierarchies: Comparative Perspectives on the Rise of the Modern Industrial Enterprise*, Harvard, Cambridge, 1980.

147–149 On the administrative side I have found most help in the tradition of German administrative history, particularly the writings of Otto Hintze and his school. See "The Origins of the Modern Ministerial System: A Comparative Study," in *The Historical Essays of Otto Hintze*, ed. Felix Gilbert, Oxford, New York, 1975, pp. 216–266. See also the studies in Otto Hintze, *Staat und Verfassung: Gesammelte Abhandlungen zur Allgemeinen Verfassungsgeschichte*, ed. Fritz Hartung, Koehler, Leipzig, 1941. Very much in Hintze's spirit is Joseph Strayer, *On the Medieval Origins of the Modern State*, Princeton, Princeton, 1973. See also J. Vicens Vives, "La struttura amministrativa statale nei secoli XVI e XVII," in E. Rotelli and P. Schiera, eds., *Lo Stato Moderno*, Il Mulino, Bologna, 1971, vol. 1, pp. 223–246; and the studies in H. Hofmann, ed., *Die Entstehung des Modernen Souveränen Staates*, Kiepenheuer, Cologne, 1967. See generally Gianfranco Poggi, *The Development of the Modern State*, Stanford, Stanford, 1978.

On *standard operating procedures and continuous hierarchy*, see Alvin   149–151
W. Gouldner, *Patterns of Industrial Bureaucracy: A Case Study of Modern Factory Administration*, Free Press, New York, 1954, pp. 215–228; Alan Fox, *Beyond Contract: Work, Power and Trust Relations*, Faber, London, 1974, pp. 13–119; M. Maurice, F. Sellier, and Jean-Jacques Silvestre, "La Production de la Hiérarchie dans l'Entreprise: Recherche d'un Effet Sociétal," *Revue Française de Sociologie*, vol. 20 (1979), pp. 331–380.

For a version of the distinction between mainstream and van-   154–158
guardist industry cast in terms of a view of stages of industrial maturation, see William J. Abernathy and James M. Utterback, "Patterns of Industrial Innovation," *Technology Review*, vol. 80 (1978), pp. 2–9; William J. Abernathy, *The Productivity Dilemma: Roadblock to Innovation in the Automobile Industry*, Johns Hopkins, Baltimore, 1978, pp. 147–174. For a contrasting version presented in sectoral terms, see Michael J. Piore and Charles Sabel, *The Second Industrial Divide*, Basic Books, New York, 1984. Many ideas crucial to this and other parts of the arguments developed in the course of conversations with Charles Sabel.

For textured descriptions of the vanguardist sector of industry,   155–156
see F. Ferreo and S. Scamuzzi, eds., *L'Industria in Italia: La Piccola Impresa*, Riuniti, Rome, 1979; George A. V. Russell, "Flexibility as a Factor in the Economic Exploitation of Some Rolling Mills and Some Technical Means for Its Realization," *Journal of the Iron and Steel Industry*, vol. 130 (1934), pp. 25–125; and especially Charles Sabel, *Work and Politics: The Division of Labor in Industry*, Cambridge, Cambridge, pp. 194–231. For the relation between the primacy of mass production and the international division of labor, see Folker Fröbel, Jürgen Heinrichs, and Otto Kreye, *The New International Division of Labor: Structural Unemployment in Industrialized Countries and Industrialization in Developing Countries*, trans. Pete Burgess, Cambridge, Cambridge, 1980, especially pp. 44–48; Rolf Dick, *Die Arbeitsteilung zwischen Industrie- und Entwicklungsländern im Maschinenbau*, Mohr, Tübingen, 1981; Michael J. Piore and Charles S. Sabel, *The Second Industrial Divide*.

For the internal generation of investment funds as a means with   159
which to compensate for instability in capital markets, see Alfred S. Eichner, *The Megacorp and Oligopoly: Micro Foundations of Macro Dynamics*, Sharpe, New York, 1976, pp. 68–70, 84–85, 111–116, 123–125.   155–156

On the extension of the distinction between the rigid and flexible   161–163
variants of rationalized collective labor to warfare, see the related contrast between attrition operations and relational-maneuver operations in Edward N. Luttwak, "The Operational Level of War,"

International Security, vol. 5 (1980–1981), pp. 61–79. For the example of tank warfare, see Field Marshal Lord Carver, *The Apostles of Mobility: The Theory and Practice of Armoured Warfare*, Weidenfeld, London, 1979; Edward N. Luttwack, "The Strategy of the Tank," in *Strategy and Politics*, Transaction, New Brunswick, N.J., 1980, pp. 295–304.

4. THE MAKING OF SOCIETY THROUGH POLITICS: IMAGINING TRANSFORMATION

Private Enterprise and Governmental Policy

177–180 For the classic American study of the early nineteenth century transformations discussed in the text, see Louis Hartz, *Economic Policy and Democratic Thought: Pennsylvania 1776–1880*, Harvard, Cambridge, 1948. On the later American developments, see Alfred D. Chandler, Jr., "Government Versus Business: An American Phenomenon," in John T. Dunlop, ed., *Business and Public Policy*, Graduate School of Business Administration, Harvard, Boston, 1980, pp. 1–11; Stephen Skowronek, *Building a New American State: The Expansion of National Administrative Capacities, 1877–1920*, Cambridge, Cambridge, 1920; William H. Becker, *The Dynamics of Business–Government Relations, 1893–1921*, Chicago, Chicago, 1982.

179   On the German and Dutch experience, see Max Barkhausen, "Staatliche Wirtschaftslenkung und freies Unternehmertum in Westdeutschen und im Nord-und Südniederländischen Raum bei der Entstehung der Neuzeitlichen Industrie im 18. Jahrhundert," *Vierteljahrschrift für Sozial- und Wirtschaftsgeschichte*, vol. 45 (1958), pp. 168–241. On the Japanese comparison see Thomas C. Smith, *Political Change and Industrial Development in Japan: Government Enterprise, 1868–1880*, Stanford, Stanford, 1955. Compare, further, the late Ch'ing Chinese experience discussed in Albert Feuerwerker, *China's Early Industrialization: Sheng Hsuan-Huai (1844–1916) and Mandarin Enterprise*, Atheneum, New York, 1970, pp. 22–26, 242–251; Wellington K. K. Chan, *Merchants, Mandarins, and Modern Enterprise in Late Ch'ing China*, Harvard, Cambridge, 1977, pp. 67–153.

The Genesis of the Work-Organization Complex: General Conception

180–183 For a simplified statement of *the conservative (classical–liberal) version of the mythical history of modern Western institutions of production and exchange*, see D. C. North and R. P. Thomas, *The Rise of the Western World: A New Economic History*, Cambridge, Cambridge, 1978.

For *the radical Marxist version of this history*, see Karl Marx, *Introduction to a Contribution to the Critique of Political Economy*, International Publishers, New York, 1970, pp. 20–21; Karl Marx and Friedrich Engels, the *Communist Manifesto*, section 1; Karl Marx,

The German Ideology, International Publishers, New York, 1970, part 1, section c, pp. 68–81; Karl Marx, *Capital*, trans. Samuel Moore and Edward Aveling, International Publishers, New York, 1967, vol. 1, chaps. 13–16, pp. 322–518.

For the development of the Marxist themes at a more detailed historiographic level, see Maurice Dobb, *Studies in the Development of Capitalism*, International Publishers, New York, 1978.

The Genesis of the Work-Organization Complex: Manufacturing

For a study of early forms of the institutions whose making this 183–187 section discusses, see Sydney Pollard, *The Genesis of Modern Management: A Study of the Industrial Revolution in Great Britain*, Arnold, London, 1965. For an analysis of the translation of this model of industrial organization and labor discipline into a managerial ideology, see Reinhard Bendix, *Work and Authority in Industry: Ideologies of Management in the Course of Industrialization*, Univ. of California, Berkeley, 1956, especially pp. 198–253. For a critique emphasizing the control aspects of the new industrial model as against its claim to represent a uniquely superior solution to technical and economic goals and constraints, see Stephen A. Marglin, "What Bosses Do? The Origins and Functions of Hierarchy in Capitalist Production," *Review of Radical Political Economics*, vol. 6 (1974), pp. 33–60. For a criticism of this thesis, see Oliver E. Williamson, "The Organization of Work: A Comparative Institutional Assessment," *Journal of Economic Behavior and Organization*, vol. 1 (1980), pp. 5–38. The last paragraph of the section in the text on "contemporary debates" defines the relation of my argument about work organization to the Marglin–Williamson debate.

On *the proto-industrialization thesis*, interpreted in the text as an 183–184 attempt to square the apparent diversity of early-modern forms of manufacturing and town–country relations with the stereotypical "English route" to economic growth, see F. F. Mendels, "Proto-Industrialization: The First Phase of the Industrialization Process," *Journal of Economic History*, vol. 32 (1972), pp. 241–261; P. Kriedte, H. Medick, and J. Schlumbohm, *Industrialization Before Industrialization: Rural Industry in the Genesis of Capitalism*, Past and Present Pub., Cambridge, 1981. For criticism of the proto-industrialization thesis, see P. Jeannin, "La Proto-Industrialization: Developpement ou Impasse?" *Annales E.S.C.*, vol. 35 (1980), pp. 52–65; Maxine Berg, Pat Hudson, and Michael Sonnenscher, "Manufacture in Town and Country Before the Factory," in M. Berg, P. Hudson, and M. Sonnenscher, eds., *Manufacture in Town and Country Before the Factory*, Cambridge, Cambridge, l983, pp. 1–32; D. C. Coleman, "Proto-Industrialization: A Concept Too Many," *Economic History Review*, 2nd series, vol. 36 (1983), pp. 435–448.

For an analysis of *suppressed and contained diversity in the industrial* institutions of modern Europe – an analysis to which this part of my argument is heavily indebted – see Charles Sabel and Jonathan Zeitlin, "Historical Alternatives to Mass Production," *Past and Present*, no. 108 (1985), pp. 133–176.

185–186   On the experiences of the West Riding, see Pat Hudson, "From Manor to Mill: The West Riding in Transition," in Maxine Berg et al., *Manufacture in Town and Country Before the Factory*, Cambridge, Cambridge, 1983; Pat Hudson, *The Genesis of Industrial Capital: A Study of the West Riding Wool Textile Industry c. 1750–1850*, Cambridge, Cambridge, 1986. On the Sheffield cutlery

186   trade, see G. I. H. Lloyd, *The Cutlery Trades*, Longmans, London, 1913. On the Lyonnaise textile industry, see Michel Laferrère, *Lyon, Ville Industrielle*, Presses Universitaires, Paris, 1960.

The petty entrepreneur and the small-scale enterprise as frustrated protagonists of a contained, alternative style of industrial organization have persistently reappeared far from the home ground of North Atlantic industrialism. See, for example, Johannes Hirschmeier, *The Origins of Entrepreneurship in Meiji Japan*, Harvard, Cambridge, 1964, pp. 44–110; Henry Rosovsky, "The Serf Entrepreneur in Russia," in *Explorations in Enterprise*, ed. Hugh G. J. Aitken, Harvard, Cambridge, 1967, pp. 341–372. In each instance these groups were condemned to remain satellites unless they established an institutional order that thoroughly fragmented both economic and governmental power.

The Genesis of the Work-Organization Complex: Agriculture

187–191   For accounts of the variety of agrarian forms in late medieval and early modern Europe that explicitly relate agricultural diversity to the troubles of the mythical history, see Robert Brenner, "Agrarian Class Structure and Economic Development in Pre-Industrial Europe," *Past and Present*, no. 70 (1976), pp. 30–75, the many critical discussions of this article in subsequent issues of *Past and Present*, and Brenner's response and restatement, "The Agrarian Roots of European Capitalism," *Past and Present*, no. 97 (1982), pp. 16–113.

189–190   For an in-depth study of one particularly successful case of deviation from the English stereotype, see Jan de Vries, *The Dutch Rural Economy in the Golden Age, 1500–1700*, Yale, New Haven, 1974, especially pp. 119–121, 236–245. See also Franklin F. Mendels, "Agriculture and Peasant Industry in Eighteenth-Century Flanders," in William N. Parker and Eric L. Jones, eds., *European Peasants and Their Markets: Essays in Agrarian Economic History*, Princeton, Princeton, 1975, pp. 179–204.

100   On the impact of alternative agrarian trajectories on industrial growth rates, see Patrick O'Brien and Coglar Keyder, *Economic Growth in Britain and France, 1780–1914: Two Paths to the Twentieth Century*, Allen, London, 1978.

For a comparative discussion of continuing agrarian diversity in the eighteenth and nineteenth centuries, see Jerome Blum, *The End of the Old Order in Rural Europe*, Princeton, Princeton, 1978. For an early twentieth century example of agrarian deconcentration in the context of general industrialization, see Ann Waswo, *Japanese Landlords: The Decline of a Rural Elite*, Univ. of California, Berkeley, 1977.

On the interplay between petty proprietorship and governmental 191 support in an American setting, see Grant McConnell, *The Decline of Agrarian Democracy*, Atheneum, New York, 1977.

For examples of the contemporary defense of small-scale family farms as a concomitant to industrialization (in the contemporary third world), see Erik Eckholm, *Land Reform and Sustainable Development*, Worldwatch Paper 30, 1979; Alain de Jainvry, *The Agrarian Question in Latin America*, Johns Hopkins, Baltimore, 1981. For a discussion of the shared hostility of traditional development theory and Marxism to small-scale private or cooperative production in the countryside, see Michael Lipton, *Why Poor People Stay Poor: Urban Bias in World Development*, Harvard, Cambridge, 1977, pp. 89–141.

Eastern Europe between the wars provides an extraordinary historical laboratory in which to study the frustrations of a petty bourgeoisie that wins parcels of state power without developing suitable models of industrialization, constitutional government, and grassroots organization. See the discussion of the peasant parties in Joseph Rothschild, *East Central Europe Between the Two World Wars*, Univ. of Washington, Seattle, 1974.

The Genesis of the Work Organization Complex: Contemporary Debates

On the key role of the artisanal or petty bourgeois classes as chal- 192–195 lengers to the dominant model of industrialism, see William H. Sewall, Jr., *Work and Revolution in France: The Language of Labor from the Old Regime to 1848*, Cambridge, Cambridge, 1980; Craig J. Calhoun, *The Question of Class Struggle: The Social Foundation of Popular Radicalism During the Industrial Revolution*, Chicago, Chicago, 1982.

For studies of particular movements that served as bearers of the 193–194 petty bourgeois ideal, see G. S. Kealey and B. D. Palmer, *Dreaming of What Might Be: The Knights of Labor in Ontario*, Cambridge, Cambridge, 1982; Dorothy Thompson, *The Chartists*, Temple Smith, London, 1984.

On the continuing role of traditional small enterprise and its 194–195 relation to the party-political self-assertion of the petty bourgeoisie, see Suzanne Berger and Michael J. Piore, *Dualism and Discontinuity in Industrial Societies*, Cambridge, Cambridge, 1981.

The Genesis of the Private-Rights Complex

On *the paradox of origin*, see the discussion of the consolidation of 198–200 absolute property rights under estatist and absolutist regimes in

Perry Anderson, *Lineages of the Absolutist State*, New Left Books, London, 1974, pp. 424–426.

On the doctrinal and intellectual background through and against which the theory of absolute property rights and its contractual counterpart developed, see Franz Wieacker, *Privatrechtsgeschichte der Neuzeit*, Vandenhoek, Göttingen, 1967, especially pp. 234–237; Stephan Buchholz, *Abstraktionsprinzip und Immobiliarecht: Zur Geschichte der Auflassung und der Grundschuld*, Klostermann, Frankfurt, 1978; P. S. Atiyah, *The Rise and Fall of Freedom of Contract*, Oxford, Oxford, 1979, especially pp. 102–138; Kenneth Vandevelde, "The New Property of the Nineteenth Century: The Development of the Modern Concept of Property," *Buffalo Law Review*, vol. 29 (1980), pp. 325–367; James Gordley, "Equality in Exchange," *California Law Review*, vol. 69 (1981), pp. 1587–1656.

The traditional doctrinal literature has often made it appear that some form of communal ownership represents the sole alternative to the system of consolidated property rights. See, for example, Otto Gierke, *Das Bürgerliche Gesetzbuch und der Deutsche Reichstag*, Hermann, Berlin, 1898.

200–204   On the paradox of specification, see, for the coexistence of classical liberal and estatist principles, Duncan Kennedy, "The Structure of Blackstone's Commentaries," *Buffalo Law Review*, vol. 28 (1979), pp. 205–382.

202–203   On the coexistence of classical liberal principles of property and contract with antiliberal forms of organizational hierarchy and surveillance, see Michel Foucault, "Two Lectures," *Power/Knowledge: Selected Interviews and Other Writings*, trans. Colin Gordon et al., Pantheon, New York, 1972, pp. 78–108.

204–207   For *the paradox of superfluity* study the literature that establishes and explores the generalization of the concept of right and its consequent loss of any implicit institutional content. See Wesley Hohfeld, "Some Fundamental Legal Conceptions as Applied in Legal Reasoning," *Yale Law Journal*, vol. 23 (1913), pp. 16–59. For the historical background, see Joseph Singer, "The Legal Rights Debate in Analytical Jurisprudence from Bentham to Hohfeld," *Wisconsin Law Review* (1982), pp. 975–1059. For an account of the paradox of superfluity and an effort to disengage legal rights and legal doctrine from the model of consolidated property, see Roberto Mangabeira Unger, *The Critical Legal Studies Movement*, Harvard, Cambridge, 1986.

The Genesis of the Governmental-Organizational Complex

213–214   For a characteristic statement of the expectation of *revolutionary change from universal suffrage*, see John Wilson Croker, *The Croker Papers* (2nd ed., rev.), ed. L. H. Jennings, Murray, London, 1885,
217–218   vol. 2, p. 113.

For the idea of the relation of modern party politics to the *suppres-*

sion or privatization of confessional disputes, see Harvey Mansfield, Jr., *Statesmanship and Party Government: A Study of Burke and Bolingbroke*, Chicago, Chicago, 1965, pp. 1–19.

For one version of the replacement of early liberal filtering-out 210 techniques by party politics, see Martin van Buren, *Inquiry into the Origin and Course of Political Parties in the United States*, Hurd, New York, 1867; Richard Hofstadter, *The Idea of a Party System: The Rise of Legitimate Opposition in the United States, 1780–1840*, Univ. of California, Berkeley, 1969.

For another version see Theodore Zeldin, *The Political System of* 210 *Napoleon III*, Norton, New York, 1958, especially, pp. 1–9, 46–65, 154–168.

Central Themes of the Institutional Genealogy

For *Marx's criticism of petty or simple commodity production*, see Karl 221–230 Marx, *Grundrisse der Kritik der Politischen Oekonomie*, Europaïsche Verlagsanstalt, Frankfurt, section on "the progressive epochs of social forms of the economy," pp. 405–411; G. A. Cohen, *Karl Marx's Theory of History*, pp. 186, 314, 332; Bob Rowthorn, "Neo-Classicism, Neo-Ricardianism and Marxism," in *Capitalism, Conflict and Inflation: Essays in Political Economy*, Lawrence, London, 1980, pp. 34–38. See also the discussion of Marx's criticism of the Gotha Program in Karl Korsch, "Introduction to the Critique of the Gotha Programme," *Marxism and Philosophy*, trans. Fred Halliday, Monthly Review, New York, 1978, pp. 145–170, emphasizing Marx's belief that Lassalle's scheme of state-supported cooperatives was unacceptable except as part of a general transformation of economic institutions.

The Making of the Communist Alternative

On the period of World War I and of its aftermath as a time of challenge to the formative contexts of European societies, see F. L. Carsten, *Revolution in Central Europe, 1918–1919*, Univ. of California, Berkeley, 1972; Charles Maier, *Recasting Bourgeois Europe: Stabilization in France, Germany, and Italy in the Decade After World War I*, Princeton, Princeton, 1975. On mid-twentieth-century adjustments of the formative institutional contexts of North Atlantic democracies, see also Margaret Weir and Theda Skocpol, "State Structure and Social Keynesianism: Responses to the Great Depression in Sweden and the United States," *International Journal of Comparative Sociology*, vol. 24 (1983), pp. 4–29.

On the *soviets* and the initial revolutionary experiments in con- 234 ciliar, direct democracy, see Oskar Anweiler, *The Soviets: The Russian Workers, Peasants, and Soldiers, 1905–1921*, Pantheon, New 238–239

York, 1974. See also Serge Bricanier, *Pannenkoek and the Workers' Councils*, trans. Malachy Carroll, Telos, St. Louis, 1978.

234–238   On the debate about alternative trajectories in the formative period of Soviet history, see the literature by and about "rightist" and "leftist" economists: E. A. Preobrazhensky, *The Crisis of Soviet Industrialization*, Sharpe, New York, 1979; Alexander Erlich, "Preobrazenski and the Economics of Soviet Industrialization," *Quarterly Journal of Economics*, vol. 64 (1950), pp. 57–88; Nikolai Bukharın, *The Politics and Economics of the Transition Period*, trans. Oliver Field, Routledge, London, 1979; Stephen E. Cohen, *Bukharin and the Bolshevik Revolution*, Knopf, New York, 1974; Rudolf Hilferding, "State Capitalism or Totalitarian State Economy?" in Julian Steinberg, ed., *Verdict of Three Decades*, Duell, New York, 1950, pp. 445, 453; Alexander Erlich, *The Soviet Industrialization Debate, 1924–1928*, Harvard, Cambridge, 1960; Moshe Lewin, *Political Undercurrents in Soviet Economic Debates*, Princeton, Princeton, 1974, pp. 97–124; Paul Costello, "Reaping the Whirlwind: Soviet Economics and Politics, 1928–1932," *Theoretical Review*, no. 27 (March–April, 1982), pp. 1–11.

234–236   On the particulars of the *grain crisis*, the transformation of agriculture, and the end of the land commune, see Moshe Lewin, *Russian Peasants and Soviet Power: A Study of Collectivization*, Norton, New York, 1968; Susan Gross Solomon, *The Soviet Agrarian Debate: A Controversy in Social Science*, Westview, Boulder, Colo., 1977; R. W. Davies, *The Socialist Offensive: The Collectivization of Soviet Agriculture, 1929–1930*, Harvard, Cambridge, 1980.

237–238   On the broader social background, see Charles Bettelheim, *Les Luttes de Classes en URSS*, part 1, 1917–1923, part 2, 1923–1930, part 3 (2 vols.), 1930–1941, Maspero, Paris, 1974.

238   On the role of the technical intelligentsia in the order resulting from the institutional settlement of the late 1920s and early 1930s see Kendall E. Bailes, *Technology and Society Under Lenin and Stalin: Origins of the Soviet Technical Intelligentsia, 1917–1941*, Princeton, Princeton, 1978.

241–246   My discussion of the Chinese Cultural Revolution has been especially influenced by Livio Maitan, *Party, Army, and Masses in China: A Marxist Interpretation of the Cultural Revolution and Its Aftermath*, trans. Gregor Benton and Marie Collitti, New Left, London, 1976, as well as by the following writings: Lowell Dittmer, *Liu Shao-ch'i and the Chinese Cultural Revolution*, Univ. of California, Berkeley, 1974; Charles Bettleheim, *Cultural Revolution and Industrial Organization in China: Changes in Management and in the Division of Labor*, trans. Alfred Ehrenfeld, Monthly Review, New York, 1974; Hong Yung Lee, *The Politics of the Chinese Cultural Revolution: A Case Study*, Univ. of California, Berkeley, 1978; Roderick MacFarquar, *The Origins of the Cultural Revolution*, Columbia, New York, vol. 1, 1974, vol. 2, 1983.

Theory of Context Making

The view of context making presented in the second part of the 246–254
chapter plays in the argument of this book a role similar to the role
played in Marxism by the theory of the evolution of modes of
production. The Marxist counterpart is the general historical materialism of the *Introduction to the Critique of Political Economy* or the
Communist Manifesto rather than the specific analysis of *Capital*. The
early pages of this commentary list sources and inspirations of the
theory of context making. The following references are almost
entirely confined to acknowledging particular intellectual debts or
suggesting where to look for more extended discussions of particular historical examples.

For the background to the example of the new artillery pieces 283–285
and flexible infantry tactics, the French revolutionary army and the
response of the German reformers, see Friedrich Meinecke, *The
Age of German Liberation, 1795–1815*, trans. Peter Paret and Helmuth
Fischer, Univ. of California, Berkeley, 1977. On the specifics,
see Peter Paret, *Yorck and the Era of Prussian Reform, 1807–1815*,
Princeton, Princeton, 1966, pp. 117–153, 173–150, and Scharn-
horst's "Three Essays on Light Troops and Infantry Tactics,"
printed as an appendix to this book, pp. 249–262. For an earlier
set of examples illustrating the same principle in the same domain, see Michael Roberts, "The Military Revolution, 1560–
1660," in *Essays in Swedish History*, Univ. of Minnesota, Minneapolis, 1967, pp. 195–225.

For three examples of conservative reforms that tried to assimilate
and reconstruct a successful technological and organizational style,
see Stanford J. Shaw, *The Ottoman Empire Under Sultan Selim III,
1789–1807*, Harvard, Cambridge, 1971, pp. 71-199, compared with
the Köprülü reforms discussed in Joseph von Hammer, *Geschichte
des Osmanischen Reiches*, Hartleben, Pest, 1830, vol. 6, pp 1–90; W.
C. Beaseley, *The Meiji Restoration*, Stanford, Stanford, 1972, pp.
350–404; Ting-yee Kuo and Kwang-ching Liu, "Self-strengthening
and the Pursuit of Western Technology," in *Cambridge History of
China*, vol. 10, *Late Ch'ing, 1800–1911*, part 1, ed. John K. Fairbank,
pp. 500–504, 517–542. In the Chinese experience, you can study
an elite that begins to understand the institutional implications of
the effort to master and reconstruct a foreign technological and
organizational style and yet refuses to go far enough. See Mary
Wright, *The Last Stand of Chinese Conservatism: The T'ung-Chih
Restoration, 1862–1874*, Stanford, Stanford, 1957, pp. 196–221; Joseph R. Levenson, *Liang Ch'i-ch'ao and the Mind of Modern China*,
Harvard, Cambridge, 1953; Hao Chang, *Liang Ch'i-ch'ao and the
Intellectual Transition in China*, Harvard, Cambridge, 1971; Benjamin Schwartz, *In Search of Wealth and Power*, Harvard, Cambridge,
1971.

The idea of coercive surplus extraction plays a central role in 285–288

Marx's social theory. See the discussion in G. A. Cohen, *Karl Marx's Theory of History*, pp. 207–215.

277 The term *negative capability* comes from a letter of Keats to his brothers, dated December 28, 1817. See *The Letters of John Keats*, ed. Maurice Forman, Oxford, Oxford, 1931, vol. 1, pp. 75–78. Although the term takes on a very different meaning in the text, a connection to Keats's meaning remains.

277–282 The thesis of *negative capability* generalizes and transforms a view that has long been familiar in many more limited versions. For one such version, see Mancur Olson, *The Rise and Decline of Nations: Economic Growth, Stagflation, and Social Rigidities*, Yale, New Haven, 1982.

286 On the particular point of *the importance of technological and or-*
302–303 *ganizational innovation relative to levels of savings and investment* in Western industrial economies, see Robert Solow, "Technical Change and the Aggregate Production Function," in *Review of Economics and Statistics*, vol. 39 (1957), pp. 312–320. For a view that emphasizes the relatively modest level of the tax burden in an agrarian-bureaucratic empire that had not yet industrialized, see Yeh-chien Wang, *Land Taxation in Imperial China, 1750–1911*, Harvard, Cambridge, 1973. For the claim that taxation levels and total government revenues under the late Ch'ing regime were roughly comparable to those of Western industrializing countries of the mid-nineteenth century see Albert Feuerwerker, *The Chinese Economy, ca. 1870–1911*, Michigan Papers in Chinese Studies, no. 5, Ann Arbor, 1969. For a polemical development of the implications, see Mark Elvin's comment on Victor Lippit, *Modern China*, vol. 4 (1978), pp. 329–330.

312–319 For the idea of *multiple pathways* and *sequential effects* as employed in contemporary evolutionary theory see, for example, Ernst Mayr, "Cladistic Analysis or Cladistic Classification?" in *Evolution and the Diversity of Life*, Harvard, Cambridge, 1976, pp. 433–476; Stephen Jay Gould, "Bushes and Ladders in Human Evolution," in *Ever Since Darwin*, Norton, New York, 1977, pp. 56–62. Remember, however, that the idea of multiple possible pathways does not go far enough in distinguishing the argument of the text from evolutionary deep-structure social theory. The argument of *False Necessity* frees the analysis of sequential effects from the appeal to a preestablished set of possible trajectories.

312–315 A good place in which to identify the theoretical ramifications of the way we understand the influence of preestablished contexts upon context change is the debate about the "transition from feudalism to capitalism." See, for an example of the influence of deep-structure moves on the understanding of sequential effects in context change, Paul Sweezy et al., *The Transition from Feudalism to Capitalism*, New Left Books, London, 1976.

332–337 The discussion of functional explanation is indebted to the exchange between Jon Elster and G. A. Cohen cited in the notes to Chapter 1.

The discussion of counterfactual explanation is equally beholden   337–340
to the exchange between Brian Barry and Jon Elster in *Political
Studies*, vol. 28 (1980): Brian Barry, "Super Fox; Review Article,"
pp. 136–143; Jon Elster, "Treatment of Counterfactuals: Reply to
Brian Barry," pp. 144–147.

5. THE PROGRAM OF EMPOWERED DEMOCRACY: THE REMAKING OF INSTITUTIONAL ARRANGEMENTS

From Explanations to Programs

For the conception of *normative argument as a historically located and*   350–355
imperfectly justifiable practice, see again my book, *Passion: An Essay
on Personality,* Free Press, 1974. Note that the overlapping practices
of internal argument and visionary justification can address either
existential projects (as in the essay to *Passion*) or social visions and
programs (as in the argument of this chapter). The two translate
into each other. Remember also that what is visionary from one
standpoint may seem internal from another.

The Justification

On the minimalist idea of democracy as a commitment to a *gov-*   369
ernment not hostage to a faction, see Joseph Schumpeter, *Capitalism,
Socialism and Democracy,* Harper, New York, 1942, pp. 269–283.
See also the skeptical elite theories of Pareto and Mosca and the
celebrated discussion of the "iron law of oligarchy," in Robert
Michels, *Political Parties: A Sociological Study of the Oligarchical Tend-
encies of Modern Democracy,* trans. Eden and Cedar Paul, Free Press,
New York, 1962, pp. 342–356.

On the idea of *the supremacy of the will* over social life as distinctive   373–374
to certain modern forms of both despotism and democracy, see
Henry Sumner Maine, *Lectures on the Early History of Institutions,*
Murray, London, 1875, lecture XIII, pp. 371–400.

On the received party-political programs, look to the platforms   377–379
of the political parties, less for their explicit commitments than for
their implicit institutional assumptions. The more discursive statements of the programmatic positions are usually just as elusive in
their institutional commitments. Some representative writings follow. For the classical liberal position, see Friedrich von Hayek, *The*   379–384
Constitution of Liberty, Gateway, Chicago, 1960. For the centrist   384–389
corporatist and communitarian view, see the interwar papal en-
cyclicals such as *Quadragesimo Anno.* See also the writing of the so-
called legal institutionalists: Albert Broderick, ed., *The French Institutionalists: Maurice Hauriou, Georges Renard, Joseph T. Delos,*
trans. Mary Welling, Harvard, Cambridge, 1970. For a recent state-   389–391
ment of the social-democratic position in a particular national setting, see David Owen, *A Future That Will Work,* Viking, London,
1984. For a detailed study of the evolution of social-democratic

ideas under the influence of office, see Kenneth Morgan, *Labor in Power, 1945–1951*, Oxford, London, 1984.

The Practice

395–397 Contemporary ideas about political practice usually fall into one of two categories. Some reflect the meeting of deep-structure and specifically Marxist assumptions with the problems of revolutionary movements. Others deal with the business-as-usual politics of redistribution or retrenchment.

Gramsci comes closest to an inclusive theory of transformative practice. See *Selections from the Prison Notebooks*, trans. Quintin Hoare and Geoffrey Nowell Smith, International Publishers, New York, 1971; *Selections from Political Writings, 1910–1920, 1921–1926*, trans. Quintin Hoare, International Publishers, New York, 1977, 1978. But his ideas remain both fragmentary in formulation and cramped by Marxist assumptions. Gramsci's activities repay analysis as much as do his doctrines. See Anthony Leeds, *Antonio Gramsci and the Revolution That Failed*, Yale, New Haven, 1977. The student of transformative practice can still learn from Machiavelli, and even more from the Machiavelli of the *Discourses* than from the Machiavelli of the *Prince*.

407 For an interesting set of studies that throws light on the problems of *a transformative movement in quest of power*, see Alain Touraine, *Mouvements Sociaux d'Aujhourd'hui: Auteurs et Analystes*, Editions Ouvrières, Paris, 1982.

415–419 For an example of the consequences of failure to deal with the problem of the cadres, see Judith Brown, *Gandhi's Rise to Power: Indian Politics, 1915–1922*, Cambridge, Cambridge, 1972, pp. 343–349.

432 For insight into the problems of *the transformative movement in power*, see writings on the transition to socialism, Serge Cristophe Kolm, *La Transition Socialiste: La Politique Economique de Gauche*, Cerf, Paris, 1977; Sergio Bitar, *Transición, Socialismo y Democracia: La Experiencia Chilena*, Siglo Veintiuno, Mexico City, 1979.

432–436 Support for the thesis of *the primacy of institutional change over redistribution* can be found in work suggesting an inverse relation between the more stable redistribution that occurs through changes in disparities among primary incomes (e.g., Netherlands, Finland, Sweden) and the less secure redistribution that takes place through tax-and-transfer (e.g., Israel, Norway). The former is likely to depend on institutional change. See J. Corinna M. van Arnhem and Geurt Schotsman, "Do Parties Affect the Distribution of Incomes? The Case of Advanced Capitalist Democracies," in Francis G. Castles, ed., *The Impact of Parties: Politics and Parties in Democratic Capitalist States*, Sage, London, 1982, pp. 283–364.

The Institutions

441–444 As stated at the outset of this commentary, three traditions of thought and practice represent the closest influences upon the programmatic argument of this chapter. The first tradition is the work of such late eighteenth and nineteenth century liberals as the makers of the American constitution, and such thinkers as Benjamin Constant, Alexis de Tocqueville, Wilhelm von Humboldt, Alexander Herzen, and John Stuart Mill. The point is to extend the impulse and enlarge the genre while revising the received institutional ideas. The second source is petty bourgeois radicalism as represented by movements like Chartism. The third source is the ultra-leftist advocacy of collective self-organization that reappears today throughout the third world.

On *the dualistic system* in the interwar European constitutions, see 444–448 Boris Mirkine-Guetzevich, *Les Nouvelles Tendances du Droit Constitutionel*, Girard, Paris, 1931. For the ideas of the architects of the dualistic system see Hugo Preuss, *Verfassungspolitische Entwicklungen in Deutschland und Westeuropa: Historische Grundlegung zu einem Staatsrecht der Deutschen Republik*, ed. Hedwig Hintze, Berlin, 1927; Hans Kelsen, *Die Verfassungsgesetze der Republik Deutschösterreich* (5 vols.), Deuticke, Vienna, 1919–22.

For a classic statement of the terms on which parties devoted to 463–464 speculative principles can be reconciled with political stability, see David Hume, "Of Parties in General," in *Essays*, Scientia Verlag, Aalen (reprint of the 1882 London edition), vol. 1, pp. 127–132. For an analysis and typology of the types of parties that result from the divorce between the style of partisan rivalry and conflict over formative contexts, see Giovanni Sartori, *Parties and Party Systems: A Framework for Analysis*, Cambridge, Cambridge, 1970.

For the discussion of an alternative to corporatist and contrac- 476–480 tualist styles of voluntary association I am indebted to Tamara Lothian.

The main contemporary inspiration to the economic part of this 491–493 program has been the literature on markets in socialist economies, if only because it invites thought about alternative market forms. See especially Włodzimierz Brus, *The Market in a Socialist Economy*, Routledge, London, 1972; Alec Nove, *The Economics of Feasible Socialism*, Unwin, London, 1983. See also the report "Into Entrepreneurial Socialism," *The Economist*, March 19, 1983, pp. 23–31. For a statement of the idea of alternative market systems, see Charles E. Lindblom, *Politics and Markets: The World's Political-Economic Systems*, Basic, New York, 1977, pp. 93–106.

Recent work has emphasized the extent to which the multidi- 494–497 visional corporation exercises, in relation to its subsidiary parts, some of the roles attributed to the capital-auctioning or capital-rationing fund under the scheme proposed in the text. See, for example, Oliver Williamson, *Markets and Hierarchies: Analysis and Antitrust Implications*, Free Press, New York, 1975, pp. 143–148; Oliver Williamson, "Corporate Governance," *Yale Law Journal*, vol. 93 (1984), pp. 1225–1226. Much the same can be said of some of the more extreme varieties of decentralization under the Soviet-model economy, such as the attempts described in the *Economist* report cited above. But the transformative significance of all such experiments is limited by the institutional framework of capital allocation and civic engagement within which they occur. Though they can serve as points of departure for the realization of the economic proposals discussed in the text, they are no substitute for more far-reaching institutional change. As a small example of the constraints the current system of capital allocation imposes upon the emergence of the capital-auctioning or capital-rationing investment fund, see, on the economic disincentives to lending to workers' cooperatives such as those existing in contemporary Western democracies, Branko Horvath, *The Political Economy of Socialism: A Marxist Social Theory*, Sharpe, New York, 1982, p. 456; Oliver Williamson, "Corporate Governance," pp. 1226–1227.

491–508   I have also found inspiration for the development of the economic proposals in the writings of nineteenth century publicists, especially Proudhon, Louis Blanc, and Lassalle. A study of Lassalle's debate with Rodbertus and Marx proved especially helpful. Lassalle, an early leader of German social democracy, criticized as impractical and demobilizing Schulze-Delitzsch's cooperativist ideas. Emphasizing the importance of access to capital, Lassalle advocated the establishment of state-supported cooperatives. Central government would supply the necessary capital and supervise the sector of producers' cooperatives, which would eventually outcompete the private-firm sector. See Ferdinand Lassalle, *Herr Bastiat-Schulze von Delitsch: Der Oekonomische Julian oder Kapital und Arbeit,* Vorwärts, Berlin, 1912 (original edition, 1893). Lassalle's program gave new life to Louis Blanc's plan for industrial social workplaces, which in turn codified ideas current among radical circles and politically engaged skilled workers in the 1830s and 1840s. See Louis Blanc, *Organisation du Travail* (enlarged version), Nouveau Monde, Paris, 1850, chap. 5, pp. 70–84; William H. Sewall, Jr., *Work and Revolution in France*, pp. 232–236. Rodbertus criticized Lassalle's proposals as both impractical (because the producers' associations would not be able to compete successfully with private firms within an economy based on current principles) and unjust (because if the proposals did succeed, they would produce a new system of group privileges). See the correspondence between Lassalle and Rodbertus: Ferdinand Lassalle, *Nachgelassene Briefe und Schriften*, ed. Gustav Mayer, Biblio, Osnabrück, 1967, vol. 6, pp. 285–381. The same series of letters is largely reproduced in Johann Karl Rodbertus, *Gesammelte Werke und Briefe*, ed. Th. Raum, Zeller, Osnabrück, 1972, vol. 6, pp. 23–109. This volume includes an interesting "fragment on the relation with Lassalle," pp. 111–117. In his parallel debate with Lassalle, Marx argued for the inefficacy of reforms that failed to change and to replace, on a societywide basis, the laws of the capitalist economy. See Ferdinand Lassalle, "Der Briefwechsel zwischen Lassale and Marx," in *Nachgelassene Briefe und Schriften*, vol. 3; and Karl Korsch's previously mentioned discussion of Marx's criticism of Lassalle. Rodbertus drew gradualistic conclusions and Marx revolutionary conclusions from what was essentially the same argument. See also George Brandes, *Ferdinand Lassalle*, trans. Bergman, New York, 1968 (original edition 1874–1875, 1881), pp. 156–167; Edward Bernstein, *Ferdinand Lassalle as a Social Reformer*, trans. Eleanor Marx Aveling, Greenwood, New York, 1969 (original edition 1891), chap. 7, pp. 134–147; Shlomo Na'aman, *Lassalle*, Verlag für Literatur and Zeitgeschehen, Hanover, 1970, pp. 635–640.

British guild socialism extended, and failed adequately to reconstruct, the tradition of Louis Blanc and Lassalle. See G. D. H. Cole, *Guild Socialism Restated*, Transaction, New Brunswick, N.J., 1980 (reprint of 1920 edition); G. D. H. Cole, *The British Cooperative Movement in a Socialist Society: A Report to the Fabian Society*, London, Allen, 1951.

The economic proposals of *False Necessity* can be viewed as a Lassallean program that has tried to absorb the force of the criticisms offered by Rodbertus and Marx. Its key move is to advocate a changed system of capital allocation and a broader set of mutually reinforcing governmental and economic arrangements. These arrangements cut through the contrasting dilemmas of self-management and statist models of economic organization. They avoid the weaknesses of the self-management approach without seeking a corrective in commanding, centralized power.

On *the design of work*, see the writings cited earlier that describe 497–499 the vanguardist sector of contemporary industry and Alan Fox, 506–508 *Beyond Contract*, pp. 134–144.

On the methods of thought and the technical legal categories that 508–539 can serve the system of *legal rights* outlined in the text, see my book, *The Critical Legal Studies Movement*. On the complex injunctions and the related legal-theoretical ideas that help inspire the concept of *destabilization rights*, see Lewis Sargentich, "Complex Enforcement" (unpublished paper on file at the Harvard Law School Library).

On *the reorganization of mass-production industry* (which the text 542–543 describes as one of several opportunities for the advancement of the program of empowered democracy), see Michael J. Piore and 554 Charles F. Sabel, *The Second Industrial Divide*, Basic, New York, 1984, pp. 258–308. On the Swedish experience (subsidization of industry as an occasion for reallocating elements of control over investment decisions), see Walter Korpi, *The Working Class in Welfare Capitalism: Work, Unions, and Politics in Sweden*, Routledge, London, 1978.

The Spirit

For the conception of empowerment and of its relation to ideals 575–585 and experiences that seem antagonistic to it, see Unger, *Passion: An Essay on Personality*.

The closest counterpart within the liberal tradition to the social 579–580 forms of empowerment described here is a conception of affirmative freedom. See, for example, T. H. Green, *Lectures on the Principles of Political Obligation*, Longmans, London, 1917, section 7, p. 9.

On the theme of fantasy and enactment, see Roland Barthes, *Sade, Fourier, Loyola*, trans. Richard Miller, pp. 163–165. On the background and intentions of Gance's *Napoleon*, see Kevin Brownlaw, *Napoleon: Abel Gance's Classic Film*, Cape, London, 1983.

For a concise statement of the classical republican vision, see Montesquieu's discussion of the democratic type of regime in *The Spirit of the Laws*, trans. Thomas Nugent, Hafner, New York, 1966, chap. 3, pp. 20–22.

Note on Aids to the Development of the Personalist Counterpart to the Institutional Program

556–570 Only a brief section of this chapter deals with the transformation of personal relations that extends the institutional program of empowered democracy. This note evokes some of the writings and studies that help inform the ideas of this section, to be developed more fully in a future Part II of *Politics*.

The argument of the fragment on cultural revolution stands in close relation to the main part of my book, *Passion: An Essay on Personality*. That essay presents a moral vision in the manner of a modernist transformation of the Christian-romantic image of man. By contrast, the discussion here addresses the personalist counterpart to an institutional program. It emphasizes certain discrete qualities of personal relations rather than, as does *Passion*, the whole individual in relation. Despite these differences in scope, concern, and form, I hope that no serious conflict of beliefs or consequences exists between the two efforts.

The ideas anticipated in the brief passage on cultural revolution have three main sources. The first source consists in the writings of certain philosophers. These writings include the middle works of Heidegger and Sartre, notably *Being and Time*, trans. John Macquarrie and Edward Robinson, Harper, New York, 1962, and *Being and Nothingness*, trans. Hazel Barnes, Philosophical Library, New York. But the assumptions of my argument differ crucially from their doctrines in its insistence upon our ability to change the relation between freedom and structure as well as in its focus on the link between an approach to personal relations and a program of social reconstruction.

Among earlier philosophers the cultural revolutionary can find guidance in Hegel and Kierkegaard. See Hegel's exploration of the convolutions of a sensibility no longer at one with allotted social stations in the later parts of *The Phenomenology of Mind*, trans. J. B. Baillie, Harper, New York, 1967. See also Kierkegaard's treatment of the problems of moral evaluation once people cease to credit conventional hierarchies of value as flawed approximations to an objective moral order: *Either/Or* (2 vols.), trans. Donald F. Swenson and Lillian Marion Swenson, Princeton, Princeton, 1959.

Only in the efforts of contemporary feminist theorists and in the occasional writings of third world ultra-leftists have I found a shared discourse that develops the speculative themes of these nineteenth and twentieth century philosophers into the beginnings of a cultural-revolutionary program.

A second source of help consists in the novels, poems, and tracts of the great modernist writers of the twentieth century, such as Proust and Joyce, Musil and Virginia Woolf. You need not read their works didactically to find in them materials for a moral psychology. The insight into personal and social possibility that these artists provide far outreaches the sentimental or cynical views dominating so much premodernist thought about human nature. Lesser modernist writers can be equally rewarding for a study of particular experiences and intentions central to the program of cultural revolution. Thus, some (such as Clarice Lispector) have probed the incongruous use of social stations while others (like Chung-shu Ch'ien) have explored the confusion of conventions that attends the clash of cultures. See also Edward Mendelson, *Early Auden*, Harvard, Cambridge, 1981, as a study of a modernist sensibility treading a long but representative itinerary of hopes for personal and social improvement.

A third inspiration is the worldwide pop culture. One way to understand its cultural-revolutionary message is to watch and compare television soap operas in different countries. These melodramas express the anxieties and longings of particular classes and communities in particular societies. They also rehearse the ancient, sentimentalized formulas of the Christian and pagan romance. But both the distinctive, local concerns and the familiar romantic tropes come out transformed by their combination with role jumbling and role defiance. See *TV Guide*.

Proper-Name Index

Abbasid regime, 90
Agincourt, 47
Alberoni, Francesco, 599
Aristotle, 353
Asiatic Near East, ancient city-states of, 88
Aztecs, 89, 338
  military life-tenants, 89

Barry, Brian, 338
Basil II, 89
Beccaria, Cesare, 202
Beckett, Samuel, 603
Bentham, Jeremy, 202
Birmingham, 185
Blackstone, William, 202, 203
Blanc, Louis, 602
Braudel, Fernand, 602
Brenner, Robert, 600
Bukharin, Nikolai Ivanovich, 237
Bukharinist cause, 231, 234, 235, 236, 238
Buren, Martin van, 210
Byzantine Empire, 90
  Basil II, 89
  bureaucracies, 138
  eleventh-century village communities, 91
  Macedonian dynasty, 602
  military farms (*ktemata stratiotikoi*), 89
  Romanus Lecapenus, 89

Calhoun, Craig J., 602
Capital, 181
Cartesian precept, 157
Catalonia, 188–189, 200
Ch'ien, Chung-shu, 631
China, 160, 246
  Ch'ing dynasty, 286
  Cultural Revolution, 85, 231, 239–245
  dynastic decline, 90
  economy of the 1970s and 1980s, 120
  Lushan Plenum of 1970, 244
  Ming-Ch'ing bureaucracy, 138
  Southern Sung dynasty, 91
  statecraft in the ancient city-states, 89
  Sung dynasty, 91
  T'ang dynasty, 90
  Toba Empire, 89, 602
Cohen, G. A., 332
Constant, Benjamin, 601
Cortés, Hernán, 239

Darwinian competition, 182
Democritean atoms, 166
Disraeli, Benjamin, 444
Durkheim, Émile, 599

Eastern Europe, 51, 239
  "feudalism" in, 142
Egypt, 285
Elbe (Europe east of), 189, 200
Elster, Jon, 333
England (Britain), 179, 187, 190, 209
  Birmingham, 185
  history, 175
  industrial development, 180
  reform bills, 210
  Sheffield cutlery industry, 185
  West Riding woolen industry, 185
Europe, 183, 190
  absolutism, 89, 132, 168
  armies before the turn of the century, 148
  constitutions of the interwar period, 72
  early modern, 198, 201
  political parties, 73

Flanders, 189
Fordist assembly line, 80, 155, 192
France, 190, 200, 209, 283–284
  Lyon and its industries, 185–186
  Orleanist regime, 186
  Revolution, 283

Galileo Galilei, 127–128
Gance, Abel, 581–582
Gandhi, Mohandas, 416, 569
General Motors, 46
Germany, 80, 179, 189, 210 ·
  Solingen cutlery industry, 185
Graeco-Roman antiquity, its city-state republics, 62, 92, 94
Gramsci, Antonio, 600
Green, Thomas Hill, 601

Hardenberg, Prince Karl August, 289
Harrington, James, 601
Hayek, F. A., 601
Hegel, G. W. F., 630
Heidegger, Martin, 603, 630
Henry V (of England), 47

Thematic Index

506.? Post-fordism?

570 And aims of Bhaskar &
     Unger critique.

ED PROSE

Journ..., Su .... *Interior, Winter* .... *Book of Illusions*, and *The New York Trilogy*, among many other works. In 2006 he was awarded the Prince of Asturias Award for Literature. Among his other honours are the Prix Médicis Étranger for *Leviathan*, the Independent Spirit Award for the screenplay of *Smoke* and the Premio Napoli for *Sunset Park*. He has also been a finalist for the International IMPAC Dublin Literary Award (*The Book of Illusions*), the PEN/Faulkner Award for Fiction (*The Music of Chance*), and the Edgar Award (*City of Glass*). He is a member of the American Academy of Arts and Letters, the American Academy of Arts and Sciences, and a Commandeur de l'Ordre des Arts et des Lettres. His work has been translated into forty-three languages. He lives in Brooklyn, New York.

Collected Prose

Autobiographical Writings,
True Stories, Critical Essays, Prefaces,
Collaborations with Artists

Paul Auster

FABER & FABER

First published in 2003
by Faber and Faber Ltd
Bloomsbury House
74–77 Great Russell Street
London WC1B 3DA
This edition published in 2014

Printed and bound by CPI Group (UK) Ltd, Croydon, CR0 4YY

A CIP record for this book
is available from the British Library

ISBN 978–0–571–21848–6

2 4 6 8 10 9 7 5 3 1

Contents

CONTENTS

THE INVENTION OF SOLITUDE

Portrait of an Invisible Man

One day there is life. A man, for example, in the best of health, not even old, with no history of illness. Everything is as it was, as it will always be. He goes from one day to the next, minding his own business, dreaming only of the life that lies before him. And then, suddenly, it happens there is death. A man lets out a little sigh, he slumps down in his chair, and it is death. The suddenness of it leaves no room for thought, gives the mind no chance to seek out a word that might comfort it. We are left with nothing but death, the irreducible fact of our own mortality. Death after a long illness we can accept with resignation. Even accidental death we can ascribe to fate. But for a man to die of no apparent cause, for a man to die simply because he is a man, brings us so close to the invisible boundary between life and death that we no longer know which side we are on. Life becomes death, and it is as if this death has owned this life all along. Death without warning. Which is to say: life stops. And it can stop at any moment.

The news of my father's death came to me three weeks ago. It was Sunday morning, and I was in the kitchen preparing breakfast for my small son, Daniel. Upstairs my wife was still in bed, warm under the quilts, luxuriating in a few extra hours of sleep. Winter in the country: a world of silence, wood smoke, whiteness. My mind was filled with thoughts about the piece I had been writing the night before, and I was looking ahead to the afternoon when I would be able to get back to work. Then the phone rang. I knew instantly that there was trouble. No one calls at eight o'clock on a Sunday morning unless it is to give news that cannot wait. And news that cannot wait is always bad news.

I could not muster a single ennobling thought.

Even before we packed our bags and set out on the three-hour drive to

3

New Jersey, I knew that I would have to write about my father. I had no plan, had no precise idea of what this meant. I cannot even remember making a decision about it. It was simply there, a certainty, an obligation that began to impose itself on me the moment I was given the news. I thought: my father is gone. If I do not act quickly, his entire life will vanish along with him.

Looking back on it now, even from so short a distance as three weeks, I find this a rather curious reaction. I had always imagined that death would numb me, immobilize me with grief. But now that it had happened, I did not shed any tears, I did not feel as though the world had collapsed around me. In some strange way, I was remarkably prepared to accept this death, in spite of its suddenness. What disturbed me was something else, something unrelated to death or my response to it: the realization that my father had left no traces.

He had no wife, no family that depended on him, no one whose life would be altered by his absence. A brief moment of shock, perhaps, on the part of scattered friends, sobered as much by the thought of capricious death as by the loss of their friend, followed by a short period of mourning, and then nothing. Eventually, it would be as though he had never lived at all.

Even before his death he had been absent, and long ago the people closest to him had learned to accept this absence, to treat it as the fundamental quality of his being. Now that he was gone, it would not be difficult for the world to absorb the fact that he was gone forever. The nature of his life had prepared the world for his death—had been a kind of death by anticipation—and if and when he was remembered, it would be dimly, no more than dimly.

Devoid of passion, either for a thing, a person, or an idea, incapable or unwilling to reveal himself under any circumstances, he had managed to keep himself at a distance from life, to avoid immersion in the quick of things. He ate, he went to work, he had friends, he played tennis, and yet for all that he was not there. In the deepest, most unalterable sense, he was an invisible man. Invisible to others, and most likely invisible to himself as well. If, while he was alive, I kept looking for him, kept trying to find the father who was not there, now that he is dead I still feel as though I must go on looking for him. Death has not changed anything. The only difference is that I have run out of time.

For fifteen years he had lived alone. Doggedly, opaquely, as if immune

4

to the world. He did not seem to be a man occupying space, but rather a block of impenetrable space in the form of a man. The world bounced off him, shattered against him, at times adhered to him—but it never got through. For fifteen years he haunted an enormous house, all by himself, and it was in that house that he died.

For a short while we had lived there as a family—my father, my mother, my sister, and I. After my parents were divorced, everyone dispersed: my mother began a new life, I went off to college, and my sister stayed with my mother until she, too, went off to school. Only my father remained. Because of a clause in the divorce agreement which stipulated that my mother still owned a share of the house and would be given half the proceeds whenever it was sold (which made my father reluctant to sell), or from some secret refusal to change his life (so as not to show the world that the divorce had affected him in a way he could not control), or simply from inertia, an emotional lethargy that prevented him from taking any action, he stayed on, living alone in a house that could have accommodated six or seven people.

It was an impressive place: old, solidly built, in the Tudor style, with leaded windows, a slate roof, and rooms of royal proportions. Buying it had been a big step for my parents, a sign of growing wealth. This was the best neighborhood in town, and although it was not a pleasant place to live (especially for children), its prestige outweighed its deadliness. Given the fact that he wound up spending the rest of his life in that house, it is ironic that my father at first resisted moving there. He complained about the price (a constant theme), and when at last he relented, it was with grudging bad humor. Even so, he paid in cash. All in one go. No mortgage, no monthly payments. It was 1959, and business was going well for him.

Always a man of habit, he would leave for work early in the morning, work hard all day, and then, when he came home (on those days he did not work late), take a short nap before dinner. Sometime during our first week in the new house, before we had properly moved in, he made a curious kind of mistake. Instead of driving home to the new house after work, he went directly to the old one, as he had done for years, parked his car in the driveway, walked into the house through the back door, climbed the stairs, entered the bedroom, lay down on the bed, and went to sleep. He slept for about an hour. Needless to say, when the new mistress of the house returned to find a strange man sleeping in her bed, she was a little surprised. But unlike Goldilocks, my father did not jump up and run away. The confusion was eventually settled, and everyone had a good laugh. Even today, it still makes me laugh. And yet, for all that, I cannot help regarding it as a pathetic story. It is one thing for a man to drive to his old house by mistake, but it is quite another, I think, for him not to notice that anything has changed inside it. Even the most tired or distracted mind has a corner of pure, animal response, and can give the body a sense of where it is. One would have to be nearly unconscious not to see, or at least not to feel, that the house was no longer the same. "Habit," as one of Beckett's characters says, "is a great deadener." And if the mind is unable to respond to the physical evidence, what will it do when confronted with the emotional evidence?

During those last fifteen years he changed almost nothing in the house. He did not add any furniture, he did not remove any furniture. The walls remained the same color, the pots and pans were not replaced, even my mother's dresses were not thrown out—but stored away in an attic closet. The very size of the house absolved him from having to make any decisions about the things it contained. It was not that he was clinging to the past, trying to preserve the house as a museum. On the contrary, he seemed to be unaware of what he was doing. It was negligence that governed him, not memory, and even though he went on living in that house all those years, he lived in it as a stranger might have. As the years went by, he spent less and less time there. He ate nearly all his meals in restaurants, arranged his social calendar so as to be busy every night, and used the house as little more than a place to sleep. Once, several years ago, I happened to mention to him how much money I had earned from my writing and translating during the previous year (a pittance by any standard, but more than I had ever made before), and his amused response was that he spent more than that just on eating out. The point is: his life was not centered around the place where he lived. His house was just one of many stopping places in a restless, unmoored existence, and this lack of center had the effect of turning him into a perpetual outsider, a tourist of his own life. You never had the feeling that he could be located.

Still, the house seems important to me, if only to the extent that it was neglected—symptomatic of a state of mind that, otherwise inaccessible, manifested itself in the concrete images of unconscious behavior. The house became the metaphor of my father's life, the exact and faithful representation of his inner world. For although he kept the house tidy and preserved it more or less as it had been, it underwent a gradual and ineluctable process of disintegration. He was neat, he always put things back in their proper place, but nothing was cared for, nothing was ever cleaned. The furniture, especially in the rooms he rarely visited, was covered with dust, cobwebs, the signs of total neglect; the kitchen stove was so encrusted with charred food that it had become unsalvageable; in the cupboard, sometimes languishing on the shelves for years: bug-infested packages of flour, stale crackers, bags of sugar that had turned into solid blocks, bottles of syrup that could no longer be opened. Whenever he prepared a meal for himself, he would immediately and assiduously do the dishes—but rinse them only, never using soap, so that every cup, every saucer, every plate was coated with a film of dingy grease. Throughout the house: the window shades, which were kept drawn at all times, had become so threadbare that the slightest tug would pull them apart. Leaks sprang and stained the furniture, the furnace never gave off enough heat, the shower did not work. The house became shabby, depressing to walk into. You felt as if you were entering the house of a blind man.

His friends and family, sensing the madness of the way he lived in that house, kept urging him to sell it and move somewhere else. But he always managed to ward them off with a non-committal "I'm happy here," or "The house suits me fine." In the end, however, he did decide to move. At the very end. In the last phone conversation we ever had, ten days before he died, he told me the house had been sold and that the closing was set for February first, about three weeks away. He wanted to know if there was anything in the house I could use, and I agreed to come down for a visit with my wife and Daniel on the first free day that opened up. He died before we had a chance to make it.

There is nothing more terrible, I learned, than having to face the objects of a dead man. Things are inert: they have meaning only in function of the life that makes use of them. When that life ends, the things change, even though they remain the same. They are there and yet not there: tangible ghosts, condemned to survive in a world they no longer belong to. What is one to think, for example, of a closetful of clothes waiting silently to be worn again by a man who will not be coming back to open the door? Or the stray packets of condoms strewn among brimming drawers of underwear and socks? Or an electric razor sitting in the bathroom, still clogged with the whisker dust of the last shave? Or a dozen empty tubes of hair coloring hidden away in a leather travelling case?—suddenly revealing things one has no desire to see, no desire to know. There is a poignancy to it, and also a kind of horror. In themselves, the things mean nothing, like the cooking utensils of some vanished civilization. And yet they say something to us, standing there not as objects but as remnants of thought, of consciousness, emblems of the solitude in which a man comes to make decisions about himself: whether to color his hair, whether to wear this or that shirt, whether to live, whether to die. And the futility of it all once there is death.

Each time I opened a drawer or poked my head into a closet, I felt like an intruder, a burglar ransacking the secret places of a man's mind. I kept expecting my father to walk in, to stare at me in disbelief, and ask me what the hell I thought I was doing. It didn't seem fair that he couldn't protest. I had no right to invade his privacy.

A hastily scrawled telephone number on the back of a business card that read: H. Limeburg—Garbage Cans of All Descriptions. Photographs of my parents' honeymoon in Niagara Falls, 1946: my mother sitting nervously on top of a bull for one of those funny shots that are never funny, and a sudden sense of how unreal the world has always been, even in its prehistory. A drawer full of hammers, nails, and more than twenty screwdrivers. A filing cabinet stuffed with canceled checks from 1953 and the cards I received for my sixth birthday. And then, buried at the bottom of a drawer in the bathroom: the monogrammed toothbrush that had once belonged to my mother and which had not been touched or looked at for more than fifteen years.

The list is inexhaustible.

It soon became apparent to me that my father had done almost nothing to prepare himself for his departure. The only signs of the impending move I could detect in the whole house were a few cartons of books—trivial books (out of date atlases, a fifty-year-old introduction to electronics, a high school Latin grammar, ancient law books) that he had been planning to give away to charity. Other than that, nothing. No empty boxes waiting to be filled. No pieces of furniture given away or sold. No arrangements made with a moving company. It was as though he had not been able to face it. Rather than empty the house, he had simply willed himself to die. Death was a way out, the only legitimate escape.

There was no escape for me, however. The thing had to be done, and

8

there was no one else to do it. For ten days I went through his things, cleared out the house, got it ready for the new owners. It was a miserable time, but also an oddly humorous time, a time of reckless and absurd decisions: sell it, throw it out, give it away. My wife and I bought a big wooden slide for eighteen-month old Daniel and set it up in the living room. He thrived on the chaos: rummaging among the things, putting lampshades on his head, flinging plastic poker chips around the house, running through the vast spaces of the gradually emptying rooms. At night my wife and I would lie under monolithic quilts watching trashy movies on television. Until the television, too, was given away. There was trouble with the furnace, and if I forgot to fill it with water, it would shut off. One morning we woke up to find that the temperature in the house had dropped to forty degrees. Twenty times a day the phone rang, and twenty times a day I told someone that my father was dead. I had become a furniture salesman, a moving man, a messenger of bad tidings.

The house began to resemble the set for a trite comedy of manners. Relatives swooped in, asking for this piece of furniture or that piece of dinnerware, trying on my father's suits, overturning boxes, chattering away like geese. Auctioneers came to examine the merchandise ("Nothing upholstered, it's not worth a nickel"), turned up their noses, and walked out. Garbage men clumped in with heavy boots and hauled off mountains of trash. The water man read the water meter, the gas man read the gas meter, the oil men read the oil gauge. (One of them, I forget which, who had been given a lot of trouble by my father over the years, said to me with savage complicity, "I don't like to say this"—meaning he did—"but your father was an obnoxious bastard.") The real estate agent came to buy some furniture for the new owners and wound up taking a mirror for herself. A woman who ran a curio shop bought my mother's old hats. A junkman came with a team of assistants (four black men named Luther, Ulysses, Tommy Pride, and Joe Sapp) and carted away everything from a set of barbels to a broken toaster. By the time it was over, nothing was left. Not even a postcard. Not even a thought.

If there was a single worst moment for me during those days, it came when I walked across the front lawn in the pouring rain to dump an armful of my father's ties into the back of a Good Will Mission truck. There must have been more than a hundred ties, and many of them I remembered from my childhood: the patterns, the colors, the shapes that had been embedded in my earliest consciousness, as clearly as my father's face had been. To see myself throwing them away like so much junk was intolerable to me, and it was then, at the precise instant I tossed them into the truck, that I came closest to tears. More than seeing the coffin itself being lowered into the ground, the act of throwing away these ties seemed to embody for me the idea of burial. I finally understood that my father was dead.

Yesterday one of the neighborhood children came here to play with Daniel. A girl of about three and a half who has recently learned that big people were once children, too, and that even her own mother and father have parents. At one point she picked up the telephone and launched into a pretend conversation, then turned to me and said, "Paul, it's your father. He wants to talk to you." It was gruesome. I thought: there's a ghost at the other end of the line, and he really does want to talk to me. It was a few moments before I could speak. "No," I finally blurted out. "It can't be my father. He wouldn't be calling today. He's somewhere else."

I waited until she had hung up the phone and then walked out of the room.

In his bedroom closet I had found several hundred photographs— stashed away in faded manila envelopes, affixed to the black pages of warped albums, scattered loosely in drawers. From the way they had been stored I gathered he never looked at them, had even forgotten they were there. One very big album, bound in expensive leather with a gold-stamped title on the cover—This is Our Life: The Austers—was totally blank inside. Someone, probably my mother, had once gone to the trouble of ordering this album, but no one had ever bothered to fill it.

Back home, I pored over these pictures with a fascination bordering on mania. I found them irresistible, precious, the equivalent of holy relics. It seemed that they could tell me things I had never known before, reveal some previously hidden truth, and I studied each one intensely, absorbing the least detail, the most insignificant shadow, until all the images had become a part of me. I wanted nothing to be lost.

Death takes a man's body away from him. In life, a man and his body are synonymous; in death, there is the man and there is his body. We say, "This is the body of X," as if this body, which had once been the man himself, not something that represented him or belonged to him, but the very man called X, were suddenly of no importance. When a man walks into a room and you shake hands with him, you do not feel that you are shaking hands with his hand, or shaking hands with his body, you are shaking hands with *him*. Death changes that. This is the body of X, not this is X. The syntax is entirely different. Now we are talking about two things instead of one, implying that the man continues to exist, but only as an idea, a cluster of images and memories in the minds of other people. As for the body, it is no more than flesh and bones, a heap of pure matter.

Discovering these photographs was important to me because they seemed to reaffirm my father's physical presence in the world, to give me the illusion that he was still there. The fact that many of these pictures were ones I had never seen before, especially the ones of his youth, gave me the odd sensation that I was meeting him for the first time, that a part of him was only just beginning to exist. I had lost my father. But at the same time, I had also found him. As long as I kept these pictures before my eyes, as long as I continued to study them with my complete attention, it was as though he were still alive, even in death. Or if not alive, at least not dead. Or rather, somehow suspended, locked in a universe that had nothing to do with death, in which death could never make an entrance.

Most of these pictures did not tell me anything new, but they helped to fill in gaps, confirm impressions, offer proof where none had existed before. A series of snapshots of him as a bachelor, for example, probably taken over a number of years, gives a precise account of certain aspects of his personality that had been submerged during the years of his marriage, a side of him I did not begin to see until after his divorce: my father as prankster, as man about town, as good time Charlie. In picture after picture he is standing with women, usually two or three, all of them affecting comical poses, their arms perhaps around each other, or two of them sitting on his lap, or else a theatrical kiss for the benefit of no one but the person taking the picture. In the background: a mountain, a tennis court, perhaps a swimming pool or a log cabin. These were the pictures brought back from weekend jaunts to various Catskill resorts in the company of his bachelor friends: play tennis, have a good time with the girls. He carried on in this way until he was thirty-four.

It was a life that suited him, and I can see why he went back to it after his marriage broke up. For a man who finds life tolerable only by staying on the surface of himself, it is natural to be satisfied with offering no more than this surface to others. There are few demands to be met, and no commitment is required. Marriage, on the other hand, closes the door. Your existence is confined to a narrow space in which you are constantly forced to reveal yourself—and therefore, constantly obliged to look into yourself, to examine your own depths. When the door is open there is never any problem: you can always escape. You can avoid unwanted confrontations, either with yourself or with another, simply by walking away.

My father's capacity for evasion was almost limitless. Because the domain of the other was unreal to him, his incursions into that domain were made with a part of himself he considered to be equally unreal, another self he had trained as an actor to represent him in the empty comedy of the world-at-large. This surrogate self was essentially a tease, a hyperactive child, a fabricator of tall tales. It could not take anything seriously.

Because nothing mattered, he gave himself the freedom to do anything he wanted (sneaking into tennis clubs, pretending to be a restaurant critic in order to get a free meal), and the charm he exercised to make his conquests was precisely what made these conquests meaningless. With the vanity of a woman he hid the truth about his age, made up stories about his business dealings, talked about himself only obliquely—in the third person, as if about an acquaintance of his ("There's a friend of mine who has this problem; what do you think he should do about it? . . ."). Whenever a situation became too tight for him, whenever he felt pushed to the verge of having to reveal himself, he would wriggle out of it by telling a lie. Eventually, the lie came automatically and was indulged in for its own sake. The principle was to say as little as possible. If people never learned the truth about him, then they couldn't turn around and use it against him later. The lie was a way of buying protection. What people saw when he appeared before them, then, was not really him, but a person he had invented, an artificial creature he could manipulate in order to manipulate others. He himself remained invisible, a puppeteer working the strings of his alter-ego from a dark, solitary place behind the curtain.

For the last ten or twelve years of his life he had one steady lady friend, and this was the woman who went out with him in public, who played the role of official companion. Every now and then there was some vague talk of marriage (at her insistence), and everyone assumed that this was the only woman he had anything to do with. After his death, however, other women began to step forward. This one had loved him, that one had worshipped him, another one was going to marry him. The principal girlfriend was shocked to learn about these other women: my father had never breathed a word about them to her. Each one had been fed a different line, and each one thought she had possessed him entirely. As it turned out, none of them knew the slightest thing about him. He had managed to elude them all.

Solitary. But not in the sense of being alone. Not solitary in the way Thoreau was, for example, exiling himself in order to find out where he was; not solitary in the way Jonah was, praying for deliverance in the belly of the whale. Solitary in the sense of retreat. In the sense of not having to see himself, of not having to see himself being seen by anyone else.

Talking to him was a trying experience. Either he would be absent, as he usually was, or he would assault you with a brittle jocularity, which was merely another form of absence. It was like trying to make yourself understood by a senile old man. You talked, and there would be no response, or a response that was inappropriate, showing that he hadn't been following the drift of your words. In recent years, whenever I spoke to him on the phone I would find myself saying more than I normally do, becoming aggressively talkative, chatting away in a futile attempt to hold his attention, to provoke a response. Afterwards, I would invariably feel foolish for having tried so hard.

He did not smoke, he did not drink. No hunger for sensual pleasures, no thirst for intellectual pleasures. Books bored him, and it was the rare movie or play that did not put him to sleep. Even at parties you would see him struggling to keep his eyes open, and more often than not he would succumb, falling asleep in a chair as the conversations swirled around him. A man without appetites. You felt that nothing could ever intrude on him, that he had no need of anything the world had to offer.

At thirty-four, marriage. At fifty-two, divorce. In one sense, it lasted years, but in fact it did not last more than a few days. He was never a married man, never a divorced man, but a life-long bachelor who happened to have had an interlude of marriage. Although he did not shirk his outward duties as a husband (he was faithful, he provided for his wife and children, he shouldered all his responsibilities), it was clear that he was not cut out to play this role. He simply had no talent for it.

My mother was just twenty-one when she married him. His conduct during the brief courtship had been chaste. No daring overtures, none of the aroused male's breathless assaults. Now and then they would hold hands, exchange a polite good-night kiss. Love, in so many words, was never declared by either one of them. By the time the wedding came, they were little more than strangers.

It was not long before my mother realized her mistake. Even before the honeymoon was over (that honeymoon, so fully documented in the photographs I found: the two of them sitting together, for instance, on a rock at the edge of a perfectly still lake, a broad path of sunlight behind them leading to the pine slope in shadow, my father with his arms around my mother, and the two of them looking at each other, smiling timidly, as if the photographer had made them hold the pose an instant too long), even before the honeymoon was over, my mother knew the marriage would not work. She went to her mother in tears and said she wanted to leave him. Somehow, her mother managed to persuade her to go back and give it a chance. And then, before the dust had settled, she found herself pregnant. And suddenly it was too late to do anything.

I think of it sometimes: how I was conceived in that Niagara Falls resort for honeymooners. Not that it matters where it happened. But the thought of what must have been a passionless embrace, a blind, dutiful groping between chilly hotel sheets, has never failed to humble me into an awareness of my own contingency. Niagara Falls. Or the hazard of two bodies joining. And then me, a random homunculus, like some dare-devil in a barrel, shooting over the falls.

A little more than eight months later, on the morning of her twenty-second birthday, my mother woke up and told my father that the baby was coming. Ridiculous, he said, that baby's not due for another three weeks—and promptly went off to work, leaving her without a car.

She waited. Thought maybe he was right. Waited a little more, then called a sister-in-law and asked to be driven to the hospital. My aunt stayed with my mother throughout the day, calling my father every few hours to ask him to come. Later, he would say, I'm busy now, I'll get there when I can.

At a little past midnight I poked my way into the world, ass first, no doubt screaming.

My mother waited for my father to show up, but he did not arrive until the next morning—accompanied by his mother, who wanted to inspect grandchild number seven. A short, nervous visit, and then off again to work.

She cried, of course. After all, she was young, and she had not expected it to mean so little to him. But he could never understand such things. Not in the beginning, and not in the end. It was never possible for him to be where he was. For as long as he lived, he was somewhere else, between here and there. But never really here. And never really there.

Thirty years later, this same little drama was repeated. This time I was there, and I saw it with my own eyes.

After my own son was born I had thought: surely this will please him. Isn't every man pleased to become a grandfather?

I had wanted to see him doting on the baby, for him to offer me proof that he was, after all, capable of demonstrating some feeling—that he did, after all, have feelings in the way other people did. And if he could show affection for his grandson, then wouldn't it be an indirect way of showing affection for me? You do not stop hungering for your father's love, even after you are grown up.

But then, people do not change. All told, my father saw his grandson only three or four times, and at no time was he able to distinguish him from the impersonal mass of babies born into the world every day. Daniel was just two weeks old when he first laid eyes on him. I can remember the day vividly: a blistering Sunday at the end of June, heat-wave weather, the country air gray with moisture. My father pulled up in his car, saw my wife putting the baby into the carriage for a nap, and walked over to say hello. He poked his head into the carriage for a tenth of a second, straightened up and said to her, "A beautiful baby. Good luck with it," and then proceeded to walk on into the house. He might just as well have been talking about some stranger's baby encountered in line at the supermarket. For the rest of his visit that day he did not look at Daniel, and not once, ever, did he ask to hold him.

All this, merely as an example.

Impossible, I realize, to enter another's solitude. If it is true that we can ever come to know another human being, even to a small degree, it is only to the extent that he is willing to make himself known. A man will say: I am cold. Or else he will say nothing, and we will see him shivering. Either way, we will know that he is cold. But what of the man who says nothing and does not shiver? Where all is intractable, where all is hermetic and evasive, one can do no more than observe. But whether one can make sense of what he observes is another matter entirely.

I do not want to presume anything.

He never talked about himself, never seemed to know there was anything he *could* talk about. It was as though his inner life eluded even him.

He could not talk about it, and therefore he passed over it in silence.

If there is nothing, then, but silence, is it not presumptuous of me to speak? And yet: if there had been anything more than silence, would I have felt the need to speak in the first place?

My choices are limited. I can remain silent, or else I can speak of things that cannot be verified. At the very least, I want to put down the facts, to offer them as straightforwardly as possible, and let them say whatever they have to say. But even the facts do not always tell the truth.

He was so implacably neutral on the surface, his behavior was so flatly predictable, that everything he did came as a surprise. One could not believe there was such a man—who lacked feeling, who wanted so little of others. And if there was not such a man, that means there was another man, a man hidden inside the man who was not there, and the trick of it, then, is to find him. On the condition that he is there to be found.

To recognize, right from the start, that the essence of this project is failure.

Earliest memory: his absence. For the first years of my life he would leave for work early in the morning, before I was awake, and come home long after I had been put to bed. I was my mother's boy, and I lived in her orbit. I was a little moon circling her gigantic earth, a mote in the sphere of her gravity, and I controlled the tides, the weather, the forces of feeling. His refrain to her was: Don't fuss so much, you'll spoil him. But my health was not good, and she used this to justify the attention she lavished on me. We spent a lot of time together, she in her loneliness and I in my cramps, waiting patiently in doctors' offices for someone to quell the insurrection that continually raged in my stomach. Even then, I would cling to these doctors in a desperate sort of way, wanting them to hold me. From the very beginning, it seems, I was looking for my father, looking frantically for anyone who resembled him.

Later memories: a craving. My mind always ready to deny the facts at the slightest excuse, I mulishly went on hoping for something that was never given to me—or given to me so rarely and arbitrarily that it seemed to happen outside the range of normal experience, in a place where I would never be able to live for more than a few moments at a time. It was not that I felt he disliked me. It was just that he seemed distracted, unable to look in my direction. And more than anything else, I wanted him to take notice of me.

Anything, even the least thing, was enough. How, for example, when the family once went to a crowded restaurant on a Sunday and we had to wait for our table, my father took me outside, produced a tennis ball (from where?), put a penny on the sidewalk, and proceeded to play a game with me: hit the penny with the tennis ball. I could not have been more than eight or nine years old.

In retrospect, nothing could have been more trivial. And yet the fact that I had been included, that my father had casually asked me to share his boredom with him, nearly crushed me with happiness.

More often, there were disappointments. For a moment he would seem to have changed, to have opened up a little, and then, suddenly, he would not be there anymore. The one time I managed to persuade him to take me to a football game (the Giants versus the Chicago Cardinals, at Yankee Stadium or the Polo Grounds, I forget which), he abruptly stood up from his seat in the middle of the fourth quarter and said, "It's time to go now." He wanted to "beat the crowd" and avoid getting stuck in traffic. Nothing I said could convince him to stay, and so we left, just like that, with the game going full tilt. Unearthly despair as I followed him down the concrete ramps, and then, even worse, in the parking lot, with the noise of the invisible crowd roaring behind me.

You could not trust him to know what you wanted, to anticipate what you might have been feeling. The fact that you had to tell him yourself vitiated the pleasure in advance, disrupted a dreamed-of harmony before a note could be played. And then, even if you did tell him, it was not at all sure that he would understand what you meant.

* * *

I remember a day very like today. A drizzling Sunday, lethargy and quiet in the house: the world at half-speed. My father was taking a nap, or had just awoken from one, and somehow I was on the bed with him, the two of us alone in the room. Tell me a story. It must have begun like that. And because he was not doing anything, because he was still drowsing in the languor of the afternoon, he did just what I asked, launching into a story without missing a beat. I remember it all so clearly. It seems as if I have just walked out of that room, with its gray light and tangle of quilts on the bed, as if, simply by closing my eyes, I could walk back into it any time I want.

He told me of his prospecting days in South America. It was a tale of high adventure, fraught with mortal dangers, hair-raising escapes, and improbable twists of fortune: hacking his way through the jungle with a machete, fighting off bandits with his bare hands, shooting his donkey when it broke its leg. His language was flowery and convoluted, probably an echo of the books he himself had read as a boy. But it was precisely this literary style that enchanted me. Not only was he telling me new things about himself, unveiling to me the world of his distant past, but he was telling it with new and strange words. This language was just as important as the story itself. It belonged to it, and in some sense was indistinguishable from it. Its very strangeness was proof of authenticity.

It did not occur to me to think this might have been a made-up story. For years afterward I went on believing it. Even when I had passed the point when I should have known better, I still felt there might have been some truth to it. It gave me something to hold on to about my father, and I was reluctant to let go. At last I had an explanation for his mysterious evasions, his indifference to me. He was a romantic figure, a man with a dark and exciting past, and his present life was only a kind of stopping place, a way of biding his time until he took off on his next adventure. He was working out his plan, figuring out how to retrieve the gold that lay buried deep in the heart of the Andes.

In the back of my mind: a desire to do something extraordinary, to impress him with an act of heroic proportions. The more aloof he was, the higher the stakes became for me. But if a boy's will is tenacious and idealistic, it is also absurdly practical. I was only ten years old, and there was no child for me to save from a burning building, no sailors to rescue at sea. On the other hand, I was a good baseball player, the star of my Little League team, and although my father had no interest in base-ball, I thought that if he saw me play, just once, he would begin to see me in a new light.

Finally he did come. My mother's parents were visiting at the time, and my grandfather, a great baseball fan, showed up with him. It was a special Memorial Day game, and the seats were full. If I was ever going to do something remarkable, this was the moment to do it. I can remem-ber catching sight of them in the wooden bleachers, my father in a white shirt with no tie and my grandfather wearing a white handkerchief on his bald head to protect him from the sun—the whole scene in my mind now drenched in this dazzling white light.

It probably goes without saying that I made a mess of it. I got no hits, lost my poise in the field, could not have been more nervous. Of all the hundreds of games I played during my childhood, this one was the worst.

Afterwards, walking to the car with my father, he told me I had played a nice game. No I hadn't, I said, it was terrible. Well, you did your best, he answered. You can't do well every time.

It was not that he was trying to encourage me. Nor was he trying to be unkind. Rather, he was saying what one says on such occasions, as if automatically. They were the right words to say, and yet they were delivered without feeling, an exercise in decorum, uttered in the same abstracted tone of voice he would use almost twenty years later when he said, "A beautiful baby. Good luck with it." I could see that his mind was somewhere else.

In itself, this is not important. The important thing is this: I realized that even if I had done all the things I had hoped to do, his reaction would have been exactly the same. Whether I succeeded or failed did not essentially matter to him. I was not defined for him by anything I did, but by what I was, and this meant that his perception of me would never change, that we were fixed in an unmoveable relationship, cut off from each other on opposite sides of a wall. Even more than that, I realized that none of this had anything to do with me. It had only to do with him. Like everything else in his life, he saw me only through the mists of his solitude, as if at several removes from himself. The world was a distant place for him, I think, a place he was never truly able to enter, and out there in the distance, among all the shadows that flitted past him, I was born, became his son, and grew up, as if I were just one more shadow, appearing and disappearing in a half-lit realm of his consciousness.

* * *

With his daughter, born when I was three and a half, it was somewhat easier for him. But in the end it was infinitely more difficult.

She was a beautiful child. Uncommonly fragile, with great brown eyes that would collapse into tears at the slightest prompting. She spent much of her time alone, a tiny figure wandering through an imaginary land of elves and fairies, dancing on tiptoe in lace-trimmed ballerina costumes, singing in a voice loud enough to be heard only by herself. She was a miniature Ophelia, already doomed, it would seem, to a life of constant inner struggle. She made few friends, had trouble keeping up in school, and was harassed by self-doubts, even at a very young age, that turned the simplest routines into nightmares of anguish and defeat. There were tantrums, fits of terrible crying, constant upheavals. Nothing ever seemed to go well for very long.

More sensitive to the nuances of the unhappy marriage around us than I was, her insecurity became monumental, crippling. At least once a day she would ask our mother if "she loved daddy." The answer was always the same: Of course I do.

It could not have been a very convincing lie. If it had been, there would not have been any need to ask the question again the next day.

On the other hand, it is difficult to see how the truth would have made things any better.

It was almost as if she gave off a scent of helplessness. One's immediate impulse was to protect her, to buffer her against the assaults of the world. Like everyone else, my father pampered her. The more she seemed to cry out for coddling, the more willing he was to give it to her. Long after she was able to walk, for example, he insisted on carrying her down the stairs. There is no question that he did it out of love, did it gladly because she was his little angel. But underneath this coddling was the implicit message that she would never be able to do anything for herself. She was not a person to him, but an angel, and because she was never compelled to act as an autonomous being, she could never become one.

My mother, however, saw what was happening. When my sister was five years old, she took her to an exploratory consultation with a child psychiatrist, and the doctor recommended that some form of therapy be started. That night, when my mother told my father the results of the meeting, he exploded in a violent rage. No daughter of mine, etc. The idea that his daughter needed psychiatric help was no different from being told she was a leper. He would not accept it. He would not even discuss it.

This is the point I am trying to make. His refusal to look into himself was matched by an equally stubborn refusal to look at the world, to accept even the most incontrovertible evidence it thrust under his nose. Again and again throughout his life he would stare a thing in the face, nod his head, and then turn around and say it was not there. It made conversation with him almost impossible. By the time you had managed to establish a common ground with him, he would take out his shovel and dig it out from under your feet.

Years later, when my sister suffered through a series of debilitating mental breakdowns, my father continued to believe there was nothing wrong with her. It was as though he were biologically unable to recognize her condition.

In one of his books R.D. Laing describes the father of a catatonic girl who on each visit to her in the hospital would grab her by the shoulders and shake her as hard as he could, telling her to "snap out of it." My father did not grab hold of my sister, but his attitude was essentially the same. What she needs, he would say, is to get a job, to clean herself up, to start living in the real world. Of course she did. But that was exactly what she could not do. She's just sensitive, he would say, she needs to overcome her shyness. By domesticating the problem to a quirk of personality, he could go on believing there was nothing wrong. It was not blindness so much as a failure of imagination. At what moment does a house stop being a house? When the roof is taken off? When the windows are removed? When the walls are knocked down? At what moment does it become a pile of rubble? She's just different, he would say, there's nothing wrong with her. And then one day the walls of your house finally collapse. If the door is still standing, however, all you have to do is walk through it, and you are back inside. It's pleasant sleeping out under the stars. Never mind the rain. It can't last very long.

Little by little, as the situation continued to get worse, he had to begin to accept it. But even then, at each stage along the way, his acceptance was unorthodox, taking on eccentric, almost self-nullifying forms. He became convinced, for example, that the one thing that could help her was a crash program in mega-vitamin therapy. This was the chemical approach to mental illness. Although it has never been proven to be an effective cure, this method of treatment has quite a large following. One can see why it would have attracted my father. Instead of having to wrestle with a devastating emotional fact, he could look upon the disease as a physical flaw, something that could be cured in the same way you cure the flu. The disease became an external force, a kind of bug that could be eradicated with an equal and opposite external force. In his eyes my sister was able to remain curiously untouched by all this. She was merely the *site* where the battle would take place, which meant that everything that was happening did not really affect *her*.

He spent several months trying to persuade her to begin this megavitamin program—even going so far as to take the pills himself, in order to prove that she would not be poisoned—and when at last she gave in, she did not take the pills for more than a week or two. The vitamins were expensive, but he did not balk at spending the money. On the other hand, he angrily resisted paying for other kinds of treatment. He did not believe that a stranger could possibly care about what happened to her. Psychiatrists were all charlatans, interested only in soaking their patients and driving fancy cars. He refused to pay the bills, which limited her to the shabbiest kind of public care. She was a pauper, with no income of her own, but he sent her almost nothing.

He was more than willing to take things into his own hands, however. Although it could not benefit either one of them, he wanted her to live in his house so that he could be the one responsible for looking after her. At least he could trust his own feelings, and he knew that he cared. But then, when she did come (for a few months, following one of her stays in the hospital), he did not disrupt his normal routine to accommodate her—but continued to spend most of his time out, leaving her to rattle around the enormous house like a ghost.

He was negligent and stubborn. But still, underneath it all, I know he suffered. Sometimes, on the phone, when he and I were discussing my sister, I could hear his voice break ever so slightly, as if he were trying to muffle a sob. Unlike everything else he ever came up against, my sister's illness finally *moved him*—but only to leave him with a feeling of utter helplessness. There is no greater sorrow for a parent than this helplessness. You have to accept it, even if you can't. And the more you accept it, the greater your despair becomes.

His despair became very great.

Wandering through the house today, without purpose, depressed, feeling that I have begun to lose touch with what I am writing, I chanced upon these words from a letter by Van Gogh: "Like everyone else, I feel the need of family and friendship, affection and friendly intercourse. I am not made of stone or iron, like a hydrant or a lamp-post."

Perhaps this is what really counts: to arrive at the core of human feeling, in spite of the evidence.

These tiniest of images: incorrigible, lodged in the mud of memory, neither buried nor wholly retrievable. And yet each one, in itself, a fleeting resurrection, a moment otherwise lost. The way he walked, for example, weirdly balanced, bouncing on the balls of his feet, as if he were about to pitch forward, blindly, into the unknown. Or the way he hunched over the table as he ate, his shoulders tensed, always merely consuming the food, never savoring it. Or else the smells that emanated from the cars he used for work: fumes, leaking oil, exhaust; the clutter of cold metal tools; the constant rattle as the car moved. A memory of the day I went driving with him through downtown Newark, no more than six years old, and he slammed down on the brakes, the jolt of it flinging my head against the dashboard: the sudden swarm of black people around the car to see if I was all right, especially the woman who thrust a vanilla ice cream cone at me through the open window, and my saying "no thank you," very politely, too stunned to know what I really wanted. Or else another day in another car, some years later, when my father spat out the window only to realize that the window had not been lowered, and my boundless, irrational delight at seeing the saliva slither down the glass. And still, as a little boy, how he would sometimes take me with him to Jewish restaurants in neighborhoods I had never seen before, dark places filled with old people, each table graced with a tinted blue seltzer bottle, and how I would grow queasy, leave my food untouched, and content myself with watching him wolf down borscht, pirogen, and boiled meats covered with horse radish. I, who was being brought up as an American boy, who knew less about my ancestors than I did about Hopalong Cassidy's hat. Or how, when I was twelve or thirteen, and wanted desperately to go somewhere with a couple of my friends, I called him at work to get his permission, and he said to me, at a loss, not knowing how to put it, "You're just a bunch of greenhorns," and how, for years afterward, my friends and I (one of them now dead, of a heroin overdose) would repeat those words as a piece of folklore, a nostalgic joke.

*   *   *

The size of his hands. Their calluses.

Eating the skin off the top of hot chocolate.

Tea with lemon.

The pairs of black, horn-rimmed glasses scattered through the house: on kitchen counters, on table tops, at the edge of the bathroom sink— always open, lying there like some strange, unclassified form of animal.

Watching him play tennis.

The way his knees sometimes buckled when he walked.

His face.

His resemblance to Abraham Lincoln, and how people always remarked on it.

His fearlessness with dogs.

His face. And again, his face.

Tropical fish.

Often, he seemed to lose his concentration, to forget where he was, as if he had lost the sense of his own continuity. It made him accident prone: smashed thumbnails from using a hammer, numerous little accidents in the car.

His absent-mindedness as a driver: to the point that it sometimes became frightening. I always thought it would be a car that did him in.

Otherwise, his health was so good that he seemed invulnerable, exempt from the physical ills that strike all the rest of us. As though nothing could ever touch him.

The way he spoke: as if making a great effort to rise up out of his solitude, as if his voice were rusty, had lost the habit of speaking. He always hemmed and hawed a lot, cleared his throat, seemed to sputter in mid-sentence. You felt, very definitely, that he was uncomfortable.

In the same way, it always amused me as a child to watch him sign his name. He could not simply put the pen against the paper and write. As if unconsciously delaying the moment of truth, he would always make a slight, preliminary flourish, a circular movement an inch or two off the page, like a fly buzzing in the air and zeroing in on its spot, before he could get down to business. It was a modified version of the way Art Carney's Norton used to sign his name on *The Honeymooners*.

He even pronounced his words a little oddly. "Upown," for example, instead of "upon," as if the flourish of his hand had its counterpart in his voice. There was a musical, airy quality to it. Whenever he answered the phone, it was a lilting "hellooo" that greeted you. The effect was not so much funny as endearing. It made him seem slightly daft, as if he were out of phase with the rest of the world—but not by much. Just a degree or two.

Indelible tics.

In those crazy, tensed-up moods he sometimes got into, he would always come out with bizarre opinions, not really taking them seriously, but happy to play devil's advocate in order to keep things lively. Teasing people put him in buoyant spirits, and after a particularly inane remark to someone he would often squeeze that person's leg—in a spot that always tickled. He literally liked to pull your leg.

Again the house.

No matter how negligent his care of it might have seemed from the outside, he believed in his system. Like a mad inventor protecting the secret of his perpetual motion machine, he would suffer no one to tamper with it. Once, when my wife and I were between apartments, we stayed in his house for three or four weeks. Finding the darkness of the house oppressive, we raised all the shades to let in the daylight. When my father returned home from work and saw what we had done, he flew into an uncontrollable rage, far out of proportion to any offense that might have been committed.

Anger of this sort rarely came out of him—only when he felt himself cornered, impinged upon, crushed by the presences of others. Money questions sometimes triggered it off. Or else some minor detail: the shades of his house, a broken plate, a little nothing at all.

Nevertheless, this anger was inside him—I believe constantly. Like the house that was well ordered and yet falling apart from within, the man himself was calm, almost supernatural in his imperturbability, and yet prey to a roiling, unstoppable force of fury within. All his life he strove to avoid a confrontation with this force, nurturing a kind of automatic behavior that would allow him to pass to the side of it. Reliance on fixed routines freed him from the necessity of looking into himself when decisions had to be made; the cliché was always quick to come to his lips ("A beautiful baby. Good luck with it") instead of words he had gone out and looked for. All this tended to flatten him out as a personality. But at the same time, it was also what saved him, the thing that allowed him to live. To the extent that he was able to live.

From a bag of loose pictures: a trick photograph taken in an Atlantic City studio sometime during the Forties. There are several of him sitting around a table, each image shot from a different angle, so that at first you think it must be a group of several different men. Because of the gloom that surrounds them, because of the utter stillness of their poses, it looks as if they have gathered there to conduct a seance. And then, as you study the picture, you begin to realize that all these men are the same man. The seance becomes a real seance, and it is as if he has come there only to invoke himself, to bring himself back from the dead, as if, by multiplying himself, he had inadvertently made himself disappear. There are five of him there, and yet the nature of the trick photography denies the possibility of eye contact among the various selves. Each one is condemned to go on staring into space, as if under the gaze of the others, but seeing nothing, never able to see anything. It is a picture of death, a portrait of an invisible man.

Slowly, I am coming to understand the absurdity of the task I have set for myself. I have a sense of trying to go somewhere, as if I knew what I wanted to say, but the farther I go the more certain I am that the path toward my object does not exist. I have to invent the road with each step, and this means that I can never be sure of where I am. A feeling of moving around in circles, of perpetual back-tracking, of going off in many directions at once. And even if I do manage to make some progress, I am not at all convinced that it will take me to where I think I am going. Just because you wander in the desert, it does not mean there is a promised land.

When I first started, I thought it would come spontaneously, in a trance-like outpouring. So great was my need to write that I thought the story would be written by itself. But the words have come very slowly so far. Even on the best days I have not been able to write more than a page or two. I seem to be afflicted, cursed by some failure of mind to concentrate on what I am doing. Again and again I have watched my thoughts trail off from the thing in front of me. No sooner have I thought one thing than it evokes another thing, and then another thing, until there is an accumulation of detail so dense that I feel I am going to suffocate. Never before have I been so aware of the rift between

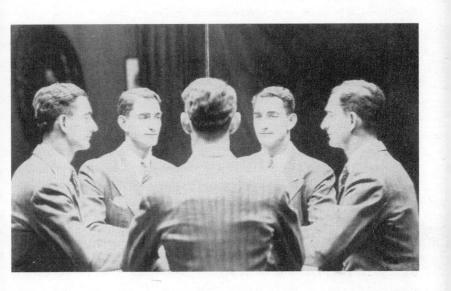

thinking and writing. For the past few days, in fact, I have begun to feel that the story I am trying to tell is somehow incompatible with language, that the degree to which it resists language is an exact measure of how closely I have come to saying something important, and that when the moment arrives for me to say the one truly important thing (assuming it exists), I will not be able to say it.

There has been a wound, and I realize now that it is very deep. Instead of healing me as I thought it would, the act of writing has kept this wound open. At times I have even felt the pain of it concentrated in my right hand, as if each time I picked up the pen and pressed it against the page, my hand were being torn apart. Instead of burying my father for me, these words have kept him alive, perhaps more so than ever. I not only see him as he was, but as he is, as he will be, and each day he is there, invading my thoughts, stealing up on me without warning: lying in the coffin underground, his body still intact, his fingernails and hair continuing to grow. A feeling that if I am to understand anything, I must penetrate this image of darkness, that I must enter the absolute darkness of earth.

Kenosha, Wisconsin. 1911 or 1912. Not even he was sure of the date. In the confusion of a large, immigrant family, birth records could not have been considered very important. What matters is that he was the last of five surviving children—a girl and four boys, all born within a span of eight years—and that his mother, a tiny, ferocious woman who could barely speak English, held the family together. She was the matriarch, the absolute dictator, the prime mover who stood at the center of the universe.

His father died in 1919, which meant that except for his earliest childhood he had no father. During my own childhood he told me three different stories about his father's death. In one version, he had been killed in a hunting accident. In another, he had fallen off a ladder. In the third, he had been shot down during the First World War. I knew these contradictions made no sense, but I assumed this meant that not even my father knew the facts. Because he had been so young when it happened—only seven—I figured that he had never been given the exact story. But then, this made no sense either. One of his brothers surely would have told him.

All my cousins, however, told me that they, too, had been given different explanations by their fathers.

No one ever talked about my grandfather. Until a few years ago, I had

never seen a picture of him. It was as though the family had decided to pretend he had never existed.

Among the photographs I found in my father's house last month there was one family portrait from those early days in Kenosha. All the children are there. My father, no more than a year old, is sitting on his mother's lap, and the other four are standing around her in the tall, uncut grass. There are two trees behind them and a large wooden house behind the trees. A whole world seems to emerge from this portrait: a distinct time, a distinct place, an indestructible sense of the past. The first time I looked at the picture, I noticed that it had been torn down the middle and then clumsily mended, leaving one of the trees in the background hanging eerily in mid-air. I assumed the picture had been torn by accident and thought no more about it. The second time I looked at it, however, I studied this tear more closely and discovered things I must have been blind to miss before. I saw a man's fingertips grasping the torso of one of my uncles; I saw, very distinctly, that another of my uncles was not resting his hand on his brother's back, as I had first thought, but against a chair that was not there. And then I realized what was strange about the picture: my grandfather had been cut out of it. The image was distorted because part of it had been eliminated. My grandfather had been sitting in a chair next to his wife with one of his sons standing between his knees—and he was not there. Only his fingertips remained: as if he were trying to crawl back into the picture from some hole deep in time, as if he had been exiled to another dimension.

The whole thing made me shake.

I learned the story of my grandfather's death some time ago. If not for an extraordinary coincidence, it never would have become known.

In 1970 one of my cousins went to Europe on a vacation with her husband. On the plane she found herself sitting next to an old man and, as people often do, they struck up a conversation to pass the time. It turned out that his man lived in Kenosha, Wisconsin. My cousin was amused by the coincidence and remarked that her father had lived there as a boy. Out of curiosity, the man asked her the name of her family. When she told him Auster, he turned pale. Auster? Your grandmother wasn't a crazy little woman with red hair, was she? Yes, that was my grandmother, my cousin answered. A crazy little woman with red hair.

And then he told her the story. It had happened more than fifty years before, and yet he still remembered the important details.

When this man returned home from his vacation, he tracked down the newspaper articles connected with the story, had them photocopied, and sent them to my cousin. This was his cover letter:

June 15, 70

Dear —— and —— .

It was good to get your letter, and altho it did look like the task might be complicated, I had a stroke of luck.—Fran and I went out to dinner with a Fred Plons and his wife, and it was Fred's father who had bought the apartment bldg on Park Ave from your family.— Mr. Plons is about three years younger than myself, but he claimed that the case (at that time) fascinated him and he remembered quite a few details.—He stated that your grandfather was the first person to be buried in the Jewish Cemetery here in Kenosha.—(Previous to 1919 the Jewish people had no cemetery in Kenosha, but had their loved ones buried either in Chicago or Milwaukee.) With this information, I had no trouble locating the plot where your grandfather is buried.—And I was able to pin point the date. The rest is in the copy I am forwarding to you.—

I only ask that your father should never learn of this knowledge that I am passing on to you—I would not want him to have any more grief than he already has suffered . . .

I hope that this will shed some light on your Father's actions over the past years.

Our fondest regards to you both—
    Ken & Fran

The newspaper articles are sitting on my desk. Now that the moment has come to write about them, I am surprised to find myself doing everything I can to put it off. All morning I have procrastinated. I have taken the trash to the dump. I have played with Daniel in the yard for almost an hour. I have read the entire newspaper—right down to the line scores of the spring training baseball games. Even now, as I write about my reluctance to write, I find myself impossibly restless: after every few words I pop up from my chair, pace the floor, listen to the wind outside as it bangs the loose gutters against the house. The least thing is able to distract me.

It is not that I am afraid of the truth. I am not even afraid to say it. My grandmother murdered my grandfather. On January 23, 1919, precisely sixty years before my father died, his mother shot and killed his father in the kitchen of their house on Fremont Avenue in Kenosha, Wisconsin. The facts themselves do not disturb me any more than might be expected. The difficult thing is to see them in print—unburied, so to speak, from the realm of secrets and turned into a public event. There are more than twenty articles, most of them long, all of them from the

Kenosha Evening News. Even in this barely legible state, almost totally obscured by age and the hazards of photocopying, they still have the ability to shock. I assume they are typical of the journalism of the time, but that does not make them any less sensational. They are a mixture of scandalmongering and sentimentality, heightened by the fact that the people involved were Jews—and therefore strange, almost by definition—which gives the whole account a leering, condescending tone. And yet, granted the flaws in style, the facts seem to be there. I do not think they explain everything, but there is no question that they explain a great deal. A boy cannot live through this kind of thing without being affected by it as a man.

In the margins of these articles, I can just manage to decipher some of the smaller news stories of that time, events that were relegated to near insignificance in comparison to the murder. For example: the recovery of Rosa Luxemburg's body from the Landwehr Canal. For example: the Versailles peace conference. And on and on, day after day, through the following: the Eugene Debs case; a note on Caruso's first film ("The situations . . . are said to be highly dramatic and filled with stirring heart appeal"); battle reports from the Russian Civil War; the funerals of Karl Liebnecht and thirty-one other Spartacists ("More than fifty thousand persons marched in the procession which was five miles long. Fully twenty percent of these bore wreaths. There was no shouting or cheering"); the ratification of the national prohibition amendment ("William Jennings Bryan—the man who made grape juice famous—was there with a broad smile"); the textile strike in Lawrence, Massachusetts, led by the Wobblies; the death of Emiliano Zapata, "bandit leader in southern Mexico"; Winston Churchill; Bela Kun; Premier Lenine (sic); Woodrow Wilson; Dempsey versus Willard.

I have read through the articles about the murder a dozen times. Still, I find it hard to believe that I did not dream them. They loom up at me with all the force of a trick of the unconscious, distorting reality in the same way dreams do. Because the huge headlines announcing the murder dwarf everything else that happened in the world that day, they give the event the same egocentric importance we give to the things that happen in our private lives. It is almost like the drawing a child makes when he is troubled by some inexpressible fear: the most important thing is always the biggest thing. Perspective is lost in favor of proportion—which is dictated not by the eye but by the demands of the mind.

I read these articles as history. But also as a cave drawing discovered on the inner walls of my own skull.

The headlines on the first day, January 24, cover more than a third of the front page.

HARRY AUSTER KILLED
WIFE HELD BY POLICE

Former Prominent Real Estate Operator is Shot to Death
in the Kitchen of the Home of His Wife
On Thursday Night Following a Family
Wrangle Over Money—and a Woman.

WIFE SAYS HUSBAND WAS A SUICIDE

Dead Man Had Bullet Wound in His Neck and in the Left Hip
and Wife Admits That Revolver With Which the Shooting Was
Done Was Her Property—Nine-Year-Old Son, Witness of the
Tragedy, May Hold Solution to the Mystery.

According to the newspaper, "Auster and his wife had separated some time ago and an action for divorce was pending in the Circuit Court for Kenosha county. They had had trouble on several occasions over money. They had also quarreled over the fact that Auster [illegible] friendly with a young woman known to the wife as 'Fanny.' It is believed that 'Fanny' figured in the trouble between Auster and his wife immediately preceding the shooting. . . ."

Because my grandmother did not confess until the twenty-eighth, there was some confusion about what really happened. My grandfather (who was thirty-six years old) arrived at the house at six o'clock in the evening with "suits of clothing" for his two oldest sons "while it was stated by witnesses Mrs. Auster was in the bedroom putting Sam, the youngest boy, into bed. Sam [my father] declared that he did not see his mother take a revolver from under the mattress as he was tucked into bed for the night."

It seems that my grandfather had then gone into the kitchen to repair an electric switch and that one of my uncles (the second youngest son) had held a candle for him to see by. "The boy declared that he became panic stricken when he heard the shot and saw a flash of a revolver and

33

fled the room." According to my grandmother, her husband had shot himself. She admitted they had been arguing about money, and "then he said, she continued, 'there is going to be an end for you or me,' and he threatened me. I did not know he had the revolver. I had kept it under the mattress of my bed and he knew it."

Since my grandmother spoke almost no English, I assume that this statement, and all others attributed to her, was invented by the reporter. Whatever it was she said, the police did not believe her. "Mrs. Auster repeated her story to the various police officers without making any decided change in it and she professed great surprise when she was told that she was to be held by the police. With a great deal of tenderness she kissed little Sam good night and then went off to the county jail.

"The two Auster boys were guests of the police department last night sleeping in the squad room and this morning the boys were apparently entirely recovered from any fright they had suffered as a result of the tragedy at their home."

Toward the end of the article, this information is given about my grandfather. "Harry Auster was a native of Austria. He came to this country a number of years ago and had resided in Chicago, in Canada, and in Kenosha. He and his wife, according to the story told the police, later returned to Austria but she rejoined her husband in this country about the time they came to Kenosha. Auster bought a number of homes in the second ward and for some time his operations were on a large scale. He built the big triple flat building on South Park avenue and another one known as the Auster flats on South Exchange street. Six or eight months ago he met with financial reverses. . . .

"Some time ago Mrs. Auster appealed to the police to aid her in watching Mr. Auster as she alleged that he had relations with a young woman which she believed should be investigated. It was in this way that the police first learned of the woman 'Fanny'. . . .

"Many people had seen and talked with Auster on Thursday afternoon and these people all declared that he appeared to be normal and that he showed no signs of desiring to take his own life. . . ."

The next day was the coroner's inquest. My uncle, as the only witness to the incident, was called on to testify. "A sad-eyed little boy, nervously twirling his stocking cap, wrote the second chapter in the Auster murder mystery Friday afternoon. . . . His attempts to save the family name were tragically pathetic. Again and again when asked if his parents were quarrelling he would answer 'They were just talking' until at last, apparently remembering his oath, he added 'and maybe quarrelling—well just a little bit.' " The article describes the jurors as "weirdly stirred by the boy's efforts to shield both his father and his mother."

The idea of suicide was clearly not going to wash. In the last paragraph the reporter writes that "developments of a startling nature have been hinted by officials."

Then came the funeral. It gave the anonymous reporter an opportunity to emulate some of the choicest diction of Victorian melodrama. By now the murder was no longer merely a scandal. It had been turned into a stirring entertainment.

WIDOW TEARLESS AT AUSTER GRAVE

Mrs. Anna Auster Under Guard Attends Funeral of Husband, Harry Auster, Sunday.

"Dry-eyed and without the least sign of emotion or grief, Mrs. Harry Auster, who is held here in connection with the mysterious death of her husband, Harry Auster, attended Sunday morning, under guard, the funeral services of the man, in connection with whose death she is being held.

"Neither at the Crossin Chapel, where she looked for the first time since Thursday night upon the dead face of her husband nor at the burial ground did she show the least sign of weakening. The only intimation which she gave of breaking under the terrific strain of the ordeal was when over the grave, after the obsequies were finished, she asked for a conference this afternoon with the Rev. M. Hartman, pastor of the B'nai Zadek Congregation. . . .

"When the rites were completed Mrs. Auster calmly tightened the fox fur collar more closely about her throat and signified to the police that she was ready to leave. . . .

"After short ritualistic ceremonies the funeral procession was formed on Wisconsin street. Mrs. Auster asked that she also be allowed to go to the burial ground and the request was granted readily by the police. She seemed very petulant over the fact that no carriage had been provided for her, perhaps remembering that short season of apparent wealth when the Auster limousine was seen in Kenosha. . . .

"... The ordeal was made exceptionally long because some delay had occurred in the preparation of the grave and while she waited she called Sam, the youngest boy, to her, and tucked his coat collar more closely around his neck. She spoke quietly to him but with this exception she was silent until after the rites were finished. ...

"A prominent figure at the funeral was Samuel Auster, of Detroit, the brother of Harry Auster. He took as his especial care the younger children and attempted to console them in their grief.

"In speeches and demonstrations Auster appeared very bitter about his brother's death. He showed clearly that he disbelieved the theory of suicide and uttered remarks which savoured of accusations of the widow. ...

"The Rev. M. Hartman ... preached an eloquent sermon at the grave. He lamented the fact that the first person to be buried in the new cemetery should be one who had died by violence and who had been killed in his prime. He paid tribute to the enterprise of Harry Auster but deplored his early death.

"The widow appeared to be unmoved by the tributes paid to her dead husband. She indifferently opened her coat to allow the patriarch to cut a gash in her knitted sweater, a token of grief prescribed by the Hebrew faith.

"Officials in Kenosha fail to give up the suspicion that Auster was killed by his wife. ..."

The paper of the following day, January 26th, carried the news of the confession. After her meeting with the rabbi, she had requested a conference with the chief of police. "When she entered the room she trembled a little and was plainly agitated as the chief provided a chair. 'You know what your little boy told us,' the latter began when he realized that the psychological moment had come. 'You don't want us to think that he's lying to us, do you?' And the mother, whose face has been for days so masked as to reveal nothing of the horror hidden behind it, tore off the camouflage, became suddenly tender, and sobbed out her awful secret. 'He isn't lying to you at all; everything he has said is true. I shot him and I want to make a confession.' "

This was her formal statement: "My name is Anna Auster. I shot Harry Auster at the city of Kenosha, Wisconsin on the 23rd day of January A.D. 1919. I have heard people remark that three shots were fired, but I do not remember how many shots were fired that day. My reason for shooting the said Harry Auster is on account of the fact that he, the said Harry Auster, abused me. I was just like crazy when I shot the said Harry Auster. I never thought of shooting him, the said Harry Auster, until the moment I shot him. I think that this is the gun I shot the said Harry Auster with. I make this statement of my own free will and without being forced to do so."

The reporter continues, "On the table before Mrs. Auster lay the revolver with which her husband was shot to death. As she spoke of it she touched it falteringly and then drew her hand back with a noticeable tremor of horror. Without speaking the chief laid the gun aside and asked Mrs. Auster if there was more she cared to say.

" 'That's all for now,' she replied composedly. 'You sign it for me and I'll make my mark.'

"Her orders—for a little moment she was almost regal again—were obeyed, she acknowledged the signature, and asked to be returned to her cell . . ."

At the arraignment the next day a plea of not guilty was entered by her attorney. "Muffled in a plush coat and a boa of fox fur, Mrs. Auster entered the court room. . . . She smiled at a friend in the crowd as she took her seat before the desk."

By the reporter's own admission, the hearing was "uneventful." But still, he could not resist making this observation: "An incident occurred upon her return to her barred room which furnished a commentary on Mrs. Auster's state of mind.

"A woman, held on a charge of association with a married man, had been brought to the jail for incarceration in an adjoining cell. Upon seeing her, Mrs. Auster asked about the newcomer and learned the particulars in the case.

" 'She ought to get ten years,' she said as the iron door clanged pitilessly. 'It was one of her kind that put me here.' "

After some intricate legal discussions concerning bail that were elaborately reported for the next few days, she was set free. " 'Have you any notion that this woman will not appear for trial?' the court asked the attorneys. It was attorney Baker who answered: 'Where could a woman with five children like these go? She clings to them and the court can see that they cling to her.' "

For a week the press was quiet. Then, on February 8th, there was a story about "the active support that the cause is being given by some of the papers published in the Jewish language in Chicago. Some of these papers contained columns arguing the case of Mrs. Auster and it is declared that these articles have strongly urged her defense . . .

"Friday afternoon Mrs. Auster with one of her children sat in the office of her attorney while portions of these articles were read. She sobbed like a child as the interpreter read to the attorney the contents of these papers . . .

"Attorney Baker declared this morning that the defense of Mrs. Auster would be one of emotional insanity . . .

"It is expected that the trial of Mrs. Auster will be one of the most interesting murder trials ever tried in the Circuit Court for Kenosha county and the human interest story that has been featured in the defense of the woman up to this time is expected to be largely developed at the trial."

Then nothing for a month. On March 10th the headlines read:

ANNA AUSTER TRIED SUICIDE

The suicide attempt had taken place in Peterboro, Ontario in 1910—by taking carbolic acid and then turning on the gas. The attorney brought this information before the court in order to be granted a delay in the trial so that he would have enough time to secure affidavits. "Attorney Baker held that at the same time the woman had endangered the lives of two of her children and that the story of the attempted suicide was important in that it would show the mental condition of Mrs. Auster."

March 27th. The trial was set for April 7th. After that, another week of silence. And then, on April 4th, as if things had been getting just a bit too dull, a new development.

AUSTER SHOOTS BROTHER'S WIDOW

"Sam Auster, brother of Harry Auster . . . made an unsuccessful attempt to avenge the death of his brother just after ten o'clock this morning when he shot at Mrs. Auster. . . . The shooting occurred just outside the Miller Grocery Store. . . .

"Auster followed Mrs. Auster outside the door and fired once at her. Mrs. Auster, though she was not struck by the shot, fell to the sidewalk and Auster returned to the store declaring according to witnesses, 'Well, I'm glad I done that.' There he calmly awaited arrest. . . .

"At the police station . . . Auster, entirely broken down nervously, gave his explanation of the shooting.

" 'That woman,' he said, 'has killed my four brothers and my mother. I've tried to help but she won't let me.' Then as he was being led down to the cell, he sobbed out, 'God's going to take my part though, I know that.'

"At his cell Auster declared that he had tried everything within his power to help the children of his dead brother. The fact that the court had refused to appoint him administrator for the estate because they declared that the widow had some rights in the case had preyed on his mind recently. . . . 'She's no widow,' he commented on that incident this morning. 'She is a murderer and should have no rights. . . .'

"Auster will not be arraigned immediately in order to make a thorough investigation of the case. The police admit that the death of his brother and subsequent events may have so preyed on his mind that he was not entirely responsible for his deed. Auster expressed several times a hope that he should die too and every precaution is being taken to prevent him from taking his own life. . . ."

The next day's paper had this to add: "Auster spent a rather troublesome night in the city lockup. Several times the officers found him sobbing in the cell and he appeared to be hysterical. . . .

"It was admitted that Mrs. Auster had suffered from a 'bad case of nerves' as a result of the fright which had attended the attack on her life on Friday, but it was declared that she would be able to be in court when the case against her is called for trial on Monday evening."

After three days the state rested its case. Contending that the murder had been premeditated, the district attorney relied heavily on the testimony of a certain Mrs. Mathews, an employee at the Miller Grocery Store, who contended that "Mrs. Auster came to the store three times on the day of the shooting to use the telephone. On one of those occasions, the witness said, Mrs. Auster called up her husband and asked him to come to the house and fix a light. She said that Auster had promised to come at six o'clock."

But even if she invited him to the house, it does not mean that she intended to kill him once he was there.

It makes no difference anyway. Whatever the facts might have been, the defense attorney shrewdly turned everything to his own advantage. His strategy was to offer overwhelming evidence on two fronts: on the one hand, to prove infidelity on the part of my grandfather, and on the other, to demonstrate a history of mental instability on the part of my grandmother—the two of them combining to produce a case of justifiable homicide or homicide "by reason of insanity." Either one would do.

Attorney Baker's opening remarks were calculated to draw every possible ounce of sympathy from the jury. "He told how Mrs. Auster had toiled with her husband to build up the home and happiness which once was theirs in Kenosha after they had passed through years of hardships. . . . 'Then after they had labored together to build up this home,' continued Attorney Baker, 'there came this siren from the city and Anna Auster was cast aside like a rag. Instead of supplying food for his family, her husband kept Fanny Koplan in a flat in Chicago. The money which she had helped to accumulate was being lavished on a more beautiful woman and after such abuse is there any wonder that her mind was shattered and that for the moment she lost control of her senses.' "

The first witness for the defense was Mrs. Elizabeth Grossman, my grandmother's only sister, who lived on a farm near Brunswick, New Jersey. "She made a splendid witness. She told in a simple manner the whole story of the life of Mrs. Auster; of her birth in Austria; of the death of her mother when Mrs. Auster was but six years of age; of the trip with her sister to this country eight years later; of long hours served as a maker of hats and bonnets in New York millinery shops; of how by this work the immigrant girl accumulated a few hundred dollars. She told of the marriage of the woman to Auster just after she reached her twenty-third birthday and of their business ventures; of their failure in a little candy store and their long trip to Lawrence, Kas., where they attempted to start over and where——, the first child was born; of the return to New York and the second failure in business which ended in bankruptcy and the flight of Auster into Canada. She told of Mrs. Auster following Auster to Canada; of the desertion by Auster of the wife and little children and how he had said that he was 'going to make way with himself' [sic] and how he had told the wife that he was taking fifty dollars so that when he was dead it might be found on him and used to give him a decent burial. . . . She said that during their residence in Canada they were known as Mr. and Mrs. Harry Ball. . . .

"A little break in the story which could not be furnished by Mrs.

Grossman, was furnished by former Chief Constable Archie Moore and Abraham Low, both of Peterboro county, Canada. These men told of the departure of Auster from Peterboro and the grief of his wife. Auster, they said, left Peterboro July 14, 1909, and the following night Moore found Mrs. Auster in a room of their shabby home suffering from the effects of gas. She and the children lay on a mattress on the floor while the gas was flowing from four open jets. Moore told of the further fact that he had found a vial of carbolic acid in the room and that traces of the acid had been found on the lips of Mrs. Auster. She was taken to a hospital, the witness declared, and was ill for many days. Both of these men declared that in their opinion there was no doubt but that Mrs. Auster showed signs of insanity at the time she attempted her life in Canada."

Further witnesses included the two oldest children, each of whom chronicled the family's domestic troubles. Much was said about Fanny, and also the frequent squabbles at home. "He said that Auster had a habit of throwing dishes and glass ware and that at one time his mother's arm had been so badly cut that it was necessary to call a physician to attend her. He declared that his father used profane and indecent language toward his mother at these times. . . ."

Another witness from Chicago testified that she had frequently seen my grandmother beat her head against the wall in fits of mental anguish. A police officer from Kenosha told how at "one time he had seen Mrs. Auster running wildly down a street. He stated that her hair was 'more or less' dishevelled and added that she acted much like a woman who had lost her mind." A doctor was also called in, and he contended that she had been suffering from "acute mania."

My grandmother's testimony lasted three hours. "Between stifled sobs and recourse to tears, she told the story of her life with Auster up to the time of the 'accident'. . . . Mrs. Auster stood the ordeal of cross questioning very well, and her story was told over three times in almost the same way."

In his summation "Attorney Baker made a strong emotional plea for the release of Mrs. Auster. In a speech lasting nearly an hour and a half he retold in an eloquent manner the story of Mrs. Auster. . . . Several times Mrs. Auster was moved to tears by the statements of her attorney and women in the audience were sobbing several times as the attorney painted the picture of the struggling immigrant woman seeking to maintain their home."

The judge gave the jury the option of only two verdicts: guilty or innocent of murder. It took them less than two hours to make their decision. As the bulletin of April 12th put it: "At four thirty o'clock this afternoon the jury in the trial of Mrs. Anna Auster returned a verdict finding the defendant not guilty."

April 14th. " 'I am happier now than I have been for seventeen years,' said Mrs. Auster Saturday afternoon as she shook hands with each of the jurors following the return of the verdict. 'As long as Harry lived,' she said to one of them, 'I was worried. I never knew real happiness. Now I regret that he had to die by my hand. I am as happy now as I ever expect to be. . . .'

"As Mrs. Auster left the court room she was attended by her daughter . . . and the two younger children, who had waited patiently in the courtroom for the return of the verdict which freed their mother. . . .

"At the county jail Sam Auster . . . while he cannot understand it all, says he is willing to abide by the decision of the twelve jurors. . . .

" 'Last night when I heard of the verdict,' he said when interviewed on Sunday morning, 'I dropped on the floor. I could not believe that she could go clear free after killing my brother and her husband. It is all too big for me. I don't understand, but I shall let it go now. I tried once to settle it in my way and failed and I can't do anything now but accept what the court has said.' "

The next day he, too, was released. " 'I am going back to my work in the factory,' Auster told the District Attorney. 'Just as soon as I get money enough I am going to raise a head stone over the grave of my brother and then I am going to give my energies to the support of the children of one of my brothers who lived in Austria and who fell fighting in the Austrian army.'

"The conference this morning brought out the fact that Sam Auster is the last of the five Auster brothers. Three of the boys fought with the Austrian army in the world war and all of them fell in battle."

In the last paragraph of the last article about the case, the newspaper reports that "Mrs. Auster is now planning to take the children and leave for the east within a few days. . . . It was said that Mrs. Auster decided to take this action on the advice of her attorneys, who told her that she should go to some new home and start life without any one knowing the story of the trial."

* * *

It was, I suppose, a happy ending. At least for the newspaper readers of Kenosha, the clever Attorney Baker, and, no doubt, for my grandmother. Nothing further is said, of course, about the fortunes of the Auster family. The public record ends with this announcement of their departure for the east.

Because my father rarely spoke to me about the past, I learned very little about what followed. But from the few things he did mention, I was able to form a fairly good idea of the climate in which the family lived.

For example, they moved constantly. It was not uncommon for my father to attend two, or even three different schools in a single year. Because they had no money, life became a series of escapes from landlords and creditors. In a family that had already closed in on itself, this nomadism walled them off entirely. There were no enduring points of reference: no home, no town, no friends that could be counted on. Only the family itself. It was almost like living in quarantine.

My father was the baby, and for his whole life he continued to look up to his three older brothers. As a boy he was known as Sonny. He suffered from asthma and allergies, did well in school, played end on the football team, and ran the 440 for the track team at Central High in Newark. He graduated in the first year of the Depression, went to law school at night for a semester or two, and then dropped out, exactly as his brothers had done before him.

The four brothers stuck together. There was something almost medieval about their loyalty to one another. Although they had their differences, in many ways did not even like one another, I think of them not as four separate individuals but as a clan, a quadruplicate image of solidarity. Three of them—the youngest three—wound up as business partners and lived in the same town, and the fourth, who lived only two towns away, had been set up in business by the other three. There was scarcely a day that my father did not see his brothers. And that means for his entire life: every day for more than sixty years.

They picked up habits from each other, figures of speech, little gestures, intermingling to such a degree that it was impossible to tell which one had been the source of any given attitude or idea. My father's feelings were unbending: he never said a word against any of his brothers. Again, it was the other defined not by what he did but by what he was. If one of the brothers happened to slight him or do something objectionable, my father would nevertheless refuse to pass judgment. He's my brother, he would say, as if that explained everything. Brotherhood was the first principle, the unassailable postulate, the one and only article of faith. Like belief in God, to question it was heresy.

As the youngest, my father was the most loyal of the four and also the one least respected by the others. He worked the hardest, was the most generous to his nephews and nieces, and yet these things were never fully recognized, much less appreciated. My mother recalls that on the day of her wedding, at the party following the ceremony, one of the brothers actually propositioned her. Whether he would have carried through with the escapade is another matter. But the mere fact of teasing her like that gives a rough idea of how he felt about my father. You do not do that sort of thing on a man's wedding day, even if he is your brother.

At the center of the clan was my grandmother, a Jewish Mammy Yokum, a mother to end all mothers. Fierce, refractory, the boss. It was common loyalty to her that kept the brothers so close. Even as grown men, with wives and children of their own, they would faithfully go to her house every Friday night for dinner—without their families. This was the relationship that mattered, and it took precedence over everything else. There must have been something slightly comical about it: four big men, each one over six feet, waiting on a little old woman, more than a foot shorter than they were.

One of the few times they came with their wives, a neighbor happened to walk in and was surprised to find such a large gathering. Is this your family, Mrs. Auster? he asked. Yes, she answered, with great smiles of pride. This is —. This is —. This is —. And this is Sam. The neighbor was a little taken aback. And these lovely ladies, he asked. Who are they? Oh, she answered with a casual wave of the hand. That's —'s. That's —'s. That's —'s. And that's Sam's.

The picture painted of her in the Kenosha newspaper was by no means inaccurate. She lived for her children. (Attorney Baker: Where could a woman with five children like these go? She clings to them and the court can see that they cling to her.) At the same time, she was a tyrant, given to screaming and hysterical fits. When she was angry, she would beat her sons over the head with a broom. She demanded allegiance, and she got it.

Once, when my father had saved the huge sum of ten or twenty dollars from his newspaper route to buy himself a new bicycle, his mother walked into the room, cracked open his piggy bank, and took the money from him without so much as an apology. She needed the money to pay some bills, and my father had no recourse, no way to air his grievance. When he told me this story, his object was not to show how his mother wronged him but to demonstrate how the good of the family was always more important than the good of any of its members. He might have been unhappy, but he did not complain.

This was rule by caprice. For a child, it meant that the sky could fall on top of him at any moment, that he could never be sure of anything. Therefore, he learned never to trust anyone. Not even himself. Someone would always come along to prove that what he thought was wrong, that it did not count for anything. He learned never to want anything too much.

My father lived with his mother until he was older than I am now. He was the last one to go off on his own, the one who had been left behind to take care of her. It would be wrong to say, however, that he was a mother's boy. He was too independent, had been too fully indoctrinated into the ways of manhood by his brothers. He was good to her, was dutiful and considerate, but not without a certain distance, even humor. After he was married, she called him often, haranguing him about this and that. My father would put the receiver down on the table, walk to the other end of the room and busy himself with some chore for a few minutes, then return to the phone, pick it up, say something innocuous to let her know he was there (uh-huh, uh-huh, mmmmmm, that's right), and then wander off again, back and forth, until she had talked herself out.

The comical side of his obtuseness. And sometimes it served him very well.

I remember a tiny, shriveled creature sitting in the front parlor of a two-family house in the Weequahic section of Newark reading the *Jewish Daily Forward*. Although I knew I would have to do it whenever I saw her, it made me cringe to kiss her. Her face was so wrinkled, her skin so inhumanly soft. Worse than that was her smell—a smell I was much later able to identify as that of camphor, which she must have put in her bureau drawers and which, over the years, had seeped into the fabric of her clothes. This odor was inseparable in my mind from the idea of "grandma."

As far as I can remember, she took virtually no interest in me. The one time she gave me a present, it was a second- or third-hand children's book, a biography of Benjamin Franklin. I remember reading it all the way through and can even recall some of the episodes. Franklin's future wife, for example, laughing at him the first time she saw him—walking through the streets of Philadelphia with an enormous loaf of bread under his arm. The book had a blue cover and was illustrated with silhouettes. I must have been seven or eight at the time.

After my father died, I discovered a trunk that had once belonged to his mother in the cellar of his house. It was locked, and I decided to force it open with a hammer and screwdriver, thinking it might contain some buried secret, some long lost treasure. As the hasp fell down and I raised the lid, there it was, all over again—that smell, wafting up toward me, immediate, palpable, as if it had been my grandmother herself. I felt as though I had just opened her coffin.

There was nothing of interest in it: a set of carving knives, a heap of imitation jewelry. Also a hard plastic dress-up pocketbook, a kind of octagonal box with a handle on it. I gave the thing to Daniel, and he immediately started using it as a portable garage for his fleet of little trucks and cars.

My father worked hard all his life. At nine he had his first job. At eighteen he had a radio repair business with one of his brothers. Except for a brief moment when he was hired as an assistant in Thomas Edison's laboratory (only to have the job taken away from him the next day because Edison learned he was a Jew), my father never worked for anyone but himself. He was a very demanding boss, far more exacting than any stranger could have been.

The radio shop eventually led to a small appliance store, which in turn led to a large furniture store. From there he began to dabble in real estate (buying, for example, a house for his mother to live in), until this gradually displaced the store as the focus of his attention and became a business in its own right. The partnership with two of his brothers carried over from one thing to the next.

Up early every morning, home late at night, and in between, work, nothing but work. Work was the name of the country he lived in, and he was one of its greatest patriots. That is not to say, however, that work was pleasure for him. He worked hard because he wanted to earn as much money as possible. Work was a means to an end—a means to money. But the end was not something that could bring him pleasure either. As the young Marx wrote: "If *money* is the bond binding me to *human life*, binding society to me, binding me and nature and man, is not money the bond of all *bonds*? Can it not dissolve and bind all ties? Is it not, therefore, the universal *agent of separation*?"

He dreamed all his life of becoming a millionaire, of being the richest man in the world. It was not so much the money itself he wanted, but what it represented: not merely success in the eyes of the world, but a way of making himself untouchable. Having money means more than being able to buy things: it means that the world need never affect you. Money in the sense of protection, then, not pleasure. Having been without money as a child, and therefore vulnerable to the whims of the world, the idea of wealth became synonymous for him with the idea of escape: from harm, from suffering, from being a victim. He was not trying to buy happiness, but simply an absence of unhappiness. Money was the panacea, the objectification of his deepest, most inexpressible desires as a human being. He did not want to spend it, he wanted to have it, to know that it was there. Money not as an elixir, then, but as an antidote: the small vial of medicine you carry in your pocket when you go out into the jungle—just in case you are bitten by a poisonous snake.

At times, his reluctance to spend money was so great it almost resembled a disease. It never came to such a point that he would deny himself what he needed (for his needs were minimal), but more subtly, each time he had to buy something, he would opt for the cheapest solution. This was bargain shopping as a way of life.

Implicit in this attitude was a kind of perceptual primitivism. All distinctions were eliminated, everything was reduced to its least common denominator. Meat was meat, shoes were shoes, a pen was a pen. It did not matter that you could choose between chuck and porterhouse, that there were throwaway ball points for thirty-nine cents and fifty-dollar fountain pens that would last for twenty years. The truly fine object was almost to be abhorred: it meant that you would have to pay an extravagant price, and that made it morally unsound. On a more general level, this translated itself into a permanent state of sensory deprivation: by closing his eyes to so much, he denied himself intimate contact with the shapes and textures of the world, cut himself off from the possibility of experiencing aesthetic pleasure. The world he looked out on was a practical place. Each thing in it had a value and a price, and the idea was to

47

get the things you needed at a price that was as close to the value as possible. Each thing was understood only in terms of its function, judged only by how much it cost, never as an intrinsic object with its own special properties. In some way, I imagine it must have made the world seem a dull place to him. Uniform, colorless, without depth. If you see the world only in terms of money, you are finally not seeing the world at all.

As a child, there were times when I became positively embarrassed for him in public. Haggling with shopkeepers, furious over a high price, arguing as if his very manhood were at stake. A distinct memory of how everything would wither up inside me, of wanting to be anywhere in the world except where I was. A particular incident of going with him to buy a baseball glove stands out. Every day for two weeks I had visited the store after school to admire the one I wanted. Then, when my father took me to the store one evening to buy it, he so exploded at the salesman I was afraid he was going to tear him to pieces. Frightened, sick at heart, I told him not to bother, that I didn't want the glove after all. As we were leaving the store, he offered to buy me an ice cream cone. That glove was no good anyway, he said. I'll buy you a better one some other time.

Better, of course, meant worse.

Tirades about leaving too many lights on in the house. He always made a point of buying bulbs with low wattage.

His excuse for never taking us to the movies: "Why go out and spend a fortune when it will be on television in a year or two?"

The occasional family meal in a restaurant: we always had to order the least expensive things on the menu. It became a kind of ritual. Yes, he would say, nodding his head, that's a good choice.

Years later, when my wife and I were living in New York, he would sometimes take us out to dinner. The script was always precisely the same: the moment after we had put the last forkful of food into our mouths, he would ask, "Are you ready to go?" Impossible even to consider dessert.

His utter discomfort in his own skin. His inability to sit still, to make small talk, to "relax."

It made you nervous to be with him. You felt he was always on the verge of leaving.

He loved clever little tricks, prided himself on his ability to outsmart the world at its own game. A niggardliness in the most trivial aspects of life, as ridiculous as it was depressing. With his cars, he would always disconnect the odometers, falsifying the mileage in order to guarantee himself a better trade-in price. In his house, he would always do his own repair work instead of hiring a professional. Because he had a gift for machines and knew how things worked, he would take bizarre shortcuts, using whatever materials were at hand to rig up Rube Goldberg solutions to mechanical and electrical problems—rather than spending the money to do it right.

Permanent solutions never interested him. He went on patching and patching, a little piece here, a little piece there, never allowing his boat to sink, but never giving it a chance to float either.

The way he dressed: as if twenty years behind the times. Cheap synthetic suits from the racks of discount stores; unboxed pairs of shoes from the bins of bargain basements. Beyond giving proof of his miserliness, this disregard of fashion reinforced the image of him as a man not quite in the world. The clothes he wore seemed to be an expression of solitude, a concrete way of affirming his absence. Even though he was well off, able to afford anything he wanted, he looked like a poor man, a hayseed who had just stepped off the farm.

In the last years of his life, this changed a little bit. Becoming a bachelor again had probably given him a jolt: he realized that he would have to make himself presentable if he wanted to have any kind of social life. It was not that he went out and bought expensive clothes, but at least the tone of his wardrobe changed: the dull browns and grays were abandoned for brighter colors; the outmoded style gave way to a flashier, more dapper image. Checkered pants, white shoes, yellow turtlenecks, boots with big buckles. But in spite of these efforts, he never looked quite at home in these costumes. They were not an integral part of his personality. It made you think of a little boy who had been dressed up by his parents.

Given his curious relationship to money (his desire for wealth, his inability to spend), it was somehow appropriate that he made his living among the poor. Compared to them, he was a man of enormous riches. And yet, by spending his days among people who had next to nothing, he could keep before his eyes a vision of the thing he most feared in the world: to be without money. It put things in perspective for him. He did not consider himself stingy—but sensible, a man who knew the value of a dollar. He had to be vigilant. It was the only thing that stood between him and the nightmare of poverty.

When the business was at its peak, he and his brothers owned nearly a hundred buildings. Their terrain was the grim industrial region of northern New Jersey—Jersey City, Newark—and nearly all their tenants were black. One says "slumlord," but in this case it would not have been an accurate or fair description. Nor was he in any way an absentee land-lord. He was *there*, and he put in hours that would have driven even the most conscientious employee to go out on strike.

The job was a permanent juggling act. There was the buying and sell-ing of buildings, the buying and repairing of fixtures, the managing of several teams of repair men, the renting of apartments, the supervision of the superintendents, listening to tenant complaints, dealing with the visits of building inspectors, constant involvement with the water and electric companies, not to speak of frequent visits to court—both as plaintiff and defendant—to sue for back rent, to answer to violations. Everything was always happening at once, a perpetual assault from a dozen directions at the same time, and only a man who took things in his stride could have handled it. On any given day it was impossible to do everything that had to be done. You did not go home because you were finished, but simply because it was late and you had run out of time. The next day all the problems would be waiting for you—and sev-eral new ones as well. It never stopped. In fifteen years he took only two vacations.

He was soft-hearted with the tenants—granting them delays in pay-ing their rent, giving clothes to their children, helping them to find work—and they trusted him. Old men, afraid of being robbed, would give him their most valuable possessions to store in his office safe. Of all the brothers, he was the one people went to with their troubles. No one called him Mr. Auster. He was always Mr. Sam.

While cleaning out the house after his death, I came across this letter at the bottom of a kitchen drawer. Of all the things I found, I am happi-est to have retrieved this. It somehow balances the ledger, provides me with living proof whenever my mind begins to stray too far from the facts. The letter is addressed to "Mr. Sam," and the handwriting is nearly illegible.

April 19, 1976

Dear Sam,

I know you are so surprised to hear from me. first of all maybe I better introduce my self to you. I'm Mrs. Nash. I'm Albert Groover Sister in law—Mrs. Groover and Albert that lived at 285 pine Street in Jersey City so long and Mrs. Banks thats my Sister too. Any way. if you can remember.

You made arrangement to get the apartment for my children and I at 327 Johnston Ave right around the Corner from Mr. & Mrs. Groover my Sister.

Anyway I move away left of owing a $40. rent. this was the year of 1964 but I didn't for get I owed this earnest debt. So now here is your money. thanks for being so very nice to the children and I at that time. this is how much I appreciated what you done for us. I hope you can recall back to the time. So you was never forgotten by me.

About 3 weeks ago I called the office but weren't in at that time. may the Good Lord ever to Bless you. I hardly comes to Jersey City if so I would stop by see you.

No matter now I am happy to pay this debt. All for now.

Sincerely

   Mrs. JB. Nash

As a boy, I would occasionally go the rounds with him as he collected rent. I was too young to understand what I was seeing, but I remember the impression it made on me, as if, precisely because I did not understand, the raw perceptions of these experiences went directly into me, where they remain today, as immediate as a splinter in the thumb.

The wooden buildings with their dark, inhospitable hallways. And behind each door, a horde of children playing in a bare apartment; a mother, always sullen, overworked, tired, bent over an ironing board. Most vivid is the smell, as if poverty were more than a lack of money, but a physical sensation, a stench that invaded your head and made it impossible to think. Every time I walked into a building with my father, I would hold my breath, not daring to breathe, as if that smell were going to hurt me. Everyone was always happy to meet Mr. Sam's son. I was given innumerable smiles and pats on the head.

Once, when I was a bit older, I can remember driving with him down a street in Jersey City and seeing a boy wearing a T-shirt I had outgrown several months before. It was a very distinctive shirt, with a peculiar combination of yellow and blue stripes, and there was no question that this was the one that had been mine. Unaccountably, I was overcome with a feeling of shame.

Older still, at thirteen, fourteen, fifteen, I would sometimes go in with him to earn money working with the carpenters, painters, and repair men. Once, on an excruciatingly hot day in the middle of summer, I was given the job of helping one of the men tar a roof. The man's name was Joe Levine (a black man who had changed his name to Levine out of gratitude to an old Jewish grocer who had helped him in his youth), and he was my father's most trusted and reliable handyman. We hauled several fifty gallon barrels of tar up to the roof and got to work spreading the stuff over the surface with brooms. The sunlight beating down on that flat black roof was brutal, and after half an hour or so I became extremely dizzy, slipped on a patch of wet tar, fell, and somehow knocked over one of the open barrels, which then spilled tar all over me.

When I got back to the office a few minutes later, my father was greatly amused. I realized that the situation was amusing, but I was too embarrassed to want to joke about it. To my father's credit, he did not get angry at me or make fun of me. He laughed, but in a way that made me laugh too. Then he dropped what he had been doing, took me to the Woolworth's across the street, and bought me some new clothes. It had suddenly become possible for me to feel close to him.

As the years went by, the business started to decline. The business itself was not at fault, but rather the nature of the business: at that particular time, in that particular place, it was no longer possible to survive. The cities were falling apart, and no one seemed to care. What had once been a more or less fulfilling activity for my father now became simple drudgery. In the last years of his life he hated going to work.

Vandalism became such a severe problem that doing any kind of repairs became a demoralizing gesture. No sooner was plumbing installed in a building than the pipes would be ripped out by thieves. Windows were constantly being broken, doors smashed, hallways gutted, fires started. At the same time, it was impossible to sell out. No one wanted the buildings. The only way to get rid of them was to abandon them and let the cities take over. Tremendous amounts of money were lost in this way, an entire life's work. In the end, at the time of my father's death, there were only six or seven buildings left. The whole empire had disintegrated.

The last time I was in Jersey City (at least ten years ago) the place had the look of a disaster area, as if it had been pillaged by Huns. Gray, desolate streets; garbage piled everywhere; derelicts shuffling aimlessly up and down. My father's office had been robbed so many times that by now there was nothing left in it but some gray metal desks, a few chairs, and three or four telephones. Not even a typewriter, not one touch of color. It was not really a work place anymore, but a room in hell. I sat down and looked out at the bank across the street. No one came out, no one went in. The only living things were two stray dogs humping on the steps.

How he managed to pick himself up and go in there every day is beyond my understanding. Force of habit, or else sheer stubbornness. Not only was it depressing, it was dangerous. He was mugged several times, and once was kicked in the head so viciously by an attacker that his hearing was permanently damaged. For the last four or five years of his life there was a faint and constant ringing in his head, a humming that never went away, not even while he was asleep. The doctors said there was nothing that could be done about it.

In the end, he never went out into the street without carrying a monkey wrench in his right hand. He was over sixty-five years old, and he did not want to take any more chances.

Two sentences that suddenly come to mind this morning as I am showing Daniel how to make scrambled eggs.

" 'And now I want to know,' the woman says, with terrible force, 'I want to know whether it is possible to find another father like him anywhere in the world.' " (Isaac Babel)

"Children have always a tendency either to depreciate or to exalt their parents, and to a good son his father is always the best of fathers, quite apart from any objective reason there may be for admiring him." (Proust)

I realize now that I must have been a bad son. Or, if not precisely bad, then at least a disappointment, a source of confusion and sadness. It made no sense to him that he had produced a poet for a son. Nor could he understand why a young man with two degrees from Columbia University should take a job after graduation as an ordinary seaman on an oil tanker in the Gulf of Mexico, and then, without rhyme or reason, take off for Paris and spend four years there leading a hand to mouth existence.

His most common description of me was that I had "my head in the clouds," or else that I "did not have my feet on the ground." Either way, I must not have seemed very substantial to him, as if I were somehow a vapor or a person not wholly of this world. In his eyes, you became part of the world by working. By definition, work was something that brought in money. If it did not bring in money, it was not work. Writing, therefore, was not work, especially the writing of poetry. At best it was a hobby, a pleasant way to pass the time in between the things that really mattered. My father thought that I was squandering my gifts, refusing to grow up.

Nevertheless, some kind of bond remained between us. We were not close, but stayed in touch. A phone call every month or so, perhaps three or four visits a year. Each time a book of my poetry was published I would dutifully send it to him, and he would always call to thank me. Whenever I wrote an article for a magazine, I would set aside a copy and make sure I gave it to him the next time I saw him. *The New York Review of Books* meant nothing to him, but the pieces in *Commentary* impressed him. I think he felt that if the Jews were publishing me, then perhaps there was something to it.

Once, while I was still living in Paris, he wrote to tell me he had gone to the public library to read some of my poems that had appeared in a recent issue of *Poetry*. I imagined him in a large, deserted room, early in the morning before going to work: sitting at one of those long tables with his overcoat still on, hunched over words that must have been incomprehensible to him.

I have tried to keep this image in mind, along with all the others that will not leave it.

The rampant, totally mystifying force of contradiction. I understand now that each fact is nullified by the next fact, that each thought engenders an equal and opposite thought. Impossible to say anything without reservation: he was good, or he was bad; he was this, or he was that. All of them are true. At times I have the feeling that I am writing about three or four different men, each one distinct, each one a contradiction of all the others. Fragments. Or the anecdote as a form of knowledge.

Yes.

The occasional flash of generosity. At those rare times when the world was not a threat to him, his motive for living seemed to be kindness. "May the good Lord ever to Bless you."

Friends called him whenever they were in trouble. A car stuck somewhere in the middle of the night, and my father would drag himself out of bed and come to the rescue. In certain ways it was easy for others to take advantage of him. He refused to complain about anything.

A patience that bordered on the superhuman. He was the only person I have ever known who could teach someone to drive without getting angry or crumpling in a fit of nerves. You could be careening straight toward a lamp post, and still he would not get excited.

Impenetrable. And because of that, at times almost serene.

Starting when he was still a young man, he always took a special interest in his oldest nephew—the only child of his only sister. My aunt had an unhappy life, punctuated by a series of difficult marriages, and her son bore the brunt of it: shipped off to military schools, never really given a home. Motivated, I think, by nothing more than kindness and a sense of duty, my father took the boy under his wing. He nursed him along with constant encouragement, taught him how to get along in the world. Later, he helped him in business, and whenever a problem came up, he was always ready to listen and give advice. Even after my cousin married and had his own family, my father continued to take an active interest, putting them up in his house at one point for more than a year, religiously giving presents to his four grand-nephews and grand-nieces on their birthdays, and often going to visit them for dinner.

This cousin was more shaken by my father's death than any of my other relatives. At the family gathering after the funeral he came up to me three or four times and said, "I ran into him by accident just the other day. We were supposed to have dinner together Friday night."

The words he used were exactly the same each time. As if he no longer knew what he was saying.

I felt that we had somehow reversed roles, that he was the grieving son and I was the sympathetic nephew. I wanted to put my arm around his shoulder and tell him what a good man his father had been. After all, he was the real son, he was the son I could never bring myself to be.

For the past two weeks, these lines from Maurice Blanchot echoing in my head: "One thing must be understood: I have said nothing extraordinary or even surprising. What is extraordinary begins at the moment I stop. But I am no longer able to speak of it."

To begin with death. To work my way back into life, and then, finally, to return to death.

Or else: the vanity of trying to say anything about anyone.

In 1972 he came to visit me in Paris. It was the one time he ever traveled to Europe.

I was living that year in a minuscule sixth-floor maid's room barely large enough for a bed, a table, a chair, and a sink. The windows and little balcony stared into the face of one of the stone angels that jutted from St. Germain Auxerrois: the Louvre to my left, Les Halles off to my right, and Montmartre in the far distance ahead. I had a great fondness for that room, and many of the poems that later appeared in my first book were written there.

My father was not planning to stay for any length of time, hardly even what you would call a vacation: four days in London, three days in Paris, and then home again. But I was pleased at the thought of seeing him and prepared myself to show him a good time.

Two things happened, however, that made this impossible. I became very ill with the flu; and I had to leave for Mexico the day after his arrival to work on a ghostwriting project.

I waited for him all morning in the lobby of the tourist hotel where he had booked reservations, sweating away with a high fever, almost delirious with weakness. When he did not show up at the appointed time, I stayed on for another hour or two, but finally gave in and went back to my room where I collapsed into bed.

Late in the afternoon he came and knocked on my door, waking me from a deep sleep. The encounter was straight out of Dostoyevsky: bourgeois father comes to visit son in a foreign city and finds the struggling poet alone in a garret, wasting away with fever. He was shocked by what he saw, outraged that anyone could live in such a room, and it galvanized him into action: he made me put on my coat, dragged me off to a neighborhood clinic, and then bought the pills that were prescribed for me. Afterwards, he refused to allow me to spend the night in my room. I was in no condition to argue, so I agreed to stay in his hotel.

The next day I was no better. But there were things to be done, and I picked myself up and did them. In the morning I took my father along with me to the vast Avenue Henri Martin apartment of the movie producer who was sending me to Mexico. For the past year I had been working on and off for this man, doing what amounted to odd jobs—

translations, script synopses—things that were only marginally connected to the movies, which anyway did not interest me. Each project
was more idiotic than the last, but the pay was good, and I needed the
money. Now he wanted me to help his Mexican wife with a book she
had been contracted to write for an English publisher: Quetzalcoatl and
the mysteries of the plumed serpent. This seemed to be pushing it a bit,
and I had already turned him down several times. But each time I said
no, his offer had gone up, until now I was being paid so much money
that I could no longer turn away. I would only be gone for a month, and
I was being paid in cash—in advance.

This was the transaction my father witnessed. For once, I could see
that he was impressed. Not only had I led him into this luxurious setting and introduced him to a man who did business in the millions, but
now this man was calmly handing me a stack of hundred dollar bills
across the table and telling me to have a pleasant trip. It was the money,
of course, that made the difference, the fact that my father had seen it
with his own eyes. I felt it as a triumph, as if I had somehow been vindicated. For the first time he had been forced to realize that I could take
care of myself on my own terms.

He became very protective, indulgent of my weakened condition.
Helped me deposit the money in the bank, all smiles and jokes. Then
got us a cab and rode all the way to the airport with me. A big hand-
shake at the end. Good luck, son. Knock 'em dead.

You bet.

Nothing now for several days. . . .

In spite of the excuses I have made for myself, I understand what is
happening. The closer I come to the end of what I am able to say, the
more reluctant I am to say anything. I want to postpone the moment of
ending, and in this way delude myself into thinking that I have only just
begun, that the better part of my story still lies ahead. No matter how
useless these words might seem to be, they have nevertheless stood
between me and a silence that continues to terrify me. When I step into
this silence, it will mean that my father has vanished forever.

The dingy green carpet in the funeral home. And the director, unctuous,
professional, suffering from eczema and swollen ankles, going down a
checklist of expenses as if I were about to buy a suite of bedroom furniture on credit. He handed me an envelope that contained the ring my

father had been wearing when he died. Idly fingering the ring as the conversation droned on, I noticed that the underside of the stone was smeared with the residue of some soapy lubricant. A few moments passed before I made the connection, and then it became absurdly obvious: the lotion had been used to remove the ring from his finger. I tried to imagine the person whose job it was to do such things. I did not feel horror so much as fascination. I remember thinking to myself: I have entered the world of facts, the realm of brute particulars. The ring was gold, with a black setting that bore the insignia of the Masonic brotherhood. My father had not been an active member for over twenty years.

The funeral director kept telling me how he had known my father "in the old days," implying an intimacy and friendship I was sure had never existed. As I gave him the information to be passed on to the newspapers for the obituary, he anticipated my remarks with incorrect facts, rushing ahead of me in order to prove how well acquainted he had been with my father. Each time this happened, I stopped and corrected him. The next day, when the obituary appeared in the paper, many of these incorrect facts were printed.

Three days before he died, my father had bought a new car. He had driven it once, maybe twice, and when I returned to his house after the funeral, I saw it sitting in the garage, already defunct, like some huge, stillborn creature. Later that same day I went off to the garage for a moment to be by myself. I sat down behind the wheel of this car, inhaling the strange factory newness of it. The odometer read sixty-seven miles. That also happened to have been my father's age: sixty-seven years. The brevity of it sickened me. As if that were the distance between life and death. A tiny trip, hardly longer than a drive to the next town.

Worst regret: that I was not given a chance to see him after he died. Ignorantly, I had assumed the coffin would be open during the funeral service, and then, when it wasn't, it was too late to do anything about it.

Never to have seen him dead deprives me of an anguish I would have welcomed. It is not that his death has been made any less real, but now, each time I want to see it, each time I want to touch its reality, I must engage in an act of imagination. There is nothing to remember. Nothing but a kind of emptiness.

When the grave was uncovered to receive the coffin, I noticed a thick orange root thrusting into the hole. It had a strangely calming effect on me. For a brief moment the bare fact of death could no longer be hidden behind the words and gestures of ceremony. Here it was: unmediated, unadorned, impossible to turn my eyes away from. My father was being lowered into the ground, and in time, as the coffin gradually disintegrated, his body would help to feed the same root I had seen. More than anything that had been said or done that day, this made sense to me.

The rabbi who conducted the funeral service was the same man who had presided over my Bar Mitzvah nineteen years earlier. The last time I had seen him he was a youngish, clean-shaven man. Now he was old, with a full gray beard. He had not known my father, in fact knew nothing about him, and half an hour before the service was to begin I sat down with him and told him what to say in the eulogy. He made notes on little scraps of paper. When it came time for him to deliver the speech, he spoke with great feeling. The subject was a man he had never known, and yet he made it sound as though he were speaking from the heart. Behind me, I could hear women sobbing. He was following what I had told him almost word for word.

It occurs to me that I began writing this story a long time ago, long before my father died.

Night after night, lying awake in bed, my eyes open in the darkness. The impossibility of sleep, the impossibility of not thinking about how he died. I find myself sweating between the sheets, trying to imagine what it feels like to suffer a heart attack. Adrenalin pumps through me, my head pounds, and my whole body seems to contract into a small area behind my chest. A need to experience the same panic, the same mortal pain.

And then, at night, there are the dreams, nearly every night. In one of them, which woke me up just hours ago, I learned from the teenage daughter of my father's lady friend that she, the daughter, had been made pregnant by my father. Because she was so young, it was agreed that my wife and I would raise the child after it was born. The baby was going to be a boy. Everyone knew this in advance.

It is equally true, perhaps, that once this story has ended, it will go on telling itself, even after the words have been used up.

The old gentleman at the funeral was my great uncle, Sam Auster, now almost ninety years old. Tall, hairless, a high-pitched, rasping voice. Not a word about the events of 1919, and I did not have the heart to ask him. I took care of Sam when he was a little boy, he said. But that was all.

When asked if he wanted anything to drink, he requested a glass of hot water. Lemon? No thank you, just hot water.

Again Blanchot: "But I am no longer able to speak of it."

From the house: a document from St. Clair County in the State of Alabama duly announcing my parents' divorce. The signature at the bottom: Ann W. Love.

From the house: a watch, a few sweaters, a jacket, an alarm clock, six tennis rackets, and an old rusted Buick that barely runs. A set of dishes, a coffee table, three or four lamps. A barroom statue of Johnnie Walker for Daniel. The blank photograph album, This Is Our Life: The Austers.

At first I thought it would be a comfort to hold on to these things, that they would remind me of my father and make me think of him as I went about my life. But objects, it seems, are no more than objects. I am used to them now, I have begun to think of them as my own. I read time by his watch, I wear his sweaters, I drive around in his car. But all this is no more than an illusion of intimacy. I have already appropriated these things. My father has vanished from them, has become invisible again. And sooner or later they will break down, fall apart, and have to be thrown away. I doubt that it will even seem to matter.

". . . here it holds good that only he who works gets the bread, only he who was in anguish finds repose, only he who descends into the under-world rescues the beloved, only he who draws the knife gets Isaac. . . . He who will not work must take note of what is written about the maid-ens of Israel, for he gives birth to the wind, but he who is willing to work gives birth to his own father." (Kierkegaard)

Past two in the morning. An overflowing ashtray, an empty coffee cup, and the cold of early spring. An image of Daniel now, as he lies upstairs in his crib asleep. To end with this.

To wonder what he will make of these pages when he is old enough to read them.

And the image of his sweet and ferocious little body, as he lies upstairs in his crib asleep. To end with this.

1979

The Book of Memory

"When the dead weep, they are beginning to recover," said the Crow solemnly.
"I am sorry to contradict my famous friend and colleague," said the Owl, "but as far as I'm concerned, I think that when the dead weep, it means they do not want to die."

Collodi, *The Adventures of Pinocchio*

He lays out a piece of blank paper on the table before him and writes these words with his pen. It was. It will never be again.

Later that same day he returns to his room. He finds a fresh sheet of paper and lays it out on the table before him. He writes until he has covered the entire page with words. Later, when he reads over what he has written, he has trouble deciphering the words. Those he does manage to understand do not seem to say what he thought he was saying. Then he goes out to eat his dinner.

That night he tells himself that tomorow is another day. New words begin to clamor in his head, but he does not write them down. He decides to refer to himself as A. He walks back and forth between the table and the window. He turns on the radio and then turns it off. He smokes a cigarette.

Then he writes. It was. It will never be again.

Christmas Eve, 1979. His life no longer seemed to dwell in the present. Whenever he turned on his radio and listened to the news of the world, he would find himself imagining the words to be describing things that had happened long ago. Even as he stood in the present, he felt himself to be looking at it from the future, and this present-as-past was so antiquated that even the horrors of the day, which ordinarily would have filled him with outrage, seemed remote to him, as if the voice in the radio were reading from a chronicle of some lost civilization. Later, in a time of greater clarity, he would refer to this sensation as "nostalgia for the present."

*   *   *

To follow with a detailed description of classical memory systems, complete with charts, diagrams, symbolic drawings. Raymond Lull, for example, or Robert Fludd, not to speak of Giordano Bruno, the great Nolan burned at the stake in 1600. Places and images as catalysts for remembering other places and images: things, events, the buried artifacts of one's own life. Mnemotechnics. To follow with Bruno's notion that the structure of human thought corresponds to the structure of nature. And therefore to conclude that everything, in some sense, is connected to everything else.

At the same time, as if running parallel to the above, a brief disquisition on the room. An image, for example, of a man sitting alone in a room. As in Pascal: "All the unhappiness of man stems from one thing only: that he is incapable of staying quietly in his room." As in the phrase: "he wrote The Book of Memory in this room."

The Book of Memory. Book One.

Christmas Eve, 1979. He is in New York, alone in his little room at 6 Varick Street. Like many of the buildings in the neighborhood, this one used to be nothing but a work place. Remnants of its former life are everywhere around him: networks of mysterious pipes, sooty tin ceilings, hissing steam radiators. Whenever his eyes fall on the frosted glass panel of his door, he can read these clumsily stencilled letters in reverse: R.M. Pooley, Licensed Electrician. People were never supposed to live here. It is a room meant for machines, cuspidors, and sweat.

He cannot call it home, but for the past nine months it is all he has had. A few dozen books, a mattress on the floor, a table, three chairs, a hot plate, and a corroded cold water sink. The toilet is down the hall, but he uses it only when he has to shit. Pissing he does in the sink. For the past three days the elevator has been out of service, and since this is the top floor, it has made him reluctant to go out. It is not so much that he dreads climbing the ten flights of stairs when he gets back, but that he finds it disheartening to exhaust himself so thoroughly only to return to such bleakness. By staying in this room for long stretches at a time, he can usually manage to fill it with his thoughts, and this in turn seems to dispel the dreariness, or at least make him unaware of it. Each time he goes out, he takes his thoughts with him, and during his absence the room gradually empties of his efforts to inhabit it. When he returns, he has to begin the process all over again, and that takes work, real spiritual work. Considering his physical condition after the climb (chest heaving like a bellows, legs as tight and heavy as tree trunks), this inner struggle takes all that much longer to get started. In the interim, in the void between the moment he opens the door and the moment he begins to reconquer the emptiness, his mind flails in a wordless panic. It is as if he were being forced to watch his own disappearance, as if, by crossing the threshold of this room, he were entering another dimension, taking up residence inside a black hole.

Above him, dim clouds float past the tar-stained skylight, drifting off into the Manhattan evening. Below him, he hears the traffic rushing toward the Holland Tunnel: streams of cars heading home to New Jersey on the night before Christmas. Next door it is quiet. The Pomponio brothers, who arrive there each morning to smoke their cigars and grind out plastic display letters—a business they keep going by working twelve or fourteen hours a day—are probably at home, getting ready to eat a holiday meal. That is all to the good. Lately, one of them has been spending the night in his shop, and his snoring invariably keeps A. awake. The man sleeps directly opposite A., on the other side of the thin wall that divides their two rooms, and hour after hour A. lies in bed, staring into the darkness, trying to pace his thoughts to the ebb and flow of the man's troubled, adenoidal dreams. The snores swell gradually, and at the peak of each cycle they become long, piercing, almost hysterical, as if, when night comes, the snorer had to imitate the noise of the machine that holds him captive during the day. For once A. can count on a calm, unbroken sleep. Not even the arrival of Santa Claus will disturb him.

Winter solstice: the darkest time of the year. No sooner has he woken up in the morning than he feels the day beginning to slip away from him. There is no light to sink his teeth into, no sense of time unfolding. Rather, a feeling of doors being shut, of locks being turned. It is a hermetic season, a long moment of inwardness. The outer world, the tangible world of materials and bodies, has come to seem no more than an emanation of his mind. He feels himself sliding through events, hovering like a ghost around his own presence, as if he were living somewhere to the side of himself—not really here, but not anywhere else either. A feeling of having been locked up, and at the same time of being able to walk through walls. He notes somewhere in the margins of a thought: a darkness in the bones; make a note of this.

By day, heat gushes from the radiators at full blast. Even now, in coldest winter, he is forced to keep the window open. At night, however, there is no heat at all. He sleeps fully clothed, with two or three sweaters, curled up tightly in a sleeping bag. During the weekends, the heat is off altogether, both day and night, and there have been times lately when he has sat at his table, trying to write, and could not feel the pen in his hand anymore. In itself, this lack of comfort does not disturb him. But it has the effect of keeping him off balance, of prodding him into a state of constant inner watchfulness. In spite of what it might seem to be, this room is not a retreat from the world. There is nothing here to welcome him, no promise of a soma holiday to woo him into oblivion. These four walls hold only the signs of his own disquiet, and in order to find some measure of peace in these surroundings, he must dig more and more deeply into himself. But the more he digs, the less there will be to go on digging into. This seems undeniable to him. Sooner or later, he is bound to use himself up.

When night comes, the electricity dims to half-strength, then goes up again, then comes down, for no apparent reason. It is as though the lights were controlled by some prankster deity. Con Edison has no record of the place, and no one has ever had to pay for power. At the same time, the phone company has refused to acknowledge A.'s existence. The phone has been here for nine months, functioning without a flaw, but he had not yet received a bill for it. When he called the other day to straighten out the problem, they insisted they had never heard of him. Somehow, he has managed to escape the clutches of the computer, and none of his calls has ever been recorded. His name is off the books. If he felt like it, he could spend his idle moments making free calls to faraway places. But the fact is, there is no one he wants to talk to. Not in California, not in Paris, not in China. The world has shrunk to the size of this room for him, and for as long as it takes him to understand it, he must stay where he is. Only one thing is certain: he cannot be anywhere until he is here. And if he does not manage to find this place, it would be absurd for him to think of looking for another.

Life inside the whale. A gloss on Jonah, and what it means to refuse to speak. Parallel text: Gepetto in the belly of the shark (whale in the Disney version), and the story of how Pinocchio rescues him. Is it true that one must dive to the depths of the sea and save one's father to become a real boy?

Initial statement of these themes. Further installments to follow.

* * *

Then shipwreck. Crusoe on his island. "That boy might be happy if he would stay at home, but if he goes abroad he will be the most miserable wretch that was ever born." Solitary consciousness. Or in George Oppen's phrase: "the shipwreck of the singular."

A vision of waves all around, water as endless as air, and the jungle heat behind. "I am divided from mankind, a solitaire, one banished from human society."

And Friday? No, not yet. There is no Friday, at least not here. Everything that happens is prior to that moment. Or else: the waves will have washed the footprints away.

First commentary on the nature of chance.

This is where it begins. A friend of his tells him a story. Several years go by, and then he finds himself thinking about the story again. It is not that it begins with the story. Rather, in the act of remembering it, he has become aware that something is happening to him. For the story would not have occurred to him unless whatever summoned its memory had not already been making itself felt. Unknown to himself, he had been burrowing down to a place of almost vanished memory, and now that something had surfaced, he could not even guess how long the excavation had taken.

During the war, M.'s father had hidden out from the Nazis for several months in a Paris *chambre de bonne*. Eventually, he managed to escape, made his way to America, and began a new life. Years passed, more than twenty years. M. had been born, had grown up, and was now going off to study in Paris. Once there, he spent several difficult weeks looking for a place to live. Just when he was about to give up in despair, he found a small *chambre de bonne*. Immediately upon moving in, he wrote a letter to his father to tell him the good news. A week or so later he received a reply: your address, wrote M.'s father, that is the same building I hid out in during the war. He then went on to describe the details of the room. It turned out to be the same room his son had rented.

It begins, therefore, with this room. And then it begins with that room. And beyond that there is the father, there is the son, and there is the war. To speak of fear, and to remember that the man who hid in that little room was a Jew. To note as well: that the city was Paris, a place A. had just returned from (December fifteenth), and that for a whole year he once lived in a Paris *chambre de bonne*—where he wrote his first book of poems, and where his own father, on his only trip to Europe, once came to see him. To remember his father's death. And beyond that, to understand—this most important of all—that M.'s story has no meaning.

Nevertheless, this is where it begins. The first word appears only at a moment when nothing can be explained anymore, at some instant of experience that defies all sense. To be reduced to saying nothing. Or else, to say to himself: this is what haunts me. And then to realize, almost in the same breath, that this is what he haunts.

He lays out a blank sheet of paper on the table before him and writes these words with his pen. Possible epigraph for The Book of Memory.

Then he opens a book by Wallace Stevens (*Opus Posthumous*) and copies out the following sentence.

"In the presence of extraordinary reality, consciousness takes the place of imagination."

Later that same day he writes steadily for three or four hours. Afterwards, when he reads over what he has written, he finds only one paragraph of any interest. Although he is not sure what to make of it, he decides to keep it for future reference and copies it into a lined notebook:

When the father dies, he writes, the son becomes his own father and his own son. He looks at his son and sees himself in the face of the boy. He imagines what the boy sees when he looks at him and finds himself becoming his own father. Inexplicably, he is moved by this. It is not just the sight of the boy that moves him, nor even the thought of standing inside his father, but what he sees in the boy of his own vanished past. It is a nostalgia for his own life that he feels, perhaps, a memory of his own boyhood as a son to his father. Inexplicably, he finds himself shaking at that moment with both happiness and sorrow, if this is possible, as if he were going both forward and backward, into the future and into the past. And there are times, often there are times, when these feelings are so strong that his life no longer seems to dwell in the present.

Memory as a place, as a building, as a sequence of columns, cornices, porticoes. The body inside the mind, as if we were moving around in there, going from one place to the next, and the sound of our footsteps as we walk, moving from one place to the next.

"One must consequently employ a large number of places," writes

Cicero, "which must be well lighted, clearly set out in order, spaced out at moderate intervals; and images which are active, sharply defined, unusual, and which have the power of speedily encountering and penetrating the psyche. . . . For the places are very much like wax tablets or papyrus, the images like the letters, the arrangement and disposition of the images like the script, and the speaking like the reading."

He returned from Paris ten days ago. He had gone there on a work visit, and it was the first time he had been abroad in more than five years. The business of traveling, of continual conversation, of too much drinking with old friends, of being away from his little son for so long, had finally worn him out. With a few days to spare at the end of his trip, he decided to go to Amsterdam, a city he had never been to before. He thought: the paintings. But once there, it was a thing he had not planned on doing that made the greatest impression on him. For no particular reason (idly looking through a guide book he found in his hotel room) he decided to go to Anne Frank's house, which has been preserved as a museum. It was a Sunday morning, gray with rain, and the streets along the canal were deserted. He climbed the steep and narrow staircase inside the house and entered the secret annex. As he stood in Anne Frank's room, the room in which the diary was written, now bare, with the faded pictures of Hollywood movie stars she had collected still pasted to the walls, he suddenly found himself crying. Not sobbing, as might happen in response to a deep inner pain, but crying without sound, the tears streaming down his cheeks, as if purely in response to the world. It was at that moment, he later realized, that The Book of Memory began. As in the phrase: "she wrote her diary in this room."

From the window of that room, facing out on the backyard, you can see the rear windows of a house in which Descartes once lived. There are children's swings in the yard now, toys scattered in the grass, pretty little flowers. As he looked out the window that day, he wondered if the children those toys belonged to had any idea of what had happened thirty-five years earlier in the spot where he was standing. And if they did, what it would be like to grow up in the shadow of Anne Frank's room.

To repeat Pascal: "All the unhappiness of man stems from one thing only: that he is incapable of staying quietly in his room." At roughly the same time these words entered the *Pensées*, Descartes wrote to a friend in France from his room in that house in Amsterdam. "Is there any country," he asked with exuberance, "in which one can enjoy freedom as enormously as one does here?" Everything, in some sense, can be read as a gloss on everything else. To imagine Anne Frank, for example, had she lived on after the war, reading Descartes' *Meditations* as a university student in Amsterdam. To imagine a solitude so crushing, so unconsolable, that one stops breathing for hundreds of years.

He notes, with a certain fascination, that Anne Frank's birthday is the same as his son's. June twelfth. Under the sign of Gemini. An image of the twins. A world in which everything is double, in which the same thing always happens twice.

Memory: the space in which a thing happens for the second time.

The Book of Memory. Book Two.

Israel Lichtenstein's Last Testament. Warsaw; July 31, 1942.

"With zeal and zest I threw myself into the work to help assemble archive materials. I was entrusted to be the custodian. I hid the material. Besides me, no one knew. I confided only in my friend Hersh Wasser, my supervisor. . . . It is well hidden. Please God that it be preserved. That will be the finest and best we achieved in the present gruesome time. . . . I know that we will not endure. To survive and remain alive after such horrible murders and massacres is impossible. Therefore I write this testament of mine. Perhaps I am not worthy of being remembered, but just for my grit in working with the Society Oneg Shabbat and for being the most endangered because I hid the entire material. It would be a small thing to give my own head. I risk the head of my dear wife Gele Seckstein and my treasure, my little daughter, Margalit. . . . I don't want any gratitude, any monument, any praise. I want only a remembrance, so that my family, brother and sister abroad, may know what has become of my remains. . . . I want my wife to be remembered. Gele Seckstein, artist, dozens of works, talented, didn't manage to exhibit, did not show in public. During the three years of war worked among children as educator, teacher, made stage sets, costumes for the children's productions, received awards. Now together with me, we are preparing to receive death. . . . I want my little daughter to be remembered. Margalit, 20 months old today. Has mastered Yiddish perfectly, speaks a pure Yiddish. At 9 months began to speak Yiddish clearly. In intelligence she is on a par with 3- or 4-year old children. I don't want to brag about her. Witnesses to this, who tell me about it, are the teaching staff of the school at Nowolipki 68. . . . I am not sorry about my life and that of my wife. But I am sorry for the gifted little girl. She deserves to be remembered also. . . . May we be the redeemers for all the rest of the Jews in the whole world. I believe in the survival of our people. Jews will not be annihilated. We, the Jews of Poland, Czechoslovakia, Lithuania, Latvia, are the scapegoat for all Israel in all the other lands."

Standing and watching. Sitting down. Lying in bed. Walking through the streets. Eating his meals at the Square Diner, alone in a booth, a newspaper spread out on the table before him. Opening his mail. Writing letters. Standing and watching. Walking through the streets. Learning from an old English friend, T., that both their families had originally come from the same town (Stanislav) in Eastern Europe. Before World War I it had been part of the Austro-Hungarian Empire; between the wars it had been part of Poland; and now, since the end of World War II, part of the Soviet Union. In the first letter from T. there is some speculation that they might, after all, be cousins. A second letter, however, offers clarification. T. has learned from an ancient aunt that in Stanislav his family was quite wealthy; A.'s family, on the other hand (and this is consistent with everything he has ever known), was poor. The story is that one of A.'s relatives (an uncle or cousin of some sort) lived in a small cottage on the property of T.'s family. He fell in love with the young lady of the household, proposed marriage, and was turned down. At that point he left Stanislav forever.

What A. finds particularly fascinating about this story is that the man's name was precisely the same as his son's.

Some weeks later he reads the following entry in the Jewish Encyclopedia:

AUSTER, DANIEL (1893–1962). Israel lawyer and mayor of Jerusalem. Auster, who was born in Stanislav (then Western Galicia), studied law in Vienna, graduated in 1914, and moved to Palestine. During World War I he served in the Austrian expeditionary force headquarters in Damascus, where he assisted Arthur Ruppin in sending financial help from Constantinople to the starving *yishuv*. After the war he established a law practice in Jerusalem that represented several Jewish-Arab interests, and served as secretary of the Legal Department of the Zionist Commission (1919, 20). In 1934 Auster was elected a Jerusalem councillor; in 1935 he was appointed deputy mayor of Jerusalem; and in 1936–38 and 1944–45 he was acting mayor. Auster represented the Jewish case against internationalization of Jerusalem brought before the United Nations in 1947–48. In 1948 Auster (who represented the Progressive Party) was elected mayor of Jerusalem, the first to hold that office in an independent Israel. Auster held that post until 1951. He also served as a member of the Provisional Council of Israel in 1948. He headed the Israel United Nations Association from its inception until his death."

All during the three days he spent in Amsterdam, he was lost. The plan of the city is circular (a series of concentric circles, bisected by canals, a cross-hatch of hundreds of tiny bridges, each one connecting to another, and then another, as though endlessly), and you cannot simply "follow" a street as you can in other cities. To get somewhere you have to know in advance where you are going. A. did not, since he was a stranger, and moreover found himself curiously reluctant to consult a map. For three days it rained, and for three days he walked around in circles. He realized that in comparison to New York (or New Amsterdam, as he was fond of saying to himself after he returned), Amsterdam was a small place, a city whose streets could probably be memorized in ten days. And yet, even if he was lost, would it not have been possible for him to ask directions of some passerby? Theoretically, yes, but in fact he was unable to bring himself to do so. It was not that he was afraid of strangers, nor that he was physically reluctant to speak. More subtly, he found himself hesitating to speak English to the Dutch. Nearly everyone speaks excellent English in Amsterdam. This ease of communication, however, was upsetting to him, as if it would somehow rob the place of its foreignness. Not in the sense that he was seeking the exotic, but in the sense that the place would no longer be itself—as if the Dutch, by speaking English, would be denied their Dutchness. If he could have been sure that no one would understand him, he would not have hesitated to rush up to a stranger and speak English, in a comical effort to make himself understood: with words, gestures, grimaces, etc. As it was, he felt himself unwilling to violate the Dutch people's Dutchness, even though they themselves had long ago allowed it to be violated. He therefore held his tongue. He wandered. He walked around in circles. He allowed himself to be lost. Sometimes, he later discovered, he would be only a few feet from his destination, but not knowing where to turn, would then go off in the wrong direction, thereby taking himself farther and farther from where he thought he was going. It occurred to him that perhaps he was wandering in the circles of hell, that the city had been designed as a model of the underworld, based on some classical representation of the place. Then he remembered that various diagrams of hell had been used as memory systems by some of the sixteenth century writers on the subject. (Cosmas Rossellius, for example, in his *Thesaurus Artificiosae Memoriae*, Venice, 1579.) And if Amsterdam was hell, and if hell was memory, then he realized that perhaps there was some purpose to his being lost. Cut off from everything that was familiar to him, unable to discover even a single point of reference, he saw that his steps, by taking him nowhere, were taking him nowhere but into himself. He was wandering inside himself, and he was lost. Far from troubling him, this state of being lost became a source of happiness, of exhilaration. He breathed it into his very bones. As if on the brink of some previously hidden knowledge, he breathed it into his very bones and said to himself, almost triumphantly: I am lost.

His life no longer seemed to dwell in the present. Each time he saw a child, he would try to imagine what it would look like as a grown-up. Each time he saw an old person, he would try to imagine what that person had looked like as a child.

It was worst with women, especially if the woman was young and beautiful. He could not help looking through the skin of her face and imagining the anonymous skull behind it. And the more lovely the face, the more ardent his attempt to seek in it the encroaching signs of the future: the incipient wrinkles, the later-to-be-sagging chin, the glaze of disappointment in the eyes. He would put one face on top of another: this woman at forty; this woman at sixty; this woman at eighty; as if, even as he stood in the present, he felt compelled to hunt out the future, to track down the death that lives in each one of us.

Some time later, he came across a similar thought in one of Flaubert's letters to Louise Colet (August 1846) and was struck by the parallel: ". . . I always sense the future, the antithesis of everything is always before my eyes. I have never seen a child without thinking that it would grow old, nor a cradle without thinking of a grave. The sight of a naked woman makes me imagine her skeleton."

Walking through the hospital corridor and hearing the man whose leg had been amputated calling out at the top of his voice: it hurts, it hurts. That summer (1979), every day for more than a month, traveling across town to the hospital, the unbearable heat. Helping his grandfather put in his false teeth. Shaving the old man's face with an electric razor. Reading him the baseball scores from the *New York Post*.

Initial statement of these themes. Further installments to follow.

Second commentary on the nature of chance.

He remembers cutting school one drizzly day in April 1962 with his friend D. and going to the Polo Grounds to see one of the first games ever played by the New York Mets. The stadium was nearly empty (attendance was eight or nine thousand), and the Mets lost soundly to the Pittsburgh Pirates. The two friends sat next to a boy from Harlem, and A. remembers the pleasant ease of the conversation among the three of them during the course of the game.

He returned to the Polo Grounds only once that season, and that was for a holiday doubleheader (Memorial Day: day of memory, day of the dead) against the Dodgers: more than fifty thousand people in the stands, resplendent sun, and an afternoon of crazy events on the field: a triple play, inside-the-park homeruns, double steals. He was with the same friend that day, and they sat in a remote corner of the stadium, unlike the good seats they had managed to sneak into for the earlier game. At one point they left their places to go to the hot dog stand, and there, just several rows down the concrete steps was the same boy they had met in April, this time sitting beside his mother. They all recognized each other and gave warm greetings, each amazed at the coincidence of meeting again. And make no mistake: the odds against this meeting were astronomical. Like the two friends, A. and D., the boy now sitting with his mother had not been to another game since that wet day in April.

Memory as a room, as a body, as a skull, as a skull that encloses the room in which a body sits. As in the image: "a man sat alone in his room."

"The power of memory is prodigious," observed Saint Augustine. "It is a vast, immeasurable sanctuary. Who can plumb its depths? And yet it is a faculty of my soul. Although it is part of my nature, I cannot understand all that I am. This means, then, that the mind is too narrow to contain itself entirely. But where is that part of it which it does not itself contain? Is it somewhere outside itself and not within it? How, then, can it be part of it, if it is not contained in it?"

* * *

The Book of Memory. Book Three.

It was in Paris, in 1965, that he first experienced the infinite possibilities of a limited space. Through a chance encounter with a stranger in a café, he was introduced to S. A. was just eighteen at the time, in the summer between high school and college, and he had never been to Paris before. These are his earliest memories of that city, where so much of his life would later be spent, and they are inescapably bound up with the idea of a room.

Place Pinel in the thirteenth arrondissement, where S. lived, was a working class neighborhood, and even then one of the last vestiges of the old Paris—the Paris one still talks about but which is no longer there. S. lived in a space so small that at first it seemed to defy you, to resist being entered. The presence of one person crowded the room, two people choked it. It was impossible to move inside it without contracting your body to its smallest dimensions, without contracting your mind to some infinitely small point within itself. Only then could you begin to breathe, to feel the room expand, and to watch your mind explore the excessive, unfathomable reaches of that space. For there was an entire universe in that room, a miniature cosmology that contained all that is most vast, most distant, most unknowable. It was a shrine, hardly bigger than a body, in praise of all that exists beyond the body: the representation of one man's inner world, even to the slightest detail. S. had literally managed to surround himself with the things that were inside him. The room he lived in was a dream space, and its walls were like the skin of some second body around him, as if his own body had been transformed into a mind, a breathing instrument of pure thought. This was the womb, the belly of the whale, the original site of the imagination. By placing himself in that darkness, S. had invented a way of dreaming with open eyes.

A former student of Vincent D'Indy's, S. had once been considered a highly promising young composer. For more than twenty years, however, none of his pieces had been performed in public. Naive in all things, but most especially in politics, he had made the mistake of allowing two of his larger orchestral works to be played in Paris during the war—*Symphonie de Feu* and *Hommage à Jules Verne*, each requiring more than one hundred-thirty musicians. That was in 1943, and the Nazi occupation was still at full strength. When the war ended, people concluded that S. had been a collaborator, and although nothing could have been farther from the truth, he was blackballed by the French music world—by innuendo and silent consent, never by direct confrontation. The only sign that any of his colleagues still remembered him was the annual Christmas card he received from Nadia Boulanger.

A stammerer, a child-man with a weakness for red wine, he was so lacking in guile, so ignorant of the world's malice, that he could not even begin to defend himself against his anonymous accusers. He simply withdrew, hiding behind a mask of eccentricity. He appointed himself an Orthodox priest (he was Russian), grew a long beard, dressed in a black cassock, and changed his name to the Abbaye de la Tour du Calame, all the while continuing—fitfully, between bouts of stupor—with the work of his life: a piece for three orchestras and four choruses that would take twelve days to perform. In his misery, in the totally abject conditions of his life, he would turn to A. and observe, stuttering helplessly, his gray eyes gleaming, "Everything is miraculous. There has never been an age more wonderful than this one."

The sun did not penetrate his room on the Place Pinel. He had covered his window with heavy black cloth, and what little light there was came from a few strategically placed and faintly glowing lamps. The room was hardly bigger than a second class train compartment, and it had more or less the same shape: narrow, high-ceilinged, with a single window at the far end. S. had cluttered this tiny place with a multitude of objects, the debris of an entire lifetime: books, photographs, manuscripts, private totems—everything that was of any significance to him. Shelves, densely packed with this accumulation, climbed up to the ceiling along each wall, each one sagging, tipping slightly inward, as if the slightest disturbance would loosen the structure and send the whole mass of things falling in on him. S. lived, worked, ate, and slept in his bed. Immediately to the left of him, fit snugly into the wall, was a set of small, cubbied shelves, which seemed to hold all he needed to get through the day: pens, pencils, ink, music paper, cigarette holder, radio, penknife, bottles of wine, bread, books, magnifying glass. To his right was a metal stand with a tray fastened to the top of it, which he could swing in and out, over the bed and away from it, and which he used as both his work table and his eating table. This was life as Crusoe would have lived it: shipwreck in the heart of the city. For there was nothing S. had not thought of. In his penury, he had managed to provide for himself more efficiently than many millionaires do. The evidence notwithstanding, he was a realist, even in his eccentricity. He had examined himself thoroughly enough to know what was necessary for his own survival, and he accepted these quirks as the conditions of his life. There was nothing in his attitude that was either faint-hearted or pious, nothing to suggest a hermit's renunciation. He embraced his condition with passion and joyful enthusiasm, and as A. looks back on it now, he realizes that he has never known anyone who laughed so hard and so often.

The giant composition, on which S. had spent the last fifteen years, was nowhere near completion. S. referred to it as his "work in progress," consciously echoing Joyce, whom he greatly admired, or else as the *Dodecalogue*, which he would describe as the-work-to-be-done-that-is-done-in-the-process-of-doing-it. It was unlikely that he ever imagined he would finish the piece. He seemed to accept the inevitability of his failure almost as a theological premise, and what for another man might have led to an impasse of despair was for him a source of boundless, quixotic hope. At some anterior moment, perhaps at his very darkest moment, he had made the equation between his life and his work, and now he was no longer able to distinguish between the two. Every idea fed into his work; the idea of his work gave purpose to his life. To have conceived of something within the realm of possibility—a work that could have been finished, and therefore detached from himself—would have vitiated the enterprise. The point was to fall short, but to do so only in attempting the most outlandish thing he could conjure for himself. The end result, paradoxically, was humility, a way of gauging his own insignificance in relation to God. For only in the mind of God were such dreams as S.'s possible. But by dreaming in the way he did, S. had found a way of participating in all that was beyond him, of drawing himself several inches closer to the heart of the infinite.

For more than a month during that summer of 1965, A. paid S. two or three visits a week. He knew no one else in the city, and S. therefore had become his anchor to the place. He could always count on S. to be in, to greet him with enthusiasm (Russian style; three kisses on the cheeks: left, right, left), and to be more than willing to talk. Many years later, at a time of great personal distress, he realized that what drew him continually to these meetings with S. was that they allowed him to experience, for the first time, what it felt like to have a father.

His own father was a remote, almost absent figure with whom he had very little in common. S., for his part, had two grown sons, and both had turned away from his example and adopted an aggressive, hard-nosed attitude towards the world. Beyond the natural rapport that existed between them, S. and A. drew together out of a congruent want: the one for a son who would accept him as he was, the other for a father who would accept him as he was. This was further underscored by a parallel of births: S. had been born in the same year as A.'s father; A. had been born in the same year as S.'s younger son. For A., S. satisfied his paternal hunger through a curious combination of generosity and need. He listened to him seriously and took his ambition to be a writer as the most natural thing a young man could hope to do with himself. If A.'s father, in his strange, self-enclosed manner of being in the world, had made A. feel superfluous to his life, as if nothing he did could ever have an effect on him, S., in his vulnerability and destitution, allowed A. to become necessary to him. A. brought food to him, supplied him with wine and cigarettes, made sure he did not starve—which was a true danger. For that was the point about S.: he never asked anyone for anything. He would wait for the world to come to him, entrusting his deliverance to chance. Sooner or later, someone was bound to turn up: his ex-wife, one of his sons, a friend. Even then, he would not ask. But neither would he refuse.

Each time A. arrived with a meal (usually roast chicken, from a charcuterie on the Place d'Italie), it was turned into a mock feast, an excuse for celebration. "Ah, chicken," S. would exclaim, biting into a drumstick. And then again, chewing away at it, the juice dribbling into his beard: "Ah, chicken," with an impish, self-deprecatory burst of laughter, as if acknowledging the irony of his need and the undeniable pleasure the food gave him. Everything became absurd and luminous in that laughter. The world was turned inside out, swept away, and then immediately reborn as a kind of metaphysical jest. There was no room in that world for a man who did not have a sense of his own ridiculousness.

Further encounters with S. Letters between Paris and New York, a few photographs exchanged, all of this now lost. In 1967: another visit for several months. By then S. had given up his priest's robes and was back to using his own name. But the costumes he wore on his little excursions through the streets of his neighborhood were just as marvelous. Beret, silk shirt, scarf, heavy corduroy pants, leather riding boots, ebony walking stick with a silver handle: a vision of Paris via Hollywood, circa 1920. It was no accident, perhaps, that S.'s younger son became a film producer.

In February 1971, A. returned to Paris, where he would remain for the next three and a half years. Although he was no longer there as a visitor, which meant that more claims were made on his time, he still saw S. on a fairly regular basis, perhaps once every other month. The bond was still there, but as time went on A. began to wonder if it was not, in fact, a memory of that other bond, formed six years earlier, which sustained this bond in the present. For it turns out that after A. moved back to New York (July 1974), he no longer wrote any letters to S. It was not that he did not continue to think of him. But it was the memory of him, more than any need to carry on contact with S. into the future, that seemed to concern A. now. In this way he began to feel, as if palpably in his own skin, the passage of time. It sufficed him to remember. And this, in itself, was a startling discovery.

Even more startling to him, however, was that when he finally went back to Paris (November 1979), after an absence of more than five years, he failed to look up S. And this in spite of the fact that he had fully intended to do so. Every morning for the several weeks of his visit, he would wake up and say to himself, I must make time today to see S., and then, as the day wore on, invent an excuse for not going to see him. This reluctance, he began to realize, was a product of fear. But fear of what? Of walking back into his own past? Of discovering a present that would contradict the past, and thus alter it, which in turn would destroy the memory of the past he wanted to preserve? No, he realized, nothing so simple. Then what? Days went by, and gradually it began to come clear. He was afraid that S. was dead. Irrationally, he knew. But since A.'s father had died less than a year before, and since S. had become important to him precisely in relation to his thoughts about his father, he felt that somehow the death of one automatically entailed the death of the other. In spite of what he tried to tell himself, he actually believed this. Beyond that he thought: if I go to see S., then I will learn he is dead; but if I stay away, it will mean he is alive. By remaining absent, therefore, A. felt that he would be helping to keep S. in the world. Day after day, he walked around Paris with an image of S. in his mind. A hundred times a day, he imagined himself entering the little room on the Place Pinel. And still, he could not bring himself to go there. It was then that he realized he was living in a state of extreme duress.

Further commentary on the nature of chance.

From his last visit to S., at the end of those years in Paris (1974), a photograph has been preserved. A. and S. are standing outside, by the doorway of S.'s house. They each have an arm around the other's shoulder, and there is an unmistakeable glow of friendship and comraderie on their faces. This picture is one of the few personal tokens A. has brought with him to his room on Varick Street.

As he studies this picture now (Christmas Eve, 1979), he is reminded of another picture he used to see on the wall of S.'s room: S. as a young man, perhaps eighteen or nineteen, standing with a boy of twelve or thirteen. Same evocation of friendship, same smiles, same arms-around-the-shoulders pose. The boy, S. had told him, was the son of Marina Tsvetayeva. Marina Tsvetayeva, who stands in A.'s mind along with Mandelstam as the greatest of Russian poets. To look at this 1974 photograph for him is to imagine her impossible life, which ended when she hanged herself in 1941. For many of the years between the Civil War and her death she had lived in the Russian emigré circles in France, the same community in which S. had been raised, and he had known her and had been a friend of her son, Mur. Marina Tsvetayeva, who had written: "It may be that a better way / To conquer time and the world / Is to pass, and not to leave a trace—/ To pass, and not to leave a shadow / on the walls . . ."; who had written: "I didn't want this, not / this (but listen, quietly, / to want is what bodies do / and now we are ghosts only) . . ."; who had written: "In this most Christian of worlds / All poets are Jews."

When A. and his wife returned to New York in 1974, they moved into an apartment on Riverside Drive. Among their neighbors in the building was an old Russian doctor, Gregory Altschuller, a man well into his eighties, who still did research work at one of the city hospitals and who, along with his wife, had a great interest in literature. Dr. Altschuller's father had been Tolstoy's personal physician, and propped up on a table in the Riverside Drive apartment was an enormous photograph of the bearded writer, duly inscribed, in an equally enormous hand, to his friend and doctor. In conversations with the younger Dr. Altschuller, A. learned something that struck him as nothing less than extraordinary. In a small village outside Prague, in the dead of winter in 1925, this man had delivered Marina Tsvetayeva's son: the same son who had grown up into the boy in the photograph on S.'s wall. More than that: this was the only baby he ever delivered in his career as a doctor.

"It was night," Dr. Altschuller wrote recently, "the last day of January, 1925. . . . The snow was falling, a terrible storm which snowed-in every-thing. A Czech boy came running to me from the village where Tsvetayeva now lived with her family, though her husband was not with her at the time. Her daughter was also away with her father. Marina was alone.

"The boy rushed into the room and said: 'Pani Tsvetayeva wants you to come to her immediately because she's already in labor! You have to hurry, it's already on the way.' What could I say? I quickly dressed and walked through the forest, snow up to my knees, in a raging storm. I opened the door and went in. In the pale light of a lonely electric bulb I saw piles of books in one corner of the room; they nearly reached the ceiling. Days of accumulated rubbish was shoveled into another corner of the room. And there was Marina, chain-smoking in bed, baby already on the way. Greeting me gaily: 'You're almost late!' I looked around the room for something clean, for a piece of soap. Nothing, not a clean handkerchief, not a piece of anything. She was lying in bed, smoking and smiling, saying: 'I told you that you'd deliver my baby. You came— and now it's your business, not mine'. . . .

"Everything went smoothly enough. The baby, however, was born with the umbilical cord wrapped around his neck so tightly that he could hardly breathe. He was blue. . . .

"I tried desperately to restore the baby's respiration and finally he started breathing; he turned from blue to pink. All this time Marina was smoking, silent, not uttering a sound, looking steadily at the baby, at me. . . .

"I came back the next day and then saw the child every Sunday for a good many weeks. In a letter (May 10, 1925), Marina wrote: 'Altschuller directs everything concerning Mur with pride and love. Before eating, Mur gets one teaspoonful of lemon juice without sugar. He's fed according to the system of Professor Czerny, who saved thousands of newborn children in Germany during the war. Altschuller sees Mur every Sunday. Percussion, auscultation, some kind of arithmetic calculation. Then he writes down for me how to feed Mur next week, what to give him, how much butter, how much lemon, how much milk, how gradually to increase the amount. Every time he comes he remembers what was given last time, without carrying any notes. . . . Sometimes I have a crazy desire just to take his hand and kiss it'. . . .

"The boy grew quickly and became a healthy child adored by his mother and her friends. I saw him for the last time when he was not yet one year old. At that time Marina moved to France and there she lived for the next fourteen years. George (Mur's formal name) went to school and soon became an ardent student of literature, music, and art. In 1936 his sister Alia, then in her early twenties, left the family and France and returned to Soviet Russia, following her father. Marina stayed now with her very young son, alone in France . . . under extreme hardship, financial and moral. In 1939 she applied for a Soviet visa and returned to Moscow with her son. Two years later, in August 1941, her life came to a tragic end. . . .

"The war was still on. Young George Efron was at the front. 'Goodbye literature, music, school,' he wrote to his sister. He signed his letter 'Mur.' As a soldier he proved to be a courageous and fearless fighter, took part in many battles, and died in July 1944, one of hundreds of victims of a battle near the village of Druika on the Western Front. He was only twenty years old."

The Book of Memory. Book Four.

Several blank pages. To be followed by profuse illustrations. Old family photographs, for each person his own family, going back as many generations as possible. To look at these with utmost care.

Afterwards, several sequences of reproductions, beginning with the portraits Rembrandt painted of his son, Titus. To include all of them: from the view of the little boy in 1650 (golden hair, red feathered hat) to the 1655 portrait of Titus "puzzling over his lessons" (pensive, at his desk, compass dangling from his left hand, right thumb pressed against his chin) to Titus in 1658 (seventeen years old, the extraordinary red hat, and, as one commentator has written, "The artist has painted his son with the same sense of penetration usually reserved for his own features") to the last surviving canvas of Titus, from the early 1660's: "The face seems that of a weak old man ravaged with disease. Of course, we look at it with hindsight—we know that Titus will predecease his father. . . ."

To be followed by the 1602 portrait of Sir Walter Raleigh and his eight-year old son Wat (artist unknown) that hangs in the National Portrait Gallery in London. To note: the uncanny similarity of their poses. Both father and son facing forward, left hands on hips, right feet pointing out at forty-five degree angles, the left feet pointing forward, and the somber determination on the boy's face to imitate the self-confident, imperious stare of the father. To remember: that when Raleigh was released after a thirteen-year incarceration in the Tower of London (1618) and launched out on the doomed voyage to Guiana to clear his name, Wat was with him. To remember that Wat, leading a reckless military charge against the Spanish, lost his life in the jungle. Raleigh to his wife: "I never knew what sorrow meant until now." And so he went back to England, and allowed the King to chop off his head.

To be followed by more photographs, perhaps several dozen: Mallarmé's son, Anatole; Anne Frank ("This is a photo that shows me as I should always like to look. Then I would surely have a chance to go to Hollywood. But now, unfortunately, I usually look different"); Mur; the children of Cambodia; the children of Atlanta. The dead children. The children who will vanish, the children who are dead. Himmler: "I have made the decision to annihilate every Jewish child from the face of the earth." Nothing but pictures. Because, at a certain point, the words lead one to conclude that it is no longer possible to speak. Because these pictures are the unspeakable.

He has spent the greater part of his adult life walking through cities, many of them foreign. He has spent the greater part of his adult life hunched over a small rectangle of wood, concentrating on an even smaller rectangle of white paper. He has spent the greater part of his adult life standing up and sitting down and pacing back and forth. These are the limits of the known world. He listens. When he hears something, he begins to listen again. Then he waits. He watches and waits. And when he begins to see something, he watches and waits again. These are the limits of the known world.

The room. Brief mention of the room and/or the dangers lurking inside it. As in the image: Hölderlin in his room.

To revive the memory of that mysterious, three-month journey on foot, crossing the mountains of the Massif Central alone, his fingers gripped tightly around the pistol in his pocket; that journey from Bordeaux to Stuttgart (hundreds of miles) that preceded his first mental breakdown in 1802.

"Dear friend . . . I have not written to you for a long time, and meanwhile have been in France and have seen the sad, lonely earth; the shepherds and shepherdesses of southern France and individual beauties, men and women, who grew up in fear of political uncertainty and of hunger. . . . The mighty element, the fire of heaven and the silence of the people, their life in nature, their confinedness and their contentment, moved me continually, and as one says of heroes, I can well say of myself that Apollo has struck me."

Arriving in Stuttgart, "deathly pale, very thin, with hollow wild eyes, long hair and a beard, and dressed like a beggar," he stood before his friend Matthison and spoke one word only: "Hölderlin."

Six months later, his beloved Suzette was dead. By 1806, schizophrenia, and thereafter, for thirty-six years, fully half his life, he lived alone in the tower built for him by Zimmer, the carpenter from Tubingen— *zimmer*, which in German means *room*.

TO ZIMMER
The lines of life are various as roads or as
The limits of the mountains are, and what we are
Down here, in harmonies, in recompense,
In peace for ever, a god will finish there.

Toward the end of Hölderlin's life, a visitor to the tower mentioned Suzette's name. The poet replied: "Ah, my Diotima. Don't speak to me about my Diotima. Thirteen sons she bore me. One is Pope, another is the Sultan, the third is the Emperor of Russia. . . ." And then: "Do you know what happened to her? She went mad, she did, mad, mad, mad."

During those years, it is said, Hölderlin rarely went out. When he did leave his room, it was only to take aimless walks through the countryside, filling his pockets with stones and picking flowers, which he would later tear to shreds. In town, the students laughed at him, and children ran away in fear whenever he approached to greet them. Towards the end, his mind became so muddled that he began to call himself by different names—Scardinelli, Killalusimeno—and once, when a visitor was slow to leave his room, he showed him the door and said, with a finger raised in warning, "I am the Lord God."

In recent years, there has been renewed speculation about Hölderlin's life in that room. One man contends that Hölderlin's madness was feigned, and that in response to the stultifying political reaction that overwhelmed Germany following the French revolution, the poet withdrew from the world. He lived, so to speak, underground in the tower. According to this theory, all of the writings of Hölderlin's madness (1806–1843) were in fact composed in a secret, revolutionary code. There is even a play that expands upon this idea. In the final scene of that work, the young Marx pays Hölderlin a visit in his tower. We are led to presume from this encounter that it was the old and dying poet who inspired Marx to write *The Economic and Philosophical Manuscripts of 1844*. If this were so, then Hölderlin would not only have been the greatest German poet of the nineteenth century but also a central figure in the history of political thought: the link between Hegel and Marx. For it is a documented fact that as young men Hölderlin and Hegel were friends. They were students together at the seminary in Tübingen.

Speculations of this sort, however, strike A. as tedious. He has no difficulty in accepting Hölderlin's presence in the room. He would even go so far as to say that Hölderlin could not have survived anywhere else. If not for Zimmer's generosity and kindness, it is possible that Hölderlin's life would have ended prematurely. To withdraw into a room does not mean that one has been blinded. To be mad does not mean that one has been struck dumb. More than likely, it is the room that restored Hölderlin to life, that gave him back whatever life it was left for him to live. As Jerome commented on the Book of Jonah, glossing the passage that tells of Jonah in the belly of the whale: "You will note that where you would think should be the end of Jonah, there was his safety."

"The image of man has eyes," wrote Hölderlin, during the first year of his life in that room, "whereas the moon has light. King Oedipus has an eye too many perhaps. The sufferings of this man, they seem indescribable, unspeakable, inexpressible. If the drama represents something like this, that is why. But what comes over me as I think of you now? Like brooks the end of something sweeps me away, which expands like Asia. Of course, this affliction, Oedipus has it too. Of course, that is why. Did Hercules suffer too? Indeed. . . . For to fight with God, like Hercules, that is an affliction. And immortality amidst the envy of this life, to share in that, is an affliction too. But this is also an affliction, when a man is covered with freckles, to be wholly covered with many a spot! The beautiful sun does that: for it rears up all things. It leads young men along their course with the allurements of its beams as though with roses. The afflictions that Oedipus bore seem like this, as when a poor man complains there is something he lacks. Son of Laios, poor stranger in Greece! Life is death, and death is a kind of life."

The room. Counter-argument to the above. Or: reasons for being in the room.

The Book of Memory. Book Five.

Two months after his father's death (January 1979), A.'s marriage collapsed. The problems had been brewing for some time, and at last the decision was made to separate. If it was one thing for him to accept this break-up, to be miserable about it and yet to understand that it was inevitable, it was quite another thing for him to swallow the consequences it entailed: to be separated from his son. The thought of it was intolerable to him.

He moved into his room on Varick Street in early spring. For the next few months he shuttled between that room and the house in Dutchess County where he and his wife had been living for the past three years. During the week: solitude in the city; on the weekends: visits to the country, one hundred miles away, where he slept in what was now his former work room and played with his son, not yet two years old, and read to him from the treasured books of the period: *Let's Go Trucks, Caps for Sale, Mother Goose*.

Shortly after he moved into the Varick Street room, the six-year old Etan Patz disappeared from the streets of that same neighborhood. Everywhere A. turned, there was a photograph of the boy (on lampposts, in shop windows, on blank brick walls), headlined by the words: LOST CHILD. Because the face of this child did not differ drastically from the face of his own child (and even if it had, it might not have mattered), every time he saw the photograph of this face he was made to think of his own son— and in precisely these terms: lost child. Etan Patz had been sent downstairs one morning by his mother to wait for the school bus (the first day following a long bus driver strike, and the boy had been eager to do this one little thing on his own, to make this small gesture of independence), and then was not seen again. Whatever it was that happened to him, it happened without a trace. He could have been kidnapped, he could have been murdered, or perhaps he simply wandered off and came to his death in a place where no one could see him. The only thing that can be said with any certainty is that he vanished—as if from the face of the earth. The newspapers made much of this story (interviews with the parents, interviews with the detectives assigned to the case, articles about the boy's personality: what games he liked to play, what foods he liked to eat), and A. began to realize that the presence of this disaster—superimposed on his own and admittedly much smaller disaster—was inescapable. Each thing that fell before his eyes seemed to be no more than an image of what was inside him. The days went by, and each day a little more of the pain inside him was dragged out into the open. A sense of loss took hold of him, and it would not let go. And there were times when this loss was so great, and so suffocating, that he thought it would never let go.

* * *

Some weeks later, at the beginning of summer. A radiant New York June: clarity of the light falling on the bricks; blue, transparent skies, zeroing to an azure that would have charmed even Mallarmé.

A.'s grandfather (on his mother's side) was slowly beginning to die. Only a year before he had performed magic tricks at A.'s son's first birthday party, but now, at eighty-five, he was so weak that he could no longer stand without support, could no longer move without an effort of will so intense that merely to think of moving was enough to exhaust him. There was a family conference at the doctor's office, and the decision was made to send him to Doctor's Hospital on East End Avenue and Eighty-eighth Street (the same hospital in which his wife had died of amniotropic lateral sclerosis—Lou Gehrig's disease—eleven years earlier). A. was at that conference, as were his mother and his mother's sister, his grandfather's two children. Because neither of the women could remain in New York, it was agreed that A. would be responsible for everything. A.'s mother had to return home to California to take care of her own gravely ill husband, while A.'s aunt was about to go to Paris to visit her first grandchild, the recently born daughter of her only son. Everything, it seemed, had quite literally become a matter of life and death. At which point, A. suddenly found himself thinking (perhaps because his grandfather had always reminded him of W.C. Fields) of a scene from the 1932 Fields film, *Million Dollar Legs:* Jack Oakey runs frantically to catch up with a departing stage coach and beseeches the driver to stop; "It's a matter of life and death!" he shouts. And the driver calmly and cynically replies: "What isn't?"

During this family conference A. could see the fear on his grandfather's face. At one point the old man caught his eye and gestured up to the wall beside the doctor's desk, which was covered with laminated plaques, framed certificates, awards, degrees, and testimonials, and gave a knowing nod, as if to say, "Pretty impressive, eh? This guy will take good care of me." The old man had always been taken in by pomp of this sort. "I've just received a letter from the president of the Chase Manhattan Bank," he would say, when in fact it was nothing more than a form letter. That day in the doctor's office, however, it was painful for A. to see it: the old man's refusal to recognize the thing that was looking him straight in the eyes. "I feel good about all this, doctor," his grandfather said. "I know you're going to get me better again." And yet, almost against his will, A. found himself admiring this capacity for blindness. Later that day, he helped his grandfather pack a small satchel of things to take to the hospital. The old man tossed three or four of his magic tricks into the bag. "Why are you bothering with those?" A. asked. "So I can entertain the nurses," his grandfather replied, "in case things get dull."

A. decided to stay in his grandfather's apartment for as long as the old man was in the hospital. The place could not remain empty (someone had to pay the bills, collect the mail, water the plants), and it was bound to be more comfortable than the room on Varick Street. Above all, the illusion had to be maintained that the old man was coming back. Until there was death, there was always the possibility there would not be death, and this chance, slight though it was, had to be credited.

A. remained in that apartment for the next six or seven weeks. It was the same place he had been visiting since earliest childhood: that tall, squat, oddly shaped building that stands on the corner of Central Park South and Columbus Circle. He wondered how many hours he had spent as a boy looking out at the traffic as it wove around the statue of Christopher Columbus. Through those same sixth floor windows he had watched the Thanksgiving Day parades, seen the construction of the Coliseum, spent entire afternoons counting the people as they walked by on the streets below. Now he was surrounded by this place again, with the Chinese telephone table, his grandmother's glass menagerie, and the old humidor. He had walked straight back into his childhood.

A. continued to hope for a reconciliation with his wife. When she agreed to come to the city with their son to stay at the apartment, he felt that perhaps a real change would be possible. Cut off from the objects and cares of their own life, they seemed to settle in nicely to these neutral surroundings. But neither one of them was ready at that point to admit that this was not an illusion, an act of memory coupled with an act of groundless hope.

Every afternoon A. would travel to the hospital by boarding two buses, spend an hour or two with his grandfather, and then return by the same route he had come. This arrangement worked for about ten days. Then the weather changed. An excruciating heat fell on New York, and the city became a nightmare of sweat, exhaustion, and noise. None of this did the little boy any good (cooped up in the apartment with a sputtering air conditioner, or else traipsing through the steamy streets with his mother), and when the weather refused to break (record humidity for several weeks running), A. and his wife decided that she and the boy should return to the country.

He stayed on in his grandfather's apartment alone. Each day became a repetition of the day before. Conversations with the doctor, the trip to the hospital, hiring and firing private nurses, listening to his grandfather's complaints, straightening the pillows under his head. There was a horror that went through him each time he glimpsed the old man's flesh. The emaciated limbs, the shriveled testicles, the body that had shrunk to less than a hundred pounds. This was a once corpulent man, whose proud, well-stuffed belly had preceded his every step through the world, and now he was hardly there. If A. had experienced one kind of death earlier in the year, a death so sudden that even as it gave him over to death it deprived him of the knowledge of that death, now he was experiencing death of another kind, and it was this slow, mortal exhaustion, this letting go of life in the heart of life, that finally taught him the thing he had known all along.

Nearly every day there was a phone call from his grandfather's former secretary, a woman who had worked in the office for more than twenty years. After his grandmother's death, she had become the steadiest of his grandfather's lady companions, the respectable woman he trotted out for public view on formal occasions: family gatherings, weddings, funerals. Each time she called, she would make copious inquiries about his grandfather's health, and then ask A. to arrange for her to visit the hospital. The problem was her own bad health. Although not old (late sixties at most), she suffered from Parkinson's disease, and for some time had been living in a nursing home in the Bronx. After numerous conversations (her voice so faint over the telephone that it took all of A.'s powers of concentration to hear even half of what she said), he finally agreed to meet her in front of the Metropolitan Museum, where a special bus from the nursing home deposited ambulatory patients once a week for an afternoon in Manhattan. On that particular day, for the first time in nearly a month, it rained. A. arrived in advance of the appointed time, and then, for more than an hour, stood on the museum steps, keeping his head dry with a newspaper, on the lookout for the woman. At last, deciding to give up, he made one final tour of the area. It was then that he found her: a block or two up Fifth Avenue, standing under a pathetic sapling, as if to protect herself from the rain, a clear plastic bonnet on her head, leaning on her walking stick, body bent forward, all of her rigid, afraid to take a step, staring down at the wet sidewalk. Again that feeble voice, and A. almost pressing his ear against her mouth to hear her—only to glean some paltry and insipid remark: the bus driver had forgotten to shave, the newspaper had not been delivered. A. had always been bored by this woman, and even when she had been well he had cringed at having to spend more than five minutes in her company. Now he found himself almost angry at her, resenting the way in which she seemed to expect him to pity her. He lashed out at her in his mind for being such an abject creature of self-absorption.

More than twenty minutes went by before he could get a cab. And then the endless ordeal of walking her to the curb and putting her into the taxi. Her shoes scraping on the pavement: one inch and then pause; another inch and then pause; another inch and then another inch. He held her arm and did his best to encourage her along. When they reached the hospital and he finally managed to disentangle her from the back seat of the cab, they began the slow journey toward the entrance. Just in front of the door, at the very instant A. thought they were going to make it, she froze. She had suddenly been gripped by the fear that she could not move, and therefore she could not move. No matter what A. said to her, no matter how gently he tried to coax her forward, she would not budge. People were going in and out—doctors, nurses, visitors—and there they stood, A. and the helpless woman, locked in the middle of that human traffic. A. told her to wait where she was (as if she could have done anything else), and went into the lobby, where he found an empty wheelchair, which he snatched out from under the eyes of a suspicious woman administrator. Then he eased his helpless companion into the chair and bustled her through the lobby toward the elevator, fending off the shouts of the administrator: "Is she a patient? Is that woman a patient? Wheelchairs are for patients only."

When he wheeled her into his grandfather's room, the old man was drowsing, neither asleep nor awake, lolling in a torpor at the edge of consciousness. He revived enough at the sound of their entering to perceive their presence, and then, at last understanding what had happened, smiled for the first time in weeks. Tears suddenly filled his eyes. He took hold of the woman's hand and said to A., as if addressing the entire world (but feebly, ever so feebly): "Shirley is my sweetheart. Shirley is the one I love."

In late July, A. decided to spend a weekend out of the city. He wanted to see his son, and he needed a break from the heat and the hospital. His wife came into New York, leaving the boy with her parents. What they did in the city that day he cannot remember, but by late afternoon they had made it out to the beach in Connecticut where the boy had spent the day with his grandparents. A. found his son sitting on a swing, and the first words out of the boy's mouth (having been coached all afternoon by his grandmother) were surprising in their lucidity. "I'm very happy to see you, Daddy," he said.

At the same time, the voice sounded strange to A. The boy seemed to be short of breath, and he spoke each word in a staccato of separate syllables. A. had no doubt that something was wrong. He insisted that they all leave the beach at once and go back to the house. Although the boy was in good spirits, this curious, almost mechanical voice continued to speak through him, as though he were a ventriloquist's dummy. His breathing was extremely rapid: heaving torso, in and out, in and out, like the breathing of a little bird. Within an hour, A. and his wife were looking down a list of local pediatricians, trying to reach one who was in (it was dinner hour on Friday night). On the fifth or sixth try they got hold of a young woman doctor who had recently taken over a practice in town. By some fluke, she happened to be in her office at that hour, and she told them to come right over. Either because she was new at her work, or because she had an excitable nature, her examination of the little boy threw A. and his wife into a panic. She sat the boy up on the table, listened to his chest, counted his breaths per minute, observed his flared nostrils, the slightly bluish tint to the skin of his face. Then a mad rush about the office, trying to rig up a complicated breathing device: a vapor machine with a hood, reminiscent of a nineteenth century camera. But the boy would not keep his head under the hood, and the hissing of the cold steam frightened him. The doctor then tried a shot of adrenalin. "We'll try this one," she said, "and if it doesn't work we'll give him another." She waited a few minutes, went through the breath-rate calculations again, and then gave him the second shot. Still no effect. "That's it," she said. "We'll have to take him to the hospital." She made the necessary phone call, and with a furious energy that seemed to gather up everything into her small body, told A. and his wife how to follow her to the hospital, where to go, what to do, and then led them outside, where they left in separate cars. Her diagnosis was pneumonia with asthmatic complications—which, after X-rays and more sophisticated tests at the hospital, turned out to be the case.

The boy was put in a special room in the children's ward, pricked and poked by nurses, held down screaming as liquid medicine was poured into his throat, hooked up to an I.V. line, and placed in a crib that was then covered by a clear plastic tent—into which a mist of cold oxygen was pumped from a valve in the wall. The boy remained in this tent for three days and three nights. His parents were allowed to be with him continuously, and they took turns sitting beside the boy's crib, head and arms under the tent, reading him books, telling him stories, playing games, while the other sat in a small reading room reserved for adults, watching the faces of the other parents whose children were in the hospital: none of these strangers daring to talk to each other, since they were all thinking of only one thing, and to speak of it would only have made it worse.

It was exhausting for the boy's parents, since the medicine dripping into his veins was composed essentially of adrenaline. This charged him with extra doses of energy—above and beyond the normal energy of a two-year old—and much of their time was spent in trying to calm him down, restraining him from breaking out of the tent. For A. this was of little consequence. The fact of the boy's illness, the fact that had they not taken him to the doctor in time he might actually have died, (and the horror that washed over him when he thought: what if he and his wife had decided to spend the night in the city, entrusting the boy to his grandparents—who, in their old age, had ceased to be observant of details, and who, in fact, had not noticed the boy's strange breathing at the beach and had scoffed at A. when he first mentioned it), the fact of all these things made the struggle to keep the boy calm as nothing to A. Merely to have contemplated the possibility of the boy's death, to have had the thought of his death thrown in his face at the doctor's office, was enough for him to treat the boy's recovery as a sort of resurrection, a miracle dealt to him by the cards of chance.

His wife, however, began to show the strain. At one point she walked out to A., who was in the adult sitting room, and said: "I give up, I can't handle him anymore"—and there was such resentment in her voice against the boy, such an anger of exasperation, that something inside A. fell to pieces. Stupidly, cruelly, he wanted to punish his wife for such selfishness, and in that one instant all the newly won harmony that had been growing between them for the past month vanished: for the first time in all their years together, he had turned against her. He stormed out of the room and went to his son's bedside.

The modern nothingness. Interlude on the force of parallel lives.

In Paris that fall he attended a small dinner party given by a friend of his, J., a well-known French writer. There was another American among the guests, a scholar who specialized in modern French poetry, and she spoke to A. of a book she was in the process of editing: the selected writings of Mallarmé. Had A., she wondered, ever translated any Mallarmé?

The fact was that he had. More than five years earlier, shortly after moving into the apartment on Riverside Drive, he had translated a number of the fragments Mallarmé wrote at the bedside of his dying son, Anatole, in 1879. These were short works of the greatest obscurity: notes for a poem that never came to be written. They were not even discovered until the late 1950s. In 1974, A. had done rough translation drafts of thirty or forty of them and then had put the manuscript away. When he returned from Paris to his room on Varick Street (December 1979, exactly one hundred years after Mallarmé had scribbled those death notes to his son), he dug out the folder that contained the handwritten drafts and began to work up final versions of his translations. These were later published in the *Paris Review*, along with a photograph of Anatole in a sailor suit. From his prefatory note: "On October 6, 1879, Mallarmé's only son, Anatole, died at the age of eight after a long illness. The disease, diagnosed as child's rheumatism, had slowly spread from limb to limb and eventually overtaken the boy's entire body. For several months Mallarmé and his wife had sat helplessly at Anatole's bedside as doctors tried various remedies and administered unsuccessful treatments. The boy was shuttled from the city to the country and back to the city again. On August 22 Mallarmé wrote to his friend Henry Ronjon 'of the struggle between life and death our poor little darling is going through . . . But the real pain is that this little being might vanish. I confess that it is too much for me; I cannot bring myself to face this idea.' "

It was precisely this idea, A. realized, that moved him to return to these texts. The act of translating them was not a literary exercise. It was a way for him to relive his own moment of panic in the doctor's office that summer: it is too much for me, I cannot face it. For it was only at that moment, he later came to realize, that he had finally grasped the full scope of his own fatherhood: the boy's life meant more to him than his own; if dying were necessary to save his son, he would be willing to die. And it was therefore only in that moment of fear that he had become, once and for all, the father of his son. Translating those forty or so fragments by Mallarmé was perhaps an insignificant thing, but in his own mind it had become the equivalent of offering a prayer of thanks

you can, with your little
hands, drag me
into the grave—you
have the right—
—I
who follow you, I
let myself go—
—but if you
wish, the two
of us, let us make . . .

an alliance
a hymen, superb
—and the life
remaining in me
I will use for——

*

no—nothing
to do with the great
deaths—etc.
—as long as we
go on living, he
lives—in us

it will only be after our
death that he will be dead
—and the bells
of the Dead will toll for
                              him

*

sail—
navigates
river,
your life that
goes by, that flows

*

for the life of his son. A prayer to what? To nothing perhaps. To his sense of life. To *the modern nothingness*.

Brief commentary on the word "radiance."

He first heard this word used in connection with his son when he had shown a photograph of the boy to his good friend, R., an American poet who had lived for eight years in Amsterdam. They were drinking in a bar that night, surrounded by a press of bodies and loud music. A. pulled the snapshot out of his wallet and handed it to R., who studied the picture for a long time. Then he turned to A., a little drunk, and said with great emotion in his voice: "He has the same radiance as Titus."

About one year later, shortly after the publication of "A Tomb for Anatole" in the *Paris Review*, A. happened to be visiting R. R. (who had grown extremely fond of A.'s son) explained to A.: "An extraordinary thing happened to me today. I was in a bookstore, leafing through various magazines, and I happened to open the *Paris Review* to a photograph of Mallarmé's son. For a second I thought it was your son. The resemblance was that striking."

A. replied: "But those were my translations. I was the one who made them put in that picture. Didn't you know that?"

And then R. said: "I never got that far. I was so struck by the picture that I had to close the magazine. I put it back on the shelf and then walked out of the store."

His grandfather lasted another two or three weeks. A. returned to the apartment overlooking Columbus Circle, his son now out of danger, his marriage now at a permanent standstill. These were probably the worst days of all for him. He could not work, he could not think. He began to neglect himself, ate only noxious foods (frozen dinners, pizza, take-out Chinese noodles), and left the apartment to its own devices: dirty clothes strewn in a bedroom corner, unwashed dishes piled in the kitchen sink. Lying on the couch, smoking cigarette after cigarette, he would watch old movies on television and read second-rate mystery novels. He did not try to reach any of his friends. The one person he did call—a girl he had met in Paris when he was eighteen—had moved to Colorado.

One night, for no particular reason, he went out to wander around the lifeless neighborhood of the West Fifties and walked into a topless bar. As he sat there at his table drinking a beer, he suddenly found himself

Setting sun
and wind
　　now vanished, and
wind of *nothing*
that breathes
(here, the modern
? nothingness)

*

death—whispers softly
—I am no one—
I do not even know who I am
(for the dead do not
know they are
dead—, nor even that they
　　　　　　　　　die
—for children
at least
　—or

heroes—sudden
deaths

for otherwise
my beauty is
made *of last*
moments—
lucidity, beauty
face—of what would be

me, without myself

*

sitting next to a voluptuously naked young woman. She sidled up to him and began to describe all the lewd things she would do to him if he paid her to go to "the back room." There was something so openly humorous and matter-of-fact about her approach that he finally agreed to her proposition. The best thing, they decided, would be for her to suck his penis, since she claimed an extraordinary talent for this activity. And indeed, she threw herself into it with an enthusiasm that fairly astonished him. As he came in her mouth a few moments later, with a long and throbbing flood of semen, he had this vision, at just that second, which has continued to radiate inside him: that each ejaculation contains several billion sperm cells—or roughly the same number as there are people in the world—which means that, in himself, each man holds the potential of an entire world. And what would happen, could it happen, is the full range of possibilities: a spawn of idiots and geniuses, of the beautiful and the deformed, of saints, catatonics, thieves, stock brokers, and high-wire artists. Each man, therefore, is the entire world, bearing within his genes a memory of all mankind. Or, as Leibniz put it: "Every living substance is a perpetual living mirror of the universe." For the fact is, we are of the same stuff that came into being with the first explosion of the first spark in the infinite emptiness of space. Or so he said to himself, at that moment, as his penis exploded into the mouth of that naked woman, whose name he has now forgotten. He thought: the irreducible monad. And then, as though taking hold of it at last, he thought of the furtive, microscopic cell that had fought its way up through his wife's body, some three years earlier, to become his son.

Otherwise nothing. He languished. He sweltered in the summer heat. Like some latter-day Oblomov curled on his couch, he did not move unless he had to.

There was a cable television in his grandfather's apartment, with more channels than A. had ever known existed. Whenever he turned it on, there seemed to be a baseball game in progress. Not only was he able to follow the Yankees and Mets of New York, but the Red Sox of Boston, the Phillies of Philadelphia, and the Braves of Atlanta. Not to speak of the little bonuses occasionally provided during the afternoon: the games from the Japanese major leagues, for example (and his fascination with the constant beating of drums during the course of the game), or, even more strangely, the Little League championships from Long Island. To

Oh! you understand
that if I consent
to live—to seem
to forget you—
it is to
feed my pain
—and so that this apparent
forgetfulness
        can spring forth more
    horribly in tears, at

    some random
    moment, in
    the middle of this
    life, when you
    appear to me

                    *

true mourning in
    the apartment
—not cemetery—

            furniture

                    *

to find *only*
absence—
—in presence
of little clothes
—etc—

                    *

    no—I will not
give up
        nothingness

        father—I
feel nothingness
    invade me

immerse himself in these games was to feel his mind striving to enter a place of pure form. Despite the agitation on the field, baseball offered itself to him as an image of that which does not move, and therefore a place where his mind could be at rest, secure in its refuge against the mutabilities of the world.

He had spent his entire childhood playing it. From the first muddy days in early March to the last frozen afternoons of late October. He had played well, with an almost obsessive devotion. Not only had it given him a feeling for his own possibilities, convinced him that he was not entirely hopeless in the eyes of others, but it had been the thing that drew him out from the solitary enclosures of his early childhood. It had initiated him into the world of the other, but at the same time it was something he could also keep within himself. Baseball was a terrain rich in potential for reverie. He fantasized about it continually, projecting himself into a New York Giants uniform and trotting out to his position at third base in the Polo Grounds, with the crowd cheering wildly at the mention of his name over the loudspeakers. Day after day, he would come home from school and throw a tennis ball against the steps of his house, pretending that each gesture was a part of the World Series game unfolding in his head. It always came down to two outs in the bottom of the ninth, a man on base, the Giants trailing by one. He was always the batter, and he always hit the game-winning homerun.

As he sat through those long summer days in his grandfather's apartment, he began to see that the power of baseball was for him the power of memory. Memory in both senses of the word: as a catalyst for remembering his own life and as an artificial structure for ordering the historical past. 1960, for example, was the year Kennedy was elected president; it was also the year of A.'s Bar Mitzvah, the year he supposedly reached manhood. But the first image that springs to his mind when 1960 is mentioned is Bill Mazeroski's homerun that beat the Yankees in the World Series. He can still see the ball soaring over the Forbes Field fence—that high, dark barrier, so densely cluttered with white numbers—and by recalling the sensations of that moment, that abrupt and stunning instant of pleasure, he is able to re-enter his own past, to stand in a world that would otherwise be lost to him.

He reads in a book: since 1893 (the year before his grandfather was born), when the pitcher's mound was moved back ten feet, the shape of the field has not changed. The diamond is a part of our consciousness.

Its pristine geometry of white lines, green grass, and brown dirt is an icon as familiar as the stars and stripes. As opposed to just about everything else in American life during this century, baseball has remained constant. Except for a few minor alterations (artificial turf, designated hitters), the game as it is played today is remarkably similar to the one played by Wee Willie Keeler and the old Baltimore Orioles: those long dead young men of the photographs, with their handlebar moustaches and heroic poses.

What happens today is merely a variation on what happened yesterday. Yesterday echoes today, and tomorrow will foreshadow what happens next year. Professional baseball's past is intact. There is a record of every game played, a statistic for every hit, error, and base on balls. One can measure performances against each other, compare players and teams, speak of the dead as if they were still alive. To play the game as a child is simultaneously to imagine playing it as an adult, and the power of this fantasy is present in even the most casual pick-up game. How many hours of his boyhood, A. wonders, were spent trying to imitate Stan Musial's batting stance (feet together, knees bent, back hunched over in a taut French curve) or the basket catches of Willie Mays? Reciprocally, for those who grow up to be professionals, there is an awareness that they are living out their childhood dreams—in effect, being paid to remain children. Nor should the depth of those dreams be minimized. In his own Jewish childhood, A. can remember confusing the last words of the Passover Seder, "Next year in Jerusalem," with the ever-hopeful refrain of disappointed fandom, "Wait till next year," as if the one were a commentary on the other: to win the pennant was to enter the promised land. Baseball had somehow become entangled in his mind with the religious experience.

It was just then, as A. was beginning to sink into this baseball quicksand, that Thurman Munson was killed. A. noted that Munson was the first Yankee captain since Lou Gehrig, that his grandmother had died of Lou Gehrig's disease, and that his grandfather's death would come quickly in the wake of Munson's.

The newspapers were filled with articles about the catcher. A. had always admired Munson's play on the field: the quick bat flicking singles to right, the stumpy body chugging around the bases, the anger that seemed to consume him as he went about his business behind the plate. Now A. was moved to learn of Munson's work with children and the troubles he had had with his own hyperactive son. Everything seemed to be repeating itself. Reality was a Chinese box, an infinite series of containers within containers. For here again, in the most unlikely of places, the theme had reappeared: the curse of the absent father. It seemed that Munson himself was the only one who had the power to calm down the little boy. Whenever he was at home, the boy's outbursts stopped, his frenzies abated. Munson was learning how to fly a plane so that he could go home more often during the baseball season to be with his son, and it was the plane that killed him.

Inevitably, A.'s memories of baseball were connected with his memories of his grandfather. It was his grandfather who had taken him to his first game, had talked to him about the old players, had shown him that baseball was as much about talk as it was about watching. As a little boy, A. would be dropped off at the office on Fifty-seventh Street, play around with the typewriters and adding machines until his grandfather was ready to leave, and then walk out with him for a leisurely stroll down Broadway. The ritual always included a few rounds of Pokerino in one of the amusement arcades, a quick lunch, and then the subway— to one of the city ball parks. Now, with his grandfather disappearing into death, they continued to talk about baseball. It was the one subject they could still come to as equals. Each time he visited the hospital, A. would buy a copy of the *New York Post*, and then sit by the old man's bed, reading to him about the games of the day before. It was his last contact with the outside world, and it was painless, a series of coded messages he could understand with his eyes closed. Anything else would have been too much.

Toward the very end, with a voice that could barely produce a sound, his grandfather told him that he had begun to remember his life. He had been dredging up the days of his Toronto boyhood, reliving events that had taken place as far back as eighty years ago: defending his younger brother against a gang of bullies, delivering bread on Friday afternoon to the Jewish families in the neighborhood, all the trivial, long-forgotten things that now, coming back to him as he lay immobilized in bed, took on the importance of spiritual illuminations. "Lying here gives me a chance to remember," he told A., as if this were a new power he had discovered in himself. A. could sense the pleasure it gave him. Little by little, it had begun to dominate the fear that had been in his grandfather's face these past weeks. Memory was the only thing keeping him alive, and it was as though he wanted to hold off death for as long as possible in order to go on remembering.

He knew, and yet he would not say he knew. Until the final week, he continued to talk about returning to his apartment, and not once was the word "death" mentioned. Even on the last day, he waited until the last possible moment to say good-bye. A. was leaving, walking through the door after a visit, when his grandfather called him back. Again, A. stood beside the bed. The old man took hold of his hand and squeezed as hard as he could. Then: a long, long moment. At last, A. bent down and kissed his grandfather's face. Neither one of them said a word.

A. remembers a schemer, a maker of deals, a man of bizarre and grandiose optimisms. Who else, after all, could have named his daughter Queenie with a straight face? But at her birth he had declared, "she'll be a queen," and could not resist the temptation. He thrived on bluff, the symbolic gesture, on being the life of the party. Lots of jokes, lots of cronies, an impeccable sense of timing. He gambled on the sly, cheated on his wife (the older he got, the younger the girls), and never lost his taste for any of it. His locutions were particularly splendid. A towel was never just a towel, but a "Turkish towel." A taker of drugs was a "dope fiend." Nor would he ever say "I saw . . .," but rather, "I've had an opportunity to observe. . . ." In so doing, he managed to inflate the world, to turn it into a more compelling and exotic place for himself. He played the bigshot and reveled in the side-effects of the pose: the head-waiters calling him Mr. B., the delivery boys smiling at his excessive tips, the whole world tipping its hat to him. He had come down to New York from Canada just after the First World War, a poor Jewish boy on the make, and in the end he had done all right for himself. New York was his passion, and in his last years he refused to move away, resisting his daughter's offer of a life in sunny California with these words, which became a popular refrain: "I can't leave New York. This is where the action is."

A. remembers a day when he was four or five. His grandparents came for a visit, and his grandfather did a magic trick for him, some little thing he had found in a novelty shop. On the next visit, when he failed to show up with a new trick, A. raised a fuss of disappointment. From then on there was always a new piece of magic: disappearing coins, silk scarves produced from thin air, a machine that turned strips of blank paper into money, a big rubber ball that became five little rubber balls when you squeezed it in your hand, a cigarette extinguished in a hand-kerchief that made no burn, a pitcher of milk poured into a cone of newspaper that made no spill. What had started out as a curiosity to amuse his grandson became a genuine calling for him. He turned him-self into an accomplished amateur magician, a deft sleight-of-hand artist, and he took special pride in his membership card from the Magician's Guild. He appeared at each of A.'s childhood birthday par-ties with his magic and went on performing until the last year of his life, touring the senior citizen clubs of New York with one of his lady friends (a blowsy woman with a pile of fake red hair) who would sing a song, accompanying herself on the accordion, that introduced him as the Great Zavello. It was only natural. His life was so steeped in the hocus-pocus of illusion, he had pulled off so many business deals by making people believe in him (convincing them that something not there was actually there, and vice versa) that it was a small matter for him to step up on stage and fool them in a more formal way. He had the ability to make people pay attention to him, and it was clear to everyone who saw him how delighted he was to be the center of their attention. No one is less cynical than a magician. He knows, and everyone else knows, that everything he does is a sham. The trick is not really to deceive them, but to delight them into wanting to be deceived: so that for the space of a few minutes the grip of cause-and-effect is loosened, the laws of nature countermanded. As Pascal put it in the *Pensées:* "It is not possible to have reasonable grounds for not believing in miracles."

A.'s grandfather, however, did not content himself merely with magic. He was equally fond of jokes, which he called "stories"—all of them written down in a little notebook that he carried around in his coat pocket. At some point during every family gathering, he would take out the notebook, skim through it quickly in some corner of the room, put it back in his pocket, sit down in a chair, and then launch into an hour's worth of verbal nonsense. Here, too, the memory is of laughter. Not, as with S., a laughter bursting from the belly, but a laughter that mean-dered outward from the lungs, a long sing-song loop of sound that began as a wheeze and dispersed, gradually, into a fainter and fainter chromatic whistle. That, too, is how A. would like to remember him: sit-ting in that chair and making everyone laugh.

His grandfather's greatest stunt, though, was neither a magic trick nor a joke, but a kind of extra-sensory voodoo that kept everyone in the family baffled for years. It was a game called the Wizard. A.'s grandfather would take out a deck of cards, ask someone to pick a card, any card, and hold it up for everyone to see. The five of hearts. Then he would go to the phone, dial a number, and ask to speak to the Wizard. That's right, he would say, I want to speak to the Wizard. A moment later he would pass around the telephone, and coming out of the receiver there would be a voice, a man's voice, saying over and over: five of hearts, five of hearts, five of hearts. Then he would thank the Wizard, hang up the phone, and stand there grinning at everyone.

Years later, when it was finally explained to A., it all seemed so simple. His grandfather and a friend had each agreed to be the Wizard for the other. The question, May I speak to the Wizard, was a signal, and the man on the other end of the line would start reeling off the suits: spade, heart, diamond, club. When he hit the right one, the caller would say something, anything, meaning go no further, and then the Wizard would go through the litany of numbers: ace, two, three, four, five, etc. When he came to the right one, the caller would again say something, and the Wizard would stop, put the two elements together, and repeat them into the phone: five of hearts, five of hearts, five of hearts.

The Book of Memory. Book Six.

He finds it extraordinary, even in the ordinary actuality of his experience, to feel his feet on the ground, to feel his lungs expanding and contracting with the air he breathes, to know that if he puts one foot in front of the other he will be able to walk from where he is to where he is going. He finds it extraordinary that on some mornings, just after he has woken up, as he bends down to tie his shoes, he is flooded with a happiness so intense, a happiness so naturally and harmoniously at one with the world, that he can feel himself alive in the present, a present that surrounds him and permeates him, that breaks through him with the sudden, overwhelming knowledge that he is alive. And the happiness he discovers in himself at that moment is extraordinary. And whether or not it is extraordinary, he finds this happiness extraordinary.

Sometimes it feels as though we are wandering through a city without purpose. We walk down the street, turn at random down another street, stop to admire the cornice of a building, bend down to inspect a splotch of tar on the pavement that reminds us of certain paintings we have admired, look at the faces of the people who pass us on the street, trying to imagine the lives they carry around inside them, go into a cheap restaurant for lunch, walk back outside and continue on our way toward the river (if this city has a river), to watch the boats as they sail by, or the big ships docked in the harbor, perhaps singing to ourselves as we walk, or perhaps whistling, or perhaps trying to remember something we have forgotten. Sometimes it seems as though we are not going anywhere as we walk through the city, that we are only looking for a way to pass the time, and that it is only our fatigue that tells us where and when we should stop. But just as one step will inevitably lead to the next step, so it is that one thought inevitably follows from the previous thought, and in the event that a thought should engender more than a single thought (say two or three thoughts, equal to each other in all their consequences), it will be necessary not only to follow the first thought to its conclusion, but also to backtrack to the original position of that thought in order to follow the second thought to its conclusion, and then the third thought, and so on, and in this way, if we were to try to make an image of this process in our minds, a network of paths begins to be drawn, as in the image of the human bloodstream (heart, arteries, veins, capillaries), or as in the image of a map (of city streets, for example, preferably a large city, or even of roads, as in the gas station maps of roads that stretch, bisect, and meander across a continent), so that what we are really doing when we walk through the city is thinking, and thinking in such a way that our thoughts compose a journey, and this journey is no more or less than the steps we have taken, so that, in the end, we might safely say that we have been on a journey, and even if we do not leave our room, it has been a journey, and we might safely say that we have been somewhere, even if we don't know where it is.

He takes down from his bookshelf a brochure he bought ten years ago in Amherst, Massachusetts, a souvenir of his visit to Emily Dickinson's house, thinking now of the strange exhaustion that had afflicted him that day as he stood in the poet's room: a shortness of breath, as if he had just climbed to the top of a mountain. He had walked around that small, sun-drenched room, looking at the white bedspread, the polished furniture, thinking of the seventeen hundred poems that were written there, trying to see them as a part of those four walls, and yet failing to do so. For if words are a way of being in the world, he thought, then even if there were no world to enter, the world was already there, in that room, which meant it was the room that was present in the poems and not the reverse. He reads now, on the last page of the brochure, in the awkward prose of the anonymous writer:

"In this bedroom-workroom, Emily announced that the soul could be content with its own society. But she discovered that consciousness was captivity as well as liberty, so that even here she was prey to her own self-imprisonment in despair or fear. . . . For the sensitive visitor, then, Emily's room acquires an atmosphere encompassing the poet's several moods of superiority, anxiety, anguish, resignation or ecstasy. Perhaps more than any other concrete place in American literature, it symbolizes a native tradition, epitomized by Emily, of an assiduous study of the inner life."

Song to accompany The Book of Memory. *Solitude*, as sung by Billie Holiday. In the recording of May 9, 1941 by Billie Holiday and Her Orchestra. Performance time: three minutes and fifteen seconds. As follows: In my solitude you haunt me / With reveries of days gone by. / In my solitude you taunt me / With memories that never die . . . Etc. With credits to D. Ellington, E. De Lange, and I. Mills.

First allusions to a woman's voice. To be followed by specific reference to several.

For it is his belief that if there is a voice of truth—assuming there is such a thing as truth, and assuming this truth can speak—it comes from the mouth of a woman.

It is also true that memory sometimes comes to him as a voice. It is a voice that speaks inside him, and it is not necessarily his own. It speaks to him in the way a voice might tell stories to a child, and yet at times this voice makes fun of him, or calls him to attention, or curses him in no uncertain terms. At times it willfully distorts the story it is telling him, changing facts to suit its whims, catering to the interests of drama rather than truth. Then he must speak to it in his own voice and tell it to stop, thus returning it to the silence it came from. At other times it sings to him. At still other times it whispers. And then there are the times it merely hums, or babbles, or cries out in pain. And even when it says nothing, he knows it is still there, and in the silence of this voice that says nothing, he waits for it to speak.

Jeremiah: "Then said I, Ah, Lord God! behold, I cannot speak: for I am a child. But the Lord said unto me, say not, I am a child: for thou shalt go to all that I shall send thee, and whatsoever I command thee thou shalt speak. . . . Then the Lord put forth his hand, and touched my mouth. And the Lord said unto me, Behold, I have put my words in thy mouth."

The Book of Memory. Book Seven.

First commentary on the Book of Jonah.

One is immediately struck by its oddness in relation to the other prophetic books. This brief work, the only one to be written in the third person, is more dramatically a story of solitude than anything else in the Bible, and yet it is told as if from outside that solitude, as if, by plunging into the darkness of that solitude, the "I" has vanished from itself. It cannot speak about itself, therefore, except as another. As in Rimbaud's phrase: "Je est un autre."

Not only is Jonah reluctant to speak (as Jeremiah is, for example), but he actually refuses to speak. "Now the word of the Lord came unto Jonah. . . . But Jonah rose up to flee from the presence of the Lord."

Jonah flees. He books passage aboard a ship. A terrible storm rises up, and the sailors fear they will drown. Everyone prays for deliverance. But Jonah has "gone down into the sides of the ship; and he lay, and was fast asleep." Sleep, then, as the ultimate withdrawal from the world. Sleep as an image of solitude. Oblomov curled on his couch, dreaming himself back into his mother's womb. Jonah in the belly of the ship; Jonah in the belly of the whale.

The captain of the ship finds Jonah and tells him to pray to his God. Meanwhile, the sailors have drawn lots, to see which among them has been responsible for the storm, ". . . and the lot fell upon Jonah.

"And then he said unto them, Take me up, and cast me forth into the sea; so shall the sea be calm unto you; for I know that for my sake this great tempest is upon you.

"Nevertheless the men rowed hard to bring it to the land; but they could not; for the sea wrought, and was tempestuous against them. . . .

"So they took up Jonah, and cast him forth into the sea; and the sea ceased from her raging."

The popular mythology about the whale notwithstanding, the great fish that swallows Jonah is by no means an agent of destruction. The fish is what saves him from drowning in the sea. "The waters compassed me about, even to the soul: the depth closed me round about, the weeds were wrapped about my head." In the depth of that solitude, which is equally the depth of silence, as if in the refusal to speak there were an equal refusal to turn one's face to the other ("Jonah rose up to flee from the presence of the Lord")—which is to say: who seeks solitude seeks silence; who does not speak is alone; is alone, even unto death—Jonah encounters the darkness of death. We are told that "Jonah was in the belly of the fish three days and three nights," and elsewhere, in a chapter of the *Zohar*, we are told, " 'Three days and three nights': which means the three days that a man is in his grave before his belly bursts apart." And when the fish then vomits Jonah onto dry land, Jonah is given back to life, as if the death he had found in the belly of the fish were a preparation for new life, a life that has passed through death, and therefore a life that can at last speak. For death has frightened him into opening his mouth. "I cried by reason of mine affliction unto the Lord, and he heard me; out of the belly of hell cried I, and thou heardest my voice." In the darkness of the solitude that is death, the tongue is finally loosened, and at the moment it begins to speak, there is an answer. And even if there is no answer, the man has begun to speak.

The prophet. As in false: speaking oneself into the future, not by knowledge but by intuition. The real prophet knows. The false prophet guesses.

This was Jonah's greatest problem. If he spoke God's message, telling the Ninevites they would be destroyed in forty days for their wickedness, he was certain they would repent, and thus be spared. For he knew that God was "merciful, slow to anger, and of great kindness."

"So the people of Ninevah believed God, and proclaimed a fast, and put on sackcloth, from the greatest of them even to the least of them."

And if the Ninevites were spared, would this not make Jonah's prophecy false? Would he not, then, be a false prophet? Hence the paradox at the heart of the book: the prophecy would remain true only if he did not speak it. But then, of course, there would be no prophecy, and Jonah would no longer be a prophet. But better to be no prophet at all than to be a false prophet. "Therefore now, O lord, take, I beseech thee, my life from me; for it is better for me to die than to live."

Therefore, Jonah held his tongue. Therefore, Jonah ran away from the presence of the Lord and met the doom of shipwreck. That is to say, the shipwreck of the singular.

* * *

Remission of cause and effect.

A. remembers a moment from boyhood (twelve, thirteen years old). He was wandering aimlessly one November afternoon with his friend D. Nothing was happening. But in each of them, at that moment, a sense of infinite possibilities. Nothing was happening. Or else one could say that it was this consciousness of possibility, in fact, that was happening.

As they walked along through the cold, gray air of that afternoon, A. suddenly stopped and announced to his friend: One year from today something extraordinary will happen to us, something that will change our lives forever.

The year passed, and on the appointed day nothing extraordinary happened. A. explained to D.: No matter; the important thing will happen next year. When the second year rolled around, the same thing happened: nothing. But A. and D. were undaunted. All through the years of high school, they continued to commemorate that day. Not with ceremony, but simply with acknowledgement. For example, seeing each other in the school corridor and saying: Saturday is the day. It was not that they still expected a miracle to happen. But, more curiously, over the years they had both become attached to the memory of their prediction.

The reckless future, the mystery of what has not yet happened: this, too, he learned, can be preserved in memory. And it sometimes strikes him that the blind, adolescent prophecy he made twenty years ago, that fore-seeing of the extraordinary, was in fact the extraordinary thing itself: his mind leaping happily into the unknown. For the fact of the matter is, many years have passed. And still, at the end of each November, he finds himself remembering that day.

Prophecy. As in true. As in Cassandra, speaking from the solitude of her cell. As in a woman's voice.

The future falls from her lips in the present, each thing exactly as it will happen, and it is her fate never to be believed. Madwoman, the daughter of Priam: "the shrieks of that ill-omened bird" from whom ". . . sounds of woe / Burst dreadful, as she chewed the laurel leaf, / And ever and anon, like the black Sphinx, / Poured the full tide of enigmatic song." (Lycophron's *Cassandra*; in Royston's translation, 1806). To speak of the future is to use a language that is forever ahead of itself, consigning things that have not yet happened to the past, to an "already" that is forever behind itself, and in this space between utterance and act, word after word, a chasm begins to open, and for one to contemplate such emptiness for any length of time is to grow dizzy, to feel oneself falling into the abyss.

A. remembers the excitement he felt in Paris in 1974, when he discovered the seventeen-hundred line poem by Lycophron (circa 300 B.C.), which is a monologue of Cassandra's ravings in prison before the fall of Troy. He came to the poem through a translation into French by Q., a writer just his own age (twenty-four). Three years later, when he got together with Q. in a cafe on the rue Condé, he asked him whether he knew of any translations of the poem into English. Q. himself did not read or speak English, but yes, he had heard of one, by a certain Lord Royston at the beginning of the nineteenth century. When A. returned to New York in the summer of 1974, he went to the Columbia University library to look for the book. Much to his surprise, he found it. *Cassandra, translated from the original Greek of Lycophron and illustrated with notes;* Cambridge, 1806.

This translation was the only work of any substance to come from the pen of Lord Royston. He had completed the translation while still an undergraduate at Cambridge and had published the poem himself in a luxurious private edition. Then he had gone on the traditional continental tour following his graduation. Because of the Napoleonic tumult in France, he did not head south—which would have been the natural route for a young man of his interests—but instead went north, to the Scandinavian countries, and in 1808, while traveling through the treacherous waters of the Baltic Sea, drowned in a shipwreck off the coast of Russia. He was just twenty-four years old.

Lycophron: "the obscure." In his dense, bewildering poem, nothing is ever named, everything becomes a reference to something else. One is quickly lost in the labyrinth of its associations, and yet one continues to run through it, propelled by the force of Cassandra's voice. The poem is a verbal outpouring, breathing fire, consumed by fire, which obliterates itself at the edge of sense. "Cassandra's word," as a friend of A.'s put it (B.: in a lecture, curiously enough, about Hölderlin's poetry—a poetry which he compares in manner to Cassandra's speech), "this irreducible sign—*deutungslos*—a word beyond grasping, Cassandra's word, a word from which no lesson is to be drawn, a word, each time, and every time, spoken to say nothing. . . ."

After reading through Royston's translation, A. realized that a great talent had been lost in that shipwreck. Royston's English rolls along with such fury, such deft and acrobatic syntax, that to read the poem is to feel yourself trapped inside Cassandra's mouth.

line 240 An oath! they have an oath in heaven!
    Soon shall their sail be spread, and in their hands
    The strong oar quivering cleave the refluent wave;
    While songs, and hymns, and carols jubilant
    Shall charm the rosy God, to whom shall rise,
    Rife from Apollo's Delphic shrine, the smoke
    Of numerous holocausts: Well pleased shall hear
    Enorches, where the high-hung taper's light
    Gleams on his dread carousals, and when forth
    The Savage rushes on the corny field
    Mad to destroy, shall bid his vines entwist
    His sinewy strength, and hurl them to the ground.

*

line 426   . . . then Greece
    For this one crime, aye for this one, shall weep
    Myriads of sons: no funeral urn, but rocks
    Shall hearse their bones; no friends upon their dust
    Shall pour the dark libations of the dead;
    A name, a breath, an empty sound remains,
    A fruitless marble warm with bitter tears
    Of sires, and orphan babes, and widowed wives!

*

line 1686 Why pour the fruitless strain? to winds, and waves,
    Deaf winds, dull waves, and senseless shades of woods
    I chaunt, and sing mine unavailing song.
    Such woes has Lepsieus heaped upon my head,
    Steeping my words in incredulity;
    The jealous God! for from my virgin couch
    I drove him amorous, nor returned his love.
    But fate is in my voice, truth on my lips;
    What must come, will come; and when rising woes
    Burst on his head, when rushing from her seat
    His country falls, nor man nor God can save,
    Some wretch shall groan, "From her no falsehood
     flowed,
    True were the shrieks of that ill-omened bird."

It intrigues A. to consider that both Royston and Q. had translated this work while still in their early twenties. In spite of the century and a half that separated them, each had given some special force to his own language through the medium of this poem. At one point, it occurred to him that perhaps Q. was a reincarnation of Royston. Every hundred years or so Royston would be reborn to translate the poem into another language, and just as Cassandra was destined never to be believed, the work of Lycophron would remain unread, generation after generation. A useless task therefore: to write a book that would stay forever closed. And still, the image rises up in his mind: shipwreck. Consciousness falling to the bottom of the sea, and the horrible noise of cracking wood, the tall masts tumbling into the waves. To imagine Royston's thoughts the moment his body smacked against the water. To imagine the havoc of that death.

The Book of Memory. Book Eight.

By the time of his third birthday, A.'s son's taste in literature had begun to expand from simple, heavily illustrated baby books to more sophisticated children's books. The illustration was still a source of great pleasure, but it was no longer crucial. The story itself had become enough to hold his attention, and when A. came to a page with no pic-ture at all, he would be moved to see the little boy looking intently ahead, at nothing, at the emptiness of the air, at the blank wall, imagin-ing what the words were telling him. "It's fun to imagine what we can't see," he told his father once, as they were walking down the street. Another time, the boy went into the bathroom, closed the door, and did not come out. A. asked through the closed door: "What are you doing in there?" "I'm thinking," the boy said. "I have to be alone to think."

Little by little, they both began to gravitate toward one book. The story of Pinocchio. First in the Disney version, and then, soon after, in the original version, with text by Collodi and illustrations by Mussino. The little boy never tired of hearing the chapter about the storm at sea, which tells of how Pinocchio finds Gepetto in the belly of the Terrible Shark.

"Oh, Father, dear Father! Have I found you at last? Now I shall never, never leave you again!"

Gepetto explains: "The sea was rough and the whitecaps overturned the boat. Then a Terrible Shark came up out of the sea and, as soon as he saw me in the water, swam quickly toward me, put out his tongue, and swallowed me as easily as if I had been a chocolate peppermint."

"And how long have you been shut away in here?"

"From that day to this, two long weary years—two years, my Pinocchio. . . ."

"And how have you lived? Where did you find the candle? And the matches to light it with—where did you get them?"

"In the storm which swamped my boat, a large ship also suffered the same fate. The sailors were all saved, but the ship went right down to the bottom of the sea, and the same Terrible Shark that swallowed me, swallowed most of it. . . . To my own good luck, that ship was loaded with meat, preserved foods, crackers, bread, bottles of wine, raisins, cheese, coffee, sugar, wax candles, and boxes of matches. With all these blessings, I have been able to live on for two whole years, but now I am at the very last crumbs. Today there is nothing left in the cupboard, and this candle you see here is the last one I have."

"And then?"

"And then, my dear, we'll find ourselves in darkness."

For A. and his son, so often separated from each other during the past year, there was something deeply satisfying in this passage of reunion. In effect, Pinocchio and Gepetto are separated throughout the entire book. Gepetto is given the mysterious piece of talking wood by the carpenter, Master Cherry, in the second chapter. In the third chapter the old man sculpts the Marionette. Even before Pinocchio is finished, his pranks and mischief begin. "I deserve it," says Gepetto to himself. "I should have thought of this before I made him. Now it's too late." At this point, like any newborn baby, Pinocchio is pure will, libidinous need without consciousness. Very rapidly, over the next few pages, Gepetto teaches his son to walk, the Marionette experiences hunger and accidentally burns his feet off—which his father rebuilds for him. The next day Gepetto sells his coat to buy Pinocchio an A-B-C book for school ("Pinocchio understood . . . and, unable to restrain his tears, he jumped on his father's neck and kissed him over and over"), and then, for more than two hundred pages, they do not see each other again. The rest of the book tells the story of Pinocchio's search for his father—and Gepetto's search for his son. At some point, Pinocchio realizes that he wants to become a real boy. But it also becomes clear that this will not happen until he is reunited with his father. Adventures, misadventures, detours, new resolves, struggles, happpenstance, progress, setbacks, and through it all, the gradual dawning of conscience. The superiority of the Collodi original to the Disney adaptation lies in its reluctance to make the inner motivations of the story explicit. They remain intact, in a pre-conscious, dream-like form, whereas in Disney these things are expressed—which sentimentalizes them, and therefore trivializes them. In Disney, Gepetto prays for a son; in Collodi, he simply makes him. The physical act of shaping the puppet (from a piece of wood that talks, that is *alive*, which mirrors Michaelangelo's notion of sculpture: the figure is already there in the material; the artist merely hews away at the excess matter until the true form is revealed, implying that Pinocchio's being precedes his body: his task throughout the book is to find it, in other words to find himself, which means that this is a story of becoming rather than of birth), this act of shaping the puppet is enough to convey the idea of the prayer, and surely it is more powerful for remaining silent. Likewise with Pinocchio's efforts to attain real boyhood. In Disney, he is commanded by the Blue Fairy to be "brave, truthful, and unselfish," as though there were an easy formula for taking hold of the self. In Collodi, there are no directives. Pinocchio simply blunders about, simply lives, and little by little comes to an awareness of what he can become. The only improvement Disney makes on the story, and this is perhaps arguable, comes at the end, in the episode of the escape from the Terrible Shark (Monstro the Whale). In Collodi, the Shark's mouth is open (he suffers from asthma and heart disease), and to organize the escape Pinocchio needs no more than courage. "Then, my dear Father, there is no time to lose. We must escape."

"Escape! How?"

"We can run out of the Shark's mouth and dive into the sea."

"You speak well, but I cannot swim, my dear Pinocchio."

"Why should that matter? You can climb on my shoulders and I, who am a fine swimmer, will carry you safely to shore."

"Dreams, my boy!" answered Gepetto, shaking his head and smiling sadly. "Do you think it possible for a Marionette, a yard high, to have the strength to carry me on his shoulders and swim?"

"Try it and see! And in any case, if it is written that we must die, we shall at least die together." Not adding another word, Pinocchio took the candle in his hand and going ahead to light the way, he said to his father: "Follow me and have no fear."

In Disney, however, Pinocchio needs resourcefulness as well. The whale's mouth is shut, and when it opens, it is only to let water in, not out. Pinocchio cleverly decides to build a fire inside the whale—which induces Monstro to sneeze, thereby launching the puppet and his father into the sea. But more is lost with this flourish than gained. For the crucial image of the story is eliminated: Pinocchio swimming through the desolate water, nearly sinking under the weight of Gepetto's body, making his way through the gray-blue night (page 296 of the American edition), with the moon shining above them, a benign smile on its face, and the huge open mouth of the shark behind them. The father on his son's back: the image evoked here is so clearly that of Aeneas bearing Anchises on his back from the ruins of Troy that each time A. reads the story aloud to his son, he cannot help seeing (for it is not thinking, really, so quickly do these things happen in his mind) certain clusters of other images, spinning outward from the core of his preoccupations: Cassandra, for example, predicting the ruin of Troy, and thereafter loss, as in the wanderings of Aeneas that precede the founding of Rome, and in that wandering the image of another wandering: the Jews in the desert, which, in its turn, yields further clusters of images: "Next year in Jerusalem," and with it the photograph in the Jewish Encyclopedia of his relative, who bore the name of his son.

A. has watched his son's face carefully during these readings of *Pinocchio*. He has concluded that it is the image of Pinocchio saving Gepetto (swimming away with the old man on his back) that gives the story meaning for him. A boy of three is indeed very little. A wisp of puniness against the bulk of his father, he dreams of acquiring inordinate powers to conquer the paltry reality of himself. He is still too young to understand that one day he will be as big as his father, and even when it is explained to him very carefully, the facts are still open to gross misinterpretations: "And some day I'll be the same tall as you, and you'll be the same little as me." The fascination with comic book super-heroes is perhaps understandable from this point of view. It is the dream of being big, of becoming an adult. "What does Superman do?" "He saves people." For this act of saving is in effect what a father does: he saves his little boy from harm. And for the little boy to see Pinocchio, that same foolish puppet who has stumbled his way from one misfortune to the next, who has wanted to be "good" and could not help being "bad," for this same incompetent little marionette, who is not even a real boy, to become a figure of redemption, the very being who saves his father from the grip of death, is a sublime moment of revelation. The son saves the father. This must be fully imagined from the perspective of the little boy. And this, in the mind of the father who was once a little boy, a son, that is, to his own father, must be fully imagined. *Puer aeternus*. The son saves the father.

* * *

Further commentary on the nature of chance.

He does not want to neglect to mention that two years after meeting S. in Paris, he happened to meet S.'s younger son on a subsequent visit—through channels and circumstances that had nothing to do with S. himself. This young man, P., who was precisely the same age as A., was working his way to a position of considerable power with an important French film producer. A. himself would later work for this same producer, doing a variety of odd jobs for him in 1971 and 1972 (translating, ghost writing), but none of that is essential. What matters is that by the mid to late seventies, P. had managed to achieve the status of co-producer, and along with the son of the French producer put together the movie *Superman*, which had cost so many millions of dollars, A. read, that it had been described as the most expensive work of art in the history of the Western world.

Early in the summer of 1980, shortly after his son turned three, A. and the boy spent a week together in the country, in a house owned by friends who were off on vacation. A. noticed in the newspaper that *Superman* was playing in a local theater and decided to take the boy, on the off-chance that he would be able to sit through it. For the first half of the film, the boy was calm, working his way through a bin of popcorn, whispering his questions as A. had instructed him to do, and taking the business of exploding planets, rocket ships, and outer space without much fuss. But then something happened. Superman began to fly, and all at once the boy lost his composure. His mouth dropped open, he stood up in his seat, spilled his popcorn, pointed at the screen, and began to shout: "Look! Look! He's flying!" For the rest of the film, he was beside himself, his face taut with fear and fascination, rattling off questions to his father, trying to absorb what he had seen, marveling, trying to absorb it again, marveling. Toward the end, it became a little too much for him. "Too much booming," he said. His father asked him if he wanted to leave, and he said yes. A. picked him up and carried him out of the theater—into a violent hail storm. As they ran toward the car, the boy said (bouncing up and down in A.'s arms), "We're having quite an adventure tonight, aren't we?"

For the rest of the summer, Superman was his passion, his obsession, the unifying purpose of his life. He refused to wear any shirt except the blue one with the S on the front. His mother sewed a cape together for him, and each time he went outside, he insisted on wearing it, charging down the streets with his arms in front of him, as if flying, stopping only to announce to each passerby under the age of ten: "I'm Superman!" A. was amused by all this, since he could remember these same things from his own childhood. It was not this obsession that struck him; nor even, finally, the coincidence of knowing the men who had made the film that led to this obsession. Rather, it was this. Each time he saw his son pretending to be Superman, he could not help thinking of his friend S., as if even the S on his son's T-shirt were not a reference to Superman but to his friend. And he wondered at this trick his mind continued to play on him, this constant turning of one thing into another thing, as if behind each real thing there were a shadow thing, as alive in his mind as the thing before his eyes, and in the end he was at a loss to say which of these things he was actually seeing. And therefore it happened, often it happened, that his life no longer seemed to dwell in the present.

The Book of Memory. Book Nine.

For most of his adult life, he has earned his living by translating the books of other writers. He sits at his desk reading the book in French and then picks up his pen and writes the same book in English. It is both the same book and not the same book, and the strangeness of this activity has never failed to impress him. Every book is an image of solitude. It is a tangible object that one can pick up, put down, open, and close, and its words represent many months, if not many years, of one man's solitude, so that with each word one reads in a book one might say to himself that he is confronting a particle of that solitude. A man sits alone in a room and writes. Whether the book speaks of loneliness or companionship, it is necessarily a product of solitude. A. sits down in his own room to translate another man's book, and it is as though he were entering that man's solitude and making it his own. But surely that is impossible. For once a solitude has been breached, once a solitude has been taken on by another, it is no longer solitude, but a kind of companionship. Even though there is only one man in the room, there are two. A. imagines himself as a kind of ghost of that other man, who is both there and not there, and whose book is both the same and not the same as the one he is translating. Therefore, he tells himself, it is possible to be alone and not alone at the same moment.

A word becomes another word, a thing becomes another thing. In this way, he tells himself, it works in the same way that memory does. He imagines an immense Babel inside him. There is a text, and it translates itself into an infinite number of languages. Sentences spill out of him at the speed of thought, and each word comes from a different language, a thousand tongues that clamor inside him at once, the din of it echoing through a maze of rooms, corridors, and stairways, hundreds of stories high. He repeats. In the space of memory, everything is both itself and something else. And then it dawns on him that everything he is trying to record in The Book of Memory, everything he has written so far, is no more than the translation of a moment or two of his life—those moments he lived through on Christmas Eve, 1979, in his room at 6 Varick Street.

The moment of illumination that burns across the sky of solitude.

Pascal in his room on the night of November 23, 1654, sewing the Memorial into the lining of his clothes, so that at any moment, for the rest of his life, he could find beneath his hand the record of that ecstasy.

In the Year of Grace 1654
On Monday, November 23rd, Feast of Saint Clement,
Pope and Martyr,
and of others in the Martyrology.
and eve of Saint Chrysogomus and other Martyrs.
From about half past ten at night until about half past twelve.

Fire
"God of Abraham, God of Isaac, God of Jacob,"
not of the philosophers and scientists.
Certainty. Certainty. Feeling. Joy. Peace.

• • •

Greatness of the human soul.

• • •

Joy, joy, joy, tears of joy.

• • •

I will not forget thy word. Amen.

• • •

Concerning the power of memory.

In the spring of 1966, not long after meeting his future wife, A. was invited by her father (an English professor at Columbia) to the family apartment on Morningside Drive for dessert and coffee. The dinner guests were Francis Ponge and his wife, and A.'s future father-in-law thought that the young A. (just nineteen at the time), would enjoy meeting so famous a writer. Ponge, the master poet of the object, who had invented a poetry more firmly placed in the outer world perhaps than any other, was teaching a course at Columbia that semester. By then A. already spoke reasonably good French. Since Ponge and his wife spoke no English, and A.'s future in-laws spoke almost no French, A. joined in the discussion more fully than he might have, given his innate shyness and penchant for saying nothing whenever possible. He remembers Ponge as a gracious and lively man with sparkling blue eyes.

The second time A. met Ponge was in 1969 (although it could have been 1968 or 1970) at a party given in Ponge's honor by G., a Barnard professor who had been translating his work. When A. shook Ponge's hand, he introduced himself by saying that although he probably didn't remember it, they had once met in New York several years ago. On the contrary, Ponge replied, he remembered the evening quite well. And then he proceeded to talk about the apartment in which that dinner had taken place, describing it in all its details, from the view out the windows to the color of the couch and the arrangement of the furniture in each of the various rooms. For a man to remember so precisely things he had seen only once, things which could not have had any bearing on his life except for a fleeting instant, struck A. with all the force of a supernatural act. He realized that for Ponge there was no division between the work of writing and the work of seeing. For no word can be written without first having been seen, and before it finds its way to the page it must first have been part of the body, a physical presence that one has lived with in the same way one lives with one's heart, one's stomach, and one's brain. Memory, then, not so much as the past contained within us, but as proof of our life in the present. If a man is to be truly present among his surroundings, he must be thinking not of himself, but of what he sees. He must forget himself in order to be there. And from that forgetfulness arises the power of memory. It is a way of living one's life so that nothing is ever lost.

It is also true that "the man with a good memory does not remember anything because he does not forget anything," as Beckett has written about Proust. And it is true that one must make a distinction between voluntary and involuntary memory, as Proust does during the course of his long novel about the past.

What A. feels he is doing, however, as he writes the pages of his own book, is something that does not belong to either one of these two types of memory. A. has both a good memory and a bad memory. He has lost much, but he has also retained much. As he writes, he feels that he is moving inward (through himself) and at the same time moving outward (toward the world). What he experienced, perhaps, during those few moments on Christmas Eve, 1979, as he sat alone in his room on Varick Street, was this: the sudden knowledge that came over him that even alone, in the deepest solitude of his room, he was not alone, or, more precisely, that the moment he began to try to speak of that solitude, he had become more than just himself. Memory, therefore, not simply as the resurrection of one's private past, but an immersion in the past of others, which is to say: history—which one both participates in and is a witness to, is a part of and apart from. Everything, therefore, is present in his mind at once, as if each element were reflecting the light of all the others, and at the same time emitting its own unique and unquenchable radiance. If there is any reason for him to be in this room now, it is because there is something inside him hungering to see it all at once, to savor the chaos of it in all its raw and urgent simultaneity. And yet, the telling of it is necessarily slow, a delicate business of trying to remember what has already been remembered. The pen will never be able to move fast enough to write down every word discovered in the space of memory. Some things have been lost forever, other things will perhaps be remembered again, and still other things have been lost and found and lost again. There is no way to be sure of any of this.

Possible epigraph(s) for The Book of Memory.

"Thoughts come at random, and go at random. No device for holding on to them or for having them. A thought has escaped: I was trying to write it down: instead I write that it has escaped me." (Pascal)

"As I write down my thought, it sometimes escapes me; but this makes me remember my own weakness, which I am constantly forgetting. This teaches me as much as my forgotten thought, for I strive only to know my own nothingness." (Pascal)

The Book of Memory. Book Ten.

When he speaks of the room, he does not mean to neglect the windows that are sometimes present in the room. The room need not be an image of hermetic consciousness, and when a man or a woman stands or sits alone in a room there is more that happens there, he realizes, than the silence of thought, the silence of a body struggling to put its thoughts into words. Nor does he mean to imply that only suffering takes place within the four walls of consciousness, as in the allusions made to Hölderlin and Emily Dickinson previously. He thinks, for example, of Vermeer's women, alone in their rooms, with the bright light of the real world pouring through a window, either open or closed, and the utter stillness of those solitudes, an almost heartbreaking evocation of the everyday and its domestic variables. He thinks, in particular, of a painting he saw on his trip to Amsterdam, *Woman in Blue*, which nearly immobilized him with contemplation in the Rijksmuseum. As one commentator has written: "The letter, the map, the woman's pregnancy, the empty chair, the open box, the unseen window—all are reminders or natural emblems of absence, of the unseen, of other minds, wills, times, and places, of past and future, of birth and perhaps of death—in general, of a world that extends beyond the edges of the frame, and of larger, wider horizons that encompass and impinge upon the scene suspended before our eyes. And yet it is the fullness and self-sufficiency of the present moment that Vermeer insists upon—with such conviction that its capacity to orient and contain is invested with metaphysical value."

Even more than the objects mentioned in this list, it is the quality of the light coming through the unseen window to the viewer's left that so warmly beckons him to turn his attention to the outside, to the world beyond the painting. A. stares hard at the woman's face, and as time passes he almost begins to hear the voice inside the woman's head as she reads the letter in her hands. She, so very pregnant, so tranquil in the imminence of motherhood, with the letter taken out of the box, no doubt being read for the hundredth time; and there, hanging on the wall to her right, a map of the world, which is the image of everything that exists outside the room: that light, pouring gently over her face and shining on her blue smock, the belly bulging with life, and its blueness bathed in luminosity, a light so pale it verges on whiteness. To follow with more of the same: *Woman Pouring Milk, Woman Holding a Balance, Woman Putting on Pearls, Young Woman at a Window with a Pitcher, Girl Reading a Letter at an Open Window.*

"The fullness and self-sufficiency of the present moment."

* * *

If it was Rembrandt and Titus who in some sense lured A. to Amsterdam, where he then entered rooms and found himself in the presence of women (Vermeer's women, Anne Frank), his trip to that city was at the same time conceived as a pilgrimage to his own past. Again, his inner movements were expressed in the form of paintings: an emotional state finding tangible representation in a work of art, as though another's solitude were in fact the echo of his own.

In this case it was Van Gogh, and the new museum that had been built to house his work. Like some early trauma buried in the unconscious, forever linking two unrelated objects (this shoe is my father; this rose is my mother), Van Gogh's paintings stand in his mind as an image of his adolescence, a translation of his deepest feelings of that period. He can even be quite precise about it, pinpointing events and his reactions to events by place and time (exact locations, exact moments: year, month, day, even hour and minute). What matters, however, is not so much the sequence of the chronicle as its consequences, its permanence in the space of memory. To remember, therefore, a day in April when he was sixteen, and cutting school with the girl he had fallen in love with: so passionately and hopelessly that the thought of it still smarts. To remember the train, and then the ferry to New York (that ferry, which has long since vanished: industrial iron, the warm fog, rust), and then going to a large exhibition of Van Gogh paintings. To remember how he had stood there, trembling with happiness, as if the shared seeing of these works had invested them with the girl's presence, had mysteriously varnished them with the love he felt for her.

Some days later, he began writing a sequence of poems (now lost) based on the canvases he had seen, each poem bearing the title of a different Van Gogh painting. These were the first real poems he ever wrote. More than a method for entering those paintings, the poems were an attempt to recapture the memory of that day. Many years went by, however, before he realized this. It was only in Amsterdam, studying the same paintings he had seen with the girl (seeing them for the first time since then—almost half his life ago), that he remembered having written those poems. At that moment the equation became clear to him: the act of writing as an act of memory. For the fact of the matter is, other than the poems themselves, he has not forgotten any of it.

Standing in the Van Gogh Museum in Amsterdam (December 1979) in front of the painting *The Bedroom*, completed in Arles, October 1888.

Van Gogh to his brother: "This time it is just simply my bed-room ... To look at the picture ought to rest the brain or rather the imagination ...

"The walls are pale violet. The floor is of red tiles.

"The wood of the bed and chairs is the yellow of fresh butter, the sheet and pillows very light lemon-green.

"The coverlet scarlet. The window green.

"The toilet table orange, the basin blue.

"The doors lilac.

"And that is all—there is nothing in this room with closed shut-ters. . . .

"This by way of revenge for the enforced rest I have been obliged to take. . . .

"I will make you sketches of the other rooms too some day."

As A. continued to study the painting, however, he could not help feeling that Van Gogh had done something quite different from what he thought he had set out to do. A.'s first impression was indeed a sense of calm, of "rest," as the artist describes it. But gradually, as he tried to inhabit the room presented on the canvas, he began to experience it as a prison, an impossible space, an image, not so much of a place to live, but of the mind that has been forced to live there. Observe carefully. The bed blocks one door, a chair blocks the other door, the shutters are closed: you can't get in, and once you are in, you can't get out. Stifled among the furniture and everyday objects of the room, you begin to hear a cry of suffering in this painting, and once you hear it, it does not stop. "I cried by reason of mine affliction . . . ." But there is no answer to this cry. The man in this painting (and this is a self-portrait, no different from a picture of a man's face, with eyes, nose, lips, and jaw) has been alone too much, has struggled too much in the depths of solitude. The world ends at that barricaded door. For the room is not a representation of soli-tude, it is the substance of solitude itself. And it is a thing so heavy, so unbreathable, that it cannot be shown in any terms other than what it is. "And that is all—there is nothing in this room with closed shutters. . . ."

Further commentary on the nature of chance.

A. arrived in London and departed from London, spending a few days on either end of his trip visiting with English friends. The girl of the ferry and the Van Gogh paintings was English (she had grown up in London, had lived in America from the age of about twelve to eighteen, and had then returned to London to go to art school), and on the first leg of his trip, A. spent several hours with her. Over the years since their graduation from high school, they had kept in touch at best fitfully, had seen each other perhaps five or six times. A. was long cured of his passion, but he had not dismissed her altogether from his mind, clinging somehow to the feeling of that passion, although she herself had lost importance for him. It had been several years since their last meeting, and now he found it gloomy, almost oppressive to be with her. She was still beautiful, he thought, and yet solitude seemed to enclose her, in the same way an egg encloses an unborn bird. She lived alone, had almost no friends. For many years she had been working on sculptures in wood, but she refused to show them to anyone. Each time she finished a piece, she would destroy it, and then begin on the next one. Again, A. had come face to face with a woman's solitude. But here it had turned in on itself and dried up at its source.

A day or two later, he went to Paris, eventually to Amsterdam, and afterwards back to London. He thought to himself: there will be no time to see her again. On one of those days before returning to New York, he was to have dinner with a friend (T., the same friend who had thought they might be cousins) and decided to spend the afternoon at the Royal Academy of Art, where a large exhibition of "Post Impressionist" paintings was on view. The enormous crush of visitors at the museum, however, made him reluctant to stay for the afternoon, as he had planned, and he found himself with three or four extra hours before his dinner appointment. He went to a cheap fish and chips place in Soho for lunch, trying to decide what to do with himself during this free time. He paid up his bill, left the restaurant, turned the corner, and there, as she stood gazing into the display window of a large shoe store, he saw her.

It was not every day that he ran into someone on the London streets (in that city of millions, he knew no more than a few people), and yet this encounter seemed perfectly natural to him, as though it were a commonplace event. He had been thinking about her only a moment before, regretting his decision not to call her, and now that she was there, suddenly standing before his eyes, he could not help feeling that he had willed her to appear.

He walked toward her and spoke her name.

Paintings. Or the collapse of time in images.

In the Royal Academy exhibition he had seen in London, there were several paintings by Maurice Denis. While in Paris, A. had visited the widow of the poet Jean Follain (Follain, who had died in a traffic accident in 1971, just days before A. had moved to Paris) in connection with an anthology of French poetry that A. was preparing, which in fact was what had brought him back to Europe. Madame Follain, he soon learned, was the daughter of Maurice Denis, and many of her father's paintings hung on the walls of the apartment. She herself was now in her late seventies, perhaps eighty, and A. was impressed by her Parisian toughness, her gravel voice, her devotion to her dead husband's work.

One of the paintings in the apartment bore a title: Madelaine à 18 mois (Madelaine at 18 months), which Denis had written out across the top of the canvas. This was the same Madelaine who had grown up to become Follain's wife and who had just asked A. to enter her apartment. For a moment, without being aware of it, she stood in front of that picture, which had been painted nearly eighty years before, and A. saw, as though leaping incredibly across time, that the child's face in the painting and the old woman's face before him were exactly the same. For that one instant, he felt he had cut through the illusion of human time and had experienced it for what it was: as no more than a blink of the eyes. He had seen an entire life standing before him, and it had been collapsed into that one instant.

O. to A. in conversation, describing what it felt like to have become an old man. O., now in his seventies, his memory failing, his face as wrinkled as a half-closed palm. Looking at A. and shaking his head with deadpan wit: "What a strange thing to happen to a little boy."

Yes, it is possible that we do not grow up, that even as we grow old, we remain the children we always were. We remember ourselves as we were then, and we feel ourselves to be the same. We made ourselves into what we are now then, and we remain what we were, in spite of the years. We do not change for ourselves. Time makes us grow old, but we do not change.

The Book of Memory. Book Eleven.

He remembers returning home from his wedding party in 1974, his wife beside him in her white dress, and taking the front door key out of his pocket, inserting the key in the lock, and then, as he turned his wrist, feeling the blade of the key snap off inside the lock.

He remembers that in the spring of 1966, not long after he met his future wife, one of the keys of her piano broke: F above Middle C. That summer the two of them traveled to a remote part of Maine. One day, as they walked through a nearly abandoned town, they wandered into an old meeting hall, which had not been used for years. Remnants of some men's society were scattered about the place: Indian headdresses, lists of names, the detritus of drunken gatherings. The hall was dusty and deserted, except for an upright piano that stood in one corner. His wife began to play (she played well) and discovered that all the keys worked except one: F above Middle C.

It was at that moment, perhaps, that A. realized the world would go on eluding him forever.

If a novelist had used these little incidents of broken piano keys (or the wedding day accident of losing the key inside the door), the reader would be forced to take note, to assume the novelist was trying to make some point about his characters or the world. One could speak of symbolic meanings, of subtext, or simply of formal devices (for as soon as a thing happens more than once, even if it is arbitrary, a pattern takes shape, a form begins to emerge). In a work of fiction, one assumes there is a conscious mind behind the words on the page. In the presence of happenings in the so-called real world, one assumes nothing. The made-up story consists entirely of meanings, whereas the story of fact is devoid of any significance beyond itself. If a man says to you, "I'm going to Jerusalem," you think to yourself: how nice, he's going to Jerusalem. But if a character in a novel were to speak those same words, "I'm going to Jerusalem," your response is not at all the same. You think, to begin with, of Jerusalem itself: its history, its religious role, its function as a mythical place. You would think of the past, of the present (politics; which is also to think of the recent past), and of the future—as in the phrase: "Next year in Jerusalem." On top of that, you would integrate these thoughts into whatever it is you already know about the character who is going to Jerusalem and use this new synthesis to draw further conclusions, refine perceptions, think more cogently about the book as a whole. And then, once the work is finished, the last page read and the book closed, interpretations begin: psychological, historical, sociological, structural, philological, religious, sexual, philosophical, either singly or in various combinations, depending on your bent. Although it is possible to interpret a real life according to any of these systems (people do, after all, go to priests and psychiatrists; people do sometimes try to understand their lives in terms of historical conditions), it does not have the same effect. Something is missing: the grandeur, the grasp of the general, the illusion of metaphysical truth. One says: Don Quixote is consciousness gone haywire in a realm of the imaginary. One looks at a mad person in the world (A. at his schizophrenic sister, for example), and says nothing. This is the sadness of a wasted life, perhaps—but no more.

Now and then, A. finds himself looking at a work of art with the same eyes he uses to look at the world. To read the imaginary in this way is to destroy it. He thinks, for example, of Tolstoy's description of the opera in *War and Peace*. Nothing is taken for granted in this passage, and therefore everything is reduced to absurdity. Tolstoy makes fun of what he sees simply by describing it. "In the second act there were cardboard monuments on the stage, and a round hole in the backdrop representing a moon. Shades had been put over the footlights and deep notes were played on the horns and contrabass as a number of people appeared from both sides of the stage wearing black cloaks and flourishing what looked like daggers. Then some other men ran onto the stage and began dragging away the maiden who had been in white and was now in pale blue. They did not take her away at once, but spent a long time singing with her, until at last they dragged her off, and behind the scenes something metallic was struck three times, and everyone knelt down and sang a prayer. All these actions were repeatedly interrupted by the enthusiastic shouts of the audience."

There is also the equal and opposite temptation to look at the world as though it were an extension of the imaginary. This, too, has sometimes happened to A., but he is loath to accept it as a valid solution. Like everyone else, he craves a meaning. Like everyone else, his life is so fragmented that each time he sees a connection between two fragments he is tempted to look for a meaning in that connection. The connection exists. But to give it a meaning, to look beyond the bare fact of its existence, would be to build an imaginary world inside the real world, and he knows it would not stand. At his bravest moments, he embraces meaninglessness as the first principle, and then he understands that his obligation is to see what is in front of him (even though it is also inside him) and to say what he sees. He is in his room on Varick Street. His life has no meaning. The book he is writing has no meaning. There is the world, and the things one encounters in the world, and to speak of them is to be in the world. A key breaks off in a lock, and something has happened. That is to say, a key has broken off in a lock. The same piano seems to exist in two different places. A young man, twenty years later, winds up living in the same room where his father faced the horror of solitude. A man encounters his old love on a street in a foreign city. It means only what it is. Nothing more, nothing less. Then he writes: to enter this room is to vanish in a place where past and present meet. And then he writes: as in the phrase: "he wrote The Book of Memory in this room."

The invention of solitude.

He wants to say. That is to say, he means. As in the French, "vouloir dire," which means, literally, to want to say, but which means, in fact, to mean. He means to say what he wants. He wants to say what he means. He says what he wants to mean. He means what he says.

Vienna, 1919.

No meaning, yes. But it would be impossible to say that we are not haunted. Freud has described such experiences as "uncanny," or *unheimlich*—the opposite of *heimlich*, which means "familiar," "native," "belonging to the home." The implication, therefore, is that we are thrust out from the protective shell of our habitual perceptions, as though we were suddenly outside ourselves, adrift in a world we do not understand. By definition, we are lost in that world. We cannot even hope to find our way in it.

Freud argues that each stage of our development co-exists with all the others. Even as adults, we have buried within us a memory of the way we perceived the world as children. And not simply a memory of it: the structure itself is intact. Freud connects the experience of the uncanny with a revival of the egocentric, animistic world-view of childhood. "It would seem as though each one of us has been through a phase of individual development corresponding to that animistic stage in primitive men, that none of us has traversed it without certain traces of it which can be re-activated, and that everything which now strikes us as 'uncanny' fulfills the condition of stirring those vestiges of animistic mental activity within us and bringing them to expression." He concludes: "An uncanny experience occurs either when repressed infantile complexes have been revived by some impression, or when the primitive beliefs we have surmounted seem once more to be confirmed."

None of this, of course, is an explanation. At best it serves to describe the process, to point out the terrain on which it takes place. As such, A. is more than willing to accept it as true. Unhomeness, therefore, as a memory of another, much earlier home of the mind. In the same way a dream will sometimes resist interpretation until a friend suggests a simple, almost obvious meaning, A. cannot prove Freud's argument true or false, but it feels right to him, and he is more than willing to accept it. All the coincidences that seem to have been multiplying around him, then, are somehow connected with a memory of his childhood, as if by beginning to remember his childhood, the world were returning to a prior state of its being. This feels right to him. He is remembering his childhood, and it has appeared to him in the present in the form of these experiences. He is remembering his childhood, and it is writing itself out for him in the present. Perhaps that is what he means when he writes: "meaninglessness is the first principle." Perhaps that is what he means when he writes: "He means what he says." Perhaps that is what he means. And perhaps it is not. There is no way to be sure of any of this.

The invention of solitude. Or stories of life and death.

The story begins with the end. Speak or die. And for as long as you go on speaking, you will not die. The story begins with death. King Shehriyar has been cuckolded: "and they ceased not from kissing and clipping and clicketing and carousing." He retreats from the world, vowing never to succumb to feminine trickery again. Later, returning to his throne, he gratifies his physical desires by taking in women of the kingdom. Once satisfied, he orders their execution. "And he ceased not to do this for three years, till the land was stripped of marriageable girls, and all the women and mothers and fathers wept and cried out against the King, cursing him and complaining to the Creator of heaven and earth and calling for succor upon Him who heareth prayer and answereth those that cry to Him; and those that had daughters left fled with them, till at last there remained not a single girl in the city apt for marriage."

At this point, Shehrzad, the vizier's daughter, volunteers to go to the King. ("Her memory was stored with verses and stories and folklore and the sayings of Kings and sages, and she was wise, witty, prudent, and well-bred.") Her desperate father tries to dissuade her from going to this sure death, but she is unperturbed. "Marry me to this king, for either I will be the means of the deliverance of the daughters of the

Muslims from slaughter, or I will die and perish as others have perished." She goes off to sleep with the king and puts her plan into action: "to tell . . . delightful stories to pass away the watches of our night . . . ; it shall be the means of my deliverance and the ridding of the folk of this calamity, and by it I will turn the king from his custom."

The king agrees to listen to her. She begins her story, and what she tells is a story about story-telling, a story within which are several stories, each one, in itself, about story-telling—by means of which a man is saved from death.

Day begins to dawn, and mid-way through the first story-within-the-story, Shehrzad falls silent. "This is nothing to what I will tell tomorrow night," she says, "if the king let me live." And the king says to himself, "By Allah, I will not kill her, till I hear the rest of the story." So it goes for three nights, each night's story stopping before the end and spilling over into the beginning of the next night's story, by which time the first cycle of stories has ended and a new one begun. Truly, it is a matter of life and death. On the first night, Shehrzad begins with The Merchant and the Genie. A man stops to eat his lunch in a garden (an oasis in the desert), throws away a date stone, and behold "there started up before him a gigantic spirit, with a naked sword in his hand, who came up to him and said, 'Arise, that I may slay thee, even as thou hast slain my son.' 'How did I slay thy son?' asked the merchant, and the genie replied, 'When thou threwest away the date stone, it smote my son, who was passing at the time, on the breast, and he died forthright.' "

This is guilt out of innocence (echoing the fate of the marriageable girls in the kingdom), and at the same time the birth of enchantment—turning a thought into a thing, bringing the invisible to life. The merchant pleads his case, and the genie agrees to stay his execution. But in exactly one year the merchant must return to the same spot, where the genie will mete out the sentence. Already, a parallel is being drawn with Sherhzad's situation. She wishes to delay her execution, and by planting this idea in the king's mind she is pleading her case—but doing it in such a way that the king cannot recognize it. For this is the function of the story: to make a man see the thing before his eyes by holding up another thing to view.

The year passes, and the merchant, good to his word, returns to the garden. He sits down and begins to weep. An old man wanders by, leading a gazelle by a chain, and asks the merchant what is wrong. The old man is fascinated by what the merchant tells him (as if the merchant's life were a story, with a beginning, middle, and end, a fiction concocted by some other mind—which in fact it is), and decides to wait and see how it will turn out. Then another old man wanders by, leading two black dogs. The conversation is repeated, and then he, too, sits down and waits. Then a third old man wanders by, leading a dappled she-mule, and once again the same thing happens. Finally, the genie appears, in a "cloud of dust and a great whirling column from the heart of the desert." Just as he is about to drag off the merchant and slay him with his sword, "as thou slewest my son, the darling of my heart!," the first old man steps forward and says to the genie: "If I relate to thee my history with this gazelle and it seem to thee wonderful, wilt thou grant me a third of this merchant's blood?" Astonishingly, the genie agrees, just as the king has agreed to listen to Sherhzad's story: readily, without a struggle.

Note: the old man does not propose to defend the merchant as one would in a court of law, with arguments, counter-arguments, the presentation of evidence. This would be to make the genie look at the thing he already sees: and about this his mind has been made up. Rather, the old man wishes to turn him away from the facts, turn him away from thoughts of death, and in so doing delight him (literally, "to entice away," from the Latin *delectare*) into a new feeling for life, which in turn will make him renounce his obsession with killing the merchant. An obsession of this sort walls one up in solitude. One sees nothing but one's own thoughts. A story, however, in that it is not a logical argument, breaks down those walls. For it posits the existence of others and allows the listener to come into contact with them—if only in his thoughts.

The old man launches into a preposterous story. This gazelle you see before you, he says, is actually my wife. For thirty years she lived with me and in all that time she could not produce a son. (Again: an allusion to the absent child—the dead child, the child not yet born—referring the genie back to his own sorrow, but obliquely, as part of a world in which life stands equal to death.) "So I took me a concubine and had by her a son like the rising full moon with eyes and eyebrows of perfect beauty. . . ." When the boy was fifteen, the old man went off to another city (he, too, is a merchant), and in his absence the jealous wife used magic to transform the boy and his mother into a calf and a cow. "Thy slave died and her son ran away," the wife told him on his return. After a year of mourning, the cow was slaughtered as a sacrifice—through the machinations of the jealous wife. When the man was about to slaughter the calf a moment later, his heart failed him. "And when the calf saw me, he broke his halter and came up to me and fawned on me and moaned and wept, till I took pity on him and said . . . 'Bring me a cow and let this calf go.' " The herdsman's daughter, also learned in the art of magic, later discovered the true identity of the calf. After the merchant granted her the two things she asked for (to marry the son and to bewitch the jealous wife, by imprisoning her in the shape of a beast— "else I shall not be safe from her craft"), she returned the son to his original form. Nor does the story quite end there. The son's bride, the old man goes on to explain, "dwelt with us days and nights and nights and days, till God took her to Himself; and after her death, my son set out on a journey to the land of Ind, which is this merchant's native country; and after a while I took the gazelle and travelled with her from place to place, seeking news of my son, till chance led me to this garden, where I found this merchant sitting weeping; and this is my story." The genie agrees that this is a marvelous story and remits to the old man a third part of the merchant's blood.

One after the other, the two remaining old men propose the same bargain to the genie and begin their stories in the same way. "These two dogs are my elder brothers," says the second old man. "This mule was my wife," says the third. These opening sentences contain the essence of the entire project. For what does it mean to look at something, a real object in the real world, an animal, for example, and say that it is something other than what it is? It is to say that each thing leads a double life, at once in the world and in our minds, and that to deny either one of these lives is to kill the thing in both its lives at once. In the stories of the three old men, two mirrors face each other, each one reflecting the light of the other. Both are enchantments, both the real and the imaginary, and each exists by virtue of the other. And it is, truly, a matter of life and death. The first old man has come to the garden in search of his son; the genie has come to the garden to slay his son's unwitting killer. What the old man is telling him is that our sons are always invisible. It is the simplest of truths: a life belongs only to the person who lives it; life itself will claim the living; to live is to let live. And in the end, by means of these three stories, the merchant's life is spared.

This is how *The Thousand and One Nights* begins. At the end of the entire chronicle, after story after story after story, there is a specific result, and it carries with it all the unalterable gravity of a miracle.

Sherhzad has borne the king three sons. Again, the lesson is made clear. A voice that speaks, a woman's voice that speaks, a voice that speaks stories of life and death, has the power to give life.

" 'May I then make bold to crave a boon of thy Majesty?'

" 'Ask, O Sherhzad,' answered he, 'and it shall be given unto thee.'

"Whereupon she cried to the nurses and the eunuchs, saying, 'Bring me my children.'

"So they brought them to her in haste, and they were three male children, one walking, one crawling, and one sucking at the breast. She took them and, setting them before the king, kissed the ground and said, 'O King of the age, these are thy children and I crave that thou release me from the doom of death, for the sake of these infants.' "

When the king hears these words, he begins to weep. He gathers the little children up into his arms and declares his love for Sherhzad.

"So they decorated the city in splendid fashion, never before was seen the like thereof, and the drums beat and the pipes sounded, whilst all the mimes and mountebanks and players plied their various arts and the King lavished on them gifts and largesse. Moreover he gave alms to the poor and needy and extended his bounty to all his subjects and the people of his realm."

Mirror text.

If the voice of a woman telling stories has the power to bring children into the world, it is also true that a child has the power to bring stories to life. It is said that a man would go mad if he could not dream at night. In the same way, if a child is not allowed to enter the imaginary, he will never come to grips with the real. A child's need for stories is as fundamental as his need for food, and it manifests itself in the same way hunger does. Tell me a story, the child says. Tell me a story. Tell me a story, Daddy, please. The father then sits down and tells a story to his son. Or else he lies down in the dark beside him, the two of them in the child's bed, and begins to speak, as if there were nothing left in the world but his voice, telling a story in the dark to his son. Often it is a fairy tale, or a tale of adventure. Yet often it is no more than a simple leap into the imaginary. Once upon a time there was a little boy named Daniel, A. says to his son named Daniel, and these stories in which the boy himself is the hero are perhaps the most satisfying to him of all. In the same way, A. realizes, as he sits in his room writing The Book of Memory, he speaks of himself as another in order to tell the story of himself. He must make himself absent in order to find himself there. And so he says A., even as he means to say I. For the story of memory is the story of seeing. And even if the things to be seen are no longer there, it is a story of seeing. The voice, therefore, goes on. And even as the boy closes his eyes and goes to sleep, his father's voice goes on speaking in the dark.

The Book of Memory. Book Twelve.

He can go no farther than this. Children have suffered at the hands of adults, for no reason whatsoever. Children have been abandoned, have been left to starve, have been murdered, for no reason whatsoever. It is not possible, he realizes, to go any farther than this.

"But then there are the children," says Ivan Karamazov, "and what am I to do with them?" And again: "I want to forgive. I want to embrace. I don't want any more suffering. And if the sufferings of children go to make up the sum of sufferings which is necessary for the purchase of truth, then I say beforehand that the entire truth is not worth such a price."

Every day, without the least effort, he finds it staring him in the face. These are the days of Cambodia's collapse, and everyday it is there, looking out at him from the newspaper, with the inevitable photographs of death: the emaciated children, the grownups with nothing left in their eyes. Jim Harrison, for example, an Oxfam engineer, noting in his diary: "Visited small clinic at kilometer 7. Absolutely no drugs or medicines— serious cases of starvation—clearly just dying for lack of food. . . . The hundreds of children were all marasmic—much skin disease, baldness, discolored hair and great fear in the whole population." Or later, describing what he saw on a visit to the 7th of January Hospital in Phnom Penh: ". . . terrible conditions—children in bed in filthy rags dying with starvation–no drugs—no food. . . . The TB allied to starva- tion gives the people a Belsen-like appearance. In one ward a boy of thirteen tied down to the bed because he was going insane—many chil- dren now orphans—or can't find families—and a lot of nervous twitches and spasms to be seen among the people. The face of one small boy of eighteen months was in a state of destruction by what appeared to be infected skin and flesh which had broken down under severe kwa- shiorkor—his eyes full of pus, held in the arms of his five-year-old sis- ter . . . I find this sort of thing very tough to take—and this situation must be applicable to hundreds of thousands of Kampuchean people today."

Two weeks before reading these words, A. went out to dinner with a friend of his, P., a writer and editor for a large weekly news magazine. It so happens that she was handling the "Cambodia story" for her publication. Nearly everything written in the American and foreign press about the conditions there had passed before her eyes, and she told A. about a story written for a North Carolina newspaper—by a volunteer American doctor in one of the refugee camps across the Thai border. It concerned the visit of the American President's wife, Rosalynn Carter, to those camps. A. could remember the photographs that had been published in the newspapers and magazines (the First Lady embracing a Cambodian child, the First Lady talking to doctors), and in spite of everything he knew about America's responsibility for creating the conditions Mrs. Carter had come to protest, he had been moved by those pictures. It turned out that Mrs. Carter visited the camp where the American doctor was working. The camp hospital was a make-shift affair: a thatched roof, a few support beams, the patients lying on mats on the ground. The President's wife arrived, followed by a swarm of officials, reporters, and cameramen. There were too many of them, and as they trooped through the hospital, patients' hands were stepped on by heavy Western shoes, I.V. lines were disconnected by passing legs, bodies were inadvertently kicked. Perhaps this confusion was avoidable, perhaps not. In any case, after the visitors had completed their inspection, the American doctor made an appeal. Please, he said, would some of you spare a bit of your time to donate blood to the hospital; even the blood of the healthiest Cambodian is too thin to be of use; our supply has run out. But the First Lady's tour was behind schedule. There were other places to go that day, other suffering people to see. There was just no time, they said. Sorry. So very sorry. And then, as abruptly as they had come, the visitors left.

In that the world is monstrous. In that the world can lead a man to nothing but despair, and a despair so complete, so resolute, that nothing can open the door of this prison, which is hopelessness, A. peers through the bars of his cell and finds only one thought that brings him any consolation: the image of his son. And not just his son, but any son, any daughter, any child of any man or woman.

In that the world is monstrous. In that it seems to offer no hope of a future, A. looks at his son and realizes that he must not allow himself to despair. There is this responsibility for a young life, and in that he has brought this life into being, he must not despair. Minute by minute, hour by hour, as he remains in the presence of his son, attending to his needs, giving himself up to this young life, which is a continual injunction to remain in the present, he feels his despair evaporate. And even though he continues to despair, he does not allow himself to despair.

The thought of a child's suffering, therefore, is monstrous to him. It is even more monstrous than the monstrosity of the world itself. For it robs the world of its one consolation, and in that a world can be imagined without consolation, it is monstrous.

He can go no farther than this.

This is where it begins. He stands alone in an empty room and begins to cry. "It is too much for me, I cannot face it" (Mallarmé). "A Belsen-like appearance," as the engineer in Cambodia noted. And yes, that is the place where Anne Frank died.

"It's really a wonder," she wrote, just three weeks before her arrest, "that I haven't dropped all my ideals, because they seem so absurd and impossible to carry out. . . . I see the world gradually being turned into a wilderness, I hear the ever-approaching thunder, which will destroy us too, I can feel the sufferings of millions and yet, if I look up into the heavens, I think that it will all come right, that this cruelty too will end. . . ."

No, he does not mean to say that this is the only thing. He does not even pretend to say that it can be understood, that by talking about it and talking about it a meaning can be discovered for it. No, it is not the only thing, and life nevertheless continues, for some, if not for most. And yet, in that it is a thing that will forever escape understanding, he wants it to stand for him as the thing that will always come before the beginning. As in the sentences: "This is where it begins. He stands alone in an empty room and begins to cry."

Return to the belly of the whale.

"The word of the Lord came unto Jonah . . . saying, Arise, go to Ninevah, that great city, and cry against it. . . ."

In this command as well, Jonah's story differs from that of all the other prophets. For the Ninevites are not Jews. Unlike the other carriers of God's word, Jonah is not asked to address his own people, but for-eigners. Even worse, they are the enemies of his people. Ninevah was the capital of Assyria, the most powerful empire in the world at that time. In the words of Nahum (whose prophecies have been preserved on the same scroll as the story of Jonah): "the bloody city . . . full of lies and rapine."

"Arise, go to Ninevah," God tells Jonah. Ninevah is to the east. Jonah promptly goes west, to Tarshish (Tartessus, on the farthest tip of Spain). Not only does he run away, he goes to the limit of the known world. This flight is not difficult to understand. Imagine an analogous case: a Jew being told to enter Germany during the Second World War and preach against the National Socialists. It is a thought that begs the impossible.

As early as the second century, one of the rabbinical commentators argued that Jonah boarded the ship to drown himself in the sea for the sake of Israel, not to flee from the presence of God. This is the political reading of the book, and Christian interpreters quickly turned it against the Jews. Theodore of Mopsuestia, for example, says that Jonah was sent to Ninevah because the Jews refused to listen to the prophets, and the book about Jonah was written to teach a lesson to the "stiff-necked peo-ple." Rupert of Deutz, however, another Christian interpreter (twelfth century), contends that the prophet refused God's command out of piety to his people, and for this reason God did not become very angry with Jonah. This echoes the opinion of Rabbi Akiba himself, who stated that "Jonah was jealous for the glory of the son (Israel) but not for the glory of the father (God)."

Nevertheless, Jonah finally agrees to go to Ninevah. But even after he delivers his message, even after the Ninevites repent and change their ways, even after God spares them, we learn that "it displeased Jonah exceedingly, and he was very angry." This is a patriotic anger. Why should the enemies of Israel be spared? It is at this point that God teaches Jonah the lesson of the book—in the parable of the gourd that follows.

"Doest thou well to be angry?" he asks. Jonah then removes himself to the outskirts of Ninevah, "till he might see what would become of the city"—implying that he still felt there was a chance Ninevah would be destroyed, or that he hoped the Ninevites would revert to their sinful ways and bring down punishment on themselves. God prepares a gourd (a castor plant) to protect Jonah from the sun, and "Jonah was exceedingly glad of the gourd." But by the next morning God has made the plant wither away. A vehement east wind blows, a fierce sun beats down on Jonah, and "he fainted, and wished himself to die, and said, it is better for me to die than to live"—the same words he had used earlier, indicating that the message of this parable is the same as in the first part of the book. "And God said to Jonah, Doest thou well to be angry for the gourd? And he said, I do well to be angry, even unto death. Then said the Lord, Thou hast had pity on the gourd, for which thou has not labored, neither madest it grow; which came up in a night and perished in a night; And should I not spare Ninevah, that great city, wherein are more than sixscore thousand persons that cannot discern between their right hand and their left hand; and also much cattle?"

These sinners, these heathen—and even the beasts that belong to them—are as much God's creatures as the Hebrews. This is a startling and original notion, especially considering the date of the story—eighth century B.C. (the time of Heraclitus). But this, finally, is the essence of what the rabbis have to teach. If there is to be any justice at all, it must be a justice for everyone. No one can be excluded, or else there is no such thing as justice. The conclusion is inescapable. This tiniest of books, which tells the curious and even comical story of Jonah, occupies a central place in the liturgy: it is read each year in the synagogue on Yom Kippur, the Day of Atonement, which is the most solemn day on the Jewish calendar. For everything, as has been noted before, is connected to everything else. And if there is everything, then it follows there is everyone. He does not forget Jonah's last words: "I do well to be angry, even unto death." And still, he finds himself writing these words on the page before him. If there is everything, then it follows there is everyone.

The words rhyme, and even if there is no real connection between them, he cannot help thinking of them together. Room and tomb, tomb and womb, womb and room. Breath and death. Or the fact that the letters of the word "live" can be rearranged to spell out the word "evil." He knows this is no more than a schoolboy's game. Surprisingly, however, as he writes the word "schoolboy," he can remember himself at eight or nine years old, and the sudden sense of power he felt in himself when he discovered he could play with words in this way—as if he had accidentally found a secret path to the truth: the absolute, universal, and unshakeable truth that lies hidden at the center of the world. In his schoolboy enthusiasm, of course, he had neglected to consider the existence of languages other than English, the great Babel of tongues buzzing and battling in the world outside his schoolboy life. And how can the absolute and unshakeable truth change from language to language?

Still, the power of rhyming words, of word transformations, cannot altogether be dismissed. The feeling of magic remains, even if it cannot be connected with a search for the truth, and this same magic, these same correspondences between words, are present in every language, even though the particular combinations are different. At the heart of each language there is a network of rhymes, assonances, and overlapping meanings, and each of these occurrences functions as a kind of bridge that joins opposite and contrasting aspects of the world with one another. Language, then, not simply as a list of separate things to be added up and whose sum total is equal to the world. Rather, language as it is laid out in the dictionary: an infinitely complex organism, all of whose elements—cells and sinews, corpuscles and bones, digits and fluids—are present in the world simultaneously, none of which can exist on its own. For each word is defined by other words, which means that to enter any part of language is to enter the whole of it. Language, then, as a monadology, to echo the term used by Leibniz. ("Since all is a plenum, all matter is connected and all movement in the plenum produces some effect on the distant bodies, in proportion to the distance. Hence every body is affected not only by those with which it is in contact, and thus feels in some way everything that happens to them; but through them it also feels those that touch the ones with which it is in immediate contact. Hence it follows that this communication extends over any distance whatever. Consequently, every body experiences everything that goes on in the universe, so much so that he who sees everything might read in any body what is happening anywhere, and even what has happened or will happen. He would be able to observe in the present what is remote in both time and space. . . . A soul, however, can read in itself only what is directly represented in it; it is unable to unfold all at once all its folds; for these go on into infinity.")

Playing with words in the way A. did as a schoolboy, then, was not so much a search for the truth as a search for the world as it appears in language. Language is not truth. It is the way we exist in the world. Playing with words is merely to examine the way the mind functions, to mirror a particle of the world as the mind perceives it. In the same way, the world is not just the sum of the things that are in it. It is the infinitely complex network of connections among them. As in the meanings of words, things take on meaning only in relationship to each other. "Two faces are alike," writes Pascal. "Neither is funny by itself, but side by side their likeness makes us laugh." The faces rhyme for the eye, just as two words can rhyme for the ear. To carry the proposition one step further, A. would contend that it is possible for events in one's life to rhyme as well. A young man rents a room in Paris and then discovers that his father had hid out in this same room during the war. If these two events were to be considered separately, there would be little to say about either one of them. The rhyme they create when looked at together alters the reality of each. Just as two physical objects, when brought into proximity of each other, give off electromagnetic forces that not only effect the molecular structure of each but the space between them as well, altering, as it were, the very environment, so it is that two (or more) rhyming events set up a connection in the world, adding one more synapse to be routed through the vast plenum of experience.

These connections are commonplace in literary works (to return to that argument), but one tends not to see them in the world—for the world is too big and one's life is too small. It is only at those rare moments when one happens to glimpse a rhyme in the world that the mind can leap out of itself and serve as a bridge for things across time and space, across seeing and memory. But there is more to it than just rhyme. The grammar of existence includes all the figures of language itself: simile, metaphor, metonymy, synecdoche—so that each thing encountered in the world is actually many things, which in turn give way to many other things, depending on what these things are next to, contained by, or removed from. Often, too, the second term of a comparison is missing. It can be forgotten, or buried in the unconscious, or somehow made unavailable. "The past is hidden," Proust writes in an important passage of his novel, "beyond the reach of intellect, in some material object (in the sensation which that material object will give us) which we do not suspect. And as for that object, it depends on chance whether we come upon it or not before we ourselves must die." Everyone has experienced in one way or another the strange sensations of forgetfulness, the mystifying force of the missing term. I walked into that room, a man will say, and the oddest feeling came over me, as if I had been there before, although I cannot remember it at all. As in Pavlov's experiments with dogs (which, at the simplest possible level, demonstrate the way in which the mind can make a connection between two dissimilar things, eventually forget the first thing, and thereby turn one thing into another thing), something has happened, although we are at a loss to say what it is. What A. is struggling to express, perhaps, is that for some time now none of the terms has been missing for him. Wherever his eye or mind seems to stop, he discovers another connection, another bridge to carry him to yet another place, and even in the solitude of his room, the world has been rushing in on him at a dizzying speed, as if it were all suddenly converging in him and happening to him at once. Coincidence: to fall on with; to occupy the same place in time or space. The mind, therefore, as that which contains more than itself. As in the phrase from Augustine: "But where is the part of it which it does not itself contain?"

Second return to the belly of the whale.

"When he recovered his senses the Marionette could not remember where he was. Around him all was darkness, a darkness so deep and so black that for a moment he thought he had been dipped head first into an inkwell."

This is Collodi's description of Pinocchio's arrival in the belly of the shark. It would have been one thing to write it in the ordinary way: "a darkness as black as ink"—as a trite literary flourish to be forgotten the moment it is read. But something different is happening here, something that transcends the question of good or bad writing (and this is manifestly not bad writing). Take careful note: Collodi makes no comparisons in this passage; there is no "as if," no "like," nothing to equate or contrast one thing with another. The image of absolute darkness immediately gives way to an image of an inkwell. Pinocchio has just entered the belly of the shark. He does not know yet that Gepetto is also there. Everything, at least for this brief moment, has been lost. Pinocchio is surrounded by the darkness of solitude. And it is in this darkness, where the puppet will eventually find the courage to save his father and thereby bring about his transformation into a real boy, that the essential creative act of the book takes place.

By plunging his marionette into the darkness of the shark, Collodi is telling us, he is dipping his pen into the darkness of his inkwell. Pinocchio, after all, is only made of wood. Collodi is using him as the instrument (literally, the pen) to write the story of himself. This is not to indulge in primitive psychologizing. Collodi could not have achieved what he does in *Pinocchio* unless the book was for him a book of memory. He was over fifty years old when he sat down to write it, recently retired from an undistinguished career in government service, which had been marked, according to his nephew, "neither by zeal nor by punctuality nor by subordination." No less than Proust's novel in search of lost time, his story is a search for his lost childhood. Even the name he chose to write under was an evocation of the past. His real name was Carlo Lorenzini. Collodi was the name of the small town where his mother had been born and where he spent his holidays as a young child. About this childhood, a few facts are available. He was a teller of tall tales, admired by his friends for his ability to fascinate them with stories. According to his brother Ippolito, "He did it so well and with such mimickry that half the world took delight and the children listened to him with their mouths agape." In an autobiographical sketch written late in life, long after the completion of *Pinocchio*, Collodi leaves little doubt that he conceived of himself as the puppet's double. He portrays himself as a prankster and a clown—eating cherries in class and stuffing the pits into a schoolmate's pockets, catching flies and putting them into someone else's ears, painting figures on the clothes of the boy in front of him: in general, creating havoc for everyone. Whether or not this is true is beside the point. Pinocchio was Collodi's surrogate, and after the puppet had been created, Collodi saw himself as Pinocchio. The puppet had become the image of himself as a child. To dip the puppet into the inkwell, therefore, was to use his creation to write the story of himself. For it is only in the darkness of solitude that the work of memory begins.

Possible epigraph(s) for The Book of Memory.

"We ought surely to look in the child for the first traces of imaginative activity. The child's best loved and most absorbing occupation is play. Perhaps we may say that every child at play behaves like an imaginative writer, in that he creates a world of his own or, more truly, he rearranges the things of his world and orders it in a new way. . . . It would be incorrect to think that he does not take this world seriously; on the contrary, he takes his play very seriously and expends a great deal of emotion on it." (Freud)

"You will not forget that the stress laid on the writer's memories of his childhood, which perhaps seem so strange, is ultimately derived from the hypothesis that imaginative creation, like day dreaming, is a continuation of and substitute for the play of childhood." (Freud)

He watches his son. He watches the little boy move around the room and listens to what he says. He sees him playing with his toys and hears him talking to himself. Each time the boy picks up an object, or pushes a truck across the floor, or adds another block to the tower of blocks growing before him, he speaks of what he is doing, in the same way a narrator in a film would speak, or else he makes up a story to accompany the actions he has set in motion. Each movement engenders a word, or a series of words; each word triggers off another movement: a reversal, a continuation, a new set of movements and words. There is no fixed center to any of this ("a universe in which the center is everywhere, the circumference nowhere") except perhaps the child's consciousness, which is itself a constantly shifting field of perceptions, memories, and utterances. There is no law of nature that cannot be broken: trucks fly, a block becomes a person, the dead are resurrected at will. From one thing, the child's mind careens without hesitation to another thing. Look, he says, my broccoli is a tree. Look, my potatoes are a cloud. Look at the cloud, it's a man. Or else, feeling the food as it touches his tongue, and looking up, with a sly glint in his eyes: "Do you know how Pinocchio and his father escape from the shark?" Pause, letting the question sink in. Then, in a whisper: "They tiptoe quietly over his tongue."

It sometimes seems to A. that his son's mental perambulations while at play are an exact image of his own progress through the labyrinth of his book. He has even thought that if he could somehow make a diagram of his son at play (an exhaustive description, containing every shift, association, and gesture) and then make a similar diagram of his book (elaborating what takes place in the gaps between words, the interstices of the syntax, the blanks between sections—in other words, unraveling the spool of connections), the two diagrams would be the same: the one would fit perfectly over the other.

During the time he has worked on The Book of Memory, it has given him special pleasure to watch the boy remember. Like all preliterate beings, the boy's memory is astonishing. The capacity for detailed observation, for seeing an object in its singularity, is almost boundless.

Written language absolves one of the need to remember much of the world, for the memories are stored in the words. The child, however, standing in a place before the advent of the written word, remembers in the same way Cicero would recommend, in the same way devised by any number of classical writers on the subject: image wed to place. One day, for example (and this is only one example, plucked from a myriad of possibilities), A. and his son were walking down the street. They ran into a nursery school playmate of the boy's standing outside a pizza parlor with his father. A.'s son was delighted to see his friend, but the other boy seemed to shy away from the encounter. Say hello, Kenny, his father urged him, and the boy managed to summon forth a feeble greeting. Then A. and his son continued on their walk. Three or four months later, they happened to be walking past the same spot together. A. suddenly heard his son muttering to himself, in a barely audible voice: Say hello, Kenny, say hello. It occurred to A. that if in some sense the world imprints itself on our minds, it is equally true that our experiences are imprinted on the world. For that brief moment, as they walked by the pizza parlor, the boy was literally seeing his own past. The past, to repeat the words of Proust, is hidden in some material object. To wander about in the world, then, is also to wander about in ourselves. That is to say, the moment we step into the space of memory, we walk into the world.

It is a lost world. And it strikes him to realize that it will be lost forever. The boy will forget everything that has happened to him so far. There will be nothing left but a kind of after-glow, and perhaps not even that. All the thousands of hours that A. has spent with him during the first three years of his life, all the millions of words he has spoken to him, the books he has read to him, the meals he has made for him, the tears he has wiped for him—all these things will vanish from the boy's memory forever.

The Book of Memory. Book Thirteen.

He remembers that he gave himself a new name, John, because all cowboys were named John, and that each time his mother addressed him by his real name he would refuse to answer her. He remembers running out of the house and lying in the middle of the road with his eyes shut, waiting for a car to run him over. He remembers that his grandfather gave him a large photograph of Gabby Hayes and that it sat in a place of honor on the top of his bureau. He remembers thinking the world was flat. He remembers learning how to tie his shoes. He remembers that his father's clothes were kept in the closet in his room and that it was the noise of hangers clicking together in the morning that would wake him up. He remembers the sight of his father knotting his tie and saying to him, Rise and shine little boy. He remembers wanting to be a squirrel, because he wanted to be light like a squirrel and have a bushy tail and be able to jump from tree to tree as though he were flying. He remembers looking through the venetian blinds and seeing his newborn sister coming home from the hospital in his mother's arms. He remembers the nurse in a white dress who sat beside his baby sister and gave him little squares of Swiss chocolate. He remembers that she called them Swiss although he did not know what that meant. He remembers lying in his bed at dusk in midsummer and looking at the tree through his window and seeing different faces in the configuration of the branches. He remembers sitting in the bathtub and pretending that his knees were mountains and that the white soap was an ocean liner. He remembers the day his father gave him a plum and told him to go outside and ride his tricycle. He remembers that he did not like the taste of the plum and that he threw it into the gutter and was overcome by a feeling of guilt. He remembers the day his mother took him and his friend B. to the television studio in Newark to see a showing of Junior Frolics. He remembers that Uncle Fred had makeup on his face, just like his mother wore, and that he was surprised by this. He remembers that the cartoons were shown on a little television set, no bigger than the one at home, and the disappointment he felt was so crushing that he wanted to stand up and shout his protests to Uncle Fred. He remembers that he had been expecting to see Farmer Gray and Felix the Cat run around on a stage, as large as life, going at each other with real pitchforks and rakes. He remembers that B.'s favorite color was green and that he claimed his teddy bear had green blood running through its veins. He remembers that B. lived with both his grandmothers and that to get to B.'s room you had to go through an upstairs sitting room where the two white-haired women spent all their time watching television. He remembers that he and B. would go scavenging through the bushes and backyards of the neighborhood looking for dead animals. He remembers burying them by the side of his house, deep in the darkness of the ivy, and that mostly they were birds, little birds like sparrows and robins and wrens. He remembers building crosses for them out of twigs and saying a prayer over their bodies as he and B. laid them in the hole they had dug in the ground, the dead eyes touching the loose damp earth. He remembers taking apart the family radio one afternoon with a hammer and screwdriver and explaining to his mother that he had done it as a scientific experiment. He remembers these were the words he used and that his mother spanked him. He remembers trying to chop down a small fruit tree in the back yard with a dull axe he had found in the garage and managing to make no more than a few dents in it. He remembers seeing the green on the underside of the bark and getting spanked for that too. He remembers sitting at his desk in the first grade away from the other children because he had been punished for talking in class. He remembers sitting at that desk and reading a book with a red cover and red illustrations with green-blue backgrounds. He remembers the teacher coming up to him from behind and very gently putting her hand on his shoulder and whispering a question into his ear. He remembers that she was wearing a white sleeveless blouse and that her arms were thick and covered with freckles. He remembers colliding with another boy during a softball game in the schoolyard and being thrown to the ground so violently that for the next five or ten minutes he saw everything as in a photographic negative. He remembers getting to his feet and walking toward the school building and thinking to himself, I'm going blind. He remembers how his panic gradually turned to acceptance and even fascination in the space of those few minutes and how, when his normal sight returned to him, he had the feeling that some extraordinary thing had taken place inside him. He remembers wetting his bed long after it was an acceptable thing to do and the icy sheets when he woke up in the morning. He remembers being invited for the first time to sleep over at a friend's house and how he stayed awake all night for fear of wetting the bed and humiliating himself, staring at the luminescent green hands of the watch he had been given for his sixth birthday. He remembers studying the illustrations in a children's Bible and accepting the fact that God had a long white beard. He remembers thinking that the voice he heard inside himself was the voice of God. He remembers going to the circus at Madison Square Garden with his grandfather and taking a ring off the finger of an eight and a half foot giant at the sideshow for fifty cents. He remembers keeping the ring on the top of his bureau beside the photograph of Gabby Hayes and that he could put four of his fingers through it. He remembers speculating that perhaps the entire world was enclosed in a glass jar and that it sat on a shelf next to dozens of other jar-worlds in the pantry of a giant's house. He remembers refusing to sing Christmas carols at school because he was Jewish and staying behind in the classroom while the other children went to rehearse in the auditorium. He remembers coming home from the first day of Hebrew school wearing a new suit and being pushed into a creek by older boys in leather jackets who called him a Jew shit. He remembers writing his first book, a detective story he composed with green ink. He remembers thinking that if Adam and Eve were the first people in the world, then everyone was related to everyone else. He remembers wanting to throw a penny out the window of his grandparents' apartment on Columbus Circle and his grandmother telling him that it would go straight through someone's head. He remembers looking down from the top of the Empire State Building and being surprised that the taxicabs were still yellow. He remembers visiting the Statue of Liberty with his mother and remembers that she got very nervous inside the torch and made him go back down the stairs sitting, one step at a time. He remembers the boy who was killed by lightning on a hike at summer camp. He remembers lying there in the rain next to him and seeing the boy's lips turn blue. He remembers his grandmother telling him how she remembered coming to America from Russia when she was five years old. He remembers that she told him she remembered waking up from a deep sleep and finding herself in the arms of a soldier who was carrying her onto a ship. He remembers that she told him this was the only thing she could remember.

The Book of Memory. Later that evening.

Not long after writing the words, "this was the only thing she could remember," A. stood up from his table and left his room. Walking along the street, feeling drained by his efforts that day, he decided to go on walking for a while. Darkness came. He stopped for supper, spread out a newspaper on the table before him, and then, after paying his bill, decided to spend the rest of the evening at the movies. It took him nearly an hour to walk to the theater. As he was about to buy his ticket, he changed his mind, put the money back in his pocket, and walked away. He retraced his steps, following the same route that had taken him there in reverse. At some point along the way he stopped to drink a glass of beer. Then he continued on his walk. It was nearly twelve when he opened the door of his room.

That night, for the first time in his life, he dreamed that he was dead.

Twice he woke up during the dream, trembling with panic. Each time, he tried to calm himself down, told himself that by changing position in bed the dream would end, and each time, upon falling back to sleep, the dream started up again at precisely the spot it had left off.

It was not exactly that he was dead, but that he was going to die. This was certain, an absolute and imminent fact. He was lying in a hospital bed, suffering from a fatal disease. His hair had fallen out in patches, and his head was half bald. Two nurses dressed in white walked into the room and told him: "Today you are going to die. It's too late to help you." They were almost mechanical in their indifference to him. He cried and pleaded with them, "I'm too young to die, I don't want to die now." "It's too late," the nurses answered. "We have to shave your head now." With tears pouring from his eyes, he allowed them to shave his head. Then they said: "The coffin is over there. Just go and lie down in it, close your eyes, and soon you'll be dead." He wanted to run away. But he knew that it was not permitted to disobey their orders. He went over to the coffin and climbed into it. The lid was closed over him, but once inside he kept his eyes open.

Then he woke up for the first time.

After he went back to sleep, he was climbing out of the coffin. He was dressed in a white patient's gown and had no shoes on. He left the room, wandered for a long time through many corridors, and then walked out of the hospital. Soon afterwards, he was knocking on the door of his ex-wife's house. "I have to die today," he told her, "there's nothing I can do about it." She took this news calmly, acting much as the nurses had. But he was not there for her sympathy. He wanted to give her instructions about what to do with his manuscripts. He went through a long list of his writings and told her how and where to have each of them published. Then he said: "The Book of Memory isn't finished yet. There's nothing I can do about it. There won't be time to finish. You finish it for me and then give it to Daniel. I trust you. You finish it for me." She agreed to do this, but without much enthusiasm. And then he began to cry, just as he had before: "I'm too young to die. I don't want to die now." But she patiently explained to him that if it had to be, then he should accept it. Then he left her house and returned to the hospital. When he reached the parking lot, he woke up for the second time.

After he went back to sleep, he was inside the hospital again, in a basement room next to the morgue. The room was large, bare, and

146

white, a kind of old-fashioned kitchen. A group of his childhood friends, now grownups, were sitting around a table eating a large and sumptuous meal. They all turned and stared at him when he entered the room. He explained to them: "Look, they've shaved my head. I have to die today, and I don't want to die." His friends were moved by this. They invited him to sit down and eat with them. "No," he said, "I can't eat with you. I have to go into the next room and die." He pointed to a white swinging door with a circular window in it. His friends stood up from their chairs and joined him by the door. For a little while they all reminisced about their childhood together. It soothed him to talk to them, but at the same time he found it all the more difficult to summon the courage to walk through the door. Finally, he announced: "I have to go now. I have to die now." One by one, with tears pouring down his cheeks, he embraced his friends, squeezing them with all his strength, and said good-bye.

Then he woke up for the last time.

Concluding sentences for The Book of Memory.

From a letter by Nadezhda Mandelstam to Osip Mandelstam, dated 10/22/38, and never sent.

"I have no words, my darling, to write this letter ... I am writing it into empty space. Perhaps you will come back and not find me here. Then this will be all you have left to remember me by. ... Life can last so long. How hard and long for each of us to die alone. Can this fate be for us who are inseparable? Puppies and children, did we deserve this? Did you deserve this, my angel? Everything goes on as before. I know nothing. Yet I know everything—each day and hour of your life are plain and clear to me as in a delirium—In my last dream I was buying food for you in a filthy hotel restaurant. The people with me were total strangers. When I had bought it, I realized I did not know where to take it, because I do not know where you are. ... When I woke up, I said to Shura: 'Osia is dead.' I do not know whether you are still alive, but from the time of that dream, I have lost track of you. I do not know where you are. Will you hear me? Do you know how much I love you? I could never tell you how much I love you. I cannot tell you even now. I speak to you, only to you. You are with me always, and I who was such a wild and angry one and never learned to weep simple tears—now I weep and weep and weep ... It's me: Nadia. Where are you?"

* * *

He lays out a piece of blank paper on the table before him and writes these words with his pen.

The sky is blue and black and gray and yellow. The sky is not there, and it is red. All this was yesterday. All this was a hundred years ago. The sky is white. It smells of the earth, and it is not there. The sky is white like the earth, and it smells of yesterday. All this was tomorrow. All this was a hundred years from now. The sky is lemon and rose and lavender. The sky is the earth. The sky is white, and it is not there.

He wakes up. He walks back and forth between the table and the window. He sits down. He stands up. He walks back and forth between the bed and the chair. He lies down. He stares at the ceiling. He closes his eyes. He opens his eyes. He walks back and forth between the table and the window.

He finds a fresh sheet of paper. He lays it out on the table before him and writes these words with his pen.

It was. It will never be again. Remember.

1980–1981

REFERENCES
(Sources of quotations not mentioned in text)

page 68   "Israel Lichtenstein's Last Testament." In *A Holocaust Reader*, edited by Lucy S. Dawidowicz. Behrman House. New York, 1976.

page 71   Flaubert. *The Letters of Gustave Flaubert*, selected, edited, and translated by Francis Steegmuller. Harvard University Press. Cambridge, 1979.

page 78   Marina Tsvetayeva. Quotations of translations by Elaine Feinstein. In *Marina Tsvetayeva: Selected Poems*. Oxford University Press, 1971.

page 78   Gregory I. Altschuller, M.D. *Marina Tsvetayeva: A Physician's Memoir*. In SUN. Volume IV, Number 3: Winter, 1980. New York.

page 80   Christopher Wright. In *Rembrandt and His Art*. Galahad Books. New York, 1975.

page 81   Hölderlin. Prose quotations translated by Michael Hamburger. In *Friedrich Hölderlin: Poems and Fragments*. University of Michigan Press. Ann Arbor, 1966.

page 82   Hölderlin. *To Zimmer*. Translated by John Riley and Tim Longville. In *What I Own: Versions of Hölderlin*. Grosseteste Review Press, 1973.

page 108 B. = André du Bouchet. In *Hölderlin Aujourd'hui*, a lecture delivered in Stuttgart, 1970.

page 110 Collodi. *The Adventures of Pinocchio*. Translated by Carol Della Chiesa. Macmillan. New York, 1925. All further quotations from this edition. Translations sometimes slightly adapted.

page 119 Edward A. Snow. *A Study of Vermeer*. University of California Press. Berkeley, 1979.

page 121 Van Gogh. *The Letters of Vincent Van Gogh*. Edited by Mark Roskill. Atheneum. New York, 1972.

page 125 Tolstoy. Ann Dunnigan's translation of *War and Peace*. New American Library. New York, 1968.

page 126 Freud. "The 'Uncanny." In *On Creativity and the Unconscious*. Harper and Row. New York, 1958.

page 127 *The Thousand and One Nights*. All quotations from *The Portable Arabian Nights*. Translated by John Payne. Edited by Joseph Campbell. Viking. New York, 1952.

page 132 Dostoyevsky. *The Brothers Karamazov*. Translated by David Magarshack. Penguin. Baltimore, 1958.

page 132 Jim Harrison. Quoted in "The End of Cambodia?" by William Shawcross. *The New York Review of Books*. January 24, 1980.

page 134 Anne Frank. *The Diary of a Young Girl*. Doubleday. New York, 1952.

page 135 Quotations of commentaries on the Book of Jonah from "Jonah, or the Unfulfilled Prophecy" in *Four Strange Books of the Bible*, by Elias Bickerman. Schocken. New York, 1967.

page 137 Leibniz. In *Monadology and Other Philosophical Essays*. Translated by Paul Schrecker and Anne Martin Schrecker. Bobbs-Merrill. Indianapolis, 1965.

page 138 Proust. *Swann's Way*. Translated by C.K. Scott Moncrieff. Random House. New York, 1928.

page 140 Freud. "The Relation of the Poet to Day-Dreaming." In *On Creativity and the Unconscious*.

page 147 Nadezhda Mandelstam. *Hope Abandoned*. Translated by Max Hayward. Collins & Harvill. London, 1974.

HAND TO MOUTH
A Chronicle of Early Failure

In my late twenties and early thirties, I went through a period of several years when everything I touched turned to failure. My marriage ended in divorce, my work as a writer foundered, and I was overwhelmed by money problems. I'm not just talking about an occasional shortfall or some periodic belt tightenings—but a constant, grinding, almost suffocating lack of money that poisoned my soul and kept me in a state of never-ending panic.

There was no one to blame but myself. My relationship to money had always been flawed, enigmatic, full of contradictory impulses, and now I was paying the price for refusing to take a clear-cut stand on the matter. All along, my only ambition had been to write. I had known that as early as sixteen or seventeen years old, and I had never deluded myself into thinking I could make a living at it. Becoming a writer is not a "career decision" like becoming a doctor or a policeman. You don't choose it so much as get chosen, and once you accept the fact that you're not fit for anything else, you have to be prepared to walk a long, hard road for the rest of your days. Unless you turn out to be a favorite of the gods (and woe to the man who banks on that), your work will never bring in enough to support you, and if you mean to have a roof over your head and not starve to death, you must resign yourself to doing other work to pay the bills. I understood all that, I was prepared for it, I had no complaints. In that respect, I was immensely lucky. I didn't particularly want anything in the way of material goods, and the prospect of being poor didn't frighten me. All I wanted was a chance to do the work I felt I had it in me to do.

Most writers lead double lives. They earn good money at legitimate professions and carve out time for their writing as best they can: early in the morning, late at night, weekends, vacations. William Carlos Williams and Louis-Ferdinand Céline were doctors. Wallace Stevens worked for an insurance company. T. S. Eliot was a banker, then a publisher. Among my own acquaintances, the French poet Jacques Dupin is codirector of an art gallery in Paris. William Bronk, the American poet, managed his family's coal and lumber business in upstate New York for over forty years. Don DeLillo, Peter Carey, Salman Rushdie, and Elmore Leonard all worked for long stretches in advertising. Other writers teach. That is probably the most common solution today, and with every major university and Podunk college offering so-called creative writing courses, novelists and poets are continually scratching and scrambling to land themselves a spot. Who can blame them? The salaries might not be big, but the work is steady and the hours are good.

My problem was that I had no interest in leading a double life. It's not that I wasn't willing to work, but the idea of punching a clock at some nine-to-five job left me cold, utterly devoid of enthusiasm. I was in my early twenties, and I felt too young to settle down, too full of other plans to waste my time earning more money than I either wanted or needed. As far as finances went, I just wanted to get by. Life was cheap in those days, and with no responsibility for anyone but myself, I figured I could scrape along on an annual income of roughly three thousand dollars.

I tried graduate school for a year, but that was only because Columbia offered me a tuition-free fellowship with a two-thousand-dollar stipend—which meant that I was actually paid to study. Even under those ideal conditions, I quickly understood that I wanted no part of it. I had had enough of school, and the prospect of spending another five or six years as a student struck me as a fate worse than death. I didn't want to talk about books anymore, I wanted to write them. Just on principle, it felt wrong to me for a writer to hide out in a university, to surround himself with too many like-minded people, to get too comfortable. The risk was complacency, and once that happens to a writer, he's as good as lost.

I'm not going to defend the choices I made. If they weren't practical, the truth was that I didn't want to be practical. What I wanted were new experiences. I wanted to go out into the world and test myself, to move from this to that, to explore as much as I could. As long as I kept my eyes open, I figured that whatever happened to me would be useful, would teach me things I had never known before. If this sounds like a rather old-fashioned approach, perhaps it was. Young writer bids farewell to family and friends and sets out for points unknown to discover what he's made of. For better or worse, I doubt that any other approach would have suited me. I had energy, a head crammed full of ideas, and itchy feet. Given how big the world was, the last thing I wanted was to play it safe.

* * *

It's not difficult for me to describe these things and to remember how I felt about them. The trouble begins only when I question why I did them and why I felt what I felt. All the other young poets and writers in my class were making sensible decisions about their futures. We weren't rich kids who could depend on handouts from our parents, and once we left college, we would be out on our own for good. We were all facing the same situation, we all knew the score, and yet they acted in one way and I acted in another. That's what I'm still at a loss to explain. Why did my friends act so prudently, and why was I so reckless?

I came from a middle-class family. My childhood was comfortable, and I never suffered from any of the wants and deprivations that plague most of the human beings who live on this earth. I never went hungry, I never was cold, I never felt in danger of losing any of the things I had. Security was a given, and yet for all the ease and good fortune in the household, money was a subject of continual conversation and worry. Both of my parents had lived through the Depression, and neither one had fully recovered from those hard times. Each had been marked by the experience of not having enough, and each bore the wound in a different way.

My father was tight; my mother was extravagant. She spent; he didn't. The memory of poverty had not loosened its hold on his spirit, and even though his circumstances had changed, he could never quite bring himself to believe it. She, on the other hand, took great pleasure in those altered circumstances. She enjoyed the rituals of consumerism, and like so many Americans before her and since, she cultivated shopping as a means of self-expression, at times raising it to the level of an art form. To enter a store was to engage in an alchemical process that imbued the cash register with magical, transformative properties. Inexpressible desires, intangible needs, and unarticulated longings all passed through the money box and came out as real things, palpable objects you could hold in your hand. My mother never tired of reenacting this miracle, and the bills that resulted became a bone of contention between her and my father. She felt that we could afford them; he didn't. Two styles, two worldviews, two moral philosophies were in eternal conflict with each other, and in the end it broke their marriage apart. Money was the fault line, and it became the single, overpowering source of dispute between them. The tragedy was that they were both good people—attentive, honest, hardworking—and aside from that one ferocious battleground, they seemed to get along rather well. For the life of me I could never understand how such a relatively unimportant issue could cause so much trouble between them. But money, of course, is never just money. It's always something else, and it's always something more, and it always has the last word.

As a small boy, I was caught in the middle of this ideological war. My mother would take me shopping for clothes, sweeping me up in the whirlwind of her enthusiasm and generosity, and again and again I would allow myself to be talked into wanting the things she offered me—always more than I was expecting, always more than I thought I needed. It was impossible to resist, impossible not to enjoy how the clerks doted on her and hopped to her commands, impossible not to be carried away by the power of her performance. My happiness was always mixed with a large dose of anxiety, however, since I knew exactly what my father was going to say when he got the bill. And the fact was that he always said it. The inevitable outburst would come, and almost inevitably the matter would be resolved with my father declaring that the next time I needed something, he was the one who would take me shopping. So the moment would roll around to buy me a new winter jacket, say, or a new pair of shoes, and one night after dinner my father and I would drive off to a discount store located on a highway somewhere in the New Jersey darkness. I remember the glare of fluorescent lights in those places, the cinder-block walls, the endless racks of cheap men's clothing. As the jingle on the radio put it: "Robert Hall this season / Will tell you the reason— / Low overhead / Bum, bum, bum / Low overhead!" When all is said and done, that song is as much a part of my childhood as the Pledge of Allegiance or the Lord's Prayer.

The truth was that I enjoyed this bargain hunting with my father as much as I enjoyed the buying sprees orchestrated by my mother. My loyalties were equally divided between my two parents, and there was never any question of pitching my tent in one camp or the other. My mother's approach was more appealing, perhaps, at least in terms of the fun and excitement it generated, but there was something about my father's stubbornness that gripped me as well, a sense of hard-won experience and knowledge at the core of his beliefs, an integrity of purpose that made him someone who never backed down, not even at the risk of looking bad in the eyes of the world. I found that admirable, and much as I adored my beautiful, endlessly charming mother for dazzling the world as she did, I also adored my father for resisting that same world. It could be maddening to watch him in action—a man who never seemed to care what others thought of him—but it was also instructive, and in the long run I think I paid more attention to those lessons than I ever realized.

As a young boy I fell into the mold of your classic go-getter. At the first sign of snow, I would run out with my shovel and start ringing doorbells, asking people if they would hire me to clear their driveways and front walks. When the leaves fell in October, I would be out there with my rake, ringing those same doorbells and asking about the lawns. At other times, when there was nothing to remove from the ground, I would inquire about "odd jobs." Straightening up the garage, cleaning out the cellar, pruning the hedges—whatever needed to be done, I was the man to do it. In the summer, I sold lemonade for ten cents a glass on the sidewalk in front of my house. I gathered up empty bottles from the kitchen pantry, loaded them in my little red wagon, and lugged them to the store to turn in for cash. Two cents for the small ones; five cents for the big. I mostly used my earnings to buy baseball cards, sports magazines, and comic books, and whatever was left over I would diligently put in my piggy bank, which was built in the shape of a cash register. I was truly the child of my parents, and I never questioned the principles that animated their world. Money talked, and to the degree that you listened to it and followed its arguments, you would learn to speak the language of life.

Once, I remember, I was in possession of a fifty-cent piece. I can't recall how I came to have that coin—which was just as rare then as it is now—but whether it had been given to me or whether I had earned it myself, I have a keen sense of how much it meant to me and what a large sum it represented. For fifty cents in those days you could buy ten packs of baseball cards, five comic books, ten candy bars, fifty jawbreakers—or, if you preferred, various combinations of all of them. I put the half-dollar in my back pocket and marched off to the store, feverishly calculating how I was going to spend my little fortune. Somewhere along the way, however, for reasons that still confound me, the coin disappeared. I reached into my back pocket to check on it—knowing it was there, just wanting to make sure—and the money was gone. Was there a hole in my pocket? Had I accidentally slid the coin out of my pants the last time I'd touched it? I have no idea. I was six or seven years old, and I still remember how wretched I felt. I had tried to be so careful, and yet for all my precautions, I had wound up losing the money. How could I have allowed such a thing to happen? For want of any logical explanation, I decided that God had punished me. I didn't know why, but I was certain that the All-Powerful One had reached into my pocket and plucked out the coin Himself.

Little by little, I started turning my back on my parents. It's not that I began to love them less, but the world they came from no longer struck me as such an inviting place to live. I was ten, eleven, twelve years old, and already I was becoming an internal émigré, an exile in my own house. Many of these changes can be attributed to adolescence, to the simple fact that I was growing up and beginning to think for myself— but not all of them. Other forces were at work on me at the same time, and each one had a hand in pushing me onto the road I later followed. It wasn't just the pain of having to witness my parents' crumbling marriage, and it wasn't just the frustration of being trapped in a small suburban town, and it wasn't just the American climate of the late 1950s—but put them all together, and suddenly you had a powerful case against materialism, an indictment of the orthodox view that money was a good to be valued above all others. My parents valued money, and where had it gotten them? They had struggled so hard for it, had invested so much belief in it, and yet for every problem it had solved, another one had taken its place. American capitalism had created one of the most prosperous moments in human history. It had produced untold numbers of cars, frozen vegetables, and miracle shampoos, and yet Eisenhower was President, and the entire country had been turned into a gigantic television commercial, an incessant harangue to buy more, make more, spend more, to dance around the dollar-tree until you dropped dead from the sheer frenzy of trying to keep up with everyone else.

It wasn't long before I discovered that I wasn't the only person who felt this way. At ten, I stumbled across an issue of *Mad* magazine in a candy store in Irvington, New Jersey, and I remember the intense, almost stupefying pleasure I felt at reading those pages. They taught me that I had kindred spirits in this world, that others had already unlocked the doors I was trying to open myself. Fire hoses were being turned on black people in the American South, the Russians had launched the first Sputnik, and I was starting to pay attention. No, you didn't have to swallow the dogma they were trying to sell you. You could resist them, poke fun at them, call their bluff. The wholesomeness and dreary rectitude of American life were no more than a sham, a halfhearted publicity stunt. The moment you began to study the facts, contradictions bubbled to the surface, rampant hypocrisies were exposed, a whole new way of looking at things suddenly became possible. We had been taught to believe in "liberty and justice for all," but the fact was that liberty and justice were often at odds with one another. The pursuit of money had nothing to do with fairness; its driving engine was the social principle of "every man for himself." As if to prove the essential inhumanity of the marketplace, nearly all of its metaphors had been taken from the animal kingdom: dog eat dog, bulls and bears, the rat race, survival of the fittest. Money divided the world into winners and losers, haves and have-nots. That was an excellent arrangement for the winners, but what about the people who lost? Based on the evidence available to me, I gathered that they were to be cast aside and forgotten. Too bad, of course, but those were the breaks. If you construct a world so primitive as to make Darwin your leading philosopher and Aesop your leading poet, what else can you expect? It's a jungle out there, isn't it? Just look at that Dreyfus lion strolling down the middle of Wall Street. Could the message be any clearer? Either eat or be eaten. That's the law of the jungle, my friend, and if you don't have the stomach for it, then get out while you still can.

I was out before I was ever in. By the time I entered my teens, I had already concluded that the world of business would have to get along without me. I was probably at my worst then, my most insufferable, my most confused. I burned with the ardor of a newfound idealism, and the stringencies of the perfection I sought for myself turned me into a pint-sized puritan-in-training. I was repulsed by the outward trappings of wealth, and every sign of ostentation my parents brought into the house I treated with scorn. Life was unfair. I had finally figured this out, and because it was my own discovery, it hit me with all the force of a revelation. As the months went by, I found it increasingly difficult to reconcile my good luck with the bad luck of so many others. What had I done to deserve the comforts and advantages that had been showered on me? My father could afford them—that was all—and whether or not he and my mother fought over money was a small point in comparison to the fact that they had money to fight over in the first place. I squirmed every time I had to get into the family car—so bright and new and expensive, so clearly an invitation to the world to admire how well off we were. All my sympathies were for the downtrodden, the dispossessed, the underdogs of the social order, and a car like that filled me with shame—not just for myself, but for living in a world that allowed such things to be in it.

My first jobs don't count. My parents were still supporting me, and I was under no obligation to fend for myself or contribute to the family budget. The pressure was therefore off, and without any pressure, nothing important can ever be at stake. I was glad to have the money I earned, but I never had to use it on nuts-and-bolts necessities, I never had to worry about putting food on the table or not falling behind with the rent. Those problems would come later. For now I was just a high school kid looking for a pair of wings to carry me away from where I was.

At sixteen, I spent two months working as a waiter at a summer camp in upstate New York. The next summer, I worked at my uncle Moe's appliance store in Westfield, New Jersey. The jobs were similar in that most of the tasks were physical and didn't require much thought. If carrying trays and scraping dishes was somewhat less interesting than installing air conditioners and unloading refrigerators from forty-foot trailer trucks, I wouldn't want to make too big a point of it. This isn't a question of apples and oranges—but of two kinds of apples, both the same shade of green. Dull as the work might have been, however, I found both jobs immensely satisfying. There were too many colorful characters around, too many surprises, too many new thoughts to absorb for me to resent the drudgery, and I never felt that I was wasting my time just to earn a paycheck. The money was an important part of it, but the work wasn't just about money. It was about learning who I was and how I fit into the world.

Even at the camp, where my coworkers were all sixteen- and seventeen-year-old high school boys, the kitchen help came from a starkly different universe. Down-and-outs, Bowery bums, men with dubious histories, they had been rounded up from the New York streets by the owner of the camp and talked into accepting their low-paying jobs—which included two months of fresh air and free room and board. Most of them didn't last long. One day they would just disappear, wandering back to the city without bothering to say good-bye. A day or two later, the missing man would be replaced by a similar lost soul, who rarely lasted very long himself. One of the dishwashers, I remember, was named Frank, a grim, surly guy with a serious drinking problem. Somehow or other, we managed to become friends, and in the evening after work was done we would sometimes sit on the steps behind the kitchen and talk. Frank turned out to be a highly intelligent, well-read man. He had worked as an insurance agent in Springfield, Massachusetts, and until the bottle got the better of him, he had lived the life of a productive, tax-paying citizen. I distinctly remember not daring to ask him what had happened, but one evening he told me anyway, turning what must have been a complicated story into a short, dry account of the events that had done him in. In the space of sixteen months, he said, every person who had ever meant anything to him died. He sounded philosophical about it, almost as if he were talking about someone else, and yet there was an undertow of bitterness in his voice. First his parents, he said, then his wife, and then his two children. Diseases, accidents, and burials, and by the time they were all gone, it was as if his insides had shattered. "I just gave up," he said. "I didn't care what happened to me anymore, so I became a bum."

The following year, in Westfield, I made the acquaintance of several more indelible figures. Carmen, for example, the voluminously padded, wisecracking bookkeeper, who to this day is still the only woman I've known with a beard (she actually had to shave), and Joe Mansfield, the assistant repairman with two hernias and a ravaged Chrysler that had wiped out the odometer three times and was now up to 360,000 miles. Joe was sending two daughters through college, and in addition to his day job at the appliance store, he worked eight hours every night as a foreman in a commercial bakery, reading comic books beside the huge vats of dough so as not to fall asleep. He was the single most exhausted man I have ever met—and also one of the most energetic. He kept himself going by smoking menthol cigarettes and downing twelve to sixteen bottles of orange soda a day, but not once did I ever see him put a morsel of food in his mouth. If he ate lunch, he said, it would make him too tired and he would collapse. The hernias had come a few years earlier, when he and two other men were carrying a jumbo refrigerator up a narrow flight of stairs. The other men had lost their grip, leaving Joe to bear the entire weight of the thing himself, and it was exactly then, as he struggled not to be crushed by the several hundred pounds he was holding, that his testicles had shot up out of his scrotum. First one ball, he said, and then the other. Pop . . . pop. He wasn't supposed to lift heavy objects anymore, but every time there was an especially large appliance to deliver, he would come along and help us—just to make sure we didn't kill ourselves.

The *us* included a nineteen-year-old redhead named Mike, a tense, wiry shrimp with a missing index finger and one of the fastest tongues I had yet encountered. Mike and I were the air conditioner installation team, and we spent a lot of time together in the store van, driving to and from jobs. I never tired of listening to the onslaught of loopy, unexpected metaphors and outrageous opinions that came pouring out of him whenever he opened his mouth. If he found one of the customers too snotty, for example, he wouldn't say "that person's an asshole" (as most would) or "that person's stuck-up" (as some would), but "that person acts as if his shit doesn't smell." Young Mike had a special gift, and on several occasions that summer I was able to see how well it served him. Again and again we would enter a house to install an air conditioner, and again and again, just as we were in the middle of the job (screwing in the screws, measuring strips of caulking to seal up the window), a girl would walk into the room. It never seemed to fail. She was always seventeen, always pretty, always bored, always "just hanging around the house." The instant she appeared, Mike would turn on the charm. It was as if he knew she was going to come in, as if he had already rehearsed his lines and was fully prepared. I, on the other hand, was always caught with my guard down, and as Mike launched into his song and dance (a combination of bullshit, razzle-dazzle, and raw nerve), I would dumbly plod on with the work. Mike would talk, and the girl would smile. Mike would talk a little more, and the girl would laugh. Within two minutes they were old friends, and by the time I'd put the finishing touches on the job, they were swapping phone numbers and arranging where to meet on Saturday night. It was preposterous; it was sublime; it made my jaw drop. If it had happened only once or twice, I would have dismissed it as a fluke, but this scene was played out repeatedly, no less than five or six times over the course of the summer. In the end, I grudgingly had to admit that Mike was more than just lucky. He was someone who created his own luck.

In September, I started my senior year of high school. It was the last year I spent at home, and it was also the last year of my parents' marriage. Their breakup had been so long in coming that when the news was announced to me at the end of Christmas vacation, I wasn't upset so much as relieved.

It had been a mismatch from the start. If they hung in together as long as they did, it was more for "the children's sake" than for their own. I don't presume to have any answers, but I suspect that a decisive moment occurred two or three years before the end, when my father took over the grocery-shopping duties for the household. That was the last great money battle my parents fought, and it stands in my mind as the symbolic last straw, the thing that finally knocked the stuffing out of both of them. It was true that my mother enjoyed filling her cart at the local Shop-Rite until it was almost too heavy to push; it was true that she took pleasure in providing the treats my sister and I asked her for; it was true that we ate well at home and that the pantry was abundantly stocked. But it was also true that we could afford these things and that the family finances were in no way threatened by the sums my mother forked over at the checkout counter. In my father's eyes, however, her spending was out of control. When he finally put his foot down, it landed in the wrong place, and he wound up doing what no man should ever do to his wife. In effect, he relieved her of her job. From then on, he was the one who took responsibility for bringing food into the house. Once, twice, even three times a week, he would stop off somewhere on the way home from work (as if he didn't have enough to do already) and load up the back of his station wagon with groceries. The choice cuts of meat my mother had brought home were replaced by chuck and shoulder. Name-brand products became generic products. After-school snacks vanished. I don't remember hearing my mother complain, but it must have been a colossal defeat for her. She was no longer in charge of her own house, and the fact that she didn't protest, that she didn't fight back, must have meant that she had already given up on the marriage. When the end came, there were no dramas, no noisy showdowns, no last-minute regrets. The family quietly dispersed. My mother moved to an apartment in the Weequahic section of Newark (taking my sister and me along with her), and my father stayed on alone in the big house, living there until the day he died.

In some perverse way, these events made me extremely happy. I was glad that the truth was finally out in the open, and I welcomed the upheavals and changes that followed as a consequence of that truth. There was something liberating about it, an exhilaration in knowing that the slate had been wiped clean. An entire period of my life had ended, and even as my body continued to go through the motions of finishing up high school and helping my mother move to her new place, my mind had already decamped. Not only was I about to leave home, but home itself had disappeared. There was nothing to return to anymore, nowhere to go but out and away.

I didn't even bother to attend my high school graduation. I offer that as proof, evidence of how little it meant to me. By the time my classmates were donning their caps and gowns and receiving their diplomas, I was already on the other side of the Atlantic. The school had granted me a special dispensation to leave early, and I had booked passage on a student boat that sailed out of New York at the beginning of June. All my savings went into that trip. Birthday money, graduation money, bar mitzvah money, the little bits I'd hoarded from summer jobs—fifteen hundred dollars or so, I can't remember the exact amount. That was the era of Europe on Five Dollars a Day, and if you watched your funds carefully, it was actually possible to do it. I spent over a month in Paris, living in a hotel that cost seven francs a night ($1.40); I traveled to Italy, to Spain, to Ireland. In two and a half months, I lost more than twenty pounds. Everywhere I went, I worked on the novel I had started writing that spring. Mercifully, the manuscript has disappeared, but the story I carried around in my head that summer was no less real to me than the places I went to and the people I crossed paths with. I had some extraordinary encounters, especially in Paris, but more often than not I was alone, at times excessively alone, alone to the point of hearing voices in my head. God knows what to make of that eighteen-year-old boy now. I see myself as a conundrum, the site of inexplicable turmoils, a weightless, wild-eyed sort of creature, slightly touched, perhaps, prone to desperate inner surges, sudden about-faces, swoons, soaring thoughts. If someone approached me in the right way, I could be open, charming, positively gregarious. Otherwise, I was walled off and taciturn, barely present. I believed in myself and yet had no confidence in myself. I was bold and timid, light-footed and clumsy, single-minded and impulsive—a walking, breathing monument to the spirit of contradiction. My life had only just begun, and already I was moving in two directions at once. I didn't know it yet, but in order for me to get anywhere, I was going to have to work twice as hard as anyone else.

The last two weeks of the trip were the strangest. For reasons that had everything to do with James Joyce and *Ulysses*, I went to Dublin. I had no plans. My only purpose in going was to be there, and I figured the rest would take care of itself. The tourist office steered me to a bed-and-breakfast in Donnybrook, a fifteen-minute bus ride from the center of town. Besides the elderly couple who ran the place and two or three of the guests, I scarcely talked to anyone in all that time. I never even found the courage to set foot in a pub. Somewhere during the course of my travels, I had developed an ingrown toenail, and while it sounds like a comical condition, it wasn't the least bit funny to me. It felt as if the tip of a knife had been lodged in my big toe. Walking was turned into a trial, and yet from early in the morning to late in the afternoon, I did little else but walk, hobbling around Dublin in my too-tight, disintegrating shoes. I could live with the pain, I found, but the effort it called for seemed to drive me ever further into myself, to erase me as a social being. There was a crotchety American geezer in full-time residence at the boardinghouse—a seventy-year-old retiree from Illinois or Indiana—and once he got wind of my condition, he started filling my head with stories about how his mother had left an ingrown toenail untended for years, treating it with patchwork home remedies—dabs of disinfectant, little balls of cotton—but never *taking the bull by the horns*, and wouldn't you know it, she came down with *cancer of the toe*, which worked its way into her foot, and then into her leg, and then spread through her whole body and eventually did her in. He loved elaborating on the small, gruesome details of his mother's demise (for my own good, of course), and seeing how susceptible I was to what he told me, he never tired of telling the story again. I'm not going to deny that I was affected. A cumbersome annoyance had been turned into a life-threatening scourge, and the longer I delayed taking action, the more dismal my prospects would become. Every time I rode past the Hospital for Incurables on my way into town, I turned my eyes away. I couldn't get the old man's words out of my head. Doom was stalking me, and signs of impending death were everywhere.

Once or twice, I was accompanied on my rambles by a twenty-six-year-old nurse from Toronto. Her name was Pat Gray, and she had checked into the bed-and-breakfast the same evening I had. I fell desperately in love with her, but it was a hopeless infatuation, a lost cause from the start. Not only was I too young for her, and not only was I too shy to declare my feelings, but she was in love with someone else—an Irishman, of course, which explained why she'd come to Dublin in the first place. One night, I recall, she came home from a date with her beloved at around half-past twelve. I was still up at that hour, scribbling away at my novel, and when she saw light coming through the crack under my door, she knocked and asked to come in. I was already in bed, working with a notebook propped against my knees, and she burst in laughing, her cheeks flushed with drink, bubbling over with excitement. Before I could say anything, she threw her arms around my neck and kissed me, and I thought: Miracle of miracles, my dream has come true. But alas, it was only a false alarm. I didn't even have a chance to kiss her back before she was drawing away from me and explaining that her Irishman had proposed to her that night and that she was the happiest girl in the world. It was impossible not to feel glad for her. This straightforward, pretty young woman, with her short hair and innocent eyes and earnest Canadian voice, had chosen me as the person to share the news with. I did my best to congratulate her, to hide my disappointment after that brief, wholly implausible rush of expectation, but the kiss had undone me, had absolutely melted my bones, and it was all I could do not to commit a serious blunder. If I managed to control myself, it was only by turning myself into a block of wood. No doubt a block of wood has good manners, but it's hardly a fitting companion for a celebration.

Everything else was solitude, silence, walking. I read books in Phoenix Park, journeyed out to Joyce's Martello Tower along the strand, crossed and recrossed the Liffey more times than I could count. The Watts riots took place then, and I remember reading the headlines at a kiosk on O'Connell Street, but I also remember a small girl singing with a Salvation Army band early one evening as people shuffled home from work—some sad, plaintive song about human misery and the wonders of God—and that voice is still inside me, a voice so crystalline as to make the toughest person fall down and weep, and the remarkable thing about it was that no one paid the slightest attention to her. The rush-hour crowd rushed past her, and she just stood on the corner singing her song in the eerie, dusky, northern light, as oblivious of them as they were of her, a tiny bird in tattered clothes chanting her psalm to the broken heart.

Dublin is not a big city, and it didn't take me long to learn my way around. There was something compulsive about the walks I took, an insatiable urge to prowl, to drift like a ghost among strangers, and after two weeks the streets were transformed into something wholly personal for me, a map of my inner terrain. For years afterward, every time I closed my eyes before going to sleep, I was back in Dublin. As wakefulness dribbled out of me and I descended into semiconsciousness, I would find myself there again, walking through those same streets. I have no explanation for it. Something important had happened to me there, but I have never been able to pinpoint exactly what it was. Something terrible, I think, some mesmerizing encounter with my own depths, as if in the loneliness of those days I had looked into the darkness and seen myself for the first time.

I started Columbia College in September, and for the next four years the last thing on my mind was money. I worked intermittently at various jobs, but those years were not about making plans, not about preparing for my financial future. They were about books, the war in Vietnam, the struggle to figure out how to do the thing I was proposing to do. If I thought about earning a living at all, it was only in a fitful, haphazard sort of way. At most I imagined some kind of marginal existence for myself—scrounging for crumbs at the far edges of the workaday world, the life of a starving poet.

The jobs I had as an undergraduate were nevertheless instructive. If nothing else, they taught me that my preference for blue-collar work over white-collar work was well founded. At one point in my sophomore year, for example, I was hired by the subdivision of a publishing company to write material for educational filmstrips. I had been subjected to a barrage of "audiovisual aids" during my childhood, and I remembered the intense boredom they invariably produced in me and my friends. It was always a pleasure to leave the classroom and sit in the dark for twenty or thirty minutes (just like going to the movies!), but the clunky images on screen, the monotone voice of the narrator, and the intermittent *ping* that told the teacher when to push the button and move on to the next picture soon took their toll on us. Before long, the room was abuzz with whispered conversations and frantic, half-suppressed giggles. A minute or two later, the spitballs would begin to fly.

I was reluctant to impose this tedium on another generation of kids, but I figured I'd do my best and see if I couldn't put some spark into it. My first day on the job, the supervisor told me to take a look at some of the company's past filmstrips and acquaint myself with the form. I picked out one at random. It was called "Government" or "Introduction to Government," something like that. He set up the spool on a machine and then left me alone to watch the film. About two or three frames into it, I came across a statement that alarmed me. The ancient Greeks had invented the idea of democracy, the text said, accompanied by a painting of bearded men standing around in togas. That was fine, but then it went on to say (*ping:* cut to a painting of the Capitol) that America was a democracy. I turned off the machine, walked down the hall, and knocked on the door of the supervisor's office. "There's a mistake in the filmstrip," I said. "America isn't a democracy. It's a republic. There's a big difference."

He looked at me as if I had just informed him that I was Stalin's grandson. "It's for little children," he said, "not college students. There's no room to go into detail."

"It's not a detail," I answered, "it's an important distinction. In a pure democracy, everyone votes on every issue. We elect representatives to do that for us. I'm not saying that's bad. Pure democracy can be dangerous. The rights of minorities need to be protected, and that's what a republic does for us. It's all spelled out in *The Federalist Papers*. The government has to guard against the tyranny of the majority. Kids should know that."

The conversation became quite heated. I was determined to make my point, to prove that the statement in the filmstrip was wrong, but he refused to swallow it. He pegged me as a troublemaker the instant I opened my mouth, and that was that. Twenty minutes after starting the job, I was given the boot.

Much better was the job I had in the summer after my freshman year—as groundskeeper at the Commodore Hotel in the Catskills. I was hired through the New York State Employment Agency in midtown Manhattan, a vast government office that found work for the unskilled and the unfortunate, the bottom dogs of society. Humble and badly paid as the position was, at least it offered a chance to get out of the city and escape the heat. My friend Bob Perelman and I signed on together, and the next morning we were dispatched to Monticello, New York, via the Short Line Bus Company. It was the same setup I'd seen three years before, and our fellow passengers were the same bums and down-and-outs I'd rubbed shoulders with during my stint as a summer camp waiter. The only difference was that now I was one of them. The bus fare was deducted from the first paycheck, as was the employment agency's fee, and unless you hung in with the job for some little time, you weren't going to make any money. There were those who didn't like the work and quit after a couple of days. They wound up with nothing—dead broke and a hundred miles from home, feeling they'd been had.

The Commodore was a small, down-at-the-heels Borscht Belt establishment. It was no match for the local competition, the Concord and Grossinger's, and a certain wistfulness and nostalgia hung about the place, a memory of rosier days. Bob and I arrived several weeks in advance of the summer season, and we were responsible for getting the grounds into shape to welcome an influx of visitors in July and August. We mowed lawns, clipped bushes, collected trash, painted walls, repaired screen doors. They gave us a little hut to live in, a ramshackle box with less square footage than a beach cabana, and bit by bit we covered the walls of our room with poems—crazy doggerel, filthy limericks, flowery quatrains—laughing our heads off as we downed endless bottles of Budweiser chug-a-lug beer. We drank the beer because there was nothing better to do, but given the food we had to eat, the hops became a necessary component of our diet as well. There were only a dozen or so workers on the premises at the time, and they gave us the low-budget treatment where culinary matters were concerned. The menu for every lunch and dinner was the same: Chun King chicken chow mein, straight out of the can. Thirty years have gone by since then, and I would still rather go hungry than put another morsel of that stuff in my mouth.

None of this would be worth mentioning if not for Casey and Teddy, the two indoor maintenance men I worked with that summer. Casey and Teddy had been palling around together for more than ten years, and by now they were a pair, an indissoluble team, a dialectical unit. Everything they did, they did in tandem, traveling from place to place and job to job as if they were one. They were chums for life, two peas in a pod, buddies. Not gay, not the least bit interested in each other sexually—but buddies. Casey and Teddy were classic American drifters, latter-day hoboes who seemed to have stepped forth from the pages of a Steinbeck novel, and yet they were so funny together, so full of wisecracks and drunkenness and good cheer, that their company was irresistible. At times they made me think of some forgotten comedy duo, a couple of clowns from the days of vaudeville and silent films. The spirit of Laurel and Hardy had survived in them, but these two weren't bound by the constraints of show business. They were part of the real world, and they performed their act on the stage of life.

Casey was the straight man, Teddy was the card. Casey was thin, Teddy was round. Casey was white, Teddy was black. On their days off they would tramp into town together, drink themselves silly, and then return for their chow mein dinner sporting identical haircuts or dressed in identical shirts. The idea was always to spend all their money in one big binge—and to spend it in exactly the same way, even-steven, penny for penny. The shirts stand out in my mind as a particularly raucous event. They couldn't stop laughing when they showed up in those twin outfits, holding their sides and pointing at each other as if they'd just played an enormous joke on the world. They were the loudest, ugliest shirts imaginable, a double insult to good taste, and Casey and Teddy were positively seized with mirth as they modeled them for me and Bob. Teddy then shuffled off to the empty ballroom on the ground floor of the main building, sat down at the piano, and launched into what he called his Port Wine Concerto. For the next hour and a half, he clanged forth tuneless improvisations, filling the hall with a tempest of inebriation and noise. Teddy was a man of many gifts, but music was not one of them. Yet there he sat, happy as a clam in the fading light, a Dada maestro at peace with himself and the world.

Teddy had been born in Jamaica, he told me, and had joined the British Navy during World War II. Somewhere along the line, his ship was torpedoed. I don't know how much time elapsed before he was rescued (minutes? hours? days?), but whenever he was found, it was an American ship that found him. From then on he was in the American Navy, he said, and by the end of the war he was an American citizen. It sounded a little fishy to me, but that's the story he told, and who was I to doubt him? In the past twenty years, he seemed to have done everything a man can possibly do, to have run the entire gamut of occupations. Salesman, sidewalk artist in Greenwich Village, bartender, skid row drunk. None of it mattered to him. A great, rumbling basso laugh accompanied every story he told, and that laugh was like an unending bow to his own ridiculousness, a sign that his only purpose in talking was to poke fun at himself. He made scenes in public places, misbehaved like a willful child, was forever calling people's bluff. It could be exhausting to be with him, but there was also something admirable about the way he caused trouble. It had an almost scientific quality to it, as if he were conducting an experiment, shaking things up for the pure pleasure of seeing where they would land once the dust had settled. Teddy was an anarchist, and because he was also without ambition, because he didn't want the things that other people wanted, he never had to play by anybody's rules but his own.

I have no idea how or where he met Casey. His sidekick was a less flamboyant character than he was, and what I remember best about him was that he had no sense of taste or smell. Casey had been in a barroom fight some years back, had received a knock on the head, and had thenceforth lost all of his olfactory functions. As a result, everything tasted like cardboard to him. Cover his eyes, and he couldn't tell you what he was eating. Chow mein or caviar, potatoes or pudding—there was no difference. Aside from this affliction, Casey was in excellent trim, a feisty welterweight with a New York Irish voice that made him sound like a Dead End Kid. His job was to laugh at Teddy's jokes and make sure his friend didn't take things too far and get himself hauled off to jail. Teddy got close to it one night that summer—standing up in a Monticello restaurant and waving around the menu as he shouted, "I ain't gonna eat this Japanese dog food!"—but Casey calmed him down, and we all managed to finish our meal. I don't suppose it's necessary to add that we weren't in a Japanese restaurant.

By any objective standard, Casey and Teddy were nobodies, a pair of eccentric fools, but they made an unforgettable impression on me, and I have never run across their likes since. That was the reason for going off to work at places like the Commodore Hotel, I think. It's not that I wanted to make a career of it, but those little excursions into the backwaters and shit holes of the world never failed to produce an interesting discovery, to further my education in ways I hadn't expected. Casey and Teddy are a perfect example. I was nineteen years old when I met them, and the things they did that summer are still feeding my imagination today.

In 1967, I signed up for Columbia's Junior Year Abroad Program in Paris. The weeks I'd spent there after finishing high school had whetted my appetite for the place, and I jumped at the chance to go back.

Paris was still Paris, but I was no longer the same person I'd been during my first visit. I had spent the past two years living in a delirium of books, and whole new worlds had been poured into my head, life-altering transfusions had reconstituted my blood. Nearly everything that is still important to me in the way of literature and philosophy I first encountered during those two years. Looking back on that time now, I find it almost impossible to absorb how many books I read. I drank them up in staggering numbers, consumed entire countries and continents of books, could never even begin to get enough of them. Elizabethan playwrights, pre-Socratic philosophers, Russian novelists, Surrealist poets. I read books as if my brain had caught fire, as if my very survival were at stake. One work led to another work, one thought led to another thought, and from one month to the next, I changed my ideas about everything.

The program turned out to be a bitter disappointment. I went to Paris with all sorts of grandiose plans, assuming I would be able to attend any lectures and courses I wanted to (Roland Barthes at the Collège de France, for example), but when I sat down to discuss these possibilities with the director of the program, he flat out told me to forget them. Out of the question, he said. You're required to study French language and grammar, to pass certain tests, to earn so many credits and half-credits, to put in so many class hours here and so many hours there. I found it absurd, a curriculum designed for babies. I'm past all that, I told him. I already know how to speak French. Why go backward? Because, he said, those are the rules, and that's the way it is.

He was so unbending, so contemptuous of me, so ready to interpret my enthusiasm as arrogance and to think I was out to insult him, that we immediately locked horns. I had nothing against the man personally, but he seemed bent on turning our disagreement into a personal conflict. He wanted to belittle me, to crush me with his power, and the longer the conversation went on, the more I felt myself resisting him. At last, a moment came when I'd had enough. All right, I said, if that's the way it is, then I quit. I quit the program, I quit the college, I quit the whole damn thing. And then I got up from my chair, shook his hand, and walked out of the office.

It was a crazy thing to do. The prospect of not getting a B.A. didn't worry me, but turning my back on college meant that I would automatically lose my student deferment. With the troop buildup in Vietnam growing at an alarming rate, I had suddenly put myself in a good position to be drafted into the army. That would have been fine if I supported the war, but I didn't. I was against it, and nothing was ever going to make me fight in it. If they tried to induct me into the army, I would refuse to serve. If they arrested me, I would go to jail. That was a categorical decision—an absolute, unbudgeable stance. I wasn't going to take part in the war, even if it meant ruining my life.

Still, I went ahead and quit college. I was utterly fearless about it, felt not the slightest tremor of hesitation or doubt, and took the plunge with my eyes wide open. I was expecting to fall hard, but I didn't. Instead, I found myself floating through the air like a feather, and for the next few months I felt as free and happy as I had ever been.

I lived in a small hotel on the rue Clément, directly across from the Marché Saint-Germain, an enclosed market that has long since been torn down. It was an inexpensive but tidy place, several notches up from the fleabag I'd stayed in two years before, and the young couple who ran it were exceedingly kind to me. The man's name was Gaston (stout, small mustache, white shirt, ever-present black apron), and he spent the bulk of his time serving customers in the café on the ground floor, a minuscule hole-in-the-wall that doubled as neighborhood hangout and hotel reception desk. That's where I drank my coffee in the morning, read the newspaper, and became addicted to pinball. I walked a lot during those months, just as I had in Dublin, but I also spent countless hours upstairs in my room, reading and writing. Most of the work I did then has been lost, but I remember writing poems and translating poems, as well as composing a long, exhaustingly complex screenplay for a silent film (part Buster Keaton movie, part philosophical tap dance). On top of all the reading I'd done in the past two years, I had also been going to the movies, primarily at the Thalia and New Yorker theaters, which were no more than a short walk down Broadway from Morningside Heights. The Thalia ran a different double feature every day, and with the price of admission just fifty cents for students, I wound up spending as much time there as I did in the Columbia classrooms. Paris turned out to be an even better town for movies than New York. I became a regular at the Cinémathèque and the Left Bank revival houses, and after a while I got so caught up in this passion that I started toying with the idea of becoming a director. I even went so far as to make some inquiries about attending IDHEC, the Paris film institute, but the application forms proved to be so massive and daunting that I never bothered to fill them out.

When I wasn't in my room or sitting in a movie theater, I was browsing in bookstores, eating in cheap restaurants, getting to know various people, catching a dose of the clap (very painful), and generally exulting in the choice I had made. It would be hard to exaggerate how good I felt during those months. I was at once stimulated and at peace with myself, and though I knew my little paradise would have to end, I did everything I could to prolong it, to put off the hour of reckoning until the last possible moment.

I managed to hold out until mid-November. By the time I returned to New York, the fall semester at Columbia was half over. I assumed there was no chance of being reinstated as a student, but I had promised my family to come back and discuss the matter with the university. They were worried about me, after all, and I figured I owed them that much. Once I had taken care of that chore, I intended to go back to Paris and start looking for a job. Let the draft be damned, I said to myself. If I wound up as a "fugitive from justice," so be it.

None of it worked out as I thought it would. I made an appointment to see one of the deans at Columbia, and this man turned out to be so sympathetic, so fully on my side, that he broke down my defenses within a matter of minutes. No, he said, he didn't think I was being foolish. He understood what I was doing, and he admired the spirit of the enterprise. On the other hand, there was the question of the war, he said. Columbia didn't want to see me go into the army if I didn't want to go, much less wind up in jail for refusing to serve in the army. If I wanted to come back to college, the door was open. I could start attending classes tomorrow, and officially it would be as if I had never missed a day.

How to argue with a man like that? He wasn't some functionary who was just doing his job. He spoke too calmly for that and listened too carefully to what I said, and before long I understood that the only thing in it for him was an honest desire to prevent a twenty-year-old kid from making a mistake, to talk someone out of fucking up his life when he didn't have to. There would be time for that later, n'est-ce pas? He wasn't very old himself—thirty, thirty-five, perhaps—and I still remember his name, even though I never saw him again. Dean Platt. When the university shut down that spring because of the student strike, he quit his job in protest over the administration's handling of the affair. The next thing I heard, he had gone to work for the UN.

The troubles at Columbia lasted from early 1968 until my class graduated the following June. Normal activity all but stopped during that time. The campus became a war zone of demonstrations, sit-ins, and moratoriums. There were riots, police raids, slugfests, and factional splits. Rhetorical excesses abounded, ideological lines were drawn, passions flowed from all sides. Whenever there was a lull, another issue would come up, and the outbursts would begin all over again. In the long run, nothing of any great importance was accomplished. The proposed site for a university gymnasium was changed, a number of academic requirements were dropped, the president resigned and was replaced by another president. That was all. In spite of the efforts of thousands, the ivory tower did not collapse. But still, it tottered for a time, and more than a few of its stones crumbled and fell to the ground.

I took part in some things and kept my distance from others. I helped occupy one of the campus buildings, was roughed up by the cops and spent a night in jail, but mostly I was a bystander, a sympathetic fellow traveler. Much as I would have liked to join in, I found myself temperamentally unfit for group activities. My loner instincts were far too ingrained, and I could never quite bring myself to climb aboard the great ship *Solidarity*. For better or worse, I went on paddling my little canoe—a bit more desperately, perhaps, a bit less sure of where I was going now, but much too stubborn to get out. There probably wouldn't have been time for that anyway. I was steering through rapids, and it took every ounce of my strength just to hold on to the paddle. If I had flinched, there's a good chance I would have drowned.

Some did. Some became casualties of their own righteousness and noble intentions, and the human loss was catastrophic. Ted Gold, one class ahead of me, blew himself to smithereens in a West Village brownstone when the bomb he was building accidentally went off. Mark Rudd, a childhood friend and Columbia dorm neighbor, joined the Weather Underground and lived in hiding for more than a decade. Dave Gilbert, an SDS spokesman whose speeches had impressed me as models of insight and intelligence, is now serving a seventy-five-year prison sentence for his involvement in the Brinks robbery. In the summer of 1969, I walked into a post office in western Massachusetts with a friend who had to mail a letter. As she waited in line, I studied the posters of the FBI's ten most wanted men pinned to the wall. It turned out that I knew seven of them.

That was the climate of my last two years of college. In spite of the distractions and constant turmoil, I managed to do a fair amount of writing, but none of my efforts ever added up to much. I started two novels and abandoned them, wrote several plays I didn't like, worked on poem after poem with largely disappointing results. My ambitions were much greater than my abilities at that point, and I often felt frustrated, dogged by a sense of failure. The only accomplishment I felt proud of was the French poetry I had translated, but that was a secondary pursuit and not even close to what I had in mind. Still, I must not have been totally discouraged. I kept on writing, after all, and when I began publishing articles on books and films in the *Columbia Daily Spectator*, I actually got to see my work in print fairly often. You have to start somewhere, I suppose. I might not have been moving as fast as I wanted to, but at least I was moving. I was up on my feet and walking forward, step by wobbly step, but I still didn't know how to run.

When I look back on those days now, I see myself in fragments. Numerous battles were being fought at the same time, and parts of myself were scattered over a broad field, each one wrestling with a different angel, a different impulse, a different idea of who I was. It sometimes led me to act in ways that were fundamentally out of character. I would turn myself into someone I was not, try wearing another skin for a while, imagine I had reinvented myself. The morose and contemplative stuffed shirt would dematerialize into a fast-talking cynic. The bookish, overly zealous intellectual would suddenly turn around and embrace Harpo Marx as his spiritual father. I can think of several examples of this antic bumbling, but the one that best captures the spirit of the time was a little piece of jabberwocky I contributed to the *Columbia Review*, the undergraduate literary magazine. For reasons that utterly escape me now, I took it upon myself to launch the First Annual Christopher Smart Award. I was a senior then, and the contest rules were published on the last page of the fall issue. I pluck these sentences from the text at random: "The purpose of the award is to give recognition to the great anti-men of our time ... men of talent who have renounced all worldly ambition, who have turned their backs on the banquet tables of the rich. ... We have taken Christopher Smart as our model ... the eighteenth-century Englishman who spurned the easy glory that awaited him as an inventor of rhymed couplets ... for a life of drunkenness, insanity, religious fanaticism, and prophetic writings. In excess he found his true path, in rejecting the early promise he showed to the academic poets of England, he realized his true greatness. Defamed and ridiculed over the past two centuries, his reputation run through the mud ... Christopher Smart has been relegated to the sphere of the unknowns. We attempt now, in an age without heroes, to resurrect his name."

The object of the competition was to reward failure. Not common, everyday setbacks and stumbles, but monumental falls, gargantuan acts of self-sabotage. In other words, I wanted to single out the person who had done the least with the most, who had begun with every advantage, every talent, every expectation of worldly success, and had come to nothing. Contestants were asked to write an essay of fifty words or more describing their failure or the failure of someone they knew. The winner would receive a two-volume boxed set of Christopher Smart's *Collected Works*. To no one's surprise but my own, not one entry was submitted.

It was a joke, of course, an exercise in literary leg pulling, but underneath my humorous intentions there was something disturbing, something that was not funny at all. Why the compulsion to sanctify failure? Why the mocking, arrogant tone, the know-it-all posturing? I could be wrong, but it strikes me now that they were an expression of fear—dread of the uncertain future I had prepared for myself—and that my true motive in setting up the contest was to declare myself the winner. The cockeyed, Bedlamite rules were a way of hedging my bets, of ducking the blows that life had in store for me. To lose was to win, to win was to lose, and therefore even if the worst came to pass, I would be able to claim a moral victory. Small comfort, perhaps, but no doubt I was already clutching at straws. Rather than bring my fear out into the open, I buried it under an avalanche of wisecracks and sarcasm. None of it was conscious. I was trying to come to terms with anticipated defeats, hardening myself for the struggles that lay ahead. For the next several years, my favorite sentence in the English language was from the Elizabethan poet Fulke Greville: "I write for those on whom the black ox hath trod."

As it happened, I wound up meeting Christopher Smart. Not the real Christopher Smart, perhaps, but one of his reincarnations, a living example of failed promise and blighted literary fortune. It was the spring of my senior year, just weeks before I was supposed to graduate. Out of nowhere, a man turned up on the Columbia campus and started causing a stir. At first I was only dimly aware of his presence, but little fragments of the stories circulating about him occasionally fell within my earshot. I'd heard that he called himself "Doc," for example, and that for obscure reasons that had something to do with the American economic system and the future of mankind, he was handing out money to strangers, no strings attached. With so many oddball doings in the air back then, I didn't pay much attention.

One night, a couple of my friends talked me into going down to Times Square with them to see the latest Sergio Leone spaghetti western. After the movie let out, we decided to cap off the evening with a little lark and repaired to the Metropole Café at Broadway and Forty-eighth Street. The Metropole had once been a quality jazz club, but now it was a topless go-go bar, complete with wall-to-wall mirrors, strobe lights, and half a dozen girls in glittering G-strings dancing on an elevated platform. We took a table in one of the back corners and started drinking our drinks. Once our eyes had adjusted to the darkness, one of my friends spotted "Doc" sitting alone in the opposite corner of the room. My friend went over and asked him to join us, and when the bearded, somewhat disheveled mystery man sat down beside me, mumbling something about Gene Krupa and what the hell had happened to this place, I turned my eyes away from the dancers for a moment and shook hands with the legendary, forgotten novelist, H.L. Humes.

He had been one of the founders of the *Paris Review* back in the fifties, had published two successful early books (*The Underground City* and *Men Die*), and then, just as he was beginning to make a name for himself, had vanished from sight. He just dropped off the literary map and was never heard from again.

I don't know the full story, but the bits and pieces I heard from him suggested that he'd had a rough time of it, had endured a long run of reversals and miseries. Shock treatments were mentioned, a ruined marriage, several stays in mental hospitals. By his own account, he'd been forced to stop writing for physical reasons—not by choice. The electroshock therapy had damaged his system, he said, and every time he picked up a pen, his legs would start to swell up, causing him unbearable pain. With the written word no longer available to him, he now had to rely on talk to get his "message" across to the world. That night, he gave a full-scale demonstration of how thoroughly he had mastered this new medium. First in the topless bar, and then on a nearly seventy-block walk up Broadway to Morningside Heights, the man talked a blue streak, rattling and rambling and chewing our ears off with a monologue that resembled nothing I had ever heard before. It was the rant of a hipster-visionary-neoprophet, a relentless, impassioned outflow of paranoia and brilliance, a careening mental journey that bounced from fact to metaphor to speculation with such speed and unpredictability that one was left dumbfounded, unable to say a word. He had come to New York on a mission, he told us. There were fifteen thousand dollars in his pocket, and if his theories about finance and the structures of capitalism were correct, he would be able to use that money to bring down the American government.

It was all quite simple, really. His father had just died, leaving Doc the aforementioned sum as an inheritance, and rather than squander the money on himself, our friend was proposing to give it away. Not in a lump, and not to any particular charity or person, but to everyone, to the whole world all at once. To that end he had gone to the bank, cashed the check, and converted it into a stack of fifty-dollar bills. With those three hundred portraits of Ulysses S. Grant as his calling cards, he was going to introduce himself to his coconspirators and unleash the greatest economic revolution in history. Money is a fiction, after all, worthless paper that acquires value only because large numbers of people choose to give it value. The system runs on faith. Not truth or reality, but collective belief. And what would happen if that faith were undermined, if large numbers of people suddenly began to doubt the system? Theoretically, the system would collapse. That, in a nutshell, was the object of Doc's experiment. The fifty-dollar bills he handed out to strangers weren't just gifts; they were weapons in the fight to make a better world. He wanted to set an example with his profligacy, to prove that one could disenchant oneself and break the spell that money held over our minds. Each time he disbursed another chunk of cash, he would instruct the recipient to spend it as fast as he could. Spend it, give it away, get it circulating, he would say, and tell the next person to do the same. Overnight, a chain reaction would be set in motion, and before you knew it, so many fifties would be flying through the air that the system would start to go haywire. Waves would be emitted, neutron charges from thousands, even millions of different sources would bounce around the room like little rubber balls. Once they built up enough speed and momentum, they would take on the strength of bullets, and the walls would begin to crack.

I can't say to what degree he actually believed this. Deranged as he might have been, a man of his intelligence surely would have known a stupid idea when he heard it. He never came out and said so, but deep down I think he understood what drivel it was. That didn't stop him from enjoying it, of course, and from spouting off about his plan at every opportunity, but it was more in the spirit of a wacko performance piece than a genuine political act. H. L. Humes wasn't some crackpot schizo taking orders from Martian command center. He was a ravaged, burnt-out writer who had run aground on the shoals of his own consciousness, and rather than give up and renounce life altogether, he had manufactured this little farce to boost his morale. The money gave him an audience again, and as long as people were watching, he was inspired, manic, the original one-man band. He pranced about like a buffoon, turning cartwheels and jumping through flames and shooting himself out of cannons, and from all I could gather, he loved every minute of it.

As he marched up Broadway that night with me and my friends, he put on a spectacular show. Between the cascading words and the barks of laughter and the jags of cosmological music, he would wheel around and start addressing strangers, breaking off in midsentence to slap another fifty-dollar bill in someone's hand and urge him to spend it like there was no tomorrow. Rambunctiousness took control of the street that night, and Doc was the prime attraction, the pied piper of mayhem. It was impossible not to get caught up in it, and I must admit that I found his performance highly entertaining. However, just as we neared the end of our journey and I was about to go home, I made a serious blunder. It must have been one or two in the morning by then. Somewhere off to my right, I heard Doc muttering to himself. "Any of you cats got a place to crash?" he said, and because he sounded so cool and nonchalant, so profoundly indifferent to the matters of this world, I didn't think twice about it. "Sure," I said, "you can sleep on my couch if you want to." Needless to say, he accepted my invitation. Needless to say, I had no idea what I had gotten myself into.

It's not that I didn't like him, and it's not that we didn't get along. For the first couple of days, in fact, things went rather smoothly. Doc planted himself on the couch and rarely stirred, rarely even brought the soles of his feet into contact with the floor. Aside from an occasional trip to the bathroom, he did nothing but sit, eat pizza, smoke marijuana, and talk. I bought the pizza for him (with his money), and after telling him five or six times that I wasn't interested in dope, he finally got the message and stopped offering it to me. The talk was incessant, however, the same repertoire of addled riffs he'd unfurled on the first night, but his arguments were more ample now, more fleshed out, more focused. Hours would go by, and his mouth never stopped moving. Even when I got up and left the room, he would go on talking, delivering his ideas to the wall, the ceiling, the light fixtures, and scarcely even notice that I was gone.

There wouldn't have been a problem if the place had been a little larger. The apartment had just two rooms and a kitchen, and since my bedroom was too small to hold anything but a bed, my work table was set up in the living room—which also happened to be where the couch was. With Doc permanently installed on the couch, it was all but impossible for me to get any work done. The spring semester was drawing to a close, and I had a number of term papers to write in order to complete my courses and graduate, but for the first two days I didn't even bother to try. I figured that I had a little margin and therefore didn't panic. Doc would be leaving soon, and once I had my desk back, I would be able to get down to work. By the morning of the third day, however, I realized that my houseguest had no intention of leaving. It wasn't that he was overstaying his welcome on purpose; the thought of leaving simply hadn't entered his head. What was I supposed to do? I didn't have the heart to kick him out. I already felt too sorry for him, and I couldn't find the courage to take such a drastic step.

The next few days were exceedingly difficult. I did what I could to cope, to see if some minor adjustments could improve the situation. In the end, things might have panned out—I don't know—but three or four days after I put Doc in the bedroom and took over the living room for myself, disaster struck. It happened on one of the most beautiful Sundays I can remember, and it was no one's fault but my own. A friend called to invite me to play in an outdoor basketball game, and rather than leave Doc alone in the apartment, I took him along with me. Everything went well. I played in the game and he sat by the side of the court, listening to the radio and yakking to himself or my friends, depending on whether anyone was within range. As we were returning home that evening, however, someone spotted us on the street. "Aha," this person said to me, "so that's where he's been hiding." I had never particularly liked this person, and when I told him to keep Doc's whereabouts under his hat, I realized that I might just as well have been talking to a lamppost. Sure enough, the buzzer of my apartment started ringing early the next morning. The campus celebrity had been found, and after his mysterious weeklong absence, H. L. Humes was more than happy to indulge his followers. All day long, groups of nineteen- and twenty-year-olds tramped into my apartment to sit on the floor and listen to Doc impart his skewed wisdom to them. He was the philosopher king, the metaphysical pasha, the bohemian holy man who saw through the lies their professors had taught them, and they couldn't get enough of it.

I was deeply pissed off. My apartment had been turned into a twenty-four-hour meeting hall, and much as I would have liked to hold Doc responsible for it, I knew that he wasn't to blame. His acolytes had come of their own accord, without invitations or appointments, and once the crowds began to gather, I could no more ask him to turn them away than I could ask the sun to stop shining. Talk was what he lived for. It was his final barrier against oblivion, and because those kids were there with him now, because they sat at his feet and hung on his every word, he could temporarily delude himself into thinking that all was not lost for him. I had no problem with that. For all I cared, he could go on talking until the next century. I just didn't want him doing it in my apartment.

Torn between compassion and disgust, I came up with a coward's compromise. It happened during one of the rare lulls of that period, at a moment when no unannounced visitors were in the apartment. I told Doc that he could stay—and that I would clear out instead. I had piles of work to do, I explained, and rather than dump him on the street before he'd found another place to live, I would go to my mother's apartment in Newark and write my school papers. In exactly one week I would return, and when I came back I expected him to be gone. Doc listened carefully as I outlined this plan to him. When I had finished, I asked him if he understood. "I dig, man," he said, speaking in his calmest, most gravelly jazzman's voice, "it's cool," and that was all there was to it. We went on to talk about other things, and somewhere in the course of our conversation that night he mentioned that many years back, as a young man in Paris, he had occasionally played chess with Tristan Tzara. This is one of the few concrete facts that has stayed with me. Over time, nearly everything else I heard from the mouth of H. L. Humes has disappeared. I can remember what his voice sounded like, but very little of what he said. All those great verbal marathons, those forced marches to the hinterlands of reason, those countless hours of listening to him unravel his plots and conspiracies and secret correspondences—all that has been reduced to a blur. The words are no more than a buzzing in my brain now, an unintelligible swarm of nothingness.

The next morning, as I was packing my bag and getting ready to leave, he tried to give me money. I turned him down, but he kept insisting, peeling off fifties from his wad like some racetrack gambler, telling me to take it, that I was a good kid, that we had to "share the wealth," and in the end I caved in to the pressure and accepted three hundred dollars from him. I felt terrible about it then and still feel terrible about it now. I had wanted to stay above that business, to resist taking part in the pathetic game he was playing, and yet when my principles were finally put on the line, I succumbed to temptation and allowed greed to get the better of me. Three hundred dollars was a large sum in 1969, and the lure of that money turned out to be stronger than I was. I put the bills in my pocket, shook Doc's hand good-bye, and hurried out of the apartment. When I returned a week later, the place was neat as a pin, and there was no sign of him anywhere. Doc had left, just as he had promised he would.

I saw him only once more after that. It was about a year later, and I was riding uptown on the number 4 bus. Just as we made the turn onto 110th Street, I spotted him through the window—standing on the corner of Fifth Avenue and the northern edge of Central Park. He appeared to be in bad shape. His clothes were rumpled, he looked dirty, and his eyes had a lost, vacant expression that had not been there before. He's slipped into hard drugs, I said to myself. Then the bus moved on, and I lost sight of him. Over the next days and weeks, I kept expecting to see him again, but I never did. Twenty-five years went by, and then, just five or six months ago, I opened *The New York Times* and stumbled across a small article on the obituary page announcing that he was dead.

Little by little, I learned how to improvise, trained myself to roll with the punches. During my last two years at Columbia, I took any number of odd freelance jobs, gradually developing a taste for the kind of literary hackwork that would keep me going until I was thirty—and which ultimately led to my downfall. There was a certain romance in it, I suppose, a need to affirm myself as an outsider and prove that I could make it on my own without kowtowing to anyone else's idea of what constituted the good life. My life would be good if and only if I stuck to my guns and refused to give in. Art was holy, and to follow its call meant making any sacrifice that was demanded of you, maintaining your purity of purpose to the bitter end.

Knowing French helped. It was hardly a rarefied skill, but I was good enough at it to have some translation jobs tossed my way. Art writings, for example, and an exceptionally tedious document from the French Embassy about the reorganization of its staff that droned on for more than a hundred pages. I also tutored a high school girl one spring, traveling across town every Saturday morning to talk to her about poetry, and another time I was collared by a friend (for no pay) to stand on an outdoor podium with Jean Genet and translate his speech in defense of the Black Panthers. Genet walked around with a red flower tucked behind his ear and rarely stopped smiling the whole time he was on the Columbia campus. New York seemed to make him happy, and he handled the attention he received that day with great poise. One night not long after that, I bumped into an acquaintance in the West End, the old student watering hole at Broadway and 114th Street. He told me that he had just started working for a pornography publisher, and if I wanted to try my hand at writing a dirty book, the price was fifteen hundred dollars per novel. I was more than willing to have a go at it, but my inspiration petered out after twenty or thirty pages. There were just so many ways to describe that one thing, I discovered, and my stock of synonyms soon dried up. I started writing book reviews instead—for a shoddily put together publication aimed at students. Sensing that the magazine wasn't going to add up to much, I signed my articles with a pseudonym, just to keep things interesting. Quinn was the name I chose for myself, Paul Quinn. The pay, I remember, was twenty-five dollars per review.

When the results of the draft lottery were announced at the end of 1969, I lucked out with number 297. A blind draw of the cards saved my skin, and the nightmare I had been girding myself against for several years suddenly evaporated. Who to thank for that unexpected mercy? I had been spared immense amounts of pain and trouble, had literally been given back control of my life, and the sense of relief was incalculable. Jail was no longer in the picture for me. The horizon was clear on all sides, and I was free to walk off in any direction I chose. As long as I traveled light, there was nothing to stop me from going as far as my legs would take me.

That I wound up working on an oil tanker for several months was largely a matter of chance. You can't work on a ship without a Merchant Seaman's card, and you can't obtain a Merchant Seaman's card without a job on a ship. Unless you know someone who can break through the circle for you, it's impossible to get in. The someone who did it for me was my mother's second husband, Norman Schiff. My mother had remarried about a year after her divorce from my father, and by 1970 my stepfather and I had been fast friends for nearly five years. An excellent man with a generous heart, he had consistently stood behind me and supported my vague, impractical ambitions. His early death in 1982 (at age fifty-five) remains one of the great sorrows of my life, but back then as I was finishing up my year of graduate work and preparing to leave school, his health was still reasonably good. He practiced law, mostly as a labor negotiator, and among his many clients at the time was the Esso Seaman's Union, for which he worked as legal counsel. That was how the idea got planted in my head. I asked him if he could swing me a job on one of the Esso tankers, and he said he would handle it. And without further ado, that was precisely what he did.

There was a lot of paperwork to take care of, trips to the union hall in Belleville, New Jersey, physical exams in Manhattan, and then an indefinite period of waiting until a slot opened up on one of the ships coming into the New York area. In the meantime, I took a temporary job with the United States Census Bureau, collecting data for the 1970 census in Harlem. The work consisted of climbing up and down staircases in dimly lit tenement buildings, knocking on apartment doors, and helping people fill out the government forms. Not everyone wanted to be helped, of course, and more than a few were suspicious of the white college boy prowling around their hallways, but enough people welcomed me in to make me feel that I wasn't completely wasting my time. I stayed with it for approximately a month, and then—sooner than I was expecting—the ship called.

I happened to be sitting in a dentist's chair at that moment, about to have a wisdom tooth pulled. Every morning since my name had gone on the list, I had checked in with my stepfather to let him know where I could be reached that day, and he was the one who tracked me down at the dentist's office. The timing couldn't have been more comical. The Novocain had already been injected into my gums, and the dentist had just picked up the pliers and was about to attack my rotten tooth when the receptionist walked in and announced that I was wanted on the phone. Extremely urgent. I climbed out of the chair with the bib still tied around my neck, and the next thing I knew, Norman was telling me that I had three hours to pack and get myself aboard the S.S. *Esso Florence* in Elizabeth, New Jersey. I stammered my apologies to the dentist and hightailed it out of there.

The tooth stayed in my mouth for another week. When it finally came out, I was in Baytown, Texas.

The *Esso Florence* was one of the oldest tankers in the fleet, a pip-squeak relic from a bygone age. Put a two-door Chevy next to a stretch limousine, and you'll have some idea of how it compared to the supertankers they build today. Already in service during World War II, my ship had logged untold thousands of watery miles by the time I set foot on it. There were enough beds on board to accommodate a hundred men, but only thirty-three of us were needed to take care of the work that had to be done. That meant that each person had his own room—an enormous benefit when you considered how much time we had to spend together. With other jobs you get to go home at night, but we were boxed in with each other twenty-four hours a day. Every time you looked up, the same faces were there. We worked together, lived together, and ate together, and without the chance for some genuine privacy, the routine would have been intolerable.

We shuttled between the Atlantic coast and the Gulf of Mexico, loading and unloading airplane fuel at various refineries along the way: Charleston, South Carolina; Tampa, Florida; Galveston, Texas. My initial responsibilities were mopping floors and making beds, first for the crew and then for the officers. The technical term for the position was "utilityman," but in plain language the job was a combination of janitor, garbage collector, and chambermaid. I can't say that I was thrilled to be scrubbing toilets and picking up dirty socks, but once I got the hang of it, the work turned out to be incredibly easy. In less than a week, I had polished my custodial skills to such a point that it took me only two or two and a half hours to finish my chores for the day. That left me with abundant quantities of free time, most of which I spent alone in my room. I read books, I wrote, I did everything I had done before—but more productively, somehow, with better powers of concentration now that there was so little to distract me. In many ways, it felt like an almost ideal existence, a perfect life.

Then, after a month or two of this blissful regimen, I was "bumped." The ship rarely traveled more than five days between ports, and nearly everywhere we docked some crew members would get off and others would get on. The jobs for the fresh arrivals were doled out according to seniority. It was a strict pecking order, and the longer you had worked for the company, the more say you had in what you were given. As low man on the totem pole, I had no say at all. If an old-timer wanted my job, he had only to ask for it, and it was his. After my long run of good luck, the boom finally fell on me somewhere in Texas. My replacement was a man named Elmer, a bovine Fundamentalist bachelor who happened to be the longest-serving, most famous utilityman of them all. What I had been able to do in two hours, Elmer now did in six. He was the slowest of the slow, a smug and untalkative mental lightweight who waddled about the ship in a world of his own, utterly ignored by the other crew members, and in all my experience I have never met a person who ate as much as he did. Elmer could pack away mountains of food—two, three, and four helpings at every meal—but what made it fascinating to watch him was not so much the scope of his appetite as the way he went about satisfying it: daintily, fastidiously, with a compulsive sense of decorum. The best part was the cleanup operation at the end. Once Elmer had eaten his fill, he would spread his napkin on the table before him and begin patting and smoothing the flimsy paper with his hands, slowly transforming it into a flat square. Then he would fold the napkin into precise longitudinal sections, methodically halving the area until it had been divided into eighths. In the end, the square would be turned into a long, rectilinear strip with all four edges exactly aligned. At that point, Elmer would carefully take hold of the edges, raise the napkin to his lips, and begin to rub. The action was all in the head: a slow back-and-forth swiveling that went on for twenty or thirty seconds. From start to finish, Elmer's hands never stirred. They would be fixed in the air as his large head turned left, right, and left again, and through it all his eyes never betrayed the slightest thought or emotion. The Cleaning of the Lips was a dogged, mechanical procedure, an act of ritual purification. Cleanliness is next to godliness, Elmer once told me. To see him with that napkin, you understood that he was doing God's work.

I was able to observe Elmer's eating habits at such close range because I had been bumped into the galley. The job of messman quadrupled my hours and made my life altogether more eventful. My responsibilities now included serving three meals a day to the crew (about twenty men), washing dishes by hand, cleaning the mess hall, and writing out the menus for the steward, who was generally too drunk to bother with them himself. My breaks were short—no more than an hour or two between meals—and yet in spite of having to work much harder than before, my income actually shrank. On the old job, there had been plenty of time for me to put in an extra hour or two in the evenings, scraping and painting in the boiler room, for example, or refurbishing rusty spots on deck, and those volunteer jobs had padded my paycheck quite nicely. Still, in spite of the disadvantages, I found working in the mess hall more of a challenge than mopping floors had been. It was a public job, so to speak, and in addition to all the hustling around that was now required of me, I had to stay on my toes as far as the men were concerned. That, finally, was my most important task: to learn how to handle the griping and rough-tempered complaints, to fend off insults, to give as good as I got.

Elmer aside, the crew was a fairly grimy, ill-mannered bunch. Most of the men lived in Texas and Louisiana, and apart from a handful of Chicanos, one or two blacks, and the odd foreigner who cropped up now and then, the dominant tone on board was white, redneck, and blue collar. A jocular atmosphere prevailed, replete with funny stories and dirty jokes and much talk about guns and cars, but there were deep, smoldering currents of racism in many of those men, and I made a point of choosing my friends carefully. To hear one of your coworkers defend South African apartheid as you sat with him over a cup of coffee ("they know how to treat niggers down there") doesn't bring much joy to the soul, and if I found myself hanging out mostly with the dark-skinned and Spanish-speaking men around me, there was a good reason for it. As a New York Jew with a college degree, I was an entirely alien specimen on that ship, a man from Mars. It would have been easy to make up stories about myself, but I had no interest in doing that. If someone asked me what my religion was or where I came from, I told him. If he didn't like it, I figured that was his problem. I wasn't going to hide who I was or pretend to be someone else just to avoid trouble. As it happened, I had only one awkward run-in the whole time I was there. One of the men started calling me Sammy whenever I walked by. He seemed to think it was funny, but as I failed to see any humor in the epithet, I told him to stop it. He did it again the next day, and once again I told him to stop it. When he did it again the day after that, I understood that polite words were not going to be enough. I grabbed hold of his shirt, slammed him against the wall, and very calmly told him that if he ever called me that again, I would kill him. It shocked me to hear myself talk like that. I was not someone who trafficked in violence, and I had never made that kind of threat to anyone, but for that one brief instant, a demon took possession of my soul. Luckily, my willingness to fight was enough to defuse the fight before it began. My tormentor threw up his hands in a gesture of peace. "It was just a joke," he said, "just a joke," and that was the end of it. As time went on, we actually became friends.

I loved being out on the water, surrounded by nothing but sky and light, the immensity of the vacant air. Seagulls accompanied us wherever we went, circling overhead as they waited for buckets of garbage to be dumped overboard. Hour after hour, they would hover patiently just above the ship, scarcely beating their wings until the scraps went flying, at which point they would plunge frantically into the foam, calling out to each other like drunks at a football game. Few pleasures can match the spectacle of that foam, of sitting at the stern of a large ship and staring into the white, churning tumult of the wake below. There is something hypnotic about it, and on still days the sense of well-being that washes through you can be overpowering. On the other hand, rough weather also holds its charms. As summer melted away and we headed into autumn, the inclemencies multiplied, bringing down some wild winds and pelting rains, and at those moments the ship felt no more safe or solid than a child's paper boat. Tankers have been known to crack in half, and all it takes is one wrong wave to do the job. The worst stretch, I remember, occurred when we were off Cape Hatteras in late September or early October, a twelve-or fifteen-hour period of flipping and flopping through a tropical storm. The captain stayed at the wheel all night, and even after the worst of it was over and the steward instructed me to carry the captain his breakfast the next morning, I was nearly blown overboard when I stepped onto the bridge with my tray. The rain might have stopped, but the wind speed was still at gale force.

For all that, working on the *Esso Florence* had little to do with high-seas adventure. The tanker was essentially a floating factory, and rather than introduce me to some exotic, swashbuckling life, it taught me to think of myself as an industrial laborer. I was one of millions now, an insect toiling beside countless other insects, and every task I performed was part of the great, grinding enterprise of American capitalism. Petroleum was the primary source of wealth, the raw material that fueled the profit machine and kept it running, and I was glad to be where I was, grateful to have landed in the belly of the beast. The refineries where we loaded and unloaded our cargo were enormous, hellish structures, labyrinthine networks of hissing pipes and towers of flame, and to walk through one of them at night was to feel that you were living in your own worst dream. Most of all, I will never forget the fish, the hundreds of dead, iridescent fish floating on the rank, oil-saturated water around the refinery docks. That was the standard welcoming committee, the sight that greeted us every time the tugboats pulled us into another port. The ugliness was so universal, so deeply connected to the business of making money and the power that money bestowed on the ones who made it—even to the point of disfiguring the landscape, of turning the natural world inside out—that I began to develop a grudging respect for it. Get to the bottom of things, I told myself, and this was how the world looked. Whatever you might think of it, this ugliness was the truth.

Whenever we docked somewhere, I made it my business to leave the ship and spend some time ashore. I had never been south of the Mason-Dixon line, and those brief jaunts onto solid ground took me to places that felt a lot less familiar or understandable than anything I'd met up with in Paris or Dublin. The South was a different country, a separate

American universe from the one I'd known in the North. Most of the time, I tagged along with one or two of my shipmates, going the rounds with them as they visited their customary haunts. If Baytown, Texas, stands out with particular clarity, that is because we spent more time there than anywhere else. I found it a sad, crumbling little place. Along the main drag, a row of once elegant movie theaters had been turned into Baptist churches, and instead of announcing the titles of the latest Hollywood films, the marquees now sported fiery quotations from the Bible. More often than not, we wound up in sailors' bars on the back streets of broken-down neighborhoods. All of them were essentially the same: squalid, low-life joints; dim drinking holes; dank corners of oblivion. Everything was always bare inside. Not a single picture on the walls, not one touch of publican warmth. At most there was a quarter-a-rack pool table, a jukebox stuffed with country-and-western songs, and a drink menu that consisted of just one drink: beer.

Once, when the ship was in a Houston dry dock for some minor repairs, I spent the afternoon in a skid row bar with a Danish oiler named Freddy, a wild man who laughed at the slightest provocation and spoke English with an accent so thick that I scarcely understood a word he said. Walking down the street in the blinding Texas sun, we crossed paths with a drunken couple. It was still early in the day, but this man and woman were already so soused, so entrenched in their inebriation, they must have been going at the booze since dawn. They wobbled along the sidewalk with their arms around each other, listing this way and that, their heads lolling, their knees buckling, and yet both with enough energy left to be engaged in a nasty, foul-mouthed quarrel. From the sound of their voices, I gathered they'd been at it for years—a pair of bickering stumblebums in search of their next drink, forever repeating the same lines to each other, forever shuffling through the same old song and dance. As it turned out, they wound up in the same bar where Freddy and I chose to while away the afternoon, and because I was not more than ten feet away from them, I was in a perfect position to observe the following little drama:

The man leaned forward and barked out at the woman across the table. "Darlene," he said, in a drawling, besotted voice, "get me another beer."

Darlene had been nodding off just then, and it took her a good long moment to open her eyes and bring the man into focus. Another long moment ticked by, and then she finally said, "What?"

"Get me a beer," the man repeated. "On the double."

Darlene was waking up now, and a lovely, fuck-you sassiness suddenly brightened her face. She was clearly in no mood to be pushed around. "Get it yourself, Charlie," she snapped back at him. "I ain't your slave, you know."

"Damn it, woman," Charlie said. "You're my wife, ain't you? What the hell did I marry you for? Get me the goddamn beer!"

Darlene let out a loud, histrionic sigh. You could tell she was up to something, but her intentions were still obscure. "Okay, darling," she said, putting on the voice of a meek, simpering wife, "I'll get it for you," and then stood up from the table and staggered over to the bar.

Charlie sat there with a grin on his face, gloating over his small, manly victory. He was the boss, all right, and no one was going to tell him different. If you wanted to know who wore the pants in that family, just talk to him.

A minute later, Darlene returned to the table with a fresh bottle of Bud. "Here's your beer, Charlie," she said, and then, with one quick flick of the wrist, proceeded to dump the contents of the bottle onto her husband's head. Bubbles foamed up in his hair and eyebrows; rivulets of amber liquid streamed down his face. Charlie made a lunge for her, but he was too drunk to get very close. Darlene threw her head back and burst out laughing. "How do you like your beer, Charlie?" she said. "How do you like your fucking beer?"

Of all the scenes I witnessed in those bars, nothing quite matched the bleak comedy of Charlie's baptism, but for overall oddness, a plunge into the deepest heart of the grotesque, I would have to single out Big Mary's Place in Tampa, Florida. This was a large, brightly lit emporium that catered to the whims of dockhands and sailors, and it had been in business for many years. Among its features were half a dozen pool tables, a long mahogany bar, inordinately high ceilings, and live entertainment in the form of quasi-naked go-go dancers. These girls were the cornerstone of the operation, the element that set Big Mary's Place apart from other establishments of its kind—and one look told you that they weren't hired for their beauty, nor for their ability to dance. The sole criterion was size. The bigger the better was how Big Mary put it, and the bigger you got, the more money you were paid. The effect was quite disturbing. It was a freak show of flesh, a cavalcade of bouncing white blubber, and with four girls dancing on the platform behind the bar at once, the act resembled a casting call for the lead role in *Moby-Dick*. Each girl was a continent unto herself, a mass of quivering lard decked out in a string bikini, and as one shift replaced another, the assault on the eyes was unrelenting. I have no memory of how I got there, but I distinctly recall that my companions that night were two of the gentler souls from the ship (Martinez, a family man from Texas, and Donnie, a seventeen-year-old boy from Baton Rouge) and that they were both just as flummoxed as I was. I can still see them sitting across from me with their mouths hanging open, doing everything they could not to laugh from embarrassment. At one point, Big Mary herself came over and sat down with us at our table. A splendid dirigible of a woman dressed in an orange pants suit and wearing a ring on every finger, she wanted to know if we were having a good time. When we assured her that we were, she waved to one of the girls at the bar. "Barbara," she yelled, belting out the word in a brassy, three-pack-a-day voice, "get your fat butt over here!" Barbara came, all smiles and good humor, laughing as Big Mary poked her in the stomach and pinched the ample rolls bulging from her hips. "She was a scrawny one at first," Mary explained, "but I've fattened her up pretty good. Ain't that so, Barbara?" she said, cackling like some mad scientist who's just pulled off a successful experiment, and Barbara couldn't have agreed with her more. As I listened to them talk, it suddenly occurred to me that I had it all wrong. I hadn't gone to sea. I'd run off and joined the circus.

Another friend was Jeffrey, the second cook (a.k.a. breakfast chef), from Bogalusa, Louisiana. We happened to have been born on the same day, and apart from the near-infant Donnie, we were the youngest members of the crew. It was the first time out for both of us, and since we worked together in the galley, we got to know each other reasonably well. Jeffrey was one of life's winners—a bright, handsome, fun-loving ladies' man with a taste for flashy clothes—and yet very practical and ambitious, a down-to-earth schemer who was quite consciously using his job on the ship to learn the ins and outs of cooking. He had no intention of making a career out of oil tankers, no desire to turn himself into an old salt. His dream was to become a chef in a high-class restaurant, maybe even to own that restaurant himself, and if nothing unexpected rose up to stop him, I don't doubt that that's exactly what he's doing today. We couldn't have been more unlike, Jeffrey and I, but we got along comfortably with each other. It was only natural that we should sometimes go ashore together when the ship was in port, but because Jeffrey was black, and because he had spent his whole life in the South, he knew that many of the places I went to with white crew members were off-limits to him. He made that perfectly clear to me the first time we planned an outing. "If you want me to go with you," he said, "you'll have to go where I can go." I tried to convince him that he could go any-where he pleased, but Jeffrey wasn't buying the argument. "Maybe up North," he said. "Down here it's different." I didn't force the issue. When I went out for beers with Jeffrey, we drank them in black bars instead of white bars. Except for the skin color of the clientele, the atmosphere was the same.

One night in Houston, Jeffrey talked me into going to a dance club with him. I never danced and never went to clubs, but the thought of spending a few hours in a place that wasn't a low-rent dive tempted me, and I decided to take my chances. The club turned out to be a splashy disco hall thronged with hundreds of young people, the hottest black nightspot in town. There was a live band onstage, psychedelic strobe lights bouncing off the walls, hard liquor available at the bar. Everything pulsed with sex and chaos and loud music. It was Saturday night fever, Texas style.

Jeffrey was dressed to the teeth, and within four minutes he struck up a conversation with one of the many stunning girls floating around the bar, and four minutes after that they were out on the dance floor together, lost in an ocean of bodies. I sat down at a table and sipped my drink, the only white person in the building. No one gave me any trou-ble, but I got some odd, penetrating looks from a number of people, and by the time I finished my bourbon, I understood that I should be shov-ing off. I phoned for a cab and then went outside to wait in the parking lot. When the driver showed up a few minutes later, he started cursing. "Goddammit," he said. "Goddammit to hell. If I'd known you were call-ing from here, I wouldn't have come." "Why not?" I asked. "Because this is the worst fucking place in Houston," he said. "They've had six murders here in the past month. Every damn weekend, somebody else gets shot."

In the end, the months I spent on that ship felt like years. Time passes in a different way when you're out on the water, and given that the bulk of what I experienced was utterly new to me, and given that I was con-stantly on my guard because of that, I managed to crowd an astonish-ing number of impressions and memories into a relatively small sliver of my life. Even now, I don't fully understand what I was hoping to prove by shipping out like that. To keep myself off balance, I suppose.

Or, very simply, just to see if I could do it, to see if I could hold my own in a world I didn't belong to. In that respect, I don't think I failed. I can't say what I accomplished during those months, but at the same time I'm certain I didn't fail.

I received my discharge papers in Charleston. The company provided airfare home, but you could pocket the money if you wanted to and make your own travel arrangements. I chose to keep the money. The trip by milk train took twenty-four hours, and I rode back with a fellow crew member from New York, Juan Castillo. Juan was in his late forties or early fifties, a squat, lumpy man with a big head and a face that looked like something pieced together with the skins and pulps of nineteen mashed potatoes. He had just walked off an oil tanker for the last time, and in appreciation of his twenty-five years of service to the company, Esso had given him a gold watch. I don't know how many times Juan pulled that watch out of his pocket and looked at it during the long ride home, but every time he did, he would shake his head for a few seconds and then burst out laughing. At one point, the ticket collector stopped to talk to us during one of his strolls down the aisle of the car. He looked very natty in his uniform, I remember, a black Southern gentleman of the old school. In a haughty, somewhat condescending manner, he opened the conversation by asking: "You boys going up North to work in the steel mills?"

We must have been a curious pair, Juan and I. I recall that I was wearing a beat-up leather jacket at the time, but other than that I can't see myself, have no sense of what I looked like or what other people saw when they looked at me. The ticket collector's question is the only clue I have. Juan had taken pictures of his shipmates to put in the family album at home, and I remember standing on the deck and looking into the camera for him as he clicked the shutter. He promised to send me a copy of the photo, but he never did.

I toyed with the idea of going out for another run on an Esso tanker, but in the end I decided against it. My salary was still being sent to me through the mail (for every two days I'd been on the ship, I received one day's pay on land), and my bank account was beginning to look fairly robust. For the past few months, I had been slowly coming to the conclusion that my next step should be to leave the country and live abroad for a while. I was willing to ship out again if necessary, but I wondered if I hadn't built up a large enough stake already. The three or four thousand dollars I'd earned from the tanker struck me as a sufficient sum to get started with, and so rather than continue in the merchant marine, I abruptly shifted course and began plotting a move to Paris.

France was a logical choice, but I don't think I went there for logical reasons. That I spoke French, that I had been translating French poetry, that I knew and cared about a number of people who lived in France— surely those things entered into my decision, but they were not deter- mining factors. What made me want to go, I think, was the memory of what had happened to me in Paris three years earlier. I still hadn't got- ten it out of my system, and because that visit had been cut short, because I had left on the assumption that I would soon be returning, I had walked around with a feeling of unfinished business, of not having had my fill. The only thing I wanted just then was to hunker down and write. By recapturing the inwardness and freedom of that earlier time, I felt that I would be putting myself in the best possible position to do that. I had no intention of becoming an expatriate. Giving up America was not part of the plan, and at no time did I think I wouldn't return. I just needed a little breathing room, a chance to figure out, once and for all, if I was truly the person I thought I was.

What comes back to me most vividly from my last weeks in New York is the farewell conversation I had with Joe Reilly, a homeless man who used to hang around the lobby of my apartment building on West 107th Street. The building was a run-down, nine-story affair, and like most places on the Upper West Side, it housed a motley collection of people. With no effort at all, I can summon forth a fair number of them, even after a quarter of a century. The Puerto Rican mailman, for example, and the Chinese waiter, and the fat blonde opera singer with the Lhasa apso. Not to mention the black homosexual fashion designer with his black fur coat and the quarreling clarinetists whose vicious spats would seep through the walls of my apartment and poison my nights. On the ground floor of this gray brick building, one of the apartments had been divided down the middle, and each half was occupied by a man con- fined to a wheelchair. One of them worked at the news kiosk on the cor- ner of Broadway and 110th Street; the other was a retired rabbi. The rabbi was a particularly charming fellow, with a pointy artist's goatee and an ever-present black beret, which he wore at a rakish, debonair angle. On most days, he would wheel himself out of his apartment and spend some time in the lobby, chatting with Arthur, the superintendent, or with various tenants getting in and out of the elevator. Once, as I entered the building, I caught sight of him through the glass door in his usual spot, talking to a bum in a long, dark overcoat. It struck me as an odd conjunction, but from the way the bum stood there and from the tilt of the rabbi's head, it was clear that they knew each other well. The bum was an authentic down-and-outer, a scab-faced wino with filthy clothes and cuts dotting his half-bald scalp, a scrofulous wreck of a man who appeared to have just crawled out of a storm drain. Then, as I pushed open the door and stepped into the lobby, I heard him speak. Accompanied by wild, theatrical gestures—a sweep of the left arm, a finger darting from his right hand and pointing to the sky—a sentence came booming out of him, a string of words so unlikely and unexpected that at first I didn't believe my ears. "It was no mere fly-by-night acquaintance!" he said, rolling each syllable of that florid, literary phrase off his tongue with such relish, such blowhard bravura, such magnificent pomposity, that he sounded like some tragic ham delivering a line from a Victorian melodrama. It was pure W. C. Fields—but several octaves lower, with the voice more firmly in control of the effects it was striving to create. W. C. Fields mixed with Ralph Richardson, perhaps, with a touch of barroom bombast thrown in for good measure. However you wanted to define it, I had never heard a voice do what that voice did.

When I walked over to say hello to the rabbi, he introduced me to his friend, and that was how I learned the name of that singular gentleman, that mightiest of fallen characters, the one and only Joe Reilly.

According to the rabbi, who filled me in on the story later, Joe had started out in life as the privileged son of a wealthy New York family, and in his prime he had owned an art gallery on Madison Avenue. That was when the rabbi had met him—back in the old days, before Joe's disintegration and collapse. The rabbi had already left the pulpit by then and was running a music publishing company. Joe's male lover was a composer, and as the rabbi happened to publish that man's work, in the natural course of things he and Joe crossed paths. Then, very suddenly, the lover died. Joe had always had a drinking problem, the rabbi said, but now he hit the bottle in earnest, and his life began to fall apart. He lost his gallery; his family turned its back on him; his friends walked away. Little by little, he sank into the gutter, the last hole at the bottom of the world, and in the rabbi's opinion he would never climb out again. As far as he was concerned, Joe was a hopeless case.

Whenever Joe came around after that, I would dig into my pocket and hand him a few coins. What moved me about these encounters was that he never let his mask drop. Blustering forth his thanks in the highly embroidered, Dickensian language that came so effortlessly to him, he would assure me that I would be paid back promptly, just as soon as circumstances allowed. "I am most grateful to you for this bounty, young man," he would say, "most grateful indeed. It's just a loan, of course, so you needn't fret about being reimbursed. As you might or might not know, I've suffered some small setbacks lately, and this generosity of yours will go a long way towards helping me back to my feet." The sums in question were never more than a pittance—forty cents here, twenty-five cents there, whatever I happened to be carrying around with me—but Joe never flagged in his enthusiasm, never once let on that he realized what an abject figure he was. There he stood, dressed in a circus clown's rags, his unwashed body emitting the foulest of stinks, and still he persisted in keeping up his pose as a man of the world, a dandy temporarily down on his luck. The pride and self-deception that went into this act were both comical and heartbreaking, and every time I went through the ritual of giving him another handout, I had trouble keeping my balance. I never knew whether to laugh or cry, whether to admire him or shower him with pity. "Let me see, young man," he would continue, studying the coins I had just put in his palm. "I have, let's see, I have here in my hand, hmmm, fifty-five cents. Add that to the eighty cents you gave me the last time, and then add that, hmmm, add that to the forty cents you gave me the time before that, and it turns out that I owe you a grand total of, hmmm, let's see, a grand total of . . . one dollar and fifteen cents." Such was Joe's arithmetic. He just plucked figures out of thin air and hoped they sounded good. "No problem, Joe," I would say. "A dollar and fifteen cents. You'll give it to me the next time."

When I came back to New York from the Esso ship, he seemed to be floundering, to have lost some ground. He looked more bruised to me, and the old panache had given way to a new heaviness of spirit, a whining, tearful sort of despair. One afternoon, he broke down in front of me as he recounted how he had been beaten up in some alleyway the night before. "They stole my books," he said. "Can you imagine that? The animals stole my books!" Another time, in the middle of a snowstorm, as I left my ninth-floor apartment and walked to the elevator down the hall, I found him sitting alone on the staircase, his head buried in his hands.

"Joe," I said, "are you all right?"

He lifted his head. His eyes were infused with sorrow, misery, and defeat. "No, young man," he said. "I'm not all right, not the least bit all right."

"Is there anything I can do for you?" I asked. "You look terrible, just terrible."

"Yes," he said, "now that you mention it, there is one thing you can do for me," and at that point he suddenly reached out and took hold of my hand. Then, looking me straight in the eye, he gathered up his strength and said, in a voice trembling with emotion, "You can take me back into your apartment, lie down on the bed, and let me make love to you."

The bluntness of his request took me completely by surprise. I had been thinking more along the lines of a cup of coffee or a bowl of soup. "I can't do that," I said. "I like women, Joe, not men. Sorry, but I don't do that kind of thing."

What he said next lingers in my mind as one of the best and most pungent statements I have ever heard. Without wasting a second, and without the slightest trace of disappointment or regret, he dismissed my answer with a shrug of the shoulders and said, in a buoyant, ringing tone of voice, "Well, you asked me—and I told you."

I left for Paris some time in the middle of February 1971. After that encounter on the staircase, I didn't see Joe again for several weeks. Then, just days before my departure, I bumped into him on Broadway. He was looking much better, and the hangdog look had disappeared from his face. When I told him I was about to move to Paris, he was off and running again, as effusive and full of himself as ever. "It's odd that you should mention Paris," he said. "Indeed, it's a most timely coincidence. Not two or three days ago, I happened to be walking down Fifth Avenue, and who should I bump into but my old friend Antoine, director of the Cunard Lines. 'Joe,' he said to me, 'Joe, you're not looking too well,' and I said, 'No, Antoine, it's true, I haven't been at my best lately,' and Antoine said that he wanted to do something for me, lend a helping hand, so to speak, and put me back on track. What he proposed, right there on Fifth Avenue the other day, was to sail me over to Paris on one of his ships and put me up at the Hôtel George V. All expenses paid, of course, with a new wardrobe thrown into the bargain. He said I could stay there as long as I liked. Two weeks, two months, even two years if I wanted. If I decide to go, which I think I will, I'll be leaving before the end of the month. Which means, young man, that we'll be in

Paris at the same time. A pleasant prospect, no? Expect to see me there. We'll have tea, dinner. Just leave a message for me at the hotel. On the Champs-Elysées. That's where we'll meet next, my friend. In Paris, on the Champs-Elysées." And then, bidding me farewell, he shook my hand and wished me a safe and happy voyage.

I never saw Joe Reilly again. Even before we said good-bye that day, I knew that I was talking to him for the last time, and when he finally disappeared into the crowd a few minutes later, it was as if he had already turned into a ghost. All during the years I lived in Paris, I thought of him every time I set foot on the Champs-Elysées. Even now, whenever I go back there, I still do.

My money didn't last as long as I thought it would. I found an apartment within a week of my arrival, and once I had shelled out for the agency commission, the security deposit, the gas and electric service, the first month's rent, the last month's rent, and the state-mandated insurance policy, I didn't have much left. Right from the start, therefore, I had to scramble to keep my head above water. In the three and a half years I lived in France, I had any number of jobs, bounced from one part-time gig to another, freelanced until I was blue in the face. When I didn't have work, I was looking for work. When I had work, I was thinking about how to find more. Even at the best of times, I rarely earned enough to feel secure, and yet in spite of one or two close calls, I managed to avoid total ruin. It was, as they say, a hand-to-mouth existence. Through it all, I wrote steadily, and if much of what I wrote was discarded (mostly prose), a fair chunk of it (mostly poems and translations) was not. For better or worse, by the time I returned to New York in July 1974, the idea of not writing was inconceivable to me.

Most of the work I landed came through friends or the friends of friends or the friends of friends of friends. Living in a foreign country restricts your opportunities, and unless you know some people who are willing to help you, it is next to impossible to get started. Not only will doors not open when you knock on them, but you won't even know where to look for those doors in the first place. I was lucky enough to have some allies, and at one time or another they all moved small mountains on my behalf. Jacques Dupin, for example, a poet whose work I had been translating for several years, turned out to be director of publications at the Galerie Maeght, one of the leading art galleries in Europe. Among the painters and sculptors shown there were Miró,

Giacometti, Chagall, and Calder, to mention just a few. Through Jacques's intervention, I was hired to translate several art books and catalogues, and by my second year in Paris, when my funds were perilously close to bottoming out, he saved the situation by giving me a room to live in—free of charge. These acts of kindness were essential, and I can't imagine how I would have survived without them.

At one point, I was steered to the Paris bureau of *The New York Times*. I can't remember who was responsible for the connection, but an editor named Josette Lazar began throwing translations my way whenever she could: articles for the Sunday *Book Review*, op-ed pieces by Sartre and Foucault, this and that. One summer, when my money was at low ebb again, she finagled a position for me as the nighttime switchboard operator at the *Times* office. The phone didn't ring very often, and mostly I just sat at a desk, working on poems or reading books. One night, however, there was a frantic call from a reporter stationed somewhere in Europe. "Sinyavsky's defected," she said. "What should I do?" I had no idea what she should do, but since none of the editors was around at that hour, I figured I had to tell her something. "Follow the story," I said. "Go where you have to go, do what you have to do, but stick with the story, come hell or high water." She thanked me profusely for the advice and then hung up.

Some jobs started out as one thing and ended up as another, like a botched stew you can't stop tinkering with. Just stir in some additional ingredients and see if it doesn't taste better. A good example would be my little adventure among the North Vietnamese in Paris, which began with an innocent phone call from Mary McCarthy to my friend André du Bouchet. She asked him if he knew of anyone who could translate poetry from French into English, and when he gave her my name, she called and invited me to her apartment to discuss the project. It was early 1973, and the war in Vietnam was still dragging on. Mary McCarthy had been writing about the war for several years, and I had read most of her articles, which I found to be among the best pieces of journalism published at the time. In the course of her work, she had come in contact with many Vietnamese from both the northern and southern halves of the country. One of them, a professor of literature, was putting together an anthology of Vietnamese poetry, and she had offered to help arrange for an English-language version to be published in America. The poems had already been translated into French, and the idea was to translate those translations into English. That was how my name had come up, and that was why she wanted to talk to me.

In her private life, Mary McCarthy was Mrs. West. Her husband was a well-to-do American businessman, and their Paris apartment was a large, richly appointed place filled with art objects, antiques, and fine furniture. Lunch was served to us by a maid in a black and white uniform. A china bell sat on the table next to my hostess's right hand, and every time she picked it up and gave it a little shake, the maid would return to the dining room to receive further instructions. There was an impressive, *grande dame* quality to the way Mary McCarthy handled these domestic protocols, but the truth was that she turned out to be everything I had hoped she would be: sharp-witted, friendly, unpretentious. We talked about many things that afternoon, and by the time I left her apartment several hours later, I was loaded down with six or seven books of Vietnamese poetry. The first step was for me to familiarize myself with their contents. After that, the professor and I would meet and get down to work on the anthology.

I read the books and enjoyed them, particularly *The Book of Kieu*, the national epic poem. The details escape me now, but I remember becoming interested in some of the formal problems presented by traditional Vietnamese verse structures, which have no equivalents in Western poetry. I was happy to have been offered the job. Not only was I going to be paid well, but it looked as if I might learn something into the bargain. A week or so after our lunch, however, Mary McCarthy called to tell me that there had been an emergency, and her professor friend had gone back to Hanoi. She wasn't sure when he would be returning to Paris, but for the time being at least, the project had been put on hold.

Such were the breaks. I pushed the books aside and hoped the job wasn't dead, even though I knew it was. Several days went by, and then, out of the blue, I received a telephone call from a Vietnamese woman living in Paris. "Professor So-and-so gave us your name," she said. "He told us you can translate into English. Is that true?" "Yes," I said, "it's true." "Good," she said. "We have a job for you."

The job turned out to be a translation of the new North Vietnamese constitution. I had no qualms about doing the work, but I found it strange that they should have come to me. You would think that a document of that sort would be translated by someone in the government—directly from Vietnamese into English, and not from French, and if from French, not by an enemy American living in Paris. I didn't ask any questions, however. I still had my fingers crossed about the anthology and didn't want to ruin my chances, so I accepted the job. The following evening, the woman came to my apartment to drop off the manuscript. She was a biologist in her mid-thirties—thin, unadorned, exceptionally reserved in her manner. She didn't say anything about a fee for the work, and from her silence I gathered that there wasn't going to be one. Given the tangled political nuances of the situation (the war between our two countries, my feelings about that war, and so on), I was hardly disposed to press her about money. Instead, I began asking her questions about the Vietnamese poems I had been reading. At one point, I got her to sit down at my desk with me and draw a diagram that explained the traditional verse forms that had piqued my curiosity. Her sketch proved to be very helpful, but when I asked her if I could keep it for future reference, she shook her head, crumpled up the paper, and put it in her pocket. I was so startled, I didn't say a word. In that one small gesture, an entire world had been revealed to me, an underground universe of fear and betrayal in which even a scrap of paper was suspect. Trust no one; cover your tracks; destroy the evidence. It wasn't that she was afraid of what I might do with the diagram. She was simply acting out of habit, and I couldn't help feeling sorry for her, sorry for both of us. It meant that the war was everywhere, that the war had tainted everything.

The constitution was eight or ten pages long, and apart from some standard Marxist-Leninist phrases ("running dogs of imperialism," "bourgeois lackeys"), it was pretty dry stuff. I did the translation the next day, and when I called my biologist friend to tell her that the work was finished, she sounded inordinately pleased and grateful. It was only then that she told me about my payment: an invitation to dinner. "By way of thanks," as she put it. The restaurant happened to be in the Fifth Arrondissement, not far from where I lived, and I had eaten there several times before. It was the simplest and cheapest Vietnamese restaurant in Paris, but also the best. The only ornament in the place was a black-and-white photograph of Ho Chi Minh hanging on the wall.

Other jobs were entirely straightforward, the essence of simplicity: tutoring a high school boy in English, serving as simultaneous translator at a small international conference of Jewish scholars (dinner included), translating material by and about Giacometti for the art critic David Sylvester. Few of these jobs paid well, but they all brought in something, and if I didn't always have great stocks of food in my refrigerator, I was rarely without a pack of cigarettes in my pocket. Still, I couldn't have sustained myself on odds and ends alone. They helped to keep me going, but add them all together, and they wouldn't have been enough to live on for more than a few weeks, a few months at most. I needed another source of income to pay the bills, and as luck would have it, I found one. To put it more accurately, it found me. For the first two years I spent in Paris, it was the difference between eating and not eating.

The story goes back to 1967. During my earlier stay as a student, an American friend had introduced me to a woman I will call Madame X. Her husband, Monsieur X, was a well-known film producer of the old style (epics, extravaganzas, a maker of deals), and it was through her that I started working for him. The first opportunity arose just a few months after I arrived. There was no telephone in the apartment I had rented, which was still the case with many Paris apartments in 1971, and there were only two ways of contacting me: by *pneumatique*, a rapid intracity telegram sent through the post office, or by coming to the apartment and knocking on the door. One morning, not long after I had woken up, Madame X knocked on the door. "How would you like to earn a hundred dollars today?" she said. The job seemed simple enough: read a movie script, then write out a six- or seven-page summary. The only constraint was time. A potential backer of the film was waiting on a yacht somewhere in the Mediterranean, and the outline had to be delivered to him within forty-eight hours.

Madame X was a flamboyant, stormy character, the first larger-than-life woman I had ever met. Mexican by birth, married since the age of eighteen or nineteen, the mother of a boy just a few years younger than I was, she lived her own independent life, drifting in and out of her husband's orbit in ways I was still too unsophisticated to understand. Artistic by temperament, she dabbled by turns at painting and writing, showing talent in both fields but with too little discipline or concentration to take those talents very far. Her true gift was encouraging others, and she surrounded herself with artists and would-be artists of all ages, hobnobbing with the known and the unknown as both a colleague and a patroness. Wherever she went, she was the center of attention, the gorgeous, soulful woman with the long black hair and the hooded cloaks and the clattering Mexican jewelry—moody, generous, loyal, her head full of dreams. Somehow or other, I had made it onto her list, and because I was young and just starting out, she counted me among those friends who needed looking after, the poor and struggling ones who required an occasional helping hand.

There were others too, of course, and a couple of them were invited along with me that morning to earn the same round figure that I had been promised. A hundred dollars sounds like pocket change today, but back then it represented more than half a month's rent, and I was in no position to turn down a sum of that magnitude. The work was to be done at the X's' apartment, an immense, palatial establishment in the Sixteenth Arrondissement with untold numbers of high-ceilinged rooms. The starting time was set for eleven o'clock, and I showed up with half an hour to spare.

I had met each of my coworkers before. One of them was an American in his mid-twenties, a fey unemployed pianist who walked around in women's high heels and had recently spent time in a hospital with a collapsed lung. The other was a Frenchman with decades of film experience, mostly as a second-unit director. Among his credits were the chariot scenes in *Ben-Hur* and the desert scenes in *Lawrence of Arabia*, but since those days of wealth and success, he had fallen on hard times: nervous breakdowns, periods of confinement in mental wards, no work. He and the pianist were major reclamation projects for Madame X, and throwing me together with them was just one example of how she operated. No matter how good her intentions were, they were invariably undermined by complex, impractical schemes, a desire to kill too many birds with a single stone. Rescuing one person is hard enough, but to think you can save the whole world at once is to ask for disappointment.

So there we were, the most mismatched trio ever assembled, gathered around the gigantic table in the dining room of the X's' gigantic apartment. The script in question was also gigantic. A work of nearly three hundred pages (three times the length of the normal script), it looked like the telephone book of a large city. Because the Frenchman was the only one with any professional knowledge of the movies, the pianist and I deferred to him and allowed him to take charge of the discussion. The first thing he did was pull out a sheet of blank paper and begin jotting down the names of actors. Frank Sinatra, Dean Martin, Sammy Davis, Jr., followed by six or seven others. When he was finished, he slapped his hands on the table with great satisfaction. "You see this piece of paper?" he asked. The pianist and I nodded our heads. "Believe it or not, this little piece of paper is worth ten million dollars." He patted the list once or twice and then pushed it aside. "Ten, maybe twelve million dollars." He spoke with the utmost conviction, betraying not the slightest hint of humor or irony. After a brief pause, he opened the manuscript to the first page. "Well," he said, "are we ready to begin?"

Almost immediately, he became excited. On the second or third line of the first page, he noticed that the name of one of the characters began with the letter Z. "Aha!" he said. "Z. This is very important. Pay close attention, my friends. This is going to be a political film. Mark my words."

Z was the title of a film by Costa-Gavras, a popular hit two years earlier. That film had most assuredly been about politics, but the screenplay we had been asked to summarize was not. It was an action thriller about smuggling. Largely set in the Sahara Desert, it featured trucks, motorcycles, several gangs of warring bad guys, and a number of spectacular explosions. The only thing that set it apart from a thousand other movies was its length.

We had been at work for approximately a minute and a half, and already the pianist had lost interest. He stared down at the table and snickered to himself as the Frenchman rambled on, lurching from one bit of nonsense to another. Suddenly, without any transition or preamble, the poor man started talking about David Lean, recalling several philosophical discussions he'd had with the director fifteen years earlier. Then, just as abruptly, he broke off from his reminiscences, stood up from the table, and walked around the room, straightening the pictures on the walls. When he was finished with that task, he announced that he was going to the kitchen to look for a cup of coffee. The pianist shrugged. "I think I'll go play the piano," he said, and just like that, he was gone as well.

As I waited for them to return, I started reading the script. I couldn't think of anything else to do, and by the time it dawned on me that neither one of them would be coming back, I had worked my way through most of it. Eventually, one of Monsieur X's associates drifted into the room. He was a youngish, good-natured American who also happened to be Madame X's special friend (the complexities of the household were fathomless), and he instructed me to finish the job on my own, guaranteeing that if I managed to produce an acceptable piece of work by seven o'clock, all three of the hundred-dollar payments would be mine. I told him I would do my best. Before I hustled out of there and went home to my typewriter, he gave me an excellent bit of advice. "Just remember," he said. "This is the movies, not Shakespeare. Make it as vulgar as you can."

I wound up writing the synopsis in the extravagant, over-heated language of Hollywood coming attractions. If they wanted vulgar, I would give them vulgar. I had sat through enough movie trailers to know what they sounded like, and by dredging up every hackneyed phrase I could think of, by piling one excess on top of another, I boiled the story down to seven pages of frantic, nonstop action, a bloodbath wrought in pulsing, Technicolor prose. I finished typing at six-thirty. An hour later, a chauffeur-driven car arrived downstairs to take me and my girlfriend to the restaurant where Madame and Monsieur X had invited us for dinner. The moment we got there, I was supposed to deliver the pages to him in person.

Monsieur X was a small, enigmatic man in his mid to late fifties. Of Russian-Jewish origin, he spoke several languages with equal fluency, often shifting from French to English to Spanish in the course of a single conversation, but always with the same cumbersome accent, as if in the end he didn't feel at home in any of them. He had been producing movies for over thirty years, and in a career of countless ups and downs, he had backed good films and bad films, big films and small films, art films and trash films. Some had made piles of money for him, others had put him miserably in debt. I had crossed paths with him only a few times before that night, but he had always struck me as a lugubrious person, a man who played things close to the vest—shrewd, hidden, unknowable. Even as he talked to you, you sensed that he was thinking about something else, working out some mysterious calculations that might or might not have had anything to do with what he was saying. It's not that they didn't, but at the same time it would have been wrong to assume that they did.

That night in the restaurant, he was noticeably edgy when I arrived. A potentially lucrative deal hinged on the work of one of his wife's arty friends, and he was anything but optimistic. I had barely settled into my seat when he asked to see the pages I had written. As the rest of us made small talk around the table, Monsieur X sat hunched in silence, reading through my florid, slam-bang paragraphs. Little by little, a smile began to form on his lips. He started nodding to himself as he turned the pages, and once or twice he was even heard to mutter the word "good" under his breath. He didn't look up, however. Not until he'd come to the last sentence did he finally raise his head and give me the verdict.

"Excellent," he said. "This is just what I wanted." The relief in his voice was almost palpable.

Madame X said something about how she'd told him so, and he confessed that he'd had his doubts. "I thought it would be too literary," he said. "But this is good. This is just right."

He became very effusive after that. We were in a large, gaudy restaurant in Montmartre, and he immediately started snapping his fingers for the flower girl. She came scurrying over to our table, and Monsieur X bought a dozen roses, which he handed to my girlfriend as an impromptu gift. Then he reached into his breast pocket, pulled out his checkbook, and wrote me a check for three hundred dollars. It was the first check I had ever seen from a Swiss bank.

I was glad to have delivered the goods under pressure, glad to have earned my three hundred bucks, glad to have been roped into the absurd events of that day, but once we left the restaurant and I returned to my apartment on the rue Jacques Mawas, I assumed that the story was over. It never once crossed my mind that Monsieur X might have further plans for me. One afternoon the following week, however, as I sat at my table working on a poem, I was interrupted by a loud knock on the door. It was one of Monsieur X's gofers, an elderly gentleman I'd seen lurking about the house on my visits there but had never had the pleasure of talking to. He wasted no time in getting to the point. Are you Paul Auster? he asked. When I told him I was, he informed me that Monsieur X wanted to see me. When? I asked. Right now, he said. There's a taxi waiting downstairs.

It was a little like being arrested by the secret police. I suppose I could have refused the invitation, but the cloak-and-dagger atmosphere made me curious, and I decided to go along to see what was up. In the cab, I asked my chaperon why I had been summoned like this, but the old man merely shrugged. Monsieur X had told him to bring me back to the house, and that was what he was doing. His job was to follow orders, not ask questions. I therefore remained in the dark, and as I mulled over the question myself, the only answer I could think of was that Monsieur X was no longer satisfied with the work I had done for him. By the time I walked into his apartment, I was fully expecting him to ask me for the money back.

He was dressed in a paisley smoking jacket with satin lapels, and as he entered the room where I'd been told to wait for him, I noticed that he was rubbing his hands together. I had no idea what that gesture meant.

"Last week," he said, "you do good works for me. Now I want to make package deal."

That explained the hands. It was the gesture of a man ready to do business, and all of a sudden, on the strength of that dashed-off, tongue-in-cheek manuscript I'd concocted for him the other day, it looked as though I was about to be in business with Monsieur X. He had at least two jobs for me right away, and if all went well with those, the implication was that others would follow. I needed the money and accepted, but not without a certain wariness. I was stepping into a realm I didn't understand, and unless I kept my wits about me, I realized that strange things could be in store for me. I don't know how or why I knew that, but I did. When Monsieur X started talking about giving me a role in one of his upcoming movies, a swashbuckling adventure story for which I would need fencing and riding lessons, I held my ground. "We'll see," I said. "The fact is, I'm not much interested in acting."

Apparently, the man on the yacht had liked my synopsis just as much as Monsieur X had. Now he wanted to take things to the next level and was commissioning a translation of the screenplay from French into English. That was the first job. The second job was somewhat less cut-and-dried. Madame X was at work on a play, Monsieur X told me, and he had agreed to finance a production at the Round House Theatre in London next season. The piece was about Quetzalcoatl, the mythical plumed serpent, and since much of it was written in verse, and since much of that verse was written in Spanish, he wanted me to turn it into English and make sure that the drama was in playable shape. Fine, I said, and that was how we left it. I did both jobs, everyone was satisfied, and two or three months later, Madame X's play was performed in London. It was a vanity production, of course, but the reviews were good, and all in all the play was quite well received. A British publisher happened to attend one of the performances, and he was so impressed by what he'd seen that he proposed to Madame X that she turn the play into a prose narrative, which he would then publish as a book.

That was where things started getting sticky between me and Monsieur X. Madame X didn't have it in her to write the book on her own, and he believed that I was the one person on earth capable of helping her. I might have accepted the job under different circumstances, but since he also wanted me to go to Mexico to do the work, I told him I wasn't interested. Why the book had to be written in Mexico was never made clear to me. Research, local color, something along those lines, I'm not sure. I was fond of Madame X, but being thrown together with her for an unspecified length of time struck me as less than a good idea. I didn't even have to think about Monsieur X's offer. I turned him down on the spot, figuring that would close the matter once and for all. Events proved me wrong. True indifference has power, I learned, and my refusal to take the job irritated Monsieur X and got under his skin. He wasn't in the habit of having people say no to him, and he became hell-bent on changing my mind. Over the next several months, he launched an all-out campaign to wear down my resistance, besieging me with letters, telegrams, and promises of ever greater sums of money. In the end, I reluctantly gave in. As with every other bad decision I've made in my life, I acted against my better judgment, allowing secondary considerations to interfere with the clarity of my instincts. In this case, what tipped the balance was money. I was having a hard time of it just then, desperately falling behind in my struggle to remain solvent, and Monsieur X's offer had grown so large, would eliminate so many of my problems at once, that I talked myself into accepting the wisdom of compromise. I thought I was being clever. Once I had climbed down from my high horse, I laid out my conditions in the toughest terms I could think of. I would go to Mexico for exactly one month, I told him— no more, no less—and I wanted full payment in cash before I left Paris. It was the first time I had ever negotiated for anything, but I was determined to protect myself, and I refused to yield on any of these points. Monsieur X was less than thrilled with my intractability, but he understood that I'd gone as far as I would go and gave in to my demands. The same day I left for Mexico, I deposited twenty-five one-hundred-dollar bills in my bank account. Whatever happened in the next month, at least I wouldn't be broke when I returned.

I was expecting things to go wrong, but not quite to the degree that they did. Without rehashing the whole complicated business (the man who threatened to kill me, the schizophrenic girl who thought I was a Hindu god, the drunken, suicidal misery that permeated every household I entered), the thirty days I spent in Mexico were among the grimmest, most unsettling days of my life. Madame X had already been there for a couple of weeks when I arrived, and I quickly learned that she was in no shape to work on the book. Her boyfriend had just left her, and this love drama had plunged her into the throes of an acute despair. It's not that I blamed her for her feelings, but she was so distraught, so distracted by her suffering, that the book was the last thing she wanted to think about. What was I supposed to do? I tried to get her started, tried to make her sit down with me and discuss the project, but she simply wasn't interested. Every time we took a stab at it, the conversation would quickly veer off onto other subjects. Again and again, she broke down and cried. Again and again, we got nowhere. After several of these attempts, I understood that the only reason she was bothering to make an effort was because of me. She knew that I was being paid to help her, and she didn't want to let me down, didn't want to admit that I had come all this way for nothing.

That was the essential flaw in the arrangement. To assume that a book can be written by a person who is not a writer is already a murky proposition, but granting that such a thing is possible, and granting that the person who wants to write the book has someone else to help with the writing of it, perhaps the two of them, with much hard work and dedication, can arrive at an acceptable result. On the other hand, if the person who is not a writer does not want to write a book, of what use is the someone else? Such was the quandary I found myself in. I was willing to help Madame X write her book, but I couldn't help her unless she wanted to write it, and if she didn't want to, there was nothing I could do but sit around and wait until she did.

So there I sat, biding my time in the little village of Tepotzolán, hoping that Madame X would wake up one morning and discover that she had a new outlook on life. I was staying with Madame X's brother (whose unhappy marriage to an American woman was on its last legs), and I filled my days with aimless walks around the dusty town, stepping over mangy dogs, batting flies out of my face, and accepting invitations to drink beers with the local drunks. My room was in a stucco outbuilding on the brother's property, and I slept under muslin netting to guard against the tarantulas and mosquitoes. The crazy girl kept showing up with one of her friends, a Central American Hare Krishna with a shaved head and orange robes, and boredom ate away at me like some tropical disease. I wrote one or two short poems, but otherwise I languished, unable to think, bogged down by a persistent, nameless anxiety. Even the news from the outside world was bad. An earthquake killed thousands of people in Nicaragua, and my favorite baseball player, Roberto Clemente, the most elegant and electrifying performer of his generation, went down in a small plane that was trying to deliver emergency relief to the victims. If anything pleasant stands out from the miasma and stupor of that month, it would be the hours I spent in Cuernavaca, the radiant little city that Malcolm Lowry wrote about in *Under the Volcano*. There, quite by chance, I was introduced to a man who was described to me as the last living descendant of Montezuma. A tall, stately gent of around sixty, he had impeccable manners and wore a silk ascot around his neck.

When I finally returned to Paris, Monsieur X arranged to meet me in the lobby of a hotel on the Champs-Elysées. Not the Hôtel George V, but another one directly across the street. I can't remember why he chose that place, but I think it had something to do with an appointment he'd scheduled there before mine, strictly a matter of convenience. In any case, we didn't talk in the hotel. The instant I showed up, he led me outside again and pointed to his car, which was waiting for us just in front of the entrance. It was a tan Jaguar with leather upholstery, and the man behind the wheel was dressed in a white shirt. "We'll talk in there," Monsieur X said. "It's more private." We climbed into the back seat, the driver started up the engine, and the car pulled away from the curb. "Just drive around," Monsieur X said to the chauffeur. I suddenly felt as if I had landed in a gangster movie.

Most of the story was known by then, but he wanted me to give him a full report, an autopsy of the failure. I did my best to describe what had happened, expressing more than once how sorry I was that things hadn't worked out, but with Madame X's heart no longer in the book, I said, there wasn't much I could do to motivate her. Monsieur X seemed to accept all this with great calm. As far as I could tell, he wasn't angry, not even especially disappointed. Just when I thought the interview was about to end, however, he brought up the subject of my payment. Since nothing had been accomplished, he said, it seemed only right that I should give him back the money, didn't it? No, I said, it didn't seem right at all. A deal is a deal, and I had gone to Mexico in good faith and had kept up my end of the bargain. No one had ever suggested that I write the book *for* Madame X. I was supposed to write it *with* her, and if she didn't want to do the work, it wasn't my job to force her to do it. That was precisely why I'd asked for the money in advance. I was afraid that something like this would happen, and I needed to know that I would be paid for my time—no matter how things turned out.

He saw the logic of my argument, but that didn't mean he was willing to back down. All right, he said, keep the money, but if you want to go on working for me, you'll have to do some more jobs to square the account. In other words, instead of asking me to return the money in cash, he wanted me to give it back in labor. I told him that was unacceptable. Our account was square, I said, I wasn't in debt to him, and if he wanted to hire me for other jobs, he would have to pay me what those jobs were worth. Needless to say, that was unacceptable to him. I thought you wanted a part in the movie, he said. I never said that, I answered. Because if you do, he continued, we'll have to clear up this business first. Once again, I told him there was nothing to clear up. All right, he said, if that's how you feel about it, then we have nothing to say to each other anymore. And with that remark he turned away from me and told the driver to stop the car.

We had been riding around for about half an hour by then, slowly drifting toward the outer fringes of Paris, and the neighborhood where the car had stopped was unfamiliar to me. It was a cold January night, and I had no idea where I was, but the conversation was over, and there was nothing for me to do but say good-bye to him and get out of the car. If I remember correctly, we didn't even shake hands. I stepped out onto the sidewalk, shut the door, and the car drove off. And that was the end of my career in the movies.

I stayed on in France for another eighteen months—half of them in Paris and half of them in Provence, where my girlfriend and I worked as caretakers of a farmhouse in the northern Var. By the time I returned to New York, I had under ten dollars in my pocket and not a single concrete plan for the future. I was twenty-seven years old, and with nothing to show for myself but a book of poems and a handful of obscure literary essays, I was no closer to having solved the problem of money than I'd been before I left America. To further complicate the situation, my girlfriend and I decided to get married. It was an impulsive move, but with so many things about to change, we figured why not go ahead and change everything at once?

I immediately began casting about for work. I made telephone calls, followed up on leads, went in for interviews, explored as many possibilities as I could. I was trying to act sensibly, and after all the ups and downs I'd been through, all the tight corners and desperate squeezes that had trapped me over the years, I was determined not to repeat my old mistakes. I had learned my lesson, I told myself, and this time I was going to take care of business.

But I hadn't, and I didn't. For all my high-minded intentions, it turned out that I was incorrigible. It's not that I didn't find a job, but rather than accept the full-time position I had been offered (as junior editor in a large publishing house), I opted for a half-time job at half the pay. I had vowed to swallow my medicine, but just when the spoon was coming toward me, I shut my mouth. Until it happened, I had no idea that I was going to balk like that, no idea how stubbornly I was going to resist. Against all the odds, it seemed that I still hadn't given up the vain and stupid hope of surviving on my own terms. A part-time job looked like a good solution, but not even that was enough. I wanted total independence, and when some freelance translation work finally came my way, I quit the job and went off on my own again. From start to finish, the experiment lasted just seven months. Short as that time might have been, it was the only period of my adult life when I earned a regular paycheck.

By every standard, the job I had found was an excellent one. My boss was Arthur Cohen, a man of many interests, much money, and a first-rate mind. A writer of both novels and essays, a former publishing executive, and a passionate collector of art, he had recently set up a little business as an outlet for his excess energies. Part hobbyhorse, part serious commercial venture, Ex Libris was a rare-book concern that specialized in publications connected with twentieth-century art. Not books *about* art, but manifestations of the art itself. Magazines from the Dada movement, for example, or books designed by members of the Bauhaus, or photographs by Stieglitz, or an edition of Ovid's *Metamorphoses* illustrated by Picasso. As the back cover of each Ex Libris catalogue announced: "Books and Periodicals in Original Editions for the Documentation of the Art of the 20th Century: Futurism, Cubism, Dada, Bauhaus and Constructivism, De Stijl, Surrealism, Expressionism, Post War Art, as well as Architecture, Typography, Photography and Design."

Arthur was just getting the operation off the ground when he hired me as his sole employee. My chief task was to help him write the Ex Libris catalogues, which were issued twice a year and ran to a little over a hundred pages. Other duties included writing letters, preparing the catalogues for bulk mailings, fulfilling orders, and making tuna fish sandwiches for lunch. Mornings I spent at home, working for myself, and at twelve o'clock I would go downstairs to Riverside Drive and take the number 4 bus to the office. An apartment had been rented in a brownstone building on East Sixty-ninth Street to store Ex Libris's holdings, and the two rooms were crammed with thousands of books, magazines, and prints. Stacked on tables, wedged onto shelves, piled high in closets, these precious objects had overwhelmed the entire space. I spent four or five hours there every afternoon, and it was a bit like working in a museum, a small shrine to the avant-garde.

Arthur worked in one room and I worked in the other, each of us planted at a desk as we combed through the items for sale and prepared our meticulous catalogue entries on five-by-seven index cards. Anything having to do with French and English was given to me; Arthur handled the German and Russian materials. Typography, design, and architecture were his domain; I was in charge of all things literary. There was a certain fusty precision to the work (measuring the books, examining them for imperfections, detailing provenances when necessary), but many of the items were quite thrilling to hold, and Arthur gave me free rein to express my opinions about them, even to inject an occasional dose of humor if I felt like it. A few examples from the second catalogue will give some idea of what the job entailed:

233. DUCHAMP, M. & HALBERSTADT, V. L'Opposition et les cases conjuguées sont réconciliées par M. Duchamp et V. Halberstadt. Editions de L'Echiquier. St. Germain-en-Laye and Brussels, 1932. Parallel text in German and English on left-hand pages. 112 double-numbered pp., with 2-color illustrations. 9 5/8 × 11". Printed paper covers.

The famous book on chess written and designed by Duchamp. (Schwarz, p. 589). Although it is a serious text, devoted to a real chess problem, it is nevertheless so obscure as to be virtually worthless. Schwarz quotes Duchamp as having said: "The endgames on which this fact turns are of no interest to any chess player; and that's the funniest thing about it. Only three or four people in the world are interested in it, and they're the ones who've tried the same lines of research as Halberstadt and myself, since we wrote the book together. Chess champions never read this book, because the problem it poses never really turns up more than once in a lifetime. These are possible endgame problems, but they're so rare that they're almost utopian." (p. 63). $1000.00

394. (STEIN, GERTRUDE). Testimony: Against Gertrude Stein. Texts by Georges Braque, Eugene Jolas, Maria Jolas, Henri Matisse, André

Salmon, Tristan Tzara. Servire Press. The Hague, February, 1935. (Transition Pamphlet no. 1; supplement to Transition 1934–1935; no. 23). 16 pp. 5 11/16 × 8 7/8". Printed paper covers. Stapled.

In light of the great Stein revival of the Seventies, the continuing value of this pamphlet cannot be denied. It serves as an antidote to literary self-serving and, in its own right, is an important document of literary and artistic history. Occasioned by the inaccuracies and distortions of fact in The Autobiography of Alice B. Toklas, Transition produced this forum in order to allow some of the figures treated in Miss Stein's book to rebut her portrayal of them. The verdict seems to be unanimous. Matisse: "In short, it is more like a harlequin's costume the different pieces of which, having been more or less invented by herself, have been sewn together without taste and without relation to reality." Eugene Jolas: "The Autobiography of Alice B. Toklas, in its hollow, tinsel bohemianism and egocentric deformations, may very well become one day the symbol of the decadence that hovers over contemporary literature." Braque: "Miss Stein understood nothing of what went on around her." Tzara: "Underneath the 'baby' style, which is pleasant enough when it is a question of simpering at the interstices of envy, it is easy to discern such a really coarse spirit, accustomed to the artifices of the lowest literary prostitution, that I cannot believe it necessary for me to insist on the presence of a clinical case of megalomania." Salmon: "And what confusion! What incomprehension of an epoch! Fortunately there are others who have described it better." Finally, the piece by Maria Jolas is particularly noteworthy for its detailed description of the early days of Transition. This pamphlet was originally not for sale separately. $95.00

437. GAUGUIN, PAUL. Noa Noa. Voyage de Tahiti. Les Editions G. Crès & Cie. Paris, 1924. 154 pp., illustrated with 22 woodcuts after Paul Gauguin by Daniel de Monfreid. 5 3/4 × 7 15/16". Illustrated paper wrappers over paper.

This is the first definitive edition, including introductory material and poems by Charles Morice. The record of Gauguin's first two years in Tahiti, remarkable not only for its significant biographical revelations, but for its insightful anthropological approach to a strange culture. Gauguin follows Baudelaire's persuasive dictum: "Dites, qu'avez vous vu?" and the result is this miracle of vision: a Frenchman, at the height of European colonialism, travelling to an "underdeveloped country" neither to conquer nor convert, but to learn. This experience is the central event of Gauguin's life, both as an artist and as a man. Also: Noa Noa, translated into English by O.F. Theis. Nicholas L. Brown. New York, 1920. (Fifth printing; first printing in 1919). 148 pp. + 10 Gauguin reproductions. 5 5/16 × 7 13/16". Paper and cloth over boards. (Some minor foxing in French edition; slight fraying of spine in both French and English editions.) $65.00

509. RAY, MAN. Mr. and Mrs. Woodman. Edition Unida. No place, 1970. Pages unnumbered; with 27 original photographs and 1 signed and numbered engraving by Man Ray. 10 1/2 × 11 7/8". Leather bound, gilt-edged cardboard pages; leather and marbleized fitted box.

One of the very strangest of Man Ray's many strange works. Mr. and Mrs. Woodman are two puppet-like wood figures constructed by Man Ray in Hollywood in 1947, and the book, composed in 1970, is a series of mounted photographs of these witty, amazingly life-like characters in some of the most contorted erotic postures imaginable. In some sense, this book can best be described as a wood-people's guide to sex. Of an edition of only 50 copies, this is number 31, signed by Man Ray. All photographs are originals of the artist and carry his mark. Inserted is an original, numbered and signed engraving, specially made by Man Ray for this edition. $2100.00

Arthur and I got along well, with no strain or conflict, and we worked together in a friendly, unruffled atmosphere. Had I been a somewhat different person, I might have held on to that job for years, but seeing that I wasn't, I began to grow bored and restless after a few months. I enjoyed looking through the material I had to write about, but I didn't have the mind of a collector, and I could never bring myself to feel the proper awe or reverence for the things we sold. When you sit down to write about the catalogue that Marcel Duchamp designed for the 1947 Surrealist exhibition in Paris, for example—the one with the rubber breast on the cover, the celebrated bare falsie that came with the admonition "*Prière de Toucher*" ("Please Touch")—and you find that catalogue protected by several layers of bubble wrap, which in turn have been swathed in thick brown paper, which in turn has been slipped into a plastic bag, you can't help but pause for a moment and wonder if you aren't wasting your time. *Prière de toucher*. Duchamp's imperative is an obvious play on the signs you see posted all over France: *Prière de ne pas toucher* (Do Not Touch). He turns the warning on its head and asks us to fondle the thing he has made. And what better thing than this spongy, perfectly formed breast? Don't venerate it, he says, don't take it seriously, don't worship this frivolous activity we call art. Twenty-seven years later, the warning is turned upside down again. The naked breast has been covered. The thing to be touched has been made untouchable. The joke has been turned into a deadly serious transaction, and once again money has the last word.

This is not to criticize Arthur. No one loved these things more than he did, and if the catalogues we mailed out to potential customers were vehicles of commerce, they were also works of scholarship, rigorous documents in their own right. The difference between us was not that I understood the issues any better than he did (if anything, it was just the opposite), but that he was a businessman and I wasn't, which explained why he was the boss and I made just a few measly dollars per hour. Arthur took pleasure in turning a profit, enjoyed the push and pull of running the enterprise and making it succeed, and while he was also a man of great sophistication and refinement, a genuine intellectual who lived in and for the world of ideas, there was no getting around the fact that he was a crafty entrepreneur. Apparently, a life of the mind was not incompatible with the pursuit of money. I understood myself well enough to know that such a thing wasn't possible for me, but I saw now that it was possible for others. Some people didn't have to choose. They didn't have to divide the world into two separate camps. They could actually live in both places at the same time.

A few weeks after I started working for him, Arthur recommended me to a friend who was looking to hire someone for a short-term job. Arthur knew that I could use the extra money, and I mention this small favor as an example of how well he treated me. That the friend turned out to be Jerzy Kosinski, and that the job involved me in editing the manuscript of Kosinski's latest book, makes the episode worth talking about a little more. Intense controversy has surrounded Kosinksi in recent years, and since a large share of it emanated from the novel I worked on (*Cockpit*), I feel that I should add my testimony to the record. As Arthur explained it to me, the job was a simple matter of looking through the manuscript and making sure that the English was in good order. Since English wasn't Kosinski's first language, it seemed perfectly reasonable to me that he should want to have the prose checked before he handed the book to his publisher. What I didn't know was that other people had worked on the manuscript before me—three or four others, depending on which account you read. Kosinski never mentioned this earlier help to me, but whatever problems the book still had were not because the English didn't sound like English. The flaws were more fundamental than that, more about the book itself than how the story was told. I corrected a few sentences here, changed a few words there, but the novel was essentially finished by the time the manuscript was given to me. If left to my own devices, I could have completed the work in one or two days, but because Kosinski wouldn't let the manuscript out of his house, I had to go to his apartment on West Fifty-seventh Street to do the work, and because he hovered around me constantly, interrupting me every twenty minutes with stories, anecdotes, and nervous chatter, the job dragged on for seven days. I don't know why, but Kosinski seemed terribly eager to impress me, and the truth was that he did. He was so thoroughly high-strung, so odd and manic in his behavior, that I couldn't help but be impressed. What made these interruptions doubly odd and intriguing was that nearly every story he told me also appeared in the book he had written—the very novel spread out before me when he came into the room to talk. How he had masterminded his escape from Poland, for example. Or how he would prowl around Times Square at two in the morning disguised as a Puerto Rican undercover cop. Or how, occasionally, he would turn up at expensive restaurants dressed in a sham military uniform (made for him by his tailor and representing no identifiable rank, country, or branch of service), but because that uniform looked good, and because it was covered with countless medals and stars, he would be given the best table in the house by the awestruck maître d'—without a reservation, without a tip, without so much as a glance. The book was supposedly a work of fiction, but when Kosinski told me these stories, he presented them as facts, real events from his life. Did he know the difference? I can't be sure, can't even begin to guess, but if I had to give an answer, I would say that he did. He struck me as too clever, too cunningly aware of himself and his effect on others not to enjoy the confusion he created. The common theme in the stories was deception, after all, playing people for fools, and from the way he laughed when he told them—as if gloating, as if reveling in his own cynicism—I felt that perhaps he was only toying with me, buttering me up with compliments in order to test the limits of my credulity. Perhaps. And then again, perhaps not. The only thing I know for certain is that Kosinski was a man of labyrinthine complexity. When the rumors started circulating about him in the mid-eighties and magazine articles began to appear with accusations of plagiarism and the use of ghost writers and false claims concerning his past, I wasn't surprised. Years later, when he took his own life by suffocating himself with a plastic bag, I was. He died in the same apartment where I had worked for him in 1974, in the same bathroom where I had washed my hands and used the toilet. I have only to think about it for a moment, and I can see it all.

Otherwise, my months at Ex Libris passed quietly. Nothing much happened, and since most of the business was conducted through the mail, it was a rare day when anyone came to the apartment and disturbed us at our work. Late one afternoon, however, when Arthur was out on an errand, John Lennon knocked on the door, wanting to look at Man Ray photographs.

"Hi," he said, thrusting out his hand at me, "I'm John."

"Hi," I said, taking hold of the hand and giving it a good shake, "I'm Paul."

As I searched for the photographs in one of the closets, Lennon stopped in front of the Robert Motherwell canvas that hung on the wall beside Arthur's desk. There wasn't much to the painting—a pair of straight black lines against a broad orange background—and after studying it for a few moments, he turned to me and said, "Looks like that one took a lot of work, huh?" With all the pieties floating around the art world, I found it refreshing to hear him say that.

Arthur and I parted on good terms, with no hard feelings on either side. I made it my business to find a replacement for myself before I quit, and that made my departure relatively simple and painless. We stayed in touch for a little while, occasionally calling each other to catch up on the news, but eventually we lost contact, and when Arthur died of leukemia several years ago, I couldn't even remember the last time I had talked to him. Then came Kosinski's suicide. Add that to John Lennon's murder more than a decade earlier, and nearly everyone associated with the months I spent in that office has disappeared. Even Arthur's friend Robert Motherwell, the good artist responsible for the bad painting that provoked Lennon's comment, is no longer with us. Reach a certain moment in your life, and you discover that your days are spent as much with the dead as they are with the living.

The next two years were an intensely busy time. Between March 1975, when I stopped working for Ex Libris, and June 1977, when my son was born, I came out with two more books of poetry, wrote several one-act plays, published fifteen or twenty critical pieces, and translated half a dozen books with my wife, Lydia Davis. These translations were our primary source of income, and we worked together as a team, earning so many dollars per thousand words and taking whatever jobs we were offered. Except for one book by Sartre (*Life/Situations*, a collection of essays and interviews), the books the publishers gave us were dull, undistinguished works that ranged in quality from not very good to downright bad. The money was bad as well, and even though our rate kept increasing from book to book, if you broke down what we did on an hourly basis, we were scarcely a penny or two ahead of the minimum wage. The key was to work fast, to crank out the translations as quickly as we could and never stop for breath. There are surely more inspiring ways to make a living, but Lydia and I tackled these jobs with great discipline. A publisher would hand us a book, we would split the work in two (literally tearing the book in half if we had only one copy), and set a daily quota for ourselves. Nothing was allowed to interfere with that number. So many pages had to be done every day, and every day, whether we felt in the mood or not, we sat down and did them. Flipping hamburgers would have been just as lucrative, but at least we were free, or at least we thought we were free, and I never felt any regrets about having left my job. For better or worse, this was how I had chosen to live. Between translating for money and writing for myself, there was rarely a moment during those years when I wasn't sitting at my desk, putting words on a piece of paper.

I didn't write criticism for money, but I was paid for most of the articles I published, and that helped pad my income to a certain degree. Still, getting by was a struggle, and from month to month we were no more than a short dry spell away from real poverty. Then, in the fall of 1975, just half a year into this tightrope walk *à deux*, my luck turned. I was given a five-thousand-dollar grant from the Ingram Merrill Foundation, and for the next little while the worst of the pressure was off. The money was so unexpected, so enormous in its ramifications, that I felt as if an angel had dropped down from the sky and kissed me on the forehead.

The man most responsible for this stroke of good fortune was John Bernard Myers. John didn't give me the money out of his own pocket, but he was the person who told me about the foundation and encouraged me to apply for the grant. The real benefactor, of course, was the poet James Merrill. In the quietest, most discreet manner possible, he had been sharing his family's wealth with other writers and artists for many years, hiding behind his middle name so as not to call attention to his astounding generosity. A committee met every six months to consider new applications and to dole out the awards. John was secretary of the committee, and although he didn't take part in choosing the recipients, he sat in on the meetings and knew how the members thought.

Nothing was sure, he said, but he suspected that they would be inclined to support my work. So I put together a sampling of my poems and sent them in. At the next semiannual meeting, John's hunch proved to be correct.

I don't think I've ever known a funnier or more effusive person than John. When I first met him, in late 1974, he had been an integral part of the New York scene for the past thirty years, most famously as director of the Tibor de Nagy Gallery in the fifties, but also as cofounder of the Artists Theatre, editor of various short-lived literary magazines, and all-around champion and impresario of young talent. John was the first to give major shows to such artists as Red Grooms, Larry Rivers, Helen Frankenthaler, and Fairfield Porter, and he published the first books of Frank O'Hara, John Ashbery, and other poets of the New York School. The plays he produced were collaborations between many of these same poets and painters—O'Hara and Rivers, for example, or James Schuyler and Elaine de Kooning, the one writing the words and the other designing the sets. The Artists Theatre didn't bring in much at the box office, but John and his partner kept it running for years, and at a time when Off Broadway had yet to come into being, it was about the only experimental theater available in New York. What set John apart from all the other dealers, publishers, and producers I've known is that he wasn't in it for the money. Truth be told, he probably wasn't much of a businessman, but he had a genuine passion for art in all its forms, rigorous standards, openness of spirit, and an immense hunger for work that was different, challenging, new. A large man of six three or six four, he often made me think of John Wayne in his physical appearance. This John, however, in that he was proudly and flagrantly homosexual, in that he gleefully mocked himself with all manner of mincing gestures and extravagant poses, in that he took delight in silly jokes and ridiculous songs and a whole repertoire of childish humor, had nothing to do with that other John. No tough guy stuff for him. This John was all enthusiasm and goodwill, a man who had dedicated his life to beautiful things, and he wore his heart on his sleeve.*

When I met him, he was just starting up a new magazine—"of words and pictures"—called *Parenthèse*. I can't remember who suggested that I send him my work, but I did, and from then on John made a point of

---

* For a vivid account of his adventures, see John's *Tracking the Marvelous: A Life in the New York Art World*, published by Random House in 1983.

putting something of mine in nearly every issue. Later, when he discontinued the magazine and began publishing books instead, the first title on the list was a collection of my poems. John's belief in my work was absolute, and he backed me at a time when few people even knew that I was alive. In the endnotes to *Parenthèse 4*, for example, buried among the dry accounts of contributors' past achievements, he took it upon himself to declare that "Paul Auster has created a stir in the literary world by his brilliant analysis of the work of Laura Riding Jackson, by his essays on French paintings, and his poetry." It didn't matter that this statement wasn't true, that John was the only one paying attention. *Someone* was behind me, and in those early days of struggle and uncertainty, of not stirring up much of anything, that encouragement made all the difference. John was the first person who took a stand for me, and I have never stopped feeling grateful to him for that.

When the grant money came, Lydia and I hit the road again. We sublet our apartment and went to the Laurentian Mountains in Quebec, holing up in the house of a painter friend for a couple of months while he was away, then returned to New York for a week or two, and then promptly packed our bags again and took a cross-country train to San Francisco. We eventually settled in Berkeley, renting a small efficiency apartment not far from the university, and lived there for six months. We weren't flush enough to stop translating, but the pace was less frantic now, and that allowed me to spend more time with my own work. I went on writing poems, but new impulses and ideas started coming as well, and before long I found myself writing a play. That led to another play, which in turn led to another play, and when I returned to New York in the fall, I showed them to John. I didn't know what to make of what I had written. The pieces had surged up unexpectedly, and the results were quite different from anything I had done before. When John told me he liked them, I felt that perhaps I had taken a step in the right direction. The farthest thing from my mind was to do anything with them in a practical sense. I had given no thought to having them performed, no thought to publishing them. As far as I was concerned, they were hardly more than spare, minimalist exercises, an initial stab at something that might or might not turn out to be real. When John said that he wanted to take the longest of the plays and mount a production of it, I was caught totally by surprise.

No one was to blame for what happened. John jumped in with his customary excitement and energy, but things kept going wrong, and after a while it began to seem that we weren't putting on a play so much as trying to prove the indestructible power of Murphy's Law. A director and three actors were found, and shortly after that a reading was scheduled to drum up financial support for the production. That was the plan, in any case. It didn't help that the actors were young and inexperienced, not up to the task of delivering their lines with conviction or true feeling, but even worse was the audience who came to hear them deliver those lines. John had invited a dozen of his richest art collector friends, and not one of these potential backers was under sixty or had the slightest interest in the theater. He was counting on the play to seduce them, to overwhelm their hearts and minds with such stunning finality that they would feel no choice but to reach into their pockets and start pulling out their checkbooks. The event was held at a posh Upper East Side apartment, and my job was to charm these wealthy patrons, to smile and chat and reassure them that they were putting their money on the right horse. The problem was that I had no talent for smiling and chatting. I arrived in a state of extreme tension, nervous to the point of being ill, and quickly downed two bourbons to undo the knot in my stomach. The alcohol had precisely the opposite effect, and by the time the reading started, I had come down with a massive headache, a blistering, brain-bending assault that grew ever more unbearable as the evening wore on. The play thudded forward, and from start to finish the rich people sat in silence, utterly unmoved. Lines that I had imagined were funny did not produce the faintest titter. They were bored by the gags, indifferent to the pathos, perplexed by the whole thing. At the end, after some grim, perfunctory applause, I could only think about how to get out of there and hide. My head was cracking with pain. I felt stabbed and humiliated, unable to speak, but I couldn't abandon John, and so for the next half hour I listened to him talk about the play to his befuddled friends, doing everything I could not to pass out on the carpet. John put up a brave front, but every time he turned to me for help, I could do no more than stare down at my shoes and mumble a brief, unintelligible comment. Finally, apropos of nothing, I blurted out some lame excuse and left.

A lesser man would have given up after such a defeat, but John was undaunted. Not a penny of aid emerged from that gruesome evening, but he went ahead and started improvising a new plan, scuttling his dream of theatrical glory for a more modest, workable approach. If we couldn't afford a real theater, he said, we would make do with something else. The play was the only thing that mattered, and even if the run was limited to just a single, invitation-only performance, there was going to be a production of my play. If not for me, he said, and if not for him, then at least for his friend Herbert Machiz, who had died that summer. Herbert had directed the plays at the old Artists Theatre, and because he had been John's companion for twenty-five years, John was determined to revive the Theatre in Herbert's memory—if only for just one night.

A man who owned a restoration studio on East Sixty-ninth Street offered John the use of his space. It happened to be just down the block from the Ex Libris office—an interesting, if minor, coincidence—but more to the point was that in its previous incarnation the carriage house where John's friend now worked had been the studio of Mark Rothko. Rothko had killed himself there in 1970, and now, less than seven years later, my play was going to be presented in that same room. I don't want to sound overly superstitious about it, but given how things turned out, it feels that we were cursed, that no matter what any of us did or didn't do, the project was bound to fail.

Preparations began. The director and the three actors worked hard, and little by little the performances improved. I wouldn't go so far as to call them good, but at least they were no longer an embarrassment. One of the actors stood out from the others, and as the rehearsals went on, I began to pin my hopes on him, praying that his inventiveness and daring might pull the production up to a reasonably competent level. A date in early March was chosen for the performance, invitations were sent out, and arrangements were made for a hundred and fifty folding chairs to be delivered to the carriage house. I should have known better, but I actually began to feel optimistic. Then, just days before the big night, the good actor came down with pneumonia, and because there were no understudies (how could there have been?), it looked as if the performance would have to be canceled. The actor, however, who had put weeks of time and effort into the rehearsals, was not about to give up. In spite of a high temperature, in spite of the fact that he was coughing up blood just hours before the play was supposed to start, he crawled out of bed, pumped his system full of antibiotics, and staggered on at the appointed time. It was the noblest of noble gestures, the gutsy act of a born trouper, and I was impressed by his courage—no, more than impressed: filled with admiration—but the sad truth was that he was in no shape to do what he did. Everything that had sparkled in the rehearsals suddenly lost its shine. The performance was flat, the timing was off, scene after scene was blown. I stood at the back of the room and watched, powerless to do a thing. I saw my little play die in front of a hundred and fifty people, and I couldn't lift a finger to stop it.

Before putting the whole miserable experience behind me, I sat down and reworked the play. The performances had been only part of the problem, and I wasn't about to palm off responsibility for what had happened on the director or the actors. The play was too long, I realized, too rambling and diffuse, and radical surgery was needed to mend it. I began chopping and trimming, hacking away at everything that felt weak or superfluous, and by the time I was finished, half of the play was gone, one of the characters had been eliminated, and the title had been changed. I typed up this new version, now called *Laurel and Hardy Go to Heaven*, put it in a folder along with the other two plays I had written (*Blackouts* and *Hide and Seek*), and stuck the folder in a drawer of my desk. My plan was to keep it there and never look inside the drawer again.

Three months after the flop of the play, my son was born. Watching Daniel come into the world was a moment of supreme happiness for me, an event of such magnitude that even as I broke down and wept at the sight of his small body and held him in my arms for the first time, I understood that the world had changed, that I had passed from one state of being into another. Fatherhood was the dividing line, the great wall that stood between youth and adulthood, and I was on the other side now forever.

I was glad to be there. Emotionally, spiritually, and even physically, there was nowhere else I wanted to be, and I was fully prepared to take on the demands of living in this new place. Financially, however, I wasn't the least bit prepared for anything. You pay a toll when you climb over that wall, and by the time I landed on the other side, my pockets were nearly empty. Lydia and I had left New York by then, moving to a house about two hours up the Hudson, and it was there that the hard times finally hit. The storm lasted for eighteen months, and when the wind died down enough for me to crawl out of my hole and inspect the damage, I saw that everything was gone. The entire landscape had been leveled.

Moving out of the city was the first step in a long series of miscalculations. We figured we could live on less money in the country, but the plain fact was that we couldn't. Car expenses, heating expenses, house repairs, and pediatrician's bills ate up whatever advantage we thought we had gained, and before long we were working so hard just to make ends meet that there was no time left for anything else. In the past, I had always managed to keep a few hours to myself every day, to push on with my poems and writing projects after spending the first part of the day working for money. Now, as our need for money rose, there was less time available to me for my own work. I started missing a day, then two days, then a week, and after a while I lost my rhythm as a writer. When I did manage to find some time for myself, I was too tense to write very well. Months went by, and every piece of paper I touched with my pen wound up in the garbage.

By the end of 1977, I was feeling trapped, desperate to find a solution. I had spent my whole life avoiding the subject of money, and now, suddenly, I could think of nothing else. I dreamed of miraculous reversals, lottery millions falling down from the sky, outrageous get-rich-quick schemes. Even the ads on matchbook covers began to hold a certain fascination. "Make Money Growing Worms in Your Basement." Now that I lived in a house with a basement, don't think I wasn't tempted. My old way of doing things had led to disaster, and I was ripe for new ideas, a new way of tackling the dilemma that had dogged me from the start: how to reconcile the needs of the body with the needs of the soul. The terms of the equation were still the same: time on the one hand, money on the other. I had gambled on being able to manage both, but after years of trying to feed first one mouth, then two mouths, and then three mouths, I had finally lost. It wasn't difficult to understand why. I had put too much of myself into working for time and not enough into working for money, and the result was that now I didn't have either one.

In early December, a friend came up from the city to visit for a few days. We had known each other since college, and he, too, had turned into a struggling writer—yet one more Columbia graduate without a pot to piss in. If anything, he was having an even rougher time of it than I was. Most of his work was unpublished, and he supported himself by bouncing from one pathetic temporary job to another, aimlessly traveling around the country in search of strange, down-and-out adventures. He had recently landed in New York again and was working in a toy store somewhere in Manhattan, part of the brigade of surplus help who stand behind the counters during the Christmas shopping season. I picked him up at the train station, and during the half-hour ride back to the house, we talked mostly about toys and games, the things he sold in the store. For reasons that still mystify me, this conversation dislodged a small pebble that had been stuck somewhere in my unconscious, an obstruction that had been sitting over a tiny pinprick hole of memory, and now that I was able to look down that hole again, I found something that had been lost for nearly twenty years. Back when I was ten or twelve, I had invented a game. Using an ordinary deck of fifty-two playing cards, I had sat down on my bed one afternoon and figured out a way to play baseball with them. Now, as I went on talking to my friend in the car, the game came rushing back to me. I remembered everything about it: the basic principles, the rules, the whole setup down to the last detail.

Under normal circumstances, I probably would have forgotten all about it again. But I was a desperate man, a man with my back against the wall, and I knew that if I didn't think of something fast, the firing squad was about to fill my body with bullets. A windfall was the only way out of my predicament. If I could rustle up a nice large chunk of cash, the nightmare would suddenly stop. I could bribe off the soldiers, walk out of the prison yard, and go home to become a writer again. If translating books and writing magazine articles could no longer do the job, then I owed it to myself and my family to try something else. Well, people bought games, didn't they? What if I worked up my old baseball game into something good, something really good, and managed to sell it? Maybe I'd get lucky and find my bag of gold, after all.

It almost sounds like a joke now, but I was in dead earnest. I knew that my chances were next to nil, but once the idea grabbed hold of me, I couldn't shake free of it. Nuttier things had happened, I told myself, and if I wasn't willing to put a little time and effort into having a go at it, then what kind of spineless shit was I?

The game from my childhood had been organized around a few simple operations. The pitcher turned over cards: each red card from ace to 10 was a strike; each black card from ace to 10 was a ball. If a face card was turned over, that meant the batter swung. The batter then turned over a card. Anything from ace to 9 was an out, with each out corresponding to the position numbers of the defensive players: Pitcher = ace (1); Catcher = 2; First Baseman = 3; Second Baseman = 4; Third Baseman = 5; Shortstop = 6; Left Fielder = 7; Center Fielder = 8; Right

Fielder = 9. If the batter turned over a 5, for example, that meant the out was made by the Third Baseman. A black 5 indicated a ground ball; a red 5 indicated a ball hit in the air (diamond = pop-up; heart = line drive). On balls hit to the outfield (7, 8, 9), black indicated a shallow fly ball, red a deep fly ball. Turn over a 10, and you had yourself a single. A jack was a double, a queen was a triple, and a king was a home run.

It was crude but reasonably effective, and while the distribution of hits was mathematically off (there should have been more singles than doubles, more doubles than home runs, and more home runs than triples), the games were often close and exciting. More important, the final scores looked like the scores of real baseball games—3 to 2, 7 to 4, 8 to 0—and not football or basketball games. The fundamental principles were sound. All I had to do was get rid of the standard deck and design a new set of cards. That would allow me to make the game statistically accurate, add new elements of strategy and decision making (bunts, stolen bases, sacrifice flies), and lift the whole thing to a higher level of subtlety and sophistication. The work was largely a matter of getting the numbers right and fiddling with the math, but I was well versed in the intricacies of baseball, and it didn't take me long to arrive at the correct formulas. I played out game after game after game, and at the end of a couple of weeks there were no more adjustments to be made. Then came the tedious part. Once I had designed the cards (two decks of ninety-six cards each), I had to sit down with four fine-tipped pens (one red, one green, one black, one blue) and draw the cards by hand. I can't remember how many days it took me to complete this task, but by the time I came to the end, I felt as if I had never done anything else. The design was nothing to brag about, but since I had no experience or talent as a designer, that was to be expected. I was striving for a clear, serviceable presentation, something that could be read at a glance and not confuse anyone, and given that so much information had to be crammed onto every card, I think I accomplished at least that. Beauty and elegance could come later. If anyone showed enough interest to want to manufacture the game, the problem could be turned over to a professional designer. For the time being, after much dithering back and forth, I dubbed my little brainchild Action Baseball.

Once again, my stepfather came to the rescue. He happened to have a friend who worked for one of the largest, most successful American toy companies, and when I showed the game to this man, he was

FOUL OUT TO C

2

STRIKE STRIKE STRIKE STRIKE

2

FOUL OUT TO C

E	DP	LDDP	SacB	SB(2)	SB(3)
2	•	• (DP)	•	•	•

SacF	SacF	EB	Inf in (3)	2 to 3
•	•	•	•	•

GROUND OUT TO 3B

5

BALL BALL BALL BALL

5

GROUND OUT TO 3B

E	DP	LDDP	SacB	SB(2)	SB(3)
5	•	•	•	•	•

SacF	SacF	EB	Inf in (3)	2 to 3
•	•	•	•	•

GROUND OUT TO 2B

4

BALL BALL BALL BALL

4

GROUND OUT TO 2B

E	DP	LDDP	SacB	SB(2)	SB(3)
4	•	•	•	•	•

SacF	SacF	EB	Inf in (3)	2 to 3
•	•	•	•	•

FOUL BALL

SWING SWING SWING SWING

6

FOUL BALL

E	DP	LDDP	SacB	SB(2)	SB(3)
6	•	•	•	•	•

SacF	SacF	EB	Inf in (3)	2 to 3
•	•	•	•	•

SINGLE
Runners advance 2 bases

SWING SWING SWING SWING

SINGLE
Runners advance 2 bases

E	DP	LDDP	SacB	SB(2)	SB(3)
6	•	•	•	•	•

SacF	SacF	EB	Inf in (3)	2 to 3
•	•	•	•	•

SINGLE
Runners advance 1 base

SWING SWING SWING SWING

SINGLE
Runners advance 1 base

E	DP	LDDP	SacB	SB(2)	SB(3)
4	•	•	•	•	•

SacF	SacF	EB	Inf in (3)	2 to 3
•	•	•	•	•

GROUND OUT TO SS

6

BALL BALL BALL BALL

6

GROUND OUT TO SS

E	DP	LDDP	SacB	SB(2)	SB(3)
6	•	•	•	•	•

SacF	SacF	EB	Inf in (3)	2 to 3
•	•	•	•	•

GROUND OUT TO P

1

BALL BALL BALL BALL

1

GROUND OUT TO P

E	DP	LDDP	SacB	SB(2)	SB(3)
1	•	•	•	•	•

SacF	SacF	EB	Inf in (3)	2 to 3
•	•	•	•	•

impressed by it, thought it had a real chance of appealing to someone. I was still working on the cards at that point, but he encouraged me to get the game in order as quickly as I could and take it to the New York Toy Fair, which was just five or six weeks down the road. I had never heard of it, but by all accounts it was the most important annual event in the business. Every February, companies from around the world gathered at the Toy Center at Twenty-third Street and Fifth Avenue to display their products for the upcoming season, take note of what the competition was up to, and make plans for the future. What the Frankfurt Book Fair is for books and the Cannes Film Festival is for films, the New York Toy Fair is for toys. My stepfather's friend took charge of everything for me. He arranged to have my name put on the list of "inventors," which qualified me for a badge and an open pass to the fair, and then, as if that weren't enough, set up an appointment for me to meet with the president of his company—at nine o'clock in the morning on the first day of the fair.

I was grateful for the help, but at the same time I felt like someone who had just been booked on a flight to an unknown planet. I had no idea what to expect, no map of the terrain, no guidebook to help me understand the habits and customs of the creatures I would be talking to. The only solution I could think of was to wear a jacket and tie. The tie was the only one I owned, and it hung in my closet for emergency use at weddings and funerals. Now business meetings could be added to the list. I must have cut a ridiculous figure as I strode into the Toy Center that morning to collect my badge. I was carrying a briefcase, but the only thing inside it was the game, which was stowed inside a cigar box. That was all I had: the game itself, along with several Xeroxed copies of the rules. I was about to go in and talk to the president of a multimillion-dollar business, and I didn't even have a business card.

Even at that early hour, the place was swarming with people. Everywhere you turned, there were endless rows of corporate stands, display booths decked out with dolls and puppets and fire engines and dinosaurs and extraterrestrials. Every kiddie amusement and gadget ever dreamed of was packed into that hall, and there wasn't one of them that didn't whistle or clang or toot or beep or roar. As I made my way through the din, it occurred to me that the briefcase under my arm was the only silent object in the building. Computer games were all the rage that year, the biggest thing to hit the toy world since the invention of the wind-up jack-in-the-box, and I was hoping to strike it rich with an old-fashioned deck of cards. Maybe I would, but until I walked into that noisy fun house, I hadn't realized how likely it was that I wouldn't.

My talk with the company president turned out to be one of the shortest meetings in the annals of American business. It didn't bother me that the man rejected my game (I was prepared for that, was fully expecting bad news), but he did it in such a chilling way, with so little regard for human decency, that it still causes me pain to think about it. He wasn't much older than I was, this corporate executive, and with his sleek, superbly tailored suit, his blue eyes and blond hair and hard, expressionless face, he looked and acted like the leader of a Nazi spy ring. He barely shook my hand, barely said hello, barely acknowledged that I was in the room. No small talk, no pleasantries, no questions. "Let's see what you have," he said curtly, and so I reached into my briefcase and pulled out the cigar box. Contempt flickered in his eyes. It was as if I had just handed him a dog turd and asked him to smell it. I opened the box and took out the cards. By then, I could see that all hope was gone, that he had already lost interest, but there was nothing to do but forge ahead and start playing the game. I shuffled the decks, said something about how to read the three levels of information on the cards, and then got down to it. One or two batters into the top half of the first inning, he stood up from his chair and extended his hand to me. Since he hadn't spoken a word, I had no idea why he wanted to shake my hand. I continued to turn over cards, describing the action as it unfolded: ball, strike, swing. "Thank you," the Nazi said, finally taking hold of my hand. I still couldn't figure out what was going on. "Are you saying you don't want to see any more?" I said. "I haven't even had a chance to show you how it works." "Thank you," he said again. "You can leave now." Without another word, he turned and left me with my cards, which were still spread out on the table. It took me a minute or two to put everything back in the cigar box, and it was precisely then, during those sixty or ninety seconds, that I hit bottom, that I reached what I still consider to be the low point of my life.

Somehow or other, I managed to regroup. I went out for breakfast, pulled myself together, and returned to the fair for the rest of the day. One by one, I visited every game company I could find, shook hands, smiled, knocked on doors, demonstrated the wonders of Action Baseball to anyone willing to spare me ten or fifteen minutes. The results were uniformly discouraging. Most of the big companies had stopped working with independent inventors (too many lawsuits), and the small ones either wanted pocket-sized computer games (beep-beep) or else refused to look at anything connected with sports (low sales). At least these people were polite. After the sadistic treatment I'd been given that morning, I found some consolation in that.

Some time in the late afternoon, exhausted from hours of fruitless effort, I stumbled onto a company that specialized in card games. They had produced only one game so far, but that one had been wildly successful, and now they were in the market for a second. It was a small, low-budget operation run by two guys from Joliet, Illinois, a back-porch business with none of the corporate trappings and slick promotional methods of the other companies at the fair. That was a promising sign, but best of all, both partners admitted to being avid baseball fans. They weren't doing much at that hour, just sitting around their little booth and chewing the fat, and when I told them about my game, they seemed more than happy to have a look at it. Not just a peek, but a thorough viewing—to sit down and play a full nine-inning contest to the end.

If I had rigged the cards, the results of the game I played with them could not have been more exciting, more true to life. It was nip and tuck the whole way, tension riding on every pitch, and after eight and a half innings of threats, rallies, and two-out strikeouts with the bases loaded, the score stood at two to one. The Joliet boys were the home team, and when they came up for their last turn at bat, they needed a run to tie and two to win. The first two batters did nothing, and quickly they were down to their last out, with no runners on base. The following batter singled, however, to keep them alive. Then, to everyone's astonishment, with the count at two balls and two strikes, the next batter hit a home run to win the game. I couldn't have asked for more than that. A two-out, two-run homer in the bottom of the ninth inning to steal a victory on the last pitch. It was a classic baseball thriller, and when the man from Joliet turned over that final card, his face lit up with an expression of pure, undisguisable joy.

They wanted to think about it, they said, to mull it over for a while before giving me an answer. They would need a deck to study on their own, of course, and I told them I would send a color Xerox copy to Joliet as soon as possible. That was how we left it: shaking hands and exchanging addresses, promising each other to be in touch. After all the dismal, demoralizing events of that day, there was suddenly cause for hope, and I walked out of the Toy Fair thinking that I might actually get somewhere with my crazy scheme.

Color Xeroxing was a new process then, and it cost me a small fortune to have the copies made. I can't remember the exact amount, but it was more than a hundred dollars, I think, perhaps even two hundred. I shipped the package off to them and prayed they would write back soon. Weeks passed, and as I struggled to concentrate on the other work I had to do, it gradually dawned on me that I was in for a disappointment. Enthusiasm meant speed, indecision meant delay, and the longer they delayed, the worse the odds would be. It took almost two months for them to answer, and by then I didn't even have to read the letter to know what was in it. What surprised me was its brevity, its utter lack of personal warmth. I had spent close to an hour with them, had felt I'd entertained them and aroused their interest, but their rejection consisted of just one dry, clumsily written paragraph. Half the words were misspelled, and nearly every sentence had a grammatical error in it. It was an embarrassing document, a letter written by dunces, and once my hurt began to wear off a little, I felt ashamed of myself for having misjudged them so thoroughly. Put your faith in fools, and you end up fooling only yourself.

Still, I wasn't quite ready to give up. I had gone too far to allow one setback to throw me off course, and so I put my head down and plunged ahead. Until I had exhausted all the possibilities, I felt duty bound to continue, to see the whole misbegotten business through to the end. My in-laws put me in touch with a man who worked for Ruder and Finn, a prominent New York public relations firm. He loved the game, seemed genuinely enthused when I showed it to him, and made an all-out effort to help. That was part of the problem. Everyone liked Action Baseball, enough people at any rate to keep me from abandoning it, and with a kind, friendly, well-connected man like this one pushing on my behalf, it wouldn't have made sense to give up. My new ally's name was George, and he happened to be in charge of the General Foods account, one of Ruder and Finn's most important clients. His plan, which struck me as ingenious, was to get General Foods to put Action Baseball on the Wheaties box as a special coupon offer. ("Hey, kids! Just mail in two Wheaties box tops and a check or money order for $3.98, and this incredible game can be yours!") George proposed it to them, and for a time it looked as if it might happen. Wheaties was considering ideas for a new promotional campaign, and he thought this one might just do the trick. It didn't. They went with the Olympic decathlon champion instead, and for the next umpteen years, every box of

Wheaties was adorned with a picture of Bruce Jenner's smiling face. You can't really fault them. It was the Breakfast of Champions, after all, and they had a certain tradition to uphold. I never found out how close George came to getting his idea through, but I must confess (somewhat reluctantly) that I still find it hard to look at a box of Wheaties without feeling a little twinge.

George was almost as disappointed as I was, but now that he'd caught the bug, he wasn't about to quit trying. He knew someone in Indianapolis who was involved with the Babe Ruth League (in what capacity I forget) and thought something good might happen if he put me in contact with this man. The game was duly shipped to the Midwest again, and then followed another inordinately long silence. As the man hastened to explain to me when he finally wrote, he wasn't entirely responsible for the delay: "I am sorry to be so late in acknowledging receipt of your June 22 letter and your game, Action Baseball. They were late reaching me because of a tornado that wiped out our offices. I've been working at home since and did not get my mail until ten days or so ago." My bad luck was taking on an almost biblical dimension, and when the man wrote again several weeks later to tell me that he was passing on my game (sadly, with much regret, in the most courtly terms possible), I barely even flinched. "There is no question that your game is unique, innovative and interesting. There may well be a market for it since it is the only table-top baseball game without a lot of trappings, which makes it faster-moving, but the consensus here is that without big league players and their statistics, the established competition is insurmountable." I called George to give him the news and thank him for his help, but enough was enough, I said, and he shouldn't waste any more time on me.

Things stalled for a couple of months after that, but then another lead materialized, and I picked up my lance and sallied forth again. As long as there was a windmill somewhere in sight, I was prepared to do battle with it. I had not the least shred of hope anymore, but I couldn't quite let go of the stupid thing I had started. My stepfather's younger brother knew a man who had invented a game, and since that game had earned him a pile of money, it seemed reasonable for me to contact him and ask for advice. We met in the lobby of the Roosevelt Hotel, not far from Grand Central Station. He was a fast-talking wheeler-dealer of around forty, a wholly antipathetical man with every kind of bluff and angle up his sleeve, but I must admit that his patter had some verve to it.

"Mail order," he said, "that's the ticket. Approach a major-league star, get him to endorse the game for a share of the profits, and then take out ads in all the baseball magazines. If enough orders come in, use the money to produce the game. If not, send the money back and call it quits."

"How much would a thing like that cost?" I asked.

"Twenty, twenty-five thousand dollars. Minimum."

"I couldn't come up with that much," I said. "Not even if my life depended on it."

"Then you can't do it, can you?"

"No, I can't do it. I just want to sell the game to a company. That's all I've ever had in mind—to make some royalties from the copies they sold. I wouldn't be capable of going into business for myself."

"In other words," the man said, finally realizing what a numskull he was talking to, "you've taken a shit, and now you want someone to flush the toilet for you."

That wasn't quite how I would have expressed it myself, but I didn't argue with him. He clearly knew more than I did, and when he went on to recommend that I find a "game broker" to talk to the companies for me, I didn't doubt that he was pointing me in the right direction. Until then, I hadn't even known of the existence of such people. He gave me the name of someone who was supposed to be particularly good, and I called her the next day. That turned out to be my last move, the final chapter of the whole muddled saga. She talked a mile a minute to me, outlining terms, conditions, and percentages, what to do and what not to do, what to expect and what to avoid. It sounded like her standard spiel, a furious condensation of years of hard knocks and cutthroat maneuvers, and for the first several minutes I couldn't get a word in edgewise. Then, finally, she paused to catch her breath, and that was when she asked me about my game.

"It's called Action Baseball," I said.

"Did you say *baseball*?" she said.

"Yes, baseball. You turn over cards. It's very realistic, and you can get through a full nine-inning game in about fifteen minutes."

"Sorry," she said. "No sports games."

"What do you mean?"

"They're losers. They don't sell, and nobody wants them. I wouldn't touch your game with a ten-foot pole."

That did it for me. With the woman's blunt pronouncement still ringing in my ears, I hung up the phone, put the cards away, and stopped thinking about them forever.

Little by little, I was coming to the end of my rope. After the grim, garbled letter from Joliet, I understood that Action Baseball was no more than a long shot. To count on it as a source of money would have been an act of pure self-deception, a ludicrous error. I plugged away at it for several more months, but those final efforts took up only a small fraction of my time. Deep down, I had already accepted defeat—not just of the game, not just of my half-assed foray into the business world, but of all my principles, my lifelong stand toward work, money, and the pursuit of time. Time didn't count anymore. I had needed it in order to write, but now that I was an ex-writer, a writer who wrote only for the satisfaction of crumpling up paper and throwing it in the garbage, I was ready to abandon the struggle and live like everyone else. Nine years of freelance penury had burned me out. I had tried to rescue myself by inventing the game, but no one had wanted the game, and now I was right back where I had been—only worse, only more burned out than ever. At least the game had represented an idea, a temporary surge of hope, but now I had run out of ideas as well. The truth was that I had dug myself into a deep, dark hole, and the only way to crawl out of it was to find a job.

I made calls, wrote letters, traveled down to the city for interviews. Teaching jobs, journalism jobs, editorial jobs—it didn't matter what it was. As long as the job came with a weekly paycheck, I was interested. Two or three things almost panned out, but in the end they didn't. I won't go into the depressing details now, but several months went by without any tangible results. I sank further into confusion, my mind almost paralyzed with worry. I had made a total surrender, had capitulated on every point I had defended over the years, and still I was getting nowhere, was losing ground with every step I took. Then, out of the blue, a grant of thirty-five hundred dollars came in from the New York State Council on the Arts, and I was given an unexpected breather. It wouldn't last long, but it was something—enough to ward off the hour of doom for another minute or two.

One night not long after that, as I lay in bed battling against insomnia, a new idea occurred to me. Not an idea, perhaps, but a thought, a little notion. I had been reading a lot of detective novels that year, mostly of the hard-boiled American school, and beyond finding them to be good medicine, a balm against stress and chronic anxiety, I had developed an admiration for some of the practitioners of the genre. The best ones were humble, no-nonsense writers who not only had more to say about American life than most so-called serious writers, but often seemed to write smarter, crisper sentences as well. One of the conventional plot gimmicks of these stories was the apparent suicide that turns out to have been a murder. Again and again, a character would ostensibly die by his or her own hand, and by the end of the story, after all the tangled strands of the intrigue had finally been unraveled, it would be discovered that the villain was in fact responsible for the character's death. I thought: why not reverse the trick and stand it on its head? Why not have a story in which an apparent murder turns out to be a suicide? As far as I could tell, no one had ever done it.

It was no more than idle speculation, a two-in-the-morning brain wave, but I couldn't fall asleep, and with my heart beginning to race and flutter in my chest, I pursued the thought a little further, trying to calm myself by cooking up a story to go with my curveball premise. I had no stake in the results, was simply groping for a sedative to tranquilize my nerves, but one piece of the puzzle kept fitting beside another, and by the time I drifted off to sleep, I had worked out the barebones plot of a mystery novel.

The next morning, it occurred to me that it might not be such a bad idea to sit down and write the damn thing. It wasn't that I had anything better to do. I hadn't written a decent syllable in months, I couldn't find a job, and my bank account was down to almost nothing. If I could crank out a reasonably good detective novel, then surely there would be a few dollars in it. I wasn't dreaming of bags of gold anymore. Just an honest wage for an honest day's work, a chance to survive.

I started in early June, and by the end of August I had completed a manuscript of just over three hundred pages. The book was an exercise in pure imitation, a conscious attempt to write a book that sounded like other books, but just because I wrote it for money doesn't mean that I didn't enjoy myself. As an example of the genre, it seemed no worse than many others I had read, much better than some. It was good enough to be published, in any case, and that was all I was after. My sole ambition for the novel was to turn it into cash and pay off as many bills as I could.

Once again, I ran straight into problems. I was doing everything in my power to prostitute myself, offering up my wares for rock-bottom prices, and still no one would have me. In this case, the problem wasn't so much what I was trying to sell (as with the game), but my own astonishing ineptitude as a salesman. The only editors I knew were the ones who hired me to translate books, and they were ill qualified to pass judgment on popular fiction. They had no experience with it, had never read or published books like mine, and were scarcely even aware that such a thing as mystery novels existed, let alone the assorted subgenres within the field: private-eye novels, police procedurals, and so on. I sent off my manuscript to one of these editors, and when he finally got around to reading it, his response was surprisingly enthusiastic. "It's good," he said, "very good. Just get rid of the detective stuff, and you'll have yourself an excellent psychological thriller."

"But that's the whole point," I said. "It's a detective novel."

"Maybe so," he said, "but we don't publish detective novels. Rework it, though, and I guarantee that we'll be interested."

Altering the book might have interested him, but it didn't interest me. I had written it in a specific way for a specific purpose, and to begin dismantling it now would have been absurd. I realized that I needed an agent, someone to shop the novel around for me while I took care of more pressing matters. The rub was that I didn't have the first idea how to find one. Poets don't have agents, after all. Translators don't have agents. Book reviewers who make two or three hundred dollars per article don't have agents. I had lived my life in the remote provinces of the literary world, far removed from the commercial center where books and money have something to say to each other, and the only people I knew were young poets whose work appeared in little magazines, publishers of small, not-for-profit presses, and various other cranks, misfits, and exiles. There was no one to turn to for help, not one scrap of knowledge or information available to me. If there was, I was too dumb to know where to find it. Quite by chance, an old high school friend mentioned that his ex-wife happened to run a literary agency, and when I told him about my manuscript, he urged me to send it to her. I did, and after waiting nearly a month for an answer, I was turned down. There wasn't enough money in this kind of thing, she said, and it wasn't worth her trouble. No one read private-eye novels anymore. They were passé, old hat, a losing proposition all around. Word for word, it was identical to the speech the game broker had given me not ten days before.

Eventually, the book was published, but that didn't happen until four years later. In the meantime, all sorts of catastrophes occurred, one upheaval followed another, and the last thing on my mind was the fate of my pseudonymous potboiler. My marriage broke up in November 1978, and the typescript of the money novel was shoved into a plastic bag, all but lost and forgotten through several changes of address. My father died just two months after that—suddenly, unexpectedly, without ever having been sick a day in his life—and for many weeks the bulk of my time was spent taking care of estate business, settling his affairs, tying up loose ends. His death hit me hard, caused immense sorrow inside me, and whatever energy I had for writing I used to write about him. The terrible irony was that he had left me something in his will. It wasn't a great amount as far as inheritances go, but it was more money than I had ever had before, and it helped see me through the transition from one life into another. I moved back to New York and kept on writing. Eventually, I fell in love and married again. In the course of those four years, everything changed for me.

Sometime in the middle of that period, in late 1980 or early 1981, I received a call from a man I had met once before. He was the friend of a friend, and since the meeting had taken place a good eight or nine years earlier, I could scarcely remember who he was. He announced that he was planning to start a publishing company and wondered if I happened to have a manuscript he could look at. It wasn't going to be just another small press, he explained, but a real business, a *commercial operation*. Hmmm, I said, remembering the plastic bag at the bottom of my bedroom closet, if that's the case, then I just might have something for you. I told him about the detective novel, and when he said that he would be interested in reading it, I made a copy and sent it to him that week. Unexpectedly, he liked it. Even more unexpectedly, he said that he wanted to go ahead and publish it.

I was happy, of course—happy and amused, but also a trifle apprehensive. It seemed almost too good to be true. Publishing books wasn't supposed to be so easy, and I wondered if there wasn't a catch to it somewhere. He was running the company out of his Upper West Side apartment, I noticed, but the contract I received in the mail was a real contract, and after looking it over and deciding that the terms were acceptable, I couldn't think of a reason not to sign it. There was no advance, of course, no money up front, but royalties would begin with the first copy sold. I figured that was normal for a new publisher just getting off the ground, and since he had no investors or serious financial support, he couldn't very well cough up money he didn't have. Needless to say, his business didn't quite qualify as a *commercial operation*, but he was hoping it would become one, and who was I to throw a wet blanket on his hopes?

He managed to bring out one book nine months later (a paperback reprint), but production of my novel dragged on for close to two years. By the time it was printed, he had lost his distributor, had no money left, and to all intents and purposes was dead as a publisher. A few copies made it into a couple of New York bookstores, hand-delivered by the publisher himself, but the rest of the edition remained in cardboard boxes, gathering dust on the floor of a warehouse somewhere in Brooklyn. For all I know, the books are still there.

Having gone that far with the business, I felt I should make one last effort and see if I couldn't conclude it once and for all. Since the novel had been "published," a hardcover edition was no longer possible, but there were still the paperback houses to consider, and I didn't want to walk away from the book until they'd had a chance to turn it down. I started looking for an agent again, and this time I found the right one. She sent the novel to an editor at Avon Books, and three days later it was accepted. Just like that, in no time at all. They offered an advance of two thousand dollars, and I agreed to it. No haggling, no counteroffer, no tricky negotiations. I felt vindicated, and I didn't care about the details anymore. After splitting the advance with the original publisher (as per contract), I was left with a thousand dollars. Deduct the ten percent agent's commission, and I wound up making a grand total of nine hundred dollars.

So much for writing books to make money. So much for selling out.

1996

TRUE STORIES

The Red Notebook

1

In 1972, a close friend of mine ran into trouble with the law. She was in Ireland that year, living in a small village not far from the town of Sligo. As it happened, I was visiting on the day a plainclothes detective drove up to her cottage and presented her with a summons to appear in court. The charges were serious enough to require a lawyer. My friend asked around and was given a name, and the next morning we bicycled into town to meet with this person and discuss the case. To my astonishment, he worked for a firm called Argue and Phibbs.

This is a true story. If there are those who doubt me, I challenge them to visit Sligo and see for themselves if I have made it up or not. I have reveled in these names for the past twenty years, but even though I can prove that Argue and Phibbs were real men, the fact that the one name should have been coupled with the other (to form an even more delicious joke, an out-and-out sendup of the legal profession) is something I still find hard to believe.

According to my latest information (three or four years ago), the firm continues to do a thriving business.

2

The following year (1973), I was offered a job as caretaker of a farmhouse in the south of France. My friend's legal troubles were well behind her, and since our on-again off-again romance seemed to be on again, we decided to join forces and take the job together. We had both run out of money by then, and without this offer we would have been compelled to return to America—which neither one of us was prepared to do just yet.

It turned out to be a curious year. On the one hand, the place was beautiful: a large, eighteenth-century stone house bordered by vineyards on one side and a national forest on the other. The nearest village was two kilometers away, but it was inhabited by no more than forty people, none of whom was under sixty or seventy years old. It was an ideal spot for two young writers to spend a year, and L. and I both worked hard there, accomplishing more in that house than either one of us would have thought possible.

On the other hand, we lived on the brink of permanent catastrophe. Our employers, an American couple who lived in Paris, sent us a small monthly salary (fifty dollars), a gas allowance for the car, and money to feed the two Labrador retrievers who were part of the household. All in all, it was a generous arrangement. There was no rent to pay, and even if our salary fell short of what we needed to live on, it gave us a head start on each month's expenses. Our plan was to earn the rest by doing translations. Before leaving Paris and settling in the country, we had set up a number of jobs to see us through the year. What we had neglected to take into account was that publishers are often slow to pay their bills. We had also forgotten to consider that checks sent from one country to another can take weeks to clear, and that once they do, bank charges and exchange fees cut into the amounts of those checks. Since L. and I had left no margin for error or miscalculation, we often found ourselves in quite desperate straits.

I remember savage nicotine fits, my body numb with need as I scrounged among sofa cushions and crawled behind cupboards in search of loose coins. For eighteen centimes (about three and a half cents), you could buy a brand of cigarettes called Parisiennes, which were sold in packs of four. I remember feeding the dogs and thinking that they ate better than I did. I remember conversations with L. in which we seriously considered opening a can of dog food and eating it for dinner.

Our only other source of income that year came from a man named James Sugar. (I don't mean to insist on metaphorical names, but facts are facts, and there's nothing I can do about it.) Sugar worked as a staff photographer for *National Geographic*, and he entered our lives because he was collaborating with one of our employers on an article about the region. He took pictures for several months, crisscrossing Provence in a rented car provided by his magazine, and whenever he was in our neck of the woods he would spend the night with us. Since the magazine also provided him with an expense account, he would very graciously slip us the money that had been allotted for his hotel costs. If I remember correctly, the sum came to fifty francs a night. In effect, L. and I became his private innkeepers, and since Sugar was an amiable man into the bargain, we were always glad to see him. The only problem was that we never knew when he was going to turn up. He never called in advance, and more often than not weeks would go by between his visits. We therefore learned not to count on Mr. Sugar. He would arrive out of nowhere, pulling up in front of the house in his shiny blue car, stay for a night or two, and then disappear again. Each time he left, we assumed that was the last time we would ever see him.

The worst moments came for us in the late winter and early spring. Checks failed to arrive, one of the dogs was stolen, and little by little we ate our way through the stockpile of food in the kitchen. In the end, we had nothing left but a bag of onions, a bottle of cooking oil, and a packaged pie crust that someone had bought before we ever moved into the house—a stale remnant from the previous summer. L. and I held out all morning and into the afternoon, but by two-thirty hunger had gotten the better of us, and so we went into the kitchen to prepare our last meal. Given the paucity of elements we had to work with, an onion pie was the only dish that made sense.

After our concoction had been in the oven for what seemed a sufficient length of time, we took it out, set it on the table, and dug in. Against all our expectations, we both found it delicious. I think we even went so far as to say that it was the best food we had ever tasted, but no doubt that was a ruse, a feeble attempt to keep our spirits up. Once we had chewed a little more, however, disappointment set in. Reluctantly—ever so reluctantly—we were forced to admit that the pie had not yet cooked through, that the center was still too cold to eat. There was nothing to be done but put it back in the oven for another ten or fifteen minutes. Considering how hungry we were, and considering that our salivary glands had just been activated, relinquishing the pie was not easy.

To stifle our impatience, we went outside for a brief stroll, thinking the time would pass more quickly if we removed ourselves from the good smells in the kitchen. As I remember it, we circled the house once, perhaps twice. Perhaps we drifted into a deep conversation about something (I can't remember), but however it happened, and however long we were gone, by the time we entered the house again the kitchen was filled with smoke. We rushed to the oven and pulled out the pie, but it was too late. Our meal was dead. It had been incinerated, burned to a charred and blackened mass, and not one morsel could be salvaged.

It sounds like a funny story now, but at the time it was anything but funny. We had fallen into a dark hole, and neither one of us could think of a way to get out. In all my years of struggling to be a man, I doubt there has ever been a moment when I felt less inclined to laugh or crack jokes. This was really the end, and it was a terrible and frightening place to be.

That was at four o'clock in the afternoon. Less than an hour later, the errant Mr. Sugar suddenly appeared, driving up to the house in a cloud of dust, gravel and dirt crunching all around him. If I think about it hard enough, I can still see the naive and goofy smile on his face as he bounced out of the car and said hello. It was a miracle. It was a genuine miracle, and I was there to witness it with my own eyes, to live it in my own flesh. Until that moment, I had thought those things happened only in books.

Sugar treated us to dinner that night in a two-star restaurant. We ate copiously and well, we emptied several bottles of wine, we laughed our heads off. And yet, delicious as that food must have been, I can't remember a thing about it. But I have never forgotten the taste of the onion pie.

3

Not long after I returned to New York (July 1974), a friend told me the following story. It is set in Yugoslavia, during what must have been the last months of the Second World War.

S.'s uncle was a member of a Serbian partisan group that fought against the Nazi occupation. One morning, he and his comrades woke up to find themselves surrounded by German troops. They were holed up in a farmhouse somewhere in the country, a foot of snow lay on the ground, and there was no escape. Not knowing what else to do, the men decided to draw lots. Their plan was to burst out of the farmhouse one by one, dash through the snow, and see if they couldn't make it to safety. According to the results of the draw, S.'s uncle was supposed to go third.

He watched through the window as the first man ran out into the snow-covered field. There was a barrage of machine-gun fire from across the woods, and the man was cut down. A moment later, the second man ran out, and the same thing happened. The machine guns blasted, and he fell down dead in the snow.

Then it was my friend's uncle's turn. I don't know if he hesitated at the doorway, I don't know what thoughts were pounding through his head at that moment. The only thing I was told was that he started to run, charging through the snow for all he was worth. It seemed as if he ran forever. Then, suddenly, he felt pain in his leg. A second after that, an overpowering warmth spread through his body, and a second after that he lost consciousness.

When he woke up, he found himself lying on his back in a peasant's cart. He had no idea how much time had elapsed, no idea of how he had been rescued. He had simply opened his eyes—and there he was, lying in a cart that some horse or mule was pulling down a country road, staring up at the back of a peasant's head. He studied the back of that head for several seconds, and then loud explosions began to erupt from the woods. Too weak to move, he kept looking at the back of the head, and suddenly it was gone. It just flew off the peasant's body, and where a moment before there had been a whole man, there was now a man without a head.

More noise, more confusion. Whether the horse went on pulling the cart or not I can't say, but within minutes, perhaps even seconds, a large contingent of Russian troops came rolling down the road. Jeeps, tanks, scores of soldiers. When the commanding officer took a look at S.'s uncle's leg, he quickly dispatched him to an infirmary that had been set up in the neighborhood. It was no more than a rickety wooden shack— a henhouse, maybe, or an outbuilding on some farm. There the Russian army doctor pronounced the leg past saving. It was too severely damaged, he said, and he was going to have to cut it off.

My friend's uncle began to scream. "Don't cut off my leg," he cried. "Please, I beg of you, don't cut off my leg!" But no one listened to him. The medics strapped him to the operating table, and the doctor picked up the saw. Just as he was about to pierce the skin of the leg, there was another explosion. The roof of the infirmary collapsed, the walls fell down, the entire place was obliterated. And once again, S.'s uncle lost consciousness.

When he woke up this time, he found himself lying in a bed. The sheets were clean and soft, there were pleasant smells in the room, and his leg was still attached to his body. A moment later, he was looking into the face of a beautiful young woman. She was smiling at him and feeding him broth with a spoon. With no knowledge of how it had happened, he had been rescued again and carried to another farmhouse. For several minutes after coming to, S.'s uncle wasn't sure if he was alive or dead. It seemed possible to him that he had woken up in heaven.

He stayed on in the house during his recovery and fell in love with the beautiful young woman, but nothing ever came of that romance. I wish I could say why, but S. never filled me in on the details. What I do know is that his uncle kept his leg—and that once the war was over, he moved to America to begin a new life. Somehow or other (the circumstances are obscure to me), he wound up as an insurance salesman in Chicago.

4

L. and I were married in 1974. Our son was born in 1977, but by the following year our marriage had ended. None of that is relevant now—except to set the scene for an incident that took place in the spring of 1980.

We were both living in Brooklyn then, about three or four blocks from each other, and our son divided his time between the two apartments. One morning, I had to stop by L.'s house to pick up Daniel and walk him to nursery school. I can't remember if I went inside the building or if Daniel came down the stairs himself, but I vividly recall that just as we were about to walk off together, L. opened the window of her third-floor apartment to throw me some money. Why she did that is also forgotten. Perhaps she wanted me to replenish a parking meter for her, perhaps I was supposed to do an errand, I don't know. All that remains is the open window and the image of a dime flying through the air. I see it with such clarity, it's almost as if I have studied photographs of that instant, as if it's part of a recurring dream I've had ever since.

But the dime hit the branch of a tree, and its downward arc into my hand was disrupted. It bounced off the tree, landed soundlessly somewhere nearby, and then it was gone. I remember bending down and searching the pavement, digging among the leaves and twigs at the base of the tree, but the dime was nowhere to be found.

I can place that event in early spring because I know that later the same day I attended a baseball game at Shea Stadium—the opening game of the season. A friend of mine had been offered tickets, and he had generously invited me to go along with him. I had never been to an opening game before, and I remember the occasion well.

We arrived early (something about collecting the tickets at a certain window), and as my friend went off to complete the transaction, I waited for him outside one of the entrances to the stadium. Not a single soul was around. I ducked into a little alcove to light a cigarette (a strong wind was blowing that day), and there, sitting on the ground not two inches from my feet, was a dime. I bent down, picked it up, and put it in my pocket. Ridiculous as it might sound, I felt certain that it was the same dime I had lost in Brooklyn that morning.

5

In my son's nursery school, there was a little girl whose parents were going through a divorce. I particularly liked her father, a struggling painter who earned his living by doing architectural renderings. His paintings were quite beautiful, I thought, but he never had much luck in convincing dealers to support his work. The one time he did have a show, the gallery promptly went out of business.

B. was not an intimate friend, but we enjoyed each other's company, and whenever I saw him I would return home with renewed admiration for his steadfastness and inner calm. He was not a man who grumbled or felt sorry for himself. However gloomy things had become for him in recent years (endless money problems, lack of artistic success, threats of eviction from his landlord, difficulties with his ex-wife), none of it seemed to throw him off course. He continued to paint with the same passion as ever, and unlike so many others, he never expressed any bitterness or envy toward less talented artists who were doing better than he was.

When he wasn't working on his own canvases, he would sometimes go to the Metropolitan Museum and make copies of the old masters. I remember a Caravaggio he once did that struck me as utterly remarkable. It wasn't a copy so much as a replica, an exact duplication of the original. On one of those visits to the museum, a Texas millionaire spotted B. at work and was so impressed that he commissioned him to do a copy of a Renoir painting—which he then presented to his fiancée as a gift.

B. was exceedingly tall (six-five or six-six), good-looking, and gentle in his manner—qualities that made him especially attractive to women. Once his divorce was behind him and he began to circulate again, he had no trouble finding female companions. I only saw him about two or three times a year, but each time I did, there was another woman in his life. All of them were obviously mad for him. You had only to watch them looking at B. to know how they felt, but for one reason or another, none of these affairs lasted very long.

After two or three years, B.'s landlord finally made good on his threats and evicted him from his loft. B. moved out of the city, and I lost touch with him.

Several more years went by, and then one night B. came back to town to attend a dinner party. My wife and I were also there, and since we knew that B. was about to get married, we asked him to tell us the story of how he had met his future wife.

About six months earlier, he said, he had been talking to a friend on the phone. This friend was worried about him, and after a while he began to scold B. for not having married again. You've been divorced for seven years now, he said, and in that time you could have settled down with any one of a dozen attractive and remarkable women. But no one is ever good enough for you, and you've turned them all away. What's wrong with you, B.? What in the world do you want?

There's nothing wrong with me, B. said. I just haven't found the right person, that's all.

At the rate you're going, you never will, the friend answered. I mean, have you ever met one woman who comes close to what you're looking for? Name one. I dare you to name just one.

Startled by his friend's vehemence, B. paused to consider the question carefully. Yes, he finally said, there was one. A woman by the name of E., whom he had known as a student at Harvard more than twenty years ago. But she had been involved with another man at the time, and he had been involved with another woman (his future ex-wife), and nothing had developed between them. He had no idea where E. was now, he said, but if he could meet someone like her, he knew he wouldn't hesitate to get married again.

That was the end of the conversation. Until mentioning her to his friend, B. hadn't thought about this woman in over ten years, but now that she had resurfaced in his mind, he had trouble thinking about any-thing else. For the next three or four days, he thought about her con-stantly, unable to shake the feeling that his one chance for happiness had been lost many years ago. Then, almost as if the intensity of these thoughts had sent a signal out into the world, the phone rang one night, and there was E. on the other end of the line.

B. kept her on the phone for more than three hours. He scarcely knew what he said to her, but he went on talking until past midnight, under-standing that something momentous had happened and that he mustn't let her escape again.

After graduating from college, E. had joined a dance company, and for the past twenty years she had devoted herself exclusively to her career. She had never married, and now that she was about to retire as a performer, she was calling old friends from her past, trying to make contact with the world again. She had no family (her parents had been killed in a car crash when she was a small girl) and had been raised by two aunts, both of whom were now dead.

B. arranged to see her the next night. Once they were together, it didn't take long for him to discover that his feelings for her were just as strong as he had imagined. He fell in love with her all over again, and several weeks later they were engaged to be married.

To make the story even more perfect, it turned out that E. was independently wealthy. Her aunts had been rich, and after they died she had inherited all their money—which meant that not only had B. found true love, but the crushing money problems that had plagued him for so many years had suddenly vanished. All in one fell swoop.

A year or two after the wedding, they had a child. At last report, mother, father, and baby were doing just fine.

6

In much the same spirit, although spanning a shorter period of time (several months as opposed to twenty years), another friend, R., told me of a certain out-of-the-way book that he had been trying to locate without success, scouring bookstores and catalogues for what was supposed to be a remarkable work that he very much wanted to read, and how, one afternoon as he made his way through the city, he took a shortcut through Grand Central Station, walked up the staircase that leads to Vanderbilt Avenue, and caught sight of a young woman standing by the marble railing with a book in front of her: the same book he had been trying so desperately to track down.

Although he is not someone who normally speaks to strangers, R. was too stunned by the coincidence to remain silent. "Believe it or not," he said to the young woman, "I've been looking everywhere for that book."

"It's wonderful," the young woman answered. "I just finished reading it."

"Do you know where I could find another copy?" R. asked. "I can't tell you how much it would mean to me."

"This one is for you," the woman answered.

"But it's yours," R. said.

"It *was* mine," the woman said, "but now I'm finished with it. I came here today to give it to you."

7

Twelve years ago, my wife's sister went off to live in Taiwan. Her intention was to study Chinese (which she now speaks with breathtaking fluency) and to support herself by giving English lessons to native Chinese speakers in Taipei. That was approximately one year before I met my wife, who was then a graduate student at Columbia University.

One day, my future sister-in-law was talking to an American friend, a young woman who had also gone to Taipei to study Chinese. The conversation came around to the subject of their families back home, which in turn led to the following exchange:

"I have a sister who lives in New York," my future sister-in-law said.

"So do I," her friend answered.

"My sister lives on the Upper West Side."

"So does mine."

"My sister lives on West 109th Street."

"Believe it or not, so does mine."

"My sister lives at 309 West 109th Street."

"So does mine!"

"My sister lives on the second floor of 309 West 109th Street."

The friend took a deep breath and said, "I know this sounds crazy, but so does mine."

It is scarcely possible for two cities to be farther apart than Taipei and New York. They are at opposite ends of the earth, separated by a distance of more than ten thousand miles, and when it is day in one it is night in the other. As the two young women in Taipei marveled over the astounding connection they had just uncovered, they realized that their two sisters were probably asleep at that moment. On the same floor of the same building in northern Manhattan, each one was sleeping in her own apartment, unaware of the conversation that was taking place about them on the other side of the world.

Although they were neighbors, it turned out that the two sisters in New York did not know each other. When they finally met (two years later), neither one of them was living in that building anymore.

Siri and I were married then. One evening, on our way to an appointment somewhere, we happened to stop in at a bookstore on Broadway to browse for a few minutes. We must have wandered into different aisles, and because Siri wanted to show me something, or because I wanted to show her something (I can't remember), one of us spoke the other's name out loud. A second later, a woman came rushing up to us. "You're Paul Auster and Siri Hustvedt, aren't you?" she said. "Yes," we said, "that's exactly who we are. How did you know that?" The woman then explained that her sister and Siri's sister had been students together in Taiwan.

The circle had been closed at last. Since that evening in the bookstore ten years ago, this woman has been one of our best and most loyal friends.

8

Three summers ago, a letter turned up in my mailbox. It came in a white oblong envelope and was addressed to someone whose name was unfamiliar to me: Robert M. Morgan of Seattle, Washington. Various post office markings were stamped across the front: *Not Deliverable, Unable to Forward, Return to Writer.* Mr. Morgan's name had been crossed out with a pen, and beside it someone had written *Not at this address.* Drawn in the same blue ink, an arrow pointed to the upper-left-hand corner of the envelope, accompanied by the words *Return to sender.* Assuming that the post office had made a mistake, I checked the upper-left-hand corner to see who the sender was. There, to my absolute bewilderment, I discovered my own name and my own address. Not only that, but this information was printed on a custom-made address label (one of those labels you can order in packs of two hundred from advertisements on matchbook covers). The spelling of my name was correct, the address was my address—and yet the fact was (and still is) that I have never owned or ordered a set of printed address labels in my life.

Inside, there was a single-spaced typewritten letter that began: "Dear Robert, In response to your letter dated July 15, 1989, I can only say that, like other authors, I often receive letters concerning my work." Then, in a bombastic, pretentious style, riddled with quotations from French philosophers and oozing with a tone of conceit and self-satisfaction, the letter-writer went on to praise "Robert" for the ideas he had developed about one of my novels in a college course on the contemporary novel.

It was a contemptible letter, the kind of letter I would never dream of writing to anyone, and yet it was signed with my name. The handwriting did not resemble mine, but that was small comfort. Someone was out there trying to impersonate me, and as far as I know he still is.

One friend suggested that this was an example of "mail art." Knowing that the letter could not be delivered to Robert Morgan (since there was no such person), the author of the letter was actually addressing his remarks to me. But that would imply an unwarranted faith in the U.S. Postal Service, and I doubt that someone who would go to the trouble of ordering address labels in my name and then sitting down to write such an arrogant, high-flown letter would leave anything to chance. Or would he? Perhaps the smart alecks of this world believe that everything will always go their way.

I have scant hope of ever getting to the bottom of this little mystery. The prankster did a good job of covering his tracks, and he has not been heard from since. What puzzles me about my own behavior is that I have not thrown away the letter, even though it continues to give me chills every time I look at it. A sensible man would have tossed the thing in the garbage. Instead, for reasons I do not understand, I have kept it on my work table for the past three years, allowing it to become a permanent fixture among my pens and notebooks and erasers. Perhaps I keep it there as a monument to my own folly. Perhaps it is a way to remind myself that I know nothing, that the world I live in will go on escaping me forever.

9

One of my closest friends is a French poet by the name of C. We have known each other for more than twenty years now, and while we don't see each other often (he lives in Paris and I live in New York), the bond between us remains strong. It is a fraternal bond, somehow, as if in some former life we had actually been brothers.

C. is a man of manifold contradictions. He is both open to the world and shut off from it, a charismatic figure with scores of friends everywhere (legendary for his kindness, his humor, his sparkling conversation) and yet someone who has been wounded by life, who struggles to perform the simple tasks that most other people take for granted. An exceptionally gifted poet and thinker about poetry, C. is nevertheless hampered by frequent writing blocks, streaks of morbid self-doubt, and surprisingly (for someone who is so generous, so profoundly lacking in mean-spiritedness), a capacity for long-standing grudges and quarrels, usually over some trifle or abstract principle. No one is more universally admired than C., no one has more talent, no one so readily commands the center of attention, and yet he has always done everything in his power to marginalize himself. Since his separation from his wife many years ago, he has lived alone in a number of small, one-room apartments, subsisting on almost no money and only fitful bouts of employment, publishing little, and refusing to write a single word of criticism, even though he reads everything and knows more about contemporary poetry than anyone in France. To those of us who love him (and we are many), C. is often a cause of concern. To the degree that we respect him and care about his well-being, we also worry about him.

He had a rough childhood. I can't say to what extent that explains anything, but the facts should not be overlooked. His father apparently ran off with another woman when C. was a little boy, and after that my friend grew up with his mother, an only child with no family life to speak of. I have never met C.'s mother, but by all accounts she is a bizarre character. She went through a series of love affairs during C.'s childhood and adolescence, each with a man younger than the man before him. By the time C. left home to enter the army at the age of twenty-one, his mother's boyfriend was scarcely older than he was. In more recent years, the central purpose of her life has been a campaign to promote the canonization of a certain Italian priest (whose name eludes me now). She has besieged the Catholic authorities with countless letters defending the holiness of this man, and at one point she even commissioned an artist to create a life-size statue of the priest—which now stands in her front yard as an enduring testament to her cause.

Although not a father himself, C. became a kind of pseudo-father seven or eight years ago. After a falling out with his girlfriend (during which they temporarily broke up), his girlfriend had a brief affair with another man and became pregnant. The affair ended almost at once, but she decided to have the baby on her own. A little girl was born, and even though C. is not her real father, he has devoted himself to her since the day of her birth and adores her as if she were his own flesh and blood.

One day about four years ago, C. happened to be visiting a friend. In the apartment there was a *Minitel*, a small computer given out for free by the French telephone company. Among other things, the *Minitel* contains the address and phone number of every person in France. As C. sat there playing with his friend's new machine, it suddenly occurred to him to look up his father's address. He found it in Lyon. When he returned home later that day, he stuffed one of his books into an envelope and sent it off to the address in Lyon—initiating the first contact with his father in over forty years. None of it made any sense to him. Until he found himself doing these things, it had never even crossed his mind that he wanted to do them.

That same night, he ran into another friend in a café—a woman psychoanalyst—and told her about these strange, unpremeditated acts. It was as if he had felt his father calling out to him, he said, as if some uncanny force had unleashed itself inside him. Considering that he had absolutely no memories of the man, he couldn't even begin to guess when they had last seen each other.

The woman thought for a moment and said, "How old is L.?," referring to C.'s girlfriend's daughter.

"Three and a half," C. answered.

"I can't be sure," the woman said, "but I'd be willing to bet that you were three and a half the last time you saw your father. I say that because you love L. so much. Your identification with her is very strong, and you're reliving your life through her."

Several days after that, there was a reply from Lyon—a warm and perfectly gracious letter from C.'s father. After thanking C. for the book, he went on to tell him how proud he was to learn that his son had grown up to become a writer. By pure coincidence, he added, the package had been mailed on his birthday, and he was moved by the symbolism of the gesture.

None of this tallied with the stories C. had heard throughout his childhood. According to his mother, his father was a monster of selfishness who had walked out on her for a "slut" and had never wanted anything to do with his son. C. had believed these stories, and therefore he had shied away from any contact with his father. Now, on the strength of this letter, he no longer knew what to believe.

He decided to write back. The tone of his response was guarded, but nevertheless it was a response. Within days he received another reply, and this second letter was just as warm and gracious as the first had been. C. and his father began a correspondence. It went on for a month or two, and eventually C. began to consider traveling down to Lyon to meet his father face to face.

Before he could make any definite plans, he received a letter from his father's wife informing him that his father was dead. He had been in ill health for the past several years, she wrote, but the recent exchange of letters with C. had given him great happiness, and his last days had been filled with optimism and joy.

It was at this moment that I first heard about the incredible reversals that had taken place in C.'s life. Sitting on the train from Paris to Lyon (on his way to visit his "stepmother" for the first time), he wrote me a letter that sketched out the story of the past month. His handwriting reflected each jolt of the tracks, as if the speed of the train were an exact image of the thoughts racing through his head. As he put it somewhere in that letter: "I feel as if I've become a character in one of your novels."

His father's wife could not have been friendlier to him during that visit. Among other things, C. learned that his father had suffered a heart attack on the morning of his last birthday (the same day that C. had looked up his address on the *Minitel*) and that, yes, C. had been precisely three and a half years old at the time of his parents' divorce. His stepmother then went on to tell him the story of his life from his father's point of view—which contradicted everything his mother had ever told him. In this version, it was his mother who had walked out on his father; it was his mother who had forbidden his father from seeing him; it was his mother who had broken his father's heart. She told C. how his father would come around to the schoolyard when he was a little boy to look at him through the fence. C. remembered that man, but not knowing who he was, he had been afraid.

C.'s life had now become two lives. There was Version A and Version B, and both of them were his story. He had lived them both in equal measure, two truths that canceled each other out, and all along, without even knowing it, he had been stranded in the middle.

His father had owned a small stationery store (the usual stock of paper and writing materials, along with a rental library of popular books). The business had earned him a living, but not much more than that, and the estate he left behind was quite modest. The numbers are unimportant, however. What counts is that C.'s stepmother (by then an old woman) insisted on splitting the money with him half and half. There was nothing in the will that required her to do that, and morally speaking she needn't have parted with a single penny of her husband's savings. She did it because she wanted to, because it made her happier to share the money than to keep it for herself.

In thinking about friendship, particularly about how some friendships endure and others don't, I am reminded of the fact that in all my years of driving I have had just four flat tires, and that on each of these occasions the same person was in the car with me (in three different countries, spread out over a period of eight or nine years). J. was a college friend, and though there was always an edge of unease and conflict in our relations, for a time we were close. One spring while we were still undergraduates, we borrowed my father's ancient station wagon and drove up into the wilderness of Quebec. The seasons change more slowly in that part of the world, and winter was not yet over. The first flat tire did not present a problem (we were equipped with a spare), but when a second tire blew out less than an hour later, we were stranded in the bleak and frigid countryside for most of the day. At the time, I shrugged off the incident as a piece of bad luck, but four or five years later, when J. came to France to visit the house where L. and I were working as caretakers (in miserable condition, inert with depression and self-pity, unaware that he was overstaying his welcome with us), the same thing happened. We went to Aix-en-Provence for the day (a drive of about two hours), and coming back later that night on a dark, back-country road, we had another flat. Just a coincidence, I thought, and then pushed the event out of my mind. But then, four years after that, in the waning months of my marriage to L., J. came to visit us again—this time in New York State, where L. and I were living with the infant Daniel. At one point, J. and I climbed into the car to go to the store and shop for dinner. I pulled the car out of the garage, turned it around in the rutted dirt driveway, and advanced to the edge of the road to look left, right, and left before going on. Just then, as I waited for a car to pass by, I heard the unmistakable hiss of escaping air. Another tire had gone flat, and this time we hadn't even left the house. J. and I both laughed, of course, but the truth is that our friendship never really recovered from that fourth flat tire. I'm not saying that the flat tires were responsible for our drifting apart, but in some perverse way they were an emblem of how things had always stood between us, the sign of some impalpable curse. I don't want to exaggerate, but even now I can't quite bring myself to reject those flat tires as meaningless. For the fact is that J. and I have lost contact, and we have not spoken to each other in more than ten years.

In 1990, I found myself in Paris again for a few days. One afternoon, I stopped by the office of a friend to say hello and was
introduced to a Czech woman in her late forties or early fifties—an
art historian who happened to be a friend of my friend. She was an
attractive and vivacious person, I remember, but since she was on the
point of leaving when I walked in, I spent no more than five or ten
minutes in her company. As usually happens in such situations, we
talked about nothing of any importance: a town we both knew in
America, the subject of a book she was reading, the weather. Then
we shook hands, she walked out the door, and I have never seen her
again.

After she was gone, the friend I had come to visit leaned back in her
chair and said, "Do you want to hear a good story?"

"Of course," I said, "I'm always interested in good stories."

"I like my friend very much," she continued, "so don't get the wrong
idea. I'm not trying to spread gossip about her. It's just that I feel you
have a right to know this."

"Are you sure?"

"Yes, I'm sure. But you have to promise me one thing. If you ever
write the story, you mustn't use anyone's name."

"I promise," I said.

And so my friend let me in on the secret. From start to finish, it
couldn't have taken her more than three minutes to tell the story I am
about to tell now.

The woman I had just met was born in Prague during the war. When
she was still a baby, her father was captured, impressed into the German
army, and shipped off to the Russian front. She and her mother never
heard from him again. They received no letters, no news to tell them if
he was alive or dead, nothing. The war just swallowed him up, and he
vanished without a trace.

Years passed. The girl grew up. She completed her studies at the university and became a professor of art history. According to my friend,
she ran into trouble with the government during the Soviet crackdown
in the late sixties, but exactly what kind of trouble was never made clear
to me. Given the stories I know about what happened to other people
during that time, it is not very difficult to guess.

At some point, she was allowed to begin teaching again. In one of her classes, there was an exchange student from East Germany. She and this young man fell in love, and eventually they were married.

Not long after the wedding, a telegram arrived announcing the death of her husband's father. The next day, she and her husband traveled to East Germany to attend the funeral. Once there, in whatever town or city it was, she learned that her now dead father-in-law had been born in Czechoslovakia. During the war he had been captured by the Nazis, impressed into the German army, and shipped off to the Russian front. By some miracle, he had managed to survive. Instead of returning to Czechoslovakia after the war, however, he had settled in Germany under a new name, had married a German woman, and had lived there with his new family until the day of his death. The war had given him a chance to start all over again, and it seems that he had never looked back.

When my friend's friend asked what this man's name had been in Czechoslovakia, she understood that he was her father.

Which meant, of course, that insofar as her husband's father was the same man, the man she had married was also her brother.

12

One afternoon many years ago, my father's car stalled at a red light. A terrible storm was raging, and at the exact moment his engine went dead, lightning struck a large tree by the side of the road. The trunk of the tree split in two, and as my father struggled to get the car started again (unaware that the upper half of the tree was about to fall), the driver of the car behind him, seeing what was about to happen, put his foot on the accelerator and pushed my father's car through the intersection. An instant later, the tree came crashing to the ground, landing in the very spot where my father's car had just been. What was nearly the end of him proved to be no more than a close call, a brief episode in the ongoing story of his life.

A year or two after that, my father was working on the roof of a building in Jersey City. Somehow or other (I wasn't there to witness it), he slipped off the edge and started falling to the ground. Once again he was headed for certain disaster, and once again he was saved. A clothesline broke his fall, and he walked away from the accident with only a few bumps and bruises. Not even a concussion. Not a single broken bone.

That same year, our neighbors across the street hired two men to paint their house. One of the workers fell off the roof and was killed.

The little girl who lived in that house happened to be my sister's best friend. One winter night, the two of them went to a costume party (they were six or seven years old, and I was nine or ten). It had been arranged that my father would pick them up after the party, and when the time came I went along to keep him company in the car. It was bitter cold that night, and the roads were covered with treacherous sheets of ice. My father drove carefully, and we made the journey back and forth without incident. As we pulled up in front of the girl's house, however, a number of unlikely events occurred all at once.

My sister's friend was dressed as a fairy princess. To complete the outfit, she had borrowed a pair of her mother's high heels, and because her feet swam in those shoes, every step she took was turned into an adventure. My father stopped the car and climbed out to accompany her to the front door. I was in the back with the girls, and in order to let my sister's friend out, I had to get out first. I remember standing on the curb as she disentangled herself from the seat, and just as she stepped into the open air, I noticed that the car was rolling slowly in reverse—either because of the ice or because my father had forgotten to engage the emergency brake (I don't know)—but before I could tell my father what was happening, my sister's friend touched the curb with her mother's high heels and slipped. She went skidding under the car—which was still moving—and there she was, about to be crushed to death by the wheels of my father's Chevy. As I remember it, she didn't make a sound. Without pausing to think, I bent down from the curb, grabbed hold of her right hand, and in one quick gesture yanked her to the sidewalk. An instant later, my father finally noticed that the car was moving. He jumped back into the driver's seat, stepped on the brake, and brought the machine to a halt. From start to finish, the whole chain of misadventures couldn't have taken more than eight or ten seconds.

For years afterward, I walked around feeling that this had been my finest moment. I had actually saved someone's life, and in retrospect I was always astonished by how quickly I had acted, by how sure my movements had been at the critical juncture. I saw the rescue in my mind again and again; again and again I relived the sensation of pulling that little girl out from under the car.

About two years after that night, our family moved to another house.

My sister fell out of touch with her friend, and I myself did not see her for another fifteen years.

It was June, and my sister and I had both come back to town for a short visit. Just by chance, her old friend dropped by to say hello. She was all grown up now, a young woman of twenty-two who had graduated from college earlier that month, and I must say that I felt some pride in seeing that she had made it to adulthood in one piece. In a casual sort of way, I mentioned the night I had pulled her out from under the car. I was curious to know how well she remembered her brush with death, but from the look on her face when I asked the question, it was clear that she remembered nothing. A blank stare. A slight frown. A shrug. She remembered nothing!

I realized then that she hadn't known the car was moving. She hadn't even known that she was in danger. The whole incident had taken place in a flash: ten seconds of her life, an interval of no account, and none of it had left the slightest mark on her. For me, on the other hand, those seconds had been a defining experience, a singular event in my internal history.

Most of all, it stuns me to acknowledge that I am talking about something that happened in 1956 or 1957—and that the little girl of that night is now over forty years old.

13

My first novel was inspired by a wrong number. I was alone in my apartment in Brooklyn one afternoon, sitting at my desk and trying to work when the telephone rang. If I am not mistaken, it was the spring of 1980, not many days after I found the dime outside Shea Stadium.

I picked up the receiver, and the man on the other end asked if he was talking to the Pinkerton Agency. I told him no, he had dialed the wrong number, and hung up. Then I went back to work and promptly forgot about the call.

The next afternoon, the telephone rang again. It turned out to be the same person asking the same question I had been asked the day before: "Is this the Pinkerton Agency?" Again I said no, and again I hung up. This time, however, I started thinking about what would have happened if I had said yes. What if I had pretended to be a detective from the Pinkerton Agency? I wondered. What if I had actually taken on the case?

To tell the truth, I felt that I had squandered a rare opportunity. If the man ever called again, I told myself, I would at least talk to him a little bit and try to find out what was going on. I waited for the telephone to ring again, but the third call never came.

After that, wheels started turning in my head, and little by little an entire world of possibilities opened up to me. When I sat down to write *City of Glass* a year later, the wrong number had been transformed into the crucial event of the book, the mistake that sets the whole story in motion. A man named Quinn receives a phone call from someone who wants to talk to Paul Auster, the private detective. Just as I did, Quinn tells the caller he has dialed the wrong number. It happens again on the next night, and again Quinn hangs up. Unlike me, however, Quinn is given another chance. When the phone rings again on the third night, he plays along with the caller and takes on the case. Yes, he says, I'm Paul Auster—and at that moment the madness begins.

Most of all, I wanted to remain faithful to my original impulse. Unless I stuck to the spirit of what had really happened, I felt there wouldn't have been any purpose to writing the book. That meant implicating myself in the action of the story (or at least someone who resembled me, who bore my name), and it also meant writing about detectives who were not detectives, about impersonation, about mysteries that cannot be solved. For better or worse, I felt I had no choice.

All well and good. I finished the book ten years ago, and since then I have gone on to occupy myself with other projects, other ideas, other books. Less than two months ago, however, I learned that books are never finished, that it is possible for stories to go on writing themselves without an author.

I was alone in my apartment in Brooklyn that afternoon, sitting at my desk and trying to work when the telephone rang. This was a different apartment from the one I had in 1980—a different apartment with a different telephone number. I picked up the receiver, and the man on the other end asked if he could speak to Mr. Quinn. He had a Spanish accent and I did not recognize the voice. For a moment I thought it might be one of my friends trying to pull my leg. "Mr. Quinn?" I said. "Is this some kind of joke or what?"

No, it wasn't a joke. The man was in dead earnest. He had to talk to Mr. Quinn, and would I please put him on the line. Just to make sure, I asked him to spell out the name. The caller's accent was quite thick, and I was hoping that he wanted to talk to Mr. Queen. But no such luck.

"Q-U-I-N-N," the man answered. I suddenly grew scared, and for a moment or two I couldn't get any words out of my mouth. "I'm sorry," I said at last, "there's no Mr. Quinn here. You've dialed the wrong number." The man apologized for disturbing me, and then we both hung up.

This really happened. Like everything else I have set down in this red notebook, it is a true story.

1992

Why Write?

1

A German friend tells of the circumstances that preceded the births of her two daughters.

Nineteen years ago, hugely pregnant and already several weeks past due, A. sat down on the sofa in her living room and turned on the television set. As luck would have it, the opening credits of a film were just coming on screen. It was *The Nun's Story*, a 1950s Hollywood drama starring Audrey Hepburn. Glad for the distraction, A. settled in to watch the movie and immediately got caught up in it. Halfway through, she went into labor. Her husband drove her to the hospital, and she never learned how the film turned out.

Three years later, pregnant with her second child, A. sat down on the sofa and turned on the television set once again. Once again a film was playing, and once again it was *The Nun's Story* with Audrey Hepburn. Even more remarkable (and A. was very emphatic about this point), she had tuned in to the film at the precise moment where she had left off three years earlier. This time she was able to see the film through to the end. Less than fifteen minutes later, her water broke, and she went off to the hospital to give birth for the second time.

These two daughters are A.'s only children. The first labor was extremely difficult (my friend nearly didn't make it and was ill for many months afterward), but the second delivery went smoothly, with no complications of any kind.

2

Five years ago, I spent the summer with my wife and children in Vermont, renting an old, isolated farmhouse on the top of a mountain. One day, a woman from the next town stopped by to visit with her two children, a girl of four and a boy of eighteen months. My daughter Sophie had just turned three, and she and the girl enjoyed playing with each other. My wife and I sat down in the kitchen with our guest, and the children ran off to amuse themselves.

Five minutes later, there was a loud crash. The little boy had wandered into the front hall at the other end of the house, and since my wife had put a vase of flowers in that hall just two hours earlier, it wasn't difficult to guess what had happened. I didn't even have to look to know that the floor was covered with broken glass and pools of water—along with the stems and petals of a dozen scattered flowers.

I was annoyed. Goddamn kids, I said to myself. Goddamn people with their goddamn clumsy kids. Who gave them the right to drop by without calling first?

I told my wife that I'd clean up the mess, and so while she and our visitor continued their conversation, I gathered up a broom, a dustpan, and some towels and marched off to the front of the house.

My wife had put the flowers on a wooden trunk that sat just below the staircase railing. This staircase was especially steep and narrow, and there was a large window not more than a yard from the bottom step. I mention this geography because it's important. Where things were has everything to do with what happened next.

I was about half finished with the clean-up job when my daughter rushed out from her room onto the second-floor landing. I was close enough to the foot of the stairs to catch a glimpse of her (a couple of steps back and she would have been blocked from view), and in that brief moment I saw that she had that high-spirited, utterly happy expression on her face that has filled my middle age with such overpowering gladness. Then, an instant later, before I could even say hello, she tripped. The toe of her sneaker had caught on the landing, and just like that, without any cry or warning, she was sailing through the air. I don't mean to suggest that she was falling or tumbling or bouncing down the steps. I mean to say that she was flying. The impact of the stumble had literally launched her into space, and from the trajectory of her flight I could see that she was heading straight for the window.

What did I do? I don't know what I did. I was on the wrong side of the banister when I saw her trip, but by the time she was midway between the landing and the window, I was standing on the bottom step of the staircase. How did I get there? It was no more than a question of several feet, but it hardly seems possible to cover that distance in that amount of time—which is next to no time at all. Nevertheless, I was there, and the moment I got there I looked up, opened my arms, and caught her.

3

I was fourteen. For the third year in a row, my parents had sent me to a summer camp in New York State. I spent the bulk of my time playing basketball and baseball, but as it was a co-ed camp, there were other activities as well: evening "socials," the first awkward grapplings with girls, panty raids, the usual adolescent shenanigans. I also remember smoking cheap cigars on the sly, "frenching" beds, and massive water-balloon fights.

None of this is important. I simply want to underscore what a vulnerable age fourteen can be. No longer a child, not yet an adult, you bounce back and forth between who you were and who you are about to become. In my own case, I was still young enough to think that I had a legitimate shot at playing in the Major Leagues, but old enough to be questioning the existence of God. I had read the Communist Manifesto, and yet I still enjoyed watching Saturday morning cartoons. Every time I saw my face in the mirror, I seemed to be looking at someone else.

There were sixteen or eighteen boys in my group. Most of us had been together for several years, but a couple of newcomers had also joined us that summer. One was named Ralph. He was a quiet kid without much enthusiasm for dribbling basketballs or hitting the cut-off man, and while no one gave him a particularly hard time, he had trouble blending in. He had flunked a couple of subjects that year, and most of his free periods were spent being tutored by one of the counselors. It was a little sad, and I felt sorry for him—but not too sorry, not sorry enough to lose any sleep over it.

Our counselors were all New York college students from Brooklyn and Queens. Wise-cracking basketball players, future dentists, accountants, and teachers, city kids to their very bones. Like most true New Yorkers, they persisted in calling the ground the "floor," even when all that was under their feet was grass, pebbles, and dirt. The trappings of traditional summer camp life were as alien to them as the I.R.T. is to an Iowa farmer. Canoes, lanyards, mountain climbing, pitching tents, singing around the campfire were nowhere to be found in the inventory of their concerns. They could drill us on the finer points of setting picks and boxing out for rebounds, but otherwise they mostly horsed around and told jokes.

Imagine our surprise, then, when one afternoon our counselor announced that we were going for a hike in the woods. He had been seized by an inspiration and wasn't going to let anyone talk him out of it. Enough basketball, he said. We're surrounded by nature, and it's time we took advantage of it and started acting like real campers—or words to that effect. And so, after the rest period that followed lunch, the whole gang of sixteen or eighteen boys along with two or three counselors set off into the woods.

It was late July, 1961. Everyone was in a fairly buoyant mood, I remember, and half an hour or so into the trek most people agreed that the outing had been a good idea. No one had a compass, of course, or the slightest clue as to where we were going, but we were all enjoying ourselves, and if we happened to get lost, what difference would that make? Sooner or later, we'd find our way back.

Then it began to rain. At first it was barely noticeable, a few light drops falling between the leaves and branches, nothing to worry about. We walked on, unwilling to let a little water spoil our fun, but a couple of minutes later it started coming down in earnest. Everyone got soaked, and the counselors decided we should turn around and head back. The only problem was that no one knew where the camp was. The woods were thick, dense with clusters of trees and thorn-studded bushes, and we had woven our way this way and that, abruptly shifting directions in order to move on. To add to the confusion, it was becoming hard to see. The woods were dark to begin with, but with the rain falling and the sky turning black, it felt more like night than three or four in the afternoon.

Then the thunder started. And after the thunder, the lightning started. The storm was directly on top of us, and it turned out to be the summer storm to end all summer storms. I have never seen weather like that before or since. The rain poured down on us so hard that it actually hurt; each time the thunder exploded, you could feel the noise vibrating inside your body. Immediately after that, the lightning would come, dancing around us like spears. It was as if weapons had materialized out of thin air: a sudden flash that turned everything a bright, ghostly white. Trees were struck, and the branches would begin to smolder. Then it would go dark again for a moment, there would be another crash in the sky, and the lightning would return in a different spot.

The lightning was what scared us, of course. It would have been stupid not to be scared, and in our panic we tried to run away from it. But the storm was too big, and everywhere we went we were met by more lightning. It was a helter-skelter stampede, a headlong rush in circles.

Then, suddenly, someone spotted a clearing in the woods. A brief dispute broke out over whether it was safer to go into the open or continue to stand under the trees. The voice arguing for the open won, and we all ran in the direction of the clearing.

It was a small meadow, most likely a pasture that belonged to a local farm, and to get to it we had to crawl under a barbed-wire fence. One by one, we got down on our bellies and inched our way through. I was in the middle of the line, directly behind Ralph. Just as he went under the barbed wire, there was another flash of lightning. I was two or three feet away, but because of the rain pounding against my eyelids, I had trouble making out what happened. All I knew was that Ralph had stopped moving. I figured that he had been stunned, so I crawled past him under the fence. Once I was on the other side, I took hold of his arm and dragged him through.

I don't know how long we stayed in that field. An hour, I would guess, and the whole time we were there the rain and thunder and lightning continued to crash down upon us. It was a storm ripped from the pages of the Bible, and it went on and on and on, as if it would never end.

Two or three boys were hit by something—perhaps by lightning, perhaps by the shock of lightning as it struck the ground near them—and the meadow began to fill with their moans. Other boys wept and prayed. Still others, fear in their voices, tried to give sensible advice. Get rid of everything metal, they said, metal attracts the lightning. We all took off our belts and threw them away from us.

I don't remember saying anything. I don't remember crying. Another boy and I kept ourselves busy trying to take care of Ralph. He was still unconscious. We rubbed his hands and arms, we held down his tongue so he wouldn't swallow it, we told him to hang in there. After a while, his skin began to take on a bluish tinge. His body seemed colder to my touch, but in spite of the mounting evidence, it never once occurred to me that he wasn't going to come around. I was only fourteen years old, after all, and what did I know? I had never seen a dead person before.

It was the barbed wire that did it, I suppose. The other boys hit by the lightning went numb, felt pain in their limbs for an hour or so, and then recovered. But Ralph had been under the fence when the lightning struck, and he had been electrocuted on the spot.

Later on, when they told me he was dead, I learned that there was an eight-inch burn across his back. I remember trying to absorb this news and telling myself that life would never feel the same to me again.

Strangely enough, I didn't think about how I had been right next to him when it happened. I didn't think, One or two seconds later, and it would have been me. What I thought about was holding his tongue and looking down at his teeth. His mouth had been set in a slight grimace, and with his lips partly open, I had spent an hour looking down at the tips of his teeth. Thirty-four years later, I still remember them. And his half-closed, half-open eyes. I remember those, too.

4

Not many years ago, I received a letter from a woman who lives in Brussels. In it, she told me the story of a friend of hers, a man she has known since childhood.

In 1940, this man joined the Belgian army. When the country fell to the Germans later that year, he was captured and put in a prisoner-of-war camp. He remained there until the war ended in 1945.

Prisoners were allowed to correspond with Red Cross workers back in Belgium. The man was arbitrarily assigned a pen pal—a Red Cross nurse from Brussels—and for the next five years he and this woman exchanged letters every month. Over the course of time they became fast friends. At a certain point (I'm not exactly sure how long this took), they understood that something more than friendship had developed between them. The correspondence went on, growing more intimate with each exchange, and at last they declared their love for each other. Was such a thing possible? They had never seen each other, had never spent a minute in each other's company.

After the war was over, the man was released from prison and returned to Brussels. He met the nurse, the nurse met him, and neither was disappointed. A short time later, they were married.

Years went by. They had children, they grew older, the world became a slightly different world. Their son completed his studies in Belgium and went off to do graduate work in Germany. At the university there, he fell in love with a young German woman. He wrote his parents and told them that he intended to marry her.

The parents on both sides couldn't have been happier for their children. The two families arranged to meet, and on the appointed day the German family showed up at the house of the Belgian family in Brussels. As the German father walked into the living room and the Belgian father rose to welcome him, the two men looked into each other's eyes and recognized each other. Many years had passed, but neither one was in any doubt as to who the other was. At one time in their lives, they had seen each other every day. The German father had been a guard in the prison camp where the Belgian father had spent the war.

As the woman who wrote me the letter hastened to add, there was no bad blood between them. However monstrous the German regime might have been, the German father had done nothing during those five years to turn the Belgian father against him.

Be that as it may, these two men are now the best of friends. The greatest joy in their lives is the grandchildren they have in common.

5

I was eight years old. At that moment in my life, nothing was more important to me than baseball. My team was the New York Giants, and I followed the doings of those men in the black-and-orange caps with all the devotion of a true believer. Even now, remembering that team which no longer exists, that played in a ballpark which no longer exists, I can reel off the names of nearly every player on the roster. Alvin Dark, Whitey Lockman, Don Mueller, Johnny Antonelli, Monte Irvin, Hoyt Wilhelm. But none was greater, none more perfect nor more deserving of worship than Willie Mays, the incandescent Say-Hey Kid.

That spring, I was taken to my first big-league game. Friends of my parents had box seats at the Polo Grounds, and one April night a group of us went to watch the Giants play the Milwaukee Braves. I don't know who won, I can't recall a single detail of the game, but I do remember that after the game was over my parents and their friends sat talking in their seats until all the other spectators had left. It got so late that we had to walk across the diamond and leave by the center-field exit, which was the only one still open. As it happened, that exit was right below the players' locker rooms.

Just as we approached the wall, I caught sight of Willie Mays. There was no question about who it was. It was Willie Mays, already out of uniform and standing there in his street clothes not ten feet away from me. I managed to keep my legs moving in his direction and then, mustering every ounce of my courage, I forced some words out of my mouth. "Mr. Mays," I said, "could I please have your autograph?"

He had to have been all of twenty-four years old, but I couldn't bring myself to pronounce his first name.

His response to my question was brusque but amiable. "Sure, kid, sure," he said. "You got a pencil?" He was so full of life, I remember, so full of youthful energy, that he kept bouncing up and down as he spoke.

I didn't have a pencil, so I asked my father if I could borrow his. He didn't have one either. Nor did my mother. Nor, as it turned out, did any of the other grown-ups.

The great Willie Mays stood there watching in silence. When it became clear that no one in the group had anything to write with, he turned to me and shrugged. "Sorry, kid," he said. "Ain't got no pencil, can't give no autograph." And then he walked out of the ballpark into the night.

I didn't want to cry, but tears started falling down my cheeks, and there was nothing I could do to stop them. Even worse, I cried all the way home in the car. Yes, I was crushed with disappointment, but I was also revolted at myself for not being able to control those tears. I wasn't a baby. I was eight years old, and big kids weren't supposed to cry over things like that. Not only did I not have Willie Mays's autograph, I didn't have anything else either. Life had put me to the test, and in all respects I had found myself wanting.

After that night, I started carrying a pencil with me wherever I went. It became a habit of mine never to leave the house without making sure I had a pencil in my pocket. It's not that I had any particular plans for that pencil, but I didn't want to be unprepared. I had been caught empty-handed once, and I wasn't about to let it happen again.

If nothing else, the years have taught me this: if there's a pencil in your pocket, there's a good chance that one day you'll feel tempted to start using it.

As I like to tell my children, that's how I became a writer.

1995

Accident Report

1

When A. was a young woman in San Francisco and just starting out in life, she went through a desperate period in which she almost lost her mind. In the space of just a few weeks, she was fired from her job, one of her best friends was murdered when thieves broke into her apartment at night, and A.'s beloved cat became seriously ill. I don't know the exact nature of the illness, but it was apparently life-threatening, and when A. took the cat to the vet, he told her that the cat would die within a month unless a certain operation was performed. She asked him how much the operation would cost. He toted up the various charges for her, and the amount came to three hundred twenty-seven dollars. A. didn't have that kind of money. Her bank account was down to almost zero, and for the next several days she walked around in a state of extreme distress, alternately thinking about her dead friend and the impossible sum needed to prevent her cat from dying: three hundred twenty-seven dollars.

One day, she was driving through the Mission and came to a stop at a red light. Her body was there, but her thoughts were somewhere else, and in the gap between them, in that small space that no one has fully explored but where we all sometimes live, she heard the voice of her murdered friend. *Don't worry*, the voice said. *Don't worry. Things will get better soon.* The light turned green, but A. was still under the spell of this auditory hallucination, and she did not move. A moment later, a car rammed into her from behind, breaking one of the taillights and crumpling the fender. The man who was driving that car shut off his engine, climbed out of the car, and walked over to A. He apologized for doing such a stupid thing. No, A. said, it was my fault. The light turned green and I didn't go. But the man insisted that he was the one to blame. When he learned that A. didn't have collision insurance (she was too poor for luxuries like that), he offered to pay for any damages that had been done to her car. Get an estimate on what it will cost, he said, and send me the bill. My insurance company will take care of it. A. continued to protest, telling the man that he wasn't responsible for the accident, but he wouldn't take no for an answer, and finally she gave in. She took the car to a garage and asked the mechanic to assess the costs of repairing the fender and the taillight. When she returned several hours later, he handed her a written estimate. Give or take a penny or two, the amount came to exactly three hundred twenty-seven dollars.

2

W., the friend from San Francisco who told me that story, has been directing films for twenty years. His latest project is based on a novel that recounts the adventures of a mother and her teenage daughter. It is a work of fiction, but most of the events in the book are taken directly from the author's life. The author, now a grown woman, was once the teenage daughter, and the mother in the story—who is still alive—was her real mother.

W.'s film was shot in Los Angeles. A famous actress was hired to play the role of the mother, and according to what W. told me on a recent visit to New York, the filming went smoothly and the production was completed on schedule. Once he began to edit the movie, however, he decided that he wanted to add a few more scenes, which he felt would greatly enhance the story. One of them included a shot of the mother parking her car on a street in a residential neighborhood. The location manager went out scouting for an appropriate street, and eventually one was chosen—arbitrarily, it would seem, since one Los Angeles street looks more or less like any other. On the appointed morning, W., the actress, and the film crew gathered on the street to shoot the scene. The car that the actress was supposed to drive was parked in front of a house—no particular house, just one of the houses on that street—and as my friend and his leading lady stood on the sidewalk discussing the scene and the possible ways to approach it, the door of that house burst open and a woman came running out. She appeared to be laughing and screaming at the same time. Distracted by the commotion, W. and the actress stopped talking. A screaming and laughing woman was running across the front lawn, and she was headed straight for them. I don't know how big the lawn was. W. neglected to mention that detail when he told the story, but in my mind I see it as large, which would have given the woman a considerable distance to cover before she reached the sidewalk and announced who she was. A moment like that deserves to be prolonged, it seems to me—if only by a few seconds—for the thing that was about to happen was so improbable, so outlandish in its defiance of the odds, that one wants to savor it for a few extra seconds before letting go of it. The woman running across the lawn was the novelist's mother. A fictional character in her daughter's book, she was also her real mother, and now, by pure accident, she was about to meet the woman who was playing that fictional character in a film based on the book in which her character had in fact been herself. She was real, but she was also imaginary. And the actress who was playing her was both real and imaginary as well. There were two of them standing on the sidewalk that morning, but there was also just one. Or perhaps it was the same one twice. According to what my friend told me, when the women finally understood what had happened, they threw their arms around each other and embraced.

3

Last September, I had to go to Paris for a few days, and my publisher booked a room for me in a small hotel on the Left Bank. It's the same hotel they use for all their authors, and I had already stayed there several times in the past. Other than its convenient location—midway down a narrow street just off the Boulevard Saint-Germain—there is nothing even remotely interesting about this hotel. Its rates are modest, its rooms are cramped, and it is not mentioned in any guidebook. The people who run it are pleasant enough, but it is no more than a drab and inconspicuous hole-in-the-wall, and except for a couple of American writers who have the same French publisher I do, I have never met anyone who has stayed there. I mention this fact because the obscurity of the hotel plays a part in the story. Unless one stops for a moment to consider how many hotels there are in Paris (which attracts more visitors than any other city in the world) and then further considers how many rooms there are in those hotels (thousands, no doubt tens of thousands), the full import of what happened to me last year will not be understood.

I arrived at the hotel late—more than an hour behind schedule—and checked in at the front desk. I went upstairs immediately after that. Just as I was putting my key into the door of my room, the telephone started to ring. I went in, tossed my bag on the floor, and picked up the phone, which was set into a nook in the wall just beside the bed, more or less at pillow level. Because the phone was turned in toward the bed, and because the cord was short, and because the one chair in the room was out of reach, it was necessary to sit down on the bed in order to use the phone. That's what I did, and as I talked to the person on the other end of the line, I noticed a piece of paper lying under the desk on the opposite side of the room. If I had been anywhere else, I wouldn't have been in a position to see it. The dimensions of the room were so tight that the space between the desk and the foot of the bed was no more than four or five feet. From my vantage point at the head of the bed, I was in the only place that provided a low enough angle of the floor to see what was under the desk. After the conversation was over, I got off the bed, crouched down under the desk, and picked up the piece of paper. Curious, of course, always curious, but not at all expecting to find anything out of the ordinary. The paper turned out to be one of those little message forms they slip under your door in European hotels. To——and From——, the date and the time, and then a blank square below for the message. The form had been folded in three, and printed out in block letters on the outer fold was the name of one of my closest friends. We don't see each other often (O. lives in Canada), but we have been through a number of memorable experiences together, and there has never been anything but the greatest affection between us. Seeing his name on the message form made me very happy. We hadn't spoken in a while, and I had had no inkling that he would be in Paris when I was there. In those first moments of discovery and incomprehension, I assumed that O. had somehow gotten wind of the fact that I was coming and had called the hotel to leave a message for me. The message had been delivered to my room, but whoever had brought it up had placed it carelessly on the edge of the desk, and it had blown onto the floor. Or else that person had accidentally dropped it (the chambermaid?) while preparing the room for my arrival. One way or the other, neither explanation was very plausible. The angle was wrong, and unless someone had kicked the message after it had fallen to the floor, the paper couldn't have been lying so far under the desk. I was already beginning to reconsider my hypothesis when something more important occurred to me. O.'s name was on the outside of the message form. If the message had been meant for me, my name would have been there. The recipient was the one whose name belonged on the outside, not the sender, and if my name wasn't there, it surely wasn't going to be anywhere else. I opened the message and read it. The sender was someone I had never heard of—but the recipient was indeed O. I rushed downstairs and asked the clerk at the front desk if O. was still there. It was a stupid question, of course, but I asked it anyway. How could O. be there if he was no longer in his room? I was there now, and O.'s room was no longer his room but mine. I asked the clerk when he had checked out. An hour ago, the clerk said. An hour ago I had been sitting in a taxi at the edge of Paris, stuck in a traffic jam. If I had made it to the hotel at the expected time, I would have run into O. just as he was walking out the door.

1999

It Don't Mean a Thing

1

We used to see him occasionally at the Carlyle Hotel. It would be an exaggeration to call him a friend, but F. was a good acquaintance, and my wife and I always looked forward to his arrival when he called to say that he was coming to town. A daring and prolific French poet, F. was also one of the world's leading authorities on Henri Matisse. So great was his reputation, in fact, that an important French museum asked him to organize a large exhibition of Matisse's work. F. wasn't a professional curator, but he threw himself into the job with enormous energy and skill. The idea was to gather together all of Matisse's paintings from a particular five-year period in the middle of his career. Dozens of canvases were involved, and since they were scattered around in private collections and museums all over the world, it took F. several years to prepare the show. In the end, there was only one work that could not be found—but it was a crucial one, the centerpiece of the entire exhibition. F. had not been able to track down the owner, had no idea where it was, and without that canvas years of travel and meticulous labor would go for naught. For the next six months, he devoted himself exclusively to the search for that one painting, and when he found it, he realized that it had been no more than a few feet away from him the whole time. The owner was a woman who lived in an apartment at the Carlyle Hotel. The Carlyle was F.'s hotel of choice, and he stayed there whenever he was in New York. More than that, the woman's apartment was located directly above the room that F. always reserved for himself—just one floor up. Which meant that every time F. had gone to sleep at the Carlyle Hotel, wondering where the missing painting could have been, it had been hanging on a wall directly above his head. Like an image from a dream.

2

I wrote that paragraph last October. A few days later, a friend from Boston called to tell me that a poet acquaintance of his was in bad shape. In his mid-sixties now, this man has spent his life in the far reaches of the literary solar system—the single inhabitant of an asteroid that orbits around a tertiary moon of Pluto, visible only through the strongest telescope. I have never met him, but I have read his work, and I have always imagined him living on his small planet like some latter-day Little Prince.

My friend told me that the poet's health was in decline. He was undergoing treatments for his illness, his money was at a low ebb, and he was being threatened with eviction from his apartment. As a way to raise some quick and necessary cash to rescue the poet from his troubles, my friend had come up with the idea of producing a book in his honor. He would solicit contributions from several dozen poets and writers, gather them into an attractive, limited-edition volume, and sell the copies by subscription only. He figured there were enough book collectors in the country to guarantee a handsome profit. Once the money came in, it would all be turned over to the sick and struggling poet.

He asked me if I had a page or two lying around somewhere that I might give him, and I mentioned the little story I had just written about my French friend and the missing painting. I faxed it to him that same morning, and a few hours later he called back to say that he liked the piece and wanted to include it in the book. I was glad to have done my little bit, and then, once the matter had been settled, I promptly forgot all about it.

Two nights ago (January 31, 2000), I was sitting with my twelve-year-old daughter at the dining room table in our house in Brooklyn, helping her with her math homework—a massive list of problems involving negative and positive numbers. My daughter is not terribly interested in math, and once we finished converting the subtractions into additions and the negatives into positives, we started talking about the music recital that had been held at her school several nights before. She had sung "The First Time Ever I Saw Your Face," the old Roberta Flack number, and now she was looking for another song to begin preparing for the spring recital. After tossing some ideas back and forth, we both decided that she should do something bouncy and up-tempo this time, in contrast to the slow and aching ballad she had just performed. Without any warning, she sprang from her chair and began belting out the lyrics of "It Don't Mean a Thing if it Ain't Got that Swing." I know that parents tend to exaggerate the talents of their children, but there was no question in my mind that her rendition of that song was remarkable. Dancing and shimmying as the music poured out of her, she took her voice to places it had rarely been before, and because she sensed that herself, could feel the power of her own performance, she immediately launched into it again after she had finished. Then she sang it again. And then again. For fifteen or twenty minutes, the house was filled with increasingly beautiful and ecstatic variations of a single unforgettable phrase: *It don't mean a thing if it ain't got that swing*.

The following afternoon (yesterday), I brought in the mail at around two o'clock. There was a considerable pile of it, the usual mixture of junk and important business. One letter had been sent by a small New York poetry publisher, and I opened that one first. Unexpectedly, it contained the proofs of my contribution to my friend's book. I read through the piece again, making one or two corrections, and then called the copy editor responsible for the production of the book. Her name and number had been provided in a cover letter sent by the publisher, and once we had had our brief chat, I hung up the phone and turned to the rest of my mail. Wedged inside the pages of my daughter's new issue of *Seventeen Magazine*, there was a slim white package that had been sent from France. When I turned it over to look at the return address, I saw that it was from F., the same poet whose experience with the missing painting had inspired me to write the short piece I had just read over for the first time since composing it in October. What a coincidence, I thought. My life has been filled with dozens of curious events like this one, and no matter how hard I try, I can't seem to shake free of them. What is it about the world that continues to involve me in such nonsense?

Then I opened the package. There was a thin book of poetry inside— what we would refer to as a chapbook; what the French call a *plaquette*. It was just thirty-two pages long, and it had been printed on fine, elegant paper. As I flipped through it, scanning a phrase here and a phrase there, immediately recognizing the exuberant and frenetic style that characterizes all of F.'s work, a tiny slip of paper fell out of the book and fluttered onto my desk. It was no more than two inches long and half an inch high. I had no idea what it was. I had never encountered a stray slip of paper in a new book before, and unless it was supposed to serve as some kind of rarefied, microscopic bookmark to match the refinement of the book itself, it seemed to have been put in there by mistake. I picked up the errant rectangle from my desk, turned it over, and saw that there was writing on the other side—eleven short words arranged in a single row of type. The poems had been written in French, the book had been printed in France, but the words on the slip of paper that had fallen out of the book were in English. They formed a sentence, and that sentence read: *It don't mean a thing if it ain't got that swing.*

3

Having come this far, I can't resist the temptation to add one more link to this chain of anecdotes. As I was writing the last words of the first paragraph in the second section printed above ("living on his small planet like some latter-day Little Prince"), I was reminded of the fact that *The Little Prince* was written in New York. Few people know this, but after Saint-Exupéry was demobilized following the French defeat in 1940, he came to America, and for a time he lived at 240 Central Park South in Manhattan. It was there that he wrote his celebrated book, the most French of all French children's books. *Le Petit Prince* is required reading for nearly every American high school student of French, and as was the case with so many others before me, it was the first book I happened to read in a language that wasn't English. I went on to read more books in French. Eventually, I translated French books as a way of earning my living as a young man, and at a certain point I lived in France for four years. That was where I first met F. and became familiar with his work. It might be an outlandish statement, but I believe it is safe to say that if I hadn't read *Le Petit Prince* as an adolescent in 1963, I never would have been in a position to receive F.'s book in the mail thirty-seven years later. In saying that, I am also saying that I never would have discovered the mysterious slip of paper bearing the words *It don't mean a thing if it ain't got that swing.*

240 Central Park South is an odd, misshapen building that stands on the corner overlooking Columbus Circle. Construction was completed in 1941, and the first tenants moved in just before Pearl Harbor and America's entrance into the war. I don't know the exact date when Saint-Exupéry took up residence there, but he had to have been among the first people to live in that building. By one of those curious anomalies that mean absolutely nothing, so was my mother. She moved there from Brooklyn with her parents and sister at the age of sixteen, and she did not move out until she married my father five years later. It was an extraordinary step for the family to take—from Crown Heights to one of the most elegant addresses in Manhattan—and it moves me to think that my mother lived in the same building where Saint-Exupéry wrote *The Little Prince*. If nothing else, I am moved by the fact that she had no

idea that the book was being written, no idea who the author was. Nor did she have any knowledge of his death some time later when his plane went down in the last year of the war. Around that same time, my mother fell in love with an aviator. As it happened, he, too, died in that same war.

My grandparents went on living at 240 Central Park South until their deaths (my grandmother in 1968; my grandfather in 1979), and many of my most important childhood memories are situated in their apartment. My mother moved to New Jersey after she married my father, and we changed houses several times during my early years, but the New York apartment was always there, a fixed point in an otherwise unstable universe. It was there that I stood at the window and watched the traffic swirling around the statue of Christopher Columbus. It was there that my grandfather performed his magic tricks for me. It was there that I came to understand that New York was my city.

Just as my mother had done, her sister moved out of the apartment when she married. Not long after that (in the early fifties), she and her husband moved to Europe, where they lived for the next twelve years. In thinking about the various decisions I have made in my own life, I have no doubt that their example inspired me to move to France when I was in my early twenties. When my aunt and uncle returned to New York, my young cousin was eleven years old. I had met him only once. His parents sent him to school at the French lycée, and because of the incongruities in our respective educations, we wound up reading Le Petit Prince at the same time, even though there was a six-year difference in our ages. Back then, neither one of us knew that the book had been written in the same building where our mothers had lived.

After their return from Europe, my cousin and his parents settled into an apartment on the Upper East Side. For the next several years, he had his hair cut every month at the barbershop in the Carlyle Hotel.

2000

GOTHAM HANDBOOK

From Double Game by Sophie Calle

THE RULES OF THE GAME
In his novel *Leviathan*, Paul Auster thanks me for having authorized him to mingle fact with fiction. And indeed, on pages 60 to 67 of his book, he uses a number of episodes from my life to create a fictive character named Maria. Intrigued by this double, I decided to turn Paul Auster's novel into a game and to make my own particular mixture of reality and fiction.

I
The life of Maria and how it influenced the life of Sophie.
In *Leviathan*, Maria puts herself through the same rituals as I did. But Paul Auster has slipped some rules of his own inventing into his portrait of Maria. In order to bring Maria and myself closer together, I decided to go by the book.

II
The life of Sophie and how it influenced the life of Maria.
The rituals that Auster "borrowed" from me to shape Maria are: *The Wardrobe, The Striptease, To Follow . . ., Suite vénitienne, The Detective, The Hotel, The Address Book*, and *The Birthday Ceremony*. *Leviathan* gives me the opportunity to present these artistic projects that inspired the author and which Maria and I now share.

III
One of the many ways of mingling fact with fiction, or how to try to become a character out of a novel.
Since, in *Leviathan*, Auster has taken me as a subject, I imagined swapping roles and taking him as the author of my actions. I asked him to invent a fictive character which I would attempt to resemble. Instead, Auster preferred to send me "Personal Instructions for SC on How to Improve Life in New York City (Because she asked . . .)". I followed his directives. This project is entitled *Gotham Handbook*.

Gotham Handbook
Personal Instructions for S.C. on How to Improve Life in New York City (Because she asked . . .)

SMILING

Smile when the situation doesn't call for it. Smile when you're feeling angry, when you're feeling miserable, when you're feeling most crushed by the world—and see if it makes any difference.

Smile at strangers in the street. New York can be dangerous, so you must be careful. If you prefer, smile only at female strangers. (Men are beasts, and they must not be given the wrong idea.)

Nevertheless, smile as often as possible at people you don't know. Smile at the bank teller who gives you your money, at the waitress who gives you your food, at the person sitting across from you on the IRT.

See if anyone smiles back at you.

Keep track of the number of smiles you are given each day.

Don't be disappointed when people don't smile back at you.

Consider each smile you receive a precious gift.

TALKING TO STRANGERS

There will be people who talk to you after you smile at them. You must be prepared with flattering comments.

Some of these people will talk to you because they feel confused or threatened or insulted by your show of friendliness. ("You got a problem, lady?") Plunge in immediately with a disarming compliment. "No, I was just admiring your beautiful tie." Or: "I love your dress."

Others will talk to you because they are friendly souls, happy to respond to the human overtures that come their way. Try to keep these conversations going as long as you can. It doesn't matter what you talk about. The important thing is to give of yourself and see to it that some form of genuine contact is made.

If you find yourself running out of things to say, bring up the subject of the weather. Cynics regard this as a banal topic, but the fact is that no subject gets people talking faster. Stop and think about it for a moment, and you'll begin to see a metaphysical, even religious quality to this preoccupation with wind-chill factors and Central Park snowfall accumulations. Weather is the great equalizer. There is nothing anyone can do about it, and it affects us all in the same way—rich and poor, black and white, healthy and sick. The weather makes no distinctions. When it rains on me, it also rains on you. Unlike most of the problems we face, it is not a condition created by man. It comes from nature, or God, or whatever else you want to call the forces in the universe we cannot control. To discuss the weather with a stranger is to shake hands and put aside your weapons. It is a sign of goodwill, an acknowledgement of your common humanity with the person you are talking to.

With so many things driving us apart, with so much hatred and discord in the air, it is good to remember the things that bring us together. The more we insist on them in our dealings with strangers, the better morale in the city will be.

BEGGARS AND HOMELESS PEOPLE

I'm not asking you to reinvent the world. I just want you to pay attention to it, to think about the things around you more than you think about yourself. At least while you're outside, walking down the street on your way from here to there.

Don't ignore the miserable ones. They are everywhere, and a person can grow so accustomed to seeing them that he begins to forget they are there. Don't forget.

I'm not asking you to give all your money to the poor. Even if you did, poverty would still exist (and have one more member among its ranks).

At the same time, it's our responsibility as human beings not to harden our hearts. Action is necessary, no matter how small or hopeless our gestures might seem to be.

Stock up on bread and cheese. Every time you leave the house, make three or four sandwiches and put them in your pocket. Every time you see a hungry person, give him a sandwich.

Stock up on cigarettes as well. Common wisdom says that cigarettes are bad for your health, but what common wisdom neglects to say is that they also give great comfort to the people who smoke them.

Don't just give one or two. Give away whole packs.

If you find your pockets can't hold enough sandwiches, go to the nearest McDonald's and buy as many meal coupons as you can afford. Give these coupons away when you're out of cheese sandwiches. You might not like the food at McDonald's, but most people do. Considering the alternatives, they give pretty good value for the money.

These coupons will be especially helpful on cold days. Not only will the hungry person be able to fill his stomach, he'll be able to go inside somewhere and get warm.

If you can't think of anything to say when you give the coupon to the hungry person, talk about the weather.

CULTIVATING A SPOT

People are not the only ones neglected in New York. Things are neglected as well. I don't just mean big things like bridges and subway tracks, I mean the small, barely noticeable things standing right in front of our eyes: patches of sidewalk, walls, park benches. Look closely at the things around you and you'll see that nearly everything is falling apart.

Pick one spot in the city and begin to think of it as yours. It doesn't matter where, and it doesn't matter what. A street corner, a subway entrance, a tree in the park. Take on this place as your responsibility. Keep it clean. Beautify it. Think of it as an extension of who you are, as a part of your identity. Take as much pride in it as you would in your own home.

Go to your spot every day at the same time. Spend an hour watching everything that happens to it, keeping track of everyone who passes by or stops or does anything there. Take notes, take photographs. Make a record of these daily observations and see if you learn anything about the people or the place or yourself.

Smile at the people who come there. Whenever possible, talk to them. If you can't think of anything to say, begin by talking about the weather.

March 5, 1994

THE STORY OF MY TYPEWRITER
(*with Sam Messer*)

Three and a half years later, I came home to America. It was July 1974, and when I unpacked my bags that first afternoon in New York, I discovered that my little Hermes typewriter had been destroyed. The cover was smashed in, the keys were mangled and twisted out of shape, and there was no hope of ever having it repaired.

I couldn't afford to buy a new typewriter. I rarely had much money in those days, but at that particular moment I was dead broke.

A couple of nights later, an old college friend invited me to his apartment for dinner. At some point during our conversation, I mentioned what had happened to my typewriter, and he told me that he had one in the closet that he didn't use anymore. It had been given to him as a graduation present from junior high school in 1962. If I wanted to buy it from him, he said, he would be glad to sell it to me.

We agreed on a price of forty dollars. It was an Olympia portable, manufactured in West Germany. That country no longer exists, but since that day in 1974, every word I have written has been typed out on that machine.

In the beginning, I didn't think about it much. A year went by, ten years went by, and not once did I consider it odd or even vaguely unusual to be working with a manual typewriter. The only alternative was an electric typewriter, but I didn't like the noise those contraptions made: the constant hum of the motor, the buzzing and rattling of loose parts, the jitterbug pulse of alternating current vibrating in my fingers. I preferred the stillness of my Olympia. It was comfortable to the touch, it worked smoothly, it was dependable. And when I wasn't pounding on the keyboard, it was silent.

Best of all, it seemed to be indestructible. Except for changing ribbons and occasionally having to brush out the ink buildup from the keys, I was absolved of all maintenance duties. Since 1974, I have changed the roller twice, perhaps three times. I have taken it into the shop for cleaning no more than I have voted in Presidential elections. I have never had

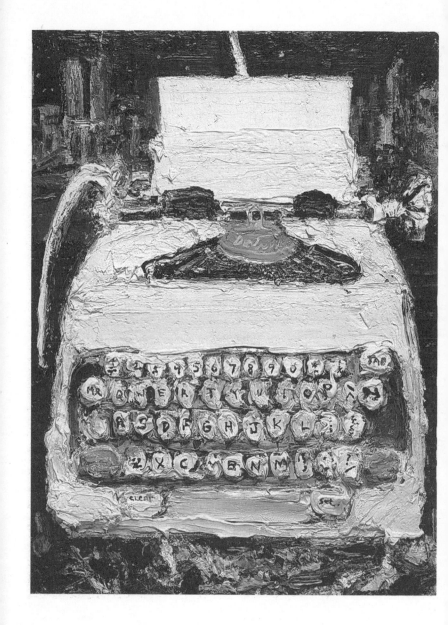

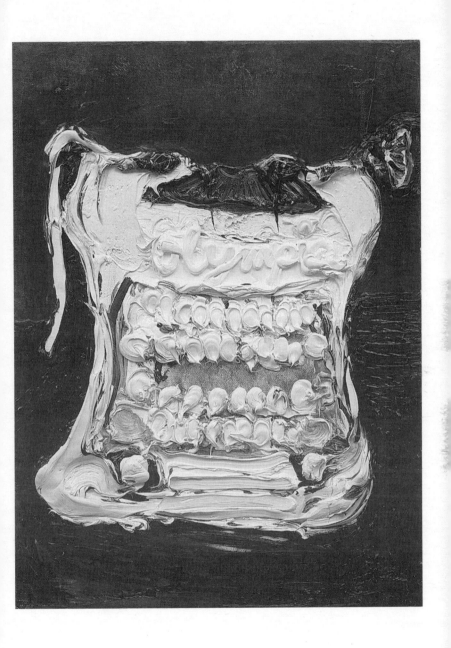

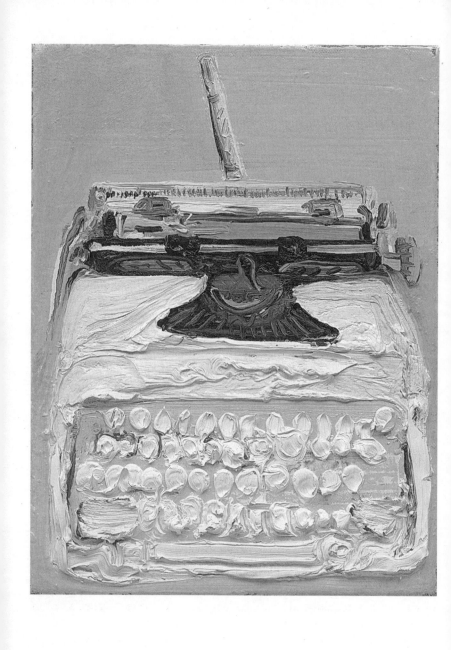

to replace any parts. The only serious trauma it has suffered occurred in 1979 when my two-year-old son snapped off the carriage return arm. But that wasn't the typewriter's fault. I was in despair for the rest of the day, but the next morning I carried it to a shop on Court Street and had the arm soldered back in place. There is a small scar on that spot now, but the operation was a success, and the arm has held ever since.

There is no point in talking about computers and word processors. Early on, I was tempted to buy one of those marvels for myself, but too many friends told me horror stories about pushing the wrong button and wiping out a day's work—or a month's work—and I heard one too many warnings about sudden power failures that could erase an entire manuscript in less than half a second. I have never been good with machines, and I knew that if there was a wrong button to be pushed, I would eventually push it.

So I held on to my old typewriter, and the 1980s became the 1990s. One by one, all my friends switched over to Macs and IBMs. I began to look like an enemy of progress, the last pagan holdout in a world of digital converts. My friends made fun of me for resisting the new ways. When they weren't calling me a curmudgeon, they called me a reactionary and a stubborn old goat. I didn't care. What was good for them wasn't necessarily good for me, I said. Why should I change when I was perfectly happy as I was?

Until then, I hadn't felt particularily attached to my typewriter. It was simply a tool that allowed me to do my work, but now that it had become an endangered species, one of the last surviving artifacts of twentieth-century *homo scriptorus*, I began to develop a certain affection for it. Like it or not, I realized, we had the same past. As time went on, I came to understand that we also had the same future.

Two or three years ago, sensing that the end was near, I went to Leon, my local stationer in Brooklyn, and asked him to order fifty typewriter ribbons for me. He had to call around for several days to scare up an order of that size. Some of them, he later told me, were shipped in from as far away as Kansas City.

I use these ribbons as cautiously as I can, typing on them until the ink is all but invisible on the page. When the supply is gone, I have little hope that there will be any ribbons left.

It was never my intention to turn my typewriter into a heroic figure.

That is the work of Sam Messer, a man who stepped into my house one day and fell in love with a machine. There is no accounting for the passions of artists. The affair has lasted for several years now, and right from the beginning, I suspect that the feelings have been mutual.

Messer seldom goes anywhere without a sketchbook. He draws constantly, stabbing at the page with furious, rapid strokes, looking up from his pad every other second to squint at the person or object before him, and whenever you sit down to a meal with him, you do so with the understanding that you are also posing for your portrait. We have been through this routine so many times in the past seven or eight years that I no longer think about it.

I remember pointing out the typewriter to him the first time he visited, but I can't remember what he said. A day or two after that, he came back to the house. I wasn't around that afternoon, but he asked my wife if he could go downstairs to my work room and have another look at the typewriter. God knows what he did down there, but I have never doubted that the typewriter spoke to him. In due course, I believe he even managed to persuade it to bare its soul.

He has been back several times since, and each visit has produced a fresh wave of paintings, drawings, and photographs. Sam has taken possession of my typewriter, and little by little he has turned an inanimate object into a being with a personality and a presence in the world. The typewriter has moods and desires now, it expresses dark angers and exuberant joys, and trapped within its gray, metallic body, you would almost swear that you could hear the beating of a heart.

I have to admit that I find all this unsettling. The paintings are brilliantly done, and I am proud of my typewriter for proving itself to be such a worthy subject, but at the same time Messer has forced me to look at my old companion in a new way. I am still in the process of adjustment, but whenever I look at one of these paintings now (there are two of them hanging on my living room wall), I have trouble thinking of my typewriter as an *it*. Slowly but surely, the *it* has turned into a *him*.

We have been together for more than a quarter of a century now. Everywhere I have gone, the typewriter has gone with me. We have lived in Manhattan, in upstate New York, and in Brooklyn. We have traveled together to California and to Maine, to Minnesota and to

Massachusetts, to Vermont and to France. In that time, I have written with hundreds of pencils and pens. I have owned several cars, several refrigerators, and have occupied several apartments and houses. I have worn out dozens of pairs of shoes, have given up on scores of sweaters and jackets, have lost or abandoned watches, alarm clocks, and umbrellas. Everything breaks, everything wears out, everything loses its purpose in the end, but the typewriter is still with me. It is the only object I own today that I owned twenty-six years ago. In another few months, it will have been with me for exactly half my life.

Battered and obsolete, a relic from an age that is quickly passing from memory, the damn thing has never given out on me. Even as I recall the nine thousand four hundred days we have spent together, it is sitting in front of me now, stuttering forth its old familiar music. We are in Connecticut for the weekend. It is summer, and the morning outside the window is hot and green and beautiful. The typewriter is on the kitchen table, and my hands are on the typewriter. Letter by letter, I have watched it write these words.

July 2, 2000

NORTHERN LIGHTS

Pages for Kafka
on the fiftieth anniversary of his death

He wanders toward the promised land. That is to say: he moves from one place to another, and dreams continually of stopping. And because this desire to stop is what haunts him, is what counts most for him, he does not stop. He wanders. That is to say: without the slightest hope of ever going anywhere.

He is never going anywhere. And yet he is always going. Invisible to himself, he gives himself up to the drift of his own body, as if he could follow the trail of what refuses to lead him. And by the blindness of the way he has chosen, against himself, in spite of himself, with its veerings, detours, and circlings back, his step, always one step in front of nowhere, invents the road he has taken. It is his road, and his alone. And yet on this road he is never free. For all he has left behind still anchors him to his starting place, makes him regret ever having taken the first step, robs him of all assurance in the rightness of departure. And the farther he travels from his starting place, the greater his doubt grows. His doubt goes with him, like breath, like his breathing between each step — fitful, oppressive — so that no true rhythm, no one pace, can be held. And the farther his doubt goes with him, the nearer he feels to the source of that doubt, so that in the end it is the sheer distance between him and what he has left behind that allows him to see what is behind him: what he is not and might have been. But this thought brings him neither solace nor hope. For the fact remains that he has left all this behind, and in all these things, now consigned to absence, to the longing born of absence, he might once have found himself, fulfilled himself, by following the one law given to him, to remain, and which he now transgresses, by leaving.

All this conspires against him, so that at each moment, even as he continues on his way, he feels he must turn his eyes from the distance that lies before him, like a lure, to the movement of his feet, appearing and disappearing below him, to the road itself, its dust, the stones that clutter its way, the sound of his feet clattering upon them, and he obeys this feeling, as though it were a penance, and he, who would have married the distance before him, becomes, against himself, in spite of himself, the intimate of all that is near. Whatever he can touch, he lingers over, examines, describes with a patience that at each moment exhausts him, overwhelms him, so that even as he goes on, he calls this going into question, and questions each step he is about to take. He who lives for an encounter with the unseen becomes the instrument of the seen: he who would quarry the earth becomes the spokesman of its surfaces, the surveyor of its shades.

Whatever he does, then, he does for the sole purpose of subverting himself, of undermining his strength. If it is a matter of going on, he will do everything in his power not to go on. And yet he will go on. For even though he lingers, he is incapable of rooting himself. No pause conjures a place. But this, too, he knows. For what he wants is what he does not want. And if his journey has any end, it will only be by finding himself, in the end, where he began.

He wanders. On a road that is not a road, on an earth that is not his earth, an exile in his own body. Whatever is given to him, he will refuse. Whatever is spread before him, he will turn his back on. He will refuse, the better to hunger for what he has denied himself. For to enter the promised land is to despair of ever coming near it. Therefore, he holds everything away from him, at arm's length, at life's length, and comes closest to arriving when farthest from his destination. And yet he goes on. And from one step to the next he finds nothing but himself. Not even himself, but the shadow of what he will become. For in the least stone touched, he recognizes a fragment of the promised land. Not even the promised land, but its shadow. And between shadow and shadow lives light. And not just any light, but this light, the light that grows inside him, unendingly, as he goes along his way.

1974

The Death of Sir Walter Raleigh

The Tower is stone and the solitude of stone. It is the skull of a man around the body of a man—and its quick is thought. But no thought will ever reach the other side of the wall. And the wall will not crumble, even against the hammer of a man's eye. For the eyes are blind, and if they see, it is only because they have learned to see where no light is. There is nothing here but thought, and there is nothing. The man is a stone that breathes, and he will die. The only thing that waits for him is death.

The subject is therefore life and death. And the subject is death. Whether the man who lives will have truly lived until the moment of his death, or whether death is no more than the moment at which life stops. This is an argument of act, and therefore an act which rebuts the argument of any word. For we will never manage to say what we want to say, and whatever is said will be said in the knowledge of this failure. All this is speculation.

One thing is sure: this man will die. The Tower is impervious, and the depth of stone has no limit. But thought nevertheless determines its own boundaries, and the man who thinks can now and then surpass himself, even when there is nowhere to go. He can reduce himself to a stone, or he can write the history of the world. Where no possibility exists, everything becomes possible again.

Therefore Raleigh. Or life lived as a suicide pact with oneself. And whether or not there is an art—if one can call it art—of living. Take everything away from a man, and this man will continue to exist. If he has been able to live, he will be able to die. And when there is nothing left, he will know how to face the wall.

It is death. And we say "death," as if we meant to say the thing we cannot know. And yet we know, and we know that we know. For we hold this knowledge to be irrefutable. It is a question for which no answer comes, and it will lead us to many questions that in their turn will lead us back to the thing we cannot know. We may well ask, then, what we will ask. For the subject is not only life and death. It is death, and it is life.

At each moment there is the possibility of what is not. And from each thought, an opposite thought is born. From death, he will see an image of life. And from one place, there will be the boon of another place. America. And at the limit of thought, where the new world nullifies the old, a place is invented to take the place of death. He has already touched its shores, and its image will haunt him to the very end. It is Paradise, it is the Garden before the Fall, and it gives birth to a thought that ranges farther than the grasp of any man. And this man will die. And not only will he die—he will be murdered. An axe will cut off his head.

This is how it begins. And this is how it ends. We all know that we will die. And if there is any truth we live with, it is that we die. But we may well ask the question of how and when, and we may well begin to ask ourselves if chance is not the only god. The Christian says not, and the suicide says not. Each of them says he can choose, and each of them does choose, by faith, or the lack of it. But what of the man who neither believes nor does not believe? He will throw himself into life, live life to the fullest of life, and then come to his end. For death is a very wall, and beyond this wall no one can pass. We will not ask, therefore, whether or not one can choose. One can choose and one cannot. It depends on whom and on why. To begin, then, we must find a place where we are alone and nevertheless together, that is to say, the place where we end. There is the wall, and there is the truth we confront. The question is: at what moment does one begin to see the wall?

Consider the facts. Thirteen years in the Tower, and then the final voyage to the West. Whether or not he was guilty (and he was not) has no bearing on the facts. Thirteen years in the Tower, and a man will begin to learn what solitude is. He will learn that he is nothing more than a body, and he will learn that he is nothing more than a mind, and he will learn that he is nothing. He can breathe, he can walk, he can speak, he can read, he can write, he can sleep. He can count the stones. He can be a stone that breathes, or he can write the history of the world. But at each moment he is the captive of others, and his will is no longer his own. Only his thoughts belong to him, and he is as alone with them as he is alone with the shadow he has become. But he lives. And not only does he live—he lives to the fullest that his confines will permit. And beyond them. For an image of death will nevertheless goad him into finding life. And yet, nothing has changed. For the only thing that waits for him is death.

But this is not all. And the facts must be considered still further. For the day comes when he is allowed to leave the Tower. He has been freed, but he is nevertheless not free. A full pardon will be granted only on the condition that he accomplish something that is flatly impossible to accomplish. Already the victim of the basest political intrigue, the butt of justice gone berserk, he will have his last fling and create his most magnificent failure as a sadistic entertainment for his captors. Once called the Fox, he is now like a mouse in the jaws of a cat. The King instructs him: go where the Spanish have rightful claim, rob them of their gold, and do not antagonize them or incite them to retaliation. Any other man would have laughed. Accused of having conspired with the Spanish thirteen years ago and put into the Tower as a result, he is now told to do a thing in such terms that they invalidate the very charge for which he was found guilty in the first place. But he does not laugh.

One must assume that he knew what he was doing. Either he thought that he could do what he set out to do, or the lure of the new world was so strong that he simply could not resist. In any case, it hardly matters now. Everything that could go wrong for him did go wrong, and from the very beginning the voyage was a disaster. After thirteen years of solitude, it is not easy to return to the world of men, and even less so when one is old. And he is an old man now, more than sixty, and the prison reveries in which he had seen his thoughts turn into the most glorious deeds now turn to dust before his eyes. The crew rebels against him, no gold can be found, the Spanish are hostile. Worst of all: his son is killed.

Take everything away from a man, and that man will continue to exist. But the everything of one man is not that of another, and even the strongest of men will have within himself a place of supreme vulnerability. For Raleigh, this place is occupied by his son, who is at once the emblem of his greatest strength and the seed of his undoing. To all things outward, the boy will bring doom, and though he is a child of love, he remains the living proof of lust—the wild heat of a man willing to risk everything to answer the call of his body. But this lust is nevertheless love, and such a love as seldom speaks more purely of a man's worth. For one does not cavort with a lady of the Queen unless one is ready to destroy one's position, one's honor, one's name. These women are the Queen's person, and no man, not even the most favored man, can approach or possess without royal consent. And yet, he shows no signs of contrition; he makes good on all he has done. For disgrace need not bring shame. He loves the woman, he will continue to love her, she will become the very substance of his life. And in this first, prophetic exile, his son is born.

The boy grows. And he grows wild. The father can do no more than dote and fret, prescribe warnings, be warmed by the fire of his flesh and blood. He writes an extraordinary poem of admonition to the boy, at once an ode to chance and a raging against the inevitable, telling him that if he does not mend his ways he will wind up at the end of a rope, and the boy sallies off to Paris with Ben Jonson on a colossal binge. There is nothing the father can do. It is all a question of waiting. When he is at last allowed to leave the Tower, he takes the boy along with him. He needs the comfort of his son, and he needs to feel himself the father. But the boy is murdered in the jungle. Not only does he come to the end his father had predicted for him, but the father himself has become the unwitting executioner of his own son.

And the death of the son is the death of the father. For this man will die. The journey has failed, the thought of grace does not even enter his head. England means the axe—and the gloating triumph of the King. The very wall has been reached. And yet, he goes back. To a place where the only thing that waits for him is death. He goes back when every-thing tells him to run for life—or to die by his own hand. For if nothing else, one can always choose one's moment. But he goes back. And the question therefore is: why cross an entire ocean only to keep an appoint-ment with death?

We may well speak of madness, as others have. Or we may well speak of courage. But it hardly matters what we speak. For it is here that words begin to fail. And if we ever manage to say what we want to say, it will nevertheless be said in the knowledge of this failure. All this, therefore, is speculation.

If there is such a thing as an art of living, then the man who lives life as an art will have a sense of his own beginning and his own end. And beyond that, he will know that his end is in his beginning, and that each breath he draws can only bring him nearer to that end. He will live, but he will also die. For no work remains unfinished, even the one that has been abandoned.

Most men abandon their lives. They live until they do not live, and we call this death. For death is a very wall. A man dies, and therefore he no longer lives. But this does not mean it is death. For death is only in the seeing of death, and in the living of death. And we may truly say that only the man who lives his life to the fullest of life will be able to see his own death. And we may truly say what we will say. For it is here that words begin to fail.

Each man approaches the wall. One man turns his back, and in the end he is struck from behind. Another goes blind at the very thought of it and spends his life groping ahead in fear. And another sees it from the very beginning, and though his fear is no less, he will teach himself to face it, and go through life with open eyes. Every act will count; even to the last act, because nothing will matter to him anymore. He will live because he is able to die. And he will touch the very wall.

Therefore Raleigh. Or the art of living as the art of death. Therefore England—and therefore the axe. For the subject is not only life and death. It is death. And it is life. And we may truly say what we will say.

1975

Northern Lights
The paintings of Jean-Paul Riopelle

PROGRESS OF THE SOUL

At the limit of a man, the earth will disappear. And each thing seen of earth will be lost in the man who comes to this place. His eyes will open on earth, and whiteness will engulf the man. For this is the limit of earth — and therefore a place where no man can be.

Nowhere. As if this were a beginning. For even here, where the land escapes all witness, a landscape will emerge. That is to say, there is never nothing where a man has come, even in a place where all has disappeared. For he cannot be anywhere until he is nowhere, and from the moment he begins to lose his bearings, he will find where he is.

Therefore, he goes to the limit of earth, even as he stands in the midst of life. And if he stands in this place, it is only by virtue of a desire to be here, at the limit of himself, as if this limit were the core of another, more secret beginning of the world. He will meet himself in his own disappearance, and in this absence he will discover the earth — even at the limit of earth.

THE BODY'S SPACE

There is no need, then, except the need to be here. As if he, too, could cross into life and take his stand among the things that stand among him: a single thing, even the least thing, of all the things he is not. There is this desire, and it is inalienable. As if, by opening his eyes, he might find himself in the world.

A forest. And within that forest, a tree. And upon that tree, a leaf. A single leaf, turning in the wind. This leaf, and nothing else. The thing to be seen.

To be seen: as if he could be here. But the eye has never been enough. It cannot merely see, nor can it tell him how to see. For when a single leaf turns, it is the entire forest that turns around it. And he who turns around himself.

He wants to see what is. But no thing, not even the least thing, has ever stood still for him. For a leaf is not only a leaf: it is the earth, it is

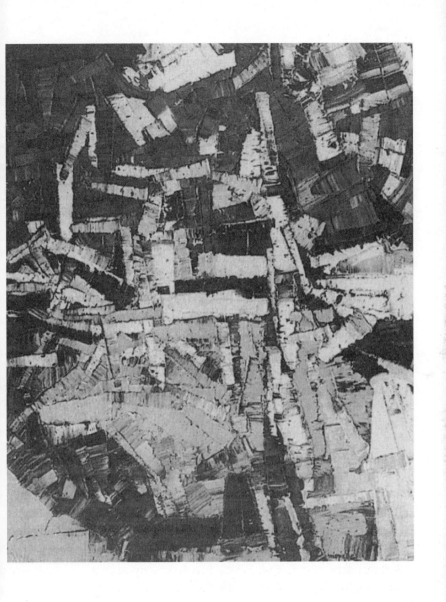

the sky, it is the tree it hangs from in the light of any given hour. But it is also a leaf. That is to say, it is what moves.

It is not enough, then, simply for him to open his eyes. If he is to see, he must begin by moving toward the thing that moves. For seeing is a process that engages the entire body. And though he begins as a witness of the thing he is not, once the first step has been taken, he becomes a participant in a motion that knows no boundaries between self and object.

Distances: what the quickness of the eye discovers, the body must then follow into experience. There is this distance to be crossed, and each time it is a new distance, a different space that opens before the eye. For no two leaves are alike. Therefore, he must feel his feet on the earth: and learn, with a patience that is the instinct of breath and blood, that this same earth is the destiny of the leaf as well.

DISAPPEARANCE

He begins at the beginning. And each time he begins, it is as if he had never lived before. Painting: or the desire to vanish in the act of seeing. That is to say, to see the thing that is, and each time to see it for the first time, as if it were the last time that he would ever see.

At the limit of himself: the pursuit of the nearly-nothing. To breathe in the whiteness of the farthest north. And all that is lost, to be born again from this emptiness in the place where desire carries him, and dismembers him, and scatters him back into earth.

For when he is here, he is nowhere. And time does not exist for him. He will suffer no duration, no continuity, no history: time is merely an alternation between being and not being, and at the moment he begins to feel time passing within him, he knows that he is no longer alive. The self flares up in an image of itself, and the body traces a movement it has traced a thousand times before. This is the curse of memory, or the separation of the body from the world.

If he is to begin, then, he must carry himself to a place beyond memory. Once a gesture has been repeated, once a road has been discovered, the act of living becomes a kind of death. The body must empty itself of the world in order to find the world, and each thing must be made to disappear before it can be seen. The impossible is that which allows him to breathe, and if there is life in him, it is only because he is willing to risk his life.

Therefore, he goes to the limit of himself. And at the moment he no longer knows where he is, the world can begin for him again. But there is no way of knowing this in advance, no way of predicting this miracle, and between each lapse, in each void of waiting, there is terror. And not only terror, but the death of the world in himself.

THE ENDS OF THE EARTH

Lassitude and fear. The endless beginning of time in the body of a man. Blindness, in the midst of life; blindness, in the solitude of a single body. Nothing happens. Or rather, everything begins to be nothing. And the world is so far from him that in each thing he sees of the world, he finds nothing but himself.

Emptiness and immobility, for as long as it takes to kill him. Here, in the midst of life, where the very density of things seems to suffocate the possibility of life, or here, in the place where memory inhabits him. There is no choice but to leave. To lock his door behind him and set out from himself, even to the ends of the earth.

The forest. Or a lapse in the heart of time, as if there were a place where a man could stand. Whiteness opens before him, and if he sees it, it will not be with the eye of a painter, but with the body of a man struggling for life. Gradually, all is forgotten, but not through any act of will: a man can discover the world only because he must — and for the simple reason that his life depends on it.

Seeing, therefore, as a way of being in the world. And knowledge as a force that rises from within. For after being nowhere at all, he will eventually find himself so near to the things he is not that he will almost be within them.

Relations. That is to say, the forest. He begins with a single leaf: the thing to be seen. And because there is one thing, there can be everything. But before there is anything at all, there must be desire, and the joy of a desire that propels him toward his very limit. For in this place, everything connects; and he, too, is part of this process. Therefore, he must move. And as he moves, he will begin to discover where he is.

NATURE

No painting captures the spirit of natural plentitude more truly than this one. Because this painter understands that the body is what sees, that there can be no seeing without motion, he is able to carry himself across the greatest distances — and come to a place of nearness and intimacy, where each thing can be set free to be what it is.

To look at one of these paintings is to enter it: to be whirled into a field of forces that is composed not only of things, but of the motion of things — of their dislocation and their harmony. For this is a man who knows the forest, and the almost inhuman energy to be found in these canvases does not speak of an abstract program to become one-with-nature, but rather, more basically, of a tangible need to be present, as if life could be lived only in the fullness of this desire. As a consequence, this work does not merely re-present the natural landscape. It is a record of an encounter, a process of penetration and mutual dependence, and, as such, a portrait of a man at the limit of himself.

This is a painter who paints in the same way that he breathes. He has never sought merely to create beautiful objects, but rather, in the act of painting, to make life possible for himself. For this reason, he has always avoided facile solutions, and whenever he has found his work becoming automatic, he has stopped work altogether — for as long as it takes for him to unmemorize his work, to block his means of access to the canvas. In effect, each burst of activity is a new beginning, the fruit of a period of unlearning the art of painting — during which time he has allowed himself to discover the world once again. His is an art of both knowledge and innocence, and the perpetual freshness of his work derives from the fact that painting is not something that he does and then divorces from himself, but a necessary struggle to gain hold of his own life and place himself in the world. It is the very substance of the man.

1976

CRITICAL ESSAYS

The Art of Hunger

> What is important, it seems to me, is not so much to defend a culture whose existence has never kept a man from going hungry, as to extract, from what is called culture, ideas whose compelling force is identical with that of hunger.
>
> Antonin Artaud

A young man comes to a city. He has no name, no home, no work: he has come to the city to write. He writes. Or, more exactly, he does not write. He starves to the point of death.

The city is Christiania (Oslo); the year is 1890. The young man wanders through the streets: the city is a labyrinth of hunger, and all his days are the same. He writes unsolicited articles for a local paper. He worries about his rent, his disintegrating clothes, the difficulty of finding his next meal. He suffers. He nearly goes mad. He is never more than one step from collapse.

Still, he writes. Now and then he manages to sell an article, to find a temporary reprieve from his misery. But he is too weak to write steadily and can rarely finish the pieces he has begun. Among his abortive works are an essay entitled "Crimes of the Future," a philosophical tract on the freedom of the will, an allegory about a bookstore fire (the books are brains), and a play set in the Middle Ages, "The Sign of the Cross." The process is inescapable: he must eat in order to write. But if he does not write, he will not eat. And if he cannot eat, he cannot write. He cannot write.

He writes. He does not write. He wanders through the streets of the city. He talks to himself in public. He frightens people away from him. When, by chance, he comes into some money, he gives it away. He is evicted from his room. He eats, and then throws everything up. At one point, he has a brief flirtation with a girl, but nothing comes of it except humiliation. He hungers. He curses the world. He does not die. In the end, for no apparent reason, he signs on board a ship and leaves the city.

These are the bare bones of Knut Hamsun's first novel, *Hunger*. It is a work devoid of plot, action, and — but for the narrator — character. By nineteenth-century standards, it is a work in which nothing happens. The radical subjectivity of the narrator effectively eliminates the basic concerns of the traditional novel. Similar to the hero's plan to make an "invisible detour" when he came to the problem of space and time in one of his essays, Hamsun manages to dispense with historical time, the basic organizing principle of nineteenth-century fiction. He gives us an account only of the hero's worst struggles with hunger. Other, less difficult times, in which his hunger has been appeased — even though they might last as long as a week — are passed off in one or two sentences. Historical time is obliterated in favor of inner duration. With only an arbitrary beginning and an arbitrary ending, the novel faithfully records the vagaries of the narrator's mind, following each thought from its mysterious inception through all its meanderings, until it dissipates and the next thought begins. What happens is allowed to happen.

This novel cannot even claim to have a redeeming social value. Although *Hunger* puts us in the jaws of misery, it offers no analysis of that misery, contains no call to political action. Hamsun, who turned fascist in his old age during the Second World War, never concerned himself with the problems of class injustice, and his narrator-hero, like Dostoevsky's Raskolnikov, is not so much an underdog as a monster of intellectual arrogance. Pity plays no part in *Hunger*. The hero suffers, but only because he has chosen to suffer. Hamsun's art is such that he rigorously prevents us from feeling any compassion for his character. From the very beginning, it is made clear that the hero need not starve. Solutions exist, if not in the city, then at least in departure. But buoyed by an obsessive, suicidal pride, the young man's actions continually betray a scorn for his own best interests.

I began running so as to punish myself, left street after street behind me, pushed myself on with inward jeers, and screeched silently and furiously at myself whenever I felt like stopping. With the help of these exertions I ended up along Pile Street. When I finally did stop, almost weeping with anger that I couldn't run any farther, my whole body trembled, and I threw myself down on a house stoop. "Not so fast!" I said. And to torture myself right, I stood up again and forced myself to stand there, laughing at myself and gloating over my own fatigue. Finally, after a few minutes I nodded and so gave myself permission to sit down; however, I chose the most uncomfortable spot on the stoop.*

He seeks out what is most difficult in himself, courting pain and

---

* All quotations are from the Robert Bly translation, Farrar, Straus, and Giroux, 1967.

adversity in the same way other men seek out pleasure. He goes hungry, not because he has to, but from some inner compulsion, as if to wage a hunger strike against himself. Before the book begins, before the reader has been made the privileged witness of his fate, the hero's course of action has been fixed. A process is already in motion, and although the hero cannot control it, that does not mean he is unaware of what he is doing.

I was conscious all the time that I was following mad whims without being able to do anything about it . . . Despite my alienation from myself at that moment, and even though I was nothing but a battleground for invisible forces, I was aware of every detail of what was going on around me.

Having withdrawn into a nearly perfect solitude, he has become both the subject and object of his own experiment. Hunger is the means by which this split takes place, the catalyst, so to speak, of altered consciousness.

I had noticed very clearly that every time I went hungry a little too long it was as though my brains simply ran quietly out of my head and left me empty. My head became light and floating, I could no longer feel its weight upon my shoulders . . .

If it is an experiment, however, it has nothing to do with the scientific method. There are no controls, no stable points of reference — only variables. Nor can this separation of mind and body be reduced to a philosophical abstraction. We are not in the realm of ideas here. It is a physical state, brought into being under conditions of extreme duress. Mind and body have been weakened; the hero has lost control over both his thoughts and actions. And yet he persists in trying to control his destiny. This is the paradox, the game of circular logic that is played out through the pages of the book. It is an impossible situation for the hero. For he has willfully brought himself to the brink of danger. To give up starving would not mean victory, it would simply mean that the game was over. He wants to survive, but only on his own terms: survival that will bring him face to face with death.

He fasts. But not in the way a Christian would fast. He is not denying earthly life in anticipation of heavenly life; he is simply refusing to live the life he has been given. And the longer he goes on with his fast, the more death intrudes itself upon his life. He approaches death, creeps toward the edge of the abyss, and once there, clings to it, unable to move either forward or backward. Hunger, which opens the void, does not have the power to seal it up. A brief moment of Pascalian terror has been transformed into a permanent condition.

His fast, then, is a contradiction. To persist in it would mean death, and with death the fast would end. He must therefore stay alive, but only to the extent that it keeps him on the point of death. The idea of ending is resisted in the interests of maintaining the constant possibility of the end. Because his fasting neither posits a goal nor offers a promise of redemption, its contradiction must remain unresolved. As such, it is an image of despair, generated by the same self-consuming passion as the sickness unto death. The soul, in its despair, seeks to devour itself, and because it cannot — precisely because it despairs — sinks further into despair.

Unlike a religious art, in which self-debasement can play an ultimately cleansing role (the meditative poetry of the seventeenth century, for example), hunger only simulates the dialectic of salvation. In Fulke Greville's poem, "Down in the depth of mine iniquity," the poet is able to look into a "fatal mirror of transgression" which "shows man as fruit of his degeneration," but he knows that this is only the first step in a two-fold process, for it is in this mirror that Christ is revealed "for the same sins dying / And from that hell I feared, to free me, come . . ." In Hamsun's novel, however, once the depths have been sounded, the mirror of meditation remains empty.

He remains at the bottom, and no God will come to rescue the young man. He cannot even depend on the props of social convention to keep him standing. He is rootless, without friends, denuded of objects. Order has disappeared for him; everything has become random. His actions are inspired by nothing but whim and ungovernable urge, the weary frustration of anarchic discontent. He pawns his waistcoat in order to give alms to a beggar, hires a carriage in search of a fictitious acquaintance, knocks on strangers' doors, and repeatedly asks the time of passing policemen, for the single reason that he fancies to do so. He does not revel in these actions, however. They remain profoundly disquieting for him. Furiously trying to stabilize his life, to put an end to his wanderings, find a room, and settle down to his writing, he is thwarted by the fast he has set in motion. Once it starts, hunger does not release its progenitor-victim until its lesson has been made unforgettable. The hero is seized against his will by a force of his own making and is compelled to respond to its demands.

He loses everything — even himself. Reach the bottom of a Godless hell, and identity disappears. It is no accident that Hamsun's hero has no name: as time goes on, he is truly shorn of his self. What names he chooses to give himself are all inventions, summoned forth on the spur of the moment. He cannot say who he is because he does not know. His name is a lie, and with this lie the reality of his world vanishes.

He peers into the darkness hunger has created for him, and what he finds is a void of language. Reality has become a confusion of thingless names and nameless things for him. The connection between self and world has been broken.

I remained for a while looking into the dark — this dense substance of darkness that had no bottom, which I couldn't understand. My thoughts could not grasp such a thing. It seemed to be a dark beyond all measurement, and I felt its presence weigh me down. I closed my eyes and took to singing half aloud and rocking myself back and forth on the cot to amuse myself, but it did no good. The dark had captured my brain and gave me not an instant of peace. What if I myself became dissolved into the dark, turned into it?

At the precise moment that he is in the greatest fear of losing possession of himself, he suddenly imagines that he has invented a new word: *Kubooa* — a word in no language, a word with no meaning.

I had arrived at the joyful insanity hunger was: I was empty and free of pain, and my thoughts no longer had any check.

He tries to think of a meaning for his word but can only come up with what it doesn't mean, which is neither "God," nor the "Tivoli Gardens," nor "cattle show," nor "padlock," nor "sunrise," nor "emigration," nor "tobacco factory," nor "yarn."

No, the word was actually intended to mean something spiritual, a feeling, a state of mind — if only I could understand it? And I thought and thought to find something spiritual.

But he does not succeed. Voices, not his own, begin to intrude, to confuse him, and he sinks deeper into chaos. After a violent fit, in which he imagines himself to be dying, all goes still, with no sounds but those of his own voice, rolling back from the wall.

This episode is perhaps the most painful in the book. But it is only one of many examples of the hero's language disease. Throughout the narrative, his pranks most often take the form of lies. Retrieving his lost pencil from a pawn shop (he had accidentally left it in the pocket of a vest he had sold), he tells the proprietor that it was with this very pencil that he had written his three-volume treatise on Philosophical

Consciousness. An insignificant pencil, he admits, but he has a sentimental attachment to it. To an old man on a park bench he recites the fantastic story of a Mr. Happolati, the inventor of the electric prayer book. Asking a store clerk to wrap his last possession, a tattered green blanket that he is too ashamed to carry around exposed to view, he explains that it is not really the blanket he wants wrapped, but the pair of priceless vases he has folded inside the blanket. Not even the girl he courts is immune from this sort of fiction. He invents a name for her, a name that pleases him for its beauty, and he refuses to call her by anything else.

These lies have a meaning beyond the jests of the moment. In the realm of language the lie has the same relationship to truth that evil has to good in the realm of morals. That is the convention, and it works if we believe in it. But Hamsun's hero no longer believes in anything. Lies and truths are as one to him. Hunger has led him into the darkness, and there is no turning back.

This equation of language and morals becomes the gist of the final episode in *Hunger*.

My brain grew clearer, I understood that I was close to total collapse. I put my hands against the wall and shoved to push myself away from it. The street was still dancing around. I began to hiccup from fury, and struggled with every bit of energy against my collapse, fought a really stout battle not to fall down. I didn't want to fall, I wanted to die standing. A wholesale grocer's cart came by and I saw it was filled with potatoes, but out of fury, from sheer obstinacy, I decided that they were not potatoes at all, they were cabbages, and I swore violent oaths that they were cabbages. I heard my own words very well, and I took the oath again and again on this lie, and swore deliberately just to have the delightful satisfaction of committing such clear perjury. I became drunk over this superb sin, I lifted three fingers in the air and swore with trembling lips in the name of the Father, the Son, and the Holy Ghost that they were cabbages.

And that is the end of it. There are only two possibilities left for the hero now: live or die; and he chooses to live. He has said no to society, no to God, no to his own words. Later that same day he leaves the city. There is no longer any need to continue the fast. Its work has been done.

Hunger: or a portrait of the artist as a young man. But it is an apprenticeship that has little in common with the early struggles of other writers. Hamsun's hero is no Stephen Dedalus, and there is hardly a word in *Hunger* about aesthetic theory. The world of art has been translated into the world of the body — and the original text has been abandoned.

Hunger is not a metaphor; it is the very crux of the problem itself. If others, such as Rimbaud, with his program for the voluntary derangement of the senses, have turned the body into an aesthetic principle in its own right, Hamsun's hero steadfastly rejects the opportunity to use his deficiencies to his own advantage. He is weak, he has lost control over his thoughts, and yet he continues to strive for lucidity in his writing. But hunger affects his prose in the same way it affects his life. Although he is willing to sacrifice everything for his art, even submit to the worst forms of debasement and misery, all he has really done is make it impossible for himself to write. You cannot write on an empty stomach, no matter how hard you try. But it would be wrong to dismiss the hero of *Hunger* as a fool or a madman. In spite of the evidence, he knows what he is doing. He does not want to succeed. He wants to fail.

Something new is happening here, some new thought about the nature of art is being proposed in *Hunger*. It is first of all an art that is indistinguishable from the life of the artist who makes it. That is not to say an art of autobiographical excess, but rather, an art that is the direct expression of the effort to express itself. In other words, an art of hunger: an art of need, of necessity, of desire. Certainty yields to doubt, form gives way to process. There can be no arbitrary imposition of order, and yet, more than ever, there is the obligation to achieve clarity. It is an art that begins with the knowledge that there are no right answers. For that reason, it becomes essential to ask the right questions. One finds them by living them. To quote Samuel Beckett:

What I am saying does not mean that there will henceforth be no form in art. It only means that there will be a new form, and that this form will be of such a type that it admits the chaos and does not try to say that the chaos is really something else . . . To find a form that accommodates the mess, that is the task of the artist now.*

Hamsun gives the portrait of this artist in the first stages of his development. But it is in Kafka's story, *A Hunger Artist*, that the aesthetics of hunger receives its most meticulous elaboration. Here the contradictions of the fast conducted by Hamsun's hero — and the artistic impasse it leads to — are joined in a parable that deals with an artist whose art consists in fasting. The hunger artist is at once an artist and not an artist. Though he wants his performances to be admired, he insists that they

* From an interview with Tom Driver, "Beckett at the Madeleine," in *The Columbia University Forum*, Summer 1961.

shouldn't be admired, because they have nothing to do with art. He has chosen to fast only because he could never find any food that he liked. His performances are therefore not spectacles for the amusement of others, but the unravelling of a private despair that he has permitted others to watch.

Like Hamsun's hero, the hunger artist has lost control over himself. Beyond the theatrical device of sitting in his cage, his art in no way differs from his life, even what his life would have been had he not become a performer. He is not trying to please anyone. In fact, his performances cannot even be understood or appreciated.

No one could possibly watch the hunger artist continuously, day and night, and so no one could produce firsthand evidence that the fast had really been rigorous and continuous; only the artist himself could know that; he was therefore bound to be the sole completely satisfied spectator of his own fast.

This is not the classic story of the misunderstood artist, however. For the very nature of the fast resists comprehension. Knowing itself from the outset to be an impossibility, and condemning itself to certain failure, it is a process that moves asymptotically toward death, destined to reach neither fruition nor destruction. In Kafka's story, the hunger artist dies, but only because he forsakes his art, abandoning the restrictions that had been imposed on him by his manager. The hunger artist goes too far. But that is the risk, the danger inherent in any act of art: you must be willing to give your life.

In the end, the art of hunger can be described as an existential art. It is a way of looking death in the face, and by death I mean death as we live it today: without God, without hope of salvation. Death as the abrupt and absurd end of life.

I do not believe that we have come any farther than this. It is even possible that we have been here much longer than we are willing to admit. In all this time, however, only a few artists have been able to recognize it. It takes courage, and not many of us would be willing to risk everything for nothing. But that is what happens in *Hunger*, a novel written in 1890. Hamsun's character systematically unburdens himself of every belief in every system, and in the end, by means of the hunger he has inflicted upon himself, he arrives at nothing. There is nothing to keep him going — and yet he keeps on going. He walks straight into the twentieth century.

1970

New York Babel

In the preface to his novel *Le Bleu du Ciel*, Georges Bataille makes an important distinction between books that are written for the sake of experiment and books that are born of necessity. Literature, Bataille argues, is an essentially disruptive force, a presence confronted in "fear and trembling" that is capable of revealing to us the truth of life and its *excessive* possibilities. Literature is not a continuum, but a series of dislocations, and the books that mean most to us in the end are usually those that ran counter to the idea of literature that prevailed at the time they were written. Bataille speaks of "a moment of rage" as the kindling spark of all great works: it cannot be summoned by an act of will, and its source is always extra-literary. "How can we linger," he says, "over books we feel the author was not compelled to write?" Self-conscious experimentation is generally the result of a real longing to break down the barriers of literary convention. But most avant-garde works do not survive; in spite of themselves, they remain prisoners of the very conventions they try to destroy. The poetry of Futurism, for example, which made such a commotion in its day, is hardly read by anyone now except scholars and historians of the period. On the other hand, certain writers who played little or no part in the literary life around them — Kafka, for example — have gradually come to be recognized as essential. The work that revives our sense of literature, that gives us a new feeling for what literature can be, is the work that changes our life. It often seems improbable, as if it had come from nowhere, and because it stands so ruthlessly outside the norm, we have no choice but to create a new place for it.

Le Schizo et les Langues by Louis Wolfson* is such a book. It is not only improbable, but totally unlike anything that has come before it. To say that it is a work written in the margins of literature is not enough: its place, properly speaking, is in the margins of language itself. Written in French by an American, it has little meaning unless it is considered an American book: and yet, for reasons that will be made clear, it is also a book that excludes all possibility of translation. It hovers somewhere in

* Published by Editions Gallimard in 1971. Preface by Gilles Deleuze.

325

the limbo between the two languages, and nothing will ever be able to rescue it from this precarious existence. For what we are presented with here is not simply the case of a writer who has chosen to write in a foreign language. The author of this book has written in French precisely because he had no choice. It is the result of brute necessity, and the book itself is nothing less than an act of survival.

Louis Wolfson is a schizophrenic. He was born in 1931 and lives in New York. For want of a better description, I would call his book a kind of third-person autobiography, a memoir of the present, in which he records the facts of his disease and the utterly bizarre method he has devised for dealing with it. Referring to himself as "the schizophrenic student of languages," "the mentally ill student," "the demented student of idioms," Wolfson uses a narrative style that partakes of both the dryness of a clinical report and the inventiveness of fiction. Nowhere in the text is there even the slightest trace of delirium or "madness": every passage is lucid, forthright, objective. As we read along, wandering through the labyrinth of the author's obsessions, we come to feel with him, to identify with him, in the same way we identify with the eccentricities and torments of Kirilov, or Molloy.

Wolfson's problem is the English language, which has become intolerably painful to him, and which he refuses either to speak or listen to. He has been in and out of mental institutions for over ten years, steadfastly resisting all cooperation with the doctors, and now, at the time he is writing the book (the late sixties), he is living in the cramped lower-middle-class apartment of his mother and stepfather. He spends his days sitting at his desk studying foreign languages — principally French, German, Russian, and Hebrew — and protecting himself against any possible assault of English by keeping his fingers stuck in his ears, or listening to foreign language broadcasts on his transistor radio with two earplugs, or keeping a finger in one ear and an earplug in the other. In spite of these precautions, however, there are times when he is not able to ward off the intrusion of English — when his mother, for example, bursts into his room shrieking something to him in her loud and high-pitched voice. It becomes clear to the student that he cannot drown out English by simply translating it into another language. Converting an English word into its foreign equivalent leaves the English word intact; it has not been destroyed, but only put to the side, and is still there waiting to menace him.

The system that he develops in answer to this problem is complex, but not difficult to follow once one has become familiar with it, since it is based on a consistent set of rules. Drawing on the several languages he has studied, he becomes able to transform English words and phrases into phonetic combinations of foreign letters, syllables, and words that form new linguistic entities, which not only resemble the English in meaning, but in sound as well. His descriptions of these verbal acrobatics are highly detailed, often taking up as many as ten pages, but perhaps the end result of one of the simpler examples will give some idea of the process. The sentence, "Don't trip over the wire!" is changed in the following manner: "Don't" becomes the German "Tu'nicht," "trip" becomes the first four letters of the French "trébucher," "over" becomes the German "über," "the" becomes the Hebrew "èth hé," and "wire" becomes the German "zwirn," the middle three letters of which correspond to the first three letters of the English word: "Tu'nicht tréb über èth hé zwirn." At the end of this passage, exhausted but gratified by his efforts, Wolfson writes: "If the schizophrenic did not experience a feeling of joy as a result of his having found, that day, these foreign words to annihilate yet another word of his mother tongue (for perhaps, in fact, he was incapable of this sentiment), he certainly felt much less miserable than usual, at least for a while."*

The book, however, is far more than just a catalogue of these transformations. They are at the core of the work, and in some sense define its purpose, but the real substance is elsewhere, in the human situation and the daily life that envelop Wolfson's preoccupation with language. There are few books that have given a more immediate feeling of what it is like to live in New York and to wander through the streets of the city. Wolfson's eye for detail is excruciatingly precise, and each nuance of his observations — whether it be the prison-like atmosphere of the Forty-Second Street Public Library reading room, the anxieties of a high school dance, the Times Square prostitute scene, or a conversation with his father on a bench in a city park — is rendered with attentiveness and authority. A strange movement of objectification is continually at work, and much of the fascination of the prose is a result of this distancing, which acts as a kind of lure, always drawing us toward what is written. By treating himself in the third person, Wolfson is able to create a space between himself and himself, to prove to himself that he exists. The French language serves much the same function. By looking out on his

* My translation.

world through a different lens, by punning his world — which is immured in English — into a different language, he is able to see it with new eyes, in a way that is less oppressive to him, as if, to some slight degree, he were able to have an effect upon it.

His powers of evocation are devastating, and in his toneless, deadpan style, he manages to present a portrait of life among the Jewish poor that is so horrendously comical and vivid that it stands comparison with the early passages of Celine's *Death on the Installment Plan*. There seems to be no question that Wolfson knows what he is doing. His aims are not aesthetic ones, but in his patient determination to record everything, to set down the facts as accurately as possible, he has exposed the true absurdity of his situation, which he is often able to respond to with an ironical sense of detachment and whimsy.

His parents were divorced when he was four or five years old. His father has spent most of his life on the periphery of the world, without work, living in cheap hotels, idling away his time in cafeterias smoking cigars. He claims that his marriage took place "with a cat in the bag," since it was not until later that he learned his wife had a glass eye. When she eventually remarried, her second husband disappeared after the wedding with her diamond ring — only to be tracked down by her and thrown into jail the moment he stepped off a plane a thousand miles away. His release was granted only on the condition that he go back to his wife.

The mother is the dominant, suffocating presence of the book, and when Wolfson speaks of his "langue maternelle," it is clear that his abhorrence of English is in direct relation to his abhorrence of his mother. She is a grotesque character, a monster of vulgarity, who ridicules her son's language studies, insists on speaking to him in English, and perseveres in doing exactly the opposite of what would make his life bearable. She spends much of her spare time playing popular songs on an electric organ, with the volume turned up full blast. Sitting over his books, his fingers stuck in his ears, the student sees the lampshade on his desk begin to rattle, to feel the whole room vibrate in rhythm to the piece, and as soon as the deafening music penetrates him, he automatically thinks of the English lyrics of the songs, which drives him into a fury of despair. (Half a chapter is devoted to his linguistic transformation of the words to *Good Night Ladies*). But Wolfson never really judges her. He only describes. And if he allows himself an occasional smirk of understatement, it would seem to be his right.

"Naturally, her optical weakness seemed in no way to interfere with the capacity of her speech organs (perhaps it was even the reverse), and she would speak, at least for the most part, in a very high and very shrill voice, even though she was positively able to whisper over the telephone when she wanted to arrange secretly for her son's entrance into the psychiatric hospital, that is to say, without his knowledge."

Beyond the constant threat of English posed by his mother (who is the very embodiment of the language for him), the student suffers from her in her role as provider. Throughout the book, his linguistic activities are counterpointed by his obsession with food, eating, and the possible contamination of his food. He oscillates between a violent disgust at the thought of eating, as if it were a basic contradiction of his language work, and terrifying orgies of gluttony that leave him sick for hours afterward. Each time he enters the kitchen, he arms himself with a foreign book, repeats aloud certain foreign phrases he has been memorizing, and forces himself to avoid reading the English labels on the packages and cans of food. Reciting one of the phrases over and over again, like a magical incantation to keep away evil spirits, he tears open the first package that comes to hand — containing the food that is easiest to eat, which is usually the least nutritional — and begins to stuff the food into his mouth, all the while making sure that it does not touch his lips, which he feels must be infested with the eggs and larvae of parasites. After such bouts, he is filled with self-recriminations and guilt. As Gilles Deleuze suggests in his preface to the book, "His guilt is no less great when he has eaten than when he has heard his mother speak. It is the same guilt."

This is the point, I feel, at which Wolfson's private nightmare locks with certain universal questions about language. There is a fundamental connection between speaking and eating, and by the very excessiveness of Wolfson's experience, we are able to see how profound this relationship is. Speech is a strangeness, an anomaly, a biologically secondary function of the mouth, and myths about language are often linked to the idea of food. Adam is granted the power of naming the creatures of Paradise and is later expelled for having eaten of the Tree of Knowledge. Mystics fast in order to prepare themselves to receive the word of God. The body of Christ, the word made flesh, is eaten in holy communion. It is as if the life-serving function of the mouth, its role in eating, had been transferred to speech, for it is language that creates us and defines us as human beings. Wolfson's fear of eating, the guilt he feels over his escapades of self-indulgence, are an acknowledgement of his betrayal of the task he has set for himself: that of discovering a language he can live with. To eat is a compromise, since it sustains him within the context of an already discredited and unacceptable world.

In the end, Wolfson's search is undertaken in the hope of one day being able to speak English again — a hope that flickers now and then through the pages of the book. The invention of his system of transformations, the writing of the book itself, are part of a slow progression beyond the hermetic agony of his disease. By refusing to allow anyone to impose a cure on him, by forcing himself to confront his own problems, to live through them alone, he senses in himself a dawning awareness of the possibility of living among others — of being able to break free from his one-man language and enter a language of men.

The book he has created from this struggle is difficult to define, but it should not be dismissed as a therapeutic exercise, as yet another document of mental illness to be filed on the shelves of medical libraries. Gallimard, it seems to me, has made a serious error in bringing out *Le Schizo et les Langues* as part of a series on psychoanalysis. By giving the book a label, they have somehow tried to tame the rebellion that gives the book its extraordinary force, to soften "the moment of rage" that everywhere informs Wolfson's writing.

On the other hand, even if we avoid the trap of considering this work as nothing more than a case history, we should still hesitate to judge it by established literary standards and to look for parallels with other literary works. Wolfson's method, in some sense, does resemble the elaborate word play in *Finnegans Wake* and in the novels of Raymond Roussel, but to insist on this resemblance would be to miss the point of the book. Louis Wolfson stands outside literature as we know it, and to do him justice we must read him on his own terms. For it is only in this way that we will be able to discover his book for what it is: one of those rare works that can change our perception of the world.

1974

Dada Bones

Of all the movements of the early avant-garde, Dada is the one that continues to say the most to us. Although its life was short — beginning in 1916 with the nightly spectacles at the Cabaret Voltaire in Zurich and ending effectively, if not officially, in 1922 with the riotous demonstrations in Paris against Tristan Tzara's play, *Le Coeur à gaz* — its spirit has not quite passed into the remoteness of history. Even now, more than fifty years later, not a season goes by without some new book or exhibition about Dada, and it is with more than academic interest that we continue to investigate the questions it raised. For Dada's questions remain our questions, and when we speak of the relationship between art and society, of art versus action and art as action, we cannot help but turn to Dada as a source and as an example. We want to know about it not only for itself, but because we feel that it will help us toward an understanding of our own, present moment.

The diaries of Hugo Ball are a good place to begin. Ball, a key figure in the founding of Dada, was also the first defector from the Dada movement, and his record of the years between 1914 and 1921 is an extremely valuable document.* *Flight Out of Time* was originally published in Germany in 1927, shortly before Ball's death from stomach cancer at the age of forty-one, and it consists of passages that Ball extracted from his journals and edited with clear and partisan hindsight. It is not so much a self-portrait as an account of his inner progress, a spiritual and intellectual reckoning, and it moves from entry to entry in a rigorously dialectical manner. Although there are few biographical details, the sheer adventure of the thought is enough to hold us. For Ball was an incisive thinker; as a participant in early Dada, he is perhaps our finest witness to the Zurich group, and because Dada marked only one stage in his complex development, our view of it through his eyes gives us a kind of perspective we have not had before.

Hugo Ball was a man of his time, and to an extraordinary degree his

* *Flight Out of Time: A Dada Diary*, edited by John Elderfield and translated by Ann Raimes (Viking Press, 1975).

life seems to embody the passions and contradictions of European society during the first quarter of this century. Student of Nietzsche's work;
stage manager and playwright for the Expressionist theatre; left-wing
journalist; vaudeville pianist; poet; novelist; author of works on
Bakunin, the German Intelligentsia, early Christianity, and the writings
of Hermann Hesse; convert to Catholicism: he seemed, at one moment
or another, to have touched on nearly all the political and artistic preoccupations of the age. And yet, despite his many activities, Ball's attitudes and interests were remarkably consistent throughout his life, and
in the end his entire career can be seen as a concerted, even feverish
attempt to ground his existence in a fundamental truth, in a single,
absolute reality. Too much an artist to be a philosopher, too much a
philosopher to be an artist, too concerned with the fate of the world to
think only in terms of personal salvation, and yet too inward to be an
effective activist, Ball struggled toward solutions that could somehow
answer both his inner and outer needs, and even in the deepest solitude
he never saw himself as separate from the society around him. He was
a man for whom everything came with great difficulty, whose sense of
himself was never fixed, and whose moral integrity made him capable
of brashly idealistic gestures totally out of keeping with his delicate
nature. We have only to examine the famous photograph of Ball reciting a sound poem at the Cabaret Voltaire to understand this. He is
dressed in an absurd costume that makes him look like a cross between
the Tin Man and a demented bishop, and he stares out from under a
high witch doctor's hat with an expression on his face of overwhelming
terror. It is an unforgettable expression, and in this one image of him we
have what amounts to a parable of his character, a perfect rendering of
inside confronting outside, of darkness meeting darkness.

In the Prologue to *Flight Out of Time* Ball presents the reader with a
cultural autopsy that sets the tone for all that follows: "The world and
society in 1913 looked like this: life is completely confined and shackled
. . . The most burning question day and night is this: is there anywhere
a force that is strong enough and above all vital enough to put an end
to this state of affairs?" Elsewhere, in his 1917 lecture on Kandinsky, he
states these ideas with even greater urgency: "A thousand-year-old culture disintegrates. There are no columns and no supports, no foundations anymore — they have all been blown up . . . The meaning of the
world has disappeared." These feelings are not new to us. They confirm
our sense of the European intellectual climate around the time of the

First World War, and echo much of what we now take for granted as having formed the modern sensibility. What is unexpected, however, is what Ball says a little further on in the Prologue: "It might seem as if philosophy had been taken over by the artists; as if the new impulses were coming from them; as if they were the prophets of rebirth. When we said Kandinsky and Picasso, we meant not painters, but priests; not craftsmen, but creators of new worlds and new paradises." Dreams of total regeneration could exist side by side with the blackest pessimism, and for Ball there was no contradiction in this: both attitudes were part of a single approach. Art was not a way of turning from the problems of the world, it was a way of directly solving these problems. During his most difficult years, it was this faith that sustained Ball, from his early work in the theater — "Only the theater is capable of creating the new society" — to his Kandinsky-influenced formulation of "the union of all artistic mediums and forces," and beyond, to his Dada activities in Zurich.

The seriousness of these considerations, as elaborated in the diaries, helps to dispel several myths about the beginnings of Dada, above all the idea of Dada as little more than the sophomoric rantings of a group of young draft-dodgers, a kind of willful Marx Brothers zaniness. There was, of course, much that was plainly silly in the Cabaret performances, but for Ball this buffoonery was a means to an end, a necessary cathar-sis: "Perfect skepticism makes perfect freedom possible . . . One can almost say that when belief in an object or a cause comes to an end, this object or cause returns to chaos and becomes common property. But perhaps it is necessary to have resolutely, forcibly produced chaos and thus a complete withdrawal of faith before an entirely new edifice can be built up on a changed basis of belief." To understand Dada, then, at least in this early phase, we must see it as a vestige of old humanistic ideals, a reassertion of individual dignity in a mechanical age of stan-dardization, as a simultaneous expression of despair and hope. Ball's particular contribution to the Cabaret performances, his sound poems, or "poems without words," bears this out. Although he cast aside ordi-nary language, he had no intention of destroying language itself. In his almost mystical desire to recover what he felt to be a prelapsarian speech, Ball saw in this new, purely emotive form of poetry a way of capturing the magical essences of words. "In these phonetic poems we totally renounce the language that journalism has abused and cor-rupted. We must return to the innermost alchemy of the word. . . ."

Ball retreated from Zurich only seven months after the opening of the Cabaret Voltaire, partly from exhaustion, and partly from disenchantment with the way Dada was developing. His conflict was principally with Tzara, whose ambition was to turn Dada into one of the many movements of the international avant-garde. As John Elderfield summarizes in his introduction to Ball's diary: "And once away he felt he discerned a certain 'Dada hubris' in what they had been doing. He had believed they were eschewing conventional morality to elevate themselves as new men, that they had welcomed irrationalism as a way toward the 'supernatural', that sensationalism was the best method of destroying the academic. He came to doubt all this — he had become ashamed of the confusion and eclecticism of the cabaret — and saw isolation from the age as a surer and more honest path toward these personal goals. . . ." Several months later, however, Ball returned to Zurich to take part in the events of the Galerie Dada and to deliver his important lecture on Kandinsky, but within a short while he was again feuding with Tzara, and this time the break was final.

In July 1917, under Tzara's direction, Dada was officially launched as a movement, complete with its own publication, manifestos, and promotion campaign. Tzara was a tireless organizer, a true avant-gardist in the style of Marinetti, and eventually, with the help of Picabia and Serner, he led Dada far from the original ideas of the Cabaret Voltaire, away from what Elderfield correctly calls "the earlier equilibrium of construction-negation" into the bravura of anti-art. A few years later there was a further split in the movement, and Dada divided itself into two factions: the German group, led by Huelsenbeck, George Grosz, and the Herzefelde brothers, which was predominantly political in approach, and Tzara's group, which moved to Paris in 1920, and which championed the aesthetic anarchism that ultimately developed into Surrealism.

If Tzara gave Dada its identity, he also robbed it of the moral purpose it had aspired to under Ball. By turning it into a doctrine, by garnishing it with a set of programmatic ideals, Tzara led Dada into self-contradiction and impotence. What for Ball had been a true cry from the heart against all systems of thought and action became one organization among others. The stance of anti-art, which opened the way for endless provocations and attacks, was essentially an inauthentic idea. For art opposed to art is nevertheless art; you can't have it both ways at once. As Tzara wrote in one of his manifestos: "The true Dadaists are against

Dada." The impossibility of establishing this as dogma is obvious, and Ball, who had the foresight to realize this contradiction quite early, left as soon as he saw signs of Dada becoming a movement. For the others, however, Dada became a kind of bluff that was pushed to further and further extremes. But the real motivation was gone, and when Dada finally died, it was not so much from the battle it had fought as from its own inertia.

Ball's position, on the other hand, seems no less valid today than it did in 1917. Of what we have come to realize were several different periods and divergent tendencies in Dada, the moment of Ball's participation, as I see it, remains the moment of Dada's greatest strength, the period that speaks most persuasively to us today. This is perhaps a heretical view. But when we consider how Dada exhausted itself under Tzara, how it succumbed to the decadent system of exchange in the bourgeois art world, provoking the very audience whose favor it was courting, this branch of Dada must be seen as a symptom of art's essential weakness under modern capitalism — locked in the invisible cage of what Marcuse has called "repressive tolerance." But because Ball never treated Dada as an end in itself, he remained flexible, and was able to use Dada as an instrument for reaching higher goals, for producing a genuine critique of the age. Dada, for Ball, was merely the name for a kind of radical doubt, a way of sweeping aside all existing ideologies and moving on to an examination of the world around him. As such, the energy of Dada can never be used up: it is an idea whose time is always the present.

Ball's eventual return to the Catholicism of his childhood in 1921 is not really as strange as it may seem. It represents no true shift in his thinking, and in many ways can be seen as simply a further step in his development. Had he lived longer, there is no reason to believe that he would not have undergone further metamorphosis. As it is, we discover in his diaries a continual overlapping of ideas and concerns, so that even during the Dada period, for example, there are repeated references to Christianity ("I do not know if we will go beyond Wilde and Baudelaire in spite of all our efforts; or if we will not just remain romantics. There are probably other ways of achieving the miracle and other ways of opposition too — asceticism, for example, the church") and during the time of his most serious Catholicism there is a preoccupation with mystical language that clearly resembles the sound poem theories of his Dada period. As he remarks in one of his last entries, in 1921: "The socialist, the aesthete, the monk: all three agree that modern bourgeois education must be destroyed. The new ideal will take its new elements from all three." Ball's short life was a constant straining toward a synthesis of these different points of view. If we regard him today as an important figure, it is not because he managed to discover a solution, but because he was able to state the problems with such clarity. In his intellectual courage, in the fervor of his confrontation with the world, Hugo Ball stands out as one of the exemplary spirits of the age.

1975

Truth, Beauty, Silence

Laura Riding was still in her thirties when she published her 477-page *Collected Poems* in 1938. At an age when most poets are just beginning to come into their own, she had already reached full maturity, and the list of her accomplishments in literature up to that time is impressive: nine volumes of poetry, several collections of critical essays and fiction, a long novel, and the founding of a small publishing house, the Seizin Press. As early as 1924, soon after her graduation from Cornell, *The Fugitive* had called her "the discovery of the year, a new figure in American poetry," and later, in Europe, during the period of her intimate and stormy relationship with Robert Graves, she became an important force of the international avant-garde. Young Auden was apparently so influenced by her poems that Graves felt obliged to write him a letter reprimanding him for his blatant Laura Riding imitations, and the method of close textual criticism developed in *A Survey of Modernist Poetry* (written in collaboration with Graves) directly inspired Empson's *Seven Types of Ambiguity*. Then, after 1938, nothing. No more poems, no more stories, no more essays. As time went on, Laura Riding's name was almost totally forgotten, and to a new generation of poets and writers it was as if she had never existed.

She was not heard from again until 1962, when she agreed to give a reading of some of her poems for a BBC broadcast and to deliver a few remarks about the philosophical and linguistic reasons for her break with poetry. Since then, there have been several appearances in print, and now, most recently, the publication of two books: a selection of her poems, which is prefaced by a further discussion of her attitude toward poetry, and *The Telling*, a prose work which she has described as a "personal evangel." Clearly, Laura Riding is back. Although she has written no poems since 1938, her new work in *The Telling* is intimately connected with her earlier writings, and in spite of her long public silence, her career is of a single piece. Laura Riding and Laura (Riding) Jackson — the married name she now uses — are in many ways mirror images of one another. Each has attempted to realize a kind of universal truth in language, a way of speaking that would somehow reveal to us our essential humanness — "a linguistically ordained ideal, every degree of fulfillment of which is a degree of express fulfillment of the hope comprehended in being, in its comprehending us within it, as human" — and if this ambition seems at times to be rather grandiosely stated, it has nevertheless been constant. The only thing that has changed is the method. Up to 1938, Laura Riding was convinced that poetry was the best way to achieve this goal. Since then, she has revised her opinion, and has not only given up poetry, but now sees it as one of the prime obstacles on this path toward linguistic truth.

When we turn to her own poetry, what is above all striking is its consistency of purpose and manner. From the very beginning, it seems, Laura Riding knew where she was going, and her poems ask to be read not as isolated lyrics, but as interconnecting parts of an enormous poetic project.

> We must learn better
> What we are and are not.
> We are not the wind.
> We are not every vagrant mood that tempts
> Our minds to giddy homelessness.
> We must distinguish better
> Between ourselves and strangers.
> There is much that we are not.
> There is much that is not.
> There is much that we have not to be.

(from "The Why of the Wind")

This is essential Riding: the abstract level of discourse, the insistence upon confronting ultimate questions, the tendency toward moral exhortation, the quickness and cleanness of thought, the unexpected juxtapositions of words, as in the phrase "giddy homelessness." The physical world is hardly present here, and when it is mentioned, it appears only as metaphor, as a kind of linguistic shorthand for indicating ideas and mental processes. The wind, for example, is not a real wind, but a way of expressing what is changeable, a reference to the idea of flux, and we feel its impact only as an idea. The poem itself proceeds as an argument rather than as a statement of feeling or an evocation of personal experience, and its movement is toward generalization, toward the utterance of what the poet takes to be a fundamental truth.

"We are not the wind." In other words, we are what does not change. For Laura Riding, this is the given of her project; it cannot be proved, but nevertheless it operates as the informing principle of her work as a whole. In poem after poem we witness her trying somehow to peel back the skin of the world in order to find some absolute and unassailable place of permanence, and because the poems are rarely grounded in a physical perception of that world, they tend, strangely, to exist in an almost purely emotional climate, created by the fervor of this metaphysical quest. And yet, in spite of the high seriousness of the poems, there are moments of sharp wit that remind us of Emily Dickinson:

> Then follows a description
> Of an interval called death
> By the living.
> But I shall speak of it
> As of a brief illness.
> For it lasted only
> From being not ill
> To being not ill.
> It came about by chance—
> I met God.
> "What," he said, "you already?"
> "What," I said, "you still?"

> (from "Then Follows," in *Collected Poems*)

In the beginning, it is difficult to take the full measure of these poems, to understand the particular kinds of problems they are trying to deal with. Laura Riding gives us almost nothing to see, and this absence of imagery and sensuous detail, of any true *surface*, is at first baffling. We feel as though we had been blinded. But this is intentional on her part, and it plays an important role in the themes she develops. She does not so much want to see as to consider the notion of what is seeable.

> You have pretended to be seeing.
> I have pretended that you saw.
> So came we by such eyes—
> And within mystery to have language.

> *

> There was no sight to see.

339

That which is to be seen is no sight.
You made it a sight to see.
It is no sight, and this was the cause.

Now, having seen, let our eyes close
And a dark blessing pass among us—
A quick-slow blessing to have seen
And said and done no worse or better.

(from "Benedictory")

The only thing that seems to be present here is the poet's voice, and it is only gradually, as we "let our eyes close," that we begin to listen to this voice with special care, to become extremely sensitive to its nuances. Malebranche said that attention is the natural prayer of the soul. In her best poems, I think, Laura Riding coaxes us into a state of rapt listening, *into* a voice to which we give our complete attention, so that we, as readers, become participants in the unfolding of the poem. The voice is not so much speaking out loud as thinking, following the complex process of thought, and in such a way that it is almost immediately internalized by us. Few poets have ever been able to manipulate abstractions so persuasively. Having been stripped of ornament, reduced to their bare essentials, the poems emerge as a kind of rhetoric, a system of pure argument that works in the manner of music, generating an interaction of themes and counter-themes, and giving the same formal pleasure that music gives.

And talk in talk like time in time vanishes.
Ringing changes on dumb supposition,
Conversation succeeds conversation,
Until there's nothing left to talk about
Except truth, the perennial monologue,
And no talker to dispute it but itself.

(from "The Talking World")

These strengths, however, can also be weaknesses. For in order to sustain the high degree of intellectual precision necessary to the success of the poems, Laura Riding has been forced to engage in a kind of poetic brinkmanship, and she has often lost more than she has won. Eventually, we come to realize that the reasons for her break with poetry are implicit in the poems themselves. No matter how much we might admire her work, we sense that there is something missing in it, that it is not really capable of expressing the full range of experience it claims to be expressing. The source of this lack, paradoxically, lies in her conception of language, which in many ways is at odds with the very idea of poetry:

> Come, words, away from mouths,
> Away from tongues in mouths
> And reckless hearts in tongues
> And mouths in cautious heads—
> Come, words, away to where
> The meaning is not thickened
> With the voice's fretting substance . . .

(from "Come, Words, Away")

This is a self-defeating desire. If anything, poetry is precisely that way of using language which forces words to remain *in* the mouth, the way by which we can most fully experience and understand "the voice's fretting substance." There is something too glacial in Laura Riding's approach to gain our sympathy. If the truth in language she is seeking is a human truth, it would seem to be contradictory to want this truth at the expense of what is human. But in trying to deny speech its physical properties — in refusing to acknowledge that speech is an imperfect tool of imperfect creatures — this seems to be exactly what she is doing.

In the 1938 preface to the *Collected Poems*, at the moment of her most passionate adherence to poetry, we can see this desire for transcendence as the motivating force behind her work. "I am going to give you," she writes, "poems written for all the reasons of poetry — poems which are also a record of how, by gradual integration of the reasons of poetry, existence in poetry becomes more real than existence in time — more real because more good, more good because more true." Thirty years later, she uses almost the same terms to justify her equally passionate opposition to poetry: "To a poet the mere making of a poem can seem to solve the problem of truth . . . But only a problem of art is solved in poetry. Art, whose honesty must work through artifice, cannot avoid cheating truth. Poetic art cheats truth to further and finer degrees than art of any other kind because the spoken word is its exclusive medium. . . ."

For all their loftiness and intensity, these statements remain curiously vague. For the truth that is referred to is never really defined, except as something beyond time, beyond art, beyond the senses. Such talk seems to set us afloat in a vast realm of Platonic idealism, and it is difficult for us to know where we are. At the same time, we are unconvinced. Neither statement is very believable to us as a statement about poetry, because, at heart, neither one *is* about poetry. Laura Riding is clearly interested in problems that extend beyond the scope of poetry, and by dwelling on these problems *as if* they were poetry's exclusive concerns, she only confuses the issue. She did not renounce poetry because of any objective inadequacy in poetry itself — for it is no more or less adequate than any other human activity — but because poetry as she conceived of it was no longer capable of saying what she wanted to say. She now feels that she had "reached poetry's limit." But what really happened, it would seem, is that she had reached her own limit in poetry.

It is appropriate, then, that her work since 1938 has been largely devoted to a more general investigation of language, and when we come to *The Telling* we find a deeper discussion of many of the same questions she had tried to formulate in her poetry. The book, which fits into no established literary category, is positively Talmudic in structure. "The Telling" itself is a short text of less than fifty pages, divided into numbered paragraphs, originally written for an issue of the magazine *Chelsea* in 1967. To this "core-text" which is written in a dense, highly abstract prose almost totally devoid of outside references, she has added a series of commentaries, commentaries on commentaries, notes, and addenda, which flesh out many of the earlier conclusions and treat of various literary, political, and philosophical matters. It is an astonishing display of a consciousness confronting and examining itself. Based on the idea that "the human utmost is marked out in a linguistic utmost," she pursues an ideal of "humanly perfect word-use" (as opposed to "artistically perfect word-use"), by which she aims to uncover the essential nature of being. Again, or rather still, she is straining toward absolutes, toward an unshakable and unified vision of the world: ". . . the nature of our being is not to be known as we know the weather, which is by the sense of the momentary. Weather is all change, while our being, in its human nature, is all constancy . . . it is to be known only by the sense of the constant." Although Laura (Riding) Jackson has put her former poet self in parentheses, she looks upon *The Telling* as the successful continuation of her efforts as a poet: "To speak as I speak in it, say such things as I say in it, was part of my hope as a poet."

The first paragraph of *The Telling* sets forth the substance of the problem that she confronts in the rest of the book:

There is something to be told about us for the telling of which we all wait. In our unwilling ignorance we hurry to listen to stories of old human life, new human life, fancied human life, avid of something to while away the time of unanswered curiosity. We know we are explainable, and not explained. Many of the lesser things concerning us have been told but the greater things have not been told; and nothing can fill their place. Whatever we learn of what is not ourselves, but ours to know, being of our universal world, will likewise leave the emptiness an emptiness. Until the missing story of ourselves is told, nothing besides told can suffice us: we shall go on quietly craving it.

What immediately strikes us here is the brilliance of the writing itself. The quiet urgency and strong, cadenced phrasing entice us to go on listening. It seems that we are about to be told something radically different from anything we have ever been told before, and of such fundamental importance that it would be in our best interests to pay careful attention to what follows. "We know we are explainable, and not explained." In the subsequent paragraphs we are shown why the various human disciplines — science, religion, philosophy, history, poetry — have not and cannot explain us. Suddenly, everything has been swept aside; the way seems to have been cleared for a totally fresh approach to things. And yet, when she reaches the point of offering her own explanations, we are once again presented with the mysterious and unbelievable Platonism we had encountered before. It seems, finally, as if she were rejecting the myth-making tendencies of previous thought only in order to present another myth of her own devising — a myth of memory, a faith in the capacity of human beings to remember a time of wholeness that preceded the existence of individual selves. "May our Manyness become All-embracing. May we see in one another the All that was once All-One re-become One." And elsewhere: "Yes, I think we remember our creation! — have the memory of it in us, to know. Through the memory of it we apprehend that there was a Before-time of being from which being passed into what would be us." The problem is not that we doubt this belief of hers. We feel, in fact, that she is trying to report back to us about a genuine mystical experience; what is hard for us to accept is that she assumes this experience to be accessible to everyone. Perhaps it is. But we have no way of knowing — and would have no way of proving it even if we did. Laura (Riding) Jackson speaks of this purely personal experience in rigorous and objective terms, and as a result mingles two kinds of incompatible discourse. Her private perceptions have been projected on to the world at large, so that when she looks out on that world she thinks she sees a confirmation of her findings. But there is no distinction made between what is asserted as fact and what is verifiable as fact. As a consequence, there is no common ground established with us, and we find no place where we would want to stand with her in her beliefs.

In spite of this, however, it would be wrong simply to dismiss the book. If *The Telling* ultimately fails to carry out its promises, it is still valuable to us for the exceptional quality of its prose and the innovations of its form. The sheer immensity of its ambitions makes it an exciting work, even when it is most irritating. More importantly, it is crucial to us for what it reveals — retroactively — about Laura Riding's earlier work as a poet. For, in the end, it is as a poet that she will be read and remembered. Whatever objections we might want to raise about her approach to poetry in general, it would be difficult not to recognize her as a poet of importance. We need not be in agreement with her to admire her.

> Roses are buds, and beautiful,
> One petal leaning toward adventure.
> Roses are full, all petals forward,
> Beauty and power indistinguishable.
> Roses are blown, startled with life,
> Death young in their faces.
> Then comes the halt, and recumbence, and failing.
> But none says, "A rose is dead."
> But men die: it is said, it is seen.
> For a man is a long, late adventure;
> His budding is a purpose,
> His fullness more purpose,
> His blowing a renewal,
> His death, a cramped spilling
> Of rash measure and miles.
> To the roses no tears:
> Which flee before the race is called.
> And to man no mercy but his will:

That he has had his will, and is done.
The mercy of truth — it is to be truth.

(from "The Last Covenant")

In one of the supplementary chapters of *The Telling*, "Extracts From Communications," she speaks of the relationship between the writer and his work in a way that seems to express her aspirations as a poet. "If what you write is true, it will not be so because of what you are as a writer but because of what you are as a being. There can be no literary equivalent to truth. If, in writing, truth is the quality of what is said, told, this is not a literary achievement: it is a simple human achievement." This is not very far from the spirit of Ben Jonson's assertion that only a good man is capable of writing a good poem. It is an idea that stands at one extreme of our literary consciousness, and it places poetry within an essentially moral framework. As a poet, Laura Riding followed this principle until she reached what she felt to be "a crisis-point at which division between craft and creed reveals itself to be absolute." In the making of poems, she concluded, the demands of art would always outweigh the demands of truth.

Beauty and truth. It is the old question, come back to haunt us. Laura Riding sacrificed here poetic career in a choice between the two. But whether she has really answered the question, as she appears to think she has, is open to debate. What we do have are the poems she left behind her, and it is not surprising, perhaps, that we are drawn to them most of all for their beauty. We cannot call Laura Riding a neglected poet, since she was the cause of her own neglect. But after more than thirty years of absence, these poems strike us with all the force of a rediscovery.

1975

From Cakes to Stones
a note on Beckett's French

Mercier and Camier was the first of Samuel Beckett's novels to be written in French. Completed in 1946, and withheld from publication until 1970, it is also the last of his longer works to have been translated into English. Such a long delay would seem to indicate that Beckett is not overly fond of the work. Had he not been given the Nobel prize in 1969, in fact, it seems likely that *Mercier and Camier* would not have been published at all. This reluctance on Beckett's part is somewhat puzzling, for if *Mercier and Camier* is clearly a transitional work, at once harking back to *Murphy* and *Watt* and looking forward to the masterpieces of the early fifties, it is nevertheless a brilliant work, with its own particular strengths and charms, unduplicated in any of Beckett's six other novels. Even at his not quite best, Beckett remains Beckett, and reading him is like reading no one else.

Mercier and Camier are two men of indeterminate middle age who decide to leave everything behind them and set off on a journey. Like Flaubert's Bouvard and Pécuchet, like Laurel and Hardy, like the other "pseudo couples" in Beckett's work, they are not so much separate characters as two elements of a tandem reality, and neither one could exist without the other. The purpose of their journey is never stated, nor is their destination ever made clear. "They had consulted together at length, before embarking on this journey, weighing with all the calm at their command what benefits they might hope from it, what ills apprehend, maintaining turn about the dark side and the rosy. The only certitude they gained from these debates was that of not lightly launching out, into the unknown." Beckett, the master of the comma, manages in these few sentences to cancel out any possibility of a goal. Quite simply, Mercier and Camier agree to meet, they meet (after painful confusion), and set off. That they never really get anywhere, only twice, in fact, cross the town limits, in no way impedes the progress of the book. For the book is not about what Mercier and Camier do; it is about what they are.

Nothing happens. Or, more precisely, what happens is what does not happen. Armed with the vaudeville props of umbrella, sack, and raincoat, the two heroes meander through the town and the surrounding countryside, encountering various objects and personages: they pause frequently and at length in an assortment of bars and public places; they consort with a warm-hearted prostitute named Helen; they kill a policeman; they gradually lose their few possessions and drift apart. These are the outward events, all precisely told, with wit, elegance, and pathos, and interspersed with some beautiful descriptive passages ("The sea is not far, just visible beyond the valleys disappearing eastward, pale plinth as pale as the pale wall of sky"). But the real substance of the book lies in the conversations between Mercier and Camier:

> If we have nothing to say, said Camier, let us say nothing.
> We have things to say, said Mercier.
> Then why can't we say them? said Camier.
> We can't, said Mercier.
> Then let us be silent, said Camier.
> But we try, said Mercier.

In a celebrated passage of *Talking about Dante*, Mandelstam wrote: "The *Inferno* and especially the *Purgatorio* glorify the human gait, the measure and rhythm of walking, the foot and its shape ... In Dante philosophy and poetry are forever on the move, forever on their feet. Even standing still is a variety of accumulated motion; making a place for people to stand and talk takes as much trouble as scaling an Alp." Beckett, who is one of the finest readers of Dante, has learned these lessons with utter thoroughness. Almost uncannily, the prose of *Mercier and Camier* moves along at a walking pace, and after a while one begins to have the distinct impression that somewhere, buried deep within the words, a silent metronome is beating out the rhythms of Mercier and Camier's perambulations. The pauses, the hiatuses, the sudden shifts of conversation and description do not break this rhythm, but rather take place under its influence (which has already been firmly established), so that their effect is not one of disruption but of counterpoint and fulfillment. A mysterious stillness seems to envelop each sentence in the book, a kind of gravity, or calm, so that between each sentence the reader feels the passing of time, the footsteps that continue to move, even when nothing is said. "Sitting at the bar they discoursed of this and that, brokenly, as was their custom. They spoke, fell silent, listened to each other, stopped listening, each as he fancied or as bidden from within."

This notion of time, of course, is directly related to the notion of *timing*, and it seems no accident that *Mercier and Camier* immediately precedes *Waiting for Godot* in Beckett's oeuvre. In some sense, it can be seen as a warm-up for the play. The music-hall banter, which was perfected in the dramatic works, is already present in the novel:

> What will it be? said the barman.
> When we need you we'll tell you, said Camier.
> What will it be? said the barman.
> The same as before, said Mercier.
> You haven't been served, said the barman.
> The same as this gentleman, said Mercier.
> The barman looked at Camier's empty glass.
> I forget what it was, he said.
> I too, said Camier.
> I never knew, said Mercier.

But whereas *Waiting for Godot* is sustained by the implicit drama of Godot's absence — an absence that commands the scene as powerfully as any presence — *Mercier and Camier* progresses in a void. From one moment to the next, it is impossible to foresee what will happen. The action, which is not buoyed by any tension or intrigue, seems to take place against a background of nearly total silence, and whatever is said is said at the very moment there is nothing left to say. Rain dominates the book, from the first paragraph to the last sentence ("And in the dark he could hear better too, he could hear the sounds the long day had kept from him, human murmurs for example, and the rain on the water") — an endless Irish rain, which is accorded the status of a metaphysical idea, and which creates an atmosphere that hovers between boredom and anguish, between bitterness and jocularity. As in the play, tears are shed, but more from a knowledge of the futility of tears than from any need to purge oneself of grief. Likewise, laughter is merely what happens when tears have been spent. All goes on, slowly waning in the hush of time, and unlike Vladimir and Estragon, Mercier and Camier must endure without any hope of redemption.

The key word in all this, I feel, is dispossession. Beckett, who begins with little, ends with even less. The movement in each of his works is toward a kind of unburdening, by which he leads us to the limits of experience — to a place where aesthetic and moral judgments become inseparable. This is the itinerary of the characters in his books, and it has also been his own progress as a writer. From the lush, convoluted, and jauny prose of *More Pricks than Kicks* (1934) to the desolate spareness of *The Lost Ones* (1970), he has gradually cut closer and closer to the bone. His decision thirty years ago to write in French was undoubtedly the crucial event in this progress. This was an almost inconceivable act. But again, Beckett is not like other writers. Before truly coming into his own, he had to leave behind what came most easily to him, struggle against his own facility as a stylist. Beyond Dickens and Joyce, there is perhaps no English writer of the past hundred years who has equalled Beckett's early prose for vigor and intelligence; the language of *Murphy*, for example, is so packed that the novel has the density of a short lyric poem. By switching to French (a language, as Beckett has remarked, that "has no style"), he willingly began all over again. *Mercier and Camier* stands at the very beginning of this new life, and it is interesting to note that in this English translation Beckett has cut out nearly a fifth of the original text. Phrases, sentences, entire passages have been discarded, and what we have been given is really an editing job as well as a translation. This tampering, however, is not difficult to understand. Too many echoes, too many ornate and clever flourishes from the past remain, and though a considerable amount of superb material has been lost, Beckett apparently did not think it good enough to keep.

In spite of this, or perhaps because of this, *Mercier and Camier* comes close to being a flawless work. As with all of Beckett's self-translations, this version is not so much a literal translation of the original as a re-creation, a "repatriation" of the book into English. However stripped his style in French may be, there is always a little extra something added to the English renderings, some slight twist of diction or nuance, some unexpected word falling at just the right moment, that reminds us that English is nevertheless Beckett's home.

> George, said Camier, five sandwiches, four wrapped and one on the side. You see, he said, turning graciously to Mr Conaire, I think of everything. For the one I eat here will give me the strength to get back with the four others.
>
> Sophistry, said Mr Conaire. You set off with your five, wrapped, feel faint, open up, take one out, eat, recuperate, push on with the others.
>
> For all response Camier began to eat.
>
> You'll spoil him, said Mr Conaire. Yesterday cakes, today sandwiches, tomorrow crusts, and Thursday stones.
>
> Mustard, said Camier.

There is a crispness to this that outdoes the French. "Sophistry" for "raisonnement du clerc," "crusts" for "pain sec," and the assonance with 'mustard' in the next sentence give a neatness and economy to the exchange that is even more satisfying than the original. Everything has been pared down to a minimum; not a syllable is out of place.

We move from cakes to stones, and from page to page Beckett builds a world out of almost nothing. Mercier and Camier set out on a journey and do not go anywhere. But at each step of the way, we want to be exactly where they are. How Beckett manages this is something of a mystery. But as in all his work, less is more.

1975

The Poetry of Exile

A Jew, born in Romania, who wrote in German and lived in France. Victim of the Second World War, survivor of the death camps, suicide before he was fifty. Paul Celan was a poet of exile, an outsider even to the language of his own poems, and if his life was exemplary in its pain, a paradigm of the destruction and dislocation of midcentury Europe, his poetry is defiantly idiosyncratic, always and absolutely his own. In Germany, he is considered the equal of Rilke and Trakl, the heir to Hölderlin's metaphysical lyricism, and elsewhere his work is held in similar esteem, prompting statements such as George Steiner's recent remark that Celan is "almost certainly the major European poet of the period after 1945." At the same time, Celan is an exceedingly difficult poet, both dense and obscure. He demands so much of a reader, and in his later work his utterances are so gnomic, that it is nearly impossible to make full sense of him, even after many readings. Fiercely intelligent, propelled by a dizzying linguistic force, Celan's poems seem to explode on the page, and encountering them for the first time is a memorable event. It is to feel the same strangeness and excitement that one feels in discovering the work of Hopkins, or Emily Dickinson.

Czernovitz, Bukovina, where Celan was born as Paul Anczel in 1920, was a multilingual area that had once been part of the Habsburg Empire. In 1940, after the Hitler-Stalin pact, it was annexed by the Soviet Union, in the following year occupied by Nazi troops, and in 1943 retaken by the Russians. Celan's parents were deported to a concentration camp in 1942 and did not return; Celan, who managed to escape, was put in a labor camp until December 1943. In 1945 he went to Bucharest, where he worked as a translator and publisher's reader, then moved to Vienna in 1947, and finally, in 1948, settled permanently in Paris, where he married and became a teacher of German literature at the Ecole Normale Supérieure. His output comprises seven books of poetry and translations of more than two dozen foreign poets, including Mandelstam, Ungaretti, Pessoa, Rimbaud, Valéry, Char, du Bouchet, and Dupin.

Celan came to poetry rather late, and his first poems were not published until he was almost thirty. All his work, therefore, was written after the Holocaust, and his poems are everywhere informed by its memory. The unspeakable yields a poetry that continually threatens to overwhelm the limits of what can be spoken. For Celan forgot nothing, forgave nothing. The death of his parents and his own experiences during the war are recurrent and obsessive themes that run through all his work.

> With names, watered
> by every exile.
> With names and seeds,
> with names dipped
> into all
> the calyxes that are full of your
> regal blood, man, — into all
> the calyxes of the great
> ghetto-rose, from which
> you look at us, immortal with so many
> deaths died on morning errands.

(from "Crowned Out . . .", 1963, trans. by Michael Hamburger)

Even after the war, Celan's life remained an unstable one. He suffered acutely from feelings of persecution, which led to repeated breakdowns in his later years — and eventually to his suicide in 1970, when he drowned himself in the Seine. An incessant writer who produced hundreds of poems during his relatively short writing life, Celan poured all his grief and anger into his work. There is no poetry more furious than his, no poetry so purely inspired by bitterness. Celan never stopped confronting the dragon of the past, and in the end it swallowed him up.

"Todesfugue" (Death Fugue) is not Celan's best poem, but it is unquestionably his most famous poem — the work that made his reputation. Coming as it did in the late forties, only a few years after the end of the war — and in striking contrast to Adorno's rather fatuous remark about the "barbarity" of writing poems after Auschwitz — "Todesfugue" had a considerable impact among German readers, both for its direct mention of the concentration camps and for the terrible beauty of its form. The poem is literally a fugue composed of words, and its pounding, rhythmical repetitions and variations mark off a terrain no less circumscribed, no less closed in on itself than a prison surrounded by barbed wire. Covering slightly less than two pages, it begins and ends with the following stanzas:

> Black milk of dawn we drink it at dusk
> we drink it at noon and at daybreak we drink it at night
> we drink and drink
> we are digging a grave in the air there's room for us all
> A man lives in the house he plays with the serpents he
>   writes
> he writes when it darkens to Germany your golden hair
>   Margarete
> he writes it and steps outside and the stars all aglisten
>   he whistles for his hounds
> he whistles for his Jews he has them dig a grave in the
>   earth
> he commands us to play for the dance

> *

> Black milk of dawn we drink you at night
> we drink you at noon death is a master from Germany
> we drink you at dusk and at daybreak we drink and we
>   drink you
> death is a master from Germany his eye is blue
> he shoots you with bullets of lead his aim is true
> a man lives in the house your golden hair Margarete
> he sets his hounds on us he gives us a grave in the air
> he plays with the serpents and dreams death is a master
>   from Germany
> your golden hair Margarete
> your ashen hair Shulamite

(trans. by Joachim Neugroschel)

In spite of the poem's great control and the formal sublimation of an impossibly emotional theme, "Todesfugue" is one of Celan's most explicit works. In the sixties, he even turned against it, refusing permission to have it reprinted in more anthologies because he felt that his poetry had progressed to a stage where "Todesfugue" was too obvious and superficially realistic. With this in mind, however, one does discover in this poem elements common to much of Celan's work: the taut energy of the language, the objectification of private anguish, the unusual distancing effected between feeling and image. As Celan himself expressed it in an early commentary on his poems: "What matters for this language . . . is precision. It does not transfigure, does not 'poetize', it names and composes, it tries to measure out the sphere of the given and the possible."

This notion of the possible is central to Celan. It is the way by which one can begin to enter his conception of the poem, his vision of reality. For the seeming paradox of another of his statements — "Reality is not. It must be searched for and won" — can lead to confusion unless one has already understood the aspiration for the real that informs Celan's poetry. Celan is not advocating a retreat into subjectivity or the construction of an imaginary universe. Rather, he is staking out the distance over which the poem must travel and defining the ambiguity of a world in which all values have been subverted.

> Speak—
> But keep yes and no unsplit,
> And give your say this meaning:
> give it the shade.
>
> Give it shade enough,
> give it as much
> as you know has been dealt out between
> midday and midday and midnight.
>
> Look around:
> look how it all leaps alive—
> where death is! Alive!
> He speaks truly who speaks the shade.
>
> (from "Speak, You Also," trans. by Michael Hamburger)

In a public address delivered in the city of Bremen in 1958 after being awarded an important literary prize, Celan spoke of language as the one thing that had remained intact for him after the war, even though it had to pass through "the thousand darknesses of death-bringing speech." "In this language," Celan said — and by this he meant German, the language of the Nazis and the language of his poems — "I have tried to write poetry, in order to acquire a perspective of reality for myself." He then compared the poem to a message in a bottle — thrown out to sea in the hope that it will one day wash up to land, "perhaps on the shore of the heart." "Poems," he continued, "even in this sense are under way: they are heading toward something. Toward what? Toward some open place that can be inhabited, toward a thou which can be addressed, perhaps toward a reality which can be addressed."

The poem, then, is not a transcription of an already known world, but a process of discovery, and the act of writing for Celan is one that demands personal risks. Celan did not write solely in order to express himself, but to orient himself within his own life and take his stand in the world, and it is this feeling of necessity that communicates itself to a reader. These poems are more than literary artifacts. They are a means of staying alive.

In a 1946 essay on Van Gogh, Meyer Schapiro refers to the notion of realism in a way that could also apply to Celan. "I do not mean realism in the repugnant, narrow sense that it has acquired today," Professor Schapiro writes, ". . . but rather the sentiment that external reality is an object of strong desire or need, as a possession and potential means of fulfillment of the striving human being, and is therefore the necessary ground of art." Then, quoting a phrase from one of Van Gogh's letters — "I'm terrified of getting away from the possible . . ." — he observes: "Struggling against the perspective that diminishes an individual object before his eyes, he renders it larger than life. The loading of the pigment is in part a reflex of this attitude, a frantic effort to preserve in the image of things their tangible matter and to create something equally solid and concrete on the canvas."

Celan, whose life and attitude toward his art closely parallel Van Gogh's, used language in a way that is not unlike the way Van Gogh used paints, and their work is surprisingly similar in spirit.* Neither Van Gogh's stroke nor Celan's syntax is strictly representational, for in the eyes of each the "objective" world is interlocked with his perception of it. There is no reality that can be posited without the simultaneous effort to penetrate it, and the work of art as an ongoing process bears witness to this desire. Just as Van Gogh's painted objects acquire a concreteness "as real as reality," Celan handles words as if they had the density of objects, and he endows them with a substantiality that enables them to become a part of the world, his world — and not simply its mirror.

---

* Celan makes reference to Van Gogh in several of his poems, and the kinship between the poet and painter is indeed quite strong: both began as artists in their late twenties after having lived through experiences that marked them deeply for the rest of their lives; both produced work prolifically, at a furious pace, as if depending on the work for their very survival; both underwent debilitating mental crises that led to confinement; both committed suicide, foreigners in France.

Celan's poems resist straightforward exegesis. They are not linear progressions, moving from word to word, from point A to point B. Rather, they present themselves to a reader as intricate networks of semantic densities. Interlingual puns, oblique personal references, intentional misquotations, bizarre neologisms: these are the sinews that bind Celan's poems together. It is not possible to keep up with him, to follow his drift at every step along the way. One is guided more by a sense of tone and intention than by textual scrutiny. Celan does not speak explicitly, but he never fails to make himself clear. There is nothing random in his work, no gratuitous elements to obscure the perception of the poem. One reads with one's skin, as if by osmosis, unconsciously absorbing nuances, overtones, syntactical twists, which in themselves are as much the meaning of the poem as its analytic content. Celan's method of composition is not unlike that of Joyce in *Finnegans Wake*. But if Joyce's art was one of accumulation and expansion — a spiral whirling into infinity — Celan's poetry is continually collapsing into itself, negating its very premises, again and again arriving at zero. We are in the world of the absurd, but we have been led there by a mind that refuses to acquiesce to it.

Consider the following poem, "Largo," one of Celan's later poems — and a typical example of the difficulty a reader faces in tackling Celan.* In Michael Hamburger's translation it reads:

> You of the same mind, moor-wandering near one:
>
> more-than-
> death-
> sized we lie
> together, autumn
> crocuses, the timeless, teems
> under our breathing eyelids,
> the pair of blackbirds hangs
> beside us, under
> our whitely drifting
> companions up there, our
>
> meta-
> stases.

---

* I am grateful to Katharine Washburn, a scrupulous reader and translator of Celan, for help in deciphering the German text of this poem and suggesting possible references.

The German text, however, reveals things that necessarily elude the grasp of translation:

> Gleichsinnige du, heidegängerisch Nahe:
> über-
> sterbens-
> gross liegen
> wir beieinander, die Zeit-
> lose wimmelt
> dir unter den atmenden Lidern,
> Das Amselpaar hängt
> neben uns, unter
> unsern gemeinsam droben mit-
> ziehenden weissen
>
> Meta-
> stasen.

In the first line, *heidegängerisch* is an inescapable allusion to Heidegger — whose thinking was in many ways close to Celan's, but who, as a pro-Nazi, stood on the side of the murderers. Celan visited Heidegger in the sixties, and although it is not known what they said to each other, one can assume that they discussed Heidegger's position during the war. The reference to Heidegger in the poem is underscored by the use of some of the central words from his philosophical writings: *Nahe, Zeit,* etc. This is Celan's way: he does not mention anything directly, but weaves his meanings into the fabric of the language, creating a space for the invisible, in the same way that thought accompanies us as we move through a landscape.

Further along, in the third stanza, there are the two blackbirds (stock figures in fairy tales, who speak in riddles and bring bad tidings). In the German one reads *Amsel* — which echoes the sound of Celan's own name, Anczel. At the same time, there is an evocation of Günter Grass's novel, *Dog Years,* which chronicles the love-hate relationship between a Jew and a Nazi during the war. The Jewish character in the story is named Amsel, and throughout the book — to quote George Steiner again — "there is a deadly pastiche of the metaphysical jargon of Heidegger."

Toward the end of the poem, the presence of "our whitely drifting / companions up there" is a reference to the Jewish victims of the Holocaust: the smoke of the bodies burned in crematoria. From early poems such as "Todesfugue" ("he gives us a grave in the air") to later poems such as "Largo," the Jewish dead in Celan's work inhabit the air, are the very substance we are condemned to breathe: souls turned into smoke, into dust, into nothing at all — "our / meta- / stases."

Celan's preoccupation with the Holocaust goes beyond mere history, however. It is the primal moment, the first cause and last effect of an entire cosmology. Celan is essentially a religious poet, and although he speaks with the voice of one forsaken by God, he never abandons the struggle to make sense of what has no sense, to come to grips with his own Jewishness. Negation, blasphemy, and irony take the place of devotion; the forms of righteousness are mimicked; Biblical phrases are turned around, subverted, made to speak against themselves. But in so doing, Celan draws nearer to the source of his despair, the absence that lives in the heart of all things. Much has been said about Celan's "negative theology." It is most fully expressed in the opening stanzas of "Psalm":

> No One kneads us anew from earth and clay,
> no one addresses our dust.
> No One.
>
> Laudeamus te, No One.
> For your sake would we
> bloom forth:
> unto
> You.
>
> Nothing
> were we, and are we and
> will be, all abloom:
> this Nothing's, this
> no-man's-rose.

(trans. by Katharine Washburn)

In the last decade of his life, Celan gradually refined his work to a point where he began to enter new and uncharted territory. The long lines and ample breath of the early poems give way to an elliptical, almost panting style in which words are broken up into their component syllables, unorthodox word-clusters are invented, and the reductionist natural vocabulary of the first books is inundated by references to science, technology, and political events. These short, usually untitled poems move along by lightning-quick flashes of intuition, and their message, as Michael Hamburger aptly puts it, "is at once more urgent and more reticent." One feels both a shrinking and an expansion in them, as if, by traveling to the inmost recesses of himself, Celan had somehow vanished, joining with the greater forces beyond him — and at the same time sinking more deeply into his isolation.

> Thread-suns
> over the gray-black wasteland.
> A tree-
> high thought
> strikes the note of light: there are
> still songs to sing beyond
> mankind.

(trans. by Joachim Neugroschel)

In poems such as this one, Celan has set the stakes so high that he must surpass himself in order to keep even with himself — and push his life into the void in order to cling to his identity. It is an impossible struggle, doomed from the start to disaster. For poetry cannot save the soul or retrieve a lost world. It simply asserts the given. In the end, it seems, Celan's desolation became too great to be borne, as if, in some sense, the world were no longer there for him. And when nothing was left, there could be no more words.

> You were my death:
> you I could hold
> when all fell away from me.

(trans. by Michael Hamburger)

1975

Innocence and Memory

From his earliest important poems, written in the trenches of the First World War, to the last poems of his old age, Giuseppe Ungaretti's work is a long record of confrontations with death. Cryptic in utterance, narrow in rage, and built on an imagery that is drawn exclusively from the natural world, Ungaretti's poetry nevertheless manages to avoid the predictable, and in spite of the limitations of his manner, he leaves an impression of almost boundless energy and invention. No word in Ungaretti's work is ever used lightly — "When I find/in this my silence/a word/it is dug into my life/like an abyss" — and the strength of his poetry comes precisely from this restraint. For a man who wrote for more than fifty years, Ungaretti published remarkably little before he died in 1970, and his collected poems amount to no more than a couple of hundred pages. Like Mallarmé before him (though in ways that are very different), Ungaretti's poetic source is silence, and in one form or another, all his work is an expression of the inexhaustible difficulty of expression itself. Reading him, one feels that he has only grudgingly allowed his words to appear on the page, that even the strongest words are in constant danger of annihilation.

Born in 1888, Ungaretti belonged to a celebrated generation of modern writers that included Pound, Joyce, Kafka, Trakl, and Pessoa. Like theirs, his importance is measured not only by his own achievement but by its effect on the history of the literature of his language. Before Ungaretti, there was no modern Italian poetry. When his first book, *Il Porto Sepolto (The Buried Port)*, appeared in 1916 in an edition of eighty copies, it seemed to have dropped from the sky, to be without precedent. These short, fragmented poems, at times hardly more ample than notes or inscriptions, announced a definitive break with the late-nineteenth-century conventions that still dominated Italian poetry. The horrible realities of the war demanded a new kind of expression, and for Ungaretti, who at that time was just finishing his poetic apprenticeship, the front was a training ground that taught the futility of all compromise.

Watch
Cima Quattro, December 23, 1915

One whole night
thrust down beside
a slaughtered comrade
his snarling
mouth
turned to the full moon
the bloating
of his hands
entering
my silence
I have written
letters full of love

Never have I held
so
fast to life*

If the brevity and hardness of his first poems seemed violent in comparison to most Italian poetry of the period, Ungaretti was no poetic rebel, and his work showed none of the spirit of self-conscious sabotage that characterized the Futurists and other avant-garde groups. His break with the past was not a renunciation of literary tradition, but a way of affirming his connection with a more distant and vital past than the one represented by his immediate predecessors. He simply cleared the ground that lay between him and what he felt to be his true sources, and like all original artists, he created his own tradition. In later years, this led him to extensive critical work, as well as translations of numerous foreign poets, including Gongora, Shakespeare, Racine, Blake, and Mallarmé.

Ungaretti's need to invent this poetic past for himself can perhaps be attributed to the unusual circumstances of his early life. By the twin accidents of his birthplace and the nature of his education, he was freed from many of the constraints of a pure Italian upbringing, and though he came from old Tuscan peasant stock, he did not set foot in Italy until he was twenty-four. His father, originally from Lucca, had emigrated to Egypt to work on the construction of the Suez Canal, and by the time of

* All quotations are translated by Allen Mandelbaum and appear in his *Selected Poems of Giuseppe Ungaretti*, published by Cornell University Press in 1975.

Ungaretti's birth he had become the proprietor of a bakery in the Arab quarter of Moharrem Bay in Alexandria. Ungaretti attended French schools, and his first real encounter with Europe took place a year before the war, in Paris, where he met Picasso, Braque, De Chirico, Max Jacob, and became close friends with Apollinaire. (In 1918, transferred to Paris at the time of the Armistice, he arrived at Apollinaire's house with the latter's favorite Italian cigars just moments after his death.) Apart from serving in the Italian army, Ungaretti did not live in Italy until 1921 — long after he had found his direction as a poet. Ungaretti was a cultural hybrid, and elements of his varied past are continually mixed into his work. Nowhere is this more concisely expressed than in "I fiumi" ("The Rivers")(1916), a long poem that concludes:

> I have gone over
> the seasons
> of my life
>
> These are
> my rivers
>
> This is the Serchio
> from whose waters have drawn
> perhaps two thousand years
> of my farming people
> and my father and my mother
>
> This is the Nile
> that saw me
> born and growing
> burning with unknowing
> on its broad plains
>
> This is the Seine
> and in its troubled flow
> I was remingled and remade
> and came to know myself
>
> These are my rivers
> counted in the Isonzo
>
> This is my nostalgia
> as it appears

in each river
now it is night
now my life seems to me
a corolla
of shadows

In early poems such as this one, Ungaretti manages to capture the past in the shape of an eternal present. Time exists, not as duration so much as accumulation, a gathering of discrete moments that can be revived and made to emerge in the nearness of the present. *Innocence and Memory* — the title given to the French edition of Ungaretti's essays — are the two contradictory aspirations embedded in his poetry, and all his work can be seen as a constant effort to renew the self without destroying its past. What concerns Ungaretti most is the search for spiritual self-definition, a way of discovering his own essence beyond the grip of time. It is a drama played out between the forces of permanence and impermanence, and its basic fact is human mortality. As in the war poem, "Watch," the sense of life for Ungaretti is experienced most fully in confronting death, and in a commentary on another of his poems, he describes this process as ". . . the knowing of being out of non-being, being out of the null, Pascalian knowing of being out of the null. Horrid consciousness."

If this poetry can be described as basically religious in nature, the sensibility that informs the poems is never monkish, and denial of the flesh is never offered as a solution to spiritual problems. It is, in fact, the conflict between the spiritual and the physical that sustains the poems and gives them their life. Ungaretti is a man of contradictions, a "man of pain," as he calls himself in one of his poems, but also a man of great passions and desires, who at times seems locked in "the glare of promiscuity," and who is able to write of ". . . the mare of your loins / Plunging you in agony / Into my singing arms." His obsession with death, therefore, does not derive from morbid self-pity or a search for other-worldliness, but from an almost savage will to live, and Ungaretti's robust sensuality, his firm adherence to the world of physical things, makes his poems tense with conflict between the irreconcilable powers of love and vanity.

In his later work, beginning with the second major collection, *Sentimento del Tempo (Sentiment of Time)* (1919–35), the distance between the present and the past grows, in the end becoming a chasm that is almost impossible to cross, either by an act of will or an act of grace. As with Pascal, as with Leopardi, the perception of the void translates itself into the central metaphor of an unappeasable agony in the face of an indifferent universe, and if Ungaretti's conversion to Catholicism in the late twenties is to be understood, it must be seen in the light of this "horrid consciousness." "La Pietà" (1928), the long poem that most clearly marks Ungaretti's conversion, is also one of his bleakest works, and it contains these lines, which can be read as a gloss on the particular nature of Ungaretti's anguish:

> You have banished me from life.
>
> And will you banish me from death?
>
> Perhaps man is unworthy even of hope.
>
> Dry, too, the fountain of remorse?
>
> What matters sin
> If it no longer leads to purity?
>
> The flesh can scarcely remember
> That once it was strong.
>
> Worn out and wild — the soul.
>
> God, look upon our weakness.
>
> We want a certainty.

Not satisfied to remain on safe ground, without the comfort of a "certainty," he continually goads himself to the edge of the abyss, threatening himself with the image of his own extinction. But rather than inducing him to succumb to despair, these acts of metaphysical risk seem to be the source of an enduring strength. In poems such as "The Premeditated Death," a sequence that serves as the hub to the whole of *Sentimento del Tempo*, and nearly all the poems in his following collection, *Il Dolore (The Grief)* (1936–47) — most notably the powerful poem written on the death of his young son, "You Shattered" — Ungaretti's determination to situate himself at the extremes of his own consciousness is paradoxically what allows him to cure himself of the fear of these limits.

By the force and precision of his meditative insight, Ungaretti manages to transcend what in a lesser poet would amount to little more than an inventory of private griefs and fears: the poems stand as objects beyond the self for the very reason that the self within them is not treated as an example of all selves or the self in general. At all times one feels the presence of the man himself in the work. As Allen Mandelbaum notes in the preface to his translations: "Ungaretti's I is grave and slow, intensive rather than far-ranging; and his longing gains its drama precisely because that I is not a random center of desperations, but a *soma* bound by weight, by earthly measure, a hard, resisting, substantial object, not wished but willed, not dreamt-upon but 'excavated'."

In the poems of his later years, Ungaretti's work comes to an astonishing culmination in the single image of the promised land. It is the promised land of both Aeneas and the Bible, of both Rome and the desert, and the personal and historical overtones of these final major poems — "Canzone," "Choruses Describing the States of Mind of Dido," "Recitative of Palinurus," and "Final Choruses for the Promised Land," — refer back to all of Ungaretti's previous work, as if to give it its final meaning. The return to a Virgilian setting represents a kind of poetic homecoming for him at the end of his career, just as the desert revives the landscape of his youth, only to leave him in a last and permanent exile:

> We cross the desert with remnants
> Of some earlier image in mind,
>
> That is all a living man
> Knows of the promised land.

Written between 1952 and 1960, the "Final Choruses" were published in *Il Taccuino del Vecchio (The Old Man's Notebook)*, and they reformulate all the essential themes of his work. Ungaretti's universe remains the same, and in a language that differs very little from that of his earliest poems, he prepares himself for his death — his real death, the last death possible for him:

> The kite hawk grips me in his azure talons
> And, at the apex of the sun,
> Lets me fall on the sand
> As food for ravens.
>
> I shall no longer bear mud on my shoulders,
> The fire will find me clean,

The cackling beaks
The stinking jaws of jackals.

Then as he searches with his stick
Through the sand, the bedouin
Will point out
A white, white bone.

1976

Book of the Dead

During the past few years, no French writer has received more serious critical attention and praise than Edmond Jabès. Maurice Blanchot, Emmanuel Levinas, and Jean Starobinski have all written extensively and enthusiastically about his work, and Jacques Derrida has remarked, flatly and without self-consciousness, that "in the last ten years nothing has been written in France that does not have its precedent somewhere in the texts of Jabès." Beginning with the first volume of *Le Livre des Questions*, which was published in 1963, and continuing on through the other volumes in the series,* Jabès has created a new and mysterious kind of literary work — as dazzling as it is difficult to define. Neither novel nor poem, neither essay nor play, *The Book of Questions* is a combination of all these forms, a mosaic of fragments, aphorisms, dialogues, songs, and commentaries that endlessly move around the central question of the book: how to speak what cannot be spoken. The question is the Jewish Holocaust, but it is also the question of literature itself. By a startling leap of the imagination, Jabès treats them as one and the same:

I talked to you about the difficulty of being Jewish, which is the same as the difficulty of writing. For Judaism and writing are but the same waiting, the same hope, the same wearing out.

The son of wealthy Egyptian Jews, Jabès was born in 1912 and grew up in the French-speaking community of Cairo. His earliest literary friendships were with Max Jacob, Paul Eluard, and René Char, and in the forties and fifties he published several small books of poetry which were later collected in *Je bâtis ma demeure* (1959). Up to that point, his reputation as a poet was solid, but because he lived outside France, he was not very well known.

---

* *Le Livre de Yukel* (1964), *Le Retour au Livre* (1965), *Yaël* (1967), *Elya* (1969), *Aély* (1972), *El, ou le dernier livre* (1973), which are followed by three volumes of *Le Livre des Resemblances*. Four books are available in English, all of them admirably translated by Rosmarie Waldrop: *The Book of Questions, The Book of Yukel, Return to the Book* (Wesleyan University Press), and *Elya* (Tree Books).

The Suez Crisis of 1956 changed everything for Jabès, both in his life and in his work. Forced by Nasser's regime to leave Egypt and resettle in France — consequently losing his home and all his possessions — he experienced for the first time the burden of being Jewish. Until then, his Jewishness had been nothing more than a cultural fact, a contingent element of his life. But now that he had been made to suffer for no other reason than that he was a Jew, he had become the Other, and this sudden sense of exile was transformed into a basic, metaphysical self-description.

Difficult years followed. Jabès took a job in Paris and was forced to do most of his writing on the Metro to and from work. When, not long after his arrival, his collected poems were published by Gallimard, the book was not so much an announcement of things to come as a way of marking the boundaries between his new life and what was now an irretrievable past. Jabès began studying Jewish texts — the Talmud, the Kabbala — and though this reading did not initiate a return to the religious precepts of Judaism, it did provide a way for Jabès to affirm his ties with Jewish history and thought. More than the primary source of the Torah, it was the writings and rabbinical commentaries of the Diaspora that moved Jabès, and he began to see in these books a strength particular to the Jews, one that translated itself, almost literally, into a mode of survival. In the long interval between exile and the coming of the Messiah, the people of God had become the people of the Book. For Jabès, this meant that the Book had taken on all the weight and importance of a homeland.

The Jewish world is based on written law, on a logic of words one cannot deny. So the country of the Jews is on the scale of their world, because it is a book . . . The Jew's fatherland is a sacred text amid the commentaries it has given rise to . . .

At the core of *The Book of Questions* there is a story — the separation of two young lovers, Sarah and Yukel, during the time of the Nazi deportations. Yukel is a writer — described as the "witness" — who serves as Jabès's alter ego and whose words are often indistinguishable from his; Sarah is a young woman who is shipped to a concentration camp and who returns insane. But the story is never really told, and it in no way resembles a traditional narrative. Rather, it is alluded to, commented on, and now and then allowed to burst forth in the passionate and obsessive love letters exchanged between Sarah and Yukel — which seem to come from nowhere, like disembodied voices, articulating what Jabès calls "the collective scream . . . the everlasting scream."

Sarah: I wrote you. I write you. I wrote you. I write you. I take refuge in my words, the words my pen weeps. As long as I am speaking, as long as I am writing, my pain is less keen. I join with each syllable to the point of being but a body of consonants, a soul of vowels. Is it magic? I write his name, and it becomes the man I love . . .

And Yukel, toward the end of the book:

And I read in you, through your dress and your skin, through your flesh and your blood. I read, Sarah, that you were mine through every word of our language, through all the wounds of our race. I read, as one reads the Bible, our history and the story which could only be yours and mine.

This story, which is the "central text" of the book, is submitted to extensive and elusive commentaries in Talmudic fashion. One of Jabès's most original strokes is the invention of the imaginary rabbis who engage in those conversations and interpret the text with their sayings and poems. Their remarks, which most often refer to the problem of writing the book and the nature of the Word, are elliptical, metaphorical, and set in motion a beautiful and elaborate counterpoint with the rest of the work.

"He is a Jew," said Reb Tolba. "He is leaning against a wall, watching the clouds go by."
"The Jew has no use for clouds," replied Reb Jale. "He is counting the steps between him and his life."

Because the story of Sarah and Yukel is not fully told, because, as Jabès implies, it *cannot* be told, the commentaries are in some sense an investigation of a text that has not been written. Like the hidden God of classic Jewish theology, the text exists only by virtue of its absence.

"I know you, Lord, in the measure that I do not know you. For you are He who comes."

Reb Lod

What happens in *The Book of Questions*, then, is the writing of *The Book of Questions* — or rather, the attempt to write it, a process that the reader is allowed to witness in all its gropings and hesitations. Like the narrator in Beckett's *The Unnamable*, who is cursed by "the inability to speak [and] the inability to be silent," Jabès's narrative goes nowhere but around and around itself. As Maurice Blanchot has observed in his excellent essay on Jabès: "The writing . . . must be accomplished in the act of interrupting itself." A typical page in *The Book of Questions* mirrors this sense of difficulty: isolated statements and paragraphs are separated by white spaces, then broken by parenthetical remarks, by italicized passages and italics within parentheses, so that the reader's eye can never grow accustomed to a single, unbroken visual field. One reads the book by fits and starts — just as it was written.

At the same time, the book is highly structured, almost architectural in its design. Carefully divided into four parts, "At the Threshold of the Book," "And You Shall Be in the Book," "The Book of the Absent," and "The Book of the Living," it is treated by Jabès as if it were a physical place, and once we cross its threshold we pass into a kind of enchanted realm, an imaginary world that has been held in suspended animation. As Sarah writes at one point: "I no longer know where I am. I know. I am nowhere. Here." Mythical in its dimensions, the book for Jabès is a place where the past and the present meet and dissolve into each other. There seems nothing strange about the fact that ancient rabbis can converse with a contemporary writer, that images of stunning beauty can stand beside descriptions of the greatest devastation, or that the visionary and the commonplace can coexist on the same page. From the very beginning, when the reader encounters the writer at the threshold of the book, we know that we are entering a space unlike any other.

"What is going on behind this door?"
"A book is shedding its leaves."
"What is the story of the book?"
"Becoming aware of a scream."
"I saw rabbis go in."
"They are privileged readers. They come in small groups to give us their comments."
"Have they read the book?"
"They are reading it."
"Did they happen by for the fun of it?"
"They foresaw the book. They are prepared to encounter it."
"Do they know the characters?"
"They know our martyrs."
"Where is the book set?"
"In the book."
"What are you?"
"I am the keeper of the house."
"Where do you come from?"
"I have wandered . . ."

The book "begins with difficulty — the difficulty of being and writing — and ends with difficulty." It gives no answers. Nor can any answers ever be given — for the precise reason that the "Jew," as one of the imaginary rabbis states, "answers every question with another question." Jabès conveys these ideas with a wit and eloquence that often evoke the logical hairsplitting — *pilpul* — of the Talmud. But he never deludes himself into believing that his words are anything more than "grains of sand" thrown to the wind. At the heart of the book there is nothingness.

"Our hope is for knowledge," said Reb Mendel. But not all his disciples were of his opinion.

"We have first to agree on the sense you give to the word 'knowledge', " said the oldest of them.

"Knowledge means questioning," answered Reb Mendel.

"What will we get out of these questions? What will we get out of all the answers which only lead to more questions, since questions are born of unsatisfactory answers?" asked the second disciple.

"The promise of a new question," replied Reb Mendel.

"There will be a moment," the oldest disciple continued, "when we will have to stop interrogating. Either because there will be no answer possible, or because we will not be able to formulate any further questions. So why should we begin?"

"You see," said Reb Mendel, "at the end of an argument, there is always a decisive question unsettled."

"Questioning means taking the road to despair," continued the second disciple. "We will never know what we are trying to learn."

Although Jabès's imagery and sources are for the most part derived from Judaism, *The Book of Questions* is not a Jewish work in the same way that one can speak of *Paradise Lost* as a Christian work. While Jabès is, to my knowledge, the first modern poet consciously to assimilate the forms and idiosyncrasies of Jewish thought, his relationship to Jewish teaching is emotional and metaphorical rather than one of strict adherence. The Book is his central image — but it is not only the Book of the Jews (the spirals of commentary around commentary in the Midrash), but an allusion to Mallarmé's ideal Book as well (the Book that contains the world, endlessly folding in upon itself). Finally, Jabès's work must be considered as part of the on-going French poetic tradition that began in the late nineteenth century. What Jabès has done is to fuse this tradition with a certain type of Jewish discourse, and he has done so with such conviction that the marriage between the two is almost imperceptible. *The Book of Questions* came into being because Jabès found himself as a writer in the act of discovering himself as a Jew. Similar in spirit to an idea expressed by Marina Tsvetaeva — "In this most Christian of worlds / all poets are Jews" — this equation is located at the exact center of Jabès's work, is the kernel from which everything else springs. To Jabès, nothing can be written about the Holocaust unless writing itself is first put into question. If language is to be pushed to the limit, then the writer must condemn himself to an exile of doubt, to a desert of uncertainty. What he must do, in effect, is create a poetics of absence. The dead cannot be brought back to life. But they can be heard, and their voices live in the Book.

1976

Reznikoff × 2

1. THE DECISIVE MOMENT

Charles Reznikoff is a poet of the eye. To cross the threshold of his work is to penetrate the prehistory of matter, to find oneself exposed to a world in which language has not yet been invented. Seeing, in his poetry, always comes before speech. Each poetic utterance is an emanation of the eye, a transcription of the visible into the brute, undeciphered code of being. The act of writing, therefore, is not so much an ordering of the real as a discovery of it. It is a process by which one places oneself between things and the names of things, a way of standing watch in this interval of silence and allowing things to be seen — as if for the first time — and henceforth to be given their names. The poet, who is the first man to be born, is also the last. He is Adam, but he is also the end of all generations: the mute heir of the builders of Babel. For it is he who must learn to speak from his eye — and cure himself of seeing with his mouth.

The poem, then, not as a telling, but as a taking hold. The world can never be assumed to exist. It comes into being only in the act of moving towards it. *Esse est percipii*: no American poet has ever adhered so faithfully to the Berkeleyan formula as Reznikoff. It is more than just the guiding principle of his work — it is *embedded* in the work, and it contains all the force of a moral dogma. To read Reznikoff is to understand that nothing can be taken for granted: we do not find ourselves in the midst of an already established world, we do not, as if by preordained birthright, automatically take possession of our surroundings. Each moment, each thing, must be earned, wrested away from the confusion of inert matter by a steadiness of gaze, a purity of perception so intense that the effort, in itself, takes on the value of a religious act. The slate has been wiped clean. It is up to the poet to write his own book.

Tiny poems, many of them barely a sentence long, make up the core of Reznikoff's work. Although his total output includes fiction, biography, drama, long narrative poems, historical meditations, and book-length documentary poems, these short lyrics are the Ur-texts of Reznikoff's imagination: everything else follows from them. Notable for their precision and simplicity, they also run counter to normal assumptions about what a poem should aspire to be. Consider these three examples:

> *April*
> The stiff lines of the twigs
> blurred by buds.

> *Moonlit Night*
> The trees' shadows lie in black pools in the lawns.

> *The Bridge*
> In a cloud bones of steel.

The point is that there is no point. At least not in any traditional sense. These poems are not trying to drum home universal truths, to impress the reader with the skill of their making, or to invoke the ambiguities of human experience. Their aim, quite simply, is clarity. Of seeing and of speaking. And yet, the unsettling modesty of these poems should not blind us to the boldness of their ambition. For even in these tiniest of poems, the gist of Reznikoff's poetics is there. It is as much an ethics of the poetic moment as it is a theory of writing, and its message never varies in any of Reznikoff's work: the poem is always more than just a construction of words. Art, then, for the sake of something — which means that art is almost an incidental by-product of the effort to make it. The poem, in all instances, must be an effort to perceive, must be a moving *outward*. It is less a mode of expressing the world than it is a way of being in the world. Merleau-Ponty's account of contemplation in *The Phenomenology of Perception* is a nearly exact description of the process that takes place in a Reznikoff poem:

. . . when I contemplate an object with the sole intention of watching it exist and unfold its riches before my eyes, then it ceases to be an allusion to a general type, and I become aware that each perception, and not merely that of sights which I am discovering for the first time, re-enacts on its own account the birth of intelligence and has some element of creative genius about it: in order that I may recognize the tree as a tree, it is necessary that, beneath this familiar meaning, the momentary arrangement of the visible scene should begin all over again, as on the very first day of the vegetable kingdom, to outline the individual idea of this tree.

Imagism, yes. But only as a source, not as a method. There is no desire on Reznikoff's part to use the image as a medium for transcendence, to make it quiver ineffably in some ethereal realm of the spirit. The progress from symbolism to imagism to objectivism is more a series of short-circuits than a direct lineage. What Reznikoff learned from the Imagists was the value — the force — of the image in itself, unadorned by the claims of the ego. The poem, in Reznikoff's hands, is an act of image-ing rather than of imagining. Its impulse is away from metaphor and into the tangible, a desire to take hold of what is rather than what is merely possible. A poem fit to the measure of the perceived world, neither larger than this world nor smaller than it. "I see something," Reznikoff stated in a 1968 interview with L. S. Dembo, "and I put it down as I see it. In the treatment of it, I abstain from comment. Now, if I've done something that moves me — if I've portrayed the object well — somebody will come along and also be moved, and somebody else will come along and say, 'What the devil is this?' And maybe they're both right."

If the poet's primary obligation is to see, there is a similar though less obvious injunction upon the poet — the duty of not being seen. The Reznikoff equation, which weds seeing to invisibility, cannot be made except by renunciation. In order to see, the poet must make himself invisible. He must disappear, efface himself in anonymity.

> I like the sound of the street—
> but I, apart and alone,
> beside an open window
> and behind a closed door.

> *

> I am alone—
> and glad to be alone;
> I do not like people who walk about
> so late; who walk slowly after midnight
> through the leaves fallen on the sidewalks.
> I do not like
> my own face
> in the little mirrors of the slot-machines
> before the closed stores.

It seems no accident that most Reznikoff poems are rooted in the city. For only in the modern city can the one who sees remain unseen, take his stand in space and yet remain transparent. Even as he becomes a part of the landscape he has entered, he continues to be an outsider. Therefore, objectivist. That is to say — to create a world around oneself by seeing as a stranger would. What counts is the thing itself, and the thing that is seen can come to life only when the one who sees it has disappeared. There can never be any movement toward possession. Seeing is the effort to create presence: to possess a thing would be to make it vanish.

And yet, it is *as if* each act of seeing were an attempt to establish a link between the one who sees and the thing that is seen. *As if* the eye were the means by which the stranger could find his place in the world he has been exiled to. For the building of a world is above all the building and recognition of relations. To discover a thing and isolate it in its singularity is only a beginning, a first step. The world is not merely an accumulation, it is a process — and each time the eye enters this world, it partakes in the life of all the disparate things that pass before it. While objectivity is the premise, subjectivity is the tacit organizer. As soon as there is more than one thing, there is memory, and because of memory, there is language: what is born in the eye, and nevertheless beyond it. In which, and out of which, the poem.

In his 1968 interview with Dembo, Reznikoff went on to say: "The world is very large, I think, and I certainly can't testify to the whole of it. I can only testify to my own feelings; I can only say what I saw and heard, and I try to say it as well as I can. And if your conclusion is that what I saw and heard makes you feel the way I did, then the poem is successful."

New York was Reznikoff's home. It was a city he knew as intimately as a woodcutter knows his forest, and in his prime he would walk between ten and twenty miles a day, from Brooklyn to Riverdale and back. Few poets have ever had such a deep feeling for city life, and in dozens of brief poems Reznikoff captures the strange and transitory beauties of the urban landscape.

> This smoky winter morning—
> do not despise the green jewel among the twigs
> because it is a traffic light.

*

> Feast, you who cross the bridge
> this cold twilight
> on these honeycombs of light, the buildings of Manhattan.

*

Rails in the subway,
what did you know of happiness
when you were ore in the earth;
now the electric lights shine upon you.

But Reznikoff's attention is focused on more than just the objects to be found in the city. He is equally interested in the people who fill the streets of New York, and no encounter, however brief, is too slight to escape his notice, too banal to become a source of epiphany. These two examples, from among many possibilities:

I was walking along Forty-Second Street as night was falling.
On the other side of the street was Bryant Park.
Walking behind me were two men
and I could hear some of their conversation:
"What you must do," one of them was saying to his companion,
"is to decide on what you want to do
and then stick to it. Stick to it!
And you are sure to succeed finally."

I turned to look at the speaker giving such good advice
and was not surprised to see that he was old,
But his companion
to whom the advice was given so earnestly,
was just as old;
and just then the great clock on top of a building across the park

began to shine.

*

The tramp with torn shoes
and clothing dirty and wrinkled—
dirty hands and face—
takes a comb out of his pocket
and carefully combs his hair.

The feeling that emerges from these glimpses of city life is roughly equivalent to what one feels when looking at a photograph. Cartier-Bresson's "decisive moment" is perhaps the crucial idea to remember in this context. The important thing is readiness: you cannot walk out into the street with the expectation of writing a poem or taking a picture, and yet you must be prepared to do so whenever the opportunity presents itself. Because the "work" can come into being only when it has been given to you by the world, you must be constantly looking at the world, constantly doing the work that will lead to a poem, even if no poem comes of it. Reznikoff walks through the city — not, as most poets do, with "his head in the clouds," but with his eyes open, his mind open, his energies concentrated on entering the life around him. Entering it precisely because he is apart from it. And therefore this paradox, lodged in the heart of the poem: to posit the reality of this world, and then to cross into it, even as you find yourself barred at all its gates. The poet as solitary wanderer, as man in the crowd, as faceless scribe. Poetry as an art of loneliness.

It is more than just loneliness, however. It is exile, and a way of coming to terms with exile that somehow, for better or worse, manages to leave the condition of exile intact. Reznikoff was not only an outsider by temperament, nurturing those aspects of himself that would tend to maintain his sense of isolation, he was also born into a state of *otherness*, and as a Jew, as the son of immigrant Jews in America, whatever idea of community he had was always ethnic rather than national (his dream as a poet was to go across the country on foot, stopping at synagogues along the way to give readings of his work in exchange for food and lodging). If his poems about the city — his American poems, so to speak — dwell on the surfaces of things, on the skin of everyday life, it is in his poems about Jewish identity that he allows himself a certain measure of lyrical freedom, allows himself to become a singer of songs.

> Let other people come as streams
> that overflow a valley
> and leave dead bodies, uprooted trees and fields of sand:
> we Jews are as dew,
> on every blade of grass,
> trodden under foot today
> and here tomorrow morning.

And yet, in spite of this deep solidarity with the Jewish past, Reznikoff never deludes himself into thinking that he can overcome the essential solitude of his condition simply by affirming his Jewishness. For not only has he been exiled, he has been exiled twice — as a Jew, and from Judaism as well.

How difficult for me is Hebrew:
even the Hebrew for *mother*, for *bread*, for *sun*
is foreign. How far I have been exiled, Zion.

*

The Hebrew of your poets, Zion,
is like oil upon a burn,
cool as oil;
after work,
the smell in the street at night
of the hedge in flower.
Like Solomon,
I have married and married the speech of strangers;
none are like you, Shulamite.

It is a precarious position, to say the least. Neither fully assimilated nor fully unassimilated, Reznikoff occupies the unstable middle ground between two worlds and is never able to claim either one as his own. Nevertheless, and no doubt precisely because of this ambiguity, it is an extremely fertile ground — leading some to consider him primarily as a Jewish poet (whatever that term might mean) and others to look on him as quintessentially American poet (whatever *that* term might mean). And yet it is safe to say, I think, that in the end both statements are true — or else that neither one is true, which probably amounts to the same thing. Reznikoff's poems are what Reznikoff is: the poems of an American Jew, or, if you will, of a hyphenated American, a Jewish-American, with the two terms standing not so much on equal footing as combining to form a third and wholly different term: the condition of being in two places at the same time, or, quite simply, the condition of being nowhere.

We have only to go on the evidence. In the two volumes of *Complete Poems* (1918–75), recently published by Black Sparrow Press, there are a surprising number of poems on Jewish themes. Poems not only about Jewish immigrant life in New York, but also long narratives on various episodes from ancient and modern Jewish history. A list of some of these titles will give a fair idea of some of Reznikoff's concerns: "King David," "Jeremiah in the Stocks: An Arrangement of the Prophecies," "The Synagogue Defeated: Anno 1096," "Palestine under the Romans," "The Fifth Book of the Maccabees," "Jews in Babylonia." In all, these poems cover more than 100 pages of the approximately 350 pages in the two volumes — or nearly a third of his total output. Given the nature of the poems he is best known for — the spare city lyrics, transcriptions of immediate sensual data — it is strange that he should have devoted so much of his writing life to works whose inspiration comes from *books*. Reznikoff, the least pretentious of all poets, never shows any inclination toward the scholarly acrobatics of some of his contemporaries — Pound, for example, or Olson — and yet, curiously, much of his writing is a direct response to, almost a translation of, his reading. By a further twist, these poems that treat of apparently remote subjects are among his most personal works.

To be schematic for a moment, a simplified explanation would be as follows: America is Reznikoff's present, Judaism is his past. The act of immersing himself in Jewish history is finally no different for him than the act of stepping out into the streets of New York. In both cases, it is an attempt to come to terms with what he is. The past, however, cannot be directly perceived: it can only be experienced through books. When Reznikoff writes about King David, therefore, or Moses, or any other Biblical figure, he is in effect writing about himself. Even in his most light-hearted moments, this preoccupation with his ancestors is always with him.

> *God and Messenger*
>
> The pavement barren
> as the mountain
> on which God spoke to Moses—
> suddenly in the street
> shining against my legs
> the bumper of a motor car.

The point is that Reznikoff the Jew and Reznikoff the American cannot be separated from one another. Each aspect of his work must be read in relation to the *oeuvre* as a whole, for in the end each point of view inhabits all the others.

> The tree in the twilit street—
> the pods hang from its bare symmetrical branches
> motionless—
> but if, like God, a century were to us
> the twinkling of an eye,
> we should see the frenzy of growth.

Which is to say: the eye is not adequate. Not even the seen can be truly seen. The human perspective, which continually thrusts us into a place where "only the narrow present is alive," is an exile from eternity, an exclusion from the fullness of human possibility. That Reznikoff, who insists so strenuously in all his work on this human perspective, should at the same time be aware of its limits, gives his work a reflexive quality, an element of self-doubt that permeates even the most straightforward lyric. For all his apparent simplicity, Reznikoff is by no means a primitive. A reductionist, perhaps, but a highly sophisticated one — who, as an adroit craftsman, always manages to make us forget that each poem is the product (as he put it in one work) of "hunger, silence, and sweat."

There is, however, a bridge between time and eternity in Reznikoff's work, a link between God and man, in the precise place where man is forced to abstain most vigorously from the demands of the self: in the idea of the Law. The Law in the Jewish sense of the word and, by extension, in the English sense. *Testimony* is a work in which reading has become the equivalent of seeing: "Note: All that follows is based on the law reports of the several states." What Reznikoff has observed, has brought to life, is the word, the language of men. So that the act of witness has become synonymous with the act of creation — and the shouldering of its burden. "Now suppose in a court of law," Reznikoff told Dembo in their interview, "you are testifying in a negligence case. You cannot get up on the stand and say, 'The man was negligent.' That's a conclusion of fact. What you'd be compelled to say is how the man acted. Did he stop before he crossed the street? Did he look? The judges of whether he is negligent or not are the jury in that case and the judges of what you say as a poet are the readers. That is, there is an analogy between testimony in the courts and the testimony of a poet."

Trained as a lawyer (though he never practiced) and for many years a researcher for a legal encyclopedia, Reznikoff used the workings of the law not only as a description of the poetic process, but also, more basically, as an aesthetic ideal. In his long autobiographical poem, *Early History of a Writer*, he explains how the study of the law helped to discipline him as a poet:

> I saw that I could use the expensive machinery
> that had cost me four years of hard work at law
> and which I had thought useless for my writing:
> prying sentences open to look at the exact meaning;

weighing words to choose only those that had meat for my purpose
and throwing the rest away as empty shells.
I, too, could scrutinize every word and phrase
as if in a document or the opinion of a judge
and listen, as well, for tones and overtones,
leaving only the pithy, the necessary, the clear and plain.

Testimony: The United States (1885–1915) Recitative is perhaps
Reznikoff's most important achievement as a poet. A quietly astonishing work, so deceptive in its making that it would be easy to misread it
as a document rather than as a piece of art, it is at once a kaleidoscopic
vision of American life and the ultimate test of Reznikoff's poetic principles. Composed of small, self-contained fragments, each the distilla-
tion of an actual court case, the overall effect is nevertheless extremely
coherent. Reznikoff has no lesson to teach, no axe to grind, no ideology
to defend: he merely wants to present the facts. For example:

> At the time of their marriage
> Andrew was worth about fifty thousand dollars;
> Polly had nothing.
> "He has gone up to the mine,
> and I wish to God he would fall down
> and break his neck.
> I just hate him.
> I just shiver when he touches me."

> "Andy, I am going to write a letter that may seem
> hardhearted:
> you know that I do not love you
> as I should
> and I know that I never can.
> Don't you think it best
> to give me a divorce?
> If you do,
> I will not have to sell the house in Denver
> that you gave me,
> and I will give you back the ranch in Delta.
> After we are divorced,
> if you care for me and I care for you,
> we will marry again. Polly."

*

Jessie was eleven years old, though some said fourteen,
and had the care of a child
just beginning to walk—
and suddenly pulled off the child's diaper
and sat the child in some hot ashes
where she had been cooking ash cakes;
the child screamed
and she smacked it on the jaw.

It would be difficult for a poet to make himself more invisible than Reznikoff does in this book. To find a comparable approach to the real, one would have to go back to the great prose writers of the turn of the century. As in Chekhov or in early Joyce, the desire is to allow events to speak for themselves, to choose the exact detail that will say everything and thereby allow as much as possible to remain unsaid. This kind of restraint paradoxically requires an openness of spirit that is available to very few: an ability to accept the given, to remain a witness of human behavior and not succumb to the temptation of becoming a judge.

The success of *Testimony* becomes all the more striking when placed beside *Holocaust*, a far less satisfying work that is based on many of the same techniques. Using as his sources the US Government publication, *Trials of the Criminals before the Nuremberg Tribunal*, and the records of the Eichmann trial in Jerusalem, Reznikoff attempts to deal with Germany's annihilation of the Jews in the same dispassionate, documentary style with which he had explored the human dramas buried in American court records. The problem, I think, is one of magnitude. Reznikoff is a master of the everyday; he understands the seriousness of small events and has an uncanny sympathy with the lives of ordinary people. In a work such as *Testimony* he is able to present us with the facts in a way that simultaneously makes us understand them; the two gestures are inseparable. In the case of *Holocaust*, however, we all know the facts in advance. The Holocaust, which is precisely the unknowable, the unthinkable, requires a treatment beyond the facts in order for us to be able to understand it — assuming that such a thing is even possible. Similar in approach to a 1960s play by Peter Weiss, *The Investigation*, Reznikoff's poem rigorously refuses to pass judgment on any of the atrocities it describes. But this is nevertheless a false objectivity, for the poem is not saying to the reader, "decide for yourself," it is saying that the decision has already been made and that the only way we can deal with these things is to remove them from their inherently emotional setting. The problem is that we cannot remove them. This setting is a necessary starting point.

Holocaust is instructive, however, in that it shows us the limits of Reznikoff's work. I do not mean shortcomings — but limits, those things that set off and describe a space, that create a world. Reznikoff is essentially a poet of *naming*. One does not have the sense of a poetry immersed in language but rather of something that takes place before language and comes to fruition at the precise moment language has been discovered — and it yields a style that is pristine, fastidious, almost stiff in its effort to say exactly what it means to say. If any one word can be used to describe Reznikoff's work, it would be humility — toward language and also toward himself.

> I am afraid
> because of the foolishness
> I have spoken.
> I must diet
> on silence;
> strengthen myself
> with quiet.

It could not have been an easy life for Reznikoff. Throughout the many years he devoted to writing poetry (his first poems were published in 1918, when he was twenty-four, and he went on publishing until his death in early 1976), he suffered from a neglect so total it was almost scandalous. Forced to bring out most of his books in private editions (many of them printed by himself), he also had to fight the constant pressures of making a living.

> After I had worked all day at what I earn my living
> I was tired. Now my own work has lost another day,
> I thought, but began slowly,
> and slowly my strength came back to me.
> Surely, the tide comes in twice a day.

It was not until he was in his late sixties that Reznikoff began to receive some measure of recognition. New Directions published a book of his selected poems, *By The Waters of Manhattan*, which was followed a few years later by the first volume of *Testimony*. But in spite of the success of these two books — and a growing audience for his works —

New Directions saw fit to drop Reznikoff from its list of authors. More years passed. Then, in 1974, Black Sparrow Press brought out *By The Well of Living & Seeing: New & Selected Poems 1918–1973*. More importantly, it committed itself to the long overdue project of putting all of Reznikoff's work back into print. Under the intelligent and sensitive editing of Seamus Cooney, the sequence so far includes the two volumes of *Complete Poems, Holocaust, The Manner Music* (a posthumous novel), the first two volumes of *Testimony*, and will go on to include more volumes of *Testimony* and a book of *Collected Plays*.

If Reznikoff lived his life in obscurity, there was never the slightest trace of resentment in his work. He was too proud for that, too busy with the work itself to be overly concerned with its fate in the world. Even if people are slow to listen to someone who speaks quietly, he knew that eventually he would be heard.

> *Te Deum*
>
> Not because of victories
> I sing,
> having none,
> but for the common sunshine,
> the breeze,
> the largess of the spring.
> Not for victory
> but for the day's work done
> as well as I was able;
> not for a seat upon the dais
> but at the common table.

1974; 1976; 1978

2. "IT REMINDS ME OF SOMETHING
THAT ONCE HAPPENED TO MY MOTHER . . ."

In 1974, I was invited by Anthony Rudolf to contribute an article to the London magazine, *European Judaism*, for an issue celebrating Charles Reznikoff's eightieth birthday. I had been living in France for the past four years, and the little piece I sent in on Reznikoff's work was the first thing I wrote after coming back to America. It seemed like a fitting way to mark my return.

I moved into an apartment on Riverside Drive in late summer. After finishing the article, I discovered that Reznikoff lived very near by—on West End Avenue—and sent him a copy of the manuscript, along with a letter asking him if it would be possible for us to meet. Several weeks went by without a response.

On a Sunday in early October I was to be married. The ceremony was scheduled to take place in the apartment at around noon. At eleven o'clock, just moments before the guests were due to arrive, the telephone rang and an unfamiliar voice asked to speak to me. "This is Charles Reznikoff," the voice said, in a sing-song tone, looping ironically and with evident good humor. I was, of course, pleased and flattered by the call, but I explained that it would be impossible for me to talk just now. I was about to be married, and I was in no condition to form a coherent sentence. Reznikoff was highly amused by this and burst out laughing. "I never called a man on his wedding day before!" he said. "Mazel tov, mazel tov!" We arranged to meet the following week at his apartment. Then I hung up the phone and marched off to the altar.

Reznikoff's apartment was on the twenty-second floor of a large building complex, with a broad, uncluttered view of the Hudson and sunlight pouring through the windows. I arrived in the middle of the day, and with a somewhat stale crumb cake set before me and numerous cups of coffee to drink, I wound up staying three or four hours. The visit made such an impression on me that even now, almost a decade later, it is entirely present inside me.

I have met some good story-tellers in my life, but Reznikoff was the champion. Some of his stories that day went on for thirty or forty minutes, and no matter how far he seemed to drift from the point he was supposedly trying to make, he was in complete control. He had the patience that is necessary to the telling of a good story—and the ability to savor the least detail that cropped up along the way. What at first seemed to be an endless series of digressions, a kind of aimless wandering, turned out to be the elaborate and systematic construction of a circle. For example: why did you come back to New York after living in Hollywood? There followed a myriad of little incidents: meeting the brother of a certain man on a park bench, the color of someone's eyes, an economic crisis in some country. Fifteen minutes later, just when I was beginning to feel hopelessly lost—and convinced that Reznikoff was lost, too—he would begin a slow return to his starting point. Then, with great clarity and conviction, he would announce: "So that's why I left Hollywood." In retrospect, it all made perfect sense.

I heard stories about his childhood, his aborted career in journalism, his law studies, his work for his parents as a jobber of hats and how he would write poems on a bench at Macy's while waiting his turn to show the store buyer his samples. There were also stories about his walks— in particular, his journey from New York to Cape Cod (on foot!), which he undertook when he was well past sixty. The important thing, he explained, was not to walk too fast. Only by forcing himself to keep to a pace of less than two miles per hour could he be sure to see everything he wanted to see.

On my visit that day, I brought along for him a copy of my first book of poems, *Unearth*, which had just been published. This evoked a story from Reznikoff that strikes me as significant, especially in the light of the terrible neglect his work suffered for so many years. His first book, he told me, had been published in 1918 by Samuel Roth (who would later become famous for pirating *Ulysses* and his role in the 1933 court case over Joyce's book). The leading American poet of the day was Edwin Arlington Robinson, and Reznikoff had sent him a copy of the book, hoping for some sign of encouragement from the great man. One afternoon Reznikoff was visiting Roth in his bookstore, and Robinson walked in. Roth went over to greet him, and Reznikoff, standing in the back corner of the shop, witnessed the following scene. Roth proudly gestured to the copies of Reznikoff's book that were on display and asked Robinson if he had read the work of this fine young poet. "Yeah, I read the book," said Robinson in a gruff, hostile voice, "and I thought it was garbage."

"And so," said Reznikoff to me in 1974, "I never got to meet Edwin Arlington Robinson."

It was not until I was putting on my coat and getting ready to leave that Reznikoff said anything about the piece I had sent him. It had been composed in an extremely dense and cryptic style, wrestling with issues that Reznikoff himself had probably never consciously thought about, and I had no idea what his reaction would be. His silence about it during our long conversation led me to suspect that he had not liked it.

"About your article," he said, almost off-handedly. "It reminds me of something that once happened to my mother. A stranger walked up to her on the street one day and very kindly and graciously complimented her on her beautiful hair. Now, you must understand that my mother had never prided herself on her hair and did not consider it to be one of her better features. But, on the strength of that stranger's remark, she spent the rest of the day in front of her mirror, preening and primping and admiring her hair. That's exactly what your article did to me. I stood in front of the mirror for the whole afternoon and admired myself."

Several weeks later, I received a letter from Reznikoff about my book. It was filled with praise, and the numerous quotations from the poems convinced me that he was in earnest—that he had actually sat down and read the book. Nothing could have meant more to me.

A few years after Reznikoff's death, a letter came to me from La Jolla, written by a friend who works in the American Poetry Archive at the University of California library—where Reznikoff's papers had recently been sold. In going through the material, my friend told me, he had come across Reznikoff's copy of *Unearth*. Astonishingly, the book was filled with numerous small notations in the margins, as well as stress marks that Reznikoff had made throughout the poems in an effort to scan them correctly and understand their rhythms. Helpless to do or say anything, I thanked him from the other side of the grave.

Wherever Edwin Arlington Robinson might be now, one can be sure that his accommodations aren't half as good as Charles Reznikoff's.

1983

The Bartlebooth Follies

Georges Perec died in 1982 at the age of forty-six, leaving behind a dozen books and a brilliant reputation. In the words of Italo Calvino, he was "one of the most singular literary personalities in the world, a writer who resembled absolutely no one else." It has taken a while for us to catch on, but now that his major work has at last been translated into English — *Life: A User's Manual* (1978) — it will be impossible for us to think of contemporary French writing in the same way again.

Born into a Jewish family from Poland that emigrated to France in the 1920s, Perec lost his father in the German invasion of 1940 and his mother to the concentration camps in 1943. "I have no memories of childhood," he would later write. His literary career began early, and by the age of nineteen he was already publishing critical notes in the *NRF* and *Les Lettres Nouvelles*. His first novel, *Les Choses*, was awarded the Prix Renadot for 1965, and from then until his death he published approximately one book a year.

Given his tragic family history, it is perhaps surprising to learn that Perec was essentially a comic writer. For the last fifteen years of his life, in fact, he was an active member of Oulipo, a strange literary society founded by Raymond Queneau and the mathematician François le Lionnais. This Workshop for Potential Literature (*Ouvroir de Littérature Potentielle*) proposes all kinds of madcap operations to writers: the S-7 method (rewriting famous poems by replacing each word with the seventh word that follows it in the dictionary), the Lipogram (eliminating the use of one or more letters in a text), acrostics, palindromes, permutations, anagrams, and numerous other "literary constraints." As one of the leading lights of this group, Perec once wrote an entire novel of more than 200 pages without using the letter "e"; this novel was followed by another in which "e" is the only vowel that appears. Verbal gymnastics of this sort seemed to come naturally to him. In addition to his literary work, he produced a notoriously difficult weekly crossword puzzle for the news magazine *Le Point*.

To read Georges Perec one must be ready to abandon oneself to a spirit of play. His books are studded with intellectual traps, allusions and secret systems, and if they are not necessarily profound (in the sense that Tolstoy and Mann are profound), they are prodigiously entertaining (in the sense that Lewis Carroll and Laurence Sterne are entertaining). In Chapter Two of "Life," for example, Perec refers to "the score of a famous American melody, 'Gertrude of Wyoming,' by Arthur Stanley Jefferson." By pure chance, I happened to know that Arthur Stanley Jefferson was the real name of the comedian Stan Laurel, but just because I caught this allusion does not mean there weren't a thousand others that escaped me.

For the mathematically inclined, there are magic squares and chess moves to be discovered in this novel, but the fact that I was unable to find them did not diminish my enjoyment of the book. Those who have read a great deal will no doubt recognize passages that quote directly or indirectly from other writers — Kafka, Agatha Christie, Melville, Freud, Rabelais, Nabokov, Jules Verne, and a host of others — but failure to recognize them should not be considered a handicap. Like Jorge Luis Borges, Georges Perec had a mind that was a storehouse of curious bits of knowledge and awesome erudition, and half the time the reader can't be sure if he is being conned or enlightened. In the long run, it probably doesn't matter. What draws one into this book is not Perec's cleverness, but the deftness and clarity of his style, a flow of language that manages to sustain one's interest through endless lists, catalogues, and descriptions. Perec had an uncanny gift for articulating the nuances of the material world, and in his hands even a worm-eaten table can become an object of fascination. "It was after he had done this that he thought of dissolving what was left of the original wood so as to disclose the fabulous aborescence within, this exact record of the worms' life inside the wooden mass: a static, mineral accumulation of all the movements that had constituted their blind existence, their undeviating single-mindedness, their obstinate itineraries; the faithful materialisation of all they had eaten and digested as they forced from their dense surroundings the invisible elements needed for their survival, the explicit, visible, immeasurably disturbing image of the endless progressions that had reduced the hardest of woods to an impalpable network of crumbling galleries."

Life: A User's Manual is constructed in the manner of a vast jigsaw puzzle. Perec takes a single apartment building in Paris, and in ninety-nine short chapters (along with a Preamble and an Epilogue) proceeds to give a meticulous description of each and every room as well as the life stories of all the inhabitants, both past and present. Ostensibly, we are watching the creation of a painting by Serge Valène, an old artist who has lived in the building for fifty-five years. "It was in the final months of his life that the artist Serge Valène conceived the idea of a painting that would reassemble his entire existence: everything his memory had recorded, all the sensations that had swept over him, all his fantasies, his passions, his hates would be recorded on canvas, a compendium of minute parts of which the sum would be his life."

What emerges is a series of self-contained but interconnecting stories. They are all briskly told, and they run the gamut from the bizarre to the realistic. There are tales of murder and revenge, tales of intellectual obsessions, humorous tales of social satire, and (almost unexpectedly) a number of stories of great psychological penetration. For the most part, Perec's microcosm is peopled with a motley assortment of oddballs, impassioned collectors, antiquarians, miniaturists, and half-baked scholars. If anyone can be called the central character in this shifting, kaleidoscopic work, it would have to be Percival Bartlebooth, an eccentric English millionaire whose insane and useless fifty-year project serves as an emblem for the book as a whole. Realizing as a young man that his wealth has doomed him to a life of boredom, he undertakes to study the art of watercolor from Serge Valène for a period of ten years. Although he has no aptitude whatsoever for painting, he eventually reaches a satisfactory level of competence. Then, in the company of a servant, he sets out on a twenty-year voyage around the world with the sole intention of painting watercolors of five hundred different harbors and seaports. As soon as one of these pictures is finished, he sends it to a man in Paris by the name of Gaspard Winckler, who also lives in the building. Winckler is an expert puzzle-maker whom Bartlebooth has hired to turn the watercolors into 750-piece jigsaw puzzles. One by one, the puzzles are made over the twenty-year period and stored in wooden boxes. Bartlebooth returns from his travels, settles back into his apartment, and methodically goes about putting the puzzles together in chronological order. By means of an elaborate chemical process that has been designed for the purpose at hand, the borders of the puzzle pieces are glued together in such a way that the seams are no longer visible, thus restoring the watercolor to its original integrity. The watercolor, good as new, is then removed from its wooden backing and sent back to the place where it was executed twenty years earlier. There, by prearrangement, it is dipped into a detergent solution that eliminates all traces of the painting, leaving Bartlebooth with a clean and unmarked sheet of paper. In other words, he is left with nothing, the same thing he started with. The project, however, does not quite go according to plan. Winckler has made the puzzles too difficult, and Bartlebooth does not live long enough to finish all five hundred of them. As Perec writes in the last paragraph of the ninety-ninth chapter: "It is the twenty-third of June nineteen hundred and seventy-five, and it is eight o'clock in the evening. Seated at his jigsaw puzzle, Bartlebooth has just died. On the tablecloth, somewhere in the crepuscular sky of the four hundred and thirty-ninth puzzle, the black hole of the sole piece not yet filled in has the almost perfect shape of an X. But the ironical thing, which could have been foreseen long ago, is that the piece the dead man holds between his fingers is shaped like a W."

Like many of the other stores in *Life*, Bartlebooth's weird saga can be read as a parable (of sorts) about the efforts of the human mind to impose an arbitrary order on the world. Again and again, Perec's characters are swindled, hoaxed, and thwarted in their schemes, and if there is a darker side to this book, it is perhaps to be found in this emphasis on the inevitability of failure. Even a self-annihilating project such as Bartlebooth's cannot be completed, and when we learn in the Epilogue that Valène's enormous painting (which for all intents and purposes is the book we have just been reading) has come no farther than a preliminary sketch, we realize that Perec does not exempt himself from the follies of his characters. It is this sense of self-mockery that turns a potentially daunting novel into a hospitable work, a book that for all its high-jinx and japery finally wins us over with the warmth of its human understanding.

1987

PREFACES

Jacques Dupin

It is not easy to come to terms with Jacques Dupin's poetry. Uncompromisingly hermetic in attitude and rigorously concise in utterance, it does not demand of us a reading so much as an absorption. For the nature of the poem has undergone a metamorphosis, and in order to meet it on its own ground, we must change the nature of our expectations. The poem is no longer a record of feelings, a song, or a meditation. Rather, it is the field in mental space in which a struggle is permitted to unfold: between the destruction of the poem and the quest for the possible poem — for the poem can be born only when all chances for its life have been destroyed. Dupin's work is the progeny of this contradiction, existing within the narrowest of confines, like an invisible seed lodged in the core of stone. The struggle is not a simple either/or conflict between this and that, either destroy or create, either speak or be silent — it is a matter of destroying in order to create, and of maintaining a silent vigil within the word until the last living moment, when the word begins to crumble from the pressure that has been placed upon it.

That which I see, and do not speak of, frightens me. What I speak of, and do not know, delivers me. Do not deliver me.

Dupin has accepted these difficulties deliberately, choosing poverty and the astringencies of denial in place of facility. Because his purpose is not to subjugate his surroundings by means of some vain notion of mastery, but to harmonize with them, to enter into relation with them, and finally, to live within them, the poetic operation becomes a process whereby he unburdens himself of his garments, his tools, and his possessions, in order to assume, in nakedness, the fullness of being. In this sense, the poem is a kind of spiritual purification. But if a monk can fashion a worldly poverty for himself in the knowledge that it will draw him nearer to his God, Dupin is not able to give himself such assurances. He takes on the distress of what is around him as a way of ending his separation from it, but there is no sign to lead him, and nothing to guarantee him salvation. Yet, in spite of this austerity, or perhaps because of it, his work holds an uncommon richness. This stems at least in part from the fact that all his poems are grounded in a landscape, firmly rooted in the palpability of the real. The problems he confronts are never posed as abstractions, but present themselves in and through this landscape, and in the end cannot be separated from it. The universe he brings forth is an alchemical itinerary through the elements, the transfiguration of the seemingly indivisible by means of the word. Similar in spirit to the cosmic correspondences revealed in the pre-Socratic fragments, it is a universe in which speech and metaphor are synonymous. Dupin has not made nature his object, he carries it within him, and when he finally speaks, it is with the force of what he already contains. Like Rilke, he finds himself in what is around him. His voice does more than conjure the presences of things, it gives them the power of speech as well. But whereas Rilke is usually passive in his relation to things — attempting to isolate the thing and penetrate its essence in transcendent stillness — Dupin is active, seeing things in their interconnectedness, as perpetually changing.

To shatter, to retake, and thus, to rebuild. In the forest we are closer to the woodcutter than to the solitary wanderer. No innocent contemplation. No high forests crossed by sunlight and the songs of birds, but their hidden future: cords of wood. Everything is given to us, but for violence, to be forced open, to be almost destroyed — to destroy us.

The solitary wanderer is Dupin himself, and each poem emerges as an account of his movements through the terrain he has staked out for himself. Dominated by stone, mountain, farm implements, and fire, the geography is cruel, built of the barest materials, and human presence can never be taken for granted in it. It must be won. Generated by a desire to join what forbids him a place and to find a dwelling within it, the Dupin poem is always on the other side: the limit of the human step, the fruit of a terrestrial harrowing. Above all, it is trial. Where all is silence, where all seems to exclude him, he can never be sure where his steps are taking him, and the poem can never be hunted systematically. It comes to life suddenly and without warning, in unexpected places and by unknown means. Between each flash there is patience, and in the end it is this that quickens the landscape — the tenacity to endure in it — even if it offers us nothing. *At the limit of strength a naked word.*

The poem is created only in choosing the most difficult path. Every advantage must be suppressed and every ruse discarded in the interests of reaching this limit — an endless series of destructions, in order to come to a point at which the poem can no longer be destroyed. For the poetic word is essentially the creative word, and yet, nevertheless, a word among others, burdened by the weight of habit and layers of dead skin that must be stripped away before it can regain its true function. Violence is demanded, and Dupin is equal to it. But the struggle is pursued for an end beyond violence — that of finding a habitable space. As often as not, he will fail, and even if he does not, success will bear its own disquiet. *The torch which lights the abyss, which seals it up, is itself an abyss.*

The strength that Dupin speaks of is not the strength of transcendence, but of immanence and realization. The gods have vanished, and there can be no question of pretending to recover the divine *logos*. Faced with an unknowable world, poetry can do no more than create what already exists. But that is already saying a great deal. For if things can be recovered from the edge of absence, there is the chance, in so doing, of giving them back to men.

1971

André du Bouchet

... this irreducible sign — deutungslos — *... a word beyond grasping, Cassandra's word, a word from which no lesson is to be drawn, a word, each time, and every time, spoken to say nothing ...*

Hölderlin aujourd'hui (*lecture delivered March 1970 in Stuttgart to commemorate the 200th anniversary of Hölderlin's birth*)

(*this joy ... that is born of nothing ...*)

Qui n'est pas tourné vers nous (1972)

Born of the deepest silences, and condemned to life without hope of life (*I found myself / free / and without hope*), the poetry of André du Bouchet stands, in the end, as an act of survival. Beginning with nothing, and ending with nothing but the truth of its own struggle, du Bouchet's work is the record of an obsessive, wholly ruthless attempt to gain access to the self. It is a project filled with uncertainty, silence, and resistance, and there is no contemporary poetry, perhaps, that lends itself more reluctantly to gloss. To read du Bouchet is to undergo a process of dislocation: here, we discover, is not here, and the body, even the physical presence within the poems, is no longer in possession of itself — but moving, as if into the distance, where it seeks to find itself against the inevitability of its own disappearance (... *and the silence that claims us, like a vast field.*) "Here" is the limit we come to. To be in the poem, from this moment on, is to be nowhere.

A body in space. And the poem, as self-evident as this body. In space: that is to say, this void, this nowhere between sky and earth, rediscovered with each step that is taken. For wherever we are, the world is not. And wherever we go, we find ourselves moving in advance of ourselves — as if where the world would be. The distance, which allows the world to appear, is also that which separates us from the world, and though the body will endlessly move through this space, as if in the hope of abolishing it, the process begins again with each step taken. We move toward an infinitely receding point, a destination that can never be reached, and in the end, this going, in itself, will become a goal, so that the mere fact of moving onward will be a way of being in the world, even as the world remains beyond us. There is no hope in this, but neither is there despair. For what du Bouchet manages to maintain, almost uncannily, is a nostalgia for a possible future, even as he knows it will never come to pass. And from this dreadful knowledge, there is nevertheless a kind of joy, a joy . . . that is born of nothing.

Du Bouchet's work, however, will seem difficult to many readers approaching it for the first time. Stripped of metaphor, almost devoid of imagery, and generated by a syntax of abrupt, paratactic brevity, his poems have done away with nearly all the props that students of poetry are taught to look for — the very difficulties that poetry has always seemed to rely on — and this sudden opening of distances, in spite of the lessons buried in such earlier poets as Hölderlin, Leopardi, and Mallarmé, will seem baffling, even frightening. In the world of French poetry, however, du Bouchet has performed an act of linguistic surgery no less important than the one performed by William Carlos Williams in America, and against the rhetorical inflation that is the curse of French writing, his intensely understated poems have all the freshness of natural objects. His work, which was first published in the early fifties, became a model for a whole generation of postwar poets, and there are few young poets in France today who do not show the mark of his influence. What on first or second reading might seem to be an almost fragile sensibility gradually emerges as a vision of the greatest force and purity. For the poems themselves cannot be truly felt until one has penetrated the strength of the silence that lies at their source. It is a silence equal to the strength of any word.

1973

Black on White
Recent paintings by David Reed

The hand of the painter has rarely instructed us in the ways of the hand. When we look at a painting, we see an accumulation of gestures, the layering and shaping of materials, the longing of the inanimate to take on life. But we do not see the hand itself. Like the God of the deists, it seems to have withdrawn from its own creation, or vanished into the density of the world it has made. It does not matter whether the painting is figurative or abstract: we confront the work as an object, and, as such, the surface remains independent of the will behind it.

In David Reed's new paintings, this has been reversed. Suddenly, the hand has been made visible to us, and in each horizontal stroke applied to the canvas, we are able to see that hand with such precision that it actually seems to be *moving*. Faithful only to itself, to the demands of the movement it brings forth, the hand is no longer a means to an end, but the substance of the object it creates. For each stroke we are given here is unique: there is no backtracking, no modeling, no pause. The hand moves across the surface in a single, unbroken gesture, and once this gesture has been completed, it is inviolate. The finished work is not a representation of this process — it is the process itself, and it asks to be *read* rather than simply observed. Composed of a series of rung-like strokes that descend the length of the canvas, each of these paintings resembles a vast poem without words. Our eyes follow its movement in the same way we follow a poem down a page, and just as the line in a poem is a unit of breath, so the line in the painting is a unit of gesture. The language of these works is the language of the body.

Some people will probably try to see them as examples of minimal art. But that would be a mistake. Minimal art is an art of control, aiming at the rigorous ordering of visual information, while Reed's paintings are conceived in a way that sabotages the idea of a preordained result. It is this high degree of spontaneity within a consciously limited framework that produces such a harmonious coupling of intellectual and physical energies in his work. No two paintings are or can be exactly alike, even though each painting begins at the same point, with the same fundamental premises. For no matter how regular or

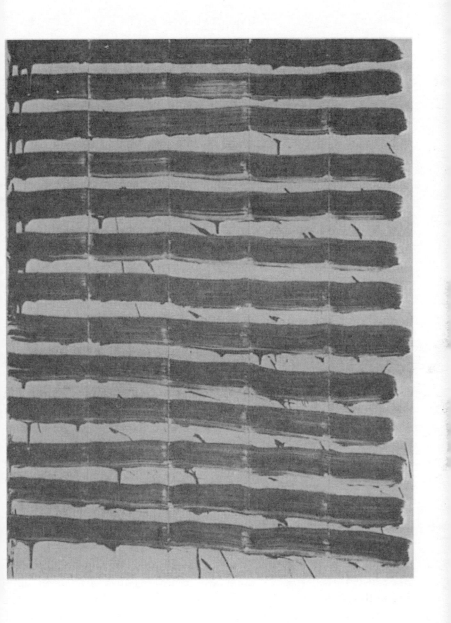

controlled the gesture may be, its field of action is unstable, and in the end it is chance that governs the result. Because the white background is still wet when the horizontal strokes are applied, the painting can never be fully calculated in advance, and the image is always at the mercy of gravity. In some sense, then, each painting is born from a conflict between opposing forces. The horizontal stroke tries to impose an order upon the chaos of the background, and is deformed by it as the white paint settles. It would surely be stretching matters to interpret this as a parable of man against nature. And yet, because these paintings evolve in time, and because our reading of them necessarily leads us back through their whole history, we are able to re-enact this conflict whenever we come into their presence. What remains is the drama: and we begin to understand that, fundamentally, these works are the statement of that drama.

In the last sentence of Maurice Blanchot's novel, *Death Sentence*, the nameless narrator writes: "And even more, let him try to imagine the hand that has written these pages: and if he is able to see it, then perhaps reading will become a serious task for him." David Reed's new work is an expression of this same desire in the realm of painting. By allowing us to imagine his hand, by allowing us to *see* his hand, he has exposed us to the serious task of seeing: how we see and what we see, and how what we see in a painting is different from what we see anywhere else. It has taken considerable courage to do this. For it pushes the artist out from the shadows, leaving him with nowhere to stand but in the painting itself. And in order for us to look at one of these works, we have no choice but to go in there with him.

1975

Twentieth-Century French Poetry

I

French and English constitute a single language.

Wallace Stevens

This much is certain: If not for the arrival of William and his armies on English soil in 1066, the English language as we know it would never have come into being. For the next three hundred years French was the language spoken at the English court, and it was not until the end of the Hundred Years' War that it became clear, once and for all, that France and England were not to become a single country. Even John Gower, one of the first to write in the English vernacular, composed a large portion of his work in French, and Chaucer, the greatest of the early English poets, devoted much of his creative energy to a translation of *Le Roman de la rose* and found his first models in the work of the Frenchman Guillaume de Machaut. It is not simply that French must be considered an "influence" on the development of English language and literature; French is a part of English, an irreducible element of its genetic make-up.

Early English literature is replete with evidence of this symbiosis, and it would not be difficult to compile a lengthy catalogue of borrowings, homages and thefts. William Caxton, for instance, who introduced the printing press in England in 1477, was an amateur translator of medieval French works, and many of the first books printed in Britain were English versions of French romances and tales of chivalry. For the printers who worked under Caxton, translation was a normal and accepted part of their duties, and even the most popular English work to be published by Caxton, Thomas Malory's *Morte d'Arthur*, was itself a ransacking of Arthurian legends from French sources: Malory warns the reader no less than fifty-six times during the course of his narrative that the "French book" is his guide.

In the next century, when English came fully into its own as a language and a literature, both Wyatt and Surrey — two of the most brilliant pioneers of English verse — found inspiration in the work of Clément Marot, and Spenser, the major poet of the next generation, not only took the title of his *Shepheardes Calender* from Marot, but two sections of the work are direct imitations of that same poet. More importantly, Spenser's attempt at the age of seventeen to translate Joachim du Bellay (*The Visions of Bellay*) is the first sonnet sequence to be produced in English. His later revision of that work and translation of another du Bellay sequence, *Ruines of Rome*, were published in 1591 and stand among the great works of the period. Spenser, however, is not alone in showing the mark of the French. Nearly all the Elizabethan sonnet writers took sustenance from the Pléiade poets, and some of them — Daniel, Lodge, Chapman — went so far as to pass off translations of French poets as their own work. Outside the realm of poetry, the impact of Florio's translation of Montaigne's essays on Shakespeare has been well documented, and a good case could be made for establishing the link between Rabelais and Thomas Nashe, whose 1594 prose narrative, *The Unfortunate Traveler*, is generally considered to be the first novel written in the English language.

On the more familiar terrain of modern literature, French has continued to exert a powerful influence on English. In spite of the wonderfully ludicrous remark by Southey that poetry is as impossible in French as it is in Chinese, English and American poetry of the past hundred years would be inconceivable without the French. Beginning with Swinburne's 1862 article in *The Spectator* on Baudelaire's *Les Fleurs du Mal* and the first translations of Baudelaire's poetry into English in 1869 and 1870, modern British and American poets have continued to look to France for new ideas. Saintsbury's article in an 1875 issue of *The Fortnightly Review* is exemplary. "It was not merely admiration of Baudelaire which was to be persuaded to English readers," he wrote, "but also imitation of him which, at least with equal earnestness, was to be urged on English writers."

Throughout the 1870s and 1880s, largely inspired by Théodore de Banville, many English poets began experimenting with French verse forms (ballades, lays, virelays and rondeaux), and the "art for art's sake" ideas propounded by Gautier were an important source for the Pre-Raphaelite movement in England. By the 1890s, with the advent of *The Yellow Book* and the Decadents, the influence of the French Symbolists became widespread. In 1893, for example, Mallarmé was invited to lecture at Oxford, a sign of the esteem he commanded in English eyes.

It is also true that little of substance was produced in English as a result of French influences during this period, but the way was prepared for the discoveries of two young American poets, Pound and Eliot, in the first decade of the new century. Each came upon the French independently, and each was inspired to write a kind of poetry that had not been seen before in English. Eliot would later write that ". . . the kind of poetry I needed, to teach me the use of my own voice, did not exist in England at all, and was only to be found in France." As for Pound, he stated flatly that "practically the whole development of the English verse-art has been achieved by steals from the French."

The English and American poets who formed the Imagist group in the years just prior to World War I were the first to engage in a *critical* reading of French poetry, with the aim not so much of imitating the French as of rejuvenating poetry in English. More or less neglected poets in France, such as Corbière and Laforgue, were accorded major status. F. S. Flint's 1912 article in *The Poetry Review* (London) and Ezra Pound's 1913 article in *Poetry* (Chicago) did much to promote this new reading of the French. Independent of the Imagists, Wilfred Owen spent several years in France before the war and was in close contact with Laurent Tailhade, a poet admired by Pound and his circle. Eliot's reading of the French poets began as early as 1908, while he was still a student at Harvard. Just two years later he was in Paris, reading Claudel and Gide and attending Bergson's lectures at the Collège de France.

By the time of the Armory show in 1913, the most radical tendencies in French art and writing had made their way to New York, finding a home with Alfred Stieglitz and his gallery at 291 Fifth Avenue. Many of the names associated with American and European modernism became part of this Paris-New York connection: Joseph Stella, Marsden Hartley, Arthur Dove, Charles Demuth, William Carlos Williams, Man Ray, Alfred Kreymborg, Marius de Zayas, Walter C. Arensberg, Mina Loy, Francis Picabia and Marcel Duchamp. Under the influence of Cubism and Dada, of Apollinaire and the Futurism of Marinetti, numerous magazines carried the message of modernism to American readers: *291, The Blind Man, Rongwrong, Broom, New York Dada*, and *The Little Review*, which was born in Chicago in 1914, lived in New York from 1917 to 1927, and died in Paris in 1929. To read the list of *The Little Review*'s contributors is to understand the degree to which French poetry had permeated the American scene. In addition to work by Pound, Eliot, Yeats and Ford Madox Ford, as well as its most celebrated contribution, James Joyce's *Ulysses*, the magazine published Breton, Éluard, Tzara, Péret, Reverdy, Crevel, Aragon and Soupault.

Beginning with Gertrude Stein, who arrived in Paris well before

World War I, the story of American writers in Paris during the twenties and thirties is almost identical to the story of American writing itself. Hemingway, Fitzgerald, Faulkner, Sherwood Anderson, Djuna Barnes, Kay Boyle, e e cummings, Hart Crane, Archibald MacLeish, Malcolm Cowley, John Dos Passos, Katherine Anne Porter, Laura Riding, Thornton Wilder, Williams, Pound, Eliot, Glenway Wescott, Henry Miller, Harry Crosby, Langston Hughes, James T. Farrell, Anäis Nin, Nathanael West, George Oppen — all of these and others either visited or lived in Paris. The experience of those years has so thoroughly saturated American consciousness that the image of the starving young writer serving his apprenticeship in Paris has become one of our enduring literary myths.

It would be absurd to assume that each of these writers was directly influenced by the French. But it would be just as absurd to assume that they went to Paris only because it was a cheap place to live. In the most serious and energetic magazine of the period, *transition*, American and French writers were published side by side, and the dynamics of this exchange led to what has probably been the most fruitful period in our literature. Nor does absence from Paris necessarily preclude an interest in things French. The most Francophilic of all our poets, Wallace Stevens, never set foot in France.

Since the twenties, American and British poets have been steadily translating their French counterparts — not simply as a literary exercise, but as an act of discovery and passion. Consider, for example, these words from John Dos Passos's preface to his translations of Cendrars in 1930: "... A young man just starting to read verse in the year 1930 would have a hard time finding out that this method of putting words together has only recently passed through a period of virility, intense experimentation and meaning in everyday life. ... For the sake of this hypothetical young man and for the confusion of Humanists, stuffed shirts in editorial chairs, anthology compilers and prize poets, sonnet writers and readers of bookchats, I think it has been worth while to attempt to turn these alive informal personal everyday poems of Cendrars' into English ..." Or T. S. Eliot, introducing his translation of *Anabasis* by Saint-John Perse that same year: "I believe that this is a piece of writing of the same importance as the later work of James Joyce, as valuable as *Anna Livia Plurabelle*. And this is a high estimate indeed." Or Kenneth Rexroth, in the preface to his translations of Reverdy in 1969: "Of all the modern poets in Western European languages Reverdy has certainly been the leading influence on my own work — incomparably more than anyone in English or American — and I have known and loved his work since I first read *Les Épaves du ciel* as a young boy."

As the list of translators included in this book shows, many of the most important contemporary American and British poets have tried their hand at translating the French, among them Pound, Williams, Eliot, Stevens, Beckett, MacNeice, Spender, Ashbery, Blackburn, Bly, Kinnell, Levertov, Merwin, Wright, Tomlinson, Wilbur — to mention just some of the most familiar names. It would be difficult to imagine their work had they not been touched in some way by the French. And it would be even more difficult to imagine the poetry of our own language if these poets had not been a part of it. In a sense, then, this anthology is as much about American and British poetry as it is about French poetry. Its purpose is not only to present the work of French poets in French, but to offer translations of that work as our own poets have re-imagined and re-presented it. As such, it can be read as a chapter in our own poetic history.

II

The French tradition and the English tradition in this epoch are at opposite poles to each other. French poetry is more radical, more total. In an absolute and exemplary way it has assumed the heritage of European Romanticism, a romanticism which begins with William Blake and the German romantics like Novalis, and via Baudelaire and the Symbolists culminates in twentieth-century French poetry, notably Surrealism. It is a poetry where the world becomes writing and language becomes the double of the world.

Octavio Paz

On the other hand, this much is also certain: If there has been a steady interest in French poetry for the past hundred years on the part of British and American poets, enthusiasm for the French has often been tempered by a certain wariness, even hostility, to literary and intellectual practices in France. This has been more true of the British than the Americans, but, nevertheless, the American literary establishment remains strongly Anglophilic in orientation. One has only to compare the dominant trends in philosophy, literary criticism, or novel-writing, to realize the enormous gulf between the two cultures.

Many of these differences reside in the disparities between the two languages. Although English is in large part derived from French, it still holds fast to its Anglo-Saxon origins. Against the gravity and substantiality to be found in the work of our greatest poets (Milton, say, or Emily Dickinson), which embodies an awareness of the contrast between the thick emphasis of Anglo-Saxon and the nimble conceptuality of French/Latin — and to play one repeatedly against the other — French poetry often seems almost weightless to us, to be composed of ethereal puffs of lyricism and little else. French is necessarily a thinner medium than English. But that does not mean it is weaker. If English writing has staked out as its territory the world of tangibility, of concrete presence, of surface accident, French literary language has largely been a language of essences. Whereas Shakespeare, for example, names more than five hundred flowers in his plays, Racine adheres to the single word "flower". In all, the French dramatist's vocabulary consists of roughly fifteen hundred words, while the word count in Shakespeare's plays runs upward of twenty-five thousand. The contrast, as Lytton Strachey noted, is between "comprehension" and "concentration." "Racine's great aim," Strachey wrote, "was to produce, not an extraordinary nor a complex work of art, but a flawless one; he wished to be all matter and no impertinence. His conception of a drama was of something swift, inevitable; an action taken at the crisis, with no redundancies however interesting, no complications however suggestive, no irrelevances however beautiful — but plain, intense, vigorous, and splendid with nothing but its own essential force." More recently, the poet Yves Bonnefoy has described English as a "mirror" and French as a "sphere," the one Aristotelian in its acceptance of the given, the other Platonic in its readiness to hypothesize "a different reality, a different realm."

Samuel Beckett, who has spent the greater part of his life writing in both languages, translating his own work from French into English and from English into French, is no doubt our most reliable witness to the capacities and limitations of the two languages. In one of his letters from the mid-fifties, he complained about the difficulty he was having in translating *Fin de partie* (*Endgame*) into English. The line Clov addresses to Hamm, "Il n'y a plus de roues de bicyclette" was a particular problem. In French, Beckett contended, the line conveyed the meaning that bicycle wheels as a category had ceased to exist, that there were no more bicycle wheels in the world. The English equivalent, however, "There are no more bicycle wheels," meant simply that there were no more bicycle wheels available, that no bicycle wheels could be found in the place where they happened to be. A world of difference is embedded here beneath apparent similarity. Just as the Eskimos have more than twenty words for snow (a frequently cited example), which means they are able to experience snow in ways far more nuanced and elaborate than we are — literally to see things we cannot see — the French live inside their language in ways that are somewhat at odds with the way we live inside English. There is no judgment of any kind attached to this remark. If bad French poetry tends to drift off into almost mechanical abstractions, bad English and American poetry has tended to be too earthbound and leaden, sinking into triviality and inconsequence. Between the two bads there is probably little to choose from. But it is helpful to remember that a good French poem is not necessarily the same thing as a good English poem.

The French have had their Academy for more than three hundred years. It is an institution that at once expresses and helps to perpetuate a notion of literature far more grandiose than anything we have ever known in England or America. As an official point of view, it has had the effect of removing the literary from the realm of the everyday, whereas English and American writers have generally been more at home in the flux of the quotidian. But because they have an established tradition to react against, French poets — paradoxically — have tended to be more rebellious than their British and American counterparts. The pressures of conformity have had the net result of producing a vigorous anti-tradition, which in many ways has actually usurped the established tradition as the major current in French literature. Beginning with Villon and Rabelais, continuing on through Rousseau, Baudelaire, Rimbaud, and the cult of the *poète maudit*, and then on into the twentieth century with Apollinaire, the Dada movement, and the Surrealists, the French have systematically and defiantly attacked the accepted notions of their own culture — primarily because they have been secure in their knowledge that this culture exists. The lessons of this anti-tradition have been so thoroughly assimilated that today they are more or less taken for granted.

By contrast, the great interest shown by Pound and Eliot in French poetry (and, in Pound's case, the poetry of other languages as well) can be read not so much as an attack on Anglo-American culture as an effort to create a tradition, to manufacture a past that would somehow fill the vacuum of American newness. The impulse was essentially conservative in nature. With Pound, it degenerated into Fascist rantings; with Eliot, into Anglican pieties and an obsession with the notion of Culture. It would be wrong, however, to set up a simple dichotomy between radicalism and conservatism, and to put all things French in the first category and all things English and American in the second. The most subversive and innovative elements of our literature have frequently surfaced in the unlikeliest places and have then been absorbed into the culture at large. Nursery rhymes, which form an essential part of every English-speaking child's early education, do not exist as such in France. Nor do the great works of Victorian children's literature (Lewis Carroll, George Macdonald) have any equivalent in French. As for America, it has always had its own, homegrown Dada spirit, which has continued to exist as a natural force, without any need of manifestoes or theoretical foundations. The films of Buster Keaton and W.C. Fields, the skits of Ring Lardner, the drawings of Rube Goldberg surely match the corrosive exuberance of anything done in France during the same period. As Man Ray (a native American) wrote to Tristan Tzara from New York in 1921 about spreading the Dada movement to America: "Cher Tzara — Dada cannot live in New York. All New York is Dada, and will not tolerate a rival . . ."

Nor should one assume that twentieth-century French poetry is sitting out there as a convenient, self-contained entity. Far from being a unified body of work that resides neatly within the borders of France, French poetry of this century is various, tumultuous and contradictory. There is no typical case — only a horde of exceptions. For the fact is, a great number of the most original and influential poets were either born in other countries or spent a substantial part of their lives abroad. Apollinaire was born in Rome of mixed Polish and Italian parentage; Milosz was Lithuanian; Segalen spent his most productive years in China; Cendrars was born in Switzerland, composed his first major poem in New York, and until he was over fifty rarely stayed in France long enough to collect his mail; Saint-John Perse was born in Guadeloupe, worked for many years in Asia as a diplomat and lived almost exclusively in Washington, D.C. from 1941 until his death in 1975; Supervielle was from Uruguay and for most of his life divided his time between Montevideo and Paris; Tzara was born in Rumania and came to Paris by way of the Dada adventures at the Cabaret Voltaire in Zurich, where he frequently played chess with Lenin; Jabès was born in Cairo and lived in Egypt until he was forty-five; Césaire is from

Martinique; du Bouchet is part American and was educated at Amherst and Harvard; and nearly all the younger poets in this book have stayed for extended periods in either England or America. The stereotypical view of the French poet as a creature of Paris, as a xenophobic purveyor of French values, simply does not hold. The more intimately one becomes involved with the work of these poets, the more reluctant one becomes to make any generalizations about them. In the end, the only thing that can be said with any certainty is that they all write in French.

An anthology, therefore, is a kind of trap, tending to thwart our access to the poems even as it makes them available to us. By gathering the work of so many poets in one volume, the temptation is to consider the poets as a group, to drown them as individuals in the great pot of literature. Thus, even before it is read, the anthology becomes a kind of cultural dinner, a smattering of national dishes served up on a platter for popular consumption, as if to say, "Here is French poetry. Eat it. It's good for you." To approach poetry in that way is to miss the point entirely — for it allows one to avoid looking squarely at the poem on the page. And that, after all, is the reader's primary obligation. One must resist the notion of treating an anthology as the last word on its subject. It is no more than a first word, a threshold opening on to a new space.

III

In the end you are weary of this ancient world.

Guillaume Apollinaire

The logical place to begin this book is with Apollinaire. Although he is neither the first-born of the poets included nor the first to have written in a consciously modern idiom, he, more than any other artist of his time, seems to embody the aesthetic aspirations of the early part of the century. In his poetry, which ranges from graceful love lyrics to bold experiments, from rhyme to free verse to "shape" poems, he manifests a new sensibility, at once indebted to the forms of the past and enthusiastically at home in the world of automobiles, airplanes and movies. As the tireless promoter of the Cubist painters, he was the figure around whom many of the best artists and writers gathered, and poets such as Jacob, Cendrars and Reverdy formed an important part of his circle. The work of these three, along with Apollinaire's, has frequently been described as Cubist. While there are vast differences among them, both in methods and tone, they nevertheless share a certain point of view, especially in the epistemogolical foundations of the work. Simultaneity, juxtaposition, an acute feeling for the jaggedness of the real — these are traits to be found in all four, and each exploits them to different poetic ends.

Cendrars, at once more abrasive and voluptuous than Apollinaire, observed that "everything around me moves," and his work oscillates between the two solutions implicit in this statement: on the one hand, the ebullient jangle of sensations in works such as *Nineteen Elastic Poems*, and on the other the snapshot realism of his travel poems (originally entitled *Kodak* but changed, under pressure from the film company of the same name, to *Documentaires*) — as if each of these poems was the record of a single moment, lasting no longer than it takes to click the shutter of a camera. With Jacob, whose most enduring work is contained in his 1917 collection of prose poems, *The Dice Cup*, the impulse is toward an anti-lyrical comedy. His language is continually erupting into playfulness (puns, parody, satire) and takes its greatest delight in unmasking the deceptions of appearances: Nothing is ever what it seems to be, everything is subject to metamorphosis, and change always occurs unexpectedly, with lightning swiftness.

Reverdy, by contrast, uses many of these same principles, but with far more somber objectives. Here an accumulation of fragments is synthesized into an entirely new approach to the poetic image. "The image is a pure creation of the mind," wrote Reverdy in 1918. "It cannot be born from a comparison but from a juxtaposition of two more or less distant realities. The more the relationship between the two juxtaposed realities is both distant and true, the stronger the image will be — the greater its emotional power and poetic reality." Reverdy's strange landscapes, which combine an intense inwardness with a proliferation of sensual data, bear in them the signs of a continual search for an impossible totality. Almost mystical in their effect, his poems are nevertheless anchored in the minutiae of the everyday world; in their quiet, at times monotone music, the poet seems to evaporate, to vanish into the haunted country he has created. The result is at once beautiful and disquieting — as if Reverdy had emptied the space of the poem in order to let the reader inhabit it.

A similar atmosphere is sometimes produced by the prose poems of Fargue, whose work predates that of any other poet included here.

Fargue is the supreme modern poet of Paris, and fully half his writings are about the city itself. In his delicate, lyrical configurations of memory and perception, which retain an echo of their Symbolist predecessors, there is an attentiveness to detail combined with a rigorous subjectivity that transforms the city into an immense interior landscape. The poem of witness is at the same time a poem of remembrance, as if, in the solitary act of seeing, the world were reflected back to its solitary source and then, once more, reflected outward as vision. With Larbaud, a close friend of Fargue's, one also finds a hint of the late nineteenth century. A. O. Barnabooth, the supposed author of Larbaud's finest book of poems (in the first edition of 1908 Larbaud's name was intentionally left off the title page), is a rich South American of twenty-four, a naturalized citizen of New York, an orphan, a world traveler, a highly sensitive and melancholy young man — a more sympathetic and humorous version of the traditional dandy hero. As Larbaud later explained, he wanted to invent a poet "sensitive to the diversity of races, people, and countries; who could find the exotic everywhere . . .; witty and 'international,' one, in a word, capable of writing like Whitman but in a light vein, and of supplying that note of comic, joyous irresponsibility which is lacking in Whitman." As in the poems of Apollinaire and Cendrars, Larbaud-Barnabooth expresses an almost euphoric delight in the sensations of travel: "I experienced for the first time all the joy of living / In a compartment of the Nord-Express . . ." Of Barnabooth André Gide wrote: "I love his haste, his cynicism, his gluttony. These poems, dated from here and there, and everywhere, are as thirst-making as a wine list . . . In this particular book, each picture of sensation, no matter how correct or dubious it may be, is made valid by the speed with which it is supplanted."

The work of Saint-John Perse also bears a definite resemblance to that of Whitman — both in the nature of his stanza and in the rolling, cumulative force of his long syntactic breaths. If Larbaud in some sense domesticates Whitman, Saint-John Perse carries him beyond universalism into a quest for great cosmic harmonies. The voice of the poet is mythical in its scope, as if, with its thunderous and sumptuous rhetoric, it had come into being for the sole purpose of conquering the world. Unlike most of the poets of his generation, who made their peace with temporality and used the notion of change as the premise of their work, Saint-John Perse's poems are quickened by an almost Platonic urge to seek out the eternal. In this respect, Milosz also stands to the side of his contemporaries. A student of the mystics and the alchemists, Milosz combines Catholicism and cabalism with what Kenneth Rexroth has described as "apocalyptic sensualism," and his work draws much of its inspiration from numerological treatment of names, transpositions of letters, anagrammatic and acronymic combinations, and other linguistic practices of the occult. But, as with the poems of Yeats, the poetry itself transcends the restrictions of its sources, displaying, as John Peck has commented, "an obsessive range of feeling, in which personal melancholy is also melancholy for a crepuscular era, that long hour before first light 'when the shadows decompose.' "

Another poet who resists categorization is Segalen. Like Larbaud, who wrote his poems through an invented persona; like Pound, whose translations stand curiously among his best and most personal works, Segalen carried this impulse toward self-effacement one step further and wrote behind the mask of another culture. The poems to be found in *Stèles* are neither translations nor imitations, but French poems written by a French poet *as if he were Chinese*. There is no attempt to deceive on Segalen's part; he never pretended these poems were anything other than original works. What at first reading might appear to be a kind of literary exoticism on closer scrutiny holds up as a poetry of solid, universal interest. By freeing himself from the limitations of his own culture, by circumventing his own historical moment, Segalen was able to explore a much wider territory — to discover, in some sense, that part of himself that was a poet.

In many ways, the case of Jouve is no less unusual. A follower of the Symbolists as a young man, Jouve published a number of books of poetry between 1912 and 1923. What he described as a "moral, spiritual, and aesthetic crisis" in 1924 led him to break with all his early work, which he never allowed to be republished. Over the next forty years he produced a voluminous body of writing — his collected poems run well over a thousand pages. Deeply Christian in outlook, Jouve is primarily concerned with the question of sexuality, both as transgression and as creative force — "the beautiful power of human eroticism" — and his poetry is the first in France to have made use of the methods of Freudian psychoanalysis. It is a poetry without predecessors and without followers. If his work was somewhat forgotten during the period dominated by the Surrealists — which meant that recognition of Jouve's achievement was delayed for almost a generation — he is now widely considered to be one of the major poets of the half-century.

Supervielle was also influenced by the Symbolists as a young man, and of all the poets of his generation he is perhaps the most purely lyrical. A poet of space, of the natural world, Supervielle writes from a position of supreme innocence. "To dream is to forget the materiality of one's body," he wrote in 1951, "and to confuse to some degree the outer and the inner world . . . People are sometimes surprised over my marvelling at the world. This arises as much from the permanency of my dreams as from my bad memory. Both lead me from surprise to surprise, and force me to be amazed at everything."

It is this sense of amazement, perhaps, that best describes the work of these first eleven poets, all of whom began writing before World War I. The poets of the next generation, however, who came of age during the war itself, were denied the possibility of such innocent optimism. The war was not simply a conflict between armies, but a profound crisis of values that transformed European consciousness, and the younger poets, while having absorbed the lessons of Apollinaire and his contemporaries, were compelled to respond to this crisis in ways that were without precedent. As Hugo Ball, one of the founders of Dada, noted in his diary in 1917: "A thousand-year-old culture disintegrates. There are no columns and no supports, no foundations anymore — they have all been blown up . . . The meaning of the world has disappeared."

The Dada movement, which began in Zurich in 1916, was the most radical response to this sense of spiritual collapse. In the face of a discredited culture, the Dadaists challenged every assumption and ridiculed every belief of that culture. As artists, they attacked the notion of art itself, transforming their rage into a kind of subversive doubt, filled with caustic humor and willful self-contradiction. "The true Dadaists are against Dada," wrote Tzara in one of his manifestoes. The point was never to take anything at face value and never to take anything too seriously — especially oneself. The Socratic ironies of Marcel Duchamp's art are perhaps the purest expression of this attitude. In the realm of poetry, Tzara was no less sly or rambunctious. This is his recipe for writing a Dada poem: "Take a newspaper. Take a pair of scissors. Select an article as long as you want your poem to be. Cut out the article. Then carefully cut out each of the words that form this article and put them in a bag. Shake gently. Then take out each scrap, one after the other. Conscientiously copy them in the order they left the bag. The poem will resemble you. And there you are, an infinitely original writer, with a charming sensibility, beyond the understanding of the vulgar." If this is a poetry of chance, it should not be confused with the aesthetics of aleatory composition. Tzara's proposed method is an assault on the sanctity of Poetry, and it does not attempt to elevate itself to the status of an artistic ideal. Its function is purely negative. This is anti-art in its earliest incarnation, the "anti-philosophy of spontaneous acrobatics."

Tzara moved to Paris in 1919, introducing Dada to the French scene. Breton, Aragon, Éluard and Soupault all became participants in the movement. Inevitably, it did not last more than a few years. An art of total negation cannot survive, for its destructiveness must ultimately include itself. It was by drawing on the ideas and attitudes of Dada, however, that Surrealism became possible. "Surrealism is pure psychic automatism," Breton wrote in his first manifesto of 1924, "whose intention is to express, verbally, in writing, or by other means, the real process of thought and thought's dictation, in the absence of all control exercised by reason and outside all aesthetic or moral preoccupations. Surrealism rests on the belief in the superior reality of certain previously neglected forms of association; in the omnipotence of dream, and in the disinterested play of thought."

Like Dada, Surrealism did not offer itself as an aesthetic movement. Equating Rimbaud's cry to change life with Marx's injunction to change the world, the Surrealists sought to push poetry, in Walter Benjamin's phrase, "to the utmost limits of possibility." The attempt was to demystify art, to blur the distinctions between life and art, and to use the methods of art to explore the possibilities of human freedom. To quote Walter Benjamin again, from his prescient essay on the Surrealists published in 1929: "Since Bakunin, Europe has lacked a radical concept of freedom. The Surrealists have one. They are the first to liquidate the liberal-moral-humanistic ideal of freedom, because they are convinced that 'freedom, which on this earth can only be bought with a thousand of the hardest sacrifices, must be enjoyed unrestrictedly in its fullness, without any kind of programmatic calculation, as long as it lasts.' " For this reason, Surrealism associated itself closely with the politics of revolution (one of its magazines was even entitled *Surrealism in the Service of the Revolution*), flirting continually with the Communist Party and playing the role of fellow traveler during the era of the Popular Front — although refusing to submerge its identity in that of pure politics. Constant disputes over principles marked the history of the Surrealists, with Breton holding the middle ground between the activist and aesthetic wings of the group, frequently shifting positions in an effort to maintain a consistent program for Surrealism. Of all the poets associated with the movement, only Péret remained faithful to Breton over the long term. Soupault, by nature averse to the notion of literary movements, lost interest by 1927. Both Artaud and Desnos were excommunicated in 1929 — Artaud for opposing Surrealism's interest in politics and Desnos for supposedly compromising his integrity by working as a journalist. Aragon, Tzara and Éluard all joined the Communist Party in the thirties. Queneau and Prévert parted amicably after a brief association. Daumal, whose work was recognized by Breton as sharing the preoccupations of the Surrealists, declined an invitation to join the group. Char, ten or twelve years younger than most of the original members, was an early adherent but later broke with the movement and went on to do his best work during and after the war. Ponge's connection was peripheral, and Michaux, in some sense the most Surrealist of all French poets, never had anything to do with the group.

This same confusion exists when one examines the work of these poets. If "pure psychic automatism" is the underlying principle of Surrealist composition, only Péret seems to have stuck to it rigorously in the writing of his poems. Interestingly, his work is the least resonant of all the Surrealists — notable more for its comic effects than for any uncovering of the "convulsive beauty" that Breton envisaged as the goal of Surrealist writing. Even in Breton's poetry, with its abrupt shifts and unexpected associations, there is an undercurrent of consistent rhetoric that makes the poems cohere as densely reasoned objects of thought. With Tzara as well, automatism serves almost as a rhetorical device. It is a method of discovery, not an end in itself. In his best work — especially the long, multifaceted *Approximate Man* — a torrent of images organizes itself into a nearly systematic argument by means of repetition and variation, propelling itself forward in the manner of a musical composition.

Soupault, on the other hand, is clearly a conscious craftsman. While limited in range, his poetry displays a charm and a humility absent in the work of the other Surrealists. He is a poet of intimacy and pathos, at times strangely reminiscent of Verlaine, and if his poems have none of the flamboyance to be found in Tzara and Breton, they are more immediately accessible, more purely lyrical. By the same token, Desnos is a poet of plain speech, whose work often achieves a stunning lyrical intensity. His output extends from early experiments with language (dexterous, often dazzling exercises in word play) to free-verse love poems of great poignancy to longer, narrative poems and works in traditional forms. In an essay published just one year before his death, Desnos described his work as an effort "to fuse popular language, even the most colloquial, with an inexpressible 'atmosphere'; with a vital use of imagery, so as to annex for ourselves those domains which . . . remain incompatible with that fiendish, plaguing poetic dignity which endlessly oozes from tongues . . ."

With Éluard, arguably the greatest of the Surrealist poets, the love poem is accorded metaphysical status. His language, as limpid as anything to be found in Ronsard, is built on syntactic structures of extreme simplicity. Éluard uses the idea of love in his work to mirror the poetic process itself — as a way both to escape the world and to understand it. It is that irrational part of man which weds the inner to the outer, rooted in the physical and yet transcending matter, creating that uniquely human place in which man can discover his freedom. These same themes are present in Éluard's later work, particularly the poems written during the German Occupation, in which this notion of freedom is carried from the realm of the individual to that of an entire people.

If Éluard's work can be read as a continuous whole, Aragon's career as a poet divides into two distinct periods. Perhaps the most militant and provocative of the French Dadaists, he also played a leading role in the development of Surrealism and, after Breton, was the group's most active theorist. Attacked by Breton in the early thirties for the increasingly propagandist tone of his poetry, Aragon withdrew from the movement and joined the Communist Party. It was not until the war that he returned to the writing of poetry — and in a manner that bears almost no relation to his earlier work. His Resistance poems brought him national fame, and they are distinguished by their force and eloquence, but in their methods they are highly traditional, composed for the most part in alexandrines and rhyming stanzas.

Although Artaud was an early participant in Surrealism (for a time he even headed The Central Bureau for Surrealist Research) and although a number of his most important works were written during that period, he is a writer who stands so defiantly outside the traditional norms of literature that it is useless to label his work in any way. Properly speaking, Artaud is not a poet at all, and yet he has probably had a greater influence on the poets who came after him than any other writer of his generation. "Where others present their works," he wrote, "I claim to do no more than show my mind." His aim as a writer was never to create aesthetic objects — works that could be detached from their creator — but to record the state of mental and physical struggle in which "words rot at the unconscious summons of the brain." There is no division in Artaud between life and writing — and life not in the sense of biography, of external events, but life as it is lived in the intimacy of the body, of the blood that flows through one's veins. As such, Artaud is a kind of Ur-poet, whose work describes the processes of thought and feeling before the advent of language, before the possibility of speech. It is at once a cry of suffering and a challenge to all our assumptions about the purpose of literature.

In a totally different way from Artaud, Ponge also commands a unique place among the writers of his generation. He is a writer of supremely classical values, and his work — most of it has been written in prose — is pristine in its clarity, highly sensitive to nuance and the etymological origins of words, which Ponge has described as the "semantical thickness" of language. Ponge has invented a new kind of writing, a poetry of the object that is at the same time a method of contemplation. Minutely detailed in its descriptions, and everywhere infused with a fine ironic humor, his work proceeds as though the object being examined did not exist as a word. The primary act of the poet, therefore, becomes the act of seeing, as if no one had ever seen the thing before, so that the object might have "the good fortune to be born into words."

Like Ponge, who has frequently resisted the efforts of critics to classify him as a poet, Michaux is a writer whose work escapes the strictures of genre. Floating freely between prose and verse, his texts have a spontaneous, almost haphazard quality that sets them against the pretensions and platitudes of high art. No French writer has ever given greater rein to the play of his imagination. Much of his best writing is set in imaginary countries and reads as a bizarre kind of anthropology of inner states. Although often compared to Kafka, Michaux does not resemble the author of Kafka's novels and stories so much as the Kafka of the notebooks and parables. As with Artaud, there is an urgency of process in Michaux's writing, a sense of personal risk and necessity in the act of composition. In an early statement about his poetry he declared: "I write with transport and for myself. a) sometimes to liberate myself from an intolerable tension or from a no less painful abandonment. b) sometimes for an imaginary companion, for a kind of alter ego whom I would honestly like to keep up-to-date on an extraordinary transition in me or in the world, which I, ordinarily forgetful, all at once believe I rediscover in, so to speak, its virginity. c) deliberately to shake the congealed and established, to invent . . . Readers trouble me. I write, if you like, for the unknown reader."

An equal independence of approach is present in Daumal, a serious student of Eastern religions, whose poems deal obsessively with the rift between spiritual and physical life. "The Absurd is the purest and most basic form of metaphysical existence," he wrote, and in his dense, visionary work, the illusions of appearance fall away only to be transformed into further illusions. "The poems are haunted by a . . . consciousness of impending death," Michael Benedikt has commented, "seen as the poet's long-lost 'double'; and also by a personification of death as a sort of sinister mother, an exacting being avaricious in her search for beings to extinguish — but only so as to place upon them perversely the burden of further metamorphoses."

Daumal is considered one of the chief precursors of the "College of Pataphysics," a mock-secret literary organization inspired by Alfred Jarry that included both Queneau and Prévert among its members. Humor is the guiding principle in the work of these two poets. With Queneau, it is a linguistic humor, based on intricate word plays, parody, feigned stupidity and slang. In his well-known prose work of 1947, for example, *Exercices de style*, the same mundane event is given in ninety-nine different versions, each one written in a different style, each one presented from a different point of view. In discussing Queneau in *Writing Degree Zero*, Roland Barthes describes this style as "white writing" — in which literature, for the first time, has openly become a problem and question of language. If Queneau is an intellectual poet, Prévert, who also adheres closely to the patterns of ordinary speech in his work, is without question a popular poet — even a populist poet. Since World War II, no one has had a wider audience in France, and many of Prévert's works have been turned into highly successful songs. Anticlerical, antimilitaristic, rebellious in political attitude and extolling a rather sentimentalized form of love between man and woman, Prévert represents one of the more felicitous marriages between poetry and mass culture, and beyond the charm of his work, it is valuable as an indicator of popular French taste.

Although Surrealism continues to exist as a literary movement, the period of its greatest influence and most important creations came to an end by the beginning of World War II. Of the second-generation

Surrealists — or those poets who found inspiration in its methods — Césaire stands out as the most notable example. One of the first black writers to be recognized in France, founder of the *négritude* movement — which asserts the uniqueness and dignity of black culture and consciousness — Césaire, a native of Martinique, was championed by Breton, who discovered his work in the late thirties. As the South African poet Mazisi Kunene has written about Césaire: "Surrealism was for him a logical instrument with which to smash the restrictive forms of language which sanctified rationalized bourgeois values. The breaking up of language patterns coincided with his own desire to smash colonialism and all oppressive forms." More vividly perhaps than in the work of the Surrealists of France, Césaire's poetry embodies the twin aspirations of political and aesthetic revolution, and in such a way that they are inseparably joined.

For many of the poets who began writing in the thirties, however, Surrealism was never a temptation. Follain, for example, whose work has proved to be particularly amenable to American taste (of all recent French poets, he is the one who has been most frequently translated), is a poet of the everyday, and in his short, exquisitely crafted works one finds an examination of the object no less serious and challenging than Ponge's. At the same time, Follain is largely a poet of memory ("In the fields / of his eternal childhood / the poet wanders / wanting to forget nothing"), and his evocations of the world as seen through a child's eyes bear within them a shimmering, epiphanic quality of psychological truth. A similar kind of realism and attention to surface detail is also to be found in Guillevic. Materialist in his approach to the world, unrhetorical in his methods, Guillevic has also created a world of objects — but one in which the object is nevertheless problematical, a reality to be penetrated, to be striven for, but which is not necessarily given. Frénaud, on the other hand, although often grouped together with Follain and Guillevic, is a far more romantic poet than his two contemporaries. Effusive in his language, metaphysical in his concerns, he has been compared at times to the Existentialists in his insistence that man's world is a creation of man himself. Despairing of certainty (*There Is No Paradise*, reads the title of one of his collections), Frénaud's work draws its force not so much from a recognition of the absurd as from the attempt to find a basis for positive values within the absurd itself.

If World War I was the crucial event that marked the poetry of the twenties and thirties, World War II was no less decisive in determining the kind of poetry written in France during the late forties and fifties. The military defeat of 1940 and the Nazi Occupation that followed were among the darkest moments in French history. The country had been devastated both emotionally and economically. In the context of this disarray, the mature poetry of René Char came as a revelation. Aphoristic, fragmented, closely allied to the thought of Heraclitus and the pre-Socratics, Char's poetry is at once a lyrical summoning of natural correspondences and a meditation on the poetic process itself. Austere in its settings (for the most part the landscape is that of Char's native Provence) and roughly textured in its language, this is a poetry that does not attempt to record or evoke feelings so much as it seeks to embody the ongoing struggle of words to ground themselves in the world. Char writes from a position of deep existential commitment (he was an important field leader in the Resistance), and his work is permeated with a sense of new beginnings, of a necessary search to rescue life from the ruins.

The best poets of the immediate postwar generation share many of these same preoccupations. Bonnefoy, du Bouchet, Jaccottet, Giroux and Dupin, all born within four years of one another, manifest in their work a vigilant hermeticism that is characterized by a consciously reduced range of imagery, great syntactical inventiveness and a refusal to ask anything but essential questions. Bonnefoy, the most classical and philosophically oriented of the five, has largely been concerned in his work with tracking the reality that haunts "the abyss of concealed appearances." "Poetry does not interest itself in the shape of the world itself," he once remarked, "but in the world that this universe will become. Poetry speaks only of presences — or absences." Du Bouchet, by contrast, is a poet who shuns every temptation toward abstraction. His work, which is perhaps the most radical adventure in recent French poetry, is based on a rigorous attentiveness to phenomenological detail. Stripped of metaphor, almost devoid of imagery, and generated by a language of abrupt, paratactic brevity, his poems move through an almost barren landscape, a speaking "I" continually in search of itself. A du Bouchet page is the mirror of this journey, each one dominated by white space, the few words present as if emerging from a silence that will inevitably claim them again.

Of these poets, it is undoubtedly Dupin whose work holds the greatest verbal richness. Tightly sprung, calling upon an imagery that seethes with hidden violence, his poems are dazzling in both their energy and their anguish. "In this infinite unanimous dissonance," he writes, in a poem entitled "Lichens," "each ear of corn, each drop of blood, speaks its language and goes its way. The torch, which lights the abyss, which seals it up, is itself an abyss." Far gentler in approach are both Jaccottet and Giroux. Jaccottet's short nature poems, which in certain ways adhere to the aesthetics of Imagism, have an Oriental stillness about them that can flare at any moment into the brightness of epiphany. "For us living more and more surrounded by intellectual schemas and masks," Jaccottet has written, "and suffocating in the prison they erect around us, the poet's eye is the battering ram that knocks down these walls and gives back to us, if only for an instant, the real; and with the real, a possibility of life." Giroux, a poet of great lyrical gifts, died prematurely in 1973 and published only one book during his lifetime. The short poems in that volume are quiet, deeply meditated works about the nature of poetic reality, explorations of the space between the world and words, and they have had a considerable impact on the work of many of today's younger poets.

This hermeticism, however, is by no means present in the work of all the poets of the postwar period. Dadelsen, for example, is an effusive poet, monologic and varied in tone, who frequently launches into slang. There have been a number of distinguished Catholic poets in France during the twentieth century (La Tour du Pin, Emmanuel, Jean-Claude Renard and Mambrino are recent examples), but it is perhaps Dadelsen, less well known than the others, who in his tormented search for God best represents the limits and perils of religious consciousness. Marteau, on the other hand, draws much of his imagery from myth, and although his preoccupations often overlap with those of, say, Bonnefoy or Dupin, his work is less self-reflective than theirs, dwelling not so much on the struggles and paradoxes of expression as on uncovering the presence of archetypal forces in the world.

Of the new work that began to appear in the early sixties, the books of Jabès are the most notable. Since 1963, when *The Book of Questions* was published, Jabès has brought out ten volumes in a remarkable series of works, prompting comments such as Jacques Derrida's statement that "in the last ten years nothing has been written in France that does not have its precedent somewhere in the texts of Jabès." Jabès, an Egyptian Jew who published a number of books of poetry in the forties and fifties, has emerged as a writer of the first rank with his more recent work — all of it written in France after his expulsion from Cairo during the Suez crisis. These books are almost impossible to define. Neither novels nor poems, neither essays nor plays, they are a combination of all these forms, a mosaic of fragments, aphorisms, dialogues, songs and commentaries that endlessly move around the central question posed by each book: How to speak what cannot be spoken. The question is the Holocaust, but it is also the question of literature itself. By a startling leap of the imagination, Jabès treats them as one and the same: "I have talked to you about the difficulty of being Jewish, which is the same as the difficulty of writing. For Judaism and writing are but the same waiting, the same hope, the same wearing out."

This determination to carry poetry into uncharted territory, to break down the standard distinctions between prose and verse, is perhaps the most striking characteristic of the younger generation of poets today. In Deguy, for example, poetry can be made from just about anything at all, and his work draws on a broad range of material: from the technical language of science to the abstractions of philosophy to elaborate play on linguistic constructions. In Roubaud, the quest for new forms has led to books of highly intricate structures (one of his volumes, Σ, is based on the permutations of the Japanese game of go), and these invented shapes are exploited with great deftness, serving not as ends in themselves but as a means of ordering the fragments they encompass, of putting the various pieces in a larger context and investing them with a coherence they would not possess on their own.

Pleynet and Roche, two poets closely connected with the well-known review *Tel Quel*, have each carried the notion of antipoetry to a position of extreme combativeness. Pleynet's jocular, and at the same time deadly serious "Ars Poetica" of 1964, is a good example of this attitude. "I. ONE CANNOT KNOW HOW TO WRITE WITHOUT KNOWING WHY. II. THE AUTHOR OF THIS ARS POETICA DOES NOT KNOW HOW TO WRITE BUT HE WRITES. III. THE QUESTION 'HOW TO WRITE' ANSWERS THE QUESTION 'WHY WRITE' AND THE QUESTION 'WHAT IS WRITING'. IV. A QUESTION IS AN ANSWER." Roche's approach is perhaps even more disruptive of conventional assumptions about literature. "Poetry is inadmissible. Besides, it does not exist," he has written. And elsewhere: ". . . the logic of modern writing demands that one should take a vigorous hand in promoting the death agonies of [this] symbolist, outmoded ideology. Writing can only symbolize what it is in its functioning, in its 'society', within the frame of its utilization. It must stick to that."

This is not to say, however, that short, lyric poems do not continue to be written in France. Delahaye and Denis, both still in their thirties, have created substantial bodies of work in this more familiar mode — mining a landscape that had first been mapped out by du Bouchet and Dupin. On the other hand, many of the younger poets, having absorbed and transmuted the questions raised by their predecessors, are now producing a kind of work that is both original and demanding in its insistence upon the textuality of the written word. Although there are significant differences among Albiach, Royet-Journoud, Daive, Hocquard and Veinstein, in one fundamental aspect of their work they share a common point of view. Their medium as writers is neither the individual poem nor even the sequence of poems, but the book. As Royet-Journoud stated in a recent interview: "My books consist only of a single text, the genre of which cannot be defined. . . . It's a *book* that I write, and I feel that the notion of genre obscures the book as such." This is as true of Daive's highly charged, psycho-erotic work, Hocquard's graceful and ironic narratives of memory, and Veinstein's minimal theaters of the creative process as it is of Royet-Journoud's obsessive "detective stories" of language. Most strikingly, this approach to composition can be found in Albiach's 1971 volume, *État*, undoubtedly the major work to be published thus far by a member of this younger generation. As Keith Waldrop has written: "The poem — it is a single piece — does not progress by images . . . or by plot. . . . The argument, if it were given, might include the following propositions: 1) everyday language is dependent on logic, but 2) in fiction, there is no necessity that any particular word should follow any other, so 3) it is possible at least to imagine a free choice, a syntax generated by desire. *État* is the 'epic' . . . of this imagination. To state such an argument . . . would be to renounce the whole project. But what is presented is not a series of emotions . . . the poem is composed mindfully; and if Anne-Marie Albiach rejects rationality, she quite obviously writes with full intelligence . . ."

IV

. . . with the conviction that, in the end, translating is madness.

Maurice Blanchot

As I was about to embark on the project of editing this anthology, a friend gave me a piece of valuable advice. Jonathan Griffin, who served as British cultural attaché in Paris after the war, and has translated several books by De Gaulle, as well as poets ranging from Rimbaud to Pessoa, has been around long enough to know more about such things than I do. Every anthology, he said, has two types of readers: the critics, who judge the book by what is *not* included in it, and the general readers, who read the book for what it actually contains. He advised me to keep this second group uppermost in my thoughts. The critics, after all, are in business to criticize, and they are familiar with the material anyway. The important thing to remember is that most people will be reading the majority of these poets for the first time. They are the ones who will get the most out of the anthology.

During the two years it has taken for me to put this book together, I have often reminded myself of these words. Frequently, however, it has been difficult to take them to heart, since I myself am all too aware of what has not been included. My original plan for the anthology was to represent the work of almost a hundred poets. In addition to more familiar kinds of writing, I had wanted to use a number of eccentric works, provide examples of concrete and sound poetry, include several collaborative poems and, in a few instances, offer variant translations when more than one good version of a poem was available. As work progressed, it became apparent that this would not be possible. I was faced with the unhappy situation of trying to fit an elephant into a cage designed for a fox. Reluctantly, I changed my approach to the book. If my choice was between offering a smattering of poems by many poets or substantial selections of work by a reduced number of poets, there did not seem to be much doubt that the second solution was wiser and more coherent. Instead of imagining everything I would like to see in the anthology, I tried to think of the poets it would be inconceivable *not* to include. In this way, I gradually whittled the list down to forty-eight. These were difficult decisions for me, and though I stand by my final selection, it is with regret for those I was not able to include.*

There are no doubt some who will also wonder about certain other exclusions. In order to keep the book focused on poetry of the

---

* Among them are the following: Pierre Albert-Birot, Jean Cocteau, Raymond Roussel, Jean Arp, Francis Picabia, Arthur Cravan, Michel Leiris, Georges Bataille, Léopold Senghor, André Pieyre de Mandiargues, Jacques Audiberti, Jean Tardieu, Georges Schéhadé, Pierre Emmanuel, Joyce Mansour, Patrice de la Tour du Pin, René Guy Cadou, Henri Pichette, Christian Dotremont, Olivier Larronde, Henri Thomas, Jean Grosjean, Jean Tortel, Jean Laude, Pierre Torreilles, Jean-Claude Renard, Jean Joubert, Jacques Réda,

twentieth century, I decided on a fixed cutoff point to determine where the anthology should begin. The crucial year for my purposes turned out to be 1876: Any poet born before that year would not be considered. This allowed me, in good conscience, to forgo the problem posed by poets such as Valéry, Claudel, Jammes and Péguy, all of whom began writing in the late nineteenth century and went on writing well into the twentieth. Although their work overlaps chronologically with many of the poets in the book, it seems to belong in spirit to an earlier time. By the same token, 1876 was a convenient date for allowing me to include certain poets whose work is essential to the project — Fargue, Jacob and Milosz in particular.

As for the English versions of the poems, I have used already existing translations whenever possible. My motive has been to underscore the involvement, over the past fifty years, of American and British poets in the work of their French counterparts, and since there is abundant material to choose from (some of it hidden away in old magazines and out-of-print books, some of it readily available), there seemed to be no need to begin my search elsewhere. My greatest pleasure in putting this book together has been in rescuing a number of superb translations from the obscurity of library shelves and microfilm rooms: Nancy Cunard's Aragon, John Dos Passos' Cendrars, Paul Bowles's Ponge, and the translations by Eugene and Maria Jolas (the editors of *transition*), to mention just a few. Also to be noted are the translations that previously existed only in manuscript. Paul Blackburn's translations of Apollinaire, for example, were discovered among his papers after his death, and are published here for the first time.

Only in cases where translations did not exist or where the available translations seemed inadequate did I commission fresh translations. In each of these instances (Richard Wilbur's version of Apollinaire's "Le Pont Mirabeau," Lydia Davis's Fargue, Robert Kelly's Roubaud, Anselm Hollo's Dadelsen, Michael Palmer's Hocquard, Rosmarie Waldrop's Veinstein, Geoffrey Young's Aragon), I have tried to arrange the marriage with care. My aim was to bring together compatible poets — so that the translator would be able to exploit his particular strengths

---

Armen Lubin, Jean Pérol, Jude Stéfan, Marc Alyn, Jacqueline Risset, Michel Butor, Jean Pierre Faye, Alain Jouffroy, George Perros, Armand Robin, Boris Vian, Jean Mambrino, Lorand Gaspar, Georges Badin, Pierre Oster, Bernard Nöel, Claude Vigée, Joseph Gugliemi, Daniel Blanchard, Michel Couturier, Claude Esteban, Alain Sueid, Mathieu Bénézet.

as a poet in rendering the original into English. The results of this matchmaking have been uniformly satisfying. Richard Wilbur's "Mirabeau Bridge," for instance, strikes me as the first acceptable version of this important poem we have had in English, the only translation that comes close to re-creating the subtle music of the original.

In general, I have followed no consistent policy about translation in making my choices. A few of the translations are hardly more than adaptations, although the vast majority are quite faithful to the originals. Translating poetry is at best an art of approximation, and there are no fixed rules to follow in deciding what works or does not. It is largely a matter of instinct, of ear, of common sense. Whenever I was faced with a choice between literalness and poetry, I did not hesitate to choose poetry. It seemed more important to me to give those readers who have no French a true sense of each poem *as a poem* than to strive for word-by-word exactness. The experience of a poem resides not only in each of its words, but in the interactions among those words — the music, the silences, the shapes — and if a reader is not somehow given the chance to enter the totality of that experience, he will remain cut off from the spirit of the original. It is for this reason, it seems to me, that poems should be translated by poets.

1981

Mallarmé's Son

Mallarmé's second child, Anatole, was born on July 16, 1871, when the poet was twenty-nine. The boy's arrival came at a moment of great financial stress and upheaval for the family. Mallarmé was in the process of negotiating a move from Avignon to Paris, and arrangements were not finally settled until late November, when the family installed itself at 29 rue de Moscou and Mallarmé began teaching at the Lycée Fontanes.

Mme Mallarmé's pregnancy had been extremely difficult, and in the first months of his life Anatole's health was so fragile that it seemed unlikely he would survive. "I took him out for a walk on Thursday," Mme Mallarmé wrote to her husband on October 7. "It seemed to me that his fine little face was getting back some of its color ... I left him very sad and discouraged, and even afraid that I would not see him anymore, but it's up to God now, since the doctor can't do anything more, but how sad to have so little hope of seeing this dear little person recover."

Anatole's health, however, did improve. Two years later, in 1873, he reappears in the family correspondence in a series of letters from Germany, where Mallarmé's wife had taken the children to meet her father. "The little one is like a blossoming flower," she wrote to Mallarmé. "Tole loves his grandfather, he does not want to leave him, and when he is gone, he looks for him all over the house." In that same letter, nine-year-old Geneviève added: "Anatole asks for papa all the time." Two years later, on a second trip to Germany, there is further evidence of Anatole's robust health, for after receiving a letter from his wife, Mallarmé wrote proudly to his friend Cladel: "Anatole showers stones and punches on the little Germans who come back to attack him in a group." The following year, 1876, Mallarmé was absent from Paris for a few days and received this anecdote from his wife: "Totol is a bad little boy. He did not notice you were gone the night you left; it was only when I put him to bed that he looked everywhere for you to say good-night. Yesterday he did not ask for you, but this morning the poor little fellow looked all over the house for you; he even pulled back the covers on your bed, thinking he would find you there." In August of that same year, during another of Mallarmé's brief absences from the family, Geneviève wrote to her father to thank him for sending her presents and then remarked: "Tole wants you to bring him back a whale."

Beyond these few references to Anatole in the Mallarmé family letters, there are several mentions of him in C. L. Lefèvre-Roujon's introduction to the *Correspondance inédite de Stephane Mallarmé et Henry Roujon* — in particular, three little incidents that give some idea of the boy's lively personality. In the first, a stranger saw Anatole attending to his father's boat and asked him, "What is your boat called?" Anatole answered with great conviction, "My boat isn't called anything. Do you give a name to a carriage?" On another occasion, Anatole was taking a walk through the Fountainebleau forest with Mallarmé. "He loved the Fountainebleau forest and would often go there with Stéphane. . . . [One day], running down a path, he came upon a very pretty woman, politely stepped to the side, looked her over from top to bottom and, out of admiration, winked his eye at her, clicked his tongue, and then, this homage to beauty having been made, continued on his child's promenade." Finally, Lefèvre-Roujon reports the following: One day Mme Mallarmé boarded a Paris bus with Anatole and put the child on her lap in order to economize on the extra fare. As the bus jolted along, Anatole fell into a kind of trance, watching a gray-haired priest beside him who was reading his breviary. He asked him sweetly: "Monsieur l'abbée, would you allow me to kiss you?" The priest, surprised and touched, answered: "But of course, my little friend." Anatole leaned over and kissed him. Then, in the suavest voice possible, he commanded: "And now, kiss mama!"

In the spring of 1879, several months before his eighth birthday, Anatole became seriously ill. The disease, diagnosed as child's rheumatism, was further complicated by an enlarged heart. The illness first attacked his feet and knees, and then, when the symptoms had apparently cleared up, his ankles, wrists, and shoulders. Mallarmé considered himself largely responsible for the child's suffering, feeling that he had given the boy "bad blood" through a hereditary weakness. At the age of seventeen, he had suffered terribly from rheumatic pain, with high fevers and violent headaches, and throughout his life rheumatism would remain a chronic problem.

In April, Mallarmé went off to the country for a few days with Geneviève. His wife wrote: "He's been a good boy, the poor little martyr, and from time to time asks me to dry his tears. He asks me often to tell little papa that he would like to write to him, but he can't move his little wrists." Three days later, the pain had shifted from Anatole's hand to his legs, and he was able to write a few words: "I think of you always. If you knew, my dear Little Father, how my knees hurt."

Over the following months, things took a turn for the better. By August, the improvement had been considerable. On the tenth, Mallarmé wrote to Robert de Montesquiou, a recently made friend who had formed a special attachment to Anatole, to thank him for sending the child a parrot. "I believe that your delicious little animal . . . has distracted the illness of our patient, who is now allowed to go to the country. . . . Have you heard from where you are . . . all the cries of joy from our invalid, who never takes his eyes . . . away from the marvelous princess held captive in her marvelous palace, who is called Sémiramas because of the stone gardens she seems to reflect? I like to think that this satisfaction of an old and improbable desire has had something to do with the struggle of the boy's health to come back; to say nothing . . . of the secret influence of the precious stone that darts out continually from the cage's inhabitant on the child. . . . How charming and friendly you have been, you who are so busy with so much, during this recent time; and it is more than a pleasure for me to announce to you, before anyone else, that I feel all our worries will soon be over."

In this state of optimism, Anatole was taken by the family to Valvins in the country. After several days, however, his condition deteriorated drastically, and he nearly died. On August 22, Mallarmé wrote to his close friend Henry Roujon:

"I hardly dare to give any news because there are moments in this war between life and death that our poor little adored one is waging when I allow myself to hope, and repent of a too sad letter written the moment before, as of some messenger of bad tidings I myself have dispatched. I know nothing anymore and see nothing anymore . . . so much have I observed with conflicting emotions. The doctor, while continuing the Paris treatment, seems to act as though he were dealing with a condemned person who can only be comforted; and persists, when I follow him to the door, in not giving a glimmer of hope. The dear boy eats and sleep a little; breathes. Everything his organs could do to fight the heart problem they have done; after another enormous attack, that is the benefit he draws from the country. But the disease, the terrible disease, seems to have set in irremediably. If you lift the blanket, you see a belly so swollen you can't look at it!

"There it is. I do not speak to you of my pain; no matter where my thought tries to lead it, this pain recoils from seeing itself worsen! But what does suffering matter, even suffering like that: the horrible thing is . . . the misfortune in itself that this little being might vanish. . . . I confess that it is too much for me; I cannot bring myself to face this idea.

"When my wife looks at the darling, she seems to see a serious illness and nothing more; I must not rob her of the courage she has found to care for the child in this quietude. I am alone here then with the hatchet blow of the doctor's verdict."

A letter from Mallarmé to Montesquiou on September 9 offers further details: "Unfortunately, after several days [in the country], everything . . . grew dark: we have been through the cruelest hours our darling invalid has caused us, for the symptoms we thought had disappeared forever have returned; they are taking hold now. The old improvements were a sham. . . . I am too tormented and too taken up with our poor little boy to do anything literary, except to jot down a few rapid notes. . . . *Tole* speaks of you, and even amuses himself in the morning by fondly imitating your voice. The parrot, whose auroral belly seems to catch fire with a whole orient of spices, is looking right now at the forest with one eye and at the bed with the other, like a thwarted desire for an excursion by her little master."

By late September there had been no improvement, and Mallarmé now centered his hopes on a return to Paris. On the twenty-fifth, he wrote to his oldest friend, Henri Cazalis: "The evening before your beautiful present came, the poor darling, for the second time since his illness began, was nearly taken from us. Three successive fainting fits in the afternoon did not, thank heaven, carry him off. . . . The belly disturbs us, as filled with water as ever. . . . The country has given us everything we could ask of it, assuming it could give us anything, milk, air, and peaceful surroundings for the invalid. We have only one idea now, to leave for a consultation with Doctor Peter. . . . I tell myself it is impossible that a great medical specialist cannot take advantage of the forces nature opposes so generously to a terrible disease. . . ."

After the return to Paris, there are two further letters about Anatole — both dated October 6. The first was to the English writer John Payne: "This is the reason for my long silence. . . . At Easter, already six hideous months ago, my son was attacked by rheumatism, which after a false

convalescence has thrown itself on his poor heart with incredible violence, and holds him between life and death. The poor friend has twice
almost been taken from us. . . . You can judge of our pain, knowing how
much I live inside my family; then this child, so charming and exquisite,
had captivated me to the point that I still include him in all my future
projects and in my dearest dreams. . . ."

The other letter was to Montesquiou. "Thanks to immense precautions, everything went well [on the return to Paris] . . . but the darling
paid for it with several bad days that drained his tiny energy. He is prey
to a horrible and inexplicable nervous cough . . . it shakes him for a
whole day and a whole night. . . . — Yes, I am quite beside myself, like
someone on whom a terrible and endless wind is blowing. All-night
vigils, contradictory emotions of hope and sudden fear, have supplanted all thought of repose. . . . My sick little boy smiles at you from
his bed, like a white flower remembering the vanished sun."

After writing these two letters, Mallarmé went to the post office to
mail them. Anatole died before his father managed to return home.

*

The 202 fragments that follow belonged to Mme E. Bonniot, the
Mallarmé heir, and were deciphered, edited, and published in a scrupulously prepared volume by the literary scholar and critic Jean-Pierre
Richard in 1961. In the preface to his book — which includes a lengthy
study of the fragments — he describes his feelings on being handed the
soft red box that contained Mallarmé's notes. On the one hand: exalta-
tion. On the other hand: wariness. Although he was deeply moved by
the fragments, he was uncertain whether publication was appropriate,
given the intensely private nature of the work. He concluded, however,
that anything that could enhance our understanding of Mallarmé
would be valuable. "And if these phrases are no more than sighs," he
wrote, "that makes them all the more precious to us. It seemed to me
that the very nakedness of these notes . . . made their distribution desirable. It was useful in fact to prove once again to what extent the famous
Mallarméan serenity was based on the impulses of a very vivid sensibility, at times even quite close to frenzy and delirium. . . . Nor was it
irrelevant to show, by means of a precise example, how this impersonality, this vaunted objectivity, was in reality connected to the most subjective upheavals of a life."

A close reading of the fragments will clearly show that they are no

more than notes for a possible work: a long poem in four parts with a
series of very specific themes. That Mallarmé projected such a work and
then abandoned it is indicated in a memoir written by Geneviève that
was published in a 1926 issue of the *N.R.F.*: "In 1879, we had the
immense sorrow of losing my little brother, an exquisite child of eight.
I was quite young then, but the deep and silent pain I felt in my father
made an unforgettable impression on me: 'Hugo,' he said, 'was happy
to have been able to speak (about the death of his daughter); for me, it's
impossible.' "

As they stand now, the notes are a kind of ur-text, the raw data of the
poetic process. Although they seem to resemble poems on the page,
they should not be confused with poetry per se. Nevertheless, more
than one hundred years after they were written, they are perhaps closer
to what we today consider possible in poetry than at the time of their
composition. For here we find a language of immediate contact, a syntax of abrupt, lightning shifts that still manages to maintain a sense, and
in their brevity, the sparse presence of their words, we are given a rare
and early example of isolate words able to span the enormous mental
spaces that lie between them — as if intelligible links could be created
by the brute force of each word or phrase, so densely charged that these
tiny particles of language could somehow leap out of themselves and
catch hold of the succeeding cliff-edge of thought. Unlike Mallarmé's
finished poems, these fragments have a startlingly unmediated quality.
Faithful not to the demands of art but to the jostling movement of
thought — and with a speed and precision that astonish — these notes
seem to emerge from such an interior place, it is as though we could
hear the crackling of the wires in Mallarmé's brain, experience each
synapse of thought as a physical sensation. If these fragments cannot be
read as a work of art, neither, I think, should they be treated simply as
a scholarly appendage to Mallarmé's collected writings. For, in spite of
everything, the Anatole notes do carry the force of poetry, and in the end
they achieve a stunning wholeness. They are a work in their own right
— but one that cannot be categorized, one that does not fit into any pre-
existent literary form.

The subject matter of the fragments requires little comment. In general, Mallarmé's motivation seems to have been the following: feeling
himself responsible for the disease that led to Anatole's death, for not
giving his son a body strong enough to withstand the blows of life, he
would take it upon himself to give the boy the one indomitable thing he

was capable of giving: his thought. He would transmute Anatole into words and thereby prolong his life. He would, *literally*, resurrect him, since the work of building a tomb — a tomb of poetry — would obliterate the presence of death. For Mallarmé, death is the consciousness of death, not the physical act of dying. Because Anatole was too young to understand his fate (a theme that occurs repeatedly throughout the fragments), it was as though he had not yet died. He was still alive in his father, and it was only when Mallarmé himself died that the boy would die as well. This is one of the most moving accounts of a man trying to come to grips with modern death — that is to say, death without God, death without hope of salvation — and it reveals the secret meaning of Mallarmé's entire aesthetic: the elevation of art to the stature of religion. Here, however, the work could not be written. In this time of crisis even art failed Mallarmé.

It strikes me that the effect of the Anatole fragments is quite close to the feeling created by Rembrandt's last portrait of his son, Titus. Bearing in mind the radiant and adoring series of canvases the artist made of the boy throughout his childhood, it is almost impossible for us to look at that last painting: the dying Titus, barely twenty years old, his face so ravaged by disease that he looks like an old man. It is important to imagine what Rembrandt must have felt as he painted that portrait; to imagine him staring into the face of his dying son and being able to keep his hand steady enough to put what he saw onto the canvas. If fully imagined, the act becomes almost unthinkable.

In the natural order of things, fathers do not bury their sons. The death of a child is the ultimate horror of every parent, an outrage against all we believe we can expect of life, little though it is. For everything, at that point, is taken away from us. Unlike Ben Jonson, who could lament the fact of his fatherhood as an impediment to understanding that his son had reached "the state he should envie," Mallarmé could find no support for himself, only an abyss, no consolation, except in the plan to write about his son — which, in the end, he could not bring himself to do. The work died along with Anatole. It is all the more moving to us, all the more important, for having been left unfinished.

1982

435

On the High Wire

The first time I saw Philippe Petit was in 1971. I was in Paris, walking down the Boulevard Montparnasse, when I came upon a large circle of people standing silently on the sidewalk. It seemed clear that something was happening inside that circle, and I wanted to know what it was. I elbowed my way past several onlookers, stood on my toes, and caught sight of a smallish young man in the center. Everything he wore was black: his shoes, his pants, his shirt, even the battered silk top hat he wore on his head. The hair jutting out from under the hat was a light red-blond, and the face below it was so pale, so devoid of color, that at first I thought he was in whiteface.

The young man juggled, rode a unicycle, performed little magic tricks. He juggled rubber balls, wooden clubs, and burning torches, both standing on the ground and sitting on his one-wheeler, moving from one thing to the next without interruption. To my surprise, he did all this in silence. A chalk circle had been drawn on the sidewalk, and scrupulously keeping any of the spectators from entering that space — with a persuasive mime's gesture — he went through his performance with such ferocity and intelligence that it was impossible to stop watching.

Unlike other street performers, he did not play to the crowd. Rather, it was somehow as though he had allowed the audience to share in the workings of his thoughts, had made us privy to some deep, inarticulate obsession within him. Yet there was nothing overtly personal about what he did. Everything was revealed metaphorically, as if at one remove, through the medium of the performance. His juggling was precise and self-involved, like some conversation he was holding with himself. He elaborated the most complex combinations, intricate mathematical patterns, arabesques of nonsensical beauty, while at the same time keeping his gestures as simple as possible. Through it all, he managed to radiate a hypnotic charm, oscillating somewhere between demon and clown. No one said a word. It was as though his silence were a command for others to be silent as well. The crowd watched, and after the performance was over, everyone put money in the hat. I realized that I had never seen anything like it before.

The next time I saw Philippe Petit was several weeks later. It was late at night — perhaps one or two in the morning — and I was walking along a quai of the Seine not far from Nôtre-Dame. Suddenly, across the street, I spotted several young people moving quickly through the darkness. They were carrying ropes, cables, tools, and heavy satchels. Curious as ever, I kept pace with them from my side of the street and recognized one of them as the juggler from the Boulevard Montparnasse. I knew immediately that something was going to happen. But I could not begin to imagine what it was.

The next day, on the front page of the *International Herald Tribune*, I got my answer. A young man had strung a wire between the towers of Nôtre-Dame Cathedral and walked and juggled and danced on it for three hours, astounding the crowds of people below. No one knew how he had rigged up his wire nor how he had managed to elude the attention of the authorities. Upon returning to the ground, he had been arrested, charged with disturbing the peace and sundry other offenses. It was in this article that I first learned his name: Philippe Petit. There was not the slightest doubt in my mind that he and the juggler were the same person.

This Nôtre-Dame escapade made a deep impression on me, and I continued to think about it over the years that followed. Each time I walked past Nôtre-Dame, I kept seeing the photograph that had been published in the newspaper: an almost invisible wire stretched between the enormous towers of the cathedral, and there, right in the middle, as if suspended magically in space, the tiniest of human figures, a dot of life against the sky. It was impossible for me not to add this remembered image to the actual cathedral before my eyes, as if this old monument of Paris, built so long ago to the glory of God, had been transformed into something else. But what? It was difficult for me to say. Into something more human, perhaps. As though its stones now bore the mark of a man. And yet, there was no real mark. I had made the mark with my own mind, and it existed only in memory. And yet, the evidence was irrefutable: my perception of Paris had changed. I no longer saw it in the same way.

It is, of course, an extraordinary thing to walk on a wire so high off the ground. To see someone do this triggers an almost palpable excitement in us. In fact, given the necessary courage and skill, there are probably very few people who would not want to do it themselves. And yet, the art of high-wire walking has never been taken very seriously.

Because wire walking generally takes place in the circus, it is automatically assigned marginal status. The circus, after all, is for children, and what do children know about art? We grownups have more important things to think about. There is the art of music, the art of painting, the art of sculpture, the art of poetry, the art of prose, the art of theater, the art of dancing, the art of cooking, the art of living. But the art of high-wire walking? The very term seems laughable. If people stop to think about the high-wire at all, they usually categorize it as some minor form of athletics.

There is, too, the problem of showmanship. I mean the crazy stunts, the vulgar self-promotion, the hunger for publicity that is everywhere around us. We live in an age when people seem willing to do anything for a little attention. And the public accepts this, granting notoriety or fame to anyone brave enough or foolish enough to make the effort. As a general rule, the more dangerous the stunt, the greater the recognition. Cross the ocean in a bathtub, vault forty burning barrels on a motorcycle, dive into the East River from the top of the Brooklyn Bridge, and you are sure to get your name in the newspapers, maybe even an interview on a talk show. The idiocy of these antics is obvious. I'd much rather spend my time watching my son ride his bicycle, training wheels and all.

Danger, however, is an inherent part of high-wire walking. When a man walks on a wire two inches off the ground, we do not respond in the same way as when he walks on a wire two hundred feet off the ground. But danger is only half of it. Unlike the stuntman, whose performance is calculated to emphasize every hair-raising risk, to keep his audience panting with dread and an almost sadistic anticipation of disaster, the good high-wire walker strives to make his audience forget the dangers, to lure it away from thoughts of death by the beauty of what he does on the wire itself. Working under the greatest possible constraints, on a stage no more than an inch across, the high-wire walker's job is to create a sensation of limitless freedom. Juggler, dancer, acrobat, he performs in the sky what other men are content to perform on the ground. The desire is at once far-fetched and perfectly natural, and the appeal of it, finally, is its utter uselessness. No art, it seems to me, so clearly emphasizes the deep aesthetic impulse inside us all. Each time we see a man walk on the wire, a part of us is up there with him. Unlike performances in the other arts, the experience of the high wire is direct, unmediated, simple, and it requires no explanation whatsoever. The art is the thing itself, a life in its most naked delineation. And if there is beauty in this, it is because of the beauty we feel inside ourselves.

There was another element of the Nôtre-Dame spectacle that moved me: the fact that it was clandestine. With the thoroughness of a bank robber preparing a heist, Philippe had gone about his business in silence. No press conferences, no publicity, no posters. The purity of it was impressive. For what could he possibly hope to gain? If the wire had snapped, if the installation had been faulty, he would have died. On the other hand, what did success bring? Certainly he did not earn any money from the venture. He did not even try to capitalize on his brief moment of glory. When all was said and done, the only tangible result was a short stay in a Paris jail.

Why did he do it, then? For no other reason, I believe, than to dazzle the world with what he could do. Having seen his stark and haunting juggling performance on the street, I sensed intuitively that his motives were not those of other men — not even those of other artists. With an ambition and an arrogance fit to the measure of the sky, and placing on himself the most stringent internal demands, he wanted, simply, to do what he was capable of doing.

After living in France for four years, I returned to New York in July of 1974. For a long time I had heard nothing about Philippe Petit, but the memory of what had happened in Paris was still fresh, a permanent part of my inner mythology. Then, just one month after my return, Philippe was in the news again — this time in New York, with his now-famous walk between the towers of the World Trade Center. It was good to know that Philippe was still dreaming his dreams, and it made me feel that I had chosen the right moment to come home. New York is a more generous city than Paris, and the people here responded enthusiastically to what he had done. As with the aftermath of the Nôtre-Dame adventure, however, Philippe kept faith with his vision. He did not try to cash in on his new celebrity; he managed to resist the honky-tonk temptations America is all too willing to offer. No books were published, no films were made, no entrepreneur took hold of him for packaging. The fact that the World Trade Center did not make him rich was almost as remarkable as the event itself. But the proof of this was there for all New Yorkers to see: Philippe continued to make his living by juggling in the streets.

The streets were his first theater, and he still takes his performances there as seriously as his work on the wire. It all started very early for him. Born into a middle-class French family in 1949, he taught himself magic at the age of six, juggling at the age of twelve, and high-wire walking a few years later. In the meantime, while immersing himself in such varied activities as horseback riding, rock-climbing, art, and carpentry, he managed to get himself expelled from nine schools. At sixteen, he began a period of incessant travels all over the world, performing as a street juggler in Western Europe, Russia, India, Australia, and the United States. "I learned to live by my wits," he has said of those years. "I offered juggling shows everywhere, for everyone — traveling around like a troubadour with my old leather sack. I learned to escape the police on my unicycle. I got hungry like a wolf; I learned how to control my life."

But it is on the high-wire that Philippe has concentrated his most important ambitions. In 1973, just two years after the Nôtre-Dame walk, he did another renegade performance in Sydney, Australia: stretching his wire between the northern pylons of the Harbour Bridge, the largest steel arch bridge in the world. Following the World Trade Center Walk in 1974, he crossed the Great Falls of Paterson, New Jersey, appeared on television for a walk between the spires of the Cathedral in Laon, France, and also crossed the Superdome in New Orleans before 80,000 people. This last performance took place just nine months after a forty-foot fall from an inclined wire, from which he suffered several broken ribs, a collapsed lung, a shattered hip, and a smashed pancreas.

Philippe has also worked in the circus. For one year he was a featured attraction with Ringling Brothers Barnum and Bailey, and from time to time he has served as a guest performer with The Big Apple Circus in New York. But the traditional circus has never been the right place for Philippe's talents, and he knows it. He is too solitary and unconventional an artist to fit comfortably into the strictures of the commercial big top. Far more important to him are his plans for the future: to walk across Niagara Falls; to walk from the top of the Sydney Opera House to the top of the Harbour Bridge — an inclined walk of more than half a mile. As he himself explains it: "To talk about records or risks is to miss the point. All my life I have looked for the most amazing places to cross — mountains, waterfalls, buildings. And if the most beautiful walks also happen to be the longest or most dangerous — that's fine. But I didn't look for that in the first place. What interests me is the performance, the show, the beautiful gesture."

When I finally met Philippe in 1980, I realized that all my feelings about him had been correct. This was not a daredevil or a stuntman, but a singular artist who could talk about his work with intelligence and humor. As he said to me that day, he did not want people to think of him as just another "dumb acrobat." He talked about some of the things he had written — poems, narratives of his Nôtre-Dame and World Trade Center adventures, film scripts, a small book on high-wire walking — and I said that I would be interested in seeing them. Several days later, I received a bulky package of manuscripts in the mail. A covering note explained that these writings had been rejected by eighteen different publishers in France and America. I did not consider this to be an obstacle. I told Philippe that I would do all I could to find him a publisher and also promised to serve as translator if necessary. Given the pleasure I had received from his performances on the street and wire, it seemed the least I could do.

On the High-Wire is in my opinion a remarkable book. Not only is it the first study of high-wire walking ever written, but it is also a personal testament. One learns from it both the art and the science of wire walking, the lyricism and the technical demands of the craft. At the same time, it should not be misconstrued as a "how to" book or an instruction manual. High-wire walking cannot really be taught: it is something you learn by yourself. And certainly a book would be the last place to turn if you were truly serious about doing it.

The book, then, is a kind of parable, a spiritual journey in the form of a treatise. Through it all, one feels the presence of Philippe himself: it is his wire, his art, his personality that inform the entire discourse. No one else, finally, has a place in it. This is perhaps the most important lesson to be learned from the treatise: the high-wire is an art of solitude, a way of coming to grips with one's life in the darkest, most secret corner of the self. When read carefully, the book is transformed into the story of a quest, an exemplary tale of one man's search for perfection. As such, it has more to do with the inner life than the high-wire. It seems to me that anyone who has ever tried to do something well, anyone who has ever made personal sacrifices for an art or an idea, will have no trouble understanding what it is about.

Until two months ago, I had never seen Philippe perform on the high-wire outdoors. A performance or two in the circus, and of course films and photographs of his exploits, but no outdoor walk in the flesh. I finally got my chance during the recent inauguration ceremony at the Cathedral of Saint John the Divine in New York. After a hiatus of several decades, construction was about to begin again on the cathedral's tower. As a kind of homage to the wire walkers of the Middle Ages — the *joglar* from the period of the great French cathedrals — Philippe had conceived of the idea of stretching a steel cable from the top of a tall apartment building on Amsterdam Avenue to the top of the Cathedral across the street — an inclined walk of several hundred yards. He would go from one end to the other and then present the Bishop of New York with a silver trowel, which would be used to lay the symbolic first stone of the tower.

The preliminary speeches lasted a long time. One after the other, dignitaries got up and spoke about the Cathedral and the historic moment that was about to take place. Clergymen, city officials, former Secretary of State Cyrus Vance — all of them made speeches. A large crowd had gathered in the street, mostly school children and neighborhood people, and it was clear that the majority of them had come to see Philippe. As the speeches droned on, there was a good deal of talking and restlessness in the crowd. The late September weather was threatening: a raw, pale gray sky; the wind beginning to rise; rain clouds gathering in the distance. Everyone was impatient. If the speeches went on any longer, perhaps the walk would have to be canceled.

Fortunately, the weather held, and at last Philippe's turn came. The area below the cable had to be cleared of people, which meant that those who a moment before had held center stage were now pushed to the side with the rest of us. The democracy of it pleased me. By chance, I found myself standing shoulder to shoulder with Cyrus Vance on the steps of the Cathedral. I, in my beat-up leather jacket, and he in his impeccable blue suit. But that didn't seem to matter. He was just as excited as I was. I realized later that at any other time I might have been tongue-tied to be standing next to such an important person. But none of that even occurred to me then. We talked about the high-wire and the dangers Philippe would have to face. He seemed to be genuinely in awe of the whole thing and kept looking up at the wire — as I did, as did the hundreds of children around us. It was then that I understood the most important aspect of the high wire: it reduces us all to our common humanity. A Secretary of state, a poet, a child: we became equal in one another's eyes, and therefore a part of one another.

A brass band played a Renaissance fanfare from some invisible place behind the Cathedral facade, and Philippe emerged from the roof of the building on the other side of the street. He was dressed in a white satin medieval costume, the silver trowel hanging from a sash at his side. He saluted the crowd with a graceful, bravura gesture, took hold of his balancing-pole firmly in his two hands, and began his slow ascent along the wire. Step by step, I felt myself walking up there with him, and gradually those heights seemed to become habitable, human, filled with happiness. He slid down to one knee and acknowledged the crowd again; he balanced on one foot; he moved deliberately and majestically, exuding confidence. Then, suddenly, he came to a spot on the wire far enough away from his starting-point that my eyes lost contact with all surrounding references: the apartment building, the street, the other people. He was almost directly overhead now, and as I leaned backward to take in the spectacle, I could see no more than the wire, Philippe, and the sky. There was nothing else. A white body against a nearly white sky, as if free. The purity of that image burned itself into my mind and is still there today, wholly present.

From beginning to end, I did not once think that he might fall. Risk, fear of death, catastrophe: these were not part of the performance. Philippe had assumed full responsibility for his own life, and I sensed that nothing could possibly shake that resolve. High-wire walking is not an art of death, but an art of life—and life lived to the very extreme of life. Which is to say, life that does not hide from death, but stares it straight in the face. Each time he sets foot on the wire, Philippe takes hold of that life and lives it in all its exhilarating immediacy, in all its joy.

May he live to be a hundred.

1982

Translator's Note
Chronicle of the Guayaki Indians
by Pierre Clastres

This is one of the saddest stories I know. If not for a minor miracle that occurred twenty years after the fact, I doubt that I would have been able to summon the courage to tell it.

It begins in 1972. I was living in Paris at the time, and because of my friendship with the poet Jacques Dupin (whose work I had translated), I was a faithful reader of *L'Éphémère*, a literary magazine financed by the Galerie Maeght. Jacques was a member of the editorial board—along with Yves Bonnefoy, André du Bouchet, Michel Leiris, and, until his death in 1970, Paul Celan. The magazine came out four times a year, and with a group like that responsible for its contents, the work published in *L'Éphémère* was always of the highest quality.

The twentieth and final issue appeared in the spring, and among the usual contributions from well-known poets and writers, there was an essay by an anthropologist named Pierre Clastres, "De l'Un sans le Multiple" ("Of the One Without the Many"). Just seven pages long, it made an immediate and lasting impression on me. Not only was the piece intelligent, provocative, and tightly argued, it was beautifully written. Clastres's prose seemed to combine a poet's temperament with a philosopher's depth of mind, and I was moved by its directness and humanity, its utter lack of pretension. On the strength of those seven pages, I realized that I had discovered a writer whose work I would be following for a long time to come.

When I asked Jacques who this person was, he explained that Clastres had studied with Claude Lévi-Strauss, was still under forty, and was considered to be the most promising member of the new generation of anthropologists in France. He had done his fieldwork in the jungles of South America, living among the most primitive stone-age tribes in Paraguay and Venezuela, and a book about those experiences was about to be published. When *Chronique des Indiens Guayaki* appeared a short time later, I went out and bought myself a copy.

It is, I believe, nearly impossible not to love this book. The care and patience with which it is written, the incisiveness of its observations, its humor, its intellectual rigor, its compassion—all these qualities reinforce one another to make it an important, memorable work. The *Chronicle* is not some dry academic study of "life among the savages," not some report from an alien world in which the reporter neglects to take his own presence into account. It is the true story of a man's experiences, and it asks nothing but the most essential questions: how is information communicated to an anthropologist, what kinds of transactions take place between one culture and another, under what circumstances might secrets be kept? In delineating this unknown civilization for us, Clastres writes with the cunning of a good novelist. His attention to detail is scrupulous and exacting; his ability to synthesize his thoughts into bold, coherent statements is often breathtaking. He is that rare scholar who does not hesitate to write in the first person, and the result is not just a portrait of the people he is studying, but a portrait of himself.

I moved back to New York in the summer of 1974, and for several years after that I tried to earn my living as a translator. It was a difficult struggle, and most of the time I was barely able to keep my head above water. Because I had to take whatever I could get, I often found myself accepting assignments to work on books that had little or no value. I wanted to translate good books, to be involved in projects that felt worthy, that would do more than just put bread on the table. *Chronicle of the Guayaki Indians* was at the top of my list, and again and again I proposed it to the various American publishers I worked for. After countless rejections, I finally found someone who was interested. I can't remember exactly when this was. Late 1975 or early 1976, I think, but I could be off by half a year or so. In any case, the publishing company was new, just getting off the ground, and all the preliminary indications looked good. Excellent editors, contracts for a number of outstanding books, a willingness to take risks. Not long before that, Clastres and I had begun exchanging letters, and when I wrote to tell him the news, he was just as thrilled as I was.

Translating the *Chronicle* was a thoroughly enjoyable experience for me, and after my labors were done, my attachment to the book was just as ardent as ever. I turned in the manuscript to the publisher, the translation was approved, and then, just when everything seemed to have been brought to a successful conclusion, the troubles started.

It seems that the publishing company was not as solvent as the world had been led to believe. Even worse, the publisher himself was a good deal less honest in his handling of money than he should have been. I know this for a fact because the money that was supposed to pay for my translation had been covered by a grant to the company by the CNRS (the French National Scientific Research Center), but when I asked for my money, the publisher hemmed and hawed and promised that I would have it in due course. The only explanation was that he had already spent the funds on something else.

I was desperately poor in those days, and waiting to be paid simply wasn't an option for me. It was the difference between eating and not eating, between paying the rent and not paying the rent. I called the publisher every day for the next several weeks, but he kept putting me off, kept coming up with different excuses. At last, unable to hold out any longer, I went to the office in person and demanded that he pay me on the spot. He started in with another excuse, but this time I held my ground and declared that I wouldn't leave until he had written out a check to me for the full amount. I don't think I went so far as to threaten him, but I might have. I was boiling with anger, and I can remember thinking that if all else failed, I was prepared to punch him in the face. It never came to that, but what I did do was back him into a corner, and at that moment I could see that he was beginning to grow scared. He finally understood that I meant business. And right then and there, he opened the drawer of his desk, pulled out his checkbook, and gave me my money.

In retrospect, I consider this to be one of my lowest moments, a dismal chapter in my career as a human being, and I am not at all proud of how I acted. But I was broke, and I had done the work, and I deserved to be paid. To prove how hard up I was during those years, I will mention just one appalling fact. I never made a copy of the manuscript. I couldn't afford to xerox the translation, and since I assumed it was in safe hands, the only copy in the world was the original typescript sitting in the publisher's office. This fact, this stupid oversight, this poverty-stricken way of doing business would come back to haunt me. It was entirely my fault, and it turned a small misfortune into a full-blown disaster.

For the time being, however, we seemed to be back on track. Once the unpleasantness about my fee was settled, the publisher behaved as if he had every intention of bringing out the book. The manuscript was sent to a typesetter, I corrected the proofs and returned them to the publisher—again neglecting to make a copy. It hardly seemed important, after all, since production was well under way by now. The book had been announced in the catalogue, and publication was set for the winter of 1977–1978.

Then, just months before *Chronicle of the Guayaki Indians* was supposed to appear, news came that Pierre Clastres had been killed in a car accident. According to the story I was told, he had been driving somewhere in France when he lost control of the wheel and skidded over the edge of a mountain. We had never met. Given that he was only forty-three when he died, I had assumed there would be ample opportunities in the future. We had written a number of warm letters to each other, had become friends through our correspondence, and were looking forward to the time when we would at last be able to sit down together and talk. The strangeness and unpredictability of the world prevented that conversation from taking place. Even now, all these years later, I still feel it as a great loss.

Nineteen seventy-eight came and went, and *Chronicle of the Guayaki Indians* did not appear. Another year slipped by, and then another year, and still there was no book.

By 1981, the publishing company was on its last legs. The editor I had originally worked with was long gone, and it was difficult for me to find out any information. That year, or perhaps the year after that, or perhaps even the year after that (it all blurs in my mind now), the company finally went under. Someone called to tell me that the rights to the book had been sold to another publisher. I called the publisher, and they told me yes, they were planning to bring out the book. Another year went by, and nothing happened. I called again, and the person I had talked to the previous year no longer worked for the company. I talked to someone else, and that person told me that the company had no plans to publish *Chronicle of the Guayaki Indians*. I asked for the manuscript back, but no one could find it. No one had even heard of it. For all intents and purposes, it was as if the translation had never existed.

For the next dozen years, that was where the matter stood. Pierre Clastres was dead, my translation had disappeared, and the entire project had collapsed into a black hole of oblivion. This past summer (1996), I finished writing a book entitled *Hand to Mouth*, an autobiographical essay about money. I was planning to include this story in the narrative (because of my failure to make a copy of the manuscript, because of the scene with the publisher in his office), but when the moment came to tell it, I lost heart and couldn't bring myself to put the words down on paper. It was all too sad, I felt, and I couldn't see any purpose in recounting such a bleak, miserable saga.

Then, two or three months after I finished my book, something extraordinary happened. About a year before, I had accepted an invitation to go to San Francisco to appear in the City Arts and Lectures Series at the Herbst Theatre. The event was scheduled for October 1996, and when the moment came, I climbed onto a plane and flew to San Francisco as promised. After my business onstage was finished, I was supposed to sit in the lobby and sign copies of my books. The Herbst is a large theater with many seats, and the line in the lobby was therefore quite long. Among all those people waiting for the dubious privilege of having me write my name in one of my novels, there was someone I recognized—a young man I had met once before, the friend of a friend. This young man happens to be a passionate collector of books, a bloodhound for first editions and rare, out-of-the-way items, the kind of bibliographic detective who will think nothing of spending an afternoon in a dusty cellar sifting through boxes of discarded books in the hope of finding one small treasure. He smiled, shook my hand, and then thrust a set of bound galleys at me. It had a red paper cover, and until that moment, I had never seen a copy of it before. "What's this?" he said. "I never heard of it." And there it was, suddenly sitting in my hands: the uncorrected proofs of my long-lost translation. In the big scheme of things, this probably wasn't such an astonishing event. For me, however, in my own little scheme of things, it was overwhelming. My hands started to tremble as I held the book. I was so stunned, so confused, that I was scarcely able to speak.

The proofs had been found in a remainder bin at a secondhand bookstore, and the young man had paid five dollars for them. As I look at them now, I note with a certain grim fascination that the pub date announced on the cover is April 1981. For a translation completed in 1976 or 1977, it was, truly, an agonizingly slow ordeal.

If Pierre Clastres were alive today, the discovery of this lost book would be a perfect happy ending. But he isn't alive, and the brief surge of joy and incredulity I experienced in the atrium of the Herbst Theatre has by now dissipated into a deep, mournful ache. How rotten that the world should pull such tricks on us. How rotten that a person with so much to offer the world should die so young.

Here, then, is my translation of Pierre Clastres's book, *Chronicle of the Guayaki Indians*. No matter that the world described in it has long since vanished, that the tiny group of people the author lived with in 1963 and 1964 has disappeared from the face of the earth. No matter that the author has vanished as well. The book he wrote is still with us, and the fact that you are holding that book in your hands now, dear reader, is nothing less than a victory, a small triumph against the crushing odds of fate. At least there is that to be thankful for. At least there is consolation in the thought that Pierre Clastres's book has survived.

1997

An Evening at Shea

I remember him well. A stocky right-hander with a sidearm delivery who wore number 26. Not much speed, but a tricky combination of sliders and sinkers that kept the hitters off balance: "give them a little air to mash at." He started when called upon, pitched in long relief, worked as a setup man, intermittently served as a closer. When he was with the New York Mets, his teammates called him Jack. As in Jack-of-All-Trades. Whatever he was asked to do, he did. He might not have impressed you, but he rarely failed to get the job done.

Terry Leach was never a star. He struggled in the minor leagues for many years before he was given a chance, and even when he performed well, his efforts went unnoticed. In a late-season start for the Mets in 1982, he pitched a one-hit, ten-inning shutout against the Phillies, but the following year he was back in the minors. As an undrafted player with an unorthodox style and less than overpowering natural skills, he had to work harder than everyone else to win a place for himself. He survived on guts, humor, and an irrational love of the game. He simply refused to take no for an answer, and in the end he built a solid career for himself. How many pitchers have had ten-game winning streaks and a season's record of 11–1? How many pitchers have come into a World Series game to face the opposing team's hottest hitter with two outs and the bases loaded and managed to strike that hitter out? Terry Leach did those things, and by the time you've read about them in this short but infinitely charming book, you will have already learned that this man is more than just an ex-pitcher. He is a born storyteller, and with Tom Clark's help he has put together one of the most engaging baseball books I have read in years.

I saw Terry Leach pitch many times, but only once in person. It was a warm August night in 1985, and at the last minute my wife and I decided to go out to Shea Stadium to watch the Mets play against the Giants. We got there just before the game began, bought our tickets at the gate, and hustled up to our seats in the right-center-field mezzanine—just in time for the national anthem. Sid Fernandez was supposed to be pitching against Vida Blue that night, but Fernandez came down sick while warming up on the mound and had to be scratched. Terry Leach was sitting in the clubhouse at that moment, dressed in his underwear and working on a crossword puzzle. Five minutes later, he threw the first of the eighty-seven pitches he would throw that night. That averages out to fewer than ten pitches an inning over nine innings, a number that signifies absolute mastery over the other team. Since Terry Leach went the full nine innings, shutting out the Giants on just three hits, I would have to rank his performance as the greatest one I have had the pleasure to witness. The Giants couldn't touch him. Late in the game, when he laid down a successful sacrifice bunt, Terry Leach was given the first standing ovation of his major-league career. My wife and I were standing with that crowd, both clapping, both shouting our heads off. Even now, fourteen and a half years later, we still talk about that night as the most beautiful night of baseball we have ever had.

December 18, 1999

The National Story Project

I never intended to do this. The *National Story Project* came about by accident, and if not for a remark my wife made at the dinner table sixteen months ago, most of the pieces in this book never would have been written. It was May 1999, perhaps June, and earlier that day I had been interviewed on National Public Radio about my most recent novel. After we finished our conversation, Daniel Zwerdling, the host of *Weekend All Things Considered*, had asked me if I would be interested in becoming a regular contributor to the program. I couldn't even see his face when he asked the question. I was in the NPR studio on Second Avenue in New York, and he was in Washington, D.C., and for the past twenty or thirty minutes we had been talking to each other through microphones and headsets, aided by a technological marvel known as fiber optics. I asked him what he had in mind, and he said that he wasn't sure. Maybe I could come on the air every month or so and tell stories.

I wasn't interested. Doing my own work was difficult enough, and taking on a job that would force me to crank out stories on command was the last thing I needed. Just to be polite, however, I said that I would go home and think about it.

It was my wife, Siri, who turned the proposition on its head. That night, when I told her about NPR's curious offer, she immediately came up with a proposal that reversed the direction of my thoughts. In a matter of thirty seconds, no had become yes.

You don't have to write the stories yourself, she said. Get people to sit down and write their own stories. They could send them in to you, and then you could read the best ones on the radio. If enough people wrote in, it could turn into something extraordinary.

That was how the *National Story Project* was born. It was Siri's idea, and then I picked it up and started to run with it.

Sometime in late September, Zwerdling came to my house in Brooklyn with Rebecca Davis, one of the producers of *Weekend All Things Considered*, and we launched the idea of the project in the form of another interview. I told the listeners that I was looking for stories. The

stories had to be true, and they had to be short, but there would be no
restrictions as to subject matter or style. What interested me most, I said,
were stories that defied our expectations about the world, anecdotes
that revealed the mysterious and unknowable forces at work in our
lives, in our family histories, in our minds and bodies, in our souls. In
other words, true stories that sounded like fiction. I was talking about
big things and small things, tragic things and comic things, any experience that felt important enough to set down on paper. They shouldn't
worry if they had never written a story, I said. Everyone was bound to
know some good ones, and if enough people answered the call to participate, we would inevitably begin to learn some surprising things
about ourselves and each other. The spirit of the project was entirely
democratic. All listeners were welcome to contribute, and I promised to
read every story that came in. People would be exploring their own
lives and experiences, but at the same time they would be part of a collective effort, something bigger than just themselves. With their help, I
said, I was hoping to put together an archive of facts, a museum of
American reality.

The interview was broadcast on the first Saturday in October, exactly
one year ago today. Since that time, I have received more than four thousand submissions. This number is many times greater than what I had
anticipated, and for the past twelve months I have been awash in manuscripts, floating madly in an ever expanding sea of paper. Some of the
stories are written by hand; others are typed; still others are printed out
from e-mails. Every month, I have scrambled to choose five or six of the
best ones and turn them into a twenty-minute segment to be aired on
Weekend All Things Considered. It has been singularly rewarding work,
one of the most inspiring tasks I have ever undertaken. But it has had
its difficult moments as well. On several occasions, when I have been
particularly swamped with material, I have read sixty or seventy stories
at a single sitting, and each time I have done that, I have stood up from
the chair feeling pulverized, absolutely drained of energy. So many
emotions to contend with, so many strangers camped out in the living
room, so many voices coming at me from so many different directions.
On those evenings, for the space of two or three hours, I have felt that
the entire population of America has walked into my house. I didn't
hear America singing. I heard it telling stories.

Yes, a number of rants and diatribes have been sent in by deranged
people, but far fewer than I would have predicted. I have been exposed

to groundbreaking revelations about the Kennedy assassination, subjected to several complex exegeses that link current events to verses from Scripture, and made privy to information pertaining to lawsuits against half a dozen corporations and government agencies. Some people have gone out of their way to provoke me and turn my stomach. Just last week, I received a submission from a man who signed his story "Cerberus" and gave his return address as "The Underworld 66666." In the story, he told about his days in Vietnam as a marine, ending with an account of how he and the other men in his company had roasted a stolen Vietnamese baby and eaten it around a campfire. He made it sound as though he were proud of what he had done. For all I know, the story could be true. But that doesn't mean I have any interest in presenting it on the radio.

On the other hand, some of the pieces from disturbed people have contained startling and arresting passages. Last fall, when the project was just getting under way, one came in from another Vietnam vet, a man serving a life sentence for murder in a penitentiary somewhere in the Midwest. He enclosed a handwritten affidavit that recounted the muddled story of how he came to commit his crime, and the last sentence of the document read, "I have never been perfect, but I am real." In some sense, that statement could stand as the credo of the *National Story Project*, the very principle behind this book. We have never been perfect, but we are real.

Of the four thousand stories I have read, most have been compelling enough to hold me until the last word. Most have been written with simple, straightforward conviction, and most have done honor to the people who sent them in. We all have inner lives. We all feel that we are part of the world and yet exiled from it. We all burn with the fires of our own existence. Words are needed to express what is in us, and again and again contributors have thanked me for giving them the chance to tell their stories, for "allowing the people to be heard." What the people have said is often astonishing. More than ever, I have come to appreciate how deeply and passionately most of us live within ourselves. Our attachments are ferocious. Our loves overwhelm us, define us, obliterate the boundaries between ourselves and others. Fully a third of the stories I have read are about families: parents and children, children and parents, husbands and wives, brothers and sisters, grandparents. For most of us, those are the people who fill up our world, and in story after story, both the dark ones and the humorous ones, I have been impressed by how clearly and forcefully these connections have been articulated.

A few high-school students sent in stories about hitting home runs and winning medals at track meets, but it was the rare adult who took advantage of the occasion to brag about his accomplishments. Hilarious blunders, wrenching coincidences, brushes with death, miraculous encounters, improbable ironies, premonitions, sorrows, pains, dreams—these were the subjects the contributors chose to write about. I learned that I am not alone in my belief that the more we understand of the world, the more elusive and confounding the world becomes. As one early contributor so eloquently put it, "I am left without an adequate definition of reality." If you aren't certain about things, if your mind is still open enough to question what you are seeing, you tend to look at the world with great care, and out of that watchfulness comes the possibility of seeing something that no one else has seen before. You have to be willing to admit that you don't have all the answers. If you think you do, you will never have anything important to say.

Incredible plots, unlikely turns, events that refuse to obey the laws of common sense. More often than not, our lives resemble the stuff of eighteenth-century novels. Just today, another batch of e-mails from NPR arrived at my door, and among the new submissions was this story from a woman who lives in San Diego, California. I quote from it not because it is unusual, but simply because it is the freshest piece of evidence at hand:

I was adopted from an orphanage at the age of eight months. Less than a year later, my adoptive father died suddenly. I was raised by my widowed mother with three older adopted brothers. When you are adopted, there is a natural curiosity to know your birth family. By the time I was married and in my late twenties, I decided to start looking.

I had been raised in Iowa, and sure enough, after a two-year search, I located my birth mother in Des Moines. We met and went to dinner. I asked her who my birth father was, and she gave me his name. I asked where he lived, and she said "San Diego," which was where I had been living for the last five years. I had moved to San Diego not knowing a soul—just knowing I wanted to be there.

It ended up that I worked in the building next door to where my father worked. We often ate lunch at the same restaurant. We never told his wife of my existence, as I didn't really want to disrupt his life. He had always been a bit of a gadabout, however, and he always had a girlfriend on the side. He and his last girlfriend were "together" for fifteen-plus years, and she remained the source of my information about him.

Five years ago, my birth mother was dying of cancer in Iowa. Simultaneously, I received a call from my father's paramour that he had died of heart complications. I called my biological mother in the hospital in Iowa and told her of his death. She died that night. I received word that both of their funerals were held on the following Saturday at exactly the same hour—his at 11 A.M. in California and hers at 1 P.M. in Iowa.

After three or four months, I sensed that a book was going to be necessary to do justice to the project. Too many good stories were coming in, and it wasn't possible for me to present more than a fraction of the worthy submissions on the radio. Many of them were too long for the format we had established, and the ephemeral nature of the broadcasts (a lone, disembodied voice floating across the American airwaves for eighteen or twenty minutes every month) made me want to collect the most memorable ones and preserve them in written form. Radio is a powerful tool, and NPR reaches into almost every corner of the country, but you can't hold the words in your hands. A book is tangible, and once you put it down, you can return to the place where you left it and pick it up again.

This anthology contains 179 pieces—what I consider to be the best of the approximately four thousand works that have come in during the past year. But it is also a representative selection, a miniaturized version of the *National Story Project* as a whole. For every story about a dream or an animal or a missing object to be found in these pages, there were dozens of others that were submitted, dozens of others that could have been chosen. The book begins with a six-sentence tale about a chicken (the first story I read on the air last November) and ends with a wistful meditation on the role that radio plays in our lives. The author of that last piece, Ameni Rozsa, was moved to write her story while listening to one of the *National Story Project* broadcasts. I had been hoping to capture bits and fragments of American reality, but it had never occurred to me that the project itself could become a part of that reality, too.

This book has been written by people of all ages and from all walks of life. Among them are a postman, a merchant seaman, a trolley-bus driver, a gas-and-electric-meter reader, a restorer of player pianos, a crime-scene cleaner, a musician, a businessman, two priests, an inmate at a state correctional facility, several doctors, and assorted housewives, farmers, and ex-servicemen. The youngest contributor is barely twenty; the oldest is pushing ninety. Half of the writers are women; half are men. They live in cities, suburbs, and in rural areas, and they come from forty-two different states. In making my choices, I never once gave a thought to demographic balance. I selected the stories solely on the basis of merit: for their humanity, for their truth, for their charm. The numbers just fell out that way, and the results were determined by blind chance.

In an attempt to make some order out of this chaos of voices and contrasting styles, I have broken the stories into ten different categories. The section titles speak for themselves, but except for the fourth section, "Slapstick," which is made up entirely of comic stories, there is a wide range of material within each of the categories. Their contents run the gamut from farce to tragic drama, and for every act of cruelty and violence that one encounters in them, there is a countervailing act of kindness or generosity or love. The stories go back and forth, up and down, in and out, and after a while your head starts to spin. Turn the page from one contributor to the next and you are confronted by an entirely different person, an entirely different set of circumstances, an entirely different worldview. But difference is what this book is all about. There is some elegant and sophisticated writing in it, but there is also much that is crude and awkward. Only a small portion of it resembles anything that could qualify as "literature." It is something else, something raw and close to the bone, and whatever skills these authors might lack, most of their stories are unforgettable. It is difficult for me to imagine that anyone could read through this book from beginning to end without once shedding a tear, without once laughing out loud.

If I had to define what these stories were, I would call them dispatches, reports from the front lines of personal experience. They are about the private worlds of individual Americans, yet again and again one sees the inescapable marks of history on them, the intricate ways in which individual destinies are shaped by society at large. Some of the older contributors, looking back on events from their childhood and youth, are necessarily writing about the Depression and World War II. Other contributors, born in the middle of the century, continue to be haunted by the effects of the war in Vietnam. That conflict ended twenty-five years ago, and yet it lives on in us as a recurrent nightmare, a great wound in the national soul. Still other contributors, from several different generations, have written stories about the disease of American racism. This scourge has been with us for more than 350 years, and no matter how hard we struggle to eradicate it from our midst, a cure has yet to be found.

Other stories touch on AIDS, alcoholism, drug abuse, pornography, and guns. Social forces are forever impinging on the lives of these people, but not one of their stories sets out to document society per se. We know that Janet Zupan's father died in a prison camp in Vietnam in 1967, but that is not what her story is about. With a remarkable eye for visual detail, she tracks a single afternoon in the Mojave Desert as her father chases after his stubborn and recalcitrant horse, and knowing what we do about what will happen to her father just two years later, we read her account as a kind of memorial to him. Not a word about the war, and yet by indirection and an almost painterly focus on the moment before her, we sense that an entire era of American history is passing in front of our eyes.

Stan Benkoski's father's laugh. The slap to Carol Sherman-Jones's face. Little Mary Grace Dembeck dragging a Christmas tree through the streets of Brooklyn. John Keith's mother's missing wedding ring. John Flannelly's fingers stuck in the holes of a stainless-steel heating grate. Mel Singer wrestled to the floor by his own coat. Anna Thorson at the barn dance. Edith Riemer's bicycle. Marie Johnson watching a movie shot in the house where she lived as a girl. Ludlow Perry's encounter with the legless man. Catherine Austin Alexander looking out her window on West Seventy-fourth Street. Juliana C. Nash's walk through the snow. Dede Ryan's philosophical martini. Carolyn Brasher's regrets. Mary McCallum's father's dream. Earl Roberts's collar button. One by one, these stories leave a lasting impression on the mind. Even after you have read through all fifteen dozen of them, they continue to stay with you, and you find yourself remembering them in the same way that you remember a trenchant parable or a good joke. The images are clear, dense, and yet somehow weightless. And each one is small enough to fit inside your pocket. Like the snapshots we carry around of our own families.

October 3, 2000

A Little Anthology of Surrealist Poems

1968. I was twenty-one, a junior at Columbia, and these poems were among my first attempts at translation. Remember the times: the war in Vietnam, the clamor of politics on College Walk, a year of unending protests, the strike that shut down the university, sit-ins, riots, the arrest of 700 students (myself among them). In the light of that tumult (that questioning), the Surrealists were a major discovery for me: poets fighting against the conventions of poetry, poets dreaming of revolution, of how to change the world. Translation, then, was more than just a literary exercise. It was a first step toward breaking free of the shackles of myself, of overcoming my own ignorance. *You must change your life.* Perhaps, Back then, it was more a question of searching for a life, of trying to invent a life I could believe in. . . .

January 22, 2002

The Art of Worry

Art Spiegelman is a one-of-a-kind quardruple threat. He is an artist who draws and paints; a chameleon who can mimic and embellish upon any visual style he chooses; a writer who expresses himself in vivid, sharply turned sentences; and a provocateur with a flair for humor in its most savage and piercing incarnations. Mix those talents together, then put them in the service of a deep political conscience, and a man can make a considerable mark on the world. Which is precisely what Art Spiegelman has done for the past ten years at *The New Yorker*.

We know him best as the author of *Maus*, the brilliant two-volume narrative of his father's nightmare journey through the camps in the Second World War. Spiegelman showed himself to be an expert story-teller in that work, and no doubt that is how history will remember him: as the man who proved that comic books are not necessarily for children, that a complex tale can be told in a series of small rectangles filled with words and pictures—and attain the full emotional and intellectual power of great literature.

But there is another side to Spiegelman as well, one which has increasingly come to dominate his energies in the post-*Maus* years: the artist as social gadfly and critic, as commentator on current events. As Spiegelman's friend and admirer, I have always found it odd that he should have found a home for that aspect of his work at *The New Yorker*. The magazine was born in the Jazz Age and has been a fixture on the American scene for more than seventy-five years, rolling off the presses every week as the country has lived through wars, depressions, and violent upheavals, steadfastly maintaining a tone that is at once cool, sophisticated, and complacent. *The New Yorker* has published some excellent journalism over the years, but incisive and disturbing as many of those reports have been, the pages on which they appear have always been flanked by advertisements for luxury goods and Caribbean vacations, adorned with blithely amusing cartoons about the foibles of middle-class life. That is *The New Yorker* style. The world might be going to hell, but once we open the pages of our favorite weekly, we understand that hell is for other people. Nothing has changed for us—and nothing ever will. We are suave, tranquil, and urbane. Not to worry.

But Spiegelman wants to worry. That is his job. He has embraced worry as his life's calling, and he frets over every injustice he perceives in the world, froths diligently at the follies and stupidities of men in power, refuses to take things in his stride. Not without wit, of course, and not without his trademark comic touch—but still, the last thing anyone could call this man is complacent. Good for *The New Yorker*, then, for having had the wisdom to put him on its payroll. And good for Spiegelman for having reinvigorated the spirit of that stodgy bastion of good taste.

Contributing both to the inside and the outside of the magazine, he has produced approximately seventy works for *The New Yorker*, toiling under the reigns of two chief editors, Tina Brown and David Remnick. These works include single-page drawings and paintings (among them a bitter sendup of *Life is Beautiful*, a film that Spiegelman abhorred), extended articles on a variety of subjects presented in comic-book form (neo-Nazi hooliganism in Rostock, Germany; homages to Harvey Kurtzman, Maurice Sendak, and Charles Schultz; an attack on George W. Bush and the bogus elections of 2000; observations on pop culture as reflected in the behavior of his own children), and close to forty covers. The outside of a magazine is its most visible feature, the signature mark of its philosophy and editorial content, the dress it wears when it goes out in public. Until Spiegelman came along, *The New Yorker* had been famous—even hilariously famous—for the blandness of its cover art. Smug and subdued, confident in the loyalty of its wide readership, issue after issue would turn up on the newsstands sporting sedate autumn scenes, snowy winter landscapes, suburban lawns, and depopulated city streets—imagery so trite and insipid as to induce drowsiness in the eye of the beholder. Then, on February 15, 1993, for an issue that fortuitously coincided with Valentine's Day, Spiegelman's first cover appeared, and *The New Yorker* exploded into a new *New Yorker*, a magazine that suddenly found itself part of the contemporary world.

It was a bad time for the city. Crown Heights, an impoverished neighborhood in Brooklyn inhabited by African-Americans and Orthodox Jews, was on the brink of a racial war. A black child had been run over by a Jew, a Jew had been murdered in retaliation by an angry mob of blacks, and for many days running a fierce agitation dominated the streets, with threats of further violence from both camps. The mayor at the time, David Dinkins, was a decent man, but he was also a cautious man, and he lacked the political skill needed to step in quickly and defuse the crisis. (That failure probably cost him victory in the next election—which led to the harsh regime of Rudolph Giuliani, who served as mayor for the next eight years.) New York, for all its ethnic diversity, is a surprisingly tolerant city, and most people make an effort most of the time to get along with one another. But racial tensions exist, often smoldering in silence, occasionally erupting in isolated acts of brutality—but here was an entire neighborhood up in arms, and it was an ugly thing to witness, a stain on the democratic spirit of New York. That was when Spiegelman was heard from, the precise moment when he walked into the battle and offered his solution to the problem. *Kiss and make up*. His statement was that simple, that shocking, that powerful. An Orthodox Jew had his arms around a black woman, the black woman had her arms around the Orthodox Jew, their eyes were closed, and they were kissing. To round out the Valentine's Day theme, the background of the picture was solid red, and three little hearts floated within the squiggly border that framed the image. Spiegelman wasn't taking sides. As a Jew, he wasn't proposing to defend the Jewish community of Crown Heights; as a practitioner of no religion, he wasn't voicing his support of the African-American community that shared that same miserable patch of ground. He was speaking as a citizen of New York, a citizen of the world, and he was addressing both groups at the same time—which is to say, he was addressing all of us. No more hate, he said, no more intolerance, no more demonizing of the other. In pictorial form, the cover's message was identical to an idea expressed by W.H. Auden on the first day of World War II: *We must love one another or die.*

Since that remarkable debut, Spiegelman has continued to confound our expectations, consciously using his inventiveness as a destabilizing force, a weapon of surprise. He wants to keep us off balance, to catch us with our guard down, and to that end he approaches his subjects from numerous angles and with countless shadings of tone: mockery and whimsy, outrage and rebuke, even tenderness and laudatory affection. The heroic construction-worker mother breast-feeding her baby on the girder of a half-finished skyscraper; turkey-bombs falling on Afghanistan; Bill Clinton's groin surrounded by a sea of microphones; college diplomas that turn out to be help-wanted ads; the weirdo hipster family as emblem of cross-generational love and solidarity; the

crucified Easter bunny impaled on an IRS tax form; the Santa Claus and the rabbi with identical beards and bellies. Unafraid to court controversy, Spiegelman has offended many people over the years, and several of the covers he has prepared for *The New Yorker* have been deemed so incendiary by the editorial powers of the magazine that they have refused to run them. Beginning with the Valentine's Day cover of 1993, Spiegelman's work has inspired thousands of indignant letters, hundreds of canceled subscriptions and, in one very dramatic instance, a full-scale protest demonstration by members of the New York City Police Department in front of the *New Yorker* offices in Manhattan. That is the price one pays for speaking one's mind—for drawing one's mind. Spiegelman's tenure at *The New Yorker* has not always been an easy one, but his courage has been a steady source of encouragement to those of us who love our city and believe in the idea of New York as a place for everyone, as the central laboratory of human contradictions in our time.

Then came September 11, 2001. In the fire and smoke of three thousand incinerated bodies, a holocaust was visited upon us, and nine months later the city is still grieving over its dead. In the immediate aftermath of the attack, in the hours and days that followed that murderous morning, few of us were capable of thinking any coherent thoughts. The shock was too great, and as the smoke continued to hover over the city and we breathed in the vile smells of death and destruction, most of us shuffled around like sleepwalkers, numb and dazed, not good for anything. But *The New Yorker* had an issue to put out, and when they realized that someone would have to design a cover—the most important cover in their history, which would have to be produced in record time—they turned to Spiegelman.

That black-on-black issue of September 24 is, in my opinion, Spiegelman's masterpiece. In the face of absolute horror, one's inclination is to dispense with images altogether. Words often fail us at moments of extreme duress. The same is true of pictures. If I have not garbled the story Spiegelman told me during those days, I believe he originally resisted that iconoclastic impulse: to hand in a solid black cover to represent mourning, an absent image to stand as a mirror of the ineffable. Other ideas occurred to him. He tested them out, but one by one he rejected them, slowly pushing his mind toward darker and darker hues until, inevitably, he arrived at a deep, unmodulated black. But still that wasn't enough. He found it too mute, too facile, too resigned, but for want of any other solution, he almost capitulated.

Then, just as he was about to give up, he began thinking about some of the artists who had come before him, artists who had explored the implications of eliminating color from their paintings—in particular Ad Reinhardt and his black-on-black canvases from the sixties, those supremely abstract and minimal anti-images that had taken painting to the farthest edge of possibility. Spiegelman had found his direction. Not in silence—but in the sublime.

You have to look very closely at the picture before you notice the towers. They are there and not there, effaced and yet still present, shadows pulsing in oblivion, in memory, in the ghostly emanation of some tormented afterlife. When I saw the picture for the first time, I felt as if Spiegelman had placed a stethoscope on my chest and methodically registered every heartbeat that had shaken my body since September 11. Then my eyes filled up with tears. Tears for the dead. Tears for the living. Tears for the abominations we inflict on one another, for the cruelty and savagery of the whole stinking human race.

Then I thought: *We must love one another or die.*

June 2002

Invisible Joubert

Some writers live and die in the shadows, and they don't begin to live for us until after they are dead. Emily Dickinson published just three poems during her lifetime; Gerard Manley Hopkins published only one. Kafka kept his unfinished novels to himself, and if not for a promise broken by his friend Max Brod, they would have been burned. Christopher Smart's Bedlamite rant, *Jubilate Agno*, was composed in the early 1760s but didn't find its way into print until 1939.

Think of how many writers disappeared when the Library of Alexandria burned in 391 AD. Think of how many books were destroyed by the Catholic Church in the Middle Ages. For every miraculous resurrection, for every work saved from oblivion by free-thinkers like Petrarch and Boccaccio, one could enumerate hundreds of losses. Ralph Ellison worked for years on a follow-up novel to *Invisible Man*, then the manuscript burned in a fire. In a fit of madness, Gogol destroyed the second part of *Dead Souls*. What we know of the work of Heraclitus and Sappho exists only in fragments. In his later years Herman Melville was so thoroughly forgotten that most people thought he was dead when his obituary appeared in 1891. It wasn't until *Moby Dick* was discovered in a second-hand bookshop in 1920 that Melville came to be recognized as one of our essential novelists.

The afterlife of writers is precarious at best, and for those who fail to publish before they die—by choice, by happenstance, by sheer bad luck—the fate of their work is almost certain doom. The American poet Charles Reznikoff reported that his grandmother threw out every one of his grandfather's poems after he died—an entire life's work discarded with the trash. More recently, the young John Kennedy Toole committed suicide over his failure to find a publisher for his book. When the novel finally appeared, it was a critical success. Who knows how many unread masterpieces are hidden away in attics or moldering in cellars? Without someone to defend a dead writer's work, that work could just as well never have been written. Think of Osip Mandelstam, murdered by Stalin in 1938. If his widow, Nadezhda, had not committed the entire body of his work to memory, he would have been lost to us as a poet.

There are dozens of posthumous writers in the history of literature, but no case is stranger or more obscure than that of Joseph Joubert, a Frenchman who wrote in the last quarter of the eighteenth century and the first quarter of the nineteenth. Not only did he not publish a single word while he was alive, but the work he left behind escapes clear definition, which means that he has continued to exist as an almost invisible writer even after his discovery, acquiring a handful of ardent readers in every generation, but never fully emerging from the shadows that surrounded him when he was alive. Neither a poet nor a novelist, neither a philosopher nor an essayist, Joubert was a man of letters without portfolio whose work consists of a vast series of notebooks in which he wrote down his thoughts every day for more than forty years. All the entries are dated, but the notebooks cannot be construed as a traditional diary, since there are scarcely any personal remarks in it. Nor was Joubert a writer of maxims in the classcial French manner. He was something far more oblique and challenging: a writer who spent his whole life preparing himself for a work that never came to be written, a writer of the highest rank who paradoxically never produced a book. Joubert speaks in whispers, and one must draw very close to him to hear what he is saying.

He was born in Montignac (Dordogne) on May 7, 1754, the son of master surgeon Jean Joubert. The second of eight surviving children, Joubert completed his local education at the age of fourteen and was then sent to Toulouse to continue his studies. His father hoped that he would pursue a career in the law, but Joubert's interests lay in philosophy and the classics. After graduation, he taught for several years in the school where he had been a student and then returned to Montignac for two years, without professional plans or any apparent ambitions, already suffering from the poor health that would plague him throughout his life.

In May 1778, just after his twenty-fourth birthday, Joubert moved to Paris, where he took up residence at the Hôtel de Bordeaux on the rue des Francs-Bourgeois. He soon became a member of Diderot's circle, and through that association was brought into contact with the sculptor Pigalle and many other artists of the period. During those early years in Paris he also met Fontanes, who would remain his closest friend for the rest of his life. Both Joubert and Fontanes frequented the literary salon of the countess Fanny de Beauharnais (whose niece later married Bonaparte). Other members included Buffon, La Harpe, and Restif de la Bretonne.

In 1785, Fontanes and Joubert attempted to found a newsletter about Paris literary life for English subscribers, but the venture failed. That same year, Joubert entered into a liaison with the wife of Restif de la Bretonne, Agnès Lebègue, a woman fourteen years his senior. But by March 1786 the affair had ended—painfully for Joubert. Later that year, he made his first visit to the town of Villeneuve and met Victoire Moreau, who would become his wife in 1793. During this period Joubert read much and wrote little. He studied philosophy, music, and painting, but the various writing projects he began—an appreciation of Pigalle, an essay on the navigator Cook—were never completed. For the most part, it seems that Joubert watched the world around him, cultivated his friendships, and meditated. As time went on, he turned more and more to his notebooks as the place to develop his thoughts and explore his inner life. By the late 1780s and early 1790s, they had become a serious daily enterprise for him. At first, he looked upon his jottings as a way to prepare himself for a larger, more systematic work, a great book of philosophy that he dreamed he had it in him to write. As the years passed, however, and the project continued to elude him, he slowly came to realize that the notebooks were an end in themselves, eventually admitting that "these thoughts form not only the foundation of my work, but of my life."

Joubert had long been a supporter of revolutionary views, and when the Revolution came in 1789, he welcomed it enthusiastically. In late 1790, he was named Justice of the Peace in Montignac, a position that entailed great responsibilities and made him the leading citizen of the town. By all accounts, he fulfilled his tasks with vigilance and fairness and was widely respected for his work. But he soon became disillusioned with the increasingly violent nature of the Revolution. He declined to stand for reelection in 1792 and gradually withdrew from politics.

After his marriage in 1793, he retired to Villeneuve, from then on dividing his time between the country and Paris. Fontanes had gone into exile in London, where he met Chateaubriand. Eventually, upon their return to Paris, Joubert and these two younger men collaborated on the magazine *Mercure de France*. Joubert would later help Chateaubriand with many passages of *Le Génie du christianisme* and give him financial help in times of trouble. During the early years of the nine-teenth century, Joubert was surrounded by many of the most successful men and women in France, deeply admired for his lucid ideas, his sharp critical intelligence, and his enormous talent for friendship.

When Joubert died in 1824 at the age of seventy, Chateaubriand, then Minister of Foreign Affairs, eulogized him in the *Journal des débats*:

He was one of those men you loved for the delicacy of his feelings, the good-ness of his soul, the evenness of his temper, the uniqueness of his character, the keenness and brilliance of his mind—a mind that was interested in everything and understood everything. No one has ever forgotten himself so thoroughly and been so concerned with the welfare of others.

Although Fontanes and Chateaubriand had both urged him to put together a book from his daily writings, Joubert resisted the temptation to publish. The first selection to appear in print, entitled *Pensées*, was compiled by Chateaubriand in 1838 and distributed privately among Joubert's friends. Other editions followed, eliciting sympathetic and passionate essays by such diverse figures as Saint-Beuve and Matthew Arnold, who compared Joubert favorably to Coleridge and remarked that "they both had from nature an ardent impulse for seeking the gen-uine truth on all matters they thought about, and an organ for finding it and recognising it when it was found." Those early editions all divided Joubert's writings into chapters with abstract headings such as "Truth," "Literature," "Family," "Society," and so on. It wasn't until 1938, in a two-volume work prepared by André Beaunier for Gallimard, that Joubert's writings were presented in the original order of their com-position. I have drawn my selections for this book from the 900 tightly printed pages of Beaunier's scrupulous edition.

No more than a tenth of Joubert's work is included here. In choosing the entries, I have been guided above all by my own contemporary and idiosyncratic tastes, concentrating my attention on Joubert's aesthetic theories, his "imaginary physics," and passages of direct autobiograph-ical significance. I have not included the lengthy reading notes that Joubert made during his study of various philosophers—Malebranche, Kant, Locke, and others—nor the frequent references to writers of his time, most of whom are unknown to us today. For convenience and economy, I have eliminated the dates that precede each entry.

I first discovered Joubert's work in 1971, through an essay written by Maurice Blanchot, "Joubert et l'espace." In it, Blanchot compares

Joubert to Mallarmé and makes a solid case for considering him to be the most modern writer of his period, the one who speaks most directly to us now. And indeed, the free-floating, questing nature of Joubert's mind, along with his concise and elegant style, has not grown old with the passage of time. Everything is mixed together in the notebooks, and reflections on literature and philosophy are scattered among observations about the weather, the landscape, and politics. Entries of unforgettable psychological insight ("Those who never back down love themselves more than they love the truth") alternate with brief, chilling comments on the turmoil around him ("Stacking the dead on top of one another"), which in turn are punctuated by sudden outbursts of levity ("They say that souls have no sex; of course they do"). The more you read Joubert, the more you want to go on reading him. He draws you in with his descretion and honesty, with his plain-spoken brilliance, with his quiet but utterly original way of looking at the world.

At the same time, it is easy to ignore Joubert. He doesn't point to himself or bang on loud rhetorical drums, and he isn't out to shock anyone with his ideas. Those of us who love his work guard him as a treasured secret, but in the 164 years since his writings were first made available to the public, he has scarcely caused a ripple in the world-at-large. This translation was first published by Jack Shoemaker of North Point Press in 1983, and the book failed to arouse anything but indifference on the part of American critics and readers. The book received just one review (in the *Boston Globe*), and sales amounted to something in the neighborhood of 800 copies. On the other hand, not long after the book was published, Joubert's relevance was brought home to me in a remarkable way. I gave a copy to one of my oldest friends, the painter David Reed. David had a friend who had recently landed in Bellevue after suffering a nervous breakdown, and when David went to visit him in the hospital, he left behind his copy of Joubert—on loan. Two or three weeks later, when the friend was finally released, he called David to apologize for not returning the book. After he had read it, he said, he had given it to another patient. That patient had passed it on to yet another patient, and little by little Joubert had made his way around the ward. Interest in the book became so keen that groups of patients would gather in the day room to read passages out loud to one another and discuss them. When David's friend asked for the book back, he was told that it no longer belonged to him. "It's our book," one of the patients said. "We need it." As far as I'm concerned, that is the most eloquent literary criticism I have ever heard, proof that the right book in the right place is medicine for the human soul.

As Joubert himself once put it in 1801: "A thought is a thing as real as a cannon ball."

August 11, 2002

Running Through Fire

I thought fast. I was lucky and got an idea. These two short sentences come toward the end of *Running Through Fire,* Zosia Goldberg's remarkable account of how she managed to live through the nightmare years of the Second World War, and they encapsulate the spirit of the entire story she tells us. Like a female Odysseus, this beautiful and resourceful young woman needed more than simple courage to overcome the dangers that surrounded her. Survival demanded cunning, quick thinking under pressure, a ferocious will to adapt to the most frightening and intolerable conditions, and sheer dumb luck—a chance encounter with the right person at the right moment, removal from one prison to another just hours before the first prison was bombed, an endless series of small, unfathomable miracles.

Why did some live when so many millions died? In Goldberg's case, it seems to have been the result of a rare and fortuitous constellation of circumstances. She was a woman, which gave her the possibility of posing as a gentile—an option not available to Jewish men—and she came from a highly assimilated secular family. Polish was the language spoken at home, not Yiddish, and therefore she could speak without having to worry that her accent would give her away. But beyond these accidents of birth and language, there was the question of character. Although just twenty-one when the Germans invaded Poland, Goldberg was no longer a girl, and to hear her talk about her experiences to her nephew, Hilton Obenzinger, she was no ordinary person. Stubborn, opinionated, sexy, fearless, with a clairvoyant's ability to read and judge the intentions of other people, she had an unbending trust in her own instincts. Early in her story, for example, when an ex-boyfriend proposes to escape from the ghetto with her and find shelter in the Aryan section of Warsaw, she hesitates. "Should I or shouldn't I?" she tells her nephew. "First of all, he was not faithful to me. He was never faithful. If he was not faithful in love, he would not be faithful for more important matters like life and death. This type of fellow I did not need."

On the other hand, she never deluded herself into thinking she could survive without the help of others. One of the most disturbing aspects of this book is where Goldberg sometimes found that help. At several perilous junctures she was aided by older German soldiers (the young ones were invariably die-hard Nazis, she discovered), and in some of those instances, even after her Jewish identity had been exposed, these men did not betray her. This contradicts nearly everything we have been told about German conduct during the war, and when you factor in the additional help she received from working-class Poles, and then combine that with the various examples she mentions of Jews betraying other Jews, the stark black-and-white picture we have drawn of the Holocaust dissolves into a muddled, terrifying gray—a world in which humanity carried on with its usual greeds and lusts, its occasional flashes of goodness and self-sacrifice, its eternal unpredictability. In one chilling passage about conditions in the ghetto, Goldberg tells us: "People hated each other. You understand, they were starving. They could kill each other for food. We had a family from Lodz in our apartment. My mother cooked. The wife of this man came and ate up my mother's soup, so my mother complained to me. The man did not like my mother complaining, so he pushed her around and beat her up. When I came home from work that day I hit him on the head with an iron pot. I got even for my mother. He got no pity from me. He never touched her anymore." And then, one paragraph down on the same page: "We were so demoralized that people became disrespectful of each other. If a married man had a sweetheart, he brought her to his house, and the wife was lucky if he did not throw her out on the street. If he gave his wife food and a place to sleep on the floor, she was considered lucky."

Eventually, Goldberg slipped out of the ghetto by way of the sewers, got herself captured on purpose, and was shipped to Germany, where she spent the rest of the war doing forced labor—in a munitions factory and on a number of farms. Every day carried the threat of denunciation, of arrest and torture, of death. But she had been given some good advice by one of her father's gentile friends before leaving the ghetto, and she learned her lessons well. "Remember one thing," the man told her. "When somebody attacks you, never show fear. Use vulgar words like anybody else, the most dirty words so that you sound sure of yourself. And attack them!" The point being, as she explains to her nephew, "if a German beats you up and you don't fight back, that means you are a Jew, that you are scared. A Gentile always strikes back."

Knowing that things could turn against her at any moment, she was constantly prepared for the worst. "I had long hair tied in a knot at the back. I had razor blades hidden in the knot in order to commit suicide in case I could not take it anymore." But Goldberg never succumbed to despair. She was interrogated by the Gestapo and badly beaten; she was often close to starvation; she suffered from hepatitis, from mange itch, from lice; and at one point she felt that her spirit had finally been broken. But it wasn't. In the end, I believe that was her most transcendent accomplishment—as great, if not greater, than the fact that she survived. *Running Through Fire* is a book filled with unspeakable horrors—but it is told without a shred of self-pity. Goldberg never complains, never bemoans her lot. She battles and endures, and in this raw, unvarnished tale of human suffering, she has given us a manual of hope.

July 2003

Hawthorne at Home

Twenty Days with Julian & Little Bunny, by Papa is one of the least known works by a well-known writer in all of literature. Buried in the seventh folio of Hawthorne's *American Notebooks*—that massive, little-read tome of treasures and revelations—the fifty pages that comprise this brief, self-contained narrative were written in Lenox, Massachusetts, between July 28 and August 16, 1851. In June of the previous year, Hawthorne and his wife had moved to a small red farmhouse in the Berkshires with their two children, Una (born in 1844) and Julian (born in 1846). A third child, Rose, was born in May 1851. A couple of months later, accompanied by her two daughters and her older sister, Elizabeth Peabody, Sophia Hawthorne left Lenox to visit her parents in West Newton, just outside Boston. Remaining in the house were Hawthorne, the five-year-old Julian, Mrs. Peters (the cook and housekeeper), and a pet rabbit who eventually came to be known as Hindlegs. That evening, after putting Julian to bed, Hawthorne sat down and wrote the first chapter of his little saga. With no intention other than to record the doings in the household during his wife's absence, he had inadvertently embarked on something that no writer had ever attempted before him: a meticulous, blow-by-blow account of a man taking care of a young child by himself.

In some ways, the situation is reminiscent of the old folk tale about the farmer and his wife who swap chores for a day. There are many versions of the story, but the outcome is always the same. The man, who has either belittled the woman for not working as hard as he does or scolded her for not doing her work well, makes a complete botch of it when he dons an apron and assumes the role of domestic manager. Depending on which variant you read, he either sets fire to the kitchen or winds up dangling from a rope attached to the family cow, who, after a long chain of misadventures, has managed to get herself onto the roof of the house. In all versions, it is the wife who comes to the rescue. Calmly planting crops in a nearby field, she hears her husband's screams and runs back home to extricate him from his predicament before he burns the place down or breaks his neck.

Hawthorne didn't break his neck, but he clearly felt that he was on rocky ground, and the tone of *Twenty Days* is at once comic, self-depre-catory, and vaguely befuddled, shot through with what the grown-up Julian would later describe as his father's "humorous gravity." Readers familiar with the style of Hawthorne's stories and novels will be struck by the clarity and simplicity of expression in the *Notebooks*. The dark, brooding obsessions of his fiction produced a complex, often ornate density to his sentences, a refinement that sometimes bordered on the fussy or obscure, and some readers of his early tales (which were mostly published unsigned) mistakenly assumed that their author was a woman. Henry James, who wrote one of the first book-length studies of Hawthorne's work, learned much from this original and delicate prose, which was unique in its ability to join the intricacies of acute psycholog-ical observation with large moral and philosophical concerns. But James was not Hawthorne's only reader, and there are several other Hawthornes who have come down to us as well: Hawthorne the alle-gorist, Hawthorne the high Romantic fabulist, Hawthorne the chroni-cler of seventeenth-century colonial New England and, most notably, Hawthorne as reimagined by Borges—the precursor of Kafka. Hawthorne's fiction can be read profitably from any one of these angles, but there is yet another Hawthorne who has been more or less forgot-ten, neglected because of the magnitude of his other achievements: the private Hawthorne, the scribbler of anecdotes and impulsive thoughts, the workman of ideas, the meteorologist and depictor of landscapes, the traveler, the letter-writer, the historian of everyday life. The pages of the *American Notebooks* are so fresh, so vivid in their articulations, that Hawthorne emerges from them not as some venerable figure from the literary past, but as a contemporary, a man whose time is still the present.

Twenty Days was not the only occasion on which he wrote about his children. Once Una and Julian were old enough to talk, he seemed to take immense pleasure in jotting down some of their zanier utterances, and the notebooks are studded with entries such as these:

"I'm tired of all sings and want to slip into God. I'm tired of little Una Hawsorne." "Are you tired of Mamma?" "No." "But are you tired of Papa?" "No. I am tired of Dora, and tired of little Julian, and tired of little Una Hawsorne."

Una—"You hurt me a little."
Julian—"Well, I'll hurt you a big."

Julian—"Mamma, why is not dinner supper?"—Mamma—"Why is not a chair a table?"—Julian—"Because it's a teapot."

I said to Julian, 'Let me take off your bib'—and he taking no notice, I repeated it two or three times, each time louder than before. At last he bellowed—"Let me take off your Head!"

On Sunday, March 19, 1848, during the period when he was employed at the U.S. Custom House in Salem, Hawthorne spent the entire day recording the activities and antics of his two offspring— one just four and the other not quite two. It is a dizzying account of some nine pages that conscientiously takes note of every whim and twist of mood that occurred in the children over the course of eleven hours. Lacking the sentimental flourishes one might expect from a nineteenth-century parent, devoid of moralizing judgments or intrusive commentary, it stands as a remarkable portrait of the reality of childhood—which, on the strength of these passages, would seem to be eternal in its sameness.

Now Una offers her finger to Julian, and they march together, the little boy aping a manly measurement of stride. Now Una proposes to play Puss in the Corner; and there is a quick tatoo of little feet all over the floor. Julian utters a complaining cry about something or other—Una runs and kisses him. Una says, "Father—*this* morning, I am not going to be naughty at all." Now they are playing with India rubber balls. Julian tries to throw the ball into the air, but usually succeeds no farther than to drop it over his head. It rolls away—and he searches for it, inquiring—"where ball?". . . . Julian now falls into a reverie, for a little space—his mind seeming far away, lost in reminiscences; but what can they be about? Recollections of a pre-existence. Now, he sits in his little chair, his chunky little figure looking like an alderman in miniature. . . . Mamma is dressing little Una in her purple pelisse, to go out with Dora. Una promises to be a very good little girl, and mind Dora—and not run away, nor step in the mud. The little boy trudges round, repeating "Go!—go!"—intimating his desire to be taken out likewise. He runs to-and-fro across the room, with a marvellous swagger—of the ludicrousness of which he seems perfectly conscious; and when I laugh, he comes to my elbow and looks up in my face, with a most humorous response. . . . He climbs into a chair at my knee, and peeps at himself in the glass—now he looks curiously on the page as I write—now, he nearly tumbles down, and is at first frightened—but, seeing that I was likewise startled, pretends to tumble again, and then laughs in my face. Enter mamma with the milk. His sits on his mother's knee, gulping the milk with grunts and sighs of satisfaction—nor ceases till the cup is exhausted, once, and again, and again—and even then asks for more. On being undressed, he is taking an airbath—he enjoys the felicity of utter nakedness—running away from Mamma with cries of remonstrance, when she wishes to put on his night-gown. Now ensues a terrible catastrophe—not to be mentioned in our seemly history. . . . Enter Una—"Where is little Julian?" "He has gone out to walk." "No; but I mean where is the place of little Julian, that you've been writing about him." So I point to the page, at which she looks with all possible satisfaction; and stands watching the pen as it hurries forward. "I'll put the ink nearer to you," says she. "Father, are you going to write all this?" she adds, turning over the book. . . . I tell her that I am now writing about herself—"That's nice writing," says she. . . . Una now proposes to him to build a block house with her; so they set about it jointly; but it has scarcely risen above its foundation, before Julian tears it down. With unwearied patience, Una begins another. "Papa! 'Ouse!" cries Julian, pointing to two blocks which he has laid together. . . . They quit the blocks, and Julian again offers to climb the chair to the bookcase; and is again forbidden by me;—whereupon he cries—Una runs to kiss and comfort him—and then comes to me with a solemn remonstrance, of no small length; the burthen being, "Father, you should not speak so loudly to a little boy who is only half years old". . . . She comes and takes her place silently in my lap, resting her head on my shoulder. Julian has clambered into a chair at the window, and appears to observe and meditate; so that we have a very quiet interval, until he disturbs it by coming and pulling off her shoe. He seldom pretermits any mischief that his hand finds to do:—for instance, finding her bare knee, he has just taken occasion to pinch it with all his might . . .

Hawthorne repeated the exercise four days later, on Thursday, March twenty-third, and six times more in 1849, covering what would amount to another thirty pages in Centenary Edition of the *Notebooks*. Adding to his descriptions of his children's games and squabbles and inner storms, he sometimes paused to make a number of more generalized remarks about their personalities. Two small passages about Una are of particular interest, since she is usually taken to be the model on which he based the character of Pearl in *The Scarlet Letter*. From January 28, 1849: "Her beauty is the most flitting, transitory, most uncertain and unaccountable affair, that ever had a real existence; it beams out when nobody expects it, it has mysteriously passed away, when you think yourself sure of it;—if you glance sideways at her, you perhaps think it is illuminating her face, but, turning full round to enjoy it, it is gone again. . . . When really visible, it is rare and precious as the vision of an angel; it is a transfiguration—a grace, delicacy, an ethereal fineness, which, at once, in my secret soul, makes me give up all severe opinions that I may have begun to form respecting her. It is but fair to conclude that, on these occasions, we see her real soul; when she seems less lovely, we merely see something external. But, in truth, one manifestation belongs to her as much as another; for, before the establishment of principles, what is character but the series and succession of moods?" From July thirtieth of the same year: ". . . There is something that almost frightens me about the child— I know not whether elfish or angelic, but, at all events, supernatural. She steps so boldly into the midst of everything, shrinks from nothing, has such a comprehension of everything, seems at times to have but little delicacy, and anon shows that she possesses the finest essence of it; now so hard, now so tender; now so perfectly unreasonable, soon again so wise. In short, I now and then catch an aspect of her, in which I cannot believe her to be my own human child, but a spirit strangely mingled with good and evil, haunting the house where I dwell. The little boy is always the same child, and never varies in relation to me."

By the summer of 1851, Hawthorne was a seasoned observer of his own children, a veteran of family life. He was forty-seven years old and had been married for close to a decade. He couldn't have known it then, but nearly every important word of fiction he would ever publish had already been written. Behind him were the two editions of *Twice-Told Tales* (1837 and 1842), *Mosses from an Old Manse* (1846), and *The Snow-Image and Other Twice-Told Tales* (already finished and planned for publication in late 1851)—his entire output as a writer of short stories. His first two novels had been published in 1850 and 1851. *The Scarlet Letter* had turned "the obscurest man of letters in America" into one of the most respected and celebrated writers of his time, and *The House of the Seven Gables* had only strengthened his reputation, prompting many critics to call him the finest writer the Republic had yet produced. Years of solitary labor had at last won him public reward, and after two decades of scrambling to make ends meet, 1851 marked the first year that Hawthorne earned enough from his writing to be able to support his family. Nor was there any reason to think that his success would not continue. Throughout the spring and early summer, he had written *A Wonder Book for Girls and Boys*, finishing the preface on July fifteenth, just two weeks before Sophia's departure for West Newton, and he was already making plans for his next novel, *The Blithedale Romance*. Looking back on Hawthorne's career now, and knowing that he would be dead just thirteen years later (a few weeks short of his sixtieth birthday), that season in Lenox stands out as one of the happiest periods of his life, a moment of sublime equipoise and fulfillment. But it was nearly August now, and for many years Hawthorne had routinely suspended his literary work during the hot months. It was a time for loafing and reflection, in his opinion, a time for being outdoors, and he had always written as little as possible throughout the dog days of the New England summers. When he composed his little chronicle of the three weeks he spent with his son, he was not stealing time from other, more important projects. It was the only work he did, the only work he wanted to do.

The move to Lenox had been precipitated by Hawthorne's disastrous experiences in Salem in 1849. As he put it in a letter to his friend Horatio Bridge, he had come to dislike the town "so much that I hate to go into the streets or to have the people see me. Anywhere else, I shall at once be entirely another man." Appointed to the post of Surveyor in the Salem Custom House in 1846 (during the Democratic administration of James Polk), Hawthorne accomplished almost nothing as a writer during the three years he held this job. With the election of Whig candidate Zachary Taylor in 1848, Hawthorne was sacked when the new administration took office in March 1849—but not without raising a great noise in his own defense, which led to a highly publicized controversy about the practice of political patronage in America. At the precise moment when this struggle was being waged, Hawthorne's mother died after a short illness. The notebook entries from those days in late July are among the most wrenching, emotionally charged paragraphs in all of Hawthorne. "Louisa pointed to a chair near the bed; but I was moved to kneel down close to my mother, and take her hand. She knew me, but could only murmur a few indistinct words—among which I understood an injunction to take care of my sisters. Mrs. Dike left the chamber, and then I found the tears slowly gathering in my eyes. I tried to keep them down; but it would not be—I kept filling up, till, for a few moments, I shook with sobs. For a long time, I knelt there, holding her hand; and surely it is the darkest hour I have ever lived."

Ten days after his mother's death, Hawthorne lost his fight to save his job. Within days of his dismissal (perhaps even the same day, if family legend is to be believed), he began writing *The Scarlet Letter*, which was completed in six months. Under great financial strain during this period, his fortunes took a sudden, unexpected turn for the better just as plans were being made by the firm of Ticknor and Fields to publish the novel. By private, anonymous subscription, friends and supporters of Hawthorne (among them, most likely, Longfellow and Lowell) "who admire your genius and respect your character . . . [and to pay] the debt we owe you for what you have done for American literature" had raised the sum of five hundred dollars to help see Hawthorne through his difficulties. This windfall allowed Hawthorne to carry out his increasingly urgent desire to leave Salem, his hometown, and become "a citizen of somewhere else."

After a number of possibilities fell through (a farm in Manchester, New Hampshire, a house in Kittery, Maine), he and Sophia eventually settled on the red farmhouse in Lenox. It was, as Hawthorne put it to one of his former Custom House co-workers, "as red as the Scarlet Letter." Sophia was responsible for finding the place, which was situated on a larger property known as Highwood, currently being rented by the Tappan family. Mrs. Tappan, née Caroline Sturgis, was a friend of Sophia's, and it was she who offered the house to the Hawthornes— free of charge. Hawthorne, wary of the complications that might arise from living off the generosity of others, struck a bargain with Mr. Tappan to pay a nominal rent of seventy-five dollars for four years.

One would assume that he was satisfied with the arrangement, but that didn't stop him from grumbling about any number of petty annoyances. No sooner did the family settle into the house than Hawthorne came down with a bad cold, which confined him to bed for several days, and before long he was complaining in a letter to his sister Louisa that the farmhouse was "the most wretched little hovel that I ever put my head in." (Even the optimistic Sophia, who tended to see every adversity in the best possible light, admitted in a letter to her mother that is was "the smallest of ten-foot houses"—barely adequate for a family of four, let alone five.) If the house displeased Hawthorne, he had even harsher things to say about the landscape that surrounded it. Sixteen months after moving in, he wrote to his publisher, James T. Fields, that "I have staid here too long and constantly. To tell you a secret, I am sick to death of Berkshire, and hate to think of spending another winter here. . . . The air and climate do not agree with my health at all; and, for the first time since I was a boy, I have felt languid and dispirited, during almost my whole residence here. Oh that Providence would build me the merest little shanty, and make me out a rood or two of garden-ground, near the sea-coast." Two years later, long after he had moved away and resettled in Concord, he was still grinding the same axe, as shown in this passage from the introduction to *Tanglewood Tales* (a second volume of Greek myths for children): "But, to me, there is a peculiar, quiet charm in these broad meadows and gentle eminences. They are better than mountains, because they do not stamp and stereotype thoughts into the brain, and thus grow wearisome with the same strong impression, repeated day after day. A few summer weeks among mountains, a lifetime among green meadows and placid slopes, with outlines forever new, because continually fading out of the memory. Such would be my sober choice." It is ironic that the area around Lenox should still be referred to as "Tanglewood." The word was Hawthorne's invention and is now indelibly associated with the music festival that takes place there every year. For a man who hated the area and ran away from it after just eighteen months, he left his mark on it forever.

Still, it was the best moment of his life, whether he knew it or not. Solvent, successfully married to an intelligent and famously devoted woman, in the middle of the most prolific writing burst of his career, Hawthorne planted his vegetable garden, fed his chickens, and played with his children in the afternoon. The shyest and most reclusive of men, known for his habit of hiding behind rocks and trees to avoid talking to people he knew, Hawthorne largely kept to himself during his stint in the Berkshires, avoiding the social activities of the local gentry and appearing in town only to collect his mail at the post office and return home. Solitude was his natural element, and considering the circumstances of his life until his early thirties, it was remarkable that he had married at all. When you were a person whose ship-captain father had died in Surinam when you were four, when you had grown up with a remote and elusive mother who had lived in a state of permanent, isolated widowhood, when you had served what is probably the most stringent literary apprenticeship on record—locking yourself up in your room for twelve years in a house you had dubbed "Castle Dismal" and leaving Salem only in the summer to go on solitary rambles through the New England countryside—then perhaps the society of your immediate family was sufficient. Hawthorne had married late to a woman who had likewise married late, and in the twenty-two years they lived together, they were rarely apart. He called her Phoebe, Dove, Beloved, Dearissima, Ownest One. "Sometimes," he had written to her during their courtship in 1840, "during my solitary life in our old Salem house, it seemed to me as if I had only life enough to know that I was not alive; for I had no wife then to keep my heart warm. But, at length, you were revealed to me, in the shadow of a seclusion as deep as my own. I drew nearer and nearer to you, and opened my heart to you, and you came to me, and will remain forever, keeping my heart warm and renewing my life with your own. You only have taught me that I have a heart,— you only have thrown a light, deep downward and upward, into my soul. You only have revealed me to myself; for without your aid my best knowledge of myself would have been merely to know my own shadow,—to watch it flickering on the wall, and mistake its fantasies for my own real actions. Do you comprehend what you have done for me?"

They lived in isolation, but visitors nevertheless came (relatives, old friends), and they were in contact with several of their neighbors. One of them, who lived six miles down the road in Pittsfield, was Herman Melville, then thirty-one years old. Much has been written about the relationship between the two writers (some of it pertinent, some of it nonsense), but it is clear that Hawthorne opened up to the younger Melville with unaccustomed enthusiasm and took great pleasure in his company. As he wrote to his friend Bridge on August 7, 1850: "I met Melville, the other day, and liked him so much that I have asked him to spend a few days with me before leaving these parts." Melville had only been visiting the area at the time, but by October he was back, acquiring the property in Pittsfield he renamed Arrowhead and installing himself in the Berkshires as a fulltime resident. Over the next thirteen months, the two men talked, corresponded, and read each other's work, occasionally traveling the six miles between them to stay as a guest at the other's house. "Nothing pleases me more," Sophia wrote to her sister Elizabeth about the friendship between her husband and Melville (whom she playfully referred to as Mr. Omoo), "than to sit & hear this growing man dash his tumultuous waves of thought against Mr. Hawthorne's great, genial, comprehending silences. . . . Without doing anything on his own, except merely *being*, it is astonishing how people make him their innermost Father Confessor." For Melville, the encounter with Hawthorne and his writings marked a fundamental turn in his life. He had already begun his story about the white whale at the time of their first meeting (projected as a conventional high-seas adventure novel), but under Hawthorne's influence the book began to change and deepen and expand, transforming itself in an unabated frenzy of inspiration into the richest of all American novels, *Moby-Dick*. As everyone who has read the book knows, the first page reads: "In token of my admiration for his genius, this book is inscribed to Nathaniel Hawthorne." Even if Hawthorne had accomplished nothing else during his stay in Lenox, he unwittingly served as Melville's muse.

The lease was good for four years, but shortly after the completion of *Twenty Days* and Sophia's return from West Newton with Una and baby Rose, Hawthorne contrived to get himself into a dispute with his landlords over a trivial matter of boundaries. The issue revolved around the question of whether he and his family had the right to pick the fruits and berries from the trees and bushes on the property. In a long, hilariously acidic letter to Mrs. Tappan dated September 5, 1851, Hawthorne set forth his case, concluding with a rather nasty challenge: "At any rate, take what you want, and that speedily, or there will be little else than a parcel of rotten plums to dispute about." A gracious, conciliatory letter from Mr. Tappan the following day—which Sophia characterized to her sister as "noble and beautiful"—seemed to settle the matter once and for all, but by then Hawthorne had already made up his mind to move, and the family soon packed up their belongings and were gone from the house on November twenty-first.

Just one week earlier, on November fourteenth, Melville had received his first copies of *Moby-Dick*. That same day, he drove his wagon over to the red farmhouse and invited Hawthorne to a farewell dinner at Curtis's Hotel in Lenox, where he presented his friend with a copy of the book. Until then, Hawthorne had known nothing about the effusive dedication to him, and while there is no record of his reaction to this unexpected tribute to "his genius," one can only surmise that he was deeply moved. Moved enough, in any case, to begin reading the book immediately upon returning home, surrounded by the chaos of boxes and packing crates as his family prepared for their departure. He must have read the book quickly and intensely, for his letter of response reached Melville on the sixteenth. All but one of Hawthorne's letters to Melville have been lost, but numerous letters from Melville to Hawthorne have survived, and his answer to this one is among the most memorable and frequently quoted letters in all of American literature: ". . . A sense of unspeakable security is in me this moment, on account of your having understood the book. I have written a wicked book, and feel spotless as the lamb. Ineffable socialities are in me. I would sit down and dine with you and all the gods in old Rome's Pantheon. . . . Whence come you, Hawthorne? By what right do you drink from the flagon of my life? And when I put it to my lips—lo, they are yours and not mine. I feel that the Godhead is broken up like the bread at the Supper, and that we are the pieces. Hence this infinite fraternity of feeling. . . . I shall leave the world, I feel, with more satisfaction for having come to know you. Knowing you persuades me more than the Bible of our immortality."

Melville makes a couple of appearances in *Twenty Days with Julian &*

Little Bunny, but the gist of the piece is the little boy himself, the daily activities of father and son, the ephemeral nothings of domestic life. No dramas are reported, the routine is fairly monotonous, and in terms of content, one can hardly imagine a duller or more pedestrian undertaking. Hawthorne kept the diary for Sophia. It was written in a separate family notebook which they both used to record material about the children (and which the children had access to as well, sometimes adding drawings and infant scribbles of their own—and, in a few instances, even tracing their pencils directly over texts written by their parents). Hawthorne intended his wife to read the little work after her return from West Newton, and it appears that she did so at the earliest opportunity. Describing the trip home to Lenox in a letter to her mother three days later (August 19, 1851), Sophia wrote, ". . . Una was very tired, and her eyes looked as cavernous as Daniel Webster's till she saw the red house; and then she began to shout, and clap her hands for joy. Mr. Hawthorne came forth with a thousand welcomes in his eyes, and Julian leaped like a fountain, and was as impossible to hold fast. . . . I found that Mr. Hawthorne had written a minute account of his and Julian's life from the hour of our departure. He had a tea-party of New York gentlemen one day, and they took him and Julian a long drive; and they all had a picnic together, and did not get home till eight o'clock. Mr. Melville came with these gentlemen, and once before in my absence. Mr. Hawthorne also had a visit from a Quaker lady of Philadelphia, Elizabeth Lloyd, who came to see the author of "The Scarlet Letter." He said that it was a very pleasant call. Mr. [G.P.R.] James also came twice, once with a great part of his family, once in a storm. Julian's talk flowed like a babbling brook, he writes, the whole three weeks, through all his meditations and reading. They spent a great deal of time at the lakes, and put Nat's ship out to sea. . . . Sometimes Julian pensively yearned for mama, but was not once out of temper or unhappy. There is a charming history of poor little Bunny, who died the morning of the day we returned. It did not appear why he should die, unless he lapped water off the bathing-room floor. But he was found stark and stiff. Mrs. Peters was very smiling, and grimly glad to see me . . ."

After Hawthorne's death in 1864, Sophia was prevailed upon by James T. Fields, Hawthorne's publisher and also the editor of the *Atlantic Monthly*, to choose excerpts from her husband's notebooks for publication in the magazine. Passages appeared in twelve successive issues in 1866, but when it came to *Twenty Days with Julian & Little*

Bunny, which Fields was hoping to include, she hesitated, claiming that Julian would have to be consulted first. Her son apparently had no objections, but still Sophia was reluctant to give her consent, and after some further reflection she decided against printing the material, explaining to Fields that Hawthorne "would never have wished such an intimate domestic history to be made public, and I am astonished at myself that I ever thought of it." In 1884, when Julian published his own book, *Nathaniel Hawthorne and His Wife*, he included a number of extracts from *Twenty Days*, commenting that the three weeks he spent alone with his father "must have been weary work, sometimes, for Hawthorne, though for the little boy it was one uninterrupted succession of halcyon days." He mentions that a full version of the diary would make "as unique and quaint a little history as was ever seen," but it wasn't until 1932, when Randall Stewart put together the first scholarly edition of the *American Notebooks*, that *Twenty Days with Julian & Little Bunny* was finally made available to the public. Not as a separate book (as Julian had suggested) but as one section in a lengthy volume of 800 pages that spans the years 1835 to 1853.

Why publish it now as an independent work? Why should this small, uneventful piece of prose command our interest more than one hundred-fifty years after it was written? I wish I could mount a cogent defense on its behalf, make some dazzling, sophisticated argument that would prove its greatness, but if the piece is great, it is great only in miniature, great only because the writing, in and of itself, gives pleasure. *Twenty Days* is a humorous work by a notoriously melancholic man, and anyone who has ever spent an extended length of time in the company of a small child will surely respond to the accuracy and honesty of Hawthorne's account.

Una and Julian were raised in an unorthodox manner, even by the standards of mid-nineteenth-century Transcendentalist New England. Although they reached school-age during their time in Lenox, neither one was sent to school, and they spent their days at home with their mother, who took charge of their education and rarely allowed them to mingle with other children. The hermetic, Eden-like atmosphere that Hawthorne and Sophia tried to establish in Concord after their marriage apparently continued after they became parents. Writing to her mother from Lenox, Sophia eloquently delineated her philosophy of childrearing: ". . . Alas for those who counsel sternness and severity instead of love towards their young children! How little they are like God, how much they are like Solomon, whom I really believe many persons prefer to imitate, and think they do well. Infinite patience, infinite tenderness, infinite magnanimity,—no less will do, and we must practise them as far as finite power will allow. Above all, no parent should feel a *pride of power*. This, I doubt not, is the great stumbling-block, and it should never be indulged. From this comes the sharp rebuke, the cruel blow, the anger. A tender sorrow, a most sympathizing regret, alone should appear at the transgression of a child ... Yet how immitigable is the judgment and treatment of these little misdemeanors often! When my children disobey, I am not personally aggrieved, and they see it, and find therefore that it is a disinterested desire that they should do right that induces me to insist. There is all the difference in the world between indulgence and tenderness."

Hawthorne, who acceded to his wife in all family and household matters, took a far less active role in raising the children. "If only papa wouldn't write, how nice it would be," Julian quoted Una as having declared one day, and according to him "their feeling about all their father's writings was, that he was being wasted in his study, when he might be with them, and there could be nothing in any books, whether his own or other authors', that could for a moment bear comparison with his actual companionship." When he finished working for the day, it seems that Hawthorne preferred acting as playmate with his children than as classic paternal figure. "Our father was a great tree-climber," Julian recalled, "and he was also fond of playing the magician. 'Hide your eyes!' he would say, and the next moment, from being there beside us on the moss, we would hear his voice descending from the sky, and behold! he swung among the topmost branches, showering down upon us a hail-storm of nuts." In her numerous letters and journal entries from that period, Sophia frequently noted glimpses of Hawthorne alone with the two children. "Mr. Hawthorne," she informed her mother, "has been lying down in the sunshine, slightly fleckered with the shadows of a tree, and Una and Julian have been making him look like the mighty Pan by covering his chin and breast with long grass-blades, that looked like a verdant, venerable beard." And again to her mother several days later: "Dear little harp-souled Una—whose love for her father grows more profound every day ... was made quite unhappy because he did not go at the same time with her to the lake. His absence darkened all the sunshine to her; and when I asked her why she could not enjoy the walk as Julian did, she replied, 'Ah, *he* does not love papa as *I* do!'. . . .

After I put Julian to bed, I went out to the barn to see about the chickens, and she wished to go. There sat papa on the hay, and like a needle to a magnet she was drawn, and begged to see papa a little longer, and stay with him. Now she has come, weary enough; and after steeping her spirit in this rose and gold of twilight, she has gone to bed. With such a father, and such a scene before her eyes, and *with eyes to see*, what may we not hope of her? I heard her and Julian talking together about their father's smile, the other day—They had been speaking of some other person's smile—Mr. Tappan's, I believe; and presently Una said, 'But you know, Julian, that there is no smile like papa's!' 'Oh no,' replied Julian. 'Not like *papa's!*' " In 1904, many years after Una's early death at the age of thirty-three, Thomas Wentworth Higginson published a memorial piece about her in *The Outlook*, a popular magazine of the period. In it, he quoted her as once having said to him about her father: "He was capable of being the gayest person I ever saw. He was like a boy. Never was such a playmate as he in all the world."

All this lies behind the spirit of *Twenty Days with Julian & Little Bunny*. The Hawthornes were a consciously progressive family, and for the most part their treatment of their children corresponds to attitudes prevalent among the secular middle-class in America today. No harsh discipline, no physical punishment, no strident reprimands. Some people found the Hawthorne children obstreperous and unruly, but Sophia, ever inclined to see them as model creatures, happily reported in a letter to her mother that at a local torchlight festival "the children enjoyed themselves extremely, and behaved so beautifully that they won all hearts. They thought that there never was such a superb child as Julian, nor such a grace as Una. 'They are neither too shy, nor bold,' said Mrs. Field, 'but just right.' " What constitutes "just right," of course, is a matter of opinion. Hawthorne, who was always more rigorous in his observations than his wife—unable, by force of instinct and habit, to allow love to color his judgments—makes no bones about how annoying Julian's presence sometimes was to him. That theme is sounded on the first page of the diary, and it recurs repeatedly throughout the twenty days they spent together. The boy was a champion chatterbox, a pint-sized engine of logorrhea, and within hours of Sophia's departure, Hawthorne was already complaining that "it is impossible to write, read, think, or even to sleep (in the daytime) so constant are his appeals to me in one way or another." By the second evening, after remarking once again on the endless stream of babble that issued from

Julian's lips, Hawthorne put him to bed and added: "nor need I hesitate to say that I was glad to be rid of him—it being my first relief from his society during the whole day. This may be too much of a good thing." Five days later, on August third, he was again harping on the same subject: "Either I have less patience to-day than ordinary, or the little man makes larger demands upon it; but it really does seem as if he had baited me with more questions, references, and observations, than mortal father ought to be expected to endure." And again on August fifth: "He continues to pester me with his inquisitions. For instance, just now, while he is whittling with my jack-knife. 'Father, if you had bought all the jack-knives at the shop, what would you do for another, when you broke them all?' 'I would go somewhere else,' say I. But there is no stumping him. 'If you had bought all the jack-knives in the world, what would you do?' And here my patience gives way, and I entreat him not to trouble me with any more foolish questions. I really think it would do him good to spank him, apropos to this habit." And once again on August tenth: "Mercy on me, was ever man before so be-pelted with a child's talk as I am!"

These little bursts of irritation are precisely what give the text its charm—and its truth. No sane person can endure the company of a high-voltage child without an occasional meltdown, and Hawthorne's admissions of less-than-perfect calm turn the diary into something more than just a personal album of summer memories. There is sweetness in the text, to be sure, but it is never cloying (too much wit, too much bite), and because Hawthorne refrains from glossing over his own faults and downcast moments, he takes us beyond a strictly private space into something more universal, more human. Again and again, he curbs his temper whenever he is on the verge of losing it, and the talk of spanking the boy is no more than a passing impulse, a way of letting off steam with his pen instead of his hand. By and large, he shows remarkable forbearance in dealing with Julian, indulging the five-year-old in his whims and escapades and cockeyed discourses with steadfast equanimity, readily allowing that "he is such a genial and good-humored little man that there is certainly an enjoyment intermixed with all the annoyance." In spite of the difficulties and possible frustrations, Hawthorne was determined not to rein in his son too tightly. After the birth of Rose in May, Julian had been forced to tiptoe around the house and speak in whispers. Now, suddenly, he is permitted to "shout and squeal just as loud as I please," and the father sympathizes with the boy's craving for commotion. "He enjoys his freedom so greatly," Hawthorne writes on the second day, "that I do not mean to restrain him, whatever noise he makes."

Julian was not the only source of irritation, however. On July twenty-ninth, the wifeless husband unexpectedly exploded, blasting forth with a splenetic tirade on one of his constant obsessions: "This is a horrible, horrible, most hor-ri-ble climate; one knows not, for ten minutes together, whether he is too cool or too warm; but he is always one or the other; and the constant result is a miserable disturbance of the system. I detest it! I detest it!! I de-test it!!! I hate Berkshire with my whole soul, and would joyfully see its mountains laid flat." On August eighth, after an excursion with Melville and others to the Shaker community in nearby Hancock, he had nothing but the most vicious and cutting remarks to offer about the sect: ". . . all their miserable pretence of cleanliness and neatness is the thinnest superficiality . . . the Shakers are and must needs be a filthy set. And then their utter and systematic lack of privacy; their close junction of man with man [two men routinely slept in one small bed], and supervision of one man over another—it is hateful and disgusting to think of; and the sooner the sect is extinct the better . . ." Then, with a kind of gloating sarcasm, he applauds Julian for answering a call of nature during their visit and defecating on the property. "All through this outlandish village went our little man, happy and dancing, in excellent spirits; nor had he been there long before he desired to confer with himself—neither was I unwilling that he should bestow such a mark of his consideration (being the one of which they were most worthy) on the system and establishment of these foolish Shakers." Less severely, perhaps, but with a noticeable touch of disdain, he also had some unkind things to say about his neighbor and landlady, Caroline Tappan—a good month before the infamous fruit-tree controversy, which would suggest a prior antipathy, perhaps one of long standing. (Some biographers have speculated that she made a pass at Hawthorne during Sophia's absence—or at least would have been willing to do so if he had given her any encouragement.) Hawthorne and Julian had given the pet rabbit to the Tappans, thinking the animal might be happier in the larger house, but for various reasons (a threatening dog, mistreatment by the Tappans' young daughter) the new arrangement had not worked out. Mrs. Tappan came to Hawthorne and "spoke of giving him to little Marshall Butler, and suggested, moreover (in reply to something I said about putting him out of existence) that he might be turned out into the woods, to shift for himself. There is something characteristic in this idea; it shows the sort of sensitiveness, that finds the pain and misery of other people disagreeable, just as it would a bad scent, but is perfectly at ease once they are removed from her sphere. I suppose she would not for the world have killed Bunny, although she would have exposed him to the certainty of lingering starvation, without scruple or remorse."

Apart from these rare instances of pique and outrage, the atmosphere of *Twenty Days* is serene, measured, bucolic. Every morning, Hawthorne and Julian went to fetch milk at a neighboring farm; they engaged in "sham battles," collected the mail at the Lenox post office in the afternoon, and made frequent trips to the lake. On the way, they would "wage war with the thistles," which was Julian's favorite sport—pretending that the thistles were dragons and beating them heartily with sticks. They collected flowers, gathered currants, and picked green beans and summer squashes from the garden. Hawthorne built a makeshift boat for Julian, using a newspaper as a sail; a drowning cat was saved from a cistern; and during their visits to the lake, they variously fished, flung stones into the water, and dug in the sand. Hawthorne gave Julian a bath every morning and then wrestled with the task of trying to curl his hair, seldom with satisfactory results. There was a bed-wetting accident on August third, a painful wasp-sting on the fifth, a stomach ache and a headache to be attended to on the thirteenth and fourteenth, and an untimely loss of bladder control during a walk home on the sixth, which prompted Hawthorne to remark "I heard him squealing, while I was some distance behind; and approaching nearer I saw that he walked wide between the legs. Poor little man! His drawers were all a-sop." Even if he wasn't completely at home with the job, the father had little by little become the mother, and by August twelfth we understand how thoroughly Hawthorne had assumed this role when, for the first time in more than two weeks, he suddenly lost track of where Julian was. "After dinner, I sat down with a book . . . and he was absent in parts unknown, for the space of an hour. At last I began to think it time to look him up; for, now that I am alone with him, I have all his mother's anxieties, added to my own. So I went to the barn, and to the currant-bushes, and shouted around the house, without response, and finally sat down on the hay, not knowing which way to seek him. But by and by, he ran round the house, holding up his little fist, with a smiling phiz, and crying out that he had something very good for me."

Barring the excursion to the Shaker Village with Melville on August eighth, the pair stayed close to home, but that outing proved to be an exhilarating experience for the little boy, and Hawthorne is at his best in capturing his enthusiasm, in being able to see the event through his son's eyes. The group lost its way on the carriage-ride home, and by the time they passed through Lenox, "it was beyond twilight; indeed, but for the full moon, it would have been quite dark. The little man behaved himself still like an old traveller; but sometimes he looked round at me from the front seat (where he sat between Herman Melville and Evert Duyckinck) and smiled at me with a peculiar expression, and put back his hand to touch me. It was a method of establishing a sympathy in what doubtless appeared to him the wildest and unprecedentedest series of adventures that had ever befallen mortal travellers."

The next morning, Julian announced to Hawthorne that he loved Mr. Melville as much as his father, his mother, and Una, and based on the evidence of a short letter that Melville sent to Julian six months later (long after the Hawthornes had left the Berkshires), it would appear that this fondness was reciprocated. "I am very happy that I have a place in the heart of so fine a little fellow as you," he wrote, and then, after commenting on the heavy snow-drifts in the woods around Pittsfield, concluded with a warm valediction: "Remember me kindly to your good father, Master Julian, and Good Bye, and may Heaven always bless you, & may you be a good boy and become a great good man."

An earlier visit from Melville to Lenox on August first (his thirty-second birthday) provided Hawthorne with what were probably his most pleasurable hours during those three weeks of bachelor life. After stopping in at the post office with Julian that afternoon, he paused on the way home in a secluded spot to read his newspapers when "a cavalier on horseback came along the road, and saluted me in Spanish; to which I replied by touching my hat, and went on with the newspaper. But the cavalier renewing his salutation, I regarded him more attentively, and saw that it was Herman Melville!" The two men walked the mile to the red house together (with Julian, "highly pleased," sitting atop Melville's horse), and then, in what are probably the most frequently quoted sentences from the *American Notebooks*, Hawthorne continues: "After supper, I put Julian to bed; and Melville and I had a talk about time and eternity, things of this world and of the next, and books, and publishers, and all possible and impossible matters, that lasted pretty deep into the night; and if truth must be told, we smoked cigars even within the sacred precincts of the sitting-room. At last, he arose, and saddled his horse (whom we had put into the barn) and rode off for his own domicile; and I hastened to make the most of what little sleeping-time remained for me."

That was the one galvanizing moment in an otherwise torpid stretch of days. When he wasn't taking care of Julian, Hawthorne wrote letters, read Fourier as he prepared to begin *The Blithedale Romance,* and took a half-hearted stab at Thackeray's *Pendennis.* The diary includes many keenly written passages about the shifting light of the landscape (few novelists looked at nature as attentively as Hawthorne did) and a handful of droll and increasingly sympathetic descriptions of Hindlegs, the pet rabbit, who unfortunately expired as the chronicle was coming to an end. More and more, however, as his solitude dragged on, Hawthorne yearned for his wife to come home. By the beginning of the final week, that feeling had been turned into a constant ache. After putting Julian to bed on the evening of August tenth, he suddenly let himself go, breaking down in a rhapsodic gush of longing and allegiance. "Let me say outright, for once, that he is a sweet and lovely little boy, and worthy of all the love that I am capable of giving him. Thank God! God bless him! God bless Phoebe for giving him to me! God bless her as the best wife and mother in the world! God bless Una, whom I long to see again! God bless Little Rosebud! God bless me, for Phoebe's and all their sakes! No other man has so good a wife; nobody has better children. Would I were worthier of her and them!" The entry then concludes: "My evenings are all dreary, alone, and without books that I am in the mood to read; and this evening was like the rest. So I went to bed at about nine, and longed for Phoebe."

He was expecting her to return on the thirteenth, then on the fourteenth, then on the fifteenth, but various delays and missed communications put off Sophia's departure from West Newton until the sixteenth. Increasingly anxious and frustrated, Hawthorne nevertheless pushed on dutifully with the diary. On the very last day, during yet another visit to the lake with Julian, he sat down at the edge of the water with a magazine, and as he read, he was moved to make the following observation, which in some sense stands as a brief and inadvertent *ars poetica,* a precise description of the spirit and methodology of all his writing: ". . . the best way to get a vivid impression and feeling of a landscape, is to sit down before it and read, or become otherwise absorbed in thought; for then, when your eyes happen to be attracted to the landscape, you seem to catch Nature at unawares, and see her before she has time to change her aspect. The effect lasts but for a single instant, and passes away almost as soon as you are conscious of it; but it is real, for that moment. It is as if you could overhear and understand what the trees are whispering to one another; as if you caught a glimpse of a face unveiled, which veils itself from every wilful glance. The mystery is revealed, and after a breath or two, becomes just as much a mystery as before."

As with landscapes, so with people, especially little people in the flush of childhood. All is change with them, all is movement, and you can grasp their essence only "at unawares," at moments when you are not consciously looking for it. That is the beauty of Hawthorne's little piece of notebook-writing. Throughout all the drudgery and tedium of his constant companionship with the five-year-old boy, Hawthorne was able to glance at him often enough to capture something of his essence, to bring him to life in words. A century and a half later, we are still trying to discover our children, but these days we do it by taking snapshots and following them around with video cameras. But words are better, I think, if only because they don't fade with time. It takes more effort to write a truthful sentence than to focus a lens and push a button, of course, but words go deeper than pictures do—which can rarely record anything more than the surfaces of things, whether landscapes or the faces of children. In all but the best or luckiest photographs, the soul is missing. That is why *Twenty Days with Julian & Little Bunny* merits our attention. In his modest, deadpan way, Hawthorne managed to accomplish what every parent dreams of doing: to keep his child alive forever.

July 2002

Night on Earth: New York

As the opening credits for *Night on Earth* begin to roll, we are informed that the film is a Locus Solus Production. A curious name, no doubt unfamiliar to most people, but one that reveals a great deal about Jim Jarmusch's sensibility—what might be called the "Jarmusch touch": that inimitable blend of deadpan humor, off-the-wall shenanigans, and exquisitely crafted images. It turns out that *Locus Solus* is the title of a novel by the eccentric, early-twentieth-century French writer Raymond Roussel, a book admired by the Surrealists and, a generation later, by the American poet John Ashbery—to such an extent that Ashbery and fellow writer Harry Mathews founded a magazine in the late fifties called . . . *Locus Solus.*

Few people know that Jim Jarmusch started out as a poet and that as a student at Columbia he served as one of the editors of the undergraduate literary magazine, the *Columbia Review.* The primary influences on his early work were Ashbery, Frank O'Hara, Kenneth Koch, Ron Padgett, and other poets of the New York School. Against the prevailing formalism and academic dryness of American poetry in the 1950s, various insurrections were taking place around the country: the Beats, the Black Mountain poets, and, most subversively of all, the gang in New York. A new aesthetic was born. Poetry was no longer perceived as a dull and ponderous quest for universal truth or literary perfection. It stopped taking itself seriously and learned to relax, to poke fun at itself, to delight in the ordinary pleasures of the world. The notion of high art was abandoned in favor of an approach marked by frequent shifts in tone, a penchant for wit and nonsense, discontinuity, and an embrace of popular culture in all its myriad forms. Suddenly, poems were filled with references to comic-strip characters and movie stars. It was a homegrown American phenomenon yet, paradoxically, the sources of this transformation largely came from Europe, in particular France.

From the start of his life as a filmmaker, Jarmusch has adhered to the principles he learned from these poets. Although his style has continued to evolve over the years, one thing has been constant throughout: his films resemble no one else's. Unlike most American directors, he has little interest in narrative per se (hence the so-called European flavor of his work), choosing instead to recount shaggy-dog stories filled with loopy asides, unpredictable digressions, and an intense focus on what is happening at each particular moment. Although his dialogue has an off-the-cuff, improvisational quality (in the manner of the New York School poets), it is in fact highly written, acutely sensitive to the nuances of spoken language, the work of a real writer. So much so that some of his most memorable characters are foreigners struggling to master English. Roberto Benigni in *Down by Law*, for example, or Armin Mueller-Stahl in the New York episode of *Night on Earth*.

Which brings me to the subject at hand. Just twenty-three minutes long, the second episode of this five-part film is quintessential Jarmusch, one of the purest, most neatly executed examples of his philosophy of filmmaking. Nothing happens, or so little in the way things traditionally happen in stories that we can almost say there is no story. A man takes a cab from Manhattan to Brooklyn. The end. But every moment of this hilarious, poignant, zany sketch is unforgettable.

The male characters in Jarmusch's films tend to be laconic, withdrawn, sorrowful mumblers (Bill Murray in *Broken Flowers*, Tom Waits in *Down by Law*, Forest Whitaker in *Ghost Dog: The Way of the Samurai*), with an occasional live-wire motormouth charging in to dominate the action. No live wire is more alive, no motormouth is in higher gear than Giancarlo Esposito in the second part of *Night on Earth*. His performance is so energetic, so tightly sprung, one feels that his entire body might explode at any second. After a languid montage of introductory shots, detailing a number of inanimate objects around the city (a glowing pay phone, a graffiti-covered truck), there he is, standing in the middle of Times Square on a freezing winter night, an oddly dressed black man wearing a grotesque fur hat with dangling earflaps, desperately trying to flag down a cab. It's a widely known fact of New York life that black men, even black men dressed in suits and ties, have great difficulty getting taxis to stop for them. Esposito shouts at each passing cab, frantically waves his arms, implores each one to stop, but his efforts appear to be doomed. Then, a miracle. A cab pulls up, but when Esposito announces that he wants to go to Brooklyn, the driver steps on the gas and speeds off. This is another widely known fact of New York life, and as a longtime resident of Brooklyn, I can vouch for its accuracy. Taxi drivers are reluctant to take passengers from Manhattan to Brooklyn. Growing more and more agitated, Esposito pulls a wad of money from his pocket and holds it up in the air, proving that his intentions are honest: he can pay; all he wants is to go home. After another cab ignores him, he calls out in frustration, "What, am I invisible, man?" Note the subtlety of the line. The word *racism* has not been mentioned, but how not to think of Ralph Ellison's novel *Invisible Man*, the classic exploration of what it means to be a black person in America? Whether Jarmusch is making a conscious or unconscious reference to the book is unimportant. The words are delivered in a natural, even humorous way—and yet they sting.

A moment later, salvation comes in the person of Armin Mueller-Stahl, a neophyte cabbie who has just started working that night. With a kind and open expression on his face, he addresses Esposito in an unmistakable foreign accent: "Come in, sir." It is a magnificent turn. From invisible man, Esposito has suddenly been transformed into a gentleman. The irony being, of course, that the person who has spoken to him in this way is ignorant of the rules. No American would use the word *sir*. It has taken a know-nothing immigrant to humanize and give dignity to our unfortunate traveler.

Then the fun begins. As the two make their way to "Brookland," the journey is marked by a steady stream of comic mishaps and verbal misunderstandings. To start with, Mueller-Stahl has no idea how to drive a car with an automatic transmission. Using both feet, he alternately presses down the gas pedal and the brake, lurching forward at a ridiculously slow pace. Esposito is so miffed that he threatens to get out and find another cab, but the sad-sack Mueller-Stahl begs him to stay. "You are my most best customer. It is very, very important to me." Esposito relents, but only on the condition that they switch places and he do the driving. When Mueller-Stahl protests that it isn't allowed, Esposito bluntly declares, "Yeah, it's allowed. This is New York."

So there we are, the two of them sitting side by side on the front seat, a former clown from East Germany by the name of Helmut and a black man from Brooklyn named YoYo, sporting nearly identical hats on their heads. From this simplest of setups, Jarmusch spins out a series of gags and inane comments worthy of Laurel and Hardy at their best, and whenever there is a lull in the conversation, we see the cab floating through a spectral New York, accompanied by Tom Waits's impressive and evocative score. Just when we have settled in for what promises to be an entertaining ride, however, a third character appears, and all hell breaks loose. There goes Rosie Perez striding down a street in lower

497

Manhattan, decked out in a black miniskirt and a bright orange jacket.
She happens to be YoYo's sister-in-law, Angela, and he is beside himself
with irritation at seeing her out alone. In one of the finest visual moments
of the film, YoYo stops the car and rushes to the corner to cut off Angela.
The point of view remains with Helmut in the taxi—a long shot of the
two Brooklynites arguing in the street—and then the camera cuts to a
close-up of Helmut, grinning in fascination at the ferocity of the quarrel.

YoYo wrestles a struggling Angela into the back of the cab, and when
he takes off again, the tone of the sequence abruptly shifts. No more odd-
couple banter from the two men in front: a war has broken out between
YoYo and Angela, an infantile shouting match that ranks as one of the sil-
liest, funniest, most rambunctious exchanges in all of Jarmusch's work.
Rosie Perez doesn't merely yell or scream—she shrieks, and in such a
high-pitched, nasalized, barely human register that one's first impulse is
to cover one's ears. *Fuck, fuck, fuck.* Nearly every word that comes from
her mouth is *fuck.* And when it isn't *fuck,* it's *asshole.* Interspersed with
such choice tidbits as "You're wearing your ass on your head." Or, notic-
ing the nearly identical hats worn by the two men: "What is this, the
fuckin' Rocky and Bullwinkle show?" Not to speak of: *shut up, shut up,
shut up.*

Nevertheless, Helmut is smitten with Angela and finds her beautiful.
When he plays her a little song on his two clown recorders, she finally
laughs. And then, almost magically, there is a brief pause as the taxi
crosses the Brooklyn Bridge. An awed hush at the beauty of everything
around them. And then the fight starts again. YoYo complains that Angela
is like a Chihuahua, always gnawing at his ankles. Angela replies that
she'll take a big fucking bite out of his big fucking ass, and Helmut smiles
and mutters to himself, "Nice family," as if he really means it.

Inevitably, the ride comes to an end. After receiving a final *Fuck you!*
from Angela, YoYo stays behind and does his best to instruct Helmut on
how to steer himself back to Manhattan. By way of response, Helmut
sticks a red clown nose on his face. The cab takes off, lurching forward
in its old brake-and-pedal two-step, and when it comes to the first intersection, it turns left instead of right. Helmut is alone, lost in an unfamiliar world. "Learn some English," he tells himself. Dark streets, sudden
bursts of light, the noise of sirens in the distance, but for the first time the
car is no longer jerking along. It appears that Helmut has overcome the
problem of the automatic transmission.

The cab is gliding through the night now, an endless night on earth, and as Helmut removes the clown nose, the expression on his face is one of fear and anxiety. He drives past a traffic accident and a number of police cars. A moment later, he whispers to himself, "New York . . . New York."

And so ends Jim Jarmusch's little poem about the city he loves.

2007

Joe Brainard

I can't remember how many times I have read *I Remember*. I discovered the book soon after it was published in 1975, and in the intervening three and a half decades, I have gone back to it once every few years, perhaps seven or eight times in all. The text is not long (just 138 pages in the original edition), but remarkably enough, in spite of these numerous rereadings, whenever I open Joe Brainard's little masterwork again, I have the curious sensation that I am encountering it for the first time. Except for a few indelible passages, nearly all of the memories recorded in the pages of *I Remember* have vanished from my own memory. There are simply too many details to hold on to over an extended period of time, too much life is packed into Brainard's shifting, swirling collage of recollections for any person to remember it in its entirety, and therefore, even if I recognize many of the entries the instant I start to reread them, there are many others that I don't. The book remains new and strange and surprising—for, small as it is, *I Remember* is inexhaustible, one of those rare books that can never be used up.

A prolific visual artist and occasional writer, Brainard stumbled upon the simple but ingenious composition method of *I Remember* in the summer of 1969. He was just twenty-seven, but a highly developed and accomplished twenty-seven, a precocious boy artist who had started exhibiting his work and winning prizes as a grade-school student in Tulsa, Oklahoma, and had landed on Manhattan's Lower East Side before he turned twenty. By 1969, he was a veteran of the New York art scene, with several one-man shows to his credit, participation in numerous group shows, cover designs for dozens of small literary magazines and books of poetry, stage decors for theater pieces by LeRoi Jones and Frank O'Hara, as well as comic-strip collaborations (most of them hilarious) with a long list of poet friends. Collages, large and small assemblages, drawings, and oil paintings—his output was varied and incessant—and on top of that, he also found time to write. Before the miraculous breakthrough of 1969 Brainard had published poems, diaries, and short prose pieces in a number of downtown literary magazines associated with the New York School, and he had already developed a distinctive style of his own—charming, whimsical, unpretentious, frequently ungrammatical, and transparent. Those qualities are all present in *I Remember*, but now, almost by accident, he had hit upon an organizing principle, and the writing takes off and soars into an altogether different register.

With typical nonchalance and acumen, Brainard described the exhilaration he felt while working on his new project in a letter written that summer to poet Anne Waldman: "I am way, way up these days over a piece I am writing called *I Remember*. I feel very much like God writing the Bible. I mean, I feel like I am not really writing it but that it is because of me that it is being written. I also feel that it is about everybody else as much as it is about me. And that pleases me. I mean, I feel like I am everybody. And it's a nice feeling. It won't last. But I am enjoying it while I can."

I remember . . . It seems so obvious now, so self-evident, so fundamental and even ancient—as if the magic formula had been known to man ever since the invention of written language. Write the words *I remember*, pause for a moment or two, give your mind a chance to open up, and inevitably you *will* remember, and remember with a clarity and a specificity that will astonish you. This exercise is now used wherever writing courses are taught, whether for children, college students, or the very old, and the results never fail to summon up long-forgotten particulars of lived experience. As Siri Hustvedt wrote in her recent book, *The Shaking Woman or a History of My Nerves*: "Joe Brainard discovered a memory machine."*

But once you discover the machine, how do you use it? How do you harness the memories that come flooding through you into a work of art, into a book that can speak to someone other than yourself? Many people have written their own versions of *I Remember* since 1975, but no one has come close to duplicating the spark of Brainard's original, of transcending the purely private and personal into a work that is about *everybody*—in the same way that all great novels are about everybody. It strikes me that Brainard's achievement is the product of several forces that operate simultaneously throughout the book: the hypnotic power of incantation; the economy of the prose; the author's courage in revealing things about himself (often sexual) that most of us would be too embarrassed to include; the painter's eye for detail; the gift for story-telling; the

* Henry Holt, New York, 2009.

reluctance to judge other people; the sense of inner alertness; the lack of self-pity; the modulations of tone, ranging from blunt assertion to elaborate flights of fancy; and then, most of all (most pleasing of all), the complex musical structure of the book as a whole.

By music, I mean counterpoint, fugue, and repetition, the interweaving of several different voices throughout the nearly fifteen hundred entries of the book. A theme is picked up for a while, then dropped, then picked up again, in the same way that a horn might sound for a few moments in an orchestral piece, then give way to a violin, which in turn will give way to a cello, and then, all but forgotten by now, the horn will suddenly return. *I Remember* is a concerto for multiple instruments, and among the various strings and woodwinds Brainard employs in his free-floating, ever-changing composition are the following:

—Family (more than seventy entries), such as "I remember my father in a tutu. As a ballerina dancer in a variety show at church"; "I remember when father seemed too formal, and daddy was out of the question, and dad too fake-casual. But, seeming the lesser of three evils, I chose fake-casual"; "I remember the only time I saw my mother cry. I was eating apricot pie."

—Food (a hundred entries), including butter and sugar sandwiches, salt on watermelon, chewy candy in movie theaters, and repeated allusions to ice cream, as in "I remember how good a glass of water can taste after a dish of ice cream."

—Clothes (roughly ninety entries), including pink dress shirts, pillbox hats, and fat ties with fish on them. (Brainard's earliest ambition was to become a fashion designer.)

—Movies, Movie Stars, TV, and Pop Music (more than a hundred entries, including references to Perry Como, Liberace, Hopalong Cassidy, Dinah Shore, Tab Hunter, Marilyn Monroe (several times), Montgomery Clift, Elvis Presley, Judy Garland, Jane Russell, Lana Turner, the Lone Ranger, and umpteen others. "I remember that Betty Grable's legs were insured for a million dollars"; "I remember rumors about what Marlon Brando had to do to get his first acting job"; "I remember Gina Lollobrigida's *very* tiny waist in *Trapeze*."

—School and Church (roughly a hundred entries), such as "I remember how much, in high school, I wanted to be handsome and popular"; "I remember an American history teacher who was always threatening to jump out of the window if we didn't quiet down. (Second floor.)"; "I remember the clock from three to three-thirty"; "'I remember two years of cheating in Spanish class by lightly penciling in the translations of words."

—The Body (more than a hundred entries), ranging from intimate personal confessions—"I remember examining my cock and balls once and finding them absolutely disgusting"—to observations of others: "I remember a very big boy named Teddy and what hairy legs his mother had. (Long black ones squashed flat under nylons.)"

—Dreams, Daydreams, and Fantasies (more than seventy entries), often pertaining to sex ("I remember sexual fantasies of making it with a stranger in the woods") but just as often not, such as "I remember day dreams of being a singer all alone on a big stage with no scenery, just one spotlight on me, singing my heart out, and moving my audience to total tears of love and affection."

—Holidays (fifty entries), centering around Christmas, Thanksgiving, Easter, Halloween, and the Fourth of July. "I remember after opening packages what an empty day Christmas is."

—Objects and Products (more than 130 entries), including driftwood lamps, pop beads, beanbag ashtrays, pearlized plastic toilet seats, jeweled bottle openers, "Ace" combs, roller skate keys, Aspergum, dented ping-pong balls, and miniature Bibles. "I remember the first ball point pens. They skipped, and deposited little balls of ink that would accumulate on the point."

—Sex (more than fifty entries), detailing early heterosexual fumblings in high school—"I remember the first time I got jerked off (never did discover it for myself). I didn't know what she was trying to do and so I just laid there like a zombie not helping one bit"—later homosexual experiences and glimpses of gay life—"I remember not liking myself for not picking up boys I probably could pick up because of the possibility of being rejected"—and more general (often touching) remarks: "I remember early sexual experiences and rubbery knees. I'm sure sex is much better now but I *do* miss rubbery knees."

—Jokes and Common Expressions (more than forty entries), including sick jokes, Mary Anne jokes—"I remember 'Mommy, Mommy, I don't like my little brother.' 'Shut up, Mary Anne, and eat what I tell you to!' "—traveling salesmen jokes, and phrases such as "to coin a phrase," "See you later alligator," "Because I say so, that's why," and "I remember, when babies fall down, 'oopsy-daisy.'"

—Friends and Acquaintances (more than ninety entries), which tend to take the form of small narratives and are generally longer than the other sections of the book. One example: "I remember my parents' bridge teacher. She was very fat and very butch (cropped hair) and she was a chain smoker. She prided herself on the fact that she didn't have to carry matches around. She lit each new cigarette from the old one. She lived in a little house behind a restaurant and lived to be very old." Another example: "I remember Anne Kepler. She played the flute. I remember her straight shoulders. I remember her large eyes. Her slightly roman nose. And her full lips. I remember an oil painting I did of her playing the flute. Several years ago she died in a fire giving a flute concert at a children's home in Brooklyn. All the children were saved. There was something about her like white marble."

—Autobiographical Fragments (twenty entries): a less insistent theme than the other subjects explored by Brainard, but fundamental to our understanding of his project, his life. We see him arriving in New York for the first time, learn of his stuttering and shyness, witness his initial encounter with the poet Frank O'Hara, are informed of his poverty and destitution during an early stay in Boston ("I remember collecting cigarette butts from the urns in front of the Museum of Fine Arts in Boston"), are told about his short, unhappy stint as a scholarship student at the Dayton Art Institute ("I remember in Dayton, Ohio the art fair in the park where they made me take down all my naked self-portraits"), are given a full account of his draft board physical and his rejection by the army after he declared himself to be a homosexual (even though he was a virgin at the time), and are exposed to his self-doubts as an artist, which surely played a role in his decision to stop exhibiting his work during the last fifteen years of his life, as in this laconic but poignant entry: "I remember when I thought I was a great artist."

—Insights and Confessions (forty entries), most of them about Brainard's inner life and character, his overpowering self-consciousness ("I remember that I never cried in front of other people"; "I remember being embarrassed to blow my nose in public"), his awkwardness in social situations ("I remember, at parties, after you've said all you can think of to say to a person—but there you both stand"), and, here and there, instances of almost blinding emotional clarity: "I remember that life was just as serious then as it is now," which could be the most important sentence in the book, the reason why the fifteen hundred fragments of I Remember ultimately cohere to form a solid and integrated work.

—Musings (more than thirty entries), which track the various stray thoughts that come flying in and out of consciousness, the bafflements or perplexities of someone trying to make sense of the world, the bizarre questions all people wind up asking themselves at one time or another. "I remember not understanding why people on the other side of the world didn't fall off"; "I remember wondering if girls fart too"; "I remember wondering how turtles 'do it'"; "I remember thinking once that flushing away pee might be a big waste. I remember thinking that pee is probably good for something and that if one could just discover what it was good for one could make a mint."

Such are the various themes and threads that comprise the totality of *I Remember*. Among its many virtues, it is a book that dwells with great focus on the sensuous details of somatic life (what it feels like to have your hair cut in a barber shop, what it feels like to "turn around and around real fast until you can't stand up," to hear water swishing around in your stomach for the first time and think you might have a tumor), that lovingly records the banal and trivial details of the American landscape of the forties, fifties, and sixties, and presents us with a portrait of a particular man—the modest, self-effacing young Joe Brainard—that is so precise and uninhibited in its telling that we as readers inevitably begin to see our own lives portrayed in his. The memories keep coming at us, relentlessly and without pause, one after the other with no strictures regarding chronology or place. One moment we are in New York, the next moment we are in Tulsa or Boston, a recollection from twenty years ago stands side by side with a memory from last week, and the farther we advance into the text, the more resonant each articulation becomes. As Brainard himself understood as he was writing *I Remember*, it is, truly, a book that belongs to everyone.

It is also interesting to consider what is *not* in Brainard's book, all the things that most of us would probably feel inclined to put in if we were to sit down and write our own versions of *I Remember*. No memories of sibling conflict, no memories of cruelty or physical violence, no eruptions of anger, no impulse to settle scores, no bitterness. Aside from fleeting references to the Kennedy assassination, "Korea" (in quotation marks), and the "I Like Ike" slogan of the Eisenhower presidential campaigns, there are no memories of political, public, or national events. Mondrian, Picasso, and Van Gogh are all mentioned, but there is nothing about Brainard's development as a visual artist, and, except for telling us that he read all of Dostoyevsky's novels in Boston, no memories of discovering the work of other writers, even though Brainard was a passionate reader of fiction. No grief, no rage, and very few tears. Only one entry ("I remember throwing my eye-glasses into the ocean off the Staten Island ferry one black night in a fit of drama and depression") gives any hint of emotional suffering or deep inner turmoil. Brainard's book was written at the precise moment when so-called confessional poetry was dominating the American literary scene. Sylvia Plath, Anne Sexton, and John Berryman (all suicides) were in vogue, and the private rant had become an acceptable, even lauded form of poetic discourse. Brainard confesses, but he does not rant, and he has no interest in mythologizing the story of his own life. He seduces us with his gentleness, his lack of pomposity, his imperturbable interest in everything the world offers up to him. He begins and ends small, but the cumulative force of so many small, exquisitely rendered observations turns his book into something great, something that will become, I believe, an enduring part of American literature.

Before *I Remember*, and after *I Remember*, and even during *I Remember* (which was composed in four separate stages between 1969 and 1973), there were, and are, the several hundred pages of Joe Brainard's other writings. Spanning nearly two decades (from the early sixties to the late seventies) this work falls more or less equally into two general categories: short texts (fiction, non-fiction, poems) and diaries or journals (Brainard used the terms interchangably). The short pieces tend to be funny—often uproariously funny. The diaries are flatter and more introspective, but not without their bursts of funniness as well. Brainard is an unclassifiable writer, but there are moments when his antic inventions recall some of the zanier stunts performed by older American humorists, in particular Ring Lardner and S. J. Perelman. Different as they are in so many ways, all three share a love of nonsense, of parody and pastiche, of disjointed narrative, and alternately exploit both raucous and deadpan approaches to the comic. In Brainard's case, one could also cite the influence of Dada and Surrealism, as filtered through the japeries and ironies of the New York School poets, as well as an occasional tip of the hat to Gertrude Stein, as in this delicious passage from an early "story" entitled "May Dye": "We found breaking bird feathers quite easy and extremely enjoyable and we enjoyed enjoyable things in the most enjoyable way you can imagine enjoyable things being enjoyed."

From the exuberant high jinks of "Back in Tulsa Again" to the irreverent and inspiriting "People of the World: Relax!" ("Take it easy and smoke a lot / Make all the noise you want to on the toilet / Other people will hear you but it does not matter / People of the world: RELAX!") to the inane brilliance of the one-sentence "No Story" ("I hope you have enjoyed not reading this story as much as I have enjoyed not writing it"), Brainard disarms us with the seemingly tossed-off, spontaneous nature of his writing and his stubborn refusal to accede to the pieties of self-importance. We must remember that he was very young when the wildest pieces in this collection were written—still in his twenties—and what these little works capture most fully, it seems to me, is precisely a sense of youth, the laughter of youth, the energy of youth, for in the end they are not really about anything so much as what it means to be young, that hopeful, anarchic time when all horizons are open to us and the future appears to be without limits.

Little by little, however, the pieces begin to take on a more somber tone, even as Brainard continues to maintain the lightness of his touch. By the mid-seventies, following his enormous exhibition of fifteen hundred collages at the Fishbach Gallery, he seems to have entered a personal and artistic crisis, leading to such troubling statements as: ". . . the person I always thought I was simply isn't anymore: *does not exist!*" (in *Nothing to Write Home About*) and then, a few sentences later in the same piece: ". . . the sky is no longer the limit . . . the temptation to wallow in one's own muck—to simply surrender—to give up—is far too appealing. And far too realistic a possibility for comfort."

In 1978, in an interview with Anne Waldman, it is clear that Brainard is already preparing to jump ship:

AW: Do you think one has a choice about being an artist?
JB: Oh yes, I think one always has a choice.
AW: When did you make that choice?
JB: I don't think I ever made it, but I think I have a choice. I think I could stop it now.
AW: Isn't it too late to stop?
JB: No, I don't really think so. I think I could stop tomorrow, I really do.

Not long after that, he did stop. No more exhibitions of his work, no more writing for publication. For the next fifteen years—until his death from AIDS in 1994 at age fifty-two—he spent his time reading books and nurturing his friendships with the many people he loved, the many people who adored him. Why he withdrew from the art world remains a mystery. Some say that he was burned out, exhausted by the frenzied pace that had fueled such an abundant outpouring of work. Others say that he was disappointed in his progress as an artist, by his failure (self-perceived failure) to master oil painting to the degree he aspired to. Others, such as poet Ann Lauterbach (a good friend of Brainard's during his last years), have reported that he felt he didn't have enough ambition, or at least not "the right kind of ambition." And then, too, there was the growing competitiveness and commercialization of the art world, which made Brainard feel increasingly uncomfortable and out of place, for as Lauterbach puts it, "Joe had no taste for this aggressive combat. Life and art were, for Joe Brainard, acts of devoted camaraderie and generative collaboration."*

All of these factors might have played a part in Brainard's decision, but it is important to note that he was not anguished by this decision, and he walked away from his career without regrets. Ron Padgett (the editor of this volume), whose friendship with Brainard began in a first-grade classroom in Tulsa, Oklahoma, and continued until the last day of Brainard's life in New York City, believes that Brainard's evolution from artist to former artist was almost inevitable. As he writes in his book about Brainard: "In a 1974 letter . . . Joe referred to what he felt was his 'basic lack of dedication to art.' For him, art was simply 'a way of life' that enabled him to fulfill his need to give people 'a present' and perhaps be loved in return. Gradually . . . Joe's need to make art diminished as his own life became his art."†

With that in mind, it strikes me as altogether fitting that Padgett should have chosen to begin and end the second part of this book with two previously unpublished pieces, "Self-Portrait on Christmas Night," written in 1961, when Brainard was just nineteen years old, and a short, untitled paragraph from January 1978, almost half a lifetime later—a glimpse, as it were, of Joe Brainard before he became Joe Brainard, followed by a glimpse of Joe Brainard when he was beginning to distance himself from the Joe Brainard of old.

"Self-Portrait on Christmas Night" is an extremely moving document, a passionate cry from the heart delivered by a very young man (still a boy, really) about his hopes and fears as an artist and as a human being. With uncanny prescience, it maps out the journey this young man is about to take, as if Brainard instinctively understood the doubts and

---

* Preface to *The Nancy Book*, by Joe Brainard, published posthumously by Siglio Press, Los Angeles, 2008.
† *Joe: A Memoir of Joe Brainard*, Coffee House Press, Minneapolis, 2004.

potential stumbling blocks that lay ahead of him. Romantic and excessive, different in tone from all of his other writings, it is both a declaration of independence and the anatomy of a soul in conflict. "I'll always know, yet will never really know. Will do great paintings, but will never do what I want. Will learn to understand and accept life, but will never know why. Will love and make love, but will know it could be greater. Will be smart, but will always know there's so much more to learn. I'm damned, but can't change."

A gush of adolescent angst, to be sure, a single paragraph that sprints along breathlessly for fourteen typewritten pages, but painfully honest and insightful, an essential key to our understanding of Brainard's work, and then, sixteen years and one month later, when the adolescent fires were nearly extinguished, the painter who was also a writer sat down to compose a small scene in words. Working calmly and patiently, with no ambition other than to depict the visual and sensual this-ness of what it feels like to sit in a room and look out the window, he offers up his impressions as a gift, since all art for Brainard is a gift to an Other, to a real or imagined someone, and that sublime little paragraph ends with these words, which were among the last words he would ever write:

Outside my window snow is falling down, against a translucent sky of deep lavender, with a touch of orange, zig-zagged along the bottom into a silhouette of black buildings. (The ice box clicks off, and shudders.) And it's as simple as this, what I want to tell you about; if perhaps not much, everything. Painting the moment for you tonight.

December 2010

OCCASIONS

A Prayer for Salman Rushdie

When I sat down to write this morning, the first thing I did was think of Salman Rushdie. I have done this every morning for almost four and a half years, and by now it is an essential part of my daily routine. I pick up my pen, and before I begin to write, I think of my fellow novelist across the ocean. I pray that he will go on living another twenty-four hours. I pray that his English protectors will keep him hidden from the people who are out to murder him—the same people who have already killed one of his translators and wounded another. Most of all, I pray that a time will come when these prayers are no longer necessary, when Salman Rushdie will be as free to walk the streets of the world as I am.

I pray for this man every morning, but deep down, I know that I am also praying for myself. His life is in danger because he wrote a book. Writing books is my business as well, and I know that if not for the quirks of history and pure blind luck, I could be in his shoes. If not today, then perhaps tomorrow. We belong to the same club: a secret fraternity of solitaries, shut-ins, and cranks, men and women who spend the better part of our time locked up in little rooms struggling to put words on a page. It is a strange way to live one's life, and only a person who had no choice in the matter would choose it as a calling. It is too arduous, too underpaid, too full of disappointments to be fit for anyone else. Talents vary, ambitions vary, but any writer worth his salt will tell you the same thing: To write a work of fiction, one must be free to say what one has to say. I have exercised that freedom with every word I have written—and so has Salman Rushdie. That is what makes us brothers, and that is why his predicament is also mine.

I can't know how I would act in his place, but I can imagine it—or at least I can try to imagine it. In all honesty, I'm not sure I would be capable of the courage he has shown. The man's life is in ruins, and yet he has continued to do the thing he was born to do. Shunted from one safehouse to another, cut off from his son, surrounded by security police, he has continued to go to his desk every day and write. Knowing how difficult it is to do this even under the best of circumstances, I can only stand in awe of what he has accomplished. A novel; another novel in the works; a number of extraordinary essays and speeches defending the basic human right to free expression. All that is remarkable enough, but what truly astonishes me is that on top of this essential work, he has taken the time to review other people's books—in some cases even to write blurbs promoting the books of unknown authors. Is it possible for a man in his position to think of anyone but himself? Yes, apparently it is. But I wonder how many of us could do what he has done with our backs against that same wall.

Salman Rushdie is fighting for his life. The struggle has gone on for nearly half a decade, and we are no closer to a solution than when the *fatwa* was first announced. Like so many others, I wish there was something I could do to help. Frustration mounts, despair sets in, but given that I have neither the power nor the influence to affect the decisions of foreign governments, the most I can do is pray for him. He is carrying the burden for all of us, and I can no longer think of what I do without thinking of him. His plight has focused my concentration, has made me reexamine my beliefs, has taught me never to take the freedom I enjoy for granted. For all that, I owe him an immense debt of gratitude. I support Salman Rushdie in his struggle to win back his life, but the truth is that he has also supported me. I want to thank him for that. Every time I pick up my pen, I want to thank him.

1993

Appeal to the Governor
of Pennsylvania

I am not here today to argue the pros and cons of the death penalty (I am fervently against it) nor to talk about the question of race relations in America (surely the central, burning issue of our culture) nor to get sidetracked into a discussion of free speech and first amendment rights. I simply want to address some words to the Honorable Thomas Ridge, Governor of Pennsylvania, who is the only person whose opinion counts anymore in the whole miserable and tragic case of Mumia Abu-Jamal.

As one American citizen to another, I would like the Governor to stop and consider the enormous power he has been given: the power to kill a man or to allow that man to go on living. Whatever the jury has decided about what Mumia Abu-Jamal did or didn't do, whatever laws might support the state of Pennsylvania's right to put Mumia Abu-Jamal to death, you have been designated by those same laws as the one person in that state with the authority to nullify the decision of the jury and save Mumia Abu-Jamal's life. That is because the law knows it isn't perfect. The law understands that it makes mistakes, that the men and women who carry out the law are imperfect creatures, and therefore the power to nullify the decisions of the law must be written into the law itself. In no instance is this more important than when the law proposes to take a man's life. That is why the appeals in such cases go directly to the governor—because the governor is assumed to be wise and just, even if the law isn't always wise and just.

Governor Ridge, you have been asked to take on the largest, most terrible task a man can be given: to decide another man's fate. Mumia Abu-Jamal's life is literally in your hands. Considering the enormous power and responsibility that have been thrust upon you, I take it for granted that you are intimately familiar with the facts of the case. Even I, an ordinary citizen with no power at all, have read endless amounts of material concerning the trial, and every report has indicated numerous irregularities and discrepancies with regard to jury selection, evidence, and the testimony of witnesses—enough for even the most cynical observer to conclude that there is far more than just a shadow of a doubt as to whether Mumia Abu-Jamal actually committed the crime he was accused of. And as long as there is a doubt, as long as a plausible argument can be made that Mumia Abu-Jamal did not do what he has been found guilty of doing, then it strikes me as monstrous that his life can be taken from him—monstrous and shameful, a sin against the laws of man and God.

Governor Ridge, we all want to live in a country we can be proud of. We all want to believe that America is a country in which there is, truly, justice for all. That is the single most important idea we have ever produced, and now it is your turn to uphold that principle and prove that America is indeed a great country worthy of the respect and admiration we want to give it. All eyes are on you, Governor Ridge. I am watching you, my fellow writers at PEN are watching you, tens of thousands of people around the world are watching you, and we are all praying that you will do what is wise and just.

Do us all proud, Governor. Save Mumia Abu-Jamal's life.

1995

The Best Substitute for War

When I was asked to write something about "the millennium," the first word that came to me was "Europe." The millennium is a European idea, after all, and it makes sense only if one refers to the European calendar, the Christian calendar. Most of the world keeps time by that calendar now, but go back a thousand years, and no one in Asia, Africa, or the Americas would have known what you were talking about if you had told him he was living in the year 1000AD. Europe is the only place on earth that has experienced this millennium from beginning to end, and when I cast about in my mind for a single, dominant image or idea that might sum up the past ten centuries of European history (when someone asks you to talk about "the millennium," you tend to take the long view), the word that kept coming back to me was "bloodshed." And by that I mean the metaphysics of violence: war, mass destruction, the slaughter of the innocent.

This is not to denigrate the glories of European culture and civilization. But in spite of Dante and Shakespeare, in spite of Vermeer and Goya, in spite of Chartres and the Declaration of the Rights of Man, it's a proven fact that scarcely a month has gone by in the past thousand years when one group of Europeans has not been intent on killing another group of Europeans. Country has fought against country (the Hundred Years War), alliances of countries have fought against other alliances of countries (the Thirty Years War), and the citizens of a single country have fought against each other (the French Religious Wars). When it comes to our own, much vaunted century of progress and enlightenment, just fill in the appropriate blanks. And lest anyone think the carnage has ended, he has only to open the paper and read about the current situation in former Yugoslavia. Not to speak of what has been happening in Northern Ireland for the past thirty years.

Mercifully, there has been peace among the major European powers since the end of World War II. For the first forty-five postwar years, that peace was tainted by another kind of war, but since the fall of the Berlin Wall and the breakup of the Soviet Union, the peace has held. This is unprecedented in European history. With a common currency on the horizon and passport-free borders already a reality, it looks as though the combatants have finally put down their arms. That doesn't mean they like each other, and it doesn't mean that nationalism is any less fervent than it used to be, but for once it seems that the Europeans have found a way to hate each other without hacking each other to pieces. This miracle goes by the name of soccer.

I don't want to exaggerate, but how else to interpret the facts? When France pulled off a surprise victory in the World Cup last summer, more than a million people gathered on the Champs-Elysées to celebrate. By all accounts, it was the largest demonstration of public happiness seen in Paris since the Liberation from the Germans in 1944.

One could only gape at the enormity of the event, the sheer excessiveness of the joy on display. It was just a sports victory, I kept telling myself, and yet there it was for everyone to see: on the same street in the same city, the same festive jubilation, the same outpouring of national pride that greeted General de Gaulle when he marched through the Arc de Triomphe fifty-four years earlier.

As I watched this scene on television, I thought of the title of a book I had read earlier in the decade: *The Soccer War*, by Ryszard Kapuściński. Was it possible that soccer had become a *substitute* for war?

Compared to American football, the European version seems rather tame, but the truth is that the history of soccer has always been steeped in violence. Legend or not, the first reference to football-playing in this millennium stems from an incident of war. In the year 1000 or thereabouts, the British were supposed to have celebrated their victory over an invading Danish chieftain by removing his head from his body and using it as a football. We don't have to believe that story, but verifiable documents confirm that by the 1100s Shrove Tuesdays were celebrated throughout England with massive football matches that pitted entire towns against one another. Five hundred players on a side. A field that could be up to several miles long. And games that lasted all day, with no fixed rules. It came to be known as "mob football," and the mayhem that resulted from these semi-organized brawls led to so many injuries, broken bones, and even deaths, that in 1314 Edward II issued an edict that banned the playing of football. "Forasmuch as there is great noise in the city, caused by hustling over large balls from which many evils might arise . . . we commend and forbid, on behalf of the King, on pain of imprisonment, such game to be used in the city in future."

Further bans were issued by Edward III, Richard II, and Henry IV.

These kings were not just disturbed by the violence of the sport, they were worried that too much "meddling in football" had cut into the time previously devoted to archery practice and that the kingdom would not be militarily prepared in the event of a foreign invasion. As far back as the first half of the millennium, then, the connection had already been made. War and football were two sides of the same coin.

With the development of firearms, archery ceased to be a required skill among soldiers, and by the late seventeenth century football was actively encouraged by Charles II. Standard rules were introduced in 1801, and as every schoolchild knows, Napoleon was defeated a decade and a half later "on the playing fields of Eton." After 1863, when the rules of present-day soccer were drawn up at Cambridge University, the game spread throughout Europe and the rest of the world. Since then, it has developed into the most popular and widely played sport in human history.

America seems to be the only country that has resisted its charms, but the importance of this game in Europe, its grip on the imagination of tens of millions of people living between Portugal and Poland, cannot be overestimated. Add together our interest in baseball, football, and basketball, then multiply by ten or twenty, and you begin to have an idea of the scope of the obsession. When you further consider that each country fields its own national team, and that these teams go head to head against each other in European and world tournaments, it isn't hard to imagine how the love of football and homeland can be turned into a cocktail for chauvinistic excess and the settling of ancient scores. No country in Europe has avoided invasion and humiliation by one or more of its neighbors during this millennium, and now, as we come to the end of these thousand years, it sometimes looks as though the entire history of the continent were being recapitulated on the soccer field. Holland versus Spain. England versus France. Poland versus Germany. An eerie memory of past antagonisms hovers over each game. Every time a goal is scored, one hears an echo of old victories and old defeats. Passions among the spectators run high. They wave their country's flag, they sing patriotic songs, they insult the supporters of the other team. Americans might look at these antics and think they're all in good fun, but they're not. They're serious business. But at least the mock battles waged by the surrogate armies in short pants do not threaten to increase the population of widows and fatherless children.

Yes, I am aware of the British football hooligans, and I know about the riots and injuries that occurred in several French cities during last year's World Cup. But these instances of extreme and violent behavior only reinforce my point. Soccer is a substitute for war. As long as countries square off against each other on the playing field, we will be able to count the casualties on the fingers of our two hands. A generation ago, they were tallied in the millions.

Does this mean that after a thousand years of bloodshed, Europe has finally found a peaceful way to settle its differences?

We'll see.

December 1, 1998

Reflections on a Cardboard Box

It's a cold and drizzly morning, eleven days before the end of the twentieth century. I am sitting in my house in Brooklyn, glad that I don't have to go out into that bleak December weather. I can sit here as long as I like, and even if I do go out at some point later in the day, I know that I will be able to return. Within a matter of minutes I will be warm and dry again.

I own this house. I bought it seven years ago by scraping together enough cash to cover one-fifth of the total price. The other 80 percent I borrowed from a bank. The bank has given me thirty years to pay off the loan, and every month I sit down and write them another check. After seven years, I have barely made a dent in the principal. The bank charges me for the service of holding the mortgage, and nearly every penny I have given them so far has gone toward reducing the interest I owe them. I don't complain. I'm happy to be spending this extra money (more than twice the amount of the loan) because it gives me a chance to live in this house. And I like it here. Especially on a raw and ugly morning like this one, I can think of no other place in the world where I'd rather be.

It costs me a lot of money to live here, but not as much as it would seem at first glance. When I pay my taxes in April, I'm allowed to deduct the entire amount I've spent on interest over the course of the year. It comes right off my income, no questions asked. The federal government does this for me, and I'm immensely grateful to them. Why shouldn't I be? It saves me thousands of dollars every year.

In other words, I accept welfare from the government. They have rigged things in such a way as to make it possible for a person like me to own a house. Everyone in the country agrees that this is a good idea, and not once have I heard of a congressman or a senator stepping forth to propose that this law be changed. In the past few years, welfare programs for the poor have been all but dismantled, but housing subsidies for the rich are still in place.

The next time you see a man living in a cardboard box, remember this. The government encourages home ownership because it is good for business, good for the economy, good for public morale. It is also the universal dream, the American dream in its purest and most essential form. America measures itself as a civilization by this standard, and whenever we want to prove how successful we are, we begin by trotting out statistics which show that a greater percentage of our citizens own their own homes than anywhere else in the world. "Housing starts" is the key economic term, the bedrock indicator of our financial health. The more houses we build, the more money we will make, and the more money we make, the happier everyone will be.

And yet, as everyone knows, there are millions of people in this country who will never own a house, who struggle every month just to come up with the rent. We also know that there are many others who fall behind with the rent and are forced out onto the streets. We call them the homeless, but what we are really talking about is people who have no money. As with everything else in America, it comes down to a question of money.

A man does not live in a cardboard box because he wants to. He might be mentally deranged, he might be addicted to drugs, or he might be an alcoholic, but he is not in the box because he suffers from these problems. I have known dozens of madmen in my time, and many of them lived in beautiful houses. Show me the book in which it is written that an alcoholic is doomed to sleep on the sidewalk. He is just as likely to be driven around town by a chauffeur in a black hat. There is no cause and effect at work here. You live in a cardboard box because you can't afford to live anywhere else.

These are difficult days for the poor. We have entered a period of enormous prosperity, but as we rush down the highway of larger and larger profits, we forget that untold numbers of people are falling by the wayside. Wealth creates poverty. That is the secret equation of a free-market economy. We don't like to talk about it, but as the rich get richer and find themselves with greater and greater amounts of money to spend, prices have been going up. No one has to be told what has happened to the New York real estate market in the past several years. Housing costs have soared beyond what anyone would have thought possible just a short time ago. Even I, proud homeowner that I am, would not be able to afford my own house if I had to buy it today. For many others, the increases have spelled the difference between having a place to live and not having a place to live. For some people, it has been the difference between life and death.

Bad luck can hit any one of us at any time. It doesn't take much imagination to think of the various things that could do us in. Every person lives with the idea of his own destruction, and even the happiest and most successful person has some dark corner in his brain where horror stories are continually played out. You imagine that your house burns down. You imagine that you lose your job. You imagine that someone who depends on you comes down with an illness, and the medical bills wipe out your savings. Or else you gamble away your savings on a bad investment or a bad roll of the dice. Most of us are only one disaster away from genuine hardship. A series of disasters can ruin us. There are men and women wandering the streets of New York who were once in positions of apparent safety. They have college degrees. They held responsible jobs and supported their families. Now they have fallen on hard times, and who are we to think that such things couldn't happen to us?

For the past several months, a terrible debate has been poisoning the air of New York about what to do with *them*. What we should be talking about is what to do with ourselves. It is our city, after all, and what happens to them also happens to us. The poor are not monsters because they have no money. They are people who need help, and it doesn't help any of us to punish them for being poor. The new rules proposed by the current administration are not just cruel in my opinion, they don't make any sense. If you sleep on the street now, you will be arrested. If you go to a shelter, you will have to work for your bed. If you don't work, you will be thrown back onto the street—and there you will be arrested again. If you are a parent, and you don't comply with the work regulations, your children will be taken from you. The people who defend these ideas all profess to be devout, God-fearing men and women. They should know that every religion in the world insists on the importance of charity—not just as something to be encouraged, but as an obligation, as an essential part of one's relationship to God. Why has no one bothered to tell these people that they are hypocrites?

Meanwhile, it is getting later. Several hours have gone by since I sat down at my desk and began writing these words. I haven't stirred in all that time. The heat is rattling in the pipes, and the room is warm. Outside, the sky is dark, and the wind is lashing the rain against the side of the house. I have no answers, no advice to give, no suggestions. All I ask is that you think about the weather. And then, if you can, that you imagine yourself inside a cardboard box, doing your best to stay warm.

On a day like today, for example, eleven days before the end of the twentieth century, out in the cold and the clamor of the New York streets.

December 20, 1999

Postcards for Georges Perec

1

Whenever I think about Georges Perec, the first word that comes to mind is *pleasure*. I know of no other contemporary writer whose work so fully captures the sense of amazement and happiness that washes over us the first time we read a book that changes the world for us, that exposes us to the infinite possibilities of what a book can be. Every passionate reader has had that experience. It usually occurs when we are quite young, and once we have lived through that moment, we understand that books are a world unto themselves—and that that world is better and richer than any one we have traveled in before. That is why we become readers. That is why we turn away from the vanities of the material world and begin to love books above all other things.

2

What I admire most about Perec is the rare combination in his work of *innocence* and *plenitude.* These qualities are almost never found together in the same writer. Cervantes had them; Swift and Poe had them; one sees flashes of them in Dickens and Kafka, perhaps in certain pages of Hawthorne and Borges. By *innocence* I mean absolute purity of purpose. By *plenitude* I mean absolute faith in the imagination. It is a literature characterized by effervescence, demonic laughter, joy. This is not the only experience we can have with books, but it is the fundamental experience, the one that makes all the others possible.

3

All critics mention the dazzling ingeniousness of Perec's writing, his cleverness. Much as I am awed by that cleverness, by the exuberant complexities of his brilliant mind, that is not what draws me to his work. What I am attracted to is his engagement with the world, his need to tell stories, his tenderness. Underneath every trick and Oulipian puzzle to be found in Perec's books there is a reservoir of human feeling, a swell of compassion, a wink of humor, an unspoken conviction that, in spite of everything, we are lucky to be alive. Restraint should never be confused with a lack of feeling. The agonizing meticulousness of *W ou le souvenir d'enfance*, for example, is the expression of a soul so wounded, a heart so shattered that anything beyond a dry recitation of the facts would have been morally impossible. And yet, for all that, I consider it to be one of the most intimate and moving books I have read in the past twenty years.

4

In David Bellos's biography *Georges Perec: A Life in Words* (an excellent book in its own right), there are several extended passages that decribe Perec's life at the Moulin d'Andé, an artists' retreat to the north of Paris. In one of them, Bellos mentions the fact that the last scene of Truffaut's film *Jules et Jim* was shot there. If one looks closely at the house in the background as the car plunges into the water, he writes, you can see "the window of the room that Georges Perec would come to live and write in for most of his weekends throughout the second half of the 1960s." I was astounded to learn this. Truffaut and Perec were almost exact contemporaries. The filmmaker, born in 1932, died in 1984, at the age of fifty-two. Perec, born in 1936, died in 1982, at the age of forty-six. Between them, they managed to live only as long as one old man. Of all French storytellers from that generation, the generation of men and women who were children during the war, they are the two who have meant the most to me, the ones whose work I have continued to go back to and from whom I will never stop learning. It moves me to know that they intersected in that singular and altogether improbable way. Six years before Perec entered that room (in which he wrote a book without once using the letter *e*), Truffaut captured it on film. Wherever they are now, I can only hope that they are talking about it.

2001

Random Notes—September 11, 2001—4 : 00 PM

Our fourteen-year-old daughter started high school today. For the first time in her life, she rode on the subway from Brooklyn to Manhattan—alone.

She will not be coming home tonight. The subways are no longer running in New York, and my wife and I have arranged for her to stay with friends on the Upper West Side.

Less than an hour after she passed under the World Trade Center, the Twin Towers crumbled to the ground.

From the top floor of our house, we can see the smoke filling the sky of the city. The wind is blowing toward Brooklyn today, and the smells of the fire have settled into every room of the house. A terrible, stinging odor: flaming plastic, electric wire, building materials.

My wife's sister, who lives in TriBeCa, just ten blocks north of what was once the World Trade Center, called to tell us about the screams she heard after the first tower collapsed. Friends of hers, who live on John Street, even closer to the site of the catastrophe, were evacuated by police after the door of their building was blown in by the impact. They walked north through the rubble and debris—which, they told her, contained human body parts.

After watching the news on television all morning, my wife and I went out for a walk in the neighborhood. Many people were wearing handkerchiefs over their faces. Some wore painters' masks. I stopped and talked to the man who cuts my hair, who was standing in front of his empty barber shop with an anguished look on his face. A few hours earlier, he said, the woman who owns the antique shop next door had been on the phone with her son-in-law—who had been trapped in his office on the 107th floor of the World Trade Center. Less than an hour after she spoke to him, the tower collapsed.

All day, as I have watched the horrific images on the television screen and looked at the smoke through the window, I have been thinking about my friend, the high-wire artist Philippe Petit, who walked between the towers of the World Trade Center in August 1974, just after construction of the buildings was completed. A small man

527

dancing on a wire more than five hundred yards off the ground—an act of indelible beauty.

Today, that same spot has been turned into a place of death. It frightens me to contemplate how many people have been killed.

We all knew this could happen. We have been talking about the possibility for years, but now that the tragedy has struck, it's far worse than anyone ever imagined. The last foreign attack on American soil occurred in 1812. We have no precedent for what has happened today, and the consequences of this assault will no doubt be terrible. More violence, more death, more pain for everyone.

And so the twenty-first century finally begins.

September 11, 2001

Underground

Riding the subway at a busy time of day—morning rush hour, evening rush hour—and having the good luck to find a seat. Counting the number of newspapers not written in English, scanning the titles of books and watching people read (the mystery of it, the impossibility of entering another person's mind), listening in on conversations, sneaking a look at the baseball scores over someone's shoulder.

The thin men with their briefcases, the voluminous women with their Bibles and devotional pamphlets, the high school kids with their forty-pound textbooks. Trashy novels, comic books, Melville and Tolstoy, *How to Attain Inner Peace*.

Looking across the aisle at one's fellow passengers and studying their faces. Marveling at the variety of skin tones and features, floored by the singularity of each person's nose, each person's chin, exulting in the infinite shufflings of the human deck.

The panhandlers with their out-of-tune songs and tales of woe; the fractious harangues of born-again proselytizers; the deaf-mutes politely placing sign-language alphabet cards in your lap; the silent men who scuttle through the car selling umbrellas, tablecloths, and cheap wind-up toys.

The noise of the train, the speed of the train. The incomprehensible static that pours through the loudspeaker at each stop. The lurches, the sudden losses of balance, the impact of strangers crashing into one another. The delicate, altogether civilized art of minding one's own business.

And then, never for any apparent reason, the lights go out, the fans stop whirring, and everyone sits in silence, waiting for the train to start moving again. Never a word from anyone. Rarely even a sigh. My fellow New Yorkers sit in the dark, waiting with the patience of angels.

October 11, 2001

NYC = USA

Every day for a year, I read stories. The stories were short, true, and personal, and they were sent to me by men and women from all over America. On the first Saturday of every month, I would gather up some of my favorite ones and read them aloud on NPR's *Weekend All Things Considered*. We called the program the *National Story Project*, and in that year (October 1999 to October 2000) I received over 4000 submissions. They were written by country people and city people, by old people and young people, by people from all walks of life: farmers and priests, housewives and ex-soldiers, businessmen and doctors, postmen and meter readers, a restorer of player pianos, a trolley-bus driver, and several inmates at state correctional facilities.

Early on, I noticed a distinct and surprising trend. The only city that anyone ever wanted to talk about was New York. Not just New Yorkers, but people from every part of the country, some of whom had lived here in the past and regretted having moved away, some of whom had visited only once. In nearly every one of their stories, New York wasn't simply the backdrop for the events that were told, *it was the subject of the story itself*. Crazy New York, inspiring New York, fractious New York, ugly New York, beautiful New York, impossible New York—New York as the ultimate human spectacle of our time. America has had a tortured, even antagonistic relationship with our city over the years, but to an astonishing number of people from Michigan, Maine, and Nebraska, the five boroughs are a living embodiment of what the United States is all about: diversity, tolerance, and equality under the law. Alone among American cities, New York is more than just a place or an agglomeration of people. It is also an idea.

I believe that idea took hold in us when Emma Lazarus's poem was affixed to the pedestal of the Statue of Liberty. Bartholdi's gigantic effigy was originally intended as a monument to the principles of international republicanism, but "The New Colossus" reinvented the statue's purpose, turning Liberty into a welcoming mother, a symbol of hope to the outcasts and downtrodden of the world. New York has continued to represent the spirit of that message, and even today, 116 years after the unveiling of the statue, we still define ourselves as a city of immigrants. With 40 percent of our current population born in foreign countries, we are a cross-section of the entire world. It is a densely crowded ethnic hodge-podge, and the potential for chaos is enormous. No one would contend that we are not bedeviled by a multitude of problems, but when you think of what ethnic differences have done to cities like Sarajevo, Belfast, and Jerusalem, New York stands out as a shining example of civic peace and order.

The murderous attacks on the World Trade Center last September were rightly construed as an assault against the United States. New Yorkers felt that way, too, but it was our city that was bombed, and even as we wrestled to understand the hateful fanaticism that could lead to the deaths of 3000 innocent people, we experienced that day as a family tragedy. Most of us went into a state of intense mourning, and we dragged ourselves around in the days and months that followed engulfed by a sense of communal grief. It was that close to all of us, and I doubt there is a single New Yorker who doesn't know someone who didn't lose at least one friend or relative in the attack. Compute the numbers, and the results are staggering. Three thousand people in addition to their immediate families, their extended families, their friends, their neighbors, and their co-workers, and suddenly you're in the millions.

Last September 11 was one of the worst days in American history, but the dreadful cataclysm that occurred that morning was also an occasion for deep reflection, a time for all of us to stop and examine who we were and what we believed in. As it happened, I spent a good deal of time on the road last fall, co-hosting events with Jacki Lyden of NPR in connection with the release of the *National Story Project* anthology, *I Thought My Father Was God*. We traveled from Boston to San Francisco and points in between, and in each city contributors to the book read their stories in public to large and attentive audiences. I talked to scores of people on those trips, perhaps hundreds of people, and nearly every one of them told me the same thing. In the aftermath of September 11, they were reassessing the values of our country, trying to figure out what separated us from the people who had attacked us. Almost without exception, the single word they used was "democracy." That is the bedrock creed of American life: a belief in the dignity of the individual, a tolerant embrace of our cultural and religious differences. No matter how often we fail to live up to those ideals, that is America at its best—the very principles that are a constant, daily reality in New York.

It has been a year now. When the Bush administration launched its War on Terrorism by invading Afghanistan, we in New York were still busy counting our dead. We watched in horror as the smoking ruins of the towers were gradually cleared; we attended funerals with empty coffins; we wept. Even now, as the international situation turns ever more perilous, we are largely preoccupied with the debate over how to build a fitting memorial to the victims of the attack, trying to solve the problem of how to reconstruct that devastated area of our city. No one is sorry that the Taliban regime has been ousted from power, but when I talk to my fellow New Yorkers these days, I hear little but disappointment in what our government has been up to. Only a small minority of New Yorkers voted for George W. Bush, and most of us tend to look at his policies with suspicion. He simply isn't democratic enough for us. He and his cabinet have not encouraged open debate of the issues facing the country. With talk of an imminent invasion of Iraq now circulating in the press, increasing numbers of New Yorkers are becoming apprehensive. From the vantage point of Ground Zero, it looks like a global catastrophe in the making.

Not long ago, I received a poetry magazine in the mail with a cover that read: USA OUT OF NYC. Not everyone would want to go that far, but in the past several weeks I've heard a number of my friends talk with great earnestness and enthusiasm about the possibility of New York seceding from the Union and establishing itself as an independent city-state. That will never happen, of course, but I do have one practical suggestion. Since President Bush has repeatedly told us how much he dislikes Washington, why doesn't he come live in New York? We know that he has no great love for this place, but by moving to our city, he might learn something about the country he is trying to govern. He might learn, in spite of his reservations, that we are the true heartland.

July 31, 2002

Remembering Beckett
on his one hundredth birthday

I moved to Paris in February 1971, a few weeks after my twenty-fourth birthday. I had been writing poetry for some time by then, and the road to my initial meeting with Beckett began with Jacques Dupin, a poet whose work I had been translating since my undergraduate days in New York. He and I became close friends in Paris, and because Jacques worked as director of publications at the Galerie Maeght, I met Jean-Paul Riopelle, the French-Canadian painter who was one of the artists of the gallery. Because of Jean-Paul, I met Joan Mitchell, the American painter he lived with in a house once owned by Monet in the town of Vétheuil. Years earlier, Joan had been married to Barney Rosset, the founder and publisher of Grove Press, and she and Beckett knew each other well. One evening, she and I happened to be discussing his work, and when she found out how important it was to me, she looked up and said, "Would you like to meet him?" "Yes," I answered. "Of course I would." "Well, just write him a letter," she announced, "and tell him I said so."

I went home and wrote the letter, and three days later I received a reply from Beckett informing me to meet him at La Closerie des Lilas the following week.

I can't remember what year it was. It might have been as early as 1972 or as late as 1974. Let's split the difference and call it 1973.

I saw him only once after that—on a subsequent visit to Paris in 1979—and over the years we exchanged a couple of dozen notes and letters. It could hardly be classified as a friendship, but given my admiration for his work (which bordered on idolatry when I was young), our personal encounters and fitful correspondence were exceedingly precious to me. Among a horde of memories, I would cite the generous help he gave me while I was putting together my *Random House Book of Twentieth-Century French Poetry* (to which he contributed translations of Apollinaire, Breton, and Éluard); the moving speech he delivered one afternoon in a Paris café about his love for France and how lucky he felt to have spent his adult life there; the kind and encouraging letters he wrote whenever I sent him something I had published: books, translations, articles about his work. There were funny moments as well: a deadpan account of his one and only stay in New York ("It was so damn hot, I was hanging onto the rails"), not to speak of the unforgettable line from our first meeting when, gesturing with his arm and failing to attract the waiter's attention, he turned to me and said, in that soft Irish brogue of his, "There are no eyes in the world harder to catch than a barman's."

All that, yes, but one remark from that afternoon at La Closerie des Lilas stands out from the others, and not only does it reveal much about Beckett the man, it speaks to the dilemma all writers must live with: eternal doubt, the inability to judge the worth of what one has created.

During the conversation, he told me that he had just finished translating *Mercier and Camier*, his first French novel, which had been written in the mid-forties. I had read the book in French and had liked it very much. "A wonderful book," I said. I was just a kid, after all, and I couldn't suppress my enthusiasm. But Beckett shook his head and said, "Oh no, no, not very good. In fact, I've cut out about twenty-five percent of the original. The English version is going to be quite a bit shorter than the French." And I said, "Why would you do such a thing. It's a wonderful book. You shouldn't have taken anything out." Again, Beckett shook his head. "No, no, not very good, not very good."

After that, we started talking about other things. Then, out of the blue, five or ten minutes later, he leaned across the table and said, "You really liked it, huh? You thought it was good?"

This was Samuel Beckett, remember, and not even he had any grasp of the value of his work. No writer ever knows, not even the best ones.

"Yes," I said to him. "I really thought it was good."

2005

The History of a Friendship
for Jacques Dupin on his eightieth birthday

1967. I have just turned twenty years old. One afternoon, I walk into the bookstore at Columbia University and buy a small anthology of contemporary French poetry. Three or four of Jacques Dupin's poems are included, and that night I read his work for the first time. It makes an immediate and lasting impression on me. *I write to bury my gold, / To close your eyes.* I tell myself: I have never encountered anything like this before.

Summer 1967. I go to Paris and manage to track down two books published by Dupin: *Cendrier du voyage* and *Gravir*. For reasons I can no longer explain, I begin translating the poems into English. Perhaps in order to understand them better. Perhaps for the pure pleasure of it. It turns out to be a singular adventure, and I spend as much time translating Dupin as I do writing my own poems.

1968. By now, I have translated nearly all of *Gravir*. I show the manuscript to an older American poet, and he suggests that I send it to a small publishing house in California that has started a series of translations of foreign poets. To my astonishment, the book is accepted. I sign a contract, and publication is scheduled for late 1969 or early 1970.

Unfortunately, the publisher goes bankrupt, and the book never appears. Nevertheless, because of this *potential* book, I write a letter to Jacques Dupin (who is delighted at the prospect of seeing his work published in English), and we begin a regular correspondence.

February 1971. Several days after my twenty-fourth birthday, I move to Paris. I will stay in France for the next three and a half years, and one of the first people I visit after my arrival is Jacques Dupin—for our long-deferred initial encounter. His wife, Christine, is out of town for a few days, so we go to a restaurant in the neighborhood with his fifteen-year-old daughter, Hélène. I am of course rather nervous at first, and after I address him as *vous* when we shake hands, he quickly puts me at my ease by insisting that I call him *tu*. Following dinner, we return to his apartment, where we sit up late into the night, drinking, smoking, and talking about everything from literature to painting to politics to God knows what else. It is the beginning of a friendship that has continued, uninterrupted, to this day. Later on, Jacques will confess to me how shocked he was when I showed up at his door. He was expecting to meet a middle-aged man—not a twenty-four-year-old boy.

Later that week, Jacques invites me to accompany him and Christine to the opening of a drawing exhibition by Henri Michaux, one of my writing heroes. At the reception afterward, I get to shake Michaux's hand and am introduced to Jacques's close friend André du Bouchet, whose work I also greatly admire and will later translate. Another long friendship begins—because of Jacques. I am unaware of it at the time, but a pattern is already being established. Nearly every good or lucky thing that happens to me during my years in France is somehow connected to Jacques.

I am poor, living on next to nothing. Again and again, Jacques and Christine invite me to their place for dinner, and again and again he and I sit up late into the night talking. One afternoon, I meet him for lunch near the Galerie Maeght (where he works as director of publications), and when he asks me how I am doing financially, I tell him that I'm waiting to receive a check for a job I have done and am quite low on cash. Without saying a word, Jacques reaches into his pocket, pulls out his wallet, and begins peeling off fifty-franc notes—one note after the other, three hundred francs in all, if I'm not mistaken. He pushes the money across the table in my direction, and when I tell him that I can't possibly accept (since I don't know when I can pay him back), he shrugs the Dupin shrug, a characteristically laconic gesture, silently telling me not to worry about it, it's only money, what are friends for? Again I refuse, but he will not take no for an answer. Take it, he says. I don't need it. Don't give it another thought.

After that, he starts giving me work. Éditions Maeght has published a number of book-length monographs on the artists who show their work at the gallery, and he hires me to translate several of them into English. The jobs are well paid. There's some talk about a British publisher being interested in bringing out the entire series, but nothing ever comes of it. By the second or third book, I understand that Jacques has manufactured this work for me. It's a way of giving me money and at the same time leaving my dignity intact.

* * *

CASIONS

Another lunch with Jacques, this time in the company of Jean-Paul
Riopelle, an artist in the Maeght stable. Riopelle and I hit it off, and after
the meal he is eager to introduce me to Joan Mitchell, the American
painter he lives with, at her studio on rue Frémicourt. Jacques returns
to work, and Jean-Paul and I climb into his car to meet Joan. On the
strength of that lunch, Jacques and Christine decide to hold a dinner at
their house. Three people are invited: Jean-Paul, Joan, and myself.

It quickly degenerates into an unforgettable and crazy evening. In her
recent book on painting, *Mysteries of the Rectangle* (Princeton Architectural
Press), my wife, Siri Hustvedt, includes an essay she wrote five years ago
on the Joan Mitchell retrospective at the Whitney Museum in New York.
The first paragraph alludes to that dinner party:

Twenty years ago, at the Musée National d'Art Moderne in Paris, I shook Joan
Mitchell's hand. I was the new wife of an old friend of hers—Paul Auster. . . . I
had been informed that Mitchell's character, like certain kinds of weather,
chanced a thunderstorm now and again, and I braced myself. But what I
remember from that day is that when Joan Mitchell saw my husband, she threw
herself into his arms and hugged him. Eleven years earlier, the then twenty-
four-year-old Paul had survived a memorable dinner party given by Jacques
Dupin and his wife, Christine. Over the course of the evening, Mitchell had
insulted Paul, not once or twice, but steadily, without respite, for hours. While
Riopelle, in a spirit of avoidance and contented oblivion, slept soundly on the
sofa, the Dupins did their best to follow the barrage of verbal missiles that were
flying across the table in English—"Who do you think you are, Lord Byron?"
But Paul's unflappable demeanor under fire (a sanguine mixture of astonishment and amusement) seemed to win the painter's affection, and after that gru-
eling but never-to-be-repeated initiation, they became friends. It was Joan who
introduced Paul to Samuel Beckett, Joan who gave him an etching of a sun-
flower for the cover of the small literary magazine, *Living Hand*, that he had
started with a friend, and Joan who wanted signed manuscripts of his poems to
keep. She got them.

By 1972, my already precarious finances have taken a turn for the
worse. I can no longer afford to keep my apartment in the fifteenth
arrondissement. When they learn of my troubles, Jacques and Christine
offer me their *chambre de bonne* on the sixth floor of their building—
rent-free, no questions asked. Is it possible that such people exist, that
such generosity exists in this miserable world? Until the Dupins enter
my life, I am convinced that acts like this one are the stuff of fairy tales.

* * *

37

It is a small room, the smallest room I have ever lived in, barely large enough to hold a bed, a desk, and a chair, but I am happy in my tiny cell, and during the year I spend in that place, I write most of the poems that make up my first published collection, *Unearth*.

I am not the only one they help, of course. The year before I move into that room, it is occupied by another penniless young poet, Philippe Denis. Strangely—but then again, perhaps not so strangely—Philippe later translates *Unearth* into French. When the book appears (1980), the illustrations are by Jean-Paul Riopelle. Needless to say, the publisher is Maeght (Collection Argile), which is to say, the publisher is Jacques Dupin. It is my first book in French.

June 1974. Under the imprint of the above-mentioned literary review—*Living Hand*, which I cofounded with a Columbia University writer friend, Mitchell Sisskind, who unexpectedly inherited a large sum of money—my translations of Jacques's poems are finally published in book form. *Fits and Starts: Selected Poems of Jacques Dupin*. Seventy-one pages (English only), handsomely printed and bound by the Compton Press in Salisbury, England. One thousand copies. As I write these words today (August 16, 2006), the edition has been out of print for more than thirty years. The book has become a much-sought-after collector's item.

One month later (July 1974), I return to New York, where I have lived ever since. But the friendship with Jacques and his family endures, undiminished. Frequent letters and telephone calls, but also numerous visits on both sides of the Atlantic: Jacques to New York, I to Paris, as well as two or three long weekends spent together in London. Most triumphant moment: after Siri and I marry, in June 1982, we go to Paris for our honeymoon. For the first time, I have enough money in my pocket to invite Jacques and Christine to a good restaurant and pay the bill myself. I feel that perhaps I am finally becoming an adult.

1992. I put together a new and much larger volume of Jacques's poetry, a bilingual edition of two hundred pages entitled *Selected Poems*, published by Wake Forest University Press (U.S.) and Bloodaxe (U.K.).

1993. Jacques writes the preface to my collected poems in French, *Disparitions,* copublished by Éditions Unes and Actes Sud.

2006. It seems impossible that so much time has passed, that the two of us have grown so old. Exactly one month before Jacques turns eighty in March, I myself will turn sixty. I study a photograph of us taken in the early seventies and am stunned by how young we look. The dark hair on our heads, the thinness of our bodies. Nearly forty years have passed since I first read a poem by Jacques Dupin, and yet it feels as if it happened only yesterday.

Dear Jacques. As I wish you a happy birthday, I also want to thank you for everything you have given me. Not only your work, not only your friendship, but the vital lessons you have taught me about what it means to be a human being, and how, for those of us who write and make art, those of us who belong to this small band of obsessed and driven souls, there is a responsibility to watch out for the ones who are struggling, the ones who are young, the ones who will not make it unless we reach out our hand and pull them back to their feet. Years ago, you gave me your hand, and I will never forget it. I think of you every day, Jacques, and every day I try to live up to your example.

2006

Talking to Strangers
Prince of Asturias Prize for Literature acceptance speech

I don't know why I do what I do. If I did know, I probably wouldn't feel the need to do it. All I can say, and I say it with utmost certainty, is that I have felt this need since my earliest adolescence. I'm talking about writing, in particular writing as a vehicle to tell stories, imaginary stories that have never taken place in what we call the real world. Surely it is an odd way to spend your life: sitting alone in a room with a pen in your hand, hour after hour, day after day, year after year, struggling to put words on pieces of paper in order to give birth to what does not exist—except in your own head. Why on earth would anyone want to do such a thing? The only answer I have ever been able to come up with is: because you have to, because you have no choice.

This need to make, to create, to invent is no doubt a fundamental human impulse. But to what end? What purpose does art, in particular the art of fiction, serve in what we call the real world? None that I can think of—at least not in any practical sense. A book has never put food in the stomach of a hungry child. A book has never stopped a bullet from entering a murder victim's body. A book has never prevented a bomb from falling on innocent civilians in the midst of war. Some like to think that a keen appreciation of art can actually make us better people—more just, more moral, more sensitive, more understanding. Perhaps that is true—in certain rare, isolated cases. But let us not forget that Hitler started out in life as an artist. Tyrants and dictators read novels. Killers in prison read novels. And who is to say they don't derive the same enjoyment from books as everyone else?

In other words, art is useless—at least when compared, say, to the work of a plumber, or a doctor, or a railroad engineer. But is uselessness a bad thing? Does a lack of practical purpose mean that books and paintings and string quartets are simply a waste of our time? Many people think so. But I would argue that it is the very uselessness of art that gives it its value—and that the making of art is what distinguishes us from all other creatures who inhabit this planet, that it is, essentially, what defines us as human beings. To do something for the pure pleasure and beauty of doing it. Think of the effort involved, the long hours of practice and discipline required to become an accomplished pianist or dancer. All the suffering and hard work, all the sacrifices in order to achieve something that is utterly and magnificently . . . useless.

Fiction, however, exists in a somewhat different realm from the other arts. Its medium is language, and language is something we share with others, that is common to us all. From the moment we learn to talk, we begin to develop a hunger for stories. Those of us who can remember our childhoods will recall how ardently we relished the moment of the Bedtime Story—when our mother or father would sit down beside us in the semidark and read from a book of fairy tales. Those of us who are parents will have no trouble conjuring up the rapt attention in the eyes of our children when we read to them. Why this intense desire to listen? Fairy tales are often cruel and violent, featuring beheadings, cannibalism, grotesque transformations, and evil enchantments. One would think this material would be too frightening for a young child, but what these stories allow the child to experience is precisely an encounter with his own fears and inner torments—in a perfectly safe and protected environment. Such is the magic of stories: they might drag us down to the depths of hell, but in the end they are harmless.

We grow older, but we do not change. We become more sophisticated, but at bottom we continue to resemble our young selves, eager to listen to the next story, and the next, and the next. For years, in every country of the Western world, article after article has been published bemoaning the fact that fewer and fewer people are reading books, that we have entered what some have called the "postliterate age." That may well be true, but at the same time this has not diminished the universal craving for stories. Novels are not the only source, after all. Films and television and even comic books are churning out vast quantities of fictional narratives, and the public continues to swallow them up with great passion. That is because human beings need stories. They need them almost as desperately as they need food, and however the stories might be presented—whether on a printed page or on a television screen—it would be impossible to imagine life without them.

Still, when it comes to the state of the novel, to the future of the novel, I feel rather optimistic. Numbers don't count where books are concerned—for there is only one reader, each and every time only one reader. That explains the particular power of the novel, and why, in my opinion, it will never die as a form. Every novel is an equal collaboration between the writer and the reader, and it is the only place in the world where two strangers can meet on terms of absolute intimacy. I have spent my life in conversations with people I have never seen, with people I will never know, and I hope to continue until the day I stop breathing.

It's the only job I've ever wanted.

October 2006

Columbia: 1968

It was the year of years, the year of craziness, the year of fire, blood, and death. I had just turned twenty-one, and I was as crazy as everyone else.

There were half a million American soldiers in Vietnam, Martin Luther King had just been assassinated, cities were burning across America, and the world seemed headed for an apocalyptic breakdown.

Being crazy struck me as a perfectly sane response to the hand I had been dealt—the hand all young men had been dealt in 1968. The instant I graduated from college, I would be drafted to fight in a war I despised to the depths of my being, and because I had already made up my mind to refuse to fight in that war, I knew that my future held only two options: prison or exile.

I was not a violent person. Looking back on those days now, I see myself as a quiet, bookish young man, struggling to teach myself how to become a writer, immersed in my courses in literature and philosophy at Columbia. I had marched in demonstrations against the war, but I was not an active member of any political organization on campus. I felt sympathetic to the aims of SDS (one of several radical student groups, but by no means the most radical), and yet I never attended its meetings and not once had I handed out a broadside or leaflet. I wanted to read my books, write my poems, and drink with my friends at the West End Bar.

Forty years ago today, a protest rally was held on the Columbia campus. The issue had nothing to do with the war but, rather, with a gymnasium the university was about to build in Morningside Park. The park was public property, and because Columbia intended to create a separate entrance for the local residents (mostly black), the building plan was deemed to be both unjust and racist. I was in accord with this assessment, but I didn't attend the rally because of the gym.

I went because I was crazy, crazy with the poison of Vietnam in my lungs, and the many hundreds of students who gathered around the sundial in the center of campus that afternoon were not there to protest the construction of the gym so much as to vent their craziness, to lash out at something, anything, and since we were all students at Columbia, why not throw bricks at Columbia, since it was engaged in lucrative research projects for military contractors and thus was contributing to the war effort in Vietnam?

Speech followed tempestuous speech, the enraged crowd roared with approval, and then someone suggested that we all go to the construction site and tear down the chain-link fence that had been erected to keep out trespassers. The crowd thought that was an excellent idea, and so off it went, a throng of crazy, shouting students charging off the Columbia campus toward Morningside Park. Much to my astonishment, I was with them. What had happened to the gentle boy who planned to spend the rest of his life sitting alone in a room writing books? He was helping to tear down the fence. He tugged and pulled and pushed along with several dozen others and, truth be told, found much satisfaction in this crazy, destructive act.

After the outburst in the park, campus buildings were stormed, occupied, and held for a week. I wound up in Mathematics Hall and stayed for the duration of the sit-in. The students of Columbia were on strike. As we calmly held our meetings indoors, the campus was roiling with belligerent shouting matches and slugfests as those for and against the strike went at one another with abandon. By the night of April 30, the Columbia administration had had enough, and the police were called in. A bloody riot ensued. Along with more than seven hundred other people, I was arrested—pulled by my hair to the paddy wagon by one cop as another cop stomped on my hand with his boot. But no regrets. I was proud to have done my bit for the cause. Both crazy and proud.

What did we accomplish? Not much of anything. It's true that the gymnasium project was scrapped, but the real issue was Vietnam, and the war dragged on for seven more horrible years. You can't change government policy by attacking a private institution. When French students erupted in May of that year of years, they were directly confronting the national government—because their universities were public, under the control of the Ministry of Education—and what they did initiated changes in French life. We at Columbia were powerless, and our little revolution was no more than a symbolic gesture. But symbolic gestures are not empty gestures, and given the nature of those times, we did what we could.

I hesitate to draw any comparisons with the present—and therefore will not end this memory piece with the word "Iraq." I am sixty-one now, but my thinking has not changed much since that year of fire and blood, and as I sit alone in this room with a pen in my hand, I realize that I am still crazy, perhaps crazier than ever.

April 2008

References

THE INVENTION OF SOLITUDE. New York, Sun Books; 1982. Reprinted by Penguin USA; 1988.

HAND TO MOUTH. New York, Henry Holt; 1997.

TRUE STORIES. "The Red Notebook" (*Granta*, 1993); "Why Write?" (*The New Yorker*, 1995); "Accident Report" (*Conjunctions*, 2000); "It Don't Mean A Thing" (*Granta*, 2000). All four pieces were later collected in *The Red Notebook*. New York, New Directions; 2002.

GOTHAM HANDBOOK. In *Double Game*, by Sophie Calle. London, Violette; 1999.

THE STORY OF MY TYPEWRITER. New York, D.A.P.; 2002.

NORTHERN LIGHTS. "Pages for Kafka" (*European Judaism*, 1974); "The Death of Sir Walter Raleigh" (*Parenthèse*, 1975); "Northern Lights" (Catalogue preface for Jean-Paul Riopelle exhibition, Galerie Maeght, Paris, 1976; *Derrière le miroir*, no. 218).

CRITICAL ESSAYS. "The Art of Hunger" (*American Letters and Commentary*, 1988); "New York Babel" (*The New York Review of Books*, 1975); "Dada Bones" (*Mulch*, 1975); "Truth, Beauty, Silence" (*The New York Review of Books*, 1975); "From Cakes to Stones" (*Commentary*, 1975); "The Poetry of Exile" (*Commentary*, 1976); "Innocence and Memory" (*The New York Review of Books*, 1976); "Book of the Dead" (*The New York Review of Books*, 1976); "Reznikoff × 2" (*Parnassus*, 1979; in *Charles Reznikoff: Man and Poet*. Orono, Maine, National Poetry Foundation; 1984); "The Bartlebooth Follies" (*The New York Times Book Review*, 1987).

PREFACES. "Jacques Dupin" (*Fits and Starts: Selected Poems of Jacques Dupin*. New York, Living Hand; 1974); "André du Bouchet" (*The Uninhabited: Selected Poems of André du Bouchet*. New York, Living Hand;

1976); "Black on White" (Leaflet distributed at Susan Cauldwell Gallery, New York, for David Reed exhibition, 1975); "Twentieth-Century French Poetry" (*The Random House Book of Twentieth-Century French Poetry*. New York, Random House; 1982); "Mallarmé's Son" (*A Tomb for Anatole*, by Stéphane Mallarmé. San Francisco, North Point Press; 1983); "Running Through Fire" (*Running Through Fire: How I Survived the Holocaust*, by Zosia Goldberg, as told to Hilton Obenzinger. San Francisco, Mercury House; 2004); "On the High Wire" (*Traité du funambulisme*, by Philippe Petit. Arles [France], Actes Sud; 1997); "Translator's Note" (*Chronicle of the Guayaki Indians*, by Pierre Clastres. New York, Zone Books; 1998); "An Evening at Shea" (*Things Happen for a Reason: The True Story of an Itinerant Life in Baseball*, by Terry Leach, with Tom Clark. Berkeley, Frog Ltd.; 2000); "The National Story Project" (*I Thought My Father Was God and Other True Tales from NPR's National Story Project*. New York, Henry Holt; 2001); "A Little Anthology of Surrealist Poems" (*A Little Anthology of Surrealist Poems*. Minneapolis, Rain Taxi; 2002. New preface for collection originally published in 1972); "The Art of Worry" (Catalogue preface for Art Spiegelman exhibition, Nuage Gallery, Brescia [Italy], 2003); "Invisible Joubert" (for reprint of *The Notebooks of Joseph Joubert*. New York, New York Review Books; 2005. Book originally published by North Point Press, San Francisco; 1983); "Hawthorne at Home" (*Nathaniel Hawthorne: Twenty Days with Julian & Little Bunny, by Papa*. New York, New York Review Books; 2003). "Night on Earth: New York" (*Night on Earth: A Film by Jim Jarmusch*. New York, The Criterion Collection; 2007).

OCCASIONS. "A Prayer for Salman Rushdie" (Op-ed piece: *The New York Times*; June 18, 1993); "Appeal to the Governor of Pennsylvania" (Delivered at a press conference at the PEN American Center, New York, on July 28, 1995. Other participants included Dennis Brutus, Thulani Davis, Cornelius Eady, and William Styron); "The Best Substitute for War" (*The New York Times Magazine*; April 1999. In response to the question: What is the best game of the millennium?); "Reflections on a Cardboard Box" (Written at the request of the New York Coalition for the Homeless—for a brochure that was never published); "Postcards for Georges Perec" (*Portrait(s) de Georges Perec*. Paris, Bibliothèque Nationale de France; 2001); "Random Notes—September 11, 2001—4:00 PM" (Commissioned by *Die Zeit*; published September 13, 2001); "Underground" (*The New York Times Magazine*; October 2001. In response to the question: Describe something about New York you love); "NYC = USA" (Op-ed piece: *The New York Times*; September 9, 2002). "Remembering Beckett" (*Beckett Remembering, Remembering Beckett: A Centenery Celebration*, edited by James and Elizabeth Knowlson. New York, Arcade Publishing; 2006); "The History of a Friendship" (*04.03: Mélanges pour Jacques Dupin*. Paris, P.O.L.; 2007); "Talking to Strangers" (Speech delivered in Oviedo, Spain; October 2006); "Columbia: 1968" (Op-ed piece: *The New York Times*; April 23, 2008).